Philosophy and Faith

A Philosophy of Religion Reader

Edited by

David Shatz

Yeshiva University

D0470248

LIBRARY
ARAPAHOE COMMUNITY COLLEGE
5900 SOUTH SANTA FE DRIVE
P.O. BOX 9002
LITTLETON, CO 80160

Boston Burr Ridge, IL Dubuque, IA Madison, WI New York San Francisco St. Louis
Bangkok Bogotá Caracas Kuala Lumpur Lisbon London Madrid Mexico City
Milan Montreal New Delhi Santiago Seoul Singapore Sydney Taipei Toronto

McGraw-Hill Higher Education

A Division of The ***McGraw-Hill*** *Companies*

PHILOSOPHY AND FAITH: A PHILOSOPHY OF RELIGION READER

Published by McGraw-Hill, a business unit of The McGraw-Hill Companies, Inc., 1221 Avenue of the Americas, New York, NY 10020. Copyright © 2002 by The McGraw-Hill Companies, Inc. All rights reserved. No part of this publication may be reproduced or distributed in any form or by any means, or stored in a database or retrieval system, without the prior written consent of The McGraw-Hill Companies, Inc., including, but not limited to, in any network or other electronic storage or transmission, or broadcast for distance learning.

Some ancillaries, including electronic and print components, may not be available to customers outside the United States.

This book is printed on acid-free paper.

3 4 5 6 7 8 9 0 QPF/QPF 0 9 8 7

ISBN 978-0-07-237689-0
MHID 0-07-237689-9

Vice president and editor-in-chief: *Thalia Dorwick*
Editorial director: *Jane E. Karpacz*
Sponsoring editor: *Monica Eckman*
Developmental editor: *Shannon Morrow*
Senior marketing manager: *Daniel M. Loch*
Senior project manager: *Susan J. Brusch*
Lead production supervisor: *Sandra Hahn*
Coordinator of freelance design: *Rick D. Noel*
Cover designer: *So Yon Kim*
Compositor: ***TECHBOOKS***
Typeface: *10/12 Times Roman*
Printer: *Quebecor World Fairfield, PA*

The credits section for this book begins on page 569 and is considered an extension of the copyright page.

Library of Congress Cataloging-in-Publication Data

Philosophy and faith : a philosophy of religion reader / [edited by] David Shatz. — 1st ed.
p. cm.
Includes index.
ISBN 0-07-237689-9
1. Religion—Philosophy. I. Shatz, David.

BL51 .P5256 2002
210—dc21

2001044138
CIP

www.mhhe.com

To Chani
with Love and Gratitude

APR 1 1 2012

Contents

PREFACE ix

INTRODUCTION: WHAT IS THE PHILOSOPHY OF RELIGION? xiv

Chapter 1 The Concept of God 1

READING 1.1
Thomas Aquinas: *The Divine Impassibility* 5

READING 1.2
Anselm of Canterbury: *How God Is Both Merciful and Impassible* 8

READING 1.3
Robert Oakes: *The Wrath of God* 9

READING 1.4
Charles Taliaferro: *Is God Vain?* 15

READING 1.5
Anne C. Minas: *God and Forgiveness* 25

READING 1.6
Peter Geach: *Omnipotence* 34

READING 1.7
William L. Rowe: *Predestination, Divine Foreknowledge, and Human Freedom* 43

READING 1.8
William Hasker: *Middle Knowledge, Foreknowledge, and the Openness of God* 54

READING 1.9
Nicholas Wolterstorff: *God Everlasting* 62

READING 1.10
John B. Cobb and David Ray Griffin: *Process Theology: God as Creative-Responsive Love* 70

Chapter 2 Talking About God: The Meaning of Religious Language 83

READING 2.1
Moses Maimonides: *Negative Theology* 85

READING 2.2
Levi Gersonides: *A Critique of Negative Theology* 88

READING 2.3
John Stuart Mill: *The Meaning of the Divine Attributes* 91

READING 2.4
Thomas Aquinas: *The Doctrine of Analogy* 93

READING 2.5
Ira M. Schnall: *Philosophy, Poetry, and the Bible* 96

READING 2.6
Averroes: *Interpreting the Koran Allegorically* 100

READING 2.7
Rudolf Bultmann: *The Task of Demythologizing* 102

READING 2.8
Howard K. Wettstein: *Poetic Imagery and Religious Belief* 106

READING 2.9
Patricia Altenbernd Johnson: *Feminist Christian Philosophy?* 114

Chapter 3 The Theistic Religious Life 126

Understanding Ritual

READING 3.1
Plato: *A Puzzle About Ritual* 129

READING 3.2
Josef Stern: *Gesture and Symbol in Ritual* 131

READING 3.3
Michael J. Murray and Kurt Meyers: *Ask and It Will Be Given to You* 137

Morality and Religion

READING 3.4
Plato: *Defining Piety* 149

READING 3.5
Janine Marie Idziak: *Divine Command Morality* 152

READING 3.6
Genesis 22: *The Binding of Isaac* 158

READING 3.7
Søren Kierkegaard: *Suspending the Ethical* 159

READING 3.8
James Rachels: *Worship and Moral Agency* 164

Chapter 4 Assessing the Case for Theism: Arguments for God's Existence 171

Ontological Arguments

READING 4.1
Anselm of Canterbury: *An Ontological Argument* 176

READING 4.2
Gaunilo: *On Behalf of the Fool* 178

READING 4.3
David Johnson: *A Modal Ontological Argument* 179

Cosmological Arguments

READING 4.4
Thomas Aquinas: *The Five Ways* 183

READING 4.5
Paul Edwards: *The Cosmological Argument* 185

READING 4.6
William Lane Craig: *Philosophical and Scientific Pointers to* Creatio ex Nihilo 194

READING 4.7
William L. Rowe: *Should We Believe the Principle of Sufficient Reason?* 204

Design Arguments

READING 4.8
David Hume: *On An Argument for Design* 206

READING 4.9
Stephen T. Davis: *Fine-Tuning: The New Design Arguments* 222

READING 4.10
Robert Hambourger: *An Argument for Design* 229

READING 4.11
John L. Mackie: **Evolution: An Alternative to the Design Hypothesis** 235

Arguments from Religious Experience

READING 4.12
Jerome I. Gellman: *From Experience to God* 237

READING 4.13
Henry Samuel Levinson and Jonathan W. Malino: *Who's Afraid of a BEE STING?: A Reply to Gellman* 246

READING 4.14
Evan Fales: *Scientific Explanations of Mystical Experiences* 251

Chapter 5 Reasons to Disbelieve: Assessing the Case for Atheism 263

The Varieties of Evil

READING 5.1
William L. Rowe: *The Problem of Evil and Some Varieties of Atheism* 267

READING 5.2
William P. Alston: *The Inductive Argument from Evil and the Human Cognitive Condition* 274

READING 5.3
Eleonore Stump: *The Mirror of Evil* 292

READING 5.4
Richard Swinburne: *A Theodicy of Heaven and Hell* 299

READING 5.5
Michael J. Murray: *Coercion and the Hiddenness of God* 305

Psychological Explanations of Religious Beliefs

READING 5.6
Xenophanes: *Gods in the Image of Humans* 314

READING 5.7
Benedict Spinoza: *How Human Ignorance Leads to Religion* 315

READING 5.8
Ludwig Feuerbach: *Religion as Projection* 317

READING 5.9
Sigmund Freud: *Religion as Wish Fulfillment* 321

READING 5.10
William L. Rowe: *Causation vs. Justification: A Critique of Freud* 327

Chapter 6 Science, Nature, and Religious Belief 331

Science and Religion

READING 6.1
John Haught: *Is Religion Opposed to Science?* 334

READING 6.2
Alvin Plantinga: *When Faith and Reason Clash: Evolution and the Bible* 342

READING 6.3
Howard J. Van Till: *When Faith and Reason Cooperate* 354

READING 6.4
Peter van Inwagen: *Genesis and Evolution* 359

READING 6.5
Robert Audi: *Theism and the Mind-Body Problem* 366

READING 6.6
Richard Swinburne: *The Future of the Soul* 374

READING 6.7
Peter van Inwagen: *The Possibility of Resurrection* 381

Miracles and God's Action in the World

READING 6.8
William P. Alston: *God's Action in the World* 385

READING 6.9
David Hume: *Of Miracles* 395

READING 6.10
Peter van Inwagen: *Of "Of Miracles"* 402

READING 6.11
John Stuart Mill: *Miracles and Undetected Natural Causes* 409

READING 6.12
David Johnson: *Mill's Challenge to Belief in Miracles* 411

READING 6.13
Stephen Griffith: *Miracles and the Shroud of Turin* 414

Chapter 7 Is There a Place for Faith? 424

Evidentialism and the Nature of Faith

READING 7.1
W. K. Clifford: *The Ethics of Belief* 429

READING 7.2
Peter van Inwagen: *"It Is Wrong, Always, Everywhere, and for Anyone, to Believe Anything upon Insufficient Evidence"* 433

READING 7.3
Alvin Plantinga: *Rationality and Religious Belief* 442

READING 7.4
Terence Penelhum: *Do Religious Beliefs Need Grounds?* 457

Pragmatic Approaches

READING 7.5
Joshua L. Golding: *Toward a Pragmatic Conception of Religious Faith* 464

READING 7.6
Blaise Pascal: *The Wager* 474

READING 7.7
William G. Lycan and George N. Schlesinger: *You Bet Your Life: Pascal's Wager Defended* 476

READING 7.8
William James: *The Will to Believe* 483

READING 7.9
Michael Martin: *An Evaluation of James's Argument* 492

On Existentialist Approaches

READING 7.10
Robert Merrihew Adams: *Kierkegaard's Arguments Against Objective Reasoning in Religion* 497

Closing Thoughts

READING 7.11
Steven M. Cahn: *Suppose God Exists* 508

Chapter 8 The Diversity of World Religions 511

READING 8.1
Avishai Margalit: *The Ring: On Religious Pluralism* 515

READING 8.2
John Hick: *Towards a Philosophy of Religious Pluralism* 521

READING 8.3
Alvin Plantinga: *A Defense of Religious Exclusivism* 531

READING 8.4
Joseph Runzo: *God, Commitment, and Other Faiths: Pluralism vs. Relativism* 540

Glossary of Technical Terms 553

Credits 569

Index 573

Preface

Few areas of philosophy have exhibited as much growth and vitality over the past two decades as the philosophy of religion. The range of topics treated has widened significantly, seemingly dead issues have been reopened and invigorated, and the philosophers contributing to the conversation about religion have come to include the best known names in the philosophical profession. Undergraduate curricula and textbooks in philosophy of religion need to keep pace with the evolving variety and richness of the field and to imaginatively expand the budget of problems and approaches they consider.

In compiling this anthology, I have tried to balance the familiar with the novel and the neglected. No collection in the field should omit the usual suspects—classics such as St. Anselm's ontological argument, David Hume's criticism of the design argument, William James's "The Will to Believe," and certain contemporary works. Accordingly, I have not sought to remake the field. Nevertheless, I have made an effort to put forth fresh topics and selections, both classical and contemporary, as well as new emphases and conceptualizations. In all, about half of the selections do not appear in other introductory textbooks. Collectively, these selections create a distinctive look and identity for the text.

The following are some of the book's salient features:

- Selections concerning the attributes of God usually confine themselves to omnipotence, omniscience, and eternity. This text also covers, however, neglected but intuitively engaging questions such as "Is God vain?" "Is it appropriate that God gets angry?" and "What could explain why God forgives sins?"
- The language used in the Bible to describe God's characteristics does not readily fit philosophers' standard conception of a perfect being. Several selections react to this gap and discuss, for example, whether biblical language should be treated as allegory, poetry, or literal truth.
- Several selections deal with ritual. Their inclusion underscores the point that religion is a way of life —not a set of beliefs alone.
- There is substantial treatment of the rapidly growing area of science and religion, including three selections on evolution and Genesis. I have embedded the subjects of miracles and the afterlife, so familiar to philosophers, in a broader treatment of religion and science.
- To help concretize issues that are abstract and laden with hypotheticals, the book presents selections that deal with vivid, actual cases — such as how to explain the patterns on the Shroud of Turin and how mystical experiences might be explained by a contemporary, science-minded nonbeliever.
- The book pays significant attention to explanations of religious beliefs given by the social sciences, which often are thought to undermine the credibility of religious belief. Although not all such accounts are covered (Emile Durkheim's, for example, is omitted), the notions that humans create God in their image (Xenophanes, Ludwig Feuerbach) and that religious beliefs are to be

explained in terms of wish fulfillment (Sigmund Freud) are represented in what I hope is a thought-provoking and accessible fashion.
- The problem of evil is often treated as if it were a problem about suffering alone. Yet there is another feature of the world that seems incompatible with the claim that God is omnipotent, omniscient, and perfectly good—namely, the fact that God's existence seems "hidden." Why would God let people be so ignorant of His existence? This challenge of divine hiddenness, which in a secular age is sensed acutely, is treated in a substantial selection. Likewise explored under the heading of explaining evil is the question of why not everyone attains heaven.

Due to limitations of space, certain areas could not be represented. Nonetheless, the overall product ranges widely and, I believe, relates to religion not only abstractly but as it is lived and experienced in the context of contemporary society. The readings are accessible and often concrete, and they link philosophy of religion to other ideas and concerns in our culture.

Many selections had to be abridged to keep the book to manageable size. My thanks to the readings' authors for their understanding.

I extend my warm thanks to several people who were involved in this project. Gregory Pence of the University of Alabama at Birmingham and Sarah Moyers, formerly philosophy editor at McGraw-Hill, invited me to undertake the reader. Monica Eckman and Jon-David Hague, subsequent philosophy editors at the press, gave wise advice and encouragement. Shannon Morrow, developmental editor, and Susan Brusch, project manager, skillfully guided the book into and through a complicated production process. Maria Maimone efficiently handled permissions to reprint materials. Gregory Pence and a team of anonymous reviewers for McGraw-Hill supplied helpful comments on an early version of some of the chapters. Catherine Fox executed the challenging task of preparing the index.

Jerome I. Gellman of Ben-Gurion University of the Negev in Beersheva, Israel, provided generous and valuable comments and suggestions on drafts of the chapter introductions. My colleague David Johnson kindly reviewed the glossary and part of the text and offered many incisive comments. Steven M. Cahn of the City University of New York supplied, as always, sage counsel on matters both philosophical and editorial. I benefited also from conversations with Matthew Bagger and Wayne Proudfoot of Columbia University and from substantial correspondence with Eleonore Stump of St. Louis University. David Berger of the history department of Brooklyn College and the Graduate Center, the City University of New York, advised me on some of the translations that appear in brackets.

I owe a few general debts as well. Sidney Morgenbesser, with whom I studied extensively as a graduate student at Columbia University, taught me that the rigor and seriousness of philosophy must never crowd out the sheer joy and fun of doing it. In this as in all my work, he is a never-ending source of inspiration and intellectual excitement. Shalom Carmy of Yeshiva University has been a wonderful interlocutor during our long friendship and has influenced my interests and way of thinking vis-á-vis many of the issues represented in this book.

Several students at Stern College for Women, Yeshiva University, played a role in the book's production. Netanella Cohen, Rebecca Feldman, and Devorah Klein ably drafted some of the introductions and study questions that accompany the selections. Meira Reinstein provided valuable reactions to many aspects of the book and assisted superbly in editing the manuscript and page proofs. My students over the years in the courses "Religion and Philosophy" and "Science and Religion" at Stern College for Women have, through their challenging questions and impressive insights, guided my planning of the volume.

I am grateful to Dr. Karen Bacon, Dean of Stern College for Women, and Dr. Morton Lowengrub, vice-president for Academic Affairs at Yeshiva University, for their steady support of my scholarly work. Dr. Norman Lamm, president of Yeshiva University, first exposed me to the complexities of theology and religious philosophy when I was a teenager, and over the years has enriched and stimulated my thinking. His continuing interest in my work is profoundly appreciated.

The rabbis of the *midrash* teach: "the very last is the most dear." Ever since she allowed herself over thirty years ago to be drawn into hearing prattle about grue emeralds, possible persons, and non-dogs, my wife Chani has shown extraordinary tolerance for the strange language and thought patterns of the philosophical profession, not to mention a remarkable ability to acclimate to the odd sense of humor it breeds. Personifying wisdom, understanding, and empathy, she is a model of steadfast devotion and love. To her I dedicate this volume, an inadequate but heartfelt gesture of appreciation for her role in shaping it—and my life.

David Shatz
New York
August 2001

Notes on the Format

- Technical terms are bolded at their first occurrence in a selection and are explained in the Glossary of Technical Terms.
- Normally, bracketed translations and notes are the editor's, except when they appear within quotations or parentheses, in which case they are the author's or translator's. Exceptions are indicated either in the selection or in the editor's introduction to it.
- Study questions preceded by an asterisk require extra reflection and thought. Other questions call for exposition based on reading the essay.
- Each chapter in this book includes suggestions for further reading. Generally, I have emphasized books, including anthologies. To economize on space, I usually have not included books from which the selections in this anthology are taken, even if other essays in those volumes are relevant. Therefore, you should check the list of credits for additional book references. For readers interested in finding still more references, an extremely useful tool is Robert G. Wolf, *Analytic Philosophy of Religion: A Bibliography 1940–1996* (Philosophy Documentation Center, 1998). For after 1996, check *The Philosopher's Index* (Philosophy Documentation Center, Charlottesville, Virginia), available in both print and CD-ROM versions. Excellent brief surveys of virtually all topics in the philosophy of religion are found in Philip L. Quinn and Charles Taliaferro, eds., A *Companion to Philosophy of Religion* (Blackwell, 1997).

Introduction: What Is the Philosophy of Religion?

Leaf through any college catalogue, and chances are that you will find a significant number of courses that treat the subject of religion. You might find "History of Religions," "Psychology of Religion," or "Sociology of Religion," along with courses about specific religions—Christianity, Islam, Judaism, Buddhism, Hinduism, Taoism. Sometimes these courses are given by a department called religion, other times they are offered by departments such as history, psychology, and sociology.

Suppose that, when you turn to the philosophy entries in the catalogue, you find a listing for "philosophy of religion" (since you are using this book, it is likely that your school offers such a course). What should you expect in the course? What will distinguish this class from others? What questions will it cover that other disciplines do not? What does philosophy seek to contribute to the study of religion that history, psychology, and sociology do not?

The beginnings of an answer to these questions may be found in the distinction between describing something and evaluating it. Whereas history, psychology, and sociology aim principally to describe their subjects, philosophy is primarily an evaluative discipline. For example, philosophy of religion does not take, as its main task, tracing the historical development of Christianity out of Judaism (that belongs to the history of religion), or determining whether people who hold religious beliefs are happier than nonbelievers are (a task of psychology of religion). It is not concerned with discovering what percentage of Americans believe in God (this is a question in the sociology of religion), or finding out how many religions there are, when they developed, and how they are distributed across the globe (which are inquiries into the history and sociology of religion). All these questions *enter into* philosophy of religion—indeed, some are covered in this book—but, when they do so, it is only because they serve a larger end that guides the discipline. That larger aim is to evaluate impartially the beliefs that are held by people who are adherents of religions. Are those beliefs true? Are they rationally justified?[1] Philosophy of religion is *the critical evaluation of religious beliefs, practices, and concepts.*[2]

"Critical evaluation" doesn't mean a negative or antagonistic evaluation; it means an evaluation conducted using the tools of reason in an impartial fashion, an analysis that may turn out either favorable or unfavorable to religious beliefs, concepts, and practices. Philosophy of religion asks such questions as: "Are there good reasons for believing in God?" and "Does the existence of evil in the world show that God does not exist?". Alone among the disciplines, it tries to see whether belief in God and other religious beliefs are supported by good reasons or whether, to the contrary, there are good reasons to *deny* the claims of religion (for example, if some of

[1]As we will see in chapter 7, the questions *is it true that p* and *is it rational to believe that p* are not the same.

[2]For the basics of this definition, I am indebted to William L. Rowe, *Philosophy of Religion: An Introduction,* 2d ed. (Belmont, CA: Wadsworth, 1993), 2. There Rowe also discusses how philosophy of religion differs from **theology**.

these claims contradict each other). It also examines the possibility that religious belief could be rational even in the absence of reasons. In addition, philosophy of religion investigates whether practices such as prayer and other rituals are rational practices. What is their meaning and purpose? Depending upon the outcome of an individual's evaluation, the person may wind up a believer in God (a theist), someone who denies that God exists (an atheist), or someone who suspends belief about the question (an **agnostic**); furthermore, different people will opt for different levels of ritual practice.

Besides assessing religious beliefs, philosophy of religion identifies major concepts in religions such as **omnipotence** (all-powerfulness), **resurrection,** faith, and miracles, and it seeks to define such terms with precision. These concepts enter into beliefs such as *God is omnipotent, resurrection is possible, faith is a virtue,* and *miracles occur.* The clarification of concepts is an important inquiry not only because it elucidates what religious people believe, but also because, by examining religious concepts and the beliefs in which they figure, we can determine whether a given concept or belief is coherent or, alternatively, self-contradictory. For example, some philosophers argue that the concept of omnipotence is self-contradictory; by this, they mean that the statement "S is omnipotent" is necessarily false for any being S.[3]

Although philosophy of religion has a distinctive focus, we must not infer that it carries on its work without the aid of history, psychology, and sociology. Far from it. In the first place, how does the philosopher choose what beliefs to examine, if not by drawing on **empirical** disciplines that describe what adherents of a religion believe and practice? Furthermore, many proposed **arguments** for God's existence begin with empirical premises.[4] For instance, some philosophers argue that the fact that many people have claimed to experience God provides adequate reason to believe that God exists. Thus, the argument begins with a description (*viz.*, of what people have reported). To evaluate this argument properly, many empirical questions must be addressed: Are the experiences reported by Christians, Jews, and Muslims sufficiently alike? Are there plausible biological, sociological, or psychological explanations of how such experiences come about, so that resorting to God's existence to explain the experiences is unnecessary? It is not at all the case, then, that philosophy of religion is *exclusively* an evaluative enterprise, with no descriptive aspect at all. But it is the case that *the philosopher is interested in empirical findings for the sake of answering a larger question.* The philosopher wants to know what empirical findings tell us about whether the claims of religion are true and/or rational.

Religion is one of those terms that is enormously difficult to define but very easy to identify examples of. One could easily name Christianity, Islam, Judaism, Hinduism, Buddhism, Shinto, and Taoism. Among the definitions we find of *religion* are:

> . . . an understanding of the universe, together with an appropriate way of living within it, which involves reference beyond the natural world to God or gods or to the Absolute or to a transcendent order or process. (John Hick, *God and the Universe of Faiths* [London: MacMillan Press, 1973], p. 133.)

> . . . a set of beliefs, actions and emotions, both personal and corporate, organized around the concept of an ultimate Reality. (Michael Peterson, William Hasker, Bruce Reichenbach, and David Basinger, *Reason and Religious Belief* [New York: Oxford University Press, 1991], p. 4.)

> . . . a conceptual system that provides an interpretation of the world and the place of human beings in it, bases an account of how life should be lived given that interpretation, and expresses this interpretation and lifestyle in a set of rituals, institutions,

[3]One such **argument** goes: suppose *S is omnipotent* is defined as *for any task t, S can perform t.* Can S create a stone that S cannot lift? If S can create such a stone, S is not omnipotent, for there is a task S cannot perform—namely, lift that stone. If S cannot create such a stone, then there is something S cannot do—namely, create such a stone. But either S can create such a stone or S cannot. If S can create such a stone, then S is not omnipotent. And, if S cannot create such a stone, then again S is not omnipotent. Either way, therefore, S is not omnipotent. What the argument seeks to show is that no being can be omnipotent.

[4]The crucial notion of an argument is clarified in the introduction to Chapter 4. For the moment, take an argument to be a line of reasoning leading to a conclusion.

> and practices. (Keith Yandell, *Philosophy of Religion: A Contemporary Introduction* [London and New York: Routledge, 1997], p. 16.)
>
> . . . a set of symbols and rituals, myths and stories, concepts and truth-claims, which a community believes gives ultimate meaning to life, via its connection to a transcendent God or Ultimate Reality *beyond* the natural order. (Joseph Runzo, in this volume, Reading 8.4)

This book will not try to improve on these definitions. We can identify the religions on which we focus without settling what the term *religion* means. There are many religions throughout the world, and many subdivisions within each religion. Nevertheless, we will concentrate on the beliefs and practices typical of *classical theism*. This term refers to the view that God exists, where God is conceived in accordance with beliefs of Christianity, Islam, and Judaism. (In the introduction to chapter 1, we will say more about the nature of God.)

Our focus on classical theism obviously is not meant to belittle the claims made by other, nontheistic religions or the way they handle some of the problems that hound classical theism (such as evil and the afterlife). Some Eastern religions adopt the view that there is an ultimate reality that is *im*personal rather than personal, as in theism. Some religions further deny that reality is differentiated, that there are distinct individuals. Instead, they assert that reality is a single whole and that differentiation and individuality are illusions. Surely these approaches are fascinating and warrant a full discussion; our Western **metaphysical** outlook is in for a rude awakening when we see alternative world views so radically opposed to it. At the same time, it is simply foolhardy to try to do justice in a single textbook both to the tremendous growth that has taken place in discussions of classical theism, ranging over problems and approaches virtually unheard of in past decades, as well as to the enormously rich structure and content of Buddhism, Hinduism, Taoism, and other Eastern religions. As it is, numerous topics and writings in classical theism had to be omitted due to space considerations. Nevertheless, the closing chapter of the book, "The Diversity of World Religions," ought to raise the consciousness of readers who come from a setting in which Christianity and Judaism dominate attention. The chapter suggests that a reflective Christian and Jew will have to ponder and reponder the existence of so many alternative world views and take account of them in understanding and justifying his or her own convictions.

Three decades ago, textbooks in philosophy of religion looked quite different from this one. Arguments for and against God's existence and questions about religious language dominated; very little was to be found about ritual or science and religion; the notion that religious belief might be justified in the absence of rational proofs had not taken root, and the question of how other religions should be regarded was rarely examined. Religion is on the rise in America, affecting much of our public life, grabbing headlines, and creating ever rising demands for more discussion and explanation. It is hoped that this text will provide you with an enhanced understanding of the intellectual underpinnings of religion and an enhanced appreciation of the power and sophistication of philosophers who have argued either for or against the claims of religion. The debate over the tenets of theism hopefully will prove to be exciting and balanced.

The structure of this book is as follows. The first chapter tackles questions about the concepts and language through which theistic traditions talk about God. The readings seek to clarify beliefs of theists about God's capacity to forgive, God's power, God's knowledge, and several other of the attributes claimed for God. In the readings for chapter 2, authors attempt to discover, more generally, whether biblical language and other descriptions of God in theistic traditions should be taken literally or instead are amenable to figurative or poetic interpretation (and, if so, what they mean). Chapter 3 moves away from beliefs and seeks to clarify and explain the practices of theists. These include both ritual practices and ethical conduct. Central in the debate that emerges about ethics is whether morality is dependent on religion or, instead, a binding ethics that is independent of religion is possible.

Chapters 4 and 5 directly assess the case for and against belief in God. The authors in chapter 4 present or contest some of the classic arguments *for* God's existence, whereas those in chapter 5 present or contest arguments *against* God's existence. The latter include the problem of evil, God's hiddenness (i.e., the fact that God's existence is not obvious), and the possibility that religious beliefs and experiences can be explained by psychological factors, such as human ignorance of natural causes, people's projection of themselves onto the world, and fear of nature.

Chapter 6 is devoted to the ways in which a theistic world view resembles and differs from a scientific view. The authors suggest how science, especially contemporary science, bears on the assessment of theistic belief, with an emphasis on the origins of the world, the prospects for life after death in the light of modern science, and the possibility of divine intervention in the world (by way of miracles).

Chapter 7 raises a question that profoundly affects how we assess the rationality of religious belief. Can a belief or set of beliefs be rational even if the believer does not have adequate evidence or argument for it? The readings in the chapter focus on the fact that there are secular beliefs that people hold for which they lack argument and adequate evidence, and on whether this situation shows that religious belief can be rational even without argument and evidence. The concluding chapter (8) explores the implications of the fact that there are so many diverse religions across the globe. How should a person who believes in one religion approach the claims of other religions? And does the existence of so many candidates for the true religion undermine the credibility of all religions?

Despite the fact that nearly eighty readings appear in this book, and that the chapter introductions and study questions raise still further points and issues, this text does not provide more than an entree into the vast field of philosophy of religion. No single text could. Never mind that there are so many religions other than theistic ones. Even in connection with theism, new problems, new issues, new insights, and new arguments arise continually in circles of professional philosophy, serving as testimony to both the immense creativity of philosophers and our rapidly changing world. The suggestions for further reading at the end of each chapter will take you further along if you so desire; more often than not, philosophical engagement with religion proves to be a life's work.

Enjoy the journey.

CHAPTER 1

The Concept of God

As noted in the general introduction to this book, much work in philosophy of religion centers on theistic religions—religions whose focus is a supreme being known as God. Adherents of these religions face the demanding question, what is this being like? What characteristics or attributes does God possess?

Over the centuries, a certain portrait of God has become deeply entrenched among philosophers.[1] God is said to be—by definition and hence necessarily—a *perfect* being. Etymologically, *perfect* means whole, complete, free of defect. Perhaps the most famous articulation of **perfect being theology** is the definition of God offered by St. Anselm of Canterbury (1033–1109): God is *the being than whom none greater can be conceived*—in other words (to use a contemporary formulation), the *greatest possible being.* Thomas V. Morris expands on this root notion:

> God is to be thought of most centrally as a being with the greatest possible array of compossible [mutually possible] great-making properties, where a great-making property is understood, roughly, as a property it is intrinsically good to have. . . . Put another way, to have a great-making property is, so far forth, to have a certain positive status or metaphysical stature which is in no way relationally derivative from external circumstances. . . . In considering candidate properties for inclusion in our overall conception of divinity, we first consult our value intuitions to determine, at least prima facie, which of those properties are to be considered great-making properties.[2]

In other words, in perfect being theology, our concept of God is constructed out of judgments concerning the intrinsic value of certain properties. We assign to God those attributes that we regard as great-making. Thus, according to perfect being theology, any attribute that is assigned to God flows logically from one core attribute: perfection. It seems fair to say, at least initially, that perfect being theology presupposes the ability of human beings to form correct value judgments about great-making properties.

Perfection can be construed in several ways, but philosophers of religion commonly start their listing of divine properties with what might be called "the three

[1]Some philosophers maintain that the expression *God* is a proper name used to *refer to* a certain beings but lacking a *connotation* or *meaning*—lacking, that is, a description or set of descriptions that *define* the word. Thus, *God* cannot be defined. This position reflects a possible application of an influential theory about proper names associated with Saul Kripke and other contemporary philosophers. Despite its interest and importance, this position will be set aside in examining the essays in this and other chapters.

[2]Thomas V. Morris, "Defining the Divine," in *Definitions and Definability: Philosophical Perspectives,* ed. James H. Fetzer, David Shatz, and George N. Schlesinger (Dordrecht, The Netherlands: Kluwer, 1991), 278.

omnis." God is necessarily all-powerful **(omnipotent);** necessarily all-knowing (**omniscient**—*scientia* is the Latin term for knowledge); and necessarily all-good **(omnibenevolent).** The three omnis, to be sure, are not endorsed by all religious thinkers. For example, the nineteenth-century British philosopher John Stuart Mill was troubled by how a being who is omnipotent, omniscient, and omnibenevolent could allow evil, so he "deprived" God of one of these attributes, omnipotence. Thereby, Mill "solved" the problem of evil, but at the price of surrendering God's claim to perfection. Other theists doubt whether the concept of omnipotence is even coherent, or whether God can know the future choices human beings will make, as omniscience seems to require. Nonetheless, the view that God is omnipotent, omniscient, and omnibenevolent and that God has these properties necessarily is, though not unanimously held, very widely accepted.

There is more to the concept of the perfect God than the three omnis, however. Theists generally agree that, in contrast to other beings, God does not come into being at one point in time and perish at another. God's existence has no beginning and no end. Furthermore, they often say that, in contrast to other things, God is a **necessary being.** Some mean by this a being whose existence is not dependent on other beings but is self-explained; others understand *God is a necessary being* to mean that the proposition *God exists* is a **necessary truth,** and that God exists in all possible worlds. Again, most theists say that God created and sustains the universe and that God has a large measure of control over events. But there is considerable controversy over whether God has certain other characteristics, because there is considerable difficulty in saying whether those characteristics reflect perfection.

Consider, for example, whether God gets angry or experiences feelings of compassion, sadness, sympathy, and regret. Certainly the Bible frequently speaks about God this way, and a literal reading of these authoritative texts would lead to the view that God has feelings like those we humans have. Yet, through a long period in the history of philosophy, major thinkers have insisted that God is **impassible**—that is, incapable of experiencing emotions or passions. Why would so many thinkers feel impelled to endorse a view that is contrary to the literal meaning of so many biblical texts? And why, for example, did the Council of Chalcedon in 451 C.E. declare that the synod "repels from the sacred assembly those who dare to say that the Godhead of the only-begotten is capable of suffering"?

The answer to this question lies in the assumptions that these thinkers made about perfection. Dating back to Plato and Aristotle, indeed earlier, the perfect was identified as that which is **immutable,** unchanging, as well as that which is impervious to external influences. Emotions necessarily involve change, and they arise in response to external circumstances. Hence, emotions are not part of the life of a perfect being such as God. As for the Bible's language implying otherwise, a theist could maintain that terms such as *merciful* refer only to God's actions or effects, not to God's inner states. Alternatively, it might be said that biblical expressions that imply **anthropopathism** (the view that God has emotions[3]) should be taken as figures of speech, not literal attributions. Human beings need a way to think about God, and drawing on the terms we use to describe human beings is our only recourse. That humans use the anthropopathic expressions says more about the users of religious language—their need for vivid imagery—than about God.

However an advocate of the view that God is impassible chooses to reconcile that view with Scripture, a more fundamental question arises. Which is better—to be changeless and impervious to external influence or to be adaptive and responsive to people and events? This value judgment will determine which attribute God is assigned—changelessness or instead change and responsiveness. Again, many philosophers say that God exists outside of time. Surely this helps make God unique and enhances God's transcendence. But is existing outside of time a perfection? Could a timeless being know which events are happening *now?* Could that being intervene at a moment in time? Here

[3]The essays in this book generally use the term *anthropomorphism* for *both* the view that God has human form *and* the view that God has human (or humanlike) emotions. Generally I shall use separate words for these distinct assertions.

again the value judgment that timelessness is a perfection can be—and has been—debated, along with whether the biblical God is depicted as timeless. In fact, in this spirit one could go back to the three omnis and ask, for example, whether the power to do *any* logically coherent task really is a great-making property. Many imaginable evil acts reflect great power in the perpetrator, but is the ability to do such acts a great-making characteristic? And does the Bible say that God can do literally *everything?*

The essays in this chapter grapple with the meanings of individual divine attributes and thereby reveal the problematics of perfection. We begin with an example of perfect being theology, the assertion of St. Thomas Aquinas that God cannot undergo passions, for God is pure **actuality,** and passions imply **potentiality.** St. Anselm of Canterbury gives a brief statement of what it means to say that God is merciful, maintaining that this phrase refers to the effects God brings about, not to God's inner states. Next, however, Robert Oakes criticizes the tradition that denies that God has emotions. He identifies arguments used to generate this view, offers refutations of them, and finally constructs an alternative notion of what it is to be infallible with regard to emotions.

The next two selections take up objections to the claim that God is perfect which derive from specific doctrines held by theists. Charles Taliaferro confronts the charge that, because God created humans in God's image, wants people to worship Him, and tries to be the one to redeem the world, God is therefore vain—surely an imperfection. Taliaferro seeks to defend God against that charge. Anne C. Minas then argues for the surprising view that a perfect being could not forgive sin; to err is human, but, in her view, to forgive is decidely not divine. Thus, if God is perfect, God cannot forgive sin; if God does forgive sin, God must be imperfect.

Return now to two other claims we noted are thought to be central to theism: that God is omnipotent and that God is omniscient. Peter Geach, a theist, argues against the attribution of omnipotence to God, for there are certain things God cannot do because of God's nature. God cannot sin, for example, or self-destruct. Therefore, Geach asserts, God is not omnipotent. Nevertheless, Geach says, God is almighty, which means that God controls all things—a distinction Geach seeks to explain.

Omniscience likewise proves to be a difficult attribute to assign to God. If God knows everything, then God has **foreknowledge** of our actions. God has known forever what each of us will do in any given slice of the future. How then can we human beings perform acts freely? To preserve human freedom, must we deny that God has foreknowledge? And, would lacking foreknowledge necessarily be an imperfection in God? William L. Rowe's essay addresses several solutions to this well-known conundrum. Expanding on the problems generated by human free will, William Hasker examines the relationship between human freedom and God's control over events. Hasker raises a variety of possibilities for understanding God's knowledge and control and shows, among other things, that the notion of simple foreknowledge is not robust enough to allow for God to control the course of events. After considering various models, Hasker advocates the idea of an **open God,** a God who voluntarily relinquishes a significant degree of control to human beings and neither can ensure that events will occur exactly as God would like, nor even—despite His omniscience!—know what human beings will choose. He cannot know, therefore, whether the future will conform to His plans. God takes risks. The "open God" idea is a significant break with perfect being theology.

The perfect being tradition regards God as immutable. This often results in God's being said to be **eternal** in the sense of *timeless,* outside of time; God has no temporal parts and is not subject to the law that no being can exist in two times at once. (Rowe mentions that some theologians invoke God's timelessness as a solution to the problem of foreknowledge and free will.) Nicholas Wolterstorff challenges the thesis that God is timeless, pointing to, among other things, its apparent inconsistency with biblical portrayals of God as being in time. Wolterstorff says that God is **everlasting** (without beginning or end) but not eternal (i.e., not outside of time).

Even more than Hasker's and Wolterstorff's, the essay by John B. Cobb and David Ray Griffin represents a sharp departure from assertions of classical theism. A fundamental aspect of reality, they assert, is *process,* and this applies even to divine reality. On the basis of this, Cobb and Griffin deny, for example, that God is immutable, but also that God is omniscient and that God controls all things. In their **process theology,** they champion a view of God as creative-responsive love. Their approach has profound implications for our understanding of evil, of prayer, and of other focal issues in the philosophy of religion.

Readers should note that all these essays reflect a concern with two criteria, philosophical cogency and fidelity to biblical teaching. But there is far more to perfect being theology than indicated to this point. For example, perfect being theology is associated with the difficult-sounding notion that God is metaphysically ***simple,*** without parts, and does not even have separate attributes. In addition, some theists resist the very attempt to characterize God, saying that God lies beyond our conceptual grasp. That approach seems to stop in its tracks any attempt to explain God's characteristics, except insofar as we preface such explanations with the words "from a human perspective, it seems that God is . . . ." Concerns such as these motivate various attempts to construe religious language in a manner that firmly establishes a difference between what we mean by, for instance, *wise* when we say "God is wise" and what we mean by *wise* when we say "Socrates is wise." But making God very distant from our conceptual range has costs of its own. These further problems and approaches toward speaking about God will be addressed in chapter 2.

READING 1.1

The Divine Impassibility

Thomas Aquinas

St. Thomas Aquinas (1225–1274) has had a monumental influence on Christian thought, in particular, on the version of Catholic philosophy and theology known as **Thomism.** *In this selection from Book One, chapter 89, of his* Summa Contra Gentiles, *Aquinas argues that God cannot have "the passions of the appetites." A perfect being is* **immutable** *(unchangeable), but a being who has passions of the appetites changes as those passions shift. In Aquinas's terms, God is perfect, and perfection excludes change and mere* **potency** *(potentiality). God is pure* **act** *(pure actuality) and is free from potency.*

Certain passions cannot belong to God not only because the **genus** *(general category) of passion is excluded from God but also because those specific passions (the* **species***) would be unbefitting for God to possess for other reasons. Aquinas explains why sorrow, pain, envy, and anger are unbefitting in God. He says also that hope cannot belong to God, for some good is not yet possessed by the being who hopes, whereas God is already perfect. Repentance (or regret) implies both sadness and a change of affection and, for that reason, cannot be attributed to God, either.*

At the selection's end, Aquinas says that joy and delight are not repugnant to the divine perfection and that these are in God. Subsequently, in the Summa Contra Gentiles *(chapters 90–91 of Book One) as well as in his* Summa Theologiae *(or* Summa Theologica*) (part 1, questions 20–21), Aquinas allows that God also has love (see study question 4). These emotions can be in God because they are not passions of the sensitive appetites—that is, of the body. Rather, they belong to the will, which Aquinas conceives of as intellective appetite. In addition, in both works he concedes that God is said to have mercy and anger but insists that these terms are used to refer to the effects of God's will, not God's inner states. This interpretation is expressed with regard to mercy by Aquinas's predecessor, St. Anselm, in the selection that follows this one. Thus, although Aquinas does not assign passions to God, in his sense of passions of the sensitive appetites, the sweeping claim that Aquinas believes emotions cannot be ascribed to God is not accurate. It all depends on which emotions are in question and on how one understands the ascription.*

CHAPTER 89.

That in God There Are Not the Passions of the Appetites

[1] From what has preceded[1] we can know that the passions of the appetites are not in God.

[2] Now, according to intellective appetite there is no passion, but only according to sensitive appetite, as is proved in *Physics* vii.[2] But no such appetite can be in God, since He does not have sensitive knowledge, as is manifest from what has been said above.[3] Therefore, there is no passion of the appetite in God.

[3] Moreover, every passion of the appetite takes place through some bodily change, for example, the contraction or distension of the heart, or something of the sort. Now, none of this can take place in God, since He is not a body to a power in a body, as was shown above.[4] There is, therefore, no passion of the appetite in Him.

[1][See the ensuing references.—Ed.]

[2]Aristotle, *Physics* vii, 3 (246b 20).

[3]Book 1, ch. 44.

[4]Book 1, ch. 20.

[4] Again, in every passion of the appetite the patient is somehow drawn out of his usual, calm, or connatural disposition. A sign of this is that such passions, if intensified, bring death to animals, But it is not possible for God to be somehow drawn outside His natural condition, since He is absolutely **immutable,** as has been shown.[5] It appears then, that such passions cannot be found in God. . . .

[6] Furthermore, every passion belongs to something existing in **potency.** But God is completely free from potency, since He is pure **act.** God, therefore, is solely agent, and in no way does any passion have a place in Him.

[7] Thus, therefore, by reason of its **genus,** passion is excluded in God.

[8] Some passions, however, are excluded from God not only by reason of their genus, but also by reason of their **species.** For every passion is specified by its object. That passion, therefore, whose subject is absolutely unbefitting to God is removed from God even according to the nature of its proper species.

[9] Such a passion, however, is *sorrow* or *pain,* for its subject is the already present evil, just as the object of *joy* is the good present and possessed. Sorrow and pain, therefore, of their very nature cannot be found in God.

[10] Furthermore, the notion of the object of a given passion is derived not only from good and evil, but also from the fact that one is disposed in a certain way towards one of them. For it is thus that *hope* and *joy* differ. If, then the mode itself in which one is disposed toward the object that is included in the notion of passion is not befitting to God, neither can the passion itself befit Him, even through the nature of its proper species. Now, although hope has as its object something good, yet it is not a good already possessed, but one to be possessed. This cannot befit God, because of His perfection, which is so great that nothing can be added to it.[6] *Hope,* therefore, cannot be found in God, even by reason of its species. And likewise, neither can the *desire* of something not possessed.

[11] Moreover, just as the divine perfection excludes from God the potency of the addition of some good to be obtained, so likewise, and all the more, does it exclude the potency to evil. *Fear* has reference to the evil that can threaten, as hope has reference to a good to be obtained. By a twofold reason of its species, therefore, is fear excluded from God: both because it belongs only to one existing in potency and because it has for its object a threatening evil.

[12] Again, *repentance* implies a change of affection. Therefore, the nature of repentance likewise is repugnant to God, not only because it is a species of sadness, but also because it implies a change of will.

[13] Furthermore, without an error of the cognitive power it is impossible that what is good be apprehended as evil. Nor is it possible that the evil of one be the good of another, except among particular goods in which "the corruption of one is the generation of another."[7] But the universal good does not lose anything because of the existence of some particular good, but is rather mirrored by each one. God, however, is the universal good, and by participating in His likeness all things are called good.[8] The evil of no thing, therefore, can be His good. Nor is it possible that what is absolutely good, and is not evil to itself, He should apprehend as something evil; for His knowledge is without error, as has been shown.[9] *Envy,* therefore, cannot be found in God, even according to the nature of its species, not only because it is a species of sadness, but also because it is saddened by the good of another and thus takes his good as its own evil.

[14] Moreover, to be saddened over a good and to seek evil are of the same nature, for the first arises because the good is judged to be evil, while the second arises because evil is judged to be good. *Anger* is the appetite of another's evil for the sake of revenge. Anger, therefore, is far from God according to the nature of its species, not only because it is an effect of sadness, but likewise because it is an appetite for revenge arising from sadness due to an injury received.

[5] Book 1, ch. 13, ¶28.
[6] See Book 1, ch. 28

[7] Aristotle, *Physics* iii, 8 (208a 10).
[8] See Book 1, ch. 29.
[9] Book 1, ch. 61.

[15] Again, whatever other passions are species of these or are caused by them, are for the same reason removed from God.

CHAPTER 90.

That in God There Are Delight and Joy, But They Are Not Opposed to the Divine Perfection

[1] There are certain passions which, though they do not befit God as passions, do not signify anything by the nature of their species that is repugnant to the divine perfection.

[2] Among these passions are *joy* and *delight.* Delight is of a present good. Neither, therefore, by reason of its object, which is a good, nor by reason of its disposition towards its object, which is possessed in act, is joy, according to the nature of its species, repugnant to the divine perfection.

[3] From this it is manifest that joy or delight is properly in God. For just as the apprehended good and evil are the object of sensible appetite, so, too, are they of intellective appetite. It belongs to both to seek good and avoid evil, whether truly or by estimation. There is the difference that the object of intellective appetite is more common than that of the sensitive appetite, because intellective appetite has reference to good and evil absolutely, whereas sensitive appetite has reference to good or evil according to the sense. So, too, the object of the intellect is more common than that of the sense. But the operations of appetite derive their species from their objects. Hence, there are found in intellective appetite, which is the will, operations that in the nature of their species are similar to the operations of the sensitive appetite, differing in that in the sensitive appetite there are passions because of its union to a bodily organ, whereas in the intellective appetite there are simple operations; for just as through the passion of fear, which resides in the sensitive appetite, someone flees a future evil, so without passion the intellective appetite does the same thing. Since, then, joy and delight are not repugnant to God according to their species, but only in so far as they are passions, and since they are found in the will according to their species but not as passions, it remains that they are not lacking even to the divine will. . . .

STUDY QUESTIONS

1. What are Aquinas's general arguments for saying that God does not have passions?
2. Aquinas writes, "Some passions, however, are excluded from God not only by reason of their genus, but also by reason of their species." What does he mean? What passions is he referring to, and why are they "excluded from God . . . also by reason of their species"?
3. Aquinas thinks that joy and delight are in God. What is his explanation of this point, based on the excerpted remarks? Do you find this explanation cogent? Why or why not? (You might want to compare your reply to this question with your reply to question 4.)
4. *As noted in the introduction to the selection, Aquinas attributes love to God, despite his denying that God has passions. In his *Summa Theologiae,* (or *Summa Theologica*) Pt. 1, question 20, article 1, he takes up the following objection:

> It seems that love does not exist in God. For in God there are no passions. Now love is a passion. Therefore love is not in God.

He replies:

> The cognitive faculty does not move except through the medium of the appetitive. . . . In ourselves, the intellectual appetite, or the will as it is called, moves through the medium of the sensitive appetite. Hence, in us the sensitive appetite is the proximate motive-force of our bodies. Some bodily change therefore always accompanies an act of the sensitive appetite. . . . Therefore acts of the sensitive appetite, inasmuch as they have annexed to them some bodily change, are called passions; whereas acts of the will are not so called. Love, therefore, and joy and delight are passions; in so far as they denote acts of the intellective appetite, they are not passions. It is in this latter sense that they are in God.

He also states that

> an act of love always tends toward two things: to the good that one wills, and to the person for whom one wills it; since to love a person is to wish that person good.

Explain these remarks as best as you can, including in your account the conception of love that you think is explicit or implicit in them. Do you find this conception cogent? Do you see any difficulties with it? If so, can you solve those difficulties? Finally, why might it be important for a theist, especially a Christian, to ascribe love to God? (The translation of the passage is from the edition of the *Summa Theologica* by the Fathers of the English Dominican Province [New York, Boston, Cincinnati, Chicago, San Francisco: Benziger Brothers, 1947].)

5. *Theists speak of the importance of *imitatio dei*, the imitation or emulation of God. Given Aquinas's views, in what respect do you think human beings should imitate God, and in what respects should they not? (In Christian thought, imitation of God is often said to be imitation or emulation of the Son, not of the Father. This question may help you understand why a Christian might draw that distinction.)

READING 1.2

How God Is Both Merciful and Impassible

Anselm of Canterbury

St. Anselm, archbishop of Canterbury (1033–1109), characterized God as a perfect being, a being than whom none greater can be conceived. Although best known for a highly controversial proof that such a being exists, known as the **ontological argument** *(see Readings 4.1–4.3), his writing also includes valuable elucidations of the attributes of God and responses to the puzzles they generate.*

Like the later figure, Thomas Aquinas, Anselm maintains that undergoing passions is inconsistent with perfection, so God is **impassible.** *If so, however, what do statements such as "God is merciful" mean? St. Anselm replies (as Aquinas does elsewhere) that, when theists say, "God is merciful," they are referring not to an emotion of mercy that God experiences but, rather, to God's acts or effects. Similarly, God is called compassionate not because God feels compassion but because an effect of God's actions is that sinners are saved. The idea that God suffers and is pained over the evils of the world likewise must be understood in terms of God's effects. In this selection, St. Anselm asserts the position but does not argue for it; however, the selection suggests a standard way for those who think God is* **impassible** *to interpret statements that ascribe passion to God.*

But how are you both merciful and **impassible?** For if you are impassible, you do not feel compassion, and if you do not feel compassion, your heart is not sorrowful out of compassion for sorrow; and that is what being merciful is. But if you are not merciful, how is it that you are such a comfort to the sorrowful?

So how, Lord, are you both merciful and not merciful? Is it not because you are merciful in relation to us but not in relation to yourself? You are indeed merciful according to what we feel, but not according to what you feel. For when you look with favor upon us in our sorrow, we feel the effect of mercy, but you do not feel the emotion of mercy. So you are merciful, because you save the sorrowful and spare those who sin against you; but you are also not merciful, because you are not affected with any feeling of compassion for sorrow.

STUDY QUESTIONS

1. St. Anselm states that God is both merciful and impassible. How does he explain this seemingly self-contradictory position?
2. Anselm explains that *God is compassionate* must be understood in terms of the effects of God's actions that we perceive. He mentions, as an example, the saving of sinners. Can you think of specific examples of compassion exemplified in the world and thus (for Anselm) attributable to God? Can you think of examples that would justify the claim *God is cruel?* If you answered yes to both questions, why should God, on St. Anselm's theory, be thought of as compassionate but not as cruel?
3. What role does the notion of divine suffering play in Christianity? (cf. reading 1.1, question 5.)
4. *Theists speak of the importance of *imitatio dei,* the imitation or emulation of God. What are the implications of St. Anselm's position for this concept? (cf. reading 1.1, question 5.)

READING 1.3

The Wrath of God

Robert Oakes

According to the tradition of perfect being theology (a tradition that boasts, among other adherents, St. Augustine, St. Anselm, St. Thomas Aquinas, and the Jewish philosopher Moses Maimonides), a being's capacity for emotion is a sign of imperfection, so God is necessarily **impassible.** *In this selection, Robert Oakes (St. Louis University) challenges the Theologically Sophisticated Thesis (TST) of divine impassibility and defends instead the Theologically Naive Thesis that it is conceptually proper to ascribe to God an affective capacity (a capacity for emotions). Oakes identifies three arguments used by TST's defenders and submits that they are not convincing. In the course of discussion, he rejects the doctrine of divine immutability and suggests that the Bible does not subscribe to this doctrine. Holding that it is conceptually proper to ascribe affective capacity to God, Oakes insists that God is affectively infallible, for God always has the appropriate affective response—God experiences the emotion appropriate to the situation, with the appropriate intensity.*

> *. . . I experience as much as anyone the uneasiness that an idea like that of God's anger inspires in modern man.*
>
> *Gabriel Marcel*

I

That God has the capacity for anger—indeed, for anger of peerless intensity—constitutes a thesis with copious Scriptural foundation. One finds in the Sacred Text many graphic and stridently unsentimental depictions of divine wrath and its (at times) catastrophic consequences. While it is true that references to God's wrath appear with greater frequency in the Hebrew Bible than in the New Testament, Revelations 19:15 speaks explicitly "of the fierceness and wrath of Almighty God."

This notwithstanding, however, the idea of divine wrath has widely been regarded as an unacceptably naive or "primitive" piece of theology, i.e., as an **anthropocentric** slur upon the divine perfection. Indeed, as will shortly be elaborated, such is pretty much the view of those philosophical theologians that have been seriously influential in shaping normative theistic **metaphysics.** Accordingly, it has standardly been contended by distinguished philosophical representatives of Judaism and Christianity that the ascription of *literal anger* to God is a flagrant breach of conceptual propriety. Moreover, this contention reflects the general doctrine that it is conceptually impermissible to ascribe *any* affective states to God. Rather (so the argument proceeds), the unsurpassable greatness of the divine nature entails that God is essentially *impassible*—that He necessarily lacks affective capacity. Accordingly, the doctrine that God can become literally wrathful reflects—so it has widely been held—an artless failure to grasp that the import of all ascription of affect to God is exclusively allegorical. In what follows, we propose to show that this long-standing theologically "sophisticated" view deserves our emphatic rejection.

II

To begin with, one needs no particular expertise in **"hermeneutics"** in order to recognize that God's wrath is portrayed in Scripture as having a distinctly *moral nexus.* That is, while a staple of Biblical monotheism is that God is "omnimerciful" or "slow to anger," He is *also* revealed in the Sacred Text as uncompromising in His demand for justice and overall moral decency. This being so, there are occasions (relatively infrequent, thank God) wherein the depth and scope of human sinfulness, i.e., of man's self-centered or willful violation of God's mandates, is of sufficient magnitude to provoke *moral outrage* in God. On such occasions, the divine requirement for justice and moral decency *overrules* (as it were) His mercy and tolerance, the result being that God then (to invert the well-worn adage) "tempers mercy with justice" by decreeing considerable suffering upon the relevant transgressors. Presumably, these "reactive decrees"—notwithstanding their harshness—are (given God's unsurpassable wisdom) precisely what is requisite for the proper *chastening* of those whose moral evil proved sufficient to provoke divine wrath. Of course, it would be misguided to suppose that God's moral outrage on the occasions in question warrants the view that He is less than infinitely *caring*[1] towards His creatures. To the contrary, Biblical monotheism requires that divine wrath be seen as a *corollary* or *function* of divine care. Alternatively, it is *because* of God's immeasurable care for mankind that human sinfulness, and, accordingly, the pain and suffering that we inflict upon one another, can provoke Him to moral outrage.

All of this notwithstanding, however, and as alluded to in our introduction, distinguished philosophical theists have tended to reject a straightforward interpretation of Scripture *vis-à-vis* God's capacity for wrath. Maimonides' analysis in this regard is instructively paradigmatic. He observes that while certain divine *actions* are "similar" to actions that *we* perform out of anger and other emotive states, one must not infer from this that there are (or can be) acts of God that result from a "similar aptitude of the soul."[2] Rather, since God is to be "exalted above every deficiency," He is entirely bereft of passion. Aquinas is in full agreement:

> Anger and the like are attributed to God on account of a likeness of effect. Thus, because to punish is properly the act of an angry man, God's punishment is metaphorically spoken of as His anger.[3]

Of course, since it is emotion *as such* that is deemed unworthy of the divine nature—not simply "negative" emotions such as anger—even "positive" or admirable feelings such as *compassion* cannot with conceptual propriety (on the canonical view) be predicated of God. In Chapter VIII of his *Proslogion,* Anselm defends the ostensibly outrageous doctrine that God is both compassionate and noncompassionate. Contradiction is eluded, however, since the sense in which Anselm maintains that God *is* compassionate turns out to be entirely **Pickwickian.** Specifically, and in his customary manner of doing

[1]Among the nonnegotiable components of canonical theism is, of course, the doctrine of divine love. Indeed, St. Thomas went so far as to identify God's *essence* with His love (cf. *Summa Theologica* I, Question 20, Article 3, Obj. 2 and Reply Obj. 2). [cf. reading 1.1, question 4—Ed.]

[2]*Guide of the Perplexed,* Part I, Chapter 54. (Pines translation [U. of Chicago Press, 1963].)

[3]*Summa Theologica* I, Question 3, Article 2, Reply Obj. 2. (English Dominican Translation.)

philosophical theology in the context of talking to God, Anselm states the following concerning God's compassion:

> Truly, thou art so in terms of our experience, but thou art not so in terms of thine own. For, when thou beholdest us in our wretchedness, we experience the effect of compassion, but thou dost not experience the feeling.[4]

Let us call this time-honored doctrine that it is conceptually improper to ascribe affective capacity to God—in, of course, a straightforward or literal sense—the *Theologically Sophisticated Thesis* (TST). In clear opposition to the TST is, of course, the claim that it is *not* conceptually improper to ascribe affective capacity to God. Let us call this latter contention the *Theologically Naive Thesis* (TNT). Needless to say that the TST has the support of many a modern theologian. For example, in discussing the **"numinous"** versus the "rational" aspects of the divine nature, Rudolph Otto supports the idea of ". . . defending the non-rational core of the Biblical conception of God from all excessive rationalization."[5] However, notwithstanding the insight displayed by those who championed such a defense, Otto maintains that—unfortunately—they "sank into **anthropomorphism**" by virtue of defending

> . . . not figurative "anger" and "emotion," but literal anger and emotion, misconceiving the numinous character of the attributes in question . . . instead of realizing that they can only be admitted as figurative indications of something essentially non-rational by means of symbols drawn from feelings that have analogy to it.

III

While the TST clearly has the weight of philosophical tradition in its corner, we hope to provide powerful justification for subscribing to the TNT over the TST. Accordingly, we intend to furnish strong philosophical vindication of a perfectly literal or straightforward construal of Scripture on the question of divine emotionality. So far as I can see—and I admit to being less than entirely clear about how to individuate arguments—it seems to me that there are three independent strands of reasoning in support of the TST that have a preliminary air of plausibility. Call them (1) *The Argument from God's Absolute* ***Immutability,*** (2) *The Argument from Divine Incorporeality,* and (3) *The Argument from Divine Infallibility.* In addition to exposing—as concisely as we can—each of them as deficient, our refutation of the third and final argument for rejecting the TNT (or accepting the TST) involves the introduction and elaboration of a concept that constitutes the core of our *positive defense* of the TNT. Hence, it turns out that our reply to the final argument for *rejecting* the TNT embodies all of the justification we need for *accepting* the TNT—and thus for rejecting the TST.

The Argument from God's Absolute Immutability, perhaps the most frequently employed polemic of those who argue for the conceptual impropriety of ascribing affective capacity to God, is rooted in the assumption that maximal greatness requires the transcendence of all changeability. This, in turn, seems to be derived from (though it seems far from clear just which idea is more "basic," if, indeed, one of them *can* properly be regarded as more basic than the other) the Aristotelian conception of Deity as necessarily devoid of **potentiality,** i.e., from the idea of God as *Pure* ***Act.*** Such a conception of God has been defended by an impressive number of theistic metaphysicians, including, of course, such luminaries of the tradition as Maimonides and Aquinas. Moreover, since it is natural to suppose that the properties *being capable of affect* and *being absolutely immutable* are incompatible, it seems eminently plausible to maintain that "X is immutable in all respects" entails "X lacks affective capacity."

Response: Why accept the thesis of God's absolute immutability? Since the literature now contains arguments (by, incidentally, very traditional theists) for rejecting this doctrine that are—or so it seems to me—as strong or definitive as one can reasonably hope for it would be gratuitous to devote

[4]*Saint Anselm: Basic Writings,* trans. by S.N. Deane with an Intro. by Charles Hartshorne, 2nd ed. (LaSalle, IL: Open Court, 1962), p. 13 (emphases mine). [See reading 1.2, which uses a different translation—Ed.]

[5]Rudolph Otto, *The Idea of the Holy* (London: Oxford University Press, 1923, 1958), p. 77.

serious space here in an effort to refute what has already (or so I believe) been refuted. Rather, we might simply note the following: one looks in vain for Scriptural support of the doctrine of God's absolute immutability. While Malachi 3:6 does tell us "For I the LORD change not—which, by the way, constitutes Aquinas's (sole) Biblical basis for subscribing to this doctrine (*Summa Theologiae,* Vol. I, Part I, Ques. 9)—a careful look at the context in which this sentence occurs, i.e., taking careful account of all that *leads up* to it (all that is said under Malachi 3:5), reveals that the sort of "immutability" in question is that of *moral constancy:* we can depend on God's unsurpassable goodness to be absolutely unwavering. Accordingly, and quite *independently* of whether one holds to the view that God is absolutely—hence **ontologically**—immutable, it is remarkably perplexing that Malachi 3:6 has been cited by influential philosophical theists as *justification* for that view. Accordingly, it is very hard to see how that passage can properly be taken to warrant a conception of God as immutable in the sense that would seem to preclude His possession of affective capacity.

Of course, it might be held that, absent *Scriptural* foundation for regarding God as immutable in all respects, there is philosophical or *conceptual* basis for doing so. It might, for example, be maintained that absolute immutability constitutes a requirement of maximal greatness. *This* contention, however, should properly be disposed of by our response to the third and final argument against the TNT. For what will have been shown thereby—assuming the success of that response—is that the possession of affective capacity is entirely compatible with maximal greatness. Accordingly, since (as noted previously) it is natural to suppose that the capacity for emotion is incompatible with absolute immutability, it is proper to conclude that *being immutable in all respects* is not a requirement of maximal greatness.

(2) *The Argument from God's Incorporeality* is rooted in the notion that a conceptually necessary condition for the possession of affective capacity is the possession of a neurophysiology. Hence, since an absolutely central component of traditional theistic metaphysics is that God is essentially incorporeal, the ascription of literal affective capacity to God (so the argument proceeds) is unacceptable.

Response: While there appears to be an ***empirically** invariant association* between the possession of affective capacity and the possession of a neurophysiology—experience seems to record no case of the former minus the latter—this clearly fails to entail that possessing a neurophysiology is *conceptually necessary* for possessing affective capacity. Moreover, it is readily seen that traditional theism entails the *denial* of the contention that one must possess a neurophysiology in order to possess affective capacity. To begin with, it is axiomatic to canonical theistic doctrine that God is both incorporeal and the subject of *mental states,* e.g., thoughts, beliefs, judgments. Accordingly, traditional theism patently entails that the possession of a neurophysiology is not a conceptual requirement for the possession of mental states. However, since their *availability to introspection* ensures that anger, sadness, joy, and the like constitute mental states no less than do knowledge, beliefs, judgments, etc., God's essential incorporeality no more precludes His possessing *affective* capacity than it precludes His possessing *intellective* capacity.

Of course, one might reject *traditional theism* by maintaining that mental states "reduce" to, or are necessarily dependent upon, physiological processes. But any such maneuver hardly constitutes a special threat to *our* thesis, i.e., that the ascription of literal affective capacity to God is entirely within the bounds of conceptual propriety. Moreover, if past attempts to establish the truth or plausibility of **materialism** are any indication of the measure of success that we can expect from *future* efforts on behalf of that **ontology,** it seems fair to conclude that traditional theism has little to fear from *that* quarter.

(3) *The Argument from Divine Infallibility* can be taken to proceed as follows: as an absolutely perfect being, nothing about God's nature, states, actions, etc. could conceivably admit of the slightest deficiency. However, if God possessed affective capacity, He would *not* be absolutely immune from deficiency. For affective reactions are notorious for often being impulsive, unmeasured or over-reactive, uncalled-for, arbitrary, and otherwise injudicious,

i.e., in many ways inappropriate to the situations that occasion them. Thus (so the argument unfolds), affective capacity carries with it the potential for a certain sort of fallibility that might properly be called "*affective* fallibility." Accordingly, since it is unimpeachable that God is essentially infallible, it is clear that He necessarily lacks affective capacity.

Response: While God's absolute perfection ensures that there could be no conceivable respect in which He was fallible, it is no way derivable from this that His nature precludes affective capacity. For the claim that it *is* so derivable assumes that affective *fallibility* is a corollary of affective *capacity.* Surely, however, any such assumption deserves to be rejected. Consider, for example, the (all too) familiar phenomenon of *intellectual* fallibility. Clearly, human persons are intellectually fallible; indeed, our proclivity for holding false beliefs and assenting to unsound arguments is legendary. Note, however, that *our* being intellectually fallible in no way legitimates the idea that *being intellectually fallible* is a corollary of the possession of intellect. Rather, the case of God illustrates the spuriousness of any such contention, i.e., intellectual *in*fallibility cannot but constitute one of God's essential attributes. Likewise, the inherent perfection of the divine nature could no more admit of *affective* deficiency than of intellective deficiency. Accordingly, that affective fallibility accompanies affective capacity *in human persons* in no way warrants the view that the ascription of affective capacity to God is conceptually improper. To the contrary, God's absolute flawlessness ensures that, necessarily, if God (exists and) possesses affective capacity, he is *affectively infallible.*

IV

What we are now positioned to see is that the concept of Affective Infallibility is just what it takes to ensure the conceptual propriety of ascribing affective capacity to God *in a perfectly straightforward or literal sense* of "affective capacity." Reference to the divine intellect should once again prove to be instructive. In observing that God's intellect is perfect, there is compelling indication that the force of the word "intellect" is—and quite properly so—entirely literal. Consider: in recognizing that God's intellect is (in glaring contradistinction to our own) maximally great, we thereby acknowledge that there obtains a staggeringly vast difference between the cognitive power of man and that of God. However, that hardly justifies the notion that, in speaking of God's intellect, the term "intellect" cannot properly be understood in its literal sense. More positively, since it is axiomatic that God's intellect could not conceivably admit of the slightest deficiency, it seems conceptually *gratuitous* to construe the divine intellect allegorically or "analogically."[6] For when we assert that God's intellect is perfect, what idea of significance is conveyed but that the capacity for cognition, reasoning, judging, etc. that we possess (or exercise) so imperfectly is *precisely* the capacity that is possessed (or always exercised) by God in an absolutely unsurpassable manner?

Likewise for the ascription of *affective* capacity to God. We have seen that the divine perfection does not preclude God's possession of such capacity, but, rather, precludes His being affectively *fallible.* Hence, just as with the case of God's intellect, it would be conceptually gratuitous to hold that, if we ascribe affective capacity to God, the "capacity" in question must be construed in figurative rather than literal terms. Rather, in recognizing that God could be nothing short of affectively infallible, we thereby recognize that *precisely* the capacity for affective response that we find in ourselves, a capacity that all too often results in emotive reactions that are (in many ways) inappropriate to the situations that occasion them, is possessed (or always exercised) by God in a manner that is consonant with His absolutely flawless nature. While this fails to entail that God actually *possesses* affective capacity, it does entail that the ascription of such capacity to God—in, of course, an entirely literal or straightforward sense—is entirely within the bounds of conceptual propriety.

Accordingly, the concept of Affective Infallibility is seen to be precisely what it takes to ensure the triumph of the TNT over the TST, i.e., it ensures that

[6][See explanations of the technical terms **allegorization** and **analogy, theory of.**—Ed.]

there is nothing conceptually problematic about the view that God can become wrathful or morally outraged in a perfectly straightforward or literal sense. Since it is evident that an affective response that was less than fully appropriate could not conceivably be an affective response *of God's,* no case of divine anger—whatever its intensity—could be impulsive, overreactive, injudicious, or in any other way inappropriate to the situation that occasioned it. Intriguingly, then, it turns out that there is nothing unduly anthropocentric about the ascription of affective capacity to God. Rather, and more than a little ironically, it is those who *deny* the conceptual propriety of ascribing such capacity to God (insofar as this denial takes its cue from the affective fallibility characteristic of *human* affective response) who are guilty of such anthropocentrism.

V

If our argument thus far has succeeded, what has been secured is that the possession of affective capacity is—*pace* [contrary to] what has traditionally been held to be the case—compatible with maximal greatness. Might it be plausible, however, to make the *stronger* claim that the possession of affective capacity is *required* by maximal greatness?[7] Briefly, it seems to me that there is profound intuitive sanction for the claim that affective capacity is *a morally significant* capacity, and, as such, constitutes an essential ingredient of moral perfection. If this is so, then—given as axiomatic that maximal greatness entails moral perfection—there is serious intuitive basis for maintaining that the possession of affective capacity is conceptually requisite for maximal greatness, and, accordingly, for its religious corollary *worship-worthiness.* While this is not, course, to suggest that "intuitive justification" constitutes *definitive* justification, the brief speculations to follow are offered in the spirit of the Kripkean principle that it is misguided not to regard our intuitions as having ("ultimately speaking") *significant* evidential value.[8]

Central to our deliberations is a consideration of what would be included in the (or a) morally called-for response by a morally perfect individual to heinous moral evil. Rather than attempting anything so elusive and problematic as a rigorous definition of the concept of moral perfection, I suggest that an Anselmian-sort of **"gedanken-experiment"** is more than adequate to the task. Imagine a case of extreme moral evil (e.g., willful genocide)—brought about by (who else?) a group of human persons—and consider the following (alternative) responses to this evil by two candidates for moral perfection. Candidate One responds by punishing severely those responsible for this evil. We might also assume that this punitive action (call it *A*) is not only morally fitting but is such that its moral fittingness—as a response to the moral evil in question—is unsurpassable. However, Candidate One is neither angered, dismayed, nor revolted by the heinous moral evil to which He has responded with action *A*. Candidate Two, however, *in addition* to responding to the case of willful genocide with action *A*—that punitive action the moral fittingness of which is unsurpassable—experiences *wrath,* i.e., is *morally outraged* by the genocidal slaughter in question. Is it not intuitively clear that—other relevant things (such as action *A*) "being equal"—Candidate Two, simply *by virtue* of Her affective responsiveness, is *morally greater* than Candidate One?

This does not, let it be clear, entail that Candidate One is to be *faulted* for not responding affectively to the case of genocide. For it might well be (let us stipulate that such is indeed the case) that Candidate One lacks affective capacity, and it seems incontestable that no one can properly be faulted for failing to respond in a way in which he/she is *unable* to respond. However, *that* in no way implies that the capacity in question does not morally enhance the nature of one who possesses it, i.e., does not significantly contribute to the level at which one weighs

[7]The argument of this final section was inspired by comments from Professor Susan Feagin after my presentation of an earlier version of this paper at the University of Missouri-Kansas City. . . .

[8]Cf. Saul A. Kripke, *Naming and Necessity* (Cambridge: Harvard University Press, 1972, 1980), p. 42.

in on the "moral greatness" scale. Analogously, while my neighbor Sam is hardly to be faulted for his lack of athletic wherewithal, it is nonetheless true that, in at least *this* respect, Babe Ruth and Willie Mays are considerably greater than Sam.

It seems to me that these speculations, while failing to yield *conclusive* justification for viewing the possession of affective capacity as an entailment of maximal greatness, ensure the *rational acceptability* of so viewing it. If so, then it is far from implausible to maintain that, necessarily, a being that lacks affective capacity is not a being than which a greater cannot be thought. What *does* seem to have been definitively or conclusively adduced, however—with, of course, a major assist from the idea of Affective Infallibility—is that the TNT triumphs over the TST; i.e., that we are entitled to hold with complete confidence that the ascription of affective capacity to God is entirely within the bounds of conceptual propriety. . . .

STUDY QUESTIONS

1. Characterize the Theologically Naive Thesis (TNT) and the Theologically Sophisticated Thesis (TST).
2. What are the three arguments for TST that Oakes considers, and how does he seek to refute them? Is his refutation convincing? Why or why not?
3. Oakes believes that affective capacity is required for maximal greatness. Why? According to him, how does God's affective capacity exemplify maximal greatness and affective infallibility?
4. Oakes believes that ascribing affective capacity to God is not anthropocentric but denying that God has affective capacity is anthropocentric. Why?
5. *God is sometimes said to be wrathful. Under what circumstances would wrath be morally required?
6. *If God has emotions, what implications might this carry for the propriety of human beings having emotions? (cf. reading 1.1, question 5 and reading 1.2, questions 3 and 4.)
7. *Relate Oakes's presentation of the TNT to Readings 1.1–1.2. Are any aspects of his presentation inaccurate? Discuss.
8. *Some philosophers argue that if God is outside of time, God cannot have emotions. What do you think the claimed connection is between timelessness and immutability?
9. *Oakes focuses on God's wrath. Under what circumstances might an affectively infallible being experience *suffering* or *sorrow?* Would the beings having those experiences signal a *need* of the being? If so, could a perfect being have needs? Discuss.
10. *Are there emotions that an affectively infallible being could *never* have? Discuss.

READING 1.4

Is God Vain?

Charles Taliaferro

The book of Genesis relates that God created human beings in God's image. But isn't an effort to clone oneself a mark of vanity? Likewise, is it not vain of God to demand that people worship Him? Finally, doesn't the Christian notion of salvation suggest a prima donna deity who can't allow creatures to effect their own salvation or a God who wants to be the talk of the town?

Charles Taliaferro (St. Olaf College) raises these neglected questions and argues that God is not vain. Creation expresses love, not vanity; and created beings are not clones of their creator but, rather, a diverse group, whose similarity to their creator lies in their capacity to love, to will, and to act. These are good states of affairs, and no vanity is involved in creating them. As for worship, Taliaferro suggests that worship, as well as love, is directed at certain characteristics—wisdom, goodness, knowledge, and power—and not per se at the possessor of those properties. With regard to the objection based on redemption, Taliaferro argues that the **Incarnation** *suggests a self-limiting love rather than vanity.*

An objection to theism which has received scant attention in the literature may be called the problem of divine vanity. It may be argued that Christian theism exults in a view of God as vain, egoistic, pompous. The problem of vanity arises in three general (broad) areas, creation, worship, and redemption. With respect to creation, God's bringing into existence creatures in His likeness is akin to bringing into being self-portraits, which is hardly a humble undertaking. God appears to be a super Narcissus who delights in His own reflection. Worship seems inescapably egoistic. God has not only created images of Himself, but expects these images to worship Him, to recount many of His greatest deeds, to be abased before the Divine glory and adore Him. We are even commanded to worship none other than God. Similarly, in salvation history God insists upon being at the center stage. Creaturely moral failure is offensive to the Creator. But instead of creatures succeeding in effecting reconciliation, God Himself does so. God may have taken on human flesh to bring about redemption, but it is still God *qua* divine and human ego who is the principal saving agent. God wants to be the talk of the town.

. . . Christians imagine God to be completely good, morally perfect and supreme, whereas the charge of the vanity objection is that He is morally inferior to His saints. This creates a problem for a Christian ethic charging us to be perfect even as our heavenly Father is perfect. If we follow our Maker's example, we find ourselves condemned by the Christian understanding of God's ordinances. God appears to flaunt preeminently the very vice God is said to abhor. I begin with preliminary reflections on the relationship between pride and humility and then address the problem of vanity under the headings creation, worship, and redemption.

PRIDE AND HUMILITY

Vanity is a form of pride. Christian ethical tradition is united in its condemnation of vanity, but it has not always condemned pride *qua* self-respect or proportionate self-regard. Common parlance appears to support a distinction between acceptable and unacceptable pride; it even reflects a quite positive approval of natural pride. Thus, in the use of the expression "false pride," there is some suggestion that real, true pride is appropriate. "False pride" is this proportionate pride in appearance only, in the same fashion as "false humility" and "false friends" are humility and friends only in appearance. When someone has false pride they have passed beyond proportionate self-regard or respect and landed themselves in egocentrism, vanity, self-aggrandizement. Even so, ordinary language is ambivalent on the matter and "pride" simpliciter may stand for either proportionate or disproportionate self-regard, a term of approval or condemnation. Ethicists have identified the former as natural or proper pride. An Aristotelian account of natural pride is that it consists in feeling a proportionate amount of pleasure in one's undertakings, character, or relationships. Vanity involves excessive, disproportionate delight as when one takes enormous pleasure in one's appearance, a pleasure which eclipses any appreciation of others, and so on.

Something like the Aristotelian account seems satisfactory, though it may be objected that vain pride or proper pride can be constituted principally by one's beliefs and not involve any feeling of pleasure and pain. Thus, a vain person may be one who tends to believe the very best of herself and the very worst of another. The Aristotelian account is not thereby utterly vitiated, however, for it seems to be essential to pride that the prideful person takes some pleasure in, or has a positive attitude toward, the object of pride. At the very least, it would be puzzling for Miriam to be prideful about X, unless she took X to be something worthy of positive regard or some pleasure. In this paper I assume an Aristotelian account of pride; pride involves some positive regard or attitude, whether or not this also involves sensory pleasure.

Vain pride does not appear to be solely a matter of having *false* beliefs about oneself. One may give great credit to oneself which is undeserved and not thereby be prideful, for one's exalted self-estimation may be grounded upon weighty evidence. Imagine Miriam has been told by otherwise reliable authorities she is the best pianist in the world. Reluctantly she believes this, but she is reticent to inform others, blushes when she thinks of her greatness and the like. In fact, she is a horrific piano player and the authorities are amusing themselves by inculcating false beliefs in innocent pianists. Miriam has self-aggrandized beliefs, but she is not vain. Vain pride appears to involve a willful self-exaltation, a self-promotion that is unwarranted. To put the matter in **epistemic** terms, we expect a humble person to employ Cliffordian standards with regard to herself and William James-type, charitable standards to others.[1] Thus, if Miriam is humble we might expect her to believe the best of another in a case where the evidence if far from overwhelming and be reluctant to believe the best of herself without some more justification. Surely a humble person need *not have* **Cartesian skepticism** about all *her positive features. Such* **pyrrhonism** may amount to servility. Be that as it may, we typically expect the healthy, humble person to have a modest degree of self-doubt. I do not take such self-doubt to be a defining feature of humility. I note simply that its absence is common among those in the grip of vain pride and its presence is common among the humble.

Vain pride and natural pride may range over many areas. One may take pride in one's scope of power, some characteristic or undergoing or even some relationship which is believed to be positive. Likewise one may have humility with respect to some relationship, characteristic, quality, degree of power or undergoing which is believed to be positive. A marked difference between the prideful and humble is that the humble person is aware of the limited nature of these features. As it happens, two people may have identical features, both having the same degree of intellectual prowess say, and yet one has pride in the degree attained whereas the other is humble in appreciating the modesty of that degree (she recognizes the comparative paltry value of such intellectual achievement over against the witness of saints). In this example we can see the close proximity of humility and proper pride. It may even be that a steadfast refusal to feel proper pride could stem from a misunderstanding of humility. A humble person may be one who knows (or has justified beliefs) that she has qualities of a certain sort and no better, but she does not thereby deny that she has the limited qualities she enjoys.

Two further aspects of pride and humility may be noted before treating the objection from vanity. First, while pride seems to be incompatible with feeling sorrow or pain in the feature one is proud about, humility is compatible with feeling such sorrow. If we are proud of getting a grant, it cannot be that we take sorrow or feel unmitigated pain and dismay over the windfall. However, if we feel humility about our moral character, having a vivid sense of past and future failings, it is possible to feel unmitigated pain and dismay over these failings. Humility need not involve pain and sorrow in this sense, but it is compatible with it. Second, pride, whether natural or unnatural, appears to involve some kind of self-regard or self-reflection in an essential way. To be proud that X occurs must involve some belief or attitude relating oneself to X. I cannot be proud of the moon unless I have some belief or attitude tying myself and the moon together, however attenuated the tie.[2] Thus, I may be proud that *my* God made it or that it is part of *my* universe. Humility may involve self-reference,

[1]W. K. Clifford insisted we not accept beliefs without sufficient, overriding evidence. William James had a more lax view, claiming that one is within one's epistemic rights to accept beliefs of a certain kind under conditions when Cliffordian standards are not met. [See Readings 7.1, 7.8 — Ed.]

[2]See David Hume, *A Treatise of Human Nature,* Book 2, part I. . . .

indeed a poignant, sharp self-awareness. But it might also be that the humble person is very unselfconscious. One who is humble may have 'died to self' and have a marked self-disregard or self-forgetfulness of the kind some of us have only rarely as when we 'lose ourselves in a book' and the like.

Initially it is difficult indeed to imagine that the God of Christianity could be humble. God is conceived of as limitless in power and knowledge, the principal Creator of all, morally perfect, and unsurpassable in all perfection. Surely it is hard to be humble if you are God, and still harder to imagine the God of Christendom is humble when one considers the specific teachings examined below of creation, worship, and redemption. Recall the refrain of a popular country song: "it's hard to be humble, when you're perfect in every way." We reproach each other with the accusation that so-and-so acts with a "holier than thou" attitude or "she thinks she is God." But what of the moral fiber of a being who actually *is* holier than ourselves? . . .

. . . The doctrine of divine **impassibility** has been taken to deny God has feelings of pain and pleasure. If vain pride involves feeling inordinate pleasure in one's own features, presumably a being incapable of any feelings of pleasure at all, cannot have vain pride. I accept a version of theism which allows that God has feelings like pleasure and pain, albeit I do not construe these as somatic or bodily undergoings. [Later in this essay] this distinction is clarified. It may be noted, too, that even contemporary defenders of Divine impassibility have not denied God experiences some emotion. In an important recent work, *Divine Impassibility,* Richard Creel argues God experiences pleasure but not sorrow.

CREATION

Creation of Divine image bearers as traditionally conceived may appear to be the height of vanity. God is pictured as creating the cosmos for his own glory and creatures are brought into being who are images or reflections of God. They are even called to so act that they come into an increasing likeness to their Maker. Certainly this suggests an extraordinary delight in self. The iconography of pride identifies the mirror as one of vanity's principal instruments. Isn't the Christian God one who loves His own reflection so much that creation is but His looking glass?

The critic may urge further that an appeal to God as Trinity does not suffice to avoid the objection from vanity. The triune life of God might appear to be a supreme model of other-regarding love and self-donation. The Father, Son and Holy Spirit are continuously united in will, forever expressing loving regard for the other. However this is spelled out, the objection of vanity can be raised in terms of the vanity of the Trinity itself. After all, a club of three members might behave in a chauvinistic, aggressively self-concerned manner even though each member of the club behaves in a perfectly other-regarding fashion to his or her fellow member. Similarly, the objection from vanity is not altered by recent discussion as to whether creation by God is voluntary as a freely chosen act or necessary as an act which was free only in the sense of being not forced by a third party, but otherwise was a necessary manifestation of God's nature as goodness.[3] All such discussion might settle is the quandary whether Divine vanity is a freely elected vice or that God is vain by His very nature.

I think that the objection from vanity is less forceful with respect to creation than with respect to worship and redemption. Briefly, a reply to the critic lies in a fuller appreciation of the nature of creation, the metaphysical distinction between God and creatures, and what is meant by being created in God's image.

If classic Christian **metaphysics** is correct, then God is the only causal agent who could be responsible for there being a contingent cosmos at all. It is a **necessary condition** of the existence of any contingent object that God exercises his creative conserving power sustaining it in existence. For God to lovingly interact with another, He must create it. Presumably both loving another and acting haughtily

[3]Cf. Norman Kretzmann, "Goodness, Knowledge, and Indeterminacy in the Philosophy of Thomas Aquinas," *Journal of Philosophy,* October 1983.

before another, requires that the other be created and conserved by God. Bare creation and conservation of a being does not entail God is vain. God was not in the position of excluding lots of other gods from creating, failing to wait His turn in line. To alter slightly one of [American philosopher Charles] Peirce's dictums: gods are not as plentiful as blackberries. Likewise it appears that neither God's failing to create nor creating entail God is vain. Just as creating may well be a necessary condition to loving, other-regarding encounter, so failing to create need not entail God is vain, for while God as trinity may (as the critic charges) image some ghastly mutual self-congratulatory club, it certainly need not do so. We can imagine treating the triune Godhead as a society of love in which other-regardingness reigns and, while accompanied by proper pride insofar as there is genuine delight in the relations and features of Godhood, it is not in excess (one is hard pressed to imagine excess here) and such self-delight is hardly a matter of harming possible creatures. Failing to create does not entail God is vain. Nor is it the case that God is vain because He creates.

But why create in one's own image? Not everything in the created order is characterized as divine image; there are rivers, mountains, volcanoes, and rocks. Only in the biological world, and specifically among sentient, thinking, active beings do we find any singling out of creatures who are Divine image bearers. And it is here that we may note the marked difference between a creature painting endless self-portraits and the Divine creating in His image. In the latter case, God brings into existence agents, creative beings distinct from Himself. Self-portraits do not love or hate their Maker and their fellow God-portraits. Our self-portraits do not hate and love, nor possess emotions in any literal sense. Creatures who are thinking, feeling agents bear a marked similarity to their creator, but it is in precisely the ways that allow them to have a life in some way independent of their maker. We, as image bearers, are not unlike Goethe's description in *Faust,* "little gods in the world."

But consider the following objection. Imagine a mad scientist, Arthur, who populates the world with thousands of clones. Despite the fact these clones are able to live in measured independence of Arthur their creator (Arthur the 500th can insult the original Arthur), isn't there something unseemly egoistic about our mad scientist's creation? Is God's creating us in His likeness analogous to Arthur's cloning creatures that resemble himself?

Yes and no. What appears to be unseemly in the thought experiment is that the mad scientist's cloning amounts to his producing creatures who narrowly resemble himself, in gender, size, race, weight, and personality features. Whatever their subsequent exercise of free will, the Arthurs are homogeneous; they are modeled after a limited, perhaps flawed, original. If we alter the thought experiment and suppose that Arthur produces a rich variety of creatures, the ego resemblance is lessened and there is less suggestion of egoism in his creative work. God does not have a specific race, gender, size, or weight to copy. Divine image bearers are persons, whatever their dimensions. Moreover, it is good for there to be persons, beings that enjoy sensation and desires and who can exercise reason, memory, imagination, and agency. Thus, it is plausible to regard the creation of such beings as good whether it be by Arthur or God. Our resemblance to God consists in our enjoyment of good making powers like agency, the capacity to love and the like; powers enabling us to be co-creators with God. Prominent Christian philosophers have identified the chief resemblance between God and Divine image bearers as the possession of will. That which makes us in God's image is that which enables us to have a will (and thus a life) independent of God (St. Bernard, William de Saint Thierry, Richard Saint-Victor, Rene Descartes, Jean-Luc Marion). I conclude that creating other agents is not by itself vain, though it may appear vain if we imagine the Creator has brought them into existence solely to complement and praise Himself. Earlier I noted that one rationale for creation is to glorify God. Insofar as God is glorified simply by there being good, created states of affairs, the problem of vanity does not arise. But what if part of what it means to glorify God is to praise and worship Him? Is one of the reasons for our creation the bestowing of "metaphysical compliments" (Hobbes' phrase) to the Almighty?

WORSHIP

If creation alone does not clinch the critic's case, Christian teaching of worship seems to do so. Isn't it the height of Divine egoism to insist creatures worship and praise God?

I place to the side one solution to this charge, namely the view that worship of God is to be understood solely in terms of creaturely regarding behavior. That is, to worship God is simply to behave as good Samaritans or in a Christ-like fashion to others. Surely any full account of Christian worship must take this into account, but I believe that there remains a distinct Christian teaching that God is to be praised and adored, which is not fully reducible to good creature-to-creature ethics.

A reply to the objection of vanity may be seen by a fuller appreciation of the nature of God's attributes and the character of worship.

There is an interesting dispute going back to Plato over whether when one loves another, Miriam loving Eric say, Miriam is loving Eric's properties or Eric himself. Eric may well ask Miriam whether she loves him for his wealth or his body or his wit. Would she love him if he lost these? I will not tease out the subtleties of this debate, the puzzles that arise if Miriam were to claim to love Eric independent of any such properties. . . . There are indeed serious problems with delimiting admirable from undesirable forms of conditional and unconditional love. What I wish to note here is that for an **Anselmian theist** the problem does not arise about whether one would love God if God were to lose one of his perfections. Perhaps it would be a defective form of fickle human love if Miriam ceased loving Eric when he lost his money. The case of God is different, however, for His metaphysical funds cannot be lost. Traditional Anselmian theism holds that God possesses His properties essentially. Thus, God could not but be limitless in power, knowledge, and goodness. In fact, the subtle doctrine of Divine **simplicity** holds that the relationship of divine attributes is so close that a perspicuous theistic metaphysics treats these attributes as distinct only from a creaturely standpoint. Really, the Divine nature is simple, without any parts, and these different Divine features are different only in the sense that the Divine manifests itself differently to the world, in some respects as **omniscient** knowledge (God's **foreknowledge**) and **omnipotent** power (God's providence) and so on. While Eric and Miriam may debate about whether each would love the other if there was a loss of money and health, the Divine object of love cannot (of metaphysical necessity) lose His richness and life.

To worship and adore God involves, in part, delighting in what we take to be the Divine properties. To love God is not to love some guy who happens to be very wise, but it is to love, adore, and delight in supreme Wisdom, Goodness, Knowledge, and Power. The question does not arise whether we would still worship God if God were to loss Goodness, Wisdom, Knowledge, and Power. A being that could lose these in *toto* would simply not be God. Thus, one important point here is that worship is not directed primarily at an ego (or three egos) but at the **instantiation** to a supreme degree of various perfections. We do not love a Divine **bare particular.** Compare the dictum about creatures: we should love the sinner and hate the sin. Whatever may be thought about loving sinners, I do not think we can love God without loving the Divine properties. To love and delight in the Divine properties is to love God.

The value of worship may now be better appreciated. Worship of God does not check creaturely narcissism because of fear that a bigger narcissist will be jealous. Rather, in worship one's attention is drawn to the features which make up the Divine Nature and constitute its excellence. It is a good thing for humans to contemplate things of high, even supreme worth. The Divine perfections are limitless and worthy of unending delight and pleasure. There is a beauty to the holiness of God. Conceivably, the prevention of creatures contemplating and adoring the divine properties may even harm them. God's self-love and our worship is not so much a matter of some fellow being lucky enough to get the Divine features while others did not—and we are stuck with delighting in *his* features. Our devotion is to the Divine perfections themselves, co-instantiated supremely in a person and so coinstantiated (or constituted) that no other being could have them. Much

Christian spiritual literature draws attention to a kind of disinterested or self-forgetful character in the high adoration of God. W. H. Auden once commented on the Narcissus myth that its lesson lies in Narcissus delighting in the reflection being *his,* and not simply in the features themselves.[4] This may be further illustrated by a complementary case described by Thomas Nagel. Nagel contends that his apprehension of the badness of pain, indeed a pain *he* is feeling, does not rest essentially upon his apprehension that the pain is his own.

> Of course he (a sufferer) wants to be rid of this pain reflectively—not because he thinks it would be good to reduce the amount of pain in the world. But at the same time his awareness of how bad it is doesn't essentially involve the thought that it is his. The desire to be rid of pain has only the pain as its object. This is shown by the fact that it doesn't even require the idea of one self in order to make sense: if I lacked or lost the conception of myself as distinct from other possible or actual persons, I could still apprehend the badness of pain, immediately.[5]

In a similar vein we may imagine delighting in certain excellences without smug self-reference.

Can God be humble in His self-delight and summoning creatures to enjoy Himself? God knows his great making features with clarity and precision; He could not think of Himself as being just one of the gods, no better than the next god. Return to a point made above about humility. Humility does not seem to be characterized solely or even essentially by having self-degrading views of the self. On the contrary, the entertainment of false beliefs about oneself is typically associated with arrogance (see, for example, "The Parson's Talk," in Chaucer's *Canterbury Tales*). It would appear to be an instance of false humility for one to believe worse of oneself in the face of evidence one has positive features, evidence which would satisfy Clifford in his most epistemically compulsive moods. God's self-love may be understood to express proper pride, not vanity.

There is a dictum common to authorities in the Christian spiritual tradition that we are to love God not for what He does for us, the rewards we might gain from it, but to love God for His own sake. Indeed this is true, but as they also note, the reward and fulfillment to be found from a non-reward conscious religious life is great. There is a sense in which such God-love is akin to God's love of Himself as traditionally conceived, for He does not love Himself for rewards like money or enslaving servile creatures. We may not conclude from our discussion of worship that God is vain, for Divine self-love and creaturely love is directed upon the divine excellences and perfection. Such may be in the domain of proper pride, but not egotism and false pride.[6] Insofar as knowledge, power, and goodness are real goods and worthy objects of enjoyment, God's love of these features is itself a good. We may understand Divine self-love in a fanciful way as goodness loving itself.

Consider a final objection. When I love God I am loving a person (or three persons), not their properties of goodness *per se* and so on. I love and reverence a person who discloses Himself to me in religious experience. Theistic **essentialism** is by no means universally accepted. Some hold that God can lose His omnipotence and omniscience, albeit by His own choice. I can still love God even if He should lose these supreme features. Therefore my love of God cannot be accounted for as an intentional attitude directed upon divine properties *per se.*

Reply: Even if we reject the thesis of Divine simplicity and theistic essentialism, it does not follow that worship is not best construed as a delight in the excellences (properties) which do constitute God. One cannot love a bare particular, a thing which has no properties whatever (one reason, I think, is that of metaphysical necessity there cannot be such

[4]W. H. Auden, cited by Henry Fairlie, *The Seven Deadly Sins Today* (Notre Dame: University of Notre Dame, 1979), p. 53.

[5]Thomas Nagel, *The View from Nowhere* (New York: Oxford University Press, 1986), p. 161. To use Nagel's terminology, I believe there are agent-relative as well as agent-neutral reasons for Divine worship. The worth of such worship is appreciable from an impersonal standpoint or the view from nowhere in particular.

[6]Immanuel Kant claimed that humility and true, noble pride are two features of proper self-respect. See his *Lectures on Ethics,* "Proper Self-Respect" and "Duties to Oneself," translated by Louis Enfield (New York: Harper and Row, 1963).

ontological items). The above critic is correct that worship does not involve sheer disinterested delight in properties *per se.* First, I believe worship of God involves reverencing the *instantiation* of these properties in a person or person-like Being. We delight in there being a supremely wise, good Creator and not simply in there being a Platonic property of Good, Wise Creator-hood. Second, we also adore the Divine lover revealed in our experience, the One who lovingly interacts with us in specific ways. This still does not circumvent the thesis that worship consists in reverent delight in supremely good or great making properties. The Hound of Heaven we may encounter in religious experience comes to us brimming over with delightful properties.

By way of a final, more fanciful, reply to our critic, consider a radically nonessentialist theistic metaphysics. Imagine (*per impossible* [what is impossible—literally, through the impossible]) God could lose his great making properties. Yahweh could have been a human being born and someone else, perhaps St. Augustine, could have been God. The roles may be reversed. There is a saying attributed to St. Augustine which allows this to be metaphysically possible. "O my God, if I were God and thou Augustine, I would wish that thou wert God and I Augustine."[7] We may consider the moral character of worship in a Rawlsian framework.[8] Let us introduce a **veil of ignorance.** Consider both Yahweh and Augustine *qua* rational creatures neither knowing which will turn out to be God. Would worship still be endorsed as appropriate so that Augustine and Yahweh would be content to endorse it independent of who will be the lucky one to wind up as God? Although this thought experiment already seems to me well beyond what can be settled with ease, I believe worship as I understand it would be so endorsed behind the veil. The delighting in wisdom, creative power, and knowledge seems to me a real good. This need in no way involve endorsing an egoistic vanity. Presumably one would desire that the person who winds up as God be given over to loving and delighting in the creature. Yahweh is not vain; if He had Augustine's position and Augustine His He would engage in divine worship without resentment. At the least, we have no reason now to think He would not do so.

My own preference is to stick to Anselmian convictions about theistic essentialism. I merely offer the above, fanciful Rawlsian story to defend the property-eyed view of worship against a nonAnselmian critic.

Does the Christian account of Salvation history suggest God is vain?

REDEMPTION

The last charge of the objection from vanity I discuss concerns the Christian account of salvation or redemption. The centrality of Christ may suggest to the critic a prima donna god who cannot bear to allow creatures to effect their own salvation. There is a peculiarity in the Gospel accounts of Jesus' sayings. On the one hand He is humble of heart and on the other He attributes to Himself a title and centrality unequalled in human literature. Who has insisted with such emphasis and force upon His centrality to the cosmos as the Christ of St. John's gospel? Christian claims about Jesus range from **cosmology** to the deepest recesses of our personality. In all such matters, Christ is to be in the limelight.

I believe the answer to this charge rests, in part, upon what I noted above about creation and worship. If the motivation for creation need not involve narcissistic vanity, neither need the motivation for the re-creation of life in redemption.

There is not space here to outline in much detail the competing theories of the atonement. The major theories insist that human creatures are unable to effect a full atonement (at-one-ment, in Anglo-Saxon) with God, owing to willful self-regard. The competing theories have different accounts of this inability. The Anselmian theory is that humans cannot effect atonement because they cannot satisfy

[7]St. Augustine as cited by E. L. Mascal in *He Who Is* (New York: Longmans, Green and Co., 1948), p. 196.

[8]Cf. [John Rawls,] *A Theory of Justice* (Cambridge: Harvard University Press, 1971).

Divine justice; the Abelardian theory [theory of Peter Abelard (1079–1142)] is that humans are so self-centered and bent upon cruelty that only a God-indwelt Christ could shock us out of moral and spiritual bondage; the ransom theory is that humans have become captive to Satan by their ill-doing and only Christ can overcome that powerful Demonic Master. As with creation, God alone is in a position to effect the re-creation of life, a restoration, or bringing about for the first time, a life of moral and spiritual health. There is some debate in the Christian tradition as to what means God was able to use in effecting redemption. Some means would seem to be unavailable (e.g., means which involve God's doing violence to innocent creatures, and so on), but, on all the competing theories, there was a fittingness to God's effecting it through incarnation. Does the atonement via incarnation itself suggest vanity? The critic may charge that God cannot leave humanity alone, but egoism prompts Him to take on human flesh as well.

The incarnation or enfleshment of God need not suggest egoism. There is as little suggestion of vanity here as there is in cases of a human lover who longs for and achieves unity with her beloved. But two Christian tenets make it harder to make a case for improper Divine egoism: the teaching of human divinization, and understanding the incarnation as a kind of Divine limiting.

The early Christian notion of divinization has received scant attention in Anglo-American philosophy. In one of the Petrine epistles we read that we are to become "partakers of the divine nature" (II Peter 1:4, RSV). In the fourth Gospel it is said that we are to be one with Christ as Christ is one with the Father. It is difficult to make sense of this within a theistic metaphysics, though William Alston in a recent paper "The Indwelling of the Holy Spirit," has advanced some intriguing suggestions of what may be involved **epistemically,** namely immediate divine-human cognitive access.[9] However this is spelled out, from an ethical standpoint the notion of divinization brings to light a problem with the vanity objection. God does not seek to *absorb* other creatures, but to have them be so linked with Him and He with them, that their action is harmonious and inextricably bound together. Recall Jesus' dictum that whoever harms or benefits the most vulnerable, harms or benefits Himself (Matthew 25:40,41). The conjoinment of wills and intent in a divine-human united life is to be one of creativity and rich in value. The divine human identification is to be so tight as to rule out any narrow self-interest or egoism. God's will is for the flourishing of all, in great, ever increasing plenitude. If we are to imagine taking pleasure in oneself in such a relationship it would be to take pleasure in God, and to take pleasure in God would be to take pleasure in God's whole creation. As we are said to dwell in God, God is said to dwell in us and share joy and sorrow. At the heart of most plausible accounts of altruism and compassion there is emphasis upon one person being affected and shaped by the well being of another. Your plight is of distress to me; you delight in some of my joys. Such sharing and extension of personal concern suggests a richly generous life. Presumably the mutual regard in Divine human life would be heightened considerably beyond the intimacy of any solely human relationships. The psychology of egoism is not in evidence.

While the Christian understanding of the incarnation suggests to the critic a vain God who cannot leave anyone alone, it can also suggest a starting image of self-limiting love. In sin creatures are bereft of God and one another and, *ex hypothesi* [by hypothesis] (given any of the plausible theories of the atonement), in need of Divine action to effect a healing. The divine enfleshment may be understood as a way to enhance the scope of human freedom and rich interplay with the supernatural. This means of grace can be thought of as a marked self-limiting of God. In a well known passage in Philippians we read that Christ did not count equality with a God a thing to be grasped but humbled Himself to take on the form of a servant.

There is not space to advance much of a Christology here. Suffice it to note that any of the current,

[9]*Philosophy and the Christian Faith,* edited by T. V. Morris (Notre Dame: University of Notre Dame Press, 1987).

plausible Christian theories of the incarnation endeavor to make some sense of the God-man living a life under considerably more limited conditions than the unincarnate God prior to incarnation.[10] In *Goods and Virtues* Michael Slote comments that humility seems to be of greater value, or to be more wonderful, the more that it is embraced by persons of greater traits and character. Thus:

> But however we are ultimately to analyze humility, it follows from the little we have already said that humility is (in the sense intended) a dependent virtue. For intuitively it seems to attain its full status as a virtue or desirable trait of character only when accompanied by other desirable traits. It is a positive virtue only in someone we have other reasons to think well of. In addition, humility can seem more wonderful, more admirable, the more highly we regard someone's other traits; . . .[11]

If this is correct, then surely the self limiting of Christ with respect to knowledge and power, His coming to live as a human being in order to effect atonement with creatures and creator might well be an act of extraordinary humility. Indeed, if we understand Divine omniscience as knowing all truths and yet claim the second member of the trinity so limited his knowledge in the earthly life as to embrace finite life, the Divine cognitive limiting might well be said to be infinite. Surely the Divine limiting and the supremely redemptive willingness to be subject to betrayal, hatred, and physical suffering may be understood as God embracing a humbled role. The God who comes to us as a servant does not strike one naturally as the god of Narcissus.

In concluding, I concede that for all I have suggested in reply to my imagined critic, at best I have shown that the vanity objection lacks clear force. There are ways to meet the objection. We may succeed in reading the notions of incarnation and divinization in salvation history as involving a real humbling of Godhead. Divine creation and worship are instances of proper pride, not vanity. Moreover, we may appeal to tenets in Christianity which appear to portray God as not in any way having defects which prompt you and me to vain pride, *viz.* low self-image, a need to show off and so on. The critic may still persist, and her persistence may stem from a sound, penetrating psychoanalysis of evil. Evil has many faces. But the critic's persistence may also stem from lack of appreciating the subtleties of the good.

STUDY QUESTIONS

1. State the three arguments Taliaferro considers that seek to show God is vain.
2. What is vanity? How does it contrast with "natural pride"?
3. What is "an Aristotelian account of natural pride"?
4. Does humility require having self-degrading views or false beliefs about oneself? If not, what is humility?
5. How does Taliaferro respond to the creation argument? *Do you think his reply is successful? Why or why not?
6. How does Taliaferro reply to the worship argument? *Do you think he is right about what "love of God" really is and about why God wants creatures to worship? Explain.
7. What does Taliaferro mean when he says that his solution to the problem of worship seems to depend on an "essentialist metaphysic"? Why does he eventually say that his solution does not, in truth, depend on an essentialist metaphysic?
8. How does Taliaferro reply to the redemption argument? *Do you think his conception of what the incarnation implies about God is correct? Why or why not?
9. Review the major theories of the atonement in Christian thought, as Taliaferro presents them.

---

[10] . . . Søren Kierkegaard beautifully portrays the incarnation as a Divine limiting and humbling, a humbling that does not overshadow or compromise the integrity and freedom of the creature. The incarnation may even be viewed along Kierkegaardian lines as part of God's enlarging and enhancing human selfhood. See especially "From on High He will draw all men unto Himself," Part III, *Training in Christianity,* translated and edited by Walter Lowrie (Princeton: Princeton University Press, 1971).

[11] Michael Slote, *Goods and Virtues* (Oxford: Clarendon Press, 1983), p. 62.

10. What is meant by "divine self-love," according to Taliaferro?

11. Suppose one accepts the doctrine of divine impassibility (that God has no emotions). How would this affect Taliaferro's essay?

12. *Compare Taliaferro's treatment of worship to the one in James Rachels's "God and Human Attitudes" in reading 3.8.

READING 1.5

God and Forgiveness

Anne C. Minas

That God forgives sin is widely thought to reflect God's perfection. Anne C. Minas (University of Waterloo) seeks to show, however, that, on the contrary, being forgiving of sin could not possibly be a divine attribute. God's perfection, she argues, logically precludes God's granting forgiveness. Minas considers various situations in which someone forgiving an agent would be appropriate (for example, learning new facts about the agent, reversing a previous judgment about the agent, or giving up resentment toward the agent) and demonstrates that none of the situations can arise for God, who is **omniscient** *and infallible in His judgments. Even forgiveness that is simply beneficent and betokens no deficiency of knowledge or judgment makes sense, Minas claims, only when there was prior harm and a feeling of personal injury and resentment. According to Minas, the latter, like cognitive mistakes, are inconsistent with God's perfect nature. Finally, forgiveness absolves sins, which in turn validates wrongdoings and leads to the dissolution of the moral system. How, then, can God forgive?*

To err is human, to forgive, divine. Most of us tend to believe this whether or not we also believe in the actual existence of a divine being. The non-believer reasons that if there were such a being he would forgive the wrong-doings of mortals, and insofar as he himself exercises forgiveness his nature approaches that which believers attribute to a deity. There is supposed to be something about being divine that makes a deity especially capable of exercising forgiveness; and, conversely, it is human frailty which prevents us from this exercise on occasions when we ought to forgive.

This belief in a connection between forgiving and being divine I want to show is mistaken, in a radical way. Far from its being the case that divine nature makes its possessor especially prone to forgive, such a nature makes forgiveness impossible. Such a being logically cannot forgive, since possession of divine attributes logically precludes conditions which are necessary for forgiveness. So, far from its being the case that human frailty makes forgiveness difficult or impossible, it is the possession of distinctly human, non-divine characteristics, that makes forgiveness appropriate for human beings. Only a human being can forgive—a divine being cannot.

In my discussion, I shall be assuming mainly that a divine being (if there is one) is perfect. He has a perfect moral sense, a perfect moral will, perfect knowledge, and perfect benevolence. I shall try not to make too many assumptions about the nature of forgiveness. The definitions given in the *Oxford English Dictionary* and the uses made of the word 'forgiveness' are varied enough to rule out any assumption that forgiveness amounts to one kind of thing in all circumstances. So I shall instead take up various kinds of actions forgiveness is, or might be, and show that not one of them is an action that could be performed by a perfect being.

I

The *OED* in some of its definitions of 'forgive' directs forgiveness upon actions that are wrong. Part of definition 3 of 'forgive' is 'to give up resentment or claim to requital for, pardon (an offence).' In this connection it mentions [Thomas] Hobbes' writing on "An Authority to Forgive, or Retain Sins," in *Leviathan* (III xlii 274); and *Isaiah* xxxiii 24, about forgiving iniquities. So let us suppose that forgiveness of one kind involves the forgiver's believing that the person forgiven has done something wrong and that it is this wrong action that the forgiveness is being directed upon.

Forgiveness of this sort may simply be retraction or modification of a previous adverse moral judgment about the act in question. The eloping couple might be forgiven in this way by their parents. The parents, in their shock and dismay when first hearing the news, censure the action harshly. Later, however, they realize that their judgment about the elopement was too severe and so they modify or abandon it, and so forgive the couple.

Now with human beings this reversal or modification of moral judgment is sometimes laudable, sometimes not. It depends on whether the original judgment was correct, or whether the person who made the judgment had good reason to believe it correct. If the parents changed their minds about the elopement, that would probably be laudable, since presumably elopement is not wrong (or not *very* wrong) and the parents had no good reason to think it was. But suppose a son had asked his parents to reverse their censure of his having murdered his sister. There would be no cause to praise them if they somehow deluded themselves into believing that the son had not done anything really wrong. They would then apparently have lost all sense of right and wrong, at least as regards their son, not to mention any special feelings they might have had about this particular victim, their daughter. Forgiveness, in the sense of reversal of moral judgment, is not always in order for human beings.

But when it is a deity considering an action, reversal of moral judgment is never in order. When contradictory judgments are made about the same action, one of them is wrong, and a being with a perfect moral sense cannot (logically cannot) make wrong moral judgments. If he was right in his second appraisal of the situation, he was wrong in his first and *vice versa.* And this is quite aside from the difficulty of how a being who is not in time can reverse his judgments, having no time in which to do so.

The situation is not appreciably changed if forgiveness, in the sense of reversal of judgment, is granted because new facts have come to light which should affect an assessment of the situation. One human being may be forgiven by another for this reason. "I didn't understand the situation fully," the forgiver says. "At first I could see no reason for your firing Smith. But since then I have learned he has had his hand in the till, and has been malicious towards his subordinates, etc. I now see you were quite right in letting him go." It is fine for a human being to make a new assessment of an action when new facts come to light. It is impossible for an **omniscient** deity, however, because, being omniscient, he always knows all the facts. For him, there can be no such thing as learning something new. And, of course, for such a being there can be no such thing as a temporary lapse of consciousness where he overlooks, or temporarily fails to remember, a relevant fact. So such things cannot be reasons for reversal of judgment in a deity, although they certainly can be for us. For this reason it is a little hard to see how some one can argue with a deity that he or someone else ought to be forgiven, by trying to bring certain facts to his attention. One of the last things Jesus said was "Father, forgive them, for they know not what they do." But how could Jesus have been trying to draw a certain fact to God's attention when God, being (as we sometimes say) omnipercipient, must have all facts in his attention all the time? He is also supposed to show perfect moral judgment in weighing facts, so it is equally insulting or, more accurately, blasphemous, to try to argue with God that a fact should have a particular moral weight in his consideration.

Sometimes it is thought that people ought to be forgiven for doing wrong for special considerations pertaining to their case. Such considerations include the motives of the agent (he stole the loaf of bread to feed his starving children), or special difficulties in which he found himself (he shot the burglar in self-defense), or any other special characteristics of the action (he went through the red light at 4 a.m. when the streets were virtually deserted). According to the rule (moral, legal, or whatever) he did something wrong, but the wrongness seems to be mitigated by special circumstances. But in cases like these, the fact of the matter is that the rule is too crude, or too general, to take the special circumstances into account. What someone who appeals to mitigating circumstances is arguing is that while the action is wrong according to the rule, it is not wrong (or not as wrong) in a more general, all things considered, sort of way. Forgiveness in this sense is really a kind of moral judgment; a recognition that the rule has only limited application to the assessment and that other factors must also be taken into account.

It is very difficult to see how God could make this kind of judgment, for what would the defective rule be for him? It could hardly be one of his own, one of the rules which he makes to define right and wrong (if this is indeed what he does) for why should he make a defective one? His only motivation, as far as I can see, would be considerations of simplicity and ease of understanding for human beings. This, however, would only function as a reason for giving human beings defective rules, and not for using them himself. Complexities being no problem for a perfectly omniscient being, he would, if he used rules at all to make moral assessments, use ones which had the degree of complexity necessary to take into account *all* morally relevant factors in a situation to be judged. Our rules would only be crude approximations to these perfectly accurate divine rules, and thus while it might appear to us as if God is making an exception to his own rules (not judging an action wrong which is wrong by our crude rules) this appearance would be delusory.

Finally, a human being may *condone* offences by others, meaning, according to *OED*, 'to forgive or overlook (an offence) so as to treat it as nonexistent.' This is especially appropriate with minor wrongdoings. For I take it that the idea of condoning is that of refusing to form an adverse moral judgment of an action, even though there may be some reason to do so. One overlooks, refuses to take account of, the immoral aspects of an action. Essentially, it is making an exception for a particular case for no reason. If this is a kind of forgiveness, as the definition suggests, it is again difficult to see how it is something a divine being can do. Being omniscient, he knows everything there is to be known, and is not able to overlook it, in the sense of refusing to know it. So in particular, he cannot do this with moral aspects of an action. In addition, condoning may show a certain lack of moral sense and so there is a second reason why a deity cannot do it. This is most clear when the immoral aspects are fairly substantial. Someone who condones mass murders shows a significant moral blindness, to say the least.

II

Reversing moral judgments, exhibiting moral blindness, and making exceptions to moral rules being impossible for perfect beings, it is time to consider other types of actions which might merit the name 'forgiveness.' In the passage quoted earlier, the *OED* mentioned giving up a claim to requital for an offence. When requital or punishment is remitted or reduced because of a new, more favourable judgment about the moral aspects of the case, then such cases become instances of the kinds discussed in the first part of this paper. This includes cases where special circumstances merit a special kind of judgment about the action. These are simply of forming judgments where all relevant circumstances are considered.

But there are also cases where punishment is remitted without reversing or modifying a judgment about the wrongdoing the punishment was supposed to be punishment for. This kind of forgiveness is akin to clemency exercised by a judge in the courts, or pardon by a high official. Someone who is in a position to mete out punishment for a wrongdoing decides to give less punishment than what is called for by the nature of the wrongdoing, or no punishment at all.

It is easy to envisage the deity in the role of a judge who makes decisions about punishments and rewards. For it is he who decides the lots of humans in life after death and these lots are often conceived of as rewards or punishments. People who are good or bad in this life get good or bad lots, respectively, in the afterlife. In addition, it is often thought that virtue is rewarded and vice punished by the deity in this life. Misfortunes, for instance, are sometimes thought of as being sent by God as a punishment for wrongdoing.

What is not so easy to envisage, however, is how a perfectly just God can remit punishment. In the first place, what would be the mechanism by which the punishment was originally assigned which was then remitted by God? With human beings the assignment and remission typically is done by two separate agencies, the remitting agency taking precedence over the assigning one. A judge (the remitter) gives a lighter punishment than that prescribed by law (the assigner). Or a high political official, a governor, say, remits a punishment assigned by the courts. But who or what assigns punishments which God then remits? God himself? He then appears to be something of a practical joker, assigning punishments which he, with perfect foreknowledge, knows he is going to remit, perhaps doing this to scare some virtue into sinners. If not he but his laws assign the original punishment, essentially the same problem arises, namely why God makes laws that he knows he is going to override.

Other problems would appear here as well. One concerns the question of whether the punishment over which the sinner is being forgiven by God was what the sinner justly deserved. If it was, then in remitting him this punishment God is not giving the sinner what he deserves, and thus not behaving in a way consistent with his being a perfectly just being. If, on the other hand, the sinner did not deserve the punishment, then it was an unjust mechanism which assigned such punishment. If this mechanism were God's laws or decrees, then once again he would not be a perfectly just being, although he certainly would be more just in remitting one of his own unjust sentences than in letting it stand. If the mechanism assigning the punishment were, on the other hand, a human one, it is difficult to see why God should pay any attention to it. Ignoring this punishment would be a much more appropriate attitude than remitting it.

Another problem has to do with God's absolving only some sinners from their punishments. For either God forgives everyone or he does not. If he only forgives some people, and not others, then he might be behaving unjustly towards those whose punishment he allows to stand. If he picks out people to forgive for no special reason, then he is acting arbitrarily and immorally. A just God does not play favourites with rewards and punishments.

So is there a reason God might have for remitting punishment in some cases but not in others? We have been assuming that these are all cases where God does not reverse his moral condemnation of the actions, so this cannot be a reason. But one reason that is often cited is repentance on the part of the sinner. This repentance would be an overt expression of the agent's realization of having done wrong, his having the appropriate feelings about his actions, and his resolve not to repeat them. So in asking for forgiveness with this attitude, the penitent is not asking God for a new judgment on his actions—as noted earlier, this smacks of blasphemy—but rather a new and more favourable judgment on *him,* as an agent. He is not the wrongdoer he once was, but has a new, reformed, character.

We, as human beings, revise our judgments about people's characters in the light of evidence that they are repentant about their past misdeeds. But for an omniscient being, such revision would not be possible. In his omniscience, God would be able to foreknow the repentance of the agent; therefore he need not make, and could not have made, a judgment about the agent's character which did not take this act of repentance into account. It is difficult to see, moreover, why God should count the end of the agent's life, the post-repentance period, more heavily than the beginning in his final assessment of the agent's character. Because God is omniscient and outside time, all parts of a human life are known to him in exactly the same way, known to him much as a number series is known to us. We do not attach any special significance to the later numbers in the series just because they are later, nor do we believe they are better representatives of the series. Similarly God should not regard an agent's later character as the best representative of his total character.

We, on the other hand, do attach special significance to an agent's later character, for at least two reasons. One is that it is the man's most recent character with which we are (presently) confronted, and with which we have to deal. And the other is that insofar as we need, or want to make, predictions about his future character, the most recent evidence will tend to be the most reliable. These two reasons have importance in a **utilitarian** justification of infliction or withholding of punishment. The utilitarian treats punishment as a method for obtaining good results, one of the foremost being improvement of the agent's character, behaviour, and motivation. Punishment is only justified to the extent it is effective in these areas. So a utilitarian would not be able to derive this kind of justification when he is considering punishing an already reformed character. The effect already having been gained, the punishment is superfluous as a method, and hence unjustified.

A utilitarian can thus consider withholding or remitting punishment for repentant, reformed agents. Now the question is, can God be such a utilitarian, consistently with his perfection, and thus exercise forgiveness in this particular way? He would be a God who uses threats and bribes to get people to behave themselves, threatening them with punishment if they misbehave, bribing them with forgiveness, remission of punishment, if they decide to behave.

It seems to me that this portrayal of God the manipulator is inconsistent with the image of divine perfection. There must be better, fairer, and more effective ways to instil into human beings a sense of right and wrong and a will to do the right. Moreover, the whole exercise of threats and bribes would presumably become inoperative at the end of an individual's life. Since he has no more opportunities to choose the wrong, there is no longer a utilitarian reason for punishing him as a threat. To condemn him to the eternal flames just as an example to mortals still on earth is not, I think, something that a just God could contemplate, particularly since these mortals seem to have no good way of knowing who has been condemned and who has not. So everyone would have to have his punishment remitted at the end of this life, i.e., everyone would have to be forgiven, a possibility that was mentioned, but not discussed, a little earlier. But then the whole activity of threats and bribes during an individual's life becomes meaningless, a little game God plays with us where everything comes out all right in the end anyway. The juiciest rewards and the most terrible punishments he can mete out would be those in the after-life, and it is just these that he can have no utilitarian reasons for conferring.

Nor, I believe, can God remit punishment for a repentant sinner for non-utilitarian reasons, as has already been noted, although he must take reformed periods of the agent's life into account in making his judgment. But to weigh (in some non-utilitarian way) the amount of punishment, if any, due to a repentant character and give him just that much would be to disregard the pre-repentance period of the agent's life and this, I have argued, a just omniscient god could not do. Far from having the special significance which they are sometimes thought to have, death-bed confessions and pleas for forgiveness would be pretty useless. If the agent spent ten minutes of his life reformed, and seventy years of his life unreformed, the seventy years should count much more heavily when God is considering what kinds of punishment to mete out.

III

The kinds of forgiveness so far considered have been essentially ones involving either a reversal of moral judgment on the actions forgiven or a reversal of judgment about punishing the agent. It may be felt that the discussion so far has missed the most central kinds of forgiveness, those, for instance, fitting this definition in the *OED:* '4. To give up resentment against, pardon (an offender).' Although pardoning an offender may mean remission of punishment, which I have already discussed, giving up resentment seems to be something different. Resentment being a kind of feeling or attitude, to give it up would be to change a feeling or attitude. This would not necessarily involve reversing a judgment. The change may be partly, or even wholly, non-cognitive.

Joseph Butler devotes two sermons to a discussion of resentment and forgiveness, viewing forgiveness as an avoidance of the abuses of resentment. He defines resentment thus: "the natural object or occasion of settled resentment then being injury as distinct from pain or loss . . . but from this [sudden anger], deliberate anger or resentment is essentially distinguished, as the latter is not naturally excited by, or intended to prevent mere harm without the appearance of wrong or injustice."[1] Resentment is a moral feeling or attitude whose object must be an action believed wrong or unjust, and not just any harm. Giving up of resentment might then mean giving up or reversing the belief that the action was wrong, as discussed in Part I of this paper; or it might mean merely giving up part or all of an accompanying feeling or attitude toward the action, while retaining the belief that it was wrong. It is forgiveness of this second sort that I want now to discuss.

Such seems to be the case of the forgiving father of the Prodigal Son. Presumably the father did not reverse his judgment of the son's prodigality deciding that the son's actions were not so bad after all. Rather, it was in spite of this judgment that he was able to forgive him.

Something of this sort seems to be the kind of forgiveness Butler urges. He does not think we ought to reverse our moral judgments about those who have wronged us (except in instances where the evidence warrants it). Nor does he recommend giving up what he calls "a due, natural sense of the injury." Some moral attitudes and feelings toward a wrongdoing may be appropriate to retain in forgiveness. What has to be given up, according to Butler, seems to be what we might call taking the wrongdoing personally. For to forgive, according to him, is just "to be affected towards the injurious person in the same way any good men, uninterested in the case, would be, if they had the same just sense, which we have supposed the injured person to have, of the fault, after which there will yet remain real goodwill towards the offender."[2] To forgive is just to cease to have any personal interest in the injury. It is to regard it as if it had happened to someone else in whom we have no special interest, other than the general interest we have in all human beings. So the father might forgive his prodigal son by ceasing to take the son's prodigality personally. He regards it no longer as a wasting of *his* money, as something *his* son has done to *him,* but instead as a mere wasting of someone's good money.

How and why can this change in feeling happen? One suggestion is that the personal feelings are gradually forgotten, or wear off in some natural manner. "Forgive and forget" is what is sometimes said, and one possibility is that forgiving is forgetting. It could be argued that personal feelings only last naturally for so long and then wear off, unless the person makes a determined effort to retain or renew them, or as Butler puts it, "resentment has taken possession of the temper and will not quit its hold," suggesting that the mechanism by which this happens is "bare obstinacy."[3]

This may be true of human beings, but it cannot be true of God, and thus this kind of forgiveness is not open to him to exercise. An omniscient being cannot (logically) forget anything, so cannot in particular forget his feelings. And all his feelings are equally alive to him at all times, this being, I think, part of what is meant in calling him **omnipercipient.** In perceiving situations, he knows them in a way in which they are fully real to him, meaning that he reacts not just by forming judgments, but also with all appropriate feelings. Then, to be omnipercipient is to have all reactions to all situations equally vivid, regardless of when they happened. So the reactions of omnipercipient beings cannot change over time. So even if God were subject to change, and this change could take place in time (even though he is supposed to exist outside time) he would not be able

[1]Joseph Butler, *Fifteen Sermons Preached at the Rolls Chapel* (London, 1967), p. 125 ff.

[2]Butler, *op. cit.,* p. 143.

[3]Butler, *op. cit.,* p. 129 ff.

to change in this particular way, since this change involves a dimming of feeling.

Let us then consider a different kind of situation where resentment, in the sense of taking an injury personally, is dispelled, not through forgetting or some other kind of natural erosion, but as a result of conscious effort on the part of the forgiver. What reasons would he have for making this kind of effort?

When an injury is taken personally, the result is a certain breach between the injured person and the person who has injured him. This breach is not wholly due to the nature of the injury, nor to the injured person's reactions by way of judgment or sense of wrongness of the action. Other people could have these same reactions without such a breach occurring. Friends of the father of the Prodigal Son could agree with him in his judgments of the son's behaviour and could react with moral indignation at the son's waste without such reactions causing estrangement from the son. They have not themselves been injured, so there is no reason to take the prodigality personally. And also their relations with the boy are not such as to be affected by resentment in the way the father's are, since he is much more involved with the boy. This involvement, I think, also makes it more important for the father that the breach should be healed.

The father's motivation for forgiveness is thus to heal the breach, and this breach presumably is virtually intolerable because of his relationship with the boy. His involvement in and regard for the relationship require that he should not spoil it by feelings of personal injury. Abandoning his feelings of personal injury is also required by a regard for the injuring party as a human being. Presumably more things should be taken into account in forming an attitude toward him than the injury he has caused. The trouble with a sense of personal injury is that it tends to swamp other considerations in the formation of attitudes. The person tends to be seen just as the agent of the injury and nothing else.

A final reason for trying to get rid of feelings of personal injury as soon as possible is that harbouring such feelings tends to be bad for the person who refuses to forgive. At least, this is what the psychologists tell us—that it is unhealthy to harbour and brood over personal resentments.

A change in attitude becomes particularly appropriate when the offender repents, shows remorse for his wrong-doing. If the remorse is genuine he has dissociated himself from the wrong-doing in the sense that if he had it to do over again he would refrain, and he censures himself for having done it in the same way as if the agent had been someone else. So, since he is no longer the kind of person who would commit such an injury, an attitude that presupposes that he is such a person is inappropriate. And a sense of personal injury is, I think, just such an attitude since it is an attitude toward a person as the agent of a certain deed. Repentance as an overt sign of remorse makes such a difference in forgiveness (as an abandonment of a sense of personal injury) that it is sometimes difficult to see how forgiveness can take place without it. The parent who is willing to forgive a child anything, despite the fact that the child shows absolutely no signs of remorse, can be regarded as indulgent at best, and, at worst, as lacking a certain sense of appropriateness in his/her relations with the child. Too much of a readiness to forgive without repentance indicates a certain lack of awareness of personal injury, which in turn indicates a general lack of awareness in personal relations. Or sometimes the injuries are so great that the person really has no redeeming features which will outbalance them. Take the operators of the furnaces at Buchenwald, for example: if they are unrepentant what possible reasons could we have for forgiving them? In the absence of remorse there may not be any basis for realigning one's attitude toward the offender. The best one can do is just forget about him, taking the method of forgiveness I previously suggested.

Now, how could God figure in this kind of forgiveness? Since it presupposes a sense of taking an injury personally (it is this attitude that is remitted in forgiveness) it is very difficult to see how God could forgive in this way. For I think it is fairly clear that taking an injury personally, as opposed to having a general sense of its wrongness, is a distinctly human failing, an imperfection. Try to imagine a god sulking or brooding, perhaps plotting revenge because someone has, say, made off with the treasure in one of his churches, and you have imagined a less than perfect being. The Olympian gods and goddesses were noted for their pettiness in their relations with each other, with regard to injuries, real or imagined, and this is one good reason why they were not and are not regarded as perfect. A god whose perspective of another god or a person is distorted by a sense of personal injury—I argued earlier that this was an accompaniment of, if not part of, resentment and so was one reason for human forgiveness, getting rid of this attitude—is at the very least not omnipercipient, and probably also not just in his assessment of the human being who committed the injury. Relations with the injuring party are also severed, I maintained, by this attitude, and surely a perfect being could not allow this to happen. And the third reason for our getting rid of feelings of personal injury also serves as a reason for God's not having them at all. They are detrimental to one's psychological wellbeing, and in extreme cases make a person a candidate for the psychiatrist's couch. This sort of thing obviously cannot (logically) happen to a perfect being.

God, then, cannot forgive personal injuries where what is given up is personal resentment (*OED*—for 'forgive'—'1. To give up, cease to harbour (resentment, wrath)') since he cannot have such feelings. But, it is sometimes said, God forgives us before we ask for forgiveness, sometimes even before we do wrong. Such a line of thinking perhaps would mean that God forgives before he resents, gives up the resentment before he has it, thus skipping the resentment phase of the process. More simply, he decides, wills not to harbour resentment. But the problem here is whether it makes any sense to make decisions where there is only one logically possible alternative. It is a little peculiar for me to make a decision about whether I am going to be the number 2, since I have only one alternative which is logically possible, and that is not to be the number 2. God presumably is in the same position with regard to harbouring resentment. Only the alternative of not harbouring it is logically open to him.

It is, however, sometimes maintained that God has all his perfections because he wills to have them, and so has made a meaningful decision in choosing them. If this is true, it would apply to a decision not (ever) to harbour resentment. But I think there are nonetheless good reasons not to count this as real forgiveness, since forgiveness has to be a giving up of something, and no one can give up something he never had. It would be as if I decided as a New Year's resolution to give up gambling, when I had never gambled. Also, repentance and remorse would lose their connection with God's forgiveness. Since he harbours no resentment anyway, there would be no point in setting matters straight by repenting. The only likely function repentance could have, in restoring a relationship with God which had been severed by a misdeed, would be if the injury made some change in the *sinner's* attitude toward God which had severed the relationship, and if this attitude could be changed back by repentance. This may well happen (although I cannot understand just how the mechanism would work), but it is clearly not a case of God's forgiving, since it is not a case of God's doing anything. Everything that is done is done by the sinner, and it is in him that the changes take place.

IV

It is, moreover, only harm, or supposed harm, to himself that a person can take personally. Even if others are harmed as well, it is only the concomitant, or resultant, harm to oneself that causes feelings of personal resentment. If a son takes insults about his parents personally, for instance, this is because he believes that, when they are insulted, he is as well. Thus, forgiveness as a ceasing to hold personal resentment can only be directed toward actions which have wronged the forgiver (or which he believes have wronged him). And I think this is true of any kind of forgiveness—it is appropriately directed only toward actions which have wronged the forgiver. It would be a bit high-handed of me, for instance, to forgive someone else's husband's excessive drinking and womanizings when his wife felt not the least inclined in that direction—high-handed because I would have to construe his behaviour as wronging me rather than her. Only in certain restricted cases can one person forgive wrongs to another by proxy, as it were. Typically this happens only when the forgiver bears a special relationship to the wronged person and the wronged person is dead. I could, for instance, conceivably forgive a wrong done to one of my dead ancestors if my relationship to him/her were such that if I were not to forgive the action, it would never be forgiven.

The implications here for God are that he can only forgive wrongs, sins, that are injuries to him. If he has universal powers of forgiveness, for all sins, sins must all have this characteristic.

Several problems arise immediately. One is how it is possible to wrong, to injure, a perfect being. His very perfection should make him immune from the kind of injury which makes forgiveness appropriate. The other problem is how even an imperfect being could construe as primarily wrongs to himself actions which seem mainly to harm someone else. On such a construction the person stolen from, raped, injured, killed, enslaved, is not really wronged at all, or at least the injury done him is rather minimal compared to that done to God by breaking his laws, contravening his wishes, or whatever. But this would have to be true if God is to forgive these actions, and especially if he is to forgive them independently of whether they have been forgiven by the ostensible injured party. To give God the first or primary right to forgive is to view him as the primary injured party.

Finally, I want to mention a kind of forgiveness which God alone is supposed to be able to exercise, which is associated with the washing away of one's sins. The idea, as nearly as I have been able to make out, is that before God forgives there are a certain number of wrongs which the person committed. Afterwards there are none. He did the actions all right, but after God's forgiveness, they are no longer wrong.

This is a little like a child's plea that a parent make things all right. The child imagines that rightness and wrongness depend wholly on the parent's say-so. So an action, or anything, might be changed from wrong to right, while remaining otherwise unchanged, because the parent first said it was wrong and then later says it is right. I think we sometimes expect God to set things right in the same way and we call this "forgiveness."

But much as we would like sometimes to retreat into these childhood fancies where God as parent makes things all right by some kind of magic, I think they embody too many confusions to make them worth considering. The first is the idea that the rightness or wrongness of an action can change without anything else about it changing. And another is the dependence of right or wrong on God's say-so. For in a situation like the ones being described it is not as if God gave us general precepts by which to live and they were right because they were expressions of the will of God. Many people have objections to the view that God's will has anything to do with right or wrong. But quite aside from these general objections, there is the problem that a god like the one being described does not impart to his decrees any generality. He literally changes wrong to right from one day to the next. This absence of generality, I think, disqualifies these changeable decrees from being *ethical* precepts. It also gives human beings considerable motivation for disobedience to God's will. If there is no telling how God is going to regard an action from one day to the next, then someone might want to take his chances on disobedience, figuring that what contravenes God's will one day will be favourably regarded the next.

With some actions, a **necessary condition** for their being wrong is an unfavourable reaction by someone affected by the action. So if the person ceases to show the reaction, the action is no longer wrong. The person to whom a promise is made can make a broken promise cease to be wrong by welcoming the fact that it was broken. The masochist, by welcoming injuries to himself, makes them cease to be injuries. Thus, if (1) all wrongs are injuries to God only and (2) they are the kind of wrongs which God eventually shows a favourable reaction to, God might be able to set all wrongs right.

I have already commented on (1) above, maintaining that it is very difficult to take the point of view that God is always the only one injured in a wrong-doing. (2), I think, is even more absurd. How could a morally sensitive and just God welcome human beings torturing, maiming, killing, and causing suffering to one another?

So we cannot without logical and/or moral absurdity say of a fully divine being that it forgives in any sense I have been able to give to "forgive."

Whether this is because divine forgiveness is beyond the scope of human understanding is another question, not the concern of this paper. I have only tried to show that divine forgiveness does appear absurd to the human understanding, or at least to mine.

STUDY QUESTIONS

1. Explain the terms *condone, remit,* and *forgive.*
2. Explain the various situations in which forgiveness is called for and why, according to Minas, it is impossible for God to forgive in any of those circumstances.
3. How is a piece of Minas's argument partly dependent on Anselm's and Aquinas's view of statements attributing emotions to God?
4. *Is Minas correct that "taking an injury personally, as opposed to having a general sense of its wrongness, is a distinctively human failing, an imperfection?" Discuss.
5. *Could someone be offended by an action without being harmed by the action? Also, could someone be offended by an action without experiencing resentment toward the offender? Discuss. If the answers to these questions are "yes," is Minas's argument affected? Explain. (See Philip Quinn, *Divine Commands and Moral Requirements,* pp. 141–43.)
6. *If we accept Minas's view, redemption and repentance are unattainable by sinners. If this conclusion were to be widely accepted by theists, what would be the likely psychological effect on human behavior?
7. *Jewish philosopher Moses Maimonides (1138–1204) writes about repentance:

> It is manifest that [belief in] repentance . . . belongs to . . . the opinions without the belief in which the existence of individuals cannot be well ordered. For an individual cannot but sin and err. . . . If then the individual believed that this fracture can never be remedied, he would persist in his error and sometimes perhaps disobey even more because of the fact that no stratagem remains at his disposal. If, however, he believes in repentance, he can correct himself and return to a better and more perfect state than the one he was in before he sinned. (*Guide of the Perplexed,* trans. Shlomo Pines [Chicago: University of Chicago Press, 1963], vol. 2, pt. III, ch. 36, p. 540).

Explain Maimonides's point. How might adopting his point affect one's assessment of Minas's argument? Compare your thoughts on this with the last paragraph of section III of Minas's essay (p. 43).

READING 1.6

Omnipotence

Peter Geach

The notion that God can do everything is a commonplace of **theology**—*but is it correct? No, argues British philosopher Peter Geach (Cambridge University). For one thing, God is bound by the laws of logic. Therefore, God cannot do anything that is logically impossible (to use an example not mentioned by Geach, God cannot create a round square). In addition, God cannot do anything that is inconsistent with God's other attributes. Thus, following Thomas Aquinas, Geach notes that God cannot sin, cannot suffer violence, and cannot break His promises. Geach implies that the concept of* **omnipotence** *is a Greek one that has been grafted onto Christian theology. He concludes that, although God is not omnipotent—God cannot do everything—God is almighty; that is, God has power over all things.*

It is fortunate for my purposes that English has the two words "almighty" and **"omnipotent,"** and that apart from any stipulation by me the words have rather different associations and suggestions. "Almighty" is the familiar word that comes in the creeds of the Church; "omnipotent" is at home rather in formal theological discussions and controversies, e.g. about miracles and about the problem of evil. "Almighty" derives by way of Latin "omnipotens" from the Greek word "*pantokratōr*"; and both this Greek word, like the more classical "*pankratēs,*" and "almighty" itself suggest God's having power *over* all things. On the other hand the English word "omnipotent" would ordinarily be taken to imply ability to *do* everything; the Latin word "omnipotens" also predominantly has this meaning in **Scholastic** writers, even though in origin it is a Latinization of "*pantocratōr.*" So there already is a tendency to distinguish the two words; and in this paper I shall make the distinction a strict one. I shall use the word "almighty" to express God's power over all things, and I shall take "omnipotence" to mean ability to do everything.

I think we can in a measure understand what God's almightiness implies, and I shall argue that almightiness so understood must be ascribed to God if we are to retain anything like traditional Christian belief in God. The position as regards omnipotence, or as regards the statement "God can do everything," seems to me to be very different. Of course even "God can do everything" may be understood simply as a way of magnifying God by contrast with the impotence of man. [J. M. E.] McTaggart described it as "a piece of theological etiquette" to call God omnipotent: Thomas Hobbes, out of reverence for his Maker, would rather say that "omnipotent" is an attribute of honour. But McTaggart and Thomas Hobbes would agree that "God is omnipotent" or "God can do everything" is not to be treated as a proposition that can figure as premise or conclusion in a serious theological argument. And I too wish to say this. I have no objection to such ways of speaking if they merely express a desire to give the best honour we can to God our Maker, whose Name only is excellent and whose praise is above heaven and earth. But theologians have tried to *prove* that God can do everything, or to derive conclusions from this thesis as a premise. I think such attempts have been wholly unsuccessful. When people have tried to read into "God can do everything" a signification not of Pious Intention but of Philosophical Truth, they have only landed themselves in intractable problems and hopeless confusions; no graspable sense has ever been given to this sentence that did not lead to self-contradiction or at least to conclusions manifestly untenable from a Christian point of view.

I shall return to this; but I must first develop what I have to say about God's almightiness, or power over all things. God is not just more powerful than any creature; no creature can compete with God in power, even unsuccessfully. For God is also the source of all power; any power a creature has comes from God and is maintained only for such time as God wills. Nebuchadnezzar submitted to praise and adore the God of heaven because he was forced by experience to realize that only by God's favour did his wits hold together from one end of a blasphemous sentence to the other end. Nobody can deceive God or circumvent him or frustrate him; and there is no question of God's trying to do anything and failing. In Heaven and on Earth, God does whatever he will. We shall see that some propositions of the form "God cannot do so-and-so" have to be accepted as true; but what God cannot be said to be able to do he likewise cannot will to do; we cannot drive a logical wedge between his power and his will, which are, as the Scholastics said, really identical, and there is no application to God of the concept of trying but failing.

I shall not spend time on citations of Scripture and tradition to show that this doctrine of God's almightiness is authentically Christian; nor shall I here develop rational grounds for believing it is a true doctrine. But it is quite easy to show that this doctrine is indispensable for Christianity, not a bit of old metaphysical luggage that can be abandoned with relief. For Christianity requires an absolute faith in the promises of God: specifically, faith in the promise that some day the whole human race will be delivered and blessed by the establishment of the Kingdom of God. If God were not almighty, he might will and not do; sincerely promise, but find fulfilment beyond his power. Men might prove untamable and incorrigible, and might kill themselves through war or pollution before God's salvific plan for them could come into force. It is useless to say that after the end of this earthly life men would live again; for as I have argued elsewhere, only the promise of God can give us any confidence that there will be an afterlife for men, and if God were not almighty, this promise too might fail. If God is true and just and unchangeable and almighty, we can have absolute confidence in his promises: otherwise we cannot—and there would be an end of Christianity.

A Christian must therefore believe that God is almighty; but he need not believe that God can do everything. Indeed, the very argument I have just used shows that a Christian must not believe that God can do everything: for he may not believe that God could possibly break his own word. Nor can a Christian even believe that God can do everything that is logically possible; for breaking one's word is certainly a logically possible feat.

It seems to me, therefore, that the tangles in which people have enmeshed themselves when trying to give the expression "God can do everything" an intelligible and acceptable content are tangles that a Christian believer has no need to enmesh himself in; the spectacle of others enmeshed may sadden him, but need not cause him to stumble in the way of faith. The denial that God is omnipotent, or able to do everything, may seem dishonouring to God; but when we see where the contrary affirmation, in its various forms, has led, we may well cry out with Hobbes: "Can any man think God is served with such absurdities? . . . As if it were an acknowledgment of the Divine Power, to say, that which is, is not; or that which has been, has not been."

I shall consider four main theories of omnipotence. The first holds that God can do everything absolutely; everything that can be expressed in a string of words that makes sense; even if that sense can be shown to be self-contradictory, God is not bound in action, as we are in thought, by the laws of logic. I shall speak of this as the doctrine that God is *absolutely* omnipotent.

The second doctrine is that a proposition "God can do so-and-so" is true when and only when "so-and-so" represents a logically consistent description.

The third doctrine is that "God *can* do so-and-so" is true just if "God does so-and-so" is logically consistent. This is a weaker doctrine than the second; for "God is doing so-and-so" is logically consistent only when "so-and-so" represents a logically consistent description, but on the other hand there may be consistently describable feats which it would involve contradiction to suppose done *by* God.

The last and weakest view is that the realm of what can be done or brought about includes all future possibilities, and that whenever "God *will* bring so-and-so about" is logically possible, "God *can* bring so-and-so about" is true.

The first sense of "omnipotent" in which people have believed God to be omnipotent implies precisely: ability to do absolutely everything, everything describable. You mention it, and God can do it. . . . At least one great philosopher, [René] Descartes, deliberately adopted and defended this doctrine of omnipotence: what I shall call the doctrine of absolute omnipotence.

As Descartes himself remarked, nothing is too absurd for some philosopher to have said it some time; I once read an article about an Indian school of philosophers who were alleged to maintain that it is only a delusion, which the wise can overcome, that anything exists at all—so perhaps it would not matter all that much that a philosopher is found to defend absolute omnipotence. Perhaps it would not matter all that much that the philosopher in question was a very great one; for very great philosophers have maintained the most preposterous theses. What does make the denial of absolute omnipotence important is not that we are thereby denying what a philosopher, a very great philosopher, thought he must assert, but that this doctrine has a live influence on people's religious thought—I should of course say, a pernicious influence. Some naive Christians would explicitly assert the doctrine; and moreover, I think McTaggart was right in believing that in popular religious thought a covert appeal to the doctrine is sometimes made even by people who would deny it if it were explicitly stated to them and its manifest consequences pointed out.

McTaggart may well have come into contact with naive Protestant defenders of absolute omnipotence when he was defending his atheist faith at his public school. The opinion is certainly not dead, as I can testify from personal experience. For many years I used to teach the philosophy of Descartes in a special course for undergraduates reading French; year by year, there were always two or three of them who embraced Descartes' defence of absolute omnipotence *con amore* [with love] and protested indignantly when I described the doctrine as incoherent. It would of course have been no good to say I was following Doctors of the Church in rejecting the doctrine; I did in the end find a way of producing silence, though not, I fear, conviction, and going on to other topics of discussion; I cited the passages of the Epistle to the Hebrews which say explicitly that God cannot swear by anything greater than himself (vi. 13) or break his word (vi. 18). Fortunately none of them ever thought of resorting to the ultimate weapon which, as I believe George Mavrodes remarked, is available to the defender of absolute omnipotence; namely, he can always say: "Well, you've stated a difficulty, but of course being omnipotent God can overcome that difficulty, though I don't see how." . . .

Let us leave these naive defenders in their entrenched position and return for a moment to Descartes. Descartes held that the truths of logic and arithmetic are freely made to be true by God's will. To be sure we clearly and distinctly see that these truths are necessary; they are necessary in our world, and in giving us our mental endowments God gave us the right sort of clear and distinct ideas to see the necessity. But though they are necessary, they are not necessarily necessary; God could have freely chosen to make a different sort of world, in which other things would have been necessary truths. The possibility of such another world is something we cannot *comprehend,* but only dimly *apprehend.* . . .

Descartes' motive for believing in absolute omnipotence was not contemptible: it seemed to him that otherwise God would be *subject to* the inexorable laws of logic as Jove was to the decrees of the Fates. The nature of logical truth is a very difficult problem, which I cannot discuss here. The easy **conventionalist** line, that it is our arbitrary way of using words that makes **logical truth,** seems to me untenable, for reasons that [Willard Van Orman] Quine among others has clearly spelled out. If I could follow Quine further in regarding logical laws as natural laws of very great generality—revisable in principle, though most unlikely to be revised, in a major theoretical reconstruction—then perhaps after all some rehabilitation of Descartes on this topic might be possible. But in the end I have to say that as we cannot say how a non-logical world would look, we cannot say how a supra-logical God would act or how he could communicate anything to us by way of revelation. So I end as I began: a Christian need not and cannot believe in absolute omnipotence.

It is important that Christians should clearly realize this, because otherwise a half-belief in absolute omnipotence may work in their minds subterraneously. As I said, I think McTaggart was absolutely right in drawing attention to this danger. One and the same man may deny the doctrine of absolute omnipotence when the doctrine is clearly put to him, and yet reassure himself that God can certainly do so-and-so by using *merely* the premise of God's omnipotence. And McTaggart is saying this is indefensible. At the very least this "so-and-so" must represent a logically consistent description of a feat; and proofs of logical consistency are notoriously not always easy. Nor, as we shall see, are our troubles at an end if we assume that God *can* do anything whose description is logically consistent.

Logical consistency in the description of the feat is certainly a ***necessary* condition** for the truth of "God can do so-and-so": if "so-and-so" represents an inconsistent description of a feat, then "God can do so-and-so" is certainly a false and impossible proposition, since it entails "It could be the case that so-and-so came about"; so, by **contraposition,** if "God can do so-and-so" is to be true, or even logically possible, then "so-and-so" must represent a logically consistent description of a feat. And whereas only a minority of Christians have explicitly believed in absolute omnipotence, many have believed that a proposition of the form "God can do so-and-so" is true whenever "so-and-so" represents a description of a logically possible feat. This is our second doctrine of omnipotence. One classic statement of this comes in the *Summa Theologica* [Part I, question 25, article 3]. Aquinas rightly says that we cannot explain "God can do everything" in terms of what is within the power of some agent; for "God can do everything any created agent can do," though true, is not a comprehensive enough account of God's power, which exceeds that of any created agent; and "God can do everything God can do" runs uselessly in a circle. So he puts forward the view that if the description "so-

and-so" is in itself possible through the relation of the terms involved—if it does not involve contradictories' being true together—then "God can do so-and-so" is true. Many Christian writers have followed Aquinas in saying this; but it is not a position consistently maintainable. As we shall see, Aquinas did not manage to stick to the position himself.

Before I raise the difficulties against this thesis, I wish to expose a common confusion that often leads people to accept it: the confusion between self-contradiction and gibberish. C. S. Lewis in *The Problem of Pain* says that meaningless combinations of words do not suddenly acquire meaning simply because we prefix to them the two other words "God can." . . . But if we take Lewis's words strictly, his point is utterly trivial, and nothing to our purpose. For gibberish, syntactically incoherent combination of words, is quite different from self-contradictory sentences or descriptions; the latter certainly have an intelligible place in our language.

It is a common move in logic to argue that a set of premises A, B, C together yield a contradiction, and that therefore A and B as premises yield as conclusion the contradictory of C; some logicians have puritanical objections to this manoeuvre, but I cannot stop to consider them; I am confident, too, that neither Aquinas nor Lewis would share these objections to ***reductio ad absurdum.*** If, however, a contradictory formula were gibberish, ***reductio ad absurdum*** certainly would be an illegitimate procedure—indeed it would be a nonsensical one. So we have to say that when "so-and-so" represents a self-contradictory description of a feat, "God can do so-and-so" is likewise self-contradictory, but that being self-contradictory it is *not* gibberish, but merely false.

I am afraid the view of omnipotence presently under consideration owes part of its attractiveness to the idea that then "God can do so-and-so" would never turn out *false,* so that there would be no genuine counterexamples to "God can do everything." Aquinas says, in the passage I just now cited: "What implies contradiction cannot be a word, for no understanding can conceive it." Aquinas, writing seven centuries ago, is excusable for not being clear about the difference between self-contradiction and gibberish; we are not excusable if we are not. It is not gibberish to say "a God can bring it about that in Alcalá there lives a barber who shaves all those and only those living in Alcalá who do not shave themselves"; this is a perfectly well-formed sentence, and not on the face of it self-contradictory; all the same, the supposed feat notoriously is self-contradictory, so this statement of what God can do is not nonsense but false.

One instance of a description of a feat that is really but not overtly self-contradictory has some slight importance in the history of conceptions of omnipotence. It appeared obvious to Spinoza that *God can bring about everything that God can bring about,* and that to deny this would be flatly incompatible with God's omnipotence (*Ethics* [Book I, Proposition 17], scholium). Well, the italicized sentence is syntactically ambiguous. "Everything that God can bring about God can bring about" is one possible reading of the sentence, and this is an obvious, indeed trivial predication about God, which must be true if there is a God at all. But the other way of taking the sentence relates to a supposed feat of *bringing about everything that God can bring about—all* of these bringable-about things *together*—and it says that God is capable of *this* feat. This is clearly the way Spinoza wishes us to take the sentence. But taken this way, it is not obvious at all; quite the contrary, it's obviously false. For among the things that are severally possible for God to bring about, there are going to be some pairs that are not ***compossible,*** pairs which it is logically impossible should both come about; and then it is beyond God's power to bring about such a pair together—let alone, to bring about all the things together which he can bring about severally.

This does not give us a description of a *logically possible* feat which God cannot accomplish. However, there is nothing easier than to mention feats which are logically possible but which God cannot do, if Christianity is true. Lying and promise-breaking are logically possible feats: but Christian faith, as I have said, collapses unless we are assured that God cannot lie and cannot break his promises.

This argument is an ***ad hominem* argument** addressed to Christians; but there are well-known logical arguments to show that on any view there must be some logically possible feats that are beyond God's power. One good example suffices: making a thing which its maker cannot afterwards destroy. This is certainly a possible feat, a feat that some human beings have performed. Can God perform the feat or not? If he cannot there is already some logically possible feat which God cannot perform. If God can perform the feat, then let us suppose that he does: . . . Then we are supposing God to have brought about a situation in which he *has* made something he cannot destroy; and in that situation destroying this thing is a *logically* possible feat that God cannot accomplish, for we surely cannot admit the idea of a creature whose destruction is logically *im*possible.

There have been various attempts to meet this argument. The most interesting one is that the proposition "God cannot make a thing that he cannot destroy" can be turned round to "Any thing that God can make he can destroy"—which does not even look like an objection to God's being able to do everything logically possible. But this reply involves the very same bracketing fallacy that I exposed a moment ago in Spinoza. There, you will remember, we had to distinguish two ways of taking "God can bring about everything that God can bring about":

A. Everything that God can bring about, God can bring about.
B. God can bring about the following feat: to bring about everything that God can bring about.

And we saw that A is trivially true, given that there is a God, and B certainly false. Here, similarly, we have to distinguish two senses of "God cannot make a thing that its maker cannot destroy":

A. Anything that its maker cannot destroy, God cannot make.
B. God cannot bring about the following feat: to make something that its maker cannot destroy.

And here A does **contrapose,** as the objectors would have it, to "Anything that God can make, its maker can destroy," which on the face of it says nothing against God's power to do anything logically possible. But just as in the Spinoza example, the B reading purports to describe a single feat, *bringing about everything that God can bring about* (this feat, I argued, is impossible for God, because logically impossible): so in our present case, the B reading purports to describe a single feat, *making something that its maker cannot destroy.* This, as I said, is a logically possible feat, a feat that men sometimes do perform; so we may press the question whether this is a feat God can accomplish or not; and either way there will be some *logically possible* feat God cannot accomplish. So this notion of omnipotence, like the Cartesian idea of absolute omnipotence, turns out to be obviously incompatible with Christian faith, and moreover logically untenable.

Let us see, then, if we fare any better with the third theory: the theory that the only condition for the truth of "God can do so-and-so" is that "God does so-and-so" or "God is doing so-and-so" must be logically possible. As I said, this imposes a more restrictive condition than the second theory: for there are many feats that we can consistently suppose to be performed but cannot consistently suppose to be performed by God. This theory might thus get us out of the logical trouble that arose with the second theory about the feat: *making a thing that its maker cannot destroy.* For though this is a logically possible feat, a feat some creatures do perform, it might well be argued that "*God* has made a thing that its maker cannot destroy" is a proposition with a buried inconsistency in it; and if so, then on the present account of omnipotence we need not say "God *can* make a thing that its maker cannot destroy."

This suggestion also, however, can easily be refuted by an example of great philosophical importance that I borrow from Aquinas. "It comes about that Miss X never loses her virginity" is plainly a logically possible proposition: and so also is "God brings it about that Miss X never loses her virginity." All the same, if it so happens that Miss X already has lost her virginity, "God *can* bring it about that Miss X never loses her virginity" is false (Part I, question 25, article 4). Before Miss X had lost her virginity, it would have been true to say this very thing; so what we can truly say about what God can do will be different at different times. This appears to imply a change in God, but Aquinas would certainly say, and I think rightly, that it doesn't really do so. It is just like the case of Socrates coming to be shorter than Theaetetus because Theaetetus grows up; here, the change is on the side of Theaetetus not of Socrates. So in our case, the change is really in Miss X not in God; something about her passes from the realm of possibility to the realm of *fait accompli,* and thus *no longer* comes under the concept of the accomplishable . . . (Aquinas, loc. cit.). I think Aquinas's position here is strongly defensible; but if he does defend it, he has abandoned the position that God can do everything that it is not **a priori** impossible *for God to do,* let alone the position that God can bring about everything describable in a logically consistent way.

Is it a priori impossible for God to do something wicked? And if not, *could* God do something wicked? There have been expressed serious doubts about this: I came across them in that favourite of modern moral philosophers, Richard Price. We must distinguish, he argues, between God's natural and his moral attributes: if God is a free moral being, even as we are, it must not be absolutely impossible for God to do something wicked. There must be just a chance that God should do something wicked: no doubt it will be a really infinitesimal chance—after all, God has persevered in ways of virtue on a vast scale for inconceivably long—but the chance must be there, or God isn't free and isn't therefore laudable for his goodness. The way this reverend gentleman commends his Maker's morals is so startling that you may suspect me of misrepresentation; I can only ask any sceptic to check in Daiches Raphael's edition of Price's work! Further comment on my part is I hope needless.

A much more restrained version of the same sort of thing is to be found in the Scholastic distinction between God's ***potentia absoluta*** **and** ***potentia ordinata.*** The former is God's power considered in abstraction from his wisdom and goodness, the latter is God's power considered as controlled in its exercise by his wisdom and goodness. Well, as regards a man it makes good sense to say: "He has the bodily and mental power to do so-and-so, but he certainly will not, it would be pointlessly silly and wicked." But does anything remotely like this make sense to say about Almighty God? If not, the Scholastic distinction I have cited is wholly frivolous.

Let us then consider our fourth try. Could it be said that the "everything" in "God can do everything" refers precisely to things that are not in the realm of *fait accompli* but of futurity? This will not do either. If God can promulgate promises to men, then as regards any promises that are not yet fulfilled we know that they certainly will be fulfilled: and in that case God clearly has not a *potentia ad utrumque*—a two-way power of either actualizing the event that will fulfil the promise or not actualizing it. God can then only do what will fulfil his promise. And if we try to evade this by denying that God can make promises known to men, then we have once more denied something essential to Christian faith, and we are still left with something that God cannot do.

I must here remove the appearance of a **fallacy.** God cannot but fulfil his promises, I argued; so he has not a two-way power, *potentia ad utrumque,* as regards these particular future events. This argument may have seemed to involve the fallacy made notorious in medieval logical treatises, of confusing the necessity by which something follows—*necessitas consequentiae*—with the necessity of that very thing which follows—*necessitas consequentis.* If it is impossible for God to promise and not perform, then if we know God has promised something we may infer with certainty that he will perform it. Surely, it may be urged, this is enough for Christian faith and hope; we need not go on to say that God *cannot not* bring about the future event in question. If we do that, are we not precisely committing the hoary **modal fallacy** I have just described?

I answer that there are various senses of "necessary." The future occurrence of such-and-such, when God has promised that such-and-such shall be, is of course not logically necessary; but it may be necessary in the sense of being, as Arthur Prior puts it, now unpreventable. If God *has* promised that Israel shall be saved, then there is nothing that anybody, even God, can do about that; this past state of affairs is now unpreventable. But it is also necessary in the same way that if God has promised then he will perform; God cannot do anything about that either—cannot make himself liable to break his word. So we have as premises "Necessarily p" and "Necessarily if p then q," in the same sense of "necessarily"; and from these premises it not merely necessarily follows that q—the conclusion in the necessitated form, "Necessarily q" with the same sense of "necessarily," follows from the premises. So if God has promised that Israel shall be saved, the future salvation of Israel is not only certain but inevitable; God must save Israel, because he cannot not save Israel without breaking his word given in the past and he can neither alter the past nor break his word.

Again, in regard to this and other arguments, some people may have felt discomfort at my not drawing in relation to God the sort of distinction between various applications of "can" that are made in human affairs: the "can" of knowing how to, the "can" of physical power to, the "can" of opportunity, the "can" of what fits in with one's plans. But of course the way we make these distinct applications of "he can" to a human agent will not be open if we are talking about God. There is no question of God's knowing how but lacking the strength, or being physically able to but not knowing how; moreover (to make a distinction that comes in a logical example of Aristotle's) though there is a right time when God may bring something about, it is inept to speak of his then having the opportunity to do it. (To develop this distinction: if "x" stands for a finite agent and "so-and-so" for an act directly in x's power, there is little difference between "At time t it is suitable for x to bring so-and-so about" and "It is suitable for x to bring so-and-so about at time t"; but if "x" means God, the temporal qualification "at time t" can attach only to what is brought about; God does not live through successive times and find one more suitable than another.)

These distinct applications of "can" are distinct only for finite and changeable agents, not for a God whose action is universal and whose mind and character and design are unchangeable. There is thus no ground for fear that in talking about God we may illicitly slip from one sort of "can" to another. What we say God can do is always in respect of his changeless supreme power.

All the same, we have to assert different propositions at different times in order to say truly what God can do. What is past, as I said, ceases to be alterable even by God; and thus the truth-value of a proposition like "God can bring it about that Miss X never loses her virginity" alters once she has lost it. Similarly, God's promise makes a difference to what we can thereafter truly say God can do; it is less obvious in this case that the real change involved is a change in creatures, not in God, than it was as regards Miss X's virginity, but a little thought should show that the promulgation or making known of God's intention, which is involved in a promise, is precisely a change in the creatures to whom the promise is made.

Thus all the four theories of omnipotence that I have considered break down. Only the first overtly flouts logic; but the other three all involve logical contradictions, or so it seems; and moreover, all these theories have consequences fatal to the truth of Christian faith. The last point really ought not to surprise us; for the absolute confidence a Christian must have in God's revelation and promises involves, as I said at the outset, both a belief that God is almighty, in the sense I explained, and a belief that there are certain describable things that God cannot do and therefore will not do.

If I were to end the discussion at this point, I should leave an impression of Aquinas's thought that would be seriously unfair to him; for although in the passage I cited Aquinas appears verbally committed to our second theory of omnipotence, it seems clear that this does not adequately represent his mind. Indeed, it was from Aquinas himself and from the *Summa Theologica* that I borrowed an example which refutes even the weaker third theory, let alone the second one. Moreover, in the other Summa ([*Summa Contra Gentiles*], Book II, ch. 25) there is an instructive list of things that *Deus omnipotens* is rightly said not to be able to do. But the mere occurrence of this list makes me doubt whether Aquinas can be said to believe, in any reasonable interpretation, the thesis that God can do everything. That God is almighty in my sense Aquinas obviously did believe; I am suggesting that here his "omnipotens" means "almighty" rather than "omnipotent." Aquinas does not say or even imply that he has given an *exhaustive* list of kinds of case in which "God can do so-and-so" or "God can make so-and-so" turns out false; so what he says here does not commit him to "God can do everything" even in the highly unnatural sense "God can do everything that is not excluded under one or other of the following heads."

I shall not explore Aquinas's list item by item, because I have made open or tacit use of his considerations at several points in the foregoing and do not wish to repeat myself. But one batch of items raises a specially serious problem. My attention was drawn to the problem by a contribution that the late Mr. Michael Foster made orally during a discussion at the Socratic Club in Oxford. Aquinas tells us that if "doing so-and-so" implies what he calls passive potentiality, then "God can do so-and-so" is false. On this ground he excluded all of the following:

> God can be a body or something of the sort.
>
> God can be tired or oblivious.
>
> God can be angry or sorrowful.
>
> God can suffer violence or be overcome.
>
> God can undergo corruption.

Foster pointed out that as a Christian Aquinas was committed to asserting the contradictory of all these theses. *Contra factum non valet ratio* [reason does not prevail against a fact]; it's no good arguing that God cannot do what God has done, and in the Incarnation God did do all these things Aquinas said God cannot do. The Word that was God *was* made flesh (and the literal meaning of the Polish for this is: The Word became a body!); God the Son *was* tired and did sink into the oblivion of sleep; he *was* angry and sorrowful; he was bound like a thief, beaten, and crucified; and though we believe his Body did not decay, it suffered corruption in the sense of becoming a corpse instead of a living body—Christ in the Apocalypse uses of himself the startling words "I became a corpse," *"egenomēn nekros,"* and the Church has always held that the dead Body of Christ during the *triduum mortis* was adorable with Divine worship for its union to the Divine Nature.

Foster's objection to Aquinas is the opposite kind of objection to the ones I have been raising against the various theories of omnipotence I have discussed. I have been saying that these theories say by implication that God *can* do certain things which Christian belief requires one to say God *cannot* do; Foster is objecting that Aquinas's account says God *cannot* do some things which according to Christian faith God *can* do and has in fact done.

It would take me too far to consider how Aquinas might have answered this objection. It would not of course be outside his intellectual milieu; it is the very sort of objection that a Jew or Moor might have used, accepting Aquinas's account of what God cannot do, in order to argue against the **Incarnation.** I shall simply mention one feature that Aquinas's reply would have had: it would have to make essential use of the particle "as," or in Latin *"secundum quod."* God did become man, so God can become man and have a human body; but God *as* God cannot be man or have a body. . . .

STUDY QUESTIONS

1. Distinguish *omnipotent* from *almighty.*
2. What are the four senses of *x is omnipotent* that Geach considers? For each definition, why does he reject the claim that God is omnipotent? *Do you find his reasons for rejection compelling? Why or why not?
3. Name some things that, at least according to Aquinas and Geach, God cannot do but a lesser being can do.
4. Explain the difference between statements A and B on page 39. What point does Geach make about these statements?
5. *Geach says that making a thing that its maker cannot afterwards destroy is a feat that some human beings have performed. What sorts of feats might Geach have in mind? Be specific.
6. *In formal logic, a dilemma is an argument of the following form: *p* or *not-p;* if *p,* then *q;* if not-*p,* then *q;* therefore, *q.* How does the following question lead to a dilemma, the conclusion of which is that no being can be omnipotent?

"Can God create a stone that God cannot lift?" What example given by Geach illustrates the same point as this question? Can you suggest a way out of the stone dilemma?

7. *Can an entity that lacks intentions, desires, and beliefs—a mechanical entity, for example—be omnipotent?
8. *Construct arguments for each of the following propositions:

   A. An omnipotent being must be omniscient.
   B. An omnipotent being cannot be omniscient. (Hint: The argument refers to certain experiences and feelings that an omnipotent being could not have.)

   Are the arguments cogent in your opinion?
9. *In the same section of *Summa Theologica* that Geach quotes (I, 25, 3), Aquinas writes that "to sin is to fall short of a perfect action; hence to be able to sin is to be able to fall short in action, which is *repugnant to omnipotence*" (my italics). Evaluate this argument, which implies that a being capable of sin is not omnipotent.
10. *In the introduction to this chapter, we saw that Aquinas and other philosophers derive God's attributes from a core attribute: perfection. How might this point help theists respond to the fact that God cannot really do everything?
11. *Do you think that power ought to be regarded as an important attribute in a perfect being? How might a feminist theologian answer this question? (See reading 2.9)

(Questions 7–11 were influenced by Charles Taliaferro's discussions in *Contemporary Philosophy of Religion* [Malden, MA and Oxford, UK: Blackwell, 1998], 61–82, 123–26.)

READING 1.7

Predestination, Divine Foreknowledge, and Human Freedom

William L. Rowe

*The existence of God—and, more specifically, the existence of divine providence—is often thought to pose severe problems for the belief in human free will. One aspect of divine providence, according to many thinkers, is that God controls or foreordains all events. If so, it would seem that human beings have no free choice as to how to act. Suppose next that God does not foreordain events but, rather, merely foreknows them (*providence *is derived from a Greek term that means to perceive beforehand). Surely no one can act contrary to the way God has always known he or she will act, so how is human free will possible?*

After briefly considering the first question—about God's foreordaining events—William L. Rowe (Purdue University) articulates the second problem in detail and describes three potential solutions. The first solution is to deny that acting freely requires the power to do otherwise than one does. The second solution maintains that, although facts that are purely about the past cannot be altered, facts that are partly about the future, such as God knew before Jones was born that Jones would mow his lawn on February 2, 2000, *can be altered (some philosophers call these* ***soft facts,*** *as opposed to* ***hard facts,*** *which cannot be altered). Thus, even if God knows how we will act in the future, we can "do otherwise." The third solution attempts to resolve the conflict by denying that God has foreknowledge. There are two versions of this solution. One version claims that statements about future human actions (what medieval philosophers called* ***future contingents****) are neither*

God has determined that something will happen it cannot be in some creature's power to prevent that thing from taking place. Therefore, if from eternity God did ordain whatever comes to pass, then there is nothing that happens which we could have prevented from happening. So, since whatever I do has been ordained by God to take place, it is never in my power to do otherwise. And if it is never in my power to do otherwise, then nothing I do is done freely. Human freedom, it seems, is inconsistent with divine predestination.

If the above argument is correct, as I'm inclined to believe it is, the theist must either abandon the belief in human freedom or the doctrine of divine predestination. And it seems reasonable that between the two, the doctrine of divine predestination should be given its walking papers. That God has *ultimate control* over the destiny of his creation and that he *knows* in advance of its happening everything that will happen are ideas that preserve the majesty of God and provide for some degree of human optimism, without requiring that God has *decreed* to happen whatever does happen. And on the surface at least, it does not appear that the doctrine of divine foreknowledge conflicts with human freedom. So perhaps the reasonable thing to do is to reject the doctrine of divine predestination, while preserving the belief in human freedom and the doctrine of divine foreknowledge.

THE CONFLICT BETWEEN HUMAN FREEDOM AND DIVINE FOREKNOWLEDGE

But if God has not ordained from eternity everything that will happen, how is it possible for him to have known from eternity everything that happens? Doesn't the doctrine of divine foreknowledge presuppose the doctrine of divine predestination? Having decreed that something will happen at a certain time would be a way in which God could know in advance that it will happen. But it is not the only way in which God might have possessed such knowledge. We possess telescopes, for example, that enable us to know what is happening at places some distance away, because by means of the telescope we can see them happening. Imagine that God has something like a *time* telescope, a telescope that enables one to see what is happening at times some distance away. By turning the lens one focuses on a certain time, say a thousand years from now, and sees the events that are occurring at that time. With some such image as this we might account for God's foreknowledge without supposing that his knowledge is derived from his prior decree that the events in question will occur. He knows in advance the events that will take place by *foreseeing* them, not by *foreordaining* them. The doctrine of divine foreknowledge, then, does not presuppose the doctrine of divine predestination. And, as we noted earlier, there does not appear to be any conflict between divine foreknowledge and human freedom. For although God's *foreordaining* something makes that something happen, his *foreknowing* does not make it happen. Things occur not because God foreknows them; rather, he foreknows them because they occur.

Unfortunately, things are not so simple as that. There is a serious problem about divine foreknowledge and human freedom. And although we may not be able to solve this problem, it will be instructive to try to understand the problem and see what the various "solutions" are that have been advanced by important philosophers and theologians. Perhaps the best way to start is by stating the problem in the form of an argument, an **argument** that begins with the doctrine of divine foreknowledge and ends with the denial of human freedom. Once we understand the major premises of the argument, as well as the reasons given in support of them, we will have come to an understanding of one of the major problems theologians have wrestled with for almost two thousand years: the problem of reconciling the doctrine of divine foreknowledge with the belief in human freedom.

1. God knows before we are born everything we will do.

2. If God knows before we are born everything we will do, then it is never in our power to do otherwise.

3. If it is never in our power to do otherwise, then there is no human freedom.

Therefore,

4. There is no human freedom.

The first premise of the argument expresses an apparent implication of the doctrine of divine foreknowledge. The third premise simply states an implication of the second idea of freedom we considered earlier. According to that idea, we do something freely only if, at the time just before we do it, it is in our power to do otherwise. Thus, we concluded that the act of staying in the room was freely done only if, at the time of the decision to stay in the room, it was in the person's power to do otherwise, that is, to leave the room. Since the door was securely bolted from the outside, we concluded that he did not *freely* stay in the room. Now premise (3) merely draws the logical conclusion from this second idea of freedom: if it is *never* in our (any human being's) power to do otherwise, then there is no human freedom. Since the argument is clearly **valid,** the remaining question concerns premise (2): if God knows before we are born everything we will do then it is never in our power to do otherwise. Why should we accept this premise? Clearly if we replaced the word *knows* with the word *ordains* the statement would be true. But the whole point of abandoning divine predestination in favor of divine foreknowledge was that although

a) If God *ordains* before we are born everything we will do, then it is never in our power to do otherwise,

seems surely true, it does not seem to be true that

b) If God *knows* before we are born everything we will do then it is never in our power to do otherwise.

Since premise 2 is the same as b why should we now accept it as true? What is the reasoning by which the proponent of this argument hopes to convince us that 2 is true?

The reasoning in support of 2 is complex, so it will be best to develop it by means of an example. Let's suppose it is 2:00 P.M. on a particular Tuesday and that you have a class in philosophy of religion that meets at 2:30. Your friends ask you to go with them to an afternoon movie, but, after considering the proposal, you somehow manage to resist temptation, and elect to attend class instead. It is now 2:45 and your instructor is carrying on about foreknowledge and free will. Somewhat bored, you now wish that you had gone to the movie instead of coming to class. You realize, however, that although you now regret your decision there is nothing that you can do about it. Of course, you could get up from your seat and rush off to see what is left of the movie. But you cannot now, at 2:45, bring it about that you did not go to class at 2:30, you cannot *now* bring it about that you actually went to the movie instead. You can regret what you did, and resolve never to make that mistake again, but, like it or not, you are stuck with the fact that instead of going to the movie you went to class at 2:30. You are stuck with it because it is *a fact about the past* and you cannot *alter the past.* Our inability to alter the past is enshrined in the colloquialism, "There's no use crying over spilt milk." Within limits, however, the future seems open, pliable; we can make it to be one way or another. You believe, for example, that on Thursday, when the class meets again, it will be in your power to go to class and it will be in your power to go to a movie instead. But the past is not open, it is closed, solid like granite, and in no way within your power to alter. As Aristotle observed:

> No one deliberates about the past but only about what is future and capable of being otherwise, while what is past is not capable of not having taken place; hence Agathon is right in saying: "For this alone is lacking, even in God, to make undone things that have once been done."[2]

There are, of course, a large number of facts about the past relative to 2:45 on Tuesday. In addition to the fact that at 2:30 you came to class, there is the fact of your birth, the fact that you became a college student, the fact that Nixon resigned from the Presidency, indeed, all the facts of past history. And what you now know is that at 2:45 it is not in your

[2]Aristotle, *Nicomachean Ethics* VII, 2. 1139[b] in *The Basic Works of Aristotle,* ed. Richard McKeon (New York: Random House, 1941).

power to alter *any* of them. There is nothing that is now in your power to do such that were you to do it, any of these facts about the past would not have been facts about the past. Pondering your powerlessness over the past, you notice that your instructor has written on the board another fact about the past:

F. Before you were born God knew that you would come to class at 2:30 this Tuesday.

If God exists and the doctrine of divine foreknowledge is true, F is certainly a fact about the past, and it has been a fact about the past at every moment of your life. It is a fact about the past now—at 2:45 on Tuesday—it was a fact about the past yesterday, and it will be a fact about the past tomorrow. At this point your instructor turns and asks: "Was it in your power at 2:00 to have refrained from coming to class today?" You certainly think that it was—indeed, you now regret that you did not exercise that power—so the instructor writes on the board:

A. It was in your power at 2:00 to do something other than come to class at 2:30 this Tuesday.

But now let's think for a bit about F and A. At 2:00, F was a fact about the past. But according to A, it was in your power at 2:00 to do something (go to a movie, say) such that had you done it, what is a fact about the past (F) would not have been a fact about the past. For, clearly, if you had *exercised* your power to refrain from coming to class at 2:30 what God would have known before you were born is not what he in fact knew, that you would come to class this Tuesday, but something quite different, that you would do something else. And this in turn means that if F is a fact about the past—as it surely is if the doctrine of divine foreknowledge is true—and if A is true, then it was in your power at 2:00 this Tuesday to *alter the past;* it was in your power to do something (go to a movie) such that had you done it, what *is* a fact about the past (F) would not have been a fact about the past. If then, *it is never in our power to alter a fact about the past,* it cannot be both that F was a fact about the past and also that it was in your power at 2:00 to refrain from coming to class at 2:30 this Tuesday.

What we have just seen is that given the doctrine of divine foreknowledge and the claim that it is in our power to have done something we did not do, it follows that it was in our power to have altered the past. For given the doctrine of divine foreknowledge it follows that *before you were born* God knew that you would come to class at 2:30 this Tuesday. And if we now claim that *at 2:00* it was in your power to have done otherwise, we imply that at 2:00 it was in your power to alter a fact about the past, the fact that before you were born God knew that you would come to class at 2:30. But we earlier concluded that we are powerless over the past, that facts about the past are not within our power to alter. If we keep to this conviction—as it seems we must—then we must conclude that if God did know before you were born that you would be in class at 2:30 (this Tuesday) then it was *not* in your power at 2:00 to do otherwise. And generalizing from this particular example, we can conclude that if it is never in our power to alter the past, then if God knows before we are born everything we will do, then it is never in our power to do otherwise.

We have worked our way through the rather complex reasoning that can be used to support premise 2 of the argument designed to show a conflict between divine foreknowledge and human freedom. That premise, as you recall, says that if God knows before we are born everything we will do, then it is never in our power to do otherwise. Reduced to its simplest terms, the reasoning given in support of 2 consists in arguing that if 2 is not true, then it is in our power to alter the past. But it is never in our power to alter the past, so 2 must be true. From

(i) God knows before we are born everything we will do and,
(ii) It is sometimes in our power to do otherwise

it follows, so the reasoning goes, that it is sometimes in our power to alter the past. Since it is never in our power to alter the past, premises (i) and (ii) can't both be true. Hence, if (i) is true then (ii) is false. But to say that (ii) is false is just to say that it is *never* in our power to do otherwise. So if (i) is true then it is *never* in our power to do otherwise—and this is exactly what premise 2 says.

SOME SOLUTIONS TO THE CONFLICT

We've had a look at perhaps the strongest argument for the view that the doctrine of divine foreknowledge, no less than the doctrine of divine predestination, is in fundamental conflict with the belief in human freedom, an argument that has troubled philosophers and theologians for centuries. It is now time to consider the various "solutions" that have been offered and to assess their strengths and weaknesses.

The argument itself limits the number of possible solutions that can be advanced to the following four:

I. *Rejection of premise 3:* denies that we do something freely only if it is in our power to do otherwise
II. *Rejection of premise 2:* denies that divine foreknowledge implies that it is never in our power to do otherwise
III. *Rejection of premise 1:* denies that God has foreknowledge of future events
IV. *Acceptance of the conclusion 4:* denies that we have human freedom

Solutions III and IV are "radical" solutions since they amount to a denial either of the doctrine of divine foreknowledge or of human freedom. No theist seriously proposes IV, so we may safely dismiss it. III, however, as we shall see, is the solution preferred by a number of important theologians, including Boethius and Aquinas. Let's consider, then, the first three solutions to this perplexing problem.

The Definition of Freedom

The first solution rejects premise 3 of the argument, charging that 3 expresses a mistaken idea of human freedom. As we saw earlier, there are two different ideas of freedom. According to the first idea, acting freely consists in no more than doing what you want or choose to do; freedom does not require the power to do otherwise. Those who accept this idea of human freedom rightly see no conflict between it and divine foreknowledge. Indeed, as we noted earlier, there is no conflict between this idea of human freedom and the doctrine of divine predestination. A solution along these lines was developed most fully by the American theologian Jonathan Edwards (1703–58). The adequacy of this solution depends entirely on whether its idea of what human freedom consists in can be defended against the criticisms philosophers have advanced against it.[3] However, having rejected this idea of freedom in favor of the second idea—the idea that we do something freely only if it is in our power to do otherwise—we shall not pursue further this first solution to the problem of divine foreknowledge and human freedom. For given the second idea of human freedom, premise 3 must be accepted as true.

Power to Alter the Past

The second major solution rejects premise 2, thereby denying that divine foreknowledge implies that it is never in our power to do otherwise. Actually, what this solution shows, if successful, is not that 2 is false, but that the reasoning given in support of it is mistaken. What is that reasoning? Well, reduced to its briefest terms, the reasoning is that if 2 is not true then it is in our power to alter facts about the past—facts about what God knew before we were even born. But, so the reasoning goes, it is never in anyone's power to alter the past, therefore 2 must be true. The second solution challenges the claim that it is never in our power to alter the past, arguing that we do have the power to alter certain facts about the past, including certain facts about what God knew before we were even born. This solution was suggested by the most influential philosopher of the fourteenth century, William of Ockham (1285–1349).

The basic point on which the second solution rests involves a distinction between two types of facts about the past: facts which are *simply* about the past,

[3]For a brilliant defense of the first idea of freedom, as well as a response to the objections raised against it, see Jonathan Edwards, *Freedom of the Will,* eds. A. S. Kaufman and W. K. Frankena (Indianapolis: The Bobbs-Merrill Co., 1969).

and facts which are *not simply* about the past.[4] To illustrate this distinction, let's consider two facts about the past, facts about the year 1941.

f_1: In 1941 Japan attacks Pearl Harbor.

f_2: In 1941 a war begins between Japan and the United States that lasts five years.

Relative to 1992, f_1 and f_2 are both *simply* about the past. But suppose we consider the year 1943. Relative to 1943, f_1 is a fact that is simply about the past, but f_2 is not simply about the past. It is a fact about the past relative to 1943, for f_2 is, in part, a fact about 1941, and 1941 lies in 1943's past. But f_2, unlike f_1, implies a certain fact about 1944; namely,

f_3: In 1944 Japan and the United States are at war.

Since f_2 implies f_3, a fact about the future relative to 1943, we can say that relative to 1943 f_2 is a fact about the past, but not simply a fact about the past. We have then three facts, f_1, f_2, and f_3, about which we can say that relative to 1992 each is a fact simply about the past. Relative to 1943, however, only f_1 is simply about the past—f_2 is about the past but not simply about the past, and f_3 is not about the past at all.

Having illustrated the distinction between a fact which, relative to a certain time *t,* is simply about the past and a fact which, relative to *t,* is not simply about the past, we are now in a position to appreciate its importance. Think of 1943 and the groups of persons then in power in both Japan and the United States. Neither group had it in its power to do anything about f_1. Both groups may have regretted the actions which brought it about that f_1 is a fact about the past. But it is abundantly clear that among all the things which, in 1943, it was in their power to do, none is such that, had they done it, f_1 would not have been a fact about the past. It makes no sense to look back upon 1943 and say that if only one of these groups had *then* done such-and-such, f_1 would never have been a fact about the past. It makes no sense precisely because, relative to 1943, f_1 is a fact *simply* about the past. Nothing that could have been done by anyone in 1943 would have in any way altered the fact that in 1941 Japan attacked Pearl Harbor.

But what about f_2, the fact that in 1941 a war begins between Japan and the United States that lasts five years? We know that in 1943 neither group did anything that altered this fact about 1941. The question, however, is whether there were things that were not done in 1943, things which, nevertheless, were in the power of one or both of the groups to do, and which, had they been done, a certain fact about 1941, f_2, would not have been a fact at all. Perhaps there were not. Perhaps the momentum of the war was such that neither group had the power to bring it to an end in 1943. Most of us, I suppose, think otherwise. We think that there probably were certain actions that were not, but could have been, taken by one or both of the groups in 1943, actions which, had they been taken, would have brought the war to an end in 1943. If what we think to be so is so, then it was in the power of one or both of the groups in 1943 to alter a fact about the past; it was in their power in 1943 to do something such that, had they done it, a certain fact about 1941, f_2, would not have been a fact about 1941. The basic reason why in 1943 f_2 may have been in their power to alter, whereas f_1 certainly was not, is that, unlike f_1, f_2 is not simply about the past relative to 1943, for f_2 implies a certain fact about 1944, that in 1944, Japan and the United States are at war (f_3).

What the above reasoning suggests is that our conviction that the past is beyond our power to affect is certainly true, so far as facts which are simply about the past are concerned. Facts which are about the past, but *not simply* about the past, may not, however, be beyond our power to affect. And what Ockham saw is that the facts about divine foreknowledge which are used as the basis for denying human freedom are facts about the past, but *not simply* about the past. Consider again the fact that before you were born, God knew that you would be in class at 2:30 this Tuesday. We want to believe that at 2:00 it was in your power to do otherwise, to refrain from coming to class at 2:30. To ascribe this power to you implies that it was in your power at 2:00 to alter a

[4][This distinction often is drawn as one between **hard facts** and **soft facts.**—Ed.]

fact about the past, the fact that before you were born God knew that you would be in class at 2:30. This fact about the past, however, is not, relative to 2:00, a fact simply about the past. For it implies a fact about the future relative to 2:00, namely, that at 2:30 you are in class. And the solution we are exploring holds that such a fact about the past was in your power to alter if it was in your power at 2:00, as we believe it was, to have gone to a movie instead of coming to class. For it was then in your power to have done something such that, had you done it, what *is* a fact about a time before you were born *would not have been* a fact at all—instead it would have been a fact that before you were born God knew that you would not be in class at 2:30. Of course, there will still be many facts about God's foreknowledge that are not in your power to alter: all those facts, for example, that relative to the time you are at, are facts simply about the past. The very fact which may have been in your power to alter at 2:00—the fact that before you were born God knew you would be in class at 2:30—is, at 2:45 when you are sitting in class regretting that you did not go to a movie, a fact that cannot *then* (at 2:45) be altered, because at 2:45 it is a fact simply about the past. And there are many facts involving divine foreknowledge that are not simply about the past, which, nevertheless, are not in your power to alter, for the facts that they imply about the future do not fall within the scope of your power. For example, God knew before you were born that the sun would rise tomorrow. This fact about the past is not simply about the past because it implies a fact about tomorrow, that the sun will rise. It is, nevertheless, a fact which is not in your power to alter.

We have been considering the second solution to the problem of divine foreknowledge and human freedom. As we saw, this solution consists in denying the reasoning supporting the second premise of the argument by means of which the problem was developed, the premise stating that if God knows before we are born everything we will do, it is never in our power to do otherwise. According to the reasoning in support of this premise, given divine foreknowledge, it is in our power to do otherwise only if it is in our power to alter some fact about the past, a fact about what God knew before we were born. The solution we have been considering accepts this point in the reasoning given in support of premise 2, but denies the next point: that it is never in our power to alter the past. The solution argues that some facts about the past are not simply about the past, that some such facts may be within our power to alter, and that the facts about divine foreknowledge used in the reasoning for premise 2 are examples of such facts. So according to the second major solution, we have no good reasons for accepting the second premise of the argument leading from divine foreknowledge to the denial of human freedom. And without such reasons, it has yet to be shown that there is any real difficulty in holding both that God knows before we are born everything we will do and that we sometimes have the power to do otherwise.

THE DENIAL OF FOREKNOWLEDGE

The third and final solution we shall consider rejects premise 1 of the argument, thereby denying that God has foreknowledge of the future events. Earlier I called this a "radical" solution since, unlike the first two solutions, instead of trying to reconcile divine foreknowledge with human freedom, it appears to deny that there is any foreknowledge at all. But, as we shall see, this was the solution preferred by a number of important theologians within the western religious tradition.

There are two different forms of the third solution. According to the first form, statements about certain events in the future, events which might or might not happen, are neither true nor false; they become true (false) when the events they are about actually occur (don't occur). For example, the statement, "You will attend class at a certain hour on a certain day next week" is, on the view we are considering not now true, nor is it false. When next week comes and the hour of that particular day occurs, then the statement will become true if you attend class, and false if you do not. This view concerning statements about the future, a view often ascribed to Aristotle, has the consequence that God does not *now*

4. How would saying that God is outside of time solve the problem of divine foreknowledge and human free will? *Are there problems with the view that God exists outside of time? (On this question, see Reading 1.9 and also questions 5 and 6 below.)
5. *In describing the third solution, Rowe mentions a view that certain statements about the future (those whose truth is dependent on human choice) are neither true nor false until the events they describe actually occur. Do you think this view is plausible?
6. *Sometimes prophets announce what will happen in the future, based on information that God communicates to them. Would the attempts Rowe considers to resolve the contradiction between *God's* foreknowledge and human free will also remove the contradiction between a *prophet's* foreknowledge and human free will? Why or why not?
7. *Suppose God knows the future completely. Some philosophers maintain that attributing such foreknowledge does not explain how God knows when to intervene in events. Do you think this is so? Explain. (Discussion can be found in Reading 1.8.)
8. *Some philosophers contend that God has what is called **middle knowledge,** the knowledge of how each possible creature would freely act in each hypothetical circumstance. Thus, suppose God creates Tom but not Tim. Acording to the doctrine of middle knowledge, God knows how Tom would act if Tom would see a person drowning in the Atlantic Ocean at time *t* and place *s*—even if Tom would never be in such a situation. God even knows how Tim, who is never even created, would act in such a situation. How is middle knowledge different from simple foreknowledge? Do you find the idea that God has middle knowledge plausible? Why or why not? (See Reading 1.8.)
9. *Rowe explains that he focuses on how God's *knowledge* affects the claim that humans have free will, not on how God's *foreordaining* of events does. Can you think of a solution to the latter problem? That is, if God controls all events, how is human free will possible? (On this problem, see reading 1.8.)
10. *Do you think that freedom requires the power to do otherwise, that is, to perform an act other than the act one actually performs? Why or why not?
11. *"Why doesn't God voluntarily decide to limit His knowledge so that human beings can have free will, just as God limits His power so that human beings can have free will?" Respond to this question.

READING 1.8

Middle Knowledge, Foreknowledge, and the Openness of God

William Hasker

This reading continues the discussion, launched by Rowe, of whether human free will is compatible with divine control and divine **foreknowledge.** *William Hasker (Huntington College) considers four views of how God controls events and, in particular, how God's providence relates to what he calls* **libertarian free will.** *In the first view,* **Calvinism** *(named for John Calvin), God determines everything and there is no libertarian free will. Hasker objects that, in this conception, God is a puppet master and further that it follows from Calvinism that God* wants *the evils of the world to take place. In the second view,* **Molinism** *(named for Jesuit thinker Luis de Molina [1535–1600]), God has* **middle knowledge.** *That is, God knows what each possible creature would freely choose to do in each possible circumstance; then God cre-*

ates the set of creatures whose free *choices would help actualize God's plan. Hasker objects here, too, that in Molinism God is an arch-manipulator; furthermore, it follows from Molinism that God plans, orders, and provides for the world's evil. In the third view,* simple foreknowledge, *God knows what each person will choose in the future. Hasker objects that this conception limits God's providential control of the world. The fourth view, the* **openness of God,** *is the view Hasker favors. God is* **omnipotent** *and* **omniscient** *but wants a world that contains genuinely free creatures. Therefore, God governs the world according to* general strategies *that are ordered for the good of creation; however, because human beings make genuinely free choices, God cannot ensure the precise result God desires. Moreover, although God is omniscient in the sense that he knows everything that logically* can *be known, future human free choices cannot be known with certainty, and God must take risks.*

Reading 1.8 omits Hasker's discussion of **process theism,** *an approach which is presented in Reading 1.10.*

THE NATURE OF FREE WILL

One of the most important questions with regard to divine providence is the nature of the free will that is attributed to human beings. Christian thinkers have almost without exception wanted to say that human beings are free in some sense. But they are deeply divided concerning the relevant sense of "free will." On the **libertarian** (or **"incompatibilist"**) understanding of free will, *an agent is free with respect to a given action at a given time if at that time it is within the agent's power to perform the action and also in the agent's power to refrain from the action.* To say that the action is "within one's power" means that nothing whatever exists that would make it impossible for the power in question to be exercised. If I am free in this sense, then whether or not the action is performed depends on me; by deciding to perform the action I bring it about that things happen in a certain way, quite different from some other, equally possible, way things might have happened had I refrained from the action.

The other main understanding of free will is the **compatibilist** conception, which may be explained as follows: *an agent is free with respect to a given action at a given time if at that time it is true that the agent can perform the action if she decides to perform it and she can refrain from the action if she decides not to perform it.* The difference between the two definitions may not be immediately apparent, but it is of fundamental importance. On the libertarian definition, in order to be free the agent must have it in her power without qualification to perform the action and also have the power to refrain from performing it. On the compatibilist definition, on the other hand, she need only have the power to perform it *if she chooses* to do so, and likewise the power to refrain.

Now, consider a situation in which she has an overwhelmingly strong desire to perform the action, and no desire whatever to refrain. (Perhaps she has just been invited by a good friend to go to a show she has been wanting to see for weeks.) She is, no doubt, free in the compatibilist sense, since if she were to decide to refrain from the action in question, she could certainly do so. (Nothing would force her to go to the show, if she decided not to.) But she is probably not free in the libertarian sense, since it is impossible for her to *desire* to refrain from the action, and thus also impossible for her to *decide* to refrain from it. On the libertarian view, in order to be truly free she must have the "inner freedom" either to act or to refrain, but on the compatibilist view she needs only the "outer freedom" to carry out the decision either way she makes it—but the decision itself may be completely determined by the psychological forces at work in her personality. As we shall see, a lot hangs on this distinction. . . .

CALVINISM

The theory of theological **determinism** to be discussed here is called Calvinism because of its association with [John] Calvin, but it by no means originated with him. The first real "Calvinist" was Augustine, and some prominent medieval theologians, notably Thomas Aquinas, held essentially deterministic views of the God-human relationship. And [Martin] Luther and [Ulrich] Zwingli were just as deterministic as was Calvin.

The central idea of Calvinism is quite simple: everything that happens, with no exceptions, is efficaciously determined by God in accordance with his eternal decrees. As Augustine said, "The will of God is the necessity of things." God's power to achieve whatever he desires is limited only by logical possibility—and that is no real limitation, for it is inconceivable that God would have an incoherent desire for a self-contradictory state of affairs. The conception of free will affirmed by a Calvinist must, of course, be a compatibilist conception: people are, in many circumstances, free to do what they chose to do, but this "freedom" has to be consistent with the fact that God has infallibly predetermined what they will choose, and there is no real possibility of their choosing otherwise.

Calvinism gives us as strong a conception of God's providential control as anyone could desire—and it might seem that this speaks decisively in its favor. It has been said that "nothing is more depressing than the thought that God is not in control"—but this, clearly, is a thought the Calvinist need never entertain. . . .

A major objection to Calvinism is found in its effect on our understanding of the personal relationship that we have with God. That believers enjoy such a relationship is a fundamental part of Christian faith—but does not Calvinism undermine this notion? (Please note that I am not denying that many Calvinists do in fact enjoy a rich and intimate relationship with their Lord. What I am suggesting is that their theory, if taken seriously at this point, undercuts the reality of the relationship that they experience.) The Calvinist understanding of the God-human relationship has been compared to a puppet-master controlling the movements of a puppet, or of a ventriloquist having a "conversation" with his dummy. Calvinists, to be sure, reject these analogies as inappropriate. Perhaps a closer comparison would be with a computer wizard who has assembled a life-like robot and, through a thorough knowledge of the robot's programming, is able to anticipate and manipulate the robot's responses to an indefinitely large variety of situations.[1] I think that reflecting on these and similar examples will convince most people that Calvinism is distinctly unappealing as an account of our personal relationship with God.

But by far the strongest objections to Calvinism are found in the phenomena of sin and moral evil. How can we say that God desires for all to be saved, when he has eternally decreed that some will be lost?[2] It is not that God "reluctantly permits" those who reject him to go their own way; rather, that is the way God wanted it all along. And in general, all the evil that is done in the world—from the murder of Abel to "ethnic cleansing" in Bosnia—is precisely what God wanted to happen. At this point Calvinists usually take refuge in the inscrutable wisdom of God—often, at the same time, lashing out indignantly at those who have the temerity to raise such questions. But all else aside, does not Calvinism attribute to God an attitude toward evil that is logically incoherent? God, the Calvinists say, is wholly good; everything that occurs God has willed to occur in preference to any other logically possible state of affairs God might have chosen. And then a just and loving God assumes toward part of what he himself has chosen to create and bring about—namely, sin and moral evil—an attitude of utter, implacable hostility. So the Calvinist must believe—but is this even coherent, let alone plausible?

[1]The robot's behavior, even if completely deterministic, would eventually escape the human roboticist's ability to anticipate it — but of course, this can never happen to God.

[2]Some Calvinists, to be sure, wish to say that God predestined the elect for salvation but did not specifically predestine others for damnation; rather, he simply "passed over" them and they are damned as a result of their own sins. This way of putting it has a softer sound, but it really does not make the situation any better. The sins they commit are the sins that God decreed they should commit, and he failed to choose them for salvation knowing that, in the absence of his choice, they will inevitably be damned. Whether or not this is described as a "decree of reprobation" is merely a verbal matter.

MOLINISM

The theory of **"middle knowledge"** was devised by the sixteenth-century Jesuit theologian Luis de Molina as a way of avoiding these difficulties.[3] Molina was convinced of the necessity of attributing to human beings free will in the libertarian sense, rather than the compatibilist free will that is consistent with theological determinism. But he also desired to maintain a strong doctrine of divine providential control, which he accomplished by attributing to God the knowledge of certain propositions that have recently come to be called **"counterfactuals** of freedom." These propositions specify, concerning every possible free agent that God might create, exactly what that agent would freely choose to do in every possible situation of (libertarian) free choice in which the agent might find itself.

This theory supplies us with an answer to the question of how God can know with certainty the future free actions of his creatures. God knows which creatures he will create and which situations those creatures will find themselves in. And in virtue of his knowledge of the counterfactuals of freedom, God knows exactly which choices will be made in each such situation, thus enabling him to know the future in its entirety.

Beyond this, however, Molinism lends itself to an extremely strong view of divine providence, probably the strongest view possible if we reject Calvinism. If human beings possess libertarian free will, then God cannot simply determine by decree what their choices shall be, as he does according to Calvinism. It seems plausible that this would introduce a kind of uncertainty and riskiness into God's plan for the world: how things ultimately turn out will depend on how free agents, such as human beings, respond to the choices that they are offered. But Molinism shows how God can entirely avoid taking any risks. Prior to his decision to create anything or to place any free agent in a situation where she would make a choice, God knows exactly what choice would be made in any possible situation. This means that God can survey all the possible ways in which things might turn out—all the "feasible worlds," as they have come to be called—and select the very one that most closely fits his desire and purpose for his creation.

God's choice is not as unconstrained as it is for Calvinism, because God is limited by the counterfactuals of freedom. If the relevant counterfactual says that, in the given situation, Adam would choose to eat the apple, then God cannot bring it about that *in that very situation* Adam freely chooses to refrain from eating it. But this is the *only* limitation on God's ability to get what he wants; in particular, there is no risk or uncertainty whatever about God's plan being executed exactly as he has conceived it. Alfred J. Freddoso, a leading contemporary Molinist, puts the point succinctly:

> God, the divine artisan, freely and knowingly plans, orders, and provides for all the effects that constitute His artifact, the created universe with its entire history, and executes His chosen plan by playing an active causal role sufficient to ensure its exact realization. Since God is the perfect artisan, not even the most trivial details escape His providential decrees.[4]

Serious questions have been raised concerning the coherence and logical possibility of Molinism, the most important of which concern the very existence of true counterfactuals of freedom.[5] These questions become very involved logically, and we cannot go into them in detail here. One way to look at the matter is this: If Adam is free with respect to eating the

[3]Molina's theory can be found in Luis de Molina, *On Divine Foreknowledge (Part IV of the Concordia),* trans. and introduction by Alfred J. Freddoso (Ithaca, N.Y.: Cornell University Press, 1988). Freddoso's introduction is the best overall exposition and defense of the doctrine in the recent literature. The modern philosophical revival of middle knowledge was initiated by Alvin Plantinga; see his *The Nature of Necessity* (New York: Oxford University Press, 1973) and, on a more popular level, his *God, Freedom and Evil* (Grand Rapids, Mich.: Eerdmans, 1977).

[4]Alfred J. Freddoso, introduction to *On Divine Foreknowledge,* p. 3.

[5]Robert M. Adams initiated this aspect of the discussion of Molinism with his article "Middle Knowledge and the Problem of Evil," *American Philosophical Quarterly* 14 (1977): 109–17; see also his recent "An Anti-Molinist Argument," *Philosophical Perspectives* 5 (1991): 343–53.

apple, then it seems reasonable to say that he *might* eat the apple, and also that he *might not* eat it. But if it is true that he might eat it, then (according to the principles of counterfactual logic) it is false that he *would not* eat it—and conversely, if it is true that he might not eat the apple, then it is false that he *would* eat it. So if he is free with respect to eating the apple, then it is true that he might eat it and also true that he might not eat it, but it is not true *either* that he (definitely) *would* eat it *or* that he (definitely) *would not* eat it. Thus, if he is free in his decision to eat or not, then there *is no* true counterfactual of freedom describing what he would do in the situation. And if there are no true counterfactuals of freedom in situations like this, the theory of middle knowledge collapses.

As I have said, these arguments become extremely complex, and if at this point the reader is bewildered rather than enlightened, he has plenty of company. But I think it is fair to say that the majority of philosophers who have considered these and similar arguments have concluded that there are serious questions about the coherence and logical possibility of middle knowledge, though this conclusion is certainly not unanimous.

As has been noted, middle knowledge can afford God a very high degree of providential control over the world. But a price must be paid for this. The effect on our understanding of a personal relationship with God is similar to what we saw for Calvinism: God becomes the archmanipulator, knowing in every case exactly "which button to push" in order to elicit precisely the desired result from his creatures. The analogy of the cyberneticist and the robot applies here also, with one change:[6] we must suppose that part of the programming of the robot was done by a third party. (This, of course, represents the counterfactuals of freedom.[7]) But the robot-master still knows all about that part of the program and is able just as before to fine-tune the situations that the robot encounters so as to achieve just the desired result. Whether the change from Calvinism to Molinism makes the situation appreciably better in this regard is left for the reader to decide.

Molinism is undeniably better off than Calvinism with respect to the problem of evil. The reason is precisely that in Molinism God has somewhat less control than he does according to Calvinism: specifically, God has no control over the counterfactuals of freedom. And this means that there may be certain logically possible states of affairs that God cannot cause to be actual—for instance, God may be unable to bring about a state of affairs in which Adam freely resists the temptation to sin. Alvin Plantinga has made use of this in order to argue that it may be impossible for God to bring about the existence of a world in which creatures have libertarian freedom to choose between good and evil, but in fact always choose good.[8] And if God could not have created such a world, then it is not a moral fault on God's part that he did not do so.

But Molinism still has plenty of trouble over the problem of evil. As Freddoso pointed out, according to Molinism God specifically "plans, orders, and provides for" each of the events that actually hap-

[6]To be sure, the human being is assumed to have libertarian free will, whereas the robot is deterministic. But given middle knowledge, this difference between the robot and the human being makes no difference with respect to the way in which they can be controlled. In either case, God knows exactly "which buttons to push" so as to obtain, within the inherent limitations of the robot or of the human being, the exact response he desires.

[7]It does make a difference how the programming was done—that is, what sorts of counterfactuals of freedom God was confronted with in the "creation situation." The counterfactuals (over which God has no control) might have been very favorable for God's purposes, so that he could create a large number of free creatures that would always, or almost always, do exactly what he wished for them to do; in that case, we might have expected him to create a world that was virtually or entirely free from sin. On the other hand, the counterfactuals might have been very unfavorable—so bad, perhaps, that God would not have chosen to create any world containing free creatures. Presumably the Molinist will not suppose that either of these extreme possibilities was realized. It seems to me that many Molinists in effect assume that while God cannot obtain just any result he desires, the creative options open to him include a feasible world that he takes as his end in the sense that he fully endorses its actualization, so that he is able to say of his creation that it is "very good."

[8]See Plantinga, *Nature of Necessity* and *God, Freedom and Evil.*

pen—the evil along with the good. So God specifically planned the Holocaust, Saddam Hussein's invasion of Kuwait, the ethnic cleansing in Bosnia—and on and on. But how, we may ask, could God intentionally bring about such horrible evils? So far as I can see, only one answer to this even begins to make sense. I believe that the Molinist is virtually compelled to affirm what Michael Peterson has termed "meticulous providence," which holds that every single instance of evil that occurs is such that God's permitting either that specific evil or some other equal or greater evil is necessary for some greater good that is better than anything God could have brought about without permitting the evil in question.[9] Peterson argues forcefully that Christians should not affirm meticulous providence, and I believe he is right. Without going into the matter at length, doesn't it strain one's credulity almost beyond limits to believe that none of the evils mentioned—or a thousand more that could have been added—could have been prevented without creating an even greater evil, or without losing some good that is great enough to outweigh those truly horrendous evils? Yet this is what the Molinist must affirm, unless he is content to say that God has deliberately arranged for these horrible evils to occur *without* there being any outweighing good that compensates for them.

SIMPLE FOREKNOWLEDGE

The theory of simple foreknowledge agrees with Molinism that human beings possess libertarian free will and that God has comprehensive knowledge of the future. But it does not accept that God possesses "middle knowledge," knowledge of the counterfactuals of freedom. (This is what makes simple foreknowledge simple!) Since they do not affirm middle knowledge, proponents of simple foreknowledge cannot avail themselves of the explanation it offers of *how* God knows the future, so they need an alternative account of this. The only plausible answer seems to be that God somehow has "direct vision" of the future—that he "sees" it as if in a telescope, or perhaps a crystal ball.

By this time it should come as no surprise that there are serious questions concerning the logical compatibility of comprehensive divine foreknowledge and libertarian free will. The idea, roughly, is this: If God knows already what will happen in the future, then God's knowing this is part of the past and is now fixed, impossible to change. And since God is infallible, it is completely impossible that things will turn out differently than God expects them to. But this means that the future event God knows is also fixed and unalterable, and it cannot be true of any human beings that they are both able to perform a certain action and able not to perform that action. If God knows that a person is going to perform it, then it is impossible that the person fail to perform it—so one does not have a free choice whether or not to perform it. . . .

There is a minor cottage industry among philosophers of religion seeking to devise an escape from this argument. I cannot go into all of this here; I will simply record my conviction . . . that none of the evasions are successful. . . .[10]

Leaving this aside for the moment, if God *did* possess simple foreknowledge, how would this affect our understanding of divine providence? The answer, rather surprisingly, is not at all! That is to say: If we assume that God has comprehensive knowledge of the past and present, including the causal powers, dispositions, tendencies and so forth of every creature, then it adds nothing at all to God's providential control over the world if we add the assumption that God possesses "simple foreknowledge" as described in this section.

To see why this is so,[11] let us begin with the example (borrowed from David Basinger) of a young woman, Susan, who is seeking God's guidance

[9]See Michael Peterson, *Evil and the Christian God* (Grand Rapids, Mich.: Baker Book House, 1982), pp. 79–99. (The definition given here is my own.)

[10][See reading 1.7—Ed.]

[11]For a more detailed development of the argument presented here, see William Hasker, *God, Time, and Knowledge* (Ithaca: Cornell University Press, 1989), chap. 3; also important is David Basinger, "Middle Knowledge and Classical Christian Thought," *Religious Studies* 22 (1986): 407–22.

show how God can logically guarantee that humans will respond to his love constitute a serious objection?

. . . In spite of all of the arguments that have been set forth and discussed, it is in the end out of the question for anyone to "prove" that a particular conception of God is the correct one. Rather, one simply finds that a particular way of understanding the things of God makes the most sense, and provides the greatest illumination, in the overall context of one's thinking and living. And so we offer a challenge to the reader, to "try and see" whether he or she cannot find a rich and satisfying understanding of Scripture, of the Christian faith generally and of our life in Christ, seen through the lens of the openness of God.

STUDY QUESTIONS

1. Explain the difference between a libertarian and a compatibilist conception of free will.
2. What is Calvinism? Why does Hasker reject it?
3. Explain Molina's doctrine that God has *middle knowledge.* In what way does God exercise control, according to Molinism? In what way does God have less control in Molinism than in Calvinism?
4. Why does Hasker reject Molinism? How do his grounds for rejecting Molinism resemble his grounds for rejecting Calvinism? Are his objections the same in both cases?
5. What is *simple foreknowledge?* Why does Hasker say that "simple foreknowledge, unlike middle knowledge, simply does not 'help' God in providentially governing the world"?
6. What is the basic idea of the "open God" approach? How does an open God theology explain the existence of moral evil—that is, evil done by human beings? What is its view of divine omniscience?
7. *Do you agree with Hasker that, in Molinism, God is the archmanipulator? After all, don't the actions people perform depend on their free choices, even according to Molinism? Explain.
8. Why is prophecy thought to be a problem for the "open God" approach? How does Hasker propose to resolve the problem? *Do you think his resolution is plausible? Why or why not?
9. *Do you see drawbacks to the open God theology? Explain.
10. *Explain and evaluate Hasker's closing paragraph.

READING 1.9

God Everlasting

Nicholas Wolterstorff

In Reading 1.7, William L. Rowe cited the idea of Boethius and Aquinas that God is timeless, existing outside of time. Nicholas Wolterstorff (Yale University) argues that this idea reveals the influence of Hellenistic thought on Christianity and is incompatible with biblical thought. The biblical God is **everlasting***—that is, existing within time but without beginning or end; yet the biblical God is not* **eternal,** *outside of time. On the contrary, in the Bible, God acts, God's acts occur in a certain sequence, and these acts are different from one another; there are thus changes on God's "time-strand." In reply, one could assert (as Aquinas did) that, although* an event that God brings about *occurs at a particular time,* God's act of bringing about that event *is not temporal. Against this view, Wolterstorff argues that, for God to know whether a certain event is occurring, was occurring, or will be occurring, God's knowing must be in time; likewise, if God plans to bring about a certain event, God's planning must exist in time. Knowing and planning are essential to God's being a redeemer, as in the Bible.*

All Christian **theologians** agree that God is without beginning and without end. The vast majority have held, in addition, that God is **eternal,** existing outside of time. Only a small minority have contended that God is **everlasting,** existing within time.[1] In what follows I shall take up the cudgels for that minority, arguing that God as conceived and presented by the biblical writers is a being whose own life and existence is temporal.

The biblical writers do not present God as some passive factor within reality but as an agent in it. Further, they present him as acting within *human* history. The god they present is neither the impassive god of the Oriental nor the nonhistorical god of the Deist. Indeed, so basic to the biblical writings is their speaking of God as agent within history that if one viewed God as only an impassive factor in reality, or as one whose agency does not occur within human history, one would have to regard the biblical speech about God as at best one long sequence of metaphors pointing to a reality for which they are singularly inept, and as at worst one long sequence of falsehoods.

More specifically, the biblical writers present God as a redeeming God. From times most ancient, man has departed from the pattern of responsibilities awarded him at his creation by God. A multitude of evils has followed. But God was not content to leave man in the mire of his misery. Aware of what is going on, he has resolved, in response to man's sin and its resultant evils, to bring about renewal. He has, indeed, already been acting in accord with that resolve, centrally and decisively in the life, death, and resurrection of Jesus Christ.

What I shall argue is that if we are to accept this picture of God as acting for the renewal of human life, we must conceive of him as everlasting rather than eternal. God the Redeemer cannot be a God eternal. This is so because God the Redeemer is a God who *changes.* And any being which changes is a being among whose states there is temporal succession. Of course, there is an important sense in which God as presented in the Scriptures is changeless: he is steadfast in his redeeming intent and ever faithful to his children. Yet, **ontologically,** God cannot be a redeeming God without there being changeful variation among his states.

If this argument proves correct the importance of the issue here confronting us for Christian **theology** can scarcely be exaggerated. A theology which opts for God as eternal cannot avoid being in conflict with the confession of God as redeemer. And given the obvious fact that God is presented in the Bible as a God who redeems, a theology which opts for God as eternal cannot be a theology faithful to the biblical witness.

Our line of argument will prove to be neither subtle nor complicated. So the question will insistently arise, why have Christian theologians so massively contended that God is eternal? Why has not the dominant tradition of Christian theology been that of God everlasting?

Our argument will depend heavily on taking with seriousness a certain feature of temporality which has been neglected in Western philosophy. But the massiveness of the God eternal tradition cannot, I am persuaded, be attributed merely to philosophical oversight. There are, I think, two factors more fundamental. One is the feeling, deep-seated in much of human culture, that the flowing of events into an irrecoverable and unchangeable past is a matter for deep regret. Our bright actions and shining moments do not long endure. The gnawing tooth of time bites all. And our evil deeds can never be undone. They are forever to be regretted. Of course, the philosopher is inclined to distinguish the mere fact of temporality from the actual pattern of the events in history and to argue that regrets about the latter should not slosh over into regrets about the former. The philosopher is right. The regrettableness of what transpires in time is not good ground for regretting that there is time. Yet where the philosopher sees the possibility and the need for a distinction, most people have seen none. Regrets over the pervasive pattern of what transpires within time have led whole societies to place the divine outside of time—freed from the "bondage" of temporality.

But I am persuaded that William Kneale is correct when he contends that the most important fac-

[1]The most noteworthy contemporary example is Oscar Cullmann, *Christ and Time* (Eng. tr., Philadelphia, 1950).

tor accounting for the tradition of God eternal within Christian theology was the influence of the classical Greek philosophers on the early theologians.[2] The distinction between eternal being and everlasting being was drawn for the first time in the history of thought by Plato (*Timaeus* 37–38), though the language he uses is reminiscent of words used still earlier by Parmenides. Plato does not connect eternity and divinity, but he does make clear his conviction that eternal being is the highest form of reality. This was enough to influence the early Christian theologians, who did their thinking within the milieu of Hellenic and Hellenistic thought, to assign eternity to God. Thus was the fateful choice made.

. . . Of course, not every bit of de**hellenization** is laudatory from the Christian standpoint, for not everything that the Greeks said is false. What is the case, though, is that the patterns of classical Greek thought are incompatible with the pattern of biblical thought. And in facing the issue of God everlasting versus God eternal we are dealing with the fundamental pattern of biblical thought. Indeed, I am persuaded that unless the tradition of God eternal is renounced, fundamental dehellenizing will perpetually occupy itself in the suburbs, never advancing to the city center. Every attempt to purge Christian theology of the traces of incompatible Hellenic patterns of thought must fail unless it removes the roadblock of the God eternal tradition. Around this barricade there are no detours. . . .

[DEFINING *X IS ETERNAL*]

For our purposes we can take as the decisive feature of temporality the exemplification of the temporal ordering-relations of precedence, succession, and simultaneity. Unless some entities did stand to each other in one or the other of these relations, there would be no temporal reality. Conversely, if there is temporal reality then there are pairs of entities whose members stand to each other in the relation of one occurring before (precedence) or one occurring after (succession) or one occurring simultaneously with (simultaneity) the other.

We must ask in turn what sort of entity is such that its examples can stand to each other in the relations of precedence, succession, and simultaneity. For not every sort of entity is such. The members of a pair of trees cannot stand in these relations. The golden chain tree outside my back door neither occurs before nor after nor simultaneously with the shingle oak outside my front door. Of course, *the sprouting of the former* stands in one of these relations to *the sprouting of the latter;* and so too does *the demise of the latter* to *the demise of the former.* But the trees themselves do not. They do not occur at all.

We have in this example a good clue, though, as to the sort of entity whose examples can stand in the relations of precedence, succession, and simultaneity. It is just such entities as *the demise of my golden chain tree* and *the sprouting of my shingle oak.* It is, in short, what I shall call events that stand in these relations.

As I conceive of an event, it consists in something's actually having some property, or something's actually performing some action, or something's actually standing in some relation to something. . . .

. . . [C]onsider some event *e* which consists in some entity *a* having some property or performing some action or standing in some relation. Let us call *a,* a *subject* of *e.* And let us call *e* an *aspect* of *a.* A given event may well have more than one subject. For example, an event consisting of my sitting under my shingle oak has both me and the shingle oak as subjects. Indeed, I think it can also be viewed as having the relation of *sitting under* as subject. I see nothing against regarding an event consisting of my sitting under my shingle oak as identical with an event consisting of the relation of *sitting under* being exemplified by me with respect to my shingle oak.

Now consider that set of a given entity's aspects such that each member bears a temporal order-relation to every member of the set and none bears a temporal order-relation to any aspect not a member of the set. Let us call that set, provided that it is not empty, the *time-strand* of that entity. . . .

Consider, next, a set of events such that each member stands to every member in one of the temporal

[2]William Kneale, "Time and Eternity in Theology," *Proceedings of the Aristotelian Society* (1961).

order-relations, and such that no member stands to any event which is not a member in any of these relations. I shall call such a set a *temporal array.* A temporal array is of course just the union of a set of time-strands such that every member of each member strand bears some temporal order-relation to every member of every other member strand, and such that no member of any member strand bears any temporal order-relation to any member of any strand which is not a member of the set. In what follows I assume that there is but one temporal array. I assume, that is, that every member of every time-strand bears a temporal order-relation to every member of every time-strand.

Now suppose that there is some entity all of whose aspects are such that they are to be found in no temporal array whatsoever. Such an entity would be, in the most radical way possible, outside of time. Accordingly, I shall define "eternal" thus:

> Def. 1: *x* is eternal if and only if *x* has no aspect which is a member of the temporal array.

An alternative definition would have been this: "*x* is eternal if and only if *x* has no time-strand." The difference between the two definitions is that, on the latter, an entity is eternal if none of its aspects bears any temporal order-relation to any of those events which are *its* aspects; whereas on the former, what is required of an entity for it to be eternal is that none of its aspects be related by any temporal order-relation to *any event whatsoever.* Of course, if every event which bears any temporal order-relation to any event whatsoever is also simultaneous with itself, then everything which fails to satisfy the "temporal array" definition of "eternal" will also fail to satisfy the "time-strand" definition. . . .

Reflecting on the consequences of the above definitions and explanations, someone might protest that the definition of eternal is altogether too stringent. For consider, say, the number 3. This, no doubt, was referred to by Euclid and also by Cantor. So, by our explanation of "aspect," *3's being referred to by Euclid* was an aspect of the number 3, and *3's being referred to by Cantor* was another aspect thereof. And of course the former preceded the latter. So, by our definition, 3 is not eternal. But—it may be protested—the fact that something is successively referred to should not be regarded as ground for concluding that it is not eternal. For after all, successive references to something do not produce any change in it. Although they produce variation among its aspects, they do not produce a changeful variation among them.

In response to this protest it must be emphasized that the concept of an eternal being is not identical with the concept of an unchanging being. The root idea behind the concept of an eternal being is not that of one which does not change but rather that of one which is outside of time. And a question of substance is whether an unchanging being may fail to be eternal. The most thoroughgoing and radical way possible for an entity to be outside of time is that which something enjoys if it satisfies our definition of "eternal." And it must simply be acknowledged that if an entity is successively referred to, then it is not in the most thoroughgoing way outside of time. There is temporal succession among its aspects.

However, the idea of change could be used by the protester in another way. It is indeed true that not every variation among the aspects of an entity constitutes change therein. Only variation among some of them—call them its *change-relevant* aspects—does so. So on the ground that the change-relevant aspects of an entity are more basic to it, we might distinguish between something being *fundamentally* noneternal and something being *trivially* noneternal. Something is *fundamentally* noneternal if it fails to satisfy the concept of being eternal by virtue of some of its change-relevant aspects. Something is *trivially* noneternal if its failure to satisfy the concept of being eternal is not by virtue of any of its change-relevant aspects.

Now in fact it will be change-relevant aspects of God to which I will appeal in arguing that he is not eternal. Thus my argument will be that God is *fundamentally* noneternal.

[THE BIBLICAL DESCRIPTION OF GOD]

It might seem obvious that God, as described by the biblical writers, is a being who changes, and who accordingly is fundamentally noneternal. For God is described as a being who *acts*—in creation, in providence, and for the renewal of mankind. He is an agent, not an impassive factor in reality. And from the manner in which his acts are described, it seems obvious that many of them have beginnings and endings, that accordingly they stand in succession relations to each other, and that these successive acts are of such a sort that their presence and absence on God's time-strand constitutes changes thereon. Thus it seems obvious that God is fundamentally noneternal.

God is spoken of as calling Abraham to leave Chaldea and later instructing Moses to return to Egypt. So does not the event of *God's instructing Moses* succeed that of *God's calling Abraham?* And does not this sort of succession constitute a change on God's time-strand—not a change in his "essence," but nonetheless a change on his time-strand? Again, God is spoken of as leading Israel through the Red Sea and later sending his Son into the world. So does not his doing the latter succeed his doing the former? And does not the fact of this sort of succession constitute a change along God's time-strand?

In short, it seems evident that the biblical writers regard God as having a time-strand of his own on which actions on his part are to be found, and that some at least of these actions vary in such a way that there are changes along the strand. It seems evident that they do not regard changes on time-strands as confined to entities in God's creation. The God who acts, in the way in which the biblical writers speak of God as acting, seems clearly to change.

Furthermore, is it not clear from how they speak that the biblical writers regarded many of God's acts as bearing temporal order-relations to events which are not aspects of him but rather aspects of the earth, of ancient human beings, and so forth? The four cited above, for example, seem all to be described thus. It seems obvious that God's actions as described by the biblical writers stand in temporal order-relations to all the other events in our own time-array.

However, I think it is not at all so obvious as on first glance it might appear that the biblical writers do in fact describe God as changing. Granted that the language they use suggests this. It is not at once clear that this is what they wished to say with this language. It is not clear that this is how they were describing God. Let us begin to see why this is so by reflecting on the following passage from St. Thomas Aquinas:

> Nor, if the action of the first agent is eternal, does it follow that His effect is eternal, . . . God acts voluntarily in the production of things, . . . God's act of understanding and willing is, necessarily, His act of making. Now, an effect follows from the intellect and the will according to the determination of the intellect and the command of the will. Moreover, just as the intellect determines every other condition of the thing made, so does it prescribe the time of its making; for art determines not only that this thing is to be such and such, but that it is to be at this particular time, even as a physician determines that a dose of medicine is to be drunk at such and such a particular time, so that, if his act of will were of itself sufficient to produce the effect, the effect would follow anew from his previous decision, without any new action on his part. Nothing, therefore, prevents our saying that God's action existed from all eternity, whereas its effect was not present from eternity, but existed at that time when, from all eternity, He ordained it (*Summa Contra Gentiles* II.35; cf. II.36, 4).

Let us henceforth call an event which neither begins nor ends an *everlasting event.* And let us call an event which either begins or ends, a *temporal event.* In the passage above, St. Thomas is considering God's acts of bringing about temporal events. So consider some such act; say, that of God's bringing about Israel's deliverance from Egypt. The temporal event in question, Israel's deliverance from Egypt, occurred (let us say) in 1225 B.C. But from the fact that what God brought about occurred in 1225 it does not follow, says Aquinas, that God's act of bringing it about occurred in 1225. In fact, it does not follow that this act had any beginning or ending whatsoever. And in general, suppose that God brings about some temporal event *e.* From the fact that *e* is temporal it does not follow, says Aquinas, that God's act of bringing about *e*'s occurrence is temporal. The temporality of the event which God brings about does not infect God's act of bringing it about. God's act of bringing it about may well be everlasting. This can perhaps more easily be seen, he says, if we remember that God, unlike us, does not have to "take steps" so as to bring about the occurrence of some event. He need only will that it occur. If God just wants it to be the case that *e* occur at *t*, *e* occurs at *t*.

Thus God can bring about changes in our history without himself changing. The occurrence of the event of Israel's deliverance from Egypt constitutes a change in our history. But there is no counterpart change among God's aspects by virtue of his bringing this event about.

Now let us suppose that the four acts of God cited above—instructing Moses, calling Abraham, leading Israel through the Red Sea, and sending his Son into the world—regardless of the impression we might gain from the biblical language used to describe them, also have the structure of God's bringing about the occurrence of some temporal event. Suppose, for example, that God's leading Israel through the Red Sea has the structure of God's bringing it about that Israel's passage through the Red Sea occurs. And suppose Aquinas is right that the temporality of Israel's passage does not infect with temporality God's act of bringing about this passage. Then what is strictly speaking the case is not that God's leading Israel through the Red Sea occurs during 1225. What is rather the case is that Israel's passage through the Red Sea occurs during 1225, and that God brings this passage about. And the temporality of the passage does not entail the temporality of God's bringing it about. This latter may be everlasting. So, likewise, the fact that the occurrence of this passage marks a change in our history does not entail that God's bringing it about marks a change among God's aspects. God may unchangingly bring about historical changes.

It is natural, at this point, to wonder whether we do not have in hand here a general strategy for interpreting the biblical language about God acting. Is it not perhaps the case that all those acts of God which the biblical writers speak of as beginning or as ending really consist in God performing the everlasting event of bringing about the occurrence of some temporal event?

Well, God does other things with respect to temporal events than bringing about their occurrence. For example, he also *knows* them. Why then should it be thought that the best way to interpret all the temporal-event language used to describe God's actions is by reference to God's action of bringing about the occurrence of some event? May it not be that the best way to interpret what is said with some of such language is by reference to one of those other acts which God performs with respect to temporal events? But then if God is not to change, it is not only necessary that the temporality of *e* not infect God's act of *bringing about* the occurrence of *e*, but also that *every* act of God such that he performs it with respect to *e* not be infected by the temporality of *e*. For example, if God *knows* some temporal event *e*, his knowledge of *e* must not be infected by the temporality of *e*.

So the best way of extrapolating from Aquinas's hint would probably be along the lines of the following theory concerning God's actions and the biblical speech about them. All God's actions are everlasting. None has either beginning or ending. Of these everlasting acts, the structure of some consists in God's performing some action with respect to some event. And at least some of the events that God acts with respect to are temporal events. However, in no case does the temporality of the event that God acts with respect to infect the event of his acting. On the contrary, his acting with respect to some temporal event is itself invariably an everlasting event. So whenever the biblical writers use temporal-event language to describe God's actions, they are to be interpreted as thereby claiming that God acts with respect to some temporal event. They are not to be interpreted as claiming that God's acting is itself a temporal event. God as described by the biblical writers is to be interpreted as acting, and as acting with respect to temporal events. But he is not to be interpreted as changing. All his acts are everlasting.

This, I think, is a fascinating theory. If true, it provides a way of harmonizing the fundamental biblical teaching that God is a being who acts in our history, with the conviction that God does not change. How far the proposed line of biblical interpretation can be carried out, I do not know. I am not aware of any theologian who has ever tried to carry it out, though there are a great many theologians who might have relieved the tension in their thought by

3. How might one argue from the mere fact that God performs different actions in a temporal sequence to the conclusion that, in biblical thought, God is not eternal? How can one reply to this argument, based on Aquinas's writing? Finally, how does Wolterstorff argue that this reply is inadequate?
4. What does Wolterstorff mean by the Hellenization of biblical thought?
5. How is the question "Does God change?" related to the question "Is God eternal?"
6. *How could the practice of petitionary prayer be cited to support Wolterstorff's view?
7. What philosophical problem did Boethius and Aquinas think the idea of God's eternality could solve? (On this, see Reading 1.7.)
8. *Wolterstorff notes that it can be argued that, if God is simple, as perfect being theology implies, then God has no parts and, hence, no *temporal* parts. Evaluate this argument.
9. *Contemporary philosopher Paul Helm has said that, if God exists in time, then God is more humanlike than if God does not exist in time. Explain this remark by thinking of the human characteristics of having memories, expectations, hopes, plans, disappointments, and frustrations. Which of these do you think an everlasting God could have without God's perfection being diminished? Which would in your opinion diminish God's perfection? Explain.
10. *Do you see a connection between God's being everlasting and God's being a necessary being? Explain.
11. *Augustine wrote the following:

> Lo, are not those men full of their old carnal nature who say to us, "What was God doing before He made heaven and earth?" "For if," they say, "He took his ease and did nothing, why did He not continue in this way henceforth and forever. . . . If any new motion arise in God, or a new will is formed in him, to the end of establishing creation, which he had never established previously, how then would there be true eternity, when a will arises that previously was not there? Yet if it were God's sempiternal [everlasting] will for the creature to exist, why is not the creature sempiternal also?" (*The Confessions of St. Augustine,* trans. John K. Ryan [New York: Doubleday and Co., 1960], book 11, chapter 10.)

How could the problem Augustine cites be used to support the view that God is eternal (in Wolterstorff's sense)?

12. *Interpret and evaluate the following argument *for* saying that God is eternal (timeless):
    - **a.** An eternal being is more perfect than an everlasting one, because the former lives a unified life.
    - **b.** An eternal being's existence is better than a noneternal being's existence, because the former never has to leave parts of life behind.
13. *It has been said that numbers have a timeless existence. Drawing on Wolterstorff's ideas, explain what might be meant by this remark. Then explain why Wolterstorff would say numbers are trivially non-eternal but fundamentally eternal.

(Note: questions 9 and 10 are discussed by Paul Helm in his article "Eternality," cited in the suggested readings. Question 12 draws on ideas in Brian Leftow, "Eternity," in *A Companion to Philosophy of Religion,* ed. Philip L. Quinn and Charles Taliaferro [Oxford: Basil Blackwell, 1997], 257–63.)

READING 1.10

Process Theology: God as Creative-Responsive Love

John B. Cobb and David Ray Griffin

Process theism *is an alternative philosophy to traditional theism that was pioneered by the British thinker Alfred North Whitehead (1861–1947) and developed, albeit within a more traditional theistic framework, by the American philosopher Charles*

Hartshorne (1897–2000). Cobb and Griffin (School of Theology at Claremont and Claremont Graduate University) here set out some fundamental tenets of process theism.

Central to process theology is a rejection of the classic conceptions that God is **immutable,** *is outside of time, is* **omniscient,** *and controls everything that happens. Development, change, growth, and responsiveness enhance rather than limit a being. Thus, God can change and can have emotions, such as sympathy and love. The core concept of God, for Cobb and Griffin, is creative-responsive love, which locates creativity not in control but in responsiveness to the world and activity within history. God seeks to "persuade" each occasion toward the best possibility but does not and cannot control it. In addition, God is not a "cosmic moralist" but, instead, aims at creatures' enjoyment. God also takes risks with the world. Since God's control is limited, the problem of evil is met. The selection ends by noting the implications of process theology for the gender of God.*

PROCESS

Process thought by definition affirms that process is fundamental. It does not assert that *everything* is in process; for that would mean that even the fact that things are in process is subject to change. There are unchanging principles of process and abstract forms. But to be *actual* is to be a process. Anything which is not a process is an abstraction from process, not a full-fledged actuality.

The bare assertion that the actual is processive has religious significance even by itself. Since the world as we experience it is a place of process, of change, of becoming, of growth and decay, the contrary notion that what is actual or fully real is beyond change leads to a devaluation of life in the world. Since our basic religious drive is to be in harmony with the fully real, belief that the fully real is beyond process encourages one or another form of escape from full participation in the world. But to understand that the process is the reality directs the drive to be "with it" into immersion in the process.

The religious implication of reality as processive is in harmony with one of the chief consequences of the Judeo-Christian vision of reality. In this tradition, God has been viewed as active within the historical process. Accordingly, historical activity has had more importance than in traditions without a doctrine of the purposive-providential presence of the sacred reality in history. Those cultures decisively affected by the Judeo-Christian view owe to it much of their vitality. . . .

THE EXISTENCE OF GOD

Process theology operates on the one side from the perspective of Christian faith and on the other in the **metaphysical** context provided by process philosophy and its doctrine of God. Arguments for the existence of God are not an essential part of its work. However, in a day when so many regard belief in God's existence as wholly irrational or view the notion of God as nonsensical, a brief comment on this question is in order.

The word "god" has partly separate histories in religion and in philosophy. In religion the gods are objects of devotion. Their **ontological** status is not directly in question. In this sense the tribe, the nation-state, or the power of sexuality may be deified. The question of existence arises only when the idea of god becomes conceptually more sophisticated, when religion moves toward philosophy. If that to which devotion is directed is thought to be an inclusive or unifying power, it becomes possible to doubt the existence of "God," for there may be no such unifying power.

The philosopher is interested in some form of ontological primacy or superiority. Thus philosophical doctrines of God vary with the view of reality expressed in the system. One cannot believe in the God of one philosopher if one accepts the conflicting understanding of reality of another philosopher.

The union of religious and philosophical concerns in classical theism gave the question of the existence of God an apparent definiteness. Much of the modern argument is about the existence of the God of classical theism, especially the God of **Thomism.** Indeed the word "theism" is often taken in this restricted sense, so that those who affirm the God of the Bible or of George Hegel deny that they are theists.

Process thought calls for a freer exploration of the question of God and a looser use of the word "theism." If the word "God" is tightly bound to any particular mode of devotion or view of reality, then in the course of events it will become clear that God does not exist. But this is not a damaging point if "God" is understood more open-endedly, for if "human being" is tightly bound to any particular definition, it eventually becomes apparent that "human beings" do not exist either. But we know that there is an actual referent for "human beings." Likewise, the fact that all conceptualities about God prove inadequate does not show that Jewish, Christian, and Islamic devotion is wholly misplaced or that ontological gradations of primacy are philosophically meaningless. Process thought continues the effort to clarify both the object of theistic worship and the formative ontological elements in reality. . . .

GOD AS RESPONSIVE LOVE

[Alfred North] Whitehead noted that whereas in a primitive religion "you study the will of God in order that He may preserve you," in a universal religion "you study his goodness in order to be like him." (*Religion in the Making* 40.) The Taoist tries to live in harmony with the Tao; the Hindu Vedantist seeks to realize the identity of Atman with Brahman; the Moslem bows to the will of Allah; the Marxist aligns with the dialectical process of history. Accordingly, the statement in Matthew 5:48, "You, therefore, must be perfect, as your heavenly Father is perfect," is a particular expression of the universal religious aspiration of humanity to participate in or be in harmony with perfection. By definition the divine reality is perfect. The question concerns the nature of this perfection.

Christian faith has held that the basic character of this divine reality is best described by the term "love." However, the meaning of the statement "God is love" is by no means self-evident. Whitehead helps us to recover much of the meaning of that phrase as it is found in the New Testament.

We are told by psychologists, and we know from our own experience, that love in the fullest sense involves a sympathetic response to the loved one. Sympathy means feeling the feelings of the other, hurting with the pains of the other, grieving with the grief, rejoicing with the joys. . . .

Nevertheless, traditional theism said that God is completely impassive, that there was no element of sympathy in the divine love for the creatures. The fact that there was an awareness that this Greek notion of divine **impassibility** was in serious tension with the Biblical notion of divine love for the world is most clearly reflected in this prayer of the eleventh-century theologian Anselm:

> Although it is better for thee to be . . . compassionate, passionless, than not to be these things; how art thou . . . compassionate, and, at the same time, passionless? For, if thou art passionless, thou dost not feel sympathy; and if thou dost not feel sympathy, thy heart is not wretched from sympathy for the wretched; but this it is to be compassionate.[1]

Anselm resolved the tension by saying: "Thou art compassionate in terms of our experience, and not compassionate in terms of thy being." In other words, God only *seems* to us to be compassionate; he is not *really* compassionate! In Anselm's words: "When thou beholdest us in our wretchedness, we experience the effect of compassion, but thou dost not experience the feeling." Thomas Aquinas in the thirteenth century faced the same problem. The objection to the idea that there is love in God was stated as follows: "For in God there are no passions. Now love is a passion. Therefore love is not in God." (*Summa Theologica* I, Question 20, article 1, objection 1.) Thomas responds by making a distinction between two elements within love, one which involves passion and one which does not. He then says, after quoting Aris-

[1][This passage appears in Reading 1.2 in a different translation—Ed.]

totle favorably, that God "loves without passion." (*Ibid.,* answer 1.)[2]

This denial of an element of sympathetic responsiveness to the divine love meant that it was entirely creative. That is, God loves us only in the sense that he does good things for us. In Anselm's words:

> Thou art both compassionate, because thou dost save the wretched, and spare those who sin against thee; and not compassionate, because thou art affected by no sympathy for wretchedness.

In Thomas' words. "To sorrow, therefore, over the misery of others belongs not to God, but it does most properly belong to Him to dispel that misery." (*Summa Theologica* I, Question 21, article 3.)

Accordingly, for Anselm and Thomas the analogy is with the father who has no feeling for his children, and hence does not feel their needs, but "loves" them in that he gives good things to them. Thomas explicitly states that "love" is to be understood in this purely outgoing sense, as active goodwill: "To love anything is nothing else than to will good to that thing." He points out that God does not love as we love. For our love is partly responsive, since it is moved by its object, whereas the divine love is purely creative, since it creates its object. (*Summa Theologica* I, Question 20, article 2, answer.)

This notion of love as purely creative has implications that are in tension with the Biblical idea of God's equal love for all persons. All persons are obviously not equal in regard to the "good things of life" (however these be defined) that they enjoy (especially in the context of traditional theism, where the majority are consigned to eternal torment). And yet, if God's love is purely creative, totally creating the goodness of the beings loved, this implies that God loves some persons more than others. As Thomas said: "No one thing would be better than another if God did not will greater good for one than for another." (*Summa Theologica* I, Question 20, article 3, answer.) This is one of the central ways in which the acceptance of the notion of divine impassibility undercuts the Biblical witness to the love of God.

[2][See Reading 1.1. Study question 4—Ed.]

Since we mold ourselves partly in terms of our image of perfect human existence, and this in turn is based upon our notion of deity, the notion of God as an Impassive Absolute whose love was purely creative could not help but have practical consequences for human existence. Love is often defined by theologians as "active goodwill." The notion of sympathetic compassion is missing. Indeed, one of the major theological treatises on the meaning of agape, or Christian love, portrays it as totally outgoing, having no element of responsiveness to the qualities of the loved one. (Anders Nygren, *Agape and Eros* [The Westminster Press, 1953], pp. 77–78.) This notion of love has promoted a "love" that is devoid of genuine sensitivity to the deepest needs of the "loved ones." Is this not why the word "charity," which is derived from *caritas* (the Latin word for agape), today has such heavily negative connotations? Also, the word "do-gooder" is a word of reproach, not because we do not want people to do good things, but because people labeled "do-gooders" go around trying to impose their own notions of the good that needs doing, without any sensitive responsiveness to the real desires and needs of those they think they are helping. This perverted view of love as purely active goodwill is due in large part to the longstanding notion that this is the kind of love which characterizes the divine reality.

This traditional notion of love as solely creative was based upon the value judgment that independence or absoluteness is unqualifiedly good, and that dependence or relativity in any sense derogates from perfection. But, . . . while perfection entails independence or absoluteness in some respects, it also entails dependence or relativity in other respects. It entails ethical independence, in the sense that one should not be deflected by one's passions from the basic commitment to seek the greatest good in all situations. But this ethical commitment, in order to be actualized in concrete situations, requires responsiveness to the actual needs and desires of others. Hence, to promote the greatest good, one must be informed by, and thus relativized by, the feelings of others. Furthermore, we do not admire someone whose enjoyment is not in part dependent upon the condition of those around them. Parents who remained in absolute bliss while their children were in agony would not be perfect—unless there are such things as perfect monsters!

In other words, while there is a type of independence or absoluteness that is admirable, there is also a type of dependence or relativity that is admirable. And, if there is an example of absoluteness that is *unqualifiedly* admirable, this means that there is a divine absoluteness; and the same holds true of relativity. Process thought affirms that both of these are true. While traditional theism spoke only of the divine absoluteness, process theism speaks also of "the **divine relativity**" (this is the title of one of Hartshorne's books).

Process theism is sometimes called **"dipolar theism,"** in contrast to traditional theism with its doctrine of divine **simplicity.** For Charles Hartshorne, the two "poles" or aspects of God are the abstract essence of God, on the one hand, and God's concrete actuality on the other. The abstract essence is eternal, absolute, independent, unchangeable. It includes those abstract attributes of deity which characterize the divine existence at every moment. For example, to say that God is omniscient means that in every moment of the divine life God knows everything which is knowable at that time. The concrete actuality is temporal, relative, dependent, and constantly changing. In each moment of God's life there are new, unforeseen happenings in the world which only then have become knowable. Hence, God's concrete knowledge is dependent upon the decisions made by the worldly actualities. God's knowledge is always relativized by, in the sense of internally related to, the world.

Whitehead's way of conceiving the divine dipolarity was not identical with Hartshorne's. Whitehead distinguished between the Primordial Nature of God and the Consequent Nature. The former will be discussed in the following section. The latter is largely identical with what Hartshorne has called God's concrete actuality. Since the Consequent Nature is God as fully actual (*Process and Reality* 524, 530), the term "consequent" makes the same point as Hartshorne's term "relative," that God as fully actual is responsive to and receptive of the worldly actualizations.

This divine relativity is not limited to a "bare knowledge" of the new things happening in the world. Rather, the responsiveness includes a sympathetic feeling with the worldly beings, all of whom have feelings. Hence, it is not merely the content of God's knowledge which is dependent, but God's own emotional state. God enjoys our enjoyments, and suffers with our sufferings. This is the kind of responsiveness which is truly divine and belongs to the very nature of perfection. Hence it belongs to the ideal for human existence. Upon this basis, Christian agape can come to have the element of sympathy, of compassion for the present situation of others, which it should have had all along.

GOD AS CREATIVE LOVE

If sympathetic responsiveness is an essential aspect of Christian love, creative activity is no less essential. Whether it be considered a theme or a presupposition, the notion that God is active in the world, working to overcome evil and to create new things, is central to the Biblical tradition. To be in harmony with the God of Israel and of Jesus is to be involved in the struggle to overcome the various impediments to the fullness of life. In Luke 4:18, Jesus quotes from Isaiah, who indicates that the Spirit of the God he worships impels one to "set at liberty those who are oppressed."

The impetus in Western civilization for individual acts and social programs aimed at alleviating human misery and injustice has come in large part from the belief that God not only loves all persons equally, and hence desires justice, but also is directly acting in the world to create just conditions. The reason is that the basic religious drive of humanity is not only to be in harmony with deity, it is also to be in contact with this divine reality. It is because God is personally present and active in the world that contact with the sacred reality does not necessitate fleeing from history. Our activity aimed at creating good puts us in harmony and contact with God. Indeed, this activity can be understood in part as God's acting through us.

Accordingly, the loss of belief in the creative side of God's love would tend to undermine the various liberation movements that have been originally inspired by belief in divine providence, since it is largely this belief which has lent importance to these movements. Cultures in which the sacred is not understood as involved in creating better conditions for life in the world have had difficulty in generating the sustained commitments necessary to bring about significant change.

It is precisely this notion of divine creative activity in the world which has been most problematic in recent centuries, both within theological circles and in the culture at large. In traditional popular Christian thought, God was understood as intervening here and there in the course of the world. The notion of "acts of God" referred to events which did not have natural causes, but were directly caused by God. In traditional theological thought, all events were understood to be totally caused by God, so all events were "acts of God." However, most events were understood to be caused by God through the mediation of worldly or natural causes. God was the "primary cause" of these events, while the natural antecedents were called "secondary causes." However, a few events were thought to be caused directly by God, without the use of secondary causes. These events were "miracles." Accordingly, while all events were in one sense acts of God, these miracles were acts of God in a special sense. Thus, both in popular and theological circles, there was meaning to be given to the idea that God was creatively active in the world.

However, there are two major problems with this notion. First, it raises serious doubt that the creative activity of God can be understood as *love,* since it creates an enormous problem of evil by implying that *every* event in the world is *totally* caused by God, with or without the use of natural causes. Second, since the Renaissance and Enlightenment, the belief has grown that there are no events which happen without natural causes. Accordingly, the notion of "acts of God" has lost all unambiguous referents. Every event termed an act of God was said also, from another perspective, to be totally explainable in terms of natural causation. This rendered the notion of "act of God" of doubtful meaning. If an event can be totally explained in terms of natural forces, i.e., if these provide a "sufficient cause" for it, what justification is there for introducing the idea of "another perspective"? This seems like special pleading in order to retain a vacuous idea.

Deism was a manifestation of the felt difficulty of speaking of divine activity in the world. God's causation was put totally at the beginning of the world process. Once created, the world was said to run autonomously, without any additional divine input. Insofar as some form of this idea has become pervasive in the culture (not to mention complete atheism), the idea that one's activity in the world could put one in harmony and contact with deity has faded.

Twentieth-century theology has reaffirmed the centrality of the idea of God's activity in history. But it has generally lacked the conceptuality for consistently explicating this belief. . . .

In Western culture generally, the problem of evil, and the widespread belief that the nexus of natural cause and effect excludes divine "intervention," have combined to render the notion of divine creative love problematic. When the leading secular thinkers then see that the leading theologians have provided no intelligible means for speaking of God's activity in the world, they are confirmed in their suspicion that this belief belongs to the myths of the past. Process theology provides a way of recovering the conviction that God acts creatively in the world and of understanding this creative activity as the expression of divine *love* for the world. The notion that there is a creative power of love behind and within the worldly process is no longer one which can only be confessed in spite of all appearances to the contrary. Instead it illuminates our experience.

DIVINE CREATIVE LOVE AS PERSUASIVE

. . . [T]raditional theism portrayed God as the Controlling Power. The doctrine of divine **omnipotence** finally meant that God controlled every detail of the world process. Some traditional theologians, such as Thomas Aquinas, muted this implication of their thought as much as possible (in order to protect the doctrine of human freedom). Others, such as Luther

history of our planet was spent in merely preparing the way for beings who are capable of the only kind of experience that really interests God.

Enjoyment is God's primary concern even with those beings who are capable of developing moral attitudes. But this is not in conflict with an emphasis on morality. God wants us to enjoy, true. But he wants us *all* to enjoy. Accordingly, he wants us to enjoy in ways that do not unnecessarily inhibit enjoyment on the part of others. That puts it negatively. Positively stated, God wants our enjoyment to be such as to increase the enjoyments of others. To be moral is to actualize oneself in such a way as to maximize the enjoyments of future actualities, insofar as these future enjoyments can be conditioned by one's present decision. Hence, although the development of moral attitudes is of extreme importance, it is a derivative concern, secondary to the primary value, which is enjoyment itself.

In traditional Christianity, morality and enjoyment were often seen as in fundamental opposition. In process thought, morality stands in the service of enjoyment. However, the question still arises of the possible tension between them. There is the possible tension between enjoying the present moment to the hilt, and forgoing some of this possible enjoyment in order to prepare for increased enjoyment in the future. Also there is the tension, in regard to the future, between my *own* future occasions of experience, and the future experiences of other enduring individuals. . . . Suffice it here to say that the creative love of God is also relevant to this problem. The divine initial aim for our human experiences is such as to transform into immediate enjoyment the intention to contribute to future good.

DIVINE CREATIVE LOVE AS ADVENTUROUS

One respect in which God's creative love is adventurous has already been discussed: since God's creative activity is persuasive, not controlling, it is a love that takes risks. Hence, each divine creative impulse into the world is adventurous, in that God does not know what the result will be.

However, there is another dimension to the divine adventurousness. Traditional theology tended to portray God as the Sanctioner of the Status Quo. The notions of "God" and "order" were closely associated. In the political realm, the connection between obedience to God and submission to the political status quo was supported by the notorious appeal to Rom., ch. 13, where Paul says that we should "be subject to the governing authorities" because they "have been instituted by God," so that "he who resists the authorities resists what God has appointed."

This notion of God is also closely connected with the notion of God as Controlling Power. Paul's statement is one of those Biblical statements which presuppose that God is in control at least of the major features of the world process. The development of traditional theism, in which God was more consistently said to be in complete control of every detail, further strengthened the conviction that the political status quo should be affirmed. For if God had not wanted those rulers in power, they would not be in power. It is largely due to this notion that those who have been in opposition to despotic rulers have also found themselves in opposition to the church, and have found it useful to espouse atheism.

In the realm of morality in general, belief in God has been closely associated with the idea of moral absolutes, especially of a negative nature. Certain kinds of actions have been said to be wrong in themselves, whether or not in a particular context they served to promote abundant life. This has focused moral attention on rules or fixed principles and distracted from consideration of what would increase the quality of life in the future. Hence the notion that Christian morality consists primarily in abstaining from certain kinds of acts that God has prohibited serves doubly to sanction the status quo. It does so directly, simply by virtue of the notion of immutable moral absolutes. It does so indirectly by diverting attention from the primary moral question of how we should act so as to increase enjoyment of life now and in the future.

The notion of God as Sanctioner of the Status Quo is closely connected with that of God as Cosmic Moralist. The focus on the development of moral attitudes, understood as being in opposition to the growth of enjoyment, distracted attention from the question of what kinds of conditions are needed in order to maximize the possibilities for enjoying existence. This question was not of ultimate importance, since moral attitudes can be developed in any situation. In fact, as some theologians have argued, the more difficult the circumstances, the greater the opportunity for developing moral qualities such as patience!

Process theology understands God precisely as the basic source of unrest in the universe. In Whitehead's words, "The pure conservative is fighting against the essence of the universe." (*Adventure of Ideas* 354.) When he speaks of the essence of the universe, Whitehead primarily has in mind the notion that actuality is process, and that at the root of process there is the Primordial Nature of God, which he sometimes calls the Divine Eros. This is conceived as "the active entertainment of all ideals, with the urge to their finite realization, each in its due season." (*AI* 357.) Not all ideal possibilities can be realized simultaneously. This is why there is process. (*Modes of Thought* 53.) But also no ideal can be repeated indefinitely without its freshness being lost. The Primordial Nature of God is the goad toward novelty in the universe (*PR* 135), stimulating us to realize new possibilities after the old ones no longer are sufficient to give zest to our enjoyment of being actual.

Order is an essential ingredient in the maximization of enjoyment. For example, the richness of human experience could emerge only on the basis of the order of the body. "It is by reason of the body, with its miracle of order, that the treasures of the past environment are poured into the living occasion." (*PR* 516.) On the other hand, excessive order can inhibit enjoyment. Hence, Whitehead speaks of "the contrast between order as the condition for excellence, and order as stifling the freshness of living." (*PR* 514.) Hence, order must not be lost, but it also must not be dominant. "The art of progress is to preserve order amid change, and to preserve change amid order." (*PR* 515.)

God is the source of order. But two important qualifications must be made. Order represents dominance of an ideal possibility which was at one time a novel element in the world. Hence God is the source of order by virtue of first being the source of novelty. Second, neither order nor novelty is understood as intrinsically good, but only as instrumental to the one intrinsic good, which is the enjoyment of intense experience. "God's purpose in the creative advance is the evocation of intensities. The evocation of societies is purely subsidiary to this absolute end." (*PR* 161.) "'Order' and 'novelty' are but the instruments of his subjective aim which is the intensification of 'formal immediacy.'" (*PR* 135.) In brief, although God is the source of order, the order is derivative from novelty, and both order and novelty are good only insofar as they contribute to the enjoyment of experience. As Whitehead puts it elsewhere, the aim toward order, which is impersonal, is subservient to the love of individuals, which is personal. Therefore, types of order are to be rated "according to their success in magnifying the individual actualities, that is to say, in promoting strength of experience." (*AI* 376.)

Hence, no type of social order is to be maintained if it no longer tends to maximize the enjoyment of the members of the society. Also, it is impossible for any form of social order to continue indefinitely to be instrumentally good. God, far from being the Sanctioner of the Status Quo, is the source of some of the chaos in the world. "If there is to be progress beyond limited ideals, the course of history by way of escape must venture along the borders of chaos in its substitution of higher for lower types of order." (*PR* 169.) (God is said to be the source of only *some* of the chaos, since only some of it can in principle lead to a higher type of order and thereby a richer form of enjoyment.)

The connection between the notion of God as the source of adventure toward novel ideals and that of divine creative love as fostering enjoyment has already been made clear. The connection with God as persuasive power is also obvious. Since God does not control the details of any worldly process, the existence of a given state of affairs does not imply that God willed it. Further, since God encourages the actualization of novel possibilities as a means to maximizing creaturely enjoyment, continuation of a state of affairs that originally resulted from a high degree of conformity to God's aims may not express

God's present will. As Henry Nelson Wieman has stressed, partly under the influence of Whitehead, we should worship the Creative Good, not the created good.

Besides the two senses already mentioned in which God's love is adventurous—that it takes risks and promotes adventure toward novelty in the world—there is a third sense. This results from combining this creative side of God's love (God as Divine Eros) with the responsive side. The result is, in Whitehead's words, "the concept of an Adventure in the Universe as One." (*AI* 380.) This is simply a way of describing God. "This Adventure embraces all particular occasions but as an actual fact stands beyond any one of them." *(Ibid.)* The point is that God's own life is an adventure, for the novel enjoyments that are promoted among the creatures are then the experiences providing the material for God's own enjoyment. "The Unity of Adventure includes the Eros which is the living urge towards all possibilities, claiming the goodness of their realization." (*AI* 381.*)* And God's life is also an adventure in the sense of being a risk, since God will feel the discord as well as the beautiful experiences involved in the finite actualizations: "The Adventure of the Universe starts with the dream and reaps tragic Beauty." (*Ibid.*)

GOD AS CREATIVE-RESPONSIVE LOVE

The traditional concept of God is in many respects stereotypically masculine. God was conceived to be active, unresponsive, impassive, inflexible, impatient, and moralistic. This being had none of the stereotypically feminine traits—it was not at all passive, responsive, emotional, flexible, patient, and it did not balance moral concern with an appreciation of beauty. This has led to a one-sided and hence unhealthy Christianity.

An overreaction resulting in a concept of God devoid of the stereotypically masculine attributes would also be destructive of authentic Christian existence. Losing the active or creative side of the divine love would undercut much of the good that Biblical faiths have brought into history, as we have already suggested. The same is true of the strong element of moral concern that has been attributed to God in the cultures decisively influenced by the Biblical faiths. Likewise, the loss of the notion of a divine purpose that at its most general level is inflexible would lead to a complete relativism. The positive aspects of these "masculine" attributes can be retained, without their destructive implications, if they are incorporated into a revolutionized concept of God into which the stereotypically feminine traits are integrated. For, in the integrated result, the former traits are changed qualitatively. . . .

The process dipolar notion of deity has some affinity with the Taoist notion of the Tao, in which the "feminine" and "masculine" (yin and yang) dimensions of reality are perfectly integrated. The Tao is spoken of as a power that works slowly and undramatically, but is finally the most effective agency in reality. Whereas there are aspects of the notion of the Tao which have unfortunate implications, the Taoist vision of deity does contain an important element which should all along have been part of the Christian vision.

STUDY QUESTIONS

1. Explain Cobb and Griffin's starting point: "To be actual is to be a process."
2. Explain Cobb and Griffin's argument for construing "theism" loosely.
3. State in a few sentences the fundamental tenets of process theology as they emerge in the selection.
4. Compare and contrast process theism with the views espoused in the following essays, which also appeared in this chapter: Aquinas, Anselm, Oakes, Minas, Geach, Hasker, Wolterstorff. Explain in particular which previous essays could be partly endorsed by a process theist and how this endorsement must be qualified and limited.
5. Cobb and Griffin state, "While there is a type of independence or absoluteness that is admirable, there is also a type of dependence or relativity that is admirable." Explain this quotation.
6. What are the several aspects of love outlined by Cobb and Griffin? How do these aspects of love

make the God of process theism different from the God of classical theism as depicted by Anselm and Aquinas?

7. What do Cobb and Griffin mean when they say, "In traditional Christianity, God has been understood as a Cosmic Moralist"? What do they propose as an alternative? *Which conception do you favor, and why?
8. What are the implications of process theology for (a) the problem of evil, (b) the practice of petitionary prayer, and (c) the question of God's gender?
9. Explain the term *dipolar theism.*
10. Compare and contrast Cobb and Griffin's notion of divine creativity with that found in the thought of Anselm and Aquinas.
11. How does process theology assess the value of order?
12. *Drawing on your own experience, illustrate how the characteristics of love you mentioned in your answer to question 6 arise in the case of human love.
13. *An attraction of classical theism is its concept of God as a perfect being. To what extent do you think Cobb and Griffin accept this concept of God? To what extent do you think they reject it?
14. Try to explain Cobb and Griffin's treatment of evil, based on what you've read. Is this treatment satisfactory in your opinion? Why or why not?
15. *To what extent does Cobb and Griffin's view of God fit the biblical depiction of God? To what extent does it not fit that depiction? Are there things that God does in the Bible that you do not think God could do according to process theism?
16. There are strong similarities between Hasker's "open God" theology (Reading 1.8) and process theism. What are they? What differences do you detect, if any?

FURTHER READING FOR CHAPTER ONE

Perfect Being Theology

MacDonald, Scott, ed. *Being and Goodness: The Concept of the Good in Metaphysics and Philosophical Theology.* Ithaca, NY, and London: Cornell University Press, 1991.

Morris, Thomas. *Anselmian Explorations.* Notre Dame, IN: Notre Dame University Press, 1987.

Divine Impassibility and Immutability

Clark, Kelly James. "Hold Not Thy Peace at My Tears: Methodological Reflections on Divine Impassibility." In *Our Knowledge of God,* edited by Kelly James Clark, 167–93. Dordrecht, The Netherlands: Kluwer, 1992.

Creel, Richard. *Divine Impassibility: An Essay in Philosophical Theology.* Cambridge, England: Cambridge University Press, 1986.

Wolterstorff, Nicholas. "Suffering Love." In *Philosophy and the Christian Faith,* edited by Thomas V. Morris, 196–237. Notre Dame, IN: Notre Dame University Press, 1988.

Forgiveness

Adams, Marilyn McCord. "Forgiveness: A Christian Model." *Faith and Philosophy* 8 (1991): 277–304.

Quinn, Philip. *Divine Commands and Moral Requirements,* 136–46. New York: Oxford University Press, 1978.

Talbott, Thomas. "Punishment, Forgiveness, and Divine Justice." *Religious Studies* 29 (1993): 151–68.

Is God Vain?

Camapana, Daniel A. "On 'The Vanity of God': A Reply to Taliaferro." *Faith and Philosophy* 9 (1992): 105–8.

Omnipotence

Mavrodes, George. "Some Puzzles Concerning Omnipotence." *Philosophical Review* 72 (1963): 221–23.

Pike, Nelson. "Omnipotence and God's Ability to Sin." *American Philosophical Quarterly* 6 (1969): 208–16.

Urban, Linwood, and Walton, Douglas N., eds. *The Power of God.* New York: Oxford University Press, 1978.

Divine Foreknowledge, Divine Control, and Human Free Will

Fischer, John Martin, ed. *God, Foreknowledge, and Freedom.* Stanford, CA: Stanford University Press, 1989.

Flint, Thomas. *Divine Providence: A Molinist Account.* Ithaca, NY: Cornell University Press, 1998.

Katzoff, Charlotte. "Divine Causality and Moral Responsibility in the Story of Joseph and His Brothers." *Iyyun: the Jerusalem Philosophical Quarterly* 47 (1998): 21–40.

Sanders, John. "Why Simple Foreknowledge Offers No More Providential Control Than the Openness of God." *Faith and Philosophy* 14, 1 (1997): 26–40.

Taliaferro, Charles. *Contemporary Philosophy of Religion,* 106–42. Malden, MA, and Oxford, England: Blackwell, 1998.

Zagzebski, Linda. *The Dilemma of Freedom and Foreknowledge.* New York: Oxford University Press, 1991.

Eternality and Timelessness

Hasker, William. *God, Time and Knowledge.* Ithaca, NY: Cornell University Press, 1989.

Helm, Paul. "Eternality." In *Philosophy of Religion: A Guide to the Subject,* edited by Brian Davies, 75–79. Washington, D.C.: Georgetown University Press, 1998.

Leftow, Brian. *Time and Eternity.* Ithaca, NY: Cornell University Press, 1991.

Pike, Nelson. *God and Timelessness.* New York: Schocken Books, 1970.

Stump, Eleonore, and Norman, Kretzmann. "Eternity." *The Journal of Philosophy* 78 (1981): 429–58.

Taliaferro, Charles. *Contemporary Philosophy of Religion,* 143–63. Malden, MA, and Oxford, England: Blackwell, 1998.

Divine Simplicity

Kretzmann, Norman, and Eleonore Stump. "Absolute Simplicity." *Faith and Philosophy* 2 (1985): 353–82.

Mann, William. "Divine Simplicity." *Religious Studies* 18 (1982): 451–71.

Wolterstorff, Nicholas. "Divine Simplicity." In *Philosophical Perspectives 5: Philosophy of Religion,* edited by James E. Tomberlin, 531–52. Atascadero, CA: Ridgeview, 1991.

Process Theism

Basinger, David. *Divine Power in Process Theism: A Philosophical Critique.* Albany, NY: SUNY Press, 1988.

Cobb, John B. *God and the World.* Philadelphia: Westminster Press, 1969.

Griffin, David Ray. *Reenchantment Without Supernaturalism: A Process Philosophy of Religion.* Ithaca, NY: Cornell University Press, 2000.

Nash, Ronald, ed. *Process Theology.* Grand Rapids, MI: Baker Book House, 1987.

Oakes, Robert. "Classical Theism and Pantheism: A Victory for Process Theism?" *Religious Studies* 13 (1977): 167–73.

CHAPTER 2

Talking About God

The Meaning of Religious Language

Theists speak freely of God's attributes, depicting God as (all-)knowing, (all-)powerful, (all-)good, compassionate, just, merciful, and the like. But *knowing, powerful, good, compassionate, just, merciful,* and other such terms are predicated of human beings as well as God. We might say, for example, that Cynthia is good or that Sam is compassionate. Do these terms mean the same thing when we speak of God as when we speak of Cynthia or Sam? Are they used **univocally** of God and humans (i.e., with the same meaning) or, instead, **equivocally** (i.e., with different meanings)?

This issue has been disputed in the history of religious thought, and understandably so. On the one hand, theists are impressed by God's otherness, uniqueness, and transcendence. This leads to a conviction, on their part, that language is utterly and hopelessly inadequate to describe God at all, let alone to capture God's nature and greatness. Often, therefore, God is said to be **ineffable,** indescribable. On the other hand, we learn language in its human context, and it is implausible that terms we apply to humans take on a totally different meaning outside that context. Moreover, human beings need knowledge of what God is, for if they lack that knowledge, what are they believing when they believe that God exists? And could it make sense for them to worship God without having knowledge of what they are worshipping?

Recall from Chapter 1 that certain terms—specifically, those that seemingly refer to emotional states of God—have been construed by some philosophers as having a different meaning when applied to God. (Anselm and Aquinas held that in God's case the term refers only to actions, not inner states.) Yet most of the readings in Chapter 1 interpreted certain other statements, such as "God knows that Jones will mow his lawn" and "God is powerful" on the assumption that *knows* and *powerful* have the same meaning as when applied to humans. Hence arose the various puzzles and paradoxes we encountered in Chapter 1. The selections that follow, however, examine explicitly and closely how to construe talk about God—univocally or equivocally.

Moses Maimonides, a towering twelfth-century Jewish thinker, champions complete equivocity. He holds that God is beyond all our conceptual powers, an idea that he elucidates using an approach called **negative theology.** We can say of God only what God is *not;* affirmative-sounding statements about God must be interpreted as, in truth, negations of entire categories of properties. Neither wisdom nor ignorance, for example, applies to God.

Maimonides's views are sharply criticized a century later by another Jewish philosopher, Levi Gersonides, who objects that, according to negative

Now to ascribe to Him—whose existence is necessary, who is truly simple, to whom **composition** cannot attach in any way—the accident of oneness is just as absurd as to ascribe to Him the accident of multiplicity. I mean to say that oneness is not a notion that is superadded to His essence, but that He is one not through oneness. . . .

[PT. I, CH. 58]

. . . Know that the description of God, may He be cherished and exalted, by means of negations is the correct description—a description that is not affected by an indulgence in facile language and does not imply any deficiency with respect to God in general or in any particular mode. On the other hand, if one describes Him by means of affirmations, one implies, as we have made clear, that He is associated with that which is not He and implies a deficiency in Him. . . . I shall make it clear to you that we have no way of describing Him unless it be through negations and not otherwise. . . .

It has already been demonstrated that God, may He be honored and magnified, is existent of necessity and that there is no composition in Him, as we shall demonstrate, and that we are only able to apprehend the fact that He is and cannot apprehend His quiddity.[4] It is consequently impossible that He should have affirmative attributes. For He has no "That" outside of His "What," and hence an attribute cannot be indicative of one of the two; all the more His "What" is not compound so that an attribute cannot be indicative of its two parts; and all the more, He cannot have accidents so that an attribute cannot be indicative of them. Accordingly He cannot have an affirmative attribute in any respect.

As for the negative attributes, they are those that must be used in order to conduct the mind toward that which must be believed with regard to Him, may He be exalted, for no notion of multiplicity can attach to Him in any respect on account of them; and, moreover, they conduct the mind toward the utmost reach that man may attain in the apprehension of Him, may He be exalted. For instance, it has been demonstrated to us that it is necessary that something exists other than those essences apprehended by means of the senses and whose knowledge is encompassed by means of the intellect. Of this thing we say that it exists, the meaning being that its nonexistence is impossible. We apprehend further that this being is not like the being of the elements, for example, which are dead bodies. We say accordingly that this being is living, the meaning being that He, may He be exalted, is not dead. We apprehend further that this being is not like the being of the heaven, which is a living body. We say accordingly that He is not a body. We apprehend further that this being is not like the being of the intellect, which is neither a body nor dead, but is caused. We say accordingly that He, may He be exalted, is eternal, the meaning being that He has no cause that has brought Him into existence. We apprehend further that the existence of this being, which is its essence, suffices not only for His being existent, but also for many other existents flowing from it, and that this overflow—unlike that of heat from fire and unlike the proceeding of light from the sun—is an overflow that, as we shall make clear, constantly procures for those existents duration and order by means of wisely contrived governance. Accordingly we say of Him, because of these notions, that He is powerful and knowing and willing. The intention in ascribing these attributes to Him is to signify that He is neither powerless nor ignorant nor inattentive nor negligent. Now the meaning of our saying that He is not powerless is to signify that His existence suffices for the bringing into existence of things other than He. The meaning of our saying that He is not ignorant is to signify that He apprehends—that is, is living, for every apprehending thing is living. And the meaning of our saying that He is not inattentive or negligent is to signify that all the existent things in question proceed from their cause according to a certain order and governance—not in a neglected way so as to be generated as chance would have it, but rather as all the things are generated that a willing being governs by means of purpose and will. We apprehend further that

[4]The statements regarding God are considered in this sentence as already demonstrated and as to be demonstrated later. This inconsistency, which may of course be explained away, cannot but strike the reader of this sentence. [Translator's note]

no other thing is like that being. Accordingly our saying that He is one signifies the denial of multiplicity.

It has thus become clear to you that every attribute that we predicate of Him is an attribute of action [this refers to Pt. I, ch. 54] or, if the attribute is intended for the apprehension of His essence and not of His action, it signifies the negation of the privation of the attribute in question. Moreover, even those negations are not used with reference to or applied to Him, may He be exalted, except from the following point of view, which you know: one sometimes denies with reference to a thing something that cannot fittingly exist in it. Thus we say of a wall that it is not endowed with sight. . . .

[PT. I, CH. 59]

Someone may ask and say: If there is no device leading to the apprehension of the true reality of His essence and if **demonstration** proves that it can only be apprehended that He exists and that it is impossible, as has been demonstrated, to ascribe to Him affirmative attributes, in what respect can there be superiority or inferiority between those who apprehend Him? If, however, there is none, Moses our Master and Solomon did not apprehend anything different from what a single individual among the pupils apprehends, and there can be no increase in this knowledge.

Now it is generally accepted . . . that there exist numerous differences of degree in this respect. Know, therefore, that this is indeed so and that the differences of degree between those who apprehend are very great indeed. For the thing of which attributes are predicated becomes more particularized with every increase in attributes that are predicated of it, and he who predicates these attributes accordingly comes nearer to the apprehension of the true reality of the thing in question. In a similar way, you come nearer to the apprehension of Him, may He be exalted, with every increase in the negations regarding Him; and you come nearer to that apprehension than he who does not negate with regard to Him that which, according to what has been demonstrated to you, must be negated. For this reason a man sometimes labors for many years in order to understand some science and to gain true knowledge of its premises so that he should have certainty with regard to this science, whereas the only conclusion from this science in its entirety consists in our negating with reference to God some notion of which it has been learnt by means of a demonstration that it cannot possibly be ascribed to God. To someone else who falls short in his knowledge of speculation, this demonstration will not be clear; and he will consider it doubtful whether or not this notion exists with reference to God. Again another one belonging to those who are struck with intellectual blindness ascribes to Him that notion which has been demonstrated should rather be negated with reference to Him. For instance, I shall demonstrate that He is not a body, whereas another man will doubt and not know whether or not He is a body, and a third one will categorically decide that He is a body and will seek to approach God by means of this belief. How great is the difference between the three individuals! The first is undoubtedly nearer to God, while the second is far away from Him, and the third still farther away. Similarly if we may suppose a fourth one to whom the impossibility of affections in Him, may He be exalted, has become clear by demonstration—whereas this was not the case with regard to the first one who denied His corporeality—this fourth individual would undoubtedly be nearer to God than the first. And so on always; so that if an individual exists to whom it has been made clear by demonstration that many things, whose existence with reference to Him or whose proceeding from Him we hold possible, are, on the contrary, impossible with reference to Him, may He be exalted—and this applies of course all the more if we believe that these things are necessarily attached to Him—that individual will undoubtedly be more perfect than we.

It has accordingly become manifest to you that in every case in which the demonstration that a certain thing should be negated with reference to Him becomes clear to you, you become more perfect, and that in every case in which you affirm of Him an additional thing, you become one who likens Him to other things and you get further away from the knowledge of His true reality. . . .

STUDY QUESTIONS

1. What does Maimonides mean by God's *oneness?* How does his belief in oneness lead to the denial that God possesses affirmative attributes?
2. Explain what Maimonides means by the following: "He exists, but not through an existence other than His essence;" "He lives, but not through life"; "He is powerful, but not through power"; "He knows, but not through knowledge"; "He is one not through oneness."
3. Apply Maimonides's negative analysis to "God is powerful."
4. What is the point of the wall example?
5. Maimonides asks what the difference is between the knowledge of God possessed by Moses or King Solomon and that possessed by an ordinary person. How does negative theology give rise to this question? How does Maimonides attempt to answer it? *Do you find the answer convincing?
6. *What difficulties would someone encounter in trying to worship Maimonides's God?
7. *Consider the following argument: "Thinkers like Maimonides hold that God is **ineffable**–that He is not describable and that no concepts apply to Him. But in saying this, they contradict themselves, for they apply a concept to God, namely, ineffability. So, the thesis that God is ineffable is self-contradictory." Can you suggest a way for the defender of the view that God is ineffable to reply to this objection?
8. *Defend or criticize Maimonides' concept of divine oneness.

READING 2.2

A Critique of Negative Theology

Levi Gersonides

Levi Gersonides (Hebrew name: Levi ben Gershom) (1288–1344) was an outstanding philosopher, scientist, talmudist, and biblical commentator. In the section of his Wars of the Lord *from which this selection is taken, Gersonides attacks Maimonides's view that the term* know *is predicated* **equivocally** *of God and of humans and is to be understood in terms of* **negative theology** *(*Guide of the Perplexed *III:20). However, Gersonides's arguments, only some of which appear in the reading, seriously threaten not only Maimonides's analysis of* know *but also negative theology generally.*

Gersonides claims that, in the negative statements about God that, for Maimonides, give the true meaning of affirmative ones, terms could not possibly be used absolutely equivocally (i.e., with totally different meanings). If they were, then if we were to say God is not a body, *we would not be contradicting the claim* God is a body. *After all, if the presumably false statement* God is a body *is taken as equivocal, it does not entail* God is not a body *in the usual sense of body. Yet, surely when we say, "God is not a body," we use that word in its ordinary sense and thereby want to exclude God's being a body in the* **univocal** *sense of that term. Indeed, if Maimonides were right to say that all assertions about God are equivocal, there would be no way to justify selecting only certain attributes to be affirmed.* God is a body *could be justified no less than* God is not a body. *In addition, all attempts to construct inferences about God are doomed to fail. One cannot, say, infer that God exists based on features of the world, since* existence *would be used in a different sense of the word, and God's existence in this other sense may not follow from the stated premises. Likewise, given a statement about an attribute of*

God, such as knowledge, nothing follows at all. Gersonides's preferred alternative is to ascribe the relevant terms to God in the primary sense and to humans in the secondary sense, meaning that God possesses them to a perfect degree and causes humans to possess them, but to a lesser degree.

[In] God knowledge is identical with His essence, whereas in anyone else knowledge is the effect of God's knowledge. In such a case the term is applied to God in a **prior sense** and to other things in a **posterior sense.** The same is true with respect to such terms as "exists," "one," "essence," and the like, i.e., they are predicated of God primarily and of other things secondarily. For His existence, unity, and essence belong to Him essentially, whereas the existence, unity, and essence of every [other][1] existent thing emanate from Him. Now when something is of this kind, the predicate applies to it in a prior sense, whereas the predicate applies in a posterior sense to the other things that are called by it insofar as they are given this property directly by the substance that has the property in the prior sense. . . . Hence, it seems that the difference between divine and human cognition is a difference in terms of greater perfection, for this is what is implied by **prior and posterior predication.** Now if what we have said is true, and since it is obvious that the most perfect knowledge is more true with respect to specificity and determinateness, it would follow that God's knowledge is more true with respect to specificity and determinateness. Hence, it cannot be that what is considered knowledge with respect to God can be called "belief," "error," or "confusion" with respect to man.

We can show in another way that the difference between divine and human cognition is not as Maimonides thought. It is evident that we proceed to affirm attributes of God from that with which we are familiar. That is, we say that God knows because of the knowledge found in us. For example, since we apprehend that the knowledge belonging to our intellect is a perfection of our intellect—without which it could not be an intellect in **act** [i.e., perfect]—we predicate of God that He knows by virtue of the fact, which we have demonstrated concerning Him, that God (may He be blessed) is indubitably an intellect in act. It is self-evident that when a predicate is affirmed of some object because it is true of some other thing, it is not predicated of both things in an absolutely **equivocal** sense, for between things that are absolutely equivocal there is no analogy. For example, just as it would be impossible to infer that man is intelligent from the fact that body is a continuous magnitude, so, too, would it be impossible [even] if we were to posit [arbitrarily] a term that is predicable of both [attributes] *intelligent* and *continuous* in an absolutely equivocal sense.[2] Hence, it is clear that the term "knowledge" is not completely equivocal when applied to God (may He be blessed) and man. Since this term cannot be applied univocally with respect to God and man, it must be predicated in the sense of priority and posteriority. The same holds for other attributes that are predicated of both God (may He be blessed) and man. Thus, the difference between divine and human knowledge is one of greater perfection, albeit exceedingly so, and this type of knowledge is more precise and clear. . . .

The inadequacy of Maimonides's contention about the [absolute] difference between our knowledge and God's knowledge can be shown in another

[1][This and subsequent bracketed interpolations are the translator's—Ed.]

[2]If inferences from effects to causes are admissible—as they are for Maimonides, e.g., proofs for God's existence—then it cannot be maintained that the terms in the inference are absolutely equivocal. For if they were, any inference would be permissible simply by using a term in the premise that is absolutely equivocal. For example, it is obvious that from the statement "All bodies are continuous" one cannot infer "All men are intelligent," even if it is true that all men have bodies. Suppose, however, that one were to replace the predicate "continuous" in "All bodies are continuous" with the predicate "intelligent," which now connotes both intelligence and continuousness; then the above inference would seem to be valid. But this is a mistake, Gersonides insists, because the term "intelligent" in the premise is absolutely equivocal, and no inferences involving absolutely equivocal premises are licit. [Translator's Note]

way. With respect to those attributes concerning which we want to know whether or not they can be predicated of God, it is evident that such predicates have one meaning regardless whether we affirm or deny them. For example, if we want to know whether God is corporeal or incorporeal, the term "corporeal" has the same meaning in some sense in either case. For if the term "body" has a completely different connotation in the negation from the meaning it has in the affirmation, these statements would not be considered genuine contradictions, as is obvious. For example, just as one could not say "I will investigate whether the wall is a body or whether it is not a color," so, too, one could not say this [i.e., "I will examine whether the wall is a body or whether it is not a color"] even if he introduces [arbitrarily] a term that [connotes both] bodies and colors, for there would be no [genuine] contradictories.[3] Hence, since it is clear when we deny attributes of God that are found in us that such attributes are not completely equivocal with respect to God (may He be blessed) and us, the same is true when we affirm of God predicates that are true of us. For example, we say that God is immovable, since if He were movable He would be a body, for all movable objects [are bodies]. Now it is evident that in this proposition the term "movable" is not completely equivocal with respect to the term "movable" when it is applied to nondivine things. For if it were, there would be no proof that God is not movable, since the movable object that must be a body is that which is movable in the domain of human phenomena, whereas the term "movable" (in the completely equivocal sense) would not imply that it is a body. Hence, since it is evident that the predicates we deny of God are not absolutely equivocal, neither are the terms that we affirm of Him. For at first we were uncertain whether to affirm or deny such predicates of God (may He be blessed). Then when the inquiry was completed, we were able to affirm or deny such predicates of Him. In general, if the terms used in affirming predicates of Him were absolutely equivocal, there would be no term applicable to things in our world that would be more appropriate to deny than to affirm of God or [more appropriate] to affirm than to deny of Him. For example, someone could say "God is a body" but not mean by the term "body," "a magnitude"; rather he would mean something that is completely equivocal with the term "body" as we usually use it. Similarly, someone could say "God does not have knowledge," since the term "knowledge" would not [on this view] have the same meaning for him in this statement as it does for us. It will not do to object that we indeed deny corporeality of God because it is an imperfection for us, whereas we affirm knowledge of Him because it is a perfection for us.[4] For the *term* "corporeality" is not [itself] an imperfection, and it is the term that we deny of Him, but the content of the term is the imperfection. Similarly, the *term* "knowledge" is not [itself] a perfection; its content is. The proof of this is as follows. If by the term "corporeality" we were to connote what the term "knowledge" connotes, and conversely, corporeality would be a perfection for us and knowledge an imperfection. Moreover, we do not affirm or deny anything of God except by determining at the outset whether it is proper or improper for *Him;* we do not ask whether or not it is a perfection for *us.* Thus, it is clear that reason shows that the term "knowledge" is not completely equivocal with respect to God (may He be blessed) and man. . . .

[3]Here Gersonides employs the logic of his earlier argument about the impossibility of making inferences when the terms of the propositions are absolutely equivocal. In the present context we are concerned with affirmative and negative statements: "S is P" and "S is not-P." Gersonides insists that in both the affirmation and the negation the predicate "P" cannot be completely equivocal, for if it were, no genuine contradiction between the affirmation and the negation would obtain. In Gersonides's own example, it is obvious that the predicates "is a body" and "is a color" are totally different, such that the affirmation "the wall is a body" and the negation "the wall is not a color" are not genuine contradictories. Suppose, however, we replace the predicate "is a color" with a new predicate that is equally true of bodies and colors: "ϕ." We would then get "the wall is ϕ" and "the wall is not ϕ," which *appear* to be contradictory statements. But they are not, Gersonides insists, since the term "ϕ" is absolutely equivocal. [Translator's Note]

[4]Maimonides, *Guide,* I:26.

STUDY QUESTIONS

1. State Gersonides's arguments against negative theology.
2. Gersonides argues that, if a term is equivocal, it cannot be used in an inference. Give examples of inferences in theology that would not be **valid** if the terms *know, body,* and *good* were equivocal.
3. *Maimonides argued for negative theology by appealing to the proposition that God is one. A God who is one, he argued, has no multiplicity. How would Gersonides's point about inferences apply in this case to create a difficulty for Maimonides's argument based on God's oneness?
4. *How would Maimonides explain Scripture's using only certain attributes for God and not others (for example, *God knows,* not *God is ignorant*)? What is Gersonides's reply to this possible explanation?

READING 2.3

The Meaning of the Divine Attributes

John Stuart Mill

John Stuart Mill (1806–1873), the most renowned British philosopher of the Victorian period, offers in this reading a sharp critique of the idea of **equivocal predication**— *that is, that a predicate means one thing when applied to human beings and something entirely different when applied to God. Mill argues that we are not entitled to say that God is good or that God is just unless the terms* good *and* just *have the same meaning in both cases. Like Gersonides, Mill holds that the difference between divine and human goodness and justice is one not of kind but of degree. The last paragraph of the selection states Mill's thesis especially powerfully. Mill casts his remarks as a critique of H. L. Mansel, a leading associate of Sir William Hamilton, whose philosophy Mill examines in the work from which this selection is excerpted.*

Here, then, I take my stand on the acknowledged principle of logic and of morality, that when we mean different things we have no right to call them by the same name, and to apply to them the same predicates, moral and intellectual. Language has no meaning for the words Just, Merciful, Benevolent, save that in which we predicate them of our fellow-creatures; and unless that is what we intend to express by them, we have no business to employ the words. If in affirming them of God we do not mean to affirm these very qualities, differing only as greater in degree, we are neither philosophically nor morally entitled to affirm them at all. If it be said that the qualities are the same, but that we cannot conceive them as they are when raised to the infinite, I grant that we cannot adequately conceive them in one of their elements, their infinity. But we can conceive them in their other elements, which are the very same in the infinite as in the finite development. Anything carried to the infinite must have all the properties of the same thing as finite, except those which depend upon the finiteness. Among the many who have said that we cannot conceive infinite space, did any one ever suppose that it is *not* space? that it does not possess all the properties by which space is characterised? Infinite Space cannot be cubical or spherical, because these are modes of being bounded: but does any one imagine that in ranging through it we might arrive at some region which was not extended; of which one part was not outside another; where, though no body intervened, motion was impossible; or where the sum of two sides of a triangle was less than the third side? The parallel assertion may be made respecting infinite goodness. What belongs to it either as Infinite or as Absolute I do not pretend to know; but I know that infinite goodness must be goodness, and that what is not consistent with goodness, is not consistent with infinite goodness. If in ascribing goodness to God I do not mean what I mean by goodness; if I do not mean the goodness of which I have some knowledge, but an incomprehensible attribute of an incomprehensible substance, which for aught I know may be a totally different quality from that which I love and venerate—and even must, if Mr. Mansel is to be believed, be in some important particulars opposed to this—what do I mean by calling it goodness? and what reason have I for venerating it? If I know nothing about what the attribute is, I cannot tell that it is a proper object of veneration. To say that God's goodness may be different in kind from man's goodness, what is it but saying, with a slight change of phraseology, that God may possibly not be good? To assert in words what we do not think in meaning, is as suitable a definition as can be given of a moral falsehood. Besides, suppose that certain unknown attributes are ascribed to the Deity in a religion the external evidences of which are so conclusive to my mind, as effectually to convince me that it comes from God. Unless I believe God to possess the same moral attributes which I find, in however inferior a degree, in a good man, what ground of assurance have I of God's veracity? All trust in a Revelation presupposes a conviction that God's attributes are the same, in all but degree, with the best human attributes.

If, instead of the "glad tidings" that there exists a Being in whom all the excellences which the highest human mind can conceive, exist in a degree inconceivable to us, I am informed that the world is ruled by a being whose attributes are infinite, but what they are we cannot learn, nor what are the principles of his government, except that "the highest human morality which we are capable of conceiving" does not sanction them; convince me of it, and I will bear my fate as I may. But when I am told that I must believe this, and at the same time call this being by the names which express and affirm highest human morality, I say in plain terms that I will not. Whatever power such a being may have over me, there is one thing which he shall not do: he shall not compel me to worship him. I will call no being good, who is not what I mean when I apply that epithet to my fellow-creatures;[1] and if such a being can sentence me to hell for not so calling him, to hell I will go. . . .

STUDY QUESTIONS

1. What view is Mill attacking in the selection, and what is his chief argument against it?
2. What is the purpose of Mill's analogy to infinite space?
3. How would you compare and/or contrast Mill's views with those of Maimonides and Gersonides?
4. Many biblical passages, especially in the books of the prophets, Psalms, and Job, imply that the suffering of righteous people seems inconsistent with God's goodness and justice. How do such passages support Mill's main contention that God's goodness and justice are not totally different from the goodness and justice of human beings?
5. *What can be said on behalf of the opposing view to Mill's—that terms do not mean the same thing when applied to God as when applied to humans?
6. In chapter 3 of this book you will encounter the idea that there is no standard of good and evil except God's will or command: what God wills or commands is by definition good, and what God wills against or prohibits is by definition evil. What is the impact of this thesis on Mill's claim?

[1]Mr. Mansel, in his rejoinder, says that this means that I will call no being good "the phenomena of whose action in any way differ from those of a good man." This is a misconstruction; he should have said "no being, the principle or rule of whose action is different from that by which a good man endeavours to regulate his actions."

READING 2.4

The Doctrine of Analogy

Thomas Aquinas

Thomas Aquinas (1225–1274) has had a monumental influence on Christian thought, inspiring in particular the version of Catholic philosophy and theology known as **Thomism.** *In this selection, Aquinas seeks to steer a middle course between two extreme theories of predication: that terms are used* **univocally** *of God and God's creatures (i.e., the terms predicated of both mean exactly the same thing in both cases) and, at the other extreme, that terms predicated of both God and creatures are used* **equivocally** *(i.e., with totally different meanings). A creature cannot have a property in the same way God does, because its* esse, *or being, is different from God's; for example, God is* simple, *without parts. Nor can terms be used equivocally of God and humans, for (as we saw in Gersonides's criticisms of Maimonides) we would be unable to explain why a particular term was selected, and we would not be able to come to know God from knowing created things.*

Aquinas's middle ground is the theory of analogical predication, whose roots lie in the philosophy of St. Augustine. There are two types of analogy:

1. **Analogy of causation:** *God's being X is the cause of the creature's being X, albeit to a lesser degree than God (this is very similar to Gersonides's approach). The terms denoting perfections apply primarily to God and secondarily to creatures.*
2. **Analogy of proportionality:** *When we say that God has a property Q, and that Socrates has Q, we mean that* $\frac{\textit{God's Q-ness}}{\textit{God's nature}}$ *as* $\frac{\textit{Socrates's Q-ness}}{\textit{Socrates's nature}}$. *The meaning of the term is adjusted according to the nature of the subject.*

Analogical interpretations are not figurative but, rather, give the correct literal understanding of a word.

In the reading, Aquinas appears to favor analogy of proportionality to understand predicates as applied to God. However, the matter is complicated. (See the essay by William Alston, "Aquinas on Theological Predication," listed under "Further Reading," especially pp. 151–60.)

It is impossible that anything should be predicated of both creatures and God **univocally.** Any effect that falls short of the power of its cause resembles its cause inadequately because it differs from it. Thus, what is found diversely and in various ways in the effect exists simply and in a single way in the cause; so, the sun by a single power produces many different kinds of lower things. In just that way, . . . all the perfections which are found among creatures in diverse and various ways preexist in God as united in one.

When we predicate of creatures some term which indicates a perfection, that term signifies the perfection as something distinct by its definition from every other perfection; for instance, when we predicate the term "wise" of some man, we signify some perfection which is distinct from the essence of the man, and also from his powers and from his existence. But when we predicate such a term of God, we do not intend to signify something which is distinct from His essence, power and existence. Also, when we predicate the term "wise" of some man, it circumscribes and isolates what is signified; but this is not so then the term "wise" is predicated of God because the reality signified by the term remains unisolated and exceeds the signification (the linguistic intention) of the term. Therefore, it is obvious that the term "wise" does not have exactly the same meaning when predicated of God and of some creature. And the same reasoning holds for all the other terms which indicate perfection. So no term is predicated of God and creatures univocally.

But the terms are not used purely **equivocally** either, as some have claimed. For, if that were so, nothing would be knowable or **demonstrable** concerning God from our knowledge of creatures; our reasoning would always commit the **fallacy of equivocation.** Such a view would be as discordant with the philosophers who demonstrate a number of things about God, as it would be with the Apostle Paul who said: "The invisible things of God are made known by the things that are made."

We have to say, then, that terms are used of creatures and God analogously, that is, according to an **ordering** between them. We can distinguish two ways in which analogy based upon the order among things can be found among terms: First, one word may be used of two things because each of them has some order or relation to a third thing. Thus we use the term "healthy" of both medicine and urine because both things have a relation to another thing, namely the health of the animal, of which the latter is the sign and the former the cause. Secondly, one word may be used of two things because of the relation the one thing has to the other; thus "healthy" is used of both the medicine and the animal because the medicine is the cause of the health in the man. In this way some terms are used of creatures and God, neither univocally nor purely equivocally, but analogously.

We are unable to speak of God except in the language we use of creatures. . . . And so, whatever is said of both creatures and God is said on the basis of the order or relation which holds between the creature and God, namely, that God is the source and cause in which all the perfections of things preexist **eminently.**

This kind of community is a middle-ground between pure equivocation and simply univocity. For among those terms which are used analogously, there is not a common or single concept, as there is among univocal terms; but neither are the concepts wholly diverse, as is the case among equivocal terms. Rather, the term which is predicated in different ways signifies different relations to some one thing; thus "healthy" when predicated of urine means "is a sign of the health of the animal," whereas when predicated of the medicine it means "is a cause of the health of the animal."

Nothing can be predicated of a creature and of God univocally. For when a term is used univocally or more than one thing, what the term signifies is common to each of the things of which it is univocally predicated. So far as the signification of the term is concerned, the things of which it is univocally predicated are undifferentiated, even though they may precede one another in being; for instance, all numbers are equally numbers although one is prior to another. But no matter how much a creature may resemble God, a point cannot be reached at which something belongs to it and to God for the same reason. For things which are in different subjects and have the same formal definition are common to the subjects in **substance** and **quiddity** but are distinct in *esse* [being]. Whatever is in God, however, is His own *esse;* for just as His essence is the same as His *esse,* so His knowledge is the same as His knowing. Since the *esse* which is proper to one thing cannot be communicated to another, it cannot happen that a creature should ever attain to having something for the same reason that God has it because it is impossible that the creature should come into possession of the same *esse* as is God's. The same is true for us; if 'man' and 'to *be* as a man' did not differ in Peter and Paul it would not be possible for the term "man" to be predicated univocally of Peter and of Paul whose *esse* is distinct.

Still, it cannot be maintained that whatever is predicated of God and a creature is predicated purely equivocally because if there were not some real resemblance between the creature and God, His essence would not be a likeness of creatures, and thus He could not understand creatures by understanding His essence. Similarly, we would not be able to come to know God from created things either; nor would it be that from among the terms which apply to creatures, one rather than another, ought to be predicated of God; for with equivocal terms it makes no difference which is applied since the term does not imply any real agreement among the things to which it applies.

So we have to say that the term "acknowledge" is predicated of God's knowledge and of ours neither wholly univocally nor purely equivocally. Instead it is predicated analogously, which is the same as proportionally.

Resemblance on account of a proportion (relation) can be of two kinds, and so two kinds of analogous community can be distinguished. There is a community between things of which one is related to another in virtue of their having a fixed distance or other determinate relationship to each other, as the number 2 to the number 1, in that the former is the double of the latter. Sometimes there is a community (or resemblance) between two things, not accounted for because the one is a function of the other but rather, because of a likeness of two relations; for instance, 6 resembles 4 in that as 6 is the double of 3, so is 4 the double of 2. The first kind of resemblance is one of proportion; the second is one of parity of proportion or proportionality.

We find something said analogically of two things in virtue of the first type of resemblance when one of them has a direct and determinate relationship to the other, as, for instance, "being" is predicated of **accident** and of substance because of the relationship which accident has to substance; and "healthy" is predicated of urine and of an animal because urine has some relation to the health of the animal. Sometimes something is predicated analogically in virtue of the second type of resemblance, as when the term insight is predicated of bodily sight and of understanding, because sight is to the eye what understanding is to the mind.

There must be some determinate (definite) relationship between things to which something is common by analogy of the first sort; consequently, it cannot be that anything is predicated of God and creatures by this type of analogy because no creature has such a determinate relationship to God. But the other type of analogy requires no determinate type of relationship between the things in which something is common by analogy; and so nothing excludes some term's being predicated analogously of God and creatures in this manner.

This can happen in two ways: sometimes the term implies that something, which cannot be common to God and a creature even in a proportionality, belongs to what it primarily designated. This is so of everything which is predicated metaphorically of God as when He is said to be a lion, the sun, and so forth, because the definitions include matter which cannot be attributed to God. In other cases, a term which is used of God and creatures has no implications in its primary uses which preclude a resemblance of the kind described between God and creatures. To this class belong all those predicates which do not imply a defect (limitation) and which do not depend upon matter for their *esse;* for instance, "being," "good," and so forth.

STUDY QUESTIONS

1. Explain why Aquinas rejects both the view that terms are predicated univocally of God and creatures and the view that they are predicated equivocally. What does Aquinas suggest as a mean between these extremes?
2. What are the two types of analogy? Explain them.
3. Which type of analogy does Aquinas say should be used to understand expressions of the form "God is Q"? Why?
4. *If we are given an equation $x/y = 3/4$, we cannot solve for either x or y; however, if we are told $x/12 = 3/4$, we know that $x = 9$. Do you see any problems that this might raise for one of the versions of analogy mentioned by Aquinas?
5. *It might be claimed that, according to the analogy of causation, we can say that God is cruel, or that God is a body. Explain this objection. Do you think it is sound?

READING 2.5

Philosophy, Poetry, and the Bible

Ira M. Schnall

In this selection, Ira M. Schnall (Bar-Ilan University, Israel) assesses different approaches to reading the Bible. Some people accept the narratives in the Bible as literally true—that is, as reporting events that actually occurred exactly as the Bible describes them. Such people are generally called fundamentalists *or* literalists. *Other people, some of them believing and practicing Jews and Christians, who hold that the Bible is the Word of God, nevertheless cannot accept the biblical narratives in this way. Medieval* **theologians,** *influenced by the ancient philosophies of Aristotle and Plotinus, believed that God is not the sort of being who could do the kinds of things the Bible describes Him as doing. Modern thinkers have found difficulty with the supernatural aspects of biblical stories, yet people from both the medieval and modern groups have felt that the Bible is a valuable (if not divine) source of inspiration. They have therefore attempted to understand the Bible in a way that preserves its status as an important document that can positively influence our lives, while rejecting its literal truth. For example, some assert that the Bible functions as poetry. Schnall exposes difficulty in this view and surveys possible ways for fundamentalists to incorporate some of the insights gained in such attempts into their own view of the Bible.*

The seventeenth-century philosopher and mathematician Blaise Pascal described the Object of his worship as "the God of Abraham, the God of Isaac, the God of Jacob, not the God of the philosophers and the learned."[1] Indeed it is common to distinguish biblical religion from philosophical **theology.** The former is characterized by assuming the existence of God, a supreme but personal Being Who created the world and enters into personal relationships with the human beings He has created. God can achieve anything by simply saying "Let it be so"; yet He commands us to behave in certain ways, and allows us to choose whether we will obey. Like a wise and loving parent, He offers us direction (often backed up by reward and punishment), but gives us the freedom to choose our path in life. He is angry with us when we do wrong, and pleased with us when we do right. He intervenes in human history, bringing down the haughty and raising up the lowly, and generally meting out justice tempered with mercy. Perhaps most importantly, He loves us and wants us to love Him.

When we look at the writings of Augustine, Aquinas, and Maimonides, as well as other classic medieval works of philosophical theology which are supposedly based on the Bible, we get an entirely different picture. We find attempts to *prove* that God exists. We find God described in terms so abstract that the theologians themselves admit that they do not know what they are talking about when they use them. God is not merely powerful, He is **omnipotent;** not just wise, but **omniscient;** not just good, but **omnibenevolent.** And far from interacting with His creatures, He is **immutable** (unchanging), **impassible** (unaffected by anything), and **eternal** (outside of time). Furthermore, these and other similarly superlative characterizations do not describe *different* properties that God *has,* the way other beings have their various properties; rather God *is* His properties and infinitely more, all rolled into one indivisible unity, unlike anything else in existence. Even God's existence is different from the existence of anything else.

[1]See his *Penseés.* Pascal was anticipated by the twelfth-century Jewish philosopher Yehuda HaLevi in his work *The Book of the Kuzari,* section IV.

Thus the God of the philosophical **theologians** is not at all what we would ordinarily call a "person"; He is *impersonal,* and so any personal relationship between Him and us is impossible.

So what is the Bible talking about?

One answer offered by philosophical theologians is that the Bible expresses theological truths in ways that are somewhat accessible to the unlearned masses. Most people are unused to abstract thinking, and can understand only what is expressed in concrete terms. One of the essential skills of a prophet, or an author of a book of the Bible, is the ability to express deep, complex, abstract, and generally difficult concepts and truths in the language of ordinary human experience. Biblical narratives and descriptions are often allegories, or parables, which (as yet) uneducated people can understand and learn; if and when they become more educated, they can "unpack" the meanings hidden in the allegories and parables, and achieve knowledge of theological truths, thus gaining the full benefit of Bible study. And if one never acquires the ability to see the literal truths at which the Bible is hinting, no great harm is done. In fact, it is another aspect of the greatness of the biblical authors (or Author) that their stories make one a better person even if one takes those stories at face value and never discovers the profound truths that lie beneath.

But once we start interpreting the biblical text allegorically, where do we stop? Which statements in the Bible are literally true, and which are *mere* allegory? Fundamentalists, i.e., those who interpret the Bible as literally true, object to many allegorical interpretations as attempting to rob us of historical truths related in the Bible. Thus, for example, Moses Nahmanides, a thirteenth-century Biblical commentator, complains of Maimonides's interpreting several biblical narratives as prophetic visions, rather than as actual events. The allegorists, on the other hand, disparage fundamentalists for taking the Bible at face value, and overlooking the deeper meanings that they hold constitute the essential message of the Bible.

However, a compromise is possible. Fundamentalists can admit the validity of allegorical interpretations of biblical narratives, while maintaining the literal truth of those narratives. For example, they can admit that the story of Abraham and Sarah in Egypt (*Genesis* 12:10–20) is a foreshadowing, or prophecy, of the experience of the Israelites in Egypt several generations later (*Exodus* 1–12). But they need not conclude that the events described in *Genesis* 12:10–20 never happened. They can say that this prophecy was "acted out" by Abraham and Sarah rather than told to them verbally. Generally, a fundamentalist can admit the importance of the moral and theological lessons taught by the various narratives in the Bible without denying that the events described really occurred. The fact that a story has a moral does not mean that it is merely a fable.

For philosophical theologians, a different kind of compromise is available. It has been suggested, by Maimonides and others, that God eternally ordains that certain miraculous events occur at certain specific times *as if* in response to human needs at those times. For example, God builds into nature that the Red Sea (or Reed Sea) should split when the Israelites encamp on its shore and find themselves pursued by the Egyptians (see *Exodus* 14). It is not that God *noticed,* at that time, that the Israelites were in trouble, and then *responded* by speaking to Moses and splitting the sea; rather it was arranged, from eternity, that the events work out this way. Generally, God does not engage in ongoing interactions with the world: rather, since He knows all of history from His timeless perspective, He (so to speak) preordained miraculous salvation and punishment, prophets' seeing visions and hearing heavenly voices, and the realization of prophecies, to occur at the appropriate times. Thus philosophical theologians can accept many of the biblical narratives as more or less literally true, while still maintaining that God is not really interacting with and responding to actions and events in the world.

What remains unclear is whether this latter view sufficiently captures the warmth of the personal relationship that many religious people feel—and many theologians think—exists between us and God. Some will feel that the idea of an impassive, immutable Being outside of time is inadequate to account for the depth of emotion that people feel for God, even if this Being somehow arranges events to occur *as if* He were responding to our situations. But others will feel that a God Who, from eternity, is there for us, providing us with what we need and deserve, with justice and yet with mercy, calls forth the most profound emotions of reverence and love of which human beings are capable.

Another suggestion about the Bible is that it is neither literal truth nor allegory, but poetic imagery, inspiring us to view the world in a certain way and to behave accordingly. For example, such biblical expressions as "God loves you" (*Deuteronomy* 23:6; see *Malachi* 1:2) and "God created man in His image" (*Genesis* 1:27) are not to be understood as expressing propositions which can be literally true or false—i.e., which can correspond or fail to correspond to facts, or to reality. Rather when we meditate on the expression "God loves you," we will come to accept life's vicissitudes with serenity, and face life's challenges with confidence. And if we keep in mind the words "We were created in God's image," we will develop a deep respect for our fellow human beings, and for ourselves, which will manifest itself in a tendency to always help and never hurt one another. But it is inappropriate to, for example, ask in exactly what way we are in God's image, or to ask for a proof or disproof of God's love for us. The meaning of such expressions is exhausted by their inspiring the appropriate attitudes and behavior; they make no factual claim.[2]

One could imagine such a suggestion coming from philosophical theologians as a way of accepting the biblical passages in question as somehow valuable, while denying that they are literally true—for example, denying that God is capable of emotions such as love, and that God has an image in which He created human beings (or that there is any similarity between God and human beings). However, it has recently come more from opponents of philosophical theology who claim that philosophical theology distorts biblical religion by analyzing it in terms of a system of propositions about God and His relation to the world, and who claim (incorrectly, in my opinion) that their suggestion is closer to the way believers view the biblical texts. It has also come from philosophical atheologians, i.e., philosophers who believe that all statements about God, taken literally, are false (atheists) or meaningless (logical empiricists), but who, for some reason, are looking for some positive role that the Bible can play in their lives. But no matter where it comes from, the suggestion is open to question.

First of all, it should be noted that the fact that biblical passages can and do, and even should, affect our attitudes and our behavior does not in any way indicate that those passages are non-propositional poetic imagery. Our propositional, or factual, beliefs affect our attitudes and behavior in much the same way as it is suggested that these poetic images do. To use the above examples, one who firmly held the factual belief that God really loves us would have the same serenity and confidence as one who meditated on the poetic imagery of God's loving us is supposed to have. His belief would be a *reason* for having such attitudes, in the sense that if someone were to ask him *why* he is so serene and confident, he could answer, "Why shouldn't I be? After all, God loves us, so whatever happens is certain to be for the best." Similarly, one who held the factual belief that we were created in God's image, i.e., that we resemble God in some specific, important way, would naturally feel respect for others and tend to behave accordingly, at least as much as someone who meditated on the poetic figure "God created man in His image."

More importantly, it is not at all clear that viewing biblical passages as non-propositional poetic imagery is consistent with being inspired by them. It is difficult to see how an expression that has no propositional content can inspire us.[3] At least it seems that if we *know,* or *believe,* that a given expression has no

[2]Such "non-cognitivist" views have been put forward by R. B. Braithwaite in *An Empiricist's View of the Nature of Religious Belief* (Cambridge University Press, 1955), George Santayana in *Reason in Religion* (New York, 1905), and more recently by Howard Wettstein in his contribution to *Midwest Studies in Philosophy* volume XXI (University of Notre Dame Press, 1997) [see also Reading 2.8—Ed.].
[3]See, e.g., William P. Alston, "Religious Language," in Paul Edwards (ed.) *The Encyclopedia of Philosophy* (New York: MacMillan, 1967), volume 7, p. 173; and Eleonore Stump, "Awe and Atheism," in *Midwest Studies in Philosophy* volume XXI (University of Notre Dame Press, 1997).

propositional content, it cannot influence our attitudes and behavior. For example, unless we believe that in actuality God loves us, how can meditating on the words "God loves us" help us accept troubles with serenity or face challenges with confidence? And if we do not believe that human beings really resemble God in any morally relevant way, then how can meditating on the words "God created man in His image" give rise to respect for human beings? It seems that to the extent that such images inspire, they must have propositional content which is believed; then the poetic expression of these propositions can further help bring about the inspirational effect.

Thus even if we view the main function of the Bible as influencing our attitudes and behavior, it is more plausible to say that it performs this function by instilling propositional beliefs than that it does so by providing us with non-propositional poetic imagery.

One might object that I underestimate the power of poetry, and of fictional literature in general, to influence us. After all, fictional literature has had profound effects on people's attitudes and behavior. For example, presumably no one believed that the events described in Stowe's *Uncle Tom's Cabin* actually occurred; yet the book is said to have had a tremendous influence on attitudes toward slavery, and to have led people to fight against slavery, in the years preceding the American Civil War. And the romantic poetry of Keats, Byron, and Shelley has changed people's lives, even though this poetry is not the propounding of propositions for the reader to believe. So perhaps the majestic prose and poetry of the Bible can influence us in the way suggested, even if it is, on the literal level, fiction.

The question of how literature influences us is much too broad and deep for us to settle here. Besides, it seems to be a question best discussed by experts in literature and psychology, as opposed to philosophy and religion. But a few brief remarks seem called for. So speaking as a philosopher, my opinion is that though fictional literature does not *state* propositions for the reader to believe, nevertheless it usually *implies* propositions for the reader to believe. For example, consider Shelley's poem "Ozymandias," in which he describes the ruined remains of a once great statue with an inscription arrogantly boasting of the grandeur of the surrounding structures, when all that remains in the area is barren sand. The poem tends to make us take less seriously our own and others' pride and ambition, and perhaps makes us pause in our pursuit of "the biggest and the best." We need not believe that the scene described in the poem ever existed. However, it is not non-propositional poetic imagery alone that influences us. Rather it is the *implied proposition* that this *sort* of thing *can* happen, and *has* happened, on one scale or another, countless times: People accomplish things of which they are so proud that they think their reputation will live forever, but in fact they are soon forgotten. The suggestive descriptions, the irony, and the other poetic devices which Shelley uses help us to conceive the implied proposition more vividly and to think of aspects of our experience that corroborate it. We believe the implied proposition, and it is this belief that primarily influences our attitudes and behavior, the poetic imagery merely facilitating that influence. I think that most cases of fictional literature's influencing us can be analyzed this way.

I may be accused of generalizing from a single, self-serving example. I plead guilty, with the excuse that I cannot do much more in this context. I recommend that all those who are interested in the issue try to apply this analysis to whatever work of fiction or poetry has influenced them, to see if they can find an implied proposition to which the primary influence can be attributed. (I suspect that **existentialist** works will pose a bit of a challenge.) But to conclude my argument: This analysis does not seem to work for "God loves us" and similar expressions. The only proposition I can see that is involved in this sentence that could give us serenity and confidence is the proposition *stated* by it—i.e., that God loves us. If I'm right, then it is only by believing the literal truth of "God loves us" that one can achieve the serenity and confidence that this central sentence of the Bible can provide.

STUDY QUESTIONS

1. In what ways is the biblical God more *personal* than the God of the medieval philosophical

theologians? Find passages and/or stories in the Bible that illustrate the concept of God as personal, involved, caring, and so on.

2. *Can you find passages in the Bible that support the medieval philosophical theologians' view of God? Discuss the ones you select.
3. *Pick a biblical narrative that involves God's personal involvement with the world, and give a purely allegorical interpretation of it.
4. *How might a philosophical theologian explain God's literally making the sun stand still for Joshua (Joshua 10:12), while maintaining God's eternity, immutability, and impassibility?
5. *Find examples of poetic imagery in the Bible, and explain how they can affect the reader.
6. According to Schnall, why is it more plausible to say that the Bible inspires by means of propositions than that it inspires by means of nonpropositional poetic images?
7. How does the influence of works of fiction support the view of biblical language as poetic imagery?
8. *Describe a modern, contemporary concept of God (or *your* concept of God). In what ways does it resemble that biblical concept? In what ways does it resemble the medieval philosophical concept? (See Readings 1.8–1.10.)
9. *Try to define, or clarify, the concept of "implying a proposition" illustrated by the example of Shelley's "Ozymandias." Cite other examples of works that *state* fictional propositions but *imply* true propositions that influence people's attitudes and behavior. Show how your definition (or clarification) applies.

READING 2.6

Interpreting the Koran Allegorically

Averroes

Known as "the Commentator" by virtue of his many commentaries on Aristotle's writings, Arabic philosopher and jurist Averroes (1126–1198), or ibn Rushd, was the chief proponent of Aristotelian **metaphysics** *in the medieval Muslim world. In the selection, Averroes addresses the gulf between the apparent meaning of the Koran and Aristotelian views such as that the world is eternal, that* **immortality** *is collective rather than individual, and that there is no providence over individuals. Averroes submits that, when the apparent meaning of Scripture contradicts the conclusions of* **demonstration** *(logical proof), the demonstrative class (philosophers, who are capable of constructing demonstrations) must interpret the problematic text allegorically or metaphorically, though always in accord with standard practices of interpretation in Arabic. In cases in which allegorical readings are used, confirmation for them will be found in other parts of Scripture. The Koran uses the mode of presentation it does in order to stimulate the learned to find the correct interpretation and, though this is not clear from the selection, to conceal the true meaning from the masses.*

Averroes's view that figurative interpretation should be used to reconcile Scripture with reason is expressed as well, with respect to the Bible, by Moses Maimonides, Thomas Aquinas, and most other philosophically inclined religious thinkers of the Middle Ages.

[CHAPTER TWO][1]

[Philosophy Contains Nothing Opposed to Islam]

[Demonstrative Truth and Scriptural Truth Cannot Conflict.]

Now since this religion is true and summons to the study which leads to knowledge of the Truth, we the Muslim community know definitely that **demonstrative** study does not lead to [conclusions] conflicting with what Scripture has given us; for truth does not oppose truth but accords with it and bears witness to it.

[If the apparent meaning of Scripture conflicts with demonstrative conclusions it must be interpreted allegorically, i.e. metaphorically.]

This being so, whenever demonstrative study leads to any manner of knowledge about any being, that being is inevitably either unmentioned or mentioned in Scripture. If it is unmentioned there is no contradiction, and it is in the same case as an act whose category is unmentioned, so that the lawyer has to infer it by reasoning from Scripture. If Scripture speaks about it, the apparent meaning of the words inevitably either accords or conflicts with the conclusions of demonstration about it. If this [apparent meaning] accords there is no argument. If it conflicts there is a call for allegorical interpretation of it. The meaning of **'allegorical interpretation'** is: extension of the significance of an expression from real to metaphorical significance, without forsaking therein the standard metaphorical practices of Arabic, such as calling a thing by the name of something resembling it or a cause or consequence or accompaniment of it, or other things such as are enumerated in accounts of the kinds of metaphorical speech.

[If the lawyer can do this, the religious thinker certainly can. Indeed these allegorical interpretations always receive confirmation from the apparent meaning of other passages of Scripture.]

[1][These and subsequent bracketed words are the translator's, except for those in the final paragraph.—Ed.]

Now if the lawyer does this in many decisions of religious law, with how much more right is it done by the possessor of demonstrative knowledge! For the lawyer has at his disposition only reasoning based on opinion, while he who would know [God] ⟨has at his disposition⟩ reasoning based on certainty. So we affirm definitely that whenever the conclusion of a **demonstration** is in conflict with the apparent meaning of Scripture, that apparent meaning admits of allegorical interpretation according to the rules for such interpretation in Arabic. This proposition is questioned by no Muslim and doubted by no believer. But its certainty is immensely increased for those who have had close dealings with this idea and put it to the test, and made it their aim to reconcile the assertions of intellect and tradition. Indeed we may say that whenever a statement in Scripture conflicts in its apparent meaning with a conclusion of demonstration, if Scripture is considered carefully, and the rest of its contents searched page by page, there will invariably be found among the expressions of Scripture something which in its apparent meaning bears witness to that allegorical interpretation or comes close to bearing witness.

[All Muslims accept the principle of allegorical interpretation; they only disagree about the extent of its application.]

In the light of this idea the Muslims are unanimous in holding that it is not obligatory either to take all the expressions of Scripture in their apparent meaning or to extend them all from their apparent meaning by allegorical interpretation. They disagree [only] over which of them should and which should not be so interpreted. . . .

[The double meaning has been given to suit people's diverse intelligence. The apparent contradictions are meant to stimulate the learned to deeper study.]

The reason why we have received a Scripture with both an apparent and an inner meaning lies in the diversity of people's natural capacities and the difference of their innate dispositions with regard to assent. The reason why we have received in

Scripture texts whose apparent meanings contradict each other is in order to draw the attention of those who are well grounded in science to the interpretation which reconciles them. This is the idea referred to in the words received from the Exalted, 'He it is who has sent down to you the Book, containing certain verses clear and definite [—they are the essence of the Book—and others ambiguous. Now those in whose hearts is mischief go after the ambiguous passages, seeking discord and seeking to interpret them allegorically. But no one knows their interpretation except God and those who are well grounded in science'.] [Koran 3:7][1]. . . .

STUDY QUESTIONS

1. Under what circumstances does Averroes maintain a text must be interpreted allegorically (though only by a member of the demonstrative class)?
2. *A question Averroes faces is how far to extend allegorical interpretation. Averroes maintains that Scripture should not be interpreted allegorically when there is no demonstration that the apparent meaning is false. Can you offer a rationale for this restriction? After all, why can't all of Scripture be understood allegorically?
3. According to Averroes in the selection, why doesn't Scripture state its meaning in literal terms, rather than use allegory? (A reason he gives elsewhere is that the scripture seeks to conceal its meaning from the masses.)
4. *It has been said of the allegorical approach that it does not leave room for the philosopher to learn anything new from Scripture that cannot be learned from philosophy and science. What do you think is meant by this criticism? Do you think it is correct?

[1][To capture Averroes's understanding of the verse, it is important to omit a comma after "God" and to end the sentence with a period after "science." So presented, the verse implies that the learned know the correct allegorical interpretation. Later in the chapter Averroes acknowledges but rejects a different reading of the verse (using a pause, or comma, after "God" and a later endpoint to the sentence), according to which the learned do not know the correct allegorical interpretation.—Ed.]

READING 2.7

The Task of Demythologizing

Rudolf Bultmann

Rudolf Bultmann (1884–1976) was a prominent liberal Protestant theologian who believed that the Bible's **cosmology** *must be rejected as mythical and primitive because it cannot be reconciled with modern science. For Bultmann, notions such as God, angels, miracles, Satan, heaven, hell, resurrection, atonement, and death as punishment for sin are false—indeed, incredible—to the modern mind. In addition, unlike "biblical man," people today do not see themselves as in the grip of outside powers—their "self-understanding" is different from that. Bultmann seeks an approach to Scripture—and, in particular, the New Testament—that recognizes this mythical character. Myth is not an objective truth but, rather, a subjective expression of human beings' relation to the world. Modern readers must undertake an* **existentialist** *interpretation and self-understanding, which stresses anthropology, the study of human beings. The approach of demythologization looks at passages detailing demonic and spiritual powers, for instance, as rooted in an understanding of existence that accepts the transcendental.*

I

A. The Problem

1. The Mythical View of the World and the Mythical Event of Redemption The **cosmology** of the New Testament is essentially mythical in character. The world is viewed as a three-storied structure, with the earth in the centre, the heaven above, and the underworld beneath. Heaven is the abode of God and of celestial beings—the angels. The underworld is hell, the place of torment. Even the earth is more than the scene of natural, everyday events, of the trivial round and common task. It is the scene of the supernatural activity of God and his angels on the one hand, and of Satan and his daemons on the other. These supernatural forces intervene in the course of nature and in all that men think and will and do. Miracles are by no means rare. Man is not in control of his own life. Evil spirits may take possession of him. Satan may inspire him with evil thoughts. Alternatively, God may inspire his thought and guide his purposes. He may grant him heavenly visions. He may allow him to hear his word of succour or demand. He may give him the supernatural power of his Spirit. History does not follow a smooth unbroken course; it is set in motion and controlled by these supernatural powers. This aeon is held in bondage by Satan, sin, and death (for "powers" is precisely what they are), and hastens towards its end. That end will come very soon, and will take the form of a cosmic catastrophe. It will be inaugurated by the "woes" of the last time. Then the Judge will come from heaven, the dead will rise, the last judgement will take place, and men will enter into eternal salvation or damnation.

This then is the mythical view of the world which the New Testament presupposes when it presents the event of redemption which is the subject of its preaching. It proclaims in the language of mythology that the last time has now come. "In the fulness of time" God sent forth his Son, a pre-existent divine Being, who appears on earth as a man. He dies the death of a sinner on the cross and makes atonement for the sins of men. His resurrection marks the beginning of the cosmic catastrophe. Death, the consequence of Adam's sin, is abolished, and the daemonic forces are deprived of their power. The risen Christ is exalted to the right hand of God in heaven and made "Lord" and "King." He will come again on the clouds of heaven to complete the work of redemption, and the resurrection and judgement of men will follow. Sin, suffering, and death will then be finally abolished. All this is to happen very soon; indeed, St. Paul thinks that he himself will live to see it.

All who belong to Christ's Church and are joined to the Lord by Baptism and the Eucharist are certain of resurrection to salvation, unless they forfeit it by unworthy behaviour. Christian believers already enjoy the first instalment of salvation, for the Spirit is at work within them, bearing witness to their adoption as sons of God, and guaranteeing their final resurrection.

2. The Mythological View of the World Obsolete All this is the language of mythology, and the origin of the various themes can be easily traced in the contemporary mythology of Jewish Apocalyptic and in the redemption myths of Gnosticism. To this extent *the **kerygma** is incredible to modern man, for he is convinced that the mythical view of the world is obsolete.* We are therefore bound to ask whether, when we preach the Gospel to-day, we expect our converts to accept not only the Gospel message, but also the mythical view of the world in which it is set. If not, does the New Testament embody a truth which is quite independent of its mythical setting? If it does, theology must undertake the task of stripping the Kerygma from its mythical framework, of "demythologizing" it.

Can Christian preaching expect modern man *to accept the mythical view of the world as true?* To do so would be both senseless and impossible. It would be senseless, because there is nothing specifically Christian in the mythical view of the world as such. It is simply the cosmology of a pre-scientific age. Again, it would be impossible, because no man can adopt a view of the world by his own volition—it is already determined for him by his place in history. Of course such a view is not absolutely unalterable, and the individual may even contribute to its change. But he can do so only when he is faced by a new set of facts so compelling as to make his previous view of the world untenable. He has then no alternative but to modify his view of the world or produce a new one. The discoveries of Copernicus and the atomic theory are instances of this, and so was romanticism, with its discovery that the human subject is richer and more complex than enlightenment or idealism had allowed, and nationalism, with its new realization of the importance of history and the tradition of peoples.

It may equally well happen that truths which a shallow enlightenment had failed to perceive are later rediscovered in ancient **myths.** Theologians are perfectly justified in asking whether this is not exactly what has happened with the New Testament. At the same time it is impossible to revive an obsolete view of the world by a mere fiat, and certainly not a mythical view. For all our thinking to-day is shaped for good or ill by modern science. A blind acceptance of the New Testament mythology would be irrational, and to press for its acceptance as an article of faith would be to reduce Christian faith to the level of a human achievement. . . . It would involve a sacrifice of the intellect which could have only one result—a curious form of schizophrenia and insincerity. It would mean accepting a view of the world in our faith and religion which we should deny in our everyday life. Modern thought as we have inherited it provides us with *a motive for criticizing the New Testament view of the world.*

Man's knowledge and mastery of the world have advanced to such an extent through science and technology that it is no longer possible for anyone seriously to hold the New Testament view of the world—in fact, there is hardly anyone who does. What meaning, for instance, can we attach to such phrases in the creed as "descended into hell" or "ascended into heaven"? We no longer believe in the three-storied universe which the creeds take for granted. The only honest way of reciting the creeds is to strip the mythological framework from the truth they enshrine—that is, assuming that they contain any truth at all, which is just the question that **theology** has to ask. No one who is old enough to think for himself supposes that God lives in a local heaven. There is no longer any heaven in the traditional sense of the word. The same applies to hell in the sense of a mythical underworld beneath our feet. And if this is so, we can no longer accept the story of Christ's descent into hell or his Ascension into heaven as literally true. We can no longer look for the return of the Son of Man on the clouds of heaven or hope that the faithful will meet him in the air. . . .

Now that the forces and the laws of nature have been discovered, we can no longer believe in *spirits, whether good or evil.* We know that the stars are physical bodies whose motions are controlled by the laws of the universe, and not daemonic beings which enslave mankind to their service. Any influence they may have over human life must be explicable in terms of the ordinary laws of nature; it cannot in any way be attributed to their malevolence. Sickness and the cure of disease are likewise attributable to natural causation; they are not the result of daemonic activity or of evil spells.[1] The *miracles of the New Testament* have ceased to be miraculous, and to defend their historicity by recourse to nervous disorders or hypnotic effects only serves to underline the fact. . . .

It is impossible to use electric light and the wireless and to avail ourselves of modern medical and surgical discoveries, and at the same time to believe in the New Testament world of daemons and spirits. We may think we can manage it in our own lives, but to expect others to do so is to make the Christian faith unintelligible and unacceptable to the modern world.

[1]It may of course be argued that there are people alive to-day whose confidence in the traditional scientific view of the world has been shaken, and others who are primitive enough to qualify for an age of mythical thought. And there are also many varieties of superstition. But when belief in spirits and miracles has degenerated into superstition, it has become something entirely different from what it was when it was genuine faith. The various impressions and speculations which influence credulous people here and there are of little importance, nor does it matter to what extent cheap slogans have spread an atmosphere inimical to science. What matters is the world view which men imbibe from their environment, and it is science which determines that view of the world through the school, the press, the wireless, the cinema, and all the other fruits of technical progress.

The mythical **eschatology** is untenable for the simple reason that the **parousia** of Christ never took place as the New Testament expected. History did not come to an end, and, as every schoolboy knows, it will continue to run its course. Even if we believe that the world as we know it will come to an end in time, we expect the end to take the form of a natural catastrophe, not of a mythical event such as the New Testament expects. And if we explain the parousia in terms of modern scientific theory, we are applying criticism to the New Testament, albeit unconsciously.

But natural science is not the only challenge which the mythology of the New Testament has to face. There is the still more serious challenge presented by *modern man's understanding of himself.*

Modern man is confronted by a curious dilemma. He may regard himself as pure nature, or as pure spirit. In the latter case he distinguishes the essential part of his being from nature. In either case, however, *man is essentially a unity.* He bears the sole responsibility for his own feeling, thinking, and willing. He is not, as the New Testament regards him, the victim of a strange dichotomy which exposes him to the interference of powers outside himself. If his exterior behaviour and his interior condition are in perfect harmony, it is something he has achieved himself, and if other people think their interior unity is torn asunder by daemonic or divine interference, he calls it schizophrenia. . . .

B. The Task Before Us

[1.] The Nature of Myth The real purpose of myth is not to present an objective picture of the world as it is, but to express man's understanding of himself in the world in which he lives. Myth should be interpreted not cosmologically, but anthropologically, or better still, existentially. Myth speaks of the power or the powers which man supposes he experiences as the ground and limit of his world and of his own activity and suffering. He describes these powers in terms derived from the visible world, with its tangible objects and forces, and from human life, with its feelings, motives, and potentialities. He may, for instance, explain the origin of the world by speaking of a world egg or a world tree. Similarly he may account for the present state and order of the world by speaking of a primeval war between the gods. He speaks of the other world in terms of this world, and of the gods in terms derived from human life.[2]

Myth is an expression of man's conviction that the origin and purpose of the world in which he lives are to be sought not within it but beyond it—that is, beyond the realm of known and tangible reality—and that this realm is perpetually dominated and menaced by those mysterious powers which are its source and limit. Myth is also an expression of man's awareness that he is not lord of his own being. It expresses his sense of dependence not only within the visible world, but more especially on those forces which hold sway beyond the confines of the known. Finally, myth expresses man's belief that in this state of dependence he can be delivered from the forces within the visible world.

Thus myth contains elements which demand its own criticism—namely, its imagery with its apparent claim to objective validity. The real purpose of myth is to speak of a transcendent power which controls the world and man, but that purpose is impeded and obscured by the terms in which it is expressed.

Hence the importance of the New Testament mythology lies not in its imagery but in the understanding of existence which it enshrines. The real question is whether this understanding of existence is true. Faith claims that it is, and faith ought not to be tied down to the imagery of New Testament mythology. . . .

[2.] An Existentialist Interpretation the Only Solution The **theological** work which such an interpretation involves can be sketched only in the broadest outline and with only a few examples. We must avoid the impression that this is a light and easy task,

[2]Myth is here used in the sense popularized by the 'History of Religions' school. Mythology is the use of imagery to express the otherworldly in terms of this world and the divine in terms of human life, the other side in terms of this side. For instance, divine transcendence is expressed as spatial distance. . . .

as if all we have to do is to discover the right formula and finish the job on the spot. It is much more formidable than that. It cannot be done single-handed. It will tax the time and strength of a whole theological generation.

The mythology of the New Testament is in essence that of Jewish apocalyptic and the Gnostic redemption myths. A common feature of them both is their basic dualism, according to which the present world and its human inhabitants are under the control of daemonic, satanic powers, and stand in need of redemption. Man cannot achieve this redemption by his own efforts; it must come as a gift through a divine intervention. Both types of mythology speak of such an intervention: Jewish apocalyptic of an imminent world crisis in which this present aeon will be brought to an end and the new aeon ushered in by the coming of the Messiah, and Gnosticism of a Son of God sent down from the realm of light, entering into this world in the guise of a man, and by his fate and teaching delivering the elect and opening up the way for their return to their heavenly home.

The meaning of these two types of mythology lies once more not in their imagery with its apparent objectivity but in the understanding of human existence which both are trying to express. In other words, they need to be interpreted existentially. . . .

Our task is to produce an **existentialist** interpretation of the dualistic mythology of the New Testament along similar lines. When, for instance, we read of daemonic powers ruling the world and holding mankind in bondage, does the understanding of human existence which underlies such language offer a solution to the riddle of human life which will be acceptable even to the non-mythological mind of to-day? Of course we must not take this to imply that the New Testament presents us with an anthropology like that which modern science can give us. It cannot be proved by logic or demonstrated by an appeal to factual evidence. Scientific anthropologies always take for granted a definite understanding of existence, which is invariably the consequence of a deliberate decision of the scientist, whether he makes it consciously or not. And that is why we have to discover whether the New Testament offers man an understanding of himself which will challenge him to a genuine existential decision.

STUDY QUESTIONS

1. What is the New Testament's presupposed view of the world?
2. What does Bultmann mean by "myth," and what is its purpose?
3. What does Bultmann offer as a resolution to the problem presented for the Bible by modern science?
4. *Do you think that the scientific evidence against biblical cosmology is as strong or conclusive as Bultmann believes?
5. *Bultmann writes, "It is impossible to use electric light and the wireless and to avail ourselves of modern medical and surgical discoveries, and at the same time to believe in the New Testament world of demons and spirits." Is this true in your opinion? Why or why not?

READING 2.8

Poetic Imagery and Religious Belief

Howard K. Wettstein

Following Jewish theologian Abraham Joshua Heschel (1907–1972), Howard K. Wettstein (University of California-Riverside) distinguishes between, on the one hand, the notion of God conveyed in philosophical theology, *especially in medieval times, and, on the other hand, the images used by the Hebrew Bible and by the rabbis who lived in the early centuries of the Christian era. The Bible and rabbis describe God anthropomorphically—that is, as having human characteristics. By contrast, medieval philosophy, in its effort to square revealed truth with reason, speaks of God abstractly as the most perfect being. Wettstein suggests that biblical and rabbinic description is poetry, rather than philosophy. Doctrine—a theory of God—is remote from their concerns. Viewing biblical and rabbinic description as poetry permits inconsistency among various images of God as judge, creator, friend, and lover. Wettstein also suggests that religious belief itself does not involve a straightforward propositional claim. You will see a direct contrast between Wettstein's essay and Schnall's (Reading 2.5).*

Religions are systems of thought. So we tend to suppose.[1] What certainly qualify as systems of thought are the products of philosophical **theology.** But there is some tension between such constellations of theological doctrine and the primary religious works—in the tradition on which I will be focused, the Hebrew Bible[2] as understood through, and supplemented by, the Rabbis of the Talmud.[3]

This tension is a product of the genesis of philosophical theology, the application of Greek philosophical thought to a very different tradition, one that emerged from a very different world. The primary religious works speak of God impressionistically. Their mode of description is as remote from definition as poetry is from mathematics. Their imagery is strikingly **anthropomorphic.**

Medieval religious philosophy, by contrast, disparages anthropomorphic description.[4] While not quite an abstract entity, God is described, even defined, in abstract terms. The flavor of this is perhaps best conveyed by an example from the Christian philosophic tradition, St. Anselm's characterization of God as "the most perfect being." This is no mere honorific supplement to the anthropomorphic characterizations. It is a definition, one that subsumes specific divine perfections.

My aim here is to explore this tension with an eye to the fate or ultimate status of the doctrinal output of the philosophers. I will argue that theological doctrine[5] is not a natural tool for thinking about Judaism, and insofar as Judaism is in this way representative, it's not a natural tool for thinking about religion. The "system of thought" model applies only with the application of force.

A. J. Heschel, an important American Jewish scholar and thinker, comments that much of his career was devoted to elucidating distinctively Jewish—as opposed to medieval Greek-inspired—modes of religious thought. "It is not an easy enterprise," Heschel notes.[6]

> The Hellenization of Jewish theology actually goes back to Philo [first century B.C.E]. . . . The impact of Philo on theology was radical. To oversimplify the matter, this approach would have Plato and Moses, for example, say the same thing, only Plato would say it in Greek. . . . This view has had a great impact on much of Jewish medieval philosophy. They talk about God in the language of the Greeks.

Perhaps we should not suppose any failure on the part of the medievals to discern the distance between biblical-rabbinic and Greek-inspired modes of theological thought. Rather, for the medievals, this was the only way to make sense of the God of the tradition; the only way to square revealed and

[1]I owe this way of formulating the tendency to Joel Gereboff, who is also skeptical about the supposition.

[2]When I speak in this essay of the Bible, I mean to refer to the Hebrew Bible. This is not quite the Old Testament of the Christian Bible, both in terms of the order of the books—the prophets come immediately after the Pentateuch in the Hebrew Bible—and the addition in the Old Testament of certain books not in the Hebrew canon, for example, Maccabees.

[3]Roughly first to fifth century of the Common Era.

[4]The role of anthropomorphism in the contrast between the two traditions constitutes a central focus of M. Halbertal and A. Margalit *Idolatry* (Cambridge, Mass. and London, 1996).

[5]I will use "doctrine" to refer to the output of philosophical theology. While I want to deny the appropriateness of doctrine, I certainly do not deny the appropriateness of religious belief or religious tenets. More on the distinction later.

[6]A. J. Heschel, *Moral Grandeur and Spiritual Audacity,* ed. S. Heschel (New York, 1996), 155–56.

philosophic truth. One who wants to make philosophical sense of biblical/rabbinic remarks about God will inevitably do so in terms of one's own idiom and conceptual repertoire. It might seem, then, that the medievals only did what we all do, what is inevitable.

Still, as Heschel sees it, Philo's innovation violates something at the heart of the tradition. The introduction of Greek modes of philosophical thought encouraged the minimization or outright rejection of anthropomorphism. The God of the Hebrew Bible is, among other things, loving, nurturing/merciful,[7] just, even angry. The Bible speaks of relations between people and God in the language of personal relationships. What grounds obligation to God, for example, is nothing very abstract. It is rather the community's historic and personal relation to God.

Such robustly anthropomorphic characterizations of God play an apparently indispensable role in the religious life. That God loves and cares are, for the religious practitioner, no throwaways. To attempt to relegate anthropomorphism to the status of a mere surface level phenomenon is to engage in an uphill battle. The burden of proof, given the character of religious life, surely seems on the other side. On the face of it, the distance between biblical/rabbinic and medieval philosophic thinking is enormous.

I. POETIC IMAGERY AND RELIGIOUS BELIEF

1. Poetic Imagery

Let's consider a somewhat lengthier list of anthropomorphic images of God in biblical/rabbinic literature: loving and nurturing, even if demanding, parent; benevolent judge/ruler who does not forget acts of loving kindness and generously and lovingly passes on the rewards to one's progeny; righteous judge who has access to our deepest secrets and who rewards and punishes accordingly; king of the universe, to be treated with lordly deference; bridegroom; husband; woman in labor; angry, regretful, even vengeful, remembering the sins of the parents and visiting them upon even distant generations. When one scans this panoply of images, doctrine seems far away. Many of the images fail to yield anything like a characterization of God that could figure in doctrine. Among the images, moreover, are striking dissonances, hardly a phenomenon friendly to doctrine.

Clearly, conceptual refinement and coherence is not a high priority in the Bible and *Aggada* [nonlegal portions of rabbinic literature]. One has the sense that one is dealing with something more like poetry; sometimes poetry per se, as in *Psalms,* other times poetic, image-laden prose.

The virtues of this poetry, any poetry, do not include the discursive articulation characteristic of philosophy. The sorts of things one seeks from poetry are brilliance and depth of perception, suggestiveness; these inextricably bound with beauty of formulation. A collection of poetry on the subject of, say, love might include pieces reflecting different attitudes, moods, experiences. The poet seeks to illuminate the phenomena, sometimes casting them in a positive light, sometimes in a negative light. Many of the images, perhaps even the most beautiful and suggestive ones, do not yield easily to anything like a philosophically adequate idea.[8] Nor would the images presumably constitute a coherent set. Imagine the folly of trying to derive any sort of theory of love from such poetry.

Doctrine—the theory of God, as it were—is equally remote from biblical/rabbinic characterizations

[7]The Hebrew word *rachamim,* often translated "mercy," might better be seen as conveying nurture or something with both dimensions. Mercy, for me at least, connotes grace, and this seems not to capture the feel of *rachamim.* The Hebrew word may be etymologically related to the word for womb, *rechem.*

[8]Such imagery often simply is not subject to explication in propositional terms without remainder, as it were. For one thing, many poetic images are propositionally indeterminate; were one to work at explicating or articulating the imagery long enough, one might see several ways it might be explicated, none of which is dictated or even suggested by the original. This is a bit like what Rudolph Carnap thought about the explication of terms of ordinary language. But analogies with Carnap's views aside, the point here is that imagery is what it is; it does not yield to propositional formulation.

of God. The point holds not only for Psalms and the like; one of the fundamental ideas of Genesis, that humans were created in God's image, provides an example from biblical prose. The idea of reflecting divinity is potent, pregnant with meaning. But it is imagery, not doctrine. Its very magnificence—literary and religious—seems to place it at some distance from doctrine.

2. The Language of Poetry

One should not suppose that literary or poetic "imagery," any more than other forms of discourse, is necessarily connected with visual or mental images. Perhaps literary imagery is more likely than is, say, a weather report, to stimulate one to form an image in one's mind. But that is not essential. We do not refer to these figures of speech as *imagery* because they induce mental images. How to characterize literary imagery—why exactly we call it "imagery"—is more difficult, something I won't explore here. But simple examples of metaphor, one form of such imagery, make it clear that mental imaging is not essential. "Sea of troubles," mentioned below, will do.

Here's *The American Heritage Dictionary*'s definition of metaphor: A figure of speech in which a word or phrase that ordinarily designates one thing is used to designate another, thus making an implicit comparison, as in "a sea of troubles." When we explain metaphor to our students—say, in connection with some philosophical metaphor—metaphorical language, we suggest, is second best. We revert to it when we are not in a position to provide literal description, when we can't do better than mere analogies, implicit comparisons. What we don't mention—because we are not really thinking about poetry and literary language—is that in literary contexts, metaphor is often used for its own sake; it is not second best.

Why is metaphorical language sometimes preferable? It goes to the heart of literary imagery—here we go beyond metaphor—that the words resonate. One might speak about this phenomenon in terms of levels or layers of meaning. But "resonance" better conveys the lingering intimations, the echoes, the movement of the mind.[9] In poetry or poetic prose, a single word or phrase may have multiple resonances. Sometimes one predominates, comes to the fore; others linger in the background. Other times one finds oneself moving between them, sometimes repeatedly. Resonances have many determinants: the occurrence of the expression in famous literary contexts; or other contexts, or other ways, in which the words are customarily used; or other words that sound alike or that come from the same root—these are a sample.

Where does meaning, significance, come in? We should not try to say what the meaning of a word in poetry consists in—a bad idea even in, as it were, straight philosophy of language. Instead, let's say that an expression's significance has everything to do with the networks of resonance in which it is embedded. A host of just such miscellaneous considerations, for example, figures in the significance of "God."

3. Mere Poetry?

Have I distanced the biblical/rabbinic literature too far from theological doctrine? If imagery is at the heart of biblical/rabbinic characterization of God, then what becomes of religious belief, of the tenets of religion?

Heschel writes, "In Biblical language the religious man is not called 'believer,' as he is for example in Islam (*mu'min*), but *yere hashem* [one who stands in awe of the Lord]."[10] In the present context this is extremely interesting; it suggests that in thinking about religion we make too much of the

[9]The superiority of "resonance" over "levels of meaning" was suggested to me by Rachel Adler.

[10]In *God in Search of Man* (New York and Philadelphia, 1959), p. 77. See also Richard Friedman, in *The Disappearance of God* (Boston, 1995):

> Indeed there is no word for "to believe" in biblical Hebrew. The word that is frequently translated as "to believe" means, in the original, something more like "to trust"; that is, it means that one can rely on this God to do what He has said He will do (e.g., Exodus 14:31). It does not mean "to believe" in the sense of belief that God exists."

doxastic dimension and too little of the affective. What I take from this is not that the concept of religious belief has no purchase in Judaism. Or that the religious life does not require appropriate beliefs. Rather belief is not at the heart of the matter; one gets a misleading picture of Jewish religiosity if one's focus is a set of beliefs. There is an analogy with the question of linguistic meaning in poetry. It's not that a linguistic expression in poetry does not mean what it ordinarily does, say, in a newspaper article. But that dimension of its meaning is often not at the heart of its function in poetry.

What then do I make of religious belief, given my emphasis on poetic imagery? My answer is that likening biblical/rabbinic remarks to poetry certainly does not imply or even suggest that these remarks involve no beliefs, no real commitments; that they are, as one might say, "just poetry." For such commitment-neutrality is surely not true of poetry itself.

Poetry may assume, for example, straightforward factual information about the world, that there are people, that they behave in certain ways, and so on. Second and more interestingly, poetry may be committal even where there is no way to formulate the relevant belief in straightforward, literal language. If we wish to formulate such belief, we do one of two things. We can approximate, extracting a piece of the picture, one that is propositionally manageable, and attributing that piece. Alternatively, we can mimic the poet, attributing belief using the very imagery she used—or related imagery. This may be a philosophical no-no; it will strike some as bizarre to suppose that such a thing counts as belief. Here as elsewhere, as Wittgenstein urged, philosophy would do well to look at actual practice rather than think about what it must be like.

In the religious literature that is my focus, many things are assumed about the world, many beliefs can be distilled from the imagery. All the old standards, as it were: belief in God, in God creating the world, creating people in his image, freeing his people from Egyptian bondage, revealing himself to Moses and giving the Torah on Mt. Sinai, and the like. How should we think about these beliefs? Are they like the straightforward propositional claims that we can often distill from poetry or are they of the second variety mentioned, claims that remain at the level of imagery? When we report someone as having such and such religious belief, to what extent are we discursively articulating propositional content; to what extent are we ourselves using religious imagery?

I'm intrigued by the idea that in speaking of the divine, intimation is the rule. Religious belief, one might then say, lives at the level of imagery. Belief ascription would then be a matter of utilizing the believer's imagery in characterizing his belief. However, I am doubtful that things are this simple and uniform, that there is a single story to tell about religious belief per se. Clearly, the matter requires much more thought, with detailed scrutiny of examples.

To return to my philosophic heterodoxy, what sort of belief is it that has no propositional content? In fact, on grounds that are completely independent of the current discussion, I think that the usual sort of philosophic thinking about belief—the propositional content model—is misconceived. Indeed, that the propositional content model is not consonant with my emphasis on religious imagery is fine with me. This is not the place to motivate my contrary conception. But we can at least see how it works out for the case of religious belief.

Let's distinguish two different ways of appreciating, say, the ideas, for example, the idea that we reflect God's image. One may appreciate this powerfully suggestive idea from the outside, as it were. Call this the Bible-as-literature approach; here one is sensitive to the idea's significance for one's religious tradition. Alternatively, one may make the divine reflection idea one's own, see the world through its imagery, declare it, for example, in prayer. The question is whether one signs on, as it were; whether the poetic resonances reflect one's own take on the world.

If one wholeheartedly endorses the divine reflection idea, then we may use this imagery to characterize her approach to the world. That is what we do when we ascribe belief, when we say, for example, that she believes that human beings reflect God's image. Don't think of this as pinning on the believer belief in another fact; it is rather using her preferred imagery to characterize her mind.

To attribute a belief is thus to kidnap a piece of the person's favored imagery, to absorb it into a different genre. It's to use the image in a new way. To ascribe such a belief to someone is like saying "This image plays a fundamental role for her."

Involved here is a sliding scale, from those parts of the imagery that are more serious and fundamental from those that are less so. Consider the imagery of God's right arm. It's as if one kidnaps the imagery of God's right arm, and then learns that one can't make straightforward use of it; it falls to go quietly into the belief ascription genre. This is so because it is an image we are happy to let go. At least we are after we learn from it. Religious Jews believe that God created the world, but not that he has a right arm. The latter is not part of the imagery with which they approach the world. It is not a constituent of the story that serves as a backdrop to their lives. So, as our belief reporting practices go, it is inappropriate to use this imagery to keep track of their religious whereabouts. This is not to say that the image has no power for them.

II. THEOLOGY

1. Philosophical Ambition

The medievals, blessed with a more-or-less stable first philosophy, lived philosophically charmed lives. There is some parallel in our attitude to, say, physics. We are not sure of the details of our physics, not confident that we have final answers, but pretty sure we are in the ballpark, playing by the right rules, very confident of some general outlines. Perhaps the medievals were even more confident about philosophy. They were, after all, looking backward towards the philosophers, while we are looking forward to a somewhat uncertain future, humbled by the history of past scientific upheavals.

Possession of philosophic truth grounded in a stable first philosophy makes many things possible: philosophy providing foundations for religious belief, philosophy clarifying the content of revealed religion, philosophy determining the nature of God, or perhaps determining that God's nature is demonstrably, as it were, beyond us. Doctrine, the propositional articulation of the religious fundamentals, is at home in such a setting.

A doctrine approach need not deny what I've been arguing about the impressionism of biblical/rabbinic characterization of God. One might argue—as Maimonides indeed suggests—that it is only because of philosophically available truths about God that we are in any position to discriminate among the images, to know which to take seriously and which not. The ordinary person has no independent access to God, so how can he discern biblical talk of God's unity and God's creation of the world from the merely figurative attribution of bodily properties to God? Absent our access to philosophical truth and we would be religiously deprived.

This seems an extreme view, one that gives more independent weight to philosophy than many of the medievals, and probably more than Maimonides himself in other moods, or literary modes. But it nicely dramatizes the contrast with our own philosophic environment. The medieval conception (or cluster of them) of how religion and philosophy might join forces seems to many of us inapplicable nowadays. The crucial philosophic truth complement seems missing in action. It is not only that the traditional proofs of God's existence are in disrepute. Nor is it merely the lack of a received view—or even a widely accepted consensus—in philosophy, substantively or methodologically. For many of us philosophy simply cannot be brought to bear on religion the way that the medievals supposed.

One might assume that this makes it natural for us to think with the Rabbis, who also carry on without a first philosophy. However, the tradition, as we have it, has acquired much medieval philosophy, much doctrine, at least semi-officially. This of course was Heschel's gripe. If we follow his lead, trying to recover what he called Jewish as opposed to Greek ways of thinking about Judaism, we are indeed led straight back to biblical/rabbinic mode of religious expression.

To reject medieval philosophic ambition is not to suggest that philosophic training is irrelevant to the understanding of religious thought, Jewish or other. In philosophy we are trained to think carefully, analytically, to be sensitive to conceptual distinctions, to extend our thinking, as it were, both vertically, persistently pressing beneath the surface, and horizontally, taking a comprehensive view of the domain. There is no reason why such virtues would be irrelevant to the understanding of religion and religious ideas. But this is a far cry from the sort of access to philosophic truth that fuels the medieval project.

2. Poetic Inconsistency

Why not start from the imagery and try to figure out what's going on with the leading figure? One of the aims of such theorizing would be to make sense of the tremendous multiplicity of roles that God plays in the imagery. What is this all about? What sort of being underlies these images and why are they fitting images for this being?

I begin with an example that shares some features with our situation. In both we begin with ideas that stand in conflict with one another. In both something short of theoretical resolution seems natural and satisfying. Indeed, theoretical resolution seems out of place.

There is a Hasidic adage that a person should carry in his pocket two pieces of paper with dissonant messages: "I am but dust and ashes," and "The world was created for me." I have often thought that the really difficult trick is to get both on the same piece of paper; to live a life that is not so compartmentalized, that integrates the superficially incompatible messages.

Maurice Friedman suggested to me that it would be better to leave them on separate sheets, maybe even in different pockets. The imagery of a single piece of paper suggested to Friedman what he took to be a bad idea: that the philosophic job is to render these insights coherent, to articulate an inclusive principle. What one needs is rather a kind of practical skill, the ability to negotiate experience respecting both truths—that is, both images, each of which illuminates human experience.

This example (and others like it) exhibits two features that are salient for us. First, there are conflicting ideas, each of which possesses a kind of truth or validity. Second, the tension is resolved not by discovering a higher order principle, but by the acquisition of a practical ability or skill, a kind of "knowing how." The agent develops a sense of balance, the ability to call upon the idea appropriate to the situation at hand.

How does the first feature apply to the sundry characterizations of God? Think of the diverse, sometimes conflicting, images of God as profiles, as views from a perspective. Each profile is crucial for the religious life. Each has validity. Each illuminates in its own way. There are situations in which the image of God as nurturing parent is salient. In other situations other imagery may be salient, perhaps God as an impartial judge, or as a friend, or as creator of heaven and earth, or as one you have wronged, or as the parent of one you have wronged.

There are still other situations in which two or more profiles of God are somehow salient. Some of these may be very pleasant; as if one were taking in several varieties of beauty at once, or through several sensory modalities. Some of these situations, though, may be troubling, confusing. Such situations, as Moshe Halbertal and Avishai Margalit point out in the first chapter of their excellent discussion in *Idolatry,* are analogous to one who works for his father-in-law, who also happens to be his teacher, landlord, and plays unnamed other roles in his life. One can readily imagine situations that become quite complicated and confusing. One doesn't quite know where one stands.

Let's turn to the second highlighted feature: the resolution of the tension between the ideas takes place on the plane of action rather than theory; it involves a practical ability or skill. Theoretical resolution in the form of a comprehensive principle seems unnecessary. This is of course the critical issue in the present context. For theoretical resolution—at least a leading candidate for such a resolution—would involve an account of the entity that lies behind the profiles, an account of how these could possibly be perspectives on the same being.

How does this apply to biblical imagery? The story here is more complicated than in the two examples. The religious life involves a combination of practical abilities or skills that are grounded in understanding, intuitive if not articulate. The religious life also involves habits, behavioral and affective. All of this requires education, training, and practice. As is our way with such things, some are more given to it, more gifted at it, some will take to it more easily than others, others may come along more slowly, but may attain greater heights in the end.

One stage in religious development is understanding the many different human relationships in terms of which these profiles of God are formulated: developing a sense of what it is to relate to another as child to parent, as subject to monarch, as defendant to judge, as creature to creator, as lover, as friend, and so on.[11] Developing a sense of these with their directions reversed is also of great utility: parent to child, monarch to subject, and so on. The more vivid one's grasp, the more deeply one sees into these relationships, the farther along one is in this stage of the training. Some of this understanding requires the accumulation—sometimes years—of experience. This education is a lifelong affair.

The next step—not that these need to be separated in time—is the application of this growing understanding to the relationships between people and God. One needs to think about and practice seeing oneself in relation to God as child to parent, with the variety of complications that entails; and to think about it from both sides of the relationship. And as lover to lover, friend to friend, judged to judge, and all the rest.

The payoff of one's work—the propriety and caring for others, the comfort and solace, the elevation and dignity that are the concomitants of developed religious character—depend upon one's ability to negotiate the world feeling and acting in ways appropriate to just such relationships. One needs to feel and act as if one has a Godly parent, a Godly lover or friend, a Godly judge who sees all, a creator of inexorable laws of nature that proceed as if we didn't exist,[12] even—I suspect—an angry, even vengeful Godly ruler—this last being more complicated and controversial.

Of course, one doesn't feel and act in these ways all the time, or all at the same time. Part of the skill—what takes training, practice, and experience—is to call upon, or be called upon by, the appropriate image at the appropriate time, sometimes a single image, sometimes multiple ones. The latter can be confusing, disconcerting, as Halbertal and Margalit point out, and it can be wonderful, sometimes both. At the death of a parent, for example, many of these images may strike: God as creator of inexorable laws of nature; God as friend and comforter; (and since belonging and community becomes so important at such times) God as focal point—glue, as it were—of Jewish community, a community that extends horizontally—the present community—and vertically—the community over time; and perhaps others.

Ritualized prayer—something that also takes training and practice if it is to be more than mechanical (and even if it is merely mechanical)—provides another example of the sometimes confusing but wonderful multiplicity. In prayer, when it works, many of the magnificent images are summoned. One is provided with the opportunity of experiencing these relationships and of reflecting upon them, seeing more deeply into them, seeing new aspects all the time.

That there are multiple images, that they seem discordant—properties that make theory seem very far away—are thus rationalized. We don't do so by finding a theoretical account of God that puts the images in their right place. Rather the miscellany, the mixed multitude of robustly anthropomorphic ideas and images, facilitate the religious life.

I will conclude with a brief return to the concept of religious belief. As I explained my approach to religious belief, the imagery that plays a fundamental role for the believer finds its way into the report of the person's belief. Belief lives at the level

[11]Cf. Halbertal and Margalit: "Our understanding of . . . God in the Bible depends on our ability to enter into the heart of these images with all their connotations of prevalent interpersonal relationships." (p. 9)

[12]Perhaps this is part of what is involved in God's *midat ha-din,* often translated, as I did earlier in this paper, as God's attribute of strict justice, but more literally translated as his attribute of law. It may be the notion of "moral law" that facilitates the transition from the literal translation to the more usual.

of imagery. I want to integrate that idea with what we have been exploring most recently, the multiplicity of discordant images. The transition from the imagery as it functions for the religious person to the imagery as it functions in the report of her belief is a very significant one. For in the original context of poetry, or image-laden prose, consistency of imagery is hardly a virtue. Indeed, the very multiplicity and variety facilitate the religious life. But once the imagery has found its way into the context of belief, into a report of someone's belief, inconsistency becomes a substantial liability. This reflects the utility of belief talk, what it does for us.

The belief idiom is a fundamental tool for locating people cognitively, for tracking their cognitive whereabouts, their take on how things stand. For that very reason, it is quite sensitive to matters of consistency. To see this, don't think of beliefs about religious matters, but about the weather, or about history, or elementary particles. When, however, we speak of belief with respect to a domain in which imagery plays such a fundamental role, the idiom has limitations. Along with talk of belief comes the suggestion that it's not a good thing to have conflicting ones. And that simply is not true, at least not in an unqualified way, of the domain in question.

I have been exploring a perspective according to which doctrine is not the heart of the religious sensibility. Indeed even religious belief—and even when not viewed as doctrinal—is not at the core. What bearers of a religious tradition have been given are directions for living the religious life. The essential constituent of such a life is a system of communal and individual practice, both ritual and ethical, informed by a narrative history interwoven with religious imagery. The imagery, in all its variety and inconsistency, along with the historical narrative provide many dimensions of meaning to the practices. And the practices in turn give definition to the otherwise abstract and elusive imagery. The constellation of practices, historical narrative, and imagery issue in a distinctive kind of life with its own substantial virtues and rewards. It seems reductive and misleading to represent this as a system of doctrine, a set of well-formed beliefs, a system of thought.

STUDY QUESTIONS

1. Explain Wettstein's contrast between medieval theology and biblical and rabbinic writing.
2. Give examples of biblical imagery about God.
3. Wettstein thinks that viewing biblical discourse as poetry enables us to understand inconsistencies in the images used about God. Why? *Do you think the supposedly inconsistent images can be rendered consistent without resorting to Wettstein's approach?
4. *Contrast Wettstein's positions with that of Ira M. Schnall. Whose approach do you think is more convincing? Why?
5. *Might the Bible be *both* poetry *and* philosophy? Discuss.
6. *Often the Bible relates stories about human beings without engaging in descriptions of God. What is the function of these stories? Discuss.
7. *What is Wettstein's conception of religious belief? Do you agree with it? Why or why not?

READING 2.9

Feminist Christian Philosophy?

Patricia Altenbernd Johnson

Patricia Altenbernd Johnson's essay continues the discussion of biblical images broached at the end of Wettstein's. Responding to a call by Alvin Plantinga for increased **autonomy,** *integrity, and boldness on the part of Christian philosophers, Johnson (University of Dayton) aims to show how feminist philosophy—and, in particular, viewing God as Mother rather than Father—can contribute positively to Christian philosophy.*

According to Johnson, the New Testament does not justify the claim that women were excluded from the community Jesus formed. Rather, Jesus sought to liberate people from patriarchal structures. Terms such as father and master are potentially destructive, as is the idea (proposed by philosophers and examined in Chapter 1) that God is lacking in emotion. Other symbols, such as Mother, along with other portrayals of God's emotional life, are needed to help Christians see loving, nurturing, and trusting in the world. Patriarchal symbols convey control and domination, obscuring other ways of dealing with danger. God need not protect us from all evils.

"There are words I cannot choose again,"
Natural Resources, 13
Adrienne Rich

[Several] years ago Alvin Plantinga offered some "Advice to Christian Philosophers." He suggested that, within the philosophical community in which we, as Christians, find ourselves, we need to display more autonomy, more integrity, and more boldness. My aim is to offer some further, but related, advice. Christian philosophers would do well to heed the voices of feminist philosophers both within and outside of the Christian community. If our philosophy is an "expression of deep and fundamental perspectives, ways of viewing ourselves and the world and God" (Plantinga, p. 271), then we must constantly examine those perspectives in order better to articulate them and to understand how those perspectives relate to our thought and our action. In this paper, I will set out the **hermeneutical** structure of the task that Plantinga recommends for Christian philosophers and show how the voices of feminism contribute to this task. . . .

I. THE HERMENEUTICAL STANCE OF THE CHRISTIAN PHILOSOPHER

Plantinga's advice helps us understand our stance as Christian philosophers in relation to the wider philosophical community. He tells us the story of a young woman (Christian in her religious commitments) who goes to college and discovers that "philosophy is the subject for her" (p. 254). As an undergraduate she learns how philosophy is currently practiced. She goes to graduate school and learns even more fully the standards and assumptions that guide contemporary philosophical thought. She learns these parameters well. She respects her mentors, and she is inclined to think that departure from these parameters is "at best marginally respectable" (p. 255). Plantinga suggests that as time goes on this young philosopher—now a professional—may "note certain tensions between her Christian belief and her way of practicing philosophy" (p. 256). She may become so concerned about these tensions that she tries to put the two together, "to harmonize them" (p. 256). Plantinga's advice to her is that she is misdirected in doing this. What she should do instead is allow her sense of tension to help her critique the presuppositions of current philosophy. Moreover, she should listen to her own voice and be emboldened to set aside the philosophical parameters of her mentors, to reject their presuppositions and begin from within her own context. She must recognize that all philosophy is engaged, is committed to a definite presuppositional stance, and she must have the Christian courage to follow through on her own engagement.

I find this story compelling for a number of reasons. It describes the **hermeneutical** process of my own philosophical development in a simple and direct manner. It speaks to me as a religious person who loves philosophy and who is schooled within contemporary philosophical parameters. Moreover, it recognizes the philosophical voice of women.

The hermeneutical process depicted by this story is one that can be called a "hermeneutic of transformation" (Johnson and Kalven, p. 165). The process is hermeneutical in the sense used by Segundo and Fiorenza. It is a process that uncovers and critiques the presuppositions of our fundamental interpretive

> which seems outwardly insignificant but which produces in woman moral and intellectual effects so profound that they appear to spring from her original nature (p. xxvi).

And so I would urge you to listen to the voices of women who reflect on their experience of invisibility and silence and who develop in their Christian faith a critique of patriarchy that challenges us to rethink our anthropology. Elizabeth Schüssler Fiorenza is one of these voices.

Fiorenza recognizes that women experience invisibility and silence within Christianity, but she also maintains that women find positive experiences within biblical religion; there is a source of strength and boldness. In *In Memory of Her: A Feminist Theological Reconstruction of Christian Origins,* she explains the goals of her work as the

> attempt to reconstruct early Christian history as women's history in order not only to restore women's stories to early Christian history but also to reclaim this history as the history of women and men. I do this not only as a feminist historian but also as a feminist theologian. The Bible is not just a historical collection but also Holy Scripture, gospel, for Christians today. As such it informs not only theology but also the commitment of many women today. Yet as long as the stories and histories of women in the beginnings of early Christianity are not theologically conceptualized as an integral part of the proclamation of the gospel, biblical texts and traditions formulated and codified by men will remain oppressive to women (pp. xiv–xv).

In order to do the reconceptualization necessary to address this oppression, she sets out a feminist critical hermeneutics that stresses the importance of identifying, acknowledging, and taking responsibility for our theoretical presuppositions. This activity is particularly important as we reflect on the Jesus tradition and scriptures. While her work is primarily theological, it is important to our work as philosophers because it examines and critiques the biblical and theological presuppositions that often go unexamined in our work.

Fiorenza argues that the theological reading that uses generic language allows women to identify with "general (male) categories and groups" such as "the poor, the lonely, the brothers." However, it does not allow women to identify themselves as in solidarity with other women. Generic (male) language serves not only to keep women as women invisible, but also conceals the message of liberation from patriarchal structures that is at the center of Jesus' message (pp. 142–143). She argues that Jesus' vision for the destitute did not separate economic exploitation and patriarchal oppression. In support of her position she presents three sets of texts from the pre-Gospel Jesus tradition:

> (1) the pre-Markian controversy stories in which Jesus challenges patriarchal marriage structures (Mark 10:2–9 and 12:18–27); (2) the texts on the a-familial ethos of the Jesus movement; and (3) the saying about domination-free relationships in the community of disciples (p. 143).

All of these are worth our careful consideration, but it is the last two sets of texts that are most helpful to my reflections on women's voice and visibility.

One presupposition that many readings of the Jesus movement perpetuate is that women were excluded from the new community that Jesus formed. The image of the disciples is of a band of itinerant men who had left family (including wives) and home behind them to live a radical ethos (p. 145) that those left at home did not live. This radical ethos is identified especially by the abandonment of traditional family relations. Fiorenza notes that Mark and Matthew mention "house, brothers, sisters, mothers, fathers, children, lands" as left behind. Only in the redactional work of Luke is the wife among those left behind. This suggests that women were not excluded from the new community. She joins this insight with a review of the texts that announce Jesus bringing "sword" to set many people against each other. She observes that nothing is said about setting wife against husband or husband against wife. (Matt. 10:34–36, "Do not think that I have come to bring peace on earth; I have not come to bring peace, but a sword. For I have come to set a man against his father, and a daughter against her mother, and a daughter-in-law against her mother-in-law; and a man's foes will be those of his own household," and

Luke 12:51–53, "Do you think that I have come to bring peace on earth? No, I tell you, but rather division; for henceforth, in one house there will be five divided, three against two and two against three; they will be divided father against son and son against father, mother against daughter and daughter against mother, mother-in-law against her daughter-in-law and daughter-in-law against her mother-in-law.") Fiorenza concludes that it is clear that Jesus did not respect patriarchal family bonds. Moreover, it would be a misreading "to claim that such a radial a-familial ethos is asked only of the male wandering charismatics" (p. 146) and not also of female disciples.

Fiorenza takes a further step in the interpretation that Jesus advocated a community of equal discipleship by looking at those texts where Jesus discusses the constitution of his true family. These texts mention brothers, sisters, and mothers, but no fathers. She examines texts from Mark:

> Jesus said, "Truly, I say to you, there is no one who has left house or brothers or sisters or mother or father or children or lands, for my sake and for the gospel, who will not receive a hundredfold now in this time, houses and brothers and sisters and mothers and children and lands, with persecutions, and in the age to come eternal life" (Mark 10:29–30).
>
> And his mother and his brothers came; and standing outside they sent to him and called him. And a crowd was sitting about him; and they said to him, "Your mother and brothers are outside, asking for you." And he replied, "Who are my mother and my brothers?" And looking around those who sat about him, he said, "Here are my mother and my brothers! Whoever does the will of God is my brother, and sister, and mother" (Mark 3:31–35).

She concludes: "The discipleship community abolishes the claims of the patriarchal family and constitutes a new familial community, one that does not include fathers in its circle" (p. 147).

Certainly this does not mean that men who participated in the procreation of children were not part of the community. But that the word "father" is not used is significant. In order to understand the implication of refraining from using the word "father," Fiorenza looks at those texts that describe the new family as one of equal discipleship (Mark 10:42–45 and 9:33–37; Matt. 20:26–27 and Luke 22:24–27; Mark 9:35–37, Matt. 18:1–4, Luke 9:48). Matt. 23:8–11 is especially significant for it is here that Jesus advocates calling "no man your father on earth." She comes to the conclusion that the discipleship of Jesus rejects the label and role of father for any human person because "it [the community of disciples] is sustained by the gracious goodness of God whom the disciples and Jesus call 'father'" (p. 150). The term "father" is not to be used to justify patriarchal relationships in the community. Reserving the term for God is intended "precisely to reject all such claims, powers, and structures" (p. 150). "Thus liberation from patriarchal structures is not only explicitly articulated by Jesus but is in fact at the heart of proclamation" (p. 151).

From her work Fiorenza proposes to draw strength for women in overcoming sexism and prejudice, especially that encountered within religion. But there are equally important implications to be drawn for Christian philosophy. If we acknowledge our roots in biblical tradition as important presuppositions to our work, then we must also acknowledge as part of our anthropological and political commitments the community of equality and the overcoming of patriarchy. More particularly, we must be committed to the visibility of women as women and be bold enough to follow out the implications of that commitment. If the name "Father" was to be reserved for God, but has been usurped by men within the family and within the church to perpetuate patriarchal structure, then how do we name God?

III. NAMING THE SACRED

In his insightful and formative work on symbols, Paul Tillich shows why we must be wary of identifying our symbols of the sacred, the ultimate, with the fullness of such a reality (pp. 41–54). Symbols point beyond themselves to the reality that they symbolize. But they also participate in that reality. It becomes easy for us to mistake that participation for the fullness of the reality. Our symbol may limit that which is symbolized and may even lead us to understand that which is symbolized in a fundamentally incorrect manner. This incorrect understanding can have destructive consequences for the religious community.

In a patriarchal society, it is very easy to slip into such problems when we use the word "Father" as a primary symbol for the sacred. While some fathers in our society take on work that has traditionally been the task of mothers, it is still the case that the title "Father" is used only of men and connotes patriarchal authority. Our concept of Father may include love, but it also includes a sense of distance and ultimate control. If we call the sacred "Father," then our image of the sacred includes these characteristics. If we limit the symbols we use of the sacred to the point that this is one of the few allowable symbols and we combine that symbol with those of Lord and Master, we define the sacred in a very limited and potentially destructive manner. The symbol serves to limit the possibility of other aspects of the sacred being present to us.

Religious feminists have addressed this problem by suggesting that we need a wide range of names for the sacred. Many do not totally reject "Father" as a way of naming the sacred, but suggest that also making use of other names will better enable us to experience the fullness of the sacred. Rosemary Ruether suggests that using the name "God/ess" would help us overcome the dualism of nature and spirit. She explains,

> The God/ess who is the foundation (at one and the same time) of our being and our new being embraces both the roots of the material substratum of our existence (matter) and also the endlessly new creative potential (spirit). The God/ess who is the foundation of our being-new being does not lead us back to a stifled, dependent self or uproot us in a spirit-trip outside the earth. Rather it leads us to the converted center, the harmonization of self and body, self and other, self and world. It is the *Shalom* of our being (p. 71).

Elizabeth Dodson Gray, who is also concerned that our images of the sacred should help us reaffirm our role in what she calls an ecological web, suggests that we image God as the power of transformation, or as "the pulse that keeps everything not only in place, but also resonating, moving, and continually transformed and new" (Johnson and Kalven, p. 55).

Letty Russell, in *Human Liberation in a Feminist Perspective—A Theology,* reminds us that we need not go outside of the Christian biblical and ecclesiastical traditions to find other names for God (pp. 98–103). She points to the image of God as servant in Genesis, Exodus, Isaiah, Mark, and Philippians. God is described as analogous to a female bird protecting her young (Ps. 17:8; 36:7; 57:1; 91:1, 4; Isa. 31:5). And finally, she reminds us that there is biblical precedent for naming God "mother" and "wife" (Ps. 51; Deut. 32:18; Isa. 46:3; 51:1; 49:14–15; Ps. 131:2).

Naming the sacred "mother" not only has Biblical basis, it also has a certain history of use. For example, there is Mary Baker Eddy's inclusive term, "Mother-Father God" (Ruether, p. 69) with which many people have grown up.[3] The name "mother" seems particularly important for helping in overcoming the continued power of patriarchal structures in Christian society.

The work of Sallie McFague outlines some of the implications of addressing the sacred as "mother." McFague tends to use the words "maternal" and "parental" interchangeably, and emphasizes that the work of parenting is done by women and men. She does suggest that one of the important effects of using mother as a model or symbol for God is that it requires Christians to focus on the acts of conception, gestation, and birth. While Christians have traditionally been comfortable with the notion of "second birth," they have tended to shy away from birth imagery for creation. She says,

> it is the imagery of gestation, giving birth, and lactation that creates an imaginative picture of creation as profoundly dependent on and cared

[3]Sallie McFague reports Herbert Richardson's story of saying his nightly prayer: "Father-Mother God, loving me, guard me while I sleep, guide my little feet up to thee" (p. 137).

> for by divine life. There is no other imagery available to us that has this power for expressing the interdependence and interrelatedness of all life with its grounds (p. 146).

If the image of mother were used more openly in the tradition, a fuller understanding of God's relation to the world might emerge. This could facilitate the experience of God as intimate and caring. (For an example of the change that this symbol can bring about, try singing "He's Got the Whole World in His Hands" changing the symbol from father to mother, "She's Got the Whole World in Her Hands.")

McFague also suggests that this model for God's agapic love is one that focuses on the importance of nurturing and fulfillment. Mother-God cares "about the most basic needs of life in its struggle to continue" (p. 147). Moreover, "God as mother is parent to *all* species and wishes all to flourish" (p. 148).

Certainly, as Tillich has cautioned, every symbol for the sacred has its limitations. The limitations of the image of father have clearly been to reinforce patriarchy and thus to alienate at least some humans from the divine. The symbol of mother will also have its limitations. But anticipation of these limitations should not prevent us from incorporating the power of this symbol into our Christian imagery.

IV. MATERNAL WORK, MATERNAL THINKING, AND MOTHER-GOD

In the context of this paper, I can neither set out nor develop all of the implications of incorporating the image of Mother-God into Christian symbolism and thus into the presuppositions of Christian philosophy arising out of the image of Mother-God. Since most of those working in Christian philosophy are men, many of whom identify with the name "father," I wish to stress that these suggestions are not intended to set mother against father. They are intended to lead to further reflection on the implications of including the image of mother.

There are many feminist philosophers who are reflecting on the **epistemological** and ethical implications of the work of mothering (see Trebilcot). These reflections come from a wide range of feminist perspectives. Sara Ruddick's recent book, *Maternal Thinking,* is not particularly aimed at the Christian community and does not discuss the issue of God language. I will, however, present aspects of her work showing how these contribute to the discussion of what it means to speak of Mother-God.

Ruddick begins her analysis from the perspective that she terms "practicalism." She explains,

> From the practicalist view, thinking arises from and is tested against practices. Practices are collective human activities distinguished by the aims that identify them and by the consequent demands made on practitioners committed to those aims (pp. 13–14).

It is from within the context of our practice that we raise questions, judge these questions to be sensible, determine criteria of truth and falsity, and determine what will count as evidence. In other words, practice and thinking are radically interconnected. Her contention is that the maternal practice gives rise to maternal thinking. She acknowledges that mothers as individuals are diverse and shaped by many practices. She focuses on the demands that all mothers must face and the disciplined reflection that arises out of the attempts to meet those demands. She, like McFague, does not restrict the activity of mothering to women. Men also perform maternal labor. She does think that mothering is far more often the work of women than of men that we should be careful not to gloss over the labor of carrying and giving birth which only women do. In order not to conceal women's role she emphasizes the importance of retaining the word "maternal" rather than using "parental."

I find her work helpful to the task of thinking about the image of Mother-God. If God is our mother, then we are imaging Mother-God as carrying out certain practices and as thinking in ways similar to humans who carry out these practices.

She suggests that maternal practice is founded on giving birth, for "To give birth is to create a new life" (p. 49). But as important as this practice is, once there is new creation all mothers are in a sense adoptive. "Mothering is a sustained response to the promise embedded in that creation" (49). Ruddick identifies three demands that all mothers face that are correlated with three sorts of maternal practice. The demands are for preservation, growth, and social acceptability. The work required is that of preservative love, nuturance, and training (p. 17). Ruddick does not idealize the role of mother in her analysis. She uses stories that emphasize that the practice of mothering is a struggle, sometimes even a struggle against our own violence.[4] Yet, she believes that out of this practice and struggle certain cognitive capacities can and do arise. Reflecting on these helps us better to understand what it means to be a mother.

The first demand, that for preservation, requires the mother to develop "cognitive capacities and virtues of protective control" (p. 71). One capacity that mothers often develop is what Ruddick calls the scrutinizing gaze. Children must be watched, but not watched too closely. It is not that mothers relinquish control. They come to think about it differently. Often because of desire to resort either to domination or passivity, mothers can come to recognize the patience required in order to exhibit appropriate control. If children are to survive they must be protected, and yet they must learn to deal with their world, both social and natural. The practice of mothering tends to lead to the development of an ability to identify danger and to deal with it, not always by eliminating that danger, but by helping the child to deal with the danger. Sometimes that means helping the child to die.

Christian philosophers may be able to use this notion of the scrutinizing gaze of Mother-God in reflections on **theodicy.** If the preservative love of Mother-God is of this sort, then we should not be expected to be protected from all evil. On the other hand, we should expect a hopeful and supportive presence to help us face and cope with our lives. If God's power is not so much that of total control as of helping us deal with the real dangers of our existence, then the concern of theodicy may be to show how a caring Mother-God helps us to confront and cope with the real dangers and griefs of our lives. The expectation is not that Mother-God will prevent all evil. Rather, the power of Mother-God is to help us preserve ourselves so that we may grow and flourish. I am not suggesting that this image will solve the problems of reconciling a good God with the existence of evil. Like human mothers, Mother-God may be experienced as destructive rather than preservative. That the image contributes to the complexity of the issue should not count against its significance.

The second demand that Ruddick identifies is for growth. This demand results in the development of ways of thinking that help the mother and child grow and change. Ruddick identifies storytelling as one of these cognitive practices (p. 101). She says

> I believe that many mothers more or less consciously recognize the importance of good maternal narratives and identify realism, compassion, and delight as among their stories' virtues (p. 101).

To tell a child a story is to help that child incorporate change into an ongoing unity. It is to help the child and the mother to share a history.

Thinking of Mother-God as storyteller seems very compatible with the image of God as presented in Christian scriptures and traditions. The stories presented there tell of a ***Heilsgeschichte,*** a history of the presence and activity of the divine in and with human history. The notion of Mother-God can augment this tradition. The contribution of this aspect of maternal work to Christian philosophy may be to direct us to focus more on narrative and the use of narrative in legitimating philosophical as well as religious presuppositions.

The third demand, that for social acceptance, requires the work of training. Ruddick describes training as a work of conscience. The work of training is to help "a child to be the kind of person whom others can accept and whom the mothers themselves

[4]Sara Ruddick tells the story of a young mother who had an infant that cried through the nights. One night she shut herself from the child's room until she was composed enough to take the child out into the night. They rode the bus all night, protected by the presence of strangers. Feeling great guilt, the mother confided her tendency to violence to another who replied that what was important was what the young mother had done. She had done what was necessary to protect the child from herself (pp. 66–67).

can actively appreciate" (p. 104). Again, mothers must struggle against the tendency to dominate. There are many pressures placed on mothers, many of whom are quite young, to have well-behaved children. I remember well the pressure on me to toilet train my son. One person claimed that all of her children were trained by nine months—so mine should be too. A mother is pushed to examine her own conscience as she tries to give guidance to her children. Perhaps the child could be trained at nine months, but what sort of power would that require and what sort of relation would it establish? The work of training requires the mother to trust herself and to be sensitive to the spirit of her child. Ruddick suggests that when this practice is developed at its best, mother becomes more trustworthy so that the child can be trustworthy. Moreover, the child comes to recognize that when trust breaks down, as it inevitably does, it is proper to protest.

If Mother-God is our trainer, our guide in coming to conscience, then she is one who is our help in the ongoing struggle to develop our human goodness and trust. We look to her not as a source of all answers or as a dominating rule to be obeyed. She is a help, a guide, a refuge. She recognizes that the work of conscience is a struggle, ongoing and often difficult. For Christian philosophy, this image might contribute to discussions of a **soul-making theodicy.** For example, this image of God supports John Hick's claim that it would be contradictory to conceive of a God as creating human beings such "that they could be guaranteed freely to respond" to God "in authentic faith and love and worship" (p. 311).

The image of Mother-God as part of the ongoing development of conscience may also contribute to **process theology.** Reflecting on how human parents change when they both trust and are trusted by their children could contribute to the process claim that God is, at least in one respect changing. Such reflection could also provide a way of understanding God as both changing and unchanging. The mothering person may be very trustworthy to begin with, but in concretely exhibiting that characteristic, by being self-reflective about trustworthiness, and by being trusted by a child, may be said to be more trustworthy. So also, Mother-God might be said to be trustworthy and yet to become more trustworthy in the process of divine-human relationships. Indeed, the image of Mother-God may be better received by process **theology** than by other forms of Christian theology because process thought is already inclined to be open to changing images of God as well as to a changing God.

V. CONCLUSION

There is much more work going on in feminist religious and philosophical thought. Most of it remains to be incorporated into the work of Christian philosophy. What I have touched on in this paper only gives some suggestions for a beginning. In Alvin Plantinga's advice, with which I began, he warned us to be "wary about assimilating or accepting presently popular philosophical ideas and procedures" (p. 271). Some of you may be wary of developing feminist Christian philosophy, thinking that you are assimilating that which comes from outside the tradition. I have chosen to look primarily at thinkers who show us the basis of feminist work from within the Christian tradition.

Reflecting on their work leads me to conclude that the autonomy, integrity, and boldness that Plantinga called for is advanced by the work of feminists. In particular, the integration of the name "Mother" for the sacred may help us relate to God in ways that enable us to develop these very virtues and thereby strengthen Christian philosophy.

BIBLIOGRAPHY

Baron, Dennis. *Grammar and Gender.* New Haven: Yale University Press, 1986.

Belenky, Mary Field, Blyth McVicker Clinchy, Nancy Rule Goldberger, and Jill Mattick Tarule. *Women's Ways of Knowing: the Development of Self, Voice, and Mind.* New York: Basic Books, 1986.

de Beauvoir, Simone. *The Second Sex.* New York: Alfred A. Knopf, 1972.

Fiorenza, Elizabeth Schüssler. *In Memory of Her: A Feminist Theological Reconstruction of Christian Origins.* New York: Crossroad, 1989.

Frank, Francine and Frank Anshen. *Language and the Sexes.* Albany: State University of New York Press, 1983.

Gray, Elizabeth Dodson. *Green Paradise Lost.* Wellesley, Massachusetts: Roundtable, 1981.

Gray, Elizabeth Dodson. *Patriarchy as a Conceptual Trap.* Wellesley, Massachusetts: Roundtable, 1982.

Heyward, Isabel Carter. *The Redemption of God: A Theology of Mutual Relation.* Lanham, Maryland: University Press of America, 1982.

Hick, John. *Evil and the God of Love.* London: Collins, 1970.

Johnson, Patricia Altenbernd, and Janet Kalven, eds. *With Both Eyes Open: Seeing Beyond Gender.* New York: The Pilgrim Press, 1988.

McFague, Sallie. "God as Mother," in *Weaving the Visions,* eds. Judith Plaskow and Carol P. Christ. San Francisco: Harper and Row, 1989.

Plantinga, Alvin. "Advice to Christian Philosophers," *Faith and Philosophy,* volume 1, number 3 (1984), pp. 253–271.

Rich, Adriene. *The Dream of a Common Language.* New York: W.W. Norton, 1978.

Ruddick, Sara. *Maternal Thinking: Toward a Politics of Peace.* Boston: Beacon, 1989.

Ruether, Rosemary Radford. *Sexism and God-Talk.* Boston: Beacon Press, 1983.

Russell, Letty M. *Human Liberation in a Feminist Perspective—A Theology.* Philadelphia: Westminster, 1974.

Segundo, Juan. *The Liberation of Theology.* Maryknoll, New York: Orbis Books, 1976.

Tillich, Paul. *Dynamics of Faith.* New York: Harper and Row, 1957.

Trebilcot, Joyce. *Mothering: Essays in Feminist Theory.* Totowa, New Jersey: Rowman and Allanheld, 1983.

Vetterling-Braggin, Mary. *Sexist Language.* New York: Littlefield, Adams, 1981.

STUDY QUESTIONS

1. Johnson says that all understanding, once engaged, carries presuppositions. What does she mean by this claim?

2. How does Christian theism carry the presupposition of patriarchy, according to Johnson?

3. What evidence does Johnson offer that the community of Jesus includes women?

4. What images of God does feminist theology emphasize?

5. *Suppose someone objects to Johnson that she is inconsistent in claiming both that Christianity is patriarchal and that Jesus included women in his community. How do you think she would respond to this objection?

6. *Does feminism cohere with the religious tradition with which you are most familiar? Explain.

7. *In your opinion, do the images of "Father" and "Master" serve a positive function? Should a feminist seek to preserve a role for them? Why or why not?

FURTHER READING FOR CHAPTER TWO

Negative Theology and the Theory of Analogy

Alston, William. "Aquinas on Theological Predication: A Look Backward and a Look Forward." In *Reasoned Faith,* edited by Eleonore Stump. Ithaca, NY: Cornell University Press, 1993.

Alston, William. *Divine Nature and Human Language.* Ithaca, NY: Cornell University Press, 1989.

Benor, Ehud. "Meaning and Reference in Maimonides' Negative Theology." *Harvard Theological Review* 88, 3 (1995):339–60.

Broadie, Alexander. "Maimonides and Aquinas on the Names of God." *Religious Studies* 23 (1987): 157–70.

Palmer, Humphrey. *Analogy: A Study of Qualification and Argument In Theology.* London: MacMillan, 1973.

Putnam, Hilary. "Thoughts Addressed to an Analytical Thomist." *The Monist* 80 (1997):487–99.

Putnam, Hilary. "On Negative Theology." *Faith and Philosophy* 14, 4 (1997):407–22.

Ross, James F. "Analogy and the Resolution of Some Cognitivity Problems." *The Journal of Philosophy* 67 (1970):725–46.

Biblical Interpretation

Fredosso, Alfred. "The 'Openness' of God: A Reply to Hasker." *Christian Scholars' Review* 28 (1998): 124–39.

Frei, Hans. *Theology and Narrative,* edited by G. Hunsinger and William C. Placher. New York: Oxford University Press, 1993.

G. R. Evans, ed., *The Language and Logic of the Bible: The Earlier Middle Ages.* Cambridge, England: Cambridge University Press, 1984.

G. R. Evans, ed., *The Language and Logic of the Bible: The Reformation.* Cambridge, England: Cambridge University Press, 1985.

Ricouer, Paul. *Essays on Biblical Interpretation.* Philadelphia: Fortress Press, 1980.

Sternberg, Meir. *The Poetics of Biblical Narrative.* Bloomington, IN: Indiana University Press, 1981, chaps. 1–5.

Stump, Eleonore and Flint, Thomas P., eds. *Hermes and Athena: Biblical Exegesis and Philosophical Theology.* Notre Dame, IN: Notre Dame University Press, 1993.

Swinburne, Richard. *Revelation.* New York: Oxford, Clarendon Press, 1992.

Wolterstorff, Nicholas. *Divine Discourse: Philosophical Reflections on the Claim that God Speaks.* Cambridge: Cambridge University Press, 1995.

Feminist Theology

Hampson, D. *Swallowing a Fishbone? Feminist Theologians Debate Christianity.* London: SPCK, 1996.

Jantzen, Grace. "Feminists, Philosophers, and Mystics." *Hypatia* 9 (1994):186–206.

Jantzen, Grace. "What's the Difference? Knowledge and Gender in Postmodern Philosophy of Religion." *Religious Studies* 32 (1996):431–48.

Suchoki, Marjorie Hewitt. "The Idea of God in Feminist Philosophy." *Hypatia* 9 (1994):56–67.

CHAPTER 3

The Theistic Religious Life

In chapters 1 and 2, we focused on clarifying some beliefs held by theists (specifically, their beliefs about the nature of God). But religions, whether theistic or nontheistic, usually demand of their adherents more than beliefs alone. Most religions prescribe certain behaviors in the form of what is called ritual. The Christian performs a baptism; the Muslim circles a cubelike structure known as the Kabah and kisses the Black stone on a pilgrimage to Mecca; the Jew blows the *shofar* (ram's horn) on the New Year; some Buddhists practice *jhanas,* prescribed stages of meditation. A widespread practice is prayer—required in Islam five times daily and in Judaism three times daily—in which worshippers thank, praise, and petition God. These and many other acts fall under the category of ritual.

In addition to rituals, religions prescribe certain emotions. For example, the Bible calls on human beings to love and to fear (or, perhaps more accurately, be in awe of) God. People are asked to love their neighbor, to forgive those who have hurt them, and to express other sentiments, at appropriate times and in appropriate circumstances.

Thus, there is more to religions than belief. A rounded religious existence, it would appear, contains all three constituents: belief, action, and emotion.

It was once fashionable for philosophers to take a **noncognitivist** view of religious statements. In this approach, religious statements such as *God is good* are not the expression of a belief in the truth of a *proposition* concerning a supernatural entity. Instead (to cite but one alternative view) such statements are an expression of a resolve to love others or to act in certain ways. **Noncognitivism,** loosely associated with the great Austrian philosopher, Ludwig Wittgenstein (1889–1951), has recently declined in popularity. It is too extreme in ignoring the cognitive component. But noncognitivism is decidely correct when it identifies components of commitment other than beliefs, and any serious treatment of religion has to confront the philosophical difficulties these components entail. In fact, even when we speak of religious belief, it is obvious that religious belief typically is of such centrality in a person's life and carries so many affective and behavioral consequences that we could hardly compare it to, say, a belief that the local grocery stocks vanilla ice cream.

RITUALS

What is a person really doing when praying, bowing, eating, or drinking as part of a ritual? What is the meaning of these practices? How are they to be explained to nonbelievers? Turning to the affective, or emotional, component of commitment, what is a believer experiencing when feeling awe or when submitting to a command of God? What are the affective and behavioral aspects of religious life—or at least theistic religious life—all about?

We begin the chapter with a challenge posed by Plato. Speaking through the character of Socrates, Plato wonders in the dialogue *Euthryphro:* why do the gods want our service? Surely we human beings cannot provide benefits to the gods. Why, then, should we serve them through sacrifice and prayer?

Plato concludes his discussion without a satisfactory answer. However, a rather obvious strategy is to reject Socrates' assumption that service of the gods is designed to benefit the gods. Perhaps rituals are, for example, meant to benefit those who perform them. Perhaps they help believers properly express certain emotions that they ought to feel, such as gratitude to God, or help them act out certain beliefs.

Josef Stern's essay suggests a variety of ways to understand rituals of Judaism as symbolic gestures. Concluding the selections on ritual, Michael J. Murray and Kurt Meyers inquire into petitionary prayer. Why does God grant certain goods to Jones only if Jones, or others who care about Jones, request these goods? Should God not give people like Jones what they need and deserve, regardless of whether they ask for it?

MORALITY AND RELIGION

Let us turn from ritual to another type of behavior associated with religion: compliance with moral principles that govern relations between people. Stealing and taking life gratuitously are prohibited by most societies. In the view of theists, they are also prohibited by God (in the Ten Commandments). Others of God's commands may require a person to experience certain emotions, have certain thoughts, or develop certain character traits; nonbelievers likewise look on those emotions, thoughts, and traits as morally good.

Why is there this convergence between moral demands and religious ones? Are God's commandments and prohibitions the basis of moral rules and value judgments? Is it the other way around—is morality the basis for God's commandments and prohibitions? Or is the convergence just a coincidence?

Many theists have maintained that morality is dependent on religion in one way or another. Ivan Karamazov, a character of Dostoevsky, suggests an especially tight dependence when he flatly declares, "If there is no God, everything is permitted." For Ivan, without a God who commands and prohibits human deeds and who approves or disapproves of our actions, there is no right and wrong. One way of developing this idea is to argue that moral terms must be defined in terms of God's command. Let us call such a view a **divine command theory of ethics.** The divine command thesis goes well beyond the claim that God's promised rewards and threatened punishments provide special incentive to act morally, so that morality depends *psychologically* on religious belief. Furthermore, the theory does not merely say that morality depends **epistemically** on religion—that is, that we need God's command to know how to act. Rather, the divine command theory submits that morality depends **metaphysically** or **ontologically** on God's issuance of commands (or, in another variant, God's adoption of attitudes). Acts simply *are not right or wrong* unless God commands (or wills) something about them. Someone once cleverly described this view as follows: subtract "God" from "Good," and you are left with "0" (a zero). To reject the divine command theory is to hold that there is, perhaps must be, a standard of ethics that is independent of God's will or command.

One of the oldest formulations of the divine command (perhaps, more accurately in this case, divine will) view is provided by the title character in Plato's dialogue *Euthyphro.* Euthyphro asserts that *by definition* "the pious is what all the gods love." Socrates, representing Plato's position, offers a famous refutation of this view. Janine Marie Idziak, in the next selection, catalogues numerous reasons for adopting or rejecting a divine command theory. As you will see from the reading by Idziak, one key issue about divine command theories concerns the nature of God. Socrates' rejection of Euthyphro's view depends on a conception of the gods as wise, rational, and nonarbitrary. Divine command theorists highlight, by contrast, the deity's freedom and power.

Earlier we noted the considerable overlap between God's commands and commonly accepted moral truths, principles, and rules. What, however, if God commands a person to do something contrary to morality? Divine command theorists think that such situations are impossible; after all, they hold, God's commands determine what is morally right and wrong. Furthermore, even those theists who believe that morality is binding independently of religion are not likely to see a command of God as truly being *in conflict with* morality, for God is morally perfect and so will not violate morality. However, the Danish philosopher Søren Kierkegaard (1813–1855) takes a position that differs from both divine command theories and the view usually taken by those who think morality is binding independently of religion. Kierkegaard acknowledges the binding nature of morality. Even so, he asserts that a certain type of person of faith, whom he calls the knight of faith, will be prepared to violate moral principles when asked by God to do so. Kierkegaard's focus is Genesis 22, where God commands Abraham to sacrifice his son Isaac on Mount Moriah. His thesis is that Abraham's readiness to carry out the command demonstrates his faith.

In sharp contrast to Kierkegaard, James Rachels maintains that a person like Abraham, who worships God and is prepared to do whatever God requests—even if it is contrary to his own moral judgment—vacates the role of moral agent. This is because such a person abandons **autonomy**—self-rule. Such a person is always prepared to submit to the will of another.

UNDERSTANDING RITUAL

READING 3.1

A Puzzle About Ritual

Plato

The works of Plato (427–347 B.C.E.) are written in the literary form known as a dialogue, or a conversation among characters, with Socrates usually occupying center stage and serving as Plato's mouthpiece. Many of Plato's dialogues are named after a central character, and several take as their central philosophical focus a question of the form "What is X?" The dialogue form helps create the back-and-forth argumentation, the **dialectic,** *characteristic of philosophical discussion.*

The dialogue Euthyphro *is named for the interlocutor (co-discussant) of that name. In the work, Socrates inquires into the nature of "piety." Euthyphro has attempted some answers to this question, and Socrates has refuted each suggestion. As the conversation continues in this selection (taken from the dialogue's second half,* viz., *12e–15c), Euthyphro suggests that piety is the care of the gods, just as cattle raising is the care of cattle (to use an analogy that Socrates deploys when he seeks to clarify the position). Care of the gods is expressed through service of them, such as prayer and sacrifice. To serve the gods, Socrates suggests, is to beg from them (as in prayer) or give to them (as in sacrifice).*

However, Socrates points out that to care for something is to achieve something for the object cared for, to benefit it in some way. He asks how the gods benefit from our service. What do pious actions achieve for them? It seems that the benefit is all one way—from them to us. Why the gods want our service is therefore puzzling, and the reading ends with no satisfactory answer.

E: I think, Socrates, that the godly and pious is the part of the just that is concerned with the care of the gods, while that concerned with the care of men is the remaining part of justice.

S: You seem to me to put that very well, but I still need a bit of information. I do not know yet what you mean by care, for you do not mean the care of the gods in the same sense as the care of other things, as, for example, we say, don't we, that not everyone knows how to care for horses, but the horse breeder does.

E: Yes, I do mean it that way.

S: So horse breeding is the care of horses.

E: Yes.

S: Nor does everyone know how to care for dogs, but the hunter does.

E: That is so.

S: So hunting is the care of dogs.

E: Yes.

S: And cattle raising is the care of cattle.

E: Quite so.

S: While piety and godliness is the care of the gods, Euthyphro. Is that what you mean?

E: It is.

S: Now care in each case has the same effect; it aims at the good and the benefit of the object cared for, as you can see that horses cared for by horse breeders are benefited and become better. Or do you not think so?

E: I do.

S: So dogs are benefited by dog breeding, cattle by cattle raising, and so with all the others. Or do you think that care aims to harm the object of its care?

E: By Zeus, no.

S: It aims to benefit the object of its care?

E: Of course.

S: Is piety then, which is the care of the gods, also to benefit the gods and make them better? Would you agree that when you do something pious you make some one of the gods better?

E: By Zeus, no.

S: Nor do I think that this is what you mean—far from it—but that is why I asked you what you meant by the care of gods, because I did not believe you meant this kind of care.

E: Quite right, Socrates, that is not the kind of care I mean.

S: Very well, but what kind of care of the gods would piety be?

E: The kind of care, Socrates, that slaves take of their masters.

S: I understand. It is likely to be a kind of service of the gods.

E: Quite so.

S: Could you tell me to the achievement of what goal service to doctors tends? Is it not, do you think, to achieving health?

E: I think so.

S: What about service to shipbuilders? To what achievement is it directed?

E: Clearly, Socrates, to the building of a ship.

S: And service to housebuilders to the building of a house?

E: Yes.

S: Tell me then, my good sir, to the achievement of what aim does service to the gods tend? You obviously know since you say that you, of all men, have the best knowledge of the divine.

E: And I am telling the truth, Socrates.

S: Tell me then, by Zeus, what is that excellent aim that the gods achieve, using us as their servants?

E: Many fine things, Socrates.

S: So do generals, my friend. Nevertheless you could easily tell me their main concern, which is to achieve victory in war, is it not?

E: Of course.

S: The farmers too, I think, achieve many fine things, but the main point of their efforts is to produce food from the earth.

E: Quite so.

S: Well then, how would you sum up the many fine things that the gods achieve?

E: I told you a short while ago, Socrates, that it is a considerable task to acquire any precise knowledge of these things, but, to put it simply, I say that if a man knows how to say and do what is pleasing to the gods at prayer and sacrifice, those are pious actions such as preserve both private houses and public affairs of state. The opposite of these pleasing actions are impious and overturn and destroy everything.

S: You could tell me in far fewer words, if you were willing, the sum of what I asked, Euthyphro, but you are not keen to teach me, that is clear. You were on the point of doing so, but you turned away. If you had given that answer, I should now have acquired from you sufficient knowledge of the nature of piety. As it is, the lover of inquiry must follow his beloved wherever it may lead him. Once more then, what do you say that piety and the pious are? Are they a knowledge of how to sacrifice and pray?

E: They are.

S: To sacrifice is to make a gift to the gods, whereas to pray is to beg from the gods?

E: Definitely, Socrates.

S: It would follow from this statement that piety would be a knowledge of how to give to, and beg from, the gods.

E: You understood what I said very well, Socrates.

S: That is because I am so desirous of your wisdom, and I concentrate my mind on it, so that no word of yours may fall to the ground. But tell me, what is this service to the gods? You say it is to beg from them and to give to them?

E: I do.

S: And to beg correctly would be to ask from them things that we need?

E: What else?

S: And to give correctly is to give them what they need from us, for it would not be skillful to bring gifts to anyone that are in no way needed.

E: True, Socrates.

S: Piety would then be a sort of trading skill between gods and men?

E: Trading yes, if you prefer to call it that.

S: I prefer nothing, unless it is true. But tell me, what benefit do the gods derive from the gifts they receive from us? What they give us is obvious to all. There is for us no good that we do not receive from them, but how are they benefited by what they receive from us? Or do we have such an advantage over them in the trade that we receive all our blessings from them and they receive nothing from us?

E: Do you suppose, Socrates, that the gods are benefited by what they receive from us?

S: What could those gifts from us to the gods be, Euthyphro?

E: What else, do you think, than honour, reverence, and what I mentioned just now, gratitude?

S: The pious is then, Euthyphro, pleasing to the gods, but not beneficial or dear to them?

E: I think it is of all things most dear to them.

S: So the pious is once again what is dear to the gods.[1]

E: Most certainly.

S: When you say this, will you be surprised if your arguments seem to move about instead of staying put? And will you accuse me of being Daedalus who makes them move, though you are yourself much more skillful than Daedalus and make them go round in a circle? Or do you not realize that our argument has moved around and come again to the same place? You surely remember that earlier the pious and the god-beloved were shown not to be the same but different from each other. Or do you not remember?

E: I do.

S: Do you then not realize now that you are saying that what is dear to the gods is the pious? Is this not the same as the god-beloved? Or is it not?

E: It certainly is.

S: Either we were wrong when we agreed before, or, if we were right then, we are wrong now.

E: That seems to be so.

S: So we must investigate again from the beginning what piety is, as I shall not willingly give up before I learn this. . . .

[1][The meaning of the rest of the passage will be clear from the other Plato selection in this chapter, Reading 3.4—Ed.]

STUDY QUESTIONS

1. How does Euthyphro define *piety* in this selection?
2. What analogies does Socrates use to explain Euthyphro's view?
3. Why does Socrates find Euthyphro's view puzzling? What question is left unanswered?
4. *Plato (and Euthyphro) seem to suppose that honor, reverence, and gratitude can make sense only if the gods benefit from these. Do you agree with this assumption? Why or why not?
5. *This question is closely connected to question 4. Develop an account of a ritual (prayer of thanksgiving is a good example to work with) that does not suppose that ritual benefits the gods.

READING 3.2

Gesture and Symbol in Ritual

Josef Stern

Josef Stern's starting point in this essay is that gestures, like words, can symbolize or refer to themes or things. Gestures in Jewish rituals refer in three main ways: (1) representation: *for example, the shofar (Ram's horn) represents or denotes the sound heard at Mount Sinai, (2)* exemplification: *the flame lit immediately after the Sabbath ends exemplifies human creative activity, which was prohibited on the Sabbath itself; and (3)* expression: *this involves metaphorical exemplification of a fea-*

ture. Kissing the Torah scroll expresses love; bowing expresses respect and submission. Stern (University of Chicago) suggests, however, that rituals are multiply symbolic, referring simultaneously to different things according to distinct modes of symbolization. Sometimes the gesture is also linked to a figurative understanding of a scriptural verse, and sometimes one ritual is linked symbolically to another.

The terms shema *and* amidah *in Stern's essay refer to two of the important prayers in Jewish practice.* Sukkot *and* Shavuot *are holidays.*

Gestures—a term that can be used for both nonverbal objects and bodily movements—are among the most distinctive elements of Jewish ritual. Only a few have a practical purpose, for example, covering the eyes with the hand in order to concentrate while reciting the first verse of the *Shema.* Most are said to symbolize themes or feelings or to refer to historical events or **eschatological** experiences. Yet while the gestures are familiar and the claim that they are symbols oft repeated, it remains to be explained how they function as symbols or vehicles of reference—reserving these two general terms to cover all ways of bearing **semanticlike relations** to objects, events, and states of affairs. That is, in what ways—assuming that there are multiple modes of symbolization—do gestures in Jewish rituals symbolize or refer to themes or things? To take some first steps toward answering this question, I will construct a taxonomy of symbolic gestures in Jewish rites, drawing on various categories of reference first distinguished by Nelson Goodman and since elaborated by Israel Scheffler.[1]

Central to this approach is a distinction between the medium of the symbol and its mode of symbolization. Gestures in all mediums—olfactory, auditory, visual, and verbal—serve as symbols in the rituals of Judaism, but in each of these mediums there also function alternative modes of symbolization, different ways in which the gestures in that medium relate to what they purport to symbolize or stand for. Three modes prove especially prominent within Jewish ritual: representation or denotation, exemplification, and expression. A few gestures symbolize by just one of these modes, but what is characteristic of ritual gestures is that they are multiply symbolic: they simultaneously refer to different things according to distinct modes of symbolization, some through simple, single-mode referential relations, others through complex chains of reference that involve different mediums as well as different modes. Indeed, a distinctive feature of Jewish ritual is a type of multimedium symbolizing that combines the symbolic interpretation of a gesture with the figurative exegesis of a scriptural text.

To analyze their symbolic functioning, we can abstract ritual gestures from the religious, historical, and social contexts in which they originated and in which they are now employed, and from the various ways in which their symbolic meaning has changed over time. Important as these issues of genesis and transformation are, the concern here will be entirely with the structure of the gestures' symbolic meaning.

The first of the modes of symbolization is gestural denotation or representation, which is the same mode of reference as that employed by names that denote their bearers and pictures that represent their subjects. (I will assume that the notions of verbal denotation and pictorial representation are sufficiently clear for the purposes of this discussion, however difficult it may be to analyze them precisely). However, while pictorial representation and verbal denotation both comprise one mode of reference, that is not to deny all differences between pictures and words; some gestures portray or depict their referents after the manner of pictures or dramatic mime, while others describe or designate them like linguistic expressions.

The many ritual gestures said to commemorate significant events, individuals, or objects in the history of Israel utilize a mode of symbolization that is

[1]See Goodman, *Languages of Art* (2nd ed., 1976); Scheffler, "Ritual and Reference," *Synthese* 46 (March 1981).

almost always denotation or representation. Some gestures, for example, circumcision, which commemorates God's covenant with Abraham, seem to denote their referents simply by virtue of the fact that the Torah decrees, in the manner of a linguistic stipulation, what they symbolize. Others secure their denotation by depicting one or more of its features, for example, the *haroset* (a mixture of mashed fruits and nuts eaten at the Passover feast) denotes the mortar the Israelites made in Egypt by depicting its color, and the *shofar* (ram's horn blown at the High Holidays) denotes what was heard at Mt. Sinai by making a like sound. And some dramatically portray what they represent, for example, the Sephardic custom for the master of the *seder* (Passover feast) to lay the wrapped *afikoman* (the "dessert" *mazah*) on his shoulder, take a few steps, and say: "This is in memory of our forefathers, who left Egypt bearing their kneading troughs wrapped in their clothes upon their shoulders." Finally, yet other gestures denote figuratively or **metonymically,** for example, the (prohibited) sinew of the thigh, which commemorates Jacob's struggle with the Angel, or the ram's horn used for the *shofar,* which commemorates the binding of Isaac. Literal or figurative, all such commemoration is generally symbolization by denotation.

A second mode of symbolization is exemplification: reference by a gesture to a selected feature of which it is a sample. When is a gesture a sample of a feature? First, it is necessary, but not sufficient, that the gesture possess the feature. The tailor's swatch of cloth is typically a sample of—or exemplifies—its color or weave but not its size or shape, though it equally possesses all of these features. Those it exemplifies are those it both possesses and refers to, but what it refers to will vary from occasion to occasion with the purpose and context of the performance.

For example, Israel is commanded to bring as a thanksgiving offering "some of every first fruit of the soil" (Deut. 26:2), though the rabbis legislate that it is necessary to bring the first fruit only of the seven species mentioned in Deuteronomy 8:8. Nevertheless, in the typical context of performance the seven species used in the ritual will exemplify all the fruit of the soil. However, a performance of that same ritual may sometimes also serve to demonstrate to others the type of ritual of which it is a performance. For how people in fact learn a ritual generally is not by mastering rules or through explicit teaching but by observing actual performances, which thereby function as samples of their type of rite. For that purpose the above gesture must exemplify only those seven species, and no others, on pain of misrepresenting the ritual.

While denotation is the preponderant mode of reference for verbal languages and exemplification is more central to the arts, the two generally function in tandem in ritual gestures. Thus, the flame lit during the *havdalah* ceremony (marking the conclusion of the Sabbath) represents, and thereby commemorates, the first fire, said to have been created by Adam with divine assistance on the night following the Sabbath of Creation (cf. Babylonian Talmud, *Pesahim* 54a); at the same time, because it is also the first thing the individual produces by his own efforts after resting on the Sabbath, it also exemplifies human creative activity. Here, moreover, these two symbolic relations interact with each other and the halakhah [Jewish law], engendering still more symbolism. Among the many accounts and myths found throughout ancient literature in which the creation of fire is used to exemplify human creativity, the talmudic version of Adam's act, aided by God and commemorated with a blessing, (Babylonian Talmud, *Berakhot* 5) is unique, especially, as the late Saul Lieberman observed, in contrast to the Prometheus myth, in which man steals the original fire from Zeus and is punished for his act. For in making a blessing over the flame he brings into being, the individual acknowledges that the product of his own apparently free, creative action is ultimately due to God. Furthermore, once this blessing has been introduced, it brings in its train additional halakhically motivated gestures. Because such a blessing of enjoyment cannot be recited unless there is actual benefit from the object blessed, the light over which the blessing is made must serve some immediate good. Hence, the practitioner folds the palm of one hand, turns its back to the light, and opens it again, using the light to distinguish the tissue of the nail from the flesh and light from shadow. Although this last gesture is possibly the most unusual in the ritual, it is, ironically, the only one that is primarily practical—though it, too, comes to symbolize the distinction between the sacred and the profane, illustrating how symbolic meanings tend to be read into gestures in context even where the gestures would never have had these meanings in themselves.

Exemplification is not, however, limited to features the symbolic object literally possesses. A third mode by which ritual gestures symbolize is metaphorical exemplification or expression. A symbolic gesture expresses a feature if it metaphorically rather than literally possesses the feature and exemplifies it. Thus, a painting that is said to express solemnity is not literally, but only metaphorically, solemn. Similarly, many ritual gestures exemplify features, such as feelings or attitudes, that can be ascribed to them only metaphorically; consequently, in this sense, they are also expressed. Thus, bowing during the *Amidah* (the eighteen benedictions recited while standing) expresses respect for God and submission to his will; beating one's breast while confessing one's sins expresses regret and contrition; and kissing the Torah or *zizit* (knotted fringe of the prayer shawl) or touching one's *tefillin* [phylacteries] while praying, express feelings of love and affection for all *mizvot* [commandments], which are as a whole literally exemplified by the individual articles.

In each instance of exemplification and expression, it should be emphasized, what is symbolized is always a feature related to the symbolic gesture itself, not to its performer or his state. When a person bows during the *Amidah,* it is his gesture that expresses humility in the presence of God regardless of what he happens to feel or intend at that moment. Not that there is no connection between the features or feelings symbolized by the gesture and those felt or had by its performer. On the contrary, the point of ritual—here possibly in contrast to works of art—is to affect its performer by making him have certain feelings and by inspiring him with certain values. But the relation between the feelings and attitudes of the performer and those his gesture symbolizes is also more subtle than identity. Frequently the feeling excited in the performer is caused by, but quite different from, that expressed by the gesture. Thus Rabbi Moses Isserles, the Rama, cites the custom of the very observant to sway while reading or studying the Torah "after the example of the Torah which was given [at Sinai] with terror and shaking" (*Shulkhan Arukh* Code of Jewish Law, 48). But if the act of swaying is meant to express those feelings, that is not to say that the person studying Torah should himself be seized with terror and shaking—a state in which all productive study is obviously impossible. Rather, the point of the ritual is achieved when its performer appreciates what the gesture symbolizes and is thereby led to regard his study of the Torah with the appropriate seriousness. Moreover, this suggests a broader moral: the feeling aroused in the performer is never simply the effect of the performance per se, but of his understanding of its significance, his reflection on its meaning, and his performance of the ritual out of a realization of what it symbolizes.

Now, with these three basic modes of symbolization—denotation, exemplification, and expression—in hand, let us turn to gestures where they function not only concurrently but in combination, linked together in chains of reference. Consider the Passover *zeroa,* or shankbone, which is said to be "in remembrance of the Paschal sacrifice." According to the earliest reference to this symbol, which is found in Babylonian tractate *Pesahim* 114a, the mode by which it commemorates the historical sacrifice is entirely unrelated to its being a shankbone. Why, then, the *zeroa?* Because that limb is said to symbolize the "outstretched arm" (*zeroa netuyah*) with which God is described as having punished the Egyptians and redeemed Israel (Deut. 26:8). The object on the seder plate exemplifies the feature of being a shankbone, the name for which (*zeroa*), when applied to God in the Torah, metaphorically denotes his might and power: thus, the shankbone symbolizes God's might, but only through the mediation of the textual verse. A chain of reference extends here from the symbolic object to an exemplified feature, from there, in turn, to a scriptural use of the term for that feature and, finally, to the metaphorical denotation of the term in its scriptural context.

In this example, the figurative interpretation of the scriptural term determines but is not itself determined by the symbolic meaning of the gesture. In other cases, though, text and gesture are so closely connected that the symbolic interpretation of each is derived from the other. One further example of a ritual chain with a scriptural link will illustrate this.

Three aspects of the *lulav* (palm frond) ritual on *Sukkot* are given symbolic interpretations: the waving itself, that it accompanies the recital of certain verses in the *Hallel* (a selection of Psalms 113–18) and not others, and that the *lulav* is pointed and waved in all four directions as well as upward and downward. To explain the first two of these, Rabbi Asher ben Yehiel (Commentary on Babylonian Talmud, *Sukkah* 3, par. 26) cites a midrash according to which the nation of Israel received the *lulav* on *Sukkot* as a sign of celebration to hold aloft and thereby proclaim publicly that, among all the nations of the world who came before God to be judged on Rosh Hashanah and Yom Kippur, it had been judged innocent. While the palm may have been generally regarded at that time as a symbol of innocence or victory, certainly in this midrash the gesture, like waving a banner, expresses Israel's victorious elation. Further, by contrasting Israel with the nations, the midrash also makes the *lulav* into a national emblem. However, Rabbi Asher hints at still other symbolic interpretations for the gesture, linked to the verse "then shall all the trees of the forest shout for joy at the presence of the Lord, for He is coming to rule the earth" (I Chron. 16:33), which he cites as a proof-text of the midrash. Just as forest trees swaying in the wind can be seen as dancing in joy, so the motion of the *lulav* can be taken to depict a dance of rejoicing. And seeing the *lulav* as a sample of nature, the gesture might also exemplify the figurative meaning of the verse and, indeed, of much of the surrounding Chronicles chapter, which describes how the entire natural universe praises God. Rabbi Asher himself, though, connects the verse to the gesture differently. He figuratively reinterprets the verse to yield a description of the rabbinically defined ritual of *lulav.* The verse, in his account, is really elliptic. What it actually means, remembering the midrash, is that with "the trees of the forest"—standing for, and exemplified by, the tree-shaped *lulav*—Israel "shall rejoice before the Lord" after he has come to judge the world, that is, after the High Holidays. Moreover, because the two subsequent verses in Chronicles, 16:34–35, parallel almost verbatim the *Hallel* passages, Ps. 118:1–4, 25, accompanying which the *lulav* is waved, Rabbi Asher interprets those verses as literally exemplifying—as a sample of—the very words in the *Hallel* Israel is to recite while waving the *lulav.* Thus, in the one direction, the scriptural passage figuratively refers to the ritual of *lulav* in all its rabbinic detail; in the other direction, the gesture symbolizes the natural, the joyous, the victorious—the literal and figurative meanings of the verse. Both gesture and verse concurrently function as symbols, each complementing and commenting on the multiple interpretations of the other.

Finally, the *lulav* is waved in all directions. To explain its symbolism, the Talmud quotes a discussion of the same gesture employed in another ritual: the Temple rite of waving the altar loaves, also in all directions, on *Shavuot.* Two explanations are given. According to Rabbi Yohanan, the gesture symbolizes—in our terminology, expresses—homage to "he who is master of the four directions and the Heavens above and the Earth below"; according to the Palestinian rabbis in the name of Rabbi Yose bar Haninah, it serves to expel or avert evil spirits, a quasi-magical function reminiscent of, and perhaps in opposition to, pagan harvest rituals in which wind deities were summoned from all directions to bless the harvest (Babylonian Talmud, *Sukkah* 37; cf. also Babylonian Talmud, *Menahot* 61a).

Now, apart from the details of these explanations, this discussion also suggests yet a fifth mode of symbolization that holds between the two rituals themselves. By appealing to the *Shavuot* ritual to explain the style and symbolism of the otherwise unrelated *Sukkot* ritual, the rabbis establish a symbolic link between the two; the one is patterned after the other and thereby indirectly refers to it. Rabbi Yossi's opinion suggests a similar, though possibly even more indirect, way in which the common gesture in the two Jewish rituals refers to the antecedent pagan rite they were instituted to counteract. This mode of indirect reference from one gesture to another is not denotation, representation, exemplification, or expression. Instead, let us say that the one alludes to the other. Allusion is one among several referential relations that hold between parallel gestures that are performances of the same or different rituals. Although intersymbolic relations like allusion are often effected through intermediate features—for example, the *Sukkot* ritual alludes to the *Shavuot* rite by virtue of the same exemplified pattern of waving—if we arranged all referential relations in a hierarchy, the ultimate terms between which relations like allusion hold would all be located on one symbolic level.

Probably the most familiar intergestural symbolic relation is reenactment. One gesture reenacts another only if the two are replicas of one another, that is, only if they are performances of the same type of ritual. However, reenactment is not merely a matter of performing another replica repeating past performances. One reenacts a ritual only if one also performs it aware that one's gesture is a replica of past performances, that the given performance belongs to a succession of parallel performances, and, with this historical perspective, that it falls within a tradition. In this specific sense of the term reenactment should not, then, be confused with commemoration. A gestural symbol, like any other singular thing, can be denoted—and thus commemorated—by another symbol, but what a given ritual performance reenacts is its replicas qua fellow performances of the same ritual type. Thus, a typical performance of the Sabbath ritual commemorates, by denoting, the creation, but it reenacts past performances of the Sabbath ritual itself. Yet what is also characteristic of many rituals in Judaism, is that, as they have historically evolved, they have explicitly incorporated within the very structure of later performances of a given ritual denotative references to earlier performances of the same ritual, performances that the present one reenacts. By thus combining commemorative denotation with reenactment, Jewish ritual achieves the sense of constantly—and quite literally—performing the old anew.

An example is the act of prostration performed as part of the recital of the *Avodah,* the description of the sacrificial service conducted in the ancient Temple, during the *Musaf* (additional) service of Yom Kippur. Three times during this narration, we tell how the congregation in the Temple court "fell upon their knees, prostrated themselves, and worshipped" when they heard "God's glorious and revered name clearly expressed by the High Priest"; and at exactly those moments it is now customary for present congregants to fall upon their faces, prostrating themselves. At least three different modes of symbolization are at work in this gesture. First, the narration as a whole commemorates—by descriptive denotation—the ancient Temple service; and the act of prostration, acting out one element in this narrative, depicts the historical gesture. However, our present prostration is not just a matter of denoting ancestral acts. Certainly a central aim of the intense poetic account is for present congregants, listening to the reader describe how the high priest pronounced the name of God, to imagine that the reader has now himself called out God's name and spontaneously, overcome with awe and emotion, prostrate themselves. The gesture, then, further expresses a feeling in its own right, though of the same type as that expressed by the historical gesture it denotes. And, finally, inasmuch as the present prostration replicates past performances of the same ritual, it also reenacts them. Like the recitation of the *Avodah,* which also parallels the actual sacrificial service (cf. Rashi, Commentary on Babylonian Talmud *Yoma* 36b, 56b), our gesture of prostration parallels, and thus indirectly refers to, all past performances of the same type. And both reenacting and historically commemorating the same ritual also creates a community with all past performers spanning Jewish history. The creation of such a community conscious of its own tradition in its present practices is a central aim of much ritual.

STUDY QUESTIONS

1. Explain the three main modes of symbolization according to Stern, and give examples of each.
2. Give examples of rituals that involve multiple modes of symbolization. Explain each mode.
3. *Must a person engaged in a ritual be aware of what the ritual symbolizes in order for his or her performance to function symbolically? Discuss.
4. *What is the difference between Stern's project and historical accounts of how particular rituals develop?

READING 3.3

Ask and It Will Be Given to You

Michael J. Murray and Kurt Meyers

The Bible is replete with instances of people petitioning God for certain events to happen. Today as well, devout people of all persuasions regularly pray for what they perceive as their needs or the needs of others they care about. In this selection, Michael J. Murray (Franklin and Marshall College) and Kurt Meyers attempt to dispel a puzzle about such **petitionary prayer.**

Consider a case in which a petitioner, or someone for whom the petitioner has prayed, receives a good from God because the petitioner requested it. Why would God bestow the good only if asked to bestow it? Why does God not grant the good irrespective of whether some person asks for it?

The authors suggest several possible reasons for God's requiring the petitioner (at least in some cases) to make the request. The act of petitioning keeps the petitioner away from "idolatry," an exaggerated sense of self-sufficiency, and it trains the petitioner to learn what God wills (the petitioner learns this by seeing which prayers are granted). In addition, drawing on the work of another philosopher, Eleonore Stump (St. Louis University), Murray and Meyers suggest that petitionary prayer creates a healthy relationship between God and humans, preventing people from being either "overwhelmed" or "spoiled" by God's having the power to grant them what God wishes. These replies are geared chiefly to the case of one's praying for one's own needs. In the case of a person praying on behalf of others, the reason that one's obtaining a certain good may be dependent on someone else's prayers is that God "has an overriding desire to sustain a harmonious interdependence amongst members of the church." For these reasons, Murray and Meyers claim, in some cases (not, they stress, all cases), God will give a person certain goods only upon being asked to give them, by either that person or others.

Consider the following situation. It is the first day of school, and the new third-grade students file into the classroom to be shown to their seats for the coming year. As they enter, the third-grade teacher notices one small boy who is particularly unkempt. He looks to be in desperate need of bathing, and his clothes are dirty, torn and tight-fitting. During recess, the teacher pulls aside the boy's previous teacher and asks about his wretched condition. The other teacher informs her that he always looks that way, even though the boy's family is quite wealthy. The reason he appears as he does, she continues, is that the family observes an odd practice according to which the children do not receive many important things—food, clothing, bathing, even shelter—unless they specifically request them. Since the boy, like many third-graders, has little interest in bathing and clean clothes, he just never asks for them.

Surely the teacher would rightly feel a certain moral revulsion at such parents. What, after all, would lead them to adopt such an odd policy? Young children are so thoroughly unfit to make judgements about what is in their own self-interest that it seems to border on abuse to administer the family's resources in such a way. One might think that the parents surely have an obligation to provide for the child's well-being, especially in light of their financial resources. Is not depriving children of their basic needs only because they fail to ask for them criminally negligent, especially in light of their relative inability to assess rightly their own needs?

THE PROBLEM

Oddly, while it appears that the parents in question are mistreating their children, the major Western theistic traditions seem to posit just such a relationship between God and His creatures. None of those in the Christian tradition are strangers to the Lord's Prayer in which believers are instructed to ask that God provide them with their 'daily bread' and deliver them from temptation. As one wonders why the parents administer goods as they do, one is led to wonder further what purpose could be served by creatures petitioning God as the Christian God asks them to? If petitions are ever **necessary conditions** of God's provision for at least some of creatures' basic needs, God seems open to the same charge raised against the parents in our above story. Yet if they are not necessary, **petitionary prayer** looks superfluous.

One might think, rightly we believe, that the second horn of this dilemma is not an option for the Christian theist since Scripture flatly asserts that prayer does have an impact on the course of earthly events. With regard to wisdom, the Christian Scriptures contend that, 'You do not have, because you do not ask' (James 4:2). So it is easy to see how one might argue that such an economy of blessings is no more just than that administered by the parents to the disheveled student.

Why is it that God, who has at His command all resources and who has the capacity for assessing His creatures' true needs far better than the creatures themselves, would make the distribution of at least some earthly blessings contingent on the creature's recognition of his needs and his request that God make provisions for them? This is the question we will address in this essay. While this problem arises for each of the major Western theistic traditions, our discussion will focus on the problem as it arises for the Christian tradition since the difficulties appear to be particularly acute there. The reason for this is that those in the Christian tradition must contend not only with the simple problem of petitionary prayer described above, what we will call 'individual petitionary prayer,' but with another related, and equally difficult, problem. This further problem arises out of particular passages in the Christian Scriptures which enjoin the believer to pray in very specific ways. Specifically, these passages declare that believers should not only petition God for their needs individually, but that they should pray for the needs of others and ask others to pray on their behalf.[1] The problem with this practice is obvious. To return to the earlier analogy, imagine that the child's parents instituted a further policy according to which each child needed not only to ask individually that his or her needs be met, but that it became a condition of receiving those needed goods that the child's siblings and friends also ask for her. Likewise, in the case of corporate prayer, what possible reason would there be for God to make provision of the believer's needs dependent on the petition of others?

While the contemporary literature on prayer is not extensive, a number of issues surrounding the practice have been discussed by contemporary philosophers. Much of this debate has focused on whether or not prayer could be efficacious in light of certain divine attributes such as **eternity, immutability, impassability,** and so on. However, little has been said about the problem we note above. For the purposes of our discussion we will assume that the more oft-discussed difficulties are resolvable. Our focus will be on the question of what might motivate an all-knowing, all-powerful, all-good Being to require His creatures to pray in order for their needs to be met.

THE PROBLEM OF INDIVIDUAL PETITIONARY PRAYER

It is surely not the case that God asks people to pray so that He might be better informed about their needs, or so that He is in any other way better enabled to grant their request. As a result, the theist must show that there is (or at least could be) some state of affairs God intends to bring about through petitionary prayer that could not be brought about through the provision alone. The solution to the problem of petitionary prayer, then, must follow one of two strategies by arguing either: (1) that there is some good which accrues as a result of the petition being made, a good significant enough to be worth forgo-

[1]For example, 'pray for each other so that you may be healed' James 5:16. See also Colossians 4:3, II Corinthians 1:11, Ezra 6:10, John 17:20, and Acts 8:15.

ing the (lesser) good of the provision being made without the request, or (2) that there is some harm which results from divine provision in the absence of the creature's petition, a harm greater than the good actualized by making the provision in the absence of the petition. We think that both strategies are applicable here and will examine each in turn.

'YOU SHALL NOT MAKE FOR YOURSELF AN IDOL . . .'

With respect to the first strategy, there are at least two goods that justify the practice of creaturely petitions. The first is that practicing petitionary prayer keeps the petitioner from a form of idolatry. In *Making Sense of It All,* Thomas Morris attempts to make some sense of the perils that readily lead people into idolatry, perils which he claims are heightened in an increasingly urban society.[2] Morris argues that as human beings are progressively withdrawn from situations in which their sustenance is derived directly from forces beyond human control, they come to see themselves as self-sufficient—masters of their own fate. When the rural, eighteenth-century farmer considered his situation it was easy for him to recognize that his continued existence was due, in large measure, to forces beyond his control. Would a late frost take the potato crop? Would a drought dry up the corn? Would a flood wash out the seed? These questions led the farmer to rely on the only Being to whom he could appeal for help in these matters. It was evident to him that he was directly dependent on the Superintendent of nature for his 'daily bread.' For the urbanite, whose water and gas come from a pipe, whose waste exits likewise, whose food comes from the grocer, shelter from the contractor, light from the bulb, etc., it can come to seem that "man is the measure of all things," that humanity is self-sufficient, that his only dependencies are on other people and the products of their hands.[3] As a result, when things go wrong (or right) people tend to look for human agents to blame (or praise). And conversely, when people are in need they tend to look to the appropriate human benefactors for their provision. In doing so, however, humans put creatures in the position reserved for God as the giver of 'every good and perfect gift,' as James describes Him [(James 1:17).]

Petitionary prayer can short-circuit this tendency by forcing the believer to consider that the goods that accrue to her do so ultimately because of forces beyond human control. While her food might still come from the grocer's hand and her drink from a tap, it is still God who brings the rain, provides the chemist and the intellect required to thwart white-fly infestations, and gives the brawn to the assembly-line worker who constructs the John Deere that harvests the wheat. With each prayer of petition, the believer is forcefully reminded that she is directly dependent on God for her provisions in life.

As a result, the creature is kept from that sort of idolatry that leads her to look only to nature or her neighbor for her daily bread rather than God. In this way, the creature remains humble in the face of the recognition that God is the ultimate source of all goods and thankful for this sustained provision.

Objection to the 'Idolatry Account'

On this account, it seems that the good that accrues to the believer as a result of prayer is purely an internal, psychological one. Its function is simply to aid the believer in keeping her thought life in order—to cause her to recognize the essential role of the Creator in her everyday life. Of course, one might object that God has already provided the believer with a mechanism for procuring this type of benefit, one that brings about the intended good in a much more direct fashion, namely, the practice of offering prayers of thanksgiving. Through prayers of thanksgiving the believer makes herself powerfully and directly aware of God's sustaining provision. In fact, reminding the believer of God and His position as provider constitutes their very purpose. Undoubtedly, one result of this expression of gratitude is that believers are kept from idolatry just as if they had petitioned God for their needs. As with petition, each instance of thanksgiving entails remembering that

[2]Thomas Morris, *Making Sense of It All* (Grand Rapids: Eerdmans, 1992), p. 44.
[3]*Ibid.*

the wheat ultimately comes by His hand, and not by that of their neighbour. It is for this very purpose that God commands the nation of Israel to remember God's provision through prayers of thanksgiving:

> When you have eaten and are satisfied, praise the Lord your God for the good land He has given you. Be careful that you do not forget the Lord your God . . . otherwise, when you eat and are satisfied . . . then your heart will become proud and you will forget the Lord your God. . . . You may say to yourself, 'My power and the strength of my hands have produced this wealth for me.' But remember the Lord your God, for it is He who gives you the ability to produce wealth, and so confirms His covenant, which He swore to your forefathers as it is today (Deuteronomy 8:10–18).

Why then is petitionary prayer required if prayers of thanksgiving serve the same purpose? It may well be the case, of course, that God has simply supplied the believer with two different means for achieving the same end. There are many different avenues by which people might improve their faith, and these different forms of prayer may simply reflect such diversity. Upon further reflection, however, there appear to be subtle differences between these practices which serve to illuminate the unique way in which they complement one another.

To see this, we ought to look for 'goods' that could be acquired through petitionary prayer which would not be available through prayers of thanksgiving alone. One of the most salient differences between these two types of prayer is the target of their resultant goods. The goal of thanksgiving seems to be strictly the enhancement of one's spiritual life. Through thanksgiving the believer acknowledges the Creator's rightful position in her life. Thus, the believer can maintain her spiritual equilibrium regarding her place in the operation of the world. Through the practice of petitionary prayer, however, the believer is also rewarded in numerous other ways. First, the believer receives those spiritual and physical goods requested in the petition that God deems suitable to provide. But in addition, God provides the petitioner with the added benefit of preservation from idolatry. Notice, then, that abandoning the practice of petitionary prayer, construed in the broadest sense, means that the believer not only suffers the loss of the attending spiritual goods, but will also suffer the loss of the physical goods on which the petitions hang. Even if the believer is consciously aware of the fact that her failure to offer thanksgiving leaves her subject to the threat of idolatry, it is simply too easy to lapse in her prayer life if prayers of thanksgiving constitute her only way of avoiding idolatry. Thus, if humans were to limit themselves only to prayers of thanksgiving, many would eventually lapse into idolatry simply because there is insufficient motivation to maintain continual prayers of thanksgiving. Through efficacious petitionary prayer, God can harness the appetites of the believer's physical body and force those appetites to serve the needs of her spirit. With this, God causes the satisfaction of the physical appetites to be dependent upon a practice that in turn feeds the spiritual life and keeps God in the forefront of the believer's mind. As a result, both the flesh and the spirit drive the believer toward this exercise which helps her avoid idolatry. Thus, efficacious petitionary prayer causes humans to persevere in their prayers in a way that prayers of thanksgivings cannot.[4] Because provision hangs on petition, petitions force humans to realize that God's provision of their bread is dependent upon them taking an active role in asking for it. If they lapse in this petition, their stomachs will pay the price. On the contrary, if they lapse in prayers of thanksgiving, only their spiritual well-being will suffer.

Furthermore, the practice of petitionary prayer not only keeps believers consistent in their prayer life, it actually serves to enhance the effectiveness of prayers of thanksgiving. The reason for this is that believers are too easily moved to take for granted goods that are gratuitously provided for them. Consider the case of a young man, Charles, who has

[4]Of course one might object here that for the spiritually mature believer prayers of thanksgiving would be sufficient to keep them from idolatry since such a believer realizes that all good things, requested or not, ultimately come from God. While this is so, not all believers are this well positioned and, as a result, God's general policy must provide for both the spiritually mature and the spiritually less mature.

grown up in a wealthy family. The father of the family generously supplies his children's every want and need. Every day, as his father brought him some new toy or gift, his mother would dutifully remind Charles that he should thank his father, something he came to do routinely. But over time what is routine degenerates into that which is rote. Charles began to take his father's generosity for granted. Realizing this, the father feared that he was no longer doing his son a favour with his indiscriminate generosity and instituted a change in his policies. No longer will these gifts be gratuitously bestowed on the children in the family. If they have a want or a need it will be up to them to make it clear and ask for their parent's help.

What would be the impact of such a policy on the children? Surely they would be more appreciative of the gifts bestowed on them, simply because they could no longer look on them as gratuitous. When they now give thanks for things that the father gives them, their thanks is genuine and sincere. They recognize that these provisions are given to them not only out of the abundance of their father's wealth, but also the goodness of his heart.

Perhaps the conjunction of these two practices brings about a good that neither could deliver on its own. Prayers of thanksgiving are important because they inspire gratitude in believers for God's provision. Through such prayers they are able to recognize their place in God's world and their dependence upon His grace. On the other hand, petitions keep people mindful of their own participation in this dependent relationship. This participation not only prevents them from falling into idolatry, it gives reality and meaning to their thanksgiving. They realize that their thanks is a meaningful result of an action performed for them out of love. Without prayers of petition, prayers of thanksgiving would likely degenerate into a pampered silence or, worse, contemptuous indifference.

One important consequence of reading the practice of petitionary prayer in this way is that its benefit cannot be realized if the petition is not efficacious. In fact, one might go so far as to say that, on this account, provision for daily needs must, to some extent, hang directly on believers' petitions. If we do not say this we turn the practice of petition into a mere meditative technique. Vincent Brümmer puts the point this way:

> [Such a move] turns petitionary prayer into a therapeutic meditation and leaves no room for it to retain an impetratory function: in petitionary prayer [on this account] we are not *asking God* to do anything, but reminding *ourselves* of our dependence on God.[5]

To do this, however, is to deny what the Scriptures appear to hold is a primary function of prayer, i.e. to be a necessary condition of God's making provisions of certain sorts for us.

Before going further, however, it is worth noting that God need not make provision of *all* goods hang on creaturely petition in order to achieve the good of preserving creature from idolatry, and this for two reasons. The first reason is that it would be (at least physically) impossible for all goods to hang on petition since certain goods are provided for us before we exist to pray for them. For example, before the first human existed, goods of food, water and materials for shelter were already in place. Second, and more to the point, even goods which we receive after we begin to exist need not invariably hang on our petitioning God for them. All that is necessary here is for God to have established an economy of blessings such that on some occasions he makes provision dependent on petitions. And these occasions must be frequent enough to achieve the good of keeping the creatures from idolatry. Yet, on these occasions, prayer must be a necessary condition of God's provision if He wishes to use it to deter His creatures from idolatry.

This line of thinking raises a troubling objection, namely, that this account entails something that is directly contrary to experience. While the claim that provision for certain needs of creatures hangs on their petitions might constitute a reasonable philosophical apologetic, one sees daily examples of people whose needs are consistently and fully supplied but who do not pray, never mind believe in God. If God has made prayer a necessary condition of provision in some cases, then it follows that those who

[5]Vincent Brümmer, *What Are We Doing When the Pray?* (London: SCM Press, 1984), p. 45.

do not pray should not in those cases get bread. However, as so many authors of Scripture point out,

> The wicked live on, reach old age, and grow mighty in power. . . . Their bull breeds without fail; their cow calves and never miscarries. They spend their days in prosperity. . . . (Job 21:7).

The fat pagans, who have all they want of caviar, much less bread, are ample in number as well as girth. They seem to be living, corpulent proof that prayer is just not efficacious, at least in the sense that it is a necessary condition for provision.

There are at least two ways one might respond to this objection. First one might hold that the cases of divine provision in view here are, in fact, necessarily dependent on petitionary prayer. Even provision which is made for the unbeliever results from prayers of petition; however, it is the prayers of the *believers* which yield the benefits for both. Thus, God causes the rain to fall and the wheat to grow in direct answer to the prayers of the believers. But a necessary and, for the unbeliever, fortuitous consequence of God answering the petitions of the believers is that those who do not pray are also able to reap the benefits. In this sense, the unbeliever 'piggybacks' on the prayers of the believer. As a result, while it might appear that the pagan and his cattle grow fat without prayer, this appearance is deceptive. The prosperity of unbeliever and believer alike hangs on the prayers of the faithful.

This account, however, only serves to raise another potentially more troubling objection. If petition is a necessary condition of provision in these instances, then God must forgo the provision in the absence of petition. But how could an omnibenevolent being, 'our Father,' allow His creatures to suffer in this way because of a simple failure to ask that their basic needs be provided? In light of such worries, many will find this account unappealing.

According to the second response, the view we favour, it is only the provision made for the believers which hangs directly on God being petitioned. In other words, on this second response, believer and unbeliever live under different economies of blessing. While the unbeliever does not need to pray for her daily bread, the believer must. The reason for this is that God has different aims for each and thus holds them accountable to different standards. The believer already recognizes God as Creator, Sustainer and Provider, and has the further responsibility of maintaining and growing in this faith. One way for God to cultivate this deeper faith is by establishing the relationship of petition-and-provision outlined above. For the unbeliever, on the other hand, such expectations on God's part would be in vain. The first order of business with the unbeliever is to bring her to faith—cultivation of that faith must come later. It is just the sort of provision that the unbeliever does not ask for that is necessary for her conversion, if not her survival. To return to our opening analogy, the parents must feed their children without being asked, at least until the children are able to talk. Until the child acquires such minimal abilities, withholding goods would not be merely absurd but utterly pointless. To withhold basic provision from those who do not believe, and who thus have no reason to pray for their daily bread, would be too cruel to be consistent with God's goodness.

'Understand What the Will of the Lord Is'

In addition to this first important benefit, there is a second general good that arises out of the institution of petitionary prayer, one that is again significant enough to justify God withholding provision of some goods in the absence of such prayers. By petitioning God for certain goods and waiting on His provision, believers can come to know God's mind concerning their circumstances. To see this more clearly, let us return to the analogy discussed at the beginning of the paper. Parents may tell their child that when there is a perceived need, he or she should come and ask what the parents can do to help meet it. The parents look on such occasions as opportunities to teach their children what is right and important and what is not. When the sixteen-year-old comes and asks for a new red Corvette, parents can use this as an opportunity to build some character. By failing to grant the request, the parents indicate to the child that there are certain things that, for various reasons, are not in their interests, contrary to the child's belief. Furthermore, when the child asks the mother for some help in making a gift for a sick elderly neighbour, the mother has the opportunity to foster important virtues in the child by granting the request.

In similar fashion, the believer is able to come to understand God's will through prayer. The believer is not merely enjoined to pray for perceived needs, but to do so with the sort of humility that permits her to say 'Thy will be done.' If the request is granted, she not only has a need fulfilled, she has continued the process of learning what sorts of things are in accordance with God's will. Likewise, if the believer prays and her request is not granted, she learns that her desires are not in accordance with God's will. Through this process, her desires and her prayers become increasingly aligned with God's, and the more closely her prayers are aligned with His will, the more likely they are to be granted. This reading of petitionary prayer helps make sense of those difficult passages which indicate that the prayers of the righteous have more standing before God: 'The prayer of a righteous man is powerful and effective' (James 5:15). The reason for this, of course, is not that the righteous enjoy greater favour with God, but that their thoughts, desires and will are increasingly aligned with God's own. By learning which prayers are effective and which are not, the believer may in turn learn to become more righteous, and thus better conformed to the image of God.

Objections to the 'God's Will' Account

However, there are some practical objections concerning exactly how this process is supposed to work. The reason for this is simply that it is difficult to tell whether or not the states of affairs that are actualized in the world come about as a result of the believer's prayer. If she prays for rain for her rosebushes and it rains, it may mean more than one thing. First, it may mean that her prayer was efficacious, and that it rained because she asked and because her rosebushes needed it. Second, it may be that it rained in answer to her neighbour's prayers, whose family would starve if his fields did not receive rain. Her rosebushes 'piggybacked' on the provision that was directly intended for the neighbour's field. Third, it may be that it was going to rain regardless of anyone's prayers, because, say, it was a natural consequence of God doing that which He is required to do in virtue of the benevolence due His creatures. Corresponding alternatives are available if the believer's prayers are not granted. Unfortunately, it appears to be impossible for believers to distinguish which of these alternatives obtains. One might then argue that because they cannot know with confidence the reason their prayer is answered (or not), the believers can never know how their specific request comports with God's will (or fails to).

But is this really the case? There are some clear cases represented in the Christian scriptures in which petitionary prayer serves as a way of instructing the believer in God's will. There is the familiar case of Paul and the 'thorn in the flesh.' In his second letter to the Corinthians, Paul tells us that he had been plagued with an infirmity which he petitioned God three times to take from him. God responded to him that the infirmity would not be removed because: 'My grace is sufficient for you, for my power is perfected in weakness' (II Corinthians 12:9). It is not known what infirmity it was that Paul was afflicted with. The suggestions range from a particular recurring temptation to opposition from enemies and even physical infirmities such as severely deficient eyesight. Whatever it might have been, here is an example in which God denies a request and the petitioner learns a direct lesson from the denial and God's attending explanation. God tells Paul that He will bring about Paul's success in spite of the infirmity and, in doing so, makes His own power evident.

Similarly, when Moses petitioned God to allow him to enter the promised land, God denied his request and told Moses to pursue the matter no further. Although God does not tell him the reason for the denial of the request at that time, He had told him earlier that he would not enter the land because of his disobedience at Meribah. Such passages record God making His will known explicitly to believers by means of His failure to grant their request. Not only did Moses learn of the grave consequence of a leader's disobedience to God's explicit command, but surely those who saw that Moses was denied his petition to enter learned this lesson in a powerful way as well.

So, at least in those cases in which God explicitly reveals the reason for granting or denying a request, one can come to know the will of God through the mechanism we propose. But since the number of such cases is exceedingly small, one is led to wonder if there are any other cases where answer to prayer provides an opportunity for better knowing the will of God. We think there are at least two such further cases.

One way that believers can come to learn the will of God through the mediation of petitionary prayer is in those cases where what is asked for is the most important event related to their request. In such cases, if God were to grant the request, it would have to be due, at least in large measure, to the nature of the believer's request. Likewise, if God failed to grant the request, this fact would have to be explained, in large measure, by the fact that the request was contrary to God's purposes in this case. Of course, one might wonder whether believers are ever positioned to know that their request is the most important factor related to the request that they make. Surely such cases are limited, but Scripture provides at least one such example and it is the case in which Jesus petitions the Father to allow Him to avoid the cross if it is the Father's will. It is known that Jesus was not spared the cross and, further, that the death of Jesus is, by comparison, the only event of any importance related to Christ's request. As a result, when it was not granted, it was clear that the primary reason was not some matter indirectly related to the request, but the fact that Christ's going to the cross was an instrumental part of God's design for the world. However, the number of such cases will also be exceedingly small since the number of cases where the believer is well-positioned enough to know that her request is the most important one among those related to the event in question is negligible.

A second way believers might learn the will of God through an answer to prayer is by their recognition that God's failure to grant it implies that the thing they asked for was not as important as they might have believed. In other words, the believer may pray for rain for her roses because she has a deep and abiding, albeit misplaced, attachment to them. God's failure to grant her petition for rain, thus allowing her roses to wither, may not mean that God directly intended that they die. What it may reveal, however, is that there are many other states of affairs attached to the presence or absence of rain which are far more important than her roses' survival. This recognition would be a sobering reminder that she has developed a degree of attachment to various objects, relationships, ideas, etc. which is out of keeping with their true importance.

Yet still none of these represents the run-of-the-mill ways in which believers claim to know that an event of one sort or another happened (or failed to happen) as a result of their petition. In fact, the believer's **epistemic** situation in making these determinations is much like ordinary situations in which we attribute certain events to certain natural agents where we are at least partly ignorant of the causal history of the event. A week ago a colleague of ours sent a message to a philosopher she knew at another university. She asked whether or not he had written a paper on a certain subject and, if he had, whether he might send a copy of it. A few days later she received through the mail a copy of a paper on that very subject from that philosopher. It seems right to say that she is quite justified in believing that this paper was sent to her in light of the message she sent, even though it might well have been the case that this other philosopher had never received the message and had sent the paper simply believing that she might find it of interest. In the same way, we suspect that believers are justified in holding that events that occur in accordance with petitions that they have made came about as a result of their prayer. As in the case of the paper, such beliefs are based on a sort of justification that is defeasible. But the belief that the believer holds is nonetheless justified, and he would surely be epistemically permitted, if not obliged, to believe that the realization of the circumstance prayed for was an 'answer' to his prayer. Of course, all of these conclusions would require that the believer believe in God and believe that God can bring about events in the world as a result of prayers being offered. Thus, in the same way that I think I can justifiably hold that the philosopher noted sent his paper to our colleague because of her request, the believer can hold that God brought about (or failed to bring about) something that was petitioned for because He wanted things to come about in that way.

'And He Was Called God's Friend'

As we noted in the introduction, there are two ways one might approach a defence of the practice of petitionary prayer. First one might look for significant goods that are acquired through petition and subsequent divine provision which could not have been acquired through provision alone. This has been the subject of the discussion above. The second approach is to look for harms which may come about from God's bestowing goods on His creatures without the believer's petition. It is to these that we turn in this section.

Eleonore Stump has described an interesting and plausible account of what such harms might consist in.[6] In general, she casts prayer as a hedge against the dangers of a 'bad friendship' between God and His creatures. Throughout Scripture there are passages that describe the type of living relationship that should exist between God and humans. Images of bride and groom, parent and child, friend, and so on are regularly employed to emphasize different facets of this relationship. Stump's contention is that in any relationship or friendship between two persons, one of whom is perfect, and the other of whom is very imperfect, there are certain obvious dangers.

Stump discusses two such dangers. The first is the danger of God 'overwhelming' the creature. When the balance of power and abilities is so monstrously uneven, the weaker member of the pair would have a notable tendency to become a pale shadow of the stronger member, losing all sense of individual personality and personal strength. She cites the paradigm example of the troubles of a friendship between a Rockefeller child and a slum child as a 'pale copy' of the potential danger between one who is divine, and one who is not. Stump argues that petitionary prayer will guard against overwhelming because it will prevent God from 'stepping on toes.' If God refrains from making provision except in response to prayer, it allows Him, in turn, to refrain from imposing His unwanted designs upon His creatures. If God were to act so as to influence the believers' lives, without being asked whether it was in their interest or not, they might become resentful, and in doing so He could rightly be viewed as overwhelming them.

Stump asks us to imagine a teacher who notices that one of her students is procrastinating on a term paper and thereby 'storing up trouble for himself.' If the teacher were to call the student at home and present him with the scheduling help he needs, Stump believes that his justified response might be, 'Who asked you?' or, 'Mind your own business.' She deems these responses to be healthy and just. However, if the student were to ask for help, then Stump asserts that the teacher could provide the student with the instruction he needs without the danger of overwhelming him. Stump claims that if humans were led to docile acceptance of God's unrequested provision, it would infringe on their **autonomy.** If believers ask for those things they are given, the God-man relationship becomes much more ask-give-take, than see-give-accept. It is only this former sort of relationship, she claims, that permits a true friendship between God and His human creatures.

Stump describes the second potential harm to the divine-human relationship as that of becoming 'spoiled.' The advantages of a friendship with a perfect Being, she argues, are likely to cause the weaker member to become willful and indulgent. Prayer helps safeguard against spoiling in that the petitioner is forced to acknowledge her need, and to further acknowledge a dependence on God for fulfillment of that need. In addition, if that prayer is answered, then the petitioner must in turn be grateful to God for His grace. This helps avoid the kinds of human pride and indulgence that might occur if God was to provide without petitionary prayer. If Stump's account is correct, then it appears that in the majority of cases God cannot provide without believers asking, if He wishes to avoid these significant harms.

In a similar vein, Vincent Brümmer notes that if God did not, at least in some cases, make provision for our needs dependent on our requests, the relationship would become 'depersonalized.' He argues that if God provided for all our needs automatically we would be akin to the potted plant on the kitchen window sill which is watered when and only when we, the caretakers, decide to do it. But just as we cannot have a personal relationship with an entity of this sort, God would be cut off from a

[6]Stump, Eleonore, 'Petitionary Prayer.' *American Philosophical Quarterly,* 16 (April 1979), 81–91.

personal relationship with His creatures without efficacious petitionary prayer.[7]

'I Will Not Leave You or Forsake You'

Thus, we can see some straightforward reasons why God might choose to administer the distribution of earthly blessings through the mediation of petitionary prayer. Before closing this discussion of individual petitionary prayer two reflections are worthy of note. First, is there anything in the above account which might allow us to explain why God ought not be held culpable for the fact that people fail to enjoy certain goods, as the parents described in our opening analogy might be for failing to provide for their own children? We think that there is. If one takes this account in conjunction with the widely held doctrine that God has knowledge of **contingent** future conditionals (or '**counterfactuals** of human freedom,' to use less scholastic, and less precise, terminology) then one can fashion a powerful response to one of the objections suggested by our opening analogy. A God who exercises providence in light of such conditional **future contingents** can be sure, prior to creation, that even in a world in which provision hangs on petitions, there will never be individuals who are unjustly denied provision because of lack of petition. This is so because God can, in light of this knowledge, know what creatures will petition for across the possible worlds. If there is some world in which there is a situation in which God knows that (a) the creature needs some good, the provision of which God has made dependent on the creature's petitioning for it, and (b) the creature will not petition for the good, then God will not actualize that world. In this way, God could make provision hang on freely offered creaturely petition with no risk that creatures will fail to petition for a good essential to their well-being. Even if God desired to create a world in which all provision hung on the believers' petitions, a God who exercises providence in this way can insure that no world is actualized in which the prayers offered will result in an unjust distribution of goods. Of course, if conditional future contingents are known prevolitionally, as **Molinists** contend, then it may turn out that no such world is actualizable. Yet, if there is no such actualizable world, the explanation for creatures being denied provision will be found in the free-will **theodicies,** since it is the creatures' failure freely to choose to pray that accounts for their un-met needs.

This makes God's relation to His creatures significantly different from the relationship of the parents and the children in our opening illustration. There, the parents who resolve to make provision for the children dependent on the children's requests are ignorant of what the children will ask for. As a result, if they intend to hold fast to their resolution, they cannot be sure whether the children will receive the basic goods they need for survival or not. God, who has access to conditional future contingents, however, is not subject to creaturely petitions in the same manner.

Second, and relatedly, since a God who has such knowledge knows perfectly how either granting or denying petitions will aid or detract from the petitioner's well-being (e.g. being kept from idolatry as opposed to being resentful, or being 'overwhelmed' as opposed to being thankful), God can know how to distinguish those goods that should depend on the petitioner's request from those which should not. In this way God can make provision depend on petitions in those cases where doing so, by either granting or denying them, would bring about the desired result in the petitioner. Parents can, and must, do something similar. They must attempt to determine when it would provide benefits to the child to withhold certain goods until they are requested as opposed to providing them routinely. But unlike the parents, God is in a position to make these discriminations perfectly, giving Him the sort of position which justifies this method of distributing goods.

THE PROBLEM OF CORPORATE PRAYER

'Pray Also for Me'

Thus, there are indeed justified reasons for God's command that believers pray for goods such as their daily bread. As we mentioned in the introduction, however, this is only one of the problems attending

[7]Brümmer, p. 47.

the Christian practice of petitionary prayer. The discussion up to this point has focused exclusively on the *individual* benefit and spiritual awareness that people may acquire through petitioning God for their daily needs. Why, then, would God require that *someone else* pray for a particular believer's needs as well? As Brümmer puts the matter:

> If intercession on behalf of other people is to be interpreted as a request to God to provide in [*sic*] their needs, then we seem to be faced with a dilemma. On the one hand, a God who is perfectly good cannot make his benevolence to someone dependent on the intercession of others. . . . On the other hand, if we were to deny that God makes his benevolence to someone dependent on the intercession of others, what is the point of intercessory prayer?[8]

The Christian Scriptures repeatedly state that this is just what is required of believers. In Paul's letters, for example, we find him not only giving explicit teaching about the efficacy of corporate prayer but also recruiting the prayers of his audience: To the Colossians he writes, 'at the same time pray for us as well that God will open to us a door for the word, that we may declare the mystery of Christ . . .' (Colossians 4:3), and to the church at Corinth, 'On Him we have set our hope that He will continue to deliver us, as you help us by your prayers' (II Cor. 1:10–11).

Stump argues that this practice, here referred to as 'corporate prayer,' is perhaps another way for God to facilitate the divine-human friendship while avoiding overwhelming the lesser member of the friendship.[9] To demonstrate the point she uses the analogy in which Jim is having trouble in school. John is Jim's friend and is aware that he is having trouble in school. Unfortunately, Jim is unwilling to ask the teacher for help on his own. As a result, John goes to the teacher to explain Jim's difficulty. Stump argues that once John intervenes on Jim's behalf, the teacher is in a position to help with 'less risk of oppressive meddling than before,'[10] because the superior member of the relationship has been asked to intervene by the inferior's well-meaning friend. Likewise, she argues, the practice of corporate petitionary prayer provides God with a mechanism for intervening in the lives of His creatures, even when they themselves may not specifically request it. As long as someone else has asked God to intervene on the believer's behalf, the danger of 'overwhelming' is eliminated or at least mitigated.

On closer examination, however, it is hard to see exactly how Stump's analogy is supposed to transfer to the relationship between God and His creatures. In the case of individual prayer, Stump raises the concern that God might overwhelm the petitioner. This worry is resolved through petitionary prayer since the believer must now ask for such assistance. The petition acts as a buffer. In the case of corporate prayer, Stump likewise believes that this buffer can be established by a petitioner on someone else's behalf. But notice that there is an important difference here. When John asks the teacher to intervene on Jim's behalf, and she does so, she can excuse her intervention by explaining that John had requested the help on his behalf. In doing this, the teacher avoids the appearance of the sort of meddling that risks 'overwhelming' the inferior member of the relationship. The problem with transferring this analogy to the God-man relationship is that the one receiving divine assistance has no opportunity to question God about His unrequested interference. Thus, the one being helped would be unable to realize that someone else had prayed for him, and so be unable to excuse God for His meddling. The relationship God and His creature have would be, as far as the creature is concerned, identical to the one which constitutes God 'overwhelming' the creature. Even if the petitioner was able to establish this so-called buffer, the one being helped would be unaware that it existed, and it is this awareness that is essential for the buffer to serve its purpose.

But there is a second problem with this account. According to Stump's analogy, the reason John must intercede is because Jim is unwilling to ask for help himself. The problem is that this makes her analogy applicable only to one sort of corporate prayer. The model of corporate prayer portrayed in Scripture indicates that corporate prayer usually takes place when the one asking for assistance from God *asks* others to intercede on his behalf. Somehow the Christian must account for the fact that even when

[8] *Ibid.*, p. 55.
[9] Stump, p. 88.
[10] *Ibid.*

one petitions on his own behalf he still needs the intercession of others. Passages such as those cited at the beginning of this section make it clear that the function of corporate prayer cannot fundamentally be to permit God to avoid charges of meddling in the way Stump describes.

So what can the Christian theist say about this? As before, we must look for some good which arises out of the practice of corporate prayer which outweighs both the good of God simply providing that which is requested, and the good of provision through the mediation of mere individual petitionary prayer. One reason why God may make provision of certain goods contingent upon corporate requests is because His creatures assisting one another in this way generates interdependence among believers—an interdependence that fosters the sort of unity God demands of the church. In Scripture, the church is often portrayed as a body. The picture is of many parts that, while all individually useful and important, depend on one another for their effectiveness. In his first letter to the Corinthians Paul writes, 'But God has combined the members of the body . . . so that there should be no division in [it], but that its parts should have equal concern for each other. If one part suffers, every part suffers with it; if one part is honored, every part rejoices with it' (12:24–6). Paul explains that spiritual gifts are distributed among members of the church so that they might realize God's purpose for the church on earth. But they are also distributed in such a way that the members of the body must rely on one another to perform their own function effectively, in the way that the parts of our own bodies do.

As a result, one of God's purposes for the church is that they recognize their interdependence and through this cultivate healthy mutual relationships within the community. Corporate prayer can serve this end by leading believers humbly to share their needs and shortcomings with others so that they might pray for them. But more than this, corporate prayer forces believers' interdependence since God has, to some extent, made the granting of petitions contingent upon them recruiting others to pray for their needs. Further, unity among the members of the church is a good significant enough for God to make many of His provisions to individuals contingent upon their prayers for others and vice-versa.

But corporate petitionary prayer not only serves to achieve the indirect benefit of fostering unity among members of the church. In addition, it serves the more direct purpose of making the community of believers aware of each other's needs so that they themselves can meet them. In this way, corporate prayer helps believers to avoid the pitfall, described by James, of deserting the cold and the hungry with the mere salutation, 'Be warmed and be filled' (James 2:16). When believers are confronted with the needs of others face-to-face they are moved not only to intercede for them but to provide for them themselves. Thus, praying for one another develops a *pathos* among the members of the community that again disposes them towards interdependence and away from independent self-reliance. . . .

CONCLUSIONS

In conclusion, we have shown that there are some considerable reasons why God might make the distribution of at least certain goods dependent on His creatures' petitions. With regard to individual prayer, God's desire to keep His creatures from idolatry and to train them in the knowledge of His will is sufficiently strong that He could justifiably make provision of certain goods hang on believers petitioning Him for them. Our claim is not that God brings about these goods as a mere side-effect of our praying for goods that He would already provide as a matter of course. Instead these benefits received from petitionary prayer are significant enough that God would be justified in withholding His provision if we failed to petition Him for them. Likewise, as Stump points out, through the practice of petitionary prayer believers can avoid certain significant pitfalls which generally attend friendships between superior and inferior beings, i.e. the pitfalls of overwhelming and spoiling. Finally, we have argued that the practice of corporate petitionary prayer can be justified in light of the fact that God has an overriding desire to cultivate and maintain a harmonious interdependence amongst members of the church. We have shown that corporate petitionary prayer can be plausibly argued to fulfill such a role. In the same way, then, God can justifiably make the procurement of various (important) goods hang on believers petitioning God in this way.

STUDY QUESTIONS

1. What problem about prayer do Murray and Meyers consider? What analogy do they use to present this problem?
2. What do Murray and Meyers mean by "idolatry"? In their opinion, why are prayers of thanksgiving not enough to rid a believer of idolatry?
3. According to Murray and Meyers, how frequently does God make the provision of a good dependent on God's being asked to provide it? Explain.
4. Suppose that Jones, an atheist, enjoys health, wealth, and good relationships with his wife and children. Smith, a devout believer, lives in poverty and ill health and is pained by her children's wayward behavior, even though she regularly prays for changes in these conditions. How would Murray and Meyers explain this? Do you find their explanation plausible? Why or why not?
5. Murray and Meyers claim that, if God makes certain goods contingent on persons' asking for them, those persons are better able to appreciate what God's will is. How does this process work? How do Murray and Meyers handle the objection that a believer cannot be sure that his or her prayer has led to the event prayed for?
6. According to Eleonore Stump, cited in the essay, petitionary prayer enhances the relationship between God and humans. How?
7. What do the authors mean by "corporate prayer"? Why doesn't Stump's account work to explain "corporate prayer"? How do Murray and Meyers explain why God might bring about a person's being cured of an illness only if another person prays for the other's health? *Do you think that—given God's way of operating, according to the authors—God is truly just? Why or why not?
8. *Some philosophers maintain that, in order for a prayer to be regarded as an "answered" prayer, the event prayed for must occur by means of a miracle. If an event can be explained by natural law, the fact that it occurs cannot be regarded as an answer to a prayer, for, in that case, it would have occurred regardless of the prayer. Do you think this argument is cogent? Why or why not? In other words, would petitionary prayer make sense in a universe without miracles?

MORALITY and RELIGION

READING 3.4

Defining Piety

Plato

This selection is from the first half of the dialogue Euthyphro *(9e–11b). Euthyphro has defined* piety *as that which is loved by the gods. Plato has elicited from him a refinement: since the gods disagree, the same act could be both pious and impious, on Euthyphro's definition. To repair the definition, Euthyphro redefines the pious as that which is loved by* all *the gods, and that is where the selection picks up the conversation.*

In his refutation, Socrates (who speaks for Plato) asks Euthyphro, "Is the pious loved by the gods because it is pious, or is it pious because it is loved by the gods?" In other words, do the gods love the pious because it has a quality that is separate and independent from their loving it? Or does the gods' loving certain acts make those acts pious? Euthyphro concurs that the former alternative is correct. Unfortunately for him, in doing so Euthyphro is admitting that there is a standard of piety independent of the gods' love, and Plato shows that this refutes Euthyphro's definition of the pious as that which is loved by the gods. For if pious means "loved by the gods," then the gods love that which is loved by the gods because it is loved by the gods. This consequence is unacceptable, Plato suggests. Interpreters believe that the problem he sees is that the gods seem to love what they love arbitrarily, without reason.

For contemporary philosophers, the significance of this exchange is that, according to Euthyphro, moral terms must be defined in purely religious ones and cannot be given a secular definition. God's attitudes are all that determines piety. This approach is associated by today's philosophers with the view that right and wrong must be defined by God's commands — **divine command theory.** *Plato's refutation offers the important objection that the gods, given this theory, appear arbitrary. (See, however, study question 6.)*

E: I would certainly say that the pious is what all the gods love, and the opposite, what all the gods hate, is the impious.

S: Then let us again examine whether that is a sound statement, or do we let it pass, and if one of us, or someone else, merely says that something is so, do we accept that it is so? Or should we examine what the speaker means?

E: We must examine it, but I certainly think that this is now a fine statement.

S: We shall soon know better whether it is. Consider this: Is the pious loved by the gods because it is pious, or is it pious because it is loved by the gods?

E: I don't know what you mean, Socrates.

S: I shall try to explain more clearly: we speak of something being carried[1] and something carrying, of something being led and something leading, of something being seen and something seeing, and you understand that these things are all different from one another and how they differ?

E: I think I do.

S: So there is something being loved and something loving, and the loving is a different thing.

E: Of course.

S: Tell me then whether that which is being carried is being carried because someone carries it or for some other reason.

E: No, that is the reason.

S: And that which is being led is so because someone leads it, and that which is being seen because someone sees it?

E: Certainly.

S: It is not seen by someone because it is being seen but on the contrary it is being seen because someone sees it, nor is it because it is being led that someone leads it but because someone leads it that it is being led; nor does someone carry an object because it is being carried, but it is being carried because someone carries it. Is what I want to say clear, Euthyphro? I want to say this, namely, that if anything comes to be, or is affected, it does not come to be because it is coming to be, but it is coming to be because it comes to be; nor is it affected because it is being affected but because something affects it. Or do you not agree?

E: I do.

S: What is being loved is either something that comes to be or something that is affected by something?

[1]This is the present participle form of the verb *pheromenon,* literally *being-carried.* The following passage is somewhat obscure, especially in translation, but the general meaning is clear. Plato points out that this participle simply indicates the object of an action of carrying, seeing, loving, etc. It follows from the action and adds nothing new, the action being prior to it, not following from it, and a thing is said to be loved because someone loves it, not vice versa. To say therefore that the pious is being loved by the gods says no more than that the gods love it. Euthyphro, however, also agrees that the pious is loved by the gods because of its nature (because it is pious), but the fact of its being loved by the gods does not define that nature, and as a definition is therefore unsatisfactory. It only indicates a quality or affect of the pious, and the pious is therefore still to be defined (11a7). [Translator's note]

E: Certainly.

S: So it is in the same case as the things just mentioned; it is not loved by those who love it because it is being loved, but it is being loved because they love it?

E: Necessarily.

S: What then do we say about the pious, Euthyphro? Surely that it is loved by all the gods, according to what you say?

E: Yes.

S: Is it loved because it is pious, or for some other reason?

E: For no other reason.

S: It is loved then because it is pious, but it is not pious because it is loved?[2]

E: Apparently.

S: And because it is loved by the gods it is being loved and is dear to the gods?

E: Of course.

S: The god-beloved is then not the same as the pious, Euthyphro, nor the pious the same as the god-beloved, as you say it is, but one differs from the other.

E: How so, Socrates?

S: Because we agree that the pious is beloved for the reason that it is pious, but it is not pious because it is loved. Is that not so?

E: Yes.

S: And that the god-beloved, on the other hand, is so because it is loved by the gods, by the very fact of being loved, but it is not loved because it is god-beloved.

E: True.

S: But if the god-beloved and the pious were the same, my dear Euthyphro, and the pious were loved because it was pious, then the god-beloved would be loved because it was god-beloved, and if the god-beloved was god-beloved because it was loved by the gods, then the pious would also be pious because it was loved by the gods; but now you see that they are in opposite cases as being altogether different from each other: the one is of a nature to be loved because it is loved, the other is loved because it is of a nature to be loved. I'm afraid, Euthyphro, that when you were asked what piety is, you did not wish to make its nature clear to me, but you told me an affect or quality of it, that the pious has the quality of being loved by all the gods, but you have not yet told me what the pious is. Now, if you will, do not hide things from me but tell me again from the beginning what piety is, whether loved by the gods or having some other quality—we shall not quarrel about that—but be keen to tell me what the pious and the impious are. . . .

STUDY QUESTIONS

1. Explain the two alternatives Plato presents to Euthyphro: do the gods love the pious because it is pious, or is it pious because it is loved by the gods?
2. Which of the alternatives in question 1 does Euthyphro agree to? Why?
3. Explain the analogies Socrates brings up: being carried, being led, being seen.
4. How does Socrates refute Euthyphro's definition based on Euthyphro's answer to the question in question 1?
5. *In what way does Socrates's rejection of Euthyphro depend on a particular conception of the gods as wise and rational? How would a conception of the gods as powerful possibly breed a different conclusion? (On this, see also Reading 3.5.)
6. *Philosophers usually say that Euthyphro maintains that *right* and *wrong* must be defined in terms of God's will. However, the term *pious* has a religious connotation. How might this point undermine the philosophers' understanding of Euthyphro's position?

[2]I quote an earlier comment of mine on this passage: " . . . it gives in a nutshell a point of view from which Plato never departed. Whatever the gods may be, they must by their very nature love the right because it is right." They have no choice in the matter. "This separation of the dynamic power of the gods from the ultimate reality, this setting up of absolute values above the gods themselves was not as unnatural to a Greek as it would be to us. . . . The gods who ruled on Olympus . . . were not creators but created beings. As in Homer, Zeus must obey the balance of Necessity, so the Platonic gods must conform to an eternal scale of values. They did not create them, cannot alter them, cannot indeed wish to do so." (*Plato's Thought,* Indianapolis: Hackett Publishing Co., 1980, pp. 152–3.) [Translator's note]

READING 3.5

Divine Command Morality

Janine Marie Idziak

In this selection, Janine Marie Idziak (Loras College) gives a brief survey of the considerations that, through the centuries, have led philosophers either to hold that morality is dependent directly and solely on God's commands or to deny this dependence. Those who espouse a **divine command theory** *of ethics stress certain characteristics of God —* **omnipotence** *and liberty, for example — along with the dependency of everything on God. Those who reject divine command theory argue that God's commands and prohibitions seem, according to those theories, arbitrary; if God were to command killing and cruelty, these actions would have to be regarded as right. The critics maintain as well that the acceptance of divine commands requires a prior moral standard. These are but a few of the many arguments Idziak considers.*

. . . Generally speaking, a "divine command moralist" is one who maintains that the content of morality (i.e., what is right and wrong, good and evil, just and unjust, and the like) is directly and solely dependent upon the commands and prohibitions of God. . . .

THE RATIONALE OF DIVINE COMMAND MORALITY

Divine command ethics has been the subject of much criticism both historically and in the recent literature. The intensity of this criticism emphasizes the question why such an ethical theory should be proposed and maintained. The literature on divine command morality suggests considerations having to do with the nature, status, and activity of God as the rationale for this ethical position.

(1) *Divine Command Morality Is a Correlate of the Divine* **Omnipotence.** This line of thought has been attributed to divine command moralists by critics of the position. After mentioning the **scholastic** divine command moralists, Ralph Cudworth asserts that "this doctrine hath been since chiefly promoted and advanced by such as think nothing so essential to the Deity, as uncontrollable power and arbitrary will, and therefore that God could not be God if there should be any thing evil in its own nature which he could not do." . . . More recently, D. Goldstick has claimed that a theist is in the position of affirming, with respect to any divinely-willed code of behavior, that "its moral rightness follows necessarily from its being willed by somebody omnipotent." . . .

(2) *Divine Command Ethics Is Involved in the Divine Liberty.* This point comes out quite clearly in Jean Gerson's *On the Consolation of Theology,* in a passage which we will subsequently discuss.

(3) *Divine Command Ethics Recognizes the Importance of the Divine Will.* We list this consideration with reservation. It may be the intended meaning of the second part of Cudworth's assertion, quoted in (1), that divine command morality was espoused "by such as think nothing so essential to the Deity, as uncontrollable power and arbitrary will." On the other hand, the phrase "arbitrary will" may simply be a reference to the divine liberty.

(4) *Divine Command Morality Must Be Espoused in the Realm of Ethics Because There Cannot Be Anything Independent of God.* Again, this view has been ascribed to divine command moralists by critics of the position. Thus A. C. Ewing states that "most theists by no means like the idea of something independent of God limiting him," and suggests that "it is for this reason chiefly that the laws of ethics have been said to be dependent on God." Within the historical literature, one finds Ralph Cudworth claiming that Descartes espoused divine command ethics for the reason that "if the natures and essences of things should not depend upon the will

of God, it would follow from hence, that something that was not God was independent upon God." . . .

(5) *Divine Command Ethics Is Related to Man's Dependency on God as Creator.* This is suggested by John Locke in his *Essays on the Law of Nature.* According to Locke, "it is proper that we should live according to the precept of His [God's] will" because "we owe our body, soul, and life—whatever we are, whatever we have, and even whatever we can be—to Him and to Him alone." In other words, since "God has created us out of nothing and, if He pleases, will reduce us again to nothing," we are, Locke suggests, "subject to Him in perfect justice and by utmost necessity."

(6) *Divine Command Ethics Satisfies the Religious Requirement That God Be the Supreme Focus of One's Loyalties.* This reason for being a divine command moralist has recently been suggested by Robert Merrihew Adams, who proposes that "If our supreme commitment in life is to doing what is right just because it is right, and if what is right is right just because God wills or commands it, then surely our highest allegiance is to God."

(7) *Divine Command Ethics Is Grounded in God's Graciousness to Man in Jesus Christ.* According to the divine command moralist Karl Barth, the basis of God's ethical claim on man lies in the fact that: "God has given us Himself." In other words, it lies in the fact that "Although He could be without us—He did not and does not will to be without us"; in the fact that "He has taken our place and taken up our cause." . . .

CRITICISM OF DIVINE COMMAND MORALITY

. . . [C]ontemporary philosophers trace the criticism of this ethical position back to Plato's *Euthyphro.*[1] The objections which have been raised against divine command morality are diverse in character.

(1) *The acceptance of divine commands as the criterion of what we ought to do requires a prior moral standard.* This line of attack carries . . . the implication that morality cannot be fundamentally dependent on God and his commands, as divine command morality claims. Patterson Brown has replied to this criticism by pointing out ways, other than moral reasoning, in which ethical standards (including divine command morality) can be acquired.

(2) *In using divine command morality to determine what we ought to do, it is necessary to resort to some other ethical principle to know what it is that God commands; thus divine command morality is in effect useless as an ethical standard.* This criticism of divine command ethics was made by Jeremy Bentham. . . . Bentham claims that the revelations of the divine will contained in Scripture stand in need of interpretation, which process of interpretation, carried on by the Church, he believes to involve ethical standards other than divine command morality. Finally, Bentham seems to discount the viability of personal revelation as a source of knowledge of divine commands in claiming that "God . . . confessedly does not now either speak or write to us."

[A] line of reply to Bentham has recently been developed by Philip L. Quinn. Quinn contends that, even if Bentham is correct in his claim that the only way we can come to know God's will is by first determining what is right, divine command morality need not be considered useless. For, according to Quinn, "ethical theories can perform other functions besides teaching us exactly where our duties lie." Specifically, Quinn suggests that "it would be theoretically interesting to find out that divine commands are **necessary and sufficient** causal conditions for moral obligations and prohibitions, regardless of the **epistemic** difficulties involved in scrutinizing the divine will."

(3) *Divine command ethics makes morality dependent on a divine choice that is arbitrary.* A. C. Ewing has recently argued this point for the **metaethical** variety of divine command morality; this criticism has also been mentioned by the twentieth century theologian Carl F. Henry. Historically, one finds Ralph Cudworth describing divine command ethics as the view that "the arbitrary will and pleasure of God" constitutes the rule of good and evil. . . . [T]his criticism does seem to have a foundation in certain statements of Luther and

[1] [See Reading 3.4—Ed.]

Calvin which are indicative of an ethics of divine commands.

Two types of reply have been made to this objection to divine command morality. Patterson Brown has developed a response based on the fact that "God is . . . defined as perfect in knowledge, justice and love." Thus Brown claims that God would "by definition will in accord with these several attributes" so that "the result would be anything but arbitrary." Heiko Oberman, on the other hand, has suggested a response which could be made on behalf of at least some scholastic divine command moralists that involves the concept of the divine simplicity:

> . . . At this point, however, we must remember Boehner's defense of [William of—Ed.] Occam mentioned earlier: the set order is for the *Venerabilis Inceptor* ["the venerable beginner," referring to Ockham—Ed.] by no means a product solely of God's will; will and intellect are two different names for God's essence. . . . Against the **Thomistic** emphasis on the priority of God's intellect, the priority of God's will is not stressed as much as the simplicity of God's being and the resulting unity of his intellect and **essence.** As the simplicity of God's being also implies a unity of essence and will, God's very essence guarantees the unbreakable relation and cooperation of intellect and will in God's *opera ad extra* [acts vis-á-vis the external world—Ed.] . . . [Gabriel—Ed.] Biel constantly tries to make clear that, whereas the will of God is the immediate cause of every act, these acts are certainly no arbitrary products of God's will alone. On the contrary, God's will operates according to God's essential wisdom, though this may be hidden from man.

. . . Finally, it should be pointed out that the particular variety of divine command morality espoused by [Nathaniel] Culverwell and by John Locke in his *Essays on the Law of Nature* can be seen as an attempt to avoid the objection of arbitrariness. For, while regarding "obligation" as dependent upon the divine will, they believe God to will in accord with the "nature of things."

(4) *God could command actions to be performed which are abhorrent and obviously immoral in character, such as murder and pointless acts of cruelty; if divine command morality were correct, such actions would have to be regarded as right.* This line of argument against divine command ethics . . . has a foundation in the divine command moralist William of Ockham, . . .

It has been suggested, however, that this criticism fails in not taking into account the fact the God who does the commanding also possesses such qualities as being "loving" and "benevolent." This line of reply has been . . . most forcefully developed by Robert Merrihew Adams.

(5) *Divine command morality reduces ethics to a matter of power.* This objection . . . could be regarded as a response to one of the reasons offered for divine command morality, namely, that this ethical position is required by the divine omnipotence.

(6) *Divine command ethics represents an infantile form of morality, in that it is* **deontological** *and* **heteronomous** *in character.* This criticism of divine command morality has been proffered by P. H. Nowell-Smith. . . .

(7) *Divine command morality is theologically unacceptable because it does not permit a coherent account of the moral attributes of God to be formulated. . . .* [Robert Merrihew] Adams formulates the problem in this way:

> . . . It is doubted that God, as an agent, can properly be called "good" in the moral sense if He is not subject to a moral law that is not of His own making. For if He is morally good, mustn't He do what is right *because* it is right? And how can He do that, if what's right is right because He wills it? Or it may be charged that divine command theories trivialize the claim that God is good. If "X is (morally) good" means roughly "X does what God wills," then "God is (morally) good" means only that God does what He wills—which is surely much less than people normally are taken to mean when they say that God is (morally) good.

Adams responds to this criticism by suggesting a meaning for the statement "God is good" which he believes to be compatible with divine command morality. Specifically, Adams suggests that when a divine command moralist claims that God is good, he is (a) expressing a favorable emotional attitude toward

God, and (b) ascribing to God certain qualities of character regarded as virtuous, such as kindness, benevolence, faithfulness, a forgiving disposition, or love. Moreover, Adams defends his proposal by arguing that the attitudinal and descriptive elements involved in his analysis of "God is good" are also part of the meaning of ascriptions of goodness to human beings.

[Philip L.] Quinn broadens the criticism discussed by Adams by calling into question the possibility of a divine command moralist attributing any moral virtue to God:

> . . . If we adopt one of the stronger divine command theories and suppose that only divine commands impose moral requirements on us, then obedience to God is a fundamental human virtue. . . . Other moral virtues will then be such that exercising them will entail being obedient to God. Thus, for example, temperance will be the disposition to obey those divine commands which require us to refrain from excesses of certain sorts. And courage will be the disposition to obey those divine commands which require us to act bravely in certain hazardous situations.
>
> But, within this framework, the divine command theorist does not seem to be able to speak coherently of God having moral virtues. For it is very odd, and perhaps unintelligible, to suppose that God, or anyone else for that matter, commands himself to do certain things and then obeys the commands he has addressed to himself. If a certain man is captain of a ship, then the crew is under his command, and he may command them and they must obey him. But he does not command himself. The admiral of the fleet addresses commands to him, and he must obey the admiral's commands. No one, then, is in a position to issue commands to God or to exact obedience from him. . . . Since no one, not even God, could be correctly said to obey or to disobey an imperative which did not originate from a source apart from himself, it is not possible for God, or for anyone else, to address commands to himself. But then, given our assumptions, since God cannot have the virtue of being obedient to God, he cannot possess any of the other human moral virtues.

And, as Quinn points out, "if God cannot have moral virtues, then it would seem that he cannot have those moral excellences which are logically necessary conditions for being worthy of worship."

Quinn's strategy of reply consists in describing divine *analogues* for human moral virtues. To take a very simple case, Quinn suggests that divine love might consist in unselfish concern for the welfare of the recipient, in which it resembles the virtue of human love; at the same time, God's love would lack two properties appropriate to human love, namely, the properties of "being commanded by God" and concomitantly of "being a moral virtue." Somewhat more complex accounts of divine analogues for the human virtues of forgiveness, mercy, and justice are also developed by Quinn.

(8) *Divine command morality is destructive of Christian beliefs about God's relationship with men.* Historically, this criticism of divine command morality was proposed by Joseph Glanvill, who found it suggested by George Rust's *A Discourse of Truth.* Glanvill believes that if morality is independent of God and reflective of the *nature of things,* there are restrictions on what God can do, viz., God "cannot lye, cannot deny himself . . . cannot act any thing that is Evil or imperfect." On the other hand, he claims that "if there be no immutable respects in things, but Just and Unjust, Honourable and Dishonourable, Good and Cruel, Faithful and Deceitful, are respects made by mere arbitrarious Will," then God could fail to abide by his promise to save those who commit themselves to Jesus Christ. Indeed, Glanvill claims that the dependency of morality on God allows for the possibility that God himself [causes] men to sin in order to assure their damnation.

(9) *Morality cannot depend solely on divine commands since nothing can be good, just, or the like, without possessing the* nature *(i.e., defining properties) of goodness, justice, etc.* This criticism is proffered by Ralph Cudworth. . . . Philip L. Quinn has perceived in Cudworth's point the claim that there are ***necessary truths*** about obligations and prohibitions, a claim which cannot be accepted by anyone who makes morality directly and solely dependent upon divine commands.

(10) *Linguistic considerations show the metaethical variety of divine command morality to be incorrect.* Specifically, the ***open question*** **argument** can

be used against definitions of moral concepts in terms of divine commands: If, e.g., the term "good" means "commanded by God," then the question "Is what God commands good?" ought to be redundant and senseless; since it is a meaningful question, the proposed definition must be wrong. A related form of argument consists in pointing out that, if divine command morality as a metaethical thesis were correct, then certain propositions (such as "God's actions are right") would be **tautologous,** insignificant, or meaningless, which they are not. . . .

Two replies to this line of argument are mentioned in the literature on divine command morality. First of all, it has been suggested that a theist might claim that definitions of moral concepts in terms of divine commands are not intended to reflect ordinary usage but constitute more adequate, **stipulative definitions** embodying the insights of the man of faith. In this way divine command **metaethics** would stand untouched by the linguistic arguments proffered against it, since these arguments are grounded in common usage. This possible move on the part of the divine command moralist has been mentioned by Kai Nielsen, who argues against it on the grounds that it both begs the question and trivializes the position of the divine command moralist.

Historically, another approach to the problem was taken by William Paley. It is claimed by Paley that divine command ethics allows for the derivation of secondary rules for judging moral situations. In fact, Paley believes that we come to use these secondary rules without thought of their origin, so that we may even judge God himself according to them. And it is this situation which accounts for the linguistic cases which seem to refute divine command metaethics.

(11) *Divine command metaethics fails in either reducing ethical statements to merely factual ones or in producing a circular definition.* This criticism has been made by A. C. Ewing, who believes the same point to be applicable to **naturalistic** definitions of ethical terms.[2]

In considering criticisms of divine command morality, mention should also be made of an alternative interpretation of evidence which seems to support divine command ethics. Specifically, it might be pointed out in favor of divine command morality that there are cases in which divine commands are acknowledged to create obligations which did not previously exist (e.g., if God should command person (or group) *X* not to eat a certain kind of food, or to move to a certain locality, or to take up a particular vocation). Both Ralph Cudworth and Richard Price, however, have argued that this sort of situation should be interpreted in the following way: Just as the laws of a civil government or the act of promising make actions obligatory which were not such before, but only because of an antecedent obligation to obey legitimate authority and to keep promises; so God's commands can create new obligations

[2][Ewing writes:

> . . . why obey God's commands? Because I ought to do so. Since 'I ought to do A' is held to mean 'God commands me to do *A*,' this can only mean that I am commanded by God to obey God's commands, which supplies no further reason whatever. Because God is good? This could only mean on the definition given that God carries out his own commands. Because I love God? This presupposes two propositions as to what I ought to do which could not without a vicious circle be validated by referring again to God's commands, i.e. that I ought to obey the commands of God if I love him and that I ought to love God. . . . Without a prior conception of God as good or his commands as right God would have no more claim on our obedience than Hitler or Stalin except that he would have more power than even they had to make things uncomfortable for those who disobey him. It is only because the notion of God (for Christians at least) already includes the notion of perfect goodness that we are inclined to think it self-evident that we ought to obey God.

He continues:

> If God is not conceived as good in a specifically ethical sense but 'good' functions just as an adjective to mean 'what God wants', ethics is reduced to a mere prudent subservience to superior power; if on the other hand in the definition of good or right as willed by God goodness in a properly ethical sense is already presupposed, the definition is a circular one and leaves undefined some fundamental ethical term. As we can find no necessary relation between goodness and obligation on the one hand and the alleged **naturalist** definitions on the other, so we can find no necessary relation between being commanded or willed by God and being obligatory or good, unless we already assume the goodness of God, thus exposing ourselves to the charge of being guilty of a vicious circle, since we should have defined both God in terms of goodness and goodness in terms of God. . . .

—Ed.]

because of another obligation we have to obey the divine authority, which obligation is not itself dependent on God. In this way an important facet of religious tradition can be preserved without resorting to divine command morality.

Finally, we wish to mention a consideration which, while not directly a criticism of divine command morality, is a caution regarding it. This consideration concerns the recent proposal of some moral philosophers that not just anything can count as a moral standard. In other words, it has been claimed that there are certain characteristics which serve to define the realm of the moral and to distinguish it from the non-moral, and concomitantly, that any norm or set of norms must possess the properties in question in order to qualify as a *moral* system. This position carries the implication that, if God's commands are to constitute a morality properly speaking, these commands must be of such a nature as to satisfy the restrictions we place on possible moral standards. . . .

[WORKS CITED] [PREPARED BY THE EDITOR BASED UPON AND IN LIEU OF THE FOOTNOTES IN THE ORIGINAL—ED.]

Adams, Robert Merrihew. "A Modified Divine Command Theory of Ethical Wrongness." In *Religion and Morality,* pp. 318–47. Ed. Gene Outka and John P. Reeder, Jr. Garden City, N. Y., 1973.

Barth, Karl. *Church Dogmatics.* Edinburgh, 1957.

Bentham, Jeremy. *An Introduction to the Principles of Morals and Legislation* (1789). London, 1970.

Brown, Patterson. "Religious Morality." *Mind* 72(1963): 235–44.

Brown, Patterson. "Religious Morality: A Reply to Flew and Campbell." *Mind* 77(1968):577–80.

Cudworth, Ralph. *Treatise Concerning Eternal and Immutable Morality,* in *The True Intellectual System of the Universe.* New York, 1838.

Culverwell, Nathaniel (1652). *An Elegant and Learned Discourse of the Light of Nature.* Ed. Robert A. Greene and Hugh MacCallum. Toronto, 1971.

Ewing, A. C. "The Autonomy of Ethics." In *Prospect for Metaphysics,* pp. 33–49. Ed. Ian Ramsey. London, 1961.

Gerson, Jean. *De Consolatione Theologiae (On the Consolation of Theology)* (1418). In *Ouevres Completes,* vol. 9. Ed. Mgr. Glorieux. Paris, 1973.

Glanvill, Joseph. *A Letter Concerning George Rust's A Discourse of Truth.* From *Two Choice and Useful Treatises.* London, 1682.

Goldstick, D. M. "Monotheism's *Euthyphro* Problem," *Canadian Journal of Philosophy* 3(1974):585–89.

Henry, Carl F. *Christian Personal Ethics.* Grand Rapids, MI, 1957.

Locke, John. *Essays on the Laws of Nature* (1664). Oxford, 1965.

Nielsen, Kai. "Some Remarks on the Independence of Morality from Religion." *Mind* 70(1961):175–86.

Nowell-Smith, P. H. "Morality: Religious and Secular." In *Christian Ethics and Contemporary Philosophy,* pp. 93–112. Ed. Ian T. Ramsey. New York, 1966.

Oberman, Heiko. *The Harvest of Medieval Theology: Gabriel Biel and Late Medieval Nominalism,* pp. 98–99. Cambriage, MA, 1963.

Paley, William. *The Principles of Moral and Political Philosophy.* 2nd ed. London, 1786.

Price, Richard. *A Review of the Principal Questions In Morals.* 3rd ed. London, 1787.

Quinn, Philip L. "Divine Command Ethics: A Causal Theory." In *Divine Command Morality,* ed. Janine Marie Idziak. pp. 305–25. New York and Toronto, 1979.

Rust, George. *A Discourse of Truth.* In Joseph Glanvill, *Two Choice and Useful Treatises.* London, 1682.

STUDY QUESTIONS

1. Explain the considerations Idziak mentions in favor of a divine command theory of ethics. *Which ones, if any, do you not find convincing? Why?
2. Explain the considerations Idziak mentions against a divine command theory of ethics. *Which ones, if any, do you not find convincing? Why?
3. Divine command theorists stress God's power and liberty. But God has other attributes, such as wisdom. What implication does this point have vis-à-vis divine command morality? (Think here of Plato's argument in Reading 3.4.)
4. *Divine command theorists argue that nothing can be independent of God; therefore, in particular, no ethical standard can exist independently of God. What does this argument seem to suggest with regard to whether truths of logic and mathematics are dependent on God? Does this implication strike you as correct?
5. *John Locke argues that, because "we owe our body, soul and life" to God, we are completely subject to God's commands. Some critics would charge that Locke's argument is inconsistent, because it itself rests on a moral principle that is independent of God's will. What principle do you think these critics would be referring to?

6. *According to divine command theory, if God were to command people to torture innocent children for fun, people would be morally obligated to do so. Critics think this result is damaging to the theory. How does the fact that God has qualities such as being loving provide a possible reply to this objection?

7. Idziak notes that, on a divine command theory, we cannot give a coherent account of God's moral attributes. God could not possess moral virtues. Why?

READING 3.6

The Binding of Isaac

Genesis 22

In Genesis 22, God commands Abraham to go up Mount Moriah and offer his son Isaac as a burnt offering. The episode is particularly poignant because Abraham's wife, Sarah, did not give birth to Isaac until the couple were elderly, and Abraham had invested all hopes of an heir in Isaac. (Shortly before the command, his other son, Ishmael, born to Hagar, had left his household.) Abraham binds Isaac and prepares him for the sacrifice; however, just as he is about to slaughter Isaac with a knife, an angel of God tells him to stay his hand because he has by now proved that he is a God-fearing person. Søren Kierkegaard viewed Abraham's willingness to comply with the command as an example of morality overriding God's command. The episode is often referred to by the Hebrew term **akedah** *(binding).*

Superscripts in this selection are verse numbers, not footnote numbers.

[1]And it came to pass after these things, that God did prove Abraham, and said unto him: 'Abraham'; and he said: 'Here am I.' [2]And He said: 'Take now thy son, thine only son, whom thou lovest, even Isaac, and get thee into the land of Moriah; and offer him there for a burnt-offering upon one of the mountains which I will tell thee of.' [3]And Abraham rose early in the morning, and saddled his ass, and took two of his young men with him, and Isaac his son; and he cleaved the wood for the burnt-offering, and rose up, and went unto the place of which God had told him. [4]On the third day Abraham lifted up his eyes, and saw the place afar off. [5]And Abraham said unto his young men: 'Abide ye here with the ass, and I and the lad will go yonder; and we will worship, and come back to you.' [6]And Abraham took the wood of the burnt-offering, and laid it upon Isaac his son; and he took in his hand the fire and the knife; and they went both of them together. [7]And Isaac spoke unto Abraham his father, and said: 'My father.' And he said: 'Here am I, my son.' And he said: 'Behold the fire and the wood; but where is the lamb for a burnt-offering?' [8]And Abraham said: 'God will provide Himself the lamb for a burnt-offering, my son.' So they went both of them together. [9]And they came to the place which God had told him of; and Abraham built the altar there, and laid the wood in order, and bound Isaac his son, and laid him on the altar, upon the wood. [10]And Abraham stretched forth his hand, and took the knife to slay his son. [11]And the angel of the Lord called unto him out of heaven, and said: 'Abraham, Abraham.' [12]And he said: 'Here am I.' And he said: 'Lay not thy hand upon the lad, neither do thou any thing unto him; for now I know that thou art a God-fearing man, seeing thou hast not withheld thy son, thine only son, from Me.' [13]And Abraham lifted up his eyes, and looked, and behold behind him a ram caught in the thicket by his horns. And Abraham went and took the ram, and offered him up for a burnt-offering in the stead of his son. [14]And Abra-

ham called the name of that place Adonaijireh; as it
is said to this day: 'In the mount where the Lord is
seen.'
15And the angel of the Lord called unto Abra-
ham a second time out of heaven,
16and said: 'By
Myself have I sworn, saith the Lord, because thou
hast done this thing, and hast not withheld thy son,
thine only son,
17that in blessing I will bless thee,
and in multiplying I will multiply thy seed as the
stars of the heaven, and as the sand which is upon
the sea-shore; and thy seed shall possess the gate of
his enemies;
18and in thy seed shall all the nations
of the earth be blessed; because thou hast hearkened
to My voice.' . . .

STUDY QUESTIONS

1. Relate the episode of the binding of Isaac.
2. What is your reaction to Abraham's willingness to obey God?
3. *In Genesis 18:20–33, when God threatens to destroy the city of Sodom because of its inhabitants' wickedness, Abraham pleads with God not to destroy the innocent together with the guilty, and God eventually agrees to spare the city if ten righteous people can be found there. Why would Abraham question God in that episode but agree to kill his son without protest or pleading?

READING 3.7

Suspending the Ethical

Søren Kierkegaard

Danish **existentialist** *philosopher Søren Kierkegaard (1813–1855), one of the major figures in philosophy of the past two centuries, construes the conflict that Abraham faces in the binding of Isaac as a clash between morality and religion. Ethically, Abraham's action (were he to kill Isaac) would be termed* murder, *but the religious term would be* sacrifice. *By choosing to obey God's command, Abraham engages in a* **teleological suspension of the ethical** *and thereby becomes a* knight of faith. *The ethical is the universal that applies to everyone (as in Immanuel Kant's philosophy). Abraham's faith is paradoxical, for he surrenders himself to the universal yet suspends it to become a singular individual. Abraham's faith cannot be communicated and is "faith by virtue of the absurd." Abraham had faith that God would not command that he kill Isaac and that he would be blessed with children, but he was willing to obey God's command to kill his son.*

Kierkegaard's view should not be confused with Euthyphro's position that morality has no validity independently of God's will. On the contrary, it is the validity and bindingness of morality that creates the conflict with God's command. In general, Kierkegaard did not deny the value of endeavors such as science, history, art, and morality, but he insisted on keeping religious commitment distinct from and, at times, opposed to these endeavors.

. . . The ethical expression for what Abraham did is that he meant to murder Isaac; the religious expression is that he meant to sacrifice Isaac—but precisely in this contradiction is the anxiety that can make a person sleepless, and yet without this anxiety Abraham is not who he is. Or if Abraham perhaps did not do at all what the story tells, if perhaps because of the local conditions of that day it was something entirely different, then let us forget him, for what is the value of going to the trouble of remembering that past which cannot become a present. Or perhaps the speaker forgot something equivalent to the ethical oversight that Isaac was the son. In other words, if faith is taken away by becoming *Nul* and *Nichts,* all that remains is the brutal fact that Abraham meant to murder Isaac, which is easy enough for anyone to imitate if he does not have faith—that is, the faith that makes it difficult for him. . . .

I wonder if anyone in my generation is able to make the movements of faith? If I am not mistaken, my generation is rather inclined to be proud of doing what it probably does not even believe me capable of—that is, the imperfect. My soul balks at doing what is so often done—talking inhumanly about the great, as if a few centuries were an enormous distance. I prefer to speak humanly about it, as if it happened yesterday, and only let the greatness itself be the distance that either elevates or judges. If I (*in the capacity of tragic hero,* for higher I cannot come) had been ordered to take such an extraordinary royal journey as the one to Mount Moriah, I know very well what I would have done. I would not have been cowardly enough to stay at home, nor would I have dragged and drifted along the road or forgotten the knife in order to cause a delay. I am quite sure that I would have been punctual and all prepared—more than likely, I would have arrived too early in order to get it over sooner. But I also know what else I would have done. The moment I mounted the horse, I would have said to myself: Now all is lost, God demands Isaac, I sacrifice him and along with him all my joy—yet God is love and continues to be that for me, for in the world of time God and I cannot talk with each other, we have no language in common. Perhaps someone in our time would be so foolish, so envious of the great, as to want to delude himself and me into believing that if I had actually done this I would have done something even greater than what Abraham did, for my immense resignation . . . would be far more ideal and poetic than Abraham's small-mindedness. But this is utterly false, for my immense resignation would be a substitute for faith. I would not be able to do more than make the infinite movement in order to find myself and again rest in myself. Neither would I have loved Isaac as Abraham loved him. That I was determined to make the movement could prove my courage, humanly speaking—that I loved him with my whole soul is the presupposition without which the whole thing becomes a misdeed—nevertheless I would not love as Abraham loved, for then I would have held back at the very last minute, without, however, arriving too late at Mount Moriah. Furthermore, by my behavior I would have spoiled the whole story, for if I had gotten Isaac again, I would have been in an awkward position. What was the easiest for Abraham would have been difficult for me—once again to be happy in Isaac!—for he who with all the infinity of his soul, *proprio motu et propriis auspiciis* [of his own accord and on his own responsibility], has made the infinite movement and cannot do more, he keeps Isaac only with pain.

But what did Abraham do? He arrived neither too early nor too late. He mounted the ass, he rode slowly down the road. During all this time he had faith, he had faith that God would not demand Isaac of him, and yet he was willing to sacrifice him if it was demanded. He had faith by virtue of the absurd, for human calculation was out of the question, and it certainly was absurd that God, who required it of him, should in the next moment rescind the requirement. He climbed the mountain, and even in the moment when the knife gleamed he had faith—that God would not require Isaac. No doubt he was surprised at the outcome, but through a double-movement he had attained his first condition, and therefore he received Isaac more joyfully than the first time. Let us go further. We let Isaac actually be sacrificed. Abraham had faith. He did not have faith that he would be blessed in a future life but that he would be blessed here in the world. God could give him a new Isaac, could restore to life the one sacrificed. He had faith by virtue of the absurd, for all human calculation ceased long ago. It is evident that sorrow can make a man mentally ill, and that is hard enough; it is also evident that there is a willpower that can haul to the wind so drastically that it rescues the understanding, even though a person becomes a little odd (and I do not intend to disparage this). But to be able to lose one's understanding and along with it everything finite, for which it is the stockbroker, and then to win the very same finitude again by virtue of the absurd—this appalls me, but that does not make me say it is something inferior, since, on the contrary, it is the one and only marvel. It is commonly supposed that what faith produces is no work of art, that it is a coarse and boorish piece of work, only for the more uncouth natures, but it is far from being that. The **dialectic** of faith is the finest and the most extraordinary of all; it has an elevation of which I can certainly form a conception, but no more than that. I can make the mighty trampoline leap whereby I cross over into infinity; my back is like a tightrope dancer's, twisted in my childhood, and therefore it is easy for me. One, two, three—I can walk upside down in existence, but I cannot make the next movement, for the marvelous I cannot do—I can only be amazed at it. Indeed, if Abraham, the moment he swung his leg over the ass's back, had said to himself: Now Isaac is lost, I could just as well sacrifice him here at home as ride the long way to Moriah—then I do not need Abraham, whereas now I bow seven times to his name and seventy times to his deed. This he did not do, as I can prove by his really fervent joy on receiving Isaac and by his needing no preparation and no time to rally to finitude and its joy. If it had been otherwise with Abraham, he perhaps would have loved God but would not have had faith, for he who loves God without faith reflects upon himself; he who loves God in faith reflects upon God.

This is the peak on which Abraham stands. The last stage to pass from his view is the stage of infinite resignation. He actually goes further and comes to faith. All those travesties of faith—the wretched, lukewarm lethargy that thinks: There's no urgency, there's no use in grieving beforehand; the despicable hope that says: One just can't know what will happen, it could just possibly be—those travesties are native to the paltriness of life, and infinite resignation has already infinitely disdained them.

Abraham I cannot understand; in a certain sense I can learn nothing from him except to be amazed. If someone deludes himself into thinking he may be moved to have faith by pondering the outcome of that story, he cheats himself and cheats God out of the first movement of faith—he wants to suck worldly wisdom out of the paradox. Someone might succeed, for our generation does not stop with faith, does not stop with miracle of faith, turning water into wine—it goes further and turns wine into water.

Would it not be best to stop with faith, and is it not shocking that everyone wants to go further? Where will it all end when in our age, as declared in so many ways, one does not want to stop with love? In wordly shrewdness, in petty calculation, in paltriness and meanness, in everything that can make man's divine origin doubtful. Would it not be best to remain standing at faith and for him who stands to see to it that he does not fall, for the movement of faith must continually be made by virtue of the absurd, but yet in such a way, please note, that one does not lose the finite but gains it whole and intact. For my part, I presumably can describe the movements of faith, but I cannot make them. In learning to go through the motions of swimming, one can be suspended from the ceiling in a harness and then presumably describe the movements, but one is not swimming. In the same way I can describe the movements of faith. If I am thrown out into the water, I presumably do swim (for I do not belong to the waders), but I make different movements, the movements of infinity, whereas faith makes the opposite movements: after having made the movements of infinity, it makes the movements of finitude. Fortunate is the person who can make these movements! He does the marvelous, and I shall never weary of admiring him; it makes no difference to me whether it is Abraham or a slave in Abraham's house, whether it is a professor of philosophy or a poor servant girl—I pay attention only to the movements. But I do pay attention to them, and I do not let myself be fooled, either by myself or by anyone else. The knights of the infinite resignation are easily recognizable—their walk is light and bold. But they who carry the treasure of faith are likely to disappoint, for externally they have a striking resemblance to bourgeois philistinism, which infinite resignation, like faith, deeply disdains.

I honestly confess that in my experience I have not found a single authentic instance, although I do not therefore deny that every second person may be such an instance. Meanwhile, I have been looking for it for many years, but in vain. Generally, people travel around the world to see rivers and mountains, new stars, colorful birds, freakish fish, preposterous races of mankind; they indulge in the brutish stupor that gawks at life and thinks it has seen something. That does not occupy me. But if I knew where a knight of faith lived, I would travel on foot to him, for this marvel occupies me absolutely. I would not leave him for a second, I would watch him every minute to see how he made the movements; I would consider myself taken care of for life and would divide my time between watching him and practicing myself, and thus spend all my time in admiring him. . . .

IS THERE A TELEOLOGICAL SUSPENSION OF THE ETHICAL?

The ethical as such is the universal, and as the universal it applies to everyone, which from another angle means that it applies at all times. It rests immanent in itself, has nothing outside itself that is its **telos** [end, purpose] but is itself the telos for everything outside itself, and when the ethical has absorbed this into itself, it goes not further. The single individual, sensately and psychically qualified in immediacy, is the individual who has his telos in the universal, and it is his ethical task continually to express himself in this, to annul his singularity in order to become the universal. As soon as the single individual asserts himself in his singularity before the universal, he sins, and only by acknowledging this can he be reconciled again with the universal. Every time the single individual, after having entered the universal, feels an impulse to assert himself as the single individual, he is in a spiritual trial . . . , from which he can work himself only by repentantly surrendering as the single individual in the universal. If this is the highest that can be said of man and his existence, then the ethical is of the same nature as a person's eternal salvation, which is his telos forevermore and at all times, since it would be a contradiction for this to be capable of being surrendered (that is, teleologically suspended), because as soon as this is suspended it is relinquished, whereas that which is suspended is not relinquished but is preserved in the higher, which is its telos. . . .

Faith is precisely the paradox that the single individual as the single individual is higher than the universal, is justified before it, not as inferior to it but as superior—yet in such a way, please note, that it is the single individual who, after being subordinate as the single individual to the universal, now by means of the universal becomes the single individual who as the single individual is superior, that the single individual as the single individual stands in an absolute relation to the absolute. This position cannot be mediated, for all mediation takes place only by virtue of the universal; it is and remains for all eternity a paradox, impervious to thought. And yet faith is this paradox, or else (and I ask the reader to bear these consequences [in mind] even though it would be too prolix for me to write them all down) or else faith has never existed simply because it has always existed, or else Abraham is lost.

It is certainly true that the single individual can easily confuse this paradox with spiritual trial . . . , but it ought not to be concealed for that reason. It is certainly true that many persons may be so constituted that they are repulsed by it, but faith ought not therefore to be made into something else to enable one to have it, but one ought rather to admit to not having it, while those who have faith ought to be prepared to set forth some characteristics whereby the paradox can be distinguished from a spiritual trial.

The story of Abraham contains just such a **teleological suspension of the ethical.** There is no dearth of keen minds and careful scholars who have found analogies to it. What their wisdom amounts to is the beautiful proposition that basically everything is the same. If one looks more closely, I doubt very much that anyone in the whole wide world will find one single analogy, except for a later one, which proves nothing if it is certain that Abraham represents faith and that it is manifested normatively in him, whose life not only is the most paradoxical that can be thought but is also so paradoxical that it simply cannot be thought. He acts by virtue of the absurd, for it is precisely the absurd that he as the single individual is higher than the universal. This paradox cannot be mediated, for as soon as Abraham begins to do so, he has to confess that he was in a spiritual trial, and if that is the case, he will never sacrifice Isaac, or if he did sacrifice Isaac, then in repentance he must come back to the universal. He gets Isaac back again by virtue of the absurd. Therefore, Abraham is at no time a tragic hero but is something entirely different, either a murderer or a man of faith. Abraham does not have the middle term that saves the tragic hero. This is why I can understand a tragic hero but cannot understand Abraham, even though in a certain demented sense I admire him more than all others.

In ethical terms, Abraham's relation to Isaac is quite simply this: the father shall love the son more than himself. But within its own confines the ethical has various gradations. We shall see whether this story contains any higher expression for the ethical that can ethically explain his behavior, can ethically justify his suspending the ethical obligation to the son, but without moving beyond the teleology of the ethical. . . .

The difference between the tragic hero and Abraham is very obvious. The tragic hero is still within the ethical. He allows an expression of the ethical to have its telos in a higher expression of the ethical; he scales down the ethical relation between father and son or daughter and father to a feeling that has its dialectic in its relation to the idea of moral conduct. Here there can be no question of a teleological suspension of the ethical itself.

Abraham's situation is different. By his act he transgressed the ethical altogether and had a higher telos outside it, in relation to which he suspended it. For I certainly would like to know how Abraham's act can be related to the universal, whether any point of contact between what Abraham did and the universal can be found other than that Abraham transgressed it. It is not to save a nation, not to uphold the idea of the state that Abraham does it; it is not to appease the angry gods. If it were a matter of the deity's being angry, then he was, after all, angry only with Abraham, and Abraham's act is totally unrelated to the universal, is a purely private endeavor. Therefore, while the tragic hero is great because of his moral virtue, Abraham is great because of a purely personal virtue. There is no higher expression for the ethical in Abraham's life than that the father shall love the son. The ethical in the sense of the moral is entirely beside the point. Insofar as the universal was present, it was cryptically in Isaac, hidden, so to speak, in Isaac's loins, and must cry out with Isaac's mouth: Do not do this, you are destroying everything.

Why, then, does Abraham do it? For God's sake and—the two are wholly identical—for his own sake. He does it for God's sake because God demands this proof of his faith; he does it for his own sake so that he can prove it. The unity of the two is altogether correctly expressed in the word already used to describe this relationship. It is an ordeal, a temptation. A temptation—but what does that mean? As a rule, what tempts a person is something that will hold him back from doing his duty, but here the temptation is the ethical itself, which would hold him back from doing God's will. But what is duty? Duty is simply the expression for God's will.

Here the necessity of a new category for the understanding of Abraham becomes apparent. Paganism does not know such a relationship to the divine. The tragic hero does not enter into any private relationship to the divine, but the ethical is the divine, and thus the paradox therein can be mediated in the universal.

Abraham cannot be mediated; in other words, he cannot speak. As soon as I speak, I express the universal, and if I do not do so, no one can understand me. As soon as Abraham wants to express himself in the universal, he must declare that his situation is a spiritual trial . . . , for he has no higher expression of the universal that ranks above the universal he violates. . . .

STUDY QUESTIONS

1. Explain what is meant by *the teleological suspension of the ethical.* How does Kierkegaard use this concept in his reading of the binding of Isaac?
2. How is Abraham's situation different from that of the tragic hero?
3. Why is Abraham's faith "faith by virtue of the absurd"?
4. *Some critics of Kierkegaard observe that, in the historical period in which the Abraham story is set, sacrificing children to God was standard practice. How might this observation undermine Kierkegaard's portrayal of Abraham's conflict?
5. *Abraham loved Isaac dearly and saw in him his only chance for an heir. Therefore, Abraham's conflict, it would seem, need not be portrayed as one between *morality* and God's command but,

rather, may be depicted as one between *parental love* and God's command. Try to develop this interpretation of his conflict and compare it with Kierkegaard's reading.

6. *Are there any details in the story of the binding (Reading 3.6) that you think support Kierkegaard? Are there any that are a problem for his position?
7. *Immanuel Kant suggested that Abraham should have doubted whether the voice he heard was God's and, therefore, Abraham should not have gone through with his actions. How would you handle this objection?
8. Study Robert Merrihew Adams's article in Reading 7.10, where he explains why Kierkegaard opposed the use of objective scientific, philosophical, and historical arguments on behalf of religion. What similarity do you see between this view of Kierkegaard and Kierkegaard's approach to the binding of Isaac?
9. *Is Kierkegaard saying that a person is *obligated* to obey God's command when it conflicts with morality, or is he only trying to characterize what is involved in leading a religious life, without passing a value judgment? Discuss based on the selection.

READING 3.8

Worship and Moral Agency

James Rachels

Theistic religions assert that a believer must worship God. In this selection, James Rachels (University of Alabama, Birmingham) maintains that, by imposing this demand, religions are asking their adherents to relinquish their roles as moral agents.

According to Rachels's definition of the term, worship requires the worshipper's total subjugation to the will of the one worshipped. By definition, a worshipper cannot view God as someone whose commands he or she may accept or reject after careful evaluation and reflection. A person cannot be a worshipper if he or she sits in judgment over whether God's command is worthy of being obeyed. If Abraham truly worships God, then, when God commands him to sacrifice his son on the altar, Abraham must submit to the divine will, no matter how offensive this deed is to Abraham's—or anyone else's—moral sensibilities. Furthermore, because worship requires such extreme submission to the will of another, no being is worthy of worship. Hence, if God is defined, in part, as a being who is worthy of worship, then God cannot exist.

Central to Rachels's argument is a conception of a moral agent that is championed by German philosopher Immanuel Kant (1724–1804). In this conception, a true moral agent is **autonomous**—*literally, self-legislating. Autonomous agents defer to no one but themselves. Thus, they worship no one, not even God, for to submit to the will of another is to act* **heteronomously** *rather than autonomously. Rachels considers but rejects several ways of reconciling moral autonomy and religious worship.*

> *Kneeling down or grovelling on the ground, even to express your reverence for heavenly things, is contrary to human dignity.*
>
> Kant

. . . It is necessarily true that God (if He exists) is worthy of worship.[1] Any being who is not worthy of worship cannot be God, just as any being who is not **omnipotent,** or who is not perfectly good, cannot be

[1] Hartshorne and Pike suggest that the formula "that than which none greater can be conceived" should be interpreted as "that than which none more worthy of worship can be conceived." Charles Hartshorne, *Anselm's Discovery* (LaSalle, Illinois, 1966), pp. 25–26, and Nelson Pike, *God and Timelessness* (London, 1970), pp. 149–160.

God. This is reflected in the attitudes of religious believers who recognize that, whatever else God may be, He is a being before whom men should bow down. Moreover, He is unique in this; to worship anyone or anything else is blasphemy. In this paper I shall present an **a priori argument** against the existence of God which is based on the conception of God as a fitting object of worship. The argument is that God cannot exist, because no being could ever *be* a fitting object of worship.

However, before I can present this argument, there are several preliminary matters that require attention. The chief of these, which will hopefully have some independent interest of its own, is an examination of the concept of worship. . . .

Worship presumes the superior status of the one worshiped. This is reflected in the logical point that there can be no such thing as mutual or reciprocal worship, unless one or the other of the parties is mistaken as to his own status. We can very well comprehend people loving one another or respecting one another, but not (unless they are misled) worshiping one another. This is because the worshiper necessarily assumes his own inferiority; and since inferiority is an asymmetrical relation, so is worship. (The nature of the "superiority" and "inferiority" involved here is of course problematic; but on the account I am presenting it may be understood on the model of superior and inferior positions within a social system. More on this later.) This is also why *humility* is necessary on the part of the worshiper. The role to which he commits himself is that of the humble servant, "not worthy to touch the hem of His garment." Compared to God's gloriousness, "all our righteousnesses are as filthy rags" (Isaiah 64:6). So, in committing oneself to this role, one is acknowledging God's greatness and one's own relative worthlessness. This humble attitude is not a mere embellishment of the ritual: on the contrary, worship, unlike love or respect, *requires* humility. Pride is a sin, and pride before God is incompatible with worshiping him.

On the view that I am suggesting, the function of worship as "glorifying" or "praising" God, which is usually taken to be its primary function, may be regarded as derivative from the more fundamental nature of worship as commitment to the role of God's Child. "Praising" God is giving him the honour and respect due to one in his position of eminence, just as one shows respect and honour in giving fealty to a King.

In short, the worshiper is in this position: He believes that there is a being, God, who is the perfectly good, perfectly powerful, perfectly wise Creator of the Universe; and he views himself as the "Child of God," made for God's purposes and responsible to God for his conduct. And the ritual of worship, which may have any number of ceremonial forms according to the customs of the religious community, has as its point the acceptance of, and commitment to, one's role as God's Child, with all that this involves. If this account is accepted, then there is no mystery as to the relation between the act of worship and the worshiper's other activity. Worship will be regarded not as an isolated act taking place on Sunday morning, with no necessary connection to one's behaviour the rest of the week, but as a ritualistic expression of and commitment to a role which dominates one's whole way of life.[2] . . .

In Genesis there are two familiar stories, both concerning Abraham, that are relevant here. The first is the story of the near-sacrifice of Isaac. We are told that Abraham was "tempted" by God, who commanded him to offer Isaac as a human sacrifice. Abraham obeyed without hesitation: he prepared an altar, bound Isaac to it, and was about to kill him until God intervened at the last moment, saying "Lay not thine hand upon the lad, neither do thou any thing unto him; for now I know that thou fearest God, seeing thou hast not withheld thy son, thine only son from me" (Genesis 22:12). So Abraham passed the test. But how could he have failed? What was his "temptation"? Obviously, his temptation was to disobey

[2]This account of worship, specified here in terms of what it means to worship God, may easily be adapted to the worship of other beings such as Satan. The only changes required are (*a*) that we substitute for beliefs about God analogous beliefs about Satan, and (*b*) that we understand the ritual of worship as committing the Satan-worshiper to a role as Satan's servant in the same way that worshiping God commits theists to the role of His servant.

God; God had ordered him to do something contrary to both his wishes and his sense of what would otherwise be right and wrong. He could have defied God; but he did not—he subordinated himself, his own desires and judgments, to God's command, even when the temptation to do otherwise was strongest.

It is interesting that Abraham's record in this respect was not perfect. We also have the story of him bargaining with God over the conditions for saving Sodom and Gomorrah from destruction. God had said that he would destroy those cities because they were so wicked; but Abraham gets God to agree that if fifty righteous men can be found there, then the cities will be spared. Then he persuades God to lower the number to forty-five, then forty, then thirty, then twenty, and finally ten. Here we have a different Abraham, not servile and obedient, but willing to challenge God and bargain with him. However, even as he bargains with God, Abraham realises that there is something radically inappropriate about it: he says, "Behold now, I have taken upon me to speak unto the Lord, which am but dust and ashes . . . O let not the Lord be angry . . ." (Genesis 18:27, 30).

The fact is that Abraham could not, consistently with his role as God's subject, set his own judgment and will against God's. The author of Genesis was certainly right about this. We cannot recognise any being *as God,* and at the same time set ourselves against him. The point is not merely that it would be imprudent to defy God, since we certainly can't get away with it; rather, there is a stronger, logical point involved—namely, that if we recognise any being *as God,* then we are committed, in virtue of that recognition, to obeying him.

To see why this is so, we must first notice that "God" is not a proper name like "Richard Nixon" but a title like "President of the United States" or "King."[3] Thus, "Jehovah is God" is a non**tautological** statement in which the title "God" is assigned to Jehovah, a particular being—just as "Richard Nixon is President of the United States" assigns the title "President of the United States" to a particular man. This permits us to understand how statements like "God is perfectly wise" can be logical truths, which is highly problematic if "God" is regarded as a proper name. Although it is not a logical truth that any particular being is perfectly wise, it nevertheless is a logical truth that if any being is God (i.e. if any being properly holds that title) then that being is perfectly wise. This is exactly analogous to saying: although it is not a logical truth that Richard Nixon has the authority to veto congressional legislation, nevertheless it is a logical truth that if Richard Nixon is President of the United States then he has that authority.

To bear the title "God," then, a being must have certain qualifications. He must, for example, be all-powerful and perfectly good in addition to being perfectly wise. And in the same vein, to apply the title "God" to a being is to recognise him as one to be obeyed. The same is true, to a lesser extent, of "King"—to recognise anyone as King is to acknowledge that he occupies a place of authority and has a claim on one's allegiance as his subject. And to recognise any being as God is to acknowledge that he has *unlimited* authority, and an unlimited claim on one's allegiance. Thus, we might regard Abraham's reluctance to defy Jehovah as grounded not only in his fear of Jehovah's wrath, but as a logical consequence of his acceptance of Jehovah *as God.* Camus was right to think that "From the moment that man submits God to moral judgment, he kills Him in his own heart."[4] What a man can "kill" by defying or even questioning God is not the being that (supposedly) *is* God, but *his own conception of that being as God.* That God is not to be judged, challenged, defied, or disobeyed, is at bottom a truth of logic; to do any of these things is incompatible with taking him as One to be worshiped.

. . . So the idea that any being could be *worthy* of worship is much more problematical than we might have at first imagined. For in admitting that a being is worthy of worship we would be recognising him as having an unqualified claim on our obedience. The question, then, is whether there could be such an

[3]Cf. Nelson Pike, "Omnipotence and God's Ability to Sin," *American Philosophical Quarterly,* VI (1969), pp. 208–9; and C. B. Martin, *Religious Belief* (Ithaca, 1959), ch. 4.

[4]Albert Camus, *The Rebel,* translated by Anthony Bower (New York, 1956), p. 62.

unqualified claim. It should be noted that the description of a being as all-powerful, all-wise, etc., would not automatically settle the issue; for even while admitting the existence of such an awesome being we might still question whether we should recognise him as having an unlimited claim on our obedience.

In fact, there is a long tradition in moral philosophy, from Plato to Kant, according to which such a recognition could never be made by a moral agent. According to this tradition, to be a moral agent is to be an autonomous or self-directed agent; unlike the precepts of law or social custom, moral precepts are imposed by the agent upon himself, and the penalty for their violation is, in Kant's words, "self-contempt and inner abhorrence." The virtuous man is therefore identified with the man of integrity, i.e. the man who acts according to precepts which he can, on reflection, conscientiously approve in his own heart. Although this is a highly individualistic approach to morals, it is not thought to invite anarchy because men are regarded as more or less reasonable and as desiring what we would normally think of as a decent life lived in the company of other men.

On this view, to deliver oneself over to a moral authority for directions about what to do is simply incompatible with being a moral agent. To say "I will follow so-and-so's directions no matter what they are and no matter what my own conscience would otherwise direct me to do" is to opt out of moral thinking altogether; it is to abandon one's role as a moral agent. And it does not matter whether "so-and-so" is the law, the customs of one's society, or God. This does not, of course, preclude one from seeking advice on moral matters, and even on occasion following that advice blindly, trusting in the good judgment of the adviser. But this is to be justified by the details of the particular case, e.g. that you cannot in that case form any reasonable judgment of your own due to ignorance or inexperience in dealing with the types of matters involved. What *is* precluded is that a man should, while in possession of his wits, adopt this style of decision-making (or perhaps we should say this style of *abdicating* decision-making) as a general strategy of living, or abandon his own best judgment in any case where he can form a judgment of which he is reasonably confident.

What we have, then, is a conflict between the role of worshiper, which by its very nature commits one to total subservience to God, and the role of moral agent, which necessarily involves **autonomous** decision-making. The point is that the role of worshiper takes precedence over every other role which the worshiper has—when there is any conflict, the worshiper's commitment to God has priority over any other commitments which he might have. But the first commitment of a moral agent is to do what in his own heart he thinks is right. Thus the following argument might be constructed:

(a) If any being is God, he must be a fitting object of worship.

(b) No being could possibly be a fitting object of worship, since worship requires the abandonment of one's role as an autonomous moral agent.

(c) Therefore, there cannot be any being who is God.

. . . The concept of moral agency underlying this argument is complex and controversial; and, although I think it is sound, I cannot give it the detailed treatment here that it requires. Instead, I will conclude by answering some of the most obvious objections to the argument.

(1) What if God lets us go our own way, and issues no commands other than that we should live according to our own consciences? In that case, there would be no incompatibility between our commitment to God and our commitments as moral agents, since God would leave us free to direct our own lives. The fact that this supposition is contrary to major religious traditions (such as the Christian tradition) doesn't matter, since these traditions could be mistaken. The answer here is that this is a mere **contingency,** and that even if God did not require obedience to detailed commands, the worshiper would still be committed to the abandonment of his role as a moral agent, *if* God required it.

(2) It has been admitted as a **necessary truth** that God is perfectly good; it follows as a corollary that He would never require us to do anything except what is right. Therefore in obeying God we would only be doing what we should do in any case. So

there is no incompatibility between obeying him and carrying out our moral commitments. Our primary commitment as moral agents is to do right, and God's commands *are* right, so that's that.

This objection rests on a misunderstanding of the assertion that (necessarily) God is perfectly good. This can be intelligibly asserted only because of the principle that *No being who is not perfectly good may bear the title "God."* We cannot determine whether some being is God without first checking on whether he is perfectly good; and we cannot decide whether he is perfectly good without knowing (among other things) whether his commands to us are right. Thus our own judgment that some actions are right, and others wrong, is logically prior to our recognition of any being as God. The upshot of this is that we cannot justify the suspension of our own judgment on the grounds that we are deferring to God's command (which, as a matter of logic, *must* be right); for if, by our own best judgment, the command is wrong, this gives us good reason to withhold the title "God" from the commander.

(3) The following expresses a view which has always had its advocates among theologians: "Men are sinful; their very consciences are corrupt and unreliable guides. What is taken for conscientiousness among men is nothing more than self-aggrandisement and arrogance. Therefore, we cannot trust our own judgment; we must trust God and do what he wills. Only then can we be assured of doing right."

This view suffers from a fundamental inconsistency. It is said that we cannot know for ourselves what is right and what is wrong; and this is because our judgment is corrupt. But how do we know that our judgment is corrupt? Presumably, in order to know that, we would have to know *(a)* that some actions are morally required of us, and *(b)* that our own judgment does not reveal that these actions are required. However, *(a)* is just the sort of thing that we can*not* know, according to this view. Now it may be suggested that while we cannot know *(a)* by our own judgment, we can know it as a result of God's revelation. But even setting aside the practical difficulties of distinguishing genuine from bogus revelation (a generous concession), there is still this problem: if we learn that God (i.e. some being that we take to be God) requires us to do a certain action, and we conclude on this account that the action is morally right, then we have *still* made at least one moral judgment of our own, namely that whatever this being requires is morally right. Therefore, it is impossible to maintain the view that we do have some moral knowledge, and that *all* of it comes from God's revelation.

(4) Many philosophers, including St. Thomas, have held that the voice of individual conscience *is* the voice of God speaking to the individual, whether he is a believer or not. This would resolve the alleged conflict because in following one's conscience one would at the same time be discharging his obligation as a worshiper to obey God. However, this manoeuvere is unsatisfying, since if taken seriously it would lead to the conclusion that, in speaking to us through our "consciences," God is merely tricking us: for he is giving us the illusion of self-governance while all the time he is manipulating our thoughts from without. Moreover, in acting from conscience we are acting under the view that our actions are right and not merely that they are decreed by a higher power. Plato's argument in the *Euthyphro* can be adapted to this point: If, in speaking to us through the voice of conscience, God is informing us of what is right, then there is no reason to think that we could not discover this for ourselves—the notion of "God informing us" is eliminable. On the other hand, if God is only giving us arbitrary commands, which cannot be thought of as "right" independently of his promulgating them, then the whole idea of "conscience," as it is normally understood, is a sham.

(5) Finally, someone might object that the question of whether any being is *worthy* of worship is different from the question of whether we *should* worship him. In general, that X is worthy of our doing Y with respect to X does not entail that we should do Y with respect to X. For example, Mrs. Brown, being a fine woman, may be worthy of a marriage proposal, but we ought not to propose to her since she is already married. Or, Seaman Jones may be worthy of a medal for heroism but perhaps there are reasons why we should not award it. Similarly, it may be that there is a being who is worthy of wor-

ship and yet we should not worship him since it would interfere with our lives as moral agents. Thus God, who is worthy of worship, may exist; and we should love, respect, and honor him, but not worship him in the full sense of the word. If this is correct, then [the preceding argument] is fallacious.

This rebuttal will not work because of an important disanalogy between the cases of proposing marriage and awarding the medal, on the one hand, and the case of worship on the other. It may be that Mrs. Brown is worthy of a proposal, yet there are circumstances in which it would be wrong to propose to her. However, these circumstances are contrasted with others in which it would be perfectly all right. The same goes for Seaman Jones's medal: there are *some* circumstances in which awarding it would be proper. But in the case of worship—if the foregoing arguments have been sound—there are *no* circumstances under which anyone should worship God. And if one should *never* worship, then the concept of a fitting object of worship is an empty one.

The above argument will probably not persuade anyone to abandon belief in God—arguments rarely do—and there are certainly many more points which need to be worked out before it can be known whether this argument is even viable. Yet it does raise an issue which is clear enough. **Theologians** are already accustomed to speaking of theistic belief and commitment as taking the believer "beyond morality," and I think they are right. The question is whether this should not be regarded as a severe embarrassment.

STUDY QUESTIONS

1. What is Rachels's definition of *worship?*
2. What conception of moral agency does Rachels deploy in the article?
3. Based on your answers to questions 1 and 2, why does Rachels believe that no being is worthy of worship?
4. How does Immanuel Kant's ethical theory influence Rachels's conception of moral agency? What other thinkers does Rachels claim support this conception?
5. For what purpose does Rachels invoke the story of the binding of Isaac? What is his opinion concerning Abraham's behavior?
6. *Suppose Abraham complied with God's command to sacrifice Isaac because he reasoned thus: "Children are on loan from God, and it is a moral principle that loans must be repaid." How would Rachels assess Abraham's behaviour in that case?
7. *Can you defend Rachels's view of moral agency? Alternatively, can you show it to be unfounded? Can you show it to be not only unfounded but false?
8. *When our opinion conflicts with that of experts—doctors, lawyers, financial advisors, and the like—we often defer to those experts. Do you think a theist can successfully defend the attitude of worship by arguing, analogously, that God is an expert on morality? Why or why not?

FURTHER READING

Ritual and Prayer

Geach, Peter. "Praying for Things to Happen." In Geach, *God and the Soul,* pp. 86–99. New York: Schocken Books, 1969, ch. 7.

Gellman, Jerome I. "In Defense of Petitionary Prayer." In *Midwest Studies in Philosophy: Volume XXI,* edited by Peter A. French, Theodore E. Uehling, Jr., and Howard K. Wettstein, pp. 83–97. Notre Dame, IN: University of Notre Dame Press, 1997.

Green, Ronald. "Religious Ritual: A Kantian Perspective." *Journal of Religious Ethics* 14 (1979): 229–38.

Hoffman, Joshua. "On Petitionary Prayer." *Faith and Philosophy* 2 (1985): 21–29.

Matthews, Gareth. "Bodily Motions and Religious Feelings." *Canadian Journal of Philosophy* 1 (1971): 75–86. Repr. as "Ritual and the Religious Feelings" in *Contemporary Philosophy of Religion,* ed. Steven M. Cahn and David Shatz (New York: Oxford, 1982), 154–66.

Penelhum, Terence. *Religion and Rationality.* New York: Random House, 1971, ch. 20.

Phillips, D. Z. *The Concept of Prayer.* New York: Schocken Books, 1966.

Scheffler, Israel. "Ritual and Reference." *Synthese* 46 (1981): 421–37.

Smart, Ninian. *The Concept of Worship.* New York: St. Martin's Press, 1979.

Stump, Eleonore. "Petitionary Prayer." *American Philosophical Quarterly* 16 (1979): 81–93.

Religion and Morality

Adams, Robert Merrihew. "Autonomy and Theological Ethics." *Religious Studies* 15 (1979). Repr. *The Virtue of Faith.* New York: Oxford University Press, 1987.

Green, Ronald. *Religious Reason: The Rational and Moral Basis of Religious Belief.* New York: Oxford University Press, 1978.

Green, Ronald. *Religion and Moral Reason: A New Method for Comparative Study.* New York: Oxford University Press, 1988.

Helm, Paul, ed. *Divine Commands and Morality.* New York: Oxford University Press, 1981.

Levenson, Jon. "Abusing Abraham" *Judaism* 47, 3 (summer 1998): 259–77.

Mann, William. "Piety: Lending a Hand to Euthyphro." *Philosophy and Phenomenological Research* 58,1 (March 1998): 123–42.

Mavrodes, George. "Religion and the Queerness of Morality."In *Rationality, Religious Belief, and Moral Commitment: Essays in the Philosophy of Religion,* edited by Robert Audi and William J. Wainwright, pp. 213–26. Ithaca, NY: Cornell University Press, 1986.

Mitchell, Basil. *Morality: Religious and Secular.* Oxford, England: Oxford University Press, 1980.

Outka, Gene, and John P. Reeder, eds. *Religion and Morality.* Garden City, NY: Anchor Books, 1973.

Perkins, Robert L., ed. *Kierkegaard's* Fear and Trembling: *Critical Appraisals.* University, ALA: University of Alabama Press, 1981.

Quinn, Philip L. *Divine Commands and Moral Requirements.* New York: Oxford University Press, 1978.

Quinn, Philip L. "The Recent Revival of Divine Command Ethics." *Philosophy and Phenomenological Research* 50, Supplement (1990): 345–65.

Rudd, A. *Kierkegaard and the Limits of the Ethical.* Oxford, England: Oxford University Press, 1993.

Sagi, Avi, and Daniel Statman. *Religion and Morality.* Amsterdam and Atlanta, GA: Rodopi, 1995.

Sharvy, Richard. "*Euthyphro* 9b–11b: Analysis and Defense in Plato and Others." *Nous* 6 (1972): 119–37.

Stout, Jeffrey. *Ethics After Babel.* Boston: Beacon Press, 1988.

CHAPTER 4

Assessing the Case for Theism

Arguments for God's Existence

Why believe that God exists? Are there good reasons to do so? Many philosophers present and past have answered the latter question in the affirmative and have put forth reasoned **arguments** for God's existence. These arguments form the heart of an enterprise called **natural theology,** the attempt to establish the truth of religion by means of human reason. This chapter presents some of these arguments, along with criticisms that have been made of them. Before we look at the intense debate surrounding the arguments themselves, we need to appreciate some points about what the chapter does and does not cover.

An argument is a set of claims, some of which are designated as premises and one other that is designated as a conclusion. It is usually assumed that, for a person to be rational in holding a belief, he or she must have a good argument for the belief. A growing chorus of philosophers maintains, however, that this is not so. In their opinion, a belief can be rational even if there is no convincing argument for it. After all, many beliefs we hold in everyday life cannot be backed up by arguments—or so the history of failed attempts by philosophers suggests. For example, the beliefs that there is a world outside of our minds, and that nature works in uniform ways, are not backed up by rationally convincing arguments. Some philosophers have urged that, just as these everyday beliefs are rational even though we lack good arguments for them, religious belief can be rational (on the theoretical plane) even if not supported by arguments.

Note, however, that, even if a belief in God could somehow be rational in the absence of good arguments to support it, we are still wise to inquire whether there are such arguments. And it is hardly pointless to find out whether they succeed or fail. For it is only by assessing the arguments that we can determine whether a theist *must* turn to the analogy to undisputed everyday beliefs in order for his or her belief to be aptly classified as rational. The approach of denying that a theist needs arguments for the view that God exists, although tremendously interesting, will be presented more fully and evaluated only later, in chapter 7. There we will consider a variety of ways in which a belief could be rational in the absence of a convincing argument (one such way is by the holding of the belief somehow benefiting the believer—for example, by providing hope and security). But that discussion should not preempt our inquiry into whether there are good arguments for God's existence.

In addition, we should make a distinction between it being rational for someone to believe a certain proposition and a *particular person's* being rational in believing that proposition. Even if there are good arguments for God's existence, these arguments are likely to be complicated and difficult, and most theists do not believe in God *because* of these arguments. Thus, in one sense, theists are not rational in believing as they do, even if there are good arguments for their view. To take an extreme case, suppose a philosopher thinks up a novel argument for God's existence and further thinks that until now no one else has come up with a good argument. If the argument is convincing, then until now no one who has believed in God has been rational in doing so, for no one has had adequate reason. Nevertheless, if the philosopher's argument is convincing, theistic belief is rational in the following sense: the proposition that theists believe can be supported by a good argument. The articles in this chapter should not be viewed as attempts to show that real-life, flesh-and-blood theists have been rational in believing in God, for the arguments to be considered are often not thought of by believers. Our inquiry is into whether theists' beliefs are supportable by good argument and are, in that sense, rational, regardless of what role these arguments play in the lives of actual theists.

Arguments can be of different types, and you should be alert to what type of reasoning is being used in each instance of an argument for God's existence. Basically, an argument consists of one or more premises and another statement called a conclusion, which is said by the arguer to follow from the premises. However, there are several distinct ways in which a premise might be defended and several senses in which a conclusion could be said to follow from given premises.

If an argument is to be rationally convincing, each premise of the argument should generally be supported in one of two ways:

1. The premise is a **necessary truth.** Truths of logic, mathematics, and geometry are generally thought to fall into this category.
2. The premise is not a necessary truth but is said to be supported by **empirical** data.[1]

And conclusions can be said to follow from premises in these senses:

1. The conclusion follows *logically* or ***deductively*** from the premises. This means that it is *logically impossible* for the premises to be true and the conclusion false. An example is the time-worn *"All men are mortal; Socrates is a man; therefore, Socrates is mortal."* When an argument's conclusion follows logically from the premises, the argument is ***valid,*** even if the premises are false. (*"All birds are immortal; Socrates is a bird; therefore, Socrates is immortal"* is a valid argument.) If in addition to an argument's being valid, the premises are true, the argument is ***sound.*** Thus, a sound argument is a valid argument with true premises. The conclusion of a sound argument is true.
2. The conclusion follows from the premises *with high probability,* although it logically could be false even if the premises are true. For present purposes, we can call such arguments inductive or probabilistic.
3. The conclusion describes a hypothesis that supplies the *best explanation* of the truths or facts described in the premises. This type of reasoning is usually called either inference to the best explanation or abductive reasoning. (This category could be assimilated to category 2, but it will be helpful for you to be alert to an inference to the best explanation as a distinctive style of argument.)

No matter whether an argument's form is deductive, inductive, or inference to the best explanation, the argument is rationally convincing only if it has true premises. In fact, even that is not enough; a premise could be true but not known to be true, in which case

[1]There is a third way to support a premise. Suppose person X tries to convince person Y that *p* by utilizing some premise *q,* which Y accepts, but in itself *q* is not supported by either method 1 or method 2. Sometimes X will do this as part of an ***ad hominem*** argument to show that Y holds inconsistent beliefs if Y does not accept X's conclusion. In **cosmological arguments** (considered below), an important premise is the Principle of Sufficient Reason. This is a principle it is difficult to show is true; but if a theist shows an atheist that the latter's overall belief system is committed to PSR, the theist might be able to use PSR as a premise in an argument.

an argument that uses the premise is not convincing. Thus, there must be a good reason for any premises used. Philosophers sometimes reserve the term *proof* or **demonstration** for arguments that are sound and have premises that are necessary truths or that deductively follow from necessarily true premises. It is for this reason that this chapter avoids the term *proof of God's existence* and favors *rationally convincing argument for God's existence*.

The four arguments to be considered in this chapter are the **ontological argument,** the **cosmological argument,** the **design argument**, and the argument from religious experience. Actually, the use of the definite article (*the*) before the name of each of these arguments is misleading. Far from there being one cosmological argument, one design argument, and so on, there are many versions of each type of argument, versions that share a certain resemblance, so we are really dealing with four families of arguments, not four arguments.

ONTOLOGICAL ARGUMENTS

Ontological arguments seek to accomplish what may seem impossible—to prove from the very concept of God or the very possibility of God that God, in fact, exists. Considering that the argument seems like sleight of hand, it has exhibited extraordinary staying power. As propounded by St. Anselm of Canterbury (there are other versions of the argument later in the history of philosophy), the argument's structure is that of a ***reductio ad absurdum;*** one starts by assuming the opposite of what one wants to prove and shows that, given that assumption, a contradiction results. Because a contradiction results, the starting point must have been false.

Anselm defines God as the greatest possible being, the being than whom none greater can be conceived. God clearly exists *in the understanding;* after all, even the fool who denies there is a god, says Anselm, has a concept of God, or that person couldn't be denying God's existence. However, if something exists in the understanding and could have existed in reality, then it might have been greater than it is. Suppose God were to exist in reality, not only in the understanding. Then God might have been greater than He is. But that surely is impossible, since God is defined as the greatest possible being. Hence, it is false that God exists only in the understanding; God must exist in reality as well as in the understanding.

Anselm's contemporary, Gaunilo, disputes the argument by showing that its logic must be flawed, for the same logic could prove, for example, the existence of the greatest possible island. Finally, David Johnson presents a different version of the ontological argument, using the machinery of contemporary **modal logic,** the branch of logic that deals with possibility and necessity.

COSMOLOGICAL ARGUMENTS

The force that propels all versions of *cosmological arguments* is the natural human quest for an understanding or explanation of the universe: the natural question you may have thought about even as a child—"Why?" What accounts for there being anything? Many people have the sense, the intuition, that the universe is ***contingent,*** that it might not have been. Ultimately, the cosmological argument enlists this intuition to postulate a **necessary being,** a being whose existence is explained by its own nature.

In a medieval version made famous by St. Thomas Aquinas (and ultimately owing to Aristotle), the cosmological argument rests on the alleged impossibility of an infinite series of causes (more exactly, of an **infinite regress**). If *X* is caused by *Y*, *Y* by *Z*, and so on, the chain must stop somewhere, and that somewhere is the First Cause, God. We shall see in the introduction to Reading 4.4 that Aquinas does not intend here to prove that the world is created but only that it is dependent on God.

Criticizing Aquinas, Paul Edwards maintains that there can be an infinite regress of causes, so the form of cosmological argument that assumes otherwise fails. But William L. Craig counters that, although a *potential infinite* is possible, an *actual infinite* is impossible, so the cosmological argument is successful.

In 1705, Samuel Clarke put forth a different version of the argument. In Clarke's version, an infinite regress of causes is possible. However, that infinite collection *as a whole* requires an explanation, and that explanation is an *independent being,* God. Following the lead of David Hume, Edwards criticizes this version on the grounds that there is no explanation *of the whole* over and apart from the explanations of the individual members. In another, far simpler version of the argument, the arguer simply says that there cannot be **brute facts** about the world. The **principle of sufficient reason** (PSR) holds true—for every fact or state of affairs, there is a reason it obtains. Thus, there must be a reason that the world exists. If it is said, as in contemporary **cosmology,** that the universe began with a Big Bang, we must explain what caused the Big Bang. This version of the argument depends crucially on the truth of PSR. The question of whether PSR is true or, instead, is a presupposition or assumption of reason, is examined in the selection by William L. Rowe. Rowe concludes that PSR might be sound—but we don't know that it is (or that it is isn't).

All sorts of questions leap to mind about these versions. Even if there is a First Cause or ultimate Cause, how do we know it is a personal being at all, let alone an **omnipotent, omniscient,** all-good one? Also, what explains God's existence? Why can't the First Cause be, say, principles of matter and energy? And, if God needs no explanation in terms of something else—if God is self-explained or, alternatively, God's existence is a brute fact—why can't the universe be self-explained, and why can't *its* explanation be a brute fact? Finally, why should we accept the principle of sufficient reason—why can't there be brute facts? All these and other questions will be grappled with in the readings.

Cosmological arguments use a combination of empirical premises—for example, *There is a world* and *There is motion in the world*—and apparently nonempirical premises, such as PSR, or *there cannot be an infinite regress of causes*. The structure of the arguments is deductive, although some of the premises are empirical.

DESIGN ARGUMENTS

In a celebrated passage in his *Natural Theology* (1802), William Paley argues that, just as from the intricate and precise way a watch's parts are put together we must conclude that the watch was made by a maker for a purpose, so, too, "every indication of contrivance, every manifestation of design, which existed in the watch, exists in the works of nature." Indeed, "the contrivances of nature surpass the contrivances of art, in the complexity, subtlety, and curiosity of the mechanism; and still more, if possible, do they go beyond them in number and variety; yet in a multitude of cases, are not less evidently mechanical, not less evidently contrivances, not less evidently accommodated to their end, or suited to their office, than are the most perfect productions of human ingenuity. . . ."

Usually, arguments of this type are called arguments *from* design, but a more accurate term is arguments *for* design. Unlike what obtains in the case of cosmological arguments, in design arguments what is crucial is not the bare fact that there is a world or the bare fact that things are in motion or that things change. Rather, the argument's focus is on what kind of world this is. The starting point is that the universe exhibits a striking degree of order, and order, it is argued—by way of *conclusion*—is brought about by intelligent design. Among the tasks that fall on a proponent of the argument are to specify precisely what is meant by *order* and to explain how we know that order of this kind is produced by design.

In a classic critique that seriously diminished the design argument's popularity among philosophers, David Hume (1711–1776) considers a version in which (a) the order is to be found in the way things in nature are constituted and (b) the correlation between order and design is based purely on our experience of human artifacts, such as watches, telescopes, and (to use an anachronistic example) computers. Hume raises many problems with the argument, including attacks on the claim that order must arise from design; objections to the effect that the order of the designer God's ideas must themselves be explained; and charges that the designer may be and indeed is probably far from the being designated God in traditional **theology.** (Hume even puts forward the possibility of multiple designers.) Some of these criticisms bear obvious parallels to weaknesses we saw in the cosmological arguments.

A century after Hume, Charles Darwin (1809–1882) propounded the theory of evolution and thereby dealt another major blow to the design argument. This theory, if true, *prima facie* destroys the design argument, for it accounts for the order of the universe in terms of initial conditions and laws of nature alone, without postulating a designer. The design hypothesis becomes superfluous—as the expression goes, we have no need of that hypothesis. However—in a striking turn—some thinkers assert that the story told by evolutionary biology actually *supports* the design hypothesis, for evolutionary biology amounts to a "just so" story. It is a story in which all sorts of things had to happen for life, intelligence, and morality to emerge, things that had a small likelihood of happening. Yet they happened. Likewise, some argue, the tiniest changes in the laws of physics or in the conditions present right at the Big Bang would have resulted long ago in the universe's destruction. That the laws of physics are what they are and the conditions at the time of the Bang Bang were what they were makes the story told by evolutionary cosmology a "just so" story, which supports a design hypothesis.

Following this line of thought, Stephen T. Davis maintains, in this chapter, that the fact that the laws of nature and the conditions of the universe at the Big Bang and thereafter were exactly what was needed for later evolution is in need of explanation, and design provides the best explanation. Robert Hambourger supports a similar line of thought using an engaging analogy. Rejecting such arguments, John L. Mackie replies, in his selection, that we have no idea how many other setups would have produced the same outcomes, so the outcome was not as unlikely as theists claim.

ARGUMENTS FROM RELIGIOUS EXPERIENCE

Many people over the course of time have claimed to see God. Jerome I. Gellman argues that the best explanation of this fact is that there is a God who reveals Himself to some people. But what of the many others who have not experienced God and did not see God even while standing in the same location as the mystic undergoing the experience? Gellman seeks to repair this seeming flaw in the argument. Several criticisms of the argument emerge in the subsequent selections. Jonathan Malino and Henry Levinson criticize Gellman for ignoring the need for **intersubjective testing** in determining the rationality of a belief based on perception. They require that any particular claim to experience God be tested intersubjectively, or at least that we have good reason to think that such testing would yield positive results. Introducing another line of attack on arguments from religious experience, Evan Fales submits that explanations of mystical experiences offered by the social sciences and by neurophysiology are superior to the explanation that such experiences are produced by God.

The four arguments in this chapter do not exhaust the reasons philosophers have given for believing in God. For example, *moral arguments* maintain that God's existence can be inferred from the existence of morality, and some maintain that God's existence can be deduced from reports of miracles (cf. Readings 6.9–6.13). Despite the omission of some arguments from this chapter, the ones we do consider raise fascinating questions, that affect not only religious belief but also other areas of philosophy and science.

ONTOLOGICAL ARGUMENTS

READING 4.1

An Ontological Argument

Anselm of Canterbury

Ordinarily, if you have a certain concept, it does not follow that a being exemplifying that concept exists in reality. For example, from your having the concept of a gremlin, you cannot conclude that a gremlin exists. However, St. Anselm (1033–1109), archbishop of Canterbury, argues that from the very definition of God it follows that God exists, so that a fool who says in his or her heart that God does not exist—and thus admits to having a concept of God—contradicts him- or herself. Anselm's attempt to go from a mere concept to a claim of existence and to show that logically God must exist—God is a **necessary being***—has always fascinated philosophers and evoked strong criticism. If Anselm is right, we can know whether God exists without making* **empirical** *observations.*

Let us define God *as* the greatest conceivable being. *Suppose, continues Anselm, that God exists only* in the understanding, *but not* in reality. *Surely we could conceive of (i.e., imagine) God's existing not only in the understanding but in reality as well. But a being who exists in reality is greater than one who exists in the understanding alone. Thus, in effect, by conceiving of God existing in reality, we are conceiving of God being greater than God is. But surely the greatest conceivable being could not have been greater than He is. Since the assumption that God exists in the understanding but not in reality has led to an absurd conclusion, it must be false; hence, God must exist both in the understanding and in reality. The form of St. Anselm's argument is* ***reductio ad absurdum:*** *assume the opposite of what you plan to prove and show it leads to contradiction.*

Empiricists *often reject the* **ontological argument** *out of hand by saying that no claim about what does or does not exist can be grounded in reason alone without experience.* **Rationalists** *reply that, on the contrary, the ontological argument, if* **sound,** *refutes the claims of empiricists.*

Brackets in this selection are the translator's.

THAT GOD TRULY EXISTS

Therefore, Lord, you who grant understanding to faith, grant that, insofar as you know it is useful for me, I may understand that you exist as we believe you exist, and that you are what we believe you to be. Now we believe that you are something than which nothing greater can be thought. So can it be that no such being exists, since "The fool has said in his heart, 'There is no God'"? (Psalm 14:1; 53:1) But when this same fool hears me say "something than which nothing greater can be thought," he surely understands what he hears; and what he understands exists in his understanding,[1] even if he does not understand that it exists [in reality]. For it is one thing for an object to exist in the understanding and quite another to understand that the object exists [in reality]. When a painter, for example, thinks out in advance what he is going to paint, he has it in his understanding, but he does not yet understand that it exists, since he has not yet painted it. But once he has painted it, he both has it in his understanding and understands that it exists because he has now painted it. So even the fool must admit that something than

[1]The word here translated "understanding" is "*intellectus.*" The text would perhaps read better if I translated it as "intellect," but this would obscure the fact that it is from the same root as the verb "*intelligere,*" "to understand." Some of what Anslem says makes a bit more sense if this fact is constantly borne in mind. [Translator's note]

which nothing greater can be thought exists at least in his understanding, since he understands this when he hears it, and whatever is understood exists in the understanding. And surely that than which a greater cannot be thought cannot exist only in the understanding. For if it exists only in the understanding, it can be thought to exist in reality as well, which is greater. So if that than which a greater cannot be thought exists only in the understanding, then that than which a greater *cannot* be thought is that than which a greater *can* be thought. But that is clearly impossible. Therefore, there is no doubt that something than which a greater cannot be thought exists both in the understanding and in reality.

THAT HE CANNOT BE THOUGHT NOT TO EXIST

This [being] exists so truly that it cannot be thought not to exist. For it is possible to think that something exists that cannot be thought not to exist, and such a being is greater than one that can be thought not to exist. Therefore, if that than which a greater cannot be thought can be thought not to exist, then that than which a greater cannot be thought is *not* that than which a greater cannot be thought; and this is a contradiction. So that than which a greater cannot be thought exists so truly that it cannot be thought not to exist.

And this is you, O Lord our God. You exist so truly, O Lord my God, that you cannot be thought not to exist. And rightly so, for if some mind could think some thing better than you, a creature would rise above the Creator and sit in judgment upon him, which is completely absurd. Indeed, everything that exists, except for you alone, can be thought not to exist. So you alone among all things have existence most truly, and therefore most greatly. Whatever else exists has existence less truly, and therefore less greatly. So then why did "the fool say in his heart, 'There is no God,'" when it is so evident to the rational mind that you of all beings exist most greatly? Why indeed, except because he is stupid and a fool.

STUDY QUESTIONS

1. Explain St. Anselm's ontological argument as a **reductio ad absurdum** argument.
2. What does Anselm mean when he says that even the fool must admit that God exists?
3. *Philosophers often try to parody Anselm's argument by creating an ontological argument for the existence of the devil, a being than whom no worse can be conceived. How do you think this parody goes? Is it an effective parody?
4. *Using Anselm's reasoning, it seems that, if God exists only in the understanding but not in reality, then a being with all of God's properties plus existence in reality would be greater than God. How do you understand this claim—after all, how does one compare an existent object with a nonexistent one? Do you agree with Anselm's claim?
5. *Many philosophers maintain that the **cosmological** and **design arguments** do not show the existence of a perfect God, since the first cause (in the cosmological argument) or the designer (in the design argument) are not shown by the arguments to be perfect. Can the same criticism be made of the ontological argument?
6. *Anselm was a follower of St. Augustine (354–430) in characterizing his philosophizing about God as "faith seeking understanding." One begins with belief in God and seeks to explain that belief philosophically. How does this point shed light on the role that the ontological argument might play in Anselm's philosophy?
7. *The late Norman Malcolm, a prominent twentieth-century philosopher, writes of the ontological argument: "I can imagine an atheist going through the argument, becoming convinced of its validity, acutely defending it against objections, yet remaining an atheist." What do you think he means, and how would you explain the phenomenon he describes? If you were to discover that people are converted by the cosmological and design arguments, but not by the ontological, how would you explain why the ontological argument is different?

READING 4.2

On Behalf of the Fool

Gaunilo

Gaunilo, an eleventh-century monk in Martmoutier, raises several criticisms of St. Anselm's argument, the most famous of which is his "lost island" parody. Speaking for Anselm's "fool," Gaunilo argues that, using the reasoning Anselm uses in his proof of God's existence, we could prove the existence of the greatest possible island (or, to go beyond his example, the greatest possible basketball player, greatest possible philosopher, and so forth). Contrary to Anselm, Gaunilo believes that, even in the case of the greatest conceivable being, one cannot infer x exists *from the mere concept of x.*

In a reply to Gaunilo, St. Anselm in effect said that the greatest conceivable island *is not a coherent concept because it lacks an intrinsic maximum. That is, there is no upper limit to how rich an island could be. Likewise, there is no upper limit to how many points the greatest conceivable basketball player could score. But* greatest possible being *is a coherent concept because such a concept does have an intrinsic maximum.*

"And when he says that this thing exists because otherwise that which is greater than everything else would not be greater than everything else, he does not fully realize whom he is addressing. For I do not yet admit—indeed, I actually deny, or at least doubt—that this greater being is greater than any real thing. Nor do I concede that it exists at all, except in the sense that something exists (if you want to call it 'existence') when my mind tries to imagine some completely unknown thing solely on the basis of a word that it has heard. How, then, is the fact that this being has been proved to be greater than everything else supposed to show me that it exists in actual fact? For I continue to deny, or at least doubt, that this has been proved, so that I do not admit that this thing exists in my understanding or thought even in the way that many doubtful and uncertain things exist there. First I must become certain that this thing truly exists somewhere, and only then will the fact that it is greater than everything else show clearly that it also subsists in itself.

"For example, there are those who say that somewhere in the ocean is an island, which, because of the difficulty—or rather, impossibility—of finding what does not exist, some call 'the Lost Island.' This island (so the story goes) is more plentifully endowed than even the Isles of the Blessed with an indescribable abundance of all sorts of riches and delights. And because it has neither owner nor inhabitant, it is everywhere superior in its abundant riches to all the other lands that human beings inhabit. Suppose that someone tells me all this. The story is easily told and involves no difficulty, and so I understand it. But if this person went on to draw a conclusion, and say, 'You cannot any longer doubt that this island, more excellent than all others on earth, truly exists somewhere in reality. For you do not doubt that this island exists in your understanding, and since it is more excellent to exist not merely in the understanding, but also in reality, this island must also exist in reality. For if it did not, any land that exists in reality would be greater than it. And so this more excellent thing that you have understood would not in fact be more excellent.'—If, I say, he should try to convince me by this argument that I should no longer doubt whether the island truly exists, either I would think he was joking, or I would not know whom I ought to think more foolish: myself, if I grant him his conclusion, or him, if he thinks he can establish the existence of that island with any degree of certainty, without first showing that its excellence exists in my understanding as a thing that truly and undoubtedly exists and not in any way like something false or uncertain."

In this way the fool might meet the objections brought against him up to this point. . . .

STUDY QUESTIONS

1. Explain Gaunilo's parody of the ontological argument.
2. *Do you agree with St. Anselm (as explained in the introduction to Reading 4.2) that *greatest conceivable being* is a concept with an intrinsic maximum? Think of the attributes **omniscience, omnipotence,** and **omnibenevolence,** and answer this question with respect to those attributes.
3. *It would seem that, when you present a parody of someone else's reasoning, you have succeeded in showing *that* the person's reasoning is wrong but have not explained *what* is wrong with the reasoning, where the faulty step is. Do you find, in the section of Gaunilo's reply to Anselm reprinted in Reading 4.2, an indication of what is wrong with Anselm's logic?

READING 4.3

A Modal Ontological Argument

David Johnson

Some philosophers believe that the particular Anselmian ontological argument we have looked at fails, but that a "modal" version of the ontological argument fares better. **Modal logic** *is the branch of formal logic that is concerned with the logic of necessity and possibility. To illustrate, the statement "if it is necessary that p, then it is not possible that not-p" (abbreviated $\Box p \rightarrow \sim\Diamond\sim p$) is a truth of modal logic. It is common to explain "it is possible that p" and "it is necessary that p" in terms of "possible worlds." "It is possible that p" is understood as "there exists a possible world in which it is the case that p," and "it is necessary that p" is understood as "in every possible world, it is the case that p."*

David Johnson's modal argument enlists the notion of an Anselmian god. *An Anselmian god is defined as whatever both necessarily exists (= exists in every possible world) and could not exist except as a god (the definition of a god given by Johnson involves familiar notions such as* **omnipotence, omniscience,** *and so forth). Johnson first argues as follows:*

> *Necessarily* (abbreviated $\Box$): if there is an Anselmian god, then necessarily there is a god.
> *Possibly* (abbreviated $\Diamond$): there is an Anselmian god. Therefore, possibly it is necessary that ($\Diamond\ \Box$) there is a god.

Using a principle that whatever is possibly necessary is necessary, Johnson (Yeshiva University) goes on to infer that necessarily there is a god, and hence that there is a god. The controversial step here is possibly there is an Anselmian god. *Johnson argues for this using the premise he calls* **Gödel's law,** *a principle enunciated by the great mathematician-logician Kurt Gödel in manuscript notes published after his death. (Some interpreters of Anselm believe that in addition to the non-modal argument Anselm presents in Reading 3.1, he used a type of modal argument.)*

The **Goldbach Conjecture** says that every even integer greater than 2 is the sum of two prime numbers. I don't know whether this conjecture is true, or untrue. And so in a certain rather weak, **epistemic** sense of 'might', the conjecture might be true, and it might be untrue. *For all I know* (as we say) it is true. But also, for all I know, it is untrue. This sort of thing is what philosophers call ***epistemic*** **possibility.**

On the usual view of the nature of mathematical truth, however, we say that if the Goldbach Conjecture is in fact true then there is no *real* possibility of its being untrue, and if it is in fact untrue then there is no real possibility of its being true. If the conjecture is true then there simply is not, in the infinite realm of the integers, any counterexample to it, nor (really) *could* there be. If the conjecture is untrue then there is at least one counterexample, nor is there any (real) possibility of things being otherwise. Real possibility is what philosophers call ***metaphysical*** **possibility.** And, as we have just seen, what is epistemically possible is sometimes not metaphysically, not really, possible.

Let us confine our attention to real possibility and, correspondingly, to real necessity, using 'it is (really) necessarily the case that p' as shorthand for 'it is not the case that it is (really) possibly the case that it is not the case that p', where (for present purposes) 'p' is a placeholder for a sentence expressing a proposition. (Henceforth the parenthetical 'real' or 'really' is to be understood, and will be omitted except for occasional emphasis.)

It has seemed to many philosophers to be a compelling principle that whatever is *possibly* the case is (furthermore) *necessarily possibly* the case. Whenever it is possibly the case that p it is (furthermore) *necessarily* the case *that it is possibly the case* that p. What (really) is possible couldn't (really) have failed to be possible. I will take this plausible principle for granted.

Now, if whatever is *possibly* the case is *necessarily possibly* the case, it follows that whatever is *possibly necessarily* the case is *necessarily* the case. Whenever it is even possibly the case that it is necessarily the case that p, it is indeed necessarily the case that p.[1] It is this (equivalent) form of our plausible principle which we will employ below.

We begin with two **stipulative definitions.** First, borrowing most of Richard Swinburne's definition, let us say that an object is a *god* if and only if it is "a person without a body (i.e. a spirit) present everywhere, the creator and sustainer of the universe, a free agent, able to do everything (i.e. **omnipotent**), knowing all things, perfectly good, a source of moral obligation, immutable, eternal . . . holy, and worthy of worship."[2] Second, let us define an Anselmian god to be whatever both necessarily exists and could not exist save as a god—so that at any given possible world, an object which exists at that world is an Anselmian god at that world, if and only if at that world it is true that at every possible world that object both exists and is a god.

A bit of formalism (which is, after all, merely abbreviation) makes it easier to see the patterns in an argument. I will use items of the form '$\Diamond$p' as abbreviations for items of the form 'it is possibly the case that p' or (synonymously) of the form 'at some possible world it is the case that p'. And I will use items of the form '$\Box$p' as abbreviations for items of the form 'it is necessarily the case that p' or (synonymously) of the form 'at every possible world it is the case that p'. Then our definitions above are designed to make the following premise obviously true:

(1) $\Box$(If there is an Anselmian god then $\Box$ there is a god)

[1]Suppose we have every instance of:
(i) If $\Diamond$p then $\Box\Diamond$p
Suppose we wish to show:
(ii) If $\Diamond\Box$q then $\Box$q
We have the following instance of (i):
(iii) If $\Diamond \sim$ q then $\Box\Diamond \sim$ q
By **contraposition** of (iii) we have:
(iv) If $\sim \Box\Diamond \sim$ q then $\sim \Diamond \sim$ q
Recalling that '$\Box$' is shorthand for '$\sim \Diamond \sim$' we thus have:
(v) If $\sim \sim \Diamond \sim \Diamond \sim$ q then $\Box$ q
And thus ('$\sim \sim \Diamond$' having the same force as '$\Diamond$'):
(vi) If $\Diamond \sim \Diamond \sim$ q then $\Box$ q
And thus (recalling again the shorthand) we have (ii).
[2]Richard Swinburne, *The Coherence of Theism* (Oxford: Oxford University Press, 1977), 2.

This premise says that the proposition expressed in the parenthesis (the **truth-functional** conditional expressed by the sentence within the round brackets) itself holds of necessity (that is, at every possible world). What would it be for (1) to be false? That would be for there to be some possible world at which the antecedent of the conditional holds—so that at that world there is an Anselmian god—but at which the consequent does not hold—so that at that world it is not *necessarily* the case that there is a god. But this cannot happen. For if, at any given world *w*, it is true at *w* that there exists an Anselmian god, then, by definition, it is true at *w* that *that* being both exists at and is a god at every possible world, so that, a fortiori, it is true at *w* that at every possible world there exists some god or other, and so it is true at *w* that: □ there is a god.

Our second premise is for now a promissory note. (We argue for it later.) It says:

(2) ◇There is an Anselmian god

(Note that, since we are concerned here with real possibility, rather than merely with the weak "for all I know" sort of possibility, (2) is not at all obviously true. As Leibniz long ago realized, and emphasized, this sort of strong modal claim requires an argument.)

From (1) and (2) it follows that:

(3) ◇□There is a god

For the pattern is the self-evidently kosher:

□(If P then Q)
◇P
———
◇Q

If at *every* world we have "If P then Q," and at *some* (that is, at least one) world we have "P," then at at least one world we have *both* "If P then Q" and "P," and so at such a world we have, by modus ponens, "Q." Thus: ◇Q.

Our next premise is an instance of the plausible principle (in its second form) embraced above:

(4) If ◇□ there is a god then □ there is a god

And hence from (3) and (4) we have:

(5) □ There is a god

and we have as well the utterly uncontroversial:

(6) If □ there is a god then there is a god

And so from (5) and (6) we have:

(7) There is a god

I believe that upon careful reflection the only controversial premise here will be (2), the claim that there (really) could be an Anselmian god. And so we now argue for this claim.

Not all properties are, in a moral or aesthetic sense, positive (morally or aesthetically wonderful, with no morally or aesthetically negative aspect). But if a certain property is positive, and nothing could have it without having a certain other property, then that other property is positive as well. (Call this ***Gödel's law.***[3] More precisely, Gödel's law says: For any properties α and β, if α is positive and necessarily whatever has α has β, then β is positive.) It follows that every *positive* property is a *possibly instantiated* property (that for any property α, if α is positive then possibly something has α). But the property of being an Anselmian god is, in a moral or aesthetic sense, positive. (Indeed, what property could be more morally or aesthetically wonderful, and without negative aspect, than the property of *being a god in every possible state of affairs?*) So,

[3] See Kurt Gödel's "Ontologischer Beweis," transcribed by Jordan Howard Sobel from notes (in Gödel's *Nachlass* kept at the Institute for Advanced Study, in Princeton) in Gödel's own hand, and printed as the second appendix to Sobel's paper, "Gödel's Ontological Proof," in Judith Jarvis Thomson, ed., *On Being and Saying: Essays for Richard Cartwright* (Cambridge, Massachusetts: MIT Press, 1987), 241–261; 256–257. (See Gödel's fourth axiom.) For helpful discussion of Gödel's law I am grateful to Joshua Abraham and to Meir Soloveichik.

possibly there is an Anselmian god.[4] And so in very truth there is a god (if Gödel's law is true).

Gödel's law is a **universal generalization** about properties. What reason is there to think that it is true? There would seem to be two reasons. First, Gödel took it to be evident. Second (if we do not wish to aver it on authority), there seem to be no evident counterexamples to it.

I have heard many purported **counterexamples** to Gödel's law, none of which I take to be evident counterexamples to it. I should note, in this regard, that I do not find it evident that the property of *being able* "to do evil" is non-positive. Or, at least, inasmuch as we construe "omnipotence" (the ability to do "everything") in some plausible and presumably restricted sense (akin to the implicit restriction on 'everything' in "Did you put everything in the refrigerator?"), such that it is indeed evident that omnipotence in that sense is positive (the ability to do *absolutely* "everything"—even *to make mistakes in arithmetic*—I do not consider to be a positive property), and inasmuch as it remains evident that necessarily whatever is omnipotent in this sense has "the ability to do evil," I do not find the property of having this latter ability to be evidently non-positive. If you could somehow persuade me that it is non-positive (I think this unlikely), you would probably at the same time persuade me either that omnipotence in the given sense is after all also non-positive (so that we had not gotten the divine property quite right), or that omnipotence in the given sense does not evidently necessitate having "the ability to do evil," in the morally or aesthetically tainted sense. It will, I think, be very hard to find an *evident* counterexample to Gödel's law.

Suppose, then, that after much trial we find no evident counterexamples to Gödel's law. Must that be at best a *weak* reason to believe that the law is true? It might seem so, since the law is a universal generalization which has infinitely many, and infinitely many *humanly inaccessible,* instances; just as the fact, that after much trial we have found no evident counterexamples to the Goldbach Conjecture, is little or no reason to believe that the conjecture is true.

However, it is certainly not the case that failure, after much trial, to find evident counterexamples to a universal generalization having an infinite number of humanly inaccessible instances is *always* at best a weak reason to believe that the generalization is true. For (even aside from our natural reluctance to decree philosophically that induction in an infinite universe must be futile) we surely quite justifiedly believe, for example, that whatever is **analytically true** (alternatively: "conceptually true," "true solely in virtue of meaning," "true by definition") is *true,* a universal generalization which has an infinite number of humanly inaccessible instances. But what can our robust confidence in such a principle be based on, except a felt absence of evident counterexamples? Our confidence certainly cannot be based simply on the claim that being true is "part of the meaning" of being analytically true, since that point would establish only that it is analytically true that

[4]I can imagine someone objecting to this argument in the following way: "Your argument is circular. If you really have established your earlier claim (that a property is positive *only if* possibly something has it) then when you now assert that the property of being an Anselmian god is positive, you are simply *presupposing* (as part of your assertion of its positivity) that possibly something has the property, and have not really proven the latter point." Such an objection, taken by itself, has no force. Consider: I show, by a little argument, that there are five syllables in 'polysyllabic' *only if* there are $e^{\pi i} + 6$ syllables in 'polysyllabic'. I then claim to know (by reflection on the matter) that there are five syllables in 'polysyllabic' and *conclude* that there are $e^{\pi i} + 6$ syllables in 'polysyllabic'. Someone objects: "Your argument is circular. If you really have established your earlier claim (that 'polysyllabic' is pentasyllabic *only if* it is $e^{\pi i} + 6$ syllabic) then, when you now assert that 'polysyllabic' is pentasyllabic, you are simply *presupposing* (as part of your assertion of its pentasyllabicity) that there are $e^{\pi i} + 6$ syllables in 'polysyllabic' and have not really proven the latter point."

$e^{\pi i} + 6$-syllabicity is not a *presupposition* in an assertion of pentasyllabicity; and possible instantiation is not *evidently* a presupposition in an assertion of positivity. Why suppose that I cannot know, directly by consideration of the property of being an Anselmian god, that it is a positive property?

Similarly, suppose I know that whatever is *conceptually true* is *true*. Suppose I then claim that a certain proposition is in fact conceptually true, and conclude that it is true. It is scarcely obvious that such an argument is circular; for it is scarcely obvious that the truth of a proposition is a *presupposition* of an assertion of its "conceptual truth."

whatever is analytically true is true, which is not what we wanted to know.

Gödel, I suppose, thought that he knew, just by reflection, that the crucial proposition here (what I have called his law) is true. If so, I see no good reason to dispute his view of the matter, or at least none that would not lead us into an epistemological abyss. So, if any philosopher knows that the above Ontological Argument is a bad argument (that it is, say, "a charming joke"), if any philosopher knows that mere thought can never prove the existence of the "immense light" of which Descartes spoke, and which Saint Anselm said flooded his being in the morning prayer—well, then that philosopher is in possession of information of which I would willingly learn the source.

STUDY QUESTIONS

1. State Johnson's argument step-by-step, and explain the justification for each step.
2. What is Gödel's law? What exactly does Johnson claim about whether it should be accepted?
3. *Some critics of modal versions of the ontological argument object that the existence of a necessary being is impossible. Can you argue for or against their contention?
4. *Ontological arguments strike some people as technical tricks. Elaborate on such a reaction. Should the appearance of a technical trick make us hesitant to accept an argument if we find no other flaw? Why or why not?

COSMOLOGICAL ARGUMENTS

READING 4.4

The Five Ways

Thomas Aquinas

Thomas Aquinas (1225–1274) is one of the most important figures in the history of Christian thought. Aquinas here asserts that God's existence can be proved in five ways; the first three, which form the selection (I have kept the customary "Five Ways" as the title), are characterized by philosophers as **cosmological arguments.**

In the first way, Aquinas argues that whatever is moved (changed) is moved by another being. If that other being is itself moved, it must likewise be moved by another, and so on. But this cannot go on to infinity. Hence, there must be a first mover, who is moved by no other, and this mover is God.

In the second way, Aquinas offers a similar argument in terms of **efficient causation***—an Aristotelian term for the type of activity that brings another into being or sustains it in being. Nothing can be an* **efficient cause** *of itself, but it cannot be that every efficient cause is itself caused by another, because the series of causes would then go on to infinity. And an* **infinite regress** *of causes is impossible. Hence, there must be a first efficient cause, "to which everyone gives the name of God."*

It is a mistake to think that Aquinas is arguing that the world was created and has a beginning in time. The movers and efficient causes of which he speaks exist simultaneously with their effects—note the example "as the staff moves only because it is moved by the hand" (and another example he gives elsewhere: the fire heats the pot; the pot heats the stew). Basically, Aquinas allows the possibility of an infinite regress of movers/efficient causes going back in time (a horizontal series*) but not the possibility of an infinite series of causes of movers/efficient causes at a given slice of time (a* vertical series*). In the former case, the cause can be removed while the effect remains; in the latter, removing the cause entails removing the effect. Whether this distinction is tenable is assessed by Paul Edwards in Reading 4.5.*

Aquinas's third proof, according to many interpreters, rests on an unstated principle that, over an infinite period of time, all possibilities must be realized. If all beings are **contingent,** *then at some point they must all go out of existence. But, if so, how can anything exist now? It follows that not all beings are contingent, and there is at least one* **necessary being.**

. . . The existence of God can be proved in five ways.

The first and more manifest way is the argument from motion. It is certain, and evident to our senses, that in the world some things are in motion. Now whatever is moved is moved by another, for nothing can be moved except it is in **potentiality** to that towards which it is moved; whereas a thing moves inasmuch as it is in act. For motion is nothing else than the reduction of something from potentiality to **actuality.** But nothing can be reduced from potentiality to actuality, except by something in a state of actuality. Thus that which is actually hot, as fire, makes wood, which is potentially hot, to be actually hot, and thereby moves and changes it. Now it is not possible that the same thing should be at once in actuality and potentiality in the same respect, but only in different respects. For what is actually hot cannot simultaneously be potentially hot; but it is simultaneously potentially cold. It is therefore impossible that in the same respect and in the same way a thing should be both mover and moved, *i.e.,* that it should move itself. Therefore, whatever is moved must be moved by another. If that by which it is moved be itself moved, then this also must needs be moved by another, and that by another again. But this cannot go on to infinity, because then there would be no first mover, and, consequently, no other mover, seeing that subsequent movers move only inasmuch as they are moved by the first mover; as the staff moves only because it is moved by the hand. Therefore it is necessary to arrive at a first mover, moved by no other; and this everyone understands to be God.

The second way is from the nature of **efficient cause.** In the world of **sensible** things we find there is an order of efficient causes. There is no case known (neither is it, indeed, possible) in which a thing is found to be the efficient cause of itself; for so it would be prior to itself, which is impossible. Now in efficient causes it is not possible to go on to infinity, because in all efficient causes following in order, the first is the cause of the intermediate cause, and the intermediate is the cause of the ultimate cause, whether the intermediate cause be several, or one only. Now to take away the cause is to take away the effect. Therefore, if there be no first cause among efficient causes, there will be no ultimate, nor any intermediate, cause. But if in efficient causes it is possible to go on to infinity, there will be no first efficient cause, neither will there be an ultimate effect, nor any intermediate efficient causes; all of which is plainly false. Therefore it is necessary to admit a first efficient cause, to which everyone gives the name of God.

The third way is taken from possibility and necessity, and runs thus. We find in nature things that are possible to be and not to be, since they are found to be generated, and to be corrupted, and consequently, it is possible for them to be and not to be. But it is impossible for these always to exist, for that which can not-be at some time is not. Therefore, if everything can not-be, then at one time there was nothing in existence. Now if this were true, even now there would be nothing in existence, because that which does not exist begins to exist only through something already existing. Therefore, if at one time nothing was in existence, it would have been impossible for anything to have begun to exist; and thus even now nothing would be in existence—which is absurd. Therefore, not all beings are merely possible, but there must exist something the existence of which is necessary. But every necessary thing either has its necessity caused by another, or not. Now it is impossible to go on to infinity in necessary things which have their necessity caused by another, as has been already proved in regard to efficient causes. Therefore we cannot but admit the existence of some being having of itself its own necessity, and not receiving it from another, but rather causing in others their necessity. This all men speak of as God. . . .

STUDY QUESTIONS

1. State each of the first three of Aquinas's "five ways," clearly identifying their premises. In the third proof, take into account the unstated premise mentioned in the introduction to the selection.
2. Aquinas asserts that whatever is moved is moved by another (first way) and that nothing is the efficient cause of itself (second way). What reasons does he give for these assertions? *Are they convincing?
3. *In the first argument, Aquinas says that all understand the first mover to be God; in the second, that all understand the first efficient cause to be God; and in the third, that all speak of the necessary being as God. How might one challenge these claims?
4. *Elsewhere in his writings, Aquinas maintains that the belief that God created the world cannot be demonstrated by reason; instead, he says, belief in creation rests on faith and revelation. How does this thesis support our claim that Aquinas's cosmological argument is concerned with vertical rather than horizontal series?
5. *Aquinas's third way has been criticized for going from "for every contingent being, there is a time when it ceases to exist" to "there is at a time at which all contingent beings cease to exist." Explain how this criticism could be met by the principle mentioned in the introduction to the selection—that over an infinite period of time all possibilities must be realized.

READING 4.5

The Cosmological Argument

Paul Edwards

In this well-known and frequently reprinted essay, Paul Edwards (Brooklyn College and the New School) examines different versions of the **cosmological argument** *and finds them all deficient. Some versions try to prove that the universe has a first cause* who created the world, *by arguing (as the early medieval Kalam philosophers did) that an* **infinite regress** *of causes going back in time is impossible. Other versions (***Thomistic** *ones) admit the possibility of an infinite causal regress going back in time but submit that there cannot be an infinite regress of simultaneous sustaining causes. Edwards holds, that, although in both such series there is no cause that can be labeled "first cause," both series can exist—there can be an infinite regress in either case. An infinite series of causes is simply one in which each member of the series is caused by a preceding member; in an infinite pile of books, for example, each book is by definition supported by one beneath it. Thus, such a pile is possible.*

*Edwards next turns to a version of the argument championed by Samuel Clarke (1675–1729), according to which, even if there is an infinite series of causes, there must be an explanation for the existence of the series as a whole. Echoing David Hume (*Dialogues Concerning Natural Religion, *IX) Edwards objects that there is no explanation of the whole beyond the sum of explanations of the individual members of the infinite series. Last, he considers the argument that the universe is* **contingent** *and that this must be explained.*

I

The so-called '**cosmological** proof' is one of the oldest and most popular arguments for the existence of God. It was forcibly criticized by Hume,[1] Kant,[2] and Mill,[3] but it would be inaccurate to consider the argument dead or even moribund. Catholic philosophers, with hardly any exception, appear to believe that it is

[1]*Dialogues Concerning Natural Religion*, Part IX.

[2]*The Critique of Pure Reason*, Transcendental Dialectic, Book II, Ch III.

[3]'Theism', Part I, in *Three Essays on Religion*.

as solid and conclusive as ever. Thus Father Copleston confidently championed it in his Third Programme debate with Bertrand Russell;[4] and in America, where Catholic writers are more sanguine, we are told by a Jesuit professor of physics that 'the existence of an intelligent being as the First Cause of the universe can be established by *rational scientific inference.*'[5]

> I am absolutely convinced [the same writer continues] that any one who would give the same consideration to that proof (the cosmological argument), as outlined for example in William Brosnan's *God and Reason*, as he would give to a line of argumentation found in the *Physical Review* or the *Proceedings of the Royal Society* would be forced to admit that the cogency of this argument for the existence of God far outstrips that which is found in the reasoning which Chadwick uses to prove the existence of the neutron, which today is accepted as certain as any conclusion in the physical sciences.[6]

Mild theists, like the late Professor Dawes Hicks[7] and Dr. [A. C.] Ewing,[8] who concede many of Hume's and Kant's criticisms, nevertheless contend that the argument possesses a certain core of truth. In popular discussions it also crops up again and again — for example, when believers address atheists with such questions as 'You tell me where the universe came from!' Even philosophers who reject the cosmological proof sometimes embody certain of its confusions in the formulation of their own position. In the light of all this, it may be worth while to undertake a fresh examination of the argument with special attention to the fallacies that were not emphasized by the older critics.

II

The cosmological proof has taken a number of forms, the most important of which are known as the 'causal argument' and 'the argument from contingency,' respectively. In some writers, in Samuel Clarke, for example, they are combined, but it is best to keep them apart as far as possible. The causal argument is the second of the 'five ways' of Aquinas and roughly proceeds as follows: we find that the things around us come into being as the result of the activity of other things. These causes are themselves the result of the activity of other things. But such a causal series cannot 'go back to infinity.' Hence there must be a first member, a member which is not itself caused by any preceding member — an uncaused or 'first' cause [see Reading 4.4-Ed.].

It has frequently been pointed out that even if this **argument** were **sound** it would not establish the existence of *God*. It would not show that the first cause is all-powerful or all-good or that it is in any sense personal. Somebody believing in the eternity of atoms, or of matter generally, could quite consistently accept the conclusion. Defenders of the causal argument usually concede this and insist that the argument is not in itself meant to prove the existence of God. Supplementary arguments are required to show that the first cause must have the attributes assigned to the deity. They claim, however, that the argument, if **valid,** would at least be an important step towards a complete proof of the existence of God.

Does the argument succeed in proving so much as a first cause? This will depend mainly on the soundness of the premise that an infinite series of causes is impossible. Aquinas supports this premise by maintaining that the opposite belief involves a plain absurdity. To suppose that there is an infinite series of causes logically implies that nothing exists now; but we know that plenty of things do exist now; and hence any theory which implies that nothing exists now must be wrong. Let us take some causal series and refer to its members by the letters of the alphabet:

$$A \rightarrow B \ldots W \rightarrow X \rightarrow Y \rightarrow Z$$

Z stands here for something presently existing, e.g., Margaret Truman. Y represents the cause or part of the cause of Z, say Harry Truman. X designates the cause or part of the cause of Y, say Harry Truman's father, etc. Now, Aquinas reasons, whenever we take away the cause, we also take away the effect: if Harry Truman had never lived, Margaret Truman would never have been born. If Harry Truman's father had never lived, Harry Truman and Margaret Truman would never have been born. If A had never existed, none of the subsequent members of the series would have come into existence. But it is precisely A that the believer in the

[4]Reprinted in the British edition of Russell's *Why I Am Not a Christian.*

[5]J. S. O'Connor, 'A Scientific Approach to Religion', *The Scientific Monthly,* 1940, p. 369; my italics.

[6]Ibid., pp. 369–70.

[7]*The Philosophical Bases of Theism*, Lecture V.

[8]*The Fundamental Questions of Philosophy*, Ch. XI.

infinite series is 'taking away.' For in maintaining that the series is infinite he is denying that it has a first member; he is denying that there is such a thing as a first cause; he is in other words denying the existence of A. Since without A, Z could not have existed, his position implies that Z does not exist now; and that is plainly false.

This argument fails to do justice to the supporter of the infinite series of causes. Aquinas has failed to distinguish between the two statements:

(1) A did not exist, and
(2) A is not uncaused.

To say that the series is infinite implies (2), but it does not imply (1). The following parallel may be helpful here: Suppose Captain Spaulding had said, 'I am the greatest explorer who ever lived,' and somebody replied, 'No, you are not.' This answer would be denying that the Captain possessed the exalted attribute he had claimed for himself, but it would not be denying his existence. It would not be 'taking him away.' Similarly, the believer in the infinite series is not 'taking A away.' He is taking away the privileged status of A; he is taking away its 'first causiness.' He does not deny the *existence* of A or of any particular member of the series. He denies that A or anything else *is the first member* of the series. Since he is not taking A away, he is not taking B away, and thus he is also not taking X, Y, or Z away. His view, then, does not commit him to the absurdity that nothing exists now, or more specifically, that Margaret Truman does not exist now. It may be noted in this connection that a believer in the infinite series is not necessarily denying the existence of supernatural beings. He is merely committed to denying that such a being, if it exists, is uncaused. He is committed to holding that whatever other impressive attributes a supernatural being might possess, the attribute of being a first cause is not among them.

The causal argument is open to several other objections. Thus, even if otherwise valid, the argument would not prove a *single* first cause. For there does not seem to be any good ground for supposing that all the various causal series in the universe ultimately merge. Hence even if it is granted that no series of causes can be infinite the possibility of a plurality of first members has not been ruled out. Nor does the argument establish the *present* existence of the first cause. It does not prove this, since experience clearly shows that an effect may exist long after its cause has been destroyed.

III

Many defenders of the causal argument would contend that at least some of these criticisms rest on a misunderstanding. They would probably go further and contend that the argument was not quite fairly stated in the first place — or at any rate that if it was fair to some of its adherents it was not fair to others. They would in this connection distinguish between two types of causes — what they call ***'causes in fieri'*** and what they call ***'causes in esse.'*** A cause *in fieri* is a factor which brought or helped to bring an effect into existence. A cause *in esse* is a factor which 'sustains' or helps to sustain the effect 'in being.' The parents of a human being would be an example of a cause *in fieri*. If somebody puts a book in my hand and I keep holding it up, his putting it there would be the cause *in fieri,* and my holding it would be the cause *in esse* of the book's position. To quote Father Joyce:

> If a smith forges a horse-shoe, he is only a cause *in fieri* of the shape given to the iron. That shape persists after his action has ceased. So, too, a builder is a cause *in fieri* of the house which he builds. In both these cases the substances employed act as causes *in esse* as regards the continued existence of the effect produced. Iron, in virtue of its natural rigidity, retains in being the shape which it has once received; and, similarly, the materials employed in building retain in being the order and arrangement which constitute them into a house.[9]

Using this distinction, a defender of the argument now reasons in the following way. To say that there is an infinite series of causes *in fieri* does not lead to any absurd conclusions. But Aquinas is concerned only with causes *in esse* and an infinite series of *such* causes is impossible. In the words of the contemporary American **Thomist,** R. P. Phillips:

> Each member of the series of causes possesses being solely by virtue of the actual present oper-

[9]*The Principles of Natural Theology,* p. 58.

ation of a superior cause. . . . Life is dependent, *inter alia,* on a certain atmospheric pressure, this again on the continual operation of physical forces, whose being and operation depends on the position of the earth in the solar system, which itself must endure relatively unchanged, a state of being which can only be continuously produced by a definite—if unknown—constitution of the material universe. This constitution, however, cannot be its own cause. That a thing should cause itself is impossible: for in order that it may cause it is necessary for it to exist, which it cannot do, on the hypothesis, until it has been caused. So it must *be* in order to cause itself. Thus, not being uncaused nor yet its own cause, it must be caused by another, which produces and preserves it. It is plain, then, that as no member of this series possesses being except in virtue of the actual present operation of a superior cause, if there be no first cause actually operating none of the dependent causes could operate either. We are thus irresistibly led to posit a first efficient cause which, while itself uncaused, shall impart causality to a whole series. . . .

> The series of causes which we are considering is not one which stretches back into the past; so that we are not demanding a beginning of the world at some definite moment reckoning back from the present, but an actual cause now operating, to account for the present being of things.[10]

Professor Phillips offers the following parallel to bring out his point:

> In a goods train each truck is moved and moves by the action of the one immediately in front of it. If then we suppose the train to be infinite, i.e., that there is no end to it, and so no engine which starts the motion, it is plain that no truck will move. To lengthen it out to infinity will not give it what no member of it possesses of itself, viz. the power of drawing the truck behind it. If then we see any truck in motion we know there must be an end to the series of trucks which gives causality to the whole.[11]

Father Joyce introduces an illustration from Aquinas to explain how the present existence of things may be compatible with an infinite series of causes *in fieri* but not with an infinite series of causes *in esse*.

> When a carpenter is at work, the series of efficient causes on which his work depends is necessarily limited. The final effect, e.g. the fastening of a nail is caused by a hammer: the hammer is moved by the arm: and the motion of his arm is determined by the motor-impulses communicated from the nerve centres of the brain. Unless the subordinate causes were limited in number, and were connected with a starting-point of motion, the hammer must remain inert; and the nail will never be driven in. If the series be supposed infinite, no work will ever take place. But if there is question of causes on which the work is not essentially dependent, we cannot draw the same conclusion. We may suppose the carpenter to have broken an infinite number of hammers, and as often to have replaced the broken tool by a fresh one. There is nothing in such a supposition which excludes the driving home of the nail.[12]

The supporter of the infinite series of causes, Joyce also remarks, is

> . . . asking us to believe that although each link in a suspended chain is prevented from falling simply because it is attached to the one above it, yet if only the chain be long enough, it will, taken as a whole, need no support, but will hang loose in the air suspended from nothing.[13]

This formulation of the causal argument unquestionably circumvents one of the objections mentioned previously. If Y is the cause *in esse* of an effect, Z, then it must exist as long as Z exists. If the argument were valid in this form it would therefore prove the present and not merely the past existence of a first cause. In this form the argument is, however, less convincing in another respect. To maintain that all 'natural' or 'phenomenal' objects — things like tables and mountains and human beings — require a cause *in fieri* is not implausible, though even here Mill and others have argued that strictly speaking only *changes* require a causal explanation. It is far from plausible, on the other

[10]*Modern Thomistic Philosophy,* Vol II, pp. 284–85.
[11]*Op. cit.*, p. 278.
[12]*Op. cit.*, pp. 67–8.
[13]*Op. cit.*, p. 82.

hand, to claim that all natural objects require a cause *in esse*. It may be granted that the air around us is a cause *in esse* of human life and further that certain gravitational forces are among the causes *in esse* of the air being where it is. But when we come to gravitational forces or, at any rate, to material particles like atoms or electrons it is difficult to see what cause *in esse* they require. To those not already convinced of the need for a supernatural First Cause some of the remarks by Professor Phillips in this connection appear merely dogmatic and **question-begging.** Most people would grant that such particles as atoms did not cause themselves, since, as Professor Phillips observes, they would in that event have had to exist before they began existing. It is not at all evident, however, that these particles cannot be uncaused. Professor Phillips and all other supporters of the causal argument immediately proceed to claim that there is something else which needs no cause *in esse*. They themselves admit thus, that there is nothing self-evident about the proposition that everything must have a cause *in esse*. Their entire procedure here lends substance to [author] Schopenhauer's gibe that supporters of the cosmological argument treat the law of universal causation like 'a hired cab which we dismiss when we have reached our destination.'[14]

But waiving this and all similar objections, the restatement of the argument in terms of causes *in esse* in no way avoids the main difficulty which was previously mentioned. A believer in the infinite series would insist that his position was just as much misrepresented now as before. He is no more removing the member of the series which is supposed to be the first cause *in esse* than he was removing the member which had been declared to be the first cause *in fieri*. He is again merely denying a privileged status to it. He is not denying the reality of the cause *in esse* labelled 'A.' He is not even necessarily denying that it possesses supernatural attributes. He is again merely taking away its 'first causiness.'

The advocates of the causal argument in either form seem to confuse an infinite series with one which is long but finite. If a book, Z, is to remain in its position, say 100 miles up in the air, there must be another object, say another book, Y, underneath it to serve as its support. If Y is to remain where it is, it will need another support, X, beneath it. Suppose that this series of supports, one below the other, continues for a long time, but eventually, say after 100,000 members, comes to a first book which is not resting on any other book or indeed on any other support. In that event the whole collection would come crashing down. What we seem to need is a first member of the series, a first support (such as the earth) which does not need another member as *its* support, which in other words is 'self-supporting.'

This is evidently the sort of picture that supporters of the First Cause argument have before their minds when they rule out the possibility of an infinite series. But such a picture is not a fair representation of the theory of the infinite series. A *finite* series of books would indeed come crashing down, since the first or lowest member would not have a predecessor on which it could be supported. If the series, however, were infinite this would not be the case. In that event every member *would* have a predecessor to support itself on and there would be no crash. That is to say: a crash can be avoided either by a finite series with a first self-supporting member or by an infinite series. Similarly, the present existence of motion is equally compatible with the theory of a first unmoved mover and with the theory of an infinite series of moving objects; and the present existence of causal activity is compatible with the theory of a first cause *in esse* as much as with the theory of an infinite series of such causes.

The illustrations given by Joyce and Phillips are hardly to the point. It is true that a carpenter would not, *in a finite time-span,* succeed in driving in a nail if he had to carry out an infinite number of movements. For that matter, he would not accomplish this goal in a finite time if he broke an infinite number of hammers. However, to make the illustrations relevant we must suppose that he has infinite time at his disposal. In that case he would succeed in driving in the nail even if he required an infinite number of movements for this purpose. As for the goods train, it may be granted that the trucks do not move unless the train has an engine. But this illustration is totally irrelevant as it stands. A relevant illustration would be that of engines, each moved by the one in front of it. Such a train would move if it were infinite. For every member of this series there would be one in front capable of drawing it along. The advocate of the infinite series of causes does not, as the original illus-

[14]*The Fourfold Root of the Principle of Sufficient Reason*, pp. 42–3. My attention to this passage was drawn by Professor C. J. Ducasse. See his excellent discussion of the arguments for the existence of God in *A Philosophical Scrutiny of Religion*.

tration suggests, believe in a series whose members are not really causally connected with one another. In the series he believes in every member is genuinely the cause of the one that follows it.

IV

No staunch defender of the cosmological argument would give up at this stage. Even if there were an infinite series of causes *in fieri* or *in esse,* he would contend, this still would not do away with the need for an ultimate, a first cause. As Father Copleston put it in his debate with Bertrand Russell:

> Every object has a phenomenal cause, if you insist on the infinity of the series. But the series of phenomenal causes is an insufficient explanation of the series. Therefore, the series has not a phenomenal cause, but a transcendent cause.[15] . . .
>
> An infinite series of contingent beings will be, to my way of thinking, as unable to cause itself as one contingent being.[16]

The demand to find the cause of the series as a whole rests on the erroneous assumption that the series is something over and above the members of which it is composed. It is tempting to suppose this, at least by implication, because the word 'series' is a noun like 'dog' or 'man.' Like the expression 'this dog' or 'this man' the phrase 'this series' is easily taken to designate an individual object. But reflection shows this to be an error. If we have explained the individual members there is nothing additional left to be explained. Supposing I see a group of five Eskimos standing on the corner of Sixth Avenue and 50th Street and I wish to explain why the group came to New York. Investigation reveals the following stories:

> Eskimo No. 1 did not enjoy the extreme cold in the polar region and decided to move to a warmer climate.
>
> No. 2 is the husband of Eskimo No. 1. He loves her dearly and did not wish to live without her.
>
> No. 3 is the son of Eskimos 1 and 2. He is too small and too weak to oppose his parents.
>
> No. 4 saw an advertisement in the New York Times for an Eskimo to appear on television.
>
> No. 5 is a private detective engaged by the Pinkerton Agency to keep an eye on Eskimo No. 4.

Let us assume that we have now explained in the case of each of the five Eskimos why he or she is in New York. Somebody then asks: 'All right, but what about the group as a whole; why is *it* in New York?' This would plainly be an absurd question. There is no group over and above the five members, and if we have explained why each of the five members is in New York we have *ipso facto* explained why the group is there. It is just as absurd to ask for the cause of the series as a whole as distinct from asking for the causes of individual members.

V

It is most unlikely that a determined defender of the cosmological line of reasoning would surrender even here. He would probably admit that the series is not a thing over and above its members and that it does not make sense to ask for the cause of the series if the cause of each member has already been found. He would insist, however, that when he asked for the explanation of the entire series, he was not asking for its *cause*. He was really saying that a series, finite or infinite, is not 'intelligible' or 'explained' if it consists of nothing but 'contingent' members. To quote Father Copleston once more:

> What we call the world is intrinsically unintelligible apart from the existence of God. The infinity of the series of events, if such an infinity could be proved, would not be in the slightest degree relevant to the situation. If you add up chocolates, you get chocolates after all, and not a sheep. If you add up chocolates to infinity, you presumably get an infinite number of chocolates. So, if you add up contingent beings to infinity, you still get contingent beings, not a **necessary being.**[17]

[15][In Russell,] *Why I Am Not a Christian*, pp. 152–53.
[16]*Ibid.*, p. 151.

[17]*Op. cit.*, p. 151.

This last quotation is really a summary of the 'contingency argument,' the other main form of the cosmological proof and the third of the five ways of Aquinas. It may be stated more fully in these words: All around us we perceive **contingent beings.** This includes all physical objects and also all human minds. In calling them 'contingent' we mean that they might not have existed. We mean that the universe can be *conceived* without this or that physical object, without this or that human being, however certain their actual existence may be. These contingent beings we can trace back to other contingent beings — e.g. a human being to his parents. However, since these other beings are also contingent, they do not provide a real or full explanation. The contingent beings we originally wanted explained have not yet become intelligible, since the beings to which they have been traced back are no more necessary than they were. It is just as true of our parents, for example, as it is of ourselves, that they might not have existed. We can then properly explain the contingent beings around us only by tracing them back ultimately to some necessary being, to something which exists necessarily, which has 'the reason for its existence within itself.' The existence of contingent beings, in other words, implies the existence of a necessary being.

This form of the cosmological argument is even more beset with difficulties than the causal variety. In the first place, there is the objection, stated with great force by Kant, that it really commits the same error as the **ontological argument** in tacitly regarding existence as an attribute or characteristic. To say that there is a necessary being is to say that it would be a self-contradiction to deny its existence. This would mean that at least one existential statement is a **necessary truth;** and this in turn presupposes that in at least one case existence is contained in a concept. But only a characteristic can be contained in a concept and it has seemed plain to most philosophers since Kant that existence is not a characteristic, that it can hence never be contained in a concept, and that hence no existential statement can ever be a necessary truth. To talk about anything 'existing necessarily' is in their view about as sensible as to talk about round squares, and they have concluded that the contingency-argument is quite absurd.

It would lead too far to discuss here the reasons for denying that existence is a characteristic. I will assume that this difficulty can somehow be surmounted and that the expression 'necessary being,' as it is intended by the champions of the contingency-argument, might conceivably apply to something. There remain other objections which are of great weight. I shall try to state these by first quoting again from the debate between Bertrand Russell and Father Copleston:

> Russell: . . . It all turns on this question of sufficient reason, and I must say you haven't defined "sufficient reason" in a way that I can understand—what do you mean by sufficient reason? You don't mean cause?
>
> Copleston: Not necessarily. Cause is a kind of sufficient reason. Only contingent being can have a cause. God is his own sufficient reason; and he is not cause of himself. By sufficient reason in the full sense I mean an explanation adequate for the existence of some particular being.
>
> Russell: But when is an explanation adequate? Suppose I am about to make a flame with a match. You may say that the adequate explanation of that is that I rub it on the box.
>
> Copleston: Well for practical purposes—but theoretically, that is only a partial explanation. An adequate explanation must ultimately be a total explanation, to which nothing further can be added.
>
> Russell: Then I can only say that you're looking for something which can't be got, and which one ought not to expect to get.
>
> Copleston: To say that one has not found it is one thing; to say that one should not look for it seems to me rather dogmatic.
>
> Russell: Well, I don't know. I mean, the explanation of one thing is another thing which makes the other thing dependent on yet another, and you have to grasp this sorry scheme of things entire to do what you want, and that we can't do.[18]

Russell's main point here may be expanded in the following way. The contingency-argument rests on a misconception of what an explanation is and does, and similarly on what it is that makes phenomena 'intelligible.' Or else it involves an obscure and arbitrary redefinition of 'explanation,' 'intelligible,' and related terms. Normally, we are satisfied that we have explained a phenomenon if we have found its cause or if we have exhibited some other uniform or near-uniform connection between it and something else. Confining ourselves to the former case, which is probably the most common, we might say that a phenomenon, Z, has been explained if it has been traced back to a group of factors, a, b, c, d, etc., which are its cause. These factors are the full

[18] *Op. cit.*, p. 150.

and real explanation of Z, quite regardless of whether they are pleasing or displeasing, admirable or contemptible, necessary or contingent. The explanation would not be adequate only if the factors listed are not really the cause of Z. If they are the cause of Z, the explanation would be adequate, even though each of the factors is merely a 'contingent' being.

Let us suppose that we have been asked to explain why General Eisenhower won the elections of 1952. 'He was an extremely popular general,' we might answer, 'while Stevenson was relatively little known; moreover there was a great deal of resentment over the scandals in the Truman Administration.' If somebody complained that this was only a partial explanation we might mention additional antecedents, such as the widespread belief that the Democrats had allowed communist agents to infiltrate the State Department, that Eisenhower was man with a winning smile, and that unlike Stevenson he had shown the good sense to say one thing on race relations in the North and quite another in the South. Theoretically, we might go further and list the motives of all American voters during the weeks or months preceding the elections. If we could do this we would have explained Eisenhower's victory. We would have made it intelligible. We would 'understand' why he won and why Stevenson lost. Perhaps there is a sense in which we might make Eisenhower's victory even more intelligible if we went further back and discussed such matters as the origin of American views on Communism or of racial attitudes in the North and South. However, to explain the outcome of the election in any ordinary sense, loose or strict, it would not be necessary to go back to prehistoric days or to the amœba or to a first cause, if such a first cause exists. Nor would our explanation be considered in any way defective because each of the factors mentioned was a 'contingent' and not a necessary being. The only thing that matters is whether the factors were really the cause of Eisenhower's election. If they were, then it has been explained although they are contingent beings. If they were not the cause of Eisenhower's victory, we would have failed to explain it even if each of the factors were a necessary being.

If it is granted that, in order to explain a phenomenon or to make it intelligible, we need not bring in a necessary being, then the contingency-argument breaks down. For a series, as was already pointed out, is not something over and above its members; and every contingent member of it could in that case be explained by reference to other contingent beings. But I should wish to go further than this and it is evident from Russell's remarks that he would do so also. Even if it were granted, both that the phrase 'necessary being' is meaningful and that all explanations are defective unless the phenomena to be explained are traced back to a necessary being, the conclusion would still not have been established. The conclusion follows from this premise together with the additional premise that *there are* explanations of phenomena in the special sense just mentioned. It is this further premise which Russell (and many other philosophers) would question. They do not merely question, as Copleston implies, whether human beings can ever obtain explanations in this sense, but whether they *exist*. To assume without further ado that phenomena have explanations or an explanation in this sense is to beg the very point at issue. The use of the same word 'explanation' in two crucially different ways lends the additional premise a plausibility it does not really possess. It may indeed be highly plausible to assert that phenomena have explanations, whether we have found them or not, in the ordinary sense in which this usually means that they have causes. It is then tempting to suppose, because of the use of the same word, that they also have explanations in a sense in which this implies dependence on a necessary being. But this is a gross ***non sequitur.***

VI

It is necessary to add a few words about the proper way of formulating the position of those who reject the main premise of the cosmological argument, in either of the forms we have considered. It is sometimes maintained in this connection that in order to reach a 'self-existing' entity it is not necessary to go beyond the universe: the universe itself (or 'Nature') is 'self-existing.' And this in turn is sometimes expanded into the statement that while all individual things 'within' the universe are caused, the universe itself is uncaused. Statements of this kind are found in Büchner, Bradlaugh, Haeckel, and other free-thinkers of the nineteenth and early twentieth century. Sometimes the assertion that the universe is 'self-existing' is elaborated to mean that *it* is the 'necessary being.' Some eighteenth-century unbelievers, apparently accepting the view that there is a necessary being, asked why Nature or the material universe could not fill the bill as well or better than God.

> Why, [asks one of the characters in Hume's *Dialogues,* (part IX)] may not the material universe be the necessarily existent Being? . . . We dare not affirm that we know all the qualities of matter; and for aught we can determine, it may contain some qualities, which, were they known, would make its non-existence appear as great a contradiction as that twice two is five.[19]

Similar remarks can be found in Holbach and several of the Encyclopedists.

The former of these formulations immediately invites the question why the universe, alone of all 'things,' is exempted from the universal sway of causation. 'The strong point of the cosmological argument,' writes Dr. Ewing, 'is that after all it does remain incredible that the physical universe should just have happened. . . . It calls out for some further explanation of some kind.'[20] The latter formulation is exposed to the criticism that there is nothing any more 'necessary' about the existence of the universe or Nature as a whole than about any particular thing within the universe.

I hope some of the earlier discussions in this article have made it clear that in rejecting the cosmological argument one is not committed to either of these propositions. If I reject the view that there is a supernatural first cause, I am not thereby committed to the proposition that there is a *natural* first cause, and even less to the proposition that a mysterious 'thing' called 'the universe' qualifies for this title. I may hold that there is no 'universe' over and above individual things of various sorts; and, accepting the causal principle, I may proceed to assert that all these things are caused by other things, and these other things by yet other things, and so on, *ad infinitum.* In this way no arbitrary exception is made to the principle of causation. Similarly, if I reject the assertion that God is a 'necessary being,' I am not committed to the view that the universe is such an entity. I may hold that it does not make sense to speak of anything as a 'necessary being' and that even if there were such a thing as the universe it could not be properly considered a necessary being.

However, in saying that nothing is uncaused or that there is no necessary being, one is not committed to the view that everything, or for that matter anything, is merely a **'brute fact.'** Ewing laments that 'the usual modern philosophical views opposed to theism do not try to give any rational explanation of the world at all, but just take it as a brute fact not to be explained.' They thus fail to 'rationalize' the universe. Theism, he concedes, cannot completely rationalize things either since it does not show 'how God can be his own cause or how it is that he does not need a cause.'[21] Now, if one means by 'brute fact' something for which there *exists* no explanation (as distinct from something for which no explanation is in our possession), then the theists have at least one brute fact on their hands, namely God. Those who adopt Büchner's formulation also have one brute fact on their hands, namely 'the universe'. Only the position I have been supporting dispenses with brute facts altogether. I don't know if this is any special virtue, but the defenders of the cosmological argument seem to think so.

STUDY QUESTIONS

1. What is the difference between *in esse* causation and *in fieri* causation? Why does Edwards think that an infinite regress of causes is possible in either case?
2. How does the version of the cosmological argument discussed in Part IV of the selection differ from Aquinas's?
3. Against which version of the cosmological argument does Edwards level the "Eskimoes" objection? What is the objection? Can you think of a reply?
4. What is a brute fact, and what do brute facts have to do with the cosmological argument?

[19][Hume], *Op. cit.,* Part IX.

[20]*Op. cit.*, p. 225.

[21]*Op. cit.*, p. 225.

READING 4.6

Philosophical and Scientific Pointers to Creatio ex Nihilo

William Lane Craig

Unlike Aquinas, William Lane Craig (Talbot School of Theology) thinks he can prove that the universe had a beginning. Responding to the by now familiar question, Why can't there be an infinite series of events going back in time?, Craig distinguishes between a potential infinite *and an* actual infinite. *An infinite collection or series cannot exist in the real world, he claims. Since a beginningless series of events in time is an actual infinite, it cannot exist. Furthermore, even if an actual infinite could exist, a collection formed by adding one member after another could not be actually infinite. The series of events in time is such a collection and hence cannot be actually infinite. There is scientific support for these conclusions, too, Craig argues. The* **Big Bang theory** *in cosmology requires the creation of matter from nothing; and, by the* **second law of thermodynamics,** *if the universe did not once begin to exist, its energy would be all used up by now. Having shown that the universe has a beginning, Craig goes on to argue that the beginning was caused and that this cause was a personal creator.*

". . . The first question which should rightly be asked," wrote Gottfried Wilhelm Leibniz, is "Why is there something rather than nothing?"[1] Think about that for a moment. Why *does* anything exist at all, rather than nothing? Why does the universe, or matter, or anything at all exist, instead of just nothing?

Many great minds have been puzzled by this problem. For example, in his biography of the renowned philosopher Ludwig Wittgenstein, Norman Malcolm reports,

> . . . he said that he sometimes had a certain experience which could best be described by saying that 'when I have it, *I wonder at the existence of the world*. I am then inclined to use such phrases as "How extraordinary that anything should exist!" or "How extraordinary that the world should exist!"'[2]

Similarly, the Australian philosopher J.J.C. Smart has said, ". . . my mind often seems to reel under the immense significance this question has for me. That anything exists at all does seem to me a matter for the deepest awe."[3]

Why *does* something exist instead of nothing? Unless we are prepared to believe that the universe simply popped into existence uncaused out of nothing, then the answer must be: something exists because there is an eternal, uncaused being for which no further explanation is possible. But who or what is this eternal, uncaused being? Leibniz identified it with God. But many modern philosophers have identified it with the universe itself. Now this is exactly the position of the atheist: the universe itself is uncaused and eternal; as [Bertrand] Russell remarks, ". . . the universe is just there, and that's all."[4] But are there reasons to think that the universe is not eternal and uncaused, that there is something more? I think that there are. For we can consider the universe by means of a series of logical alternatives:

[1]G. W. Leibniz, . . . in *Leibniz Selections*, ed. Philip P. Wiener, The Modern Student's Library (New York: Charles Scribner's Sons, 1951), p. 527.

[2]Norman Malcolm, *Ludwig Wittgenstein: A Memoir* (London: Oxford University Press, 1958), p. 70.

[3]J.J.C. Smart, "The Existence of God," *Church Quarterly Review* 156 (1955): 194.

[4]Bertrand Russell and F. C. Copleston, "The Existence of God," in *The Existence of God* (Problems of Philosophy Series), ed. with an Introduction by John Hick (New York: Macmillan, 1964), pp. 174, 176.

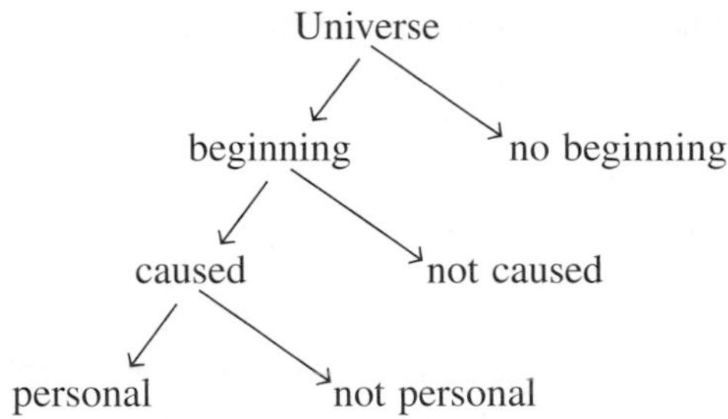

By proceeding through these alternatives, I think we can demonstrate that it is reasonable to believe that the universe is not eternal, but that it had a beginning and was caused by a personal being, and that therefore a personal Creator of the universe exists.

DID THE UNIVERSE BEGIN?

The first and most crucial step to be considered in this argument is the first: that the universe began to exist. There are four reasons why I think it is more reasonable to believe that the universe had a beginning. First, I shall expound two philosophical arguments and, second, two scientific confirmations.

The First Philosophical Argument:

1. An actual infinite cannot exist.
2. A beginningless series of events in time is an actual infinite.
3. Therefore, a beginningless series of events in time cannot exist.

A collection of things is said to be actually infinite only if a part of it is equal to the whole of it. For example, which is greater? 1, 2, 3, . . . or 0, 1, 2, 3, . . . According to prevailing mathematical thought, the answer is that they are equivalent because they are both actually infinite. This seems strange because there is an extra number in one series that cannot be found in the other. But this only goes to show that in an actually infinite collection, a part of the collection is equal to the whole of the collection. For the same reason, mathematicians state that the series of even numbers is the same size as the series of all natural numbers, even though the series of all natural numbers contains all the even numbers plus an infinite number of odd numbers as well. So a collection is actually infinite if a part of it is equal to the whole of it.

Now the concept of an *actual* infinite needs to be sharply distinguished from the concept of a *potential* infinite. A potential infinite is a collection that is increasing without limit but is at all times finite. The concept of potential infinity usually comes into play when we add to or subtract from something without stopping. Thus, a finite distance may be said to contain a potentially infinite number of smaller finite distances. This does not mean that there actually are an infinite number of parts in a finite distance, but rather it means that one can keep on dividing endlessly. But one will never reach an "infinitieth" division. Infinity merely serves as the limit to which the process approaches. Thus, a potential infinite is not truly infinite—it is simply indefinite. It is at all points finite but always increasing.

To sharpen the distinction between an actual and a potential infinite, we can draw some comparisons between them. The concept of actual infinity is used in set theory to designate a set which has an actually infinite number of members in it. But the concept of potential infinity finds no place in set theory. This is because the members of a set must be definite, whereas a potential infinite is indefinite—it acquires new members as it grows. Thus, set theory has only either finite or actually infinite sets. The proper place for the concept of the potential infinite is found in mathematical analysis, as in infinitesimal calculus. There a process may be said to increase or diminish to infinity, in the sense that the process can be continued endlessly with infinity as its terminus. The concept of actual infinity does not pertain in these operations because an infinite number of operations is never actually made. According to the great German mathematician David Hilbert, the chief difference between an actual and a potential infinite is that a potential infinite is always something growing toward a limit of infinity, while an actual infinite is a completed totality with an actually infinite number of things.[5] A good example contrasting these two

[5]David Hilbert, "On the Infinite," in *Philosophy of Mathematics,* ed. with an Introduction by Paul Benacerraf and Hilary Putnam (Englewood Cliffs, NJ: Prentice-Hall, 1964), pp. 139, 141.

types of infinity is the series of past, present, and future events. For if the universe is eternal, as the atheist claims, then there have occurred in the past an actually infinite number of events. But from any point in the series of events, the number of future (that is, subsequent) events is potentially infinite. Thus, if we pick 1845, the birth year of Georg Cantor, who discovered infinite sets, as our point of departure, we can see that past events constitute an actual infinity while future events constitute a potential infinity. This is because the past is realized and complete, whereas the future is never fully actualized, but is always finite and always increasing. In the following discussion, it is exceedingly important to keep the concepts of actual infinity and potential infinity distinct and not to confuse them.

A second clarification that I must make concerns the word "exist." When I say that an actual infinite cannot exist, I mean "exist in the real world" or "exist outside the mind." I am not in any way questioning the legitimacy of using the concept of actual infinity in the realm of mathematics, for this is a realm of thought only. What I am arguing is that an actual infinite cannot exist in the real world of stars and planets and rocks and men. What I will argue in no way threatens the use of the actual infinite as a concept in mathematics. But I do think it is absurd that an actual infinite could exist in the real world.

I think that probably the best way to show this is to use examples to illustrate the absurdities that would result if an actual infinite could exist in reality. For suppose we have a library that has an actually infinite number of books on its shelves. Imagine furthermore that there are only two colors, black and red, and these are placed on the shelves alternately: black, red, black, red, and so forth. Now if somebody told us that the number of black books and the number of red books is the same, we would probably not be too surprised. But would we believe someone who told us that the number of black books is the same as the number of black books *plus* red books? For in this latter collection there are all the black books plus an infinite number of red books as well. Or imagine there are three colors of books, or four, or five, or a hundred. Would you believe someone if he told you that there are as many books in a single color as there are in the whole collection? Or imagine that there are an infinite number of colors of books. You would probably think that there would be one book per color in the infinite collection. You would be wrong. If the collection is actually infinite then, according to mathematicians, there could be for each of the infinite colors an infinite number of books. So you would have an infinity of infinities. And yet it would still be true that if you took all the books of all the colors and added them together, you wouldn't have any more books than if you had taken just the books of a single color.

Suppose each book had a number printed on its spine. Because the collection is actually infinite, that means that *every possible number* is printed on some book. Now this means that we could not add another book to the library. For what number would we give to it? All the numbers have been used up! Thus, the new book could not have a number. But this is absurd, since objects in reality can be numbered. So *if* an infinite library could exist, it would be impossible to add another book to it. But this conclusion is obviously false, for all we have to do is tear out a page from each of the first hundred books, add a title page, stick them together, and put this new book on the shelf. It would be easy to add to the library. So the only answer must be that an actually infinite library could not exist.

But suppose we *could* add to the library. Suppose I put a book on the shelf. According to the mathematicians, the number of books in the whole collection is the same as before. But how can this be? If I put the book on the shelf, there is one more book in the collection. If I take it off the shelf, there is one less book. I can see myself add and remove the book. Am I really to believe that when I add the book there are no more books in the collection and when I remove it there are no less books? Suppose I add an infinity of books to the collection. Am I seriously to believe there are no more books in the collection than before? Suppose I add an infinity of infinities of books to the collection. Is there not now one single book more in the collection than before? I find this hard to believe.

But now let's reverse the process. Suppose we decide to loan out some of the books. Suppose we loan out book number 1. Isn't there now one less book in the collection? Suppose we loan out all the odd-numbered books. We have loaned out an infinite number of books, and yet mathematicians would say there are no less books in the collection. Now when we loaned out all these books, that left an awful lot of gaps on the shelves. Suppose we push all the books together again and close the gaps. All these gaps added together would add up to an infinite distance. But according to mathematicians, after you pushed the books together, the shelves will still be full, the same as before you loaned any out! Now suppose once more we loaned out every other book. There would still be no less books in the collection than before. And if we pushed all the books together again, the shelves would still be full. In fact, we could do this an infinite number of times, and there would never be one less book in the collection, and the shelves would always remain full. But suppose we loaned out book numbers 4, 5, 6, . . . out to infinity. At a single stroke, the collection would be virtually wiped out, the shelves emptied, and the infinite library reduced to finitude. And yet, we have removed exactly the same number of books this time as when we first loaned out all the odd numbered books! Can anybody believe such a library could exist in reality?

These examples serve to illustrate that *an actual infinite cannot exist* in the real world. Again I want to underline the fact that what I have argued in no way attempts to undermine the theoretical system bequeathed by Cantor to modern mathematics. Indeed, some of the most eager enthusiasts of transfinite mathematics, such as David Hilbert, are only too ready to agree that the concept of an actual infinite is an idea only and has no relation to the real world. So we can conclude the first step: an actual infinite cannot exist.

The second step is: *a beginningless series of events in time is an actual infinite*. By "event" I mean something that happens. Thus, this step is concerned with change, and it holds that if the series of past events or changes just goes back and back and never had a beginning, then, considered all together, these events constitute an actually infinite collection. Let me provide an example. Suppose we ask someone where a certain star came from. He replies that it came from an explosion in a star that existed before it. Suppose we ask again, where did that star come from? Well, it came from another star before it. And where did that star come from?—From another star before it; and so on and so on. This series of stars would be an example of a beginningless series of events in time. Now if the universe has existed forever, then the series of all past events taken together constitutes an actual infinite. This is because for every event in the past, there was an event before it. Thus, the series of past events would be infinite. Nor could it be potentially infinite only, for we have seen that the past is completed and actual; only the future can be described as a potential infinite. Therefore, it seems pretty obvious that a beginningless series of events in time is an actual infinite.

But that leads us to our conclusion: *therefore, a beginningless series of events in time cannot exist*. We have seen that an actual infinite cannot exist in reality. Since a beginningless series of events in time is an actual infinite, such a series cannot exist. That means the series of all past events must be finite and have a beginning. But because the universe *is* the series of all events, this means that the universe must have had a beginning.

Let me give a few examples to make the point clear. We have seen that if an actual infinite could exist in reality, it would be impossible to add to it. But the series of events in time is being added to every day. Or at least so it appears. If the series were actually infinite, then the number of events that have occurred up to the present moment is no greater than the number of events up to, say, 1789. In fact, you can pick any point in the past. The number of events that have occurred up to the present moment would be no greater than the number of events up to that point, no matter how long ago it might be.

Or take another example. Suppose Earth and Jupiter have been orbiting the sun from eternity. Suppose that it takes the Earth one year to complete one orbit, and that it takes Jupiter three years to complete one orbit. Thus, for every one orbit Jupiter completes, Earth completes three. Now here is the question: if they have been orbiting from eternity, which has completed more orbits? The answer is: they are equal. But this seems absurd, since the longer they went, the farther and farther Jupiter got behind, since every time Jupiter went around the sun once, Earth went around three times. How then could they possibly be equal?

Or, finally, suppose we meet a man who claims to have been counting from eternity, and now he is finishing: −5, −4, −3, −2, −1, 0. Now this is impossible. For, we may ask, why didn't he finish counting yesterday or the day before or the year before? By then an infinity of time had already elapsed, so that he should have finished. The fact is, we could never find anyone completing such a task because at any previous point he would have already finished. But what this means is that there could never be a point in the past at which he finished counting. In fact, we could never find him counting at all. For he would have already finished. But if no matter how far back in time we go, we never find him counting, then it cannot be true that he has been counting from eternity. This shows once more that the series of past events cannot be beginningless. For if you could not count numbers from eternity, neither could you have events from eternity.

These examples underline the absurdity of a beginningless series of events in time. Because such a series is an actual infinite, and an actual infinite cannot exist, a beginningless series of events in time cannot exist. This means that the universe began to exist, which is the point that we set out to prove.

The Second Philosophical Argument:

1. The series of events in time is a collection formed by adding one member after another.
2. A collection formed by adding one member after another cannot be actually infinite.
3. Therefore, the series of events in time cannot be actually infinite.

This argument does not argue that an actual infinite cannot exist. But it does argue that an actual infinite cannot come to exist by the members of a collection being added one after the other.

The series of events in time is a collection formed by adding one member after another. This point is pretty obvious. When we consider the collection of all past events, it is obvious that those events did not exist simultaneously—all at once—but they existed one after another in time: we have one event, then another after that, then another, then another, and so on. So when we talk about the collection of "all past events," we are talking about a collection that has been formed by adding one member after another.

The second step is the crucial one: *a collection formed by adding one member after another cannot be actually infinite.* Why? Because no matter how many members a person added to the collection, he could always add one more. Therefore, he would never arrive at infinity. Sometimes this is called the impossibility of counting to infinity. For no matter how many numbers you had counted, you could always count one more. You would never arrive at infinity. Or sometimes this is called the impossibility of traversing the infinite. For you could never cross an infinite distance. Imagine a man running up a flight of stairs. Suppose everytime his foot strikes the top step, another step appears above it. It is clear that the man could run forever, but he would never cross all the steps because you could always add one more step.

Now notice that this impossibility has nothing to do with the amount of time available. It is of the very nature of the infinite that it cannot be formed by adding one member after another, regardless of the amount of time available. Thus, the only way an infinite collection could come to exist in the real world would be by having all the members created simultaneously. For example, if our library of infinite books were to exist in the real world, it would have to be created instantaneously by God. God would say, "Let there be . . . !" and the library would come into existence all at once. But it would be impossible to form the library by adding one book at a time, for you would never arrive at infinity.

Therefore, our conclusion must be: *the series of events in time cannot be actually infinite.* Suppose there were, for example, an infinite number of days prior to today. Then today would never arrive. For it is impossible to cross an infinite number of days to reach today. But obviously, today has arrived. Therefore, we know that prior to today, there cannot have been an infinite number of days. That means that the number of days is finite and therefore the universe had a beginning. Contemporary philosophers have shown themselves to be impotent to refute this reasoning. Thus, one of them asks,

> If an infinite series of events has preceded the present moment, how did we get to the present moment? How could we get to the present moment—where we obviously are now—if the present moment was preceded by an infinite series of events?[6]

Concluding that this difficulty has not been overcome and that the issue is still in dispute, Hospers passes on to another subject, leaving the argument unrefuted. Similarly, another philosopher comments rather weakly, "It is difficult to show exactly what is wrong with this argument," and with that remark moves on without further ado.[7]

Therefore, since the series of events in time is a collection formed by adding one member after another, and since such a collection cannot be actually infinite, the series of events in time cannot be actually infinite. And once more, since the universe is nothing else than the series of events, the universe must have had a beginning, which is precisely the point we wanted to prove.

The First Scientific Confirmation: The Evidence from the Expansion of the Universe

Prior to the 1920s, scientists assumed that the universe as a whole was a stationary object. But in 1929 an astronomer named Edwin Hubble contended that this was not true. Hubble observed that the light from distant galaxies appeared to be redder than it should be. He explained this by proposing that the universe is expanding. Therefore, the light from the stars is affected since they are moving away from us. But this is the interesting part: Hubble not only showed that the universe is expanding, but that *it is expanding the same in all directions*. To get a picture of this, imagine a balloon with dots painted on it. As you blow up the balloon, the dots get further and further apart. Now those dots are just like the galaxies in space. Everything in the universe is expanding outward. Thus, the relations in the universe do not change, only the distances.

Now the staggering implication of this is that . . . at some point in the past, *the entire known universe was contracted down to a single point*, from which it has been expanding ever since. The farther back one goes in the past, the smaller the universe becomes, so that one finally reaches a point of *infinite density* from which the universe began to expand. That initial event has come to be known as the **"big bang."**

How long ago did the big bang occur? Only during the 1970s [did] accurate estimates become available. In a very important series of six articles published in 1974 and 1975, Allan Sandage and G. A. Tammann estimate that the big bang occurred about 15 billion years ago. Therefore, according to the big bang model, the universe began to exist with a great explosion from a state of infinite density about 15 billion years ago. Four of the world's most prominent astronomers describe that event in these words:

> The universe began from a state of infinite density. Space and time were created in that event and so was all the matter in the universe. It is not meaningful to ask what happened before the big bang; it is somewhat like asking what is north of the north pole. Similarly, it is not sensible to ask where the big bang took place. The point-universe was not an object isolated in space; it was the entire universe, and so the only answer can be that the big bang happened everywhere.[8]

This event that marked the beginning of the universe becomes all the more amazing when one reflects on the fact that a state of "infinite density" is synonymous with "nothing." There can be no object that possesses infinite density, for if it had any size at all, it would not be *infinitely* dense. Therefore, as astronomer Fred Hoyle points out, the big bang theory requires the creation of matter from nothing. This is because as one goes back in time, he reaches a point at which, in Hoyle's words, the

[6]John Hospers, *An Introduction to Philosophical Analysis,* 2nd ed. (London: Routledge & Kegan Paul, 1967), p. 434.

[7]William L. Rowe, *The Cosmological Argument* (Princeton, NJ: Princeton University Press, 1975), p. 122.

[8]J. Richard Gott III, James E. Gunn, David N. Schramm, Beatrice M. Tinsley, "Will the Universe Expand Forever?," *Scientific American,* March 1976, p. 65. This article is a popular rewrite of their article, "An Unbound Universe?," *Astrophysical Journal* 194 (1974): 543–53.

universe was "shrunk down to nothing at all."[9] Thus, what the big bang model requires is that the universe had a beginning and was created out of nothing.

Now some people are bothered with the idea that the universe began from nothing. This is too close to the Christian doctrine of creation to allow atheistic minds to be comfortable. But if one rejects the big bang model, he has apparently only two alternatives: the steady state model or the oscillating model. Let's examine each of these.

The **steady-state** model holds that the universe never had a beginning but has always existed in the same state. Ever since this model was first proposed in 1948, it has never been very convincing. According to S. L. Jaki, this theory never secured "a single piece of experimental verification."[10] It always seemed to be trying to explain away the facts rather than explain them. According to Jaki, the proponents of this model were actually motivated by "openly anti-theological, or rather anti-Christian motivations."[11] A second strike against this theory is the fact that a count of galaxies emitting radio waves indicates that there were once more radio sources in the past than there are today. Therefore, the universe is not in a steady state after all. But the real nails in the coffin for the steady state theory came in 1965, when A. A. Penzias and R. W. Wilson discovered that the entire universe is bathed with a background of microwave radiation. This radiation background indicates that the universe was once in a very hot and very dense state. In the steady-state model no such state could have existed, since the universe was supposed to be the same from eternity. Therefore, the steady-state model has been abandoned by virtually everyone. . . .

But what of the oscillating model of the universe? John Gribbin describes this model,

> The biggest problem with the big bang theory of the origin of the universe is philosophical—perhaps even theological—what was there before the bang? This problem alone was sufficient to give a great initial impetus to the steady-state theory, but with that theory now sadly in conflict with the observations, the best way round this initial difficulty is provided by a model in which the universe expands, collapses back again, and repeats the cycle indefinitely.[12]

According to this model, the universe is sort of like a spring, expanding and contracting from eternity. It is only in the last three or four years that this model has been discredited. The key question here is whether the universe is "open" or "closed." If it is "closed," then the expansion will reach a certain point, and then the force of gravity will pull everything together again. But if the universe is "open," then the expansion will never stop, but will just go on and on forever. Now clearly, if the universe is open, then the oscillating model is false. For if the universe is open, it will never contract again.

Scientific evidence seems to indicate that the universe is open. The crucial factor here is the density of the universe. Scientists have estimated that if there are more than about three hydrogen atoms per cubic meter on the average throughout the universe, then the universe would be closed. That may not sound like very much, but remember that most of the universe is just empty space. I shall not go into all the technicalities of how scientists measure the density of the universe, but let me simply report their conclusions. According to the evidence, the universe would have to be at least ten times denser than it is for the universe to be closed.[13] Therefore, the universe is open by a wide margin. Let me share with you the conclusion of Alan Sandage: (1) the universe is open, (2) the expansion will not reverse, and (3) *the universe has happened only once* and the expansion will never stop.[14]

[9]Fred Hoyle, *Astronomy and Cosmology: A Modern Course* (San Francisco: W. H. Freeman, 1975), p. 658.

[10]Stanley L. Jaki, *Science and Creation* (Edinburgh and London: Scottish Academic Press, 1974), p. 347.

[11]Jaki, *Science and Creation,* p. 347.

[12]John Gribbin, "Oscillating Universe Bounces Back," *Nature* 259 (1976): 15.

[13]J. Richard Gott III and Martin J. Rees, "A Theory of Galaxy Formation and Clustering," *Astronomy and Astrophysics* 45 (1975): 365–76; S. Michael Small, "The Scale of Galaxy Clustering and the Mean Matter Density of the Universe," *Monthly Notices of the Royal Astronomical Society* 172 (1975): 23p–26p.

[14]Sandage and Tammann, "Steps Toward the Hubble Constant. VI," p. 276; Allan Sandage, "The Redshift Distance Relation. VIII," *Astrophysical Journal* 202 (1975): 563–82.

The evidence therefore appears to rule out the oscillating model, since it requires a closed universe. But just to drive the point home, let me add that the oscillating model of the universe is only a *theoretical* possibility, not a *real* possibility. As Dr. Tinsley of Yale observes [in a personal letter], in oscillating models

> even though the mathematics *says* that the universe oscillates, there is no known physics to reverse the collapse and bounce back to a new expansion. The physics seems to say that those models start from the big bang, expand, collapse, then end.

Hence, it would be impossible for the universe to be oscillating from eternity. Therefore, this model is doubly impossible.

The Second Scientific Confirmation: The Evidence from Thermodynamics

According to the **second law of thermodynamics,** processes taking place in a closed system always tend toward a state of equilibrium. In other words, unless energy is constantly being fed into a system, the processes in the system will tend to run down and quit. For example, if I had a bottle that was a sealed vacuum inside, and I introduced into it some molecules of gas, the gas would spread itself out evenly inside the bottle. It is virtually impossible for the molecules to retreat, for example, into one corner of the bottle and remain. This is why when you walk into a room, the air in the room never separates suddenly into oxygen at one end and nitrogen at the other. It is also why when you step into your bath you may be confident that it will be pleasantly warm instead of frozen solid at one end and boiling at the other. It is clear that life would not be possible in a world in which the second law of thermodynamics did not operate.

Now our interest in the law is what happens when it is applied to the universe as a whole. The universe is a gigantic closed system, since it is everything there is and there is nothing outside it.[15] What this seems to imply then is that, given enough time, the universe and all its processes will run down and the entire universe will slowly grind to a halt. This is known as the heat death of the universe. Once the universe reaches this state, no further change is possible. The universe is dead.

There are two possible types of heat death for the universe. If the universe is "closed," then it will die a hot death. Tinsley describes such a state:

> If the average density of matter in the universe is great enough, the mutual gravitational attraction between bodies will eventually slow the expansion to a halt. The universe will then contract and collapse into a hot fireball. There is no known physical mechanism that could reverse a catastrophic big crunch. Apparently, if the universe becomes dense enough, it is in for a hot death.[16]

If the universe is closed, it is in for a fiery death from which it will never reemerge. But suppose, as is more likely, the universe is "open." Tinsley describes the final state of this universe:

> If the universe has a low density, its death will be cold. It will expand forever, at a slower and slower rate. Galaxies will turn all of their gas into stars, and the stars will burn out. Our own sun will become a cold, dead remnant, floating among the corpses of other stars in an increasingly isolated milky way.[17]

Eventually, equilibrium will prevail throughout, and the entire universe will reach its final state from which no change will occur.

Now the question that needs to be asked is this: If given enough time, the universe will reach heat death, then why is it not in a state of heat death now if it has existed forever, from eternity? If the universe

[15] In saying the universe is a closed system, I do not mean it is closed in the sense that its expansion will eventually contract. I rather mean that there is no energy being put into it. Thus, in the thermodynamic sense, the universe is closed, but in the sense of its density the universe is open. One must not confuse "open" and "closed" in thermodynamics with "open" and "closed" in expansion models.
[16] Beatrice M. Tinsley, "From Big Bang to Eternity?," *Natural History Magazine,* October 1975, p. 103.
[17] Tinsley, "From Big Bang to Eternity?," p. 185.

did not begin to exist, then it should now be in a state of equilibrium. Its energy should be all used up. For example, I have a very loud wind-up alarm clock. If I hear that the clock is ticking—which is no problem, believe me—then I know that at some point in the recent past, it was wound up and has been running down since then. It is the same with the universe. Since it has not yet run down, this means, in the words of one baffled scientist, "In some way the universe must have been wound up."

Some scientists have tried to escape this conclusion by arguing that the universe oscillates back and forth from eternity and so never reaches a final state of equilibrium. I have already observed that such a model of the universe is a physical impossibility. But suppose it were possible. The fact is that the thermodynamic properties of this model imply the very beginning of the universe that its proponents seek to avoid. For as several scientists have pointed out, each time the model universe expands it would expand a little further than before. Therefore, if you traced the expansions back in time they would get smaller and smaller and smaller. Therefore, in the words of one scientific team, "The multicycle model has an infinite future, but only a finite past." As yet another writer points out, this implies that the oscillating model of the universe still requires an origin of the universe prior to the smallest cycle.[18]

Traditionally, two objections have been urged against the thermodynamic argument. First, the argument does not work if the universe is infinite. I have two replies to this. (a) The universe is not, in fact, infinite. An actually spatially infinite universe would involve all the absurdities entailed in the existence of an actual infinite. But if space-time is torus-shaped, then the universe may be both open and finite. The objection is therefore irrelevant. (b) Even if the universe were infinite, it would still come to equilibrium. As [English scientist Paul Davies] explained in a letter to me, if every finite region of the universe came to equilibrium, then the whole universe would come to equilibrium. This would be true even if it had an infinite number of finite regions. This is like saying that if every part of a fence is green, then the whole fence is green, even if there are an infinite number of pickets in the fence. Since every single finite region of the universe would suffer heat death, so would the whole universe. Therefore, the objection is unsound.

The second objection is that maybe the present state of the universe is just a fluctuation in an overall state of equilibrium. In other words, the present energy is like just the ripple on the surface of a still pond. But this objection loses all sense of proportion. Fluctuations are so tiny, they are important only in systems where you have a few atoms. In a universe at equilibrium, fluctuations would be imperceptible. A chart showing fluctuations in such a universe would be simply a straight line. Therefore, since the present universe is in *dis*equilibrium, what are we to conclude? According to . . . Davies, the universe must have been created a finite time ago and is in the process of winding down.[19] He says the present disequilibrium cannot be a fluctuation from a prior state of equilibrium, because prior to this creation event the universe simply did not exist. Thus, Davies concludes, even though we may not like it, we must conclude that the universe's energy "was simply 'put in' at the creation as an initial condition."

Thus, we have two philosophical arguments and two scientific confirmations of the point we set out to defend: the universe began to exist. In light of these four reasons, I think we are amply justified in affirming the first alternative of our first disjunction: *the universe had a beginning*.

WAS THE BEGINNING CAUSED?

Having concluded that the evidence points to a beginning of the universe, let's now turn to our second set of alternatives: the beginning of the universe was either caused or not caused. I am not going to give a lengthy defense of the point that the beginning of the universe must have been caused. I do not think I need to. For probably no one in his right mind *sincerely* believes

[18]Gribbin, "Oscillating Universe," p. 16.

[19]Davies, *The Physics of Time Asymmetry* (London: Survey University Press, 1974), p. 104.

that the universe could pop into existence uncaused out of nothing. Even the famous skeptic David Hume admitted that it is preposterous to think anything could come into existence without a cause.[20] This is doubly true with regard to the entire universe. As the English philosopher C. D. Broad confessed, "I cannot really *believe in* anything beginning to exist without being caused by something else which existed before and up to the moment when the thing in question began to exist."[21] As still another philosopher has said, "It seems quite inconceivable that our universe could have sprung from an absolute void. If there is anything we find inconceivable it is that something could arise from nothing."[22] The old principle that "out of nothing, nothing comes" is so manifestly true that a sincere denial of this point is practically impossible.

This puts the atheist on the spot. For as Anthony Kenny explains, "A proponent of [the big bang] theory, at least if he is an atheist, must believe that the matter of the universe came from nothing and by nothing." That is a pretty hard pill to swallow. In terms of sheer "believability," I find it intellectually easier to believe in a God who is the cause of the universe than in the universe's popping into existence uncaused out of nothing or in the universe's having existed for infinite time without a beginning. For me these last two positions are intellectually inconceivable, and it would take *more* faith for me to believe in them than to believe that God exists. But at any rate, we are not dependent upon just "believability," for we have already seen that both philosophical and empirical reasoning points to a beginning for the universe. So the alternatives are only two: either the universe was caused to exist or it sprang into existence wholly uncaused out of nothing about fifteen billion years ago. The first alternative is eminently more plausible.

It is interesting to examine the attitude of scientists toward the philosophical and theological implications of their own big bang model. It is evident that there are such implications, for as one scientist remarks, "The problem of the origin (of the universe) involves a certain metaphysical aspect which may be either appealing or revolting."[23] Unfortunately, the man of science is, as Albert Einstein once observed, "a poor philosopher." For these implications seem either to escape or not to interest most scientists. Since no **empirical** information is available about what preceded the big bang, scientists simply ignore the issue. Thus, Hoyle, after explaining that the big bang model cannot inform us as to where the matter came from or why the big bang occurred, comments, "It is not usual in present day cosmological discussions to seek an answer to this question; the question and its answer are taken to be outside the range of scientific discussion."[24] But while this attitude may satisfy the scientist, it can never satisfy the philosopher. For as one scientist admits, the big bang model only *describes* the initial conditions of the universe, but it cannot *explain* them.[25] As yet another astronomer concludes, "So the question 'How was the matter created in the first place?' is left unanswered."[26] Thus, science begs off answering the really ultimate question of where the universe came from. Scientific evidence points to a beginning of the universe; as rigorous scientists we may stop there and bar further inquiry, but as thinking people must we not inquire further until we come to the cause of the beginning of the universe?

Either the universe was caused to exist or it just came into existence out of nothing by nothing. Scientists refuse to discuss the question; but philosophers admit that it is impossible to believe in something's coming to exist uncaused out of nothing. Therefore, I think that an unprejudiced inquirer will have to agree that the beginning of the universe

[20]David Hume to John Stewart, February 1754, in *The Letters of David Hume,* Vol. 1, ed. J.Y.T. Greig (Oxford, Engl.: Clarendon Press, 1932), p. 187.

[21]C. D. Broad, "Kant's Mathematical Antinomies," *Proceedings of the Aristotelian Society* 55 (1955): 10.

[22][P. J. Zwart, *About Time* (Amsterdam and Oxford, Engl: North Holland Publishing Co., 1976)], p. 240.

[23]Hubert Reeves, Jean Audouze, William A. Fowler, and David N. Schramm, "On the Origin of Light Elements," *Astrophysical Journal* 179 (1973): 909–30.

[24]Fred Hoyle, *Astronomy Today* (London: Heinemann, 1975), p. 166.

[25]Adrian Webster, "The Cosmic Background Radiation," *Scientific American,* August 1974, p. 31.

[26]J. V. Narlikar, "Singularity and Matter Creation in Cosmological Models," *Nature: Physical Science* 242 (1973): 136.

was caused, which is the second point we set out to prove: *the universe was caused to exist.*

Now this is a truly remarkable conclusion. For this means that the universe was caused to exist by something beyond it and greater than it. . . .

PERSONAL OR IMPERSONAL CREATOR?

I think there is good reason to believe that the cause of the universe is a personal creator. This is our third set of alternatives: *personal or not personal.*

The first event in the series of past events was, as we have seen, the beginning of the universe. Furthermore, we have argued that the event was caused. Now the question is: If the cause of the universe is eternal, then why isn't the universe also eternal, since it is the effect of the cause? Let me illustrate what I mean. Suppose we say the cause of water's freezing is the temperature's falling below 0 degrees. Whenever the temperature is below 0 degrees, the water is frozen. Therefore, if the temperature is always below 0 degrees, the water is always frozen. Once the cause is given, the effect must follow. So if the cause were there from eternity, the effect would also be there from eternity. If the temperature were below 0 degrees from eternity, then any water around would be frozen from eternity. But this seems to imply that if the cause of the universe existed from eternity then the universe would have to exist from eternity. And this we have seen to be false.

One might say that the cause came to exist just before the first event. But this will not work, for then the cause's coming into existence would be the first event, and we must ask all over again for its cause. But this cannot go on forever, for we have seen that a beginningless series of events cannot exist. So there must be an absolutely first event, before which there was no change, no previous event. We have seen that this first event was caused. But the question then is: How can a first event come to exist if the cause of that event is always there? Why isn't the effect as eternal as the cause? It seems to me that there is only one way out of this dilemma. That is to say that the cause of the universe is personal and chooses to create the universe in time. In this way God could exist changelessly from eternity, but choose to create the world in time. By "choose" I do not mean God changes his mind. I mean God intends from eternity to create a world in time. Thus, the cause is eternal, but the effect is not. God chooses from eternity to create a world with a beginning; therefore, a world with a beginning comes to exist. Hence, it seems to me that the only way a universe can come to exist is if a Personal Creator of the universe exists. And I think we are justified in calling a Personal Creator of the universe by the name "God.". . .

STUDY QUESTIONS

1. Craig offers two philosophical and two scientific arguments for the claim that the universe had a beginning. Explain each argument carefully.
2. Craig's argument requires establishing two additional claims. What are they? How does he try to establish each of them?
3. *Are any of the steps in any of Craig's arguments dubious or wrong, in your opinion? Explain.

READING 4.7

Should We Believe the Principle of Sufficient Reason?

William L. Rowe

The **principle of sufficient reason** *(PSR) plays a crucial role in the* **cosmological argument.** *The principle can be variously formulated*—every being must have an explanation, every fact must have an explanation, every positive fact must have an explanation, every event must have an explanation—*but somewhere along the way a proponent of the cosmological argument will need the principle of sufficient reason to justify the quest for an explanation. William L. Rowe (Purdue University) distinguishes between saying that PSR is known to be true and saying that PSR is a presupposition of reason. He then points out the impact of each of these formulations for the question of whether we should accept the argument. Rowe makes the interesting point that, if PSR were not known to be true but were true, the cosmological argument would be* **sound** *and yet would not provide good grounds for believing in God.*

. . . Why, after all, should we accept the idea that every being and every positive fact must have an explanation? Why, in short, should we believe PSR? These are important questions, and any final judgment of the Cosmological Argument depends on how they are answered.

Most of the theologians and philosophers who accept PSR have tried to defend it in either of two ways. Some have held that PSR is (or can be) known *intuitively* to be true. By this they mean that if we fully understand and reflect on what is said by PSR we can see that it must be true. Now, undoubtedly, there are statements which are known intuitively to be true. "Every triangle has exactly three angles" or "No physical object can be in two different places in space at one and the same time" are examples of statements whose truth we can apprehend just by understanding and reflecting on them. The difficulty with the claim that PSR is intuitively true, however, is that a number of very able philosophers fail to apprehend its truth, and some even claim that the principle is false. It is doubtful, therefore, that many of us, if any, know intuitively that PSR is true.

The second way philosophers and theologians who accept PSR have sought to defend it is by claiming that although it is not known to be true, it is, nevertheless, a presupposition of reason, a basic assumption that rational people make, whether or not they reflect sufficiently to become aware of the assumption. It's probably true that there are some assumptions we all make about our world, assumptions which are so basic that most of us are unaware of them. And, I suppose, it might be true that PSR is such an assumption. What bearing would this view of PSR have on the Cosmological Argument? Perhaps the main point to note is that even if PSR is a presupposition we all share, the premises of the **Cosmological Argument** could still be false. For PSR itself could still be false. The fact, if it is a fact, that all of us *presuppose* that every existing being and every positive fact has an explanation does not imply that no being exists, and no positive fact obtains, without an explanation. Nature is not bound to satisfy our presuppositions. As the American philosopher William James once remarked in another connection, "In the great boarding house of nature, the cakes and the butter and the syrup seldom come out so even and leave the plates so clear."

Our study of the first part of the Cosmological Argument[1] has led us to the fundamental principle on which its premises rest, the Principle of Sufficient Reason. Since we do not seem to know that PSR is true, we cannot reasonably claim to know that the premises of the Cosmological Argument are true. They might be true. But unless we do know them to be true they cannot *establish* for us the conclusion that there exists a being that has the explanation of its existence within its own nature. If it were shown, however, that even though we do not *know* that PSR is true we all, nevertheless, *presuppose* PSR to be true, then, whether PSR is true or not, to be consistent we should accept the Cosmological Argument. For, as we've seen, its premises imply its conclusion and its premises do seem to follow from PSR. But no one has succeeded in *showing* that PSR is an assumption that most or all of us share. So our final conclusion must be that although the Cosmological Argument might be a ***sound* argument** (**valid** with true premises), it does not provide us with good rational grounds for believing that among these beings that exist there is one whose existence is accounted for by its own nature. . . . [E]ven if it succeeded in showing that a self-existent being would have the other attributes of the theistic God,

[1][Not included in this book—Ed.]

the Cosmological Argument would still not provide us with good rational grounds for belief in God, having failed . . . to provide us with good rational grounds for believing that there is a self-existent being.

STUDY QUESTIONS

1. What are the two ways of viewing PSR, according to Rowe?
2. What difference does it make to the cosmological argument which view of PSR we adopt?
3. *What examples can you think of to illustrate that people use PSR?
4. *If we maintain that PSR is a presupposition of reason, what motivation might we have for presupposing it?
5. *Some philosophers have examined the possibility that PSR is a principle based on empirical observation. Can you think of why most philosophers reject this understanding of PSR? (Hint: think of whether PSR is actually corroborated by **empirical** observation—that is, whether empirically speaking every fact has been found to have an explanation.)
6. *Could an event happen by chance but not violate PSR? Discuss. If you are familiar with quantum physics, assess an example from that domain.

DESIGN ARGUMENTS

READING 4.8

On An Argument for Design

David Hume

David Hume's (1711–76) Dialogues Concerning Natural Religion *contains a classic formulation and critique of a* **design argument.** *(***Natural religion** *refers to religion that is accepted because of reason and experience; it contrasts with* revealed religion, *or religion accepted because of revelation.) A version of the design argument is presented by a character named Cleanthes. Cleanthes represents a new style of* **theologian** *that emerged in the seventeenth and eighteenth centuries, one who is willing to use* ***a posteriori,*** *probabilistic,* **inductive arguments** *for God's existence, as opposed to the* ***a priori,*** *demonstrative,* **deductive arguments** *favored by the older, medieval type of theologian, represented by the character Demea. A third character, Philo, functions primarily as a critic and commentator (an astute "kibitzer," one might say). When scholars allude to "Hume's" objections to the design argument, they refer mostly to Philo's clever and penetrating criticisms.*

Cleanthes proposes that the world's order, the "curious adapting of means to ends," resembles that of a machine, and like effects have like causes. Since the cause of a machine's order is intelligent design, so, too, is intelligent design the cause of the universe's order. Philo's criticisms of this argument by analogy can be summarized as follows. First, in part II, he says that the analogy between the world and a machine is defective; there are too many dissimilarities. To have a good basis for inference, we would need experience of other worlds. Second, in part IV, he objects that if, as Cleanthes claims, order must be explained by intelligent design, would we not have to infer a second designer for the orderly ideas of Cleanthes' designer, and then a third designer for that designer's ideas, and so on ad infinitum? *Cleanthes attempts a reply, that one need not find the cause of the designer's ideas because "even in common life" we do not trace causes all the way back. Philo rejects this reply. Third, in part V, Philo suggests that even if the argument were successful in showing the world is designed, it would not show that this designer is perfect and infinite, that there was one designer rather than many, or that the designer got it right the first time—"many a world might have been botched and bungled, throughout an eternity, ere this system was struck out." Philo does not mean to accept any of these hypotheses, but rather to show that there are too many possibilities to allow inferring the traditional God. Cleanthes responds that all these alternate design hypotheses still concede design. Fourth, however, Philo goes on to construct various hypotheses that do not involve design. In part VII, Philo proposes the alternate hypothesis that the world arose through "generation and vegetation"—that is, the operation of natural laws. This hypothesis is at least as well supported as the design hypothesis and, in fact, Philo argues, is better, for reasons found in the selection. He suggests that the plausibility we attribute to the design hypothesis results from human beings' extrapolating from their own way of producing order (namely, through design). If spiders could reason, he suggests, they would infer from the design of the world that it was spun out, like a web, by a giant spider. Fifth and finally, in part VIII, Philo presents a further nondesign hypothesis: that particles are inherently in motion but eventually, by chance, become arranged in a stable, ordered pattern. This hypothesis is remarkably like the theory of* ***natural selection*** *propounded by Charles Darwin a century later. Again, Philo does not endorse this or his other hypotheses, but merely wants to show that the design hypothesis is but one among many. "A total suspense of judgment," he states, "is here our only reasonable resource."*

PART II

Not to lose any time in circumlocutions, said Cleanthes, addressing himself to Demea, much less in replying to the pious declamations of Philo, I shall briefly explain how I conceive this matter. Look round the world, contemplate the whole and every part of it: you will find it to be nothing but one great machine, subdivided into an infinite number of lesser machines, which again admit of subdivisions to a degree beyond what human senses and faculties can trace and explain. All these various machines, and even their most minute parts, are adjusted to each other with an accuracy which ravishes into admiration all men who have ever contemplated them. The curious adapting of means to ends, throughout all nature, resembles exactly, though it much exceeds, the productions of human contrivance—of human design, thought, wisdom, and intelligence. Since therefore the effects resemble each other, we are led to infer, by all the rules of analogy, that the causes also resemble, and that the Author of nature is somewhat similar to the mind of man, though possessed of much larger faculties, proportioned to the grandeur of the work which he has executed. By this argument ***a posteriori,*** and by this argument alone, do we prove at once the existence of a Deity and his similarity to human mind and intelligence.

I shall be so free, Cleanthes, said Demea, as to tell you that from the beginning I could not approve of your conclusion concerning the similarity of the Deity to men, still less can I approve of the mediums by which you endeavour to establish it. What! No demonstration of the Being of God! No abstract **arguments!** No proofs ***a priori!*** Are these which have hitherto been so much insisted on by philosophers all fallacy, all sophism? Can we reach no farther in this subject than experience and probability? I will not say that this is betraying the cause of a Deity; but surely, by this affected candour, you give advantages to atheists which they never could obtain by the mere dint of argument and reasoning.

What I chiefly scruple in this subject, said Philo, is not so much that all religious arguments are by Cleanthes reduced to experience, as that they appear not to be even the most certain and irrefragable of that inferior kind. That a stone will fall, that fire will burn, that the earth has solidity, we have observed a thousand and a thousand times; and when any new instance of this nature is presented, we draw without hesitation the accustomed inference. The exact similarity of the cases gives us a perfect assurance of a similar event, and a stronger evidence is never desired nor sought after. But wherever you depart, in the least, from the similarity of the cases, you diminish proportionably the evidence, and may at last bring it to a very weak *analogy,* which is confessedly liable to error and uncertainty. After having experienced the circulation of the blood in human creatures, we make no doubt that it takes place in Titius and Maevius; but from its circulation in frogs and fishes it is only a presumption, though a strong one, from analogy that it takes place in men and other animals. The analogical reasoning is much weaker when we infer the circulation of the sap in vegetables from our experience that the blood circulates in animals; and those who hastily followed that imperfect analogy are found, by more accurate experiments, to have been mistaken.

If we see a house, Cleanthes, we conclude, with the greatest certainty, that it had an architect or builder because this is precisely that species of effect which we have experienced to proceed from that species of cause. But surely you will not affirm that the universe bears such a resemblance to a house that we can with the same certainty infer a similar cause, or that the analogy is here entire and perfect. The dissimilitude is so striking that the utmost you can here pretend to is a guess, a conjecture, a presumption concerning a similar cause; and how that pretension will be received in the world, I leave you to consider.

It would surely be very ill received, replied Cleanthes; and I should be deservedly blamed and detested did I allow that the proofs of a Deity amounted to no more than a guess or conjecture. But is the whole adjustment of means to ends in a house and in the universe so slight a resemblance? the economy of final causes? the order, proportion, and arrangement of every part? Steps of a stair are plainly contrived that human legs may use them in mounting; and this inference is certain and infallible. Human legs are also contrived for walking and mounting; and this inference, I allow, is not altogether so certain because of the dissimilarity which you remark; but does it, therefore, deserve the name only of presumption or conjecture?

Good God! cried Demea, interrupting him, where are we? Zealous defenders of religion allow that the proofs of a Deity fall short of perfect evidence! And you, Philo, on whose assistance I depended in proving the adorable mysteriousness of the Divine Nature, do you assent to all these extravagant opinions of Cleanthes? For what other name can I give them? or, why spare my censure when such principles are advanced, supported by such an authority, before so young a man as Pamphilus?

You seem not to apprehend, replied Philo, that I argue with Cleanthes in his own way, and, by showing him the dangerous consequences of his tenets, hope at last to reduce him to our opinion. But what sticks most with you, I observe, is the representation which Cleanthes has made of the argument *a posteriori;* and, finding that that argument is likely to escape your hold and vanish into air, you think it so disguised that you can scarcely believe it to be set in its true light. Now, however much I may dissent, in other respects, from the dangerous principle of Cleanthes, I must allow that he has fairly represented that argument, and I shall endeavour so to state the matter to you that you will entertain no further scruples with regard to it.

Were a man to abstract from everything which he knows or has seen, he would be altogether incapable, merely from his own ideas, to determine what kind of scene the universe must be, or to give the preference to one state or situation of things above another. For as nothing which he clearly conceives could be esteemed impossible or implying a contradiction, every chimera of his fancy would be upon an equal footing; nor could he assign any just reason why he adheres to one idea or system, and rejects the others which are equally possible.

Again, after he opens his eyes and contemplates the world as it really is, it would be impossible for him at first to assign the cause of any one event, much less of the whole of things, or of the universe. He might set his fancy a rambling, and she might bring him in an infinite variety of reports and representations. These would all be possible, but, being all equally possible, he would never of himself give a satisfactory account for his preferring one of them to the rest. Experience alone can point out to him the true cause of any phenomenon.

Now, according to this method of reasoning, Demea, it follows (and is, indeed, tacitly allowed by Cleanthes himself) that order, arrangement, or the adjustment of **final causes,** is not of itself any proof of design, but only so far as it has been experienced to proceed from that principle. For aught we can know *a priori,* matter may contain the source or spring of order originally within itself, as well as mind does; and there is no more difficulty in conceiving that the several elements, from an internal unknown cause, may fall into the most exquisite arrangement, than to conceive that their ideas, in the great universal mind, from a like internal unknown cause, fall into that arrangement. The equal possibility of both these suppositions is allowed. But, by experience, we find (according to Cleanthes) that there is a difference between them. Throw several pieces of steel together, without shape or form, they will never arrange themselves so as to compose a watch. Stone and mortar and wood, without an architect, never erect a house. But the ideas in a human mind, we see, by an unknown, inexplicable economy, arrange themselves so as to form the plan of a watch or house. Experience, therefore, proves that there is an original principle of order in mind, not in matter. From similar effects we infer similar causes. The adjustment of means to ends is alike in the universe, as in a machine of human contrivance. The causes, therefore, must be resembling.

I was from the beginning scandalized, I must own, with this resemblance which is asserted between the Deity and human creatures, and must conceive it to imply such a degradation of the Supreme Being as no sound theist could endure. With your assistance, therefore, Demea, I shall endeavour to defend what you justly call the adorable mysteriousness of the Divine Nature, and shall refute this reasoning of Cleanthes, provided he allows that I have made a fair representation of it.

When Cleanthes had assented, Philo, after a short pause, proceeded in the following manner.

That all inferences, Cleanthes, concerning fact are founded on experience, and that all experimental reasonings are founded on the supposition that similar causes prove similar effects, and similar effects similar causes, I shall not at present much dispute with you. But observe, I entreat you, with what extreme caution all just reasoners proceed in the transferring of experiments to similar cases. Unless the cases be exactly similar, they repose no perfect confidence in applying their past observation to any particular phenomenon. Every alteration of circumstances occasions a doubt concerning the event; and it requires new experiments to prove certainly that the new circumstances are of no moment or importance. A change in bulk, situation, arrangement, age, disposition of the air, or surrounding bodies—any of these particulars may be attended with the most unexpected consequences. And unless the objects be quite familiar to us, it is the highest temerity to expect with assurance, after any of these changes, an event similar to that which before fell under our observation. The slow and deliberate steps of philosophers here, if anywhere, are distinguished from the precipitate march of the vulgar, who, hurried on by the smallest similitude, are incapable of all discernment or consideration.

But can you think, Cleanthes, that your usual phlegm and philosophy have been preserved in so wide a step as you have taken when you compared to the universe houses, ships, furniture, machines, and, from their similarity in some circumstances, inferred a similarity in their causes? Thought, design, intelligence, such as we discover in men and other animals, is no more than one of the springs and principles of the universe, as well as heat or cold, attraction or repulsion, and a hundred others which fall under daily observation. It is an active cause by which some particular parts of nature, we find, produce alterations on other parts. But can a conclusion, with any propriety, be transferred from parts to the whole? Does not the great disproportion bar all comparison and inference? From observing the growth of a hair, can we learn anything concerning the generation of a man? Would the manner of a leaf's blowing, even though perfectly known, afford us any instruction concerning the vegetation of a tree?

But allowing that we were to take the *operations* of one part of nature upon another for the foundation of our judgment concerning the *origin* of the whole (which never can be admitted), yet why select so minute, so weak, so bounded a principle as the reason and design of animals is found to be upon this planet? What peculiar privilege has this little agitation of the brain which we call *thought,* that we must thus make it the model of the whole universe? Our partiality in our own favour does indeed present it on all occasions, but sound philosophy ought carefully to guard against so natural an illusion.

So far from admitting, continued Philo, that the operations of a part can afford us any just conclusion concerning the origin of the whole, I will not allow any one part to form a rule for another part if the latter be very remote from the former. Is there any reasonable ground to conclude that the inhabitants of other planets possess thought, intelligence, reason, or anything similar to these faculties in men? When nature has so extremely diversified her manner of operation in this small globe, can we imagine that she incessantly copies herself throughout so immense a universe? And if thought, as we may well suppose, be confined merely to this narrow corner and has even there so limited a sphere of action, with what propriety can we assign it for the original cause of all things? The narrow views of a peasant who makes his domestic economy the rule for the government of kingdoms is in comparison a pardonable sophism.

But were we ever so much assured that a thought and reason resembling the human were to be found throughout the whole universe, and were its activity elsewhere vastly greater and more commanding than it appears in this globe, yet I cannot see why the operations of a world constituted, arranged, adjusted, can with any propriety be extended to a world which is in its embryo state, and is advancing towards that constitution and arrangement. By observation we know somewhat of the economy, action, and nourishment of a finished animal, but we must transfer with great caution that observation to the growth of a fœtus in the womb, and still more to the formation of an animalcule in the loins of its male parent. Nature, we find, even from our limited experience, possesses an infinite number of springs and principles which incessantly discover themselves on every change of her position and situation. And what new and unknown principles would actuate her in so new and unknown a situation as that of the formation of a universe, we cannot, without the utmost temerity, pretend to determine.

A very small part of this great system, during a very short time, is very imperfectly discovered to us; and do we thence pronounce decisively concerning the origin of the whole?

Admirable conclusion! Stone, wood, brick, iron, brass, have not, at this time, in this minute globe of earth, an order or arrangement without human art and contrivance; therefore, the universe could not originally attain its order and arrangement without something similar to human art. But is a part of nature a rule for another part very wide of the former? Is it a rule for the whole? Is a very small part a rule for the universe? Is nature in one situation a certain rule for nature in another situation vastly different from the former?

And can you blame me, Cleanthes, if I here imitate the prudent reserve of Simonides, who, according to the noted story, being asked by Hiero, *What God was?* desired a day to think of it, and then two days more; and after that manner continually prolonged the term, without ever bringing in his definition or description? Could you even blame me if I had answered, at first, *that I did not know,* and was sensible that this subject lay vastly beyond the reach of my faculties? You might cry out **sceptic** and rallier, as much as you pleased; but, having found in so many other subjects much more familiar the imperfections and even contradictions of human reason, I never should expect any success from its feeble conjectures in a subject so sublime and so remote from the sphere of our observation. When two *species* of objects have always been observed to be conjoined together, I can *infer,* by custom, the existence of one wherever I *see* the existence of the other; and this I call an argument from experience. But how this argument can have place where the objects, as in the present case, are single, individual, without parallel or specific resemblance, may be difficult to explain. And will any man tell me with a serious countenance that an orderly universe must arise from some thought and art like the human because we have experience of it? To ascertain this reasoning it were requisite that we had experience of the origin of worlds; and it is not sufficient, surely, that we have seen ships and cities arise from human art and contrivance.

Philo was proceeding in this vehement manner, somewhat between jest and earnest, as it appeared to me, when he observed some signs of impatience in Cleanthes, and then immediately stopped short. What I had to suggest, said Cleanthes, is only that you would not abuse terms, or make use of popular expressions to subvert philosophical reasonings. You know that the vulgar often distinguish reason from experience, even where the question relates only to matter of fact and existence, though it is found, where that *reason* is properly analyzed, that it is nothing but a species of experience. To prove by experience the origin of the universe from mind is not more contrary to common speech than to prove the motion of the earth from the same principle. And a caviller might raise all the same objections to the Copernican system which you have urged against my reasonings. Have you other earths, might he say, which you have seen to move? Have . . .

Yes! cried Philo, interrupting him, we have other earths. Is not the moon another earth, which we see to turn round its centre? Is not Venus another earth, where we observe the same phenomenon? Are not the revolutions of the sun also a confirmation, from analogy, of the same theory? All the planets, are they not earths which revolve about the sun? Are not the satellites moons which move round Jupiter and Saturn, and along with these primary planets round the sun? These analogies and resemblances, with others which I have not mentioned, are the sole proofs of the Copernican system; and to you it belongs to consider whether you have any analogies of the same kind to support your theory.

In reality, Cleanthes, continued he, the modern system of astronomy is now so much received by all inquirers, and has become so essential a part even of our earliest education, that we are not commonly very scrupulous in examining the reasons upon which it is founded. It is now become a matter of mere curiosity to study the first writers on that subject who had the full force of prejudice to encounter, and were obliged to turn their arguments on every side in order to render them popular and convincing. But if we peruse Galileo's famous *Dialogues*[1] concerning the system of the world, we shall find that that great genius, one of the sublimest that ever existed, first bent all his endeavours to prove that there was no foundation for the distinction commonly made between elementary and celestial substances. The [medieval] schools, proceeding from the illusions of sense, had carried this distinction very far; and had established the latter substances to be ingenerable, incorruptible, unalterable, impassible; and had assigned all the opposite qualities to the former. But Galileo, beginning with the moon, proved its similarity in every particular to the earth: its convex figure, its natural darkness when not illuminated, its density, its distinction into solid and liquid, the variations of its phases, the mutual illuminations of the earth and moon, their mutual eclipses, the inequalities of the lunar surface, etc. After many instances of this kind, with regard to all the planets, men plainly saw that these bodies became proper objects of experience, and that the similarity of their nature enabled us to extend the same arguments and phenomena from one to the other.

In this cautious proceeding of the astronomers you may read your own condemnation, Cleanthes, or rather may see that the subject in which you are engaged exceeds all human reason and inquiry. Can you pretend to show any such similarity between the fabric of a house and the generation of a universe? Have you ever seen nature in any such situation as resembles the first arrangement of the elements? Have worlds ever been formed under your eye, and have you had leisure to observe the whole progress of the phenomenon, from the first appearance of order to its final consummation? If you have, then cite your experience and deliver your theory. . . .

PART IV

It seems strange to me, said Cleanthes, that you, Demea, who are so sincere in the cause of religion, should still maintain the mysterious, incomprehensible nature of the Deity, and should insist so strenuously that he has no manner of likeness or resemblance to human creatures. The Deity, I can readily allow, possesses many powers and attributes of which we can have no comprehension; but, if our ideas, so far as they go, be not just and adequate and correspondent to his real nature, I know not what there is in this subject worth insisting on. Is the name, without any meaning, of such mighty importance? Or how do you mystics, who maintain the absolute incomprehensibility of the Deity, differ

[1][*Dialogue on the Great World Systems (1632).*]

from sceptics or atheists, who assert that the first cause of all is unknown and unintelligible? Their temerity must be very great if, after rejecting the production by a mind—I mean a mind resembling the human (for I know of no other)—they pretend to assign, with certainty, any other specific intelligible cause; and their conscience must be very scrupulous, indeed, if they refuse to call the universal unknown cause a God or Deity, and to bestow on him as many sublime eulogies and unmeaning epithets as you shall please to require of them.

Who could imagine, replied Demea, that Cleanthes, the calm philosophical Cleanthes, would attempt to refute his antagonists by affixing a nickname to them, and, like the common bigots and inquisitors of the age, have recourse to invective and declamation instead of reasoning? Or does he not perceive that these topics are easily retorted, and that *anthropomorphite* is an appellation as invidious, and implies as dangerous consequences, as the epithet of *mystic* with which he has honoured us? In reality, Cleanthes, consider what it is you assert when you represent the Deity as similar to a human mind and understanding. What is the soul of man? A composition of various faculties, passions, sentiments, ideas—united, indeed, into one self or person, but still distinct from each other. When it reasons, the ideas which are the parts of its discourse arrange themselves in a certain form or order which is not preserved entire for a moment, but immediately gives place to another arrangement. New opinions, new passions, new affections, new feelings arise which continually diversify the mental scene and produce in it the greatest variety and most rapid succession imaginable. How is this compatible with that perfect **immutability** and **simplicity** which all true theists ascribe to the Deity? By the same act, say they, he sees past, present, and future; his love and hatred, his mercy and justice, are one individual operation; he is entire in every point of space, and complete in every instant of duration. No succession, no change, no acquisition, no diminution. What he is implies not in it any shadow of distinction or diversity. And what he is this moment he ever has been and ever will be, without any new judgment, sentiment, or operation. He stands fixed in one simple, perfect state; nor can you ever say, with any propriety, that this act of his is different from that other, or that this judgment or idea has been lately formed and will give place, by succession, to any different judgment or idea.

I can readily allow, said Cleanthes, that those who maintain the perfect simplicity of the Supreme Being, to the extent in which you have explained it, are complete mystics, and chargeable with all the consequences which I have drawn from their opinion. They are, in a word, atheists, without knowing it. For though it be allowed that the Deity possesses attributes of which we have no comprehension, yet ought we never to ascribe to him any attributes which are absolutely incompatible with that intelligent nature essential to him. A mind whose acts and sentiments and ideas are not distinct and successive, one that is wholly simple and totally immutable, is a mind which has no thought, no reason, no will, no sentiment, no love, no hatred; or, in a word, is no mind at all. It is an abuse of terms to give it that appellation, and we may as well speak of limited extension without figure, or of number without composition.

Pray consider, said Philo, whom you are at present inveighing against. You are honouring with the appellation of *atheist* all the sound, orthodox divines, almost, who have treated of this subject; and you will at last be, yourself, found, according to your reckoning, the only sound theist in the world. But if idolaters be atheists, as, I think, may justly be asserted, and Christian theologians the same, what becomes of the argument, so much celebrated, derived from the universal consent of mankind?

But, because I know you are not much swayed by names and authorities, I shall endeavour to show you, a little more distinctly, the inconveniences of that **anthropomorphism** which you have embraced, and shall prove that there is no ground to suppose a plan of the world to be formed in the Divine mind, consisting of distinct ideas, differently arranged, in the same manner as an architect forms in his head the plan of a house which he intends to execute.

It is not easy, I own, to see what is gained by this supposition, whether we judge of the matter by *reason* or by *experience.* We are still obliged to mount higher in order to find the cause of this cause which you had assigned as satisfactory and conclusive.

If *reason* (I mean abstract reason derived from inquiries *a priori*) be not alike mute with regard to all questions concerning cause and effect, this sentence at least it will venture to pronounce: that a mental world or universe of ideas requires a cause as much as does a material world or universe of objects, and, if similar in its arrangement, must require a similar cause. For what is there in this subject which should occasion a different conclusion or inference? In an abstract view, they are entirely alike; and no difficulty attends the one supposition which is not common to both of them.

Again, when we will needs force *experience* to pronounce some sentence, even on these subjects which lie beyond her sphere, neither can she perceive any material difference in this particular between these two kinds of worlds, but finds them to be governed by similar principles, and to depend upon an equal variety of causes in their operations. We have specimens in miniature of both of them. Our own mind resembles the one; a vegetable or animal body the other. Let experience, therefore, judge from these samples. Nothing seems more delicate, with regard to its causes, than thought; and as these causes never operate in two persons after the same manner, so we never find two persons who think exactly alike. Nor indeed does the same person think exactly alike at any two different periods of time. A difference of age, of the disposition of his body, of weather, of food, of company, of books, of passions—any of these particulars, or others more minute, are sufficient to alter the curious machinery of thought and communicate to it very different movements and operations. As far as we can judge, vegetables and animal bodies are not more delicate in their motions, nor depend upon a greater variety or more curious adjustment of springs and principles.

How, therefore, shall we satisfy ourselves concerning the cause of that Being whom you suppose the Author of nature, or, according to your system of anthropomorphism, the ideal world into which you trace the material? Have we not the same reason to trace that ideal world into another ideal world or new intelligent principle? But if we stop and go no farther, why go so far? Why not stop at the material world? How can we satisfy ourselves without going on *in infinitum?* And, after all, what satisfaction is there in that infinite progression? Let us remember the story of the Indian philosopher and his elephant. It was never more applicable than to the present subject. If the material world rests upon a similar ideal world, this ideal world must rest upon some other, and so on without end. It were better, therefore, never to look beyond the present material world. By supposing it to contain the principle of its order within itself, we really assert it to be God; and the sooner we arrive at that Divine Being, so much the better. When you go one step beyond the mundane system, you only excite an inquisitive humour which it is impossible ever to satisfy.

To say that the different ideas which compose the reason of the Supreme Being fall into order of themselves and by their own nature is really to talk without any precise meaning. If it has a meaning, I would fain know why it is not as good sense to say that the parts of the material world fall into order of themselves and by their own nature. Can the one opinion be intelligible, while the other is not so?

We have, indeed, experience of ideas which fall into order of themselves and without any *known* cause. But, I am sure, we have a much larger experience of matter which does the same, as in all instances of generation and vegetation where the accurate analysis of the cause exceeds all human comprehension. We have also experience of particular systems of thought and of matter which have no order; of the first in madness, of the second in corruption. Why, then, should we think that order is more essential to one than the other? And if it requires a cause in both, what do we gain by your system, in tracing the universe of objects into a similar universe of ideas? The first step which we make leads us on for ever. It were, therefore, wise in us to limit all our inquiries to the present world, without looking farther. No satisfaction can ever be attained by these speculations which so far exceed the narrow bounds of human understanding.

It was usual with the **Peripatetics,** you know, Cleanthes, when the cause of any phenomenon was demanded, to have recourse to their *faculties* or *occult qualities,* and to say, for instance, that bread nourished by its nutritive faculty, and senna purged by its purgative. But it has been discovered that this subterfuge was nothing but the disguise of ignorance, and that these philosophers, though less ingenuous, really said the same thing with the sceptics or the vulgar who fairly confessed that they knew not the cause of these phenomena. In like manner, when it is asked, what cause produces order in the ideas of the Supreme Being, can any other reason be assigned by you, anthropomorphites, than that it is a *rational* faculty, and that such is the nature of the Deity? But why a similar answer will not be equally satisfactory in accounting for the order of the world, without having recourse to any such intelligent creator as you insist on, may be difficult to determine. It is only to say that *such* is the nature of material objects, and that they are all originally possessed of a *faculty* of order and proportion. These are only more learned and elaborate ways of confessing our ignorance; nor has the one hypothesis any real advantage above the other, except in its greater conformity to vulgar prejudices.

You have displayed this argument with great emphasis, replied Cleanthes: You seem not sensible how easy it is to answer it. Even in common life, if I assign a cause for any event, is it any objection, Philo, that I cannot assign the cause of that cause, and answer every new question which may incessantly be started? And what philosophers could possibly submit to so rigid a rule?—philosophers who confess ultimate causes to be totally unknown, and are sensible that the most refined principles into which they trace the phenomena are still to them as inexplicable as these phenomena themselves are to the vulgar. The order and arrangement of nature, the curious adjustment of final causes, the plain use and intention of every part and organ—all these bespeak in the clearest language an intelligent cause or author. The heavens and the earth join in the same testimony: The whole chorus of nature raises one hymn to the praises of its Creator. You alone, or almost alone, disturb this general harmony. You start abstruse doubts, cavils, and objections; you ask me what is the cause of this cause? I know not; I care not; that concerns not me. I have found a Deity; and here I stop my inquiry. Let those go farther who are wiser or more enterprising.

I pretend to be neither, replied Philo; and for that very reason I should never, perhaps, have attempted to go so far, especially when I am sensible that I must at last be contented to sit down with the same answer which, without further trouble, might have satisfied me from the beginning. If I am still to remain in utter ignorance of causes and can absolutely give an explication of nothing, I shall never esteem it any advantage to shove off for a moment a difficulty which you acknowledge must immediately, in its full force, recur upon me. Naturalists indeed very justly explain particular effects by more general causes, though these general causes themselves should remain in the end totally inexplicable, but they never surely thought it satisfactory to explain a particular effect by a particular cause which was no more to be accounted for than the effect itself. An ideal system, arranged of itself, without a precedent design, is not a whit more explicable than a material one which attains its order in a like manner; nor is there any more difficulty in the latter supposition than in the former.

PART V

But to show you still more inconveniences, continued Philo, in your anthropomorphism, please to take a new survey of your principles. *Like effects prove like causes.* This is the experimental argument; and this, you say too, is the sole **theological** argument. Now it is certain that the liker the effects are which are seen and the liker the causes which are inferred, the stronger is the argument. Every departure on either side diminishes the probability and renders the experiment less conclusive. You cannot doubt of the principle; neither ought you to reject its consequences.

All the new discoveries in astronomy which prove the immense grandeur and magnificence of the works of nature are so many additional arguments for a Deity, according to the true system of theism; but, according to your hypothesis of experimental theism, they become so many objections, by removing the effect still farther from all resemblance to the effects of human art and contrivance. . . .

. . . If this argument, I say, had any force in former ages, how much greater must it have at present when the bounds of Nature are so infinitely enlarged and such a magnificent scene is opened to us? It is still more unreasonable to form our idea of so unlimited a cause from our experience of the narrow productions of human design and invention.

The discoveries by microscopes, as they open a new universe in miniature, are still objections, according to you, arguments, according to me. The further we push our researches of this kind, we are still led to infer the universal cause of all to be vastly different from mankind, or from any object of human experience and observation.

And what say you to the discoveries in anatomy, chemistry, botany? . . . These surely are no objections, replied Cleanthes; they only discover new instances of art and contrivance. It is still the image of mind reflected on us from innumerable objects. Add a mind *like the human,* said Philo. I know of no other, replied Cleanthes. And the liker, the better, insisted Philo. To be sure, said Cleanthes.

Now, Cleanthes, said Philo, with an air of alacrity and triumph, mark the consequences. *First,* by this method of reasoning you renounce all claim to infinity in any of the attributes of the Deity. For, as the cause ought only to be proportioned to the effect, and the effect, so far as it falls under our cognizance, is not infinite, what pretensions have we, upon your suppositions, to ascribe that attribute to the Divine Being? You will still insist that, by removing him so much from all similarity to human creatures, we give in to the most arbitrary hypothesis, and at the same time weaken all proofs of his existence.

Secondly, you have no reason, on your theory, for ascribing perfection to the Deity, even in his finite capacity, or for supposing him free from every error, mistake, or incoherence, in his undertakings. There are many inexplicable difficulties in the works of nature which, if we allow a perfect author to be proved *a priori,* are easily solved, and become only seeming difficulties from the narrow capacity of man, who cannot trace infinite relations. But according to your method of reasoning, these difficulties become all real, and, perhaps, will be insisted on as new instances of likeness to human art and contrivance. At least, you must acknowledge that it is impossible for us to tell, from our limited views, whether this system contains any great faults or deserves any considerable praise if compared to other possible and even real systems. Could a peasant, if the *Æneid* were read to him, pronounce that poem to be absolutely faultless, or even assign to it its proper rank among the productions of human wit, he who had never seen any other production?

But were this world ever so perfect a production, it must still remain uncertain whether all the excellences of the work can justly be ascribed to the workman. If we survey a ship, what an exalted idea must we form of the ingenuity of the carpenter who framed so complicated, useful, and beautiful a machine? And what surprise must we feel when we find him a stupid mechanic who imitated others, and copied an art which, through a long succession of ages, after multiplied trials, mistakes, corrections, deliberations, and controversies, had been gradually improving? Many worlds might have been botched and bungled, throughout an eternity, ere this system was struck out; much labour lost, many fruitless trials made, and a slow but continued improvement carried on during infinite ages in the art of world-making. In such subjects, who can determine where the truth, nay, who can conjecture where the probability lies, amidst a great number of hypotheses which may be proposed, and a still greater which may be imagined?

And what shadow of an argument, continued Philo, can you produce from your hypothesis to prove the unity of the Deity? A great number of men join in building a house or ship, in rearing a city, in framing a commonwealth; why may not several deities combine in contriving and framing a world? This is only so much greater similarity to human affairs. By sharing the work among several, we may so much further limit the attributes of each, and get rid of that extensive power and knowledge which must be supposed in one deity, and which, according to you, can only serve to weaken the proof of his existence. And if such foolish, such vicious creatures as man can yet often unite in framing and executing one plan, how much more those deities or demons, whom we may suppose several degrees more perfect!

To multiply causes without necessity is indeed contrary to true philosophy,[1] but this principle applies not to the present case. Were one deity antecedently proved by your theory who were possessed of every attribute requisite to the production of the universe, it would be needless, I own, (though not absurd) to suppose any other deity existent. But while it is still a question whether all these attributes are united in one subject or dispersed among several independent beings, by what phenomena in nature can we pretend to decide the controversy? Where we see a body raised in a scale, we are sure that there is in the opposite scale, however concealed from sight, some counterpoising weight equal to it; but it is still allowed to doubt whether that weight be an aggregate of several distinct bodies or one uniform united mass. And if the weight requisite very much exceeds anything which we have ever seen conjoined in any single body, the former supposition becomes still more probable and natural. An intelligent being of such vast power and capacity as is necessary to produce the universe, or, to speak in the language of ancient philosophy, so prodigious an animal exceeds all analogy and even comprehension.

But further, Cleanthes: Men are mortal, and renew their species by generation; and this is common to all living creatures. The two great sexes of male and female, says Milton, animate the world. Why must this circumstance, so universal, so essential, be excluded from those numerous and limited deities? Behold, then, the theogeny of ancient times brought back upon us.

And why not become a perfect anthropomorphite? Why not assert the deity or deities to be corporeal, and to have eyes, a nose, mouth, ears, etc.? Epicurus maintained that no man had ever seen reason but in a human figure; therefore, the gods must have a human figure. And this argument, which is deservedly so much ridiculed by Cicero, becomes, according to you, solid and philosophical.

In a word, Cleanthes, a man who follows your hypothesis is able, perhaps, to assert or conjecture that the universe sometime arose from something like design; but beyond that position he cannot ascertain one single circumstance, and is left afterwards to fix every point of his theology by the utmost license of fancy and hypothesis. This world, for aught he knows, is very faulty and imperfect, compared to a superior standard, and was only the first rude essay of some infant deity who afterwards abandoned it, ashamed of his lame performance; it is the work only of some dependent, inferior deity, and is the object of derision to his superiors; it is the production of old age and dotage in some superannuated deity, and ever since his death has run on at adventures, from the first impulse and active force which it received from him. You justly give signs of horror, Demea, at these strange suppositions; but these, and a thousand more of the same kind, are Cleanthes' suppositions, not mine. From the moment the attributes of the Deity are supposed finite, all these have place. And I cannot, for my part, think that so wild and unsettled a system of theology is, in any respect, preferable to none at all.

These suppositions I absolutely disown, cried Cleanthes: they strike me, however, with no horror, especially when proposed in that rambling way in which they drop from you. On the contrary, they give me pleasure when I see that, by the utmost indulgence of your imagination, you never get rid of the hypothesis of design in the universe, but are obliged at every turn to have recourse to it. To this concession I adhere steadily; and this I regard as a sufficient foundation for religion. . . .

PART VII

But here, continued Philo, in examining the ancient system of the soul of the world there strikes me, all on a sudden, a new idea which, if just, must go near to subvert all your reasoning, and destroy even your first inferences on which you repose such confidence. If the universe bears a greater likeness to animal bodies and to vegetables than to the works of human art, it is more probable that its cause resembles the cause of the former than that of the latter, and its origin ought rather to be ascribed to generation or vegetation than to reason or design. Your con-

[1] ["**Ockham's razor**" tells us not to multiply entities without necessity—Ed.]

clusion, even according to your own principles, is therefore lame and defective.

Pray open up this argument a little further, said Demea, for I do not rightly apprehend it in that concise manner in which you have expressed it.

Our friend Cleanthes, replied Philo, as you have heard, asserts that, since no question of fact can be proved otherwise than by experience, the existence of a Deity admits not of proof from any other medium. The world, says he, resembles the works of human contrivance; therefore its cause must also resemble that of the other. Here we may remark that the operation of one very small part of nature, to wit, man, upon another very small part, to wit, that inanimate matter lying within his reach, is the rule by which Cleanthes judges of the origin of the whole; and he measures objects, so widely disproportioned, by the same individual standard. But to waive all objections drawn from this topic, I affirm that there are other parts of the universe (besides the machines of human invention) which bear still a greater resemblance to the fabric of the world, and which, therefore, afford a better conjecture concerning the universal origin of this system. These parts are animals and vegetables. The world plainly resembles more an animal or a vegetable than it does a watch or a knitting-loom. Its cause, therefore, it is more probable, resembles the cause of the former. The cause of the former is generation or vegetation. The cause, therefore, of the world we may infer to be something similar or analogous to generation or vegetation.

But how is it conceivable, said Demea, that the world can arise from anything similar to vegetation or generation?

Very easily, replied Philo. In like manner as a tree sheds its seed into the neighbouring fields and produces other trees, so the great vegetable, the world, or this planetary system, produces within itself certain seeds which, being scattered into the surrounding chaos, vegetate into new worlds. A comet, for instance, is the seed of a world; and after it has been fully ripened, by passing from sun to sun, and star to star, it is, at last, tossed into the unformed elements which everywhere surround this universe, and immediately sprouts up into a new system.

Or if, for the sake of variety (for I see no other advantage), we should suppose this world to be an animal: a comet is the egg of this animal; and in like manner as an ostrich lays its egg in the sand, which, without any further care, hatches the egg and produces a new animal, so . . . . I understand you, says Demea. But what wild, arbitrary suppositions are these! What *data* have you for such extraordinary conclusions? And is the slight, imaginary resemblance of the world to a vegetable or an animal sufficient to establish the same inference with regard to both? Objects which are in general so widely different ought they to be a standard for each other?

Right, cries Philo: This is the topic on which I have all along insisted. I have still asserted that we have no *data* to establish any system of **cosmogony.** Our experience, so imperfect in itself and so limited both in extent and duration, can afford us no probable conjecture concerning the whole of things. But if we must needs fix on some hypothesis, by what rule, pray, ought we to determine our choice? Is there any other rule than the greater similarity of the objects compared? And does not a plant or an animal, which springs from vegetation or generation, bear a stronger resemblance to the world than does any artificial machine, which arises from reason and design?

But what is this vegetation and generation of which you talk? said Demea. Can you explain their operations, and anatomize that fine internal structure on which they depend?

As much, at least, replied Philo, as Cleanthes can explain the operations of reason, or anatomize that internal structure on which it depends. But without any such elaborate disquisitions, when I see an animal, I infer that it sprang from generation; and that with as great certainty as you conclude a house to have been reared by design. These words *generation, reason* mark only certain powers and energies in nature whose effects are known, but whose essence is incomprehensible; and one of these principles, more than the other, has no privilege for being made a standard to the whole of nature.

In reality, Demea, it may reasonably be expected that the larger the views are which we take of things, the better will they conduct us in our conclusions concerning such extraordinary and such magnificent subjects. In this little corner of the world alone, there are four principles, *reason, instinct, generation, vegetation,* which are similar to each other, and are the causes of similar effects. What a number of other principles may we naturally suppose in the immense extent and variety of the universe could we travel from planet to planet, and from system to system, in order to examine each part of this mighty fabric? Any one of these four principles above mentioned (and a hundred others which lie open to our conjecture) may afford us a theory by which to judge of the origin of the world; and it is a palpable and egregious partiality to confine our view entirely to that principle by which our own minds operate. Were this principle more intelligible on that account, such a partiality might be somewhat excusable; but reason, in its internal fabric and structure, is really as little known to us as instinct or vegetation; and, perhaps, even that vague, undeterminate word *nature* to which the vulgar refer everything is not at the bottom more inexplicable. The effects of these principles are all known to us from experience; but the principles themselves and their manner of operation are totally unknown; nor is it less intelligible or less conformable to experience to say that the world arose by vegetation, from a seed shed by another world, than to say that it arose from a divine reason or contrivance, according to the sense in which Cleanthes understands it.

But methinks, said Demea, if the world had a vegetative quality and could sow the seeds of new worlds into the infinite chaos, this power would be still an additional argument for design in its author. For whence could arise so wonderful a faculty but from design? Or how can order spring from anything which perceives not that order which it bestows?

You need only look around you, replied Philo, to satisfy yourself with regard to this question. A tree bestows order and organization on that tree which springs from it, without knowing the order; an animal in the same manner on its offspring; a bird on its nest; and instances of this kind are even more frequent in the world than those of order which arise from reason and contrivance. To say that all this order in animals and vegetables proceeds ultimately from design is begging the question; nor can that great point be ascertained otherwise than by proving, *a priori,* both that order is, from its nature, inseparably attached to thought and that it can never of itself or from original unknown principles belong to matter.

But further, Demea, this objection which you urge can never be made use of by Cleanthes, without renouncing a defence which he has already made against one of my objections [in Part IV]. When I inquired concerning the cause of that supreme reason and intelligence into which he resolves everything, he told me that the impossibility of satisfying such inquiries could never be admitted as an objection in any species of philosophy. *We must stop somewhere,* says he; *nor is it ever within the reach of human capacity to explain ultimate causes or show the last connections of any objects. It is sufficient if any steps, so far as we go, are supported by experience and observation.* Now that vegetation and generation, as well as reason, are experienced to be principles of order in nature is undeniable. If I rest my system of cosmogony on the former, preferably to the latter, it is at my choice. The matter seems entirely arbitrary. And when Cleanthes asks me what is the cause of my great vegetative or generative faculty, I am equally entitled to ask him the cause of his great reasoning principle. These questions we have agreed to forbear on both sides; and it is chiefly his interest on the present occasion to stick to this agreement. Judging by our limited and imperfect experience, generation has some privileges above reason; for we see every day the latter arise from the former, never the former from the latter.

Compare, I beseech you, the consequences on both sides. The world, say I, resembles an animal; therefore it is an animal, therefore it arose from generation. The steps, I confess, are wide, yet there is some small appearance of analogy in each step. The world, says Cleanthes, resembles a machine; therefore it is a machine, therefore it arose from design. The steps are here equally wide, and the analogy less striking. And if he pretends to carry on *my* hypothesis a step further, and to infer design or reason from the great principle of generation on which I insist, I may, with better authority, use the same freedom to push further *his* hypothesis, and infer a divine generation or theogony from his principle of reason. I have at least some faint shadow of experience, which is the utmost that can ever be attained in the present subject. Reason, in innumerable instances, is observed to arise from the principle of generation, and never to arise from any other principle.

Hesiod and all the ancient mythologists were so struck with this analogy that they universally explained the origin of nature from an animal birth, and copulation. Plato, too, so far as he is intelligible, seems to have adopted some such notion in his *Timœs*.

The Brahmins assert that the world arose from an infinite spider, who spun this whole complicated mass from his bowels, and annihilates afterwards the whole or any part of it, by absorbing it again and resolving it into his own essence. Here is a species of **cosmogony** which appears to us ridiculous because a spider is a little contemptible animal whose operations we are never likely to take for a model of the whole universe. But still here is a new species of analogy, even in our globe. And were there a planet wholly inhabited by spiders (which is very possible), this inference would there appear as natural and irrefragable as that which in our planet ascribes the origin of all things to design and intelligence, as explained by Cleanthes. Why an orderly system may not be spun from the belly as well as from the brain, it will be difficult for him to give a satisfactory reason.

I must confess, Philo, replied Cleanthes, that, of all men living, the task which you have undertaken, of raising doubts and objections, suits you best and seems, in a manner, natural and unavoidable to you. So great is your fertility of invention that I am not ashamed to acknowledge myself unable, on a sudden, to solve regularly such out-of-the-way difficulties as you incessantly start upon me, though I clearly see, in general, their fallacy and error. And I question not, but you are yourself, at present, in the same case, and have not the solution so ready as the objection, while you must be sensible that common sense and reason are entirely against you, and that such whimsies as you have delivered may puzzle but never can convince us.

PART VIII

What you ascribe to the fertility of my invention, replied Philo, is entirely owing to the nature of the subject. In subjects adapted to the narrow compass of human reason there is commonly but one determination which carries probability or conviction with it; and to a man of sound judgment all other suppositions but that one appear entirely absurd and chimerical. But in such questions as the present, a hundred contradictory views may preserve a kind of imperfect analogy, and invention has here full scope to exert itself. Without any great effort of thought, I believe that I could, in an instant, propose other systems of cosmogony which would have some faint appearance of truth, though it is a thousand, a million to one if either yours or any one of mine be the true system.

For instance, what if I should revive the old Epicurean hypothesis? This is commonly, and I believe justly, esteemed the most absurd system that has yet been proposed; yet I know not whether, with a few alterations, it might not be brought to bear a faint appearance of probability. Instead of supposing matter infinite, as Epicurus did, let us suppose it finite. A finite number of particles is only susceptible of finite transpositions; and it must happen, in an eternal duration, that every possible order or position must be tried an infinite number of times. This world, therefore, with all its events, even the most minute, has before been produced and destroyed, and will again be produced and destroyed, without any bounds and limitations. No one who has a conception of the powers of infinite, in comparison of finite, will ever scruple this determination.

But this supposes, said Demea, that matter can acquire motion without any voluntary agent or first mover.

And where is the difficulty, replied Philo, of that supposition? Every event, before experience, is equally difficult and incomprehensible; and every event, after experience, is equally easy and intelligible. Motion, in many instances, from gravity, from elasticity, from electricity, begins in matter, without any known voluntary agent; and to suppose always, in these cases, an unknown voluntary agent is mere hypothesis and hypothesis attended with no advantages. The beginning of motion in matter itself is as conceivable *a priori* as its communication from mind and intelligence.

Besides, why may not motion have been propagated by impulse through all eternity, and the same stock of it, or nearly the same, be still upheld in the universe? As much is lost by the composition of motion, as much is gained by its resolution. And whatever the causes are, the fact is certain that matter is and always has been in continual agitation, as far as human experience or tradition reaches. There is not probably, at present, in the whole universe, one particle of matter at absolute rest.

And this very consideration, too, continued Philo, which we have stumbled on in the course of the argument suggests a new hypothesis of cosmogony that is not absolutely absurd and improbable. Is there a system, an order, an economy of things, by which matter can preserve that perpetual agitation which seems essential to it, and yet maintain a constancy in the forms which it produces? There certainly is such an economy, for this is actually the case with the present world. The continual motion of matter, therefore, in less than infinite transpositions, must produce this economy or order, and, by its very nature, that order, when once established, supports itself for many ages if not to eternity. But wherever matter is so poised, arranged, and adjusted, as to continue in perpetual motion, and yet preserve a constancy in the forms, its situation must, of necessity, have all the same appearance of art and contrivance which we observe at present. All the parts of each form must have a relation to each other and to the whole; and the whole itself must have a relation to the other parts of the universe, to the element in which the form subsists, to the materials with which it repairs its waste and decay, and to every other form which is hostile or friendly. A defect in any of these particulars destroys the form, and the matter of which it is composed is again set loose, and is thrown into irregular motions and fermentations till it unite itself to some other regular form. If no such form be prepared to receive it, and if there be a great quantity of this corrupted matter in the universe, the universe itself is entirely disordered, whether it be the feeble embryo of a world in its first beginnings that is thus destroyed or the rotten carcass of one languishing in old age and infirmity. In either case, a chaos ensues till finite though innumerable revolutions produce, at last, some forms whose parts and organs are so adjusted as to support the forms amidst a continued succession of matter.

Suppose (for we shall endeavour to vary the expression) that matter were thrown into any position by a blind, unguided force; it is evident that this first position must, in all probability, be the most confused and most disorderly imaginable, without any resemblance to those works of human contrivance which, along with a symmetry of parts, discover an adjustment of means to ends and a tendency to self-preservation. If the actuating force cease after this operation, matter must remain for ever in disorder and continue an immense chaos, without any proportion or activity. But suppose that the actuating force, whatever it be, still continues in matter, this first position will immediately give place to a second which will likewise, in all probability, be as disorderly as the first, and so on through many successions of changes and revolutions. No particular order or position ever continues a moment unaltered. The original force, still remaining in activity, gives a perpetual restlessness to matter. Every possible situation is produced, and instantly destroyed. If a glimpse or dawn of order appears for a moment, it is instantly hurried away and confounded by that never-ceasing force which actuates every part of matter.

Thus the universe goes on for many ages in a continued succession of chaos and disorder. But is it not possible that it may settle at last, so as not to lose its motion and active force (for that we have supposed inherent in it), yet so as to preserve an uniformity of appearance, amidst the continual motion and fluctuation of its parts? This we find to be the case with the universe at present. Every individual is perpetually changing, and every part of every individual; and yet the whole remains, in appearance, the same. May we not hope for such a position or rather be assured of it from the eternal revolutions of unguided matter; and may not this account for all the appearing wisdom and contrivance which is in the universe? Let us contemplate the subject a little, and we shall find that this adjustment if attained by matter of a seeming stability in the forms, with a real and perpetual revolution or motion of parts, affords a plausible, if not a true, solution of the difficulty.

It is in vain, therefore, to insist upon the uses of the parts in animals or vegetables, and their curious adjustment to each other. I would fain know how an animal could subsist unless its parts were so adjusted? Do we not find that it immediately perishes whenever this adjustment ceases, and that its matter, corrupting, tries some new form? It happens indeed that the parts of the world are so well adjusted that some regular form immediately lays claim to this corrupted matter; and if it were not so, could the world subsist? Must it not dissolve, as well as the animal, and pass through new positions and situations till in great but finite succession it fall, at last, into the present or some such order?

It is well, replied Cleanthes, you told us that this hypothesis was suggested on a sudden, in the course of the argument. Had you had leisure to examine it, you would soon have perceived the insuperable objections to which it is exposed. No form, you say, can subsist unless it possess those powers and organs requisite for its subsistence; some new order or economy must be tried, and so on, without intermission, till at last some order which can support and maintain itself is fallen upon. But according to this hypothesis, whence arise the many conveniences and advantages which men and all animals possess? Two eyes, two ears are not absolutely necessary for the subsistence of the species. Human race might have been propagated and preserved without horses, dogs, cows, sheep, and those innumerable fruits and products which serve to our satisfaction and enjoyment. If no camels had been created for the use of man in the sandy deserts of Africa and Arabia, would the world have been dissolved? If no loadstone had been framed to give that wonderful and useful direction to the needle, would human society and the human kind have been immediately extinguished? Though the maxims of nature be in general very frugal, yet instances of this kind are far from being rare; and any one of them is a sufficient proof of design—and of a benevolent design—which gave rise to the order and arrangement of the universe.

At least, you may safely infer, said Philo, that the foregoing hypothesis is so far incomplete and imperfect, which I shall not scruple to allow. But can we ever reasonably expect greater success in any attempts of this nature? Or can we ever hope to erect a system of cosmogony that will be liable to no exceptions, and will contain no circumstance repugnant to our limited and imperfect experience of the analogy of nature? Your theory itself cannot surely pretend to any such advantage, even though you have run into *anthropomorphism,* the better to preserve a conformity to common experience. Let us once more put it to trial. In all instances which we have ever seen, ideas are copied from real objects, and are ectypal, not archetypal, to express myself in learned terms. You reverse this order and give thought the precedence. In all instances which we have ever seen, thought has no influence upon matter except where that matter is so conjoined with it as to have an equal reciprocal influence upon it. No animal can move immediately anything but the members of its own body; and, indeed, the equality of action and reaction seems to be an universal law of nature; but your theory implies a contradiction to this experience. These instances, with many more which it were easy to collect (particularly the supposition of a mind or system of thought that is eternal or, in other words, an animal ingenerable and immortal)—these instances, I say, may teach all of us sobriety in condemning each other, and let us see that as no system of this kind ought ever to be received from a slight analogy, so neither ought any to be rejected on account of a small incongruity. For that is an inconvenience from which we can justly pronounce no one to be exempted.

All religious systems, it is confessed, are subject to great and insuperable difficulties. Each disputant triumphs in his turn, while he carries on an offensive war, and exposes the absurdities, barbarities, and pernicious tenets of his antagonist. But all of them, on the whole, prepare a complete triumph for the *sceptic,* who tells them that no system ought ever to be embraced with regard to such subjects: for this plain reason that no absurdity ought ever to be assented to with regard to any subject. A total suspense of judgment is here our only reasonable resource. And if every attack, as is commonly observed, and no defence among theologians is successful, how complete must be *his* victory who remains always, with all mankind, on the offensive, and has himself no fixed station or abiding city which he is ever, on any occasion, obliged to defend? . . .

STUDY QUESTIONS

1. Summarize Cleanthes's design argument.
2. Cleanthes's argument is unpalatable to Demea (in the paragraph beginning "I shall be so free . . .") for two reasons: it is *a posteriori* and it is anthropomorphic. Explain each of these objections by referring to what you know of medieval theology from chapters 1 and 2 of this book and from the selections on the cosmological argument.
3. Formulate in detail Philo's objections in parts II, IV, V, VII, and VIII. What is Cleanthes' reply to each?
4. What is the point of the discussion of astronomy in part II?
5. How is Philos' objection in part IV akin to the "hired cab" objection we encountered in Reading 4.5?
6. In part V's final paragraph, what is Cleanthes' reply to Philo's wild-sounding design hypotheses, such as the multiple gods hypothesis? Is this reply adequate in your opinion?
7. In part VII, in the paragraph beginning "Compare, I beseech you . . . ," Philo maintains that his argument for the hypothesis of generation and vegetation is *better than* Cleanthes' design hypothesis. Read the paragraph carefully, and explain Philo's argument. An important ingredient of the argument is that Cleanthes might combat the generation and vegetation hypothesis by asking who designed the laws of generation and vegetation.
8. In part VII, what is the point of Hume's spider example?
9. Explain the hypothesis Philo puts forth in part VIII. How does it resemble Charles Darwin's theory of natural selection?
10. *Do you think Philo is denying the design hypothesis in the selection? Or is he just trying to show that it is one hypothesis among many equally plausible ones? Cite textual evidence.
11. *Read parts III and XII of Hume's *Dialogues Concerning Natural Religion* (not included in this book). What discrepancies do you see when you compare parts III and XII with what you read in Reading 4.8? Can you resolve these discrepancies?

READING 4.9

Fine-Tuning: The New Design Arguments

Stephen T. Davis

According to the theory of biological evolution originally promulgated by Charles Darwin, existing species evolved from lower forms of life through a process involving random genetic changes, **natural selection,** *and* self-replication. *Further extending the evolutionary viewpoint, contemporary* **cosmologists** *maintain that the stars and planets emerged over a long period through the operation of natural law on a set of initial objects and conditions. It may seem that evolutionary accounts destroy the design argument (DA) by providing an alternative explanation of order. However, as Stephen T. Davis (Claremont McKenna College) explains, proponents of contemporary DAs argue that evolutionary accounts actually* support *the design hypothesis.*

This support arises from the observation that the universe is "fine-tuned." The laws of nature and cosmological constants are minutely adjusted to allow for life and even intelligent life. If the constants were different in the tiniest way, life would not have emerged. Focusing on cosmology, Davis surveys items in the universe that seem uniquely conducive to the emergence of life and even intelligent life. He then responds to two objections to the new design arguments. (To avoid confusion, you should take note that, although Davis mentions a version of what is called the anthropic principle *that is part of a rebuttal to the new DAs, often a form of the anthropic principle is cited to* support *the fine-tuning idea. See the entry for* **Anthropic Principle** *in the Glossary of Technical Terms.)*

EVOLUTION AS A CRITICISM OF THE DESIGN ARGUMENT (DA)

. . . I[n] 1859 Darwin published *The Origin of Species* expounding his theory of biological evolution. It had an immediate and powerful impact upon both **theology** and the philosophy of religion. One aspect of this impact was that many people concluded that the DA was no longer viable. The reason was that Darwin provided a way of explaining apparent design and complexity in organisms that involved no reference to intelligent design.

Three central aspects of Darwin's theory were: (1) random genetic change (these changes occur mainly through mutations; sometimes by random genetic drift); (2) **natural selection** (in competition for scarce resources, those species and organisms that are the fittest will survive); and (3) **self-replication** (genetic structures are passed on to offspring; and because of natural selection, genetic structures that provide competitive advantages survive). These three factors, Darwin said—together of course with the natural laws and regularities in the universe—have produced, over long periods of time, complex and sophisticated organisms.

If Darwin is right, it is possible for the universe to produce apparently designed biological systems blindly, that is, without an intelligent designer or any sort of **teleology.** Darwin's great gift to enemies of the DA is that he provided a *theory* which allowed as much. By now Darwin's theory is well developed and, to most people, persuasive. It is an entirely **naturalistic** theory; it does not mention God or any intelligent designer. The importance of this result for the DA and belief in a designer of the universe is well captured by Richard Dawkins, a contemporary scientist and defender of Darwin: 'Although atheism might have been intellectually tenable before Darwin, Darwin made it possible to be an intellectually fulfilled atheist'.[1]

In the early aftermath of Darwin's theory, the DA had few intellectually first rate defenders. But it is quite mistaken to think that evolution refutes the DA. This was shown, among others, by the work of British theologian F. R. Tennant (1866–1957), whose 'wider teleological argument' was the first important version of what I am calling newer DAs, and whose argument presupposes evolution.[2] For reasons of space, I will not explore Tennant's argument here. Let me simply note that like all newer DAs, it stressed not specific cases of adaptedness (which evolution can explain) but the general order of nature and the fitness of the inorganic environment (which cannot evolve) for life.

NEWER VERSIONS OF THE DA

. . . Most of the arguments fall under the heading of what is called **'fine-tuning.'** The central idea is that the basic regularities or laws of nature and cosmological constants are minutely adjusted to allow for life and even intelligent life. Some newer DAs (like Tennant's) presuppose evolution; some reject it entirely; some accept parts of the theory but not others (for example, by suggesting divine guidance of the process of evolution at various points); and some by-pass evolution entirely. All argue, however,

[1]Richard Dawkins, *The Blind Watchmaker: Why the Evidence of Evolution Reveals a Universe Without Design* (New York: W. W. Norton and Co., 1986), p. 10.

[2]See F. R. Tennant, *Philosophical Theology,* 2 vols. (New York: Cambridge University Press, 1928).

for the existence of an intelligent designer of the universe.

Like early DAs, the contemporary versions are probabilistic as opposed to **deductive.** That is, the premises are designed to provide support for the conclusion, or make it more probable, rather than strictly entail it. The main differences are (1) (as noted) the newer DAs appeal to general examples of fine-tuning or overall order rather than to specific cases of biological complexity or adaptedness; (2) they primarily emphasise facts in physics, astronomy and chemistry rather than facts in the life sciences (which might be susceptible to Darwinian explanation); (3) they make little appeal to specific purposes ('the eye was designed for the purpose of seeing,' etc.) but rather emphasise only the general purpose of producing life or intelligent life; and (4) they are not primarily arguments from analogy but rather inferences to the best explanation.

Very many points are made by contemporary design arguers, and in several different areas of science. It is only possible to mention a few. Indeed, the *many* items that look to be fine-tuned for life—so far as I can tell, there are over fifty such items that are discussed in the literature—constitutes one of the great strengths of newer DAs. There is an impressive cumulative case that can be built up.

Most newer DAs emphasise the cosmic constants, or the fundamental constants of physics. These are items like the gravitational constant, the speed of light, the strong force, the weak force, the basic properties of elementary particles (for example, mass, charge, spin), Planck's constant, etc. The general point is that all these constants, the values of which could easily have been quite different from what they are, and which in most cases are causally quite unrelated to each other, must have values that fall within a very narrow range if life is to be possible. If any one of them were changed, even slightly, life (as least as we know it) would not have emerged.

(1) The Rate of Expansion of the Big Bang

The speed at which bits of matter flew apart from other bits of matter soon after the Big Bang (it took time for individual particles to form) seems to be finely turned in relation to the density of the universe, that is, the exact amount of matter that exists. Galaxies (and thus stars, and thus planets) would have been impossible had the expansion rate and the total mass of the universe not been finely tuned to each other. Too rapid a rate of expansion relative to the total mass would have overpowered the gravitational attraction of the various bits of matter to each other, and no gases could have been formed, let alone the galaxies that the gases later became. Too slow a rate of expansion relative to the total mass would have caused too much gravitational attraction, and the universe would have collapsed back into itself billions of years ago. The expansion rate lies perilously close to the borderline between recollapse into a crunch and total dispersal of all matter. Philosopher of science J. P. Moreland summarises the point as follows: 'A reduction by one part in a million million would have led to collapse before the temperature could fall below ten thousand degrees. An early increase by one part in a million would have prevented the growth of galaxies, stars, and planets.' Design arguers take this fine-tuning as evidence of an intelligent designer who had the aim of producing life in mind.

(2) The Strong Force

The strong nuclear force is what binds together the various elementary particles (for example, the quarks in neutrons and protons, and the neutrons and protons themselves) in the nuclei of atoms. It appears that either a 1 per cent increase or a 1 per cent decrease in the power of the strong force would have made impossible the stellar nucleosynthesis of carbon. A slight increase would have led to all the carbon being burned into oxygen; a slight decrease would have led to a universe consisting only of hydrogen. And of course carbon is necessary to life.

(3) The Weak Force

The weak nuclear force is what is responsible for such nuclear processes as radioactive decay, fission and fusion; this includes energy from the sun. Very many points have been made about fine-tuning in relation to the weak force. I will mention just one. Just after the Big Bang, the universe had a brief period of nuclear fusion during which helium was formed. It appears that had the weak force been stronger, the burning produced by the Big Bang would have, as [John] Leslie says, 'proceeded past helium and all the way to iron. Fusion-powered stars would then be impossible.'[3] That is, there would have been no hydrogen for them to burn. But had the weak force been much weaker, then the universe would consist entirely of helium.

(4) Isotropy

Isotropy means smoothness or evenness in all directions; here it refers to the surprising and puzzling fact that the background temperature in the universe varies only slighly from region to region, something like only one part in a hundred thousand. The puzzle is how to account for this fact, since the various regions are far too distant from each other to have any causal influence on each other. Even at the early stages of the Big Bang, the regions were separating from each other at too high a rate for there to have been causal influence.

In addition, the matter that exists is amazingly isotropic in its distribution throughout the universe. The universe looks pretty much the same no matter which direction we look from the earth. On a smaller scale there are exceptions to this point; for example, astronomers are aware of immense bubbles in space which contain galaxies at their edges but little matter in their interiors. Still, the universe must have been amazingly isotropic at its early stage; this is evident from the uniform 'background radiation' that bathes the entire universe and is an artifact of the Big Bang. The uniformity is not exact—there are slight variations from region to region—but some such **anisotropy** is needed for the formation of galaxies.

But the main point is that slight variations either in background temperature or in distribution of matter would make life impossible. If the early universe were significantly anisotropic—which surely seems possible—the matter of the universe would have collapsed into black holes. If it were almost completely isotropic, it would have been destroyed by the heat resulting from the smoothing out of anisotropic regions. The problem is how to explain the fact that the universe has precisely the highly improbable delicate balance necessary for the formation of the universe as we know it. Paul Davies places 'the odds against a starry cosmos' at 'one followed by a thousand billion billion zeroes, at least.'[4]

(5) The Thermal Properties of the Earth

The earth has certain properties, many of them causally unrelated to each other, which make it thermally hospitable to life. Changing any of them, even slightly, would have made life impossible. Let me mention just three. The earth is just the right distance from the sun to ensure that the temperatures on its surface will be right for life. Michael Hart performed some admittedly incomplete computer simulations (not all the relevant factors are yet known), which nevertheless produced the conclusion that if the earth were either 5 per cent closer or 1 per cent farther from the the sun, life would not be possible on it.[5] The earth also possesses an atmosphere which protects it from ultra-violet radiation and other dangers such as extreme temperatures. It also contains vast oceans over much of its surface, which serve as a thermostat for the earth, also shielding it from extreme temperatures.

(6) Water

The existence of water, essential as it is to carbon-based life, is another example of the fine-tuning which design arguers take to be evidence of intelligent design. There are other elements that are

[3]John Leslie, *Universes* (London: Routledge, 1989), p. 34.

[4]For many of these points, see Paul Davies, *Other Worlds* (London: Dent, 1980), pp. 56, 160–61, 168–69.

[5]See Michael Hart, 'Atmospheric Evolution, the Drake Equation, and DNA: Sparse Life in an Infinite Universe,' in John Leslie (ed.), *Physical Cosmology and Philosophy* (New York: MacMillan, 1990).

necessary to life, for example carbon dioxide, carbolic acid, and chlorophyll, but the unique properties of water make it a special case. Water has a very high melting point, boiling point, and vapourising point (this last property makes water an excellent coolant by evaporation, which many living creatures take advantage of through perspiration). Ice floats because (very unusually, compared to other substances) in its solid stage water is less dense than it is in its liquid phase. This causes ice to serve as a protective skin on the surface of bodies of water (if ice were denser than water it would sink to the bottom of the lakes and oceans and eventually freeze them). Water can store heat efficiently because it has a high specific heat, and this (as noted) serves to stabilise temperatures. Since living bodies consist mainly of water, its high specific heat keeps chemical reactions in them fairly stable (a low specific heat would mean that living bodies would die by 'boiling over' very readily).

Again, we could mention many more such points, but this is enough to provide a sense of what design arguers mean by 'fine-tuning.' While all these points (and as noted, many others) are mentioned by newer design arguers, there seems to be a consensus that items that have to do with general laws of nature and basic cosmological constants are stronger evidences of design that the items than have to do with the physical conditions necessary to life.

But the general conclusion that newer design arguers draw from all these points is that if the initial conditions or fundamental constants in the universe were even slightly different than they in fact are, it is most unlikely that life or anything like it would have emerged. Note also that unless some 'Theory of Everything' (TOE) that says otherwise is proposed and gains acceptance, the values of most of the constants that we have discussed are quite independent of each other. We are talking, then, not just about each of many different constants falling within a certain narrow range (which in itself powerfully points to a designer), but about precise and narrow ratios of interactions between the various forces—all of which are necessary to life.

William L. Craig likens the emergence of life in the universe apart from intelligent guidance not to a roulette wheel yielding a certain number, but to all the roulette wheels in Monte Carlo, quite unrelated to each other, simultaneously yielding numbers within narrow limits and bearing certain precise mathematical relations among them.[6] In other words, a universe without life, or at least carbon-based life, is far, far more probable than one with it. Design arguers accordingly conclude that what we have here is either a grand coincidence, so mathematically improbable as to be virtually impossible, or else evidence of fine-tuning by an intelligent designer whose aim was the emergence of life, perhaps even intelligent, conscious, morally aware life.

CRITICISMS OF NEWER DAs

Now most of the items of fine-tuning that design arguers emphasise are points that will have been discovered or reported by scientists. Most of the scientists who write about such matters have found the case for fine-tuning to be impressive. But not all of them believe in God, let alone a designer of the universe, and very many philosophers are atheists as well. So naturally the question emerges: How do those folk who refuse to accept the existence of a designer respond to the case for fine-tuning? What is the atheist's counter-attack to the newer DAs?

The answer is that there are several such responses. Some deny that there is any problem here to be explained—the numbers are wrong; the laws could be different; life is possible under many conditions. But the idea that there is nothing unusual here is refuted by the simple fact that atheists feel a strong need to come up with an argument that responds to all the apparent fine-tuning. The *appearance,* at least, of cosmic teleology is pretty obvious. Others suggest (as Hume did) that the universe is in some sense self-organising (and thus far this is only a vague and unsupported suggestion). But I will

[6]William L. Craig, 'The Teleological Argument and the Anthropic Principle,' in William L. Craig and Mark S. McLeod (eds.), *The Logic of Rational Theism: Exploratory Essays* (Lewiston, ME: The Edwin Mellen Press, 1990), p. 134.

focus on the two most popular responses, the **anthropic principle** and the idea of many universes.

(1) The Anthropic Principle

There are several versions of 'the anthropic principle.' Let us focus simply on what is called the weak version (WAP). Here is [John] Barrow and [Frank] Tipler's version of it:

> WAP: The observed values of all physical and cosmological quantities are not equally probable, but they take on values restricted by the requirement that there exist sites where carbon-based life can evolve and by the requirement that the Universe be old enough for it to have already done so.[7]

In other words, given our presence in the universe as observers, it necessarily follows that the requisite conditions for intelligent life are met. We should accordingly expect *only* to observe values that are compatible with our existence; our existence is a selection effect in assessing the various laws and constants.

The upshot of this argument is as follows: *We should not be surprised that we observe a universe with laws and constants that allow for intelligent life.* In other words, no explanation for apparent design is required or should be expected, for if the universe were other than it is, we would not be here. Since we *are* here, we must expect the universe to be much as it is.

Is this a good argument? Hardly; indeed, it is not difficult to refute. It is surely true that if the universe is observed by observers who exist in it, then it must have whatever properties are necessary for the existence of those observers. But this trivial observation does nothing to negate the idea that there is apparent design, nor does it explain the apparent design that we see. If our existence depends on certain basic conditions being met, then, since we *do* exist, we should not be surprised that those conditions are met. True enough. But this does nothing to rule out the need for an explanation of the fact that the conditions are met.

Several philosophers have pointed out the error at work here through stories like the following from Richard Swinburne:

> Suppose that a madman kidnaps a victim and shuts him in a room with a card-shuffling machine. The machine shuffles ten packs of cards simultaneously and then draws a card from each pack and exhibits simultaneously the ten cards. The kidnapper tells the victim that he will shortly set the machine to work and it will exhibit its first draw, but that unless the draw consists of an ace of hearts from each pack, the machine will simultaneously set off an explosion which will kill the victim, in consequence of which he will not see which cards the machine drew. The machine is set to work, and to the amazement and relief of the victim the machine exhibits an ace of hearts drawn from each pack.[8]

Suppose the victim were to respond, 'No explanation is required why the ten aces of hearts appeared, since if they hadn't appeared, I would not be here.' This would obviously be an inadequate response. It is not true that the cards came up as they did *because* the victim survived. So clearly something puzzling remains to be explained—why the machine drew the ten aces of hearts (thus allowing the victim to live) in the first place.

Similarly, the problem of explaining why the universe shows the fine-tuning that it does remains. It is true that we should not be surprised that we do not observe conditions in the universe which allow no life to emerge. That is, we should not be surprised that we do not observe a universe that is incompatible with our existence. But we *should* be surprised that we *do* observe that we as living and intelligent creatures exist. What is surprising, and what still requires explanation is this: the fact that the extremely improbable conditions for life were all in fact satisfied.

(2) Many Universes

The other main position taken by those who grant fine-tuning but deny the existence of a fine-tuner is

[7]Barrow and Tipler, *The Anthropic Cosmological Principle* (Oxford: Oxford University Press, 1986).

[8]Swinburne, *The Existence of God* (Oxford University Press, 1979), p. 138.

the hypothesis of many universes, or the 'World Ensemble,' as it is sometimes called. (The hypothesis is sometimes combined with the WAP.) The idea is that our observable universe is only one of many—maybe even an infinite number of—possible or actual universes. Now there is a terminological issue here, having to do with the term 'universe,' but it can easily be sidestepped. As noted earlier, most people think of the universe as everything real, everything that there is. And if we accept that usage then by definition there cannot be 'other universes.' However, many physicists are comfortable with talk about other universes, for reasons that we will see, and so they use the term 'universe' in different ways. Perhaps it would refer to the reality that follows from any particular Big Bang, or to whatever exists in any one observable area, or to whatever exists in any one of many parallel realities. So the issue cannot be settled against these theories merely by definition.

There are several ways in which the World Ensemble thesis can be developed. We will consider three (there are others).

(a) It might be said that the universe is oscillating and that there have been many big bangs and ensuing universes, and that each cycle emerges with a new set of laws and constants. (b) It might be said that there are many causally unrelated regions of the present universe where the laws and constants are different from the way they are in our region. (c) Or the 'many worlds' interpretation of **quantum physics** might be adopted. In any quantum interaction, it is said, all possible states are actualised in some universe or other, with universes constantly splitting off into new universes. The various parallel universes have no contact with each other; each observer observes but one universe. All universes are as equally real as all the others. Davies summarises the theory as follows:

> We must envision every atom in every galaxy as continually engaging in this type of scattering activity, thereby splitting the world again and again into a stupendous number of near-carbon-copies of itself. The universe must therefore be likened to a tree, which branches and rebranches. Nearby branches differ little from each other, perhaps distinguished only by the arrangements of a few individual atoms. However, amid the infinite array of parallel worlds will be examples representing all possible physical universes.[9]

The crucial point, in the case of each theory, is that all or many possible combinations of natural laws and cosmic constants are actualised somewhere; most of them do not produce intelligent life; but it is not surprising that some few of them do (including our universe).

There are problems with each of these views. All three, for example, face the objection that there is virtually no evidence for them apart from fine-tuning, the existence of intelligent life, and the desire to avoid a cosmic designer. Accordingly, they have an air of desperation about them.

(a) With the oscillating universe, it is not clear that there is enough density in the universe to overcome the initial impetus of the Big Bang and cause a 'Big Crunch.' Moreover, even if there does exist enough such matter, it is not clear that an implosion would produce a subsequent Big Bang. Craig says that 'there is no known physics which would cause the universe to oscillate.'[10] And how do we know that the basic laws and constants will be reshuffled each time (which of course is required if this theory is to constitute a viable alternative to theistic interpretations of fine tuning)? And since time supposedly began with the Big Bang, how are the various universes that follow their own Big Bangs related temporally? The physics here are murky, to say the least.

(b) There are indeed causally unrelated regions of space in the existing universe, but there is no evidence at all that the basic physical laws and constants differ from region to region. And that is what is needed if this theory is to constitute a viable atheistic interpretation of fine-tuning. Only if there are innumerably many such regions, each with its own laws and constants, will it no longer be surprising that in *some* regions (including ours) the laws and constants allow for life. But, in fact, the reverse is the case; all the evidence supports the claim that the basic laws and con-

[9]Davies, *The Accidental Universe* (Cambridge University Press, 1982), p. 125.

[10]William L. Craig, 'The Teleological Argument . . . ,' p. 143. Craig is actually quoting the late astronomer Beatrice Tinsley.

stants are the same throughout the universe. The discipline of astrophysics is based upon that assumption.

(c) The many-worlds interpretation is favoured by a minority of physicists. It seems fanciful and speculative to many, especially since there is no known causal mechanism that could cause the splitting. And is there supposed to be a kind of timeless superspace in which all the parallel universes exist? If so, what is it? What are its properties? Moreover, the theory also seems to violate respected philosophical principles like parsimony (if two theories are equal in explanatory power, accept the simpler of the two) and **Ockham's razor** (do not posit the existence of more entities than are strictly necessary).

CONCLUSION

. . . [T]he DA does two things. First, it presents evidence of apparent intelligent design. Second, it asks, in the light of the evidence presented, which is the more sensible conclusion: Alternative 1 or Alternative 2. *Alternative 1* says that the world is fine-tuned as it is due to entirely blind forces and natural causes, apart from any intelligent designer. *Alternative 2* says that the world is as it is because it was designed this way by an intelligent designer.

Design arguers will claim that Alternative 2 is by far the most sensible of the two, especially given the severe weakness of the arguments based on the anthropic principle and of the World Ensemble models. Accordingly, design arguers will insist that the hypothesis of a designer of the universe is much stronger, relative to either naturalism or supernaturalism, given the evidence of fine-tuning, than it is apart from that evidence.

Finally, a point that is more related to the **cosmological argument** than the DA. Alternative 2 can answer questions like 'Why is there a universe at all?' and 'Why is there anything instead of nothing?' None of the theories that fit under Alternative 1 can do so. The existence of a reality at all must be, from the point of view of the friends of Alternative 1, an unexplained **brute fact.**

STUDY QUESTIONS

1. Review the scientific data that Davis cites in his attempt to show that the universe is fine-tuned for the production of life and even intelligent life.
2. *Often, events that are improbable occur. Thus, it is improbable that you would win the Pennsylvania lottery if you were to buy just one ticket; however, if you were to win, no one would say that an explanation in terms of design is called for. Why, then, would the fine-tuned universe require an explanation in terms of design?
3. *Some people argue that, for any actual situation, the obtaining of *that exact situation* is improbable. What do you think is meant by this claim? If true, how would it undermine the fine-tuning argument?

READING 4.10

An Argument for Design

Robert Hambourger

Like Stephen T. Davis, Robert Hambourger (North Carolina State University) thinks that, if the laws and initial conditions of the universe produced the world as we know it, this calls for an explanation in terms of intelligent purpose. What Hambourger adds, however, is an argument as to why **fine-tuning** *calls for an explanation. After all, don't the laws of nature and the conditions of the universe suffice to explain how life and intelligence arose? Hambourger gives an example in which a nativity scene is formed by frost on a window. Scientists succeed in finding natural events that led up to the frost's forming this pattern. Would we not attribute the formation to intelligent design, Hambourger asks, even though we can provide a natural explanation in terms of prior events and laws of nature? Analogously, we* *must invoke design to explain the world's having laws of nature and initial conditions that produce impressive characteristics.*

Hambourger then argues that evolution does not provide a satisfying explanation of order, in part because the genetic mechanisms that pass on the characteristics of "fit" parents to their children cannot themselves be explained in terms of evolution. Also, too many "chance" events would have to occur. Although he does not use the terminology, Hambourger is presenting the fine-tuning argument, using biological rather than (as in Davis) cosmological data.

. . . Suppose that I happen by chance to be standing up at the moment you read this sentence. Can one then hope to explain why I stand as you read? I think it would be natural to answer in the negative. There is no reason why I was standing as you read; things just happened to work out that way. However, someone who takes seriously the **principle of sufficient reason,** that every truth has an explanation, will not accept this reply as the last word. Rather, I think, he will want to say that all one has to do to explain the occurrence in question in the sense *he* has in mind is to conjoin explanations of why, at a certain time, I was standing and why, at the same time, you were reading the sentence you were. Corresponding to these two possible answers, let me say that a **conjunction** of two or more states of affairs, or the co-occurrence of the states of affairs, has a *basic explanation* when and only when each state in the conjunction has an explanation, and I shall say that a basic explanation of a conjunction is a conjunction of explanations of its conjuncts. Further, let me say that the states in a conjunction of two or more states of affairs have an *explanation in common* when and only when explanations of any two states in the conjunction contain a significant part in common. . . .

Now there are two points I would like to make using these distinctions. First, there would seem to be no logical guarantee that two logically independent states of affairs will have an explanation in common. Things often happen by chance, and a supporter of the principle of sufficient reason can hope for no more than that every conjunction will have a basic explanation. Secondly, however, there are cases in which, as an **epistemological** matter of fact, we simply would not believe that certain states of affairs had occurred together by chance. And it is on this second point that the argument I shall present is based. For I believe there are natural phenomena which it would be extremely hard to believe occurred together by chance but which, it would seem, could only have an explanation in common if at least some of them were created by design. And thus, I think, by a two-step argument we might be able to prove that some natural phenomena are created intentionally.

I shall not offer an example of the sort of phenomena I have in mind until later. First let me illustrate the reasoning I hope to use with a fictitious example which, if my memory has not deceived me, is adapted from one I was given a number of years ago by [Elizabeth] Anscombe.

Suppose that one day a perfect picture, say, of a nativity scene were formed by the frost on someone's window. I think we almost certainly would believe that this occurrence was brought about by design,[1] though not necessarily by the design of a divine being. And if we were asked why, I think we would probably respond that if this were not so, there would be no way to explain why ice formed on the window in the pattern it did. However, if by an explanation, we have in mind a basic explanation, this might well not be true.

Supposedly, in normal cases, various facts about weather conditions, the make-up of a pane of glass, the temperature and humidity in the room in which the pane is installed and the like, cause ice to form in the way it does on a window pane. And also, supposedly, there are possible conditions which, if they

[1]Anyone who believes a nativity scene could appear on a window without having been designed may substitute a more elaborate example for the one I am presenting. For example, it might be supposed that numerous perfect nativity scenes appear one Christmas morning on the windows of many practising Christians living in cold climates. Remarks similar to those I make below could then be made in connection with this example.

were to obtain, might cause ice to form a nativity scene on a given pane. Of course, these conditions might be very strange, but we do not know this. Suppose, in fact, that the nativity scene in our example arose by natural means from conditions that appeared quite normal, that those conditions themselves arose from normal-seeming conditions, etc. Then we can imagine that scientists could give a perfectly good basic explanation of why the pattern formed by the ice in our example was one that constituted a nativity scene.

First, one would explain why ice formed in the pattern it did on the relevant window in the way that one might hope to do so in normal cases, that is, by explaining why ice crystals of various sorts formed on various spots of the window. Then one would explain why the pattern that was formed made up a nativity scene, using facts about geometry, about basic human perceptual mechanisms, perhaps, and the like. The result would be a basic explanation of why the pattern that formed was a nativity scene.

What I think is interesting here, though, is this. If we were given such an explanation of the nativity scene in our example, we would still, I think, be no less inclined than before to believe that it resulted from design. If anything, by showing that the scene arose from processes that were, so to speak, part of the course of nature, such an explanation would make us more inclined to believe that it was designed by a being deserving of our worship and not merely by someone who had made a technological breakthrough over ice.[2]

The question, then, I think, is: what reasoning do we use when we conclude that the nativity scene in our example was produced by design? And the answer, I believe, is the following. First, I think, we believe that ice could not form a nativity scene on a window merely by chance. That is, in our example, there must be an explanation in common of the fact that ice formed the pattern it did on a certain window and the fact that that pattern constitutes a nativity scene. Why we believe this is not completely clear. Ice very often forms beautiful patterns on window panes, and yet we are content to accept that it is by chance that the patterns that are formed are ones that strike us as beautiful. However, that we would not be content to hold similarly that a nativity scene resulted from chance I think is clear.

But if this is true, then the fact that the ice formed a certain pattern on the pane in our example and the fact that that pattern constitutes a nativity scene must share a significant part of their causes in common. And, therefore, either one of the facts is a significant part of the cause of the other, or a third state of affairs is a significant part of the cause of both. However, the fact that a certain pattern forms a nativity scene is a very general one. It results from facts about geometry, about what counts as a nativity scene, and, perhaps, about what patterns we see when we encounter various sorts of objects. And many of these facts are not caused at all, while the remainder, it would seem, as an **empirical** matter of fact, could be caused neither by the fact that ice formed in a certain pattern on a particular pane of glass nor by the sort of facts, for example, about local weather conditions and the make-up of a pane, that would cause ice to form in such a pattern. And, therefore, it seems that neither the fact that ice formed in a certain pattern nor causes of that fact could be significant parts of what caused the pattern to be a nativity scene.

However, in this case it must be that the fact that a certain pattern constitutes a nativity scene was an important part of what brought it about that the pattern appeared on the window in our example. And this, again as an empirical matter, seems to be something that could not happen unless the pattern was produced by design. For the fact that a pattern forms a nativity scene could give a designer reason to bring it about that it appeared on a window and, thus, play a significant role in an explanation of such a fact. However, if the pattern in our example was not

[2]It should be noted that an analogous point could be made about the argument from design. Someone holding that certain natural phenomena were designed need not deny that the phenomena resulted from a chain of purely natural causes extending indefinitely far in the past. And, again, if a natural phenomenon one believes to have been produced by design turns out to have resulted from such a chain of causes, that fact may count as evidence for the eminence of its designer.

brought about by design, then it seems out of the question to think that the fact that it constitutes a nativity scene might have been an important part of the cause of the very specific conditions holding in and around a particular piece of glass on a particular night that caused it to be formed in ice. And, thus, it seems that the nativity scene in our example must have been produced by design.

The case of the nativity scene, of course, is fictitious, but I believe that similar reasoning might well be able to show that in many actual cases natural phenomena have been produced by design. For in many cases complex states of affairs have come together in ways that have produced noteworthy features of the universe, and one might argue that it could not simply be by chance that they came together in ways that had such impressive results. That is, one might think that there must be an explanation in common of the facts that certain states of affairs have occurred and that, by having done so, they have produced the impressive results they have. However, the fact that various states of affairs would produce impressive results, if they occurred together, cannot, it would seem, be explained by the fact that the states actually did occur, nor by the sort of facts that would cause them to occur. And, therefore, the only alternative is that the fact that the states would produce impressive results helps to explain their occurrence. But, again, it would seem that this could not happen unless the states were caused to occur by a designer acting to produce their impressive results. . . .

Let me move on, then, to objection (iii). I think many people today are taken by a certain picture of the origin of life in which the theory of evolution plays a large part. As things are represented by this picture, it was simply a matter of good fortune that the earth came to provide an environment suitable for living creatures, though the good fortune here was not particularly surprising. For in a universe as vast as ours there are many stars like the sun, and—often enough—such stars should have planets whose size, composition, and orbit are similar to those of the earth. Then, once the earth afforded the proper environment, the first primitive organisms came into existence as results of what, it is hoped, were not too improbable series of chemical reactions. Again, here, it was simply by chance that the chemical processes that occurred were ones that produced living creatures. Finally, once the first organisms were in existence, it is thought that the theory of evolution can account for the rest and that the mechanisms of chance mutation and **natural selection** embodied in the theory led to the development of more and more highly developed creatures until, finally, beings evolved that were capable of reason.

This picture of the origin of life seems to be widely held today. Indeed, I believe its popularity is an important feature of the intellectual history of the present age. Nonetheless, I think the picture is flawed. For one thing, we might believe that various chemical processes could produce very simple living creatures, even if the fact that they produced such creatures had nothing to do with the fact the processes came about. But we would not accept that very complex creatures could come about in this way. However, as [Peter T.] Geach has noted,[3] the process of natural selection itself seems to presuppose the existence of creatures with highly developed genetic mechanisms and, so, cannot be used to explain their origin. And, therefore, we must find another plausible account of the origin of these mechanisms.

Natural selection can only take place among creatures that bear offspring that closely resemble their parents without resembling them too closely. For if offspring are exactly like their parents, then natural selection can occur only among characteristics already in existence and, thus, will not lead to the development of new characteristics. On the other hand, if offspring do not closely resemble their parents, then even if certain parents have highly adaptive characteristics and bear many more children than others, their children will not be very likely to inherit the characteristics, and the process will stop.

Of course, in fact creatures do have genetic mechanisms that facilitate natural selection, but the mechanisms are very complicated, and though they

[3]P. T. Geach, 'An Irrelevance of Omnipotence,' *Philosophy* vol. 48, No. 186 (1973), 327–33.

might themselves have evolved to some extent by natural selection, it would seem that any mechanism that led to offspring that resembled their parents closely enough but not too closely would have to be very complicated. And so, one would have to ask how they could come about, if not by design. As Geach writes:

> There can be no origin of *species,* as opposed to an Empedoclean chaos of varied monstrosities, unless creatures reproduce pretty much after their kind; the elaborate and ostensibly **teleological** mechanism of this reproduction logically cannot be explained as a product of evolution by natural selection from among chance variations, for unless the mechanism is presupposed there cannot be any evolution.[4]

Thus, there is much that is noteworthy about the development of living beings that cannot be explained by the theory of evolution. But even if this problem can be surmounted without recourse to a designer, there is a second difficulty.

Simplified accounts of the theory of evolution might make it appear inevitable that creatures evolved with the sorts of impressive and obviously adaptive features that might otherwise be thought to have been designed. For over a sufficient period, one might think, a few individuals would develop such features by chance mutation, and once some creatures had them, the obvious desirability of the features would be enough to explain their proliferation. However, this impression of inevitability, I think, is quite misleading.

Evolutionary change generally proceeds very slowly. We can be confident, for example, that no ancestors of birds suddenly came by wings in a single step and, likewise, that no ancestor of man came to have a brain capable of reason because of one chance mutation. Instead, these sorts of noteworthy and obviously adaptive features come about only as results of long series of evolutionary changes, each of which has to be adaptive and has to become dominant among members of a species, and the noteworthy features themselves cannot come about unless all the others do. Further, these smaller evolutionary changes cannot be counted on to be obviously adaptive, nor always to be adaptive for the same reasons that the larger, more noteworthy changes are. And most importantly, as the term 'adaptive' itself suggests, very often these small changes will be adaptive only because of fine details of, and changes in, the relationship between members of a species and their environment.

Consider the following passage from a recent biology textbook, for example:

> There is . . . good evidence that during the period in which *Australopithecus* lived there existed considerable expanses of lush savannah with scattered shrubs, trees, and grasses. There were berries and roots in abundance, and because such areas were suitable for grazing, these savannahs were well stocked with game. These areas provided new habitats, abundant in food, and so we surmise the australopithecines came down from the trees in which their own apelike ancestors lived in order to avail themselves of these new sources of food. . . . Although descent from the trees does not always result in evolution of upright posture in primates . . . , through a lucky combination of anatomy and habits, these ape-men became bipedal. Being bipedal meant that the hands were freed from locomotor function and could be employed in manipulative skills such as carrying and dragging objects, fashioning tools and weapons, and so on.[5]

This, in turn, led to improvements in the primitive tool-making ability that had preceded upright posture. And finally, 'with the advent of toolmaking, hunting for big game became a possibility, and the brain and the hand were now subject to the molding force of natural selection.'[6]

Now whether the precise details of the picture presented in this passage turn out to be true is not important here. What is important is that something of this sort almost certainly was true. Had not the grass in a certain area grown to the proper height,

[4]P. T. Geach, *Ibid*, p. 330.

[5]I. W. Sherman and V. G. Sherman, *Biology: A Human Approach* (OUP, New York, 1975), p. 456.

[6]I. W. Sherman and V. G. Sherman, *Ibid.* p. 456.

had not a certain food source become available or unavailable, had not various predators been present or absent, had not climatic conditions been what they were, etc. as ancestors of man developed, human beings would not have come into existence. And if they had not, there seems to be no reason to think other beings capable of reason would have evolved instead. After all, useful as intelligence is, no other species has come into existence with such a high level of it.

Furthermore, seemingly chance occurrences like these did not play a role only in the final stages of the evolution of human beings. It is likely that, at nearly every step in the evolutionary chain that led from the most primitive of creatures to people, similar sorts of occurrences played a role. In fact, without specific evidence one cannot assume even that it was inevitable that mammals, vertebrates, or even multi-celled creatures would evolve.

But then, one might ask, again, whether it could have been simply by chance that so many seemingly unconnected occurrences came together in just the way that would lead to the evolution of creatures capable of reason, and I think that one might well conclude that it could not have been.[7] At least, it would be very strange, if the myriad occurrences needed to produce human beings came about in just the right way simply by chance and equally strange if the occurrences had an explanation in common, but the fact that they would produce intelligent beings had nothing to do with the fact that they came about. However, one might wonder how so many different sorts of occurrences could have an explanation in common and, indeed, have an explanation in common with the fact that they would lead to the evolution of beings capable of reason, unless they were produced by design?

Of course, I must admit that I cannot prove that the occurrences that led to the development of beings capable of reason could not have taken place by chance. To do so in a fully satisfactory manner, I think, would require a method for distinguishing those conjunctions of states of affairs which require explanations in common from those which do not, and this I do not know how to provide.[8] However, I find it hard to believe that so much could have happened simply by chance, and yet I think this is exactly what one must believe, if one believes that the universe was not created by design. I think, then, that it is safe to conclude that those who fear that the secular view of things, common today among so many intellectuals, robs the world of its mystery are quite mistaken.

STUDY QUESTIONS

1. What is Hambourger's example of the nativity scene supposed to illustrate? How does it do so?
2. What is Hambourger's criticism of purely evolutionary explanations?
3. *In Reading 4.8 by Hume (with Cleanthes speaking in part IV), and, in Reading 4.5 by Edwards, we encountered the idea that explanations of events need not be complete. To explain something, you don't have to go all the way back in the causal chain. This may furnish one response to Ham-

[7]Of course, one might conclude that such occurrences could have come together by chance. In particular one might argue that, unlikely as it may be that all the conditions needed to produce beings capable of reason should have arisen on earth, still in a universe as vast as ours we can expect that it should have happened somewhere, and earth just happens to be a place where it did happen. However, I think this argument is little more than an appeal to **scepticism.** One could as well argue that we do not know that the speed of light is constant in a vacuum, because if the speed of light were random one still would expect it to appear constant in some region or other of a large enough universe. The point in both cases is the same. Random processes can be imagined and—in a large enough universe—expected to mimic controlled processes, but when phenomena of the right sort would be sufficiently improbable if they occurred by chance, we have a right to conclude that they did not occur by chance.

[8]The problem here, I think, is closely connected with *one* of the problems of induction. If a coin is tossed 1,000 times, and the results form certain patterns of heads and tails (for example, if the coin lands heads on all and only the prime numbered tosses), then we will believe that the pattern that was formed did not occur by chance, and we will expect future losses to result in a similar pattern. On the other hand, other patterns of heads and tails would strike us as 'random,' and one would not expect them to be repeated by future tosses. But how do we distinguish the random patterns from the others?

bourger's nativity scene example. How? Do you think the response is effective? Why or why not?

4. *Your winning a large lottery is improbable. Even so, if you win, we would not ascribe this to intelligent design (i.e., rigging). Under what circumstances would your winning such a lottery require an explanation in terms of design, according to Hambourger? Do you agree that an explanation in terms of design *would* be called for in that case?

5. *(A) Suppose (as I'm told once happened) a woman in a large state wins the state lottery two years in a row. Should this be explained by intelligent design? Why or why not? (B) (Adapted from an article by George N. Schlesinger:) Suppose Joe, seemingly randomly, picks a series of letters and numbers. Sue takes out a dollar bill that has exactly that number. Is an explanation in terms of design called for, in your opinion? Why or why not?

READING 4.11

Evolution: An Alternative to the Design Hypothesis

John L. Mackie

This selection, by the late British philosopher John L. Mackie, expresses a viewpoint opposite to that put forth by Stephen T. Davis and Robert Hambourger in Readings 4.9 and 4.10. Theists ask, as we saw, why the laws of nature and the initial conditions of the world are such that they can give rise to life and complex organisms, as well as to galaxies containing stars and planetary systems. Is it not striking that things just "happened" to be right to produce life, evolution, and consciousness? Mackie's response is that we do not know what other possibilities there were such that we could declare the actual laws and initial conditions to be "a uniquely fruitful set." Hence, there may be no surprise in the fact that the world as we know it evolved. He maintains also that atomic and nuclear physics do not involve reciprocal adjustments that could be taken as a sign of purposiveness.

. . . [S]ome of the alternative explanations, [to design] deserve to be taken very seriously indeed. For example, if the order in the world which is supposed to be a mark of design is located in, say, the regular working of the solar system, then we can point out that if Newton's laws represent ways of working which are natural to objects with mass, we need only find some sequence of events—perhaps, as has been suggested, a near-collision between the sun and some other star—which might leave behind a group of bodies with the appropriate relative motions; from there the thing will run on of its own accord. *Given Newton's laws,* it is really quite easy to make a solar system; certainly no great ingenuity is required. If, as modern astronomy might suggest, the order is located not in the solar system but in the multiplicity of galaxies, then what we naturally look for is a **cosmological** history that will account for the phenomena; but again it seems likely that the solution will lie in laws, not in ingenuity. If the order is located in plant and animal bodies, then plainly the immediate explanation of this order in the organisms that are around now lies in what Hume called 'generation and vegetation,' the simple and obvious fact that each individual organism is produced by its parents and then grows. However, this is only an outline explanation; a more adequate immediate explanation would identify and trace the laws and mechanisms and processes of generation and vegetation. If a further explanation is sought, we can now offer the evolutionary one towards which Hume could only make rather fumbling gestures. . . . As Darwin so convincingly argued, there are many details which his hypothesis explains while that of special creation does not.

. . . [S]ince Darwin wrote, anyone who wants to use an argument for design must locate elsewhere the order which the designer is postulated to explain. On the assumption that a full account of the development of life from inorganic materials, and of the gradual evolution of more and more complex organisms, can be given, using as data only the general laws of physics and chemistry and some astronomically understandable initial conditions, this argument for theism will have to take, as the order to be explained, either the atomic and subatomic structure of inorganic materials or the basic laws which govern their workings and interactions. Again, after modern developments in **cosmology,** anyone who wants to use anything like the astronomical variant of the argument must locate the order to be explained in some initial set-up—perhaps somewhere inside the **'big bang.'** This shift, however, is sometimes made in a way that attempts, unfairly, to cancel the necessary concession. It may be said that we still have to explain why there should be materials and laws which are *such that* they can give rise to life and the evolution of complex organisms, or again why there should be an initial cosmological set-up which is *such that* it can generate galaxies containing stars and planetary systems. This is misleading in two ways. On the one hand, it invites us to **beg the question** by supposing that these future developments are not only causally latent within the initial situation—that is, that it will eventually lead to them or bring them about—but are also already *envisaged* at its formation. On the other hand, it suggests that a *potentiality* for the producing of these developments is part of what still needs to be explained. But this suggestion is unfair. If, as we are supposing, the future developments are accounted for by the initial conditions and materials and laws alone, then it is only for those initial conditions and materials and laws as they are in themselves that any further explanation could reasonably be sought. We must not overload the **explanandum** by adding to it, even as a potentiality, the developments which we can presume it to have accounted for already.

But it may be argued that there is still something that calls for further explanation. With the various basic materials and physical constants as they contingently are, life and evolution and consciousness are naturally possible; but things might so easily have been different. Is it not remarkable and intrinsically surprising that things happen to be just right for the possibility of these developments? . . .

I suspect, however, that this objection also is being presented in a **question-begging** way. Though some small variation from the actual initial materials and constants would, perhaps, eliminate the possibility of life's having developed as it did, we really have no idea of what other interesting possibilities might have been latent within others of the endless range of possible initial conditions. We are not in a position, therefore, to regard the actual initial materials and constants as a uniquely fruitful set, and as surprising and as specially calling for further explanation on that account.

Once these matters are cleared up, we can see that the shift of topic due to the work of Darwin and his successors greatly diminishes the plausibility of the argument for design. The reciprocal adjustments of structures and functions in myriads of different organisms are indeed so delicate and complicated as to be initially surprising in the extreme, and not merely to invite but to require a search for *some* further explanation; and then the hypothesis of design is at least one to be considered among others. But we find nothing comparable to this in sub-atomic particles or the laws that govern them. Atomic and nuclear physics are, no doubt, intricate enough to be of theoretical as well as practical interest, but we cannot see them as involving reciprocal adjustments which might plausibly be taken as signs of purposiveness.

The shift produced by modern cosmology is less important in this respect, not because any initially surprising reciprocal adjustments have to be postulated in a proposed starting-point of cosmic history, but because none was to be found even in the developed universe. The eighteenth-century thinkers drew quite the wrong conclusion from Newtonian gravitational astronomy. It should, as I have said, have told them not that a solar system is a marvellously coherent machine with mutually assisting and mutually adjusted components (like a watch, only more so), but rather that it is something that, given the gravitational laws, could be botched up with no forethought at all, or that could emerge from a fortuitous concourse of masses. It takes ingenuity to make an orrery, an artificial model of the solar system, precisely because it cannot use the gravitational laws, but no such ingenuity is needed to make a gravitationally governed solar system. . . .

STUDY QUESTIONS

1. How does Darwin's theory of evolution threaten the design argument?
2. How might a theist seek to defuse the threat mentioned in question 1?
3. Why does Mackie think the theist would be wrong to respond in the way mentioned in question 2?
4. What point does Mackie make about atomic and nuclear physics? What does this point add to his argument?
5. *Mackie's position clearly contradicts that of Stephen T. Davis and Robert Hambourger in Readings 4.9 and 4.10. Who do you think is right? Why?

ARGUMENTS FROM RELIGIOUS EXPERIENCE

READING 4.12

From Experience to God

Jerome I. Gellman

In this selection, Jerome I. Gellman (Ben-Gurion University, Israel) defends the argument from religious experience. Gellman argues that there are certain principles about how to rationally connect experience with reality, which, in our everyday assessment of claims, we implicitly accept as authoritative. When these principles are applied to alleged experiences of God, Gellman claims, the rational conclusion to draw is that God exists.

Gellman appeals to two principles. First is the Best Explanation of Experience (BEE): if a person, S, has an experience, E, which seems to be of a particular object, O, then, everything else being equal, the best explanation of S's having E is that S has experienced O, rather than something else or nothing at all. Applying this principle to alleged experiences of God, the best explanation for a person who seems to have had an experience of God, everything else being equal, is that the person has experienced God, rather than something else or nothing at all. Second is the principle of Strength in Number Greatness (STING): the presumption created by BEE that a seeming experience of an object, O, is, in fact, an experience of O is strengthened the more "sightings" there are of O and the more variable the circumstances under which O has been sighted. There have been many accounts of people who claim to have experienced God, occurring under highly variable circumstances. According to BEE, if we consider even one such account, it is rational to believe that this person did, indeed, experience God and that, therefore, God exists. According to STING, the fact that there are many and varied accounts of experiencing God strengthens the presumption created by any individual's experience of God. It is not rational to believe that this person was experiencing something other than God, or that the person was not experiencing anything at all and that God does not exist.

Gellman considers an important objection to his argument, which was raised by Michael Martin against a similar argument formulated by Richard Swinburne. Martin says that the best explanation for an experience that a person has of the absence of an object is that that person is experiencing the absence of that object (Gellman calls this principle BEEN). Thus, if someone appears to experience the absence of God—an experience many have had—then the best explanation is that the person is experiencing the absence of God.

Gellman replies that we must draw a distinction between (a) a person's actually observing the absence of an object and (b) a person failing to observe the presence of that object after searching thoroughly for it. In the case of experiencing God, the only way we can know that (a) rather than (b) is the case is if we apply BEE and STING first in order to determine the circumstances under which God can be experienced.

Gellman then raises a version of BEEN (BEEN.A), which says that, if a person has searched thoroughly for an object and has failed to observe that object, the best explanation of that experience is that the object is absent. Gellman points out that, in order to know what constitutes "searching thoroughly" for God, one must first know in what situations God can be experienced. Since we have no knowledge as to what are the sufficient circumstances under which God can be experienced, BEEN.A, like BEEN, is not applicable to the case of experiencing God.

There are certain principles about how to connect experience with reality that we implicitly recognize as authoritative. We regularly appeal to these rules when wanting to determine in a rational way the connection between experience and reality in contexts other than the experience of God. I will not be arguing for these principles, other than to claim that we *in fact* recognize their authority to govern our relevant, rational deliberations. My argument thus starts with them.

My principles yield what I call strong rationality. [A belief in *p* is strongly rational if and only if the belief that *p* is rational while a belief *that not-p* is not.] At the same time, though, at least because of the clause "everything else being equal" which they contain, not every reasonable, proper application of them, even when considering the same evidence, need yield the same results. Reasonable, informed human beings could conceivably reach different conclusions from these same principles . . . because they could reasonably differ over whether everything else *was* equal. Hence, we do not claim that *all* reasonable, proper applications of these principles would show, with regard to a belief *that p,* that it was rational and that the belief *that not-p* was not.

I

I begin my argument with the following principle, connecting experience to reality:

> If a person, S, has an experience, E, which seems (**phenomenally**) to be of a particular object, O (or of an object of kind, K), then *everything else being equal* the best explanation of S's having E is that S has experienced O (or an object of kind, K), rather than something else or nothing at all.[1]

Let us call this principle, the principle of the "Best Explanation of Experience," or "BEE."

I clarify a number of features of BEE:

1. BEE is meant to apply only to what can be judged by what is phenomenally present to S.

[1]Those familiar with the literature on the evidential value of putative experiences of God will recognize BEE as first cousin to a principle formulated by Richard Swinburne, the "Principle of Credulity" ("PC"). Swinburne writes, "It is a principle of rationality that (in the absence of special considerations) if it seems (**epistemically**) to a subject that x is present, then probably x is present." (Richard Swinburne, *The Existence of God,* Revised Edition, (Oxford: Clarendon Press, 1991), p. 254.) In the "epistemic" sense of "seems," "It seems to S that O is present," means that S is inclined to believe O is present on the basis of his present perception. (Swinburne, *The Existence of God,* p. 245.)

Although we are indebted to Swinburne for our principle and for the direction of our argument, at the same time, there are differences between BEE and PC. The main differences between them are that, first, PC applies only when it seems *to S* that O is present. BEE has no such limitation, as explained in number 2 below. And secondly, in PC Swinburne speaks of what is "probable" whereas in BEE we prefer to speak of the "best explanation" of what S is experiencing. The use of "probable" here can be misleading, suggesting a statistical form of argument.

This excludes cases where, for example, it seems that O is present to S only on the basis of S's hunch or inner conviction of some sort.

2. In BEE it is required only *that* S seem to have an experience of a certain sort. It is not necessary that it seem *to S* that she is having an experience of that sort. S may not realize that what she is experiencing is O. S may describe an experience of hers to someone else who may then have good reason to assert that S seems to have had an experience of O while S herself did not realize that her experience was of O.
3. In BEE I am thinking of perception along the lines of an Appearance Theory of Perception. On this theory, sensory perception does not consist merely of experiencing certain "qualities," caused by an object, the identity of which we set out, as it were, to determine in order to know what object we have perceived. Rather, the experience is phenomenally constituted in the first place by an act-object form. Hence, in BEE we consider S to be having an "of-O" experience as given phenomenally. But I do not believe that anything in my argument hinges upon this way of thinking of perception, because, as I will argue below, the rational status of BEE does not depend upon the truth of any particular philosophical theory about perception.
4. That S's experiencing O is the "best explanation" of what S has experienced is meant to entail that it is a perfectly good explanation and does not mean just that it beats all other explanations but might itself be rather weak.
5. If S seems to experience O, then on BEE this creates a *presumption* that S has experienced O, and thus of O's existing. Thus on BEE an apparent experience of O is *evidence* for O's presence and existence. Since, however, BEE carries the condition, "everything else being equal," that the experience really is of O can be overturned or defeated by considerations stronger than the presumption the putative experience creates on its own behalf. So a putative experience of O is in itself neither self-validating nor neutral as to what it is really an experience of, if anything.
6. The logic of the clause "everything else being equal" in BEE (and in the further principle to be introduced below) is such that the burden of proof is not upon the one who claims that everything else is equal, but on the one who would argue that everything else is *not* equal. Or to put it differently, everything else being equal everything else is equal.
7. The presumption which according to BEE a putative experience of O carries for its being a real experience of O is independent of knowledge of a prior correlation between putative experiences of O and the actual presence of O being experienced, or of any other correlation which would imply that one. According to BEE it is rational in and of itself to take a putative experience of O as best explained as being really of O, everything else being equal. This includes the very first time a person seems to experience an object O. It is then "already" rational to assume, everything else being equal, that O is present to the subject as an object of experience.
8. BEE relates to what is the best explanation of S's putative experience of O, choosing between saying either that S has experienced O or that S has experienced something other than O or that S has experienced nothing at all. Among the three, BEE affirms that the best (and good) explanation is, everything else being equal, that S has experienced O. BEE does not relate directly to such questions as how it is that O was there to be experienced, or how it is that S came to be in a position or place to have an apparent experience of O or came to have the concepts necessary to form the belief, if she did form it, that it was O that was being experienced. And so on.

   On the other hand, BEE has implications for explanations not covered by it directly. For example, it follows from BEE that any explanation of any of these other matters, such as how S came to be in a position to have an apparent experience of O, which implied that S did *not* have a real experience of O, is to be rejected, everything else being equal, in favor of an explanation which did not have such an implication.
9. According to BEE, that the best explanation of S's having the experience she has is that S has experienced O, is the best explanation *simpliciter,* and

not only for S. Assuming we can trust S's report of her experience, S's experience counts as evidence for its authenticity for all others besides S.

BEE implies that if a person seems to be seeing a tree in front of him, then the best (and good) explanation of that person's having that experience, everything else being equal, is that there is indeed a tree in front of him which he sees, rather than something else or nothing at all. And that means that everything else being equal it is rational to believe that the person is seeing a tree, and not rational to believe that he isn't. And BEE implies that if a person seems to see a flying saucer, then the best explanation of that fact, everything else being equal, is that there is a flying saucer up there which he sees. So it is rational, everything else being equal, to believe he does and not rational to believe that he does not. This latter example illustrates that in any given case, admitting that S seems to see O and accepting BEE does not commit one to accepting that S really does see O, since the clause "everything else being equal" may point us in precisely the opposite direction. But it does illustrate that unless everything else is not equal an experience counts in favor of its own objectivity.

I claim that BEE is a principle of rationality widely recognized as governing our everyday rational discourse connecting experience to reality. As such its rationality is independent of its being shown to be so by philosophical argumentation. A clear indication of its status in our thinking is that when a person has had a putative experience of something and we do not wish to accept what would follow were the experience to be veridical, we feel obligated to come up with a *reason* for thinking that the experience should not be accepted at face value. We do not deem ourselves free simply to ignore the experiential claim. But that is tantamount to recognizing that a putative experience counts in favor of its own veracity and that unless we have a better reason to reject it, then the experience should be accepted as being *of* reality.

II

Having presented and explained BEE, I now present the first part of my argument, the application of BEE to alleged experiences of God:

I maintain that BEE applies just as much to putative experiences of God as to putative perceptions of a material object. No matter which **epistemological** theory we may favor, it is intuitively plausible to maintain that, *everything else being equal,* that a person has an apparent experience of God is best explained (and well explained) by saying that the person experienced God, rather than something else or nothing at all.

Whether BEE, along with the principle soon to be introduced, confers *as much* rationality upon belief in God as it does on belief in physical objects is a matter to be considered in its own right. However the question of the over-all rationality of the one experience as compared to the other is an entirely different issue from the fact that when a person seems to experience God, that creates the presumption, *everything else being equal,* that God is experienced by that person.

Now there is no doubt that very many people throughout history have had experiences, each of which *seems* on a phenomenal basis to be an experience of God. The traditions of Judaism, Christianity, and Islam are saturated by the sense of the presence and reality of God on the part of their adherents. There exists, furthermore, a most impressive array of first-hand reports of vivid experiences of various sorts each of which is best described as a putative experience of God. This is more so in some religious traditions than in others and in some denominations more than others within the same religious tradition, yet a pervasive feature of them all. That God exists is not just an "idea" of these religions, but is believed to be disclosed in a living awareness of God, more vividly amongst great spiritual souls, less vividly amongst less spiritually endowed adherents.

In the contemporary world as well, many people of diverse cultural backgrounds and religious (and some of non-religious) persuasions likewise seem to have had experiences of God, or do have such experiences regularly.

Now consider just one such apparent experience of God, "G." From BEE it follows that everything else being equal the best (and good) explanation of G is that God is being experienced, rather than nothing or something else instead. Hence, everything else being equal BEE renders it rational to believe that God is experienced and exists, and not rational to believe that God is not experienced, or that God doesn't exist.

G can be a type of experience in which it seems to the subject that God *as* God is present. It would follow from BEE that if in G it seemed to a subject, S, that God was (phenomenally) present to her then the best explanation of that, everything else being equal, is that S was indeed experiencing God.

Or G could be a perception of God in which S is aware of God in some way or other, but in which it did not seem *to* S that God was present to her or being experienced. This could be, for example, because S lacks the conceptual equipment to make the relevant judgments. Based upon previous perceptions of God the genuineness of which was attested to by BEE, persons other than S could be in a position to judge rationally that S was aware of God even if S herself wasn't aware that it was God. They could make this judgment on the basis of what S reports of the phenomenal content of her experience together with their knowledge of what has been disclosed in previous experiences of God. S's experience would thus seem to *others* to be an experience of God, and on BEE, everything else being equal, the best explanation of S's experience would be that S was experiencing God.

Up to this point, I have been focusing upon the evidential value of a single apparent perception of God, arguing that it is strongly rational to believe that *it* was an experience of God, and thus that God exists. But we are not limited in our argument to the evidential value provided by a single apparent experience or even to a small number of them.

This brings us to a second principle governing the rationality of reasoning from experience to reality:

> If a person, S, has an experience, E, which seems (phenomenally) to be of a particular object, O (or of an object of kind, K), then our belief that S's having experienced O (or an object of kind, K) is the best explanation (everything else being equal) of E, is strengthened in proportion to the number of purported experiences of O there are and in proportion to the variability of circumstances in which such experiences occur.

Let us call this the principle of "Strength in Number Greatness," or, STING. According to STING, the presumption created by BEE that a seeming experience of an object, O, is a true experience of O, is strengthened the more "sightings" of O there are, and the more variable the circumstances under which O is sighted. That means that the presumption created together by *many* experiences of O in varied circumstances is stronger than the presumption created by any individual perception of O. And for that reason any counter-argument to the presumption of truth is going to have to be stronger than it would have to have been had an experience been backed by a single experience or by a very few.

In addition, the more *varied* the conditions in which O is sighted the more difficult it will be to find a defeater of the presumption of truth, since the defeater will have to be true of all of the varied circumstances in which the experience takes place. The more varied the circumstances, the harder this will be to find.[2]

. . . Considering the large number of [reports of] perceptions of God [both in the past and contemporary times in the traditions of Judaism, Christianity, and Islam], STING much strengthens the belief that the best explanation, everything else being equal, of a person's seeming to experience God is that the person really is experiencing God.

Furthermore, given the richly varied circumstances in which such experiences take place, by STING the conclusion is strengthened further. The experience of God is reported across widely different cultures and religions over a wide span of time and by individuals of greatly differing temperament, education, social status, and immediate, personal circumstances. This makes it all the more difficult to

[2]STING is first cousin to a line of reasoning endorsed by C.D. Broad: When there is a nucleus of agreement between the experiences of men in different places, times, and traditions, and when they all tend to put much the same kind of interpretation on the cognitive content of these experiences, it is reasonable to ascribe this agreement to their all being in contact with a certain objective aspect of reality *unless* there be some positive reason to think otherwise. (C.D. Broad, *Religion, Philosophy and Psychical Research* [London: Routledge, and Kegan Paul, 1953.])

come up with some wholesale considerations which would defeat the evidential value of such experiences as a class. And it also makes it more difficult to come up with counter-considerations against the genuineness of a specific experience, backed as it is by a large number of similar experiences for which there might not be any counter-considerations.

Hence, the overall conclusion to be reached is that each individual experience allegedly of God that has occurred has a strong presumption in its favor of being in fact an experience of God, everything else being equal. Hence BEE and STING show that it is rationally well-grounded, everything else being equal, to believe that God exists and not rational to believe that God does not exist.

IV

. . . Michael Martin has objected to Richard Swinburne's claim that alleged experiences of God contribute to showing that God exists. Martin's objection, if correct, would be telling against our argument as well. In what follows, therefore, I will present a reconstituted argument of Martin's.

Martin's argument (recast) is founded on the claim that a principle equally legitimate and equally convincing as BEE would mark the connection between what seems to be *absent* and what really is absent, as follows:

> If a person, S, has an experience, E, which seems (phenomenally) to be of the absence of a particular object, O (or of an object of kind, K), then *everything else being equal* the best explanation of S's having E is that S has experienced the absence of O (or of an object of kind, K).[3]

Let us call this "negative" version of BEE, "BEEN."

Martin argues for parity between BEE and BEEN by example. He says, "The experience of a chair is a good ground for believing that the chair is present. [And] the experience of the absence of a chair is a good ground for supposing that a chair is absent."[4]

Martin next notes that "many people have tried to experience God and have failed." Therefore, the application of BEEN to their experiences should count for God's being absent no less than the application of BEE to experiences of God counts for the presence of God. However, if God exists then He exists everywhere, as it were. Hence if God is perceived to be absent anywhere, then God is absent everywhere, i.e., does not exist. Hence the application of BEEN yields the conclusion that God does not exist no less than BEE yields the result that God does exist.

Thus does Martin wish to argue that putative experiences of God's absence, i.e., God's nonexistence, neutralize or overweigh whatever evidential value there may be in putative experiences of God's presence, i.e., God's existence.

An obvious reply to Martin would be to argue that BEEN is not applicable to the case of God. . . . The Non-Applicability Reply begins by noting the distinction to be made between:

> (A) S observes the absence of O.

and

> (B) S fails to observe the presence of O after searching thoroughly for O.

In some cases (A) and (B) are equivalent, for all practical purposes. If a chair were reported present in an average furnished room and S searched the room thoroughly for a chair and found none, we may say not only that S "failed to find" a chair, but also that S "discovered there was no chair" in the room. We may even say that S "saw that there was no chair" in the room. In this situation it would be quite natural to assert that S had observed the absence of a chair. In a case such as this, (A) and (B) coincide.

But in other cases (A) and (B) diverge. Consider where S conducts a search for a reported mouse in the same furnished household room, but fails to observe a mouse. This would not count for the same as S observing that the mouse was absent. And the reason

[3]See: Michael Martin, *Atheism: A Philosophical Justification* (Philadelphia: Temple University Press, 1990), p. 170, principle "(NPC)."

[4]M. Martin, *Atheism,* p. 170.

for this is that from what we know of mice they are quite successful in hiding in difficult to reveal places and in moving around quickly and silently from place to place, only to reappear when least expected. Hence, that S has failed to come up with a mouse may give some ground for *inferring* that there is no mouse, depending on how well and how long S has searched and perhaps on S's success record in the past in uncovering mice or some such objects. But S's failure to see a mouse in the room would not be tantamount to S's having *observed* that there was no mouse in the room.[5] In this situation (A) and (B) diverge.

The Non-Applicability Reply against Martin continues by asking how we know, in any given case, whether or not (A) is tantamount to (B). How can we tell in a particular instance whether failing to experience O, after searching thoroughly, is tantamount or not to experiencing its absence?

Suppose some biologists report sighting an animal never before seen. Others look for it and fail to find it. Have the latter experienced the *absence* of the animal or have they merely failed to find it? There are cases where we won't be able to say because not enough will be known about the animal being reported. We may not know what sizes it comes in. We might not know whether it is sluggish or swift, cunning or dull, shy or daring. We may not know its mode of locomotion or habits of appearing, by day, by night, by full moon, etc. As the object is sighted more often we will presumably learn more that will be relevant to coming to know the difference between experiencing its absence and failing to experience its presence. For example, if those who claim to have sighted the animal profess to have sighted that it is stable and doesn't move around much, that it appears quite regularly in a certain area, etc., etc., then the conditions for experiencing its absence will have improved. But if those who have seen it report on how elusive it is, etc., then it will be harder to identify genuine instances of observing its absence.

This illustration shows that knowing whether we have experienced the absence of something or merely failed to experience its presence is parasitic upon experiences of its presence, or at the least of the presence of objects similar to it in relevant ways. It is only by taking the latter at face value, everything else being equal, that we learn enough about the object in question to make out the distinction between (A) and (B), if at all.

How, then, do we in fact *know* when we fail to see a mouse that it is not the same as seeing that there is no mouse there? And how do we in fact *know* when we fail to see a chair, in most ordinary cases, that it is tantamount to seeing that there is no chair there? The answer is that we know these things by relying upon BEE and STING. It is because of our taking many and varied alleged experiences of mice and of chairs (and of other, similar, objects as well), respectively, as true experiences of mice and chairs (and of those other objects) that we come to know about their habits of coming and going. It is on the basis of BEE that we know, for example, that chairs stay put and do not hide. That is why if we scan an ordinary room and see no chairs, that counts as seeing that there is no chair. And it is on the basis of BEE that we know about mice moving around quietly and not being easily detected. And so that's how we know that if someone searches an ordinary room, with an ordinary amount of furniture and bookcases, say, the fact that they do not see the mouse is not tantamount to their seeing that there is no mouse there.

So we are beholden to BEE to give us knowledge about the presence of O in general, before we can even begin to formulate applications of BEEN. That is because BEEN applies to cases where a subject has "an experience which seems to be of the absence" of O. But we can identify such cases only via depending on BEE. Were we not to grant epistemic priority to BEE we would never be able to tell in any case whether our failure to observe O was or was not the same as observing the absence of O. We could not as much as make the distinction between (A) and (B). So BEE has a logical priority to BEEN.

Now suppose it happens that from the very start most people who sight O report sighting it only sporadically. Few report regular sightings. Perhaps some report rough conditions that from their experience

[5]No doubt when S sees no chair in the room some inferences are involved, but they are sufficiently implicit for it to be natural to say that S "sees that there is no chair" in the room.

seem, normally, to be *necessary* for sighting O. But none have any idea what **sufficient conditions** for O's being observable might be like. O is reported to make an impression of being quite elusive. In the main, sightings are reported from time to time, but without any discernible pattern, making reliable prediction possible. And let us suppose that from sightings of O not enough is known to compare O to other known objects from which we could make informed predictions about O on the basis of relevant similarities to their behavior.

In such circumstances, the Non-Applicability Reply concludes that there would not be [enough] information available to apply BEEN. And that is because applying BEEN requires S's putative observation that O is absent. But in the described circumstances there would not be enough to go on to distinguish between (A) "S observes the absence of O" and (B) "S fails to observe the presence of O after searching thoroughly for O." In the described circumstances, when a person, S, does not see O after a thorough search we may not know enough to be able to say whether S is observing the absence of O or only has failed to observe the presence of O. Not enough will be known about O to make this distinction. We could not (yet) apply BEEN.

But consider now a weaker analog of BEEN, BEEN.A:

> If a person, S, has searched thoroughly for O (or for an object of kind, K) and has failed to observe O (or an object of kind, K), then *everything else being equal* the best explanation of S's failure to observe O (or object of kind, K) is that O (or an object of kind, K) is absent.

BEEN.A applies where BEEN itself doesn't. Would BEEN.A apply in our hypothetical case?[6] BEEN.A would not apply there any more than BEEN does. And the reason still is that we would not know enough of what would count as *searching thoroughly* for O, for we would not have enough knowledge of when or where or how O could be expected to appear were it to be present.

But in our hypothetical case, BEE would well apply. Positive sightings of O would count, everything else being equal, in favor of O being present. And if there were an impressive number of sightings in different circumstances then STING would strengthen the results of applying BEE.

The moral of the story is that BEEN, and its weaker analog BEEN.A, are not on a par with BEE. Sometimes BEE will apply where BEEN and BEEN.A do not.

The Non-Applicability Reply concludes by applying the above findings to putative experiences of God. Such putative experiences have been and continue to be reported across several of the world's religions and cultures and across wide periods of time. BEE and STING support the conclusion, therefore, that these are truly experiences of God, everything else being equal. But from what we know of these reports, relying on BEE and STING, the experience of God comes only to some individuals and not to others. And to those to whom it does comes it does so, in the main, only sporadically, though some saintly souls report a life lived constantly in the presence of God. In addition, judging from those who have had such experiences we are not able to say what conditions are *sufficient* to experience God. From what is disclosed about God in such experience everything points to God's not being able to be coerced into appearing. In fact, judging from the reports of some of the world's greatest mystics, sometimes God is experienced only when one does not "try" to experience Him. God makes the impression of being quite elusive.

. . . It is true that there exist mystical traditions which teach a path to the experience of God, a path of arduous training and self-deprivation. But typically these traditions do not look upon such techniques as guarantees of having such experiences. And in any case a great number of reported putative perceptions of God seem to occur outside of organized mystical traditions.

And finally, God appears to be so unlike any other known object that there is no basis upon which to make even educated guesses about when God will or will not appear by reference to them.

[6]Even if it would, we should note that BEEN.A is evidentially weaker than BEEN. That's why we quickly give up the search for a chair in a room where someone has failed to find one, yet sometimes set mouse traps even where a thorough search has failed to find a mouse.

In light of all of these considerations, the conclusion which emerges is that based on putative experiences of God supported by BEE and STING, we just do not know enough about the sufficient conditions under which God appears and does not appear, to be able to determine with any assurance when we should say that "S has experienced God's absence," and when we should say instead "S has failed to experience God." Thus BEEN cannot be applied in the case of God, since BEEN applies solely to putative instances of experiencing God's absence.

Similarly, BEEN.A is not effective in the case of putative experiences of God. That is because not enough is known about the conditions under which God appears, to be able to give sufficient meaning to the notion of "thoroughly searching" for Him, that would confer good evidential weight upon the *failure* to find Him. On the basis of experiences of God attested to by BEE and STING, we do not know enough about what one must do in order to thoroughly search for God in order for us to know that such a search has failed. So when Martin affirms that "many people have tried to experience God and have failed," if he means to be referring to searching thoroughly for God, then Martin's argument fails.

But perhaps Martin means to be referring to something less than a "thorough search" for God. Perhaps he means that lots of people have just "made an effort," some effort, to experience God and have failed. But what does Martin think people do when they try to experience God? He does not tell us.

. . . We can point to what might amount to making an effort to experience God which would not count as searching thoroughly for Him. . . . One guise under which God is experienced, in various degrees of clarity and fullness, is that of a "maximally valuable being" or "absolutely perfect being." In this type of experience, a value perception lies at the very heart of recognizing God as God, a value perception the subject must be capable of acknowledging. For to acknowledge God as a maximally valuable being, involves acknowledging that it be fit and proper for God to be the center of one's entire value orientation. And this acknowledgement requires a decentering of one's own self, and what is of earthly importance to one, as the focus of one's value orientation. This is why persons who experience God are often profoundly shaken, and greatly transformed in the way they subsequently assess the value of various aspects of their life.

Indeed it is a widely held teaching in the world's religions that in seeking God one should labor hard to erase one's self-centered and selfish stance in the world, to abandon one's own self as one's value center, so that God can become the value center of one's life. And typically, the mystic "path" is shaped and formed precisely by such a goal. In light of this, it may be proposed that a strong, determined effort to [at least minimally detach oneself from self-centeredness] should count, at least, as "trying" to experience God. If so, then where God had been sought in this way and not found, perhaps a weaker form of BEEN.A, reformulated for cases of "trying" to experience O, would yield at least *some* evidence that God was absent, to a degree our Non-Applicability Reply has been interested to deny.

This suggestion is not successful, however. A determined effort at decentering the self coupled with the failure to have experienced God cannot count as evidence of the absence of God, since from what is known about God from alleged experiences of Him, He cannot be coerced to appear. God's hand cannot be forced. Decentering of the self only conduces to having an experience of God from the side of the subject, making the subject a proper vessel for receiving God's self-disclosure. Hence, that one has tried to decenter oneself and failed to experience God counts no more against God's existence than does just going to where there is some light and failing to see a mouse counts against there being a mouse in the vicinity.

In addition, it is very difficult to say when a true effort to perceive God by an attempt at self-decentering has taken place. It is notoriously difficult, after all, to determine a person's authentic stance in the world. It is extremely difficult for a person, and surely others looking in on him, to determine when he really has made an authentic, non-compromising effort at a decentering of the self. Hence, it would be extremely difficult in any given case to establish that one had truly tried hard to decenter and hence had to that extent tried to perceive

comments about BEE, Gellman does assert that "If S seems to experience O, then on BEE this creates a *presumption* that S has experienced O, and thus of O's existence. *Thus* [italics added] on BEE an apparent experience of O is *evidence* for O's presence and existence." Talk of presumption and evidence [is] certainly a step in the right direction, but we remain curious as to how strong a presumption and how much evidence BEE is being claimed to provide. . . .

Gellman's . . . use of [presumption] seems odd. One doesn't normally infer that one has evidence because there is a presumption. Quite the contrary; talk of a presumption implies that it is not necessary to accumulate evidence to support what is being presumed. This aside, since BEE is a principle of rationality, it would seem that its conclusion should be directly stated in terms of evidence, probability, or rationality, and not, as Gellman does here, in terms of presumption from which the other **epistemic** notions are inferred.

[Shortly thereafter,] we do, however, get our answer. Applying BEE first to a person's seeing a tree, and then to seeing a flying saucer, Gellman claims that in both cases BEE yields the conclusion that everything else being equal, it is rational to believe that the person is seeing what he seems to see. And a few more pages on we read: "Now consider just one such apparent experience of God, 'G.' From BEE it follows that, everything else being equal, the best (and good) explanation of G is that God is being experienced, rather than nothing or something else instead. *Hence* [italics added], everything else being equal, BEE renders it rational to believe that God is experienced and exists, and not rational to believe that God is not experienced, or that God doesn't exist." As he did initially, Gellman formulates the consequent of BEE directly in terms of what is the best explanation of an experience, rather than in terms of the evidence for such a belief or its rationality. But the answer to our main question nonetheless emerges by implication: BEE, alone, other things being equal, supports strong rationality. Finally, . . . we are told that "each individual experience allegedly of God that has occurred has a *strong* [italics added] presumption in its favor of being in fact an experience of God, everything else being equal."

Having satisfied our curiosity about how powerful he thinks BEE is, Gellman has stirred an even deeper curiosity. How do we know that BEE, so understood, is a principle of rationality at all? Gellman devotes surprisingly little space to this question. As far as we can tell, his entire argument is contained in the following paragraph.

> [I] claim that BEE is a principle of rationality widely recognized as governing our everyday rational discourse connecting experience to reality. As such its rationality is independent of its being shown to be so by philosophical argumentation. A clear indication of its status in our thinking is that when a person has had a putative experience of something and we do not wish to accept what would follow were the experience to be veridical, we feel obligated to come up with a *reason* for thinking that the experience should not be accepted at face value. We do not deem ourselves free simply to ignore the experiential claim. But that is tantamount to recognizing that a putative experience counts in favor of its own veracity and that unless we have a better reason to reject it, then the experience should be accepted as being *of* reality.

Suppose we go along with Gellman in accepting the existence of the practice he describes. When someone reports a putative experience of something, if we want to reject its **veridicality** we need to provide a "better reason" to reject it. But how does this show that BEE is the principle that governs this practice? Won't that depend on what counts as a "better reason"? Suppose, for example, we claim that a good reason to reject the veridicality of a putative experience of O is that either there are no (or too few) **intersubjective tests** for its veridicality, or there exist tests, but we lack any reason to believe that, were they to be performed, they would come out positive. How would this underwrite BEE as Gellman construes its evidential force? According to BEE, Gellman tells us, if a person seems to see a flying saucer, then everything else being equal, it is strongly rational to believe this experience is veridical, just as it is if a person seems to see a tree. But if we accept the above suggestion for a good reason to reject the veridicality of a putative experience, then even if other things are equal in both the case of the person who seems to see a tree and in the case of the person who seems to see a flying saucer, it will be strongly rational to believe in the veridicality of the putative tree experience, but not rational to believe in the veridicality of the putative flying saucer experience. The upshot is that absent an account of what are good reasons for rejecting putative experiences, Gellman has made no case for BEE as he interprets it.

We will consider below the question of how one might defend one account of "good reasons" over another.[1] Intuitions no doubt play a role, and Gellman apparently finds it intuitive to accord strong rationality (other things being equal) to both the putative tree experience and the putative flying saucer experience. We do not. Nor, accordingly, do we find it plausible that the practice Gellman describes is best interpreted as being governed by BEE. As an alternative to BEE, we propose the following, call it BEEV:

> If a person, S, has an experience, E, which seems (phenomenally) to be of a particular object, O (or of an object of kind K), then it is rational to believe and not rational not to believe that S's having experienced O (or an object of kind K) is the best explanation *everything else being equal* of E, if there are (a sufficient number of) intersubjective tests for the veridicality of E (or of an object of kind K) which have been performed and turned out positive, or which there is reason to believe would turn out positive if they were performed.

Though we reject BEE as a principle which establishes strong rationality (other things being equal), we do believe that in the above argument for BEE (and even more powerfully in the following chapter), Gellman has made a compelling case that a putative experience E does, all on its own (and other things being equal), carry evidential weight. Thus, in addition to BEEV, we accept what we will call BEEP:

> If a person, S, has an experience, E, which seems (phenomenally) to be of a particular object, O (or of an object of kind K), then the belief that S's having experienced O (or an object of kind K) is the best explanation *everything else being equal* of E has *a small degree* of evidential support.

One who favors BEEV and BEEP over BEE, as noted earlier, would hardly react in the same way to a report of an experience of a tree and a report of an experience of a flying saucer. In both cases, of course, BEEP would warrant attributing *some* evidential support to the report, other things being equal. But even if one cannot show that other things are not equal in either case, one has no basis for claiming it is strongly rational to believe in the veridicality of the alleged flying saucer experience, while one does have such a basis in the alleged tree experience. In the alleged tree experience, even if one does not run through any intersubjective tests of its veridicality, there is reason, utterly absent in the alleged flying saucer experience, to believe such tests would turn out positive. The sheer ordinariness of the alleged tree experience, and the mountain of evidence of the reliability of such reports based on past experience, establishes a *strong presumption* in favor of any such report. The presumption can, of course, be overturned if it turns out that other things are not equal, or if one should attempt, but fail, to confirm the report via familiar intersubjective tests.

Replacing BEE with BEEV and BEEP would seem to substantially undermine Gellman's argument for God's existence. While BEEP allows us to infer that God's existence has some evidential support from religious experience (other things being equal), the conditions for rationality which BEEV demands of experiences of God cannot be met.[2] . . .

. . . [W]e must comment briefly on Gellman's use of his second principle, STING. As we noted earlier, STING is a principle whose application makes it possible to strengthen the belief in the veridicality of experiences of God. But is it essential to Gellman's argument for strong rationality? It's not so easy to tell. Sometimes Gellman talks as though BEE alone does the trick; at other times, he explicitly states that BEE along with STING does it. The second way of

[1][This part of the article is not included in this excerpt—Ed.]

[2][The authors' attempt to show this is not included here—Ed.]

talking, of course, does not contradict the first, but it does make it hard to be sure exactly what Gellman intends. Here's our best take on what Gellman has in mind. BEE alone is sufficient to establish the strong rationality of theistic belief (other things being equal). STING increases the likelihood of theistic belief (other things being equal) beyond the minimum degree of rationality that is necessary for its strong rationality. STING also makes it harder to show that other things are not equal (for example, any reductive explanation of experience of God has to cope with its quantity, variety, etc.). Finally, STING enables experiences of God to satisfy principles which are more demanding than BEE. Given the multiplicity of roles which STING apparently plays, we will have to argue that even with STING, experiences of God cannot meet the demands placed before it when BEE is replaced by BEEV.

. . . Gellman begins his response to objections by considering an objection presented by Michael Martin. The objection "charges that the result of applying BEE to putative experiences of God is neutralized or outweighed by an equally valid principle applying to instances where people have tried to experience God and have failed." Since our objection, unlike this one, claims that we have no reason to believe that experience of God provides sufficient evidence unless it satisfies BEEV, Gellman's reply to Martin's objection would seem to be utterly irrelevant to our own. Ironically, however, Gellman's reply to Martin reinforces our objection. For in arguing against the applicability of the principles Martin relies on, Gellman insists that "we don't know enough to be able to say when a person has experienced God's absence and we don't know enough to be able to say when a person has searched thoroughly for God, or even has made a really genuine effort to perceive God." Gellman further substantiates these observations by what we know from relying on BEE and STING, namely, that "the experience of God comes only to some individuals and not to others. And to those to whom it does come it does so, in the main, only sporadically, though some saintly souls report a life lived constantly in the presence of God. In addition, judging from those who have had such experiences we are not able to say what conditions are **sufficient** to experience God. From what is disclosed about God in such experiences everything points to the fact that God cannot be coerced into appearing." In short, according to Gellman, the kinds of intersubjective tests which BEEV calls for are not only not, in fact, available; they contradict the nature of God as this is revealed in experiences of God. . . .

STUDY QUESTIONS

1. Explain the difference between "the best explanation of S's having E is that S has experienced O" and "it is strongly rational to believe that S has experienced O."
2. Formulate BEE, BEEV, and BEEP. Why do Levinson and Malino suggest replacing BEE with BEEP or BEEV?
3. Levinson and Malino argue that Gellman's reply to Martin concedes their point about the need for intersubjective testing. Why?
4. *Levinson and Malino place great emphasis on the requirement of intersubjective testing. Do you agree with this requirement? How would accepting it affect the question of whether to accept one person's report of a miracle? Can you think of cases in which we accept beliefs that are not subject to intersubjective testing? What could Levinson and Malino say about such cases?
5. *It would seem that no belief can be exhaustively tested intersubjectively. Suppose I claim to see a zebra. We test the belief by asking you if *you* see the zebra, by taking a photograph, and so on. But your perception, no less than mine, has to be tested intersubjectively; also, our belief that the camera produces pictures of what is really there has to be tested, and so on. Thus, the belief can't be tested intersubjectively. How might Levinson and Malino respond to this objection to the requirement of intersubjective testing?

READING 4.14

Scientific Explanations of Mystical Experiences

Evan Fales

As we saw in Readings 4.12–4.13, a crucial claim in the argument from religious experience is that the existence of God provides the best explanation of such experiences. Evan Fales (University of Iowa) disputes this contention by laying out what he regards as the superior explanatory power possessed by **naturalistic** *accounts of religious experiences. Contrary to theists such as William Alston, Fales thinks that mystical phenomena are accessible to scientific understanding. He invokes, in particular, social anthropologist I. M. Lewis, who treats mystical experience as a strategy used by marginalized groups or individuals for gaining social or political power. It is not persuasive, Fales says, to tack on a theistic hypothesis to supplement Lewis's, for that will force the theist either to postulate all the gods, spirits, and demons of other cultures or to see God at work in all mystical experiences of all cultures. In the latter case, the question arises as to why God gives the Hindu, Zulu, and Black Carib an experience that leads them to believe in something other than God. Thus, unlike the theistic hypothesis, Lewis's theory works very well for nontheistic religious experiences. In addition, theism has no way to supply insight into the correlations between ecstasy and social context. In order to solve an* **empirical** *challenge to Lewis, Fales also refers to explanations of mystical experiences in terms of neurophysiology. In chapter 8, there will be more selections that address the diversity of religious experience. (See Readings 8.2 and 8.4.)*

Unprejudiced reflection upon religious visions, mystical experiences, and the like might reasonably lead one, initially at least, to the conclusion that such episodes can provide *prima facie* perceptual evidence for the existence and nature of God (and of other supernatural beings—e.g. the risen Jesus and Mary); and that the character and weight of this evidence is similar to that which sense experience provides to science and common sense. Matters are not in the end so straightforward, however. For one thing, the supernaturalistic claims said to be confirmed by mystical experiences have wildly divergent, or even contradictory, contents. For another, there exist multiple and highly sophisticated means of cross-checking empirical claims based on ordinary sense perception, whereas nothing really analogous exists for the corresponding religious claims. In view of these considerations, it seems especially critical to ask whether there are any good explanations of the occurrence and content of mystical experiences; and in particular, whether theistic explanations have more plausibility than any purely **naturalistic** explanations that may be in the offing.

Thus William P. Alston (1991), for example, argues not only that the various scientific disciplines do not have anything to offer by way of plausible competitors to the theistic view of mystical experience, but that there is no real prospect of their ever doing so (pp. 228–34). Is Alston right about this? Setting aside for the moment the question of future prospects, is it true that there are at present no serious naturalistic competitors to theism?

The social anthropologist I. M. Lewis, in his *Ecstatic Religion,* finds that mystical experiences occur primarily in two categories of persons, but are used in every case as a strategy for gaining greater access to social or political power. It is employed by disenfranchised, marginalized groups (who are involuntarily possessed by allegedly malignant spirits that through their unwilling hosts may unleash considerable havoc) to recruit or demand attention and concessions from those who oppress them. And, under certain competitive conditions, it is employed by aspirants to high or central status in whom involuntary possession by a central deity can confer authority, sanctity, and the ability to recruit followers. So mystical possession battens at the doors to power, and provides a route to social legitimation.

While Lewis develops his theory primarily by considering data from primitive societies, in (1996a) I took, as an exemplar to test the theory, one prominent Christian mystic—Teresa of Avila. How well, I wondered, does Lewis's theory, with its home in the study of pagan cultures, generalize to her case? The results are, I believe, quite striking. More completely than one would have expected, Teresa might be said to provide a flagship confirming instance for Lewis' view, while at the same time suggesting some theoretical improvements and extensions of his work.

At this point, however, several issues remain to be addressed. These include (1) filling a gap in Lewis's theory—*viz.* explaining how social circumstances translate into the experiences of individual mystics, (2) considering evidence which may be thought to disconfirm Lewis's theory, (3) showing that a theistic **etiology** for mystical experiences cannot plausibly be grafted onto the theory, so that Lewis and theists supply competing accounts for the same phenomena, and finally (4) a comparison of the evidential strengths of Lewis's theory and the theistic alternative.

PSYCHOLOGICAL ISSUES

To raise these questions is to point the way to a more general problem. Like many sociological theories, Lewis's theory has little to say about the psychological processes occurring within the actors in these social dramas. It simply formulates a pattern of correlations among social variables. Nevertheless, it seems obvious that no account of mystical states could hope to be complete unless it had something to say about the psychology of the mystic. If mystical experience has social causes, what exactly are the causal pathways leading from them to the subjective state?

Unlike most social anthropologists, Lewis is sufficiently alive to this question to devote a chapter to it. . . . But for our purposes, his discussion is hardly adequate, for he fails to explain the content of mystical experiences. How do social circumstances, including a particular religious ideology and iconography, get translated into a *particular* ecstatic content in the mind of the mystic? Here I shall propose and discuss five possibilities. Each of these is compatible with Lewis's social analysis, and, on the evidence, it seems more than likely that one will apply to some cases, another to other cases. A fundamental question is whether the mystic really does fall into trance, and really does have the unusual experiences he or she reports having. Philosophers who discuss mysticism have by and large tended naively to assume that the self-reports of mystics are sincere and to be taken pretty much at face value. Lewis, on the other hand, recognizes that much of what falls under this heading involves a calculated strategy which need not be accompanied by any genuine ecstasy at all, no matter how convincing the mystic's behavior or descriptions may seem. One possibility, therefore, is simply calculated deception.

Philosophers who are interested in the evidential significance of mystical experience for theism will of course simply toss out the cases of deception. If a "mystic" does not actually experience any **theophany,** mystical union, or the like, then there is no relevant experience to be explained, by appeal to divine action or in any other way. But of course the possibility of deception does still pose a problem. By what means are we to sort out the genuine mystics from the frauds?[1] What are the patterns, if any, exhibited by genuine mystical experience; and how often do they occur? Indeed, are there *any* cases to which the religious evidentialist (who is not herself a genuine mystic) can point with assurance as putative experiences of the divine? Does Teresa provide us with such a case?

[1]The Spanish Inquisition was fully alive to these questions, as, therefore, of necessity, were the Reformation mystics themselves. Even a superficial look at the historical data will impress one with the need to take the possibility of fraud seriously.

At one extreme lies the radical skepticism of Spanos (1989), who doubts that trance is a genuine state. More reasonable, I believe, is Lewis's verdict that it is, sometimes, quite genuine. But before discussing ecstatic experience as something which simply happens to a passive subject, we need to consider, as a second possibility, that delicately nuanced range of cases in which self-deception may be at work, either in the mystic's efforts to induce ecstasy and to judge that it has been achieved, or in his interpretation and description of the experience. Here, given the cultural conventions and strong motivations which Lewis details, the opportunities are many. Thus this second possibility deserves to be taken quite seriously, however poorly we may at present understand the mechanisms of self-deception.

A third possibility is that certain kinds of social tension simply cause individuals with certain personalities to become susceptible to trance and ecstatic experience. Such experiences, besides perhaps being intrinsically beneficial because of their cathartic effects, may become integrated into broader social strategies to address the sources of tension. Here, calculation (conscious or unconscious) need play no role in the production of ecstasy itself. While the psychological mechanisms that might mediate such a process are not yet well understood, there is little reason to think they will not eventually be so. Lewis himself cites with some circumspection Freud's work on hysteria, and favors this general sort of explanation for many cases.

A fourth possibility is that, especially with respect to the descriptions of mystics from cultures rather different from our own, we may be seriously misunderstanding what the content of their experiences is. This kind of difficulty is one to which the interpretation of religious language generally seems particularly prone. Here is a non-mystical example. Philosophers have been perennially mystified by such beliefs as the belief allegedly found among certain Australian tribal people (e.g. the Arunta) that their souls reside in certain sticks which they keep carefully hidden. Among these tribes' souls, as well as being treated as if they "reside" in the sticks, are successively incarnated by members of the tribe in accordance with certain lineage rules: roughly, if you replace your grandfather by filling the position he once occupied in the clan structure, then you inherit his soul. The sticks in question are actually flat boards (sometimes stones) called *churinga;* they have elaborately painted designs which include a record of man's lineage, and are inherited along with the soul. Though this is something of an oversimplification, it does not take a very clever reading of the classic ethnographic work by Spencer and Gillen to realize that, if the Arunta term translated into English as 'soul' really means 'social position or role,' and if the *churinga* are—as they clearly appear to be—the certificates of legitimacy and insignia of office for the holders of those positions, then the Arunta are being just as sensible (and mundane) as you please. The interpretation which generated the alleged philosophical puzzle is just, I suggest, mistaken. Similarly, if a mystic is describing something rather more mundane than we have supposed, the mystic's reasons for making the assertions she makes may not involve any belief that she is in contact with something supernatural (as we understand the term). I have argued elsewhere (1976, 1977) that mistakes in interpretation of this kind render impenetrable much religious discourse, and especially references to the spirit world and the supernatural. For example, if claims concerning souls entering or leaving a person in association with mystical experiences are correctly to be understood as claims concerning changes in social status or role, then this will have significant implications for the interpretation of mystical discourse. Perhaps it is not terribly plausible that we have misunderstood Teresa as badly as this; but with the mysticism indigenous to more alien cultures, I regard it a genuine possibility.

Fifth and finally, certain cases such as *sar* possession in Somalia clearly suggest the functionality, not of deception, but of a publicly maintained fiction. Unhappy women possessed by malicious spirits are able to exert pressure upon their husbands for attention without being held responsible for the mayhem they cause. Their husbands, on the other hand, are able, by the same token, to accede to their wives' demands without losing face. Of course, the charade can only be pursued by a wife so far before husbandly patience wears thin and a sound beating unmasks the real understanding husband and wife have of their culture's conventional devices. That is, the fiction can perform its mediating function only so long as all parties agree to play along. This is not deception so much as a form of mutual accommodation.

This completes the presentation of scientific approaches to mystic union. We are now in a position to consider how successful such explanations can hope to be, and, in particular, how they stack up against the theistic notion that (certain) mystical experiences are veridical. I shall then conclude by evaluating some data that might appear to conflict with Lewis's views.

THEISTIC STRATEGIES

Alston offers several general arguments designed to show (1) that mystical phenomena are not amenable to scientific study, and (2) that even if science uncovers physical or psychological mechanisms which underlie mystical experience, these do not exclude a divine cause which would underwrite their claim to be **veridical** perceptions of the supreme being (1991, 228–34).

Alston discharges the first task with some dispatch. Let me quote him in full:

> Mystical experience poses severe problems for **empirical** research. In addition to the difficulties in determining when we have a case thereof, it is something that cannot be induced at the will of the researcher and so is not amenable to experiment. Attempts to get around this by substituting drug-induced analogues are of little value, since it is an open question whether findings concerning these analogues can be extrapolated to spontaneous cases. Since the states are usually short-lived, the researcher must rely on autobiographical reports. Hence the data are subject to all the well-known problems that attach to such reports; we can't expect a researcher to hang around a person on the off chance that he might happen to have a mystical experience. Moreover, the most prominent theories in the field invoke causal mechanisms that themselves pose thus far insoluble problems of identification and measurement: unconscious psychological processes like repression, identification, regression, and mechanisms of defense; social influences on ideology and on belief and attitude formation. It is not surprising that theories like those of Freud, Marx, and Durkheim rest on a slender thread of evidential support and generalize irresponsibly from such evidence as they can muster. Nor do the prospects seem rosy for significant improvement (230).

Perhaps the first thing to remark about this litany of difficulties is that two of them—determining which cases are genuine, and the possible inaccuracy of reports—present the scientist with no more difficulty than they present the **theologian.** Indeed it is ironic that the theistic literature on the subject has tended to rely heavily upon reports of isolated, often long-past experiences, whereas it is scientists who have acquainted themselves with these phenomena first-hand in the field. Perhaps theistic philosophers need to be reminded that the phenomena they seek are no further away than the next Sunday and the nearest Pentecostal church or Quaker meeting.

This last fact also belies the claim that mystical experiences are neither reliably reproducible nor controllable. Indeed Sargant observed that the degree of "excitement" (as he put it) in a Pentecostal church was controlled by the minister's hand-clapping rate. When his students, who had been invited with him to attend the service, "took over" the hand clapping, it was *they* who could control the action of the Holy Spirit upon members of the congregation (Sargant 1974, 183–4).

No doubt some theists will want to disqualify such controllable experiences as illusory, on the grounds that we know that the Holy Spirit would not allow its activity to be thus controlled. But to claim such knowledge on the basis of revelation would be to **beg the question** here, unless some independent basis for that conclusion (whether from revelation or not) could be shown to outweigh the *prima facie* evidence Pentecostals have to the contrary. After all, why shouldn't the Spirit be responsive to sincere individuals who make themselves receptive and available by means of such techniques? It certainly *seems* to Pentecostals that they have been touched by the Spirit. However, such considerations are in any case entirely beside the point. Theists are welcome to whatever criteria of genuineness they may wish to use; but since the present topic is not theistic explanations but scientific ones, it must be pointed out that—unless scientists were talking about some obviously different range of experiences entirely—there is no earthly reason why they should have to be bound by theistically imposed criteria or taxonomies.

In this connection drug-induced mystical experiences deserve mention. Wainwright (1981) provides an elaborate argument for discounting such hallucinogenic states, on the grounds that they fall outside his typology for genuine theophanies. But as far as I can see, mystical states produced by psychotropic chemicals, variable as they are, as a class show no more difference from spontaneous experiences than the differences the latter display among themselves. It is a familiar fact that many religious traditions incorporate the use of psychedelics into their mystical practices for just this reason.

However, Wainwright's main reason for excluding drug-induced experiences is that they are mostly **extroverted** (as he puts it) rather than **introverted:** that is, they involve the sensory appearances of what are presented as external objects, rather than the inward impressions to which Wainwright assigns the most exalted status in his typology of states.[2] In this estimation he is joined by a number of other philosophers, including Alston and Davis. The most explicit motive for this evaluation is that, since God has no body, the most **veridical** apprehensions of Him would not be ones that represent Him as an object of sensory or quasi-sensory perception. A less explicit motive (for W. T. Stace and Ninian Smart, but not for Wainwright) is that the most easily identified differences between mystical states are differences in sensory content. Thus, when attention is restricted to introverted states which (largely) lack such content, one can claim to find universal similarities which cut across cultures. And, on the other side, one can, by demoting extroverted experiences, relegate the ones of dramatically different content found in other cultures to peripheral **epistemic** status.

But this marginalization of extroverted experiences is as tendentious as the marginalization, noted earlier, of experiences which can be voluntarily brought on, controlled, or otherwise influenced by discipline of practice. For one thing, it would marginalize an enormous number of Christian mystical experiences, including many of those regarded most authoritative by the tradition (e.g., most of the Old Testament theophanies, Paul's conversion experience as recorded in Acts, Stephen's dying vision (Acts 7), and the entire book of Revelations). What is worse, a great many Christian theophanies have as their object Jesus, who, even in his risen condition, has a visible (if spiritual) body. Virtually all of Teresa's experiences were taken by her to establish a communion with Jesus. So Wainwright's point about psychedelic experiences carries no real weight.

But even if Wainwright were right, the striking similarities between mystical states and some psychedelic states invites a strong argument from analogy—*viz.* that mystical states, like psychedelic ones, are mediated by neurochemical processes, and that anything which can suitably influence those processes will produce the states in question.

Why then shouldn't a theist grant this but claim that, in veridical mystical perception, it is *God* who influences the neural substrates of perceptual consciousness? I shall return to this important question in a moment. But first, let's take stock of Alston's arguments that science cannot hope to capture the causes of mystical experiences. Since the real proof of this pudding is in the eating, it should be a sufficient refutation of the claim to have presented Lewis's theory, and to point out how rich and powerful it is. (Indeed, I shall go on to argue that it is much more powerful than any theory theists can hope to field.) But the main lesson to emphasize is simply that mystical phenomena are not nearly as inaccessible to scientific understanding as Alston supposes.

[2]Of the introverted states, only some are supposed to be theistic in content. Wainwright thinks the existence of drug-induced introverted theistic states has not been demonstrated.

Let's return now to the question whether a theistic explanation of mystical experience can't be tacked on to a scientific account. Both Wainwright and Alston find this an attractive possibility.[3] Naturally, how plausible the insertion of divine agency into the causal story is will depend upon the scientific theory into which it has to be grafted. Lewis's theory being presently at issue, it is in terms of it that I shall pose the question.

In approaching a question of this kind, it can be a salutary exercise to gain some distance from the home culture by posing it in an unfamiliar context. So take an imaginary trip to Belize, where the Black Carib practice a syncretistic blend of African and Indian religion, with an admixture of Christian idioms.[4] Black Carib women become possessed, in a manner by now familiar, with a variety of mischievous demonic spirits. Of these, the most ominous is the malignant belzing bug, which is apprehended by these women while in trance. Lewis's theory, coupled with one or another of the psychological mechanisms I have suggested, can account for these experiences. But now imagine a Black Carib woman protesting that Lewis's theory is all well and good—even convincing to her—but that, in any case, the belzing bug most certainly exists (she has seen it, after all!), and plays a crucial role in the production of her possession experiences. What shall we say to her? Skepticism about belzing bugs aside, won't we be entirely within our rights to demand an account of just how and where, in the context of Lewis's story, the bug exerts its demonic influence? If our Carib protester inserts the bug's operation at some point where the anthropological causal story is as yet incomplete (a bug-of-the-gaps ploy, as it were), we shall surely be justified in asking what independent evidence she has for the view that just *that* is the bug's *modus operandi.* And in any case, we shall want to point out that, in spite of its present incompleteness in places, Lewis's theory doesn't have any foreseeable *need* of the bug's machinations. Belzing bugs need not apply. *Nous n'avons besoin de cette hypothese,* we have no need of that hypothesis.

I also want to bring out a different point. It isn't just that theists would have to specify YHWH's mode of action within the context of a Lewisian story. They will have to decide also whether YHWH is to be held responsible only for those mystical experiences which are acknowledged to be experiences of Him, or whether He is equally responsible for Dinka experiences of the god Flesh, belzing bug possession, and the like.

Suppose a theist adopts the former view. What, then, explains the non-Yahwistic experiences? Is the world to be populated with all the gods, spirits, and demons required to plug the gaps in Lewis's story as it applies within these other cultures? Or is the field to be abandoned entirely to Lewis's theory in those cases? But if Lewis's causal factors can perform their explanatory task satisfactorily without supernatural assistance in the pagan cases, why does such assistance have to be invoked to help explain what happens to Christian mystics? Is it that Christian mystical experience is relevantly different? In exactly what way?

Consider, then, the alternative: the hand of YHWH is crucially at work in all mystical experiences. Some theists with ecumenical inclinations are tempted by this possibility,[5] focussing upon allegedly universal features in mystical experience. But that line becomes implausible when the real range of mystical experience comes into view. As Lewis shows, the similarities lie at the level of structure and context much more than at the level of content. Furthermore, it would do violence to Lewis's theory to impose upon it the typologies of these theists.

[3]It may be noted that Alston, who advocates a **direct realist theory of perception,** is loath to speak of God's presence as *explaining* a mystical perceptual experience. Yet Alston concedes that having the experience is distinct from God's action (and from the fact of God's being present), and that, just as a perceptual experience as of the Washington Monument wouldn't be a perceiving of the Monument unless the Monument played a suitable causal role in the production of the experience, so too a perception as of God wouldn't be a perception of God unless God played such a causal role. But then, God is the object of a perceptual experience only if God's presence (causally) explains the experience.

[4]The Black Caribs are the descendants of African slaves who escaped from Caribbean plantations and intermarried to a small degree with Island Carib Indians. They were rather unsuccessfully missionized by Christian churches.

[5][See Reading 8.2—Ed.]

But in any case, how is a theist to explain the strange transformations to which YHWH is subject when He travels to foreign cultures? Either it is YHWH's will that these deceptively distorted apprehensions of His divine nature occur in the Hindu, Zulu, and Black Carib, or else this is somehow the result of a defect on the part of these mystics.

The former is incompatible with the Christian commitment to divine goodness and honesty, so we must suppose the problem lies with the non-monotheistic mystics. Some Christians have been quite willing to embrace this conclusion. Calvin attributed the inability of heathens to apprehend God properly to their sinful, unredeemed wills. But it is hard to see how the pagan will could so effectively resist God's efforts, and harder still to understand why, given God's failure to make Himself properly understood in this way, He would not resort to a different method, or give up entirely (cp. Rom. 1:24–28). Better the pagan should have no mystical visions at all, than ones which lead him or her deeper into sin. Theological difficulties aside, it is virtually impossible to see how such claims as this could be made anthropologically respectable. What evidence could Calvin give, absent special pleading, that Teresa, but not the Dinka Master of the Fishing Spear, was a recipient of the grace which allowed her to apprehend correctly the divine nature? No such claim as that could be grafted into Lewis's theory, for it would destroy precisely the bases for the generalizations he has to offer concerning the relationship between social context and access to divinity.

I suggest therefore, that, at least in the case of Lewis's theory, "tacking on" is not a plausible maneuver for the theist to offer. It follows, then, that Lewis's theory provides a genuine competitor to the theist's view that Christian mystical experiences, at least, are more or less veridical apprehensions of God. . . .

THEISM OR NATURALISM: WHICH MAKES THE STRONGER CASE?

If that is correct, then we are in a position to frame and address the question whether the Lewis theory does better as an explanation of Christian mystical experience, and whether it is better supported by the data relevant to it, than is a theistic explanation. Let us for a moment suppose—I shall return to this issue in my concluding remarks—that Lewis's theory can explain Christian mysticism. What then?

In that case, Lewis's theory explains the data regarded by theists to be relevant, in the fashion I've described. But Lewis's theory goes much further: it illuminates connections between social conventions and Christian mystical claims, between social context and these claims, and between all of these and the behavior of mystics. How well does a theistic explanation fare on that score? Theists can certainly claim to provide an understanding of the connections between ecstasy and subsequent behavior (as well as inner transformation). But theism does not, so far as I can see, have the resources to supply similarly powerful insights into the **empirically** discovered correlations between ecstasy and social context and convention. Theists can argue that God (generally) chooses to appear to humans in a form that observes cultural conventions. But Lewis can give a much more nuanced explanation of why these conventions take the forms they do. Theists can claim, for example, that in certain societies God appears only to those seeking "big man" status; but why would God restrict Himself in that peculiar way? Furthermore, it is common wisdom among Christians that the greatest susceptibility to (adult) conversion occurs precisely at times of personal crisis, times when an individual is most likely to feel a strong or desperate need for the support of a community which affirms his or her individual worth and dignity. At such times, the welcoming arms of a congregation are a tremendously powerful invitation; but the price of admission, in some congregations, is the visible, public, and dramatic reception of an invasion of the Holy Spirit. If that is correct, then Lewis's theory has an advantage in terms of fertility and power.

However by far the most damaging consideration for theism is the problem posed by the competing claims to veridicality of the disparate mystical traditions. In the present context the difficulty is doubly damaging. Not only do the claims of the Black Carib, Zulu, and Dinka weaken the plausibility of orthodox Christian claims by opposing them, but these same claims *support* Lewis's theory. What is a massive problem for theists, in other words, is just so much more welcome data for Lewis. Because the relevant body of such data is enormous, there seems to be no prospect of theism gaining a comparable degree of confirmation, as an explanation of Christian mystical states.

PUBLIC AND PRIVATE MYSTICISM

But might there not be more private, personal, and sporadic instances of mystical experience which persist, as it were, below or barely at the threshold of social significance—in which case Lewis's theory, with its emphasis on dramatic forms of epiphany that attract public attention, will tell us little about them?

Some of the data from broader studies of mystical experience fit Lewis's account nicely. Stark and Glock (1968) report that a sizable percentage of religious individuals in the U. S. report having "religious experiences," the number varying with denomination. While their surveys did not measure any of the demographic and social variables relevant to testing Lewis's hypotheses, we may observe that high incidence appears to correlate with membership in those denominations (e.g. Southern Baptists and "sects") which appeal heavily to the socially marginal, and that low incidence (e.g. among Congregationalists) occurs among those less likely to be marginalized. Similarly, Starbuck (1912), upon whom William James relied heavily for examples in his classic study, *The Varieties of Religious Experience,* notes that religious conversion—which is often associated with mystical experiences—peaks sharply during adolescence; and he suggests that this may have something to do with the stress and emotional turmoil which commonly characterize that age in the U.S.. Lewis might here observe that U.S. teenagers, who are neither children nor adults, and who have to negotiate the transition from one to the other over several years with no clear rite of passage, are among the most socially marginalized of groups within American culture.

Nonetheless, the most puzzling data, from the Lewisian perspective, come from two surveys, one conducted in the U.S. and one in Britain. Summarizing some of the findings of the former, Greeley (1975) writes,

> If mystics came from socially oppressed groups, one would expect them to be disproportionately young, female, black, lower income. In fact, however, mystics are more likely to be over forty, male, college-educated, and making over $10,000 a year. They are, however, substantially more likely to be black and to be Protestant. (p. 59)

Hay and Morisy (1978) report similar results for Great Britain.

A major difficulty with both these surveys is that the questions used to probe respondents' religious experiences were vague and ambiguous; in fact, it has been shown that they are not diagnostic of the kind of religious ecstacy at issue here (see Fales 1996b). An even more serious problem is that both surveys did not consider at what age, how often, or how recently subjects had such experiences. They thus fail to measure the socioeconomic status of their respondents at the time of the experiences; and incautious use of these data can ignore the possibility that within marginalized communities (e.g., among blacks), ecstasy may reflect what Lewis calls central possession.

Still, the picture these surveys—and my own experience with mystics—provides of mystical experience in the U.S. and Britain suggests that the complexity of the situation in modern industrial societies may not be entirely accounted for by Lewis's approach: in the U.S., the more dramatic possession-traditions (e.g. Pentecostalism) certainly have their historical roots in marginalized subcultures, but have become increasingly mainstream; in Britain, the disdain for mysticism shown by many working-class people may reflect the influence of socialism.

Certainly, there is abundant evidence that the capacity for ecstatic experience is a natural human endowment, but one whose manifestations are highly sensitive to social and cultural forces. It may be that Lewis's account generalizes quite successfully to industrialized societies; but even if it does, it would not be surprising if there were sporadic occurrences of ecstasy which do not fit that picture: random effervescence, as it were, of the human potential for dissociative states. We can call mystics of this sort, the sort with which Lewis is concerned, *public* mystics. What, however, about *private* mystics—mystics who keep knowledge of their intensely personal mystical lives to themselves, or share them only with close friends? Can a naturalistic account accommodate mystical experiences that fall outside the purview of Lewis's approach?

Neuropsychological Explanations

We can see that such "rogue" experiences are quite compatible with Lewis's account by picking up the suggestion that a tendency toward ecstatic experience has neurophysiological underpinnings and is fairly randomly distributed through human populations. In social contexts that provide avenues for the deployment of ecstasy in negotiations for social goods, some of those gifted with a capacity for ecstasy will cultivate it for that purpose. . . . But a variety of factors, both social and personal, might lead the ecstasies of a mystically gifted individual to remain socially invisible. Such an individual will have a neurophysiological propensity for ecstasy; and when that propensity is triggered, the resulting experience may be heavily conditioned by cultural context, but it will not enter the social arena.

There is, in fact, a considerable body of research which has begun to uncover the neurophysiological underpinnings of mystical experience. In the 1950's, Wilder Penfield, a neurosurgeon, discovered, in the course of surgically treating epilepsy, that some patients would report vivid mystical experiences when certain areas of their brains were electrically stimulated. Subsequent work indicates that mystical experiences are initiated by microseizures in the temporal lobes of the brain, seizures less severe than those that produce epileptic convulsions. This work has even produced plausible hypotheses concerning how some of the specific phenomenological qualities of mystical experience—e.g., the profound sense of realism—are generated.[6] A significant proportion of the general (and otherwise normal) population is subject to such protoepileptic seizures; they can also be triggered, it seems, by certain sorts of trauma.[7]

It is probably significant that the locus of these seizures is the temporal lobes and the associated structures, the hippocampus and amygdala. It is known that this area of the brain integrates cognition and emotion, so it is not surprising that seizures there would be experienced in ways that could be conditioned by the subject's belief-system, and also have powerful affective components. It further appears that stimulus to this region imparts to the consequent experiences a powerful sense that what is experienced is real.

All this could, of course, provoke from the theist a retort that invokes the familiar **God-of-the-gaps** strategy: inducing protoepileptic seizures is just God's way of directly communicating with us. But that strategy will suffer from all the infirmities I have detailed concerning a similar theistic strategy for piggybacking on Lewis: for example, it will have difficulty explaining the protoepileptic seizures of polytheists and nontheists, and it is just otiose.

If we flesh out Lewis's analysis of how mysticism "works" in the social arena with the neuropsychological picture, we get the following synthesis. Mystical states are produced with a certain frequency in the general population by a variety of stimuli, which may operate perhaps in each case by provoking microseizures in the temporal lobes and to which

[6]See e.g. Penfield (1955), Persinger (1984) and (1993), and Munro and Persinger (1992).

[7]Another massive, but popularized treatment of the neurological basis of mystical experience is Austin (1998); see also the brief discussion and bibliography of Cardena et al. (2000). See Persinger and Makarec (1987) for the distribution of temporal lobe abnormalities in the general population. Susan Blackmore (1993) has argued that they account for near-death experiences, which share certain features with some mystical experiences.

some may be much more susceptible than others.[8] For some, mystical states have profound personal significance but remain essentially private. Others cultivate these states in contexts in which there is a social and ideological framework which permits the mystic who has such experiences, suitably interpreted and acted upon, to gain stature and authority. (Of course, we need not assume that everyone who is socially accepted as a mystic actually has such experiences.) It goes without saying that many of the details of this general picture—especially as concerns the neurophysiology of mysticism—remain to be supplied. But there is no reason to think those details can't be, or won't be, naturalistically filled in.

This approach reaps an additional benefit, since it can address the longstanding dispute between those who insist upon the culture-specificity of mystical experience, and those who focus upon features that appear to be universal or culture-neutral.[9] For the neurophysiological explanation is one that shows how the content of such experiences can be culturally conditioned, while also leading us to expect certain culture-neutral features dependent only upon brain physiology.

It can hardly be claimed that we have at present conclusive evidence for Lewis's theory (or any other naturalistic account of mystical experience). Yet it is worth remembering how far we have come. If we take David Hume's pioneering work, *The Natural History of Religion,* as inaugurating the scientific study of religion, we have a field that is only about 200 years old. It has grown by fits and starts. Serious empirical research into mystical experience is much more recent; little can be found that predates the last half-century. By contrast, theistic interpretations of such experiences can be traced back for two millennia or more. What have theists to offer in the way of a detailed (let alone testable) account of the etiology of mystical experiences? As the new kids on the block, the sciences can point already to a promising and impressive record of achievement.

Let me then draw some conclusions. First, Alston's claim that mystical experience is by its very nature not amenable to scientific explanation is borne out neither by the data nor by the record of what has been achieved. Alston's pessimism about what science can hope for here, and the suggestion he and Wainwright make that divine action can be spliced into a natural-causal account, both reflect the same strategy. I suggest that the prospects for such a strategy are unpromising.

Second, according to Alston, Davis, and other theists, the claim that (some) mystical experiences are veridical is better justified (or at least not less well justified) than naturalistic accounts on which they are unveridical. But these theists are mistaken. Theism cannot hope to match the explanatory power or empirical backing of Lewis's theory.

REFERENCES

Alston, William P. (1991). *Perceiving God: The Epistemology of Religious Experience.* Ithaca, NY: Cornell University Press.

Austin, James H. (1998). *Zen and the Brain: Toward an Understanding of Meditation and Consciousness.* Cambridge, MA: MIT Press.

Blackmore, Susan (1993). *Dying to Live: Near-Death Experiences.* Buffalo, NY: Prometheus Books.

Cardena, Etzel, Steven Jay Lynn, and Stanley Krippner, eds. (2000). *Varieties of Anomalous Experience: Examining the Scientific Evidence.* Washington, D.C.: The American Psychological Association.

Davis, Caroline Franks (1989). *The Evidential Force of Religious Experience.* Oxford, England: Clarendon Press.

Fales, Evan (1976). "Truth, Tradition, and Rationality," *Philosophy of the Social Science* 6, 97–113.

[8]Seizures may be "spontaneous," or they may be triggered by such well-known trance-inducing stimuli as meditation, the use of percussive sounds and dancing, or hallucinogens. Mystical states are also often associated with the onset of certain sorts of mental illness, and mystics are often people who have had "close encounters" with mental disturbance but who have regained some mental balance. It is however not entirely easy to assess when experiences described by subjects in mystical terms are associated with abnormal neural states, and when they are simply occurrences of intense religious feeling. It seems likely that those who are strongly religious, and have certain beliefs, expectations, and cultural background, may, from time to time and perhaps especially at moments of personal crisis, experience moments of heightened feeling which they understand to be epiphanies. But this capacity for intense, often introverted affective states, however interpreted, is by no means unique to the religious.

[9]See the dispute between Katz (1978, 1983) and Foreman (1990).

——— (1977). "The Ontological Status of Social Roles," *Philosophy of the Social Sciences* 7, 139–161.

——— (1996a). "Scientific Explanations of Mystical Experience, Part I: The Case of St Teresa," *Religious Studies* 32, 143–163.

——— (1996b). "Scientific Explanations of Mystical Experience, Part II: The Challenge to Theism," *Religious Studies* 32, 297–313.

Foreman, R. (1990). *The Problem of Pure Consciousness.* Oxford: Oxford University Press.

Greeley, Andrew M. (1975). *The Sociology of the Paranormal: A Reconnaissance.* Beverly Hills, CA: Sage Publications.

Hay, David and Ann Morisy (1978). "Reports of Ecstatic, Paranormal, or Religious Experience in Great Britain and the United States—a Comparison of Trends," *Journal for the Scientific Study of Religion* 17, 255–268.

Katz, Steven T. (1978). "Language, Epistemology, and Mysticism," in Steven Katz, ed., *Mysticism and Philosophical Analysis.* NY: Oxford University Press, 22–74.

Katz, Steven T. (1983). "The 'Conservative' Character of Mysticism," in Steven Katz, ed., *Mysticism and Religious Traditions.* Oxford: Oxford University Press, 3–60.

Lewis, I. M. (1989)[1971]. *Ecstatic Religion,* 2nd ed. London: Routledge.

Munro, Catherine and M. A. Persinger (1992). "Relative Right-Lobe Theta Activity Correlates with Vingiano's Hemispheric Quotient and 'Sensed Presence,'" *Perceptual and Motor Skills* 75:899–903.

Penfield, Wilder (1955). "The Role of the Temporal Cortex in Certain Psychical Phenomena," *The Journal of Mental Science* 101:451–465.

Persinger, M. A. (1984). "Propensity to Report Paranormal Experiences Is Correlated with Temporal Lobe Signs," *Perceptual and Motor Skills* 59:583–586.

——— (1993). "Paranormal and Religious Beliefs May Be Mediated Differentially by Subcortical and Cortical Phenomenological Processes of the Temporal (Limbic) Lobes," *Perceptual and Motor Skills* 76:247–251.

——— and K. Makarec (1987). "Temporal Lobe Epileptic Signs and Correlative Behaviours Displayed by Normal Populations," *Journal of General Psychology* 114:1179–1195.

Sargant, William (1974). *The Mind Possessed: A Physiology of Possession, Mysticism and Faith Healing.* Philadelphia: J. B. Lippincott.

Spanos, Nicholas P. (1989). "Hypnosis, Demonic Possession, and Multiple Personality," in Colleen A. Ward, ed., *Altered States of Consciousness and Mental Health: A Cross-cultural Perspective.* Newbury Park, CA: Sage Publications.

Spencer, Baldwin and F. J. Gillen (1899). *Native Tribes of Central Australia.* London: Macmillan & Co.

Starbuck, Edwin D. (1912). *The Psychology of Religion: An Empirical Study of the Growth of Religious Consciousness.* 3rd ed. NY: Charles Scribner's Sons.

Stark, Rodney and Charles Y. Glock (1968). *American Piety: The Nature of Religious Commitment.* Berkeley: University of California Press.

Wainwright, William J. (1981). *Mysticism: A Study of Its Nature, Cognitive Value and Moral Implications.* Madison, WI: The University of Wisconsin Press.

STUDY QUESTIONS

1. State Fales's main point in a sentence or two, and contrast it with the view he cites from Alston's writing.
2. What is Lewis's theory of mystical experience?
3. What gap in Lewis's theory does Fales try to fill? How does he do this? (There are several ways.)
4. What does Wainwright say about drug-induced mystical experiences? How does Fales criticize this approach?
5. According to Fales, how does the experience of the possessed Black Carib women undercut the theist?
6. What does Fales mean when he distinguishes the structure of mystical experience from its content?
7. How does the occurrence of private mystical experiences threaten Lewis's theory? What solution does Fales suggest?
8. *Do you find gaps in Fales's account of religious experience? If so, what are they?

FURTHER READING

All Arguments for God's Existence

Davis, Stephen. *God, Reason and Theistic Proofs.* Grand Rapids, MI: Erdmans, 1997.

Gale, Richard. *On the Existence and Nature of God.* Cambridge, England: Cambridge University Press, 1991.

Harrison, Jonathan. *God, Freedom, and Immortality.* Aldershot, England: Ashgate, 1999.

Hick, John. *Arguments for the Existence of God.* London: MacMillan, 1971.

Hick, John, ed. *The Existence of God.* London: MacMillan, 1964.

Martin, Michael. *Atheism: A Philosophical Justification.* New York: Temple University Press, 1990.

Swinburne, Richard. *The Existence of God.* Oxford, England: Clarendon Press, 1993.

Ontological Arguments

Barnes, Jonathan. *The Ontological Argument.* New York: St. Martin's Press, 1972.

Davis, Stephen T. "Anselm and Gaunilo on the Lost Island." *The Southern Journal of Philosophy* 13 (1975):435–48.

Findlay, J. N. "Can God's Existence Be Disproved?" *Mind* n. s. 57 (1948):176–83. Repr. in *New Essays in Philosophical Theology,* edited by Anthony Flew and Alasdair MacIntyre, pp. 47–56. New York: Macmillan, 1955.

Haight, David, and Marjorie Haight. "An Ontological Argument for the Devil." *The Monist* 54 (1970):218–20.

Hartshorne, Charles. *Anselm's Discovery: A Re-examination of the Ontological Proof of God's Existence.* LaSalle, IL: Open Court, 1965.

Oppy, Graham. *Ontological Arguments and Belief in God.* Cambridge, England and New York: Cambridge University Press, 1995.

Plantinga, Alvin. *God, Freedom and Evil.* New York: Harper & Row, 1974,

Plantinga, Alvin, ed. *The Ontological Argument: From St. Anselm to Contemporary Philosophers.* Garden City, NY: Anchor Books, 1965.

Rowe, William L. *Philosophy of Religion: An Introduction,* 2d ed. Belmont, CA: Wadsworth, 1993, 29–43.

Cosmological Arguments

Burrill, Donald, ed. *The Cosmological Arguments.* Garden City, NY: Doubleday, 1967.

Craig, William Lane. *The Kalam Cosmological Argument.* New York: Barnes & Noble, 1979.

Craig, William Lane. *The Cosmological Argument from Plato to Leibniz.* New York: Barnes & Noble, 1980.

Craig, William Lane, and Quentin Smith. *Theism, Atheism, and Big Bang Cosmology.* Oxford, England: Oxford University Press, 1993.

Rowe, William. *The Cosmological Argument.* Princeton, NJ: Princeton University Press, 1975.

Taylor, Richard. *Metaphysics,* 4th ed. Englewood Cliffs, NJ: Prentice-Hall, 1992. Chapter 11.

Design Arguments

Barrow, John D., and Frank Tipler. *The Anthropic Cosmological Principle.* Oxford, England: Clarendon Press, 1986.

Collins, Robin. "The Fine-Tuning Argument." In *Reason for the Hope Within,* edited by Michael Murray, 47–75. Grand Rapids, MI: Eerdsmans, 1998.

Leslie, John. *Universes.* London: Routledge, 1989.

Plantinga, Alvin. *God and Other Minds.* Ithaca, NY: Cornell University Press, 1967.

Schlesinger, George. *New Perspectives on Old-Time Religion.* Oxford, England: Clarendon Press, 1988. Chapter 5.

Mysticism and Arguments from Religious Experience

Alston, William P. *Perceiving God.* Ithaca, NY: Cornell University Press, 1991.

Bagger, Matthew C. *Religious Experience, Justification and History.* New York: Cambridge University Press, 1999.

Broad, C. D. *Religion, Philosophy and Psychical Research.* London: Routledge & Kegan Paul, 1930.

Gutting, Gary. *Religious Belief and Religious Skepticism.* Notre Dame, IN: Notre Dame University Press, 1982.

James, William. *Varieties of Religious Experience.* New York: Modern Library, 1902.

Katz, Steven T., ed. *Mysticism and Philosophical Analysis.* New York: Oxford University Press, 1978.

Katz, Steven T., ed. *Mysticism and Religious Traditions.* New York: Oxford University Press, 1983.

Martin, Charles B. *Religious Belief.* Ithaca, NY: Cornell University Press, 1959. Chapter 5.

Mavrodes, George. *Belief in God.* New York: Random House, 1970. Chapter 3.

Pojman, Louis. *Philosophy of Religion.* Mountain View, CA: Mayfield, 2001. Chapter 5.

Proudfoot, Wayne. *Religious Experience.* Berkeley: University of California Press, 1985.

Stace, William, ed. *The Teachings of the Mystics.* New York: American Library, 1960.

Wainwright, William. *Mysticism: A Study of Its Nature, Cognitive Value, and Moral Implications.* Madison: University of Wisconsin Press, 1981.

Yandell, Keith. *The Epistemology of Religious Experience.* Cambridge, England: Cambridge University Press, 1993.

"Cumulative Case" Arguments

Mitchell, Basil. *The Justification of Religious Belief.* New York: Seabury, 1973.

CHAPTER 5

Reasons to Disbelieve

Assessing the Case for Atheism

In this chapter, we will examine the case for atheism—that is, alleged reasons for believing that God does not exist. We will look at three parts of the atheist's arsenal: the existence of evil, the hiddenness of God, and psychological explanations of religious belief.

Stephen J. Wykstra writes that "many of us—believers as well as nonbelievers, car mechanics as well as philosophers—have at some times in our lives felt instances of suffering in the world to be evidence against theism" ("The Humean Obstacle to Evidential Arguments from Suffering: On Avoiding the Evils of 'Appearance'" *International Journal of the Philosophy of Religion* 16 [1984]: 73–93). The world is full of evils, both *moral* evils (evils caused by human actions, such as murders, acts of torture and oppression, thefts, and wars) and *physical,* or *natural,* evils (evils caused by natural forces, such as earthquakes, tornadoes, and diseases). Moral evils also include evil thoughts and desires; physical evils include, besides suffering and death, conditions such as mental incapacity and ignorance, which do not always bring about suffering. The catalogue of evils in the world is depressing and much celebrated by writers such as Voltaire and Dostoevsky. Moreover—and this is an important point in understanding the problem of evil—theistic traditions themselves acknowledge that there is at least ostensible evil in the world. Prophets such as Habakuk, as well as the Psalmist and the author of Job, all raise the problem of how God allows evil, implying thereby that in their view evil exists. Theists, then, do not deny evils; they face up to the question of why God allows them.

Despite its apparent force, articulating the problem of evil in a philosophically rigorous and convincing way is no simple matter. Philosophers generally agree that we should distinguish between two forms of the problem: logical and evidential. The **logical problem** maintains that there is a logical incompatibility, a contradiction, between the proposition *God exists* and the proposition *evil exists.* The **evidential problem,** by contrast, maintains only that, if evil exists, the existence of God is *improbable* or *unlikely* but not 100 percent ruled out.

Let us represent the alleged logical problem as an attempt to show that, if God were to exist, there would be no evil. The argument proceeds:

1. If God exists, He is (according to theists), an **omniscient, omnipotent,** and all-good being.
2. An omniscient, omnipotent, and all-good being would not allow any evil and would prevent all evils from occurring. (The idea here is that such a being can never plead ignorance of, or an inability to do anything about,

a bad situation; further, if God is all-good, God will want to remove the evil.)

3. Therefore, if God exists, there is no evil.
4. But there is evil.
5. Therefore, God does not exist.

The problem with this argument is that we cannot establish (2). For what if an omnipotent, omniscient, all-good being has a morally adequate justification for allowing evil? What if the evil results in a good that outweighs the evil (a "greater good"), and that is *logically necessary* for the good to be brought about? What if it is deserved by the person who endures it? We may not know what the greater good is, or why the evil is deserved, but the fact that we have not thought of a justification does not entail that there is none. And if an atheist asks, "Couldn't an omnipotent, omniscient being bring about the so-called greater good without allowing the evil?" the theist will call the atheist's attention to the words "and that is *logically necessary* for the good to be brought about." Some tasks are logically impossible, not merely **empirically** impossible; if an omnipotent being cannot perform those tasks, if the task is logically incoherent, that being is nonetheless omnipotent (see chapter 1 for more on this point). To take an example, suffering and other evils may be logically necessary for the development of sympathy and benevolence; danger, for the development of courage. Thus, some goods may be such that they are *logically* impossible to achieve without there being evil. And maybe the evils God allows are all either deserved or logically necessary for a greater good.[1] For this reason, (2) must be replaced by

2′. An omniscient, omnipotent, and all-good being would not allow any *unjustified* evil and would prevent all *unjustified* evils from occurring.

Theists grant (2′); however, from (1) and (2′), what follows is not

3. Therefore, there is no evil.

but, rather,

3′. Therefore, there is no unjustified evil.

And, once we make this change, the atheist needs to establish not

4. There is evil,

which the theist agrees to, but, rather,

4′. There is unjustified evil.

And why should a theist have to admit to (4′)? Surely (4′), unlike (4), is not a claim to which theism is committed. Nor is it necessarily true.

Thus, the logical problem evaporates. And it evaporates without the theist's having to propose a **theodicy**—that is, an explanation of why God allows evil.[2]

Thanks to work done in the 1960s by Nelson Pike and Alvin Plantinga, philosophers have achieved some consensus that the charge of logical incompatibility fails for the reason sketched in the

[1]The following emendation is called for, however. Consider the claim that sympathy is a greater good that logically entails the existence of suffering. This isn't so, one could object, because God could mislead people into believing that suffering is occurring without the suffering actually occurring; in that case, people could respond with sympathy. If so, the greater good will be attained without the suffering. To this a theist would respond that such a world would have an evil of its own—namely, massive error—and the evilness of massive error would outweigh the good of sympathy. Thus, the development of a greater good (viz., sympathy) logically requires an evil—either suffering or massive error. In addition, in such a world people could not be genuinely *benevolent,* because their efforts to remove evil won't be removing an evil. Thus, the good of benevolence is eliminated. Note that the sympathy case is just an *example* of how a greater good may logically require an evil. At this point, the theist does not have to specify what the greater good is and what evils it requires; he or she needs only to point to the *possibility* that the evil is needed for the good.

[2]For simplicity's sake, I have not presented the refutation of the charge of logical contradiction in its most rigorous form. In that rigorous form, the key technical point is that, in order to show that *God exists* and *evil exists* are contradictory, we require some further statement or statement that is a *necessary truth.* Thus, to show that (1) and (4) are contradictory, (2) must be a necessary truth. But (2) is not a necessary truth; and, when we replace (2) with (2′), we lose (4). See William L. Rowe, *Philosophy of Religion: An Introduction,* Belmont, CA (Wadsworth, 2d ed. 1993), 73–79. Also, notice that if (2) were a statement accepted by theists, but not a necessary truth, then theists would be stuck with an inconsistent triad of statements. But (2) is not accepted by theists.

preceding paragraphs.[3] Nevertheless, the evidential form of the argument from evil escapes this weakness, for it asserts only that it is likely (highly probable) that there is unjustified evil. Once the charge is improbability, as opposed to logical incompatibility, the theist cannot simply refuse to concede that there is unjustified evil by saying that it is *possible* that every seemingly unjustified evil has a justification that no human has thought of. Rather, the theist can turn back the charge of improbability only by suggesting justifications for the existence of evil that are (at the least) plausible. Many philosophers would add that, since the atheist has the burden of proof here, it suffices for theists to suggest a justification that the atheist cannot show to be improbable. In this view, the theist need not show that the justification is probable, only that it is not *im*probable. A "tie" goes to the theist.

In the first selection in this chapter, William L. Rowe elaborates on the evidential argument. If we consider the suffering of a fawn burned in a forest fire and now in agony, it does not appear that there is a justification for this state of affairs. Rowe believes this case renders the existence of God unlikely. Nevertheless, for reasons you will see, he grants that an atheist may find theism rational even while the atheist rejects theism.

William P. Alston replies to Rowe by considering a number of theodicies and arguing that we lack enough knowledge to reject any of them. The selection by Alston serves a dual purpose in this chapter: it summarizes various theodicies, and it replies to the evidential form of the problem of evil. Next, Eleonore Stump provides an interesting account of how seeing horrendous evils may ultimately enable a person to perceive goodness and feel God's presence. Richard Swinburne discusses a specific ostensible evil described by theistic traditions—the exclusion of nonbelievers or at least of those individuals who do not inquire honestly into religious belief. He offers a rationale for God's limiting who goes to heaven, while rejecting the thesis that God might subject evildoers to eternal torment in hell.

Does the amount of evil in the world affect the strength of the theist's case? As a start, notice that, if the logical problem of evil is compelling, the existence of even one instance of evil is enough to establish the claimed incompatibility. If the suffering of one innocent child is incompatible with God's existence, reference to the suffering of millions of innocent people will not generate a new argument. However, if we shift our attention to what is likely or unlikely, atheists might argue that, the greater the quantity of evil, the more unlikely it is that *all* the evil is justified evil. This is not to say that we have a firm idea of how much evil is too much.

The second challenge to theism arises from divine hiddenness. If God is all-powerful, all-knowing, and all good, why would God not make God's existence known to all people? Why does God not provide evidence that will convince everyone of God's existence—for example, by a massive revelation? As this formulation suggests, it is useful to think of divine hiddenness as an aspect of the problem of evil: the specific evil in question is atheism, the failure of people to believe in God. Michael J. Murray's essay develops a response to this challenge based on the idea that, if God were to make His existence manifest, human beings would lose their free will. This explanation of divine hiddenness fits well with theodicies that explain God's allowing evil in terms of God's wishing to preserve human free will.

The final challenge put forth by the atheist is that religious belief can be explained in terms of purely psychological causes—causes that, once known, cast the truth of the belief into doubt. In the seventeenth century, Benedict Spinoza claimed that religious belief arises from people's ignorance of the real causes of things; in the eighteenth century, Ludwig Feuerbach said that God is just a projection of desirable human qualities (an ancient writer, Xenophanes, advances something somewhat like this idea). A century later, Sigmund Freud offered the most celebrated of all psychological accounts of religion's origins. Religion arises, Freud said, from the human need for a father figure. People need to feel

[3]See, e.g., Pike, "Hume on Evil," The *Philosophical Review* 72 (1963):180–197; Plantinga, *God and Other Minds* (Ithaca, NY: Cornell University Press, 1967).

protection from and a sense of control over the terrifying forces of nature. In addition, they need to be reconciled to the sacrifices, the curbing of instinct, that civilization demands of them. Religious belief is a form of wishful thinking, then. Other thinkers not represented in this chapter likewise sought to explain religious belief in psychological terms—Karl Marx (1818–83) taught that religion is the opiate of the masses, the longing of oppressed people, and Emile Durkheim (1858–1917), a sociologist, suggests that the real object of religious worship is society.

It may seem at first that theists must refute every one of these theories in order for their belief in God to be rational. But William L. Rowe gives us reason to maintain that this is not so. In general, it is a fallacy—known as the **genetic fallacy**—to reason that, since one's belief that *p* was formed in a certain way that does not involve the truth of *p,* it is therefore false. The fallacy is still a fallacy even if everyone who believes that *p* formed this belief in a way that does not involve the truth of *p*. The success of a Freudian or any other account of religious belief does not mean it is *false* that God exists; nor does it mean, Rowe argues, that no *good* reasons can be given for such a belief.

THE VARIETIES OF EVIL

READING 5.1

The Problem of Evil and Some Varieties of Atheism

William L. Rowe

William L. Rowe (Purdue University) does three things in this article. He provides an argument against theism based on the existence of evil; he suggests how a theist could defend the rationality of theistic belief in the face of this argument; finally, he suggests how an atheist could view this theistic defense.

In terms developed in this chapter's introduction, Rowe's argument from evil can be described as **inductive** *or* **evidential,** *rather than as* **deductive** *or* **logical.** *He focuses on a case of a fawn burned by lightning, which suffers horrible agony for days before dying. If this case were an instance of unjustified suffering—suffering that is not needed to bring about a greater good or to prevent an equally bad or worse evil—then an* **omniscient, omnipotent,** *and wholly good being would not allow it; hence, if such an evil exists, God does not. Rowe concedes that it cannot be* proved *that this is a case of unjustified evil, since there always may be some justification that we have not thought of. Nevertheless, he insists, it is* rational *to believe that it is not justified and, hence, rational to believe that God does not exist.*

A theist could meet this challenge by using the **"G. E. Moore shift"** *(the origin of the term is described in the article). Whereas the atheist argues,* "Unjustified evil exists, therefore God does not," *the theist argues,* "God exists [presumably the theist has grounds for this belief]; therefore, it is not the case that there are unjustified evils." *Both arguments are* **valid**—*that is, their conclusion follows from their premise. Hence, if an atheist concedes that the theist has rational grounds for believing in God, then, even though the atheist regards that belief as false, the atheist should be "friendly" and admit that the theist's belief is rational. This position is called friendly atheism.*

This paper is concerned with three interrelated questions. The first is: Is there an **argument** for atheism based on the existence of evil that may rationally justify someone in being an atheist? To this first question I give an affirmative answer and try to support that answer by setting forth a strong argument for atheism based on the existence of evil.[1] The second question is: How can the theist best defend his position against the argument for atheism based on the existence of evil? In response to this question I try to describe what may be an adequate rational defense for theism against any argument for atheism based on the existence of evil. The final question is: What position should the informed atheist take concerning the rationality of theistic belief? Three different answers an atheist may give to this question serve to distinguish three varieties of

[1]Some philosophers have contended that the existence of evil is *logically inconsistent* with the existence of the theistic God. No one, I think, has succeeded in establishing such an extravagant claim. Indeed, granted **incompatibilism,** there is a fairly compelling argument for the view that the existence of evil is logically consistent with the existence of the theistic God. (For a lucid statement of this argument see Alvin Plantinga, *God, Freedom, and Evil* [New York: Harper & Row, 1974], pp. 29–59.) There remains, however, what we may call the *evidential* form—as opposed to the *logical* form—of the problem of evil: the view that the variety and profusion of evil in our world, although perhaps not logically inconsistent with the existence of the theistic God, provides, nevertheless, *rational support* for atheism. In this paper I shall be concerned solely with the evidential form of the problem, the form of the problem which, I think, presents a rather severe difficulty for theism.

familiar good outweighing the fawn's suffering to which that suffering is connected in a way we do not see. Furthermore, there may well be unfamiliar goods, goods we haven't dreamed of, to which the fawn's suffering is inextricably connected. Indeed, it would seem to require something like omniscience on our part before we could lay claim to *knowing* that there is no greater good connected to the fawn's suffering in such a manner that an omnipotent, omniscient being could not have achieved that good without permitting that suffering or some evil equally bad or worse. So the case of the fawn's suffering surely does not enable us to *establish* the truth of (1).

The truth is that we are not in a position to prove that (1) is true. We cannot know with certainty that instances of suffering of the sort described in (1) do occur in our world. But it is one thing to *know* or *prove* that (1) is true and quite another thing to have *rational grounds* for believing (1) to be true. We are often in the position where in the light of our experience and knowledge it is rational to believe that a certain statement is true, even though we are not in a position to prove or to know with certainty that the statement is true. In the light of our past experience and knowledge it is, for example, very reasonable [in 1979] to believe that neither Goldwater nor McGovern will ever be elected President, but we are scarcely in the position of knowing with certainty that neither will ever be elected President. So, too, with (1), although we cannot know with certainty that it is true, it perhaps can be rationally supported, shown to be a rational belief.

Consider again the case of the fawn's suffering. Is it reasonable to believe that there is some greater good so intimately connected to that suffering that even an omnipotent, omniscient being could not have obtained that good without permitting that suffering or some evil at least as bad? It certainly does not appear reasonable to believe this. Nor does it seem reasonable to believe that there is some evil at least as bad as the fawn's suffering such that an omnipotent being simply could not have prevented it without permitting the fawn's suffering. But even if it should somehow be reasonable to believe either of these things of the fawn's suffering, we must then ask whether it is reasonable to believe either of these things of *all* the instances of seemingly pointless human and animal suffering that occur daily in our world. And surely the answer to this more general question must be no. It seems quite unlikely that *all* the instances of intense suffering occurring daily in our world are intimately related to the occurrence of greater goods or the prevention of evils at least as bad; and even more unlikely, should they somehow all be so related, that an omnipotent, omniscient being could not have achieved at least some of those goods (or prevented some of those evils) without permitting the instances of intense suffering that are supposedly related to them. In the light of our experience and knowledge of the variety and scale of human and animal suffering in our world, the idea that none of this suffering could have been prevented by an omnipotent being without thereby losing a greater good or permitting an evil at least as bad seems an extraordinarily absurd idea, quite beyond our belief. It seems, then, that although we cannot *prove* that (1) is true, it is, nevertheless, altogether *reasonable* to believe that (1) is true, that (1) is a *rational* belief.[5]

[5]One might object that the conclusion of this paragraph is stronger than the reasons given warrant. For it is one thing to argue that it is unreasonable to think that (1) is false and another thing to conclude that we are therefore justified in accepting (1) as true. There are propositions such that believing them is much more reasonable than disbelieving them, and yet are such that *withholding judgment* about them is more reasonable than believing them. To take an example of [Roderick] Chisholm's: it is more reasonable to believe that the Pope will be in Rome (on some arbitrarily picked future date) than to believe that he won't; but it is perhaps more reasonable to suspend judgment on the question of the Pope's whereabouts on that particular date, than to believe that he will be in Rome. Thus, it might be objected that, while we've shown that believing (1) is more reasonable than disbelieving (1), we haven't shown that believing (1) is more reasonable than withholding belief. My answer to this objection is that there are things we know which render (1) probable to the degree that it is more reasonable to believe (1) than to suspend judgment on (1). What are these things we know? First, I think, is the fact that there is an enormous variety and profusion of intense human and animal suffering in our world. Second is the fact that much of this suffering seems quite unrelated to any greater goods (or the absence of equal or greater evils) that might justify it. And, finally, there is the fact that such suffering as is related to greater goods (or the absence of equal or greater evils) does not, in many cases, seem so intimately related as to require its permission by an omnipotent being bent on securing those goods (the absence of those evils). These facts, I am claiming, make it more reasonable to accept (1) than to withhold judgment on (1).

Returning now to our argument for atheism, we've seen that the second premise expresses a basic belief common to many theists and nontheists. We've also seen that our experience and knowledge of the variety and profusion of suffering in our world provides *rational support* for the first premise. Seeing that the conclusion "There does not exist an omnipotent, omniscient, wholly good being" follows from these two premises, it does seem that we have *rational support* for atheism, that it is reasonable for us to believe that the theistic God does not exist.

II

Can theism be rationally defended against the argument for atheism we have just examined? If it can, how might the theist best respond to that argument? Since the argument from (1) and (2) to (3) is valid, and since the theist, no less than the nontheist, is more than likely committed to (2), it's clear that the theist can reject this atheistic argument only by rejecting its first premise, the premise that states that there are instances of intense suffering which an omnipotent, omniscient being could have prevented without thereby losing some greater good or permitting some evil equally bad or worse. How, then, can the theist best respond to this premise and the considerations advanced in its support?

There are basically three responses a theist can make. First, he might argue not that (1) is false or probably false, but only that the reasoning given in support of it is in some way *defective.* He may do this either by arguing that the reasons given in support of (1) are *in themselves* insufficient to justify accepting (1), or by arguing that there are other things we know which, when taken in conjunction with these reasons, do not justify us in accepting (1). I suppose some theists would be content with this rather modest response to the basic argument for atheism. But given the validity of the basic argument and the theist's likely acceptance of (2), he is thereby committed to the view that (1) is false, not just that we have no good reasons for accepting (1) as true. The second two responses are aimed at showing that it is reasonable to believe that (1) is false. Since the theist is committed to this view I shall focus the discussion on these two attempts, attempts which we can distinguish as "the direct attack" and "the indirect attack."

By a direct attack, I mean an attempt to reject (1) by pointing out goods, for example, to which suffering may well be connected, goods which an omnipotent, omniscient being could not achieve without permitting suffering. It is doubtful, however, that the direct attack can succeed. The theist may point out that some suffering leads to moral and spiritual development impossible without suffering. But it's reasonably clear that suffering often occurs in a degree far beyond what is required for character development. The theist may say that some suffering results from free choices of human beings and might be preventable only by preventing some measure of human freedom. But, again, it's clear that much intense suffering occurs not as a result of human free choices. The general difficulty with this direct attack on premise (1) is twofold. First, it cannot succeed, for the theist does not know what greater goods might be served, or evils prevented, by each instance of intense human or animal suffering. Second, the theist's own religious tradition usually maintains that in this life it is not given to us to know God's purpose in allowing particular instances of suffering. Hence, the direct attack against premise (1) cannot succeed and violates basic beliefs associated with theism.

The best procedure for the theist to follow in rejecting premise (1) is the indirect procedure. This procedure I shall call "the **G. E. Moore shift,**" so-called in honor of the twentieth century philosopher, G. E. Moore, who used it to great effect in dealing with the arguments of the **skeptics.** Skeptical philosophers such as David Hume have advanced ingenious arguments to prove that no one can know of the existence of any material object. The premises of their arguments employ plausible principles, principles which many philosophers have tried to reject directly, but only with questionable success. Moore's procedure was altogether different. Instead of arguing directly against the premises of the skeptic's arguments, he simply noted that the premises implied, for example, that he (Moore) did not know of the existence of a pencil. Moore then proceeded indirectly against the skeptic's premises by arguing:

If the skeptic's principles are correct I cannot know of the existence of this pencil.

∴ The skeptic's principles (at least one) must be incorrect.

Moore then noted that his argument is just as **valid** as the skeptic's, that both of their arguments contain the premise "If the skeptic's principles are correct Moore cannot know of the existence of this pencil," and concluded that the only way to choose between the two arguments (Moore's and the skeptic's) is by deciding which of the first premises it is more rational to believe—Moore's premise "I do know that this pencil exists" or the skeptic's premise asserting that his skeptical principles are correct. Moore concluded that his own first premise was the more rational of the two.[6]

Before we see how the theist may apply the G. E. Moore shift to the basic argument for atheism, we should note the general strategy of the shift. We're given an argument: *p, q,* therefore, *r.* Instead of arguing directly against *p,* another argument is constructed—not-*r; q,* therefore, not-*p*—which begins with the denial of the conclusion of the first argument, keeps its second premise, and ends with the denial of the first premise as its conclusion. Compare, for example, these two:

I.	II.
p	not-*r*
q	*q*
r	not-*p*

It is a truth of logic that if I is valid II must be valid as well. Since the arguments are the same so far as the second premise is concerned, any choice between them must concern their respective first premises. To argue against the first premise *(p)* by constructing the counter argument II is to employ the G. E. Moore shift.

Applying the G. E. Moore shift against the first premise of the basic argument for atheism, the theist can argue as follows:

Not-3. There exists an omnipotent, omniscient, wholly good being.

2. An omniscient, wholly good being would prevent the occurrence of any intense suffering it could, unless it could not do so without thereby losing some greater good or permitting some evil equally bad or worse.

Therefore,

not-1. It is not the case that there exist instances of intense suffering which an omnipotent, omniscient being could have prevented without thereby losing some greater good or permitting some evil equally bad or worse.

We now have two arguments: the basic argument for atheism from (1) and (2) to (3), and the theist's best response, the argument from (not-3) and (2) to (not-1). What the theist then says about (1) is that he has rational grounds for believing in the existence of the theistic God (not-3), accepts (2) as true, and sees that (not-1) follows from (not-3) and (2). He concludes, therefore, that he has rational grounds for rejecting (1). Having rational grounds for rejecting (1), the theist concludes that the basic argument for atheism is mistaken.

III

We've had a look at a forceful argument for atheism and what seems to be the theist's best response to that argument. If one is persuaded by the argument for atheism, as I find myself to be, how might one best view the position of the theist? Of course, he will view the theist as having a false belief, just as the theist will view the atheist as having a false belief. But what position should the atheist take concerning the *rationality* of the theist's belief? There are three major positions an atheist might take, positions which we may think of as some varieties of atheism. First, the atheist may believe that no one is rationally justified in believing that the theistic God exists. Let us call this position "unfriendly atheism." Second, the atheist may hold no belief concerning whether any theist is or isn't rationally justified in believing that the theistic God exists. Let us call this

[6]See, for example, the two chapters on Hume in G. E. Moore, *Some Main Problems of Philosophy* (London: Allen & Unwin, 1953).

view "indifferent atheism." Finally, the atheist may believe that some theists are rationally justified in believing that the theistic God exists. This view we shall call "friendly atheism." In this final part of the paper I propose to discuss and defend the position of friendly atheism.

If no one can be rationally justified in believing a false proposition, then friendly atheism is a paradoxical, if not incoherent, position. But surely the truth of a belief is not a necessary condition of someone's being rationally justified in having that belief. So in holding that someone is rationally justified in believing that the theistic God exists, the friendly atheist is not committed to thinking that the theist has a true belief. What he is committed to is that the theist has rational grounds for his belief, a belief the atheist rejects and is convinced he is rationally justified in rejecting. But is this possible? Can someone, like our friendly atheist, hold a belief, be convinced that he is rationally justified in holding that belief, and yet believe that someone else is equally justified in believing the opposite? Surely this is possible. Suppose your friends see you off on a flight to Hawaii. Hours after take-off they learn that your plane has gone down at sea. After a twenty-four hour search, no survivors have been found. Under these circumstances they are rationally justified in believing that you have perished. But it is hardly rational for you to believe this, as you bob up and down in your life vest, wondering why the search planes have failed to spot you. Indeed, to amuse yourself while awaiting your fate, you might very well reflect on the fact that your friends are rationally justified in believing that you are now dead, a proposition you disbelieve and are rationally justified in disbelieving. So, too, perhaps an atheist may be rationally justified in his atheistic belief and yet hold that some theists are rationally justified in believing just the opposite of what he believes.

What sort of grounds might a theist have for believing that God exists? Well, he might endeavor to justify his belief by appealing to one or more of the traditional arguments: **Ontological, Cosmological, Teleological [Design],** Moral, etc.[7] Second, he might appeal to certain aspects of religious experience, perhaps even his own religious experience. Third, he might try to justify theism as a plausible theory in terms of which we can account for a variety of phenomena. Although an atheist must hold that the theistic God does not exist, can he not also believe, and be justified in so believing, that some of these "justifications of theism" do actually rationally justify some theists in their belief that there exists a supremely good, omnipotent, omniscient being? It seems to me that he can.

If we think of the long history of theistic belief and the special situations in which people are sometimes placed, it is perhaps as absurd to think that no one was ever rationally justified in believing that the theistic God exists as it is to think that no one was ever justified in believing that a human being would never walk on the moon. But in suggesting that friendly atheism is preferable to unfriendly atheism, I don't mean to rest the case on what some human beings might reasonably have believed in the eleventh or thirteenth century. The more interesting question is whether some people in modern society, people who are aware of the usual grounds for belief and disbelief and are acquainted to some degree with modern science, are yet rationally justified in accepting theism. Friendly atheism is a significant position only if it answers this question in the affirmative.

It is not difficult for an atheist to be friendly when he has reason to believe that the theist could not reasonably be expected to be acquainted with the grounds for disbelief that he (the atheist) possesses. For then the atheist may take the view that some theists are rationally justified in holding to theism, but

[7]Suppose that I add a long sum of numbers three times and get result *x*. I inform you of this so that you have pretty much the same evidence I have for the claim that the sum of the numbers is *x*. You then use your calculator twice over and arrive at result *y*. You, then, are justified in believing that the sum of the numbers is *not x*. However, knowing that your calculator has been damaged and is therefore unreliable, and that you have no reason to think that it is damaged, *I* may reasonably believe not only that the sum of the numbers is *x*, but also that you are justified in believing that the sum is not *x*. Here is a case, then, where you have all of my evidence for *p*, and yet I can reasonably believe that you are justified in believing not-*p*—for I have reason to believe that your grounds for not-*p* are not as telling as you are justified in taking them to be.

would not be so were they to be acquainted with the grounds for disbelief—those grounds being sufficient to tip the scale in favor of atheism when balanced against the reasons the theist has in support of his belief.

Friendly atheism becomes paradoxical, however, when the atheist contemplates believing that the theist has all the grounds for atheism that he, the atheist, has, and yet is rationally justified in maintaining his theistic belief. But even so excessively friendly a view as this perhaps can be held by the atheist if he also has some reason to think that the grounds for theism are not as telling as the theist is justified in taking them to be.[8]

In this paper I've presented what I take to be a strong argument for atheism, pointed out what I think is the theist's best response to that argument, distinguished three positions an atheist might take concerning the rationality of theistic belief, and made some remarks in defense of the position called "friendly atheism." I'm aware that the central points of the paper are not likely to be warmly received by many philosophers. Philosophers who are atheists tend to be tough minded—holding that there are no good reasons for supposing that theism is true. And theists tend either to reject the view that the existence of evil provides rational grounds for atheism or to hold that religious belief has nothing to do with reason and evidence at all. But such is the way of philosophy.

STUDY QUESTIONS

1. Explain the argument Rowe gives for atheism.
2. Explain why Rowe does not think the argument in question 1 *proves* that atheism is true. What does the argument achieve, according to him?
3. What is the G. E. Moore shift in its original context? How does Rowe seek to apply it to the problem of evil?
4. Rowe distinguishes among unfriendly, indifferent, and friendly atheism. Explain these categories.
5. *Do you find friendly atheism tenable? Why or why not?
6. *Rowe says that the friendly atheist regards the theist's belief as rational. Is Rowe's sense of "rational" too weak to make *significant* the atheist's concession that the theist is rational?
7. *In what way is the suffering of an animal more difficult to explain than the suffering of a human being? (You will be in a better position to answer this question after you have read William P. Alston's article in this chapter, but you may be able now to think of some theodicies that would not explain the fawn's suffering in Rowe's example.)

[8][See chapter 4—Ed.]

READING 5.2

The Inductive Argument from Evil and the Human Cognitive Condition

William P. Alston

William P. Alston's essay seeks to provide a reply to Rowe's argument in Reading 5.1. In the process, it offers a useful survey of **theodicies.** *The theodicies that Alston (Syracuse University) considers are (1) suffering is punishment for sin; (2) suffering is necessary for "soul making," since it allows, and is logically necessary for, the development of traits such as patience, courage, and compassion; (3) suffering educates onlookers; (4) suffering is a consequence of free will; and (5) suffering* *results from the operation of a lawful natural order. Alston's main contention is that our* ***cognitive*** *powers are too limited to allow us to claim that, in specific cases that may trouble us, God would not allow suffering for any of the reasons proposed. Even if these theodicies do not explain the suffering in all cases, we cannot ever be sure that, in the troublesome cases, we have exhausted all possibilities. (It bears repeating that these theodicies claim that evil is logically necessary for the greater good achieved, so that even an* ***omnipotent*** *God cannot bring about the greater good without allowing the evil.)*

I

The recent outpouring of literature on the problem of evil has materially advanced the subject in several ways. In particular, a clear distinction has been made between the "logical" *argument against the existence of God* ("atheological argument") from evil, which attempts to show that evil is logically incompatible with the existence of God, and the "**inductive**" ("**empirical,**" "**probabilistic**") **argument,** which contents itself with the claim that evil constitutes (sufficient) empirical evidence against the existence of God. It is now acknowledged on (almost) all sides that the logical argument is bankrupt,[1] but the inductive argument is still very much alive and kicking.

In this paper I will be concerned with the **inductive argument.** More specifically, I shall be contributing to a certain criticism of that argument, one based on a low estimate of human **cognitive** capacities in a certain application. To indicate the point at which this criticism engages the argument, I shall use one of the most careful and perspicuous formulations of the argument in a recent essay by William Rowe.

1. There exist instances of intense suffering which an **omnipotent, omniscient** being could have prevented without thereby losing some greater good or permitting some evil equally bad or worse.
2. An omniscient, wholly good being would prevent the occurrence of any intense suffering it could, unless it could not do so without thereby losing some greater good or permitting some evil equally bad or worse.
3. There does not exist an omnipotent, omniscient, wholly good being.[2]

Let's use the term 'gratuitous suffering' for any case of intense suffering, E, that satisfies premise 1, that is, which is such that an omnipotent, omniscient being could have prevented it without thereby losing some greater good or permitting some evil equally bad or worse. . . . I will oscillate freely between speaking of a particular case of suffering, E, being gratuitous, and speaking of the impossibility of God's having a sufficient reason for permitting E. I shall call a proponent of an inductive argument from evil the "critic."

The criticism I shall be supporting attacks the claim that we are rationally justified in accepting 1, and it does so on the grounds that our **epistemic** situation is such that we are unable to make a sufficiently well grounded determination that 1 is the case. I will call this, *faute de mieux* [for want of anything better], the **agnostic** thesis, or simply *agnosticism.* The criticism claims that the magnitude or complexity of the question is such that our powers, access to data, and so on are radically insufficient to provide sufficient warrant for accepting 1. And if that is so, the inductive argument collapses.

How might one be justified in accepting 1? The obvious way to support an existential statement is to establish one or more **instantiations** and then use **existential generalization.** This is Rowe's tack, and I don't see any real alternative. Thus Rowe considers one or another case of suffering and argues, in the case of each, that it instantiates 1. I will follow him in this approach. Thus to argue that we cannot

[1][See the chapter introduction—Ed.]

[2][See reading 5.1—Ed.]

be justified in asserting 1, I shall argue that we cannot be justified in asserting any of its instantiations, each of which is of the form

> 1A. E is such that an omnipotent, omniscient being could have prevented it without thereby losing some greater good or permitting some evil equally bad or worse.

In the sequel when I speak of being or not being justified in accepting 1, it must be remembered that this is taken to hang on whether one is, or can be justified, in accepting propositions of the form 1A. . . .

II

. . . As already noted, Rowe does not argue for 1 by staying on its level of unspecificity; rather he takes particular examples of suffering and argues in the case of each that it is gratuitous; from there it is a short step of existential generalization to 1. In (1979 [reading 5.1]) and subsequent papers Rowe focuses on the case of a fawn trapped in a forest fire and undergoing several days of terrible agony before dying (hereinafter 'Bambi'). In (1988) he adds to this a (real life) case introduced by Bruce Russell (1989), a case of the rape, beating, and murder by strangulation of a 5-year-old girl ('Sue') by her mother's boyfriend. Since I am specifically interested in criticizing Rowe's argument I will argue that we are not justified, and cannot be justified, in judging these evils to be gratuitous. It will turn out that some of my discussion pertains not to Rowe's cases but to others. . . .

. . . Rowe obviously supposes, as premise 2 makes explicit, that cases of "gratuitous" evil count decisively against the existence of God. That is, he takes it that an omnipotent, omniscient, and perfectly good God would not permit any gratuitous evil; perhaps he regards this as conceptually or metaphysically necessary. Thus he holds that God could have no other reason for permitting suffering except that preventing it would involve losing some greater good or permitting some equally bad or worse evil. But this is highly controversial. It looks as if there are possible divine reasons for permitting evil that would be ruled out by (2). (i) Suppose that God could bring about a greater good only by permitting any one of several equally bad cases of suffering. Then no one is such that by preventing it He would lose that greater good. And if we stipulate that God has a free choice as to whether to permit any of these **disjuncts,** it is not the case that to prevent it would be to permit something equally bad or worse; that might or might not ensue, depending on God's choice. But if we are to allow that being necessary for a greater good can justify permission of evil, it looks as if we will have to allow this case as well. (ii) More importantly, human free will complicates God's strategies for carrying out His purposes. As we will be noting later in the paper, if God has a policy of respecting human free will, He cannot guarantee human responses to His initiatives where those responses would be freely made if at all. Hence if God visits suffering on us in an attempt to turn us from our sinful ways, and a particular recipient doesn't make the desired response, God could have prevented that suffering without losing any greater good (no such good was forthcoming), even though we might reasonably take God to be justified in permitting the suffering, provided that was His best strategy in the situation, the one most likely to get the desired result. (iii) Look at "general policy" **theodicies.** Consider the idea that God's general policy of, e.g., usually letting nature take its course and not interfering, even when much suffering will ensue, is justified by the overall benefits of the policy. Now consider a particular case of divine non-intervention to prevent intense suffering. Clearly, God could have intervened in this case without subverting the general policy and losing its benefits. To prevent this particular suffering would not be to lose some greater good or permit something worse or equally bad. And yet it seems that general policy considerations of the sort mentioned could justify God in refraining from intervening in this case. For if it couldn't, it could not justify His non-intervention in any case, and so He would be inhibited from carrying out the general policy.

Since my central aim in this paper is not to refine principles like 2 in microscopic detail, I will take a shortcut in dealing with these difficulties. (i) can be handled by complicating the formula to allow the permission of any member of a **disjunction,** some member of which is necessary for a greater good.

Consider it done. (ii) and (iii) can be accommodated by widening the sphere of goods for which the evil is necessary. For cases of the (ii) sort, take the greater good to be having as great a chance as possible to attain salvation, and let's say that this good is attained whatever the response. As for (iii), we can say that E is permitted in order to realize the good of maintaining a beneficial general policy except where there are overriding reasons to make an exception, and the reasons in this case are not overriding. With these modifications we can take Rowe to have provided a plausible formulation of **necessary conditions** for divine sufficient reasons for permitting E. But if you don't think I have successfully defended my revision of Rowe, then you may think in terms of an unspecific substitute for 1 like "There are instances of suffering such that there is no sufficient reason for God to allow them." That will still enable me to argue that no one is in a position to justifiably assert that God could have no sufficient reason for allowing E.

III

Clearly the case for 1 depends on an inference from "So far as I can tell, p" to "p" or "Probably, p." And, equally clearly, such inferences are sometimes warranted and sometimes not. Having carefully examined my desk I can infer 'Jones' letter is not on my desk' from 'So far as I can tell, Jones' letter is not on my desk.' But being ignorant of **quantum mechanics** I cannot infer 'This treatise on quantum mechanics is well done' from 'So far as I can tell, this treatise on quantum mechanics is well done.' I shall be contending that our position vis-á-vis 1 is like the latter rather than like the former.

I am by no means the first to suggest that the **atheological** argument from evil is vitiated by an unwarranted confidence in our ability to determine that God could have no sufficient reason for permitting some of the evils we find in the world. . . . Wykstra points out that our cognitive capacities are much more inferior to God's than is a small child's to his parents; and in the latter case the small child is often unable to understand the parents' reasons for inflicting punishment or for requiring him to perform tasks that are distasteful to him (88). Ahern points out that our knowledge of the goods and evils in the world (54–5) and of the interconnections between things (57, 72–3) are very limited. Fitzpatrick adduces the deficiencies in our grasp of the divine nature (25–28). This is all well taken and, I believe, does provide support for the agnostic thesis. But then why am I taking pen in hand to add to this ever swelling stream of literature? For several reasons. First, I will not be proceeding on the basis of any general **skepticism** about our cognitive powers either across the board or generally with respect to God. I will, rather, be focusing on the peculiar difficulties we encounter in attempting to provide adequate support for a certain very ambitious **negative existential claim,** viz., that there is (can be) no sufficient divine reason for permitting a certain case of suffering, E. I will be appealing to the difficulties of defending a claim of this particular kind, rather than to more generalized human cognitive weaknesses. . . .

IV

Now, at last, I am ready to turn to my central project of arguing that we cannot be justified in accepting 1A. As already noted, I will be emphasizing the fact that this is a negative existential claim. It will be my contention that to be justified in such a claim one must be justified in excluding all the live possibilities for what the claim denies to exist. . . .

Thus I shall first consider theodical suggestions that seem clearly not to apply to Bambi or Sue. Here I shall be thinking instead of an adult sufferer from a painful and lengthy disease (fill in the details as you like) whom I shall call 'Sam.' Having argued that we are not in a position to exclude the possibility that God has reasons of these sorts for permitting Sam's suffering, I shall pass on to other suggestions that do constitute genuine possibilities for Bambi and/or Sue.

V

I begin with a traditional theme, that human suffering is God's punishment for sin. Though it hardly applies to Bambi or Sue, it may be a live possibility in other cases, and so I will consider it. The punishment motif has tended to drop out of theodicies in our "soft-on-criminals" and "depravity-is-a-disease" climate, but it has bulked large in the Christian tradition. It often draws the criticism that, so far as we can see, degree or extent of suffering is not nicely proportioned to degree of guilt. Are the people of Vietnam, whose country was ravaged by war in this century, markedly more sinful than the people of Switzerland, whose country was not? But, remembering the warnings of the last section, that does not show that this is never God's reason for permitting suffering, and here we are concerned with a particular case, Sam. Let's say that it seems clear, so far as we can tell, that Sam's suffering is not in proportion to his sinfulness. Sam doesn't seem to have been a bad sort at all, and he has suffered horribly. Can we go from that to "Sam's suffering was not a punishment for sin," or even to "It is reasonable to suppose that Sam's suffering was not a punishment for sin"? I suggest that we cannot.

First, we are often in a poor position to assess the degree and kind of a certain person's sinfulness, or to compare people in this regard. Since I am thinking of the inductive argument from evil as directed against Christian belief in God, it will be appropriate to understand the punishment-for-sin suggestion in those terms. Two points about sin are particularly relevant here. (1) Inward sins—one's intentions, motives, attitudes—are more serious than failings in outward behavior. (2) The greatest sin is a self-centered refusal or failure to make God the center of one's life. (2) is sharply at variance with standard secular bases for moral judgment and evaluation. Hence the fact that X does not seem, from that stand point, more wicked than Y, or doesn't seem wicked at all, does nothing to show that God, on a Christian understanding of God, would make the same judgment. Because of (1) overt behavior is not always a good indication of a person's condition, sin-wise. This is not to say that we could not make a sound judgement of a person's inner state if we had a complete record of what is publicly observable concerning the person. Perhaps in some instances we could, and perhaps in others we could not. But in any event, we rarely or never have such a record. Hence, for both these reasons our judgements as to the relation between S's suffering and S's sinfulness are usually of questionable value.

Second, according to Christianity, one's life on earth is only a tiny proportion of one's total life span. This means that, knowing nothing about the immeasurably greater proportion of Sam's life, we are in no position to deny that the suffering qua punishment has not had a reformative effect, even if we can see no such effect in his earthly life.

I might be accused of **begging the question** by dragging in Christian convictions to support my case. But that would be a misunderstanding. I am not seeking to prove, or give grounds for, theism or Christianity. I am countering a certain argument against Christian theism. I introduce these Christian doctrines only to spell out crucial features of what is being argued against. The Christian understanding of sin, human life, God's purposes, and so on, go into the determination of what the critic must be justified in denying if she is to be justified in the conclusion that Sam's suffering would not have been permitted by God.

VI

I have led off my survey of theodical suggestions with the punishment motif, despite the fact that it is highly controversial and the reverse of popular. Nor would I want to put heavy emphasis on it were I constructing a theodicy. I have put my worst foot forward in order to show that even here the critic is in no position to show that Sam's suffering is not permitted by God for this reason. If the critic can't manage even this, he will presumably be much worse off with more plausible suggestions for divine reasons, to some of which I now turn.

One of the most prominent theodical suggestions is that God allows suffering because He is interested in a "vale of **soul making.**" He takes it that by confronting difficulties, hardships, frustrations, perils, and even suffering and only by doing this, we have a chance to develop such qualities of character as patience, courage, and compassion, qualities we would otherwise have no opportunity to develop. This line has been set forth most forcefully in our time by John Hick in *Evil and the God of Love* (revised edition, 1978), a book that has evoked much discussion. To put the point most generally, God's purpose is to make it possible for us to grow into the kind of person that is capable of an eternal life of loving communion with Himself. To be that kind of person one will have to possess traits of character like those just mentioned, traits that one cannot develop without meeting and reacting to difficulties and hardships, including suffering. To show that E would not be permitted by God, the critic has to show that it does not serve the "soul-making" function.

To get to the points I am concerned to make I must first respond to some standard objections to this theodicy. (1) God could surely just create us with the kind of character needed for fellowship with Himself, thereby rendering the hardships and suffering unnecessary. Hick's answer is that what God aims at is not fellowship with a suitably programmed robot, but fellowship with creatures who freely choose to work for what is needed and to take advantage of the opportunity thus engendered. God sees the realization of this aim for some free creatures, even at the cost of suffering and hardship for all, as being of much greater value than any alternative, including a world with no free creatures and a world in which the likes of human beings come off the assembly line pre-sanctified. As usual, I am not concerned to defend the claim that this is the way things are, but only to claim that we are in no position to deny that God is correct in this judgment. (For a discussion of difficulties in carrying out comparative evaluation of total universes, see the end of section IX.)

(2) "If God is using suffering to achieve this goal, He is not doing very well. In spite of all the suffering we undergo, most of us don't get very far in developing courage, compassion, etc." There are two answers to this. First, we are in no position to make that last judgment. We don't know nearly enough about the inner springs of peoples' motivation, attitudes, and character, even in this life. And we know nothing about any further development in an after-life. Second, the theism under discussion takes God to respect the free will of human beings. No strategy consistent with that can guarantee that all, or perhaps any, creatures will respond in the way intended. Whether they do is ultimately up to them. Hence we cannot argue from the fact that such tactics often don't succeed to the conclusion that God wouldn't employ them. When dealing with free creatures God must, because of self-imposed limitations, use means that have some considerable likelihood of success, not means that cannot fail. It is amazing that so many critics reject theodicies like Hick's on the grounds of a poor success rate. I don't say that a poor success rate could not, under any circumstances, justify us in denying that God would permit E for the sake of soul making. If we really did know enough to be reasonably sure that the success rate is very poor *and* that other devices open to God would be seen by omniscience to have a significantly greater chance of success, *then* we could conclude that Hick's line does not get at what God is up to. But we are a very long way indeed from being able to justifiably assert this.

We cannot take the kind of reason stressed by Hick to be a live possibility for the Bambi and Sue cases. The former is much more obvious than the latter, but even in the latter case Sue has no chance to respond to the suffering in the desired way, except in an afterlife, and it strains credulity to suppose that God would subject a 5-year old to *that* for the sake of character building in the life to come. Hence once more, and until further notice, we will stick with Sam.

Let's stipulate that Sam's suffering does not appear, on close examination, to be theistically explainable as aimed by God at "soul-making." He seems already to have more of the qualities of character in question than most of us, or the amount of suffering seems to be too much for the purpose, or to be so great as to overwhelm him and make character development highly unlikely. And so our best judgment is that God wouldn't be permitting his suffering for that reason. But that judgment is made in ignorance of much relevant information. Perhaps a more penetrating picture of Sam's spiritual condition would reveal that he is much more in need of further development than is apparent to us from our usual superficial perspective on such matters. Since we don't see his career after death, we are in a poor position to determine how, over the long run, he reacts to the suffering; perhaps if we had that information we would see that this suffering is very important for his full development. Moreover, we are in a poor position, or no position, to determine what is the most effective strategy for God to use in His pursuit of Sam. We don't know what alternatives are open to God, while respecting Sam's freedom, or what the chances are, on one or another alternative, of inducing the desired responses. We are in a poor position to say that this was too much suffering for the purpose, or to say how much would be just right. And we will continue to be in that position until our access to relevant information is radically improved.

Thus we cannot be justified in holding that Sam's suffering is not permitted by God in order to further His project of soul-making. There is an allied, but significantly different theodical suggestion by Eleonore Stump concerning which I would make the same points. Briefly, and oversimply, Stump's central suggestion is that the function of **natural evil** in God's scheme is to bring us to salvation, or, as she likes to put it, to contribute to the project of "fixing our wills," which have been damaged by original sin. Natural evil tends to prod us to turn to God, thereby giving Him a chance to fix our wills.

> Natural evil—the pain of disease, the intermittent and unpredictable destruction of natural disasters, the decay of old age, the imminence of death—takes away a person's satisfaction with himself. It tends to humble him, show him his frailty, make him reflect on the transience of temporal goods, and turn his affections towards other-worldly things, away from the things of this world. No amount of moral or natural evil, of course, can *guarantee* that a man will seek God's help. If it could, the willing it produced would not be free. But evil of this sort is the best hope, I think, and maybe the only effective means, for bringing men to such a state (Stump, 1985, p. 409).

Objections will be raised somewhat similar to those that have been made to Hick. A perfectly good God wouldn't have let us get in this situation in the first place. God would employ a more effective technique. There's too much suffering for the purpose. It is not distributed properly. And so on. These will be answered in the same way as the analogous objections to Hick. As for Sam, if we cannot see how his suffering was permitted by God for the reason Stump suggests, I will do a rerun of the parallel points concerning Hick's soul making suggestion.

Closely related suggestions have been made by Marilyn McCord Adams in her essay, "Redemptive Suffering: A Christian Solution to the Problem of Evil" (1986). She takes martyrdom as her model for redemptive suffering, though she by no means wishes to limit her discussion to martyrdom strictly so called. ". . . [T]he redemptive potential of many other cases that, strictly speaking, are not martyrdoms can be seen by extrapolation" (p. 261). In other words her suggestion is that the benefits for the martyr and others that can flow from martyrdom in the strict sense, can also flow from suffering that does not involve undergoing persecution for the faith. Her bold suggestion is that "martyrdom is an expression of God's righteous love toward the onlooker, the persecutor, and even the martyr himself" (257). Here I want to focus on her account of the benefits to the martyr. ". . . [T]he threat of martyrdom is a time of testing and judgment. It makes urgent the previously abstract dilemma of whether he loves God more than the temporal goods that are being extracted as a price . . . the martyr will have had to face a deeper truth about himself and his relations to God and temporal goods than ever he could in fair weather . . . the time of trial is also an opportunity for building a relationship of trust between the martyr and that to which he testifies. Whether because we are fallen or by the nature of the case, trusting relationships have to be built up by a history of interactions. If the martyr's loyalty to God is tested, but after a struggle he holds onto his allegiance to God and God delivers him (in his own time and way), the relationship is strengthened and deepened" (259). Adams is modest in her claims. She does not assert that all cases of suffering are analogous to martyrdom in these respects. "Some are too witless to have relationships that can profit and mature through such tests of loyalty. Some people are killed or severely harmed too quickly for such moral struggles to take place. At other times the victim is an unbeliever who has no explicit relationship with God to wrestle with." However none of these disqualifications apply to her boldest suggestion, that given the Christian doctrine of the suffering of God incarnate on the cross, "temporal suffering itself is a vision into the inner life of God" (264), a theme that she takes from Christian mysticism. That value of suffering, if such it be, can be enjoyed by any sufferer, whatever the circumstances. To be sure, one might not realize at the time that the suffering has that significance. But if one reaches the final term of Christian development, "he might be led to reason that the good aspect of an experience of deep suffering [the aspect just pointed to] is great enough that, from the standpoint of the beatific vision, the victim would not wish the experience away from his life history, but would, on the contrary, count it as an extremely valuable part of his life" (265). It should also be noted that Adams does not suggest that God's reasons for permitting suffering in any particular case are restricted to one of the considerations she has been presenting, or indeed to all of the points she makes.

If we were to try to decide whether Sam's suffering is permitted by God for any of these reasons, we would be in a poor position to make a negative judgment for reasons parallel to those brought out in the discussion of Hick. Given the limits of our access to the secrets of the human heart and the course of the after life, if any, we are, in many instances, in no position to assert with any confidence that this suffering does not have such consequences, and hence that God does not permit it (at least in part) for the sake of just those consequences.

VII

Thus far I have been restricting myself to conceivable divine reasons for suffering that involve the use of that suffering to bring about good for the sufferer. This is obvious except for the punishment reason. As for that one, this claim is equally obvious if we are thinking of punishment in terms of reformation of the punishee, but what about a "retributive" theory, according to which the rationale of punishment is simply that the sinner *deserves* to suffer for his sin, that justice demands this, or that a proportionate suffering for wickedness is intrinsically good? Well, though one might balk at describing this as a *good* for the sufferer, it remains that such good as is aimed at and effected by the punishment, on this conception, terminates with the sufferer and does not extend to the welfare of others.

Where divine reasons are restricted this narrowly, the critic is operating on the most favorable possible terrain. If he has any hope of making his case it will be here, where the field of possibilities that must be excluded is relatively narrow. What we have seen is that wherever the reasons we have canvassed are live possibilities, even this is too much for his (our) powers. Our ignorance of relevant facts is so extensive, and the deficiencies in our powers of discernment are so fundamental, as to leave us without any sufficient basis for saying, with respect to a particular case of suffering, that God does not permit it for reasons such as these.

To be sure, this is cold comfort for the critic of Rowe's argument since, as noted earlier, the possibilities we have been canvassing do not seem to be live possibilities for Bambi or Sue. The only real chance for an exception is Adams' suggestion that the experience of suffering constitutes a vision of the inner life of God. Since this is not confined to those who identify it as such, it could apply to Sue, and perhaps to Bambi as well, though presumably only Sue would have a chance to recognize it and rejoice in it, retrospectively, in the light of the beatific vision. However, I don't want to insist on this exception. Let us say that a consideration of the theodicies thus far canvassed does nothing to show that we can't be justified in affirming an instantiation of 1 for Bambi or Sue.

Nevertheless, that does *not* show that we can be justified in excluding the possibility that God has no patient-centered reason for permitting Bambi's or Sue's suffering. It doesn't show this because we are not warranted in supposing that the possible reasons we have been extracting from theodicies exhaust the possibilities for patient-centered reasons God might have for permitting Bambi's or Sue's suffering.

Perhaps, unbeknownst to us, one or the other of these bits of suffering is necessary, in ways we cannot grasp, for some outweighing good of a sort with which we are familiar, e.g., supreme fulfillment of one's deepest nature. Or perhaps it is necessary for the realization of a good of which we as yet have no conception. And these possibilities are by no means remote ones. "There are more things in heaven and earth, Horatio, than are dreamt of in your philosophy." Truer words were never spoken. They point to the fact that our cognitions of the world, obtained by filtering raw data through such conceptual screens as we have available for the nonce, acquaint us with only some indeterminable fraction of what is there to be known. The progress of human knowledge makes this evident. No one explicitly realized the distinction between concrete and abstract entities, the distinction between **efficient** and **final causes,** the distinction between knowledge and opinion, until great creative thinkers adumbrated these distinctions and disseminated them to their fellows. The development of physical science has made us aware of a myriad of things hitherto undreamed of, and developed the concepts with which to grasp them—gravitation, electricity, electromagnetic fields, space-time curvature, irrational numbers, and so on. It is an irresistible **induction** from this that we have not reached the final term of this process, and that more realities, aspects, properties, structures remain to be discerned and conceptualized. And why should values, and the conditions of their realization, be any exception to this generalization? A history of the apprehension of values could undoubtedly be written, parallel to the history just adumbrated, though the archeology would be a more difficult and delicate task.

Moreover, remember that our topic is not the possibilities for future human apprehensions, but rather what an omniscient being can grasp of modes of value and the conditions of their realization. Surely it is eminently possible that there are real possibilities for the latter that exceed anything we can anticipate, or even conceptualize. It would be exceedingly strange if an omniscient being did not immeasurably exceed our grasp of such matters. Thus there is an unquestionably live possibility that God's reasons for allowing human suffering may have to do, in part, with the appropriate connection of those sufferings with goods in ways that have never been dreamed of in our theodicies. Once we bring this into the picture, the critic is seen to be on shaky ground in denying, of Bambi's or Sue's suffering, that God could have any patient-centered reason for permitting it, even if we are unable to suggest what such a reason might be.

This would be an appropriate place to consider Rowe's argument that we can be justified in excluding the possibility that God permits one or another case of suffering in order to obtain goods of which we have no conception. In his latest article on the subject (1988) Rowe claims that the variant of 1 there put forward:

Q. No good state of affairs is such that an omnipotent, omniscient being's obtaining it would morally justify that being in permitting E1 or E2.[3]

can be derived probabilistically from:

P. No good state of affairs we know of is such that an omnipotent, omniscient being's obtaining it would morally justify that being's permitting E1 or E2.

I have been arguing, and will continue to argue, that Rowe is not justified in asserting P, since he is not justified in supposing that none of the particular goods we have been discussing provide God with sufficient reason for permitting the suffering of Bambi and Sue. But even if Rowe were justified in asserting P, what I have just been contending is that the argument from P to Q does not go through. In defending the argument Rowe says the following.

> My answer is that we are justified in making this inference in the same way we are justified in making the many inferences we constantly make from the known to the unknown. All of us are constantly inferring from the A's we know of to the A's we don't know of. If we observe many A's and all of them are B's we are justified in

[3]E1 is Bambi's suffering and E2 is Sue's suffering.

> believing that the A's we haven't observed are also B's. If I encounter a fair number of pit bulls and all of them are vicious, I have reason to believe that all pit bulls are vicious (1988, pp. 123–24).

But it is just not true that Rowe's inference from known goods to all goods is parallel to inductive inferences we "constantly make." Typically when we generalize from observed instances, at least when we are warranted in doing so, we know quite a lot about what makes a sample of things like that a good base for general attributions of the properties in question. We know that temperamental traits like viciousness or affectionateness are often breed-specific in dogs, and so when a number of individuals of a breed are observed to exhibit such a trait it is a good guess that it is characteristic of that breed. If, on the other hand, the characteristic found throughout the sample were a certain precise height or a certain sex, our knowledge indicates that an inference that all members of that breed are of that height or of that sex would be foolhardy indeed. But, as I have been arguing, an inference from known goods lacking J to all goods (including those we have never experienced and even those of which we have no conception) is unlike both the sorts just mentioned in the way they resemble one another, viz., our possession of knowledge indicating which characteristics can be expected to be (fairly) constant in the larger population. We have no background knowledge that tells us the chances of J's being a "goods-specific" characteristic, one that can reasonably be expected to be present in all or most goods if it is found in a considerable sample. Hence we cannot appeal to clearly warranted generalizations in support of this one. Rowe's generalization is more like inferring from the fact that no one has yet produced a physical theory that will unify relativity and quantum mechanics, to the prediction that no one will ever do so, or inferring, in 1850, from the fact no one has yet voyaged to the moon that no one will ever do so. We have no way of drawing boundaries around the total class of goods; we are unable to anticipate what may lie in its so-far-unknown sub-class, just as we are unable to anticipate future scientific developments and future artistic innovations. . . .

VIII

It is now time to move beyond the restriction on divine reasons to benefits to the sufferer. The theodical suggestions we will be discussing from here on do not observe this restriction. Since I am moving onto territory less favorable to my opponent, I must give some indication of what might justify dropping the restriction. For my central purposes in this paper I do not need to show that the restriction is unjustified. I take myself to have already shown that the critic is not entitled to his "no sufficient divine reasons" thesis even with the restriction. But I do believe that the restriction is unwarranted, and I want to consider how the land lies with respect to conceivable divine reasons of other sorts. As a prelude to that I will point out the main reasons for and against the restriction to benefits to the sufferer.

On the pro side by far the main consideration is one of justice and fairness. Why should suffering be laid on me for the sake of some good in which I will not participate, or in which my participation is not sufficient to justify my suffering? Wouldn't God be sacrificing me to His own ends and/or to the ends of others if that were His modus operandi, and in that case how could He be considered perfectly good?

> Undeserved suffering which is uncompensated seems clearly unjust; but so does suffering compensated only by benefits to someone other than the sufferer . . . other things being equal, it seems morally permissible to allow someone to suffer involuntarily only in case doing so is a necessary means or the best possible means in the circumstances to keep the sufferer from incurring even greater harm.[4]

I agree with this to the extent of conceding that a perfectly good God would not wholly sacrifice the welfare of one of His intelligent creatures simply in order to achieve a good for others, or for Himself. This would be incompatible with His concern for the welfare of each of His creatures. Any plan that God would implement will include provision for each of us having a life that is, on balance, a good thing, and

[4]Stump (1990), p. 66. . . .

one in which the person reaches the point of being able to see that his life as a whole is a good for him. Or at least, where free creaturely responses have a significant bearing on the overall quality of the person's life, any possible divine plan will have to provide for each of us to have the chance (or perhaps many chances) for such an outcome, if our free responses are of the right sort. Nevertheless, this is compatible with God having as part of his reason for permitting a given case of suffering that it contributes to results that extend beyond the sufferer. So long as the sufferer is amply taken care of, I can't see that this violates any demands of divine justice, compassion, or love. After all, parents regularly impose sacrifices on some of their children for the overall welfare of the family. Of course, in doing so they are acting out of a scarcity of resources, and God's situation is enormously different in this respect. Nevertheless, assuming that Sue's suffering is necessary even for God to be able to achieve a certain good state of affairs, then, provided that Sue is taken care of in such a way that she will eventually come to recognize the value and justifiability of the proceeding and to joyfully endorse it (or at least has ample opportunities to get herself into this position), I cannot see that God could be faulted for setting things up this way.

From now on I will be considering possible divine reasons that extend beyond benefit to the sufferer. Though in line with the previous paragraph I will not suppose that any of these (so far as they exclusively concern persons other than the sufferer) could be God's whole reason for permitting a bit of suffering, I will take it as a live possibility that they could contribute to a sufficient divine reason. The theodicies to be considered now will give us more specific suggestions for Bambi and Sue.

I will begin with the familiar **free will theodicy,** according to which God is justified in permitting creaturely wickedness and its consequences because he has to do so if he is to bestow on some of his creatures the incommensurable privilege of being responsible agents who have, in many areas, the capacity to choose between alternatives as they will, without God, or anyone or anything else (other than themselves), determining which alternative they choose. The suggestion of this theodicy is that it is conceptually impossible for God to create free agents and also determine how they are to choose, within those areas in which they are free. If He were so to determine their choices they would, ipso facto, not be free. But this being the case, when God decided to endow some of His creatures, including us, with free choice, He thereby took the chance, ran the risk, of our sometimes or often making the wrong choice, a possibility that has been richly realized. It is conceptually impossible for God to create free agents and not subject Himself to such a risk. Not to do the latter would be not to do the former. But that being the case, He, and we, are stuck with whatever consequences ensue. And this is why God permits such horrors as the rape, beating, and murder of Sue. He does it not because that particular wicked choice is itself necessary for the realization of some great good, but because the permission of such horrors is bound up with the decision to give human beings free choice in many areas, and that (the capacity to freely choose) is a great good, such a great good as to be worth all the suffering and other evils that it makes possible.

This theodicy has been repeatedly subjected to radical criticisms that, if sound, would imply that the value of creaturely free will is not even a possible reason for God's allowing Sue's attacker to do his thing. For one thing, it has been urged that it is within God's power to create free agents so that they always choose what is right. For another, it has been denied or doubted that free will is of such value as to be worth all the sin and suffering it has brought into the world. In accord with my general policy in this paper, I will not attempt to argue that this theodicy does succeed in identifying God's reasons for permitting wrongdoing and its results, but only that the possibility of this cannot be excluded. Hence I can confine myself to arguing that these criticisms do not dispose of that possibility. Though lack of space prevents a proper discussion, I will just indicate what I would say in such a discussion. On the first point, if we set aside **middle knowledge** as I am doing in this paper, it is logically impossible for God to create beings with genuine freedom of choice and also guarantee that they will always choose the right. And even granting middle knowledge, Plantinga (1974) has established the *possibility* that God could not actualize a world containing free creatures that always do the right thing. As for the second point, though it may be beyond our powers to show that free will has sufficient value to carry the theodical load, it is surely equally beyond our powers to show that it does not.[5]

Thus we may take it to be a live possibility that the maintenance of creaturely free will is at least part of God's reason for permitting wrongdoing and its consequences. But then the main reason one could have for denying that this is at least part of why God would allow the attack on Sue is that God could, miraculously or otherwise, prevent any one incipient free human action without losing the value of human free will. Clearly a divine interference in normal human operations in this one instance is not going to prevent even Sue's attacker from being a free moral agent in general, with all that that involves. This point is supported by the consideration that, for all we know, God does sometimes intervene to prevent human agents from doing wicked things they would otherwise have done, and, so the free will theodicist will claim, even if that is the case we do enjoy the incommensurable value of free choice. We can also think of it this way. It is perfectly obvious that the scope of our free choice is not unlimited. We have no effective voluntary control over, e.g., our genetic constitution, our digestive and other biological processes, and much of our cognitive operations. Thus whatever value the human capacity for free choice possesses, that value is compatible with free choice being confined within fairly narrow limits. But then presumably a tiny additional constriction such as would be involved in God's preventing Sue's attacker from committing that atrocity would not render things radically different, free-will-wise, from what they would have been without that. So God could have prevented this without losing the good emphasized by this theodicy. Hence we can be sure that this does not constitute a sufficient reason for His not preventing it.

[5]On this point, see the discussion in the next section of our inability to make evaluative comparisons on the scale required here.

To be sure, if God were to act on this principle in every case of incipient wrongdoing, the situation would be materially changed. Human agents would no longer have a real choice between good and evil, and the surpassing worth that attaches to having such a choice would be lost. Hence, if God is to promote the values emphasized by the free will theodicy, He can intervene in this way in only a small proportion of cases. And how are these to be selected? I doubt that we are in a position to give a confident answer to this question, but let's assume that the critic proposes that the exceptions are to be picked in such a way as to maximize welfare, and let's go along with that. Rowe's claim would then have to be that Sue's murder was so horrible that it would qualify for the class of exceptions. But that is precisely where the critic's claims far outrun his justification. How can we tell that Sue falls within the most damaging n% of what would be cases of human wrongdoing apart from divine intervention? To be in a position to make such a judgment we would have to survey the full range of such cases and make reliable assessments of the deleterious consequences of each. Both tasks are far beyond our powers. We don't even know what free creaturely agents there are beyond human beings, and with respect to humans the range of wickedness, past, present, and future, is largely beyond our ken. And even with respect to the cases of which we are aware we have only a limited ability to assess the total consequences. Hence, by the nature of the case, we are simply not in a position to make a warranted judgment that Sue's case is among the n% worst cases of wrongdoing in the history of the universe. No doubt, it strikes us as incomparably horrible on hearing about it, but so would in-numerable others. Therefore, the critic is not in a position to set aside the value of free will as at least part of God's reason for permitting Sue's murder.

IX

Next I turn to theodicies that stress benefit to human beings other than the sufferer or to humanity generally. And first let's return to Marilyn Adams' discussion of martyrdom in (1986). In addition to her account, already noted, of martyrdom as a vehicle of God's goodness to the martyr, she discusses "Martyrdom as a vehicle of God's goodness to the onlooker." "For onlookers, the event of martyrdom may function as a prophetic story, the more powerful for being brought to life. The martyr who perseveres to the end presents an inspiring example. Onlookers are invited to see in the martyr the person they ought to be and to be brought to a deeper level of commitment. Alternatively, onlookers may see themselves in the persecutor and be moved to repentance. If the onlooker has ears to hear the martyr's testimony, he may receive God's redemption through it" (p. 257). She also suggests that martyrdom may be redemptive for the persecutor. "First of all, the martyr's sacrifice can be used as an instrument of divine judgment, because it draws the persecutor an external picture of what he is really like—the more innocent the victim, the clearer the focus . . . In attempting to bring reconciliation out of judgment, God may find no more promising vehicle than martyrdom for dealing with the hard-hearted" (p. 258). (Again, in making these suggestions for a theodicy of suffering, Adams is not restricting their scope to martyrdom strictly so called.) To be sure, sometimes there is no persecutor, but often there is, as in child and wife abuse. And there is always the possibility, and usually the actuality, of onlookers.

Can the critic be justified in holding that Sue's suffering, e.g., would not be permitted by God at least in part for reasons of these sorts? Once more, even if we cannot see that Sue's suffering brings these kinds of benefits to her attacker or to onlookers, our massive ignorance of the recesses of the human heart and of the total outcomes, perhaps through eternity, for all such people, renders us poor judges of whether such benefits are indeed forthcoming. And, finally, even if no goods of these sorts eventuate, there is once more the insoluble problem of whether God could be expected to use a different strategy, given His respect for human free will. Perhaps that was (a part of) the strategy that held out the best chance of evoking the optimal response from these particularly hard-hearted subjects.

Next I want to consider a quite different theodicy that also sees God's reasons for permitting suffering in terms of benefits that are generally distributed, viz., the appeal to the benefits of a lawlike natural order, and the claim that suffering will be an inevitable byproduct of any such order. I choose the exposition of this theodicy in Bruce Reichenbach in *Evil and a Good God* (1982).

> . . . creation, in order to make possible the existence of moral agents . . . had to be ordered according to some set of natural laws (p. 101).

The argument for this is that if things do not happen in a lawlike fashion, at least usually, agents will be unable to anticipate the consequences of their volitions, and hence will not be able to effectively make significant choices between good and evil actions. Reichenbach continues:

> Consequently, the possibility arises that sentient creatures like ourselves can be negatively affected by the outworkings of these laws in nature, such that we experience pain, suffering, disability, disutility, and at times the frustration of our good desires. Since a world with free persons making choices between moral good and evil and choosing a significant amount of moral good is better than a world without free persons and moral good and evil, God in creating had to create a world which operated, according to natural laws to achieve this higher good. Thus, his action of creation of a natural world and a natural order, along with the resulting pain and pleasure which we experience, is justified. The natural evils which afflict us—diseases, sickness, disasters, birth defects—are all the outworking of the natural system of which we are a part. They are the byproducts made possible by that which is necessary for the greater good (100–01).

This is a theodicy for natural evil, not for the suffering that results from human wickedness. Hence it has possible application to Bambi, but not to Sue, and possible application to any other suffering that results from natural processes that are independent of human intentional action.

Let's agree that significant moral agency requires a natural lawful order. But that doesn't show that it is even possible that God had a sufficient reason to allow Bambi's suffering. There are two difficulties that must be surmounted to arrive at that point.

First, a natural order can be regular enough to provide the degree of predictability required for morally significant choice even if there are exceptions to the regularities. Therefore, God could set aside the usual consequences of natural forces in this instance, so as to prevent Bambi's suffering, without thereby interfering with human agents' reasonable anticipations of the consequences of their actions. So long as God doesn't do this too often, we will still have ample basis for suppositions as to what we can reasonably expect to follow what. But note that by the same line of reasoning God cannot do this too often, or the desired predictability will not be forthcoming. Hence, though any one naturally caused suffering could have been miraculously prevented, God certainly has a strong prima facie reason in each case to refrain from doing this; for if He didn't He would have no reason for letting nature usually take its course. And so He has a possible reason for allowing nature to take its course in the Bambi case, a reason that would have to be overridden by stronger contrary considerations.

This means that in order to be justified in supposing that God would not have a sufficient reason to refrain from intervening in this case, we would have to be justified in supposing that God would have a sufficient reason to make, in this case, an exception to the general policy. And how could we be justified in supposing that? We would need an adequate grasp of the full range of cases from which God would have to choose whatever exceptions He is going to make, if any, to the general policy of letting nature take its course. Without that we would not be in a position to judge that Bambi is among the n% of the cases most worthy of being miraculously prevented.[6] And it is abundantly clear that we have and can have no such grasp of this territory as a whole. We are quite unable, by our natural powers, of determining just what cases, or even what kinds of cases, of suffering there would be throughout the history of the universe if nature took its course. We just don't know enough about the constituents of the universe even at present, much less throughout the past and future, to make any such catalogue. And we could not make good that deficiency without an enormous enlargement of our cognitive capacities. Hence we are in no position to judge that God does not have sufficient reason (of the Reichenbach sort) for refraining from interfering in the Bambi case.

But all this has to do with whether God would have interfered with the natural order, as it actually exists, to prevent Bambi's suffering. And it will be suggested, secondly, that God could have instituted a quite different natural order, one that would not involve human and animal suffering, or at least much less of it. Why couldn't there be a natural order in which there are no viruses and bacteria the natural operation of which results in human and animal disease, a natural order in which rainfall is evenly distributed, in which earthquakes do not occur, in which forests are not subject to massive fires? To be sure, even God could not bring into being just the creatures we presently have while subjecting their behavior to different laws. For the fact that a tiger's natural operations and tendencies are what they are is an essential part of what makes it the kind of thing it is.[7] But why couldn't God have created a world with different constituents so as to avoid subjecting any sentient creatures to disease and natural disasters? Let's agree that this is possible for God. But then the critic must also show that at least one of the ways in which God could have done this would have produced a world that is better on the whole than the actual world. For even if God could have instituted a natural order without disease and natural disasters, that by itself doesn't show that He would have done so if He existed. For if that world had other undesirable features and/or lacked desirable features in such a way as to be worse, or at least no better than, the actual world, it still doesn't follow that God would have chosen the former over the latter. It all

[6]There are also questions as to whether we are capable of making a reasonable judgment as to which cases from a given field have the strongest claim to being prevented. Our capacity to do this is especially questionable where incommensurable factors are involved, e.g., the worth of the subject and the magnitude of the suffering. But let this pass.

[7]Reichenbach, 110–11.

depends on the overall comparative worth of the two systems. Once again I am not concerned to argue for Reichenbach's theodicy, which would, on the rules by which we are playing, require arguing that no possible natural order is overall better than the one we have. Instead I merely want to show that the critic is not justified in supposing that some alternative natural order open to God that does not involve suffering (to the extent that we have it) is better on the whole.

There are two points I want to make about this, points that have not cropped up earlier in the paper. First, it is by no means clear what possibilities are open to God. Here it is important to remember that we are concerned with **metaphysical possibilities** (necessities . . .), not merely with conceptual or logical possibilities in a narrow sense of 'logical.' The critic typically points out that we can consistently and intelligibly conceive a world in which there are no diseases, no earthquakes, floods, or tornadoes, no predators in the animal kingdom, while all or most of the goods we actually enjoy are still present. He takes this to show that it is possible for God to bring about such a world. But, as many thinkers have recently argued,[8] consistent conceivability (conceptual possibility) is by no means sufficient for metaphysical possibility, for what is possible given the **metaphysical** structure of reality. To use a well worn example, it may be metaphysically necessary that the chemical composition of water is H_2O since that is what water essentially is, even though, given the ordinary concept of water, we can without contradiction or unintelligibility, think of water as made of up of carbon and chlorine. Roughly speaking, what is conceptually or logically (in a narrow sense of 'logical') possible depends on the composition of the concepts, or the meanings of the terms, we use to cognize reality, while metaphysical possibility depends on what things are like in themselves, their essential natures, regardless of how they are represented in our thought and language.

It is much more difficult to determine what is metaphysically possible or necessary than to determine what is conceptually possible or necessary. The latter requires only careful reflection on our concepts. The former requires—well, it's not clear what will do the trick, but it's not something we can bring off just by reflecting on what we mean by what we say, or on what we are committing ourselves to by applying a certain concept. To know what is metaphysically possible in the way of alternative systems of natural order, we would have to have as firm a grasp of this subject matter as we have of the chemical constitution of familiar substances like water and salt. It is clear that we have no such grasp. We don't have a clue as to what essential natures are within God's creative repertoire, and still less do we have a clue as to which combinations of these into total lawful systems are doable. We know that you can't have water without hydrogen and oxygen and that you can't have salt without sodium and chlorine. But can there be life without hydrocarbons? Who knows? Can there be conscious, intelligent organisms with free will that are not susceptible to pain? That is, just what is metaphysically required for a creature to have the essential nature of a conscious, intelligent, free agent? Who can say? Since we don't have even the beginnings of a canvass of the possibilities here, we are in no position to make a sufficiently informed judgment as to what God could or could not create by way of a natural order that contains the goods of this one (or equal goods of other sorts) without its disadvantages.

One particular aspect of this disability is our inability to determine what consequences would ensue, with metaphysical necessity, on a certain alteration in the natural order. Suppose that predators were turned into vegetarians. Or rather, if predatory tendencies are part of the essential natures of lions, tigers, and the like, suppose that they were replaced with vegetarians as much like them as possible. How much like them is that? What other features are linked to predatory tendencies by metaphysical necessity? We may know something of what is linked to predation by natural necessity, e.g., by the structure and **dispositional** properties of genes. But to what extent does metaphysical possibility go beyond natural possibility here? To what extent could God institute a different system of heredity such that what is inseparable from predation in the actual

[8]See, e.g., Kripke (1972), Plantinga (1974).

genetic code is separable from it instead? Who can say? To take another example, suppose we think of the constitution of the earth altered so that the subterranean tensions and collisions involved in earthquakes are ruled out. What would also have to be ruled out, by metaphysical necessity? (Again, we know something of what goes along with this by natural necessity, but that's not the question.) Could the earth still contain soil suitable for edible crops? Would there still be mountains? A system of flowing streams? We are, if anything, still more at a loss when we think of eradicating all the major sources of suffering from the natural order. What metaphysical possibilities are there for what we could be left with? It boggles the (human) mind to contemplate the question.

The second main point is this. Even if we could, at least in outline, determine what alternative systems of natural order are open to God, we would still be faced with the staggering job of comparative evaluation. How can we hold together in our minds the salient features of two such total systems sufficiently to make a considered judgment of their relative merits? *Perhaps* we are capable of making a considered evaluation of each feature of the systems (or many of them), and even capable of judicious comparisons of features two-by-two. For example, we might be justified in holding that the reduction in the possibilities of disease is worth more than the greater variety of forms of life that goes along with susceptibility to disease. But it is another matter altogether to get the kind of overall grasp of each system to the extent required to provide a comprehensive ranking of those systems. We find it difficult enough, if not impossible, to arrive at a definitive comparative evaluation of cultures, social systems, or educational policies. It is far from clear that even if I devoted my life to the study of two primitive cultures, I would thereby be in a position to make an authoritative pronouncement as to which is better on the whole. How much less are we capable of making a comparative evaluation of two alternative natural orders, with all the indefinitely complex ramification of the differences between the two.[9]

Before leaving this topic I want to emphasize the point that, unlike the theodicies discussed earlier the natural law theodicy bears on the question of animal as well as human suffering. If the value of a lawful universe justifies the suffering that results from the operation of those laws, that would apply to suffering at all levels of the great chain of being.

X

I have been gleaning suggestions from a variety of theodicies as to what reasons God might have for permitting suffering. I believe that each of these suggestions embody one or more sorts of reasons that God might conceivably have for some of the suffering in the world. And I believe that I have shown that none of us are in a position to warrantedly assert, with respect to any of those reasons, that God would not permit some cases of suffering for that reason. Even it I am mistaken in supposing that we cannot rule out some particular reason, e.g. that the suffering is a punishment for sin, I make bold to claim that it is extremely unlikely that I am mistaken about all those suggestions. Moreover, I have argued, successfully I believe, that some of these reasons are at least part of possible divine reasons for Rowe's cases, Bambi and Sue, and that hence we are unable to justifiably assert that God does not have reasons of these sorts for permitting Rowe-like cases.

However that does not suffice to dispose of Rowe's specific argument, concerned as it is with the Bambi and Sue cases in particular. For I earlier conceded, for the sake of argument, that (1) none of

[9]This point cuts more than one way. For example, theodicists often confidently assert, as something obvious on the face of it, that a world with free creatures, even free creatures who often misuse their freedom, is better than a world with no free creatures. But it seems to me that it is fearsomely difficult to make this comparison and that we should not be so airily confident that we can do so. Again, to establish a natural law theodicy along Reichenbach's lines one would have to show that the actual natural order is at least as beneficial as any possible alternative; and the considerations I have been adducing cast doubt on our inability to do this. Again, please note that in this paper I am not concerned to defend any particular theodicy.

the sufferer-centered reasons I considered could be any part of God's reasons for permitting the Bambi and Sue cases, and (2) that nonsufferer-centered reasons could not be the whole of God's reasons for allowing any case of suffering. This left me without any specific suggestions as to what might be a fully sufficient reason for God to permit those cases. And hence showing that no one can be justified in supposing that reasons of the sort considered are not at least part of God's reasons for one or another case of suffering does not suffice to show that no one can be justified in supposing that God could have no sufficient reason for permitting the Bambi and Sue cases. And hence it does not suffice to show that Rowe cannot be justified in asserting 1.

This lacuna in the argument is remedied by the point that we cannot be justified in supposing that there are no other reasons, thus far unenvisaged, that would fully justify God in permitting Rowe's cases. That point was made at the end of section VII for sufferer-centered reasons, and it can now be made more generally. Even if we were fully entitled to dismiss all the alleged reasons for permitting suffering that have been suggested, we would still have to consider whether there are further possibilities that are undreamt of in our theodicies. Why should we suppose that the theodicies thus far excogitated, however brilliant and learned their authors, exhaust the field? The points made in the earlier discussion about the impossibility of anticipating future developments in human thought can be applied here. . . . [S]uppose that God, if such there be, has more tricks up His sleeve than we can envisage. Since it is in principle impossible for us to be justified in supposing that God does not have sufficient reasons for permitting E that are unknown to us, and perhaps unknowable by us, no one can be justified in holding that God could have no reasons for permitting the Bambi and Sue cases, or any other particular cases of suffering.

This last point, that we are not warranted in supposing that God does not have sufficient reasons unknown to us for permitting E, is not only an essential part of the total argument against the justifiability of 1. It would be sufficient by itself. Even if all my argumentation prior to that point were in vain and my opponent could definitively rule out all the specific suggestions I have put forward, she would still face the insurmountable task of showing herself to be justified in supposing that there are no further possibilities for sufficient divine reasons. That point by itself would be decisive.

XI

In the case of each of the theodical suggestions considered I have drawn on various limits to our cognitive powers, opportunities, and achievements in arguing that we are not in a position to deny that God could have that kind of reason for various cases of suffering. In conclusion it may be useful to list the cognitive limits that have formed the backbone of my argument.

1. *Lack of data.* This includes, inter alia, the secrets of the human heart, the detailed constitution and structure of the universe, and the remote past and future, including the afterlife if any.
2. *Complexity greater than we can handle.* Most notably there is the difficulty of holding enormous complexes of fact—different possible worlds or different systems of natural law—together in the mind sufficiently for comparative evaluation.
3. *Difficulty of determining what is metaphysically possible or necessary.* Once we move beyond conceptual or semantic modalities (and even that is no piece of cake) it is notoriously difficult to find any sufficient basis for claims as to what is metaphysically possible, given the essential natures of things, the exact character of which is often obscure to us and virtually always controversial. This difficulty is many times multiplied when we are dealing with total possible worlds or total systems of natural order.
4. *Ignorance of the full range of possibilities.* This is always crippling when we are trying to establish negative conclusions. If we don't know whether or not there are possibilities beyond the ones we have thought of, we are in a very bad position to show that there can be no divine reasons for permitting evil.

5. *Ignorance of the full range of values.* When it's a question of whether some good is related to E in such a way as to justify God in permitting E, we are, for the reason mentioned in 4., in a very poor position to answer the question if we don't know the extent to which there are modes of value beyond those of which we are aware. For in that case, so far as we can know, E may be justified by virtue of its relation to one of those unknown goods.
6. *Limits to our capacity to make well considered value judgments.* The chief example of this we have noted is the difficulty in making comparative evaluations of large complex wholes.

It may seem to the reader that I have been making things too difficult for the critic, holding him to unwarrantedly exaggerated standards for **epistemic** justification. "If we were to apply your standards across the board," he may complain, "it would turn out that we are justified in believing little or nothing. That would land us in a total skepticism. And doesn't that indicate that your standards are absurdly inflated?" I agree that it would indicate that if the application of my standards did have that result, but I don't agree that this is the case. The point is that the critic is engaged in attempting to support a particularly difficult claim, a claim that there isn't something in a certain territory, while having a very sketchy idea of what is in that territory, and having no sufficient basis for an estimate of how much of the territory falls outside his knowledge. This is very different from our more usual situation in which we are forming judgments and drawing conclusions about matters concerning which we antecedently know quite a lot, and the boundaries and parameters of which we have pretty well settled. Thus the attempt to show that God could have no sufficient reason for permitting Bambi's or Sue's suffering is quite atypical of our usual cognitive situation; no conclusion can be drawn from our poor performance in the former to an equally poor performance in the latter.

I want to underline the point that my argument in this paper does not rely on a general skepticism about our cognitive powers, about our capacity to achieve knowledge and justified belief. On the contrary, I have been working with what I take to be our usual non-skeptical standards for these matters, standards that I take to be satisfied by the great mass of our beliefs in many areas. My claim has been that when these standards are applied to the kind of claim exemplified by Rowe's 1, it turns out this claim is not justified and that the prospects for any of us being justified in making it are poor at best. This is because of the specific character of that claim, its being a negative existential claim concerning a territory about the extent, contents, and parameters of which we know little. My position no more implies, presupposes, or reflects a general skepticism than does the claim that we don't know that there is no life elsewhere in the universe. . . .

REFERENCES

1. Adams, Marilyn McCord, "Redemptive Suffering: A Christian Approach to the Problem of Evil," in *Rationality, Religious Belief, and Moral Commitment*, ed. R. Audi & W. J. Wainwright (Ithaca, NY: Cornell U. Press, 1986).
2. Ahern, M. B., *The Problem of Evil* (London: Routledge & Kegan Paul, 1971).
3. Fitzpatrick, F. J., "The Onus of Proof in Arguments About the Problem of Evil," *Religious Studies*, 17 (1981).
4. Kripke, Saul A., "Naming and Necessity," in *Semantics of Natural Language*, ed. Donald Davidson & Gilbert Harman (Dordrecht: D. Reidel Pub. Co., 1972).
5. Plantinga, Alvin, *The Nature of Necessity* (Oxford: Clarendon Press, 1974).
6. Reichenbach, Bruce, *Evil and a Good God* (New York: Fordham U. Press, 1982).
7. Rowe, William, "Evil and Theodicy," *Philosophical Topics* 16, 2 (Fall 1988).
8. Russell, Bruce, "The Persistent Problem of Evil," *Faith and Philosophy*, 6, no. 2 (April, 1989).
9. Stump, Eleonore, "The Problem of Evil," *Faith and Philosophy*, 2, no. 4 (Oct., 1985).
10. Stump, Eleonore, "Providence and Evil," in *Christian Philosophy*, ed. Thomas P. Flint (Notre Dame, IN: U. of Notre Dame Press, 1990).
11. Wykstra, Stephen, "The Humean Obstacle to Evidential Arguments from Suffering: On Avoiding the Evils of 'Appearance,' " *International Journal for the Philosophy of Religion,* 16 (1984).

STUDY QUESTIONS

1. What is Alston's main point about Rowe's argument?

2. Alston surveys numerous theodicies. (a) Explain each theodicy. (b) Classify each as sufferer-centered or nonsufferer-centered. (c) Explain each objection he considers to each theodicy. (d) Explain Alston's reply to each objection.
3. Alston concedes that the theodicies he mentions do not explain the suffering of Bambi and Sue in Rowe's cases. Why? What does he say to handle such cases? *Do you find his stance convincing?
4. *At the end of the essay, Alston considers the reply by an atheist that Alston's standards for knowledge are too high and would preclude knowing many other things that we obviously do know. How does Alston respond to this reply? Do you think he has answered the challenge satisfactorily?
5. Evaluate the following objections to the "soul-making theodicy," which are not considered in the article. The objections are related, and you may prefer to respond to them as a unit:

   a. According to the soul-making theodicy, God allows evils because they are logically necessary for the development of such good traits as courage, sympathy, compassion, and benevolence. But this response is untenable because it suggests a double standard. Human beings would not be justified in allowing a human being to suffer on the grounds that the person will develop courage in the process or that others will develop sympathy. How, then, can such reasoning justify God's allowing evil?
   b. Suppose a theist says that evil is valuable because it promotes a certain good response, such as courage, sympathy, compassion, or faith. It would seem that, by eliminating a particular evil, a person would be preventing the emergence of the good traits that this evil may promote. It follows that, according to the theist, people should not try to eliminate evils, for by doing so they are stifling good responses. Thus, theists should not provide state aid for the needy, should not try to eliminate war, and so on.
   c. Following the thought in *b,* theists should regret the discovery of the Salk polio vaccine because Dr. Salk, in one blow, destroyed infinite possibilities of moral good.

(These objections are adapted from H. J. McCloskey, "God and Evil," *Philosophical Quarterly* 10 [1960]: 97–114).

READING 5.3

The Mirror of Evil

Eleonore Stump

In this moving essay, written as an autobiographical reflection on her personal religious path, Eleonore Stump (St. Louis University) tries to show how a confrontation with evil can lead a person to God. Stump focuses on moral evil, evil done by human beings to each other. Moral evils of the world, however atrocious, are a mirror through which we see ourselves, members of a species capable of such loathsome acts. However, unless we are, as in J. R. R. Tolkien's story, "hobbits," who forget the evils they have seen, it is precisely through this mirror, she suggests, that we may come to "taste and see" the goodness of God. (cf. I Corinthians 13:12: "We see as through a mirror darkly.") Having witnessed the horrible evils, we are all the more startled and moved by true goodness when we find it and all the more convinced that there is a reason God allows the evils, even though we cannot locate that reason. In the end, although we must not withdraw from social action, we are able to accept evils with the confidence that God is good. A salient feature of Stump's analysis is its interweaving of biblical texts, such as Ecclesiastes and Job, to illuminate religious perspectives.

. . . For reflective people, contemplation of human suffering tends to raise the problem of evil. If there is an **omnipotent, omniscient,** perfectly good God, how can it be that the world is full of evil? This response to evil is normal and healthy. I have discussed this problem myself in print and tried to find a solution to it. But there is another way to think about evil.

Consider just these examples of human suffering, which I take from my morning newspaper. Although the Marines are in Somalia, some armed Somalis are still stealing food from their starving neighbors, who are dying by the thousands. Muslim women and girls, some as young as ten years old, are being raped and tortured by Serb soldiers. In India, Hindus went on a rampage that razed a mosque and killed over 1,000 people. In Afghanistan, gunmen fired into a crowded bazaar and shot ten people, [including] two children. Closer to home, the R. J. Reynolds company is trying to defend itself against charges that it is engaged in a campaign to entice adolescents to smoke. The recently defeated candidate for governor in my state [Missouri], as well as lawyers and doctors employed by the state as advocates for disabled workers, are charged with stealing thousands of dollars from the fund designed for those workers. A high school principal is indicted on charges of molesting elementary and middle school boys over a period of twenty years. A man is being tried for murder in the death of a nine-year-old boy; he grabbed the boy to use as a shield in a gunfight. I could go on—racism, rape, assault, murder, greed and exploitation, war and genocide—but this is enough. By the time you read these examples, they will be dated, but you can find others just like them in your newspaper. There is no time, no part of the globe, free from evil. The crust of the earth is soaked with the tears of the suffering.

This evil is a mirror for us. It shows us our world; it also shows us ourselves. How could anyone steal at gunpoint food meant for starving children? How could anyone rape a ten-year-old girl? How could anyone bear to steal money from disabled workers or get rich by selling a product he knows will damage the health of thousands? But people do these things, and much worse things as well. We ourselves—you and I, that is—are members of the species that does such things, and we live in a world where the wrecked victims of this human evil float on the surface of all history, animate suffering flotsam and jetsam. The author of Ecclesiastes says, "I observed all the oppression that goes on under the sun: the tears of the oppressed with none to comfort them; and the power of their oppressors—with none to comfort them. Then I accounted those who died long since more fortunate than those who are still living" (4:1–2).

Some people glance into the mirror of evil and quickly look away. They take note, shake their heads sadly, and go about their business. They work hard, they worry about their children, they help their friends and neighbors, and they look forward to Christmas dinner. I don't want to disparage them in any way. [J. R. R.] Tolkien's hobbits are people like this. There is health and strength in their ability to forget the evil they have seen. Their good cheer makes them robust.

But not everybody has a hobbit's temperament. Some people look into the mirror of evil and can't shut out the sight. You sit in your warm house with dinner on the table and your children around you, and you know that not far from you the homeless huddle around grates seeking warmth, children go hungry, and every other manner of suffering can be found. Is it human, is it decent, to enjoy your own good fortune and forget their misery? But it's morbid, you might say, to keep thinking about the evils of the world; it's depressive; it's sick. Even if that were true, how would you close your mind to what you'd seen once you'd looked into the mirror of evil?

Some people labor at obliviousness. They drown their minds in drinking, or they throw themselves into their work. At certain points in his life, [Albert] Camus seems to have taken this tack. He was at Le Chambon writing feverishly, and obliviously, while the Chambonnais were risking their lives rescuing Jews. Jonathan Swift, whose mordant grasp of evil is evident in his writings, was chronically afflicting with horror at the world around him; he favored violent exercise as an antidote. The success of this sort of strategy, if it ever really does succeed, seems clearly limited.

Some people believe that evil can be eliminated, that Eden on earth is possible. Whatever it is in human behavior or human society that is responsible for the misery around us can be swept away, in their view. They are reformers on a global scale. The moral response to suffering, of course, is the Good Samaritan's: doing what we can to stop the suffering, to help those in need. Global reformers are different from Good Samaritans, though; global reformers mean to remove the human defects that produced the evil in the first place. The failure of the great communist social experiment is a sad example of the problems with this approach to evil. Every good family runs on the principle "from each according to his ability; to each according to his need." The extended human family in Eastern Europe intended to run on this principle and turned it instead into "from each according to his weakness; to each according to his greed." Ecclesiastes sums up the long-term prospects for global reform in this way: "I observed all the happenings beneath the sun, and I found that all is futile and pursuit of wind; a twisted thing that cannot be made straight, a lack that cannot be made good" (1:14–15).

And don't reason and experience suggest that Ecclesiastes has the right of it? The author of Ecclesiastes says, "I set my mind to study and to probe with wisdom all that happens under the sun . . . and I found that all is futile . . . as wisdom grows, vexation grows; to increase learning is to increase heartache" (1:13, 14, 18). This is a view that looks pathological to the hobbits of the world. But whether it *is* pathological depends on whose view of the world is right, doesn't it? A hobbit in a leper colony in a cheerful state of denial, oblivious to the disease in himself and others, wouldn't be mentally healthy either, would he? Ecclesiastes recognizes the goodness of hobbits. The author says over and over again, "eat your bread in gladness, and drink your wine in joy; . . . enjoy happiness with a woman you love all the fleeting days of life that have been granted to you under the sun" (9:7, 9). But the ability to eat, drink, and be merry in this way looks like a gift of God, a sort of blessed irrationality. For himself, Ecclesiastes says, "I loathed life. For I was distressed by all that goes on under the sun, because everything is futile and pursuit of wind" (2:17).

So, some people react with loathing to what they can't help seeing in the mirror of evil—loathing of the world, loathing of themselves. This malaise of spirit is more likely to afflict those living in some prosperity and ease, inhabitants of the court, say, or college students on scholarship, if you've just been fired or told you have six months to live or have some other large and urgent trouble, you're likely to think that you would be happy and life would be wonderful if only you didn't have *that* particular affliction. Given the attitude of Ecclesiastes, it's not surprising that the book was attributed to Solomon, who was as known for wealth and power as for wisdom.

The misery induced by the mirror of evil is vividly described by Philip Hallie in his book on Le Chambon.[1] Hallie had been studying cruelty for years and was working on a project on the Nazis. His focus was the medical experiments carried out on Jewish children in the death camps. Nazi doctors broke and rebroke "the bones of six- or seven- or eight-year old Jewish children in order, the Nazis said, to study the processes of natural healing in young bodies" (p. 3). "Across all these studies," Hallie says, "the pattern of the strong crushing the weak kept repeating itself and repeating itself, so that when I was not bitterly angry, I was bored at the repetition of the patterns of persecution. . . . My study of evil incarnate had become a prison whose bars were my bitterness toward the violent, and whose walls were my horrified indifference to slow murder. Between the bars and the walls I revolved like a madman. . . . [O]ver the years I had dug myself into Hell" (p. 2).

Hallie shares with the author of Ecclesiastes an inability to look away from the loathsome horrors in the mirror of evil. The torment of this reaction to evil is evident, and it seems the opposite of what we expect from a religious spirit. It's no wonder that some people think Ecclesiastes has no place in the canonical Scriptures. To see why this view of Ecclesiastes is mistaken, we have to think not just about our reactive attitudes toward evil but also about our recognition of evil.

How does Hallie know—how do we know—that the torture of Jewish children by Nazi doctors is evil?

By reason, we might be inclined to answer. But that answer is not entirely right. It's true that our moral principles and our ethical theories rely on reason. But we build those principles and theories, at least in part, by beginning with strong intuitions

[1]Philip Hallie, *Lest Innocent Blood Be Shed* (Philadelphia: Harper and Row, 1979).

about individual cases that exemplify wrongdoing, and we construct our ethical theories around those intuitions. We look for what the individual cases of wrongdoing have in common, and we try to codify their common characteristics into principles. Once the principles have been organized into a theory, we may also revise our original intuitions until we reach some point of **reflective equilibrium,** where our intuitions and theories are in harmony. But our original intuitions retain an essential primacy. If we found that our ethical theory countenanced those Nazi experiments on children, we'd throw away the theory as something evil itself.

But what exactly are these original intuitions? What cognitive faculty produces them? Not reason, apparently, since reason takes them as given and reflects on them. But equally clearly, not memory: We aren't remembering that it is evil to torture children. And not sense perception either. When we say that we just see the wrongness of certain actions, we certainly don't mean that it's visible.

At this stage in our understanding of our own minds and brains, we don't know enough to identify the **cognitive** faculty that recognizes evil intuitively. But it would be a mistake to infer that there is no such faculty. It's clear that we have many other cognitive faculties that similarly can't be accounted for by the triad of reason, memory, and perception. We have the abilities to tell mood from facial expression, to discern affect from melody of speech. We have the ability to recognize people from seeing their faces. When I see my daughter's face, I know who she is, and not by reason, memory, or perception. There are people who suffer from prosopagnosia. In them, reason functions well, and so do memory and perception; they perform normally on standard tests for all those faculties. Furthermore, the links among reason, memory, and perception also seem intact. Prosopagnosics can remember what they've perceived and thought; they can reason about what they remember and what they're perceiving. Nonetheless, they can't recognize people they know on the basis of visual data acquired by seeing their faces. So it is plain that reason, memory, and perception no more exhaust the list of our cognitive faculties than animal, vegetable, and mineral exhaust the list of material objects in the world. That we have no idea *what* faculty has been damaged or destroyed in prosopagnosia obviously doesn't mean that there is no such faculty. Furthermore, there is no reason for being particularly skeptical about the reliability of such peculiar cognitive faculties. It seems to me that our cognitive faculties come as a set. If we accept some of them—such as reason—as reliable, on what basis would we hold skeptically aloof from any others? So I think it is clear that we have cognitive faculties that we don't understand much about but regularly and appropriately rely on, such as the ability to recognize people from their faces.

Our ability to recognize certain things as evil seems to me like this. We don't understand much about the faculty that produces moral intuitions in us, but we all regularly rely on it anyway. The vaunted cultural relativity of morality doesn't seem to me an objection. The diversity of moral opinions in the world masks a great underlying similarity of view; and perhaps a lot of the diversity is attributable not to moral differences but to differences in beliefs about **empirical** and **metaphysical** matters. I think, then, that we have some cognitive faculty for discerning evil in things, and that people in general treat it as they treat their other cognitive faculties: as basically reliable, even if fallible and subject to revision.

It also seems clear that this cognitive faculty can discern differences in kind and degree. For example, there is a great difference between ordinary wrongdoing and real wickedness. A young Muslim mother in Bosnia was repeatedly raped in front of her husband and father, with her baby screaming on the floor beside her. When her tormentors seemed finally tired of her, she begged permission to nurse the child. In response, one of the rapists swiftly decapitated the baby and threw the head in the mother's lap. This evil is different, and we feel it immediately. We don't have to reason about it or think it over. As we read the story, we are filled with grief and distress, shaken with revulsion and incomprehension. The taste of real wickedness is sharply different from the taste of garden-variety moral evil, and we discern it directly, with pain.

What is perhaps less easy to see is that this faculty also discerns goodness. We recognize acts of generosity, compassion, and kindness, for example, without needing to reflect much or reason it out. And when the goodness takes us by surprise, we are sometimes moved to tears by it. Hallie describes his first acquaintance with the acts of the Chambonnais in this way: "I came across a short article about a little village in the mountains of southern France. . . . I was reading the pages with an attempt at objectivity . . . trying to sort out the forms and elements of cruelty and of resistance to it. . . . About halfway down the third page of the account of this village, I was annoyed by a strange sensation on my cheeks. The story was so simple and so factual that I had found it easy to concentrate upon *it,* not upon my own feelings. And so, still following the story, and thinking about how neatly some of it fit into the old patterns of persecution, I reached up to my cheek to wipe away a bit of dust, and I felt tears upon my fingertips. Not one or two drops; my whole cheek was wet" (p. 3). Those tears, Hallie says, were "an expression of moral praise" (p. 4); and that seems right.

With regard to goodness, too, I think we readily recognize differences in kind and degree. We are deeply moved by the stories of the Chambonnais. People feel the unusual goodness of Mother Teresa and mark it by calling her a living saint. We sense something special in the volunteers who had been in Somalia well before the Marines came, trying to feed the starving. We don't have a single word for the contrary of wickedness, so 'true goodness' will have to do. True goodness tastes as different from ordinary instances of goodness as wickedness does from ordinary wrongdoing; and we discern true goodness, sometimes, with tears.

Why tears, do you suppose? A woman imprisoned for life without parole for killing her husband had her sentence unexpectedly commuted by the governor, and she wept when she heard the news. Why did she cry? Because the news was good, and she had been so used to hearing only bad. But why cry at good news? Perhaps because if most of your news is bad, you need to harden your heart to it. So you become accustomed to bad news, and to one extent or another, you learn to protect yourself against it, maybe by not minding so much. And then good news cracks your heart. It makes it feel keenly again all the evils to which it had become dull. It also opens it up to longing and hope, and hope is painful because what is hoped for is not yet here.

For the same reasons, we sometimes weep when we are surprised by true goodness. The latest tales of horror in the newspaper distress us but don't surprise us. We have all heard so many stories of the same sort already. But true goodness is unexpected and lovely, and its loveliness can be heartbreaking. The stories of the Chambonnais rescuing Jews even on peril of their own imprisonment and death went through him like a spear, Hallie says. Perhaps if he had been less filled with the vision of the mirror of evil, he would have wept less over Le Chambon.

Some people glimpse true goodness by seeing it reflected in other people, as Hallie did. Others approach it more indirectly through beauty, the beauty of nature or mathematics or music. But I have come to believe that ultimately all true goodness of the heartbreaking kind is God's. And I think that it can be found first and most readily in the traces of God left in the Bible.

The biblical stories present God as the glorious creator of all the beauty of heaven and earth, the majestic ruler and judge of the world. But Rebecca feels able to turn to Him when she doesn't understand what's happening in her womb, Hannah brings Him her grief at her childlessness, and Deborah trusts Him for victory in a pitched battle with her people's oppressors. Ezekiel presents Him at his most uncompromisingly angry, filled with righteous fury at human evil. But when God commands the prophet to eat food baked in human excrement as a sign to the people of the coming disasters, the shocked prophet tells Him, "I can't!", and almighty God rescinds His command (Ez. 4:12–15). When His people are at their repellent moral worst, God addresses them in this way: "They say if a man put away his wife and she go from him and become another man's, shall he return to her again? . . . [Y]ou have played the harlot with many lovers; yet return again to me, says the Lord" (Jer. 3:1). And when we won't come to Him, He comes to us, not to rule and command, but to be despised and rejected, to bear our griefs and sorrows, to be stricken for our sake, so that we might be healed by His suffering.

There is something feeble about attempting to describe in a few lines the moving goodness of God that the biblical stories show us; and the attempt itself isn't the sort of procedure the biblical narratives encourage, for the same reason, I think, that the Bible is conspicuously lacking in proofs for the existence of God.[2] Insofar as the Bible presents or embodies any method for comprehending the goodness of God or coming to God, it can be summed up in the Psalmist's invitation to individual listeners and readers: Taste and see that the Lord is good.

The Psalmist's mixed metaphor seems right. Whether we find it in the Chambonnais or in the melange of narrative, prayer, poetry, chronicle, and epistle that constitute the Bible, the taste of true goodness calls to us, wakes us up, opens our hearts. If we respond with surprise, with tears, with gratitude, with determination not to lose the taste, with commitment not to betray it, that tasting leads eventually to seeing, to some sight of or insight into God.

Hallie left his college office and his family and went seeking the villagers of Le Chambon. He concluded his study of the Chambonnais years later this way:

> We are living in a time, perhaps like every other time, when there are many who, in the words of the prophet Amos, "turn judgment to wormwood." Many are not content to live with the simplicities of the prophet of the ethical plumbline, Amos, when he says in the fifth chapter of his Book: "Seek good, and not evil, that ye may live: and so the Lord, the God of Hosts, shall be with you." . . . We are afraid to be "taken in," afraid to be credulous, and we are not afraid of the darkness of unbelief about important matters. . . . But perplexity is a luxury in which I cannot indulge. . . . For me, as for my family, there is the same *kind* of urgency as far as making ethical judgments about Le Chambon is concerned as there was for the Chambonnais when they were making their ethical judgments upon the laws of Vichy and the Nazis. . . . For me [the] awareness [of the standards of goodness] is my awareness of God. I live with the same sentence in my mind that many of the victims of the concentration camps uttered as they walked to their deaths: *Shema Israel, Adonoi Elohenu, Adonoi Echod.* [Hear, O Israel, The Lord is our God, The Lord is one] (pp. 291–293)

So, in an odd sort of way, the mirror of evil can also lead us to God. A loathing focus on the evils of our world and ourselves prepares us to be the more startled by the taste of true goodness when we find it and the more determined to follow that taste until we see where it leads. And where it leads is to the truest goodness of all—not to the boss of the universe whose word is moral law or to sovereignty that must not be dishonored, but to the sort of goodness of which the Chambonnais's goodness is only a tepid aftertaste. The mirror of evil becomes translucent, and we can see through it to the goodness of God. There are some people, then, and I count myself among them, for whom focus on evil constitutes a way to God. For people like this, Ecclesiastes is not depressing but deeply comforting.

If we taste and see the goodness of God, then the vision of our world that we see in the mirror of evil will look different, too. Start just with the fact of evil in the world, and the problem of evil presents itself forcefully to you. But start with a view of evil and a deep taste of the goodness of God, and you will know that there must be a morally sufficient reason for God to allow evil—not some legal and ultimately unsatisfying sort of reason, but the sort of reason that the Chambonnais would recognize and approve of, a reason in which true goodness is manifest. People are accustomed to say that Job got no answer to his anguished demand to know why God had afflicted him. But they forget that in the end Job says to God, "now I see you." If you could see the loving face of a truly good God, you would have an answer to the question why God had afflicted you. When you see the deep love in the face of a person you suppose has betrayed you, you know you were wrong. Whatever happened was done out of love for you by a heart that would never betray you and a mind bent on your good. To answer a mistaken charge of betrayal, someone who loves you can explain the misunderstanding or he can show his

[2]Arguments for God's existence certainly have their place, but for most people that place is after, not before, coming to God. I have explained and defended this attitude toward arguments for God's existence in "Aquinas on Faith and Goodness," in *Being and Goodness,* ed. Scott MacDonald (Ithaca, N.Y.: Cornell University Press, 1991), pp. 179–207.

face. Sometimes showing his face heals the hurt much faster.

If a truly good God rules the world, then the world has a good mother, and life is under the mothering guidance of God. Even the most loathsome evils and the most horrendous suffering are in the hand of a God who is truly good. All these things have a season, as Ecclesiastes says, and all of them work together for good for those who love God—for those who are finding their way to the love of God, too, we might add.[3]

Nothing in this thought makes evil less evil. Suffering remains painful; violence and greed are still execrable. We still have an obligation to lessen the misery of others, and our own troubles retain their power to torment us. But it makes a great difference to suppose that the sufferers of evil, maybe ourselves included, are in the arms of a mothering God.

Although, as Ecclesiastes is fond of saying, we often cannot understand the details of the reason why God does what He does in the world, when we see through the mirror of evil and taste the goodness of the Lord, we do understand the general reason, just as Job must have done when he said, "now I see you." Like a woman in childbirth, then, as Paul says, we feel our pains of the moment, but they are encircled by an understanding that brings peace and joy.

And so in an Alice-through-the-looking-glass way, the mirror of evil brings us around to the hobbit's way of seeing things at the end. "Go," says Ecclesiastes, "eat your bread in gladness and drink your wine in joy; for your action was long ago approved by God" (9:7). If God is mothering the earth and if its evils are in His hands, then you may be at peace with yourself and your world. You can be grateful for the good that comes your way without always contrasting it with the ghastliness elsewhere. This road to quiet cheerfulness is the long way to the goal, but perhaps for some people it is also the only way there.

Nothing in this view, of course, is incompatible with a robust program of social action. "Send your bread forth upon the waters; for after many days you will find it," Ecclesiastes says. "Distribute portions to seven or even to eight, for you cannot know what misfortune may occur on earth" (11:1–2). If you are moved by goodness, then you will want to ally yourself with it, to diminish evils in the world, to alleviate suffering. Those who love God will hate evil, the psalmist says (97:10). There is no love of God, I John says, in those without compassion for the world's needy (3:17). A good part of true religion, James says, is just visiting "the fatherless and the widows in their affliction" (1:27).

The spirit with which you respond to the evil around you will be different, though, if you see through it to the goodness of God on the other side. Someone asked Mother Teresa if she wasn't often frustrated because all the people she helped in Calcutta died. "Frustrated?" she said, "no—God has called me to be faithful, not successful." If God is the world's mother, then Mother Teresa doesn't have to be. Quiet cheer and enjoyment of the small pleasures of the world are compatible with succouring the dying in Calcutta in case the suffering ones are in the hands of a God who is truly good. Maybe that's why the Psalmist follows his line "Taste and see that the Lord is good" with "blessed is the man that trusts in him."

Even our own evils—our moral evils, our decay and death—lose their power to crush us if we see the goodness of God. The ultimate end of our lives is this, Ecclesiastes says: "the dust returns to the ground as it was, and the lifebreath returns to God who bestowed it" (12:7)—to God who loves us as a good mother loves her children. In the unending joy of that union, the suffering and sorrow of this short life will look smaller to us, as Paul says (Rom. 8:18). Nothing in this view of our relation to God makes *joie de vivre* seem any less crazy; sin and death are still real evils. But tasting the goodness of God makes seeing the world's evils and our own compatible with joy in the Lord.

I think the Psalmist is speaking for people who take this long way round to peace and cheer when he says, "I have taught myself to be contented like a weaned child with its mother; like a weaned child am I in my mind" (131:2). How can a child who is being weaned understand the evil of the weaning?

[3]In other work, I have argued that God uses suffering to further the redemption of the sufferer. . . .

What he wants is right there; there is nothing bad about his having it—it costs his mother nothing to satisfy him; the pain of doing without it is sharp and urgent. And so, for a while, the child will be overwhelmed by the evil of his situation. But sooner or later in his thrashing he will also see his mother, and that makes all the difference. His desire for what she will not give him is still urgent, and the pain of the deprivation remains sharp. But in seeing her, he feels her love of him. He senses her goodness, and he comes to trust her. As Isaiah puts it, he sucks consolation to the full in another way (66:11). That is how he can be both weaned and also resting peacefully by her side.

And doesn't it seem likely that he comes to see his mother as he does just because he finds the evil of weaning intolerable? How much did he see her when his focus was himself and what he wanted, the comfort of the breast and the taste of the milk? The evil of the weaning, which seems to separate him from her, in fact drives him toward recognizing her as a person, and a person who loves him.

For Hallie, for the author of Ecclesiastes, and for me, too, the ghastly vision in the mirror of evil becomes a means to finding the goodness of God, and with it peace and joy. I don't know any better way to sum it up than Habakkuk's. Habukkuk has the Ecclesiastes temperament. He begins his book this way: "How long, O lord, shall I cry out and You not listen, shall I shout to You, 'Violence!' and You not save? Why do You make me see iniquity, why do You look upon wrong? Raiding and violence are before me, Strife continues and contention goes on. That is why decision fails and justice never emerges" (1:1–4). But he ends his book this way. He presents the agricultural equivalent of nuclear holocaust: the worst sufferings imaginable to him, the greatest disaster for himself and his people. And he says this: "Though the fig tree does not bud, and no yield is on the vine, though the olive crop has failed, and the fields produce no grain, though sheep have vanished from the fold, and no cattle are in the pen, yet will I rejoice in the Lord, exult in the God who delivers me. My Lord God is my strength" (3:17–19). . . .

STUDY QUESTIONS

1. What does Stump mean by the phrase "the mirror of evil"?
2. Describe the process by which, according to Stump, confronting and witnessing evil leads to an appreciation of goodness and God. In what way does the mirror of evil eventually lead to the hobbit's way of seeing things, as Stump claims? And in what way can the mirror of evil allow for "quiet cheer and enjoyment of the small pleasures of the world"?
3. What does Stump say is the origin of our moral views of good and evil? Do you find this account plausible?
4. Stump insists that viewing the world as good should not influence a person to withdraw from social action. What is her basis for saying this? *Do you concur with this argument?
5. *Stump remarks that, when one sees the goodness of God, one will become confident that all evils exist for a good reason. Compare this approach with the G. E. Moore shift described in William L. Rowe's article, Reading 5.1.

READING 5.4

A Theodicy of Heaven and Hell

Richard Swinburne

According to traditional Christian teaching, people go to heaven if—but only if—they have the right beliefs and a readiness to act in the right way (a good will). The others go to hell. Many **theologians** *today maintain that honest inquiry, rather than true belief, is all that is required along with a good will. However, even with this modification, asks Richard Swinburne, why would God punish someone for not* *honestly seeking true religious beliefs, if a person could get to heaven without having such beliefs? Why is God not good to both good and bad people by giving both the joys of heaven?*

Swinburne answers that heaven is not a reward but, rather, a home where people who wish to perform worthwhile tasks of supreme value forever can do so while having true beliefs about the value of their actions and situation. Only a person of a certain character will be happy in heaven. It is compatible with the goodness of God that God allows some people to put themselves beyond the possibility of salvation, because a good God might allow one to choose the sort of person he or she wants to be. Swinburne adds that, if one pursues heaven for the wrong reasons, such as a desire to attain happiness or to live forever, and does not pursue the tasks of supreme value for their own sake, one will not be happy in heaven and therefore will not attain it.

A remaining question is whether inflicting eternal physical pain in hell as punishment for bad actions on earth is consistent with God's goodness. Swinburne suggests that the answer is no.

I

Most theistic religions have a doctrine of the afterlife in which the eternal fate of a man depends on how he has led his life on earth. A doctrine of traditional Christianity, as of some other theistic religions, is that the good go to heaven and the bad are permanently barred from heaven. . . . I wish to investigate whether the permanent separation of the good and bad is consonant with the supposed goodness of God. . . .

. . . [W]hy should God insist either on right belief or on good will as an entry condition for heaven?[1] To start with, what is the justice in someone losing his eternal salvation merely for having the wrong beliefs? After all, he may never have heard of the Christian Gospel, or if he has, he may never have heard of good reason for believing it. . . . [W]hat is the justice in punishing the man who disbelieves, despite sincere inquiry into the relative merits of such religions as he is acquainted with? Surely all honest inquirers with sufficient love ought to go to heaven.

Most Christians today, I think, hold that God takes such honest inquirers to heaven. That he would do so was proclaimed as official Catholic doctrine by the Second Vatican Council. The latter declared that all men who strive to live a good life and who through no fault of their own "do not know the Gospel of Christ and his Church . . . . can attain to everlasting salvation." This possibility is open not only to theists but even to those who, through no fault of their own, "have not yet arrived at an explicit knowledge of God." This was, I believe, a claim made in effect also by many earlier **theologians** and implicit in the gospel itself. What matters is that people shall honestly seek after the truth, but if they do not find the truth (i.e., the Christian faith) in this life, that shall not debar them from heaven. However, if you can get to heaven without having true religious beliefs, why does it matter so much that people shall honestly seek after such beliefs? And the question remains: Why are the men of bad will excluded from heaven? Would not a generous God give the joys of heaven to good and bad alike? . . . Or at least give [bad people] a second chance? What is the justice of a man's fate being sealed at death? . . .

Before we can ask why certain people should not go to heaven and why true belief matters, we need to ask what heaven is and why certain people should go to heaven.

II

Heaven is a place where people enjoy eternally a supremely worthwhile happiness. But what is that, and why are the traditional occupations of heaven likely to provide it?

[1][In material omitted here, Swinburne shows that right belief and good will are conditions for heaven according to both Catholics and Protestants—Ed.]

Happiness is not basically a matter of having pleasant sensations. . . . Basically a man's happiness consists in doing what he wants to be doing and having happen what he wants to have happen. The man who is happy playing golf is happy because he is doing what he wants to be doing. Someone who is having pleasant sensations may indeed be happy for that reason, but he will not be happy if he does not want to have these sensations, e.g., if he wants to try and do without such things for a period.

Unfortunately men so often have conflicting wants, e.g., wants to have the pleasurable sensations caused by heroin and wants to avoid heroin addiction. Sometimes these conflicts are explicitly acknowledged; sometimes they are ones of which we are only half-conscious; and sometimes they are suppressed from consciousness altogether. A man will only be fully happy if he has no conflicting wants; if he is doing what he wants to be doing and wants in no way to be doing anything else. A man who does have conflicting wants may nevertheless still be on balance happy—especially if he is doing what he really thinks to be most worthwhile.

However, although someone may be fully happy doing some action or having something happen, this happiness may arise from a false factual belief or from doing an action or being in a situation which, objectively, is not really a very good one. Happiness is surely more to be prized according as the happy man has true beliefs about what is happening and according as what is happening is in fact of great value or only of little value. A man who is happy because he believes that his son is making a success of the business, when in fact he is not, has a happiness which is not as worth having as the happiness of the man who has a true belief that his son is making a success of the business. We can see this by asking ourselves which we would choose if faced with a choice of much happiness with a false belief that something marvellous was so, or small happiness with a true belief that some small good thing was so. Further, a man who is happy because he is watching a pornographic film by himself, or because he has made men sneer at some companion, has a happiness which is less to be prized than the happiness of a man enjoying a drink in company or watching the performance of a great work of art. That this is so can be seen by those of us capable of enjoying all such pleasures, comparing them for their worth. Insofar as happiness is to be prized, I shall call it deep, and I shall contrast deep happiness with shallow happiness which is to be prized less.

It follows that a man's deepest happiness is to be found in pursuing successfully a task of supreme value and being in a situation of supreme value, when he has true beliefs about this and wants to be only in that situation doing those actions. What are the most worthwhile actions, the most worthwhile tasks to pursue? I suggest that they are developing our understanding of the world and beautifying it, developing our friendship with others, and helping others toward a deeply happy life. And what are the most worthwhile situations? The having of pleasurable sensations is desirable, but they are the better for coming from the doing of worthwhile actions. People want the sensations of sexual pleasure through the development of a personal relationship, not by themselves. It is better to drink alcohol in company than alone. And so on. And a worthwhile situation will be one in which the good triumphs in the world, and one's own contribution toward this is recognized.

If all this is correct, the occupations of the inhabitants of the heaven depicted by traditional Christian theologians would be supremely worthwhile, and so would their situation be. If the world depends for its being on God, a personal ground of being, the fullest development of understanding will be growth in the understanding of the nature of God himself. Friendship is of great value to a man when his friends are good people, who take an interest in him and are enjoyable company in virtue of their kindness and ability to keep him interested. Friendship with God would be of supreme value, for he is (by definition) perfectly good and, being (by definition) **omnipotent** and **omniscient,** will ever be able to hold our interest by showing us new facets of reality and above all his own nature. According to Christian **theology** God takes an interest in his creatures and exercises that ability to show us ever-new facets of reality. The principal occupation of heaven is the enjoyment of the friendship of God. This has been traditionally described as the "Beatific Vision" of God. Aquinas stresses that this "vision" is an act of ours, not merely something that happens to us. Knowledge in heaven will be more sure than on earth. On earth people depend on sense organs and nervous systems that may lead them astray or let them down. Christian theology assures people of a more direct grasp on reality in the hereafter. God will be present to the inhabitants of heaven as intimately as their own thoughts. Friendship with persons involves acknowledgment of their worth. So friendship with God, the supremely good source of being, involves adoration and worship. According to Christian tradition heaven will also comprise friendship with good finite beings, including those who have been our companions on earth. The task of comprehending and worshipping God will be a cooperative one, one in cooperation with those who have shared a man's lesser tasks on earth. Christian theology has always stressed both that heaven will include a renewal of earthly acquaintance and also that the enjoyment of such acquaintance will not be its main point. And, of course, one always enjoys acquaintance the better if it serves some further point, if one and one's fellows are working together to attain a goal. Even friendship with God would involve his helping us toward understanding himself and fulfilling other heavenly tasks. The main other such task, according to traditional theology, is helping others toward their deepest happiness (and perhaps also beautifying the world). According to Christian tradition the saints have work to do (by intercession or other means) in bringing others into the sphere of God's love. These others may be like many on earth, half-developed beings ignorant of their capacities for these tasks, with wounds of body and soul to be healed. But the relation of those in heaven to those others will be of a different kind from the bodily relation which we have to our fellows on earth. A man seeks friendship with others not only for his own sake but for theirs, as part of helping others toward a deeply happy life. The most worthwhile such helping would be helping others toward their own deepest happiness, and thus seeking this sort of friendship also indirectly contributes to the seeker's own happiness.

I suspect that only that sort of life would be worth living forever. Only a task which made continued progress valuable for its own sake but which would take an infinite time to finish would be worth doing forever; only a situation which would be evermore worth having would be worth living in for ever. The growing development of a friendship with God who (if he is the sort of God pictured by Christian theology) has ever-new aspects of himself to reveal, and the bringing of others into an ever-developing relationship with God, would provide a life worth living for ever. A man who desired only to do the good (and had a right idea of what was good) would want that sort of life for ever. Most earthly occupations indeed pall after a time, but the reason why they pall is that there are no new facets to them which a man wants to have. And also most earthly occupations are rightly judged only to be worth a finite amount of interest, because there are not ever-new facets to them which are greatly worthwhile having. A man who has molded his desires so as to seek only the good and its continuation would not, given the Christian doctrine of God, be bored in eternity.

. . . The inhabitants of a Christian heaven will be performing actions of supreme worth and be in a situation of supreme worth, and they will know that they are doing such actions and in such a situation. Hence they will have this worthwhile happiness—so long as they want to be in that situation, doing those actions, and do not want in any way to be anywhere else or doing anything else. That is, the only people who will be happy in heaven will be people with a certain character.

The Christian doctrine—Catholic and Protestant—is that heaven is not a reward for good action (for, as we have seen, even on the Catholic view a man can go there without having done any); rather, it is a home for good people. This view receives abundant biblical support in the parable of the laborers in the vineyard (Matthew 20:1–16). Entry to the kingdom of heaven is compared to a situation where the same reward is given to those who have worked the whole day and to those who have worked only one hour. What determines whether they get their reward is their status as workers, that they are developing the vineyard (having accepted the challenge to work when it came), not how many hours work they have done.

The character needed for the inhabitants of heaven is that of perfect goodness. To have a worthwhile happiness in the situation and occupations of heaven a man needs to want to be there doing those things and also to hold true beliefs that that situation and those actions are of supreme value. He must, that is, both desire the good and also have a true belief about where it is to be found.

III

This point enables us to answer the question about why true religious belief matters for getting to heaven. People who come to have different beliefs about whether there is a God, what he is like, and what he has done, will, if they are pursuing the good, do different actions. If they come to believe that there is a God, they will worship God and will seek to make others worshipping people; if they come not to believe, they will not do these things. Someone with a theistic creed different from the Christian one will have a different view about the kind of reverence to be paid to God. If you think that God walked on earth, you are likely to have a different kind of reverence for him than if you think of him merely as a philosopher's first principle, and also a different kind of reverence for men, of whom God became one. A man with a different creed will meditate on different things and practice different kinds of human relationship (e.g., Islam commends a different pattern of family life from that of Christianity). Thereby, even if both are basically seeking the good, the character of a non-Christian will be different from that of a Christian. If the Christian creed is the true one and so the Christian way to behave the right one, the non-Christian would have to acquire true beliefs and practice different actions before he could enjoy the worthwhile happiness of the Christian heaven. (And, of course, if the Islamic creed is the true one, the reverse change would be required.)

So you need true beliefs simply in order to know which actions are most worth doing—which is necessary before you start doing those actions, and so start on the road to doing them naturally and spontaneously (and so desiring to do them). And you need true beliefs about your situation (e.g., of being redeemed, etc.) if you are to be truly blessed, for then you know wherein to rejoice.

So it is important that we acquire true beliefs, and so we ought to set about so doing. A man who seeks the good will seek to discover what is most worthwhile. Such an honest inquirer may discover the answer on earth. But he may not. Yet since such a person is seeking the good, he has embarked on the way to heaven and would enjoy heaven when he is given information on how to do so. As he will need to make no further choice, God may well give him the information when this earthly life is over. But a man not seeking true beliefs about what is worth doing is not a man of good will. . . .

So the answer to my original question is that right religious belief matters because only with it will a man know how he should live, and only if he does live in the right way can he attain the happiness of heaven. For heaven is the community of those who live in the right way and get happiness out of it because they want to live in the right way. By pursuit of the good they have so molded themselves that they desire to do the good. So the answer why God would send the men of natural good will and true belief to heaven is that they are fitted for it.

. . . But what of those who do not seek the good, who choose to do what is morally bad, and not through a false belief that it is really good but because their will is bad? . . .

Clearly there is no point in God sending the bad to heaven as they are, for they would not be happy there. The man who wants to be applauded for what he has not done, who wishes to see the good humiliated and to get pleasure out of the company of similarly malevolent persons, would not be happy pursuing the occupations of heaven. . . .

IV

. . . Strangely, it would not necessarily help someone attain the happiness of heaven if God did make it crystal clear to him that heaven existed and provided happiness for the good. For Christian theology emphasizes that the happiness of heaven is something which begins on earth for the man who pursues the Christian way. This is because the pursuit of that way on earth involves starting to do the tasks of heaven—for a short time with limited tools and understanding, with many obstacles including the desires for other things. The Christian on earth has begun to understand the divine nature (by Bible reading, receiving religious instruction, etc.), to worship (in the Eucharist with music, poetry, art, etc.), and to show the divine love to others. But his tools are poor—his mind and his instructors provide weak understanding of the divine nature; his organs and choirs are poor things; and he has many desires to do other things, which need to be eradicated before the Christian way can be enjoyed. Now, given all that, if a man did not seek such a life on earth, why should he seek it if he comes to learn that it can go on forever and provide deep happiness? Either because he wants to live forever or because he wants the happiness. But while someone is seeking to live the good life for those reasons, he will not find the happiness of heaven. For the happiness of heaven is not simply happiness. It is, as we have seen, a special kind of happiness. It is a happiness which comes from doing actions which you know to be supremely good because you want to be doing those supremely good actions. A man who sought the happiness of heaven for *its* own sake could not find it while that was his goal, for it is the happiness which comes from doing certain actions for *their* own sake. The happiness of heaven is a happiness which comes to those who are not seeking it.

True, the news of heaven might provide an initial incentive for a bad man to pursue the good way, which he might later come to pursue for better reasons. (Heaven and hell have often been preached for this purpose.) But clearly, if you encourage a man to pursue happiness (or everlasting life), he is likely to continue to do so. In this way, by pursuing happiness (or everlasting life) rather than goodness, he might fail to find the happiness which he might otherwise have got.

There are good reasons other than to provide an incentive for the bad why God should tell men about heaven. The news of heaven would, for example, show people that God was good and so provide further reason for giving particular content to the good life—that is, for worshipping God. It would also provide encouragement for those who sought to live the good life anyway to know that they could go on doing so forever under circumstances where the obstacles to living that life had been removed.

Perhaps the best compromise would be for God to let people know that there is *some chance* of their going to heaven if they lead a good life (and of "losing their soul" in some sense if they lead a bad life), but only some chance—to avoid to some extent the danger of men pursuing heaven for the wrong reasons and so losing it. And indeed the knowledge situation of most people in most societies has been just this. True, in our secular society someone might not know even that. Yet, as we have already seen, that is not necessarily a bad thing; and also there is the most important point that if one insists that agents had to know that there were such chances before they could be deprived of heaven, this would have the consequence that God would have to promulgate the Gospel independently of the activities of men. If men, in a particular church, are to make known the possibility of heaven, there must be those who otherwise would live in total ignorance of that possibility. It is good that the fate of men should depend in small part on the activity of other men—that men should carry the enormous responsibility of the care of the souls of others.

I conclude that a good God might well allow a man to put himself beyond the possibility of salvation, even without revealing to him the depth of eternal happiness which he was losing. The doctrine of the majority of Christian theologians down the centuries is not, however, merely this, but that such persons suffer eternal physical pain in hell as a punishment for their sins. Now certainly such persons may deserve much punishment. For God gave them life and the opportunity of salvation, but they ignored their creator, hurt his creatures, damaged his creation, and spent their lives seeking trivial pleasures for themselves. But for God to subject them to literally *endless* physical pain (*poena sensus* in medieval terminology) does seem to me to be incompatible with the goodness of God. It seems to have the character of a barbarous vengeance; whatever the evil, a finite number of years of evildoing does not deserve an infinite number of years of physical pain as punishment. The all-important punishment is to be deprived of eternal happiness. . . . This deprivation, I have suggested, is plausibly an inevitable fate of those who have finally rejected the good. It seems to me that the central point of New Testament teaching is that an eternal fate is sealed, at any rate for many, at death, a good fate for the good and a bad fate for the bad. . . . [I]t is compatible with the goodness of God that he should allow a man to put himself beyond possibility of salvation, because it is indeed compatible with the goodness of God that he should allow a man to choose the sort of person he will be.

STUDY QUESTIONS

1. What problem do the concepts of heaven and hell raise about God's goodness?
2. What does Swinburne regard as "a supremely worthwhile happiness"? What does he mean by "deep happiness"? What does he mean by "friendship with God"?
3. What does Swinburne mean by "good" people? According to Swinburne, why is heaven a place of supremely worthwhile happiness only for good people, not for bad ones? How does this answer his original problem?
4. *Swinburne argues that the most important punishment for a bad person is to be deprived of eternal happiness. Would a person who did not appreciate the happiness derived from earthly worthwhile tasks be able to appreciate the deprivation of happiness suffered by those in hell? If the answer is yes, would not that person be in the same position as the good person is to appreciate and enjoy heaven? Would it be inconsistent with God's goodness to deprive such a person of the joys of heaven?
5. *In a section of the article omitted in this text, Swinburne asks why God does not mold bad people's character so as to make them good, enabling them to attain heaven. How would *you* answer this question?
6. *Swinburne thinks that the notion of hell as eternal pain is inconsistent with God's goodness and that the notion of hell as nonexistence is consistent with such goodness. Do you agree? Is nonexistence a "better" fate than eternal pain? If so, how would you explain why capital punishment is thought of as a worse sentence for the evildoer than a lifetime in prison?
7. *Do you agree that it is important for people to be allowed to be the sorts of people they want to be? Why or why not?
8. *Swinburne concentrates on whether traditional teachings about heaven and hell are compatible with God's "goodness." However, "goodness" entails both love and justice. Does the fact that God is loving make hell harder to understand? Or can Swinburne's explanation of the afterlife be convincing even if God's love is taken into account?

READING 5.5

Coercion and the Hiddenness of God

Michael J. Murray

If God exists, why doesn't He "part the Heavens to show Himself"—that is, why doesn't God provide unambiguous evidence of God's existence? Michael J. Murray (Franklin and Marshall College) points out that this question about divine hiddenness is a form of the problem of evil and asserts that a variant of the free will **theodicy** *provides an explanation of hiddenness. If a person is to exercise free will in a morally significant manner, he or she must not act under coercion—that is, must not act only in response to a significant threat. But God threatens to consign to hell those who disobey Him—an exceptionally strong threat. If people were fully persuaded of God's existence, therefore, they would not have free will with regard to* *whether to obey God. To protect human freedom, God must hide His existence to a degree that will protect the freedom of even the "least wanton" individual—that is, the individual most likely to respond to a threat. Why, though, doesn't God tailor the degree of hiddenness to each individual? Why doesn't God provide each person with an additional revelation to make up for the lack of a general revelation? Murray responds to these questions at the end of the selection.*

But if I go to the east, he is not there;
if I go to the west I do not find him.
When he is at work in the north, I do not see him;
when he turns to the south. I catch no glimpse of him.

—Job 23:8–9

I

The sentiments expressed by Job in the above epigram are ones that have been expressed by the sophisticated atheist as well as the typical churchgoer. Most of us, in fact, have wondered at one time or another why it is that God does not reveal Himself in some dramatic fashion if He actually exists. Yet, while this question is widely entertained, it has received surprisingly little attention in the philosophical literature. In addition to puzzling many theists, the fact of divine **hiddenness** has prompted some non-theists to challenge the theist to provide some explanation for God's apparent silence. The problem they have raised can be roughly stated as follows: If, as most theists claim, belief in God is essential to ultimate human fulfillment, one would expect that God would provide us with unambiguous evidence for His existence. However, such evidence is not forthcoming. Therefore, it is unlikely that the theist's God exists. . . .

. . . The argument is made . . . forcefully by [Friedrich] Nietzsche in the following section:

> A god who is all-knowing and all powerful and who does not even make sure his creatures understand his intention—could that be a god of goodness? Who allows countless doubts and dubities to persist, for thousands of years, as though the salvation of mankind were unaffected by them, and who on the other hand holds out the prospect of frightful consequences if any mistake is made as to the nature of truth? Would he not be a cruel god if he possessed the truth and could behold mankind miserably tormenting itself over the truth?—But perhaps he is a god of goodness notwithstanding—and merely *could* express himself more clearly! Did he perhaps lack the intelligence to do so? Or the eloquence? So much the worse! For then he was perhaps also in error as to that which he calls his 'truth,' and is himself not so very far from being the 'poor deluded devil'! Must he not then endure almost the torments of Hell to have to see his creatures suffer so, and go on suffering even more through all eternity, for the sake of knowledge of him, and *not* be able to help and counsel them, except in the manner of a deaf and dumb man making all kinds of ambiguous signs when the most fearful danger is about to befall on his child or his dog? . . . All religions exhibit traces of the fact that they owe their origin to an early, immature intellectuality in man—they all take astonishingly *lightly* the duty to tell the truth: they as yet know nothing of a *Duty of God* to be truthful towards mankind and clear in the manner of his communications.[1]

The challenge to the theist is to explain this heavenly silence.

II

In order to understand the nature of the problem of divine hiddenness it is important to ask exactly what the objector to theism finds problematic here. The real problem, as I see it, is the fact that the hiddenness of God seems to be closely tied to disbelief. For most Christian theists, disbelief is a form of sin, possibly the most damaging form. As a result, the prob-

[1]Friedrich Nietzsche, *Daybreak,* trans. R. J. Hollingdale (Cambridge: Cambridge University Press, 1982), pp. 89–90. . . .

lem appears to reduce to the fact that God's self-imposed obscurity seems to be indirectly, or possibly directly, responsible for an important form of evil. The atheist's challenge, then, amounts to this: why has God established conditions, or at least allowed conditions to prevail, which seem to lead to the occurrence of a significant amount of evil, especially evil of such a grave sort? Seen in this way, the problem is similar to a number of others which fall under the traditional problem of evil. One might thus be led to consider, first, whether or not the hiddenness of God might simply be treated as a species of the problem of evil and thus be resolved by appealing to certain traditional **theodicies** regarding this problem. What I intend to show here is that certain traditional theodicies do seem to provide some interesting resolutions to the problem of God's hiddenness. I will begin in this section with a discussion of the traditional free-will defense and show how it can be brought to bear on this vexing problem.

Briefly, a **free-will theodicy** claims that the existence of free-will causes, allows, or presupposes the possibility of certain evils. However, there are two distinct species of free-will theodicies, both of which I will make use of in the course of this discussion. The first type of free-will theodicy argues that one of the consequences of endowing creatures with free-will is that these beings have the option to choose evil over good. As a result, it is impossible that God actualize a world such that there are both free beings and also no possibility of these beings undertaking evil actions. I call theodicies of this type *consequent free-will theodicies.* They are "consequent" in the sense that evil is to be accounted for in terms of conditions that arise as a consequence of the existence of free-will in our world. It is this sort of theodicy that is most often invoked by theists in order to account for the existence of moral evil in the world.

However, the type of free-will theodicy I am going to be concerned with first is somewhat different. The theodicy that is important here argues that there are certain *antecedent* conditions that must necessarily hold or fail to hold if beings endowed with freedom are to be able to exercise this freedom in a morally significant manner. For example, [Richard] Swinburne, and others, have argued that any world which is such that free beings can exercise their freedom in a morally significant manner must also be a world in which there are stable natural regularities of some sort. If this were not the case, it is argued, free creatures could never come to understand that there are regular connections between their undertakings and the consequence of their undertakings. So, for example, if there were no stable natural regularities, firing a gun at another person's head at point-blank range may, on one occasion, give them a haircut, whereas on another occasion it may kill them. But it seems clear that one could not be said to be morally responsible for their actions if they had no way of knowing that their undertaking, in this case firing the gun, would have the undesirable consequence of taking another life. As a result, free creatures must be created in a world in which such stable connections between undertakings and the consequences of undertakings obtain. And it seems plausible to suppose that such a world requires a set of stable natural regularities to insure the stability of this very connection. It is only when we can be assured that, for example, gun-firings result in certain predictable consequences, that we can be responsible for the outcomes of such actions.

However, the **argument** continues, the existence of stable natural laws may also lead to other events which result in natural evil, for example, hurricanes, earthquakes, and so on. Thus, if one can argue that there is some overriding reason why God should create a world with beings that are free and also able to exercise that freedom in a morally significant fashion, then the existence of these laws which give rise to natural evil are justified.

This argument strategy thus contends that certain antecedent conditions must obtain if free creatures are to be able to exercise their freedom in the most robust sense. And since there is good reason for creating creatures who can exercise their freedom in this fashion, there is good reason to create the necessary antecedent conditions which would allow for such exercising of freedom. One can then argue that even though certain evil states of affairs might result from these antecedent conditions obtaining, such is necessary if God is going to be able to bring about the greater good of actualizing a world in which free creatures can exercise their freedom in a thoroughly robust manner.

Clearly, theodicies of this sort differ from theodicies of the consequent type in that they argue that there are certain antecedent conditions which are requisite for free beings to be able to exercise their freedom and that such conditions may incidentally lead to certain other evil states of affairs. However, it is argued, the circumstances for which these antecedent conditions are necessary are sufficiently good to justify the evil which arises as a result of their obtaining. I will refer to this class of theodicies as *antecedent free-will theodicies*.

In addition to arguing that certain conditions must *obtain* for free creatures to be able to exercise their freedom, it can also be shown that certain conditions must *fail to obtain* if free beings are to be able to exercise their freedom in a morally significant manner. Specifically, it appears that one cannot act freely when one is in the condition of *compulsion by another in the context of a threat.* Under conditions that I will specify below, it seems clear that fully robust and morally significant free-will cannot be exercised by someone who is compelled by another in the context of a threat. Further, I will argue that if God does not remain "hidden" to a certain extent, at least some of the free creatures He creates would be in the condition of being compelled in the context of a threat and, as a result, such creatures could not exercise their freedom in this robust, morally significant manner.

It seems at least *prima facie* plausible to claim that morally significant freedom cannot be exercised by an individual who is being told to perform a certain action in the context of a significant threat, say, hand over his money to one holding a gun to his head and threatening to shoot. The threatened individual is compelled by another in such a way that morally significant free-will cannot be exercised. This claim, however, is certainly not uncontroversial. Adequately defending this position would require a separate treatment on the nature of coercion and its relation to freedom, a task too great given the limitations of this essay. However, a few things need to be said here about the relationship between a significant threat and freedom. First of all, I am certainly not claiming that freely willed acts are metaphysically impossible in the context of a significant threat. There is even no *physical* impossibility involved in the case of one refusing to comply with the demands of the robber described above. But if this is so, what *is* going on in cases where we are threatened?

There are at least three alternative answers. The first possibility is that we *are* free in such cases but that under the circumstances no rational person would choose to act contrary to the demands of the threatener. We might say, further, that as a result of the threat, our ability to rationally deliberate about alternatives is blocked because the threatener has brought it about that there can only be one rational choice. If we look at the matter in this way what is surrendered in such cases is the *deliberative* or *reasoned* exercise of freedom. On this account the external threat of an intentional agent has limited the rational possibilities of action to just one. And in such circumstances, one may hold we are not able to fully exercise our freedom.

The second thing one might say is that we are not free at all. It is a common view amongst **libertarians** that a free action requires that neither **metaphysically necessary truths,** the history of the world, nor the laws of nature prevent us from choosing between more than one option. One might hold, however, that there are cases in which certain operative psychological laws make only one alternative *psychologically* possible. When such laws are operative we are in a state where we cannot view physically possible alternative courses of action as legitimate possibilities for action for us at that time. In such cases, these psychological laws make it the case that one psychologically could not choose to fail to act in accordance with the threatener's demands. As a result, in cases such as these the libertarian might legitimately hold that we are not free in the most fundamental sense.

Finally, one might argue that what is not possible in these threat contexts, is free actions that are *morally significant.* One adopting this approach might argue that freedom has not been lost here because the threatened can consider the alternatives and choose what, in that instance, is the most rational course of action. What the threat does provide, however, are excuses for the behavior—excuses which suffice to relieve the threatened of moral responsibility for the action committed. Traditional Christian theists often argue that it is not only freedom, but morally significant freedom which is desirable for free creatures. [Alvin] Plantinga argues, for example, that the moral significance of the free actions is important because God desires to increase the diversity and amount of good in His creation. One way to accomplish this is to create free beings who can exercise this freedom in a morally significant manner, thus creating a world containing *moral good* in addition to just, say, **metaphysical** goodness, the sort of goodness that attaches to something's mere existence or being. If this is correct, one might argue that praise and blame are not justified in the context of significant threats because such threats provide adequate moral excuses for the behavior performed. Suppose that the individual being robbed in the case described above, call him Barney, had been sent by his friend, Fred, to make a deposit to Fred's savings account. On his way to drop off the deposit, Barney is stopped by our robber and promptly hands over the cash. In such a case it seems clear that we would not feel that Barney is morally culpable for giving up the money as we would if he were simply to hand it to some passerby. The fact that there was a significant threat provides an excuse which is sufficient to make Barney no longer morally culpable for an act he would have been responsible for had the significant threat not been present. Because praise or blame [is] not justifiably imputed in such cases of compulsion it would appear that although freedom *simpliciter* is not eliminated, the moral significance of the action performed is.

Whichever interpretation one wishes to place on such cases of compulsion, the fact remains that the prospect of being in such circumstances is quite unsavory. If one thinks that such threats make the threatened unable to act freely, then threatening destroys freedom. But even if one concludes that the threatened is still free, there is still something defective about the activity of the threatened in such a case. Whatever this defect might be explains why we legislate against such coercive behavior and do not allow robbers to excuse their action by claiming that they do nothing wrong since the victim "gave his money over freely." For the purposes of this essay I will not argue for any of these three views about the relationship between threats and freedom. Instead I will simply note that such cases do put the threatened in an unsavory position, one which in some way interferes with their exercising morally significant freedom in a fully robust manner.

III

There is, however, an ambiguity regarding exactly what constitutes a "significant threat." Not just any threat counts as a compelling one since, for example, one would not feel compelled to hand their money over to a robber who simply threatened to call them a dirty word. What would be helpful is a list of **necessary and sufficient conditions** which would suffice to clarify exactly what constitutes a threat significant enough to eliminate the possibility of morally significant, rational freedom. Unfortunately, the subject matter here does not allow for such precision. However, there are certain factors which jointly determine "threat significance." Below I will discuss these factors in an effort to provide a clearer picture of how threats give rise to compulsion and how this compulsion affects the exercise of morally significant free-will.

The three factors that are important for my analysis are what I will call *threat strength, threat imminence,* and *wantonness of the threatened.* By threat strength I mean the degree to which the threatened person feels the consequences of the threat to be harmful to him. By threat imminence I mean the degree to which the threatened perceives that the threat will inevitably follow given that the conditions for the threatened consequences being enacted are met. The notion of "inevitably follows" is ambiguous here and intentionally so. Below I will explain that this notion must be carefully unpacked since the notion of threat imminence is multi-faceted. Finally, by wantonness of the threatened I have in mind a characteristic of the individual threatened to disregard personal well-being in the fact of threats to his freedom. My claim is that the degree of compulsion is *directly proportional* to threat strength and imminence and *inversely proportional* to wantonness. I will now discuss these conditions in more careful detail.

It should be obvious that the degree of compulsion is directly proportional to the degree of threat strength. The degree to which I feel compelled to do an act that I would not otherwise do (say, to give all my money to a stranger) would be much greater if the threatener held a gun to my back than if he threatened to call me a dirty word if I failed to comply with his wish.

It is more difficult to see exactly how threat imminence relates to compulsion simply because it is less easy to characterize. By examining a few cases I think it will become clear that the notion of the consequences of a threat "inevitably following" when the threatened fails to satisfy the conditions of a threat must be cashed out in more than one way. There are, in fact, at least three distinct senses of threat imminence which must be distinguished for my purposes.

The first type of threat imminence is what I will call *probabilistic* threat imminence. Consider the standard robber case above in which I am threatened with being shot if I fail to hand over my wallet to the thief. In this case I would consider it highly probable that the thief would shoot me if I failed to comply with the conditions of the threat. As a result, the probabilistic threat imminence would be high in this case. However, consider another case in which certain prisoners are allowed to spend recreation time in an enclosed prison yard. Surrounding the yard are high barbed wire fences which are periodically punctuated by guard towers. The prisoners have been told that the guards have orders to shoot if any of the prisoners attempt to escape. As a result we have a case which, in important respects, is similar to the standard robber case. Most importantly, in both cases the threatened individuals are under a threat of the same strength, namely, being shot if the conditions of the threat are not satisfied. However, in the prison-yard case, a prisoner might be more tempted to attempt to escape because he might feel that there is some significant probability that the threat would not be successfully carried out because, for example, the guards might miss him at that distance, or because they may fail to see him since they are so busy watching the other prisoners. Thus, in this case the degree of compulsion is somewhat lower than in the standard robber case because the *probability* that the threat will be carried out is somewhat less even though the threat strength is identical.

The second type of threat imminence is what I call *temporal* threat imminence. With this type of threat imminence, compulsion is greater in those cases in which the threat will be carried out with more temporal immediacy, once the conditions of the threat have not been met. To show this consider the standard robber case once again. In such a case the temporal threat imminence is high since I know that if I fail to comply with the robber's demands I will be shot on the spot. Compare this, however, to a case in which the robber tells me that he has a blow gun with darts which he will shoot at me if I fail to hand over my money. Furthermore, the robber tells me that these darts contain a poison which has no antidote and will lead to my certain death in fifty years. In the former case, compulsion is higher because the *temporal imminence* of the threat is greater. Differing degrees of temporal threat imminence may also explain phenomena such as the fact that some individuals choose to eat high fat foods which they know, in the long run, are very likely to cause, say, fatal arteriosclerosis, while these same individuals would not ingest antifreeze, which although quite sweet tasting, is very likely to be immediately fatal. Ingesting both types of substances makes death likely; but ingesting high fat foods makes death likely sometime in the future, whereas ingesting ethylene glycol makes death immediately likely.

Finally, there is ***epistemic*** threat imminence. This type of imminence is also quite difficult to characterize but it is one with which I believe that we are all familiar. It is this third type of imminence that explains why we believe that massive advertising campaigns are effective in reducing the incidence of smoking or drinking and driving. In both of these cases it seems that few engaging in the behaviors really believes that it is not bad for them; they are usually quite well aware that they are so. Clearly, then, the purpose of such advertising campaigns is not to *inform* the individuals engaging in these behaviors that they are bad for them. What then is their purpose? It can only be to make the fact that these behaviors are dangerous more **epistemically** *forceful.* Somehow, by repeating the message over and over we become more powerfully aware of just how harmful such behaviors potentially are. As a result, the more epistemically forceful the danger is, the more likely we are to not act in such a way. Likewise, when we are discussing compulsion, the more epistemically imminent a threat, the more compelled the threatened individual will feel.

However, these two factors of strength and imminence alone are not sufficient to explain compulsion by another in the context of a threat completely. This is evident when we look again at our prison-yard case. Why, one might wonder, do certain prisoners try to escape, while others in similar circumstances do not, even though threat strength and imminence are the same for all prisoners? Assuming that none of them wishes to remain in prison, why do they not all try to escape? This question points to the need for a third factor, and this factor is the wantonness of the threatened. Again, this factor is difficult to define precisely. However, it does seem clear that different individuals under the same threat and with the same degree of threat imminence can feel compelled to different degrees depending on a certain internal character trait which can be described as incorrigibility or threat indifference. This trait can be roughly characterized as a feeling of indifference for one's well-being in cases where that well-being is threatened should there be a refusal to submit to the terms of some restriction on one's freedom.

These, then, are the factors which must be taken into account when we consider the degree to which a threat prevents the exercise of robust morally significant freedom. While it is surely impossible to quantify these characteristics in order to define exactly what constitutes a threat which overwhelms freedom, it can be said that the degree to which freedom is compromised is directly proportional to threat strength and imminence and inversely proportional to wantonness.

IV

One feature of the major Western theistic traditions is that they seem to involve the issuing of both temporal and eternal threats for disobedience to the divine will. Passages from, for example, the Hebrew and Christian scriptures, such as the following, represent both aspects of this threatened punishment:

> A man who remains stiff-necked after many rebukes will suddenly be destroyed—without remedy. (Prov. 29:1).

and

> But because of your stubbornness and your unrepentant heart you are storing up wrath against yourself for the day of God's wrath. (Rom. 2:5).

As a result, those who are aware of such threats and are convinced of their veracity are in a state where their freedom is at risk. What this creates, simply, is some degree of compulsion by another in the context of the threat. Specifically, it is compulsion by God in the context of a threat of both temporal and eternal punishment. Consequently, on the picture painted by these traditions, God has issued threats, both temporal and eternal, which will be carried out if one fails to submit to Him, in action or belief, in certain ways. Here I will focus particularly on the Christian tradition and the notion of a threat contained therein.

Since these appear to be quite significant threats, the theist must provide some explanation for how this threat can be mitigated so as to prevent the compromising of human freedom. To do this, one of the three factors of compulsion must be mitigated in some way. I will now look at each one to see where the force of compulsion could be averted.

Certainly, with regard to the factor of threat strength, the threat posed by the prospect of eternal damnation is equal to the strongest imaginable threat. One, of course, might wonder why God does not simply eliminate the threat of hell for disobedience and in doing so eliminate or severely limit the threat strength and thus the compulsion. This is an interesting question but not one I will address here. My goal here is to determine whether the traditional, orthodox

Christian position can be reconciled with the fact that God does not reveal himself in the manner [critics] might wish. Since the existence of hell is, I take it, a presumption of the traditional Christian view, I will take it for granted at this point. By doing so, however, we also preclude the possibility of mitigating compulsion by attenuating threat strength.

As a result, unless one of the other two factors can be appropriately controlled, it would seem that morally significant exercise of human free-will would be precluded. What about wantonness? It is unlikely that this factor will provide what is required to avoid the consequence of compulsion which eliminates free-will. The reason for this is that it seems likely that the development and functioning of traits such as wantonness is something which falls within the domain of the freedom of the individual. To attempt to argue for this claim in any complete way would lead into the complex psychological question of whether such personality traits in general are acquired by heredity, environment or elements of individual free choice. Another area that would need to be addressed is how we develop character traits relating to wantonness. Aristotelian views on the development of virtues by the willful cultivation of habits of right-acting, for example, would support the view I hold above in my claim that wantonness is a factor that God cannot manipulate if He desires to preserve free-will. As a result, my claim is that if God were to preserve human free-will, manipulating this element of the picture would not be an option.

This leaves us with the possibility of controlling the degree of threat imminence. Let's begin by looking at *probabilistic* threat imminence. This condition seems to provide little help since, on the Christian story, it is nothing less than certain that the threat will be carried out if the conditions of the threat are not met.

What about *temporal* threat imminence? Clearly this condition has some relevance to our case since carrying out the threat does not follow immediately upon failure to obey the conditions of the threat. There is no trap door to hell that opens upon one's first sin or willful failure to assent to the Christian plan of redemption. Yet merely reducing the temporal imminence of the threat does not appear to be sufficient guarantee that creature's freedom is not compromised by divine compulsion. Given the strength of the threat involved it does not seem that merely delaying the carrying out of the threat temporally is sufficient to mitigate compulsion. If it were, it appears that we should be content to say that God could appear in the sky . . . , issuing the relevant temporal and eternal threats, and yet not have the actions of free creatures be compelled by the issuing of such threats. Yet, it seems that the actions of such free creatures clearly *would be* compelled if they were to be confronted by such obvious threats.

We are left then with *epistemic* threat imminence as the final factor which can be attenuated if God desires to preserve the exercise of morally significant freedom by creatures. My claim is that the hiddenness of God is required in order for free beings to be able to exercise their freedom in a morally significant manner given the strength of the threat implied by knowledge of the threat implicit in the traditional Christian story. If God revealed his existence in a more perspicuous fashion we would be in a situation very much like the one in the standard robbery case, i.e., strong threat strength and strong threat imminence such that the level of wantonness of most, if not all, individuals would not significantly diminish their feeling compelled to act in accordance with the demand of the threatener. However, if God desires that there be individuals with free-will who can use it in morally significant ways, then He must decrease the threat imminence of eternal and temporal punishment and He, in fact, does so by making the existence of the threat epistemically ambiguous. It is this epistemic ambiguity that we call the problem of the hiddenness of God.

This may make it clear why God does not, say, open the sky and give a world-wide, unambiguous proclamation of his existence. However, it does not seem to explain why there is *the particular degree* of divine hiddenness that there is. An objector may reply here that God may not be able to "open the sky" without the loss of morally significant freedom on the part of humans: yet, must that also mean that merely one more unit of divine manifestation in the world would cause the fabric of significant moral freedom to collapse? The answer is no. What this argument is intended to provide is a response to the question of why God does not provide a grand, universal display of general revelation.[2] But why then does God provide the fairly low general level of revelation that he does? Since God is concerned with preserving the freedom of each individual, the level of general revelation must be such as not to preclude the possibility of anyone's exercising his or her free-will in a morally significant fashion. Since threat strength is constant, God must tailor the degree of general revelation to the individual most likely to be compelled by a threat, namely, the least wanton individual. If this is correct, the degree of threat imminence, and consequently the degree of divine manifestation in the world, must be appropriately moderated. And, the degree of moderation here is likely to be great, with the result that the amount of unambiguous general revelation that God can provide is likely to be fairly minimal.

V

. . . [T]he solution offered above does not answer the whole question with respect to the hiddenness of God because it does not address the possibility that God could supplement his general revelation by individual revelation that would be such that each individual is maximally aware of God's existence to the extent possible *for that individual* without such revelation impugning the possibility of the exercise of free-will. If, for example, as [John] Calvin taught, there is a sense of the divine, or *sensus divinitatus,* in each of us, making us aware of the divine presence, why is God not able to make up the lack of general revelation at an individual level and thereby avoid the difficulty of having to cater to the least common denominator with respect to wantonness?

. . . [T]he antecedent free-will theodicy I have chosen . . . however, can be supplemented by a consequence free-will theodicy combined with a second theodicy, i.e., an Augustinian-style punishment theodicy. . . .

Let us assume that it is correct that God does supplement general revelation through a *sensus divinitatus* which provides each individual with knowledge of God yielding a maximal threat imminence without thereby eliminating the possibility for the morally significant exercise of that individual's free will. How could one then account for the hiddenness of God? The consequence free-will theodicy claims that part of the hiddenness of God can be accounted for as a result of some act which prevents the individual from interpreting this revelation properly or giving the properly interpreted evidence the appropriate epistemic weight. As a result, one might argue that one source of God's hiddenness is that free individuals can turn away from the less ambiguous internal evidence that God has provided for his existence. These theories are sometimes characterized as "human-defectiveness" approaches to the hiddenness of God.

Not only does the corruptness of human nature contribute to the hiddenness of God, but it also seems clear that the Jewish and Christian traditions represent God, in some cases, as veiling His existence and **"hardening"** the epistemic capacity that is normally used to understand the revelation He gives. This hardening is usually a punishment which results from some form of moral disobedience. As such, this explanation for the hiddenness of God can be subsumed under the punishment theodicy which claims that some evil (in this case, some divine hiddenness) is the result of justified punishment for sin.[3]

The view that humans can orient themselves in such a way as to make divine revelation less readily understood, either by a direct act or as a result of cultivating a sinful character, as well as the claim that God sometimes withdraws revelation or the ability to properly interpret revelation, combine to give a potential solution to the problem of "individual" divine hiddenness. These supplement the earlier argument as to why God's general revelation is as ambiguous as it is by showing that even if individual revelation were originally intended to be at its

[2]By general revelation I have in mind revelation given to all, or a very large number of, individuals.

[3]Passages such as the following indicate instances when such hardening occurred. "[Because the Israelites worshipped the golden calf] God turned away and gave them over to the worship of heavenly bodies . . . " (Acts 7:42), and, "But my people would not listen to me; Israel would not submit to me. So I gave them over to their stubborn hearts to follow their own devices" (Psalm 81:11–12).

maximum, while still allowing morally significant employment of free-will, it may still be the case that divine hardening as punishment for sin and/or a self-induced human blindness with regard to divine revelation may cause one to find divine exposure non-compelling. . . .

STUDY QUESTIONS

1. What is the problem of divine hiddenness?
2. Murray suggests that the solution to divine hiddenness is a form of the free will theodicy that he calls antecedent free will theodicy. Explain the distinction between antecedent and consequent free will theodicies, and apply it to clarify Murray's solution to the problem of hiddenness.
3. What are Murray's three criteria for determining the significance of a threat? Which of these factors must God control in the case of God's threat to send sinners to hell? Why?
4. Why does Murray feel the need to introduce the idea of human defectiveness?
5. *It would seem that, on Murray's account, God places sinners in an unfair situation. If they disobey God, God will send them to hell; however, by hiding Himself, God makes it difficult for sinners to believe God exists and, hence, difficult for them to take the threat seriously. How might you respond to this objection on Murray's behalf?
6. *Murray admits that God could remove the need to hide Himself were God to eliminate the threat of hell. Murray declines, however, to examine why God does not preserve freedom by simply eliminating the threat. What is a plausible reason for God's keeping the threat of hell intact?
7. *Compare and contrast Murray's remarks on hell with Swinburne's view in Reading 5.4.

PSYCHOLOGICAL EXPLANATIONS OF RELIGIOUS BELIEF

READING 5.6

Gods in the Image of Humans

Xenophanes

This fragment by Greek philosophical poet Xenophanes (c. 570–478 B.C.E.) is the first in a series of selections that try to explain belief in God as due to certain psychological mechanisms—rather than to the truth of what is believed. Xenophanes attacked and even ridiculed the **anthropomorphism** *of Greek religion and such beliefs as transmigration of the soul. He went on to say that the true god is the world. In this reading, he suggests that people form their image of God according to their own physical appearance.*

The Ethiopians make their gods black and snub-nosed; the Thracians say theirs have blue eyes and red hair. Yes, and if oxen and horses or lions had hands, and could paint with their hands, and produce works of art as men do, horses would paint the forms of the gods like horses, and oxen like oxen, and make their bodies in the images of their several kinds.

STUDY QUESTIONS

1. How do conceptions of God arise, according to Xenophanes?
2. *Do you think that Xenophanes is attacking religion by showing that each person fashions a god in his or her own image? Or is he explaining how religious belief arises, without implying that it is false? Or is the passage ambiguous on this point?

READING 5.7

How Human Ignorance Leads to Religion

Benedict Spinoza

The heresies attributed to Benedict (Baruch) Spinoza (1632–1677) led to his excommunication in 1654 by the Jewish community in Amsterdam. In part I of his posthumously published work, Ethics, *Spinoza argues that God is the whole of nature, not, as in traditional theism, a creator who oversees the world and controls its workings through occasional direct interventions. In the appendix from which this selection is taken, Spinoza maintains that the traditional belief in a deity who acts for a purpose, and whose purpose is the welfare of human beings, stems from human ignorance of the true causes of things, coupled with a type of self-centeredness. In Spinoza's analysis, when an event occurs whose causes are not known, human beings wrongly tend to assume that the causes resemble the way in which they, human beings, produce effects—namely, through "***final causes***" (intelligent purposes). They explain disasters as punishments inflicted by an angry deity, even though such phenomena strike "the godly and ungodly alike without discrimination." In truth, the explanation of such events lies in the impersonal causes in nature, and they should not be assumed to be responses to human deeds. (Spinoza's argument for his view about nature, which occupies much of Book I of the* Ethics, *is not included in the selection.)*

. . . Now all the prejudices which I intend to mention here turn on this one point, the widespread belief among men that all things in Nature are like themselves in acting with an end in view. Indeed, they hold it as certain that God himself directs everything to a fixed end; for they say that God has made everything for man's sake and has made man so that he should worship God. So this is the first point I shall consider, seeking the reason why most people are victims of this prejudice and why all are so naturally disposed to accept it. Secondly, I shall demonstrate its falsity; and lastly I shall show how it has been the source of misconceptions about good and bad, right and wrong, praise and blame, order and confusion, beauty and ugliness, and the like.

However, it is not appropriate here to demonstrate the origin of these misconceptions from the nature of the human mind. It will suffice at this point if I take as my basis what must be universally admitted, that all men are born ignorant of the causes of things, that they all have a desire to seek their own advantage, a desire of which they are conscious. From this it follows, firstly, that men believe that they are free, precisely because they are conscious of their volitions and desires; yet concerning the causes that have determined them to desire and will they do not think, not even dream about, because they are ignor-ant of them. Secondly, men act always with an end in view, to wit, the advantage that they seek. Hence it happens that they are always looking only for the **final causes** of things done, and are satisfied when they find them, having, of course, no reason for further doubt. But if they fail to discover them from some external source, they have no recourse but to turn to themselves, and to reflect on what ends would normally determine them to similar actions, and so they necessarily judge other minds by their own. Further, since they find within themselves and outside themselves a considerable number of means very convenient for the pursuit of their own advantage—as, for instance, eyes for seeing, teeth for chewing, cereals and living creatures for food, the sun for giving light, the sea for breeding fish—the result is that they look on all the things of Nature as means to their own advantage. And realising that these were found, not produced by them, they come to believe that there is someone else who produced these means for their use. For looking on things as means, they could not believe them to be self-created, but on the analogy of the means which they are accustomed to produce for themselves, they were bound to conclude that there was some governor or governors of Nature, endowed with human freedom, who have attended to all their needs and made everything for their use. And having no information on the subject, they also had to estimate the character of these rulers by their own, and so they asserted that the gods direct everything for man's use so that they may bind men to them and be held in the highest honour by them. So it came about that every individual devised different methods of worshipping God as he thought fit in order that God should love him beyond others and direct the whole of Nature so as to serve his blind cupidity and insatiable greed. Thus it was that this misconception developed into superstition and became deep-rooted in the minds of men, and it was for this reason that every man strove most earnestly to understand and to explain the final causes of all things. But in seeking to show that Nature does nothing in vain—that is, nothing that is not to man's advantage—they seem to have shown only this, that Nature and the gods are as crazy as mankind.

Consider, I pray, what has been the upshot. Among so many of Nature's blessings they were bound to discover quite a number of disasters, such as storms, earthquakes, diseases and so forth, and they maintained that these occurred because the gods were angry at the wrongs done to them by men, or the faults committed in the course of their worship. And although daily experience cried out against this and showed by any number of examples that blessings and disasters befall the godly and the ungodly alike without discrimination, they did not on that account abandon their ingrained prejudice. For they found it easier to regard this fact as one among other mysteries they could not understand and thus maintain their innate condition of ignorance rather than to demolish in its entirety the theory they had constructed and devise a new one. Hence they made it axiomatic that the judgment of the gods is far beyond man's understanding. Indeed, it is for this reason, and this reason only, that truth might have evaded mankind forever had not Mathematics, which is concerned not with ends but only with the essences and properties of figures, revealed to men a different standard of truth. And there are other causes too—there is no need to mention them here—which could have made men aware of these widespread misconceptions and brought them to a true knowledge of things. . . .

I must not fail to mention here that the advocates of this doctrine, eager to display their talent in assigning purpose to things, have introduced a new style of argument to prove their doctrine, i.e., a reduction, not to the impossible, but to ignorance, thus revealing the lack of any other argument in its favour. For example, if a stone falls from the roof on somebody's head and kills him, by this method of arguing they will prove that the stone fell in order to kill the man; for if it had not fallen for this purpose by the will of God, how could so many circumstances (and there are often many coinciding circumstances) have chanced to concur? Perhaps you will reply that the event occurred because the wind was blowing and the man was walking that way. But they will persist in asking why the wind blew at that time and why the man was walking that way at that very time. If you again reply that the wind sprang up at that time because on the previous day the sea had begun to toss after a period of calm and that the man had been invited by a friend, they will again persist—for there is no end to questions—"But why did the sea toss, and why was the man invited for that time?" And so they will go on and on asking the causes of causes, until you take refuge in the will of God—that is, the sanctuary of ignorance. Similarly, when they consider the structure of the human body, they are astonished, and being ignorant of the causes of such skillful work they conclude that it is fashioned not by mechanical art but by divine or supernatural art, and is so arranged that no one part shall injure another.

As a result, he who seeks the true causes of miracles and is eager to understand the works of Nature as a scholar, and not just to gape at them like a fool, is universally considered an impious heretic. . . .

When men become convinced that everything that is created is created on their behalf, they were bound to consider as the most important quality in every individual thing that which was most useful to them, and to regard as of the highest excellence all those things by which they were most benefited. Hence they came to form these abstract notions to explain the natures of things:—Good, Bad, Order, Confusion, Hot, Cold, Beauty, Ugliness; and since they believed that they are free, the following abstract notions came into being:—Praise, Blame, Right, Wrong. . . .

STUDY QUESTIONS

1. How does religious belief originate, according to Spinoza? *Do you find his explanation convincing? Why or why not?
2. According to Spinoza, in what two distinct ways do humans see the world in terms of themselves?
3. *Nowadays many scientists deny that God exists, whereas many others (an estimated 40 percent) affirm it. Given Spinoza's views about the human tendency to find explanations in terms of purpose, how might he assess the psychological mindset of each of these groups?
4. *Spinoza believes that good and bad are humans' misconceived categorizations of events, based on how they are affected by them. How could this claim be used to solve the problem of evil?

READING 5.8

Religion as Projection

Ludwig Feuerbach

Ludwig Feuerbach (1804–1872) was a German philosopher, a critic of George Hegel (1770–1831) who influenced Karl Marx (1818–83) and Friedrich Engels (1820–1895). In this selection, Feuerbach argues that God is merely a projection of the human self-consciousness of humans' own *infinite nature. The human being possesses reason, will, and affection, but projects those characteristics onto another—God. "He who makes God act humanly, declares human nature to be divine." To contemplate God is really to contemplate* human *nature. (Animals do not have religion because animals are conscious only of themselves as individuals, not of the species.)*

Religion thus understood requires **alienation** *from the human self. For God is thought to possess good qualities, which, in fact, are human—and humans, not realizing this, are left ascribing the* bad *qualities to themselves. "Man denies as to himself only what he attributes to God." When human beings attribute more and more good qualities to themselves, healthy development and freedom arrive.*

This selection is from The Essence of Christianity; *in other writings, Feuerbach gives a different account of religion (as dependence).*

Religion has its basis in the essential difference between man and the brute—the brutes have no religion. . . .

But what is this essential difference between man and the brute? The most simple, general, and also the most popular answer to this question is—consciousness:—but consciousness in the strict sense; for the consciousness implied in the feeling of self as an individual, in discrimination by the senses, in the perception and even judgment of outward things according to definite sensible signs, cannot be denied to the brutes. Consciousness in the strictest sense is present only in a being to whom his species, his essential nature, is an object of thought. The brute is indeed conscious of himself as an individual—and he has accordingly the feeling of self as the common centre of successive sensations—but not as a species: hence, he is without that consciousness which in its nature, as in its name, is akin to science. Where there is this higher consciousness there is a capability of science. Science is the cognisance of species. . . . [O]nly a being to whom his own species, his own nature, is an object of thought, can make the essential nature of other things or beings an object of thought. . . .

Religion being identical with the distinctive characteristic of man, is then identical with self-consciousness—with the consciousness which man has of his nature. But religion, expressed generally, is consciousness of the infinite; thus it is and can be nothing else than the consciousness which man has of his own—not finite and limited, but infinite nature. A really finite being has not even the faintest adumbration, still less consciousness, of an infinite being, for the limit of the nature is also the limit of the consciousness. . . .

What, then, *is* the nature of man, of which he is conscious, or what constitutes the specific distinction, the proper humanity of man? Reason, Will, Affection. To a complete man belong the power of thought, the power of will, the power of affection. The power of thought is the light of the intellect, the power of will is energy of character, the power of affection is love. Reason, love, force of will, are perfections—the perfections of the human being—nay, more, they are absolute perfections of being. To will, to love, to think, are the highest powers, are the absolute nature of man as man, and the basis of his existence. Man exists to think, to love, to will. Now that which is the end, the ultimate aim, is also the true basis and principle of a being. But what is the end of reason? Reason. Of love? Love. Of will? Freedom of the will. We think for the sake of thinking; love for the sake of loving; will for the sake of willing—*i.e.,* that we may be free. True existence is thinking, loving, willing existence. That alone is true, perfect, divine, which exists for its own sake. But such is love, such is reason, such is will. The divine trinity in man, above the individual man, is the unity of reason, love, will. Reason, Will, Love, are not powers which man possesses, for he is nothing without them, he is what he is only by them; they are the constituent elements of his nature, which he neither has nor makes, the animating, determining, governing powers—divine, absolute powers—to which he can oppose no resistance. . . .

. . . Man denies as to himself only what he attributes to God. Religion abstracts from man, from the world; but it can only abstract from the limitations, from the phenomena; in short, from the negative, not from the essence, the positive, of the world and humanity: hence, in the very abstraction and negation it must recover that from which it abstracts, or believes itself to abstract. And thus, in reality, whatever religion consciously denies—always supposing that what is denied by it is something essential, true, and consequently incapable of being ultimately denied—it unconsciously restores in God. Thus, in religion man denies his reason; of himself he knows nothing of God, his thoughts are only worldly, earthly; he can only believe what God reveals to him. But on this account the thoughts of God are human, earthly thoughts: like man, he has plans in his mind, he accommodates himself to circumstances and grades of intelligence, like a tutor with his pupils; he calculates closely the effect of his gifts and revelations; he observes man in all his doings; he knows all things, even the most earthly, the commonest, the most trivial. In brief, man in relation to God denies his own knowledge, his own thoughts, that he may place them in God. Man gives up his personality; but in return, God, the Almighty, infinite, unlimited being, is a person; he denies human dignity, the human *ego;* but in return God is to him a selfish, egoistical being, who in all things seeks only himself, his own honour, his own ends; he represents God as simply seeking the satisfaction of his own selfishness, while yet he frowns on that of every other being; his God is the very luxury of egoism. Religion further denies goodness as a quality of human nature; man is wicked, corrupt, incapable of good; but, on the other hand, God is only good—the Good Being. Man's nature demands as an object goodness, personified as God; but is it not hereby declared that goodness is an essential tendency of man? If my heart is wicked, my understanding perverted, how can I perceive and feel the holy to be holy, the good to be good? Could I perceive the beauty of a fine picture if my mind were aesthetically an absolute piece of perversion? Though I may not be a painter, though

I may not have the power of producing what is beautiful myself, I must yet have aesthetic feeling, aesthetic comprehension, since I perceive the beauty that is presented to me externally. Either goodness does not exist at all for man, or, if it does exist, therein is revealed to the individual man the holiness and goodness of human nature. That which is absolutely opposed to my nature, to which I am united by no bond of sympathy, is not even conceivable or perceptible by me. The holy is in opposition to me only as regards the modifications of my personality, but as regards my fundamental nature it is in unity with me. The holy is a reproach to my sinfulness; in it I recognise myself as a sinner; but in so doing, while I blame myself, I acknowledge what I am not, but ought to be, and what, for that very reason, I, according to my destination, can be; for an "ought" which has no corresponding capability does not affect me, is a ludicrous chimaera without any true relation to my mental constitution. But when I acknowledge goodness as my destination, as my law, I acknowledge it, whether consciously or unconsciously, as my own nature. Another nature than my own, one different in quality, cannot touch me. I can perceive sin as sin, only when I perceive it to be a contradiction of myself with myself—that is, of my personality with my fundamental nature. As a contradiction of the absolute, considered as another being, the feeling of sin is inexplicable, unmeaning. . . .

As with the doctrine of the radical corruption of human nature, so is it with the identical doctrine, that man can do nothing good, *i.e.,* in truth, nothing of himself—by his own strength. For the denial of human strength and spontaneous moral activity to be true, the moral activity of God must also be denied; and we must say, with the Oriental **nihilist** or **pantheist:** the Divine being is absolutely without will or action, indifferent, knowing nothing of the discrimination between evil and good. But he who defines God as an active being, and not only so, but as morally active and morally critical,—as a being who loves, works, and rewards good, punishes, rejects, and condemns evil,—he who thus defines God only in appearance denies human activity, in fact, making it the highest, the most real activity. He who makes God act humanly, declares human activity to be divine; he says: A god who is not active, and not morally or humanly active, is no god; and thus he makes the idea of the Godhead dependent on the idea of activity, that is, of human activity, for a higher he knows not.

Man—this is the mystery of religion—projects his being into objectivity, and then again makes himself an object to this projected image of himself thus converted into a subject; he thinks of himself [as] an object to himself, but as the object of an object, of another being than himself. Thus here. Man is an object to God. That man is good or evil is not indifferent to God; no! He has a lively, profound interest in man's being good; he wills that man should be good, happy—for without goodness there is no happiness. Thus the religious man virtually retracts the nothingness of human activity, by making his dispositions and actions an object to God, by making man the end of God—for that which is an object to the mind is an end in action; by making the divine activity a means of human salvation. God acts, that man may be good and happy. Thus man, while he is apparently humiliated to the lowest degree, is in truth exalted to the highest. Thus, in and through God, man has in view himself alone. It is true that man places the aim of his action in God, but God has no other aim of action than the moral and eternal salvation of man: thus man has in fact no other aim than himself. The divine activity is not distinct from the human.

How could the divine activity work on me as its object, nay, work in me, if it were essentially different from me; how could it have a human aim, the aim of ameliorating and blessing man, if it were not itself human? Does not the purpose determine the nature of the act? When man makes his moral improvement an aim to himself, he has divine resolutions, divine projects; but also, when God seeks the salvation of man, he has human ends and a human mode of activity corresponding to these ends. Thus in God man has only his own activity as an object. But for the very reason that he regards his own activity as objective, goodness only as an object, he necessarily receives the impulse, the motive not from himself, but from this object. He contemplates his nature as external to himself, and this nature as goodness; thus it is self-evident, it is mere tautology to say that the impulse to good comes only from thence where he places the good.

God is the highest subjectivity of man abstracted from himself; hence man can do nothing of himself, all goodness comes from God. The more subjective God is, the more completely does man divest himself of his subjectivity, because God is, *per se,* his relinquished self, the possession of which he however again vindicates to himself. As the action of the arteries drives the blood into the extremities, and the action of the veins brings it back again, as life in general consists in a perpetual systole and diastole; so is it in religion. In the religious systole man propels his own nature from himself, he throws himself outward; in the religious diastole he receives the rejected nature into his heart again. God alone is the being who acts of himself,—this is the force of repulsion in religion; God is the being who acts in me, with me, through me, upon me, for me, is the principle of my salvation, of my good dispositions and actions, consequently my own good principle and nature,—this is the force of attraction in religion.

The course of religious development which has been generally indicated consists specifically in this, that man abstracts more and more from God, and attributes more and more to himself.

Religion is the disuniting of man from himself; he sets God before him as the antithesis of himself. God is not what man is—man is not what God is. God is the infinite, man the finite being; God is perfect, man imperfect; God eternal, man temporal; God almighty, man weak; God holy, man sinful. God and man are extremes: God is the absolutely positive, the sum of all realities; man the absolutely negative, comprehending all negations.

But in religion man contemplates his own latent nature. Hence it must be shown that this antithesis, this differencing of God and man, with which religion begins, is a differencing of man with his own nature.

This inherent necessity of this proof is at once apparent from this,—that if the divine nature, which is the object of religion, were really different from the nature of man, a division, a disunion could not take place. If God is really a different being from myself, why should his perfection trouble me? Disunion exists only between beings who are at variance, but who ought to be one, who can be one, and who consequently in nature, in truth, are one. On this general ground, then, the nature with which man feels himself in disunion must be inborn, immanent in himself, but at the same time it must be of a different character from that nature or power which gives him the feeling, the consciousness of reconciliation, of union with God, or, what is the same thing, with himself.

This nature is nothing else than the intelligence—the reason or the understanding. God as the antithesis of man, as a being not human, *i.e.,* not personally human, is the objective nature of the understanding. The pure, perfect divine nature is the self-consciousness of the understanding; the consciousness which the understanding has of its own perfection. The understanding knows nothing of the sufferings of the heart; it has no desires, no passions, no wants, and, for that reason, no deficiencies and weaknesses, as the heart has. Men in whom the intellect predominates, who, with one-sided but all the more characteristic definiteness, embody and personify for us the nature of the understanding, are free from the anguish of the heart, from the passions, the excesses of the man who has strong emotions; they are not passionately interested in any finite, *i.e.,* particular object; they do not give themselves in pledge; they are free. "To want nothing, and by this freedom from wants to become like the immortal gods";—"not to subject ourselves to things, but things to us";—"all is vanity";—these and similar sayings are the mottoes of the men who are governed by abstract understanding. The understanding is that part of our nature which is neutral, impassible, not to bribed, not subject to illusions—the pure, passionless light of the intelligence. It is the categorical, impartial consciousness of the fact as fact, because it is itself of an objective nature. It is the consciousness of the uncontradictory, because it is itself the uncontradictory unity, the source of logical identity. It is the consciousness of law, necessity, rule, measure, because it is itself the activity of law, the necessity of the nature of things under the form of spontaneous activity, the rule of rules, the absolute measure, the measure of measures. Only by the understanding can man judge and act in contradiction with his dearest human, that is, personal feelings, when the God of the understanding,—law, necessity, right,—commands it. The father who, as a judge, condemns his own son to death because he knows him to be guilty, can do this only as a rational, not as an emotional being. The understanding shows us the faults and weaknesses even of our beloved ones; it shows us even our own. It is for this reason that it so often throws us into painful collision with ourselves, with our own hearts. We do not like to give reason the upper hand: we are too tender to ourselves to carry out the true, but hard, relentless verdict of the understanding. The understanding is the power which has relation to species: the heart represents particular circumstances, individuals,—the understanding, general circumstances, universals; it is the superhuman, *i.e.,* the impersonal power in man. Only by and in the understanding has man the power of abstraction from himself, from his subjective being,—of exalting himself to general ideas and relations, of distinguishing the object from the impressions which it produces on his feelings, of regarding it in and by itself without reference to human personality. Philosophy, mathematics, astronomy, physics, in short, science in general, is the practical proof, because it is the product of this truly infinite and divine activity. Religious **anthropomorphisms,** therefore, are in contradiction with the understanding; it repudiates their application to God; it denies them. But this God, free from **anthropomorphisms,** impartial, passionless, is nothing else than the nature of the understanding itself regarded as objective. . . .

STUDY QUESTIONS

1. Describe Feuerbach's notion of religion as a projection. What assessment of human qualities does it entail? What are the three essential qualities of human beings in this theory?
2. Why is religion a form of alienation from self, according to Feuerbach?
3. Why is religion only a stage in the history of humanity, according to Feuerbach? What replaces it?
4. What role does Feuerbach assign to the understanding?
5. *It has been said that Feuerbach substitutes anthropology for theology. How do you understand this remark?
6. *Give your own assessment of Feuerbach's ideas.

READING 5.9

Religion as Wish Fulfillment

Sigmund Freud

*Sigmund Freud (1856–1939), the celebrated founder of psychoanalysis, presents in this selection his account of how religious beliefs originate. Essentially, religious ideas are created to protect human beings against the dangers of nature and fate (*Moira*). Children tend to think of their fathers as powerful and as able to protect and provide for them. When they grow older, they realize that their fathers are not very powerful and cannot control nature so as to be protected and protect others from its dangers. They seek a figure to provide protection—a (father-) figure, who if placated and prayed to can provide for them; and that figure is God (or the gods). When the gods themselves come to be thought of as subject to fate, religion stresses the gods' role in evening out the evils of civilization by providing precepts and (via promises of reward and threats of punishment) reconciling people to the sacrifices and privations they must endure in civilization for the sake of others. Eventually, just as the child matures and achieves independence from the father, so, too, the* *human race will eventually acquire* **autonomy,** *will exercise reason, and will rid itself of the God-figure.*

Freud claims that, by declaring religion an **illusion,** *he is not evaluating its truth but is only giving a psychological account of the religious idea as an "illusion," that is, a belief deriving from human wishes. Even so, the selection bears indications that he thinks religion is not likely to be true. (See also the quotations from Freud in Reading 5.10.)*

[THE ORIGIN OF RELIGIOUS IDEAS]

In what does the peculiar value of religious ideas lie?

We have spoken of the hostility to civilization which is produced by the pressure that civilization exercises, the renunciations of instinct which it demands. If one imagines its prohibitions lifted—if, then, one may take any woman one pleases as a sexual object, if one may without hesitation kill one's rival for her love or anyone else who stands in one's way, if, too, one can carry off any of the other man's belongings without asking leave—how splendid, what a string of satisfactions one's life would be! . . .

But how ungrateful, how short-sighted after all, to strive for the abolition of civilization! What would then remain would be a state of nature, and that would be far harder to bear. It is true that nature would not demand any restrictions of instinct from us, she would let us do as we liked; but she has her own particularly effective method of restricting us. She destroys us—coldly, cruelly, relentlessly, as it seems to us, and possibly through the very things that occasioned our satisfaction. It was precisely because of these dangers with which nature threatens us that we came together and created civilization, which is also, among other things, intended to make our communal life possible. . . . [T]he principal task of civilization, its actual *raison d'être,* is to defend us against nature.

We all know that in many ways civilization does this fairly well already, and clearly as time goes on it will do it much better. But no one is under the illusion that nature has already been vanquished; and few dare hope that she will ever be entirely subjected to man. There are the elements, which seem to mock at all human control: the earth, which quakes and is torn apart and buries all human life and its works; water, which deluges and drowns everything in a turmoil; storms, which blow everything before them; there are diseases, which we have only recently recognized as attacks by other organisms; and finally there is the painful riddle of death, against which no medicine has yet been found, nor probably will be. With these forces nature rises up against us, majestic, cruel and inexorable; she brings to our mind once more our weakness and helplessness, which we thought to escape through the work of civilization. One of the few gratifying and exalting impressions which mankind can offer is when, in the face of an elemental catastrophe, it forgets the discordancies of its civilization and all its internal difficulties and animosities, and recalls the great common task of preserving itself against the superior power of nature.

For the individual, too, life is hard to bear, just as it is for mankind in general. The civilization in which he participates imposes some amount of privation on him, and other men bring him a measure of suffering, either in spite of the precepts of his civilization or because of its imperfections. To this are added the injuries which untamed nature—he calls it Fate—inflicts on him. One might suppose that this condition of things would result in a permanent state of anxious expectation in him and a severe injury to his natural narcissism. We know already how the individual reacts to the injuries which civilization and other men inflict on him: he develops a corresponding degree of resistance to the regulations of civilization and of hostility to it. But how does he defend himself against the superior powers of nature, of Fate, which threaten him as they threaten all the rest?

Civilization relieves him of this task; it performs it in the same way for all alike; and it is noteworthy that in this almost all civilizations act alike. Civilization does not call a halt in the task of defending man against nature, it merely pursues it by other means. The task is a manifold one. Man's self-regard, seriously menaced, calls for consolation; life and the universe must be robbed of their terrors; moreover his curiosity, moved, it is true, by the strongest practical interest, demands an answer.

A great deal is already gained with the first step: the humanization of nature. Impersonal forces and destinies cannot be approached; they remain eternally remote. But if the elements have passions that rage as they do in our own souls, if death itself is not something spontaneous but the violent act of an evil Will, if everywhere in nature there are Beings around us of a kind that we know in our own society, then we can breathe freely, can feel at home in the uncanny and can deal by psychical means with our senseless anxiety. We are still defenceless, perhaps, but we are no longer helplessly paralysed; we can at least react. Perhaps, indeed, we are not even defenceless. We can apply the same methods against these violent supermen outside that we employ in our own society; we can try to adjure them, to appease them, to bribe them, and, by so influencing them, we may rob them of a part of their power. A replacement like this of natural science by psychology not only provides immediate relief, but also points the way to a further mastering of the situation.

For this situation is nothing new. It has an infantile prototype, of which it is in fact only the continuation. For once before one has found oneself in a similar state of helplessness: as a small child, in relation to one's parents. One had reason to fear them, and especially one's father; and yet one was sure of his protection against the dangers one knew. Thus it was natural to assimilate the two situations. Here, too, wishing played its part, as it does in dream-life. The sleeper may be seized with a presentiment of death, which threatens to place him in the grave. But the dream-work knows how to select a condition that will turn even that dreaded event into a wish-fulfilment: the dreamer sees himself in an ancient Etruscan grave which he has climbed down into, happy to find his archaeological interests satisfied. In the same way, a man makes the forces of nature not simply into persons with whom he can associate as he would with his equals—that would not do justice to the overpowering impression which those forces make on him—but he gives them the character of a father. He turns them into gods, following in this, as I have tried to show, not only an infantile prototype but a **phylogenetic** one.

In the course of time the first observations were made of regularity and conformity to law in natural phenomena, and with this the forces of nature lost their human traits. But man's helplessness remains and along with it his longing for his father, and the gods. The gods retain their threefold task: they must exorcize the terrors of nature, they must reconcile men to the cruelty of Fate, particularly as it is shown in death, and they must compensate them for the sufferings and privations which a civilized life in common has imposed on them.

But within these functions there is a gradual displacement of accent. It was observed that the phenomena of nature developed automatically according to internal necessities. Without doubt the gods were the lords of nature; they had arranged it to be as it was and now they could leave it to itself. Only occasionally, in what are known as miracles, did they intervene in its course, as though to make it plain that they had relinquished nothing of their original sphere of power. As regards the apportioning of destinies, an unpleasant suspicion persisted that the perplexity and helplessness of the human race could not be remedied. It was here that the gods were most apt to fail. If they themselves created Fate, then their counsels must be deemed inscrutable. The notion dawned on the most gifted people of antiquity that Moira [Fate] stood above the gods and that the gods themselves had their own destinies. And the more autonomous nature became and the more the gods withdrew from it, the more earnestly were all expectations directed to the third function of the gods—the more did morality become their true domain. It now became the task of the gods to even out the defects and evils of civilization, to attend to the sufferings which men inflict on one another in their life together and to watch over the fulfilment of the precepts of civilization, which men obey so imperfectly. Those precepts themselves were credited with a divine origin; they were elevated beyond human society and were extended to nature and the universe.

And thus a store of ideas is created, born from man's need to make his helplessness tolerable and built up from the material of memories of the helplessness of his own childhood and the childhood of the human race. It can clearly be seen that the possession of these ideas protects him in two directions—against the dangers of nature and Fate, and against the injuries that threaten him from human society itself. Here is the gist of the matter. Life in this world serves a higher purpose; no doubt it is not easy to guess what that purpose is, but it certainly signifies a perfecting of man's nature. It is probably the spiritual part of man, the soul, which in the course of time has so slowly and unwillingly detached itself from the body, that is the object of this elevation and exaltation. Everything that happens in this world is an expression of the intentions of an intelligence superior to us, which in the end, though its ways and byways are difficult to follow, orders everything for the best—that is, to make it enjoyable for us. Over each one of us there watches a benevolent Providence which is only seemingly stern and which will not suffer us to become a plaything of the overmighty and pitiless forces of nature. Death itself is not extinction, is not a return to inorganic lifelessness, but the beginning of a new kind of existence which lies on the path of development to something higher. And, looking in the other direction, this view announces that the same moral laws which our civilizations have set up govern the whole universe as well, except that they are maintained by a supreme court of justice with incomparably more power and consistency. In the end all good is rewarded and all evil punished, if not actually in this form of life then in the later existences that begin after death. In this way all the terrors, the sufferings and the hardships of life are destined to be obliterated. Life after death, which continues life on earth just as the invisible part of the spectrum joins on to the visible part, brings us all the perfection that we may perhaps have missed here. And the superior wisdom which directs this course of things, the infinite goodness that expresses itself in it, the justice that achieves its aim in it—these are the attributes of the divine beings who also created us and the world as a whole, or rather, of the one divine being into which, in our civilization, all the gods of antiquity have been condensed. The people which first succeeded in thus concentrating the divine attributes was not a little proud of the advance. It had laid open to view the father who had all along been hidden behind every divine figure as its nucleus. Fundamentally this was a return to the historical beginnings of the idea of God. Now that God was a single person, man's relations to him could recover the intimacy and intensity of the child's relation to his father. But if one had done so much for one's father, one wanted to have a reward, or at least to be his only beloved child, his Chosen People. . . .

[ILLUSIONS]

. . . [Religious ideas,] which are given out as teachings, are not precipitates of experience or end-results of thinking: they are **illusions,** fulfilments of the oldest, strongest and most urgent wishes of mankind. The secret of their strength lies in the strength of those wishes. As we already know, the terrifying impression of helplessness in childhood aroused the need for protection—for protection through love—which was provided by the father; and the recognition that this helplessness lasts throughout life made it necessary to cling to the existence of a father, but this time a more powerful one. Thus the benevolent rule of a divine Providence allays our fear of the dangers of life; the establishment of a moral world-order ensures the fulfilment of the demands of justice, which have so often remained unfulfilled in human civilization; and the prolongation of earthly existence in a future life provides the local and temporal framework in which these wish-fulfilments shall take place. . . . It is an enormous relief to the individual psyche if the conflicts of its childhood arising from the father-complex—conflicts which it has never wholly overcome—are removed from it and brought to a solution which is universally accepted.

When I say that these things are all **illusions,** I must define the meaning of the word. An illusion is not the same thing as an error; nor is it necessarily an error. . . . What is characteristic of illusions is that they are derived from human wishes. In this respect they come near to psychiatric delusions. But they differ from them, too, apart from the more complicated structure of delusions. In the case of delusions, we emphasize as essential their being in contradiction with reality. Illusions need not necessarily be false—that is to say, unrealizable or in contradiction to reality. For instance, a middle-class girl may have the illusion that a prince will come and marry her. . . . Thus we call a belief an illusion when a wish-fulfilment is a prominent factor in its motivation, and in doing so we disregard its relations to reality, just as the illusion itself sets no store by verification.

Having thus taken our bearings, let us return once more to the question of religious doctrines. We can now repeat that all of them are illusions and insusceptible of proof. No one can be compelled to think them true, to believe in them. Some of them are so improbable, so incompatible with everything we have laboriously discovered about the reality of the world, that we may compare them—if we pay proper regard to the psychological differences—to delusions. Of the reality value of most of them we cannot judge; just as they cannot be proved, so they cannot be refuted. . . .

To assess the truth-value of religious doctrines does not lie within the scope of the present enquiry. It is enough for us that we have recognized them as being, in their psychological nature, illusions. But we do not have to conceal the fact that this discovery also strongly influences our attitude to the question which must appear to many to be the most important of all. We know approximately at what periods and by what kind of men religious doctrines were created. If in addition we discover the motives which led to this, our attitude to the problem of religion will undergo a marked displacement. We shall tell ourselves that it would be very nice if there were a God who created the world and was a benevolent Providence, and if there were a moral order in the universe and an after-life; but it is a very striking fact that all this is exactly as we are bound to wish it to be. And it would be more remarkable still if our wretched, ignorant and downtrodden ancestors had succeeded in solving all these difficult riddles of the universe. . . .

[RELIGION AND CIVILIZATION]

. . . Religion has clearly performed great services for human civilization. It has contributed much towards the taming of the asocial instincts. But not enough. It has ruled human society for many thousands of years and has had time to show what it can achieve. If it had succeeded in making the majority of mankind happy, in comforting them, in reconciling them to life and in making them into vehicles of civilization, no one would dream of attempting to alter the existing conditions. But what do we see instead? We see that an appallingly large number of people are dissatisfied with civilization and unhappy in it, and feel it as a yoke which must be shaken off; and that these people either do everything in their power to change that civilization, or else go so far in their hostility to it that they will have nothing to do with civilization or with a restriction of instinct. At this point it will be objected against us that this state of affairs is due to the very fact that religion has lost a part of its influence over human masses precisely because of the deplorable effect of the advances of science. We will note this admission and the reason given for it, and we shall make use of it later for our own purposes; but the objection itself has no force.

It is doubtful whether men were in general happier at a time when religious doctrines held unrestricted sway; more moral they certainly were not. They have always known how to externalize the precepts of religion and thus to nullify their intentions. The priests, whose duty it was to ensure obedience to religion, met them half-way in this. God's kindness must lay a restraining hand on His justice. One sinned, and then one made a sacrifice or did penance and then one was free to sin once more. Russian introspectiveness has reached the pitch of concluding that sin is indispensable for the enjoyment of all the blessings of divine grace, so that, at bottom, sin is pleasing to God. It is no secret that the priests could only keep the masses submissive to religion by making such large concessions as these to the instinctual nature of man. Thus it was agreed: God alone is strong and good, man is weak and sinful. In every age immorality has found no less support in religion than morality has. If the achievements of religion in respect to man's happiness, susceptibility to culture and moral control are no better than this, the question cannot but arise whether we are not overrating its necessity for mankind, and whether we do wisely in basing our cultural demands upon it. . . .

Civilization has little to fear from educated people and brainworkers. In them the replacement of religious motives for civilized behaviour by other, secular motives would proceed unobtrusively;

moreover, such people are to a large extent themselves vehicles of civilization. But it is another matter with the great mass of the uneducated and oppressed, who have every reason for being enemies of civilization. So long as they do not discover that people no longer believe in God, all is well. But they will discover it, infallibly, even if this piece of writing of mine is not published. And they are ready to accept the results of scientific thinking, but without the change having taken place in them which scientific thinking brings about in people. Is there not a danger here that the hostility of these masses to civilization will throw itself against the weak spot that they have found in their task-mistress? If the sole reason why you must not kill your neighbour is because God has forbidden it and will severely punish you for it in this or the next life—then, when you learn that there is no God and that you need not fear His punishment, you will certainly kill your neighbour without hesitation, and you can only be prevented from doing so by mundane force. Thus either these dangerous masses must be held down most severely and kept most carefully away from any chance of intellectual awakening, or else the relationship between civilization and religion must undergo a fundamental revision. . . .

Our knowledge of the historical worth of certain religious doctrines increases our respect for them, but does not invalidate our proposal that they should cease to be put forward as the reasons for the precepts of civilization. On the contrary! Those historical residues have helped us to view religious teachings, as it were, as neurotic relics, and we may now argue that the time has probably come, as it does in an analytic treatment, for replacing the effects of **repression** by the results of the rational operation of the intellect. We may foresee, but hardly regret, that such a process of remoulding will not stop at renouncing the solemn transfiguration of cultural precepts, but that a general revision of them will result in many of them being done away with. In this way our appointed task of reconciling men to civilization will to a great extent be achieved. We need not deplore the renunciation of historical truth when we put forward rational grounds for the precepts of civilization. The truths contained in religious doctrines are after all so distorted and systematically disguised that the mass of humanity cannot recognize them as truth. The case is similar to what happens when we tell a child that new-born babies are brought by the stork. Here, too, we are telling the truth in symbolic clothing, for we know what the large bird signifies. But the child does not know it. He hears only the distorted part of what we say, and feels that he has been deceived; and we know how often his distrust of the grown-ups and his refractoriness actually take their start from this impression. We have become convinced that it is better to avoid such symbolic disguisings of the truth in what we tell children and not to withhold from them a knowledge of the true state of affairs commensurate with their intellectual level.

STUDY QUESTIONS

1. Explain Freud's notion of an "illusion."
2. Summarize Freud's account of how religious belief originates.
3. *Are there nontheistic religions whose origins cannot be captured by Freud's account? Are there theistic conceptions of God that cannot be captured by Freud's view of God as a father-figure?
4. Freud emphasizes the psychological benefits that religion brings to the individual. But religion also requires hardship and sacrifice. Can you suggest a way for Freud to account for this last fact?
5. *Do you think religion claims to afford people control over nature to the degree Freud implies? Explain.
6. According to Freud, what role do the gods serve besides offering protection from nature? Explain.
7. *Philosophers often argue that our beliefs that there is an external world and that the world follows uniform laws cannot be proved. To what extent can these beliefs be viewed as a product of wishful thinking? How would regarding them as products of wishful thinking affect your evaluation of Freud's account of religious beliefs?
8. *If Freud's account is true, does it show that religious beliefs are false? (This question is taken up by William L. Rowe in Reading 5.10.)

READING 5.10

Causation vs. Justification: A Critique of Freud

William L. Rowe

Freud, as we saw, offers a psychological explanation of how people come to believe in God. If his account is true, would that show that people's belief in God is false? No, argues William L. Rowe (Purdue University). To have found psychological causes of a belief is not to have shown that the belief is false. Truth or falsehood must be judged by considering reasons for and against the belief. Only in some cases is the cause of a belief highly relevant to the question of truth. But, in general, to reason from a belief's causes to its truth or falsehood is to commit the "**genetic fallacy.**"

Freud himself explains that an "**illusion,**" *as opposed to a "delusion," need not be false and professes not to have shown that religious beliefs are false by virtue of their origin. Even so, Rowe suggests, one could argue, based on a passage in Freud, that religious beliefs are false because they are formed by wishful thinking, and beliefs formed in this way tend to be false. However, Rowe does not find this* **argument** *compelling, partly because some individuals might have good reasons for beliefs that others hold only because of wishful thinking.*

If Rowe is correct, then not only does Freud's explanation of religious belief not show those beliefs to be false, but neither do any of the other explanations we have studied (Spinoza, Feuerbach), nor any other social scientific explanation, show those beliefs to be false.

. . . Does Freud's account of the emergence of religious beliefs provide him or us with rational grounds for thinking that the basic beliefs of theistic religion are false?

Let's suppose that Freud has made a good case for the view that religious beliefs are **illusions,** that they owe their origin and continuing appeal to the fact that they satisfy people's deepest wishes. Let's also suppose that not only would religious people cling to these beliefs in the absence of rational grounds for them, but that most people do not in fact have good rational grounds for their religious beliefs. Does Freud think that in showing that religious beliefs are illusions he has succeeded in showing that they are *false?* This question must be answered in the negative for two reasons. First, . . . Freud is careful to explain that an illusion need not be false. Thus the mere fact that religious beliefs are illusions is insufficient to establish that they are false. Second, Freud is careful to point out that the question of the truth or falsity of religious ideas is not a question that his investigations are able to answer. Thus he remarks:

> Of the reality value of most of them we cannot judge; just as they cannot be proved, so they cannot be refuted. We still know too little to make a critical approach to them.[1]

And again he says:

> To assess the truth-value of religious doctrines does not lie within the scope of the present enquiry. It is enough for us that we have recognized them as being, in their psychological nature, illusions.[2]

Thus it seems clear that Freud did not take himself to have shown that religious beliefs are false.

Of course, if Freud's explanation of the emergence of the idea of God is correct, then what causes

[1]*The Future of An Illusion* [Anchor Books, 1964], p. 50. [p. 325 above]

[2]Ibid., p. 52. [p. 325 above]

the appearance of this idea, as well as its acceptance by continuing generations, has nothing to do with any immediate divine activity or force; the causes lie within the natural world. But this would show that the belief in God is false only if we had some conclusive reason for thinking that if God exists, then the cause of someone's coming to believe in his existence would have to be supranatural. And there does not seem to be any good reason for thinking that God's existence rules out natural causes for the belief that he exists.

Still, someone might object, if the causes of the belief in God are purely natural, due to a longing for the father-figure, doesn't that somehow throw doubt on the issue of God's existence? To the extent that we think that it does, we are probably falling into a way of thinking that logicians have called "the **genetic fallacy.**" We commit the genetic fallacy whenever we fallaciously infer that a belief is true or false from a premise stating the causal origin of that belief. Sometimes what causes us to hold a belief is highly relevant to the truth or falsehood of the belief. "What caused me to believe that Purdue defeated Michigan is the fact that I saw the game and the final score." Here the cause of my belief has a direct bearing on its truth. But often, what causes someone to take up a belief has little or nothing to do with what justifies one in holding that belief. Perhaps what caused me to believe that the earth is not flat was my mother's telling me so. But I would hardly try to justify that belief by appealing to what caused me to accept it. There is, then, an important distinction between the *causation of belief* and the *justification of belief.* To ignore this distinction, to suppose that from whatever is the *cause* of someone's holding a belief we can determine whether the belief is true or false, is to commit the genetic fallacy. Although he does not discuss this fallacy, it's clear that Freud has not committed it.

Although Freud's causal explanation of religious ideas does not, by itself, show these ideas to be false, there are, I believe, some special features about his account that perhaps render it somewhat unlikely that religious ideas are true. Indeed, there is, I think, an interesting argument against the truth of religion that can be developed out of Freud's view that religious beliefs are wish-fulfillments. Although he does not explicitly develop the argument Freud alludes to it. Directly after pointing out that assessing the truth-value of religious doctrines lies beyond the scope of his work, that it is enough to have shown them to be illusions, Freud remarks:

> But we do not have to conceal the fact that this discovery also strongly influences our attitude to the question which must appear to many to be the most important of all. We know approximately at what periods and by what kind of men religious doctrines were created. If in addition we discover the motives which led to this, our attitude to the problem of religion will undergo a marked displacement. We shall tell ourselves that it would be very nice if there were a God who created the world and was a benevolent Providence, and if there were a moral order in the universe and an after-life; but it is a very striking fact that all this is exactly as we are bound to wish it to be. And it would be more remarkable still if our wretched, ignorant and downtrodden ancestors had succeeded in solving all these difficult riddles of the universe.[3]

The question which "must appear to many to be the most important of all" is, of course, the question of whether religious beliefs are true or false, whether God exists or does not exist. And in the passage quoted there is, I think, an unexpressed argument for the view that religious beliefs are false. Let's state it as follows:

1. Among those beliefs which we come to accept, not on the basis of rational proof, but because they satisfy certain profound wishes, the majority turn out to be false.
2. Religious beliefs are beliefs which we come to accept, not on the basis of rational proof, but because they satisfy certain profound wishes.

Therefore,

3. Probably, religious beliefs are false.

[3]Ibid., pp. 52–53. [p. 325 above]

Insofar as Freudian psychology provides any reason for thinking that religious ideas are false, its reason, I think, is expressed in the above argument. The second premise merely expresses Freud's view that religious beliefs are illusions. The first premise is based on the conviction that reality does not often conform to our wishes. It would be nice if reality were exactly as we are bound to wish it to be, but if experience has taught us anything about our wishes it is that only infrequently does reality satisfy them. Freud adds that the beliefs in question are even more doubtful since they were formulated by our ignorant ancestors.

The argument I've attributed to Freud is not especially compelling. Aside from the question of whether Freud has succeeded in establishing that religious beliefs are illusions, his argument, at best, shows only that it is unlikely, strange, or odd that religious beliefs should be true. Perhaps it is, but it is doubtful that any religious believer would find this in itself surprising. One of the features of religion is that it is out of the ordinary, strange, and wonderful. Consequently, many religious thinkers would allow that Freud's reasoning shows that it is somewhat "striking" or unlikely that religious beliefs are true, but contend that this is not a sufficient reason for rejecting those beliefs. Futhermore, we must not forget that Freud has not considered the reasons that sophisticated religious thinkers such as Anselm or Aquinas give for their religious beliefs. [See Readings 4.1, 4.4.] Hence, he has not shown that no one has good grounds for these beliefs, only that many who accept them do not. If a belief is a wish-fulfilment, and if we show that *no one* has good reasons for accepting it, we will perhaps have some reason for thinking that it will likely turn out to be a false belief. But Freud has not shown that no one has good reasons for religious beliefs, only that many do not. Thus his argument is not as compelling as, at first glance, it may appear to be.

STUDY QUESTIONS

1. According to Rowe, why wouldn't the truth of Freud's account of how religious beliefs originate show that those beliefs are false?
2. Give an example in which knowing the cause of a belief *does* properly lead us to form a belief about its truth or falsehood.
3. Give your own examples of the genetic fallacy.
4. *Rowe proposes the following thought question in the book from which Reading 5.10 is taken. How would you reply?

   > Discuss the following argument: The importance of Freud's work for religion is that he has uncovered the mechanism by which God creates an idea of himself in the human mind. Religion has long taught that the relation of the good father to his children is like the relation of God to his creatures. Instead of rejecting Freud's view, the theologian can embrace it as providing an explanation of how God works through natural means to enable us to form a correct idea of our creator.

5. *Imagine that a teenager has been accused of a terrible crime. In truth, he is innocent. His mother, because of her love for the boy, does not believe the accusation is true. To help him be acquitted in court, she investigates thoroughly and finds strong evidence of his innocence. On the basis of this evidence, a jury (correctly) finds him not guilty. How might this example (which is adapted from an article by philosopher Keith Lehrer on a different subject) be used to illustrate the point Rowe makes at the end of the selection?

FURTHER READING

The Problem of Evil

Adams, Marilyn McCord. *Horrendous Evils and the Goodness of God.* Ithaca, NY: Cornell University Press, 1999.

Adams, Marilyn McCord, and Robert Merrihew Adams, eds. *The Problem of Evil.* New York: Oxford University Press, 1990.

Gale, Richard. *On the Nature and Existence of God.* Cambridge: Cambridge University Press, 1991, Ch. 4.

Griffin, David Ray. *Evil Revisited: Responses and Reconsiderations.* Albany, NY: SUNY Press, 1991.

Hick, John. *Evil and the God of Love.* New York: Harper & Row, 1977.

Lewis, C. S. *The Problem of Pain.* London: Geoffrey Bles, 1940.

Mackie, John L. *The Miracle of Theism.* Oxford: Oxford University Press, 1982. Ch. 9.

Martin, Michael. *Atheism.* Philadelphia: Temple University Press, 1990. Chs. 14–17.

Peterson, Michael, ed. *The Problem of Evil: Selected Readings.* Notre Dame, IN: University of Notre Dame Press, 1992.

Pike, Nelson, ed. *God and Evil: Readings on the Theological Problem of Evil.* Englewood Cliffs, NJ: Prentice-Hall, 1964.

Plantinga, Alvin. *God, Freedom and Evil.* New York: Harper & Row, 1974.

Russel, Bruce and Stephen Wykstra. "The 'Inductive' Argument From Evil: a Dialogue." *Philosophical Topics* 16, 2 (1988): 133–60.

Schlesinger, George N. "Suffering and Evil." In *Contemporary Philosophy of Religion,* pp. 25–31. Edited by Steven M. Cahn and David Shatz. New York: Oxford University Press, 1982.

Snyder, Daniel, ed. *The Evidential Argument from Evil.* Bloomington and Indianapolis: University of Indiana Press, 1996.

Swinburne, Richard. *Is There a God?* New York: Oxford University Press, 1996, pp. 95–111.

Tracy, Thomas F. "Victimization and the Problem of Evil: A Response to Ivan Karamazov." *Faith and Philosophy* 9 (1992): 301–19.

Wolterstorff, Nicholas. *Lament for a Son.* Grand Rapids, MI: Eerdmans, 1987.

Divine Hiddenness

McKim, Robert. "The Hiddenness of God." *Religious Studies* 26 (1990): 141–61.

Morris, Thomas V. "The Hidden God." *Philosophical Topics* 16, 2 (1988): 5–22.

Schellenberg, J. L. *Divine Hiddenness and Human Reason.* Ithaca, NY: Cornell University Press, 1993.

Heaven and Hell

Adams, Marilyn McCord. "Hell and the God of Justice." *Religious Studies* 11 (1975): 433–47.

Davis, Steven. "Universalism, Hell, and the Fate of the Ignorant." *Modern Theology* 6 (1990): 173–86.

Kvanvig, John. *The Problem of Hell.* New York: Oxford University Press, 1993.

Social Scientific Explanations of Religious Belief

Alston, William. "Psychoanalytic Explanations of Religious Experience." In *God and the Philosophers,* edited by John Hick. New York: St. Martin's Press, 1964, pp. 63–102.

Gordon, Jeffrey. "Freud's Religious Scepticism Resurrected." *Religious Studies* 27 (1991): 309–17.

Jung, Carl Gustav. "Freud and Jung—Contrasts." In *Modern Man in Search of a Soul,* pp. 132–42. London: K. Paul, Trench, Trubner and Co., 1933.

Smart, Ninian. *The Philosophy of Religion.* New York: Oxford University Press, 1979, pp. 167–88.

CHAPTER 6

Science, Nature, and Religious Belief

To many people, as John Haught remarks in the opening selection of this chapter, the historical relationship between science and religion is one of perpetual warfare. From the Church's condemnation of Galileo for teaching that the earth and other planets revolve around the sun, to the efforts of biblical literalists today to prevent the teaching of evolution in schools (or at least to give "creationism" equal time in the curriculum), strife and conflict are very much in evidence. If anything, one would expect that tensions today would be worse than ever, for today more than ever we live in an age of science. As a trip through exhibits at Disneyworld will suggest, the march of scientific knowledge today is producing dramatic effects in areas that theists have long believed are God's domain. For centuries, God was invoked to explain phenomena for which natural explanations were lacking—diseases, earthquakes, weather patterns, and the very existence of the world. The deity was, in a famous phrase, the "**God-of-the-gaps.**" With the advance of scientific understanding, there is less and less space available for God to fill. As Owen Gingerich, a religiously committed astronomer, put it, "Where, in the world, is God?" We have dealt with one aspect of this question in the introduction to chapter 4, when treating the cosmological argument; there we heard William L. Craig argue that God is needed to explain the **big bang.** But certainly as we contemplate everyday life the feeling that "we have no need of that hypothesis" intensifies the more we come to understand nature's ways.

It is not only God who has been squeezed out by advancing scientific knowledge. Theists have long believed in a **dualist** theory of the person; each person is the union of a physical entity—a body—and a nonphysical thinking and experiencing entity—the soul. However, as neuroscientists discover more and more correlations between states of mind and states of the brain and nervous system, we need to ask whether belief in a soul is credible. The soul looks like a soul-of-the-gaps. If so, the theist's vision of human **immortality** is shattered.

Are the prospects for harmonization or peaceful coexistence as bleak as they seem? In the first selection in this chapter, John Haught lays out four ways of conceiving of the relationship between science and religion. Although one could see the relationship in terms of conflict, science and religion could alternatively be thought of as independent of each other on the grounds that they posit different aims. For example, it sometimes is said that science tries to describe the **empirical** world, while religion is occupied with issues of meaning; or that science is concerned with the question *how,* while religion asks *why.* Some forms of interaction are possible, too. Science and religion can be brought together in dialogue on specific issues, Haught claims. (**Natural theology**—that is, arguing for God's existence based on empirical premises drawn from the sciences—is only one example of dialogue.) Further, religion can be invoked to undergird the rationality of scientific inquiry. Science has faith or trust that the universe is coherent, rational and ordered and that the human mind can fathom its workings. Religion provides what Haught calls confirmation for this trust.

Haught's article is followed by three selections by theists on the hotly contested topic of the seeming conflict between Genesis and the theory of evolution. Alvin Plantinga points to weaknesses in the theory of evolution that could be remedied, in his opinion, by embracing the theistic doctrine of **special creations** by God of the various species. Howard Van Till resists this move from a theistic perspective and, unlike Plantinga, sees science and religion cooperating in this area, rather than clashing. Peter van Inwagen accepts that certain statements in Genesis about the origins of the universe are false in light of modern science, yet he notes that the Bible was meant to address people across time and therefore could not present the science accurately.

Following these selections on evolution are three on the nature of the mind and the prospects for an afterlife. Robert Audi addresses the mind-body relationship. Audi explains how in his opinion the theistic conception of mind and of a nonphysical but minded God can be harmonized with contemporary neurophysiology. Richard Swinburne then argues that the soul depends on the brain for its functioning, albeit not for its existence. Finally, Peter van Inwagen speculates on how resurrection might take place. The problem he addresses is that it is difficult to justify regarding the resurrected person as identical with the one who died. After all, the body has since decomposed.

No discussion of science and religion can be complete without examining whether belief in divine intervention and miracles can be incorporated into an outlook that accepts laws of nature. The religious doctrine of divine providence submits that God not only knows the future but also arranges events and, on occasion, intervenes in nature. Events occur in consonance with God's plan. From a theologian's standpoint, should we ever explain events in terms of natural causes?

The seventeenth-century Christian thinker Nicholas Malebranche (1638–1715) argued against the very idea that natural objects can cause anything; the only true cause is the divine will. Regularities in nature, no less than miracles, must be understood as effects of the divine, for to believe otherwise is paganism. William Alston suggests in his article, however, that, although miracles are possible, it is a live possibility that God acts through the natural order and that there is no *direct* divine intervention except in special cases.

But from a scientific standpoint, can we believe in miracles? A **theologian** frames the challenge this way:

> The traditional conception of miracle is irreconcilable with our modern understanding of both science and history. Science proceeds on the assumption that whatever events occur in the world can be accounted for in terms of other events that also belong within the world; and if on some occasions we are unable to give a complete account of some happening—and presumably all our accounts fall short of completeness—the scientific conviction is that further research will bring to light further factors in the situation, but factors that will turn out to be just as immanent and this-worldly as those already known. (John MacQuarrie, *Principles of Christian Theology,* 2d ed. [New York: Scribners, 1977], 247–48.)

The author adds that appealing to miracles and supernatural interventions "belongs to the mythological outlook and cannot commend itself in a post-mythological climate of thought."

Is this true? Several selections debate the question: Under what circumstances, if any, is it reasonable to believe that a miracle has occurred?

Attacks on belief in miracles proceed along four levels:

1. It can be questioned whether the concept of a miracle is coherent. A miracle might be defined as a violation of a law of nature. But how can the alleged law be a law if there is

a violation? How can the theist have it both ways—the law is a law and the violation is a violation? This question is only touched on in the selections; one answer to this. Although a theist conceives of a miracle as a violation of a law of nature, the theist adds that the violation is due to a special cause, the intervention of a *supernatural* agent. Therefore, if a miracle occurs, the law of nature remains a law despite the violation, for the law describes what always happens when only natural causes are operative—not what happens when supernatural causes are introduced.

2. Even if the concept of a miracle is coherent, it can be questioned whether it can *ever* be rational to believe that events thought by observers to be miracles really have occurred.
3. Even if one is willing to grant, in response to point 2, that it can be rational to believe that events of an *apparently* miraculous type occurred, it can be questioned whether it is ever rational to believe that those events are truly miracles; perhaps they have a natural explanation.
4. Even if it is granted that under some *imaginable* circumstances it is rational to believe that a miracle has occurred, it can be questioned whether the *particular events* that religious traditions *actually* report as miracles really did occur and whether, if they did occur, they are due to natural causes.

The selections cover the points under 2 and 3 extensively and pay some attention to number 4. David Hume, in a famous essay, argues that, when there is a report of a miracle, the testimony to the miracle is outweighed by the accumulated testimony to the law of nature that the alleged miracle would violate. Peter van Inwagen objects to Hume's conditions, arguing that they force us to reject perfectly persuasive testimony to unusual events, such as Charles Linbergh's solo flight across the Atlantic. John Stuart Mill argues that, even if we accept testimony to a seemingly miraculous event, we can never know there isn't a natural cause lurking, undiscovered. David Johnson attacks Mill's appeal to possible undiscovered causes, arguing, for instance, that such a logic would have precluded our accepting the existence of the particles known as neutrinos. Finally, Stephen Griffith discusses the Shroud of Turin, on which some think there miraculously has appeared the image of a crucified man, presumed to be Jesus. Griffith's essay makes the theoretical contributions of Hume, van Inwagen, Mill, and Johnson relevant to a concrete, real-life situation.[1]

These essays barely scratch the surface of the science-religion relationship. The books by Barbour and Huchingson listed at the end of this chapter under "Further Reading," as well as the book by Haught from which Reading 6.1 is excerpted, will take you into fascinating historical and philosophical discussions of **cosmology,** evolution, sociobiology, **quantum physics,** and more.

[1]The concept of miracle could be expanded to include cases that do not seem to us to involve violations of laws of nature. For example, suppose a child falls down on railroad tracks just as a train is approaching. Rounding a curve, the driver doesn't see the child, and the train would surely hit the child under normal circumstances. But the driver suddenly faints for a reason having nothing to do with the child's presence (e.g., as the result of something he ate); and the brakes are applied automatically as the driver's hand ceases to exert pressure on the control lever. The train stops a few feet short of the child, who escapes unhurt. We—and certainly the child's mother—might speak of the child's surviving as a "miraculous escape," even though no natural law seems to have been violated. (This case is adapted from R. F. Holland, "The Miraculous," cited under Further Reading.) Here it is not the events themselves, but their *timing*—the *coincidence* of the fainting occurring just as the train was about to hit the child—that suggest to the theist that God's hand is present, and to the atheist that the child and its parents benefited from pure luck. Cf. the selection by Hume (6.9), note 2. For other ways in which special acts of God might occur within a natural order, see Reading 6.8 by William Alston.

SCIENCE AND RELIGION

READING 6.1

Is Religion Opposed to Science?

John Haught

John Haught describes four ways of understanding the relationship between religion and science. Many people believe that science and religion are irreconcilable. Haught calls this the conflict *model. But there are three other models as well. The* contrast *approach holds that religion and science are responding to different questions and therefore do not conflict. The* contact *model asserts that religion and science enter into dialogue and exert mutual impact. Finally, the* confirmation *approach maintains that religion supports the scientific enterprise because the belief in a rational, orderly universe created by God nurtures the quest for scientific knowledge and instills confidence that such knowledge is attainable. In the selection, Haught presents these approaches abstractly; however, in the remainder of the book from which the selection is taken, he provides illustrations of each position with respect to challenges posed by* **cosmology,** *evolution, neuroscience, and other areas of modern science.*

When we hear the words "science" and "religion" we immediately think of the stormy history of their relationship. But the chronicle of religion's encounter with science is by no means one of warfare only. Throughout these pages we shall observe that there are at least four distinct ways in which science and religion can be related to each other.

1) *Conflict*—the conviction that science and religion are fundamentally irreconcilable;
2) *Contrast*—the claim that there can be no genuine conflict since religion and science are each responding to radically different questions;
3) *Contact*—an approach that looks for dialogue, interaction, and possible "consonance" between science and religion, and especially for ways in which science shapes religious and theological understanding;
4) *Confirmation*—a somewhat quieter, but extremely important perspective that highlights the ways in which, at a very deep level, religion supports and nourishes the entire scientific enterprise. . . .

I. CONFLICT

Many scientific thinkers are quite certain that religion can never be reconciled with science. If you are a scientist, they say, it is hard to imagine how you could honestly also be religious, at least in the sense of believing in God. Their main reason for drawing this conclusion is that religion apparently cannot demonstrate the truth of its ideas in a straightforward way, whereas science can. Religion tries to sneak by without providing any concrete evidence of God's existence. Science, on the other hand, is willing to test all of its hypotheses and theories against "experience." Religion cannot do this in a way that is satisfying to an impartial witness, **skeptics** claim, so there must be a "conflict" between the scientific and the religious ways of understanding.

Both historical and philosophical considerations seem to substantiate such a grim verdict. Historically, we need only recall the obvious examples: the church's persecution of Galileo in the seventeenth century, and the widespread religious and theological aversion to Darwin's evolutionary theory in the nineteenth and twentieth. The slow pace by which religious thought comes to terms with such scientific ideas, and the fact that many theists still have a distaste for them, suggest that religion will never get along with science. Since so many believers in God have resisted the findings of astronomy, physics, and biology, is it any wonder that religion comes across as inherently hostile to science?

More important than these historical considerations, however, are the imposing philosophical (specifically **epistemological**) obstacles that religion and **theology** present to scientific skeptics. The main problem here is that religious ideas seem to be experientially untestable. That is, they apparently exempt themselves from the rigors of public examination, whereas science always submits its ideas to open experimentation. If **empirical** scrutiny shows a scientific hypothesis to be mistaken, then science willingly discards it and tries out alternatives, subjecting these also to the same rigorous process of inspection.

But can you do the same with religious teachings? Don't they dodge all attempts to demonstrate their truth observationally? Don't theists, for example, go on believing in God no matter what they observe in the world, including enormous suffering and evil? Doesn't Judaism, for example, say of its Lord: "Even though He slay me, yet shall I trust in Him"? [Job 13:15] And aren't all religious interpretations of the world, for that matter, fundamentally unaffected by the contradictions to them that we actually experience?

Putting this another way, it seems to skeptics that religious teachings are "unfalsifiable." Karl Popper, one of the most renowned philosophers of this century, argued that genuine science must strive to come up with evidence that will show its ideas to be mistaken. That is, science has to risk the "falsification" of its various claims.[1] For example, since relativity theory predicts that light waves will always bend in the presence of gravitational fields, scientists should look for possible instances in which this prediction might not be true. Then if they cannot find any evidence to the contrary, this means that relativity is a pretty strong theory for weathering all attempts at falsification. **Falsifiability** is the mark of a theory's scientific status. A willingness to allow its ideas to be falsified purifies science and shows it to be a truly open and honest way of learning about the nature of things.

But can religion display a comparable openness? Scientific skeptics (i.e. those who reject religion in the name of science) declare that religion lacks the robust probity of science. The God-hypothesis, for example, seems to be completely beyond falsification, so it cannot pass muster before the courts of science. Can you imagine any situations and experiences that might lead you to deny God's existence? If you cannot, then the idea of God must be unfalsifiable—and therefore is not to be taken seriously.

Religion is based, skeptics often claim, on ***a priori*** assumptions, or "faith," whereas science takes nothing for granted. In addition, religion relies heavily on untamed imagination, whereas science sticks to observable facts. And religion is highly emotional, passionate and subjective, whereas science strives to remain disinterested, dispassionate and objective. These antitheses seem to add up to nothing less than an insuperable mutual hostility between science and religion.

. . . [W]e should note here, at least in passing, that the skeptics are not the only ones to insist that religion clashes with science. Biblical literalists (people who think the words of the Bible are literally true) also often see a conflict between their faith and some well established scientific theories. Whenever scientific ideas do not correspond with the letter of the Bible (which is quite often), biblical literalists argue that science must be wrong and religion right. This is especially the case with regard to evolution, but also with miracles, the creation of the universe, the origin of life, and other issues. Many Christians in the United States and elsewhere maintain that the Bible teaches the "true" science and that secular science should be rejected if it does not correspond with the letter of scripture.

In addition to biblical literalists, there are still other critics who think that science is the enemy of religion. They argue that it was the coming of science that caused most of the emptiness and meaninglessness in modern life and culture. When science separated the experience of "facts" from our human need for eternal "values," they argue, it emptied the cosmos of any real meaning. And since the main business of religion is to teach us the meaning of things, it cannot be reconciled with science. We would be better off if the scientific revolution had never occurred. . . .

II. CONTRAST

Many scientists and **theologians,** on the other hand, find no such opposition between religion and

[1] Karl Popper, *Conjectures and Refutations,* Second Edition (Routledge and Kegan Paul, 1965), pp. 33–39.

science. Each is valid, they argue, though only in its own clearly defined sphere of inquiry. We should not judge religion by the standards of science, nor vice versa, because the questions each asks are so completely disparate, and the content of their answers so distinct, that it makes no sense to compare them with each other. If religion and science were both trying to do the same job, then they might be incompatible. But they have radically dissimilar tasks, and if we just keep them in their separate jurisdictions, preventing them from invading each other's territory, there can never be any real "problem" of science and religion.

According to this "contrast" approach, the impression that religion conflicts with science is almost always rooted in a previous confusion, or "conflation," of science with either a religious or a secular belief system. ("Conflation," a term that appears often in the pages ahead, simply means the collapsing of distinct items in such a way that their differences are apparently lost.) . . . The church's failure to acknowledge the separate domains of science and religion led its officials to condemn Galileo's novel ideas as though they were an invasion of their own territory. This, of course, was a most unfortunate misunderstanding, leading as it did to much of the hostility that many scientists still feel toward religion.

However, we should now know better: religion and science have no business meddling in each other's affairs in the first place. To avoid possible combat, our second approach claims, we should carefully *contrast* science with religion. Science and religion are such completely independent ways of understanding reality that it is meaningless to place them in opposition to each other.

Conflation, in this view, is an unsatisfactory attempt to avoid conflict by carelessly commingling science with belief. Instead of respecting the sharp differences between science and religion, conflation weaves them into a single fabric where they fade into each other, almost to the point of becoming indistinguishable. Today, for instance, many conservative Christians argue that since the Bible is divinely inspired and inerrant, it gives us the most reliable *scientific* information about the beginnings of the universe and life. Some of them call their fusion of science and belief "creation science," and they renounce the Darwinian theory of evolution in favor of a literalist interpretation of the biblical accounts of the world's creation. They insist that since the biblical stories are "scientific" they should be taught in public schools as the best alternative to evolutionary biology.

Another common brand of conflation is "concordism." Rather than rejecting science outright, concordism forces the biblical text to correspond, at least in a loose way, with the contours of modern **cosmology.** In order to salvage the literal truth of the biblical book of Genesis, for example, some religious scientists match the six days of creation with what they consider to be six corresponding epochs in the scientific account of cosmic evolution. Religion, in this interpretation, must be made to look scientific at all costs if it is to be intellectually respectable today. In his book *Genesis and the Big Bang* the physicist Gerald Schroeder, for example, argues that relativity theory, with its challenge to the common sense notion of absolute simultaneity, once again allows us to take literally the six-day sequence of creation as depicted in the Bible. He attempts to show that what appears as a single day from one frame of reference may, from another, be billions of years. So the Bible agrees with science after all, and physicists can now embrace religion! . . .

. . . [A]dvocates of [the contrast] approach typically emphasize that the "game" science plays is one of examining the natural world **empirically,** while religion's is that of expressing the ultimate meaning that transcends (lies beyond) the empirically known world. Science is concerned with *how* things happen in nature, religion with *why* there is anything at all rather than nothing. Science is about *causes,* religion about *meaning.* Science deals with solvable *problems,* religion with unsolvable *mystery.* Science answers specific questions about the *workings* of nature, whereas religion expresses concern about the ultimate *ground* of nature. Science is concerned with particular truths; religion is interested in explaining why we should seek truth at all.

Where many theologians allow for clear logical distinctions between the tasks of science and religion, the contrast approach sees such differences as a reason for sharply *segregating* the two. Only by drawing an unbroken line between them can we avoid the conflation that leads to conflict. Contrast envisages science and religion as independent, autonomous ways of knowing. Only by putting them in separate camps, it insists, can we prevent eventual warfare between them. . . .

Another reason for the appeal of the contrast approach, however, is that the contrast approach also allows us to distinguish science from the assumptions that underlie scientific skepticism. For it is not just creationists and benighted religious believers who practice the questionable art of conflation. Scientific skeptics typically also conflate science with a belief system of their own. Their belief system is not theism, of course, but rather **"scientism."**

Scientism may be defined as "the *belief* that science is the only reliable guide to truth." Scientism, it must be emphasized, is by no means the same thing as science. For while science is a modest, reliable, and fruitful method of learning some important things about the universe, *scientism* is the assumption that science is the *only* appropriate way to arrive at the totality of truth. Scientism is a philosophical *belief* (strictly speaking an "epistemological" one) that enshrines science as the only completely trustworthy method of putting the human mind in touch with "objective" reality.

According to our "contrasters" such a doctrinaire conviction is itself by no means the product of any detached, objective, or neutral process of scientific knowing. Rather, it is a kind of faith-commitment not entirely unlike the kind we find in religion. Devotees of scientism place their trust in scientific method itself, but no more than religious believers can they scientifically demonstrate the truth of this faith. They trust deeply in the power of science to clear up all confusion about the world, but they cannot scientifically justify this trust without logical circularity.

Skeptics often trust in science almost as though, like the gods of religion, it were our savior from the original sin of prescientific ignorance. As the contrasters are quick to point out, however, there is no possible way you could set up a scientific experiment to demonstrate that science is the only reliable guide to truth. For such an experiment would already presuppose belief in the effectiveness of science to lead us to the right conclusions. Thus scientism is in fact no less a conflation of science with belief than is "scientific creationism."

Hence, if theism is flawed because the God-hypothesis is unfalsifiable, then it seems only fair to ask whether scientism can itself meet the falsification test. To do so its advocates must be able to state under what conditions it could be falsified. They must actively look for ways to show that science is inadequate. Instead of doing so, however, they steadfastly *assume* it to be true, no matter what. At least in this respect their faith in science looks suspiciously like the religion they reject for being unfalsifiable. . . .

III. CONTACT

. . . The urge to discover the coherence of all our ways of knowing is too powerful for us to suppress indefinitely, and so I suggest here that we consider a third approach, one that I shall simply call *contact.*

This way of relating religion to science is not willing to leave the world divided into the two realms defined by the contrast position. Yet it does not wish to revert to the superficial harmony of conflation either. It agrees that science and religion are logically and linguistically distinct, but it knows that in the real world they cannot be as easily compartmentalized as the contrast position supposes. After all, religion in the West has helped shape the history of science, and scientific cosmology has in turn influenced theology. It is impossible to separate them completely, even though we can try to make clear logical distinctions in our definitions of them.

In addition, it seems unlikely that just any old cosmology will be compatible with just any old theology, as the contrast position would seem to allow. The kind of world described by evolutionary biology and **big bang** physics, for example, cannot peacefully coexist with the picture of God that Newton, Descartes, and perhaps even Thomas Aquinas idealized. Whether they are aware of it or not, theologians always bring at least implicit cosmological assumptions to their talk about

God, and it is only honest that they acknowledge this fact. It often happens, however, that their cosmological assumptions are scientifically out of date. The contact approach, therefore, is concerned that theology always remain positively "consonant" with cosmology.[2] Theology cannot rely too heavily on science, but it must pay attention to what is going on in the world of scientists. It must seek to express its ideas in terms that take the best of science into account lest it become intellectually irrelevant.

For this reason, the contact approach looks for an open-ended conversation between scientists and theologians. The term "contact" implies coming together without necessarily fusing. It allows for interaction, dialogue, and mutual impact but forbids both conflation and segregation. It insists on preserving differences, but it also cherishes relationship.

Contact proposes that scientific knowledge can broaden the horizon of religious faith and that the perspective of religious faith can deepen our understanding of the universe. It does not strive to prove God's existence from science but is content simply to interpret scientific discoveries within the framework of religious meaning. It does not seek to shore up religious doctrines by appealing to scientific concepts that may on the surface seem to point directly to a divine designer. The days in which scientific ideas could be used to seal arguments for God's existence are over. Still, it is convinced that, without in any way interfering with scientists' own proper methods, religious faith can flourish alongside of science in such a way as to co-produce with it a joint meaning that is more illuminating than either can provide on its own.

The kind of religion we are discussing . . . characteristically strives to instill in its followers a special way of looking at things, and this perspective, as it turns out, is ideally suited to frame recent developments in biology and physics. Rooted in the story of Abraham, the prophetic faith traditions invite their followers to look for the *promise* that lies in all things. Judaism, Christianity, and Islam think of genuine "faith" as a confidence that new life and undreamed of possibilities are latent even in the most desperate of situations. The authentic religious attitude, then, is a steadfast conviction that the future is open and that an incalculable fulfillment awaits the entire cosmos.

At first sight such a hopeful orientation of consciousness would seem to be anything but compatible with the "realism" that science demands of us. And yet . . . many religious thinkers have found what they consider to be a remarkable accord between a faith-perspective shaped by a sense of reality's promise, and the universe now coming to light as a consequence of new developments in science. . . .

. . . [W]e should mention here that in recent philosophical discussions of the nature of science, the ways of science and theology do not appear nearly so divergent as either the conflict or the contrast position insinuates. Science no longer appears quite so pure and objective as we used to think, nor theology so impure and subjective. Both science and theology generate imaginative metaphors and theories to interpret certain kinds of "data," but in neither case is it always clear just where metaphor or theory leaves off and "fact" begins. Indeed the consensus of philosophers today is that there are no uninterpreted facts. And so we are now more aware than ever before that in both science and theology there is an aspect of human "construction" which we previously failed to notice. This does not mean that our ideas are therefore inevitably unobjective, but it does mean that we cannot enshrine as absolutely unrevisable any particular forms of expression that we employ in our quest for truth.

Recent examinations of the culturally and historically conditioned nature of scientific understanding, for example, make us question whether we can simply assume that science is the pure model of objectivity that scientific textbooks make it out to be. Scientific textbooks, as Thomas Kuhn has pointed out, tend to "mask" or cover up the squabbles and conflicts that underlie the evolution of scientific understanding. They give students the impression that scientific method is a straight-arrow way to the truth, whereas the actual history of science indicates

[2]The search for "consonance" between theology and science is advocated by Ernan McMullin, Ted Peters, and Robert Russell among others. See Ted Peters, ed., *Cosmos as Creation: Theology and Science in Consonance* (Nashville: Abingdon Press, 1989).

that growth in knowledge is not nearly that direct.[3] It may be harder now to draw as sharp a line between science and other ways of thinking as we used to.

Nevertheless, though scientific "facts" are always in some sense our own constructs, and are inevitably theory-laden, they are not simply wild guesses that have no reference to a real world existing independently of our preferences. In some way, though chastened by our new understanding of the social nature of knowing, we may still trust that both scientific and religious ideas refer to a real world, one that transcends mere wishing. This appreciation of the mind's capacity to put us in touch—in an always provisional way—with the real world is known as **"critical realism."** Critical realism, as distinct from naive realism, maintains that our understanding, both scientific and religious, may be oriented toward a real world, whether the universe or God, but that precisely because the universe and God are always too colossal for the human mind to encompass, our thoughts in both science and religion are also always open to correction.

Science and religion make meaningful contact with each other, therefore, only when they agree to play by the rules of what we are calling critical realism. Good science, in this covenant, hopes to approximate, more or less, the way things are in nature, but it is always willing to be critical of its ways of representing the world. And a theological method committed to the same principles of critical realism allows that our religious symbols and ideas are also always in need of constant correction, but that in a finite way they too may point toward a Transcendent Reality, one that is infinitely elusive but also always truly "there."

Scientific theories and religious metaphors, in this epistemological contract, are not just imaginative concoctions, as much modern and postmodern thought asserts. Rather, they bear an always tentative relationship to a *real* world and its ultimate ground. This world beyond our representations is always only incompletely grasped, and its presence constantly "judges" our hypotheses, inviting us continually to deepen our understanding both in science and religion. So it is their mutual sharing in this critical openness to the real that provides the basis for genuine "contact" between science and religion.

[3]Thomas Kuhn, *The Structure of Scientific Revolutions,* 2d ed. (Chicago: University of Chicago Press, 1970).

IV. CONFIRMATION

. . . I envisage an even more intimate relationship of religion to science than any of the first three approaches has yet explicitly acknowledged. I shall propose here, . . . that religion is in a very deep way supportive of the entire scientific enterprise.

. . . My proposal is simply that religion essentially fortifies the humble desire to know. That is, it confirms the very drive that gives rise to science in the first place. I call this fourth approach "confirmation," a term equivalent to "strengthening" or "supporting," because it holds that religion, when carefully purged of idolatrous implications, fully endorses and even undergirds the scientific effort to make sense of the universe.

I am aware that science has come under heavy criticism today. Many critics even think that it is responsible for most of the ills of the modern world. Were it not for science, they say, we would have no nuclear threat, no global pollution of the air, soil and water. We and our planet would probably be better off without it. Science, they claim, is at root an assault upon nature, a crushing exercise in control. It is a Faustian effort to wrest all mystery from the cosmos so that we can be the masters of it. Some even argue that science is inherently patriarchal, an exploitation of nature closely tied to our culture's oppression of women.

Obviously theology would not wish to endorse science if it were inherently connected to these evils. But I suspect that much criticism of science mistakenly identifies it with trends and motives that can, at least in principle, be clearly distinguished from science itself. *Essentially* speaking, I consider science to be a modest but fruitful attempt to grasp empirically, and as much as possible with mathematical clarity, some small part of the totality of reality. Any pretensions to **omniscience** such as we find in scientism are not a part of science at all. . . .

Most criticisms of science fail to acknowledge that at root science flows out of a simple, humble desire to know. We must distinguish this fundamental longing for truth from other human desires—such as the will to pleasure, power, or security—that place science in servitude to impulses that have nothing to do with truth-seeking. When I say that religion supports science, therefore, I am not arguing that it favors all the twisted ways in which science is exploited and conflated. I am simply saying that the disinterested desire to know, out of which science grows and flourishes, finds its deepest confirmation in a religious interpretation of the universe. . . .

The *confirmation* approach may be stated as follows: religion's claim that the universe is a finite, coherent, rational, ordered totality, grounded in an ultimate love and promise, provides a general vision of things that consistently nurtures the scientific quest for knowledge and liberates science from association with imprisoning ideologies.

Science, to be more specific, cannot even get off the ground without rooting itself in a kind of **a priori** "faith" that the universe is a rationally ordered totality of things. Scientists always rely on a tacit faith (which they seldom reflect on in an explicitly conscious way) that there is a real world "out there," that this real world hangs together intelligibly, that the human mind has the capacity to comprehend at least some of the world's intelligibility, and that no matter how far we probe there will still be further intelligibility to uncover. Without this kind of trust there could be no incentive to look for the order present in nature or to keep looking deeper into the specifics of this order.

Even in the mind's spontaneous quest for insight, coherence, and truth there is a dynamism not far removed from what we may call "faith." As we see plainly in modern physics, but also in other fields, a fundamental objective of the scientific quest is to find whatever it is that unifies or holds together the universe that we are exploring. Science, no less than religion, is borne along by this quest for a unifying knowledge. But at the roots of a scientist's irrepressible desire to make coherent sense of things there lies a basic confidence, nothing less than a "faith," that reality will eventually yield to our desire to find in it the unity of some kind of order.

Thus faith, in the sense of a basic trust in the limitless rationality of the real, is not opposed to science but is its very wellspring. . . .

What then is the precise connection of religion to this prerequisite trust? We must be careful not to let religion intrude into the actual work of science, but it is my conviction that religion does provide *confirmation* of the trusting that inevitably underlies science. Religion, I repeat, cannot add anything to the list of scientific discoveries. It is not in the business of disclosing things about nature that science can arrive at on its own. Rather, religion by its very nature is concerned that we put our trust in reality's overall rationality. And in this sense religion is much more intimately connected to the epistemological *roots* of scientific inquiry than the other approaches have enunciated. Religion, taken as a confirmation of the faith assumptions out of which science springs, and not as an alternative source of scientific hypotheses, will not obstruct, but only promote, the work of science.

Religion comes about in human culture because of our awareness of the fact that trust can fail, and its central mission is continually to revive this trust. It does not initiate our trust, since a capacity to trust in reality seems native to us, but instead functions to revive our trust when it fails. Religion, Schubert Ogden correctly notes, is best understood as "re-assurance," a re-plenishing of the basic confidence we may have lost in the course of living. Religion exists because our reliance on reality is subject to constant erosion by the pain, tragedy, hostility, absurdity, and death with which the world confronts us.[4] There are any number of experiences that can lead us to doubt the intelligibility of the universe. The point of religion, though, is to encourage us to trust anyway. It seeks to restore our hope in the face of despair, to help us cling to the conviction that there is a final meaning and promise to things, a meaning

[4]Schubert Ogden, *The Reality of God* (New York: Harper & Row, 1977), pp. 32ff.

and promise that can light up even those experiences that seem to make the universe absurd. The word "God" points us toward this mysterious meaning and promise, toward that which guarantees the world's ultimate coherence and trustworthiness.[5]

Religious symbols, stories, and teachings persuade us that there is an infinitely wider perspective than our own, and that our own minds are not encompassing enough to take in the whole horizon of being at any given moment, but that nonetheless things do make sense in terms of an ultimate frame of reference. Religion implies therefore that we need continually to press onward, beyond the narrowness of current understanding, and go in search of this transcending breadth and depth. Such an impetus, I am saying, can also quietly energize the enterprise of scientific discovery. Scientists can be theists, in other words, because their discipline thrives on the conviction that the world does finally make sense.

Religion, I have said, invites us to assume a posture of trust in the ultimate intelligibility of things. Abandoning ourselves to such trust, I would then argue, does not lead us into conflict with science but instead prepares our consciousness for the journey of scientific discovery. "Confirmation" goes further than the "contact" approach by attaching itself directly onto the faith that scientists have to possess as they embark on their forays into the world's endless intelligibility. The place to locate religion in relation to scientific discourse, therefore, is not as the answer to specific scientific questions (since this would be conflation), but as a response to the root question concerning why we should go forth on the adventure of truth-seeking in the first place. The business of religion is not to place itself alongside of science as a competing set of "answers" to scientific questions, but to confirm the scientist's trust in reality's coherence.

Skepticism has rightly exposed the naiveté of associating religion with the solving of problems that are more suitably left to science. Whenever we submit religious teachings as the answers to specific scientific puzzles, skeptics quite rightly chastise us. For example, when the **scientific creationist** offers a biblical story of creation as a better scientific account of origins than evolutionary theory, the skeptic rightly reacts by pointing out that religion is trying here to subvert honest scientific inquiry. However, if we read the biblical accounts of creation not as an alternative and competing body of scientific information, but as an invitation to experience the ultimate trustworthiness of reality, then there need be no conflict.

In our attempts to clarify the relationship of religion to science we can avoid both unnecessary conflation and dualism if we keep to the view that religious expression is most appropriately concerned with grounding our trust, not with solving scientific questions. For when we situate religion in this way we see how it functions as the confirmation rather than the contradiction of science. Religion then is deeply related to science without being conflated with it. Religion's implications for science are much more radical, intimate, and nourishing than the other three approaches have allowed us to see. . . .

[5]Ibid.

STUDY QUESTIONS

1. Describe in detail each of the four models Haught presents. In explaining the contrast model, specify what contrasts are alleged to exist between religion and science.
2. How does religion "confirm" science in the sense intended by the "confirmation" approach?
3. Haught cautions against "conflating" religion and science. What does he mean by the term, and what examples does he give?
4. *Where would you place **natural theology** (the attempt to show by reason that God exists) on Haught's spectrum of approaches?
5. *Haught objects to concordism's attempts to find contemporary scientific theories in the biblical text. Contrary to Haught, however, a believer might argue that, since the Bible presents truth, it

should be no surprise to find in it assertions that we today regard as scientific truth. Can you think of reasons that a believer should nonetheless shun concordism?

6. *Construct a reply to the "confirmation" approach.
7. *Which of the models Haught considers do you think is the most plausible? Which is the least plausible? Why?

READING 6.2

When Faith and Reason Clash: Evolution and the Bible

Alvin Plantinga

In the next two selections, Alvin Plantinga (Notre Dame) and Howard Van Till (Calvin College), both committed theists, debate whether evolutionary theory as propounded by scientists is compatible with the Bible. Plantinga accepts the idea of an ancient earth and certain claims about what species existed before others. However, he rejects the thesis that human beings are descendants of members of other species, the claim that there is a **naturalistic** *explanation of the development of life from simple to complex forms through* **natural selection** *operating on random genetic mutations, and the thesis that life developed from nonliving matter by laws of nature. Instead, Plantinga maintains that God created humanity, other kinds of animals, and plants in acts of special and separate creation. From a nontheistic and naturalistic perspective, evolution is more probable than its alternatives. Furthermore, natural science will not accept a hypothesis that invokes special creation; reference to God's activity makes the theory unscientific. However, according to Plantinga, although evolution may be the best* scientific *hypothesis, it is not the best hypothesis overall. Rather, theism is the best* overall *hypothesis. Plantinga concludes with a call for* theistic *science and a Christian critique of the prevailing culture of evolution. The debate makes plain that theists disagree with one another over the role of God in creation.*

A. EVOLUTION RELIGIOUSLY NEUTRAL?

According to a popular contemporary myth, science is a cool, reasoned, wholly dispassionate attempt to figure out the truth about ourselves and our world, entirely independent of religion, or ideology, or moral convictions, or theological commitments. I believe this is deeply mistaken. Following Augustine (and Abraham Kuyper, Herman Dooyeweerd, Harry Jellema, Henry Stob and other **Reformed** thinkers), I believe that there is conflict, a battle between the *Civitas Dei,* the City of God, and the City of the World. As a matter of fact, what we have, I think, is a three-way battle. On the one hand there is Perennial **Naturalism,** a view going back to the ancient world, a view according to which there is no God, nature is all there is, and mankind is to be understood as a part of nature. Second, there is what I shall call 'Enlightenment Humanism': we could also call it 'Enlightenment Subjectivism' or 'Enlightenment **Antirealism**': this way of thinking goes back substantially to the great eighteenth-century enlightenment philosopher Immanuel Kant. According to its central tenet, it is really we human beings, we men and women, who structure the world, who are responsible for its fundamental outline and lineaments. Naturally enough, a view as startling as this comes in several forms. According to Jean Paul Sartre and his existentialist friends, we do this world-structuring freely and individually; according to Ludwig Wittgenstein and his followers we do it communally and by way of language; according to Kant himself it is done by the transcendental ego which, oddly enough, is neither one nor many, being itself the source of the one-many structure of the world. So two of the parties to this three-way contest are Perennial Naturalism and Enlightenment Humanism; the third party, of course, is Christian theism. Of course there are many unthinking and ill-conceived combinations, much blurring of lines, many cross currents and eddies, many halfway houses, much halting between two opinions. Nevertheless I think these are the three basic contemporary Western ways of looking at reality, three basically *religious* ways of viewing ourselves and the world. The conflict is real, and of profound importance. The stakes, furthermore, are high; this is a battle for men's souls.

Now it would be excessively naive to think that contemporary science is religiously and theologically neutral, standing serenely above this battle and wholly irrelevant to it. Perhaps *parts* of science are like that: mathematics, for example, and perhaps physics, or parts of physics—although even in these areas there are connections. Other parts are obviously and deeply involved in this battle: and the closer the science in question is to what is distinctively human, the deeper the involvement.

To turn to the bit of science in question, the theory of evolution plays a fascinating and crucial role in contemporary Western culture. The enormous controversy about it is what is most striking, a controversy that goes back to Darwin and continues full force today. Evolution is the regular subject of courtroom drama; one such trial—the spectacular Scopes trial of 1925—has been made the subject of an extremely popular film. Fundamentalists regard evolution as the work of the Devil. In academia, on the other hand, it is an idol of the contemporary tribe; it serves as a shibboleth, a litmus test distinguishing the ignorant and bigoted fundamentalist goats from the properly acculturated and scientifically receptive sheep. Apparently this litmus test extends far beyond the confines of this terrestrial globe: according to the Oxford biologist Richard Dawkins, "If superior creatures from space ever visit earth, the first question they will ask, in order to assess the level of our civilization, is: 'Have they discovered evolution yet'?" Indeed many of the experts—for example, Dawkins, William Provine, Stephen Gould—display a sort of revulsion at the very idea of **special creation** by God, as if this idea is not merely not good science, but somehow a bit obscene, or at least unseemly; it borders on the immoral; it is worthy of disdain and contempt. In some circles, confessing to finding evolution attractive will get you disapproval and ostracism and may lose you your job; in others, confessing doubts about evolution will have the same doleful effect. In Darwin's day, some suggested that it was all well and good to discuss evolution in the universities and among the *cognoscenti;* they thought *public* discussion unwise, however; for it would be a shame if the lower classes found out about it. Now, ironically enough, the shoe is sometimes on the other foot; it is the devotees of evolution who sometimes express the fear that public discussion of doubts and difficulties with evolution could have harmful political effects.

So why all the furor? The answer is obvious: evolution has deep religious connections; deep connections with how we understand ourselves at the most fundamental level. Many evangelicals and fundamentalists see in it a threat to the faith; they don't want it taught to their children, at any rate as scientifically established fact, and they see acceptance of it as corroding proper acceptance of the Bible. On the other side, among the secularists, evolution functions as a **myth,** in a technical sense of that term: a shared way of understanding ourselves at the deep level of religion, a deep interpretation of ourselves to ourselves, a way of telling us why we are here, where we come from, and where we are going.

It was serving in this capacity when Richard Dawkins (according to Peter Medawar, "one of the most brilliant of the rising generation of biologists") leaned over and remarked to A. J. Ayer at one of those elegant, candle-lit, bibulous Oxford dinners that he couldn't imagine being an atheist before 1859 (the year Darwin's *Origin of Species was* published); "although atheism might have been logically tenable before Darwin," said he, "Darwin made it possible to be an intellectually fulfilled atheist."[1] . . . Dawkins goes on:

> All appearances to the contrary, the only watchmaker in nature is the blind forces of physics, albeit deployed in a very special way. A true watchmaker has foresight: he designs his cogs and springs, and plans their interconnections, with a future purpose in his mind's eye. **Natural selection,** the blind, unconscious automatic process which Darwin discovered, and which we now know is the explanation for the existence and apparently purposeful form of all life, has no purpose in mind. It has no mind and no mind's eye. It does not plan for the future. It has no vision, no foresight, no sight at all. If it can be said to play the role of watchmaker in nature, it is the blind watchmaker (p. 5).

Evolution was functioning in that same mythic capacity in the remark of the famous zoologist G. G. Simpson: after posing the question "What is man?" he answers, "The point I want to make now is that all attempts to answer that question before 1859 are worthless and that we will be better off if we ignore them completely."[2] Of course it also functions in that capacity in serving as a litmus test to distinguish the ignorant fundamentalists from the properly enlightened *cognoscenti;* it functions in the same way in many of the debates, in and out of the courts, as to whether it should be taught in the schools, whether other views should be given equal time, and the like. Thus Michael Ruse: "the fight against creationism is a fight for all knowledge, and that battle can be won if we all work to see that Darwinism, which has had a great past, has an even greater future."[3]

The essential point here is really Dawkins' point: Darwinism, the Grand Evolutionary Story, makes it possible to be an intellectually fulfilled atheist. What he means is simple enough. If you are Christian, or a theist of some other kind, you have a ready answer to the question, how did it all happen? How is it that there are all the kinds of floras and faunas we behold; how did they all get here? The answer, of course, is that they have been created by the Lord. But if you are not a believer in God, things are enormously more difficult. How did all these things get here? How did life get started and how did it come to assume its present multifarious forms? It seems monumentally implausible to think these forms just popped into existence; that goes contrary to all our experience. So how did it happen? Atheism and Secularism need an answer to this question. And the Grand Evolutionary Story gives the answer: somehow life arose from nonliving matter by way of purely natural means and in accord with the fundamental laws of physics; and once life started, all the vast profusion of contemporary plant and animal life arose from those early ancestors by way of common descent, driven by random variation and natural selection. I said earlier that we can't automatically identify the deliverances of reason with the teaching of current science because the teaching of current science keeps changing. Here we have another reason for resisting that identification: a good deal more than reason goes into the acceptance of such a theory as the Grand Evolutionary Story. For the nontheist, evolution is the only game in town; it is an essential part of any reasonably complete nontheistic way of thinking; hence the devotion to it, the suggestions that it shouldn't be discussed in public, and the venom, the **theological** odium with which dissent is greeted.

B. THE LIKELIHOOD OF EVOLUTION

Of course the fact that evolution makes it possible to be a fulfilled atheist doesn't show either that the theory isn't true or that there isn't powerful evidence for it. Well then, how likely is it that this theory is true? Suppose we think about the question from an explicitly theistic and Christian perspective; but suppose we temporarily set to one side the evidence,

[1]Richard Dawkins, *The Blind Watchmaker* (London and New York: W. W. Norton and Co., 1986), pp. 6 and 7.

[2]Quoted in Richard Dawkins, *The Selfish Gene* (Oxford: Oxford University Press, 1976), p. 1.

[3]*Darwinism Defended,* pp. 326–327.

whatever, exactly it is, from early Genesis. From this perspective, how good is the evidence for the theory of evolution?

The first thing to see is that a number of *different* large-scale claims fall under this general rubric of evolution. First, there is the claim that the earth is very old, perhaps some 4.5 billion years old: The *Ancient Earth Thesis,* as we may call it. Second, there is the claim that life has progressed from relatively simple to relatively complex forms of life. In the beginning there was relatively simple unicellular life, perhaps of the sort represented by bacteria and blue green algae, or perhaps still simpler unknown forms of life. (Although bacteria are simple compared to some other living beings, they are in fact enormously complex creatures.) Then more complex unicellular life, then relatively simple multicellular life such as seagoing worms, coral, and jelly fish, then fish, then amphibia, then reptiles, birds, mammals, and finally, as the culmination of the whole process, human beings: the *Progress Thesis,* as we humans may like to call it (jelly fish might have a different view as to where the whole process culminates). Third, there is the *Common Ancestry Thesis:* that life originated at only one place on earth, all subsequent life being related by descent to those original living creatures—the claim that, as Stephen Gould puts it, there is a "tree of evolutionary descent linking all organisms by ties of genealogy."[4] According to the Common Ancestry Thesis, we are literally cousins of all living things—horses, oak trees and even poison ivy—distant cousins, no doubt, but still cousins. (This is much easier to imagine for some of us than for others.) Fourth, there is the claim that there is a (**naturalistic**) *explanation* of this development of life from simple to complex forms; call this thesis *Darwinism,* because according to the most popular and well-known suggestions, the evolutionary mechanism would be natural selection operating on random genetic mutation (due to copy error or ultra violet radiation or other causes); and this is similar to Darwin's proposals. Finally, there is the claim that life itself developed from non-living matter without any special creative activity of God but just by virtue of the ordinary laws of physics and chemistry: call this the *Naturalistic Origins Thesis.* These five theses are of course importantly different from each other. They are also logically independent in pairs, except for the third and fourth theses: the fourth entails the third, in that you can't sensibly propose a mechanism or an explanation for evolution without agreeing that evolution has indeed occurred. The combination of all five of these theses is what I have been calling 'The Grand Evolutionary Story'; the Common Ancestry Thesis together with Darwinism (remember, Darwinism isn't the view that the mechanism driving evolution is just what Darwin says it is) is what one most naturally thinks of as the Theory of Evolution.

So how shall we think of these five theses? First, let me remind you once more that I am no expert in this area. And second, let me say that, as I see it, the **empirical** or scientific evidence for these five different claims differs enormously in quality and quantity. There is excellent evidence for an ancient earth: a whole series of interlocking different kinds of evidence, some of which is marshalled by Howard Van Till in *The Fourth Day.* Given the strength of this evidence, one would need powerful evidence on the other side—from Scriptural considerations, say—in order to hold sensibly that the earth is young. There is less evidence, but still good evidence in the fossil record for the Progress Thesis, the claim that there were bacteria before fish, fish before reptiles, reptiles before mammals, and mice before men (or wombats before women, for the feminists in the crowd). The third and fourth theses, the Common Ancestry and Darwinian Theses, are what is commonly and popularly identified with evolution; I shall return to them in a moment. The fourth thesis, of course, is no more likely than the third, since it includes the third and proposes a mechanism to account for it. Finally, there is the fifth thesis, the Naturalistic Origins Thesis, the claim that life arose by naturalistic means. This seems to me to be for the most part mere arrogant bluster; given our present state of knowledge, I believe it is vastly less probable, on our present evidence, than is its denial. Darwin thought this claim very chancy; discoveries

[4]"Evolution as Fact and Theory" in *Hen's Teeth and Horse's Toes* (New York: Norton, 1983).

since Darwin and in particular recent discoveries in molecular biology make it much less likely than it was in Darwin's day. I can't summarize the evidence and the difficulties here.

Now return to evolution more narrowly so-called: the Common Ancestry Thesis and the Darwinian Thesis. Contemporary intellectual orthodoxy is summarized by the 1979 edition of the *New Encyclopedia Britannica,* according to which "evolution is accepted by all biologists and natural selection is recognized as its cause. . . . Objections . . . have come from **theological** and, for a time, from political standpoints" (Vol 7). It goes on to add that "Darwin did two things; he showed that evolution was in fact contradicting Scriptural legends of creation and that its cause, natural selection, was automatic, with no room for divine guidance or design." According to most of the experts, furthermore, evolution, taken as the Thesis of Common Ancestry, is not something about which there can be sensible difference of opinion. Here is a random selection of claims of certainty on the part of the experts. Evolution is certain, says Franciso J. Ayala, as certain as "the roundness of the earth, the motions of the planets, and the molecular constitution of matter."[5] According to Stephen J. Gould, evolution is an established fact, not a mere theory; and no sensible person who was acquainted with the evidence could demur.[6] According to Richard Dawkins, the theory of evolution is as certainly true as that the earth goes around the sun. This comparison with Copernicus apparently suggests itself to many; according to Philip Spieth, "A century and a quarter after the publication of the Origin of Species, biologists can say with confidence that universal genealogical relatedness is a conclusion of science that is as firmly established as the revolution of the earth about the sun."[7] Michael Ruse, trumpets, or perhaps screams, that "evolution is Fact, FACT, **FACT !**" If you venture to suggest doubts about evolution, you are likely to be called ignorant or stupid or worse. In fact this isn't merely *likely;* you have already *been* so-called: in a recent review in the *New York Times,* Richard Dawkins claims that "It is absolutely safe to say that if you meet someone who claims not to believe in evolution, that person is ignorant, stupid or insane (or wicked, but I'd rather not consider that)." (Dawkins indulgently adds that "You are probably not stupid, insane or wicked, and ignorance is not a crime. . . .")

Well then, how should a serious Christian think about the Common Ancestry and Darwinian Theses? The first and most obvious thing, of course is that a Christian holds that all plants and animals, past as well as present, have been created by the Lord. Now suppose we set to one side what we take to be the best understanding of early Genesis. Then the next thing to see is that God could have acomplished this creating in a thousand different ways. It was entirely within his power to create life in a way correspon-ding to the Grand Evolutionary scenario: it was within his power to create matter and energy, as in the **Big Bang,** together with laws for its behavior, in such a way that the outcome would be first, life's coming into existence three or four billion years ago, and then the various higher forms of life, culminating, as we like to think, in humankind. This is a semi**deistic** view of God and his workings: he starts everything off and sits back to watch it develop. (One who held this view could also hold that God constantly *sustains* the world in existence—hence the view is only *semi*deistic—and even that any given causal transaction in the universe requires specific divine concurrent activity.) On the other hand, of course, God could have done things very differently. He has created matter and energy with their tendencies to behave in certain ways—ways summed up in the laws of physics—but perhaps these laws are *not* such that given enough time, life would automatically arise. Perhaps he did something different and special in the creation of life. Perhaps he did some-

[5]"The Theory of Evolution; Recent Sucesses and Challenges," in *Evolution and Creation,* ed. Ernan McMullin (Notre Dame: University of Notre Dame Press, 1985), p. 60.

[6]"Evolution as Fact and Theory" in *Hen's Teeth and Horse's Toes* (New York: W. W. Norton and Company, 1980), pp. 254–55.

[7]"Evolutionary Biology and the Study of Human Nature," presented at a consultation on Cosmology and Theology sponsored by the Presbyterian (USA) Church in Dec. 1987.

thing different and special in creating the various kinds of animals and plants. Perhaps he did something different and special in the creation of human beings. Perhaps in these cases his action with respect to what he has created was different from the ways in which he ordinarily treats them.

How shall we decide which of these is initially the more likely? That is not an easy question. It is important to remember, however, that the Lord has not merely left the Cosmos to develop according to an initial creation and an initial set of physical laws. According to Scripture, he has often intervened in the working of his cosmos. This isn't a good way of putting the matter (because of its deistic suggestions); it is better to say that he has often treated what he has created in a way different from the way in which he ordinarily treats it. There are miracles reported in Scripture, for example; and, towering above all, there is the unthinkable gift of salvation for humankind by way of the life, death, and resurrection of Jesus Christ, his son. According to Scripture, God has often treated what he has made in a way different from the way in which he ordinarily treats it; there is therefore no initial edge to the idea that he would be more likely to have created life in all its variety in the broadly deistic way. In fact it looks to me as if there is an initial probability on the other side; it is a bit more probable, before we look at the scientific evidence, that the Lord created life and some of its forms—in particular, human life—specially.

From this perspective, then, how shall we evaluate the evidence for evolution? Despite the claims of Ayala, Dawkins, Gould, Simpson and the other experts, I think the evidence here has to be rated as ambiguous and inconclusive. The two hypotheses to be compared are (1) the claim that God has created us in such a way that (a) all of contemporary plants and animals are related by common ancestry, and (b) the mechanism driving evolution is natural selection working on random genetic variation and (2) the claim that God created mankind as well as many kinds of plants and animals separately and specially, in such a way that the thesis of common ancestry is false. Which of these is the more probable, given the empirical evidence and the theistic context? I think the second, the special creation thesis, is somewhat more probable with respect to the evidence (given theism) than the first.

There isn't the space, here, for more than the merest hand waving with respect to marshalling and evaluating the evidence. But according to Stephen Jay Gould, certainly a leading contemporary spokesman,

> our confidence that evolution occurred centers upon three general arguments. First, we have abundant, direct observational evidence of evolution in action, from both field and laboratory. This evidence ranges from countless experiments on change in nearly everything about fruit flies subjected to artificial selection in the laboratory to the famous populations of British moths that became black when industrial soot darkened the trees upon which the moths rest. . . . [8]

Second, Gould mentions **homologies:** "Why should a rat run, a bat fly, a porpoise swim, and I type this essay with structures built of the same bones," he asks, "unless we all inherited them from a common ancestor?" Third, he says, there is the fossil record:

> transitions are often found in the fossil record. Preserved transitions are not common . . . but they are not entirely wanting. . . . For that matter, what better transitional form could we expect to find than the oldest human, *Australopithecus afrarensis,* with its apelike palate, its human upright stance, and a cranial capacity larger than any ape's of the same body size but a full 1000 cubic centimeters below ours? If God made each of the half-dozen human species discovered in ancient rocks, why did he create in an unbroken temporal sequence of progressively more modern features, increasing cranial capacity, reduced face and teeth, larger body size? Did he create to mimic evolution and test our faith thereby?[9]

Here we could add a couple of other commonly cited kinds of evidence: (a) we along with other animals display vestigial organs (appendix, coccyx, muscles that move ears and nose); it is suggested that the best explanation is evolution. (b) There is alleged

[8] *Hen's Teeth and Horse's Toes,* p. 257.
[9] *Op. cit.,* pp. 258–259.

evidence from biochemistry: according to the authors of a popular college textbook, "All organisms . . . employ DNA, and most use the citric acid cycle, cytochromes, and so forth. It seems inconceivable that the biochemistry of living things would be so similar if all life did not develop from a single common ancestral group.[10] There is also (c) the fact that human embryos during their development display some of the characteristics of simpler forms of life (for example, at a certain stage they display gill-like structures). Finally, (d) there is the fact that certain patterns of geographical distribution—that there are orchids and alligators only in the American south and in China, for example—are susceptible to a nice evolutionary explanation.

Suppose we briefly consider the last four first. The arguments from vestigial organs, geographical distribution and embryology are suggestive, but of course nowhere near conclusive. As for the similarity in biochemistry of all life, this is reasonably probable on the hypothesis of special creation, hence not much by way of evidence against it, hence not much by way of evidence for evolution.

Turning to the evidence Gould develops, it too is suggestive, but far from conclusive; some of it, furthermore, is seriously flawed. First, those famous British moths didn't produce a new species; there were both dark and light moths around before, the dark ones coming to predominate when the industrial revolution deposited a layer of soot on trees, making the light moths more visible to predators. More broadly, while there is wide agreement that there is such a thing as microevolution, the question is whether we can extrapolate to macroevolution, with the claim that enough microevolution can account for the enormous differences between, say, bacteria and human beings. There is some experiential reason to think not; there seems to be a sort of envelope of limited variability surrounding a species and its near relatives. Artificial selection can produce several different kinds of fruit flies and several different kinds of dogs, but, starting with fruit flies, what it produces is only more fruit flies. As plants or animals are bred in certain direction, a sort of barrier is encountered; further selective breeding brings about sterility or a reversion to earlier forms. Partisans of evolution suggest that, in nature, genetic mutation of one sort or another can appropriately augment the reservoir of genetic variation. That it can do so sufficiently, however, is not known; and the assertion that it does is a sort of Ptolemaic epicycle attaching to the theory.

Next, there is the argument from the fossil record; but as Gould himself points out, the fossil record shows very few transitional forms. "The extreme rarity of transitional forms in the fossil record," he says, "persists as the trade secret of paleontology. The evolutionary trees that adorn our textbooks have data only at the tips and nodes of their branches; the rest is inference, however reasonable, not the evidence of fossils."[11] Nearly all species appear for the first time in the fossil record fully formed, without the vast chains of intermediary forms evolution would suggest. Gradualistic evolutionists claim that the fossil record is woefully incomplete. Gould, Eldredge and others have a different response to this difficulty: **punctuated equilibrium,** according to which long periods of evolutionary stasis are interrupted by relatively brief periods of very rapid evolution. This response helps the theory accommodate some of the fossil data, but at the cost of another Ptolemaic epicycle.[12] And still more epicycles are

[10]Claude A. Villee, Eldra Pearl Solomon, P. William Davis, *Biology* (Saunders College Publishing, 1985), p. 1012. Similarly, Mark Ridley *The Problems of Evolution* (Oxford: Oxford University Press, 1985) takes the fact that the genetic code is universal across all forms of life as proof that life originated only once; it would be extremely improbable that life should have stumbled upon the same code more than once.

[11]*The Panda's Thumb* (New York: 1980), p. 181. According to George Gaylord Simpson (1953): "Nearly all categories above the level of families appear in the record suddenly and are not led up to by known, gradual, completely continuous transitional sequences."

[12]And even so it helps much less than you might think. It does offer an explanation of the absence of fossil forms intermediate with respect to closely related or adjoining species; the real problem, though, is what Simpson refers to in the quote in the previous footnote: the fact that nearly all categories above the level of families appear in the record suddenly, without the gradual and continuous sequences we should expect. Punctuated equilibriumism does nothing to explain the nearly complete absence, in the fossil record, of intermediates between such major divisions as, say, reptiles and birds, or fish and reptiles, or reptiles and mammals.

required to account for puzzling discoveries in molecular biology during the last twenty years.[13] And as for the argument from homologies, this too is suggestive, but far from decisive. First, there are of course many examples of architectural similarity that are not attributed to common ancestry, as in the case of the Tasmanian wolf and the European wolf; the anatomical givens are by no means conclusive proof of common ancestry. And secondly, God created several different kinds of animals; what would prevent him from using similar structures?

But perhaps the most important difficulty lies in a slightly different direction. Consider the mammalian eye: a marvelous and highly complex instrument, resembling a telescope of the highest quality, with a lens, an adjustable focus, a variable diaphragm for controlling the amount of light, and optical corrections for spherical and chromatic aberration. And here is the problem: how does the lens, for example, get developed by the proposed means—random genetic variation and natural selection—when at the same time there has to be development of the optic nerve, the relevant muscles, the retina, the rods and cones, and many other delicate and complicated structures, all of which have to be adjusted to each other in such a way that they can work together? Indeed, what is involved isn't, of course, just the eye; it is the whole visual system, including the relevant parts of the brain. Many different organs and suborgans have to be developed together, and it is hard to envisage a series of mutations which is such that each member of the series has adaptive value, is also a step on the way to the eye, and is such that the last member is an animal with such an eye.

We can consider the problem a bit more abstractly. Think of a sort of space, in which the points are organic forms (possible organisms) and in which neighboring forms are so related that one could have originated from the other with some minimum probability by way of random genetic mutation. Imagine starting with a population of animals without eyes, and trace through the space in question all the paths that lead from this form to forms with eyes. The chief problem is that the vast majority of these paths contain long sections with adjacent points such that there would be no adaptive advantage in going from one point to the next, so that, on Darwinian assumptions, none of them could be the path in fact taken. How could the eye have evolved in this way, so that each point on its path through that space would be adaptive and a step on the way to the eye? (Perhaps it is possible that some of these sections could be traversed by way of steps that were not adaptive and were fixed by genetic drift; but the probability of the population's crossing such stretches will be much less than that of its crossing a similar stretch where natural selection is operative.) Darwin himself wrote, "To suppose that the eye, with all its inimitable contrivances . . . could have been formed by natural selection seems absurd in the highest degree." "When I think of the eye, I shudder" he said (3–4). And the complexity of the eye is enormously greater than was known in Darwin's time.

We are never, of course, given the *actual* explanation of the evolution of the eye, the actual evolutionary history of the eye (or brain or hand or whatever). That would take the form: in that original population of eyeless life forms, genes A_1–A_n mutated (due to some perhaps unspecified cause), leading to some structural and functional change which was adaptively beneficial; the bearers of A_1–A_n thus had an advantage and came to dominate the population. Then genes B_1–B_n mutated in an individual or two, and the same thing happened again; then gene C_1–C_n, etc. Nor are we even given any possibilities of these sorts. (We couldn't be, since, for most genes, we don't know enough about their functions.) We are instead treated to broad brush scenarios at the macroscopic level: perhaps reptiles gradually developed feathers, and wings, and warm-bloodedness, and the other features of birds. We are given possible evolutionary histories, not of the detailed genetic sort mentioned above, but broad macroscopic scenarios: what Gould calls "just-so stories."

And the real problem is that we don't know how to evaluate these suggestions. To know how to do *that* (in the case of the eye, say), we should have to start with some population of animals without eyes; and then we should have to know the rate at which mutations occur for that population; the proportion

[13]Here see Michael Denton, *Evolution: A Theory in Crisis* (London: Burnet Books, 1985), chapter 12.

of those mutations that are on one of those paths through that space to the condition of having eyes; the proportion of *those* that are adaptive, and, at each stage, given the sort of environment enjoyed by the organisms at that stage, the rate at which such adaptive modifications would have spread through the population in question. Then we'd have to compare our results with the time available to evaluate the probability of the suggestion in question. But we don't know what these rates and proportions are. No doubt we *can't* know what they are, given the scarcity of operable time-machines; still, the fact is we don't know them. And hence we don't really know whether evolution is so much as biologically possible: maybe there is no path through that space. It is ***epistemically* possible** that evolution has occurred: that is, we don't know that it hasn't; for all we know, it has. But it doesn't follow that it is *biologically* possible. (Whether every even number is the sum of two primes is an open question; hence it is epistemically possible that every even number is the sum of two primes, and also epistemically possible that some even numbers are not the sum of two primes; but one or the other of those epistemic possibilities is in fact mathematically impossible.) Assuming that it *is* biologically possible, furthermore, we don't know that it is not prohibitively improbable (in the statistical sense), given the time available. But then (given the Christian faith and leaving to one side our evaluation of the evidence from early Genesis) the right attitude towards the claim of universal common descent is, I think, one of a certain interested but wary skepticism. It is *possible* (epistemically possible) that this is how things happened; God could have done it that way; but the evidence is ambiguous. That it is *possible* is clear; that it *happened* is doubtful; that it is *certain,* however, is ridiculous.

But then what about all those exuberant cries of certainty from Gould, Ayala, Dawkins, Simpson and the other experts? What about those claims that evolution, universal common ancestry, is a rock-ribbed certainty, to be compared with the fact that the earth is round and goes around the sun? What we have here is at best enormous exaggeration. But then what accounts for the fact that these claims are made by such intelligent luminaries as the above? There are at least two reasons. First, there is the cultural and religious, the mythic function of the doctrine; evolution helps make it possible to be an intellectually fulfilled atheist. From a naturalistic point of view, this is the only answer in sight to the question "How did it all happen? How did all this amazing profusion of life get here?" From a nontheistic point of view, the evolutionary hypothesis is the only game in town. According to the thesis of universal common descent, life arose in just one place; then there was constant development by way of evolutionary mechanisms from that time to the present, this resulting in the profusion of life we presently see. On the alternative hypothesis, different forms of life arose independently of each other; on that suggestion there would be many different genetic trees, the creatures adorning one of these trees genetically unrelated to those on another. From a nontheistic perspective, the first hypothesis will be by far the more probable, if only because of the extraordinary difficulty in seeing how life could arise even once by any ordinary mechanisms which operate today. That it should arise many different times and at different levels of complexity in this way, is quite incredible.

From a **naturalist** perspective, furthermore, many of the arguments for evolution are much more powerful than from a theistic perspective. (For example, *given* that life arose naturalistically, it is indeed significant that all life employs the same genetic code.) So from a naturalistic, nontheistic perspective the evolutionary hypothesis will be vastly more probable than alternatives. Many leaders in the field of evolutionary biologists, of course, *are* naturalists—Gould, Dawkins, and Stebbins, for example; and according to William Provine, "very few truly religious evolutionary biologists remain. Most are atheists, and many have been driven there by their understanding of the evolutionary process and other science."[14] If Provine is right or nearly right, it becomes easier to see why we hear this insistence that the evolutionary hypothesis is certain. It is also easy to see how this attitude is passed on to graduate students, and, indeed, how accepting the view that evolution is certain is itself adaptive for life in graduate school and academia generally.

[14] *Op. Cit.*, p. 28.

There is a second and related circumstance at work here. We are sometimes told that natural science is *natural* science. So far it is hard to object: but how shall we take the term 'natural' here? It could mean that natural science is science devoted to the study of nature. Fair enough. But it is also taken to mean that natural science involves a *methodological naturalism* or provisional atheism:[15] no hypothesis according to which God has done this or that can qualify as a *scientific* hypothesis. It would be interesting to look into this matter: is there really any compelling or even decent reason for thus restricting our study of nature? But suppose we irenically concede, for the moment, that natural science doesn't or shouldn't invoke hypotheses essentially involving God. Suppose we restrict our explanatory materials to the ordinary laws of physics and chemistry; suppose we reject divine special creation or other hypotheses about God as *scientific* hypotheses. Perhaps indeed the Lord has engaged in special creation, so we say, but that he has (if he has) is not something with which natural science can deal. So far as natural science goes, therefore, an acceptable hypothesis must appeal only to the laws that govern the ordinary, day-to-day working of the cosmos. As natural scientists we must eschew the supernatural—although, of course, we don't mean for a moment to embrace naturalism.

Well, suppose we adopt this attitude. Then perhaps it looks as if by far the most probable of all the properly scientific hypotheses is that of evolution by common ancestry: it is hard to think of any other real possibility. The only alternatives, apparently, would be creatures popping into existence fully formed; and that is wholly contrary to our experience. Of all the scientifically acceptable explanatory hypotheses, therefore, evolution seems by far the most probable. But if this hypothesis is vastly more probable than any of its rivals, then it must be certain, or nearly so.

But to reason this way is to fall into confusion compounded. In the first place, we aren't just given that one or another of these hypotheses is in fact correct. Granted: if we *knew* that one or another of those scientifically acceptable hypotheses were in fact correct, then perhaps this one would be certain; but of course we don't know that. One real possibility is that we don't have a very good idea how it all happened, just as we may not have a very good idea as to what terrorist organization has perpetrated a particular bombing. And secondly, this reasoning involves a confusion between the claim that of all of those *scientifically* acceptable hypotheses, that of common ancestry is by far the most plausible, with the vastly more contentious claim that of all the acceptable hypotheses *whatever* (now placing no restrictions on their kind) this hypothesis is by far the most probable. Christians in particular ought to be alive to the vast difference between these claims; confounding them leads to nothing but confusion.

From a Christian perspective, it is dubious, with respect to our present evidence, that the Common Ancestry Thesis is true. No doubt there has been much by way of microevolution: Ridley's gulls are an interesting and dramatic case in point. But it isn't particularly likely, given the Christian faith and the biological evidence, that God created all the flora and fauna by way of some mechanism involving common ancestry. My main point, however, is that Ayala, Gould, Simpson, Stebbins and their coterie are wildly mistaken in claiming that the Grand Evolutionary Hypothesis is *certain.* And hence the source of this claim has to be looked for elsewhere than in sober scientific evidence.

So it could be that the best scientific hypothesis was evolution by common descent—i.e., of all the hypotheses that conform to methodological naturalism, it is the best. But of course what we really want to know is not which hypothesis is the best from some artificially adopted standpoint of naturalism, but what the best hypothesis is *overall.* We want to know what the *best* hypothesis is, not which of some limited class is best—particularly if the class in question specifically excludes what we hold to be the basic truth of the matter. It could be that the best scientific hypothesis (again supposing that a scientific hypothesis must be naturalistic in the above sense) isn't even a strong competitor in *that* derby.

[15]"Science must be provisionally atheistic or cease to be itself." Basil Whilley "Darwin's Place in the History of Thought" in M. Banton, ed., *Darwinism and the Study of Society* (Chicago: Quadrangle Books, 1961).

Judgments here, of course, may differ widely between believers in God and non-believers in God. What for the former is at best a methodological restriction is for the latter the sober **metaphysical** truth; her naturalism is not merely provisional and methodological, but, as she sees it, settled and fundamental. But believers in God can see the matter differently. The believer in God, unlike her naturalistic counterpart, is free to look at the evidence for the Grand Evolutionary Scheme, and follow it where it leads, rejecting that scheme if the evidence is insufficient. She has a freedom not available to the naturalist. The latter accepts the Grand Evolutionary Scheme because from a naturalistic point of view this scheme is the only visible answer to the question *what is the explanation of the presence of all these marvelously multifarious forms of life?* The Christian, on the other hand, knows that creation is the Lord's; and she isn't blinkered by *a priori* dogmas as to how the Lord must have accomplished it. Perhaps it was by broadly evolutionary means, but then again perhaps not. At the moment, 'perhaps not' seems the better answer.

Returning to methodological naturalism, if indeed natural science is essentially restricted in this way, if such a restriction is a part of the very essence of science, then what we need here, of course, is not natural science, but a broader inquiry that can include *all* that we know, including the truths that God has created life on earth and could have done it in many different ways. "Unnatural Science," "Creation Science," "Theistic Science"—call it what you will: what we need when we want to know how to think about the origin and development of contemporary life is what is most plausible from a Christian point of view. What we need is a scientific account of life that isn't restricted by that methodological naturalism.

C. WHAT SHOULD CHRISTIAN INTELLECTUALS TELL THE REST OF US?

Alternatively, how can Christian intellectuals—scientists, philosophers, historians, literary and art critics, Christian thinkers of every sort— . . . best serve the Christian community in an area like this? How can they—and since we are they, how can we—best serve the Christian community, the Reformed community of which we are a part, and, more importantly, the broader general Christian community? One thing our experts can do for us is help us avoid rejecting evolution for stupid reasons. The early literature of Creation-Science, so called, is littered with arguments of that eminently rejectable sort. Here is such an argument. Considering the rate of human population growth over the last few centuries, the author points out that even on a most conservative estimate the human population of the earth doubles at least every 1000 years. Then if, as evolutionists claim, the first humans existed at least a million years ago, by now the human population would have doubled 1000 times. It seems hard to see how there could have been fewer than two original human beings, so at that rate, by the inexorable laws of mathematics, after only 60,000 years or so, there would have been something like 36 quintillion people, and by now there would have to be 2^{1000} human beings. 2^{1000} is a large number; it is more than 10^{300}, 1 with 300 zeros after it; if there were that many of us the whole universe would have to be packed solid with people. Since clearly it isn't, human beings couldn't have existed for as long as a million years; so the evolutionists are wrong. This is clearly a lousy argument; I leave as homework the problem of saying just where it goes wrong. There are many other bad arguments against evolution floating around, and it is worth our while to learn that these arguments are indeed bad. We shouldn't reject contemporary science unless we have to, and we shouldn't reject it for the wrong reasons. It is a good thing for our scientists to point out some of those wrong reasons.

But I'd like to suggest, with all the diffidence I can muster, that there is something better to do here—or at any rate something that should be done in addition to this. And the essence of the matter is fairly simple, despite the daunting complexity that arises when we descend to the nitty-gritty level where the real work has to be done. The first thing to see, as I said before, is that Christianity is indeed engaged in a conflict, a battle. There is indeed a battle between the Christian community and the forces of unbelief. This contest or battle rages in many areas of contemporary culture—the courts, in the so-called media and the like—but perhaps most particularly in academia. And the second thing to see is that important cultural forces such as science are not neutral with respect to this conflict—though of course certain parts of contemporary science and many contemporary scientists might very well be. It is of the first importance that we discern in detail just *how* contemporary science—and contemporary philosophy, history, literary criticism and so on—is involved in the struggle. This is a complicated, many-sided matter; it varies from discipline to discipline, and from area to area within a given discipline. One of our chief tasks, therefore, must be that of cultural criticism. We must *test* the spirits, not automatically welcome them in because of their great academic prestige. Academic prestige, wide, even nearly unanimous acceptance in academia, declarations of certainty by important scientists—none of these is a guarantee that what is proposed is true, or a genuine deliverance of reason, or plausible from a theistic point of view. Indeed, none is a guarantee that what is proposed is not animated by a spirit wholly antithetical to Christianity. We must discern the religious and ideological connections; we can't automatically take the word of the experts, because their word might be dead wrong from a Christian standpoint.

Finally, in all the areas of academic endeavor, we Christians must think about the matter at hand from a Christian perspective; we need Theistic Science. Perhaps the discipline in question, as ordinarily practiced, involves a methodological naturalism; if so, then what we need, finally, is not answers to our questions from *that* perspective, valuable in some ways as it may be. What we really need are answers to our questions from the perspective of *all* that we know—what we know about God, and what we know by faith, by way of revelation, as well as what we know in other ways. In many areas, this means that Christians must rework, rethink the area in question from this perspective. This idea may be shocking, but it is not new. Reformed Christians have long recognized that science and scholarship are by no means religiously neutral. In a way this is our distinctive thread in the tapestry of Christianity, our instrument in the great symphony of Christianity. This recognition underlay the establishment of the Free University of Amsterdam in 1880; it also underlay the establishment of Calvin College. Our forebears recognized the need for the sort of work and inquiry I've been mentioning, and tried to do something about it. What we need from our scientists and other academics, then, is both cultural criticism and Christian science.

We must admit, however, that it is our *lack* of real progress that is striking. Of course there are good reasons for this. To carry out this task with the depth, the authority, the competence it requires is, first of all, enormously difficult. However, it is not just the *difficulty* of this enterprise that accounts for our lackluster performance. Just as important is a whole set of historical or sociological conditions. You may have noticed that at present the Western Christian community is located in the twentieth-century Western world. We Christians who go on to become professional scientists and scholars attend twentieth-century graduate schools and universities. And questions about the bearing of Christianity on these disciplines and the questions within them do not enjoy much by way of prestige and esteem in these universities. There are no courses at Harvard entitled "Molecular Biology and the Christian View of Man." At Oxford they don't teach a course called "Origins of Life from a Christian Perspective." One can't write his Ph.D. thesis on these subjects. The National Science Foundation won't look favorably on them. Working on these questions is not a good way to get tenure at a typical university; and if you are job hunting you would be ill-advised to advertise yourself as proposing to specialize in them. The entire structure of contemporary university life is such as to discourage serious work on these questions.

This is therefore a matter of uncommon difficulty. So far as I know, however, no one in authority has promised us a rose garden; and it is also a matter of absolutely crucial importance to the health of the Christian community. It is worthy of the very best we can muster; it demands powerful, patient, unstinting and tireless effort. But its rewards match its demands; it is exciting, absorbing and crucially important. Most of all, however, it needs to be done. I therefore commend it to you.

STUDY QUESTIONS

1. Which theses associated with evolutionary theory does Plantinga accept? Which does he reject? Why?
2. What alternative does Plantinga propose to the theses of Common Ancestry, Darwinism, and Naturalistic Origins?
3. Plantinga claims that, although evolution may be the best *scientific* hypothesis, it is not the best hypothesis *overall.* What does he mean by this?
4. *Plantinga says that scientists do not regard as scientific any hypothesis that includes God as a cause. He calls for the development of theistic science. Do you think that scientists are justified in limiting the scope of science to the discovery of *natural* causes? Why or why not?

READING 6.3

When Faith and Reason Cooperate

Howard J. Van Till

This essay is a reply to Reading 6.2, by Plantinga. Howard J. Van Till (Calvin College), a physicist who also writes on the relations between science and **theology,** *disagrees with Plantinga's portrayal of "conflict" between evolution and the Bible. He rejects the claim that God's special creation of individual species is the only acceptable reading of Genesis. In Van Till's view, the world created by God is marked by* functional integrity. *This means that it has no gaps which would require that God act immediately (directly); rather, at each stage of creation, the capacities God has given things produce the next stage, thanks to God's enabling power. Belief in God does not entail the impossibility of genealogical continuity as described by scientists. Furthermore, the sciences study only the relations between members of the created universe, not between God and the universe. God's creative action is not a component among others in the economy of the created world: it* undergirds *all that occurs.*

As beneficiaries of the same **Reformed** Christian heritage, Alvin Plantinga and I are likely to articulate our **theological** positions in similar conceptual vocabularies, view many issues from nearby standpoints, and hold numerous important beliefs in common. With little difficulty I could use my allotted space to reflect appreciatively on the sizeable intersection of our commitments and perspectives. However, at the risk of appearing excessively contentious, most of this response will concern those areas where there is some disagreement and those matters that need further development. Even in this endeavor I shall have to be both selective and brief.

FAITH, REASON AND CONFLICT

I have long been sorely vexed at the frequency with which the warfare metaphor has been employed in the discussion of the relationship of natural science and Christian belief. And my irritation seems to be irreversibly amplified each time I observe the proponents of "**creation-science**" or the preachers of modern Western **naturalism** resonantly encourage one another in the perpetuation of this conflict thesis in the service of their own polemical agendas.[1]

Hence, with all due respect for the long history of the faith-versus-reason discussion, I believe it was most inappropriate for Plantinga to employ the conflict metaphor as frequently as he did in his paper. In fact, I would strongly contest the idea that a Christian critique of the scientific concept of evolution can fruitfully be conducted in the arena of the historical faith-versus-reason tension. As persons already committed to faith in God, our concern is not with faith *versus* reason, nor is it with the unambiguous teaching of the Bible *versus* the "teachings" (Plantinga's term) of contemporary natural science. Rather, it is our earnest desire to bring into consonance our reasoned understanding of the Scriptures and our reasoned understanding of the Creation. At a number of points Plantinga acknowledged this, but all too often the emotion-laden rhetoric of faith *versus* reason appeared, thereby clouding the atmosphere of fruitful response to the question, "How shall we think about this matter?"

Perhaps my complaint is primarily with Plantinga's use of the term *faith.* In most instances in this paper the term does not refer to one's personal commitment to act in the warranted confidence that the object of one's faith is trustworthy (e.g., to have faith that God will provide lovingly for our needs); rather, Plantinga employs the term principally as an abbreviated version of "a deliverance of the faith." And, in the context of the issue at hand, I take this to be a reference to some specific belief concerning what the Scriptures require a Christian to affirm, a belief held mostly for the reason that it constitutes an element in the received Christian tradition (e.g., the belief that the Bible teaches the concept of special creation). In fairness, however, we should note the possibility that belief in such a "deliverance of the faith" might well be strengthened as a result of contemporary reexamination.

As I see it, the real challenge that stands before us is not to resolve some *conflict* between Christian faith and scientific reasoning, but instead to promote a *cooperative effort* of Christian scientists and biblical scholars as together we seek to grow in our understanding of what Scripture requires of us and of what the Creation's formative history was like. My version of McGonagall's rhyme would be:

> When faith and reason appear to clash,
> 'tis the appearance must go to smash. . . .

. . . [I]s the concept of **special creation** required of all persons who profess trust in the Creator-God revealed in Scripture? While most Christians in my acquaintance who are engaged in either scientific or biblical scholarship have concluded that the special creationist picture of the world's formation is *not* a necessary component of Christian belief, the larger North American Christian community is deeply divided over this issue. But questions regarding the relationship between the scientific concept of evolutionary development and biblical proclamations concerning creation can not legitimately be framed in the faith-versus-reason rhetoric unless we are agreed (on the basis of something far more substantial than unexamined tradition or "folk exegesis") either that the concept of special creation is required or that the concept of biological evolution is excluded by faithful biblical exegesis. Furthermore, it could well be argued that to hold the special creationist interpretation of early Genesis is not so much a manifestation of faith in God as it is a manifestation of uncritical acceptance of a particular exegetical tradition. Hence the faith-versus-reason discussion soon degenerates into a contest between rigid traditionalism and open inquiry.

Personally, I heartily agree with those biblical scholars who conclude that the concept of special creation (immediate formation of creatures not genealogically related) is *not* biblically warranted. Furthermore, it is my firm conviction that the Bible does not at all exclude a full evolutionary development of lifeforms in a manner similar to that envisioned by modern biological theory. . . . I say this

[1]For an extended expression of my irritation relative to this issue see chapter 8 of Van Till, Snow, Stek and Young, *Portraits of Creation: Biblical and Scientific Perspectives on the World's Formation* (Grand Rapids: Eerdmans, 1990), pp. 266–77.

not by "deciding in advance what Scripture can speak on," but in large part by respecting God's choice for the historical and cultural contexts in which the biblical text was to be written. Was it not God's choice to accommodate this mode of revelation to the historically and culturally limited conceptual vocabularies of the day? The human writers inspired by God had no vocabulary for concepts like galactic redshift, thermonuclear fusion, plate tectonics, spacetime metrics, radiometric dating, stellar evolution, ionizing radiation, chemical reactions, atomic spectra, deoxyribonucleic acid, proteinoid microspheres, genetic drift, molecular clocks, configurational entropy, microevolution, macroevolution, etc., etc., etc. Hence, to expect the Scriptures to provide us with the kind of statements that would be directly relevant to the evaluation of contemporary scientific theories on the world's formative history strikes me as profoundly misguided. . . .

SHOULD CHRISTIAN SCHOLARSHIP REJECT METHODOLOGICAL NATURALISM?

In the section titled "The Likelihood of Evolution," . . . Plantinga presents his evaluation of selected **empirical** evidence relevant to the macroevolutionary scenario and he concludes that as a Christian he finds the concept of special creation more credible. My own inclinations, on the other hand, are toward an evolutionary picture—not only because it provides a coherent means of integrating a broad array of empirical evidence (I will leave Plantinga's handling of specific empirical matters for Christian biologists to evaluate), but also because it comports with the theological position that the world created by the God who reveals himself in Scripture is a world characterized by what I shall call *functional integrity.*

By this term I mean to denote a created world that has no functional deficiencies, no gaps in its economy of the sort that would require God to act immediately, temporarily assuming the role of creature to perform functions within the economy of the creation that other creatures have not been equipped to perform. When the Creator says, "Let the land produce vegetation," or "Let the water teem with living creatures," or "Let the land produce living creatures," a world created with functional integrity will, by the enabling power and directing governance of God, be able to respond obediently and employ its capacities to carry out the intentions of the Creator.

This theological position is stated clearly by John Stek in his contribution to *Portraits of Creation.* Concerning the creation as God's Kingdom Stek says,

> *It possesses its own integral and integrating economy.* Each of its components has its own internal economy (e.g., the biological economy of plants and animals), and all of its components were created to fill out and integrate the economy of the whole. . . . Furthermore, the internal economy of the created realm is neither incomplete nor defective. That is to say, it contains no gaps that have to be filled with continuous or sporadic *immediate* operations of divine power; God is not himself a component within the internal economy of his creaturely realm.[2]

From this theological starting point, drawn from a thorough exegetical study of Scripture, Stek is led to state a number of implications regarding human knowledge of the created world. One especially relevant observation is that:

> Since the created realm is replete with its own economy that is neither incomplete (God is not a component within it) nor defective, *in our understanding of the economy of that realm so as to exercise stewardship over it . . . we must methodologically exclude all notions of immediate divine causality.* As stewards of the creation we must methodologically honor the principle that creation interprets creation. . . . In pursuit of a stewardly understanding of the creation, we may not introduce a "**God of the gaps**. . . ." We may not do so (1) because God is not an internal component within the economy of the created realm, and (2) because to do so would be to presume to exercise power over God—the presumptuous folly of those in many cultures

[2]John Stek, in *Portraits of Creation,* p. 254.

who have claimed to be specialists in the manipulation of divine powers.[3]

In *Christian Belief in a Postmodern World,* a lucid and helpful work on the constructive relationship of Christian faith and careful reasoning, philosopher Diogenes Allen articulates similar concepts of the created world and scientific descriptions of it. Concerning the limits of the competence of scientific investigation he reminds us that

> our natural sciences seek to describe and explain the relations *between* the members of the universe, not their origin. The existence of the universe and its basic constituents are taken for granted by our sciences. . . . When we consider the whole of nature, the relations we find within nature cannot tell us why the universe exists nor why it is the kind of universe that it is. The continuing increase of scientific knowledge, which discovers the relations that exist within our universe, does not get us closer to an answer to either question.[4]

Hence, as Christians we do *not* look for gaps either in the present-day functioning of the universe or in its formative history—gaps into which the immediate action of God might be inserted. Says Allen,

> This is theologically improper because God, as creator of the universe, is not a member of the universe. God can never properly be used in scientific accounts, which are formulated in terms of the relations between the members of the universe, because that would reduce God to the status of a creature. According to a Christian conception of God as creator of a universe that is rational through and through, there are no missing relations between the members of nature. If, in our study of nature, we run into what seems to be an instance of a connection missing between members of nature, the Christian doctrine of creation implies that we should keep looking for one. [p. 45]

Applying this approach to questions regarding biological evolution, Allen rejects the view, rooted largely in Aristotle, that species must be fixed—a view that would force Christians to reject any concept of genealogical continuity in favor of special creationism. "But," says Allen, "The Christian conviction that God is the Creator is the claim that nature's order is intended by God, not the claim that present-day life forms arose directly from God's action." [p. 59] To argue, as do some contemporary proponents of special creationism, that belief in God as Creator logically entails the impossibility of genealogical continuity in the formative history of living creatures is, according to Allen, "contrary to the Christian conviction that a rational God creates a universe with members that are coherently connected. Rather than defending Christianity against science, it contradicts a fundamental Christian conviction" [p. 59].

Given my theologically-rooted conviction that the created world is characterized by functional integrity, both in its present operation and in its formative history, and given my judgment that speciation within the bounds of genealogical continuity would constitute a remarkably elegant expression of that functional integrity, I expect the scientific search for evolutionary accounts of the history of life forms to be an increasingly fruitful enterprise. As Allen notes, "Christianity rightly endorses the search for such accounts on the ground that the source of the universe is rational and so there are connections to be found between its members" [p. 59].

With Stek, Allen and others, I understand the natural sciences to be properly engaged in, and limited to, a study of the properties, behavior and interrelationships among the diverse members of the created world. As such, science does not make explicit mention of God's creative activity as the source and sustainer of the world's existence, or as the architect of the particular dynamic order exhibited by the world, or as the One whose enabling power and blessing are necessary for all components of the world to act as they do in carrying out his intentions for their being. "There is a discontinuity," says Allen, "between God and our scientific explanations because God's relation to the universe is that

[3]Stek, in *Portraits of Creation,* p. 261.

[4]Diogenes Allen, *Christian Belief in a Postmodern World* (Louisville: Westminster/John Knox Press, 1989), p. 53.

of Creator [to the created] and the sciences study [only] the relations between the members of the universe" [p. 75]. Science does not have either the competence or the calling to study the creative relationship between the universe and God. Neither do the sciences have the right to bring God's creative activity down to the level of creaturely action and treat God as if he were a component in the economy of the created world.

But the scientific approach that I have here described (as have others elsewhere) is characterized by Plantinga as the strategy of "methodological naturalism" or "provisional atheism"—a strategy that he judges to be inferior because it seems arbitrarily to exclude explicit reference to God's immediate action from its theoretical explanations. "What we need," says Plantinga, "is a scientific account of life that isn't restricted by methodological naturalism. . . . We need Theistic Science."

My criticism will concern both the terminology and substance of this claim. With Stek and Allen I believe there are good theological reasons for keeping *scientific* accounts within the bounds of creaturely phenomena alone; God's creative activity is not an empirically accessible component within the economy of the created world. Hence I find Plantinga's use of terms like "methodological naturalism" and "provisional atheism" highly pejorative. As I see it, granting the limited competence of natural science is not a concession to naturalism; rather, it is simply a recognition that we have empirical access only to creaturely phenomena. And constructing scientific accounts of the formative history of life forms without explicit appeal to immediate acts of the Creator is not a capitulation to atheism; rather, it is a theologically-based recognition that God is not one component among many others in the economy of the created world—God's creative action, operating at a level different from creaturely action, undergirds *all* that occurs, not only that which eludes our first efforts toward scientific description.

Posing the possibility that all of the present floras and faunas developed over an extended period of time in a genealogically continuous manner from earlier forms, or even proposing that the first living structure formed from inanimate components, in no way denies or even calls into question the creative work of God; rather, it should call us to consider the incomprehensible creativity required of God to give being to a world with such a degree of functional integrity that it could, with God's blessing, so respond in obedience to his "Let the land bring forth. . . ."

Methodological naturalism? Provisional atheism? Highly pejorative terms that function only to cloud the issue. It would be far more fitting, I believe, to think of the approach that I have described simply as natural science performed within the arena permitted by biblical theism—science recognized as providing an incomplete picture of reality because of its inability to probe beyond the creaturely realm (I deplore **scientism** as much as Plantinga does), science that needs to be placed within the framework of an all-emcompassing, biblically informed, theistic worldview that does indeed draw from *all* that we know about God, his creation and his revelation. Call this broader activity of placing the results of natural science in the framework of theism by the name *Theistic Science* if you like, but contrary to Plantinga's vision for it I propose that it should differ from ordinary science not by the occasional insertion of immediate divine acts into a world whose internal economy is either deficient or defective, but rather by its recognition that every aspect of the world's functionally complete economy is radically dependent on the Creator's ceaseless activity as the world's Originator, Sustainer, Governor and Provider.

Plantinga placed his reflections on evolution and the Bible in the framework of the faith versus reason debate—"when faith and reason clash." I see no hope for progress in that approach. As I see it, progress in this discussion will come only when we work communally toward growth in our reasoned understanding of the Scriptures and in our reasoned understanding of the Creation—when faith and reason cooperate.

STUDY QUESTIONS

1. Explain Van Till's notion of functional integrity. Why is the doctrine of functional integrity congenial to the theory that human beings arose through naturalistic evolution rather than special creation?

2. What advantages does Van Till see in thinking of creation as unfolding through the natural capacities of created things rather than through special creation?
3. *Contrast Van Till's notion of science with Plantinga's notion of theistic science. Whose conception do you favor? Why?

READING 6.4

Genesis and Evolution

Peter van Inwagen

In this reading, Peter van Inwagen (Notre Dame) advocates an approach to reading Genesis that does not take the creation narrative to be affirming literal truth. Van Inwagen accepts that the earth is thousands of millions of years old, contrary to the literal meaning of Genesis. But he explains this by arguing that an "abstract Genesis," a version of Genesis that is correct in its scientific details, would not be pedagogically useful. Readers in the ancient Near East, for example, could not have understood it. The Bible wishes to convey certain truths that are more important than the truths of science, and, with regard to those more important matters, the Bible states things accurately. Van Inwagen claims that the notion that reading scriptural truth non-literally is heresy does not predate the Reformation.

. . . I shall describe, and invent names for, two positions that I believe correspond to *some* of the things said by people who are popularly called 'fundamentalists' and *some* of the things said by people who are popularly called 'secular humanists.' I shall call the one 'Genesiac literalism' (or literalism for short) and the other 'saganism'—after one of its most illustrious and talkative ornaments (Carl Sagan).

I begin with a statement of Genesiac literalism. (I say Genesiac rather than *biblical* literalism, because I believe that the early chapters of the book of Genesis are a very special part of the Bible, and I mean to talk about them only. Nothing I say should be regarded as having any implications whatever for questions about how to read, say, Job or the Gospels or Revelation.)

"The planet earth came into existence about six thousand years ago, when God created it in a series of six twenty-four-hour days. On the third, fifth, and sixth of these days, God created all the various species of living things, concluding with a single pair of human beings, the first man and the first woman. Any appearance to the contrary in the geological record is due to a worldwide flood that occurred about forty-five hundred years ago; the geological distortions caused by that vast deluge created phenomena that the clever and perverse have—like someone finding internal evidence of Baconian authorship in *Hamlet*—interpreted as showing that the earth is not thousands but thousands of *millions* of years old, its present geological features supposedly being due to the effects of various natural processes that have been at work over this immense stretch of time.

"We know the facts I have outlined concerning the beginning of the earth and life and man because God revealed them to Moses thousands of years later and Moses wrote them down in the book we call Genesis, a book that God has ensured is historically accurate in every respect because it is a part of His Holy Scripture. It is true that Scripture contains metaphor and hyperbole—as, for example, when it tells us that the soldiers of the kings of Canaan were as numerous as the grains of sand on the shore of the sea—but any reasonably intelligent and well-intentioned reader can tell when metaphor or hyperbole are intended by Scriptural writers, and the main historical statements of Genesis are clearly intended to be taken literally."

So says the literalist.

The saganist tells another story: "The cosmos, the totality of the distribution of matter and radiation in space-time, is 'all that is or was or ever will be.' Ten thousand million years ago or more, it was concentrated in a very tiny volume of space, which was, nevertheless, all the space there was. This tiny volume expanded very rapidly, and certain processes, which we are beginning to understand, led, after a few minutes, to the three-to-one ratio of hydrogen to helium nuclei that we observe today. A few hundred thousand years later, the density of the expanding universe had fallen to a point at which electrons could arrange themselves around the hydrogen and helium nuclei, and the space between the atoms thus formed was suddenly filled with free radiation, radiation which, vastly attenuated, is still detectable. Gravitational effects caused matter to be concentrated in stars and stars to be collected into galaxies. In the stars, new elements like carbon and oxygen were formed and were dispersed when these stars came to the ends of their lives and exploded. The scattered atoms of these elements eventually became parts of new stars and of solid planets circling them.

"On at least one planet, but presumably on many, natural processes led to the formation of a complex molecule capable of replicating itself with variations. Owing entirely to the operation of **natural selection,** the descendants of this molecule achieved a sufficient level of internal organization for us to feel comfortable about thinking of them as living organisms. The blind but, in appearance, creative processes of natural selection continued to operate, and produced the cell, the multicellular organism, sexual dimorphism, and, eventually, representatives of all the phyla we see today (and some that we don't). In due course, owing to the interplay of variation and selection over hundreds of millions of years, intelligence appeared. (The broad outlines of the latter part of this narrative, the part dealing with biological evolution, have been accepted by every serious scientist since about 1870. Opposition to it is due entirely to **theological** obscurantism.) A short time later, perhaps through a social analogue of natural selection, intelligence developed *science,* a powerful, self-correcting mechanism for understanding the cosmos. Various older and much less efficient competitors with science—notably religion—survive, but, having tried and failed to destroy their new and dangerous rival in its infancy, they are steadily losing ground to it and will soon go the way of the saber-toothed tiger. Perhaps the final nail in their coffin will be the discovery of intelligent life elsewhere in the universe, a shock they are too narrow-minded and parochial to survive. . . ."

Well, here are two extreme positions. Probably every position one could take on the relation between the book of Genesis and the scientific study of the origins of the universe, the earth, and humanity lies on the continuum between them. One possible position, for example, is ***deism,*** which accepts most of the saganists' story but rejects its contention that there is nothing besides the cosmos. Deism postulates an intelligent Creator who set the universe in motion and then sat back to watch the show. (Like the typical Hollywood producer, this Creator seems to have rather a taste for shows that involve sex and violence—especially violence. It is, however, doubtful whether he shares Hollywood's taste for happy endings.)

What I mean to do in the rest of this essay is, first, to set forth a position on the relation between Genesis and scientific accounts of the history of the universe that is radically different from literalism and saganism (and from deism). I shall then offer critiques of both literalism and saganism from the point of view afforded by this position. I pick these two positions to criticize because, first, they have been getting the lion's share of the publicity, and, secondly, as a consequence of the fact that they are extremes between which most if not all the other possible positions on this issue lie, what I would say about other positions may perhaps be gleaned from what I say about the extremes.

Now a word as to my own religious beliefs. I am a Christian. More exactly, I am an Episcopalian, and I fully accept the teaching of my denomination that "the Holy Scriptures of the Old and New Testaments are the revealed Word of God"; that they "contain all things necessary to salvation and are the rule and ultimate standard of faith"; that "God inspired their human authors and still speaks to us through the Bible." But I am not constructing a position that I recommend only to Episcopalians. I recommend this position to any Christian—and to any Jew—who regards the book of Genesis as divinely inspired and who, nevertheless, rejects, as I do, Genesiac literalism. I will add that a Christian is not logically committed, by the very fact of being a Christian, to regarding the Bible as being divinely inspired throughout. . . .

While one might want to qualify this statement in various ways, in the light of such things as Martin Luther's remarks about the Letter of James, it seems roughly correct to say that all Christians whose witness on the matter has survived have regarded the Bible as being divinely inspired throughout, and I have no intention of separating myself from this cloud of witnesses. How, then, shall those who agree with me and the literalists that Genesis is the inspired word of God and who also agree with me and the saganists that life and the earth and the cosmos have histories that are measured in thousands of millions of years explain themselves? This question is not, in its essentials, a new one. A lot of people seem to think that all Christians were literalists before the geological discoveries of the early nineteenth century. Under the impact of these discoveries and the Darwinian account of evolution that was built upon them (the story goes) some Christians began desperately to scramble about to try to devise some way of reconciling science and the Bible.

This is historically false. Let us consider the greatest of all Christian theologians, St. Augustine (whose death in the year 430 places him at a comfortable remove from the impact of nineteenth-century science). Augustine argued that the "six days" account of creation in Genesis could hardly be literally correct, since (among other reasons he gives) it asserts that day and night existed before the sun was made. (Let me assure you parenthetically that if the author of Genesis 1 did not know much about geology, he certainly did know that daylight was due to the sun.) Now if Genesis is not a literally correct account of the Creation—Augustine reasoned—then it must belong to one of the many non-literal modes of presentation recognized by the science of rhetoric (which, as we should say today, was Augustine's area of professional competence). But I do not propose to discuss Augustine's **hermeneutical** theories; I am more interested in the account he gave of what he took to be the literal reality behind the non-literal presentation.[1] Augustine held that God had created the universe all at once, and that, at the moment of its creation, the universe was, by present standards, without form, and was empty of things of the kinds it now contains. But there was *latent* form and there were things in which that form was latent. He calls these things *seed-principles,* using a botanical trope, as we use a political trope when we speak of the laws of nature. The newly created universe subsequently, by its own inner necessity, evolved into its present highly differentiated state, this present state having been implicit in its original state much as a field of grain is implicit in a mixture of seed and water and earth. (Or, at any rate, many aspects of the present state of the world were in this strong sense implicit in the initial state. Others may have been due to miraculous actions by God subsequent to the beginning of things. But if miracles did play a part in the

[1]Augustine's views on Genesis are found in his *De genesi ad litteram* ("On Genesis according to the Letter"). The standard English translation by J. H. Taylor (New York: Newman, 1982) is titled *On the Literal Meaning of Genesis.* The "literal meaning" of the English title refers not to what we would today call "the literal meaning of the text" but to what I have called 'the literal reality behind the non-literal mode of presentation.' To read an inspired text *ad litteram,* for Augustine, is to read it with an eye toward discovering what its human author intended to convey; one could also read an inspired text *allegorically,* with an eye toward discovering types or foreshadowings of persons or events of later sacred history (which, if they are objectively present in the inspired text, were presumably unknown to its human author). In the discussion of Augustine in the text of this essay, I use the word 'literal' in its customary present-day sense. In this discussion, I have drawn heavily on Ernan McMullin's introduction to the collection *Evolution and Creation* (South Bend: University of Notre Dame Press, 1985). In this account of Augustine's views, I have glossed over several important matters—such as the relation of the timeless reality of God to the unfolding temporal processes of the created world—that are irrelevant to our purposes.

development of the world, these miracles were not local acts of creation **ex nihilo;** they rather consisted in the miraculous activation of potentialities that had existed from the beginning.) This is not to say that Augustine believed in anything like what *we* call "evolution." He did not believe that elephants were remotely descended from fish. The idea of the mutability of species would have been quite foreign to his **Platonism.** Rather, elephants arose from one seed-principle and mackerel from another. The "days" of Genesis, Augustine says, represent *aspects* of the development of the world; perhaps—he is rather tentative about this—what is represented is six successive stages of the angelic understanding of creation. Augustine's science may strike us as quaint, but it is evident that his account of the origin and development of the universe is no more consistent with Genesiac literalism than is an article covering the same ground in last month's *Scientific American.* Nor is Augustine an isolated example of a non-literalist in the ancient world: the Alexandrian theologians, Gregory of Nyssa, and St. Jerome (who produced the Latin translation of the Bible that was the Church's standard for fourteen hundred years) were non-literalists. . . . Non-literalism was, of course, *rejected* by many important authorities in the Western Church. St. Thomas Aquinas, for example, was a literalist who explicitly stated that the Creation took place over a period of six successive twenty-four-hour days. What is important to note about Aquinas, however, is that, in his discussion of Augustine's "opinion that all the days that are called seven are one day represented in a sevenfold aspect," Augustine is, in the words of Jaroslav Pelikan "criticized but not hereticized." Pelikan goes on to say, "It took the Reformation to change that."[2]

I agree, although perhaps my "agreeing" on a point of church history with one of our greatest church historians has its comic aspect. Literalism before the Reformation was no doubt the majority opinion. The theory that the Bible is literally and in every sentence and in every respect inerrant is, after all, the simplest and most natural theory of the "reliability" of the Bible that must in some sense be a consequence of the doctrinal statement that the Bible is the revealed word of God—just as **geocentrism** is the simplest and most natural theory of the causes of observed celestial motions. But *militant* literalism, the literalism that makes the denial of plenary verbal inerrancy a heresy to be destroyed before any other is a child of the Reformation. . . .

To establish the credentials of non-literalism, however, is not to establish its possibility. How can the Bible be the revealed word of God if, to take one example among many, it says that birds and fish came into existence on the same day, when the plain truth is that there were fish for hundreds of millions of years before there were birds? Well, I don't *know* the answer to this question, but I will do what St. Augustine did: I will present an answer that I find plausible and which I am willing to recommend. To do this, I must discuss both the content of Genesis and its formation. These two matters are intimately related, but I shall begin by treating them separately.

First, as to content. Suppose that someone who had never heard of the Bible and had never so much as thought about the beginning of the world were one day to read the book of Genesis and were to take everything it contained in a pretty literal sense and were to believe every word of it. This person would thereby come to believe many true things and many false things. Among the false things there would be two that we have already mentioned: the proposition that the alternation of day and night existed before the sun, and the proposition that Aves and Pisces are **coevals.** We could make quite a list of such false propositions. Here are some of the true ones. That the world is finite in space and time—at least time past. That it has not always been as it is now but has changed from a primal chaos into its present form. That it owes its existence and its features to an immeasurably powerful being who made it to serve His purposes. That it was originally not evil and not neutral as between good and evil and not a mixture of good and evil but simply good. That human beings are part of this world and are formed from its elements—that they were not separately created and

[2]Jaroslav Pelikan, "Darwin's Legacy: Emanation, Evolution, and Development," in *Darwin's Legacy: Nobel Conference XVIII,* ed. Charles L. Hamrum (San Francisco, Harper & Row, 1983), p. 81. . . .

then placed in it like figurines in a china cabinet. That the stars and the moon are inanimate objects and are without any religious significance—that, at least in relation to human beings, their main purpose is to mark the hours and the seasons. That it is not only kings but all men and women who are images of the divine. That human beings have been granted a special sort of authority over the rest of nature. That these divine images, the stewards of all nature, have, almost from their creation, disobeyed God, and have thereby marred the primal goodness of the world and have separated themselves from God and now wander as exiles in a realm of sin and death.

So our imaginary credulous reader of Genesis comes to believe some true things and some false things. The first (but not the last) point to note about the credulous reader's situation is that the true things are much more important than the false things. In fact, the true things are among the most important there are, and the false things are not very important at all. Someone who believes that the world began six thousand years ago is wrong; so is someone who believes that Columbus was the first European to reach North America. For the life of me, however, I can't see that it is much more important to get the age of the earth right than it is to get the identity of the first European voyager to reach North America right. I can expect a protest at this point from both the literalists and the saganists. Each will tell me that the question of the age of the earth is of very great importance. The literalist will say that it is important because a mistake about the age of the earth could lead one to reject the Word of God, and the saganist will say that it is important because a mistake about the age of the earth could lead one to reject science and reason. But these protests rest on a misunderstanding. I am talking about the *intrinsic* importance of a mistake in this area, not about its *extrinsic* importance. Clearly any false belief whatever, however trivial its subject matter, *could* have disastrous consequences in special circumstances. We could easily imagine circumstances in which a woman's mistaken belief that her husband had stopped to buy a newspaper on his way home from work led her to suspect that he was lying to her about his movements and eventually destroyed their marriage. And, of course, a false belief about the age of the earth could lead to disastrous repudiation of the reliability of something that *is* reliable and whose reliability is important. It could, in fact, lead one to devote a large portion of one's life to defending the indefensible—as, no doubt, false beliefs about Columbus have done. What I am saying is that the matter of the age of the earth is of little importance in itself. This is far from an empty platitude. The last few hundred years have seen thinkers who overestimate the intrinsic value of scientific knowledge as absurdly as Matthew Arnold and F. R. Leavis overestimated the intrinsic value of a well-honed literary sensibility. Here is a quotation from the Nobel Prize-winning physicist Steven Weinberg that illustrates the evaluation I am deprecating:

> The more the universe seems comprehensible, the more it also seems pointless.
>
> But if there is no solace in the fruits of our research, there is at least some consolation in the research itself. Men and women are not content to comfort themselves with tales of gods and giants, or to confine their thoughts to the daily affairs of life; they also build telescopes and satellites and accelerators, and sit at their desks for endless hours working out the meaning of the data they gather. The effort to understand the universe is one of the very few things that lifts human life a little above the level of farce, and gives it some of the grace of tragedy.[3]

Against this, I would set the following statements of the "great champion of the obvious," Dr. Johnson:

> [W]e are perpetually moralists, but we are geometricians only by chance. . . . our speculations upon matter are voluntary and at leisure.
>
> [Scientific knowledge] is of such rare emergence that one man may know another half his life without being able to estimate his skill in hydrostatics or astronomy; but his moral and prudential character immediately appears.

[3]Steven Weinberg, *The First Three Minutes: A Modern View of the Origin of the Universe* (London: Andre Deutsch, 1977), p. 155.

> [T]he innovators whom I oppose are turning off attention from life to nature. They seem to think that we are placed here to watch the growth of plants, or the motions of the stars.[4]

Well, I have set before you a choice of values. If you think that the evaluation of scientific knowledge that is implicit in my quotation from Weinberg is the right one and that Johnson's belongs to the rubbish of history and good riddance to it, you will not believe a word of anything I am going to say. But at least don't mistake my position: I am not saying that science is unimportant; I am only denying scientific knowledge the central place in the proper scheme of human values that Weinberg gives it. I also deny this central place to a knowledge and appreciation of history or music or literature, each of which is neither more nor less important than scientific knowledge.

My first step in reconciling the thesis that Genesis is the revealed Word of God with the findings of science is, therefore, to contend that what Genesis is right about is of great intrinsic importance and that what it is wrong about is of little intrinsic importance. This contention, however, raises the question why Genesis, if it is the Word of God, is wrong about *anything*. I said that I should discuss questions both of content and of formation. I have said something about content. To discuss the question I have now raised I introduce some points having to do with the formation of the Genesis narrative—the genesis of Genesis, as it were.

What is the purpose of the first chapters of Genesis? What is their purpose in relation to the Hebrew Bible as a whole? The Hebrew Bible is mainly the narrative of God's covenant relationship with His people Israel. The opening chapters of Genesis are intended to set the stage for the story of that covenant. They are intended to describe and explain the relations between God and humanity as they stood when God made a covenant with Abraham. Thus, Genesis begins with an account of the creation of the world and of human beings, an account that displays God as the maker and sovereign of the world and the ordainer of the place of humanity in the world, and which does that in a way that militates against various disastrous **theological** misconceptions current among Israel's neighbors and conquerors—as that divinity is divided among many beings whose wills are often in conflict; or that the lights in the sky are objects of worship; or that the image of divinity is present in a few human beings—kings—but not in ordinary people. But then why doesn't Genesis get it right? I say that Genesis does get it right—in essence. W. J. Bryan may have been a fool in many respects,[5] but he had a more accurate picture of the cosmos than Carl Sagan (who, if we may trust the Fourteenth Psalm, is also a fool). Bryan believed that the world had been created by God, and that by itself is enough to outweigh all the matters of detail in which Sagan is right and Bryan wrong. But why doesn't Genesis get it right not only in essence but in detail? Why doesn't Genesis get it wholly right? After all, we expect a reliable source to get even relatively unimportant details right, insofar as it is able, and God knows all the details. The beginning, but not the end, of the answer to this question is that if Genesis did get it right in every detail, most people couldn't understand it. Never mind the fact that only a person with years of rigorous formal training in mathematics can fully understand the current theories about the first three minutes of the existence of the cosmos. Consider only the *age* of the cosmos: more than ten thousand million years. You and I can in a sense grasp numbers like 10^{10}: we know how to do arithmetic with them. But how could the age of the universe be conveyed to most people at most times? Suppose the Bible began, "Ten thousand million years ago, God created . . . ." Suppose you are a missionary trying to explain the Genesis narrative to a tribe of Amazonian Indians. How shall you explain these words to them? Shall you leave off teaching them about important things like the sover-

[4]. . . The quotations are from Johnson's essay "Milton," in his *Lives of the English Poets.*

[5]But not nearly so big a fool as the character who bears his name in the almost wholly fictional movie *Inherit the Wind.* The popular account of the Scopes trial is one of the two great legends of the saganist history of Darwinism, the other being the story (as it is usually told) of the confrontation between T. H. Huxley and Bishop Wilberforce in 1860. Of course, each of these legends, like Piltdown Man, was put together from pieces of real things.

eignty of God till you have taught them about unimportant things like the decimal system? (Do not suppose that teaching them the decimal system will be the work of an afternoon, for there is no basis in their culture for using the kinds of numbers it gives access to.) And most cultures have been like our imaginary Amazonian culture in that respect. A scientifically accurate rewriting of Genesis, therefore, would turn it into something all but useless, for the result would be inaccessible to most people at most places and times. Only a few people like you and me—who are simply freaks from the historical and anthropological point of view—could penetrate even its surface. I wonder how many of us believe, at some level, that God—if there is a God—regards scientifically educated people as being somehow the human norm and therefore regards Amazonian Indians or elementary-school dropouts as being less worthy of his attention than we; I wonder whether many of us aren't disposed to think that if the Bible were divinely inspired it would be written with the preoccupations of the scientifically educated in mind? I will not bother to quote the very clear dominical and Pauline repudiations of the values that underlie this judgment. Everyone is of equal value to God and the Bible is addressed to everyone. A Bible that was made easy for kings to understand at the cost of making it hard for peasants to understand would be in violation of this principle—if only because there are a lot more peasants than kings. And, of course, there are a lot more people who could not understand a scientifically accurate rewriting of Genesis than there are people who could.

To this I can expect the skeptic to reply along the following lines: "That's beside the point. Of course the universe is so complex—no doubt any *possible* universe would *have* to be so complex—that only a few highly trained people in a few very special cultures could understand a *detailed* account of its origin and development. But the writer of Genesis could have described the early history of the cosmos very *abstractly*. He could have included all of the theses that you regard as 'important truths,' and, nevertheless, everything he said about the development of the physical universe could have been true as far as it went. When God inspired the author of Genesis, why didn't He inspire him to write it that way?"

The answer to this question is threefold. One of the three parts I am not going to explore. I will simply mention it and leave it. I do this because I think it is very important, but that it could not be adequately discussed within the scope of this essay. It is this: not all the truths that are revealed in Genesis can be said; some (to employ a distinction of the early Wittgenstein) can only be shown. These truths, I believe, truths relating to sin and knowledge, can be shown only by telling a very concrete story. I believe that as a result of knowing the story of the fruit of the knowledge of good and evil, I know something important that I cannot articulate; something that could not have been conveyed in discursive prose and which perhaps did not have to be conveyed by a story about trees and a serpent but which certainly had to be conveyed parabolically—that is, by means of *some* story about the actions of concrete, picturable beings.

I pass with relief to the two more straightforward points I want to make. First, that an abstract version of Genesis would have little pedagogical value for most people at most times. Even if it contained all the correct lessons, the lessons would not be learned—or would be learned only by rote, as "lessons" in the schoolroom sense. Secondly, the idea of God's inspiring Moses (or whomever) to write an "abstract" Genesis purged of all harmless error seems either to presuppose a primitive "dictation" model of inspiration or else to imagine God as purging His revelation of harmless error at a very high cost to the recipients of that revelation. I will illustrate these points with a parable.

Imagine that a doctor visits our Amazonian Indians with the intention of teaching them some useful medicine—say, some elementary principles of first aid and hygiene and antisepsis, and such pharmacological lore and simple surgical procedures as they can be trusted with in the absence of continuing supervision. What would be the best way to teach such things? One might give one's pupils a précis of a medical encyclopedia, deleting whatever material was not applicable to their condition. But this précis, because it was presented in a form that was without model or precedent in their culture, might well be forgotten or ignored or even be sung as a chant to accompany the application of traditional tribal medical procedures. Another, and perhaps more effective technique, would be to revise and purify and extend the existing medical lore of one's pupils, making use of literary and mnemonic devices indigenous to their culture. In applying this technique, one might simply not bother to correct parts of the existing medical lore that were harmlessly wrong. If one's pupils believed that childbirth fever was caused by demons, why should one not teach them that the demons must make their way into the bodies of new mothers via the hands of midwives, and that this path could be blocked by a scrupulous ritual washing before the delivery? If this teaching would lead to the same behavior on the part of midwives as a much longer lesson that involved an introduction to the germ theory of disease, and if the extra time required by the longer lesson were time that could be devoted to a lesson about making effective splints—well, one would have to ascribe a very high value indeed to truth in the abstract to recommend the longer lesson. . . .

The human author or authors of Genesis, whatever their historical period may have been, would have had no natural disposition to tell a story like our imaginary abstract Genesis, a story utterly at variance with every model provided by their own culture and every other culture I know of. People are not naturally inclined to divest a story they want to tell of the concrete details that give that story its character, and the ancient Hebrews had very concrete minds indeed—as did all their contemporaries. No doubt the continued influence of the Holy Spirit could *eventually* have produced an abstract Genesis. I have no idea how long this would have taken, but certainly longer than it took to produce the concrete, suggestive, effective Genesis that we have. And what would have been the value of this costly thing? Only this: that a few saganists in our own time would have had to find some other excuse to reject the Word of God than its disagreement with the fossil record. I do not see why God, who values any six holders of endowed chairs neither more nor less than He values any six agricultural laborers in ancient Palestine, should have thought the price worth paying.

This completes my outline of the position that I oppose both to Genesiac literalism and to saganism. . . .

STUDY QUESTIONS

1. Describe briefly the conflicting views of the saganists and biblical literalists as to the origins of the universe.
2. In van Inwagen's opinion, what true assertions are found in the Genesis narrative?
3. According to van Inwagen, what assertions in the Genesis narrative are false if taken literally?
4. How does van Inwagen account for the absence of a true "abstract Genesis"?
5. What role do van Inwagen's references to church history play in his argument?
6. *Do you agree with van Inwagen's value judgments about the relative importance of the various truths he discusses? Why or why not? Do you agree with all the statements that he regards as important truths? Why or why not?
7. *Van Inwagen writes that an abstract Genesis containing accurate science would be too difficult for many readers of the Bible. It might be suggested, however, that, by the same token, the Bible gives us **philosophical** ideas that are false. After all, what if, like scientific truth, philosophical truth is too difficult for us to grasp? Why, then, should we take the Bible's *philosophy* as literal truth?

READING 6.5

Theism and the Mind-Body Problem

Robert Audi

Traditional theism maintains that what we call a person is an entity involving two fundamentally different types of substances: mind and body. This view is known as **dualism,** *or more exactly* **substance dualism.** *By contrast, many scientists endorse* *versions of* **materialism.** *Broadly speaking, materialists maintain that only physical entities and properties exist. According to materialists, mental entities and properties are in truth physical. Besides threatening dualism, such a conception of mind threatens the theistic understanding of God as a spiritual (nonmaterial) being.*

In this essay, Robert Audi (University of Nebraska, Lincoln) addresses this serious challenge to theism, arguing that theism can be harmonized with a scientific conception of mind. Audi criticizes several versions of materialism and then suggests that there is no decisive reason to rule out a brand of substance dualism. In Audi's version of substance dualism, mental states depend in many respects on physical states, even though the former can cause the latter and are dependent on them. God could have a body, he suggests; perhaps the world can be God's body, for example.

Audi's essay contains brief characterizations of the major views in philosophy concerning the nature of mind.

The relation between religion and science has long been a major concern of the philosophy of religion, particularly since Darwin. There are many elements in the relation, but the most important may be those connected with the concept of mind. In an unqualified form, the central question here is whether the truth of theism can be squared with a scientific conception of mind, or, to change at least the emphasis of the question, whether there is a scientifically acceptable conception of mind that squares with a plausible theistic concept of a person—human or divine. . . .

SOME SCIENTIFIC PERSPECTIVES ON THE NATURE OF MIND

. . . [N]either psychologists nor biological scientists interested in mind need countenance any *substance* that can be called "the mind." Rather, talk of the mind—for example of someone's having a good mind—may be considered a kind of discourse about people and their mental properties, such as thinking. To have a good mind, on this view, is not to possess something like a mental organ that functions well; it is (roughly) to have a nature in virtue of which, as a person, one functions well in intellectual activities.

To be sure, many educated people tend to think of the mind as the brain. This is not, however, a considered view: it comes of oversimplifying the multitude of connections between our brains and our mental properties, and (outside philosophy) it is not often put to the basic test it must pass as a serious identity claim: every property of the brain must be a property of the mind and vice versa. Do we want to assign the mind a weight in grams? Could it be dyed bright red, as the brain could? Can we, as in the case of the brain, remove parts of the mind, hold them in our hands, and discard them, without affecting its mental function? And when the mind is wholly occupied with the relation between religion and science, must the brain be so occupied also? Given everything we know about what the brain must do to keep us alive, the answers are surely negative. It must, for instance, control heartbeat and respiration in order to sustain thought; but exercising that control, in the automatic way in question, is not thinking, nor can any clearly mental process be plausibly identified with the brain's exercising the relevant kind of control over heartbeat and respiration or over other involuntary bodily processes.

There may be a few who will dig in their heels and defend the view that the mind is the brain. Rather than continue to discuss this, we would do better to note that what, in a scientifically minded person, motivates the brain-mind identity view is the desire to construe a person as a physical system. *That* desire, however, can be accommodated by simply taking every mental property to be some kind of brain property—a view commonly called the ***identity theory.*** The identity theory goes well with a **materialistic** conception of the universe, and that, in turn, seems to go well with a scientific worldview.

Physics, for instance, is commonly taken to understand phenomena in terms of matter and motion, especially contacts between concrete material entities. This conception is, however, naive: even Newtonian physics countenanced action at a distance, and the relevant gravitational forces do not require a stream of material particles traversing the entire distance between the mutually attracting bodies.

As scientists report progressively smaller and less "corpuscular" elementary particles, we may wonder how material the basic entities postulated by current physics *are.* We might also ask what scientists, as such, must say about the status of numbers, which are indispensable for their work. The number 3 is not a numeral or even a set of numerals (destroying them all would not destroy it, or undermine the truths in which it figures). Granted, a scientific **materialist** may care only about concrete entities; but even if all of these can be conceived as material, numbers and properties (such as the property of being square) are at best not easily interpreted as such. The point is that while materialist **metaphysicians** want to conceive everything real as material, this aim is not essential to science, which, arguably, presupposes rather than seeking to explain, the nature and truth of pure mathematics, and appears quite uncommitted to restricting its posited entities to those properly conceived as material.

There are two broad conceptions of science that are not commonly distinguished and that we must not allow to be conflated. One, which perhaps deserves to be called the loose and popular conception, takes science to be concerned with accounting for everything that is real. This in turn is often identified with everything "in the world" or "in the universe." The second, more guarded view, takes science to be concerned with accounting for everything that is **empirical,** in the sense of being accessible, directly or through the use of instruments, to normal human sensory experience. The paradigms of what is empirical are physical, but psychological phenomena are often included as well. On the first, but not the second, conception, science must apparently account for abstract entities such as numbers. On the second conception, science must give an account of psychological phenomena, but is not committed to identifying them with physical phenomena, particularly if explaining their interrelations and their role in producing overt behavior does not require that identification.

A natural step to take here is to distinguish the material from the physical and to maintain simply that mental properties are physical. Now, however, the contrast between the mental and the canonical basic elements of science is weakened. Suppose, for example, that physical properties are understood as those having causal and explanatory power with respect to observable events. "Mentalists"—those who believe that mental properties like thinking and sensing are real—will respond that, clearly, mental properties have this kind of power.

But, one might ask, how can a mental phenomenon like a decision, cause a physical phenomenon like my telephoning a friend? With action at a distance, there are two physical phenomena in a causal relation; here, the relation is cross-categorial, at least in its linking of physical properties that are not material to those that, like the moving of a hand, are material. There may be no obviously cogent answer to this question, but it should help to recall that physics itself seems to be appealing to less and less familiar kinds of entities in explaining observable events. It should also be said that if there is something mysterious here, a mystery is not an impossibility. Indeed, there is, as David Hume saw, something mysterious about causation of any kind once we look for more than a mere regularity linking causes to their effects.

Suppose, however, that it should be true that a scientifically minded thinker must opt for the identity theory. Is there good reason to think the theory true? It has been ably and plausibly attacked in the literature and is presently not held by most scientifically minded philosophers who count themselves physicalists. There are many other conceptions of the mental available to such philosophers. Two should be noted here: *philosophical* ***behaviorism,*** roughly the view that mental properties are behavioral (and hence physical) properties; and ***eliminative materialism,*** roughly the view that there are no mental properties, and, hence, mental terms represent false postulations (it is usually coupled with the hypothesis that neuropsychology will ultimately enable us to do without those terms in explaining behavior). Philosophical behaviorism is widely agreed to have been refuted, in part because it seems to undermine the distinction between convincingly pretending to be in a mental state, such as pain, and actually being in that state. Eliminative materialism, though currently defended by a small number of theorists, does not provide a positive conception of the mental that can be readily used in pursuing the problem central here. Even if it should be successful in showing that certain apparently mental concepts are empty, its proponents have not provided a plausible general account of the concept of the mental and shown that this broad concept is empty.

A view that may promise to avoid the pitfalls of both behaviorism on one side and the identity theory on the other is ***functionalism,*** roughly the thesis that mental properties are to be understood in terms of certain input-output relations; for example, to be in pain is to be in a state of the kind caused by a burn and causing outcries. Mental properties are, as it were, *role defined* rather than defined in terms of any quality they have or type of material constituting them. On this view, a person has only physical and functional properties, and the latter are defined in terms of relations among the former. This may be taken to leave open precisely how functional properties are to be classified in the physical-nonphysical dimension, but it undermines the view that any of them are either irreducibly mental or commit us to positing mental substances as their possessors.

Functionalism is defensible, but is widely (though not universally) agreed to leave us at least unsatisfied with respect to understanding qualities of experience, such as the painfulness of pain and the redness of an afterimage. Whereas the identity theory could claim that the experience of (say) being in pain is identical with a brain state, functionalism must maintain that there is nothing it "is like" to be in pain, no intrinsic character of the experience: talk of the experience is talk of mediation between inputs and outputs, and that mediation has no intrinsic character. Thus, if my sensory impressions of red and green were inverted with respect to those of normal people, functionalism would apparently have to say that I am still having the same experience (am in the same perceptual mental state) when I approach a red light because, being taught in the same way as everyone else, I respond to red stimuli as they do regardless of my internally "seeing green."

These and other difficulties with the identity theory and functionalism have led a number of scientifically minded philosophers to maintain a **nonreductive materialism:** mental properties are grounded in (supervene on, in a currently much-discussed terminology) physical ones, but are not identical with them, hence not reducible to them. This view allows us to anchor the mental in the physical and biological world without either the difficulties of identifying mental with physical properties or those of trying to account for qualities of experience.

Granting that nonreductive materialism does not have to countenance mental *substances,* such as **Cartesian** minds, it remains a ***property dualism.*** It will thus be unsatisfactory to those who take physical properties to be the only kind there are, as well as those who do not see how mental phenomena as such can have any explanatory power if they are not really physical. If, for example, my decision to telephone someone merely *depends* on my brain properties and is identical with none of them, how does my decision produce my physical behavior, as opposed to being, say, a mere shadow of the real productive work done by something in my brain that really has the power to move my fingers over the buttons?

It may help to stress that whatever **supervenience** relation obtains in the mental case is, like the physical instance, also presumably a causal or **nomic** relation. Perhaps, then, the mental elements inherit causal power from the base elements, as the magnetism of iron, say, apparently inherits its causal power from the base properties in virtue of which iron is magnetic. Let me develop this idea.

On the assumption that causation is a **transitive relation,** if certain physical events cause certain mental ones, and the latter apparently cause certain further events, both mental and physical, it would be natural to think there is a causal chain. Granted, **epiphenomenalism,** taken to be roughly the view that mental events are effects of physical events but causes of nothing, cannot be ruled out **a priori.** But apart from arguments for it that to my knowledge have not been offered, its plausibility is matched or exceeded by the implausibility of supposing that physical events produce events that themselves have no causal power. Indeed, there are surely no uncontroversial examples of *any* concrete events that clearly have no causal power; and such models of causation as we best understand seem to involve what it is natural to call *transfers* of power or energy from cause to effect: think of pushing, pulling, heating, freezing, coloring, wetting, crushing, and inflating. Not only is something affected in these cases; it also acquires or at least retains causal power (not all of these relations are transitive, of course, but a non-transitive relation can imply a transitive one).

When we add to these points that it is partly by virtue of its content that the mental plays the role it does in explaining action, we can see how the mental might be a crucial link in any causal chain from the physical to action: through the map provided by their content, mental factors such as beliefs give direction to physical forces that, so far as we can tell, would otherwise be blind. Granted that mental factors might have no causal power apart from their nonmental bases, they might both exercise the power they derive from the latter and, in so doing, direct that power. Desire might move our limbs in part because of its roots in our brains; but this does not entail that it has no causal power itself: a lever that can move a stone only when anchored still moves the stone.

This kind of problem is receiving much discussion, and nonreductive materialism is still in development. What has not been generally noticed that is highly relevant to our problem is that if there should be mental substances, their mental properties might still depend on physical ones in much the way posited by nonreductive materialists: nothing prevents my mind from being integrated with my body so as to respond to neural stimuli, say from my color perception, just as reliably as, for an identity theorist, the brain responds to them by going into "color states." If the nonphysical property of having a red sensation or being in pain can depend on a brain property, then in principle it can do this even if it is a property of a Cartesian mind. Descartes famously said (in Meditation VI), "I am not lodged in my body as a pilot in a vessel, but . . . am very closely united to it, and so to speak so intermingled with it that I seem to compose with it one whole." If one thinks there are mental-physical causal interactions, one might well suppose that the mental depends on the physical even if it also has causal powers over (other) physical phenomena. Reflection on this sort of possibility may lead to the hypothesis that in the end one must either live with a deep mystery in nonreductive materialism or choose between a version of the identity theory and a version of substance dualism.

Is a **substance dualism** compatible with a scientific worldview? If such a worldview includes the metaphysical drive for **monism,** and especially for materialism (or at least physicalism) that is so prominent among philosophers of science (and indeed other thinkers in and outside of science), it is not. But if one conceives science as seeking a testable, explanatory account of the phenomena we experience and appealing to causal connections with underlying states or processes as basic, then there is no strict incompatibility. Indeed, one can do psychology, and scientifically connect the brain with our mental life, in all the ways psychologists do, without presupposing either that substance dualism is right or that it is wrong. For neither the kinds of laws one seeks, say those linking mental states to each other or to behavior, nor the empirical criteria for the application of mental terms, need be affected by this metaphysical assumption. Pain properties, for instance, may be linked to other **phenomenal** properties and to behavior whether they supervene on physical ones or are identical to certain of the latter.

In framing an overall conception of the human person, much depends on the status of the principle of intellectual economy **(Occam's razor),** which tells us not to multiply kinds of entity beyond necessity. This is a widely accepted principle, especially among the scientifically minded. But when is it *necessary* to posit a kind of entity? That is simply not obvious. The jury seems to be still out on the question of what philosophy of mind, taken together with all the scientific data, best harmonizes with this principle. This is not to say that a philosophy of mind that does not harmonize well with this principle must be either false or at least not a rational position. The point is that there is apparently no decisive reason to think the harmony cannot be achieved.

THEISM, MIND, AND BODY

We may assume (for our purposes here) that standard Western theism centers on a personal God, a God conceived as having a sufficiently rich set of mental properties to count as a person of a special kind. Usually, God is conceived as a spiritual being; commonly, God is also considered a nonphysical substance. If, however, one wants to say that in the "typical" view, God is a kind of Cartesian mind, this would go too far. Those who speak, religiously and not philosophically, of the divine mind do not conceive it as identical with God but as essential to God. It is not common, however, for believers—apart from special cases like the incarnation of Jesus—to speak of God as embodied, and here we may leave the incarnation aside in order to avoid presupposing any specific **theology.**

Still, any theist convinced that a person must have a body can make a case for God's having a body—for instance, the physical world as a whole. At least three points are important if this view is to be taken seriously: God can move any part of the physical world at will, as we can move our limbs at will (roughly, without the mediation of any other action, such as a prior movement of special muscles that in turn control our limb muscles); God has noninferential knowledge (roughly, knowledge not based on premises) of the position of every part of the physical world, as we (often) have such knowledge of the position of certain of our limbs; and insofar as God has experiences (which might be taken to be a matter wholly up to God), the entire physical world might be experienced in the divine mind in something like a perceptual way, producing the appropriate sensations with as rich phenomenal qualities as God wishes them to have. An **omnipotent** God can bring it about that divine knowledge of the physical world be through, or accompanied by, sensory states or more purely **cognitive,** and in either case it might be noninferential.

To be sure, it is not clear how the states of the divine mind would have to *depend* on anything physical, as our perceptual states often do; on one view, they would immediately depend on the physical, as where a divine perception is produced by my moving my head, but *ultimately* depend on God, as (at least the sustaining) creator of everything physical. The view in question—that the physical world is God's body—also implies that we human beings are part of God. This consequence brings its problems, but most of them, such as the harmony between divine sovereignty and human freedom, are already with us.

Still another possibility is that the notion of a body need not be tied to that of physical matter. As some philosophers imagine **resurrection,** it takes place not by disembodiment of the mind or soul and the person's survival therein, but through God's providing a resurrection body in place of the physical one (note that in 1 Corinthians 15:43–44, Paul speaks of a "spiritual body" as what is "raised"). Matter as we know it is not required, for instance, for having a perceptual point of view, for mobility of that point of view in space, or even for perceptibility construed as a causal potentiality to affect other persons (those who perceive one); and it would also seem that functional divisions of "the mind" into, say, intellect, imagination, and will does not require materiality. Theism as such, however, does not immediately entail the possibility of personal resurrection; it entails this only on the assumption that such resurrection is logically possible. If one's philosophy of mind forced one to conclude that it is not, unless some suitable physical embodiment occurred, then one could harbor a hope of resurrection only insofar as one took God to supply an appropriate body. That, however, is apparently logically possible, as are various kinds of embodiment on the part even of God.

So far, our discussion has presupposed a kind of **realism:** that there are things, such as physical objects, whose existence is mind-independent and material. For **idealists,** such as [George] Berkeley, this view is a mistake; and some current **antirealisms** also reject such views. One intelligible form of antirealism would be, like Berkeley's, theistic: the primary reality would then be not only mental but also constituted by the divine mind. The divine mind would sustain the physical (as opposed to material) world that other minds perceive. **Idealism** need not, however, be theistic, and it is arguable that each person's experience can be as vivid and stable on an idealist view as on the realism usually thought to be a commitment of common sense.

An idealist view, with or without the idea that the world is God's "body," can make sense of both the relation of God to human persons and the commonsense world known through perception and scientific investigation. The central problem here is to make good sense of the regularity and familiar features of experience, and this can in principle be done without taking perceptual experience to reflect the causal impact of mind-independent objects. If the picture is as coherent as it seems, the task is arguably quite within the scope of omnipotence.

COMPATIBILITY, HARMONY, AND MUTUAL SUPPORT

Several points seem clear from our discussion above: that standard Western theism, taken apart from specific **theological** commitments that cannot be addressed here, provides considerable latitude in the conception of God, that there is no universally acceptable notion of science that rules out the existence of God, and that most of the leading views in the philosophy of mind are either not materialist at all or at least not reductively so. Even reductive materialism is not strictly incompatible with theism: God could have created us as material systems, and God could also have a body some of whose properties would be the physical identicals of divine mental properties. Even **omniscience, omnipotence,** and **omnibenevolence** may not be simply assumed to be by their nature properties of a nonphysical being. Granted, if there is an independent argument that they can belong only to minds and that minds are necessarily mental substances, then they could not belong to a nonphysical being; but apart from such a general (and highly contestable) argument, theism has the option in principle of taking God to have a body.

I am speaking, of course, about sheer logical compatibility between theism and various conceptions of mind and thereby going well beyond theological plausibility in any tradition of standard Western theism. As important as compatibility by itself is, one naturally wants to ask whether there can be something more: a harmony between theism and the scientific conception of mind.

Here we might begin with a question so far left in the background: Does a scientific conception of *anything,* mental or physical, require the assumption that all explanations of its existence and career must be natural? It is by no means clear that this is so, in part because it is not clear what counts as a natural explanation. It is certainly not clear that if a mental property, such as my making a decision, is not identical with a physical one, then that property's explaining something, such as my telephoning a friend, is not natural, or indeed not a case of a naturalistic explanation. The natural need not be identified with the physical; it should be a substantive question, not to be resolved by stipulation, what counts as natural—or at least this is a plausible assumption if we take natural properties and events to be the kind fundamental in the natural world: the world of hills, brooks, standing lakes and groves, and of people and animals.

Suppose, then, that a divine decision explains a physical event. It might be said that this *must* be a non-natural explanation because it is supernatural. That may seem true if God has no body, but even on that assumption there is a danger of going too fast. If it is even possible that we human beings are essentially mental substances, then the way events in our minds cause physical events could be a model for one way in which divine decisions do: cross-categorially. This could be harmonized with the view that we are created in God's image: for us, too, there are causal interactions between the mental and the physical, and our actions, too, represent just such a thrust from the mental to the physical.

There remains the disanalogy concerning the different kind of dependence of our mental states on the physical and of God's mental states on the physical (or anything else outside God). But it is not clear that a scientific approach to the world—as opposed to certain **metaphysical** interpretations of such an approach—cannot accommodate that disanalogy. Causation across different metaphysical categories may be mysterious, but (as noted earlier) causation—taken to be something more than Humean **constant conjunction**—may be somewhat mysterious in any case. If a scientific worldview is possible without it, that would at least not be a typical case of such a view. To many scientifically minded people, moreover, it would seem explanatorily impoverished.

At least four further responses to our problem should be mentioned if we are to indicate the range of main options. The appeal of these different responses will depend on one's intellectual and other priorities, but all of them show that the proverbial stark choice between science and theism is not inevitable for people inclined toward worldviews incorporating both.

First, a person attracted both to theism and to a scientific conception of mind and unable to harmonize them could **agnosticize**: simply hold theism as a perhaps ultimately unknowable hypothesis deserving regular reflection and meriting certain responses in one's daily life. Some people in this intellectual position are capable of living their day-to-day lives in a substantially religious manner. They might act on a kind of presumption of theism without believing (or, of course, disbelieving) that it is true or even that it is better confirmed than its negation.

Second, one could treat one's favorite position in the philosophy of mind similarly, being agnostic about that while taking one's theism to be true. This would certainly permit one's comfortably *doing* science, including psychology; it would simply require suspending judgment about certain philosophical theses regarding the mental.

Third, one could opt for theological ***noncognitivism,*** roughly the view that religious language is expressive rather than assertive: providing a picture of the world and prescriptions for human life, but not describing how reality in fact is. Here the task is to harmonize religious *attitudes* with scientific *beliefs,* rather than to harmonize two sets of beliefs having apparently disparate kinds of content. The former task is less demanding, intellectually at least, than the one we have been exploring.

Fourth, one could try to work out a **naturalistic** conception of God harmonious with one's scientific outlook. Unless this conception proceeds through taking God to be embodied, as it often does not in the theologians in question, it tends to lose contact with the idea of God as a person. That tends to make it an unattractive option for many committed to a version of standard Western theism, but an ingenious **naturalism** can be adapted to preserve certain elements in that tradition and can, in any case, be argued to be a version of theism. God need not be identified with nature, but can be seen as a power felt in human experience and sustaining us in ways similar to those traditionally associated with divine conservation.

There is a bolder approach for those who want to be both theists and scientifically minded: to employ the points made here (and others) in working toward not only a harmony between the two sets of commitments but also mutual support between them. From this perspective, scientific discovery is viewed as a *prima facie* indication of God's structuring of the world; divine sovereignty is seen as an assurance that the search for truth will tend to lead to valuable results; the intimate connection between one's physical and one's mental life, and especially our autonomy in directing our conduct, are conceived as possibly reflecting free agency in a sense that is applicable to divine sovereignty over the world. For people proceeding in this way, scientific results may lead to revisions in theology, as theology may lead to scientific hypotheses or changes in scientific direction. Different people with different theologies and philosophies of science will proceed in diverse ways; but so far as we can see, the compatibility between the two worldviews is clear, and possibilities for harmonious interactions between them are wide.

STUDY QUESTIONS

1. Review the conceptions of mind that Audi identifies in the section titled "Some Scientific Perspectives on the Nature of Mind." Review his criticism of each view.
2. Explain the suggestion that the world is God's body.
3. Explain the suggestion that the notion of a body need not be tied to that of physical matter.
4. Audi sketches various ways in which there can be harmony between theism and a scientific conception of the mind. What are those ways?
5. *Which suggestions of Audi's do you find most plausible? least plausible? Why?

READING 6.6

The Future of the Soul

Richard Swinburne

Richard Swinburne (Oxford University) argues that, even if the soul can exist after death, its functioning depends on a functioning brain. Thus, after death, the soul would cease to function. Evidence from **parapsychology** *does not refute this, he claims; nor can it be shown, as Plato and others tried to show, that by its very nature the soul survives death. At the same time, it cannot be shown that the soul* cannot *survive death. And Swinburne suggests that an* **omnipotent** *God could bring about survival after death by plugging the soul into another body. Perhaps there are other processes, too, that would bring about this result.*

When the body dies and the brain ceases to function, the evidence . . . suggests that the soul will cease to function also. For that evidence suggests that the soul functions only when the brain has rhythms of certain kinds, and at death the brain ceases to function altogether. If the soul does not function before there is a functioning brain, or during deep sleep, when the brain is not functioning at a certain level, surely it will not function after there ceases to be a functioning brain? However, there are **arguments** and evidence of less usual kinds which purport to show that things are different after death from what they are before birth.

Before we face the question of whether the soul can function without the functioning of the brain currently connected with it, we must consider the question of whether, after death, the brain which ceases to function at death can be made to function again and whether thereby the soul can be revived.

CAN THE BRAIN BE REACTIVATED?

A crucial problem is that we do not know how much of the brain that was yours has to be reassembled and within what time interval in order that we may have *your* brain and so your soul function again. . . .

Suppose you die of a brain haemorrhage which today's doctors cannot cure, but your relatives take your corpse and put it straight into a very deep freeze in California. Fifty years later your descendents take it out of the freeze; medical technology has improved and the doctors are able quickly to mend your brain, and your body is then warmed up. The body becomes what is clearly the body of a living person, and one with your apparent memory and character. Is it you? Although we might be mistaken, the satisfaction of the criterion of apparent memory[1] (together with the—at any rate partial—satisfaction of the criterion of brain continuity) would suggest that we ought to say 'Yes.' So long as the same brain is revived, the same functioning soul would be connected with it—whatever the time interval. But what if the brain is cut up into a million pieces and then frozen? Does the same hold? Why should there be any difference? Suppose that the brain is reduced to its component atoms; and then these are reasembled either by chance or because they have been labelled radioactively. Again, if the subsequent person makes your memory claims, surely we ought to say that it is you. But how many of the original atoms do we need in the original locations? That we do not know. So long as the subsequent person had many similar atoms in similar locations in his brain, he would claim to have been you. So, the criterion of apparent memory will be satisfied. Total non-satisfaction of the brain criterion would defeat the claims of apparent memory (in the absence of any general failure of coincidence in results between these criteria). But it remains unclear and indeed insoluble exactly how much of the orig-

[1][See Glossary of Technical Terms under "**memory criterion of personal identity**"—Ed.]

inal brain is needed to provide satisfaction of the brain criterion. . . .

Nevertheless, although neurophysiology cannot tell us which part of his brain is physically necessary for the embodiment of a given man, it does tell us, as I argued earlier [in the book from which this selection is taken], that some of the brain is thus necessary. For the functioning of a given human soul, there has to be a man whose brain contains certain of the matter of his original brain (but which matter we do not know), similarly arranged. A certain amount of the original brain matter has to be reassembled in a similar arrangement and reactivated by being joined to other brain matter and a body if the soul is to function again. And how likely is it that physical processes will bring about such a reassembly? As the time since death increases, and brain cells and then brain molecules are broken up, burnt by fire, or eaten by worms—it becomes very, very unlikely indeed that chance will reassemble them; or even that human agents can do so for they will not be able to re-identify the atoms involved. (One must, however, be careful here about the possibilities for technology in the twenty-second century. Maybe a brain map could be constructed and a process of labelling constituent atoms devised, which would make possible a reassembly after many years. But the possible development of such a technology seems to me very unlikely.) When the original atoms are reduced to packets of energy, then since these perhaps cannot be individuated, reassembly finally becomes not merely physically very, very improbable, but totally impossible physically. (But the word is 'perhaps'; it is a difficult question in the philosophy of physics whether bursts of energy can be individuated.) I conclude that it is very, very unlikely (and with increasing time virtually impossible) that after death souls will again have reassembled the brain basis which we know makes them function.

Is there any good reason to suppose that the soul continues to function without the brain functioning? Arguments to show that the soul continues to function without the brain functioning may be divided into three groups, involving different amounts of theoretical structure, to reach their conclusions. First, we may consider arguments which purport to show that certain men have survived death, in the sense that their souls have functioned without their brains functioning, directly—i.e. without needing first to establish anything about the nature of the soul or any more systematic **metaphysical** structure. Arguments of this kind may be called parapsychological arguments.

ARGUMENTS FROM PARAPSYCHOLOGY

First, there is the alleged evidence of **reincarnation,** that souls function in new bodies with new brains on Earth. There are Indian children who claim to remember having lived a certain past life, and whose memory claims coincide with the events of some real past life about which—allegedly—they could not have learnt by what they were told or had read. Now, it is of course open to serious question whether perhaps those Indian children had read or were told or learnt in some other perfectly normal way the details of those past lives. But even if for a few Indian children there was this coincidence between their memory claims and the events of a certain past person's life, without there being any normal cause of the accuracy of their memory claims that would not be enough evidence to show their identity with those persons. For, . . . given the general coincidence of sameness of memory with continuity of brain, we must take continuity of brain as a criterion of identity; and the nonsatisfaction of that in the case of the few Indian children (who do not have the same brain matter as the cited past persons), must remain substantial evidence against the supposition that they are those persons.

Next, there is the alleged evidence of spiritualism, that souls function without bodies or with new bodies and brains in another world. Mediums purport to have telepathic communication with dead persons. The evidence that they do is allegedly provided by the knowledge of the details of the dead person's life on Earth (not obtainable by the medium by normal means) which the medium's reports of the telepathic communications reveal. In the reincarnation case there is no doubt that there exists in the present a living conscious person; the debatable question concerns his identity with the past person. In the spiritualism case the crucial issue concerns whether there is a conscious person with whom the medium is in communication.

A serious issue in medium cases, like the similar issue in the supposed reincarnation cases, concerns the source of the mysterious knowledge. Perhaps the medium gets her knowledge from some spy who has done research on the dead person's life. But even if investigation showed clearly that the mediums had gained their knowledge of the past lives of dead person[s] by no normal route, the evidence would still, I suggest, not support the hypothesis of telepathic communication with the dead. For also compatible with the evidence would be the hypothesis that the mediums have clairvoyance—they see directly into the past and acquire their knowledge thus. (Adopting the latter hypothesis would involve supposing either that the mediums were deceiving us about the kind of experiences they were having (apparent two-way traffic with a living person), or that they were deceiving themselves, or that their experiences were illusory.) On the choice between the two hypotheses there seem to me to be two important reasons for preferring the clairvoyance hypothesis. First, there are no cross-checks between mediums about the alleged present experiences of the dead in the afterlife. Mediums never give independently verifiable reports on this. Secondly, their reports about the present alleged experiences of the dead are themselves very banal. Yet one would expect because of the total lack of dependence of the dead on their past bodies, that they would live in a very different world, and that this would emerge in their reports on that world.

Finally, there is the interesting and recently published alleged evidence that souls function while their bodies are out of action. There has been careful analysis of the experiences of those who clinically were as good as dead and then recovered. Such experiences are often called 'near-death experiences.'[2] Fifteen per cent of subjects resuscitated after being in such a condition report strange experiences of one of two kinds. Many of them report the following 'transcendental experiences':

> an initial period of distress followed by profound calm and joy; out-of-the-body experiences with the sense of watching resuscitation events from a distance; the sensation of moving rapidly down a tunnel or along a road, accompanied by a loud buzzing or ringing noise or hearing beautiful music; recognising friends and relatives who have died previously; a rapid review of pleasant incidents from throughout the life as a panoramic playback (in perhaps twelve per cent of cases); a sense of approaching a border or frontier and being sent back; and being annoyed or disappointed at having to return from such a pleasant experience—"I tried not to come back," in one patient's words. Some describe frank transcendent experiences and many state that they will never fear death again. Similar stories have been reported from the victims of accidents, falls, drowning, anaphylaxis, and cardiac or respiratory arrest.[3]

Resuscitated patients other than those who had transcendental experiences have undergone 'a wide variety of vivid dreams, hallucinations, nightmares and delusions,' but some of those who had transcendental experiences also experienced these and sharply distinguished between the two kinds of experience. The 'dreams' were regarded as dreams, and were quickly forgotten; the 'supposed glimpses of a future life' were regarded as real and permanently remembered. These glimpses were reported as having occurred at moments when 'breathing had ceased, the heart had stopped beating, and the patients showed no visible signs of life.' The principle of credulity might suggest that we ought to take such apparent memories seriously, especially in view of the considerable coincidences between them, as evidence that what subjects thought they experienced, they really did. But although the subjects

[2]There is a brief and well-balanced survey of this evidence in Paul and Linda Badham, *Immortality or Extinction?*, Macmillan, London, 1982, ch. 5. My summary of the evidence is based on this chapter, but I also make use of a very careful and balanced account of a new programme of investigations by Michael B. Sabom, *Recollections of Death,* Harper and Row, New York, 1982.
[3]*Lancet,* 24 June 1978, quoted in Badham, op. cit.

referred these experiences to moments at which the heart had stopped beating, etc., I do not know of any evidence that at these moments their brains had ceased to function. And if the brain was still functioning then, what the evidence would show is not that the soul may function when the brain does not, but only that its perceptual experiences (i.e. sensations and acquisitions of belief about far away places) are not dependent on normal sensory input.

The same conclusion will follow with respect to the considerable but not overwhelming evidence of those resuscitated patients who had experiences of the other strange kind, 'out-of-body-experiences,' i.e. being able to view their own bodies and events in the operating theatre from a distance, obtaining thereby information which they would not have been able to obtain by normal means (e.g. having visual experiences of events which they would not have got from use of their eyes, such as views of parts of the theatre hidden from their eyes).[4] This again suggests that the subject's acquisition of information is dependent on some factor quite other than normal sensory input to the brain. But again I know of no evidence that these experiences occurred while the brain was not functioning; and so the available evidence does not support the suggestion that the soul can function without the brain functioning.

My conclusion on parapsychology is that it provides no good evidence that the soul continues to function without the brain to which it is currently connected, functioning.

ARGUMENTS FOR NATURAL SURVIVAL

The second class of arguments purporting to show that the soul survives death purport to show from a consideration of what the soul is like when it functions normally that its nature is such that the failure of the brain to function would make no difference to the operation of the soul. Such arguments verge from very general arguments of what the soul must be like to be conscious at all to arguments which appeal to particular empirical data.

Dualist philosophers of the past have usually affirmed the natural **immortality** of the soul—that the soul has such a nature, or the laws of nature are such, that (barring suspension of natural laws) it will continue to function forever. There have been a variety of general arguments for the natural immortality of the soul. Each argument has, in my view, its own fallacies; and the fallacies being fairly evident today, there is no need for any extensive discussion of such arguments. (Expositions of the arguments do, incidentally, usually suffer from confusing the existence of the soul with its functioning; wrongly supposing that when it exists, necessarily it will function.)

To illustrate the fallacies of such arguments, I take just one famous argument, put forward by Plato.[5] Plato argues that the soul being an immaterial thing is unextended, and so does not have parts; but the destruction of a thing consists in separating from each other its parts; whence it follows that souls cannot be destroyed and must continue to exist forever.

Now certainly the normal way by which most material objects cease to exist is that they are broken up into parts. The normal end of a table is to be broken up; likewise for chairs, houses, and pens. But this need not be the way in which a material object ceases to exist. Things cease to exist when they lose their essential properties. The essential properties of a table include being solid. If a table was suddenly liquified, then, even if its constituent molecules remained arranged in the shape of a table by being contained in a table-shaped mould, the table would have ceased to exist. So if even material objects can cease to exist without being broken up into parts, souls surely can cease to exist by some other route than by being broken up into parts.

Nor are the more **empirically** based arguments of traditional dualists any more successful at showing that the soul has a nature such as to survive death.

[4]On this, see Sabom, op. cit., chs. 3, 6, 7, and 8.

[5]*Phaedo,* 78b–80e. See also, for example, George Berkeley: 'We have shown that the soul is indivisible, incorporeal, unextended, and it is consequently incorruptible'—G. Berkeley, *Principles of Human Knowledge,* § 141.

In *The Analogy of Religion,* Joseph Butler pointed out that many men die of disease, when in full possession of powers of thought; and this, he considered, suggested that weakening of powers of body has no effect at all on many powers of soul:

> as it is evident our present powers and capacities of reason, memory, and affection do not depend upon our gross body in the manner in which perception by our organs of sense does; so they do not appear to depend upon it at all in any such manner as to give ground to think that the dissolution of this body will be the destruction of these our present powers of reflection, as it will of our powers of sensation; or to give ground to conclude, even that it will be so much as a suspension of the former.[6]

But, although it is true that weakening of certain bodily faculties does not affect powers of thought, the evidence is manifest that other bodily damage or disease or mere sleep does affect powers of thought. Drugs and alcohol affect clarity of thought, and . . . there is no reason to suppose that any conscious events occur during periods of deep sleep.

The failure of the above arguments is, I suggest, typical of the failure of dualist arguments to show that the soul has an immortal nature or at any rate a nature such that it is able to go on functioning 'under its own steam.' We need a form of dualism which brings out that the soul does not have a *nature* so as to function on its own.[7]

IS THE SOUL NATURALLY EMBODIED?

If it cannot be shown that the soul has a nature so as to survive death without its connected brain functioning, can it be shown that the soul has a nature such that its functioning is dependent on that of the brain with which it is connected? Can we show that there is a natural law which (i) connects consciousness of a soul with the functioning of some material system, and (ii) connects the consciousness of each soul with the functioning of a particular material system; so that of natural necessity a soul can only function if the brain or other complex system with which it is at some time connected continues to function?

The answer . . . is that this cannot be shown. It has not been shown and probably never can be shown that there is any naturally necessary connection of these kinds between soul and body. All we are ever likely to get is correlations—between this kind of brain-event and that kind of mental event. And in the absence of a theory which explains why a material system of this kind is needed to produce a soul, how this sort of physical change will produce this kind of mental state, how just so much of the brain and no more is needed for the continuity of a certain soul (as opposed to the mere functioning of a soul with similar apparent memories), we have no grounds for saying that souls *cannot* survive the death of their brains. We do not know and are not likely to find out what if any natural necessity governs the functioning of souls.

The situation is simply that the fairly direct kinds of evidence considered so far give no grounds for supposing that anyone has survived death, but we know of no reason to suppose that it is not possible for anyone to survive death. The situation is thus similar to that in many areas of enquiry when no one has yet found a so-and-so but no one has shown that so-and-sos do not exist. Maybe there are living persons on other planets, naturally occurring elements with atomic numbers of over 1,000, or magnetic monopoles; but as yet no one has found them. Someone may argue that failure to find something when you have looked for it is evidence that it does not exist. But that is so only if you would recognize the

[6]*The Analogy of Religion,* 1. 1. 3.

[7]Although Aquinas like most other dualists taught that the soul has a natural immortality (see *Summa Theologiae,* Ia. 75. 6), he did claim the powers which its nature gave to a bodiless soul are less than those which it has when embodied, and less even than those which Butler ascribed to it—although understanding and will remain, Aquinas claimed, memory does not. (See *Summa Contra Gentiles,* 2. 81. 11 and 14, translated as *On the Truth of the Catholic Faith,* Book II, *Creation,* by James F. Anderson, Image Books, New York, 1956.)

object when you found it, and if there is a limited region within which the object can exist and you have explored quite a lot of the region. Failure to find oil in the English Channel after you have drilled in most parts of it, or to find the Abominable Snowman if you have explored most of the Himalayas, is indeed evidence that the thing does not exist. But that is hardly the case with souls whose brains have ceased to function. Maybe they are reincarnate in new bodies and brains on Earth but, as they have lost their memories, the evidence of their identity has gone. Or maybe they are where we cannot at present look. They may still function without being embodied . . . and so there [would] be no place which they occupy. Or if they are re-embodied in another body with another brain, they may be anywhere in this universe or some other. Failure to find souls who have survived death shows no more than that if they do exist, they are not in the very few places where we have looked for them or that if they are, the marks of their identity (e.g. apparent memories of past lives) have been removed. In the absence of any further evidence as to whether souls do survive death we can only remain **agnostic** and wait until further evidence does turn up.

EVIDENCE OF SURVIVAL VIA METAPHYSICAL THEORY

There is however a third kind of evidence about whether men survive death which we have not yet considered. This is evidence of a wide ranging character which is most simply explained by a very general **metaphysical** theory of the world, which has as its consequence that human souls survive death as a result of their nature or as a result of the predictable action of some agent who has the power to bring them to life.

One such theory is the Hindu-Buddhist metaphysic of **karma,** a deep law of retribution in nature whereby an agent who lives a life thereafter lives another in which he gets the deserts (reward or punishment) for the previous life. (The establishment of such a system would have the consequence that, despite the lack of evidence for this . . . souls exist before birth; in order to be reborn they must then normally lose much of the character which, I have argued, comes to characterize the soul by the time of death.)

Another such theory is of course Christian theism. The theist has first to argue for the existence of God, a person (in a wide sense) of infinite power, wisdom, goodness, and freedom. He may argue that the existence of God provides the simplest explanation of the existence of the universe, the virtual total regularity of its behaviour in its conformity to natural laws, and various more particular phenomena within the universe. It would then follow that God, being **omnipotent,** would have the power to give to souls life after death (and if there is no natural law which ties the functioning of a soul to the operation of a brain, God would not need to suspend natural laws in order to do this). The Christian theist will need further to show that God intends to bring souls to function after death. He could show this either by showing that it was an obligation on an omnipotent being to do such a thing, and so that, being good, God would do it; or by showing that God had announced his intention of doing this (e.g. by doing something which God alone could do such as suspending a law of nature, in connection with the work of a prophet as a sign that the prophet who had said that God so intended was to be trusted).

It will be evident that any argument via metaphysical theory to the survival of death by human souls will have a lengthy and complicated structure. But of course those who produce such arguments are equally concerned about most of the other things which need to be proved on the way. Few people are interested in the existence of God solely for its value in proving life after death. And if I am right in my claim that we cannot show that the soul has a nature such that it survives 'under its own steam,' and that we cannot show that it has a nature such that it cannot survive without its sustaining brain, the only kind of argument that can be given is an argument which goes beyond nature, i.e. that shows there is something beyond the natural order embodied in laws of nature, and that the operation of that something is to some extent predictable.

If God did give to souls life after death in a new body or without a body, he would not in any way be violating natural laws—for, if I am right, there are no natural laws which dictate what will happen to the soul after death. The soul doesn't have a nature which has consequences for what will happen to it subsequent to the dissolution of its links to the body.

. . . I argued earlier that the human soul at death had a structure, a system of beliefs and desires which might be expected to be there to some degree in the soul if that soul were to be revived. If a man does survive death, he will take his most central desires and beliefs with him, which is the kind of survival for which, I suspect, most men hope. In hoping to survive death, a man hopes not only that subsequent to his death, he will have experiences and perform actions. He hopes also to take with him a certain attitude to the world. That attitude certainly does not always include all aspects of a man's present character. Much, no doubt, many a man would be happy to dispense with. But it does include some of his character, and that part just because it is the part which he desires should continue, is the most central part.

Note that if there does occur a general resurrection of souls with new bodies in some other world, yet with apparent memories of their past lives (or a general reincarnation on Earth with such memories), they would have grounds for reidentifying each other correctly. For then the general failure of the results of the criterion of bodily continuity to coincide with those of apparent memory would . . . justifiably lead us to abandon the former criterion and rely entirely on the latter. Not merely is a general **resurrection** logically possible but it would be known by the subjects to have occurred.

CONCLUSION

The view of the evolved human soul which I have been advocating may be elucidated by the following analogy. The soul is like a light bulb and the brain is like an electric light socket. If you plug the bulb into the socket and turn the current on, the light will shine. If the socket is damaged or the current turned off, the light will not shine. So, too, the soul will function (have a mental life) if it is plugged into a functioning brain. Destroy the brain or cut off the nutriment supplied by the blood, and the soul will cease to function, remaining inert. But it can be revived and made to function again by repairing or reassembling the brain—just as the light can be made to shine again by repairing the socket or turning on the current. But now, my analogy breaks down slightly (as all analogies do—else they would not be analogies). Humans can repair light sockets. But there is a practical limit to the ability of humans to repair brains; the bits get lost. Humans can move light bulbs and put them into entirely different sockets. But no human knows how to move a soul from one body and plug it into another; nor does any known natural force do this. Yet the task is one involving no contradiction and an omnipotent God could achieve it; or maybe there are other processes which will do so. And just as light bulbs do not have to be plugged into sockets in order to shine (loose wires can be attached to them), maybe there are other ways of getting souls to function than by plugging them into brains. But investigation into the nature of the soul does not reveal those ways. And humans cannot discover what else is needed to get souls to function again, unless they can discover the ultimate force behind nature itself.

STUDY QUESTIONS

1. Why does Swinburne consider it "very, very unlikely (and with increasing time virtually impossible) that after death souls will again have reassembled the brain basis which we know makes them function"?
2. What kinds of evidence do some thinkers bring from parapsychology to show that souls function in new bodies with new brains? Why does Swinburne deny that the evidence they cite supports the suggestion that the soul can exist without a functioning brain?
3. Why does Swinburne reject the argument that the soul, by its nature, survives death?
4. How can religious beliefs bear on the suggestion that souls can be reactivated after death?
5. *What is your opinion about whether the soul, if it exists, can survive the death of the brain?
6. *Do you think it is plausible to believe that souls exist? Why or why not?

READING 6.7

The Possibility of Resurrection

Peter van Inwagen

The doctrine of the **resurrection** *of the dead is problematic. How could a body that has been "resurrected" and now appears on the scene be identical with a body that long ago decomposed? Peter van Inwagen (Notre Dame) rejects the "Aristotelian story" often used to solve this problem. On that view, God collects the atoms that used to constitute that person and then reassembles them in their original arrangement. Van Inwagen offers several arguments against the "Aristotelian position" and suggests instead that resurrection can be accomplished only if, contrary to appearances, God preserves the person's body. In a postcript, van Inwagen admits that the story he suggests as to* how *God preserves the body is not the only way God could do so, and probably is not true. He nevertheless inclines to the view that resurrection would occur by God* somehow *preserving a remnant of each person.*

It has been said that the Christian doctrine of the **Resurrection** of the Dead faces the following philosophical difficulty: There is no criterion that anyone could use to determine whether a given post-Resurrection man was Caesar or Socrates or anyone else who had long ago lived and died and returned to the dust. But the real philosophical problem facing the doctrine of the Resurrection does not seem to me to be that there is no criterion that the men of the new age could apply to determine whether someone then alive was the same man as some man who had died before the Last Day; the problem seems to me to be that there *is* such a criterion and (given certain facts about the present age) it would, of necessity, yield the result that many men who have died in our own lifetime and earlier will not be found among those who live *after* the Last Day.

Let us consider an analogy. Suppose a certain monastery claims to have in its possession a manuscript written in Saint Augustine's own hand. And suppose the monks of this monastery further claim that this manuscript was burned by Arians in the year 457. It would immediately occur to me to ask how *this* manuscript, the one I can touch, could be the very manuscript that was burned in 457. Suppose their answer to this question is that God miraculously recreated Augustine's manuscript in 458. I should respond to this answer as follows: The deed it describes seems quite impossible, even as an accomplishment of **omnipotence.** God certainly might have created a perfect duplicate of the original manuscript, but it would not be *that one;* its earliest moment of existence would have been after Augustine's death; it would never have known the impress of his hand; it would not have been a part of the furniture of the world when he was alive; and so on.

Now suppose our monks were to reply by simply asserting that the manuscript now in their possession *did* know the impress of Augustine's hand; that it *was* a part of the furniture of the world when the saint was alive; that when God re-created or restored it, he (as an indispensable component of accomplishing this task) saw to it that the object he produced had all these properties.

I confess I should not know what to make of this. I should have to tell the monks that I did not see how what they believed could *possibly* be true. They might of course reply that their belief is a mystery, that God had *some* way of restoring the lost manuscript but that the procedure surpasses human understanding. Now I am sometimes willing to accept such answers; for example, in the case of the doctrine of the Trinity. But there are cases in which I would never accept such an answer. For example, if there were a religion that claimed that God had created two adjacent mountains without thereby bringing into existence an intermediate valley, I should regard any attempt to defend this doctrine as a "mystery" as so much whistle-talk. After all, I can hardly expect to be able to understand the Divine

Nature, but I do understand mountains and valleys. And I understand manuscripts, too. I understand them sufficiently well to be quite confident that the monks' story is impossible. Still, I wish to be reasonable. I admit that one can be mistaken about conceptual truth and falsehood. I know from experience that a proposition that seems to force itself irresistibly upon the mind as a conceptual truth can turn out to be false. (If I had been alive in 1890, I should doubtless have regarded the Galilean law of the addition of velocities and the unrestricted comprehension principle in set theory as obvious conceptual truths.) Being reasonable, therefore, I am willing to listen to any ***argument*** the monks might have for the conclusion that what they believe is possible. Most arguments for the conclusion that a certain proposition is possibly true take the form of a story that (the arguer hopes) the person to whom the argument is addressed will accept as possible and which (the arguer attempts to show) entails the proposition whose **modal** status is in question.

Can such a story be told about the manuscript of Augustine? Suppose one of the monks is, in a very loose sense, an Aristotelian. He tells the following story (a version of a very popular tale): "Augustine's manuscript consisted of a certain parcel of matter upon which a certain form had been impressed. It ceased to exist when this parcel of matter was radically deformed. To re-create it, God needed only to collect the matter (in modern terms, the atoms) that once composed it and reimpress that form upon it (in modern terms, cause these atoms to stand to one another in the same spatial and chemical relationships they previously stood in)."

This story is defective. The manuscript God creates in the story is not the manuscript that was destroyed, since the various atoms that compose the tracings of ink on its surface occupy their present positions not as a result of Augustine's activity but of God's. Thus what we have is not a manuscript in Augustine's hand. (Strictly speaking, it is not even a *manuscript.*) (Compare the following conversation: "Is that the house of blocks your daughter built this morning?" "No, I built this one after I accidentally knocked hers down. I put all the blocks just where she did, though. Don't tell her.")

I think the philosophical problems that arise in connection with the burned manuscript of Saint Augustine are very like the problems that arise in connection with the doctrine of the Resurrection. If a man should be totally destroyed, then it is very hard to see how any man who comes into existence thereafter could be the *same* man. And I say this not because I have no criterion of identity I can employ in such cases but because I have a criterion of identity for men and it is, or *seems* to be, violated. And the popular quasi-Aristotelian story that is often supposed to establish the conceptual possibility of God's restoring to existence a man who has been totally destroyed does not lead me to think that I have got the wrong criterion or that I am misapplying the right one. The popular story, of course, is the story according to which God collects the atoms that once composed a certain man and restores them to the positions they occupied relative to one another when that man was alive; thereby (the storyteller contends) God restores the man himself. But this story, it seems to me, does not "work." The atoms of which I am composed occupy at each instant the positions they do because of the operations of certain processes within me (those processes that, taken collectively, constitute my being alive). Even when I become a corpse—provided I decay slowly and am not, say, cremated—the atoms that compose me will occupy the positions relative to one another that they do occupy *largely* because of the processes of life that *used* to go on within me: or this will be the case for at least some short period. Thus a former corpse in which the processes of life have been "started up again" may well be the very man who was once before alive, provided the processes of dissolution did not progress too far while he was a corpse. But if a man does not simply die but is totally destroyed (as in the case of cremation) then *he* can never be reconstituted, for the causal chain has been irrevocably broken. If God collects the atoms that used to constitute that man and "reassembles" them, they will occupy the positions relative to one another they occupy because of God's miracle and not because of the operation of the natural processes that, taken collectively, were the life of that man. (I should also be willing to defend the following theses: The thing such an action of God's would produce would not be a member of our species and would not speak a language or have memories of any sort, though, of course, he—or it—would *appear* to have these features.)

This much is analogous to the case of the burned manuscript. Possibly no one will find what I have said very convincing unless he thinks very much like me. Let me offer three arguments against an "Aristotelian" account of the Resurrection that have no analogues in the case of the manuscript and which will perhaps be more convincing to the generality of philosophers. Arguments (a) and (b) are **ad hominems,** directed against Christians who might be inclined toward the "Aristotelian" theory. Argument (c) attempts to show that the "Aristotelian" theory has an impossible consequence.

A. The atoms of which I am composed cannot be destroyed by burning or the natural processes of decay, but they *can* be destroyed, as can atomic nuclei and even subatomic particles. (Or so it would seem: The principles for identity through time for subatomic particles are very hazy; physical theory has little if anything to say on the subject.) If, in order to raise a man on the Day of Judgment, God had to collect the "building blocks"—atoms, neutrons, or what have you—of which that man had once been composed, then a wicked man could hope to escape God's wrath by seeing to it that all his "building blocks" were destroyed. But according to Christian theology, such a hope is senseless. Thus, unless the nature of the ultimate constituents of matter is different from what it appears to be, the "Aristotelian" theory is inimical to a central point of Christian theology.

B. The atoms (or what have you) of which I am composed may very well have been parts of other people at some time in the past. Thus, if the "Aristotelian" theory is true, there could be a problem on the day of the Resurrection about *who* is resurrected. In fact, if that theory were true, a wicked man who had read his Aquinas might hope to escape punishment in the age to come by becoming a life-long cannibal. But again, the possibility of such a hope cannot be admitted by any Christian.

C. It is possible that none of the atoms that are now parts of me were parts of me when I was ten years old. It is therefore possible that God could collect all the atoms that were parts of me when I was ten, without destroying me, and restore them to the positions they occupied relative to one another in 1952. If the "Aristotelian" theory were correct, this action would be sufficient for the creation of a boy who could truly say, "I am Peter van Inwagen." In fact, he and I could stand facing one another and each say truly to the other, "I am you." But this is conceptually impossible and therefore the "Aristotelian" theory is *not* correct.

No story other than our "Aristotelian" story about how it might be that a man who was totally destroyed could live again seems even superficially plausible. I conclude that my initial judgment is correct and that it is absolutely impossible, even as an accomplishment of God, that a man who has been burned to ashes or been eaten by worms should ever live again. What follows from this about the Christian hope of resurrection? Very little of any interest, I think. All that follows is that if Christianity is true, then what I earlier called "certain facts about the present age" are *not* facts.

It is part of the Christian faith that all men who share in the sin of Adam must die. What does it mean to say that I must die? Just this: that one day I shall be composed entirely of nonliving matter; that is, I shall be a corpse. It is not part of the Christian faith that I must at any time be totally annihilated or disintegrate. (One might note that Christ, whose story is supposed to provide the archetype for the story of each man's resurrection, became a corpse but did not, even in his human nature, cease to exist.) It is of course true that men apparently cease to exist: those who are cremated, for example. But it contradicts nothing in the creeds to suppose that this is not what really happens, and that God preserves our corpses contrary to all appearance. Perhaps at the moment of each man's death, God removes his corpse and replaces it with a simulacrum, which is what is burned or rots. Or perhaps God is not quite so wholesale as this: Perhaps he removes for "safe-keeping" only the "core person"—the brain and central nervous system—or even some special part of it. These are details.

I take it that this story shows that the Resurrection is a feat an almighty being could accomplish. I think this is the *only* way such a being could accomplish it. Perhaps I'm wrong, but that's of little importance. What *is* important is that God can accomplish it this way or some other. Of course one might wonder why God would go to such lengths to make it look as if most people not only die but pass into complete nothingness. This is a difficult question. I think it can be given a plausible answer, but not apart from a discussion of the nature of religious belief. I will say just this: If corpses inexplicably disappeared no matter how carefully they were guarded or inexplicably refused to decay and were miraculously resistant to the most persistent and ingenious attempts to destroy them, then we should be living in a world in which observable events that were *obviously* miraculous, *obviously* due to the intervention of a power beyond nature, happened with monotonous regularity. In such a world we should all believe in the supernatural: Its existence would be the best explanation for the observed phenomena. If Christianity is true, God wants us to believe in the supernatural. But experience shows us that if there is a God, he does not do what he very well *could* do: provide us with a ceaseless torrent of public, undeniable evidence of a power outside the natural order. And perhaps it is not hard to think of good reasons for such a policy. [Cf. reading 5.5.]

POSTSCRIPT (1997)

If I were writing a paper on this topic today, I should not make the definite statement, "I think this is the *only* way such a being could accomplish it." My goal in "The Possibility of Resurrection" was to argue for the **metaphysical possibility** of the Resurrection of the Dead. My method was to tell a story, a story I hoped my readers would grant was a metaphysically possible story, in which God accomplished the Resurrection of the Dead. But I was, I now think, too ready to identify the possibility of the Resurrection with the story I told to establish it. I am now inclined to think that there may well be other ways in which an omnipotent being could accomplish the Resurrection of the Dead than the way that was described in the story I told, ways I am unable even to form an idea of because I lack the conceptual resources to do so. An analogy would be this: A medieval philosopher, or even a nineteenth-century physicist, could have formed no idea of the mechanisms by which the sun shines, not because these mechanisms are a mystery that surpasses human understanding but simply because some of the concepts needed to describe them were not available before the twentieth century.

This analogy can be pressed a bit. Despite overwhelming evidence (provided by the fossil record) that there had been life on the earth for hundreds of millions of years, the great nineteenth-century physicist Lord Kelvin insisted that the sun had been shining for at most 20 million years. He maintained that the only conceivable mechanism of solar radiation was this: The sun is undergoing very gradual gravitational contraction, and solar radiation is due to the resulting gradual transformation of gravitational potential energy into radiant energy. When you plug the sun's mass, radius, and surface temperature into the appropriate equations (Kelvin contended), you will find that the sun cannot have been putting out radiant energy at anything like its current level for more than 20 million years. So (he concluded) the geologists and paleontologists—who are, after all, mere "stamp collectors" and not real *scientists*—have, demonstrably, drawn a false conclusion from their fossils and sedimentary layers.

Lord Kelvin's calculations were (I understand) correct: Given his premise about the mechanism of solar radiation, his conclusion follows. Twentieth-century nuclear physics, however, has supplied the real mechanism of solar radiation, and we now know that Kelvin's premise and conclusion were both wrong and that the conclusion the despised "stamp collectors" drew from the fossil record was right. Even in the nineteenth century, however, it would have been possible to show that Kelvin's premise and conclusion were not indisputable. Even within the confines of classical physics, it would have been possible to tell "just-so stories" according to which the sun has been shining for hundreds of millions of years. Here is the beginning of one: The sun is made up of rapidly spinning atoms; continual collisions between these atoms result in their kinetic energy of rotation being gradually transformed into radiant energy.

If one continues the story by specifying (for some particular moment in the past) the right average rotational kinetic energy for the solar atoms and the right average linear velocity and mean free path of the atoms between collisions and the right average loss of rotational kinetic energy in each collision, the resulting filled-out story will have the consequence that the sun has been producing light and heat at its present level for hundreds of millions of years—or for any period one likes.

This is, of course, a "just-so story": Although it serves to establish a possibility, it isn't *true.* In fact—as Kelvin would certainly have been quick to point out—it's a preposterous story, for no imaginable physical mechanism could have produced the initial conditions (the enormous rotational kinetic energy of the solar atoms) the story postulates. And yet, in a way, the story *is* true. There is one very abstract—and very important—feature that the sun-in-the-story shares with the real sun: Most of the energy that the sun gives off in the form of light and heat was not stored before it was radiated as gravitational potential energy, but rather was stored in the inner dynamics of the atoms of which the sun is composed (in the story, as kinetic energy of rotation; in the real world, as nuclear binding energy).

I am inclined now to think of the description that I gave in "The Possibility of Resurrection" of how an omnipotent being could accomplish the Resurrection of the Dead as a "just-so story": Although it serves to establish a possibility, it probably isn't true. (And it is easy to see why someone might think it was preposterous, although it might be questioned whether any of us is in an **epistemic** position to make a judgment of this sort.) But I am also inclined to think that even if the story is not true, even if it gets the "mechanism" of Resurrection wrong, it nevertheless *is* true—in a way. That is, I am inclined to think that even if the story is wrong about the specifics of the Resurrection, the Resurrection-in-the-story, like the sun-in-the-story, nevertheless shares some important but very abstract feature of the real thing. My inclination is to believe that God will somehow—in the way I have imagined or in some way I lack the conceptual resources to imagine, "in this way or some other"—preserve a remnant of each person, a *gumnos kókkos* (a naked kernel: 1 Cor. 15:37), which will be sown in corruption and raised in incorruption.

STUDY QUESTIONS

1. What is the philosophical problem in the doctrine of resurrection?
2. What is the "Aristotelian solution" to the problem, as presented by van Inwagen?
3. For what three reasons does van Inwagen reject the solution in question 2?
4. What is van Inwagen's contention in the "Postscript"? What is the point of the sun analogy?
5. *Do you think that van Inwagen is justified in believing that resurrection is possible, though he does not know *how* God performs it? Why or why not?
6. *Suppose you have been resurrected, but the body that the "resurrected you" has is not the same as the body you once occupied. Could it still be that it is you, but now in that different body? If so, how?
7. *Compare and contrast van Inwagen's position with that of Swinburne in Reading 6.6.

MIRACLES AND GOD'S ACTION IN THE WORLD

READING 6.8

God's Action in the World

William P. Alston

Augustine, Aquinas, John Calvin, and Martin Luther held that God governs everything in the world and is the agent of every happening. It would seem that this thesis, called by William

P. Alston (Syracuse University) **omnidetermination,** *is incompatible with the thesis that everything that happens is determined to happen by natural causes, which Alston calls* causal **determinism.** *Alston argues, however, that, although direct divine action is possible, direct divine action is not necessary for God's correctly being thought of as acting in the world. Rather, as long as God has set up the world to accomplish God's purposes, even events that are brought about by natural causes reflect divine agency.*

Alston draws a line, however: he denies that God could be the agent of free human choices and of happenings they naturally cause. In order to preserve divine agency while affirming free choice, Jesuit **theologian** *Luis de Molina held that God has "***middle knowledge,***" or knowledge of how different possible free agents would choose to act in all possible circumstances. On the basis of this knowledge, God creates certain people and adjusts the natural order to realize His will. (See also reading 1.8.) Alston rejects the doctrine of middle knowledge, but he mentions ways God can ensure that events do not deviate too widely from His intentions.*

In a part of the essay not included here (5), Alston continues the discussion he launched in part 4, namely, how, even within a framework mostly devoid of direct divine action, some acts of God can be singled out as specially significant.

---

1. THE PROBLEM

In this essay I seek an understanding of the notion of God's acting in the world, where this is to be understood as going beyond God's creation and preservation of the world, and as involving God's intentionally producing various particular effects in the world. The general notion covers a wide variety of putative cases. On the one hand, there is a variety of ways in which God is thought to deal "directly" with human beings: communicating messages to them, judging them, forgiving them, sustaining them, enlightening or guiding them. Then there are more public displays, the Cecil B. De Mille spectaculars, such as parting the waters of the Sea of Reeds, sending the plagues on Egypt, and raising the dead to life. In my discussion I will be taking this whole spectrum into account, though at times I will narrow the focus.

It goes without saying that this problem will assume different forms, depending on how we view God and how we view the world. Let me explain the setting within which I am raising the question. God is the ultimate source of being for everything other than himself: everything other than God exists only because of the divine creative activity. It is not simply that God initially brings each creature into existence; God's creative or sustaining activity is continually required to keep the creature in being. God's existence, on the other hand, depends on nothing outside Himself. . . .

. . . I think of God as literally a personal agent. By a "personal agent" I mean a being that acts in the light of knowledge to achieve purposes, a being whose actions express attitudes and are guided by standards and principles, a being that enters into communication and other forms of personal relations with other personal agents. In saying that God *literally* acts in the light of knowledge and purposes, I do not mean to imply that knowledge, intention, and other psychological states and processes are realized in God in the same way they are realized in human beings. What it is for God to intend something may be, and undoubtedly is, radically different from what it is for a human being to intend something. But this is quite compatible with the basic sense of terms like 'know' and 'intend' holding constant across the divine-human gap. For example, despite the radical differences in divine and human nature, the existence of an intention (together with the power to carry it out) can have the same sorts of implications in both cases. Thus, from "God intends to establish his kingdom on earth," together with "God is **omnipotent,**" we can infer that God's kingdom will be established on earth. . . .

I will not say much about the world. I use the term to designate the whole of creation, the totality of everything that exists other than God. In this essay I will be focusing on the physical universe, including human beings, leaving to one side whatever else there may be to creation. . . .

2. DETERMINISM AND DIVINE AGENCY

The most basic issue that arises when, against this background, we try to understand the action of God in the world in this. Must we think of *everything* that happens in the world, including those happenings that are due to natural causes, as actions of God, as something that God does? Or is it only some, perhaps very small, subclass of happenings that deserves that appellation? We are pulled both ways here. On the one hand, as we shall see in a moment, there is a considerable case to be made for the thesis that everything that happens in the world (with the possible exception of free voluntary acts of created agents) is God's doing. But, on the other hand, it seems that when we take some particular occurrence to be an action of God, we mean to be contrasting it with more humdrum happenings that are purely the work of created agents. When the waters of the Sea of Reeds part to let the Israelites through, but close when the Egyptians seek to follow, that is seen as an act of God. But the normal rippling of the water before and after this event is not thought of as God's doing, at least not in the same way. We single out an act of God against a massive background of the purely worldly. In the remainder of this section I will look at the case for holding that everything, or almost everything, is done by God. The rest of the paper will be devoted to exploring the idea that happenings of some relatively small subset are actions of God in some special sense.

There is a widespread view in Christian **theology** that I will call "**omnidetermination.**" This is the thesis that God wills, intentionally brings about, every detail of creation. It can boast such distinguished adherents as Augustine, Aquinas, Calvin, and Luther. For example, Aquinas argues that all things are subject to the divine government, including **contingent events** and things that happen by chance.[1] To say that something happens by chance is simply to say that it is not determined by some particular kind of natural causes; to say that something happens contingently is to say that its **proximate causes** are not sufficient to determine it uniquely.[2] But nothing falls outside the order instituted by the divine will. God, as first cause and first mover, is responsible for all existence and all activity. And since God's causation is by His will, guided by His intellect, every activity in the world was willed by God and so carries out a divine intention. This even includes human volition, which, Aquinas insists, is free, but free in the sense that no created being outside the agent causes the agent to will one alternative rather than another, and contingent in that its proximate cause, the created will in question, is not determined by its nature to will in just one way.[3] Since God wills every created happening, God is the agent of every happening. "God works in every agent."[4]

Thus Aquinas seeks to establish omnidetermination, and hence universal divine agency, from very general considerations concerning the nature of God and the relations He must have to *any* created world. I do not find the arguments convincing, but to explain why, I would have to go deeply into **Thomistic** theology and philosophy, something I have no time for in this essay. I shall simply assume that the fundamental nature of God, as briefly adumbrated at the beginning of this section, leaves open the extent to which God determines every detail of His creation. God could determine everything; He has the power to do so. But He also has a choice as to whether to be omnidetermining. His nature does not constrain Him either way. It is quite conceivable that He proceeds as Augustine, Aquinas, and others suppose, but it is also quite conceivable that God has deliberately refrained from deciding certain details, for example, the free voluntary choices of human beings.

Proceeding in that spirit, I shall explore the prospects for universal divine agency on one or another assumption about the universe. And first I shall indicate how universal divine agency follows from a certain possible feature of the universe, namely, *causal* ***determinism.*** Determinism is the thesis that everything that happens in the universe is uniquely determined to happen in just that way by

[1]Aquinas, *Summa Theologiae (ST),* Ia, Q [= Question] 103, art [= article] 5, Aquinas, *Summa Contra Gentiles (SCG),* III, 64.
[2]*ST,* Ia, Q. 103, art. 7. *SCG,* III, 72, 74.
[3]*ST,* Ia, Q. 105, art. 4. *SCG,* III, 89, 90.
[4]*ST,* Ia, Q. 105, art. 5. *SCG,* III, 67, 70.

natural causes. Thinking of the universe in this way, let us consider a particular naturally determined event. A cow eats some grass and is thereby sustained. We would say, of course, that the cow is nourished by the grass and that the grass does the nourishing. Does that rule out God's doing the nourishing? By no means. After all, God instituted and maintains the natural order by which this nourishing takes place. God created the entities involved and established the laws by which their behavior is governed. Since He did this knowingly and since He acts purposefully, we must suppose that He set all this up in order, inter alia, that this cow should be nourished by this grass at this time.[5] Thus we must hold that God used the grass to nourish the cow and hence that God is the ultimate doer of the deed, just as when I use a hammer to drive in a nail, it is I who drove in the nail, even though I used a hammer to do so. In the latter case I intentionally bring about certain **dispositions** of the hammer vis-à-vis the nail in order to get the nail imbedded in the wood. In the former case God, via creating and sustaining the natural order, intentionally brings about a certain disposition of the grass vis-à-vis the cow in order to get the cow nourished. Thus in both cases the agent who intentionally brings about the immediate cause of E in order to produce E is rightly said to have produced E. Indeed, God has, if anything, a better right to be regarded as the nourisher of the cow than I have to be regarded as the driver of the nail, for He is more fully responsible than I for the intended effect. I merely make use of an instrument I find ready to hand, whereas God is responsible for the existence of His instrument. Even if I forged the hammer, I merely transformed preexisting materials. I did not bring them into existence out of nothing.

Indeed, we do not even need the doctrine of continuous divine preservation to arrive at the conclusion that God brings about every effect. Suppose that God simply brings created substances into existence, ordains deterministic laws that govern their behavior, and then leaves them alone. It is still the case that God intentionally set up the natural order as He did, knowing how it would work out at every time and place. We can hardly deny that He did this in order to accomplish His purpose, and hence that in exercising His creative activity, He was intentionally bringing about what ensues in the world. We have as much reason, on this hypothesis, to say that God nourished the cow as we have for saying that the person who booby-trapped a car killed the driver. In both cases some arrangements were made in order to lead to a result, and after a passage of time they did lead to that result, even though the agent did not actively intervene after the initial arrangements were made. If God continuously sustains everything in being, this gives His agency, so to say, more immediacy, but it is not required for the pervasive reality of divine agency.

Note that the doctrine of divine agency in the world, as I have been presenting it, is not simply the doctrine of creation and preservation expressed differently. The thesis that God is the intentional agent of all worldly happenings follows from the doctrine of divine creation (and preservation) *provided* that it is conjoined with (a) the thesis of determinism and (b) the assumption that it is God's purpose to bring about all that He does bring about.

To be sure, since God's claim to have nourished the cow rests on the fact that God intentionally and knowingly brought about a state of affairs that led to that nourishment, we cannot limit the instrument God used for this action to the grass ingested. For God no more directly brought about the ingestion than he did the resultant bovine metabolism. That herbaceous ingestion was itself brought about by the use of a previous state of affairs, and that, in turn, all the way back to the **Big Bang,** or back indefinitely if the universe is temporally infinite. But it is hardly a matter for surprise that God should use instruments on a cosmic scale.

It is sometimes thought that universal divine agency is incompatible with the reality of created agency, so that if we hold that God nourished the

[5]Of course it may be that God didn't really care whether *this* cow ate *this* grass at *this* time. Perhaps he cared about cows being nourished but wasn't specifically concerned about precisely how it is carried out in each instance. In that case the particular details of this ingestion constitute a foreseen but unintended result of the natural order. If this is the right way to look at it we will have to modify the strong statement in the text; but there will still be plenty of aspects of the world that do constitute a carrying out of divine purposes. . . .

cow, we must deny that the grass did. To dispel this impression we only need note that the action involves different roles for different agents and that the filling of one role by no means implies that the others are empty. Whenever an agent uses an instrument to do something, both the (ultimate) agent and the instrument are doing something, and if they were not both doing their job, the effect would not be forthcoming, at least not in that way. The hammer will not pick itself up and drive in the nail, but neither can I drive the nail by my bare hands. Just so, the grass will not nourish the cow unless God endows it with its properties and sustains it in being. To be sure, God could perfectly well bring it about that the cow is sustained without using grass or any other created agency. However, if God chooses to nourish the cow by the ingestion of grass, the grass must do its thing metabolically if God is to do it that way. Similarly, suppose that I could drive the nail with my bare hands if I so choose. Even so, when I choose to use the hammer, the hammer has an essential role to play; if the hammer did not knock the nail in (propelled and guided by me), then I would not drive the nail in that way, by using a hammer. Thus we must reject the theological version of the National Rifle Association principle: "Diseases don't kill people; God kills people." We can recognize that both God and the disease kill, both God and the grass nourish, each in its distinctive way.

Thus far I have been proceeding on the assumption of determinism. Here the case for universal divine agency, on the assumptions of classical theism, is quite straightforward. But many thinkers today hold that the results of **quantum mechanics** show that no physical events are strictly causally determined, though for macroscopic events the chances of things having come out differently are negligible. It would be interesting to explore the bearing of a quantum mechanical point of view on the case for universal divine agency. Could we think of God as having nourished the cow if he used means that are only very, very, very likely to bring it about? I would think so. But here I want to concentrate on another kind of possible exception to causal determinism, human voluntary actions. If they are causally determined, the above account of bovine nourishment applies equally to them. We would all be divine instruments in the same straightforward sense as the grass. But what if, as **libertarians** think, human voluntary actions are not causally determined? On that assumption can God be said to perform those actions? Aquinas, as we have seen, insists that God intentionally brings about every event, whether uniquely determined by natural causes or not. But having set aside that position, we want to know what follows concerning divine agency of human voluntary actions, from the tenets of classical theism as set out in Section 1, plus a libertarian account of human voluntary action.

There is no doubt but that the situation is significantly different from what it is on the thesis of complete determinism. Here we cannot say that God instituted the natural order knowing that it would lead to my freely choosing to become a professional philosopher. Hence we lack that reason for holding that God is the agent of that choice. Even if God foreknows all free human actions, it does not follow that He intentionally brought them about in order to achieve his purpose. It is true that God cannot escape all responsibility for a given naturally undetermined event, for example, that choice of mine. For, being omnipotent, He could have made it impossible, either by creating a wholly deterministic universe that excluded it, by refraining from allowing some of the conditions of its possibility (for example, not endowing me with the capacity to make such a choice), or by interfering before I could bring it off. Thus God bears the kind of responsibility for naturally undetermined events that I bear for something I could have prevented but did not, for example, my small child's beating his fists on the wall in rage. But the fact that I could have prevented that action does not imply that I did it, that *I* beat my son's fists against the wall; the same point holds for God and human free action.

This last result underlines the point that the doctrines of divine omnipotence and continuous divine conservation do not by themselves imply that everything that happens in the world is done by God. For free **autonomous** created agents, as much as other creatures, exist and exercise their powers only because God continuously sustains them in existence. And the divine omnipotence extends to them as much as to other creatures; God could have refrained from creating them as autonomous agents, and He can interfere with their activities at any time. But despite all that, the above considerations show that God is not properly regarded as the agent of their actions.

I cannot discuss the status of human voluntary actions in this essay, but I want to consider the bearing of the libertarian position on the extent of divine agency. I have already noted that causally undetermined human actions or volitions cannot be regarded as divine actions in a full sense. But, in addition, the libertarian position greatly complicates the case for divine agency of causally determined happenings. Recall that the case for universal divine agency, given universal determinism, rested on the thesis that every worldly happening issued from the order God instituted in order to produce those happenings. But in allowing some created agents a say in what they do, God is also giving them a share in causally determining other sorts of events. Human voluntary actions themselves have effects as much as any other worldly happenings. At least on or near the surface of the earth very little happens that is totally causally independent of past human activity. That leaves the rest of the universe; yet apart from the prospects for human exploration outside our solar system, if there are free created agents elsewhere in the universe, a like situation obtains there. To be sure, there are gross features of the environment that are, thus far, independent of human manipulation. We have not yet altered the cycle of the seasons or the location of the seas. But even here the precise details of the weather or of the sea level are affected by our doings. So there are a vast number of causally determined happenings whose causal determinants did not stem solely from God's choice. In fact, the above-mentioned bovine nourishment is undoubtedly one of them. Assuming that this is a domesticated cow, she would not have been in just that place, in a position to eat just that grass, apart from the voluntary activity of husbandmen. So what is the case for divine agency of those causally determined happenings that are influenced by free human choices?

Let us remind ourselves that we have a problem here because the earlier case for universal divine agency depended on the assumption that God *chose* *all* worldly happenings by creating the constituents of the world and ordaining laws governing their interaction. But since that cow would not be eating that grass if some human had not made certain choices that God did not determine, even indirectly, the previous argument does not apply. So what is God's role in a happening that partly depends on free human choices? It is still true that God partly determines the event; human choices make a partial contribution at most. If God had not endowed cows and grass and numerous other things with the powers they have, no cow would be eating any grass anywhere. But the crucial difficulty here comes not from the extent of divine causal involvement in the outcome, but rather from divine intentions. Can we think of God's having intended just this outcome, considering the role of human free choice in producing it? We cannot, as before, hold that God knew that this result would be forthcoming just by instituting the natural order. Of course, it is conceivable that God acts directly to shape the situations that are influenced by human voluntary activity. But at this point we are confining ourselves to happenings that are determined by natural causes.

Let us make a fresh start. It seems clear that God can intentionally produce an effect that is completely determined by created causes only by way of His institution of the causal order. Is there any way in which God could do that if other, independent sources of determination are involved? (Even if those sources owe their independent voice to God's permission, they still make their contribution in ways not specifically chosen by God.) This could happen if God could foresee those independent contributions *and on the basis of that* adjust the details of the natural order so that the outcomes of those creaturely choices would always be in line with His intentions: not necessarily in line with what He would have chosen had He been calling all the shots (His antecedent will), but at least in accordance with His intentions, given that free created agents will act as they will (His consequent will). But if God is to adjust the natural order in light of this knowledge, it cannot be direct intuitive knowledge of the actual occurrence of the free actions, whether this is a contemporaneous awareness of them in the divine eternal now (on the assumption that God is timeless) or a special **cognitive** power of directly intuiting what will happen in the future (if God is temporal). For the direct intuition of the actual occurrence of the free choice is logically posterior to that choice; it presupposes the constitution of that choice. But that means that it also presupposes the constitution of the causal order that produced the situation in which the choice was made. Human free choices, even if not uniquely determined by their natural environment, are surely heavily influenced by that environment. If my natural environment were different from what it is in certain respects, I would not even have the same alternatives from which to choose. In an appropriately different environment I would not have the opportunity to choose whether to be a professional philosopher. Moreover, given those alternatives, various features of my situation determine what influences me one way or the other. Hence if God's only "**foreknowledge**" of human free choices is an intuitive awareness of the actual choices, this "comes too late" to permit Him to adjust the natural order so as to carry out His intentions in the light of those choices. He would already be stuck with one natural order rather than another.

Thus it seems that if God is to produce intentionally the sustenance of the cow, via the institution of the natural order, He will have to know how free created agents *would* act in various possible situations, as well as knowing how they will act in actual situations. That is, He will have to have "**middle knowledge.**"[6] (God's "middle knowledge" is his conditional knowledge of future contingent events. The controversial doctrine of *scientia media* was devised originally by [Luis de] Molina in an attempt to secure both God's foreknowledge and the reality of human freedom, the latter of which he thought to be undermined by the standard Thomistic accounts.) I myself am dubious about the possibility of such knowledge, not because I think God might be limited in his cognitive powers, but because I doubt that there are any true-or-false propositions, any facts of the matter to be known, about how free agents would act in this or that situation. There may well be truths to the effect that the probability of a given free agent doing A in situation S is so-and-so. But I doubt that there are any truths as to precisely what a free agent would do in a given situation. How could there be such truths if the agent does indeed have a free choice in such a situation? How could there be such a truth if the agent were not somehow determined to do A in that kind of situation? But be that as it may, it would seem that only if God has middle knowledge could He adjust the laws of nature in the light of human free choices. God needs that knowledge of how the agent would act in various situations if He is to have a realm of possibilities within which the free choice and the laws of nature can be mutually adjusted so as to produce consequences in line with His intentions.

But even in the absence of middle knowledge, and given libertarian assumptions about human voluntary action, it can still be true that God intentionally brings about various not completely specific features of causally determined states of affairs influenced by human voluntary action. God can limit the scope of human free choice, so as to prevent it from threatening various features of His world He wishes to preserve. And He can see to it that His world contains enough counterinfluences to prevent the most disastrous possible consequences of human sin. But on those assumptions God would not unqualifiedly be the agent of all naturally determined happenings.

Let me summarize the results of this section. Given an unrestricted thesis of determinism, there is a straightforward derivation of universal divine agency of worldly happenings from the classical theism we are presupposing. If there are naturally undetermined happenings, whether human voluntary actions or otherwise, this line of argument does not apply to them, and God is not their agent unless He directly produces them. Furthermore, it is only on the assumption that God has "middle knowledge" that He could be the agent of naturally determined

[6]This term was introduced by the sixteenth-century Jesuit theologian Luis de Molina. For a discussion of this type of knowledge, together with historical references, see R. M. Adams, "Middle Knowledge and the Problem of Evil," *American Philosophical Quarterly,* 14 (April 1977), 109–17. [See also Reading 1.8—Ed.]

happenings that are causally influenced by naturally undetermined happenings. Finally, even where God is not, in the full sense, the agent of certain happenings, He could still see to it that they do not deviate too widely from His intentions.

4. IS DIRECT DIVINE INTERVENTION REQUIRED?[7]

. . . [T]hough I consider it a live possibility that God sometimes directly produces effects in the world, I am not at all inclined to restrict myself to this way of marking out those occurrences that are acts of God in some specially significant way. I also take it as a live possibility that God always acts through the natural order, and so I want to consider how to mark out the "special" acts of God on that assumption. There are several reasons for not restricting ourselves to the "direct intervention" account, even if we are not prepared to rule out its possibility.

First, even though divine intervention is possible, it is by no means clear that it ever does happen. I do not go along with Hume's argument in his famous essay on miracles that it is in principle impossible to be justified in believing that something has happened outside the usual course of nature,[8] but I do recognize that we are rarely, if ever, in a position to justify conclusively such a claim. No matter how unusual or outlandish the occurrence, we cannot rule out the possibility that it was brought about by natural causes in a way that we do not currently understand. It is a truism that with respect to some occurrences attributed at one time to supernatural intervention we are, at a later time, in a position to give a scientific explanation, or at least to see the gross outlines of such an explanation. Mental illness and recovery therefrom is a signal case in point. We can be justified in dismissing the possibility of a **naturalistic** explanation only if we have (a) a complete description of the particular case and (b) a complete inventory of natural causes of that sort of occurrence. Armed with that, we might be able to show that there were no available natural causes that could have produced that result. But when are we in a position to do that? If we insist that what makes something a "special" act of God is that it is a direct act of God on the world, we cannot be assured that there are any "special" acts of God.

Second, not all the occurrences we feel inclined to treat as special acts of God even appear to be independent of natural causes. The contrary impression is fostered by preoccupation with the standard biblical "superspectacular" miracles: the parting of the waters of the Sea of Reeds, walking on water, changing water into wine, and so on. These do *appear* to stem from special divine intervention, whatever our final judgment. But other cases do not immediately strike us that way. Think of all the cases in which one takes oneself to have been guided or strengthened by God. When I take God to have guided me in making a decision, or to have enabled me to meet a crisis without collapsing, the **phenomenology** of the situation may present nothing outlandish. On the surface nothing untoward happens. In the guidance case I weigh the alternatives, think about them, pray about the problem, try to imagine alternative outcomes, and so on. In the strengthening case I simply meet the crisis, doing what seems called for at each point, perhaps frequently calling on God for help. Or consider a case in which I take God to have spoken to me. This *may* involve an apparent miracle—the clouds open and a booming voice seems to emerge from the empyrean vault. But more commonly we get something like the following: I ask God in prayer what I should concentrate on in my work, after which the thought forms in my mind that I should give priority to administration rather than scholarship, accompanied by a strong conviction that this is God's message for me. Again, on the surface nothing happens in a way that seems outside the order of natural causality. In all these cases we have events of quite ordinary sorts, occurring in contexts in which they frequently occur. Or again, consider events taken to be "providential," like the boy's emerging unhurt from the accident in which all others perished. This may be mildly unusual, but it is by no means unprecedented. It is easy to think of natural factors that would produce

[7][In the omitted section (3), Alston argues that direct divine intervention is possible—Ed.]

[8][See Hume's essay in Reading 6.9 and Mill's in Reading 6.11—Ed.]

such a result—place and angle of impact, positioning of passengers, what each encounters in being propelled from his/her position. In all these cases one may believe that God is working outside the ordinary course of nature to strengthen one, to preserve the person from harm, or whatever, but one is not forced into this belief by an apparent absence of the right kind of natural causes. For all we can tell by an examination of the situation itself, these thoughts, capacities, or whatever were just as much produced by natural causes as other effects of those sorts.

Third, even where we believe that God is acting outside the natural order, that belief is by no means always crucial to our taking the occurrence to be an act of God in a specially significant way. Sometimes it *is* crucial. Here we must draw some distinctions within this vaguely demarcated class of "special" acts of God. The distinctions have to do with the special role or function we take the act in question to have, what sort of thing we take God to be up to in performing it, or, more generally, what we take to be so special about it. One historically important kind of specialness that does depend on divine intervention is the way in which an act of God is supposed to authenticate some person's claim to authority, to be delivering a divine message, or to be acting under divine instructions. Thus, according to Exodus 4, when God gave Moses his commission in the wilderness, He empowered Moses to validate his claims by performing certain miracles, for example, turning a staff into a snake and then back into a staff and turning water from the Nile into blood. God confirmed Elijah's claims to authority by sending fire from heaven to consume the offering made on Mt. Carmel. Jesus' status was confirmed, for many, by the wonders he performed. When this is taken to be the special significance of an act of God, it is essential that the act be thought of as direct. The reasoning presumably runs like this. Moses did something that he could not do by his own natural powers; indeed, it was something that no creature could bring off by its natural powers. This could only happen if the creator and controller of the natural order set aside the usual rules in this particular instance and endowed Moses with special supernatural powers.[9] But He would not have done this had He not wished thereby to endorse Moses' claims. Therefore . . . . [ellipses original-ed.]

If an occurrence is to elicit this reasoning, it must not only *be* outside the course of nature but must seem to be so. In fact, the latter is presumably sufficient in itself. If and only if the occurrence runs counter to what is generally believed to be the natural outcome of the antecedent situation will it be taken as an authentication of prophetic claims. Furthermore, it must be a publicly observed occurrence if it is to be effective. In this connection we should note that the effectiveness of this procedure depends on a certain cast of mind in the audience; in particular, it presupposes that the audience will be disposed to take direct divine intervention as the correct explanation of anything that strongly runs counter to what is confidently believed to be the course of nature. Hence it will fall flat with a contemporary **scientistic** audience that is predisposed to take such surprising occurrences as an indication that our scientific theories need to be revised. If *they* were to witness fire falling from heaven at Elijah's request on Mt. Carmel, their reaction would be, not "God has confirmed Elijah's authority," but rather "Back to the drawing board."

However, many occurrences are taken to be special acts of God in a way that does not require the assumption of direct divine intervention. For one thing, there are God's "personal dealings" with creatures of which we spoke earlier—God's strengthening, guiding, enlightening, empowering, and speaking to the person. Again, there are all the cases that fall under the rubric of "providential care," personal and corporate. This includes, on the personal level, recovery from

[9]It does not matter whether we think of God as endowing Moses with supernatural powers or think of God as turning the staff into a serpent himself. In either case God has acted outside the natural order—either to bring about an event in the universe directly or to endow some creature with supernatural powers. In either case the direct action of God, in connection with the claims made by the human being, is taken to validate those claims. Some miracles are more naturally viewed in one of these ways, and some in the other. It is more natural to think of *Moses* as turning the staff into a serpent (having been granted the special power to do so by God), whereas it is more natural to think of God sending down the fire on the sacrifice, after Elijah calls on Him to do so.

illness, survival of accidents, and the building of a career in ways not anticipated in advance. On the corporate level we have the rise and fall of nations, the preservation of a people from destruction, and the growth of the Church. In all these cases what is taken to be "specially significant" is the nature of the outcome, not merely as happening somehow or other but *as a carrying out of God's purposes.* We may believe in some or all such cases that God has brought about the outcome apart from natural causes, but that belief is not essential for our singling out these occurrences in the way we do. What we take to be special about them is simply that God has acted in such a way as to effect *this result,* that *this* is something that God *intended* to bring about. How God chose to do this is not the heart of the matter; it will be special in the relevant way whatever that choice. In these cases we are centrally interested in the character of the result whereas in the "authentication" cases the result could be, and often was, quite indifferent in itself, its significance residing in its being a sign of divine favor.

Many people think, and I myself at one time thought, that the belief that God enters into active interaction with His creatures, a belief crucial to the Judeo-Christian tradition, requires us to suppose that God directly intervenes in the world, acting outside the course of nature. But the considerations of this essay clearly indicate otherwise. Just by virtue of creating and sustaining the natural order God is in as active contact with his creatures as one could wish. Merely by the use of natural causes God carries out His purposes and intentions with respect to creatures, and this surely counts as genuine action toward them. If God speaks to me, or guides me, or enlightens me by the use of natural causes, He is as surely in active contact with me as if He had produced the relevant effects by a direct fiat. Indeed, as I suggested above, we do not even need the doctrine of continuous divine preservation in order to achieve that result; although if God is actively sustaining everything in being at every moment, this does, so to speak, give God's instrumental actions more immediacy. But even without that, God is still intentionally doing everything done by the natural order he creates. After all, when one human being directly interacts with another, by speaking to or embracing the other, the agent is making use of aspects of the natural order, exploiting physical and psychological regularities; we do not know how to do it otherwise. And surely this does not imply that we are not in active contact with each other in such transactions. However necessary direct intervention may be for the authentication of messengers, it is not required for genuine divine-human interaction. Thus we can think of God's action in the world as pervasive, if not all-pervasive, whether or not anything ever happens outside the ordinary course of nature. . . .

STUDY QUESTIONS

1. What is meant by *omnidetermination?* Which philosophers adopted it?
2. According to Alston, why is omnidetermination compatible with—indeed, on theistic premises follows from—causal determinism?
3. What does Alston say concerning events that are not strictly determined—can God be the agent of those?
4. What is Molina's doctrine of middle knowledge? How does the doctrine purport to reconcile omnidetermination by God with human free will?
5. What reason does Alston give for rejecting Molinism?
6. *Do you think Alston has made a plausible case for having divine agency in the framework of a natural order? Why or why not?
7. *Compare Alston's essay with William Hasker's in Reading 1.8. What similarities do you see? What differences?

READING 6.9

Of Miracles

David Hume

This essay by David Hume (1711–1776) has stood at the center of the philosophical discussion of miracles for over two centuries. Hume understands a miracle as "a transgression of a law of nature by a particular volition of the Deity, or by the interposition of some invisible agent." Given this conception of a miracle as a violation of nature's laws, Hume argues that, whenever we assess the credibility of a report of a miracle, we must weigh two facts against each other: the fact that human testimony is generally reliable and the fact that if the reported event occurred it would be contrary to the course of all previous experience. In the concluding paragraph of the first part of the essay, Hume does not say which of these is the weightier fact; however, in the preceding paragraph and in part II there are strong indications that he would almost always reject the testimony. He further maintains that the testimony that exists for miracles' actually having occurred in history *is weak because, among other things, education and integrity are lacking in the witnesses, and reports of miracles in one religion destroy the testimonial evidence for miracles in every other religion. The essay begins with an approving reference to an argument given by John Tillotson (1630–94), a Presbyterian* **theologian,** *against the "real presence," i.e. the presence of the body and blood of Jesus in the bread and wine of the Eucharist.*

PART I.

There is, in Dr. Tillotson's writings, an argument against the *real presence* which is as concise and elegant and strong as any argument can possibly be supposed against a doctrine so little worthy of a serious refutation. It is acknowledged on all hands, says that learned prelate, that the authority either of the Scripture or of tradition is founded merely in the testimony of the Apostles who were eyewitnesses to those miracles of our Savior by which he proved his divine mission. Our evidence, then, for the truth of the *Christian* religion is less than the evidence for the truth of our senses, because even in the first authors of our religion it was no greater; and it is evident it must diminish in passing from them to their disciples, nor can anyone rest such confidence in their testimony as in the immediate object of his senses. But a weaker evidence can never destroy a stronger; and, therefore, were the doctrine of the real presence ever so clearly revealed in scripture, it would be directly contrary to the rules of just reasoning to give our assent to it. It contradicts sense, though both the Scripture and tradition, on which it is supposed to be built, do not carry such evidence with them as sense, when they are considered merely as external evidences and are not brought home to everyone's breast by the immediate operation of the Holy Spirit.

Nothing is so convenient as a decisive argument of this kind, which must at least *silence* the most arrogant bigotry and superstition and free us from their impertinent solicitations. I flatter myself that I have discovered an argument of a like nature which, if just, will, with the wise and learned, be an everlasting check to all kinds of superstitious delusion and consequently will be useful as long as the world endures. For so long, I presume, will the accounts of miracles and prodigies be found in all history, sacred and profane.

Though experience is our only guide in reasoning concerning matters of fact, it must be acknowledged that this guide is not altogether infallible, but in some cases is apt to lead us into errors. One who in our climate should expect better weather in any week of June than in one of December would reason frequently observed to happen. But it is a miracle that a dead man should come to life, because that has never been observed in any age or country. There must, therefore, be a uniform experience against every miraculous event; otherwise the event would not merit that appellation. And as a uniform experience amounts to a proof, there is here a direct and full *proof,* from the nature of the fact, against the existence of any miracle, nor can such a proof be destroyed or the miracle rendered credible but by an opposite proof which is superior.[2]

The plain consequence is (and it is a general maxim worthy of our attention): that no testimony is sufficient to establish a miracle, unless the testimony is of such a kind that its falsehood would be more miraculous than the fact which it endeavors to establish; and even in that case there is a mutual destruction of arguments and the superior only gives us an assurance suitable to that degree of force which remains after deducting the inferior. When anyone tells me that he saw a dead man restored to life, I immediately consider with myself whether it is more probable that this person should either deceive or be deceived or that the fact which he relates should really have happened. I weigh the one miracle against the other and, according to the superiority which I discover, I pronounce my decision and always reject the greater miracle. If the falsehood of his testimony would be more miraculous than the event which he relates, then, and not until then, can he pretend to command my belief or opinion.

PART II.

In the foregoing reasoning we have supposed that the testimony upon which a miracle is founded may possibly amount to an entire proof and that the falsehood of that testimony would be a real prodigy. But it is easy to show that we have been a great deal too liberal in our concession and that there never was a miraculous event established on so full an evidence.

For *first,* there is not to be found, in all history, any miracle attested by a sufficient number of men of such unquestioned good sense, education, and learning, as to secure us against all delusion in themselves; of such undoubted integrity as to place them beyond all suspicion of any design to deceive others; of such credit and reputation in the eyes of mankind as to have a great deal to lose in case of their being detected in any falsehood, and at the same time attesting facts performed in such a public manner and in so celebrated a part of the world as to render the detection unavoidable—all which circumstances are requisite to give us a full assurance in the testimony of men.

Secondly, we may observe in human nature a principle which, if strictly examined, will be found to diminish extremely the assurance which we might, from human testimony, have in any kind of prodigy. The maxim by which we commonly conduct ourselves in our reasonings is that the objects of which we have no experience, resemble those of which we have; that what we have found to be most usual is always most probable; and that where there is an opposition of arguments, we ought to give the preference to such as are founded on the greatest number of past observations. But though, in proceeding by this rule, we readily reject any fact which is unusual and incredible in an ordinary degree, yet in advancing further, the mind does not observe always the same rule; but when anything is affirmed utterly absurd and miraculous, it rather the more readily admits of such a fact upon account of that very circumstance which ought to destroy all its authority.

[2]Sometimes an event may not, *in itself, seem* to be contrary to the laws of nature, and yet, if it were real, it might, by reason of some circumstances, be denominated a miracle; because, in *fact,* it is contrary to these laws. Thus if a person, claiming a divine authority, should command a sick person to be well, a healthful man to fall down dead, the clouds to pour rain, the winds to blow, in short, should order many natural events, which immediately follow upon his command; these might justly be esteemed miracles, because they are really, in this case, contrary to the laws of nature. For if any suspicion remain, that the event and command concurred by accident, there is no miracle, and a transgression of these laws; because nothing can be more contrary to nature than that the voice or command of a man should have such an influence. A miracle may be accurately defined, *a transgression of a law of nature by a particular volition of the Deity, or by the interposition of some invisible agent.* A miracle may either be discoverable by men or not. This alters not its nature and essence. The raising of a house or ship into the air is a visible miracle. The raising of a feather, when the wind wants ever so little of a force requisite for that purpose, is as real a miracle, though not so sensible with regard to us.

The passion of *surprise* and *wonder,* arising from miracles, being an agreeable emotion, gives a sensible tendency towards the belief of those events from which it is derived. And this goes so far that even those who cannot enjoy this pleasure immediately, nor can believe those miraculous events of which they are informed, yet love to partake of the satisfaction at secondhand or by rebound, and place a pride and delight in exciting the admiration of others.

With what greediness are the miraculous accounts of travelers received, their descriptions of sea and land monsters, their relations of wonderful adventures, strange men, and uncouth manners? But if the spirit of religion joins itself to the love of wonder, there is an end of common sense and human testimony in these circumstances loses all pretensions to authority. A religionist may be an enthusiast and imagine he sees what has no reality. He may know his narrative to be false and yet persevere in it with the best intentions in the world, for the sake of promoting so holy a cause. Or even where this delusion does not have place, vanity, excited by so strong a temptation, operates on him more powerfully than on the rest of mankind in any other circumstances, and self-interest with equal force. His auditors may not have and commonly do not have sufficient judgment to canvass his evidence. What judgment they have, they renounce by principle in these sublime and mysterious subjects. Or if they were ever so willing to employ it, passion and a heated imagination disturb the regularity of its operations. Their credulity increases his impudence and his impudence overpowers their credulity. . . .

The many instances of forged miracles and prophecies and supernatural events, which, in all ages, have either been detected by contrary evidence or which detect themselves by their absurdity, prove sufficiently the strong propensity of mankind to the extraordinary and the marvelous and ought reasonably to beget a suspicion against all relations of this kind. . . .

Thirdly, it forms a strong presumption against all supernatural and miraculous relations that they are observed chiefly to abound among ignorant and barbarous nations; or if a civilized people has ever given admission to any of them that people will be found to have received them from ignorant and barbarous ancestors, who transmitted them with that inviolable sanction and authority which always attend received opinions. When we peruse the first histories of all nations, we are apt to imagine ourselves transported into some new world where the whole frame of nature is disjointed and every element performs its operations in a different manner from what it does at present. Battles, revolutions, pestilence, famine, and death are never the effect of those natural causes which we experience. Prodigies, omens, oracles, judgments quite obscure the few natural events that are intermingled with them. But as the former grow thinner every page, in proportion as we advance nearer the enlightened ages, we soon learn that there is nothing mysterious or supernatural in the case, but that all proceeds from the usual propensity of mankind towards the marvelous, and that, though this inclination may at intervals receive a check from sense and learning, it can never be thoroughly extirpated from human nature. . . .

I may add, as a *fourth* reason which diminishes the authority of prodigies, that there is no testimony for any, even those which have not been expressly detected, that is not opposed by an infinite number of witnesses, so that not only the miracle destroys the credit of testimony, but the testimony destroys itself. To make this the better understood, let us consider that in matters of religion whatever is different is contrary and that it is impossible the religions of ancient Rome, of Turkey, of Siam, and of China should all of them be established on any solid foundation. Every miracle, therefore, pretended to have been wrought in any of these religions (and all of them abound in miracles), as its direct scope is to establish the particular system to which it is attributed, so it has the same force, though more indirectly, to overthrow every other system. In destroying a rival system, it likewise destroys the credit of those miracles on which that system was established, so that all the prodigies of different religions are to be regarded as contrary facts and the evidences of these prodigies, whether weak or strong, as opposite to each other. According to this method of reasoning, when we believe any miracle of Mahomet or his successors, we have for our warrant the testimony of a few barbarous Arabians. And, on the other hand, we are to regard the authority of Titus Livius [Livy], Plutarch, Tacitus, and, in short, of all the authors and witnesses, Greek, Chinese, and Roman Catholic, who have related any miracle in their particular religion—I say, we are to regard their testimony in the same light as if they had mentioned that Mahometan miracle and had in express terms contradicted it with the same certainty as they have for the miracle they relate. This argument may appear over subtle and refined, but is not in reality different from the reasoning of a judge who supposes that the credit of two witnesses maintaining a crime against anyone is destroyed by the testimony of two others who affirm him to have been two hundred leagues distant at the same instant when the crime is said to have been committed. . . .

There surely never was a greater number of miracles ascribed to one person than those which were lately said to have been wrought in France upon the tomb of Abbé Paris, the famous Jansenist, with whose sanctity the people were so long deluded. The curing of the sick, giving hearing to the deaf and sight to the blind, were everywhere talked of as the usual effects of that holy sepulcher. But what is more extraordinary, many of the miracles were immediately proved upon the spot, before judges of unquestioned integrity, attested by witnesses of credit and distinction, in a learned age, and on the most eminent theater that is now in the world. Nor is this all: A relation of them was published and dispersed everywhere, nor were the *Jesuits,* though a learned body supported by the civil magistrate and determined enemies to those opinions in whose favor the miracles were said to have been wrought, ever able distinctly to refute or detect them. Where shall we find such a number of circumstances agreeing to the corroboration of one fact? And what have we to oppose to such a cloud of witnesses but the absolute impossibility or miraculous nature of the events which they relate? And this, surely, in the eyes of all reasonable people, will alone be regarded as a sufficient refutation. . . .

Upon the whole, then, it appears that no testimony for any kind of miracle has ever amounted to a probability, much less to a proof; and that, even supposing it amounted to a proof, it would be opposed by another proof derived from the very nature of the fact which it would endeavor to establish. It is experience only which gives authority to human testimony and it is the same experience which assures us of the laws of nature. When, therefore, these two kinds of experience are contrary, we have nothing to do but subtract the one from the other and embrace an opinion either on one side or the other with that assurance which arises from the remainder. But according to the principle here explained, this subtraction with regard to all popular religions amounts to an entire annihilation and, therefore, we may establish it as a maxim that no human testimony can have such force as to prove a miracle and make it a just foundation for any such system of religion.

I beg the limitations here made may be remarked, when I say that a miracle can never be proved so as to be the foundation of a system of religion. For I admit that otherwise there may possibly be miracles or violations of the usual course of nature of such a kind as to admit of proof from human testimony; though perhaps it will be impossible to find any such in all the records of history. Thus, suppose all authors, in all languages, agree that from the first of January 1600 there was a total darkness over the whole earth for eight days; suppose that the tradition of this extraordinary event is still strong and lively among the people—that all travelers who return from foreign countries bring us accounts of the same tradition without the least variation or contradiction—it is evident that our present philosophers, instead of doubting the fact, ought to receive it as certain and ought to search for the causes from which it might be derived. The decay, corruption, and dissolution of nature is an event rendered probable by so many analogies that any phenomenon which seems to have a tendency towards that catastrophe comes within the reach of human testimony, if that testimony is very extensive and uniform.

But suppose that all the historians who treat of England should agree that on the first of January 1600, Queen Elizabeth died; that both before and after her death she was seen by her physicians and the whole court, as is usual with persons of her rank; that her successor was acknowledged and proclaimed by the parliament; and that, after being interred a month, she again appeared, resumed the throne, and governed England for three years—I must confess that I should be surprised at the concurrence of so many odd circumstances, but should not have the least inclination to believe so miraculous an event. I should not doubt of her pretended death and of those other public circumstances that followed it; I should only assert it to have been pretended, and that it neither was nor possibly could be real. You would in vain object to me the difficulty and almost impossibility of deceiving the world in an affair of such consequence; the wisdom and solid judgment of that renowned queen, with the little or no advantage which she could reap from so poor an artifice—all this might astonish me, but I would still reply that the knavery and folly of men are such common phenomena that I should rather believe the most extraordinary events to arise from their concurrence than admit of so signal a violation of the laws of nature.

But should this miracle be ascribed to any new system of religion, men in all ages have been so much imposed on by ridiculous stories of that kind that this very circumstance would be a full proof of a cheat and sufficient, with all men of sense, not only to make them reject the fact, but even reject it without further examination. Though the Being to whom the miracle is ascribed is in this case Almighty, it does not, upon that account, become a whit more probable, since it is impossible for us to know the attributes or actions of such a Being otherwise than from the experience which we have of his productions in the usual course of nature. This still reduces us to past observation and obliges us to compare the instances of the violation of truth in the testimony of men with those of the violation of the laws of nature by miracles, in order to judge which of them is most likely and probable. As the violations of truth are more common in the testimony concerning religious miracles than in that concerning any other matter of fact, this must diminish very much the authority of the former testimony and make us form a general resolution, never to lend any attention to it, with whatever specious pretense it may be covered. . . .

What we have said of miracles may be applied without any variation to prophecies; and, indeed, all prophecies are real miracles and as such only can be admitted as proofs of any revelation. If it did not exceed the capacity of human nature to foretell future events, it would be absurd to employ any prophecy as an argument for a divine mission or authority from heaven. So that, upon the whole, we may conclude that the Christian religion not only was at first attended with miracles, but even at this day cannot be believed by any reasonable person without one. Mere reason is insufficient to convince us of its veracity. And whoever is moved by faith to assent to it is conscious of a continued miracle in his own person which subverts all the principles of his understanding and gives him a determination to believe what is most contrary to custom and experience.

STUDY QUESTIONS

1. How does Hume define *miracle?* See Hume's footnotes 1 and 2.
2. *Is it coherent to speak of a "violation of a law of nature"? After all, if there is a violation, how can we speak of a law? (The problem was discussed in the introduction to this chapter.)
3. What method does Hume propose for evaluating reports of (supposed) miracles?
4. *Is Hume attacking the view that miracles are possible? Or instead is he attacking only the view that we can ever *know* that a miracle has occurred? Explain.
5. Is Hume's willingness to accept the reports in his example of the prolonged total eclipse consistent with the lead principles of his essay? Explain. Why is the case of the eclipse different, in his opinion, from the case of Queen Elizabeth's reported death?
6. Famous British religious writer C. S. Lewis (1898–1963) criticized Hume as follows:

   > Now of course we must agree with Hume that if there is absolutely "uniform experience" against miracles, if in other words, they have never happened, why then they never have. Unfortunately we know the experience against them to be uniform only if we know that all the reports of them are false. And we can know all the reports to be false only if we know already that miracles have never

occurred. In fact, we are arguing in a circle. (*Miracles: A Preliminary Study* [New York: Simon & Schuster, 1996], 134)

Explain what circle Lewis has in mind. Do you agree with the criticism? Why or why not?

7. *Reflecting on your own experience, do you agree with Hume that human beings like to believe in extraordinary events? You might consider such things as conspiracy theories and reports of the paranormal.
8. *Hume rejects reports of the miracles in France at the tomb of the Abbé Paris, denying that the events reported ever occurred. Alternatively, however, he could have accepted the occurrence of the events but suggested that they had a natural explanation. Would such an approach be justified, in your opinion? Why or why not?
9. *Do you agree with Hume that the reports of miracles claimed in one religion destroy the evidence for miracles claimed in another religion? Why or why not?
10. *Some interpreters maintain that Hume objects only to using reports of miracles as the foundation of a religion, not to believing in miracles per se. Explain what difference this distinction might make to the assessment of miracle reports. What evidence can you find in Hume's essay for this interpretation?
11. *(For students familiar with the main points of Hume's philosophy.) In his *Treatise of Human Nature* and *Enquiry Concerning Human Understanding,* Hume denied that there is any logically convincing way of getting from past experiences of sequences in nature to a belief that nature is uniform. In what way does "Of Miracles" seem inconsistent with that thesis? How can "Of Miracles" be reconciled with his denial that **inductive** reasoning can be justified logically?
12. *Would the availability of photographs and videotape affect Hume's argument? Why or why not?

READING 6.10

Of "Of Miracles"

Peter van Inwagen

Contemporary philosopher Peter van Inwagen (Notre Dame) focuses on Hume's contention that we should not accept a report that is "contrary to experience." This would imply, van Inwagen says, that no one should have accepted the first reports that someone had run the four-minute mile, that someone had climbed Mount Everest, and that Lindbergh had flown across the Atlantic without a copilot. For this reason, van Inwagen rejects Hume's argument.

. . . What, exactly, is the conclusion of the central argument of "Of Miracles"? It is a commonplace that Hume's conclusion is not **ontological:** He does not claim to show that there are no miracles. His conclusion is **epistemological.** But it is not that one should not believe that there are miracles. It is not so general as that. It has to do with the attitude one should take toward any (supposed, putative) report of a miracle one might encounter. It is something like this: If one hears a report of a miracle, one should not believe it (or one should believe it only in very special circumstances, circumstances so special that no one has in fact ever been in them). But this formulation of Hume's conclusion raises two important questions. First, what counts as a "report of a miracle"? Secondly, does "one should not believe it" mean "one should reject it" or "one should refrain from accepting it"—or perhaps some third thing?

Let us say that a report of a miracle (or a miracle-report) is any narrative, presented as historical or factual, such that (a) it does not follow logically from that narrative that a miracle has occurred, and (b) if the narrative were true, the only reasonable conclusion would be that at least one of the events it recounted was a miracle. The following story

> Jill was about to cross Sixth Avenue in New York when, all in an instant, she was miraculously translated to Sydney,

does not satisfy the terms of this definition, since it follows logically from the story that a miracle has occurred. Here, by way of contrast, are two stories that—whatever other features they may have—do not logically entail that a miracle has occurred:

> Jill was about to cross Sixth Avenue in New York when, without any sensation of motion, she suddenly found herself in Sydney.[1]
>
> And when he got into the boat his disciples followed him. And behold there arose a great storm on the sea, so that the boat was being swamped by the waves; but he was asleep. And they went and woke him, saying, "Save us, Lord, for we are perishing." And he said to them, "Why are you afraid, O men of little faith?" Then he rose and he rebuked the wind and the sea, and there was a great calm. And the men marveled, saying, "What manner of man is this that even the wind and the wave obey him?" (Matt. 8:23–27).[2]

Whether either of these two stories satisfies condition (b) in our definition of 'miracle-report'—and thereby qualifies as a miracle-report—is an epistemological question: Given that the story was true, would the only reasonable conclusion be that one of the events recounted in the story was a miracle?[3] It would be possible to argue, some no doubt have argued, that one should never believe of any story (unless it logically entails the occurrence of a miracle) that if that story is true, some of the events it recounts were miracles. One should rather believe (the argument might continue) that if the story is true, there is *some* explanation of the events it relates that is consistent with the laws of nature and this explanation is the correct explanation. (It is not hard to provide gestures at such explanations. Take the story of the stilling of the storm. This story could be embedded in a logically consistent science fiction novel according to which Christianity was "founded" by extraterrestrial beings as an adjunct to a project involving the manipulation of human history; it might be that, in the novel, all the "miracles" related in the New Testament actually happened—at least as far as appearances went—but were the products of an advanced technology rather than true miracles.)

I shall not attempt to answer the (instrinsically very interesting) question whether there in fact are any stories that satisfy the terms of the above definition of 'miracle-report,' for the cogency of Hume's **argument** does not depend on what the right

[1]It does not follow from our definition of 'miracle-report' that if a miracle-report is true, the people whose deeds and experiences are related in that report should believe that they have witnessed or been involved in a miracle. Consider the story of Jill's translation to Sydney (the second version, the version in which the translation is not described as miraculous). Suppose that we who hear the story should conclude that if the story is true, it recounts a miracle. (It follows from this supposition that the story is a miracle-report.) And suppose that the story *is* true. It does not follow that *Jill* should conclude from her experience that a miracle has happened. *We* know that if the story is true, Jill was translated instantaneously to Sydney. But it is not evident that Jill knows (or that she will presently come to know) that she has been translated instantaneously to Sydney—or even that it would be reasonable for her to believe that she has been. Perhaps she should believe that she is still in New York but dreaming or mad or that she was never in New York in the first place.

[2]To continue the theme of the previous note: It may or may not be true that we should believe that if the events related in this story really happened, at least one of them was a miracle. But if this is what we should believe, it does not follow that if these events really happened, those who witnessed them should have regarded at least one of them as a miracle. For one thing, it is extremely doubtful whether anyone in the first century A.D. possessed the concept expressed by the modern word 'miracle.'

[3]It will simplify the statement of our argument if in applying this definition we assume that 'miracle' and 'violation of a law of nature' are interchangeable. The equation of 'miracle' and 'violation' would be objectionable if my purpose were to defend the thesis that it was sometimes reasonable to believe that a miracle had occurred. This would be objectionable because it might be reasonable to believe that an event of type X had occurred and reasonable to believe that the occurrence of an event of type X required the violation of a law of nature, but *not* reasonable to believe that the "transgression of a law of nature" required by the occurrence of X was a consequence of a "particular volition of the Deity." My purpose, however, is to show that Hume's argument does not establish its conclusion, and not that this conclusion is false. And Hume's conclusion is (roughly) that it is unreasonable to believe any report of an event that would require a violation of a law—*whatever* the reason for that violation might be.

should proceed to "search for the causes whence it might be derived"—and hence they should presumably *not* regard the darkness as a miracle as the term is "accurately defined" ("A transgression of a law of nature by a particular volition of the Deity, or by the interposition of some invisible agent") but only in the loose and much weaker sense he has supplied: as a violation of the usual course of nature. He then argues that various (unspecified) analogies with known events suggest that a universal eight-day darkness "comes within the reach of human testimony, if that testimony be very extensive and uniform." And this statement implies that other imaginable events might not come within the reach of any testimony, however extensive and uniform. This argument is immediately followed by an example of such an imaginable event: the death and "resurrection" of Elizabeth I. It seems likely, therefore, that Hume would maintain that no imaginable human testimony could be such that its falsity would be what we are calling a very large contravention. And from this and our two epistemological premises, it follows that any imaginable miracle-report should be dismissed.

Even if I have not interpreted Hume correctly, however, even if, in his view, there are imaginable miracle-reports that should not be *dismissed,* it does not follow from this that any imaginable miracle-report should be *accepted.* (I do not believe that the story of King Alfred and the cakes is false—that is, I do not assent to the proposition that the story of King Alfred and the cakes is false. And I do not think that the probability of this story's being true is so low as to be insignificant. I therefore do not *dismiss* the story of Alfred and the cakes. But I certainly do not assent to the proposition that the story is *true*—and, in fact, I think it's very unlikely to be true.) And I think that it would certainly be Hume's position that none should be: Whether or not every imaginable miracle-report should be dismissed, no imaginable miracle-report should be accepted. No imaginable miracle-report should be accepted because a miracle-report, no matter what testimony might support it, is a very large contravention, and no testimonial evidence in favor of a very large contravention could be so good as to make it worthy of belief—even if it were possible for there to be testimonial evidence good enough to lead the judicious reasoner not to dismiss it. (In the most favorable possible case, there would be, as Hume says, "a mutual destruction of arguments.") And, of course, if we leave the realm of the merely imaginable and turn to the actual and historical, it is clear—this is the import of our "historical" premise—that Hume believes that all actual miracle-reports should be dismissed.[4]

Is Hume's argument, as I have reconstructed it, cogent? I think not. My defense of this judgment begins with an examination of E1, the premise that any miracle-report must be a very large contravention. That is, for any story about the past one might hear, one should refuse to make the following judgment about it:

> If that story is true, then some of the events it relates involve violations of the laws of nature,

unless one is also willing to make the following judgment:

> That story is contrary to my experience—and *as* contrary to my experience as the "shaman" story.

In order to evaluate this premise, we must turn to a question we have so far glossed over. What is it for a story to be "contrary to one's experience"? Hume generally writes as if the following were true: A story is contrary to one's experience if that story involves something's having the property F and the property G and one has observed many things having the property F and has observed that all of them had the **complement** of G. For example, on this account, a story about a man's returning from the dead is contrary to my experience owing simply to the fact that I have known of a very large number of people who have died and all of them have the property "not having returned from the dead." But this account of what it is for a story to be contrary to one's experience is

[4]Even the "memorable story related by Cardinal de Retz" and the accounts of those miracles "which were lately said to have been wrought in France upon the tomb of Abbé Paris. . . . " "And what have we [Hume asks after telling these two stories] to oppose to such a cloud of witnesses, but the absolute impossibility or miraculous nature of the events, which they relate." . . .

useless for Hume's purposes, since it will classify far too many stories as contrary to one's experience. Suppose for example, that I know of many visits that Tom has made to his mother over the past ten years; it is all but inevitable that if I hear a detailed account of his latest visit to her, this account will ascribe to this visit some property that all of the others lacked. And this will be true even if we do not "count" the *date* of the latest visit as a relevant property. It may, for example, be that the story I have been told of his latest visit includes the information that he arrived on her doorstep at 3:21 P.M. and that the comprehensive diary I have for some reason kept of his earlier visits reveals that on all the other occasions on which he has visited her he arrived at some other time. No doubt we could play a lengthy game of "**counterexample** and revision" with the above account of what it is for a story to be contrary to experience. But I do not know of any way of "improving" this account that will enable it to avoid consequences like the following: The first reports of someone's making a solo flight across the Atlantic or running a four-minute mile or reaching the summit of Mount Everest were contrary to the experience of those who heard them.

But might Hume not reply that these consequences are acceptable? Might he not argue that such reports would indeed be a *bit* contrary to the experience of those who heard them? Might he not go on to say, "But it would be *more* contrary to the experience of those who heard them if all the reports of these events were false, and that is why it was proper for those who heard the reports to believe them"? Perhaps so. But how, then, are we to understand the relevant notion of *degree* of contrariety? If I hear on Monday that Lindbergh has flown across the Atlantic without a copilot and on Tuesday that a rival has flown across the Atlantic without an aircraft, on what basis am I to judge that the second story is more contrary to my experience (is a larger contravention) than the first? My experience tells me that all previous transatlantic flights have involved an aircraft of some sort, but it also tells me that all previous transatlantic flights have involved two or more pilots. There simply do not seem to be any materials in the "property-complement" account of a story's being contrary to experience from which to construct an account of the concept of one story's being "more contrary to experience" than another is.

Let us consider an actual example (at least I believe it to be actual, although, unfortunately, I no longer remember where I heard or read it) of someone's applying the "property-complement" account of this concept. Thomas Jefferson was once told that in a museum in Cambridge (Massachusetts) there was exhibited a stone that had fallen from the sky. Jefferson declined to believe this story on the ground that although he had never known a stone to fall from the sky, he had often known a Yankee parson—the staff of Harvard College in those days comprised Congregational ministers—to prevaricate. (He had observed the sky on many occasions, and on each of those occasions, it had the property "not being the source of a falling stone"; he had observed many Yankee parsons making assertions, and on many of these occasions, the assertions had the property "being a lie." He concluded that stones falling from the sky were contrary to his experience and lying Yankee parsons were not.) Now even if Jefferson's statement about his experience of the New England clergy was something of an exaggeration, he was no doubt telling the truth when he said he had never known a stone to fall from the sky. But there were many, many things he had "never known" that he wouldn't have been disinclined to believe reports of, even reports from Yankee parsons. If he thought the story unlikely on the basis of his experience, it cannot have been simply because such a thing had never happened in his experience. If the story was indeed "contrary to his experience," it cannot have been simply because events of the type related in the story were not included in the totality of his experience to date. This observation might lead us to conclude that the "property-complement" account of an event's being contrary to experience must be replaced by some other account.

Was there *any* sense in which the story Jefferson was told was contrary to his experience? Well, suppose that Jefferson had fallen asleep like Rip van Winkle and had slept till the existence and nature of meteors was common knowledge. Suppose that, on awakening, he was given an encyclopedia article on the subject to read and had afterward received the testimony of several eminent (Virginian) astronomers that what the article said was true. Would he have been in a position to complain that his eighteenth-century experience was misleading—that it had somehow "told" him that stones never fell from the sky when stones in fact sometimes *do* fall from the sky? Certainly not. No doubt Descartes was wrong in holding that the testimony of experience was never false, but it does not seem to have testified falsely to Jefferson on this point. Experience may have testified to some persons at some points in history that the earth is at the center of the universe or that maggots are spontaneously generated in dung, but it has never testified to anyone that stones do not fall from the sky (or, for most people, that they do—not "directly," not otherwise than via the testimony of other people; for most people, "direct" experience has had nothing to say about whether stones fall from the sky). Although experience may have testified that if stones ever fall from the sky, their doing so is a very uncommon event, it has not testified that stones never fall from the sky.

It is very hard indeed to find a sense in which experience testifies in any direct or immediate sense that events of some sort never happen—or in which stories of events of some sort are contrary to experience. If direct, immediate experience testifies to anything (truly or falsely) its testimony seems to be essentially "positive": It testifies that events of certain sorts *do* happen. One might of course point out that it is *reasonable to believe* of events of various sorts that events of those sorts never happen, and that the reasonableness of such beliefs must ultimately be based on experience. Having made this observation, one might propose an account of what it is for a story to be "contrary to experience" that is based on what it is reasonable to believe. It would go something like this: A story is contrary to one's experience if that story involves the occurrence of events of sorts such that given one's experience at the time one hears the story, it is reasonable for one to believe that events of those sorts never happen—or perhaps that it is highly improbable that such events ever happen (or, more simply, a story is contrary to one's experience if, given one's experience at the time one hears the story, it is reasonable for one to believe that the story is false or is highly improbable). And one might go on to spell out the concept "more contrary to one's experience" in terms of its being more unreasonable to believe one proposition than another. (One might say that p is more contrary to one's experience than q just in the case that although what it is reasonable to believe, on the basis of one's experience, is that p and q are both false, one should also believe that if one or the other of them is, after all, true, it is q. Thus, or so I would judge, Calvin's story about the handprints on the sofa is "more contrary to experience" than my story about the mileage my Cadillac got, and the "shaman" story is "more contrary to experience" than the story of Sally's quick mastery of French.)

I think, however, that it is reasonably clear that this is not what Hume means by "contrary to experience" and "more contrary to experience." Whatever he means by these phrases and the related phrases he uses, he means something much more concrete, much more immediate than this. For Hume, if one judges that a story of a man's rising from the dead is "contrary to one's experience," the experience that the story is contrary to is one's experience of the dead's staying dead, not the totality of one's experience of the world to date. But at least in my view, what it is now *reasonable for me to believe* about men's rising from the dead must be based on pretty nearly the whole of my experience to date (e.g., those experiences that are relevant to the truth or falsity of the principles of thermodynamics and the truth or falsity of judgments about the historical reliability of the New Testament and the authority of the Church). In any case, if this is what "contrary to experience" and "more contrary to experience" mean, there seems to me to be no very compelling reason for anyone to accept E1.

It may be reasonable to believe that if the Matthean story of the stilling of the storm is historical, then a miracle, a violation of the laws of nature, occurred. I certainly think that this would be the reasonable conclusion to draw from the truth of the story. But I do not think that this story is, by the terms of the definition we are considering, at least as contrary to experience as the "shaman" story is. In fact, I think that the Matthean story is *true* (and, of course, I think I am being reasonable in thinking that it is true), and I think that anyone who heard and believed the "shaman" story and whose experience of the world was otherwise like mine would be very unreasonable indeed. I am not trying to convince you, the reader, that these epistemological judgments are correct. I am saying only that nowhere in "Of Miracles" do I find any reason to suppose they are not correct. Hume's argument, after all, is of this general form: *Because* certain propositions are contrary to experience—*very* contrary to experience—it is unreasonable to accept them. And it is, to say the least, very hard to see how an argument of this form could be cogent if 'contrary to experience' *means* 'unreasonable to believe.'

I can think of no other plausible sense that can be given to the phrase 'contrary to experience.' I conclude, provisionally, that Hume's argument is a failure, owing to the fact that there is no sense that can be given to 'contrary to experience' such that E1 is compelling when 'contrary to experience' is interpreted in that sense. It should be noted that I do not claim to have shown that anyone is ever justified in believing a miracle-report. Indeed, I do not even claim to have addressed this question. It is perfectly consistent with everything I have said to suppose that anyone who believed any story that could conceivably count as a miracle-report (such as the Matthean story of the stilling of the storm) would be wholly unreasonable. I claim to have shown only that the argument of "Of Miracles" (as I understand the argument) does not establish either this conclusion or any other negative conclusion about the reasonableness of accepting miracle-reports.

STUDY QUESTIONS

1. Explain the difference between the ontological and epistemological interpretations of Hume's position. Which interpretation does van Inwagen think is correct?
2. What difficulty does van Inwagen see in Hume's argument, using Hume's notion of an event being "contrary to experience"?
3. *Intuitively, we do not react the same to reports of Lindbergh's flying across the Atlantic without a copilot as we do to reports of Lindbergh's flying across the Atlantic without an aircraft. How might one distinguish between these cases and thereby perhaps rescue Hume from van Inwagen's objection? How might van Inwagen reply to this counter?
4. Do you think there is a difference between the situations of someone who thinks he or she has *seen* a miracle him- or herself and someone who hears a report of *someone else's* having seen a miracle? Why or why not?

READING 6.11

Miracles and Undetected Natural Causes

John Stuart Mill

In Reading 6.9, Hume emphasized the question of whether, when we hear a report of a miracle, we should believe that the reported event really happened. In Reading 6.11, John Stuart Mill stresses a different question, also touched upon by Hume: assuming the event happened, do we know that it has no natural explanation? Perhaps the event is due to an as yet unknown law of nature or a "hidden fact." Mill distinguishes between the situation of one who already believes in God and one who does not, pointing out that the former may have greater reason than the latter to think that God produced the event. Even then, argues Mill, the event would have to accord with what can reasonably be surmised about the ways of God. The problem with determining whether this accord obtains is that the believer must hold that not only events beneficial to people, but also events harmful to people, are consistent with God's workings. Mill suggests as well that, although a miracle can be tested by a challenge to repeat it, "recorded miracles were seldom or never put to this test."

[In the case of an alleged miracle,] the event is supposed not to have been produced at all through physical causation, while there is no direct evidence to connect it with any volition. The ground on which it is ascribed to a volition is only negative, because there is no other apparent way of accounting for its existence.

But in this merely speculative explanation there is always another hypothesis possible, viz., that the event may have been produced by physical causes, in a manner not apparent. It may either be due to a law of physical nature not yet known, or to the unknown presence of the conditions necessary for producing it according to some known law. Supposing even that the event, supposed to be miraculous, does not reach us through the uncertain medium of human testimony but rests on the direct evidence of our own senses; even then so long as there is no direct evidence of its production by a divine volition, like that we have for the production of bodily movements by human volitions—so long, therefore, as the miraculous character of the event is but an inference from the supposed inadequacy of the laws of physical nature to account for it,—so long will the hypothesis of a natural origin for the phenomenon be entitled to preference over that of a supernatural one. The commonest principles of sound judgment forbid us to suppose for any effect a cause of which we have absolutely no experience, unless all those of which we have experience are ascertained to be absent. Now there are few things of which we have more frequent experience than of physical facts which our knowledge does not enable us to account for, because they depend either on laws which observation, aided by science, has not yet brought to light, or on facts the presence of which in the particular case is unsuspected by us. Accordingly when we hear of a prodigy we always, in these modern times, believe that if it really occurred it was neither the work of God nor of a demon, but the consequence of some unknown natural law or of some hidden fact. Nor is either of these suppositions precluded when, as in the case of a miracle properly so called, the wonderful event seemed to depend upon the will of a human being. It is always possible that there may be at work some undetected law of nature which the wonder-worker may have acquired, consciously or unconsciously, the power of calling into action; or that the wonder may have been wrought (as in the truly extraordinary feats of jugglers) by the employment, unperceived by us, of ordinary laws: which also need not necessarily be a case of voluntary deception; or, lastly, the event may have had no connection with the volition at all, but the coincidence between them may be the effect of craft or accident, the miracle-worker having seemed or affected to produce by his will that which was already about to take place, as if one were to command an eclipse of the sun at the moment when one knew by astronomy that an eclipse was on the point of taking place. In a case of this description, the miracle might be tested by a challenge to repeat it; but it is worthy of remark, that recorded miracles were seldom or never put to this test. No miracle-worker seems ever to have made a *practice* of raising the dead: that and the other most signal of the miraculous operations are reported to have been performed only in one or a few isolated cases, which may have been either cunningly selected cases, or accidental coincidences. There is, in short, nothing to exclude the supposition that every alleged miracle was due to natural causes: and as long as that supposition remains possible, no scientific observer, and no man of ordinary practical judgment, would assume by conjecture a cause which no reason existed for supposing to be real, save the necessity of accounting for something which is sufficiently accounted for without it.

Were we to stop here, the case against miracles might seem to be complete. But on further inspection it will be seen that we cannot, from the above considerations, conclude absolutely that the miraculous theory of the production of a phenomenon ought to be at once rejected. We can conclude only that no extraordinary powers which have ever been alleged to be exercised by any human being over nature, can be evidence of miraculous gifts to any one to whom the existence of a supernatural Being, and his interference in human affairs, is not already a *vera causa* [true cause, i.e., true position]. The existence of God cannot possibly be proved by miracles, for unless a God is already recognized, the apparent miracle can always be accounted for on a more probable hypothesis than that of the interference of a Being of whose very existence it is supposed to be the sole evidence. Thus far Hume's argument is conclusive. But it is far from being equally so when the existence of a Being who created the present order of Nature, and, therefore, may well be thought to have power to modify it, is accepted as a fact, or even as a probability resting on independent evidence. Once admit a God, and the production by his direct volition of an effect which in any case owed its origin to his creative will, is no longer a purely arbitrary hypothesis to account for the fact, but must be reckoned with as a serious possibility. . . .

. . . To those who already believe in supernatural power, the supernatural hypothesis may appear more probable than the natural one; but only if it accords with what we know or reasonably surmise respecting the ways of the supernatural agent. Now all that we know, from the evidence of nature, concerning his ways, is in harmony with the natural theory and repugnant to the supernatural. There is, therefore, a vast preponderance of probability against a miracle, to counterbalance which would require a very extraordinary and indisputable congruity in the supposed miracle and its circumstances with something which we conceive ourselves to know, or to have grounds for believing, with regard to the divine attributes.

This extraordinary congruity is supposed to exist when the purpose of the miracle is extremely beneficial to mankind, as when it serves to accredit some highly important belief. The goodness of God, it is supposed, affords a high degree of antecedent probability that he would make an exception to his general rule of government, for so excellent a purpose. For reasons, however, which have already been entered into,[1] any inference drawn by us from the goodness of God to what he has or has not actually done, is to the last degree precarious. If we reason directly from God's goodness to positive facts, no misery, nor vice nor crime ought to exist in the world. . . .

STUDY QUESTIONS

1. What is Mill's objection to accepting claims of miracles? How does this objection differ from Hume's main one?
2. According to Mill, why is the believer in a different situation than the nonbeliever with regard to belief in miracles?
3. At the end of the selection, what problem does Mill pose to the believer with regard to establishing that a certain event is due to God's activity?
4. Explain Mill's rationale for the requirement that a miracle be repeatable.* Do you agree with this requirement? Why or why not? Do you know of reported miracles that satisfy this condition?

[1][Elsewhere in the work—Ed.]

READING 6.12

Mill's Challenge to Belief in Miracles

David Johnson

Mill held we should not infer to a cause of which we have no prior experience until it has been ascertained that all those causes of which we have experience are absent. David Johnson (Yeshiva University) replies, however, that, if we were to follow Mill's approach, the postulation of neutrinos by physicist Enrico Fermi would not have been justified; yet clearly Fermi was *justified in believing in neutrinos. Johnson next argues, using an example of a giant billiard table, that we can infer a supernatural explanation of an event even if the event is not repeatable.*

. . . Mill claims that the "commonest principles of sound judgment forbid us to suppose for any effect a cause of which we have absolutely no experience, unless all those of which we have experience are ascertained to be absent." But, given what he says earlier in the passage, "ascertained to be absent" must be taken in rather a strong sense, since it is allowed that the effect "may either be due to a law of physical nature not yet known, or to the unknown presence of the conditions necessary for producing it according to some known law." But how then is this "principle of sound judgment" followed even in science? When Enrico Fermi (following Wolfgang Pauli) postulated the existence of "a cause of which we [had] absolutely no experience"—the neutrino (the "little neutral one")—to explain a certain effect (Beta decay), how had he "ascertained" that the then familiar particles were not *somehow* producing the effect by way of "a law of physical nature not yet known"? How is it that he rightly postulated the existence of an otherwise unknown cause, rather than postulate the existence of otherwise unknown *powers* of the familiar particles? Fermi was of course perfectly justified, but it will be very difficult for Mill to explain why. In science, there are always logically possible alternative hypotheses for explaining any effect, especially if we are given a free hand vis-à-vis "a law of physical nature not yet known, or . . . the unknown presence of the conditions necessary for producing it according to some known law." The explainer who is free with *law* and free with *conditions* is free indeed. So how will we ever get to the neutrino?

Of course, Fermi's explanation was somehow *better* than the (ever-present) logically possible alternatives, in a way philosophers of science find hard to specify. It was *simpler,* or more *natural* (which of course does not mean "natural" in Mill's sense) than its gerrymandered competitors (which were equally "natural" in Mill's sense). But if considerations of "simplicity" or of "naturalness" (or, as one sometimes hears, of "beauty" or "the ring of truth"), whatever these may mean exactly, can give preference to one scientific explanation over (at least) its gerrymandered competitors, why might not such considerations give preference to a theological or supernatural explanation over its gerrymandered **naturalistic** competitors? When Mill says that the "existence of God cannot possibly be proved by miracles," this is, taken in a certain sense, perhaps trivially true, given what Mill means by 'miracle'. But then the claim is hardly significant. More to the point is the question of whether the existence of God can be proved by miracles (in my sense)—by those extraordinary physical occurrences such as the parting of or walking on a sea, or the reappearance, vigorously alive, of those who recently had been crucified, spear-pierced, and entombed—the *happening* of which Mill has given us no reason at all to dispute. Why might not the best explanation of such a miracle be a theological or supernatural explanation? Mill needs to say why this *cannot* be so, without invoking over-strong and implausible and unsupported "principles of sound judgment."

For my own part I do not see why the same sort of considerations (of "simplicity," "naturalness," etc.) which properly lead one to explain a certain physical effect in terms of the existence of an otherwise unknown entity, a neutrino (rather than in terms of unknown logically possible powers of familiar particles), *might* not also properly lead one to explain a certain physical effect in terms of the existence of an otherwise unknown intelligent and powerful entity, a deity (rather than in terms of unknown logically possible powers of natural objects). As for Mill's remark that a miracle "might be tested by a challenge to repeat it," I don't see how *repetition* is relevant to the point now at issue. Repetition, if relevant to anything, is relevant to the question of the reality of the effect, not (in any obvious way) to its explanation. But the reality of the *physical effect* is at present being taken for granted. (If Mill is here taking up again the earlier discussion, and now wants to claim that testimony to unrepeated extraordinary physical effects should not be given credence, such a claim is in need of the very sort of cogent Humean argument which we have not found in Mill.) If the claim is that, in the absence of repetition, *coincidence* is a logically possible "explanation" of the effect, that (if it is an explanation at all) remains logically possible after ever so many repetitions. If the claim is that, in the absence of repetition, coincidence must always be at least as plausible an explanation of the effect as is any supernatural explanation, that claim wants an argument.

Perhaps Mill is assuming (as *perhaps* Hume holds in the *Dialogues Concerning Natural Religion*—but see the remarkable third dialogue and the rejoinder there by Cleanthes, which Philo never answers) that a *single, unique* physical event can never, as it were, demand an explanation other than coincidence. This is far from being obvious. Suppose that in England there is an enormous billiard table, ten thousand million square feet in area. Racked up on this table in random order are one thousand million billiard balls labeled from '1' to '1,000,000,000.' There is also a massive cue ball and an enormous and powerful "cue stick," with which the balls will be "broken." Suppose that for political or financial reasons this can only be done once. So there is a single physical event, unique of its kind: the Big Break. Suppose, further, that the table's surface is divided into ten thousand million little squares, each one square foot in area, and each bearing the name of some natural number from 0 to 9, with one thousand million of each of these ten kinds, and these randomly distributed over the surface. The Big Break occurs. We find that the ball labeled '1' lands on a square labeled '1', the ball labeled '2' lands on a square labeled '4', the ball labeled '3' lands on a square labeled '1', the ball labeled '4' lands on a square labeled '5', and so forth, spelling out the first one thousand million digits of π after the decimal point. Would not the Big Break, though unique, cry out for some explanation other than coincidence?

My second remark about the Mysterious Passage [the passage under discussion —Ed.] will be brief. It is just a little story. Recall the account from the fourteenth chapter of *Matthew,* about Jesus walking on the sea. Suppose that Mill and I have gone back in time and are sitting discreetly in the boat. In the fourth watch of the night comes Jesus walking on the sea. Peter goes out, takes a few steps, and then begins to sink. Jesus rescues him and the two get into the boat; then some or all of the disciples say to Jesus, "Surely you are the Son of God." I say to Mill that I quite agree with them. Mill then turns to me and says: "Look, whatever these ignorant and incompetent people may say, you—as a man of modern times—should see that you have no evidence at all for this theological claim. You are overlooking the possibility that this business of walking on the sea was the result of conspiring unknown natural circumstances, perhaps a natural *coincidence* of some sort; or perhaps this wonder-worker cunningly played on known natural laws, as in the truly extraordinary feats of jugglers."

STUDY QUESTIONS

1. How does Johnson justify our positing causes of which we have no prior experience before we ascertain that "all those [causes] of which we have experience are absent"?
2. Explain Johnson's objection to Mill's repeatibility requirement.
3. *Under what conditions do you think Johnson would believe that a miracle has occurred? Under what conditions would he reject such a report?
4. *In footnote 1 of the introduction to this chapter, we noted that sometimes an event might be described as a "miracle" even when it has a natural explanation—namely, when the *timing* of events in the context seems remarkable. Is it ever rational to attribute remarkable coincidences of this sort to the intervention of a supernatural being? Why or why not? The example we gave in the introduction was of a train stopping just before hitting a child on the tracks (the driver suddenly faints due to natural causes that are unrelated to the child being there, activating the brakes). You might find other useful points and examples in the selection by Johnson, in Hume's essay [Reading 6.9, footnote 2] and in selections 4.9–4.11.

READING 6.13

Miracles and the Shroud of Turin

Stephen Griffith

Stephen Griffith's article examines a real-life instance of a purported miracle. The Shroud of Turin is a cloth that bears the image of a crucified man and is thought by some to be the burial shroud of Jesus. It seems that the image could have arisen out of (1) human artistry, (2) the transfer of an image to the cloth by a crucified corpse, or (3) supernatural means. Griffith (Lycoming College) maintains that the first two possibilities are unlikely, given the current state of evidence. Nevertheless, he does not think we should conclude that the explanation of the image definitely is supernatural. There is no direct evidence that it is, and the state of the evidence may change. Also, perhaps the event is scientifically inexplicable but is not a miracle. Scientific evidence, therefore, cannot provide proof that the shroud is Jesus's burial shroud and that the image arose by supernatural means.

. . . The Shroud of Turin is a sizable piece of linen cloth which bears the image of a recently crucified man. It is known to have been in existence since at least 1354 A.D. and is believed by some to be the actual burial shroud of Jesus of Nazareth. Because Jesus died more than nineteen centuries ago, public interest in the Shroud waned significantly when it was announced that carbon-14 dating tests conducted by three supposedly reliable laboratories had indicated that the Shroud was only a little more than six centuries old. Prior to the carbon dating tests, however, scientists had subjected the Shroud to numerous non-destructive tests and measurements in an effort to determine both the nature and the origin of the image which it bears. For most of these scientists, and for others who understand the implications of their work, the results of the carbon dating tests simply deepen the mystery of the image on the Shroud.

Marvin Mueller is a research physicist at the Los Alamos National Laboratory. He is familiar with many of the visual characteristics of the image on the Shroud, but unfamiliar with the results of many of the scientific tests performed on it. Even before the carbon dating tests were done, Mueller was convinced that the Shroud was a medieval work of art. In a published paper, he says the following:

> There are only three classes of possibilities for the image formation: by human artifice, through natural processes transferring the image to the linen from a real crucified corpse, or by supernatural means.[1]

As a scientist, he immediately rejects the possibility that the image was produced by supernatural means, because he believes that if we take this possibility seriously, "all scientific discussion and all rational discourse must perforce cease." He then goes on to say that, based on the visible characteristics of the image itself, "natural processes . . . can be ruled out *definitively* [his italics] . . . ," presumably on theoretical grounds of an extremely general kind. In other words, he argues for the first leg of his trichotomy, i.e., for the claim that the Shroud is a work of art, primarily by rejecting the other two. The problem is that the STURP scientists[2] who have worked most closely with the Shroud, are almost unanimous in rejecting any possibility of human artifice, simply because the best interpretations of the substantial

[1]Marvin Mueller, "The Shroud of Turin: A Critical Appraisal," *The Skeptical Inquirer* VI, 3, (Spring 1982): 27.

[2]The team of scientists I am referring to here is a loosely organized group of forty scientists who eventually began referring to themselves as the Shroud of Turin Research Project, or STURP for short. I shall henceforth refer to them collectively as the "STURP scientists."

data which they have collected count strongly against this possibility.

Let us now suppose that the trichotomy suggested by Mueller is legitimate, as it certainly seems to be. Let us further suppose that Mueller can justify, on scientific grounds, his rejection of the possibility that the image on the Shroud was produced naturally without human artifice. Finally, let us suppose that the STURP scientists can justify, again on scientific grounds, their rejection of the possibility that the image was produced by human artifice. In other words, let us suppose that we have strong scientific grounds for rejecting both the possibility that the image is the result of human artifice and the possibility that it is the result of natural processes not involving human artifice. Would we then be justified in regarding the Shroud image as "scientifically inexplicable," and would we then have strong scientific grounds for accepting the third leg of Mueller's trichotomy and believing that the image was produced by supernatural means?

Let us begin by examining Mueller's trichotomy more carefully. Although Mueller talks as if he is referring simply to different sorts of processes (of image formation), it is clear from the context that he is thinking primarily of *explanations*. But this presupposes that there are objective facts here which need to be explained. Is this really true?

With regard to the image on the Shroud, it is clear that it is not a purely subjective phenomenon like the visions of Mary and Jesus often reported by believers. Although faint, it is nonetheless visible to the naked eye for normally sighted human beings and can be photographed using any standard (and many non-standard) photographic techniques. It is, in short, a completely objective feature of the cloth. Moreover, although it is logically possible that the image is just an "accidental" feature of the cloth in the same way that outcroppings of rock sometimes look like human faces in profile, this possibility does not deserve serious consideration in the case of the Shroud. The image, when examined closely, is simply too anatomically accurate and too detailed to be "explained away" in this manner. It would thus appear that the existence of the image on the Shroud of Turin is an objective fact which, like any other physical phenomenon which cannot be regarded as due simply to chance, must have an explanation.

We must now ask whether Mueller's trichotomy exhausts all possibilities of explanation. Given the common understanding of the term "supernatural," it is clear that all possible explanations must be either supernatural or naturalistic.[3] Ignoring the possibility of a supernatural explanation for the moment, it would seem that any naturalistic explanation must explain the nature and origin of the image completely in terms of such things as the substance(s) of which it is now composed and the various purely physical events involving the Shroud which have occurred throughout its natural history. Assuming, as we surely must, that the cloth itself antedates the image, there are only two possibilities concerning the composition of the image itself. One possibility is that it consists of a colored substance which has adhered to the cloth in just those places necessary to account for the image which we see. The other possibility is that some physical process has transformed certain fibers of the cloth itself in such a way as to discolor them, thus producing the image. To explain the image is thus, in the former case, to explain how the colored substance got onto the Shroud, and in the latter case, to explain how the fibers were transformed. If a human artist initiated either of these processes in order to produce the image, the Shroud is a work of art, and otherwise not. But since we are justified in assuming that the image is an objective and non-accidental feature of the Shroud, the only conceivable hypothesis concerning image-formation in the absence of human artifice would surely be one involving interaction between the Shroud and a

[3]Although Mueller does not explain what he means by the term "supernatural," it is clear from the context that he would regard a "supernatural explanation" of a physical event as an explanation in terms of agents or entities which are not part of the physical universe but which nevertheless have physical effects within the physical universe. An explanation in terms of the activities of "extraterrestrials," i.e., physical beings from some distant part of the physical universe, would thus not be considered supernatural; whereas an explanation in terms of the activities of such beings as God or angels (fallen or otherwise) would be.

human body. Thus all naturalistic explanations are either explanations in terms of human artifice or explanations involving such interaction, and Mueller's trichotomy is established.

Initially, it seems overwhelmingly probable that the Shroud is a work of art. After all, there is a clear sense in which the image on the Shroud is a two-dimensional image of a three-dimensional entity, and there are extraordinarily few examples of such things which are not due to artistic endeavor of some sort.[4] Jesus has probably been artistically depicted more often and in a greater variety of ways than any other figure in Western civilization, and the fact that various bodily features, such as wounds, correspond to the events described in the Biblical narrative can readily be explained in terms of the intentions of an informed artist. Besides, no other naturalistic explanation for something like the image springs readily to mind.

This helps to explain why most people, like Mueller, are so quick to assume that the Shroud is a work of art. It also explains why the STURP team began by attempting to confirm or disconfirm this hypothesis, rather than the naturalistic hypothesis rejected by Mueller. In particular, they initially assumed that the image on the Shroud was a painting and attempted, by means of various tests and measurements, to determine how it was painted and with what. As previously mentioned, this hypothesis initially seemed by far the most probable, but the **epistemic** probability of a given hypothesis being true depends on what else we know or have good reason to believe. As it turns out in the case of the Shroud, most of the available scientific data concerning the image on the Shroud of Turin tend to disconfirm the hypothesis that it is a work of art, and nearly all of the STURP scientists have essentially ruled out this hypothesis. They do not claim to have *proven* that the Shroud is not a work of art. Their claim is rather that this hypothesis has been shown to be highly improbable.[5]

How can an hypothesis which is *prima facie* the most probable become highly improbable? It would be beyond the scope of this paper to attempt to cover all of the details of the scientific investigation which leads to this conclusion, but some of the more accessible details can be readily given. In the first place, the clearly visible details of the image itself raise suspicions as to why an artist would have created it with the features that it has. It consists, for example, of both a dorsal and a ventral image arranged longwise on the cloth and placed head to head, a most peculiar artistic rendering of a human figure. In the second place, the image has all the shading and contrast of a "negative" image, as if the Shroud were a photographic negative waiting to be developed, and we know that the image was in existence many centuries before the invention of photography. Why would a medieval or classical artist create a "photographically negative" image?

The results of the scientific tests, however, are by far the most telling evidence against the hypothesis that the Shroud is a work of art. Various tests, for example, indicate the presence of blood, probably human, on the Shroud. More precisely, although there is no single scientific test which is definitive for the presence of blood, what appears to be blood on the Shroud gives a positive reading on twelve different standard tests for blood. This implies that the substance on the Shroud which appears to be blood is either blood or a mixture of twelve other substances, each of which gives a positive reading for one of the twelve different tests.[6] The likelihood that these twelve substances would be mixed together deliberately by an artist or occur together naturally in some sort of artistic medium is vanishingly small, so

[4]The only example that comes readily to mind is the "permanent shadows" of physical objects which appeared on walls as a result of the atomic bombs dropped on Hiroshima and Nagasaki at the end of World War II. Even in this case, the "shadows" were the result of deliberate human action, but at least they were not one of the intended results.

[5]I once asked one of the STURP physicists what he would conclude if the carbon dating (which had not yet been done at that time) indicated a fourteenth century origin for the Shroud, and he said that he would conclude that someone had been crucified and wrapped in the Shroud in the fourteenth century. I took this to be a measure of his confidence that the image had a naturalistic but non-artistic origin.

[6]John H. Heller and Alan D. Adler, "Blood on the Shroud of Turin," *Applied Optics* 19, 16, (14 August 1980): 2742 – 2744.

if what appear to be blood stains on the Shroud were put there by an artist, the artist must have used real blood. Moreover, tests have shown that some of the blood found on the Shroud is pre-mortem blood, and some, especially that found on the area of the cloth corresponding to the side wound on the image (supposedly from the spear wound inflicted by one of the executioners), is post-mortem blood. In addition, x-ray fluoroscopy indicates the presence of serum albumin on the Shroud in those areas of the image where one would expect to find it if the ostensible blood stains on the Shroud were in fact due to wounds on a human body. If the Shroud is simply a work of art, the artist must have applied not only both pre-mortem and post-mortem blood, but also serum albumin in the appropriate places on the Shroud. The application of serum albumin by an artist would be especially remarkable, in view of the fact that it is a colorless liquid which remains invisible and leaves physical effects visible only under ultraviolet light. Finally, it has been determined that the blood on the Shroud was there before the image was.[7] If both the apparent bloodstains and the image on the Shroud were put there by an artist, he or she must have begun by putting blood and serum on the Shroud in various locations with the idea of subsequently creating the image—a very unlikely scenario.

With regard to the image itself, as opposed to the apparent bloodstains, there are even greater difficulties for the hypothesis that it was created by an artist. Microscopic examination reveals that there are no brushstrokes, and no capillary action within the fibrils of the cloth (which would necessarily have occurred if any liquid medium had been used to create the image). Moreover, no pigment or other substance of an appropriate kind and of sufficient amount to account for the image was detected. This implies not only that the image is not a painting or drawing of any kind, but also that it is not a rubbing, since this would also require that some sort of colored particles adhere to the cloth. The scientific investigation of the image shows that it is extraordinarily superficial and consists of nothing but submicroscopic oxidized cellulose fibrils. In other words, the image was produced when some physical process slightly oxidized certain fibrils. The problem is that there is no known physical process sufficiently subject to human control to enable an artist to create such an image. The application of a liquid oxidizing agent would show the effects of capillary action, even more than most liquid artistic media, and the use of a solid would have left some residue and could not have been controlled well enough to produce such a precise image. Finally, although various forms of radiant energy are capable of oxidizing cloth, none of them can be controlled well enough by human beings to produce a precise image like that on the Shroud. This seems to exhaust the possibilities of artistic creation, but there is still at least one more bit of scientific data indicating that the image cannot be a work of art.

The most intriguing scientific data pertaining to the image on the Shroud is that obtained by means of the VP-8 image analyzer. The VP-8 was developed by NASA to obtain "photographs" of celestial objects in outer space. Unlike ordinary cameras, which rely on the diffused light available within the earth's atmosphere to create an albedo image, the VP-8 must rely entirely on light which emanates or is reflected directly in straight lines from the object being photographed. Since the intensity of light decreases as it travels through space, the VP-8 is programmed to create realistic images of objects by treating their distances from the lens of the VP-8 as a function of the intensity of the light reaching it from those objects. In other words, if the intensity of the light reaching the VP-8 from object A is less than that reaching it from object B, the VP-8 will create a picture which makes it look like object A is further away from the camera than object B. The same principle applies to a single three-dimensional object in that the part of that object that seems the farthest away in the picture created by the VP-8 will be that part from which light of the lowest intensity is detected by the VP-8.

The VP-8 is fairly effective at producing realistic images of three-dimensional objects in outer space, but because of the effects of diffusion, it

[7]John H. Heller, *Report on the Shroud of Turin* (Boston: Houghton Miffin, 1983), 203.

produces remarkably distorted images when its lenses are trained on ordinary two-dimensional representations of three-dimensional objects. In other words, a photograph of a realistic painting taken by the VP-8 will not normally look realistic, nor will VP-8 photographs of ordinary photographs. Photographs taken by the VP-8 of the image on the Shroud, however, while they lack the resolution of ordinary photographs, do look realistic, at least in the sense that there is no spatial distortion of the sort to be expected. This may not seem important to a typical layperson, but to the physicists investigating the Shroud, it was an important fact which needed to be explained. The most intriguing fact is that the VP-8 takes into account differences in light intensity that are far too small to be detected by human beings with the naked eye. Artists who were commissioned to attempt to duplicate the physical appearance of the image on the Shroud were unable to produce images which did not produce distortion when photographed by the VP-8 even though these images were, to the naked eye, almost indistinguishable from the Shroud image. Given the range and accuracy of the VP-8 in detecting different light intensities, the likelihood that a human artist would accidentally create an image which does not produce distortion is extremely small.

These considerations and many others like them have convinced nearly all of the STURP scientists that the image on the Shroud cannot be a work of art. As previously mentioned, they do not claim to have *proven* that it is not a work of art, but scientists seldom if ever claim to have proven anything absolutely. What they do say in this case is that it is *highly improbable* that the Shroud is a work of art, which is to say that they regard the hypothesis that it is *not* as *highly confirmed.*

The STURP scientists, of course, as scientists, are still committed to the view that there must be a naturalistic explanation for the image, so they have turned to the other naturalistic leg of Mueller's trichotomy and are attempting to explain the image in terms of some sort of physical interaction between the cloth and the body of a recently crucified man. This sort of explanation, however, is precisely the sort that Mueller claims can be "ruled out *definitively.*"[8] The problem is that there are strong theoretical considerations which seem to count against any image-formation hypothesis consistent with both the known facts and with currently accepted scientific theory. Explanations in terms of funereal oils and bodily secretions can be ruled out due to the previously mentioned lack of capillarity displayed by the image, and lack of residues rules out powdered oxidizing agents. The clarity of the image rules out oxidizing vapors as a source of the image. Given the results of the VP-8 investigation, the best naturalistic hypothesis is that the image was created by some form of radiation emanating from a human body, but there is no explanation of how this radiation could have been produced, nor is there any known form of radiation which would have all the requisite image-producing characteristics. One of the STURP scientists sums up the status of the scientific attempt to explain the image in the following way:

> Briefly stated, we seem to know what the image is chemically, but how it got there remains a mystery. The dilemma is not one of choosing from among a variety of likely transfer mechanisms, but rather that no technologically credible process has been postulated that satisfies all the characteristics of the existing image.[9]

It might be appropriate at this point to reconsider the results of the carbon dating tests. If these tests had shown conclusively that the Shroud came into existence only six or seven centuries ago, then we certainly would have been justified in concluding that it could not have been the burial shroud of Jesus. This would also have lent significant support

[8]He is by no means alone in this assessment. Steven Schafersman is another scientist who is not a member of STURP and believes that the Shroud must be a work of art simply because "the perfection of the image rules out [. . .] the possibility of its being formed by any conceivable [his italics] natural process . . ." "Science, the Public, and the Shroud of Turin," *The Skeptical Inquirer* VI, 3, (Spring 1982): 41.

[9]Eric J. Jumper, et al.," A Comprehensive Examination of Various Stains and Images on the Shroud of Turin," *ACS Advances in Chemistry,* No. 205, *Archaeological Chemistry* III, ed. Joseph B. Lambert (1984):456.

to the skeptical view that the Shroud was, after all, nothing but a medieval work of art. There are several problems with this view. In the first place, the carbon-14 dating results are by no means conclusive. The methods used are very controversial in archaeological circles, especially when applied to cloth, since the method has often produced results which are many centuries off when applied to samples of known age. In addition, there are special problems in this particular case. The sample used was apparently taken from a narrow strip along one side of the cloth which might well have been added in the fourteenth century to center the image for its first public display. Extreme heat from a fire which almost destroyed the Shroud in 1532 could have resulted in ion exchange which would have invalidated the results of the carbon dating tests, as would various forms of radiation, which is significant if the image was produced by a form of radiation. Finally, it has recently been reported that the laboratories which conducted the tests may have failed to cleanse the Shroud fragments of invisible, submicroscopic fungi, the presence of which would also invalidate the results of a carbon-dating test. More importantly for our present purposes, however, the results of the carbon-dating tests, *even if completely accurate,* do *nothing* to explain how the image was formed! If the Shroud itself came into existence in the fourteenth century, then the image was produced no earlier than that, but how? Every bit of data which indicates that the Shroud is not a work of art is completely unaffected by the carbon-14 data, and the hypothesis that the image was produced by contact with a crucified body becomes less likely than it would otherwise be, since it is less likely that anyone was crucified in the fourteenth century. We still have no naturalistic explanation of how the image was formed, and the "contact" hypotheses currently favored by the STURP scientists are now even less plausible than they would otherwise be. This explains why the results of the carbon dating tests, far from resolving anything, actually make the situation more confusing than ever to knowledgeable sindonologists.

Let us now summarize our discussion so far. It would seem that if we assume that the image on the Shroud of Turin is neither subjective nor an accidental phenomenon, then the only naturalistic explanations of its nature and existence are that it is a work of art or that it is the natural effect of a natural interaction between the cloth and a human body. There is a strong body of scientific evidence which counts against the hypothesis that it is a work of art, and there are strong theoretical considerations which count against its being the result of a natural interaction. No one has claimed that either of these hypotheses has been conclusively disproven, but it could be argued that they have both been scientifically disconfirmed to such an extent that they have become unreasonable to believe. But what then *is* reasonable to believe about the image? If it really is "scientifically inexplicable," are we to believe simply that it has no explanation, or should we believe that the correct explanation, if we are willing to call it an "explanation," is that a supernatural event has occurred? Within the context of the theistic framework sketched earlier in this paper, why not simply conclude that God changed the inherent properties of some of the theons composing the Shroud in order to produce the image? If we decide to reject the results of the carbon dating tests, why not simply conclude that the image was produced when God changed the causal powers of the theons composing the body of Jesus at the moment of the Resurrection?

As of this writing, it is tempting to regard the image on the Shroud of Turin as scientifically inexplicable in the stronger of the two senses described above. In the first place, far from not having enough data, we seem to have enough to know exactly what the image consists in, even though we have no idea what produced it. In the second place, far from having too many possible explanations to choose from, we currently have none consistent both with what we know about the image and with currently accepted scientific theory. Finally, although we have not mentioned this previously, the Shroud image appears to be unique. If the Shroud is a burial garment, it is the only one among thousands of extant specimens which bears a recognizable image (although there are many with decomposition stains and bloodstains on them), and if it is a work of art, it is the only one which has many of the physical features previously described. It thus appears that it might satisfy all of the conditions mentioned for something's being scientifically inexplicable in the strong sense mentioned above.

The fact that no satisfactory scientific explanation of the Shroud image has been given does not imply that none can be, and no scientists, including the members of STURP, have concluded that the Shroud image is scientifically inexplicable. For one thing, despite everything that has been said above, it is nevertheless true that the facts about the Shroud of Turin are not all in, and never will be. Besides, it is always possible that some of the data referred to earlier will prove to be faulty, or that someone will discover a fairly simple naturalistic hypothesis that has been overlooked, in which case the Shroud of Turin may lose its air of mystery. It is also possible, however, that the data will *not* prove to be faulty, and that the origin of the image will never be naturalistically explained. In any case, it would appear, as of this writing at least, that science has given us good reason to believe that the image on the Shroud of Turin is scientifically inexplicable in a fairly strong sense of the term. A fairly intensive scientific investigation has given us no good scientific reason to believe that the image is a work of art, and many scientific reasons to believe that it is not. Moreover, despite extensive knowledge of the physical nature of this particular image and of the various processes which are capable of producing images on cloth, this same scientific investigation has produced *no* credible hypothesis concerning the formation of the image. Moreover, scientists have more or less ruled out entire classes of potential explanations, and it is difficult to see how more data would help. In recent years, each new batch of data has simply deepened the mystery. As the scientific grounds for rejecting both of the first two legs of Mueller's trichotomy continue to accumulate, must there not be some point at which it is simply unreasonable to believe that the image on the Shroud has a completely naturalistic explanation? And would it not then become reasonable to infer that it must have a supernatural explanation?

The answer to this question at present is at best a "qualified maybe." To see why, we must reexamine the argument derived from Mueller's trichotomy. Simply put, the argument has the following logical form:

(1) The Shroud image is either a work of art, a result of a natural interaction between a human body and the cloth, or a supernatural phenomenon.
(2) The Shroud image is not a work of art.
(3) The Shroud image is not a result of a natural interaction between a human body and the cloth. Therefore,
(4) The Shroud image is a supernatural phenomenon.

This is a **valid** form of argument, and we have already established that (1) is true. If we could establish the truth of (2) and (3) to the same degree of credibility as (1), we could then be confident of the truth of (4). Assuming that supernatural phenomena are almost always scientifically inexplicable, we could then regard the Shroud image as scientifically inexplicable in an "absolute" sense of the term. As it turns out, of course, we never can establish the truth of (2) and (3) to the same degree of credibility as (1), but it would at least appear that (2) and (3) might be rendered increasingly probable by further scientific research, in which case the probability of (4) would presumably be increased as well. Thus it would seem that science itself might indeed present us with good grounds for believing that a scientifically inexplicable event has occurred. To put it another way, the scientific evidence which we have concerning the image on the Shroud of Turin is of considerable weight, and gives us much more reason to believe that the image is scientifically inexplicable than we would otherwise have. Moreover, it might even turn out that when all is said and done, the most reasonable explanation, all things considered, for the image on the Shroud of Turin is that a miraculous event has occurred, or perhaps even that the image was produced by the resurrection of Jesus from the dead.

Even if, however, science can provide us with good grounds for believing that a scientifically inexplicable event has occurred, it does not follow that science can *prove* that this has happened, nor does it follow that science in itself can show that such an event must be miraculous. In the first place, just as there can be violations of scientific law which are not miraculous, there can be scientifically inexplicable events which are not miraculous. Although we might have good grounds for regarding a scientifically inexplicable spontaneous remission of an ordinarily fatal disease as miraculous, we would presumably not so regard a scientifically inexplicable recurrence (or first occurrence) of such a disease. The point here is that even in those cases where an event's being scientifically inexplicable is an important reason for its being regarded as miraculous, it is never a **sufficient condition** for so regarding it. The concept of a miracle must obviously be defined at least partly in terms of divine agency and purpose, but the nature of God precludes a direct **empirical** discovery of either of these things. Thus, even in those cases where a theistic explanation seems to be the most reasonable, science itself cannot provide direct evidence of divine involvement, and any inferences to such involvement, even if justified in some sense, is not *scientifically* justified.[10]

More importantly, all claims concerning scientific inexplicability are necessarily **defeasible,** so that what is scientifically inexplicable today might not be scientifically inexplicable tomorrow. This is *not* to say that we are never justified in believing that something is scientifically inexplicable, nor is it to say that nothing can be permanently or absolutely scientifically inexplicable. It is simply to say that even in those cases in which the most reasonable thing to say is that something is scientifically inexplicable, it is nevertheless possible that this might not always be the case. Everything science tells us is provisional. This is inherent in the nature of science. With regard to the Shroud of Turin, for example, no matter how probable (2) and (3) become relative to available evidence and then-current scientific theory, it will always be at least possible that either (2) or (3) is false, so that (4) can never be conclusively established by means of this argument. We will always be free to withhold judgment while we continue to attempt to discredit either (2) or (3), and this is precisely what the STURP scientists have done and will probably continue to do.

Any attempt to enlist science as the handmaiden of theology in this case thus runs into two difficulties. In the first place, it must acknowledge that science can at best provide indirect, circumstantial support for the claim that a miracle has occurred. Even if science could somehow conclusively demonstrate the truth of both (2) and (3), non-scientific considerations would also have to be introduced to justify the conclusion that a miracle had occurred. In the second place, it must acknowledge that, to the extent that science can at best show (2) and (3) to be highly probable, any conclusion based on them will also be only probable, and these probabilities can change dramatically with the accumulation of new data and the evolution of scientific theory. Finally, it would seem that the conclusions reached here in the case of the Shroud of Turin can easily be generalized. Science deals only with the physical world; divinity is inaccessible to it. It can therefore neither confirm nor disconfirm claims involving the existence, nature, or agency of God. Moreover, even in those cases where physical evidence (or the lack thereof) seems to suggest divine agency or presence, this evidence, to the extent that it is provided by science, must be probabilistic at best.

David Hume, in his famous chapter on miracles, says the following:

> . . . we may establish it as a maxim, that no human testimony can have such force as to prove a miracle, and make it a just foundation for any such system of religion. I beg the limitations here made may be remarked, when I say, that a miracle can never be proved, so as to be the foundation of a system of religion. For I own, that otherwise, there may possibly be miracles, or violations of the usual course of nature, of such a kind as to admit of proof from human testimony . . . [See Reading 6.9—Ed.]

It is not entirely clear what Hume means by this, nor are his motives for saying it as clear as we might hope. What is clear is that he would countenance a belief that "a violation of the usual course of nature"

[10]It should also be noted that we have said nothing about the possibility of non-theistic supernatural explanations. It would be beyond the scope of this paper to attempt to describe and assess either the possibility or the relative merits of such explanations, but it seems clear that science would be of no help in this regard in any case.

had occurred more readily if it were not used as a "foundation" for religious belief. In other words, we may need better reasons to base a religion on presumed empirical facts than we need simply to believe those facts in themselves. Hume may have been somewhat confused and misguided concerning both the nature and the possibility of miracles, but, ironically enough, he may have been on the right track in this instance at least.

STUDY QUESTIONS

1. Explain the evidence against the hypothesis that the Shroud of Turin is a piece of artistry, as well as the evidence against the hypothesis that the image arose naturally without artistry.
2. Explain why Griffith does not think the evidence in question 1 proves that the image on the shroud arose supernaturally.
3. Explain Griffith's distinction between *scientifically inexplicable* and *miraculous.*
4. Summarize Griffith's main point.
5. *What is your opinion about the cause of the image on the shroud?
6. *Are there any circumstances under which Griffith would regard an event as a miracle?
7. *Explain the distinction Hume makes in the paragraph quoted at the end of the reading. How would these remarks apply to the shroud?

FURTHER READING

Science and Religion

Badham, Paul and Badham, Linda, eds. *Immortality or Extinction?* New York: Barnes and Noble, 1981.

Barbour, Ian. *Myths, Models, and Paradigms.* New York: Harper & Row, 1974.

Barbour, Ian. *Religion and Science: Historical and Contemporary Issues.* Revised edition. San Francisco: HarperSanFrancisco, 1997.

Dawkins, Richard. *The Blind Watchmaker: Why the Evidence of Evolution Reveals a Universe Without Design.* New York: W. W. Norton and Co., 1986.

Gingerich, Owen. "Where In the World is God." In *Man and Creation: Perspectives on Science and Theology,* ed. M. Bauman and L. Roche; pp. 209–29. Hillsdale, MI: Hillsdale College Press, 1993.

Huchingson, James E. ed. *Religion and the Natural Sciences: The Range of Engagement.* Orlando, FL: Harcourt Brace, 1993.

McMullin, Ernan. "Evolution and Special Creation." *Zygon* 28 (1993): 299–335.

Miller, Kenneth R. *Finding Darwin's God: A Scientist's Search for Common Ground Between God and Evolution.* New York: Harper Collins, 1999.

Richardson, Mark W. and Wildman, Wesley J. *Religion and Science: History, Method, Dialogue.* New York and London: Routledge, 1996.

Schroeder, Gerald. *The Science of God; The Convergence of Scientific and Biblical Wisdom.* New York: The Free Press, 1997.

Soloveitchik, Joseph B. *The Lonely Man of Faith.* New York: Doubleday, 1992.

Stanesby, Derek. *Science, Reason and Religion.* New York: Routledge, 1998.

Swinburne, Richard. *The Evolution of the Soul.* Oxford, England: Clarendon, 1996.

Van Till, Howard. *The Fourth Day: What the Bible and the Heavens Are Telling Us About the Creation.* Grand Rapids, MI: Eerdmans, 1994.

The Journal *Zygon* (University of Chicago Press) is devoted to problems of science and religion.

Providence and Divine Action

Flint, Thomas. *Divine Providence: The Molinist Account.* Ithaca, NY: Cornell University Press, 1998.

Geach, Peter T. *Providence and Evil.* Cambridge, England: Cambridge University Press, 1977.

Hebblethwaite, Brian and Edward Henderson, eds. *Divine Action.* Edinburgh: T & T Clark, 1990.

Helm, Paul. *The Providence of God.* Downers Grove, IL: InterVarsity Press, 1994.

Mavrodes, George I. "Is There Anything Which God Does Not Do?" *Christian Scholars' Review* 16 (1987): 384–91.

Morris, Thomas, ed. *Divine & Human Action: Essays in the Metaphysics of Theism.* Ithaca, NY: Cornell University Press, 1988.

Shatz, David. "Hierarchical Theories of Freedom and the Hardening of Hearts." *Midwest Studies in Philosophy XXI: The Philosophy of Religion,* Ed. Peter A. French, Theodore E. Vehling Jr. and

Howard K. Wettstein, pp. 202–24. Notre Dame, IN: University of Notre Dame Press, 1987.

Taliaferro, Charles. *Consciousness and the Mind of God.* New York: Cambridge University Press, 1994.

Thomas, Owen, ed. *God's Activity in the World.* Atlanta, GA: Scholars Press, 1983.

Tracy, Thomas F. ed. *The God Who Acts: Philosophical and Theological Explorations.* University Park, PA: Pennsylvania State University Press, 1994.

Miracles

Basinger, David and Basinger, Randall. *Philosophy and Miracle: The Contemporary Debate.* Lewiston, New York: Edwin Mellen Press, 1986.

Broad, Charles Dunbar. "Hume's Theory of the Credibility of Miracles." *Proceedings of the Aristotelian Society,* New Series XVII (1916–17), 77–94.

Earman, John. *Hume's Abject Failure: The Argument Against Miracles.* New York: Oxford University Press, 2000.

Flew, Antony. "Miracles." *The Encyclopedia of Philosophy,* edited by Paul Edwards. 5:346–53. New York: Macmillan, 1967.

Holland, R. F. "The Miraculous." *American Philosophical Quarterly* 2(1965): 43–51.

Houston, Joseph. *Reported Miracles: A Critique of Hume.* Cambridge, England: Cambridge University Press, 1994.

Lewis, C. S. *Miracles.* New York: MacMillan, 1947.

Swinburne, Richard, ed. *The Concept of Miracle.* New York: St. Martin's Press, 1970.

Swinburne, Richard, ed. *Miracles.* New York: MacMillan, 1989.

CHAPTER 7

Is There a Place for Faith?

In chapters 4 and 5, as well as parts of other chapters, we assessed the case for and against theism. We did so by evaluating the evidence, reasons, and **arguments** that may be proffered for and against theism's claims. However, many theists would object that such an approach to the claims of theism is inappropriate and irrelevant. For religious belief is and/or should be based not on reason, but on faith.

What do theists mean when they say this? Why is evaluating reasons and arguments alleged to be inappropriate and irrelevant in the case of theism? What is faith, and why should one have it? In this chapter, we will explore attempts by theists to answer these questions.

DESCRIPTIVE FIDEISM

A theist might claim that, in point of fact, theists who believe in God do not have reasons for their belief but, rather, believe "on faith." What is faith in this context? It is, precisely, belief without evidence, reason, or argument. Thus, even if arguments for the existence of God succeed, they are irrelevant to why believers believe as they do. And, if the arguments fail, they are likewise irrelevant to why believers believe as they do. On this view, theists simply do not think in terms of evidence and arguments at all. We can call this position *descriptive* **fideism:** the position that theists are correctly described as believing on faith *(fide),* not because of reasons.

One problem with descriptive fideism is that many theists do have reasons for what they believe. Their reasons may be good or bad, but in either case their belief is held on the basis of reasons. To this objection, a theist could respond that, even when believers have reasons for their belief, the reasons are not the *basis* for the belief. To adapt an example given by philosopher Keith Lehrer in another context, suppose the son of an attorney is accused of a heinous crime. The lawyer may have faith that her son is innocent of the charges, but to defend her son in court she will need to gather evidence and present, in court, an argument that is cogent. Does the lawyer have good reasons for believing that her son is innocent? Yes. Does she *base* her belief on those reasons? No—for she would believe in his innocence even if she did not have reasons for that belief. The belief does not *depend* on the reasons. Just so, theists who have reasons for their beliefs, a descriptive fideist would say, do not base their belief on those reasons but, instead, on faith.

The notion that many believers fit the preceding description is, a descriptive fideist might argue, plausible. But surely, not all believers fit the characterization. Occasionally people convert to a theistic religion because they think they have come upon a proof of God's existence or have experienced a particular revelation. Presumably the nonbelievers who are thus won over do not base their belief on faith but would, rather, give up religious belief were there not good enough reason to hold it. Still and all, the descriptive fideist could claim that *many* believers base their belief on faith. Many of them do not think about why they should believe; they just believe.

Supposing that descriptive fideism is true to some extent, does it really help theists defend their beliefs? Hardly. For, even if we grant that believers actually do base their belief on faith, we must confront the **normative,** prescriptive issue: are theists *entitled* to base their belief on faith—that is, is there some true **epistemological** principle (a principle about knowledge, justification, or rationality) that *permits* them to base their belief on faith? If not, theists who base their belief on faith are simply irrational. If you say that you believe in gremlins based on your faith, is that a rational way of believing? Are you entitled to hold the belief *gremlins exist* without reasons? Surely not. So a religious person cannot claim to be rational just by saying he or she believes on faith.

The problem facing the theist who says he or she believes on faith is exacerbated if there is evidence against theism—for example, if the theist has no reply to the objection based on the existence of evil in the world or to objections based on the incompatibility of certain divine attributes. For it is bad enough to believe in gremlins without evidence that gremlins exist. It is still worse to believe that gremlins exist even after one has found evidence against the existence of gremlins and even after someone has shown that the description of gremlins given by the believer is logically inconsistent. In fact, when a descriptive fideist says that religious belief is (as a descriptive matter) based on faith, the theist seems not to be successfully defending him- or herself but, quite the contrary, to be conceding to critics what they have asserted all along—that theistic belief is not rational.

EVIDENTIALISM VS. NORMATIVE FIDEISM

How, then, is an appeal to faith supposed to serve as a defense against criticism? Supposing that theists do, in fact, believe on faith, isn't it wrong of them to do so? If there is no good evidence or argument for theism, isn't a theist irrational, no matter how strong his or her faith? Should we not say that, the stronger the faith, the greater the irrationality of believing on faith?

Let us use the term **evidentialism** to denote the position that it is wrong to hold a belief that is not based on adequate evidence. The words of nineteenth-century thinker W. K. Clifford are a classic statement of evidentialism:

> It is wrong always, everywhere, and for anyone to believe anything on insufficient evidence. (Reading 7.1)

As long as evidentialism is accepted, theists cannot say that it is irrelevant if they have no reasons for their belief. If theists have no good evidence, no reasons, no good arguments, then it is wrong for theists to be theists, to believe what they cannot establish by rational methods. Hence, if theists are to make room for belief on faith, if they want to show that theists are entitled or permitted to believe on faith—that they are within their **epistemic** rights—they have no choice but to reject evidentialism.

The essays in this chapter by theists should be viewed as various ways to attack evidentialism and to defend the possibility of holding a rational belief without having good reasons for the belief. The view that religious belief can properly and legitimately be based on faith, that it is not irrational or epistemically wrong to believe based on faith, can be called *normative fideism.* Normative fideism can be divided into five categories.

Reformed Epistemology

Reformed epistemology maintains that beliefs about God can be rational even if not supported by evidence or argument because (according to the version of the approach most prevalent today) they are *properly basic.* It is easiest to grasp this position and follow the selection by Alvin Plantinga (reading 7.3) in terms of a theory called **foundationalism.**

Foundationalism argues as follows: suppose that a person holds a belief that *p*. This belief may be derived from another belief—namely, the belief that *q*. The belief that *q* may be derived from another belief—namely, the belief that *r*. And the belief that *r*, in turn, may be derived from the belief that *s*. But, says the foundationalist, this cannot go on infinitely; the chain of justification must eventually come to a stop. There must be a belief that is accepted without reasons. A belief system thus requires foundations or basic beliefs. Let us suppose a theist accepts this foundationalist position. The theist could hold theistic beliefs such as *God exists* not because the theist *infers* that God exists from other beliefs (as *p* is inferred from *q* and *q* from *r* in our example). Rather, *God exists* is a foundation of belief—other beliefs are derived from it, not it from them. In this way, we can understand how a belief based on faith might be regarded as rational. A belief based on faith is a foundational, or basic, belief. Critics like Clifford have no good case for excluding this belief from the foundations, Plantinga maintains.

Although there may be other ways to develop the position, the argument that religious beliefs are foundational, or basic, is certainly one way to explicate the Reformed school of epistemology in Protestantism. The approach's most significant advocate today is Alvin Plantinga. Plantinga actually writes that a belief is rational if it is *properly* basic, meaning that the belief is formed by the proper operation of one's faculties in the right circumstances. If I believe that *God is speaking to me, God has created all this,* or *God forgives me,* these propositions are properly basic in the right circumstances. (Plantinga prefers to take these beliefs, rather than the belief *God exists,* as examples of basic beliefs.)

Unfortunately, as stated so far, Reformed epistemology meets up with an obvious problem. Any belief, no matter how bizarre, could be defended just by saying that it is properly basic. In addition, even if a person is rational in holding a certain basic belief, this does not itself show that the belief is true. A belief can be rational without being true. People who once believed the earth was flat held a belief that was false but, nonetheless, was rational relative to their other beliefs.

Parity Arguments

Some beliefs that are unquestionably rational, and universally regarded as such, cannot be justified by reasons and arguments. These beliefs are familiar to anyone who has studied the position known as **skepticism.** Skeptics try to show that our most widespread commonsense beliefs (that is, beliefs held to be rational and true by common consensus) are not justified. These beliefs include

> The belief that there is a world outside of our minds (as philosophers call it, the external world)
>
> The belief that our memories are reliable
>
> The belief that there are other minds besides one's own
>
> The belief that the regularities we observe in nature are uniform—they operate everywhere and at all times.

Consider also particular instances of these general beliefs:

> There is a computer on the desk in front of me.
>
> I had cereal for breakfast every day this week.
>
> Joe has a mind.
>
> After I put this match to this paper, the paper will burn.

These beliefs, both the general and the particular ones, are clearly rational and indeed true. Yet many philosophers believe that these beliefs cannot be proved, or established on the basis of evidence. If so, why should belief in God be singled out as irrational for lacking sufficient evidence or argument? Parity dictates that these beliefs be treated as rational, just as are the beliefs that there is an external world, that memory is reliable, and the other beliefs we listed earlier.

Parity arguments can lead to epistemological anarchy, to an "anything goes" situation, a wholesale license for looney beliefs. Why can't any belief whatsoever that is lacking in evidence be defended by saying, "Well, many eminently rational beliefs can't be defended"? Further, several differences come to mind between religious beliefs and the commonsense beliefs we considered above. No person can live a life without the commonsense beliefs, but people can lead lives without religious beliefs. The commonsense beliefs are held universally; the religious ones are not. There is no good evidence against commonsense beliefs, but there is ostensibly good evidence against religious beliefs (to wit, evil). Defenders of the parity argument will have to argue that these differences are irrelevant. For example, they might say, exactly why should the fact that a belief is held universally make it rational when otherwise it would not be? Why should universal agreement create justification?

Not all parity arguments play off of general skepticism about the external world, memory, other minds, and induction. For example, Peter van Inwagen (reading 7.2), in criticizing W. K. Clifford (reading 7.1), mentions that, in philosophy and politics, it is permissible for people to hold beliefs that are not based on sufficient evidence. He rejects the notion that the assessment of religion should proceed any differently. Van Inwagen's examples clearly do not involve beliefs that are universally held—political and philosophical views are not in that category. Nor are they beliefs that people cannot live without. However, they are rational beliefs.

In both Reformed epistemology and the parity argument, the theist might be confronted with the question of whether atheism no less than theism could be taken as properly basic (Reformed epistemology) or as on a par with commonsense beliefs (in the parity arguments). The simplest answer for a defender of those strategies to give is that, yes, atheism no less than theism could be rational on this view. Terence Penelhum (Reading 7.4) evaluates this response.

Wittgensteinian Fideism

Wittgensteinian fideism is championed by some followers of the great philosopher Ludwig Wittgenstein (1889–1951)—notably, Norman Malcolm (1911–1990) and D. Z. Phillips (1934–). On this view, religion is a *form of life*. One cannot evaluate a form of life from the outside; it has its own language game, with its own rules and logic. Religious belief is not a hypothesis that can be tested as a scientific hypothesis would be, and it does not stand in need of justification. The language game can be described but not evaluated. It is in order as it is.

These formulations cry out for elucidation, and one critic refers to some characteristic statements of Wittgensteinian fideists as "dark sayings." Nevertheless, the overall intent is clear enough for our purposes, and that is to establish that religious commitment can only be understood by someone within the religious system, a participant in this form of discourse; further, this form of discourse sets its own criteria of coherence, rationality, and intelligibility. Wittgensteinian fideism is not represented in the selections, but we may compare it to Reformed epistemology at least with regard to one potential criticism. Specifically, the problem of abuse lurks here, too—could not any belief system protect itself against criticism by insisting it is a form of life with its own rules and therefore cannot be criticized from the outside?

Pragmatic Responses

Sometimes a belief is not supported by evidence, but holding it achieves certain goals that a person wishes to attain. For example, the seventeenth-century mathematician and philosopher Blaise Pascal (Reading 7.6) reasoned that, even if a person's evidence does not support the belief that God exists, the person should take into account the potential rewards of believing that God exists and the potential costs of not believing that God exists. If God exists, the reward for belief is infinite bliss, and the punishment (cost) of disbelief is infinite suffering. The smart money is to bet on God. At the turn of the twentieth century, American philosopher William James (reading 7.8) rejected certain aspects of Pascal's discussion but affirmed nonetheless that, under certain conditions, a person may decide to believe what religion asserts based on the potential benefits of this belief and the potential harms brought on by non-belief.

Underlying the pragmatic approach is the idea that rationality is of two types, theoretical and practical. As a rough, preliminary definition, we can say that

> A belief that *p* is theoretically rational for person *S* if and only if it is adequately supported by *S*'s evidence. (This is stated as a **necessary and sufficient condition.** For a belief to be theoretically rational, it must satisfy this condition; and satisfying the condition itself suffices for the belief being theoretically rational.)

> A belief that *p* is pragmatically rational for person *S* if and only if holding it leads to certain goals *S* has, besides the goal of acquiring truth. (This too is stated as a necessary and sufficient condition.)

The characterization of *pragmatically rational belief* is modeled after the definition of rational *action:* person *S* is rational in doing an action *A* if and only if doing *A* leads to goals that *S* has.

Many questions arise about our definition of *pragmatically rational belief:* is it really enough that holding a belief that *p* leads to *S*'s attaining *S*'s goals, or should we also require that *S*'s goals are themselves rational to pursue? If so, how do we understand what a "rational goal" is? Also, can a belief be pragmatically rational even if the evidence points in the direction of *not-p?* Can a person really *will to believe*—can *S* believe that *p* while knowing that this belief is held for pragmatic reasons alone and is not theoretically rational? These questions will come up in the readings.

Existentialist Fideism

Existentialist fideism holds that religious belief, by its very nature, requires a leap of faith; a belief based on evidence is not a *religious* belief. One point that seems to favor this claim is that religion requires sacrifice and risk, and a belief that follows the evidence involves no sacrifice or risk. It is useful to distinguish between moderate existentialist fideism and extreme existentialist fideism. Moderate existentialist fideism says that, for person *S* to hold a belief as a *religious* belief, *S* must not have evidence to support the belief. Extreme existentialist fideism says that, for *S* to hold a belief as a *religious* belief, S must have evidence that the belief is false. The extreme version must explain how to distinguish religion from impassioned insanity; and both it and the moderate version need to explain why people should be praised for having faith, as if irrationality were a virtue. Some existentialist fideists have sought to address these problems.

OUTLINE OF THE READINGS

In the readings in this chapter, W. K. Clifford articulates evidentialism; Peter van Inwagen argues against it, using examples from philosophy and politics. Alvin Plantinga, also criticizing Clifford, holds that religious beliefs are properly basic when they are formed in the right circumstances. Terence Penelhum assesses parity arguments.

Next, Joshua L. Golding develops a conception of religious belief in terms of the concept *acting as if,* which helps support a pragmatic approach. Blaise Pascal, who also counsels *acting as if* theism is true, presents his wager argument. William G. Lycan and George N. Schlesinger defend the wager argument against objections. William James defends a form of pragmatism that is different from Pascal's, and his position is criticized by Michael Martin.

Søren Kierkegaard thought that, for a belief or commitment to properly be called religious, the believer must lack objectively adequate evidence for the belief (according to some of Kierkegaard's reasoning, the believer must even have evidence against the belief). In his essay, Robert Merrihew Adams offers a critique of these arguments. Finally, Steven M. Cahn's essay bridges the essays in chapter 4 with those in this chapter and chapter 8. Cahn suggests that, no matter how religious belief is defended by a philosopher, whether by theoretical or **pragmatic** considerations, the religious believer will not be able to know how to act in concrete situations—there are too many possibilities and no way to choose among them. This naturally leads to the question of how one knows what religion to adopt, which is the subject of chapter 8.

EVIDENTIALISM AND THE NATURE OF FAITH

READING 7.1

The Ethics of Belief

W. K. Clifford

In this 1879 essay, a classic statement of **evidentialism,** *W. K. Clifford argues, "It is wrong always, everywhere, and for anyone, to believe anything upon insufficient evidence." To prove his point, Clifford gives an example of a shipowner who believes without adequate evidence that his ship is safe for travel and allows it to depart. The shipowner is culpable for any deaths that ensue as a result of his unjustified belief. If his belief is true and the ship travels safely, but the person has no right to hold the belief, he is still culpable. (Clifford gives a second example, involving religious persecution, to make the same point.) It will not do to say that we judge negatively only the shipowner's action, not his belief; for beliefs influence action. In addition, believing on insufficient evidence makes a person credulous and has a bad influence on others. The implications for religious belief are obvious, though left understated: It is wrong to hold religious beliefs without "sufficient" evidence.*

A shipowner was about to send to sea an emigrant-ship. He knew that she was old, and not over-well built at the first; that she had seen many seas and climes, and often had needed repairs. Doubts had been suggested to him that possibly she was not seaworthy. These doubts preyed upon his mind, and made him unhappy; he thought that perhaps he ought to have her thoroughly overhauled and refitted, even though this should put him to great expense. Before the ship sailed, however, he succeeded in overcoming these melancholy reflections. He said to himself that she had gone safely through so many voyages and weathered so many storms that it was idle to suppose she would not come safely home from this trip also. He would put his trust in Providence, which could hardly fail to protect all these unhappy families that were leaving their fatherland to seek for better times elsewhere. He would dismiss from his mind all ungenerous suspicions about the honesty of builders and contractors. In such ways he acquired a sincere and comfortable conviction that his vessel was thoroughly safe and seaworthy; he watched her departure with a light heart, and benevolent wishes for the success of the exiles in their strange new home that was to be; and he got his insurance-money when she went down in mid-ocean and told no tales.

What shall we say of him? Surely this, that he was verily guilty of the death of those men. It is admitted that he did sincerely believe in the soundness of his ship; but the sincerity of his conviction can in no wise help him, because *he had no right to believe on such evidence as was before him.* He had acquired his belief not by honestly earning it in patient investigation, but by stifling his doubts. And although in the end he may have felt so sure about it that he could not think otherwise, yet inasmuch as he had knowingly and willingly worked himself into that frame of mind, he must be held responsible for it.

Let us alter the case a little, and suppose that the ship was not unsound after all; that she made her voyage safely, and many others after it. Will that diminish the guilt of her owner? Not one jot. When an action is once done, it is right or wrong for ever; no accidental failure of its good or evil fruits can possibly alter that. The man would not have been innocent, he would only have been not found out. The question of right or wrong has to do with the origin of his belief, not the matter of it; not what it was, but how he got it; not whether it turned out to be true or false, but whether he had a right to believe on such evidence as was before him.

There was once an island in which some of the inhabitants professed a religion teaching neither the doctrine of original sin nor that of eternal punishment. A suspicion got abroad that the professors of this religion had made use of unfair means to get their doctrines taught to children. They were accused of wresting the laws of their country in such a way as to remove children from the care of their natural and legal guardians; and even of stealing them away and keeping them concealed from their friends and relations. A certain number of men formed themselves into a society for the purpose of agitating the public about this matter. They published grave accusations against individual citizens of the highest position and character, and did all in their power to injure these citizens in the exercise of their professions. So great was the noise they made, that a Commission was appointed to investigate the facts; but after the Commission had carefully inquired into all the evidence that could be got, it appeared that the accused were innocent. Not only had they been accused on insufficient evidence, but the evidence of their innocence was such as the agitators might easily have obtained, if they had attempted a fair inquiry. After these disclosures the inhabitants of that country looked upon the members of the agitating society, not only as persons whose judgment was to be distrusted, but also as no longer to be counted honourable men. For although they had sincerely and conscientiously believed in the charges they had made, *yet they had no right to believe on such evidence as was before them*. Their sincere convictions, instead of being honestly earned by patient inquiring, were stolen by listening to the voice of prejudice and passion.

Let us vary this case also, and suppose, other things remaining as before, that a still more accurate investigation proved the accused to have been really guilty. Would this make any difference in the guilt of the accusers? Clearly not; the question is not whether their belief was true or false, but whether they entertained it on wrong grounds. They would no doubt say, "Now you see that we were right after all; next time perhaps you will believe us." And they might be believed, but they would not thereby become honourable men. They would not be innocent, they would only be not found out. Every one of them, if he chose to examine himself *in foro conscientiae* [in the forum of conscience], would know that he had acquired and nourished a belief, when he had no right to believe on such evidence as was before him; and therein he would know that he had done a wrong thing.

It may be said, however, that in both of these supposed cases it is not the belief which is judged to be wrong, but the action following upon it. The shipowner might say, "I am perfectly certain that my ship is sound, but still I feel it my duty to have her examined, before trusting the lives of so many people to her." And it might be said to the agitator, "However convinced you were of the justice of your cause and the truth of your convictions, you ought not to have made a public attack upon any man's character until you had examined the evidence on both sides with the utmost patience and care."

In the first place, let us admit that, so far as it goes, this view of the case is right and necessary; right, because even when a man's belief is so fixed that he cannot think otherwise, he still has a choice in regard to the action suggested by it, and so cannot escape the duty of investigating on the ground of the strength of his convictions; and necessary, because those who are not yet capable of controlling their feelings and thoughts must have a plain rule dealing with overt acts.

But this being premised as necessary, it becomes clear that it is not sufficient, and that our previous judgment is required to supplement it. For it is not possible so to sever the belief from the action it suggests as to condemn the one without condemning the other. No man holding a strong belief on one side of a question, or even wishing to hold a belief on one side, can investigate it with such fairness and completeness as if he were really in doubt and unbiased; so that the existence of a belief not founded on fair inquiry unfits a man for the performance of this necessary duty.

Nor is that truly a belief at all which has not some influence upon the actions of him who holds it. He who truly believes that which prompts him to an action has looked upon the action to lust after it, he has committed it already in his heart. If a belief is not realized immediately in open deeds, it is stored up for the guidance of the future. It goes to make a part of that aggregate of beliefs which is the link between sensation and action at every moment of all our lives, and which is so organized and compacted together that no part of it can be isolated from the rest, but every new addition modifies the structure of the whole. No real belief, however trifling and fragmentary it may seem, is ever truly insignificant; it prepares us to receive more of its like, confirms those which resembled it before, and weakens others; and so gradually it lays a stealthy train in our inmost thoughts, which may some day explode into overt action, and leave its stamp upon our character for ever.

And no one man's belief is in any case a private matter which concerns himself alone. Our lives are guided by that general conception of the course of things which has been created by society for social purposes. Our words, our phrases, our forms and processes and modes of thought, are common property, fashioned and perfected from age to age; an heirloom which every succeeding generation inherits as a precious deposit and a sacred trust to be handed on to the next one, not unchanged but enlarged and purified, with some clear marks of its proper handiwork. Into this, for good or ill, is woven every belief of every man who has speech of his fellows. An awful privilege, and an awful responsibility, that we should help to create the world in which posterity will live.

In the two supposed cases which have been considered, it has been judged wrong to believe on insufficient evidence, or to nourish belief by suppressing doubts and avoiding investigation. The reason of this judgment is not far to seek: it is that in both these cases the belief held by one man was of great importance to other men. But forasmuch as no belief held by one man, however seemingly trivial the belief, and however obscure the believer, is ever actually insignificant or without its effect on the fate of mankind, we have no choice but to extend our judgment to all cases of belief whatever. Belief, that sacred faculty which prompts the decisions of our will, and knits into harmonious working all the compacted energies of our being, is ours not for ourselves, but for humanity. It is rightly used on truths which have been established by long experience and waiting toil, and which have stood in the fierce light of free and fearless questioning. Then it helps to bind men together, and to strengthen and direct their common action. It is desecrated when given to unproved and unquestioned statements, for the solace and private pleasure of the believer; to add a tinsel splendour to the plain straight road of our life and display a bright mirage beyond it; or even to drown the common sorrows of our kind by a self-deception which allows them not only to cast down, but also to degrade us. Whoso would deserve well of his fellows in this matter will guard the purity of his belief with a very fanaticism of jealous care, lest at any time it should rest on an unworthy object, and catch a stain which can never be wiped away.

It is not only the leader of men, statesman, philosopher, or poet, that owes this bounden duty to mankind. Every rustic who delivers in the village alehouse his slow, infrequent sentences, may help to kill or keep alive the fatal superstitions which clog his race. Every hard-worked wife of an artisan may transmit to her children beliefs which shall knit society together, or rend it in pieces. No simplicity of mind, no obscurity of station, can escape the universal duty of questioning all that we believe.

It is true that this duty is a hard one, and the doubt which comes out of it is often a very bitter thing. It leaves us bare and powerless where we thought that we were safe and strong. To know all about anything is to know how to deal with it under all circumstances. We feel much happier and more secure when we think we know precisely what to do, no matter what happens, than when we have lost our way and do not know where to turn. And if we have supposed ourselves to know all about anything, and to be capable of doing what is fit in regard to it, we naturally do not like to find that we are really ignorant and powerless, that we have to begin again at the beginning, and try to learn what the thing is and how it is to be dealt with—if indeed anything can be learnt about it. It is the sense of power attached to a sense of knowledge that makes men desirous of believing, and afraid of doubting.

This sense of power is the highest and best of pleasures when the belief on which it is founded is a true belief, and has been fairly earned by investigation.

For then we may justly feel that it is common property, and hold good for others as well as for ourselves. Then we may be glad, not that *I* have learned secrets by which I am safer and stronger, but that *we men* have got mastery over more of the world; and we shall be strong, not for ourselves, but in the name of Man and in his strength. But if the belief has been accepted on insufficient evidence, the pleasure is a stolen one. Not only does it deceive ourselves by giving us a sense of power which we do not really possess, but it is sinful, because it is stolen in defiance of our duty to mankind. That duty is to guard ourselves from such beliefs as from a pestilence, which may shortly master our own body and then spread to the rest of the town. What would be thought of one who, for the sake of a sweet fruit, should deliberately run the risk of bringing a plague upon his family and his neighbours?

And, as in other such cases, it is not the risk only which has to be considered; for a bad action is always bad at the time when it is done, no matter what happens afterwards. Every time we let ourselves believe for unworthy reasons, we weaken our powers of self-control, of doubting, of judicially and fairly weighing evidence. We all suffer severely enough from the maintenance and support of false beliefs and the fatally wrong actions which they lead to, and the evil born when one such belief is entertained is great and wide. But a greater and wider evil arises when the credulous character is maintained and supported, when a habit of believing for unworthy reasons is fostered and made permanent. If I steal money from any person, there may be no harm done by the mere transfer of possession; he may not feel the loss, or it may prevent him from using the money badly. But I cannot help doing this great wrong towards Man, that I make myself dishonest. What hurts society is not that it should lose its property, but that it should become a den of thieves; for then it must cease to be society. This is why we ought not to do evil that good may come; for at any rate this great evil has come, that we have done evil and are made wicked thereby. In like manner, if I let myself believe anything on insufficient evidence, there may be no great harm done by the mere belief; it may be true after all, or I may never have occasion to exhibit it in outward acts. But I cannot help doing this great wrong towards Man, that I make myself credulous. The danger to society is not merely that it should believe wrong things, though that is great enough; but that it should become credulous, and lose the habit of testing things and inquiring into them; for then it must sink back into savagery.

The harm which is done by credulity in a man is not confined to the fostering of a credulous character in others, and consequent support of false beliefs. Habitual want of care about what I believe leads to habitual want of care in others about the truth of what is told to me. Men speak the truth to one another when each reveres the truth in his own mind and in the other's mind; but how shall my friend revere the truth in my mind when I myself am careless about it, when I believe things because I want to believe them, and because they are comforting and pleasant? Will he not learn to cry, "Peace," to me, when there is no peace? [Jeremiah 6:14, 8:11] By such a course I shall surround myself with a thick atmosphere of falsehood and fraud, and in that I must live. It may matter little to me, in my cloud-castle of sweet illusions and darling lies; but it matters much to Man that I have made my neighbours ready to deceive. The credulous man is father to the liar and the cheat; he lives in the bosom of this his family, and it is no marvel if he should become even as they are. So closely are our duties knit together, that whoso shall keep the whole law, and yet offend in one point, he is guilty of all.

To sum up: it is wrong always, everywhere, and for anyone, to believe anything upon insufficient evidence.

If a man, holding a belief which he was taught in childhood or persuaded of afterwards, keeps down and pushes away any doubts which arise about it in his mind, purposely avoids the reading of books and the company of men that call in question or discuss it, and regards as impious those questions which cannot easily be asked without disturbing it—the life of that man is one long sin against mankind.

If this judgment seems harsh when applied to those simple souls who have never known better, who have been brought up from the cradle with a horror of doubt, and taught that their eternal welfare depends on *what* they believe, then it leads to the very serious question, *Who hath made Israel to sin?*

It may be permitted me to fortify this judgment with the sentence of Milton—

> A man may be a heretic in the truth; and if he believe things only because his pastor says so, or the assembly so determine, without knowing other reason, though his belief be true, yet the very truth he holds becomes his heresy.

And with this famous aphorism of Coleridge—

> He who begins by loving Christianity better than Truth, will proceed by loving his own sect or Church better than Christianity, and end in loving himself better than all.

Inquiry into the evidence of a doctrine is not to be made once for all, and then taken as finally settled. It is never lawful to stifle a doubt; for either it can be honestly answered by means of the inquiry already made, or else it proves that the inquiry was not complete.

"But," says one, "I am a busy man; I have no time for the long course of study which would be necessary to make me in any degree a competent judge of certain questions, or even able to understand the nature of the arguments." Then he should have no time to believe.

STUDY QUESTIONS

1. Explain Clifford's examples of the shipowner and the people who were falsely accused, as well as the conclusion he draws from those examples.
2. *Why does Clifford introduce the thesis that belief leads to action? Does belief always lead to action? Discuss.
3. *Can you think of examples that refute Clifford's famous saying, "It is wrong always, everywhere, and for anyone, to believe anything upon insufficient evidence"? (Readings 7.2–7.4 point out weaknesses in Clifford's thesis.)
4. *How explicitly does Clifford criticize religious believers? Explain. (See Reading 7.2.)

READING 7.2

"It Is Wrong, Always, Everywhere, and for Anyone, to Believe Anything upon Insufficient Evidence"

Peter van Inwagen

Peter van Inwagen (Notre Dame) argues against Clifford's position. If Clifford's position (quoted in the title of van Inwagen's essay) were applied to areas such as philosophy and politics, van Inwagen argues, the result would be **skepticism** *or* **agnosticism,** *for, although philosophical and political beliefs have important effects on behavior—just as in Clifford's examples of the shipowner and the explorer—those who believe a proposition in these areas cannot produce adequate justification and argument. Equally competent authorities hold diametrically opposed positions in these spheres, yet such beliefs are justified for the people who hold them. Van Inwagen maintains that to hold religious beliefs to a stricter evidential standard than beliefs in philosophy and politics—a practice he describes as widespread—is to embrace a double standard. If what justifies belief in the cases of philosophy and politics is not evidence and arguments alone but something else—perhaps an "incommunicable insight"—then religious beliefs can be justified the same way.*

My title is a famous sentence from W. K. Clifford's celebrated lecture, "The Ethics of Belief" [Reading 7.1]. What I want to do is not so much to challenge (or to vindicate) the principle this sentence expresses as to examine what the consequences of attempting consistently to apply it in our lives would be. Various philosophers have attempted something that might be described in these words, and have argued that a strict adherence to the terms of the principle would lead to a chain of requests for further evidence that would terminate only in such presumably unanswerable questions as "What evidence have you for supposing that your sensory apparatus is reliable?," or "Yes, but what considerations can you adduce in support of the hypothesis that the future *will* resemble the past?"; and they have drawn the conclusion that anyone who accepts such propositions as that one's sensory apparatus is reliable or that the future will resemble the past must do so in defiance of the principle. You will be relieved to learn that an investigation along these lines is not on the program tonight. I am not going to raise the question whether a strict adherence to the principle would land us in the one of those very abstract sorts of **epistemological** predicaments exemplified by uncertainty about the reliability of sense perception or induction. I shall be looking at consequences of accepting the principle that are much more concrete, much closer to our concerns as **epistemically** responsible citizens—citizens not only of the body politic but of the community of philosophers. . . .

. . . Philosophers do not agree about anything to speak of. That is, it is not very usual for agreement among philosophers on any important philosophical issue to be describable as being, in a quite unambiguous sense, common. Oh, this philosopher may agree with that philosopher on many philosophical points; for that matter, if this philosopher is a former student of that philosopher, they may even agree on *all* philosophical points. But you don't find universal or near-universal agreement about very many important theses or arguments in philosophy. Indeed, it would be hard to find an important philosophical thesis that, say, 95 percent of, say, American analytical philosophers born between 1930 and 1950 agreed about in, say, 1987.

And why not? How can it be that equally intelligent and well-trained philosophers can disagree about the freedom of the will or **nominalism** or the **covering-law model** of scientific explanation when each is aware of all of the arguments and distinctions and other relevant considerations that the others are aware of? How—and now I will drop a broad hint about where I am going—how can we philosophers possibly regard ourselves as justified in believing much of anything of philosophical significance in this embarrassing circumstance? How can *I* believe (as I do) that free will is incompatible with **determinism** or that unrealized possibilities are not physical objects or that human beings are not four-dimensional things extended in time as well as in space, when David Lewis—a philosopher of truly formidable intelligence and insight and ability—rejects these things I believe and is already aware of and understands perfectly every argument that I could produce in their defense?

Well, I *do* believe these things, and I believe that I am justified in believing them. And I am confident that I am right. But how can I take these positions? I don't know. That is itself a philosophical question, and I have no firm opinion about its correct answer. I suppose my best guess is that I enjoy some sort of philosophical insight (I mean in relation to these three particular theses) that, for all his merits, is somehow denied to Lewis. And this would have to be an insight that is incommunicable—at least *I* don't know how to communicate it—for I have done all I can to communicate it to Lewis, and he has understood perfectly everything I have said, and he has not come to share my conclusions. But maybe my best guess is wrong. I'm confident about only one thing in this area: the question must have some good answer. For not only do my beliefs about these questions seem to me to be undeniably *true,* but (quite independent of any consideration of which theses it is that seem to me to be true), I don't want to be forced into a position in which I can't see my way clear to accepting any philosophical thesis of any consequence. Let us call this unattractive position "philosophical skepticism." (Note that I am not using this phrase in its usual sense of "comprehensive and general **skepticism** based on philosophical argument." . . . I think that any philosopher who does not wish to be a philosophical skeptic—I know of no philosopher who *is* a philosophical skeptic—must agree with me that this question has some good answer: whatever the reason, it must be possible for one to be justified in accepting a philosophical thesis when there are philosophers who, by *all* objective and external criteria, are at least equally well qualified to pronounce on that thesis and who reject it.)

Will someone say that philosophical theses are theses of a very special sort, and that philosophy is therefore a special case? That adequacy of evidential support is much more easily achieved in respect of philosophical propositions than in respect of geological or medical or historical propositions? Perhaps because nothing really hangs on philosophical questions, and a false or unjustified philosophical opinion is therefore harmless? Or because philosophy is in some sense not about matters of **empirical** fact? As to the first of these two suggestions, I think it is false that nothing hangs on philosophical questions. What people have believed about the philosophical theses advanced by—for example—Plato, Locke, and Marx has had profound effects on history. I don't know what the world would be like if everyone who ever encountered philosophy immediately became, and thereafter remained, a philosophical skeptic, but I'm willing to bet it would be a vastly different world. . . . In a more general, theoretical way, Clifford has argued, and with some plausibility, that it is *in principle* impossible to claim on behalf of any subject-matter whatever—on the ground that mistaken beliefs about the things of which that subject-matter treats are harmless—exemption from the strict **epistemic** standards to which, say, geological, medical, and historical beliefs are properly held. He argues,

> [That is not] truly a belief at all which has not some influence upon the actions of him who holds it. He who truly believes that which prompts him to an action has looked upon the action to lust after it, he has committed it already in his heart. If a belief is not realized immediately in open deeds, it is stored up for the guidance of the future. It goes to make a part of that aggregate of beliefs which is the link between sensation and action at every moment of all our lives, and which is so organized and compacted together that no part of it can be isolated from the rest, but every new addition modifies the structure of the whole. No real belief, however trifling and fragmentary it may seem, is ever truly insignificant; it prepares us to receive more of its like, confirms those which resembled it before, and weakens others; and so gradually it lays a stealthy train in our inmost thoughts, which may some day explode into overt action, and leave its stamp upon our character forever. . . . And no one man's belief is in any case a private matter which concerns himself alone . . . no belief held by one man, however seemingly trivial the belief, and however obscure the believer, is actually insignificant or without its effect on the fate of mankind.

Whether or not you find this general, theoretical argument convincing, it does in any case seem quite impossible to maintain, given the actual history of the relation between philosophy and our social life, that it makes no real difference what people believe about philosophical questions.

The second suggestion—that philosophy is "different" (and that philosophers may therefore properly, in their professional work, observe looser epistemic standards than geologists or physicians observe in theirs) because it's not about matters of empirical fact—is trickier. Its premise is not that it doesn't make any difference what people believe about philosophical questions; it's rather that the world would look exactly the same whether any given philosophical thesis were true or false. I think that that's a dubious assertion. If the declarative sentences that philosophers characteristically write and speak in their professional capacity are meaningful at all, then many of them express propositions that are ***necessary* truths** or *necessary* falsehoods, and it's at least a very doubtful assertion that the world would look the same if some necessary truth were a falsehood or if some necessary falsehood were a truth. (Would anyone argue that mathematicians may properly hold themselves to looser epistemic standards than geologists because the world would look the same whether or not there was a greatest prime?) And even if it were true that philosophy was, in no sense of this versatile word, "about" matters of empirical fact, one might well raise the question why this should lend any support to the suggestion that philosophers were entitled to looser epistemic standards than geologists or physiologists, given that philosophical beliefs actually do have important effects on the behavior of those who hold them.

Rather than address the issues that these speculations raise, however, I will simply change the subject.

Let us consider politics.

Almost everyone will admit that it makes a difference what people believe about politics—I am using the word in its broadest possible sense—and it would be absurd to say that propositions like "Capital punishment is an ineffective deterrent" or "Nations that do not maintain a strong military capability actually increase the risk of war" are not about matters of empirical fact. And yet people disagree about these propositions (and scores of others of equal importance), and their disagreements about them bear a disquieting resemblance to the disagreements of philosophers about nominalism and free will and the covering-law model. That is, their disagreements are matters of interminable debate, and impressive authorities can be found on both sides of many of the interminable debates.

It is important to realize that this feature of philosophy and politics is not a universal feature of human discourse. It is clear, for example, that someone who believes in astrology believes in something that is simply indefensible. It would be hard to find a philosopher—I *hope* this is true—who believed that every philosopher who disagreed with his or her position on nominalism held a position that was indefensible in the same way that a belief in astrology was indefensible. It might be easier to find someone who held the corresponding position about disputed and important political questions. I suspect there really are people who think that those who disagree with them about the deterrent effect of capital punishment or the probable consequences of unilateral disarmament are not only mistaken but hold beliefs that are indefensible in the way that a belief in astrology is indefensible. I can only say that I regard this attitude as ludicrous. On each side of many interminably debated political questions—it is not necessary to my argument to say *all*—one can find well-informed (indeed, immensely learned) and highly intelligent men and women who adhere to the very highest intellectual standards. And this is simply not the case with debates about astrology. In fact, it is hardly possible to suppose that there could be a very *interesting* debate about the truth-values of the claims made by astrologers.

Everyone who is intellectually honest will admit this, will admit that there are interminable political debates with highly intelligent and well-informed people on both sides. And yet few will react to this state of affairs by becoming political skeptics, by declining to have any political beliefs that are disputed by highly intelligent and well-informed people. But how can this rejection of political skepticism be defended? How can responsible political thinkers believe that the Syndicalist Party is the last, best hope for Ruritania when they know full well that there are well-informed (even immensely learned) and highly intelligent people who argue vehemently—all the while adhering to the highest intellectual standards—that a Syndicalist government would be the ruin of Ruritania? Do the friends of Syndicalism claim to see gaps in the arguments of their opponents, "facts" that they have cited that are not really facts, real facts that they have chosen not to mention, a hidden agenda behind their opposition to Syndicalism? No doubt they do. Nevertheless, if they are intelligent and intellectually honest, they will be aware that if these claims were made in public debate, the opponents of Syndicalism would probably be able to muster a very respectable rebuttal. The friends of Syndicalism will perhaps be confident that they could effectively meet the points raised in this rebuttal, but, if they are intelligent and intellectually honest, they will be aware . . . and so, for all practical purposes, *ad infinitum*.

I ask again, what could it be that justifies us in rejecting political skepticism? How can *I* believe that my political beliefs are justified when these beliefs are rejected by people whose qualifications for engaging in political discourse are as impressive as David Lewis's qualifications for engaging in philosophical discourse? These people are aware of (at least) all the evidence and all the arguments that I am aware of, and they are (at least) as good at evaluating evidence and arguments as I. How, then, can I maintain that the evidence and arguments I can adduce in support of my beliefs actually justify these beliefs? If this evidence and these arguments are capable of that, then why aren't they capable of convincing these other people that these beliefs are correct? Well, as with philosophy, I am inclined to think that I must enjoy some sort of incommunicable insight that the others, for all their merits, lack. I am inclined to think that "the evidence and arguments I can adduce in support of my beliefs" do not constitute the totality of my justification for these beliefs. But all that I am willing to say for sure is that *something* justifies me in rejecting political skepticism, or at least that it is *possible* that something does: that it is not a **necessary truth** that one is not justified in holding a political belief that is controverted by intelligent and well-informed political thinkers.

I have now accomplished one of the things I wanted to do in this chapter. I have raised the question how it is possible to avoid philosophical and political skepticism. In the remainder of this essay, I am going to turn to questions about religious belief. My point in raising the questions I have raised about philosophy and politics was primarily to set the stage for comparing religious beliefs with philosophical and political beliefs. But I think that the questions I have so far raised are interesting in their own right. Even if everything I say in the remainder of the essay is wrong, even if my comparisons of philosophical and political beliefs with religious beliefs turn out to be entirely wide of the mark, the interest of the questions I have raised so far will remain. How can we philosophers, when we consider the matter carefully, avoid the uncomfortable suspicion that the following words of Clifford might apply to *us:* "Every one of them, if he chose to examine himself *in foro conscientiae* [in the forum of conscience–Ed.] would know that he had acquired and nourished a belief, when he had no right to believe on such evidence as was before him; and therein he would know that he had done a wrong thing."?

Now as to religion: is religion different from philosophy and politics in the respects we have been discussing? Should religious beliefs perhaps be held to a stricter evidential standard than philosophical and political beliefs? Or, if they are to be held to the same standard, do typical religious beliefs fare worse under this standard than typical philosophical or political beliefs? It is an extremely popular position that religion *is* different. Or, at least, it must be that many antireligious philosophers and other writers hostile to religious belief hold this position, for it seems to be presupposed by almost every aspect of their approach to the subject of religious belief. And yet this position seems never to have been explicitly formulated, much less argued for. Let us call it the Difference Thesis . . . : Either religious beliefs should be held to a stricter epistemic standard than beliefs of certain other types—of which philosophical and political beliefs are the paradigms—or, if they are to be held to the same epistemic standard as other beliefs, they typically fare worse under this standard than typical beliefs of most other types, including philosophical and political beliefs. I use this **disjunctive** either-or formulation because, while I think I see some sort of difference thesis at work in much of the hostile writing on the epistemic status of religious belief, the work of this thesis is generally accomplished at a subliminal level and it is hard to get a clear view of it. I suspect that some of the writers I have alluded to are thinking in terms of one of the **disjuncts** and some in terms of the other.

A good example of the Difference Thesis at work is provided by Clifford's lecture. One of the most interesting facts about "The Ethics of Belief" is that nowhere in it is religious belief explicitly discussed. There are, to be sure, a few glancing references to religion in the lecture, but the fact that they are references to religion, while it doubtless has its polemical function, is never essential to the point that Clifford professes to be making. Clifford's shipowner, for example, comes to his dishonest belief partly because he puts his trust in Providence, but Clifford could have made the same philosophical point if he had made the shipowner come to his dishonest belief because he had put his trust in his brother-in-law. Clifford's other main illustrative case is built round an actual Victorian scandal (described in coyly abstract terms: "There was once a certain island in which . . .") involving religious persecution. But he could have made the same philosophical point if he had described a case of purely secular persecution, such as those that attended the investigations of Senator McCarthy; his illustration turned simply on the unwillingness of zealous agitators, convinced that the right was on their side, to examine certain matters of public record and to obtain easily available testimony. In both of Clifford's illustrative cases, there is a proposition that is dishonestly accepted, accepted without sufficient attention to the available evidence. In neither case is it a religious or theological proposition. And at no point does Clifford come right out and say that his arguments have any special connection with religious beliefs. It would, however, be disingenuous in the extreme to say that "The Ethics of Belief" is simply about the ethics of belief in general and is no more directed at religious belief than at any other kind of belief. "Everyone knows," as the phrase goes, that Clifford's target is religious belief. . . . The real thesis of Clifford's lecture, its subtext, as our friends in the literature departments say, is that religious beliefs—belief in God; belief in an afterlife, belief in the central historical claims of Judaism or Christianity or Islam—are always or almost always held in ways that violate the famous ethico-epistemic principle whose quotation-name is my title: It is wrong always, everywhere, and for anyone, to believe anything upon insufficient evidence. If, moreover, he is of the opinion that beliefs in any other general category are always or almost always (or typically or rather often) held in ways that violate his principle, this is certainly not apparent.

This conviction that Clifford's specific target is religious belief is no knee-jerk reaction of overly sensitive religious believers or of antireligious polemicists eager to find yet another stick to beat churchgoers with. If the conviction is not supported by his argument, in the strictest sense of the word, it is well grounded in his rhetoric. For one thing, the lecture abounds in biblical quotations and echoes, which is not a usual feature of Clifford's prose. For another, there are the inessential religious elements in both of his illustrative examples. Much more importantly, however, there are two passing allusions to religious belief, which, although they go by rather quickly, are nevertheless writ in letters that he who runs may read. First, one of the dishonest comforts provided by certain beliefs that are not apportioned to evidence is said to be this: they "add a tinsel splendor to the plain straight road of our life and display a bright mirage beyond it." Secondly, when Clifford raises the question whether it is fair to blame people for holding beliefs that are not supported by evidence if they hold these beliefs as a result of their having been trained from childhood not to raise questions of evidence in certain areas, he refers to these unfortunates as "those simple souls . . . who have been brought up from the cradle with a horror of doubt, and taught that their eternal welfare depends on what they believe."

Let us call Clifford's principle—"It is wrong always, everywhere, and for anyone . . ."—Clifford's Principle, which seems an appropriate enough name for it. I should note that there seems to be another principle that Clifford seems sometimes to be appealing to and which he neither articulates nor distinguishes clearly from Clifford's Principle. Call it Clifford's Other Principle. It is something very much like this: "It is wrong always, everywhere, and for anyone to ignore evidence that is relevant to his beliefs, or to dismiss relevant evidence in a facile way." Clifford's Other Principle is obviously not Clifford's Principle. It is very doubtful whether someone who satisfied the requirements of Clifford's Principle would necessarily satisfy the requirements of Clifford's Other Principle (it could be argued that it would be possible to have evidence that justified one's accepting a certain proposition even though one had deliberately chosen not to examine certain other evidence that was relevant to the question whether to accept that proposition) and it is pretty certain that someone who satisfied the requirements of Clifford's Other Principle would not necessarily satisfy the requirements of Clifford's Principle. I suspect that Clifford tended to conflate the two principles because of a combination of his antireligious agenda with an underlying assumption that the evidence, such as it is, that people have for their religious beliefs is inadequate because it is incomplete, and incomplete because these believers have declined to examine certain evidence relevant to their beliefs, owing to a subconscious realization that examination of this evidence would deprive even them of the power to continue to hold their cherished beliefs. However this may be, having distinguished Clifford's Other Principle from Clifford's Principle, I am not going to discuss it further, beyond pointing out that there does not seem to be any reason to suppose, whatever Clifford may have thought, that those who hold religious beliefs are any more likely to be in violation of Clifford's Other Principle than those who hold philosophical or political beliefs. We all know that there are a lot of people who have violated Clifford's Other Principle at one point or another in the course of arriving at their political beliefs and a few who have not. As to philosophy, well, I'm sure that violations of Clifford's Other Principle are quite rare among professional philosophers. . . .

It is interesting to note that Clifford's Principle is almost never mentioned by writers subsequent to Clifford except in hostile examinations of religious belief, and that the antireligious writers who mention it never apply it to anything but religious beliefs. (With the exception of illustrative examples—like Clifford's example of the irresponsible shipowner—that are introduced in the course of explaining its content and arguing for it.) It is this that provides the primary evidence for my contention that many antireligious philosophers and other writers against religion tacitly accept the Difference Thesis: the fact that they apply Clifford's Principle only to religious beliefs is best explained by the assumption that they accept the Difference Thesis. The cases of Marxism and Freudianism are instructive examples of what I am talking about. It is easy to point to philosophers who believe that Marxism and Freudianism are nonsense: absurd parodies of scientific theories that get the real world wildly wrong. Presumably these philosophers do not believe that Marxism and Freudianism were adequately supported by the evidence that was available to Marx and Freud—or that they are adequately supported by the evidence that is available to any of the latter-day adherents of Marxism and Freudianism. But never once has any writer charged that Marx or Freud blotted his epistemic escutcheon by failing to apportion belief to evidence. I challenge anyone to find me a passage (other than an illustrative passage of the type I have mentioned) in which any devotee of Clifford's Principle has applied it to anything but religious belief. And yet practically all philosophers—the literature will immediately demonstrate this to the most casual inquirer—subscribe to theses an obvious logical consequence of which is that the world abounds in gross violations of Clifford's Principle that have nothing to do with religion.

An explanation of the widespread tacit acceptance of the Difference Thesis among those who appeal to Clifford's Principle in their attacks on religious belief is not far to seek. If Clifford's Principle were generally applied in philosophy (or in politics or history or even in many parts of the natural sciences), it would have to be applied practically everywhere. If its use became general, we'd all be constantly shoving it in one another's faces. And there would be no comfortable reply open to most of the recipients of a charge of violating Clifford's Principle. Use every man after his desert, and who shall scape whipping? If, for example, I am an archaeologist who believes that an artifact found in a neolithic tomb was a religious object used in a fertility rite, and if my rival, Professor Graves—a professor, according to the German aphorism, is someone who thinks otherwise—believes that it was used to wind flax, how can I suppose that my belief is supported by the evidence? If my evidence really supports my belief, why doesn't it convert Professor Graves, who is as aware of it as I am, to my position? This example, of course, is made up. But let me mention a real and not entirely dissimilar example that I recently came across in a review (by Malcolm W. Browne) of several books about the Neanderthals in the *New York Times Book Review* (4 July 1993, p. 1). The review includes the following quotation from the recent book *The Neandertals* by Erik Trinkhaus and Pat Shipman. The authors are discussing a debate between two people called Stringer and Wolpoff, who are leading experts on the Neanderthals. "What is uncanny—and disheartening—is the way in which each side can muster the fossil record into seemingly convincing and yet utterly different syntheses of the course of human evolution. Reading their review papers side by side gives the reader a distinct feeling of having awakened in a Kafka novel." Assuming that this description of the use Stringer and Wolpoff make of their evidence is accurate, can it really be that their beliefs are adequately supported by this evidence? Will someone say that Stringer and Wolpoff are scientists, and that scientists do not really *believe* the theories they put forward, but rather bear to them some more tentative sort of **doxastic** relation? "Regard as the best hypothesis currently available," or some such tentative attitude as that? Well, that is certainly not the way the author of the review sees the debate. Stringer, one of the parties in the debate, has written his own book, also discussed in the review, of which the reviewer says, "*In Search of the Neanderthals* is built around Mr. Stringer's underlying (and highly controversial) belief that the Neanderthals were an evolutionary dead end, that they simply faded away after a long and unsuccessful competition with their contemporaries, the direct ancestors of modern man." (That the Neanderthals were an evolutionary dead end is, by the way, the proposition that was at issue in the debate between Stringer and Wolpoff that was said to give the reader the feeling of having awakened in a novel by Kafka.) Later in the review, summarizing the book of another expert on human origins, the reviewer says, "In another section of the book, Mr. Schwartz defends his belief that modern human beings are more closely related to orangutans than to either chimpanzees or gorillas." It is hard to see how to avoid the conclusion that it is very common for scientists *qua* scientists to have beliefs that are vehemently rejected by other equally intelligent scientists who possess the same scientific qualifications and the same evidence. Even in the more austere and abstract parts of science, even in high-energy physics, the current queen of the sciences, where there is some real plausibility in the thesis that investigators typically hold some more tentative attitude than belief toward the content of the controversial theories they champion, it is possible to find clear examples of this. To find them, one need only direct one's attention away from the *content* of the theories to the judgments that physicists make *about* the theories, their judgments about such matters as the usefulness of the theories, their "physical interest," and their prospects. A former colleague at Syracuse University, an internationally recognized quantum-gravity theorist, has told me, using a simple declarative sentence that contained no hedges whatever, that superstring theory would come to nothing. Many prominent physicists (Sheldon Glashow, for example) agree. They really *believe* this. And many prominent physicists (such as Steven Weinberg and Edward Witten) vehemently disagree. They really *believe* that superstring theory has provided the framework within which the development of fundamental physics will take place for a century.

But let us leave the sciences and return to our central examples, philosophy and politics. If we applied Clifford's Principle generally, we'd all have to become skeptics or agnostics as regards most philosophical and political questions—or we'd have to find some reasonable answer to the challenge. "In what sense can the evidence you have adduced support or justify your belief when there are many authorities as competent as you who regard this evidence as unconvincing?" But no answer to this challenge is evident, and religion seems to be the only area of human life in which very many people are willing to be **agnostics** about the answers to very many questions. (When I say "very many people," I mean very many people like *us:* people who write books. It is, of course, false that a very high proportion of the world population consists of people who are willing to be agnostics about religious questions.)

It might, however, be objected that what I have been representing as obvious considerations are obvious only on a certain conception of the nature of evidence. Perhaps the Difference Thesis is defensible because the evidence that some people have for their philosophical and political (and archaeological and historical . . .) beliefs consists partly of the deliverances of that incommunicable "insight" that I speculated about earlier. This objection would seem to be consistent with everything said in "The Ethics of Belief," for Clifford nowhere tells his readers what evidence is. . . .

If, however, "evidence" can include "insight" or some other incommunicable element—my private experience and my memories are not necessarily incommunicable—it may be that some of the philosophical and political beliefs of certain people are justified by the evidence available to them. (This, as I have said, is the view I find most attractive, or least unattractive.) But if evidence is understood in this way, how can anyone be confident that some of the religious beliefs of some people are not justified by the evidence available to them? . . . If evidence can include incommunicable elements, how can anyone be confident that all religious believers are in violation of Clifford's Principle? If "evidence" can include the incommunicable, how can the Difference Thesis be defended?

What I have said so far amounts to a polemic against what I perceive as a widespread double standard in writings about the relation of religious belief to evidence and argument. This double standard consists in setting religious belief a test it could not possibly pass, and in studiously ignoring the fact that very few of our beliefs on any subject could possibly pass this test.

Let me summarize this polemic by setting out some Socratic questions; a complex, in fact, of alternative lines of Socratic questioning laid out in a sort of flowchart.

Either you accept Clifford's Principle or not. If not, game ends. If so, either you think that religious belief stands convicted of some epistemic impropriety under Clifford's Principle or not. If not, game ends. If so, do you think that other important categories of belief stand convicted of similar epistemic impropriety under Clifford's Principle—preeminently philosophical and political belief? If you do, are you a skeptic as regards these categories of belief, a philosophical and political skeptic (and, in all probability, a skeptic in many other areas)? If not, why not? If you do think that the only important category of belief that stands convicted of epistemic impropriety under Clifford's Principle is religious belief—that is, if you accept the Difference Thesis—how will you defend this position? Do you accept my disjunctive formulation of the Difference Thesis: "Either religious beliefs should be held to a stricter epistemic standard than beliefs of certain other types—of which philosophical and political beliefs are the paradigms—or, if they are to be held to the same epistemic standard as other beliefs, they typically fare worse under this standard than typical beliefs of most other types, including philosophical and political beliefs"? If not, how would *you* formulate the Difference Thesis (and how would you defend the thesis you have formulated)? If you do accept my disjunctive formulation of the Difference Thesis, which of the disjuncts do you accept? And what is your defense of that disjunct? In formulating your defense, be sure to explain how you understand evidence. Does "evidence" consist entirely of objects that can be publicly examined (photographs and pointer readings), or that can, at least for purposes of setting out descriptions of the evidence available for a certain thesis, be adequately described in public language (sensations and memories, perhaps)? Or may what is called "evidence" be, or be somehow contained in or accessible to the subject in the form of, incommunicable states of mind of the kind I have rather vaguely called "insight"? If the former, and if you have chosen to say that a single standard of evidence is appropriate to both religious beliefs (on the one hand) and philosophical and political beliefs (on the other), and if you have decided that religious beliefs fare worse under this one standard than philosophical and political beliefs—well, how can you suppose that philosophical and political beliefs *are* supported by that sort of evidence, public evidence, to any significant degree? If the evidence available to you provides adequate support for, say, your adherence to a certain brand of **functionalism** and if it is evidence of this straightforward public sort, then it is no doubt readily available to most philosophers who have paid the same careful attention to questions in the philosophy of mind that you have. But then why aren't most of these philosophers functionalists of your particular stripe? (Why, some respectable philosophers of mind aren't even functionalists at all, shocking as that may seem to some of us.) Wouldn't the possession and careful consideration of adequate, really *adequate,* evidence for a proposition induce belief in that proposition? Or, if evidence that provided adequate support for a philosophical proposition was readily available throughout a sizable population of careful, qualified philosophers, wouldn't this fact at least induce a significant uniformity of opinion as regards that proposition among those philosophers?

If you take the other option as to the nature of evidence, if you grant that evidence may include incommunicable insight, can you be sure, have you any particular reason to suppose, that it is false that there are religious believers who have "insight" that lends the same sort of support to their religious beliefs that the incommunicable insight that justifies *your* disagreement with [Saul] Kripke or [W. V. O.] Quine or [Donald] Davidson or [Michael] Dummett or [Hilary] Putnam lends to *your* beliefs?

This is the end of my Socratic flowchart. I will close with an attempt to forestall two possible misinterpretations. First, I have not challenged Clifford's Principle, or not unless to point out that most of us would find it awkward to live by a certain principle is to challenge it. Clifford's Principle could be correct as far as anything I have said goes. Secondly, I have not argued that religious beliefs—any religious beliefs of anyone's—*are* justified or enjoy any particular warrant or positive epistemic status or whatever your own favorite jargon is. (For that matter, I have not argued that philosophical and political beliefs—any philosophical or political beliefs of anyone's—are justified or enjoy any particular warrant or positive epistemic status. I have recorded my personal conviction that some philosophical and political beliefs are justified, but I have not *argued* for this conclusion. I do not mind—just for the sake of literary symmetry—recording my personal conviction that some religious beliefs are justified, but that they are is not a part of my thesis.)

There is one important question that bears on the epistemic propriety of religious belief that I have not even touched on: whether some or all religious beliefs may go clean contrary to the available evidence—as many would say the belief in a loving and all-powerful deity goes clean contrary to the plain evidence of everyone's senses. To discuss this question was not my project. My project has been to raise certain points about the relevance of Clifford's Principle to the problem of the epistemic propriety of religious belief. These are different questions: it suffices to point out that the philosopher who argues that some religious belief—or some belief of any sort—should be rejected because it goes contrary to some body of evidence is not appealing to Clifford's Principle. If what I have said is correct, then philosophers who wish to mount some sort of evidential or epistemic attack on religious belief (or, more likely, not on religious belief in general, but on particular religious beliefs) should set Clifford's Principle aside and argue that religious belief (or this or that religious belief) is refuted by the evidence they present.

STUDY QUESTIONS

1. According to van Inwagen, what implication does Clifford's principle have with respect to philosophical and political beliefs? Why?
2. *Do you think that when there is a dispute among equally competent authorities about a given philosophical or political view, there isn't sufficient evidence for either side because there is disagreement? Defend your answer by using examples.
3. Van Inwagen says that there are examples in science that do not meet the evidentialist's standards. Explain these examples.
4. What is the Difference Thesis, and what is van Inwagen's assessment of it?
5. Explain why van Inwagen introduces the notion of "incommunicable insight."
6. *Suppose the problem of evil cannot be overcome logically by a theist. Would van Inwagen's criticism of Clifford's principle serve as a response to the critic? Why or why not?
7. *Besides religious beliefs, what other kinds of beliefs could be justified by van Inwagen's argument? Do you think his argument leads to an excessively permissive list of justified beliefs?

READING 7.3

Rationality and Religious Belief

Alvin Plantinga

Criticizing Clifford's doctrine of **evidentialism,** *Alvin Plantinga (Notre Dame) argues that religious beliefs can be rational even if they lack supporting evidence. Plantinga maintains that an evidentialist will subscribe to* **foundationalism.** *This is the view that knowledge is ultimately based on a set of beliefs that are not justified by reference to other beliefs. Instead, these beliefs are properly basic. Beliefs about God could be part of the foundations of one's "***noetic** *[intellectual] struc-*

ture," Plantinga suggests, and as such not have to be justified by evidence. If the evidentialist objects that religious beliefs proposed by the theist as properly basic lack the characteristics of being self-evident or **incorrigible,** *or being evident to the senses, how will the foundationalist support the belief that only propositions that meet these criteria are properly basic? This latter belief, Plantinga says, is neither self-evident nor incorrigible, as the foundationalist must require.*

The position that beliefs about God (e.g., God is speaking to me.*) are properly basic represents a Protestant tradition known as* **Reformed epistemology** *associated with John Calvin (1509–64). Plantinga insists that such beliefs are not groundless; rather, a belief is properly basic when it is formed in certain conditions. Beliefs such as* God is speaking to me *or* God forgives me *are properly basic when formed in the right circumstances. At the end of the selection, Plantinga replies to the objection that any belief—for example, the belief that the Great Pumpkin returns every Halloween—could be taken as properly basic.*

What I mean to discuss in this paper is the question: "Is it rational, or reasonable, or rationally acceptable, to believe in God?" I mean to *discuss* this question, not answer it. My initial aim is not to argue that religious belief *is* rational (although I think it is) but to try to understand this question.

The first thing to note is that I have stated the question misleadingly. What I really want to discuss is whether it is rational to believe that God exists—that there is such a person as God. Of course there is an important difference between believing that God exists and believing *in* God. To believe that God exists is just to accept a certain proposition—the proposition that there really is such a person as God—as true. According to the book of James (2:19) the devils believe this proposition, and they tremble. To believe *in* God, however, is to trust him, to commit your life to him, to make his purposes your own. The devils do not do that. So there is a difference between believing in God and believing that he exists; for purposes of economy, however, I shall use the phrase "belief in God" as a synonym for "belief that God exists."

I. THE EVIDENTIALIST OBJECTION

Our question, therefore, is whether belief in God is rational. This question is widely asked and widely answered. Many philosophers—most prominently, those in the great tradition of **natural theology**—have argued that belief in God is rational; they have typically done so by providing what they took to be ***demonstrations*** or *proofs* of God's existence. Many others have argued that belief in God *is ir*rational. If we call those of the first group "natural theologians," perhaps we should call those of the second "natural atheologians." (That would at any rate be kinder than calling them "unnatural theologians.") J. L. Mackie, for example, opens his statement of the problem of evil as follows: "I think, however, that a more telling criticism can be made by way of the traditional problem of evil. Here it can be shown, not merely that religious beliefs lack rational support, but that they are positively irrational."[1] And a very large number of philosophers take it that a central question—perhaps *the* central question—of philosophy of religion is the question whether religious belief in general and belief in God in particular is rationally acceptable.

Now an apparently straightforward and promising way to approach this question would be to take a definition of rationality and see whether belief in God conforms to it. The chief difficulty with this appealing course, however, is that no such definition of rationality seems to be available. If there *were* such a definition, it would set out some conditions for a belief's being rationally acceptable—conditions that are **severally necessary** and **jointly sufficient.** That is, each of the conditions would have to be met by a belief that is rationally acceptable; and if a belief met all the conditions, then it would

[1]"Evil and Omnipotence," *Mind* 64 (1955), pp. 203–4.

follow that it is rationally acceptable. But it is monumentally difficult to find any non-trivial **necessary conditions** at all. Surely, for example, we cannot insist that S's belief that *p* is rational only if it is *true*. For consider Newton's belief that if *x, y* and *z* are moving colinearly, then the motion of *z* with respect to *x* is the sum of the motions of *y* with respect to *x* and *z* with respect to *y*. No doubt Newton was rational in accepting this belief; yet it was false, at least if contemporary physicists are to be trusted. And if they aren't—that is, if they are wrong in contradicting Newton—then *they* exemplify what I'm speaking of; they rationally believe a proposition which, as it turns out, is false.

Nor can we say that a belief is rationally acceptable only if it is possibly true, not necessarily false in the broadly logical sense. For example, I might do the sum 735 + 421 + 9,216 several times and get the same answer: 10,362. I am then rational in believing that 735 + 421 + 9,216 = 10,362, even though the fact is I've made the same error each time—failed to carry a "1" from the first column—and thus believe what is necessarily false. Or I might be a mathematical neophyte who hears from his teacher that every continuous function is differentiable. I need not be irrational in believing this, despite the fact that it is necessarily false. Examples of this sort can be multiplied.

So this question presents something of an initial enigma in that it is by no means easy to say what it is for a belief to be rational. And the fact is those philosophers who ask this question about belief in God do not typically try to answer it by giving **necessary and sufficient conditions** for rational belief. Instead, they typically ask whether the believer has *evidence* or *sufficient evidence* for his belief; or they may try to argue that in fact there is sufficient evidence for the proposition that there is *no* God; but in any case they try to answer this question by finding evidence for or against theistic belief. Philosophers who think there are sound arguments for the existence of God—the **natural theologians**—claim there is good evidence *for* this proposition; philosophers who believe that there are sound arguments for the non-existence of God naturally claim that there is evidence *against* this proposition. But they concur in holding that belief in God is rational only if there is, on balance, a preponderance of evidence for it—or less radically, only if there is not, on balance, a preponderance of evidence against it.

The nineteenth-century philosopher W. K. Clifford provides a splendid if somewhat strident example of the view that the believer in God must have evidence if he is not to be irrational. Here he does not discriminate against religious belief; he apparently holds that a belief of any sort at all is rationally acceptable only if there is sufficient evidence for it. And he goes on to insist that it is wicked, immoral, monstrous, and perhaps even impolite to accept a belief for which one does not have sufficient evidence:

> Whoso would deserve well of his fellows in this matter will guard the purity of his belief with a very fanaticism of jealous care, lest at any time it should rest on an unworthy object, and catch a stain which can never be wiped away.

He adds that if a

> belief has been accepted on insufficient evidence, the pleasure is a stolen one. Not only does it deceive ourselves by giving us a sense of power which we do not really possess, but it is sinful, because it is stolen in defiance of our duty to mankind. That duty is to guard ourselves from such beliefs as from a pestilence which may shortly master our body and spread to the rest of the town.

And finally:

> To sum up: it is wrong always, everywhere, and for anyone to believe anything upon insufficient evidence. [Reading 7.1]

(It is not hard to detect, in these quotations, the "tone of robustious pathos" with which William James credits him.) Clifford finds it utterly obvious, furthermore, that those who believe in God do indeed so believe on insufficient evidence and thus deserve the above abuse. A believer in God is, on his view, at best a harmless pest and at worst a menace to society; in either case he should be discouraged.

Here Clifford is urging *the* **evidentialist** *objection to theistic belief*—the claim that belief in God is irrational, or unreasonable, or **noetic**ally substandard because, so goes the claim, there is insufficient evidence for it. Suppose we take a deeper look at this position. What is essential to it is the claim that we must evaluate the rationality of belief in God by examining its relation to *other* propositions. We are directed to estimate its rationality by determining whether we have *evidence* for it—whether we know, or at any rate rationally believe, some other propositions which stand in the appropriate relation to the proposition in question. And belief in God is rational, or reasonable, or rationally acceptable, on this view, only if there are other propositions with respect to which it is thus evident.

According to the Cliffordian position, then, there is a set of propositions E such that my belief in God is rational if and only if it is evident with respect to E—if and only if E constitutes, on balance, evidence for it. But what propositions are to be found in E? Do we know that belief in God is not itself in E? If it *is,* of course, then it is certainly evident with respect to E. How does a proposition get into E anyway? How do we decide which propositions are the ones such that my belief in God is rational if and only if it is evident with respect to them? Should we say that E contains the propositions that I *know?* But then, for our question to be interesting, we should first have to argue or agree that I don't know that God exists—that I only *believe* it, whether rationally or irrationally. This position is widely taken for granted, and indeed taken for granted by theists as well as others. But why should the latter concede that he doesn't know that God exists—that at best he rationally believes it? The Bible regularly speaks of *knowledge* in this context—not just rational or well-founded belief. Of course it is true that the believer has *faith*—faith in God, faith in what He reveals—but this by no means settles the issue. The question is whether he doesn't also *know* that God exists. Indeed, according to the Heidelberg Catechism, knowledge is an essential element of faith, so that one has true faith that *p* only if he knows that *p:*

> True faith is not only a certain (i.e., sure) knowledge whereby I hold for truth all that God has revealed in His word, but also a deep-rooted assurance created in me by the Holy Spirit through the gospel that not only others but I too have had my sins forgiven, have been made forever right with God and have been granted salvation.

So from this point of view a man has true faith that *p* only if he knows that *p,* and also meets a certain further condition: roughly (where *p* is a universal proposition) that of accepting the **universal instantiation** of *p* with respect to himself. Now of course the theist may be unwilling to concede that he does not have true faith. But if he does have true faith, then, at least according to the Catechism, he has a "certain (i.e., sure) knowledge" of such revealed truths as that, e.g., "God so loved the world that he gave his only son, that whoever believes in him should not perish but have everlasting life" (John 3:16)—a truth that self-evidently entails that God exists. Accordingly the theist may be unwilling to concede that he does not know but only believes that God exists.

II. CLASSICAL FOUNDATIONALISM

Now of course the evidentialist will not be at all eager to agree that belief in God belongs in E. But why not? To answer we must take a deeper look at his position. The evidentialist objection is nearly always rooted in *classical* ***foundationalism,*** an enormously popular picture or total way of looking at faith, knowledge, justified belief, rationality and allied topics. This picture has had a long and distinguished career in the history of philosophy, including among its adherents Plato, Aristotle, Aquinas, Descartes, Leibniz, Locke, and, to leap to the present, Professor Roderick Chisholm; its near relatives, perhaps, remain the dominant ways of thinking about these topics. We may think of the classical foundationalist as beginning with the observation that some of one's beliefs may be *based upon* others; it may be that there are a pair of propositions *A* and *B* such that I believe *A on the basis of B*. Although this relation isn't easy to characterize in a revealing and non-trivial fashion, it is nonetheless familiar. I believe that the word "umbrageous" is spelled u-m-b-r-a-g-e-o-u-s: this belief is based on another belief of mine; the belief that that's how the dictionary says it's spelled. I believe that $72 \times 71 = 5112$. This belief is based upon several other beliefs I hold: that $1 \times 72 = 72$; $7 \times 2 = 14$; $7 \times 7 = 49$; $49 + 1 = 50$; and others. Some of my beliefs, however, I accept but don't accept on the basis of any other beliefs. Call these beliefs *basic*. I believe that $2 + 1 = 3$, for example, and don't believe it on the basis of other propositions. I also believe that I am seated at my desk, and that there is a mild pain in my right knee. These too are basic for me; I don't believe them on the basis of any other propositions. According to the classical foundationalist, some propositions are *properly* or *rightly* basic for a person and some are not. Those that are not, are rationally accepted only on the basis of *evidence,* where the evidence must trace back, ultimately, to what is properly basic.

Suppose we say that the assemblage of beliefs a person holds, together with the various logical and **epistemic** relations that hold among them, constitutes that person's noetic structure; and let's say that the *foundations* of S's noetic structure (call it "F") is the set of propositions that are *basic* for S and *properly* basic for him.

And from the foundationalist point of view, our question must be restated: Is belief in God evident with respect to the foundations of my noetic structure? Clifford, as I say, takes it to be obvious that the answer is no. But is this obvious? To restate my earlier question: Might it not be that my belief in God is itself in the foundations of my noetic structure? Perhaps it is a member of F, in which case, of course, it will automatically be evident with respect to F.

Here the classical foundationalist goes further. Not just any belief can properly be in the foundations of a person's noetic structure; to be in F a belief must meet some fairly specific conditions. It must be capable of functioning foundationally; it must be capable of bearing its share of the weight of the entire noetic structure. The propositions in F, of course, are not inferred from other propositions and are not accepted on the basis of other propositions. I *know* the propositions in the foundations of my noetic structure, but not by virtue of knowing other propositions; for these are the ones I start with. And so the question the foundationalist asks about belief in God—namely, what is the evidence for it?—is not properly asked about the members of F; these items don't require to be evident with respect to other propositions in order to be rationally believed. Accordingly, says the foundationalist, not just any proposition is capable of functioning foundationally; to be so capable, with respect to a person S, a proposition must not need the evidential support of other propositions; it must be such that it is possible that S know p but have no evidence for p.

Well, suppose all this is so; what kind of propositions can function foundationally? Here different foundationalists give different answers. Aristotle and Aquinas, for example, held that self-evident propositions—ones like *all black dogs are black*—belong in the foundations. Aquinas, at least, seems also to hold that propositions "evident to the senses," as he puts it—propositions like *some things change*—belong there. For he believed, of course, that the existence of God is **demonstrable;** and by this I think he meant that God's existence can be deduced from foundational propositions. He holds, furthermore, that God's existence can be demonstrated "from his effects"—from **sensible** objects; and in each of the five ways there is a premise that, says Aquinas, is "evident to the senses." I therefore believe Aquinas meant to include such propositions among the foundations. You may think it strange, incidentally, to count Aquinas among the Cliffordians. On this point, however, he probably belongs with them; he held that belief in God is rational only if supported by the foundations. Of course he differs from Clifford in holding that in fact God's existence *is* supported by them; he thinks it follows from members of F by argument forms that are themselves in F. This, indeed, is the burden of his five ways [See Reading 4.4.]

According to Aquinas, therefore, self-evident propositions and those evident to the senses belong in the foundations. And when he speaks of propositions of the latter sort, he means such propositions as

(1) there's a tree over there,
(2) there is an ashtray on my desk,
(3) that tree's leaves have turned yellow,

and

(4) this fender has rusted through.

Modern foundationalists—Descartes, for example—argue that what goes into the foundations, in addition to self-evident propositions, are not propositions that, like (1)–(4), entail the existence of such material objects as ashtrays, trees, leaves, and fenders, but more cautious claims; for example:

(5) I seem to see a red book,
(6) it seems to me that I see a book with a red cover,
(7) I seem to see something red,

or even, as Professor Chisholm put it,

(8) I am appeared redly to.

The modern foundationalist who opts for propositions like (5)–(8) rather than (1)–(4) has a prima facie plausible reason for doing so: Belief in a proposition of the latter sort seems to have a sort of immunity from error not enjoyed by belief in one of the former. I may believe that there is a red ashtray on my desk, or that I see a red ashtray on my desk, when the fact is there is no red ashtray there at all: I am color-blind, or hallucinating, or the victim of an illusion of some sort or other. But it is at the least very much harder to see that I could be wrong in believing that I *seem* to see a red ashtray on my desk—that, in Chisholm's language, I am appeared redly (or red-ashtrayly) to. There are plenty of possible worlds in which I mistakenly believe that there is a red book on my desk; it is at least plausible to hold that there are no possible worlds in which I mistakenly believe that I seem to see a red book there. And this immunity from error may plausibly be taken to provide a reason for distinguishing between propositions like (5)–(8) and (1)–(4), admitting the former but not the latter to the foundations.

There is a small problem here, however: Every necessarily true proposition—every proposition true in all **possible worlds**—is such that there is no possible world in which I mistakenly believe it. [See **contingent truth vs. necessary truth**–Ed.] Yet presumably the foundationalist will not be inclined to hold that every necessary proposition I believe is in the foundations of my noetic structure. Consider, for example, **Goldbach's Conjecture** that every even number greater than two is the sum of two primes. This proposition is either necessarily true or necessarily false, although it isn't presently known which. Suppose it is in fact true, and I believe it, but not because I have found a proof of it; I simply believe it. The foundationalist will presumably hold, in this case, that my belief in Goldbach's Conjecture is necessarily true but not a good candidate for the foundations. Here I truly believe but do not know the proposition in question; so it does not belong among the foundations, and this despite the fact that there is no possible world in which I mistakenly believe it.

Presumably, then, the modern foundationalist will not hold that just any necessarily true belief is automatically among the foundations. He may argue instead that what characterizes propositions like (5)–(8) is not just that it is not possible to believe them mistakenly, but that it is not possible to be mistaken about them. That is to say, a proposition of this sort is like a necessary proposition in that it is not possible for me to believe it mistakenly; it is unlike a necessary proposition, however, in that it is also not possible for me to believe its *denial* mistakenly. If I believe that I am appeared to redly, then it follows that I *am* appeared to redly; but if I believe that I am not appeared to redly, it follows equally that I am not thus appeared to. We might say that propositions meeting this condition are *incorrigible* for me; perhaps we can explain this notion thus:

(9) p is incorrigible for S at t iff [if and only if] there is no possible world in which S mistakenly believes p at t and no possible world in which S mistakenly believes not-p at t.[2]

According to our paradigm Cliffordian, then, a belief is properly in the foundations of my noetic

[2]Philip Quinn has pointed out (in correspondence) that, according to (9), false propositions will be **incorrigible** for me now: Although I do not now seem to see something green, the proposition *I seem to see something green* is incorrigible for me now. I'm not certain this feature of the definition is a defect; if it is, it can be repaired by adding the clause "p is true" to the **definiens** or, as Quinn suggests, by adding "S believes p at t."

structure only if it is either self-evident or incorrigible for me. So suppose we take a look at self-evidence. What is it? Under what conditions is a proposition self-evident? What kinds of propositions are self-evident? Examples would include very simple arithmetical truths such as

(10) $2 + 1 = 3$,

simple truths of logic such as

(11) no man is both married and unmarried,

perhaps the generalizations of simple truths of logic, such as

(12) for any proposition *p*, the **conjunction** of *p* with its denial is false,

and certain propositions expressing identity and diversity; for example:

(13) Redness is distinct from greenness,
(14) the property of being prime is distinct from the property of being composite,

and

(15) the proposition *all men are mortal* is distinct from the proposition *all mortals are men.*[3]

There are others; Aquinas gives as examples:

(16) the whole is greater than the part,

where, presumably, he means by "part" what we mean by "proper part," and, more dubiously,

(17) man is an animal.[4]

Still other candidates—candidates which may be less than entirely uncontroversial—come from many other areas; for example:

(18) if *p* is necessarily true and *p* entails *q*, then *q* is necessarily true,
(19) if e^1 occurs before e^2 and e^2 occurs before e^3, then e^1 occurs before e^3,

and

(20) it is wrong to cause unnecessary (and unwanted) pain just for the fun of it.

What is it that characterizes these propositions? According to the tradition, the outstanding characteristic of a self-evident proposition is that one simply sees it to be true upon grasping or understanding it. Understanding a self-evident proposition is sufficient for apprehending its truth. Of course this notion must be relativized to *persons;* what is self-evident to you might not be to me. Very simple arithmetical truths will be self-evident to nearly all of us; but a truth like $17 + 18 = 35$ may be self-evident only to some. And of course a proposition is self-evident to a person only if he does in fact grasp it; so a proposition will not be self-evident to those who do not apprehend the concepts involved in the proposition. As Aquinas says, some propositions are self-evident only to the learned; his example is the truth that immaterial substances do not occupy space. Among those propositions whose concepts not everyone grasps, some are such that anyone who *did* grasp them would see their truth; for example:

(21) A model of a first order theory *T* assigns truth to the axioms of *T*.

Others—$17 + 13 = 30$, for example—may be such that some but not all of those who apprehend them also see that they are true.

But how shall we understand this "seeing that they are true"? Those who speak of self-evidence explicitly turn to this visual metaphor and expressly explain self-evidence by reference to vision. There are two important aspects to the metaphor and two corresponding components to the idea of self-evidence. First, there is the **epistemic** component: a proposition *p* is self-evident to a person *S* only if *S* has *immediate* knowledge of *p*—i.e., knows *p*, and does not know *p* on the basis of his knowledge of other propositions. Consider a simple arithmetic truth such as $2 + 1 = 3$ and compare it with one like $24 \times 24 = 576$. I know each of these propositions; and I know the second but not the first on the basis of computation, which is a kind of inference. So I have immediate knowledge of the first but not the second.

[3]Examples of these kinds are given by Locke, *Essay Concerning Human Understanding,* Book IV, chap. *7.*
[4]*Summa Theologica* 1, Q[= Question] 1 a [= article] 2; *Summa Contra Gentiles* 1, chap. 10.

The epistemic component of self-evidence, therefore, is immediate knowledge; it follows, of course, that any proposition self-evident to a person is true.

But there is also a **phenomenological** component. Consider again our two propositions; the first but not the second has about it a kind of luminous aura or glow when you bring it to mind or consider it. Locke speaks, in this connection, of an "evident luster"; a self-evident proposition, he says, displays a kind of "clarity and brightness to the attentive mind." Descartes speaks instead of "clarity and distinctness"; each, I think, is referring to the same phenomenological feature. And this feature is connected with another: Upon understanding a proposition of this sort one feels a strong inclination to accept it; this luminous obviousness seems to compel or at least impel assent. Aquinas and Locke, indeed, held that a person, or at any rate a normal well-formed human being, finds it impossible to withhold assent when considering a self-evident proposition. The phenomenological component of the idea of self-evidence, then, seems to have a double aspect: There is the luminous aura that 2 + 1 = 3 displays, and there is also an experienced tendency to accept or believe it. Perhaps, indeed, the luminous aura *just is* the experienced impulsion towards acceptance; perhaps these are the very same thing. In that case the phenomenological component would not have the double aspect I suggested it did have; in either case, however, we must recognize this phenomenological aspect of self-evidence.

Now suppose we return to the main question: Why shouldn't belief in God be among the foundations of my noetic structure? Can belief in God be properly basic for a person? If not, why not? The answer, on the part of the modern foundationalist was that even if this belief is *true,* it does not have the characteristics a proposition must have to deserve a place in the foundations. There is no room in the foundations for a proposition that can be known only on the basis of other propositions. A proposition is properly basic for a person only if he knows it immediately—i.e., knows it, and does not know it on the basis of other propositions. The proposition that God exists, however, is at best truly believed, not known, and even if it were known, it wouldn't be known immediately. The only propositions that meet this condition of immediate knowledge are those that are self-evident or incorrigible. Since this proposition is neither, it is not properly basic for anyone; that is, no well-formed, rational noetic structure contains this proposition in its foundations.

But why should the theist concede these things? Suppose he grants that there is a foundation to his noetic structure: a set F of propositions such that (1) he knows each member of F *immediately* and (2) whatever else he knows is evident with respect to the members of F. Suppose he concedes, further, that he does know other things, and knows them on the basis of his knowledge of these basic propositions. Suppose, in a particularly irenic and conciliatory frame of mind, he concedes still further that much of what he believes, he believes but does not know; and that the rationality of these beliefs is to be tested or measured by way of their connections with those propositions that are basic for him. Why should he not combine these concessions with the claim that his belief in God is properly basic for him?

Because, says the modern foundationalist, belief in God is neither self-evident nor incorrigible. But now we must look more closely at this fundamental principle of the foundationalist's position:

(22) a proposition *p* is properly basic for a person *S* if and only if *p* is either self-evident to *S* or incorrigible for *S;*

that is, the foundations of a well-formed, rational noetic structure will contain propositions that are self-evident or incorrigible and will not contain any propositions that do not meet this condition.

And here we must ask a question that has been clamoring for attention. How does the foundationalist know—how does anyone know—that, indeed, a given proposition *is* self-evident? How do we tell? Isn't it possible that a proposition should seem to me to be self-evident when in fact it is not? Consider an analogy. Suppose the theist claims that a proposition *p* is properly basic for a person *S* if *S* knows *p immediately;* and suppose he adds that one of the things he immediately knows is that God exists. The foundationalist, presumably, will want to reply as follows: you *say* you have immediate knowledge of this proposition, but perhaps you are mistaken; perhaps you only *believe* and do not *know* that God exists; perhaps, indeed, God does *not* exist. How do you know that you have immediate knowledge of this proposition? What leads you to think so?

Here the theist may be hard put to give an answer; but the foundationalist may find a similar question similarly embarrassing. How does he know that a given proposition—7 + 5 = 12, for example—*is* self-evident? Might we not be mistaken in our judgment of self-evidence? It seems obviously possible that there should be a race of persons—on some other planet, let's say—who think they find *other* propositions self-evident, some of these others being the denials of propositions *we* find self-evident. Perhaps this race invariably makes mistakes about what is self-evident. But might not the same thing be true of us? A proposition is self-evident, after all, only if it is *true;* and it certainly seems possible that we should believe a proposition self-evident when in fact it is not.

Nor need we rest content with the mere possibility that we should mistakenly find a proposition self-evident. Here the [Bertrand] Russell **paradoxes** are peculiarly instructive. It seems self-evident to many that some properties—e.g., that of being a horse—do not exemplify themselves, while others—e.g., that of being a property—do. It seems self-evident, furthermore, that if some properties exemplify themselves and others do not, then there is such a property as *self-exemplification:* a property enjoyed by the properties in the first group but lacked by those in the second. But it also seems self-evident that if there is such a property as *self-exemplification,* then there is such a property as *non-self-exemplification:* the property a property has if and only if it does not exemplify itself. And of course it seems self-evident that if there is such a property as *non-self-exemplification,* then either it exemplifies itself or it does not. But if it does exemplify itself, it has the property of non-self-exemplification, in which case it does not exemplify itself. So if it does exemplify itself, it does not exemplify itself. But of course it is also true that if it does exemplify itself, then it does; so if it exemplifies itself, it both does and does not exemplify itself. Hence it does not exemplify itself. If, on the other hand, non-self-exemplification does not exemplify itself, then it does not have the property of non-self-exemplification, in which case it must have the property of self-exemplification, i.e., it exemplifies itself. So if it does not exemplify itself, it does exemplify itself. But it is also true that if it does not exemplify itself, then it does not exemplify itself; so if it does not exemplify itself, it both does and does not exemplify itself. Hence it is false that it does not exemplify itself, and true that it does. But now from propositions that seem self-evident we have deduced, by arguments that seem self-evidently right, that non-self-exemplification both exemplifies itself and does not exemplify itself; and this seems self-evidently false. The conclusion must be that at least one proposition that *seems* self-evident, is not *in fact* self-evident.

We must distinguish, therefore, what *appears* to be self-evident from what really *is*. Suppose we say that a proposition *seems* or *appears* self-evident to a person if he understands it, and if it displays the phenomenological feature referred to above—the "evident luster" of which Locke speaks—when he attentively considers it. How, then, does the foundationalist determine which propositions really *are* self-evident for him? By noting, of course, which ones appear self-evident to him; he has nothing else to go on. Of course he cannot sensibly hold that *whatever* appears self-evident, really is; that is the lesson of the Russell paradoxes. Perhaps, however, he can retreat to a weaker principle; perhaps he can hold that whatever seems self-evident has, as we might put it, the presumption of self-evidence in its favor. What appears to be self-evident ought to be taken to be self-evident unless there are reasons to the contrary—unless, for example, it appears self-evident that the proposition in question conflicts with *other* apparently self-evident propositions. And perhaps he will support this injunction by appeal to some such principles as

(24) Whatever seems self-evident is very likely true

or

(25) most propositions that *seem* self-evident *are* self-evident (and hence true).

But why should we accept (24) and (25)? Why does the foundationalist accept them? We should note, first of all, that neither of these propositions seems self-evident. One who understands them can nonetheless wonder whether they are true and in fact reject them. They do not possess that evident luster; and there certainly seem to be thinkable alternatives. Impressed with evolutionary theory, for example, we might suppose that the **disposition** to find these propositions self-evident is a trait emerging in the course of a long evolutionary development—a trait that has a certain survival value, but is at best fortuitously connected with truth, so that many or most of the propositions that appear self-evident to us are in fact false. Or, remembering our Descartes, we might speculate that we have been created by a being who delights in deception and produces in us a powerful tendency to accept certain false propositions as self-evident. Or we might speculate, in a Kierkegaardian vein, that our noetic endowment, once pristine and totally reliable, has been corrupted by some primal cataclysm befalling the human race. So (24) and (25) are not themselves apparently self-evident.

The important point here, however, lies in a different direction. Suppose these principles—(24) and (25)—*were* apparently self-evident. That is, suppose the proposition

(26) most propositions that display the phenomenological feature are true

itself displayed this feature. Would that be a relevant answer to the question of what reason, if any, there is for believing that most propositions displaying this feature are true? It is hard to see how. The question is whether a proposition's displaying this feature is a reason for thinking it true; to reply that (26) itself displays this feature is simply to invite the question again. Here the appeal to self-evidence seems entirely unsatisfactory. It is as if the theist were to reply to the question: "Why believe in God?" by pointing out that God requires us to believe in Him, and requires us to believe only what is true. This may indeed be so; but it does not supply a reason for belief for anyone who does not already believe. Similarly, the claim that (24) and (25) are apparently self-evident, may or may not be true; but it can serve as a reason for accepting them only for someone who already accepts them. And hence it cannot serve as a reason, for the foundationalist, for accepting them.

The fact of the matter is, I think, that the foundationalist has no reason at all for accepting (24) and (25). They do not appear to be self-evident; and of course they are not incorrigible. But if the foundationalist *does* have a reason for them, that reason must trace back, ultimately, to the foundations; that is, the foundationalist has a reason, on his own view, for (24) and (25) only if they are evident with respect to propositions that are properly basic for him—propositions that are self-evident or incorrigible. It is hard to see how (24) or (25) could be evident with respect to such propositions.

Accordingly, the foundationalist accepts (24) and (25) but has no reason for so doing. He isn't *obliged* to accept them; there are alternatives. He simply commits himself to them. We might say that he commits himself to the trustworthiness of his noetic equipment. More elegantly, he commits himself to the reliability of his epistemic endowment. If, with an older tradition, we think of reason as an organ, or power, or faculty—the faculty whereby we discern what is self-evident—then the foundationalist commits himself to the basic reliability of reason. He doesn't do so, of course, as a result of (broadly speaking) scientific or rational investigation; he does so in advance of such investigation. For he has no reasons for accepting (24) and (25); but he does accept them, and he uses them to determine the acceptability of *other* propositions. In other words, (24) and (25) are members of the foundation of his noetic structure.

The foundationalist, therefore, commits himself to the basic reliability of reason. I do not say this by way of criticism; it is a commitment I share. The theist is by no means obliged to reject this commitment. Augustine, indeed, argued that reason is ultimately reliable just because God has created us and is not a deceiver. He has created us in such a way that certain propositions appear self-evident to us; and because he is a God of goodness and truth, he would not create us in such a way that *false* propositions should appear self-evident. Had Augustine been apprised of the Russell paradoxes, he might have expressed himself more guardedly; but his basic point remains. One who believes in God can certainly accept (24) and (25); and he, unlike the foundationalist, can give a reason for doing so.

Since the theist can properly concur with the foundationalist on (24) and (25), he can agree with the latter that apparently self-evident and incorrigible propositions are properly basic for S. But the foundationalist *credo,* we have seen, contains *two* elements, a positive and a negative. The foundationalist holds, positively, that

(27) self-evident and incorrigible propositions are properly basic for S,

and he adds, negatively, that

(28) *only* propositions of those sorts are properly basic for S.

But why should we accept this negative element? What is there to be said in favor of it? Do we have anything more than the foundationalist's word for (28)?

The fact is we have *less* than the foundationalist's word for it. For consider (28). (28) is neither self-evident nor incorrigible; nor does it appear to follow from propositions that are. It is, therefore, basic for the foundationalist. So he holds that self-evident and incorrigible propositions are the only viable candidates for the foundations of his noetic structure, but he himself accepts (28) as basic, which is neither self-evident nor incorrigible. Accordingly, the foundationalist is hoist on his own petard; his characteristic claim is self-referentially incoherent.[5] Is there then any reason at all for believing (28)? If so, it is hard to see what it might be. (28) certainly does not appear to be self-evident; it is certainly not incorrigible. It is very hard to see, furthermore, that it either follows from or is evident with respect to propositions that are self-evident or incorrigible. So it is hard to see that there is any reason for accepting (28), even from a roughly foundationalist point of view. Why then should we accept it? Why should the theist feel any obligation to believe it?

The answer, I believe, is that there is no reason at all for accepting (28); it is no more than a bit of intellectual imperialism on the part of the foundationalist. He means to commit himself to reason and to nothing more; he therefore declares irrational any noetic structure that contains more—belief in God, for example—in its foundations. But here there is no reason for the theist to follow his example.

III. IS BELIEF IN GOD PROPERLY BASIC?

Now many Reformed theologians[6] and thinkers have rejected natural theology (thought of as the attempt to provide proofs or arguments for the existence of God). They have held not merely that the proffered arguments are unsuccessful, but that the whole enterprise is in some way radically misguided. I've argued elsewhere[7] that the Reformed rejection of natural theology is best construed as an inchoate and unfocused rejection of classical foundationalism. What these Reformed thinkers really mean to hold, I think, is that belief in God need not be based on argument or evidence from other propositions at all. They mean to hold that the believer is entirely within his intellectual rights in believing as he does even if he doesn't know of any good theistic argument (**deductive** or non-deductive), even if he doesn't believe that there is any such argument, and even if in fact no such argument exists. They hold that it is perfectly rational to accept belief in God without accepting it on the basis of any other beliefs or propositions at all. In a word, they hold that *belief in God is properly basic.* And insofar as they mean to reject clas-

[5](28), of course, is stated for modern foundationalism, but precisely similar remarks apply to the ancient and medieval foundationalism embraced Aristotle and Aquinas.

[6]A Reformed theologian is one whose intellectual sympathies lie with the Protestant tradition going back to John Calvin (not someone who was formerly a theologian and has since seen the light).

[7]"The Reformed Objection to Natural Theology," *Proceedings of the American Catholic Philosophical Association,* 1980.

sical foundationalism, they are to be applauded; classical foundationalism is eminently rejectable. Of course it does not follow that belief in God *is* properly basic; perhaps the class of properly basic propositions is broader than classical foundationalists think, but still not broad enough to admit belief in God. But why think so? What might be the objections to the Reformed view that belief in God is properly basic? I wish to examine two such objections.

It is sometimes claimed that if I have no evidence for the existence of God, then if I accept that proposition my belief will be groundless, or gratuitous, or arbitrary. I think this is an error; let me explain. Suppose we consider perceptual beliefs, memory beliefs, and beliefs ascribing mental states to other persons: such beliefs as

(29) I see a tree,
(30) I had breakfast this morning,

and

(31) That person is angry.

Although beliefs of this sort are typically and properly taken as basic, it would be a mistake to describe them as *groundless.* Upon having an experience of a certain sort, I believe that I am perceiving a tree. In the typical case, I do not hold this belief on the basis of other beliefs; it is nonetheless not groundless. My having that characteristic sort of experience—to use Professor Chisholm's language, my being appeared treely to—plays a crucial role in the formation and justification of that belief. We might say this experience, together, perhaps, with other circumstances, is what *justifies* me in holding it; this is the *ground* of my justification, and, by extension, the ground of the belief itself.

If I see someone displaying typical pain behavior, I take it that he or she is in pain. Again, I don't take the displayed behavior as *evidence* for that belief; I don't infer that belief from others I hold; I don't accept it on the basis of other beliefs. Still, my perceiving the pain behavior plays a unique role in the formation and justification of that belief; as in the previous case, it forms the ground of my justification for the belief in question. The same holds for memory beliefs. I seem to remember having breakfast this morning; that is, I have an inclination to believe the proposition that I had breakfast, along with a certain past-tinged experience that is familiar to all but hard to describe. Perhaps we should say that I am appeared to pastly; but perhaps that insufficiently distinguishes the experience in question from that accompanying beliefs about the past not grounded in my own memory. The **phenomenology** of memory is a rich and unexplored realm; here I have no time to explore it. In this case as in the others, however, there is a justifying circumstance present, a condition that forms the ground of my justification for accepting the memory belief in question.

In each of these cases, a belief is taken as basic, and in each case properly taken as basic. In each case there is some circumstance or condition that confers justification; there is a circumstance that serves as the *ground* of justification. So in each case there will be some true proposition of the sort:

(32) In condition *C, S* is justified in taking *p* as basic.

Of course *C* will vary with *p*. For a perceptual judgment such as

(33) I see a rose-colored wall before me,

C will include my being appeared to in a certain fashion. No doubt *C* will include more. If I'm appeared to in the familiar fashion but know that I'm wearing rose-colored glasses, or that I am suffering from a disease that causes me to be thus appeared to, no matter what the color of the nearby objects, then I'm not justified in taking (33) as basic. Similarly for memory. Suppose I know that my memory is unreliable; it often plays me tricks. In particular, when I seem to remember having breakfast, then, more often than not, I *haven't* had breakfast. Under these conditions I am not justified in taking it as basic that I had breakfast, even though I seem to remember that I did.

So being appropriately appeared to, in the perceptual case, is not **sufficient** for justification; some further condition—a condition hard to state in detail—is clearly necessary. The central point here, however, is that a belief is properly basic only in certain conditions; these conditions are, we might say, the ground of its justification and, by extension, the ground of the belief itself. In this sense, basic beliefs are not, or are not necessarily, *groundless* beliefs.

Now similar things may be said about belief in God. When the Reformers claim that this belief is properly basic, they do not mean to say, of course, that there are no justifying circumstances for it, or that it is in that sense groundless or gratuitous. Quite the contrary. Calvin holds that God "reveals and daily discloses himself in the whole workmanship of the universe," and the divine art "reveals itself in the innumerable and yet distinct and well ordered variety of the heavenly host." God has so created us that we have a tendency or disposition to see his hand in the world about us. More precisely, there is in us a disposition to believe propositions of the sort *this flower was created by God* or *this vast and intricate universe was created by God* when we contemplate the flower or behold the starry heavens or think about the vast reaches of the universe.

Calvin recognizes, at least implicitly, that other sorts of conditions may trigger this disposition. Upon reading the Bible, one may be impressed with a deep sense that God is speaking to him. Upon having done what I know is cheap, or wrong, or wicked, I may feel guilty in God's sight and form the belief *God disapproves of what I've done*. Upon confession and repentance, I may feel forgiven, forming the belief *God forgives me for what I've done*. A person in grave danger may turn to God, asking for his protection and help; and of course he or she then forms the belief that God is indeed able to hear and help if he sees fit. When life is sweet and satisfying, a spontaneous sense of gratitude may well up within the soul; someone in this condition may thank and praise the Lord for his goodness, and will of course form the accompanying belief that indeed the Lord is to be thanked and praised.

There are therefore many conditions and circumstances that call forth belief in God: guilt, gratitude, danger, a sense of God's presence, a sense that he speaks, perception of various parts of the universe. A complete job would explore the phenomenology of all these conditions and of more besides. This is a large and important topic; but here I can only point to the existence of these conditions.

Of course, none of the beliefs I mentioned a moment ago is the simple belief that God exists. What we have instead are such beliefs as

(34) God is speaking to me,
(35) God has created all this,
(36) God disapproves of what I have done,
(37) God forgives me,

and

(38) God is to be thanked and praised.

These propositions are properly basic in the right circumstances. But it is quite consistent with this to suppose that the proposition *there is such a person as God* is neither properly basic nor taken as basic by those who believe in God. Perhaps what they take as basic are such propositions as (34)–(38), believing in the existence of God on the basis of propositions such as those. From this point of view, it isn't exactly right to say that it is belief in God that is properly basic; more exactly, what are properly basic are such propositions as (34)–(38), each of which self-evidently entails that God exists. It isn't the relatively high level and general proposition *God exists* that is properly basic, but instead propositions detailing some of his attributes or actions.

Suppose we return to the analogy between belief in God and belief in God and belief in the existence of perceptual objects, other persons, and the past. Here too it is relatively specific and concrete propositions rather than their more general and abstract colleagues that are properly basic. Perhaps such items as

(39) There are trees,
(40) There are other persons,

and

(41) The world has existed for more than five minutes

are not in fact properly basic; it is instead such propositions as

(42) I see a tree,
(43) That person is pleased,

and

(44) I had breakfast more than an hour ago

that deserve that accolade. Of course, propositions of the latter sort immediately and self-evidently entail propositions of the former sort; and perhaps there is thus no harm in speaking of the former as properly basic, even though so to speak is to speak a bit loosely.

The same must be said about belief in God. We may say, speaking loosely, that belief in God is properly basic; strictly speaking, however, it is probably not that proposition but such propositions as (34)–(38) that enjoy that status. But the main point, here, is this: belief in God or (34)–(38), are properly basic; to say so, however, is not to deny that there are justifying conditions for these beliefs, or conditions that confer justification on one who accepts them as basic. They are therefore not groundless or gratuitous.

A second objection I've often heard: If belief in God is properly basic, why can't *just any* belief be properly basic? Couldn't we say the same for any bizarre aberration we can think of? What about voodoo or astrology? What about the belief that the Great Pumpkin returns every Halloween? Could I properly take *that* as basic? And if I can't, why can I properly take belief in God as basic? Suppose I believe that if I flap my arms with sufficient vigor, I can take off and fly about the room; could I defend myself against the charge of irrationality by claiming this belief is basic? If we say that belief in God is properly basic, won't we be committed to holding that just anything, or nearly anything, can properly be taken as basic, thus throwing wide the gates to irrationalism and superstition?

Certainly not. What might lead one to think the **Reformed epistemologist** is in this kind of trouble? The fact that he rejects the criteria for proper basicality purveyed by classical foundationalism? But why should *that* be thought to commit him to such tolerance of irrationality? Consider an analogy. In the palmy days of **positivism,** the positivists went about confidently wielding their **verifiability criterion** and declaring meaningless much that was obviously meaningful. Now suppose someone rejected a formulation of that criterion—the one to be found in the second edition of A. J. Ayer's *Language, Truth and Logic,* for example. Would that mean she was committed to holding that

(45) " 'Twas brillig; and the slithy toves did gyre and bymble in the wabe,"

contrary to appearances, makes good sense? Of course not. But then the same goes for the Reformed epistemologist; the fact that he rejects the classical foundationalist's criterion of proper basicality does not mean that he is committed to supposing just anything is properly basic.

But what then is the problem? Is it that the Reformed epistemologist not only rejects those criteria for proper basicality, but seems in no hurry to produce what he takes to be a better substitute? If he has no such criterion, how can he fairly reject belief in the Great Pumpkin as properly basic?

This objection betrays an important misconception. How do we rightly arrive at or develop criteria for meaningfulness, or justified belief, or proper basicality? Where do they come from? Must one have such a criterion before one can sensibly make any judgments—positive or negative—about proper basicality? Surely not. Suppose I don't know of a satisfactory substitute for the criteria proposed by classical foundationalism; I am nevertheless entirely within my rights in holding that certain propositions are not properly basic in certain conditions. Some propositions seem self-evident when in fact they are not; that is the lesson of some of the Russell paradoxes. Nevertheless it would be irrational to take as basic the denial of a proposition that seems self-evident to you. Similarly, suppose it seems to you that you see a tree; you would then be irrational in taking as basic the proposition that you don't see a tree, or that there aren't any trees. In the same way, even if I don't know of some illuminating criterion of meaning, I can quite properly declare (45) meaningless.

And this raises an important question—one Roderick Chisholm has taught us to ask. What is the status of criteria for knowledge, or proper basicality, or justified belief? Typically, these are universal statements. The modern foundationalist's criterion for proper basicality, for example, is doubly universal:

(46) For any proposition *A* and person *S, A* is properly basic for *S* if and only if *A* is incorrigible for S or self-evident to *S*.

But how could one know a thing like that? What are its credentials? Clearly enough, (46) isn't self-evident or just obviously true. But if it isn't, how does one arrive at it? What sorts of arguments would be appropriate? Of course a foundationalist might find (46) so appealing, he simply takes it to be true, neither offering argument for it, nor accepting it on the basis of other things he believes. If he does so, however, then, as we have seen in connection with (28), his noetic structure will be self-referentially incoherent. (46) itself is neither self-evident nor incorrigible; hence in accepting (46) as basic, the modern foundationalist violates the condition of proper basicality he himself lays down in accepting it. On the other hand, perhaps the foundationalist will try to produce some argument for it from premisses that are self-evident or incorrigible; it is exceedingly hard to see, however, what such an argument might be like. And until he has produced such arguments, what shall the rest of us do—we who do not find (46) at all obvious or compelling? How could he use (46) to show us that belief in God, for example, is not properly basic? Why should we believe (46), or pay it any attention?

The fact is, I think, that neither (46) nor any other revealing necessary and sufficient condition for proper basicality follows from clearly self-evident premisses by clearly acceptable arguments. And hence the proper way to arrive at such a criterion is, broadly speaking, **inductive.** We must assemble examples of beliefs and conditions such that the former are obviously properly basic in the latter, and examples of beliefs and conditions such that the former are obviously *not* properly basic in the latter. We must then frame hypotheses as to the necessary and sufficient conditions of proper basicality and test these hypotheses by reference to those examples. Under the right conditions, for example, it is clearly rational to believe that you see a human person before you: a being who has thoughts and feelings, who knows and believes things, who makes decisions and acts. It is clear, furthermore, that you are under no obligation to reason to this belief from others you hold; under those conditions that belief is properly basic for you. But then (46) must be mistaken; the belief in question, under those circumstances, is properly basic, though neither self-evident nor incorrigible for you. Similarly, you may seem to remember that you had breakfast this morning, and perhaps you know of no reason to suppose your memory is playing you tricks. If so, you are entirely justified in taking that belief as basic. Of course it isn't properly basic on the criteria offered by classical foundationalists; but that fact counts not against you but against those criteria.

Accordingly, criteria for proper basicality must be reached from below rather than above; they should not be presented *ex cathedra* but argued and tested by a relevant set of examples. But there is no reason to assume, in advance, that everyone will agree on the examples. The Christian or Jew will of course suppose that belief in God is entirely proper and rational; if he doesn't accept this belief on the basis of other propositions, he will conclude that it is basic for him and quite properly so. Followers of Bertrand Russell and Madelyn Murray O'Hare may disagree, but how is that relevant? Must my criteria, or those of the believing community, conform to their examples? Surely not. The theistic community is responsible to *its* set of examples, not to theirs.

Accordingly, the Reformed epistemologist can properly hold that belief in the Great Pumpkin is not properly basic, even though he holds that belief in God *is* properly basic, and even if he has no full-fledged criterion of proper basicality. Of course he is committed to supposing that there is a relevant *difference* between belief in God and belief in the Great Pumpkin, if he holds that the former but not the latter is properly basic. But this should prove no great embarrassment; there are plenty of candidates. These candidates are to be found in the neighborhood of the conditions I mentioned that justify and ground belief in God. Thus, for example, the Reformed epistemologist may concur with Calvin in holding that God has implanted in us a natural tendency to see his hand in the world around us; the same cannot be said for the Great Pumpkin, there being no Great Pumpkin and no natural tendency to accept beliefs about the Great Pumpkin.

By way of conclusion then, the evidentialist objection, insofar as it is based upon classical foundationalism, is bankrupt; being self-evident, or incorrigible, or evident to the senses is not a necessary condition of proper basicality. Furthermore, one who holds that belief in God *is* properly basic is not thereby committed to the idea that belief in God is groundless, or gratuitous, or without justifying circumstances. And even if he lacks a general criterion of proper basicality, he is not obliged to suppose that just any or nearly any belief—belief in the Great Pumpkin, for example—is properly basic. Like everyone should, he begins with examples; and he may take belief in the Great Pumpkin as a paradigm of irrational basic belief.

STUDY QUESTIONS

1. What is evidentialism? What is foundationalism? How does Plantinga connect evidentialism to foundationalism?
2. Plantinga suggests that a foundationalist might say that beliefs that imply God's existence cannot be properly basic because they lack a feature of proper basicality: being self-evident, being incorrigible, or being evident to the senses. How does he reply to this contention?
3. Which religious beliefs does Plantinga think can be properly basic? What makes them properly basic? What is the status of *God exists*—is it properly basic?
4. Contrast Plantinga's view with natural theology.
5. *Critics of Plantinga have charged that he has improperly shifted the burden of proof from the theist onto critics of theism. What do you think is meant by this charge of an improper shift?
6. *Many people do not take belief in God or other theistic propositions as properly basic. Either they deny that God exists, or they give arguments such as the cosmological, design, and ontological arguments. How might Plantinga respond to this objection?
7. *Some critics believe that Plantinga's position amounts to the conclusion that "everything goes"—*any* belief can be defended by saying it is properly basic. It is in reply to this concern that Plantinga broaches the Great Pumpkin example. Should Plantinga's critics accept his reply? If not, how can they criticize it?

READING 7.4

Do Religious Beliefs Need Grounds?

Terence Penelhum

An argument often used by theists (and encountered in Readings 7.2 and 7.3) is that, even if belief in God cannot be supported by good grounds—in other words, even if it cannot be shown true by means of argument and evidence—it is justified and rational. For aren't there other beliefs that are widely regarded as justified and rational but have not been shown true by evidence and argument? Among such beliefs are beliefs of common sense (that is, common consensus): (1) that sense perceptions are generally reliable, (2) that there are other thinking and feeling beings besides oneself, and (3) that, in the future, nature will follow the same course as in the past. Terence Penelhum (University of Calgary) dubs the preceding argument "the **parity argument,**" *because the theist argues that there is parity between religious beliefs and beliefs of common sense, so that the former should be deemed justified, because the latter are. Penelhum distinguishes between two forms of this argument. In one, associated with Blaise Pascal and Søren Kierkegaard, the argument says that atheists are inconsistent in accepting the commonsense beliefs while rejecting belief in God for lack of grounds. In the other argument (the permissive version), the contention is only that theists are not irrational in holding religious beliefs as well as commonsense beliefs.*

David Hume sought to upset the claimed parity by reference to, among other things, the point that, unlike religious belief, the commonsense beliefs mentioned in the parity argument are universal and unavoidable. Penelhum rejects Hume's objection and likewise criticizes the suggestion that the situations are different because commonsense beliefs are indispensable, whereas religious beliefs are not. Penelhum then turns to the parity argument as wielded by Plantinga and by Norman Malcolm, a follower of Ludwig Wittgenstein. Penelhum accepts the permissive form of the argument, which says that the religious believer is not guilty of irrationality merely because he or she lacks grounds for believing in God. But this argument comes at a cost, for, by the same token, atheists are not guilty of irrationality if they reject theism, leaving us with a standoff. In contrast to the permissive parity argument, those who undertake **natural theology** *are asserting that nonbelief is irrational. Because advocates of the parity argument allow nonbelief to be as rational as belief, such theists cannot attribute nonbelief to sinfulness.*

I

. . . Many philosophers, when discussing religion, have assumed it to be their task to see whether or not there are good grounds for believing the claims religious persons urge upon them. It is tacitly assumed here that if there are no such grounds, it is somehow irrational to accept those claims and, *a fortiori,* to urge them upon others. This assumption does not imply that everyone who has religious beliefs can be expected to have adopted them because they have *considered* these grounds: religion, after all, is for everyone, and not everyone has the talent or opportunity to engage in philosophical reflection. But the assumption does imply that grounds for religious belief are, in some sense, *there;* so that those who are religious, if they are rational in being so, have come, for whatever reason, to hold beliefs for which some good grounds are available and can be given by someone competent to rehearse them. The presentation of such grounds is the traditional task of **natural theology,** as practised, for example, by St. Thomas Aquinas.

In presenting such grounds, natural theologians have not assumed that they amount in every case to proof, though they have usually thought that it is possible to prove *some* of the claims of religion. It is hard to say what 'proof' means, but I suggest that to prove a religious claim to be true is, in part, to show it to be irrational *not* to accept it. Natural theologians have thought that they could show it to be irrational not to accept some of the truths of religion; though they have settled for far less about many of the others. . . .

It is news to no one that the arguments of natural theologians have been attacked severely by philosophers in modern times, and that it is now common to say they are all inadequate; even that no one can prove them, or even offer grounds sufficient to show it is more reasonable than not to accept them. If one thinks this, one is then open to the argument I want to discuss. This argument assumes that no one has yet managed to provide grounds for religious belief in the way natural theologians have tried to do, and that no one is likely to manage it in the future. But it argues that this should not make us reject religious beliefs, saying they are irrational because of this. For, it is said, the history of philosophy makes it very clear to us that exactly the same situation obtains with regard to the basic beliefs of common sense. Everyone takes it for granted in daily life that his or her sense-perceptions are generally reliable guides to the state of the immediate environment. Everyone takes it for granted that there are, occupying the human organisms he sees around him, thinking and feeling individuals like himself. Everyone assumes that in certain general respects the future course of nature will be exactly like the past course of nature. But although we all assume these things, we assume them without ever having considered the philosophical grounds that might be offered for them. And this is just as well, for we find that the philosophical grounds that have been offered for them are weak. If we waited to find good grounds for these beliefs before agreeing to them, we should be unable to function in our world and would die from starvation or anxiety. Not only are there no satisfying grounds on hand for our basic common-sense beliefs, in spite of the best efforts of Descartes or Locke or Kant; these efforts are all designed to refute **skeptical** *objections* to common sense, and their conspicuous failure means that these skeptical objections stand unrefutted. Very properly, sane people do not let this bother them. In spite of all the skeptical arguments about bent sticks and perspectival distortion and jaundice, they go on trusting their eyesight and having spectacles fitted if it deteriorates. In spite of all the suggestions of a world full of robots or deceivers, they go on talking to their friends. And in spite of all the anxieties about the next billiard ball exploding or melting instead of rolling away, they go on playing games and making scientific predictions. But this situation is exactly parallel (the argument goes) to the situation of religion. In spite of the fact that natural theology has been such a failure, there is no reason to call religious believers irrational, unless you are prepared to apply this description to absolutely everyone at the common-sense level. . . .

I call this argument the *Parity Argument*. It attempts to defend religious belief against the charge of irrationality, but it does so . . . by accepting the skeptical claims that there are no cogent philosophical grounds for accepting the basic beliefs of common sense. . . .

II

The first fact to note about the Parity Argument, in this context, is that although it is usually used in situations where one and only one body of religious beliefs is under consideration, its force is very limited. For the same line of reasoning could be offered in favour of any one of an indefinite number of systems of thought, theistic or not. . . . The Argument does not offer a positive reason for accepting any given one of them rather than another. It merely tells us that none of them is in any worse position in relation to reason than the commitments of common sense, so that to restrict oneself to the commitments of common sense is arbitrary.

But although the force of the Parity Argument is limited, it is not negligible. Someone who wishes to answer it is best advised to find characteristics of secular common sense which distinguish it from faith in a way that provides some rational ground for not moving from the one to the other. One way of doing this is to say that the commitments of common sense are in some way indispensable, whereas those of religious faith are not. Another is to say that the demands of faith are psychologically damaging in ways that those of common sense are not. A third is to suggest that the commitments of common sense entail consequences that undermine the claims of faith, so that the two kinds of commitment are inconsistent with each other. We find all three arguments in Hume's philosophy of religion, which, as I read it, is designed in part to answer the Parity Argument systematically. For Hume took the view that our most basic common-sense beliefs are not as a result of philosophical argument, and that no philosophical argument can provide good grounds for them; but he also held that they are, fortunately, beliefs that we are unable to suspend judgement about in the manner the **Sceptic** recommends. Yet Hume devotes some of his finest critical argument to the task of undermining religious faith. He does not only do this by destroying the credentials of traditional natural theology; he also seems to think that in destroying these credentials he is undermining the claim of faith on us. So his philosophical system is a perfect target for the Parity Argument, since he tries to behave like the Sceptics with regard to religion, but to reject Scepticism about common sense. He is fully aware of this difficulty, and it is a useful start for our enquiry to look at the ways in which he tries to meet it.

There is, first of all, a psychological argument, which can be reconstructed by putting together things he says in the *Treatise of Human Nature,* the *Enquiry Concerning Human Understanding,* and the account of religion he gives in the *Natural History of Religion*. It amounts to saying that the commitments of common sense are commitments that we cannot avoid making: we can trace their causes, and we can see that these causes lie deep in our natures in such a way that we are biologically programmed (as we might now say) to hold these beliefs. They are universal and unavoidable. But if one turns to the causes of religion, one will find that these lie in the effects which the mysteries and dangers of the world of primitive man have upon his thoughts and attitudes; they are primarily environmental causes. The result of this is that those who are fortunate enough to live in a cultured and scientific environment, unhaunted by fears of the unknown, can avoid committing themselves to religious beliefs altogether. Let us suppose that these psychological claims are true. Do they help? I do not think they help very much. If someone is being accused of inconsistency when he accepts one proposition, *p,* but rejects another proposition, *q,* because he has reasons for rejecting *p* that are very similar to those that have made him reject *q,* how does he help his case by showing that he is psychologically unable to reject *p,* but is psychologically able to reject *q?* Well, if the reasons for rejecting each of them are good reasons, then all he has offered is an excuse for accepting *p* in spite of the arguments, namely that he cannot help it; but the inconsistency remains, and the whole weight of his case regarding *q* has to lie in the reasons against it. If, on the other hand, the reasons for rejection are less good than this (if, for example, they merely amount to the fact that there are no cogent arguments in favour of *p* or of *q*), then the charge of inconsistency is still unaffected; whether our subject's inability to reject *p* and ability to reject *q* then provides an excuse for his accepting the one, or an excuse for his rejecting another, will depend on what you think of some general philosophical principle, such as the principle that it is always best to reject a proposition if you do not have cogent philosophical grounds for accepting it.

So Hume's appeal to psychology here is not very useful. But, closely related to it, he has another argument. He thinks that our common-sense beliefs are *indispensable* in a special way: that we cannot think or talk about scientific or practical matters without *presupposing* them. He says, for instance, that it is 'vain' to wonder 'whether there be body or not?' We have to take this for granted in all our reasoning, he says. It is clear that he does not think this is true for religious beliefs. We do not have to take God's existence for granted in all our reasonings. Now this does not remove the inconsistency the Parity Argument emphasizes, but it does, now, give a *reason* for it. The reason is that if we want to respond to life's practical demands, or satisfy our scientific curiosity, we must assume these beliefs are true and go on from there. . . . Now it is importantly true, I think, that the existence of God is not something we have to take for granted in *all* our reasonings in the way in which the existence of physical bodies is. But although it is not indispensable for daily business and natural science, it *is* indispensable for *religious* actions and reasonings. In both cases there is a system of thought and action which can only go forward if the basic beliefs on which it is founded are presupposed. In both cases, there is, by hypothesis, no independent philosophical justification for the basic beliefs that are required. In the one case, the lack of justification presents no hindrance, since natural forces and demands activate the system without it. In the other, the forces and demands that activate the system in some do not activate it in others, because they are deflected by competing environmental influences. But there is still an obvious inconsistency in permitting this to happen. Unless, of course, one says something else—something Hume clearly does believe, and says in other places: that the religious life is socially and personally unpleasant and undesirable. But this moves the dispute into a completely different plane, and I will not follow it.

III

I do not think that Hume lays the Parity Argument to rest. . . . I would like to look at two recent presentations of it. . . .

[Alvin] Plantinga [Reading 7.3] seeks to defend belief in God against the criticism that it is irrational if adequate grounds are not given for it. This criticism, he says, is based upon a position he calls ***foundationalism.*** Foundationalism is the theory that our beliefs, if they are rational ones, can be divided into two classes: those that depend upon others, and those that do not depend upon others. The latter ones he calls **basic beliefs.** According to the foundationalist, every rational belief must either be justifiable by reference to a basic one, or must *be* a basic one. But what beliefs are basic? Traditional philosophical views about this, he says, say that a belief is basic (or is *properly* basic, or *ought* to be basic) if it is either self-evident or incorrigible: roughly it is properly basic if anyone who understands it sees it is beyond doubt (such as the statement that I am now thinking), or if anyone who sincerely states it cannot be mistaken (such as the statement that I have a mild headache now). Now anyone who insists that *only* statements like these should be allowed as basic is telling us something that he cannot possibly justify. For what he says is not self-evident and is not incorrigible; it can easily be doubted. Nor can it be proved to be true on the basis of statements that are self-evident or incorrigible. In fact, he says, any claim that only certain beliefs and not others can be basic is bound to be arbitrary. Traditional natural theologians thought they had to justify belief in God by proving it on the basis of something more basic; but why suppose this? Why can it not be rational to hold there is a God as one of my basic beliefs—one, roughly, that I start from, not one I have to justify.

[Norman] Malcolm's argument is similar to this,[1] though he bases it on some claims made by Wittgenstein in his late work, *On Certainty*. Among these is the claim that we can only raise doubts within a framework of beliefs which we acquire without question and without proof. Each of us, therefore, has a number of groundless beliefs which are fundamental to the questions and answers we frame during our lives. Malcolm gives as an example the belief that things do not vanish without explanation. He suggests it is quite conceivable that there should be a culture in which this possibility is not excluded, although in our culture we are not able to entertain it seriously, and we frame all our thinking, and answer all our questions about physical objects, in a manner which simply excludes it from consideration. He quotes Wittgenstein as offering the principle of the uniformity of nature as another example of such a framework-principle.

Each of us, then, lives within a group of framework beliefs which Wittgenstein calls a 'system,' which is presupposed without reflection, and without which our doubts cannot arise and our assertions cannot be made. Malcolm says that religious beliefs are framework-beliefs, in that it is out of place to demand justification of them. The system for which religious beliefs form the framework can require no justification, and the demand for one is based on misunderstanding: a misunderstanding that has generated the enterprise of natural theology. Justification may have its place *within* a religion; but internal disputes, like those about the status of some controversial doctrine, belong within a system whose framework beliefs are not subject to justification themselves. A result of this, which Malcolm accepts, and which seems independently to be plausible, is that one and the same fact may quite rationally have religious significance for someone whose thinking goes on within such a religious context, but have none at all for someone whose thinking does not.

There are interesting differences between these two arguments. But I am concerned with a core argument that is common to both. This I think may be called a *permissive* version of the Parity Argument. The older versions of the Parity Argument that we find in Pascal and Kierkegaard accuse *the unbeliever* of inconsistency in accepting common sense and denying religion. If I understand them correctly, Plantinga and Malcolm say something less than this. They say that *the believer* is *not* guilty of irrationality merely because he does not have grounds or justifications for believing in God. They argue this because rational disputes all presuppose *some* basic, or framework, beliefs, and it is arbitrary to insist that belief in God cannot function for believers as one of these. They do not say that an unbeliever is irrational merely because belief in God does not so function for *him*. Their view may be *part* of the one we find in Pascal and Kierkegaard, but is more modest.

What are we to make of the permissive Parity Argument? I assume, first, that however one uses the very difficult notion of rationality, we can agree that it is irrational to hold inconsistent beliefs; so that no rational being could hold as basic beliefs, or as framework beliefs, two or more beliefs which contradicted one another. I also assume that even though religious beliefs may not be based on grounds, they are, in an obvious way, *fruitful:* that is, that if one accepts them, one is able to offer interpretations of

[1]Norman Malcolm, 'The Groundlessness of Belief', in Norman Malcolm, *Thought and Knowledge* (Cornell University Press, Ithaca, 1977).

facts and events in one's life that would not be available without this.

Given these assumptions, I think it is fair to say that the permissive Parity Argument is successful. By this I mean that if it is true that each of us must make some intellectual commitments that cannot be justified without circularity, then someone who holds a religious commitment, such as belief in God, as one of these, cannot be convicted of irrationality merely because belief in God could not be justified by arguments to someone who did *not* have it as one of *his* fundamental intellectual commitments.

IV

What point have we reached? This, I think; the Parity Argument, as used by apologists such as Pascal and Kierkegaard, suggests that secular unbelievers are inconsistent to accept common sense and deny belief in God, if on the one hand they deny belief in God because there are no cogent philosophical grounds for it, yet have no cogent grounds to support their acceptance of common sense. The classic example of someone who represents this combination is Hume; and I do not think that any of his attempts to evade this charge of inconsistency are successful. Recent presentations of the Parity Argument, found in Plantinga and Malcolm, are less ambitious. They are designed, not to convict the unbeliever of inconsistency, but to defend the believer against the charge of irrationality. They hold that, whatever philosophers may suppose, all of us have to accept *some* beliefs as basic or ungrounded ones, and say that, in these circumstances, it is arbitrary to say that believers have no intellectual right to include belief in God among these. One can use this permissive version of the Parity Argument without seeking to use the more aggressive version; for one can hold that *both* the believer *and* the unbeliever are functioning *rationally,* that is, are functioning not irrationally.

This, of course, conjures up the picture of a multitude of worldviews, each rational in its own fashion, and each immune to the charge of irrationality. Before returning to this, and its religious implications, I would like to tidy up the unfinished discussion of the aggressive Parity Argument. I think I have now mentioned facts which can actually provide a defence for someone like Hume, even though he does not himself use this defence as far as I can tell.

Hume needs a special reason for treating the claims of religion differently from those of common sense, other than the groundlessness of belief in God. It is ready to hand if we notice that the believer's belief system does not involve the rejection of common sense. The religious believer does not reject the belief in the reality of objects of perception or the regularity of nature. He accepts them. What he does is to *add* to them. The unbeliever can now charge him with inconsistency in adding to them. The unbeliever can say that the secular intellectual commitment of common sense has borne fruit in the development of a large body of common sense and scientific knowledge, and that in arriving at this body of knowledge we have not only built it up by assembling positive evidence. We have also refrained from adopting beliefs, however secular in character, if they *exceeded* the evidence. One of the standards we have used is that of economy, or simplicity. It may be hard to formulate it very exactly, but it is very familiar. And it is clearly violated by adding religious beliefs to the system, given (as it is by hypothesis) that there is no independent body of evidence that establishes them. So adding belief in God represents an abandonment of the standard of simplicity that we have gained so much by following in science.

How good would this argument be? Well, the believer . . . can say that the standard of simplicity has to yield when faced with certain kinds of experience; or that it has to be understood as applying only to nature and not to the supernatural; or that it has to give place to the need for certain sorts of explanatory *depth*. Certainly there are reasons he can give for not letting it prevent his adding his religious commitments into his common-sense ones. But this would only show that *he* is not irrational to add these things on. It would *not* show that the unbeliever is inconsistent, or irrational in any other fashion, in *refusing* to add them on. So the charge of irrationality as this is levelled against *un*believers by writers like Pascal and Kierkegaard is not sustained, and Hume's position, though not the only rational possibility, is not an irrational or inconsistent one after all.

If this is right, then we are left with the situation that the permissive version of the Parity Argument presents: that it is not irrational to hold religious beliefs as basic or groundless ones. But this **epistemological** permission is bought at the price of recognizing that it is not irrational not to, either. This is an epistemological stand-off. In the absence of any cogent grounds for religious belief, this stand-off I have described is our actual intellectual situation. It is not as bad for the believer as many unbelievers think it is, intellectually speaking. But the same is true, equally, the other way around. The Parity Argument is victorious, but its victory is a Pyrrhic victory for religion.

V

Another way of expressing the situation I have described is to say that our world is *religiously ambiguous*. We live in a world where believers and unbelievers cannot successfully accuse one another of irrationality, merely because each holds beliefs without justification. Now a world like this is a world in which one can rationally believe; but it is also one in which one can rationally disbelieve. Clearly, many do one and many do the other.

I would like to suggest, as my conclusion, that there is something about this situation that ought to be disturbing to the believer. As a believer, it *is* disturbing to me.

Plantinga and Malcolm appear to think that traditional natural theology rests on a mistake: the mistake of thinking that religious belief has to have justification, and then seeking to offer that justification. I think that their permissive Parity Argument undermines that supposition—if natural theologians were making it. But I am not sure that this captures the real point of natural theology. Of course, writers like Aquinas did think they could give good grounds for religion. But Aquinas, at least, was quite clear that someone whose religious beliefs are not the results of entertaining these grounds, is not believing irrationally. What exactly were they trying to do? What would actually be involved if one of the natural theologian's arguments were successful? It would show that the believer's key commitment, say to the existence of God, could be derived from information that he and the unbeliever both agreed upon, using standards that he and the unbeliever both shared. (For example, what Cleanthes in Hume's *Dialogues* tries unsuccessfully to do is to show God's existence to be an overwhelmingly likely scientific hypothesis [See Reading 4.8]). A successful argument along such lines would show that the unbeliever ought to believe, on pain of violating *his own criteria* of rationality, and on pain of being inconsistent with *his own* belief system—for example, without violating the principle of simplicity. In such a situation, the Parity Argument could not be used to shield the unbeliever from what would then be the manifest obligation to accept the existence of God. If such an argument were successful, the world of the believer and the unbeliever would be dis-ambiguated. It would no longer be possible, with equal rationality, either to believe or not. I think it is quite clear from the literature that the traditional natural theologians were indeed trying to do something as strong as this. They were not offering arguments in support of religion because they felt that without them religion would stand convicted of irrationality. They were on the attack: they wanted to show that it is irrational *not* to believe in the existence of God, and the fact of creation, and the providential governance of the world. In their own words, they were trying to *prove* that there is a God, that there is creation, that the world is under Providence. They were trying to establish that religion is rational in a stronger sense than the Parity Argument shows it to be: namely, that denying it is *not* rational.

So, what if they were? Well, if their enterprise were ever successful, something of great religious importance would follow. Someone who has had the existence of God proved to him has had all reasonable ground for not believing in God taken away. Even if he is still worried by the problem of evil, for example, once God's existence is proved to him, he knows quite well that the problem of evil has to have a solution, even if he does not know yet what it is. On the other hand, someone who lives in a world where it is rational to believe, but also rational not to believe, has a reasonable ground for not believing in God, whether the problem of evil worries him or not. This ground is the simple fact that there are no cogent grounds for believing. It does not prove God does *not* exist; but it makes it quite reasonable not to believe he does. There are perfectly good excuses for unbelief in a religiously ambiguous world such as ours.

Now believers are very prone (and this is especially true, ironically, of believers like Pascal and Kierkegaard) to say that unbelief is due to sinfulness or corruption; that if we do not believe in God it is because we *will* not [to]. They say it costs us too much. But this claim is one which can never be substantiated in a world in which it is reasonable to disbelieve.

For even if unbelievers *are* all people who do not *want* to believe, in a religiously ambiguous world they have a decent excuse for not contending with their evil disinclinations. But a world in which God's existence were *proved* to them would be one in which they did not have any such excuse; for that sort of world *would* be one in which unbelief could be due only to nonintellectual factors, like sinfulness.

If this is right, it seems to me that **theologians** should abandon the lamentable and fashionable practice of rejoicing in the fact that no one has yet succeeded in proving God's existence. They should *deplore* this failure, and try to rectify it.

There is a standard response to this, familiar and ready to hand. If God's existence were proved to us, we could not help believing it. Our freedom would be taken away. Our submission to God would be compelled. God's existence has to be uncertain for the acceptance of it to be free.

There is no merit in this argument. It is the easiest thing in the world for something to be proved to me that I will not accept. All I need to do is to be determined about going back to the premisses of the argument and questioning them, or denying the cogency of the steps that lead from the evidence to the conclusion. I can deceive myself, readily, about the facts the proof is based on, or the logic of the reasoning that concludes with it. All I need is a little training in philosophy. The world is full of people who deny things they know perfectly well.

I have not argued that if God's existence were proved to us, we would all believe in it. Very likely it would have no effect on the extent of religious belief at all. But it *would* then be clear that unbelief was deliberate, and was a product of self-deception; so that we had no excuse for not believing. And what theological merit could there be in the fact that there is an excuse for not believing now? More simply, if religion is true, why is it not more *obviously* true?

STUDY QUESTIONS

1. Summarize the parity argument.
2. Penelhum accepts one form of the parity argument and rejects another. Which does he accept, and which does he reject? Why?
3. Why does Penelhum think that the permissive parity argument does not do enough for theists? Do you agree? *How might theists reply?
4. *Penelhum asserts that the fact that religious beliefs are avoidable, universal, and indispensable, whereas our major commonsense beliefs are not, does not refute the parity argument for regarding religious beliefs as rational. Do you agree? Why or why not?
5. *What might Penelhum say about a parity argument for the existence of the Great Pumpkin of Plantinga's article (Reading 7.3)?

PRAGMATIC APPROACHES

READING 7.5

Toward a Pragmatic Conception of Religious Faith

Joshua L. Golding

Joshua L. Golding (Bellarmine College) argues in this selection that religious faith should be understood as an "action-guiding assumption." The religious person, Golding says, has a certain goal—to have a good relationship with God. However, whereas someone who believes that he or she already has such a relationship clearly believes that God exists, someone who is merely trying to attain such a relationship does not necessarily believe that God exists. Just as a person might enter a lottery while not believing he or she will win, or a doctor might try to cure a deathly ill patient while not believing the patient will be cured, so may one act as if God exists while not believing that God exists—in fact, while believing it unlikely that God exists. The religious person is committed only to the belief that there is a chance that God exists; however, he or she assumes for practical purposes that God exists and acts as if this belief were true.

Golding argues that it is pragmatically rational for a person to make an action-guiding assumption. He maintains that not only how one acts but also how one interprets events and experiences are affected by one's action-guiding assumption that God exists.

INTRODUCTION

. . . [T]he question of whether it is (or can be) rational to have faith is of special interest precisely because we want to know whether it is (or can be) rational *to be religious*. After all, if faith were not in some way a necessary part of the religious life, we would not be so interested in determining whether it is (or can be) rational. For [this and other] reasons, then, it is constructive to focus the debate about religious faith on the question, What stance is a religious person committed to take on the proposition "God exists"?

The present paper aims to provide an answer to this question. It does not aim to provide a *full* answer to the question, What is religious faith? For faith may involve more than some stance on the proposition "God exists." However, to the extent that faith does involve some such stance, this paper aims to provide a *partial* answer to the question, What is religious faith?

Now it is obvious that the nature of this stance can be settled only in the context of some conception of what it is to be a religious person. Accordingly, this paper begins with an attempt to work out such a conception. The bulk of this paper then expounds and defends the view that a religious person is committed to making a certain sort of "assumption for practical purpose" that God exists. The notion of an "assumption for practical purpose" is often used in ordinary speech, and occurs in philosophical discussions as well, particularly in contexts where a claim is made to the effect that some such "assumption for practical purpose" is rationally justified.[1] Doubtless there are several senses this notion can take, yet it is rarely explicated with precision. Hence, it will be necessary to work out the notion of an "assumption for practical purpose" in some detail, and to contrast it with other neighborhood notions such as "belief" and "hope." I shall then formulate a general condition under which it is *pragmatically rational* for a person to make such an assumption, which will facilitate the argument that a religious person is committed to taking precisely this sort of stance on the proposition "God exists." For the sake of clarification, I shall then contrast this view with other accounts of religious faith expounded in recent literature. Finally, I shall briefly discuss the implications of this view for the problem of whether it is (or can be) rational to have religious faith.

1. THE RELIGIOUS PERSON

Quite obviously, it is possible to propose different and perhaps even mutually incompatible conceptions of what it is to be a religious person. Nevertheless, it is legitimate to demand that any such proposal meet the following criteria. Firstly, it must characterize a great

[1]For example, [Immanuel] Kant attempts to justify what he calls "postulates of practical reason" in the *Critique of Practical Reason*, Book II, chapter II: secs. IV–VI. Also, in *The Scientific Image* (Oxford: Clarendon Press, 1980), B. C. van Fraassen argues that we are justified in "accepting" (but not believing) scientific theories. Finally, James C. S. Wernham has reconstructed James' "Will to Believe" as an attempt to justify not the *belief* but rather the "gamble" that God exists. See *James' Will to Believe Doctrine: A Heretical View* (Kingston and Montreal: McGill-Queen's University Press, 1987). . . .

bulk of people who are designated as "religious" in ordinary speech, and it must fail to characterize a great bulk of people who are not so designated. Secondly, the proposal should be fruitful in giving us some handle on **normative** questions as to whether it is good or bad, rational or irrational to be religious.

I propose the following. *A person is religious if and only if he pursues the goal of having a good relationship with God. . . .*

What requires . . . elaboration here is the notion of *pursuing a goal,* in this case the goal of having a good relationship with God. The following rough analysis will apply, *mutatis mutandis* [the necessary changes having been made], to the pursuit of *any* goal; for the sake of brevity let's confine our discussion to the religious case. Firstly, a person may pursue the goal of having a good relationship with God only if he has some *conception* of what that goal is like. This means, of course, that he must have some conception of God and of what makes for a good relationship with God. Secondly, a person may pursue that goal only if he *desires* to have a good relationship with God. This desire may be "impure" or "pure," that is, it may or may not be a desire that is in turn motivated by a desire for something ulterior, such as, the desire to maintain family tradition. Or, it may be a mixture of both. In any case, this desire alone is not sufficient for *pursuing* a good relationship with God; another condition is that one *acts* on that desire by doing (or refraining from) those actions which one believes are more (rather than less) likely to result in one's having that relationship. Now the *extent* to which one does (or refrains from) those actions may vary from "always" to "sometimes" to "once in a while"; this will determine the *extent* to which one pursues a good relationship with God. Finally, implicit in "acting on the desire" for a good relationship with God is yet another condition, namely, that in the first place one *believes* that some actions are more (rather than less) likely to result in one's having that relationship. If one believes that no matter what one does (or refrains from), one is just as likely to succeed in having that relationship, one cannot properly be said to "act on a desire" to have that relationship. Precisely what it means to "act on a desire" is a tricky question, but for our purposes we need not carry the analysis further. In sum, we may say that a person pursues the goal of having a good relationship with God if and only if:

a) he has some conception of God and of what makes for a good relationship with God,
b) he desires to have that relationship,
c) he believes that some actions are more (rather than less) likely to result in his having that relationship, and,
d) he acts on his desire to have that relationship by (to some extent) doing (or refraining from) those actions.

Now there is an important distinction to be made between two classes of people who may be said to pursue this goal. Firstly, there are those who believe they already have a good relationship with God and are trying to maintain or perhaps improve that relationship. Secondly, there are those who do not believe they have that relationship, but who are trying to attain it in the first place. Of course, the boundary of this distinction is not so sharp: a person may not be sure whether his relationship with God is good. Moreover, the same person may drift from one of these classes to the other.

So much for elaboration of the proposal that a person is religious if and only if he pursues the goal of having a good relationship with God. I submit that this proposal meets the above criteria for an adequate conception of what it is to be a religious person. Firstly, it characterizes a great bulk of people who are designated "religious" in ordinary speech, and does not characterize a great bulk of people who are not so designated. Of course, it would be preposterous to claim that it fits every occasion on which the phrase "religious person" is used. Most notably, although many would describe polytheists and Zen Buddhists as "religious," neither group can be said to "pursue the goal of having a good relationship with God." But the proposal covers not only "monotheists" such as Jews, Christians, and Muslims, but indeed anyone who pursues a good relationship with a being whom he or she considers radically supreme. Secondly, this proposal is fruitful in giving us a handle on normative questions about the religious life. We can now ask, for example, whether the conception in (a), the desire in (b), the belief in (c), and the policy in (d) are, respectively, coherent or incoherent, good or bad, true or false, rational or irrational. In what follows, we shall adopt this proposal in order to work out what stance a religious person is committed to take on the proposition "God exists."

2. MUST THE RELIGIOUS PERSON BELIEVE THAT GOD EXISTS?

It is clear that whether or not God exists, there certainly are religious persons. It is equally clear that no religious person can succeed in his goal of having a good relationship with God if God does not exist. Whether a religious person is committed to *believe* that God exists is a matter to which we now turn our attention. Recall that there are two classes of religious persons. Firstly, there are those who believe they have a good relationship with God and are trying to maintain or perhaps improve that relationship. Secondly, there are those who do not believe they have that relationship, but are trying to attain it in the first place. Now it is patent that the first class of persons are committed to believing that God exists, for it would be irrational or incoherent to believe that one has a good relationship with God without believing that God exists. In general, if one believes that one has a relationship with X, one is committed to believing that X exists. . . .

Now consider the second class of religious persons, namely, those who do not believe they have a good relationship with God, but are trying to attain it in the first place. Of course, such persons *may* believe that God exists. But they are not *committed* to the belief that God exists. Quite often, we desire and pursue goals for which we do not believe that conditions are such that we will succeed. For example, we pursue such goals as winning a lottery, or curing a deathly ill patient. And there is nothing inherently irrational about our doing so. Furthermore, there is nothing inherently irrational about a person who pursues the goal of having some relationship with X even whilst not having the belief that X exists. For example, consider a scientist who pursues the goal of communicating with extra-terrestrial life. Following our analysis in the previous section of what it is to pursue a goal, such a scientist

a′) has a conception of extra-terrestrial life and of what it is to communicate with extra-terrestrial life,
b′) desires to communicate with extra-terrestrial life,
c′) believes that some actions are more (rather than less) likely to result in his communicating with extra-terrestrial life, and,
d′) he acts on his desire by (to some extent) doing (or refraining from) those actions.

It would be perfectly plausible for such a scientist not to have the belief that there exists extra-terrestrial life. In fact, in the extreme case such a scientist might even believe that it is extremely unlikely that there exists such life; still there is nothing inherently irrational about this scientist. Similarly, it is not inherently irrational for a person to pursue a good relationship with God, even whilst not having the belief that God exists, or for that matter, even whilst having the belief that it is extremely unlikely that God exists.

However, there does seem to be something irrational about pursuing a goal which one does not believe there is at least some chance (however small) of attaining. And indeed, given the analysis sketched previously of what it is involved in pursuing a goal, we can pinpoint the irrationality. Recall that in order to pursue a goal, one must believe that some actions are more (rather than less) likely to result in one's attaining that goal. But if one believes this, one is rationally committed to believe that there is at least some chance (however small) that one will attain the goal. And it follows that one is rationally committed to believe that there is some chance (however small) that there exists whatever is necessary for obtaining the goal. Thus the scientist in the example above must at least believe that there is some chance (however small) that extra-terrestrial life exists. Similarly, all religious persons are rationally committed to the belief that *there is some chance (however small) that God exists.*

Precisely what it means to believe that *there is some chance that p* is a matter of philosophical controversy, and there is no room here to enter this debate. Suffice it to say that the belief that *there is some chance that God exists* is quite different from the belief that *God exists*. In normal usage, the statement "John believes P" implies that "John is more confident of P than not-P." But the statement "John believes there is some chance that P" does *not* imply that "John is more confident of P than not-P." Thus, a person who believes that *God exists* is more confident of *God exists* than of *God does not exist*. However, a person who believes *there is some chance that God exists* may in fact be more confident of *God does not exist* than *God exists*.

We may sum up the conclusions of this section as follows. Those religious persons who believe that they have a good relationship with God are rationally committed to believe that God exists, and *a fortiori* they are committed to believe that there is at least some chance that God exists. Those religious persons who do not believe that they have a good relationship with God are not committed to believe that God exists. But, all religious persons are committed to believe that there is at least some chance (however small) that God exists.

At this point, one might be tempted to conclude that the stance which a religious person is committed to take on the proposition "God exists" has been resolved: a religious person is committed to believe that there is at least some chance (however small) that God exists. However, this would be quite odd—if only for the fact that many (and perhaps most) people who are *not* religious believe that there is some small chance that God exists! Indeed, in the remaining sections we shall see that there is a much stronger stance which the religious person must take on the proposition "God exists."

3. THE NOTION OF AN "ASSUMPTION FOR PRACTICAL PURPOSE"

The view I propose to articulate and defend is that a religious person is committed to "act on the assumption" or "assume for practical purpose" that God exists. Now obviously there are different ways of explicating what is an "assumption for practical purpose." In this section I present one way of doing so.

To begin with, two general comments are in order. Firstly, the notion of an "assumption that P for practical purpose" (where P is some proposition) is not restricted to the religious dimension. There are many sorts of propositions which we can assume for practical purpose. For example, one might assume for practical purpose that it will not rain tomorrow, that the future will be like the past, or that nature is uniform. This *kind* of assumption is obviously not peculiar to religion.

Secondly, it is obvious that an "assumption that P for practical purpose" makes reference to some goal or goals in virtue of which the assumption is made by some person. A point that is less obvious but equally important is that different persons may assume the very same proposition P for the purpose of pursuing different goals; indeed, even the very same person may assume P for the purpose of pursuing different goals. We must also distinguish between an assumption that is made by someone for the purpose of pursuing a single goal or set of goals on the one hand, and an assumption that someone makes, as the saying goes, for "all practical purposes," or, as we may say, for the purpose of pursuing all of his goals. Hence, in place of speaking of an "assumption for practical purpose that P" it is more explicit (and less misleading) to distinguish an "assumption that P for the purpose of pursuing goal G"—where G is some specified goal or set of goals—from an "assumption that P for the purpose of pursuing all of one's goals." Clearly, though, an analysis of the latter will depend on an analysis of the former.

Having made these preliminary points, we may now proceed to explicate the notion of an "assumption that P for the purpose of pursuing goal G." Of course, there are various ways of doing this. The particular sort of assumption I have in mind may also be dubbed an "action-guiding" assumption. The **necessary and sufficient conditions** for a person's making such an assumption are as follows:

> Given that person N pursues goal G, N makes *an action-guiding assumption that P for the purpose of pursuing G* if and only if insofar as N pursues G he tries to do those things which are, if P is true, more (rather than less) likely to result in his attaining G.

This somewhat cumbersome definition is best grasped by means of example. Suppose that Dr. Jones pursues the goal of curing a patient of a tumor, and that several medical options are available, such as, chemical treatments, surgical procedures, and dietary regimens. Suppose also that Jones believes that if the tumor is benign, chemical treatments are more (rather than less) likely to result in the patient's cure (i.e., the patient is more likely to be cured if he is chemically treated than if he is not chemically treated). Furthermore, Jones believes that surgical procedures are somewhat dangerous, and are unnecessary if the tumor is benign. However, Jones also believes that if the tumor is malignant, chemical treatments will be completely ineffectual, and in this case surgical procedures are more (rather than less) likely to result in the patient's cure (i.e., the patient is more likely to be cured if surgery is done than if surgery is not done). Now, we may say that Jones makes an action-guiding assumption that "the tumor is benign" for the purpose of trying to cure the patient if and only if, insofar as he pursues this goal, he tries to do those things which are, if the tumor is benign, more (rather than less) likely to cure the patient. In our case, this would involve his employing the chemical treatments and not the surgical procedures. But it may involve more than that. For example, depending on other particular facts about the patient and the nature of the tumor, Jones may also conclude that if the tumor is benign, certain dietary regimens are more (rather than less) likely to cure the patient. The particular actions which are dictated by Jones' action-guiding assumption that the tumor is benign will depend on the particular circumstances of the case.

In effect, there is both a "**cognitive**" and a "practical" component involved in an action-guiding assumption that P for the purpose of pursuing G. A person who makes such an assumption engages in a research program designed to *figure out* what things promote (i.e., render it more likely that he will attain) goal G if proposition P is true. Secondly, based on his background beliefs as well as the information gleaned from this research, he tries to *do* those things that promote his attaining G if P is true.[2]

So much for clarification of the necessary and sufficient conditions for making what I have called an "action-guiding" assumption. This appears to be one of the ways in which the phrase "assumption for practical purpose" is used. No doubt there are other uses as well, and it would be nice to spell them out. Here we shall concentrate further on this particular use. It is important to contrast an "action-guiding assumption that P for the purpose of pursuing G" with the *hope that P* and the *belief that P,* as well as with some other neighboring notions. We begin with the notion of "hope that P." Roughly speaking, a person who "hopes that P" desires or wants it to be the case that P, but does not know that P and does not know that not-P. It is easy to see that an "action-guiding assumption that P for the purpose of pursuing G" differs from a "hope that P." To begin with, a person who hopes that P need not be pursuing a goal for which he guides his actions on the assumption that P. For example, I may hope that someday I will own a million dollars but not pursue any goal on the assumption that I will own a million dollars. Nor does it follow from the fact that one assumes that P for the purpose of pursuing some goal G that one also hopes that P. For example, in the case described earlier, Dr. Jones may assume that "the tumor is malignant" for the purpose of curing his patient, without *hoping* that the tumor is malignant. In short, hopes need not be action guiding, and action-guiding assumptions need not constitute things hoped for.

Another notion worth considering here is that of "acting to pursue some goal G *in the hope* that P." This notion may seem close to the notion of an action-guiding assumption, but our previous example (concerning Dr. Jones) also shows that one can be involved in doing the latter without doing the

[2]It is necessary to insert the phrase ". . . insofar as N pursues G . . ." in the **definiens** of an action-guiding assumption since N may try to promote *other* goals, and, what promotes goal G may not promote some other goal; moreover, what promotes G *if P is true* may not promote another goal. For example, Dr. Jones may believe that if the tumor is benign his patient is more likely to be cured if he is put on a liquid diet for a year. However, putting the patient on such a diet may conflict with Jones' other goal of not causing his patient unnecessary pain. But we would not want to say that Jones has failed to assume that "the tumor is benign" for the purpose of curing his patient just if he fails to order the liquid diet. Here, he neglects to order the liquid diet because he has other goals aside from curing the patient. Thus our definition has built in the restriction that it concerns what N does "insofar as he pursues G."

former. Similarly, one can act to pursue some goal G *in the hope that P* without guiding one's actions on the assumption that P. For example, Jones may pursue the goal of curing his patient *in the hope* that the tumor is benign, even though he makes an action-guiding assumption that the tumor is malignant.

Next, let us consider the difference between an *action-guiding assumption that P for the purpose of pursuing G* and a *belief that P*. Certainly it is quite compatible for someone both to believe that P and to make an action-guiding assumption that P for the purpose of pursuing some goal G. However, the one does not require or entail the other. Consider once again the example mentioned above. Even though Jones may not *believe* that the tumor is malignant, he may *still* decide to make the action-guiding assumption that it is malignant for the purpose of curing his patient. Indeed, he may doubt *very much* that the tumor is malignant, and *still* assume so for that specific goal.

Conversely, a person may believe that P, without making an action-guiding assumption that P for the purpose of pursuing G. This may happen simply because the person happens not to pursue G, or because although he pursues G, he deems the truth or falsity of P as irrelevant to the pursuit of G. In neither case has the person made an action-guiding assumption that P. In sum, one may believe that P without assuming it for some specific goal G, and, conversely, one may assume that P for some goal G without believing that P.

Moreover, the notion of an action-guiding assumption that P for the purpose of pursuing G is not to be confused with the notion of "believing that there is some chance that P." Firstly, given two individuals who believe there is the exact same chance that P, one may assume P for some goal G and one may not. This may happen because the latter happens not to pursue G, or because although he pursues G he regards the truth or falsity of P as irrelevant to the pursuit of goal G. Moreover, the very same individual who believes there is some chance that P may assume P for one of his goals but not for another.[3]

[3]It is not clear to me whether a person can make an action-guiding assumption that P without believing that there is some chance (however small) that P. However, it would seem irrational to do so.

Let us consider next the contrast between the notion of an action-guiding assumption that P for the purpose of pursuing goal G and the notion of "acting to pursue goal G in the belief that P." Obviously the two differ at least to the extent that, as we have already seen, the notion of an action-guiding assumption that P differs from the notion of a belief that P. But, it also seems that someone who "pursues goal G in the belief that P" is someone who pursues G on the action-guiding assumption that P (although not necessarily *vice versa*). This leads us to pose the following question. Where the goal is identical, to what extent would the *actions* involved in "acting in the belief that P" and "acting on an assumption that P" differ? Compare, for example, a defense strategist who attempts to construct a secure defense policy merely on the *assumption* that the Russians are cheating on the latest arms-treaty, with another strategist—exactly alike in all other respects, but—who makes the same attempt not only on the assumption but also in the *belief* that the Russians are cheating. Our question is, insofar as they pursue the stated goal, would their actions differ? It is tempting to say that, in any realistic case, their actions would not differ at all.

It is worthwhile in this context to comment on the rather common phrase, "acting as if one believes." In the case just described, it seems reasonable to say that the first strategist is "acting as if he believes" that the Russians are cheating. This is an accurate turn of phrase here, as long as it is kept in mind that it is only with respect to a limited range of his behavior that he "acts as if he believes" that the Russians are cheating. That is, he "acts as if he believes" insofar as he pursues the goal of constructing a secure defense policy. He need not "act as if he believes" with respect to his other goals (such as, the goal of forming warm personal ties with Russian diplomats).

Moreover, in spite of the above example, it is emphatically *not* always the case that a person who pursues G in the belief that P and a person who merely assumes that P for the purpose of pursuing G act in the same way, *even* with respect to actions that are oriented toward G. This may occur in cases where the fact that a person believes P is itself relevant to determining how that person pursues G. Let us return to our example concerning the doctor and patient. Imagine that although Dr. Jones is a skilled surgeon and usually does his own operations, he gets too nervous to operate if he believes that a patient's life depends on successful surgery, and he refers any such cases to another surgeon. Suppose also that Dr. Jones believes that the life of any patient with a malignant tumor depends on successful surgery. Under these circumstances, there will be an important difference between the case where Dr. Jones pursues the goal of curing his patient in the *belief* that the tumor is malignant, and the case where he pursues this same goal only on the *assumption* that the tumor is malignant. In the former case, he will refer the patient elsewhere for operation; in the latter case, he will be confident enough to operate. And in the latter case, it would be quite mistaken to say that Dr. Jones is "acting as if he believes" that the tumor is malignant; if he believed the tumor were malignant, he wouldn't operate! Hence, there are some cases where a person who pursues G *in the belief* that P acts differently from a person who pursues G merely *on the action-guiding assumption* that P—*even* with respect to those actions that are oriented toward G. And in such cases it is wrong to describe the latter as "acting as if he believes" that P.

We may summarize the discussion of the last several pages as follows. The notion of an action-guiding assumption that P for the purpose of pursuing some goal G is different from any of the following:

a) hoping that P
b) acting to pursue G in the hope that P
c) believing that P
d) assuming that P for the purpose of pursuing *all* goals
e) believing that there is some chance that P
f) acting to pursue G in the belief that P

In addition, we have found that in some cases, a person who makes an action-guiding assumption that P for the purpose of pursuing G need not act in the same way (to attain goal G) as a person who pursues the very same goal G *in the belief* that P. These conclusions will be important later, when we turn to the topic of religious faith.

Before doing so, it is necessary to formulate a principle which describes one condition under which it is *pragmatically rational* to make an action-guiding assumption. I call it the *Principle of Rational Assumption* (or *PRA*). I shall first state the principle, then give two examples of its application, and then attempt to defend it.

> *PRA:* Given a person N who pursues goal G and believes that he will attain G only if P is true, it is *pragmatically rational* for person N to make an action-guiding assumption that P for the purpose of pursuing G.

An example of the application of *PRA* is as follows. Suppose that Dr. Jones pursues the goal of curing his patient of a tumor, *and* that he believes he will succeed only if the tumor is benign. *PRA* dictates that under these circumstances, it is pragmatically rational for Jones to make an action-guiding assumption that the tumor is benign for the purpose of trying to cure his patient. Thus if Jones believes that, if the tumor is benign, he is more likely to cure his patient by chemical treatments than by surgery, *PRA* dictates that it is pragmatically rational for him to use the treatments rather than the surgery. Another example is as follows. Suppose that Smith pursues the goal of winning the next election against the incumbent, *and* that Smith believes he will win only if there is currently widespread dissatisfaction with the incumbent. *PRA* dictates that under such circumstances, it is pragmatically rational for Smith to make an action-guiding assumption that there is widespread dissatisfaction with the incumbent for the purpose of pursuing the goal of winning the election. For example, Smith may believe that if there is widespread dissatisfaction with the incumbent, it is more likely that Smith will win if he espouses radically new policies than if he does not do so. If so, *PRA* says that, insofar as Smith pursues the goal of winning the election, the pragmatically rational thing for him to do is to espouse radically new policies.

From these examples it is easy to see that *PRA* is, at the very least, intuitively plausible. Jones believes he will cure the patient only if the tumor is benign. So (given his other beliefs) there is no point in his doing the surgery, and his only sensible strategy is to use chemical treatments. True, Jones believes that if the tumor is malignant the chemical treatments are unlikely to help; but Jones believes that if the tumor is malignant he will not cure the patient anyhow.

Similarly, Smith believes that he will win only if there is widespread dissatisfaction with the incumbent. In trying to win the election, he does well to guide his actions on the assumption that there is such dissatisfaction. In general, then, *PRA* seems valid.

A more rigorous defense of *PRA* requires us first to comment on the notion of "pragmatic rationality." It would take us far afield to dissect this notion. However, it seems plausible to say that given a person N who pursues goal G, it is *pragmatically rational* for person N to try to do action A if it follows from some of N's beliefs that of all his available options, it is most likely that he will attain G if he does action A. To take a simple example, suppose N has the goal of getting to Chicago by train, and that N believes that of two available trains, it is more likely that train One is going to Chicago than train Two. It follows from N's beliefs that of all his available options, he is most likely to attain his goal if he takes train One. We may say, then, that given N's goal of getting to Chicago, it is pragmatically rational for him to try to take train One. Now I caution the reader that we have defined a course of action as "pragmatically rational" in such a way that it does not matter whether N's goal is good or bad, rational or irrational (if goals can be evaluated in this way). Nor does it matter whether N's relevant belief is true or false, rational or irrational. For example, suppose that N pursues the goal of traveling backward in time, and that he (irrationally) believes it is more likely that he will do so if he fasts for three days. Our definition yields that it is pragmatically rational for N to fast for three days. One might balk at this result, since from an "objective" point of view, it is *not* rational for N to fast for three days. However, this does not mean that our notion of pragmatic rationality is in itself "subjective." It is neither subjective nor objective. The matter may be put as follows. If N's goal and the relevant belief are objectively rational, then the course of action will be objectively pragmatically rational. And if N's goal or his relevant belief is not objectively rational, then the course of action will be only subjectively pragmatically rational.

To return to *PRA*. Given this conception of "pragmatic rationality" we can now see that *PRA* is valid. If a person N pursues goal G and believes he will attain G only if P is true, it follows from N's beliefs that he is more likely to attain G if he makes an action-guiding assumption that P than if he does not. Using our earlier example, given Dr. Jones' goal of curing his patient, and his belief that he will cure the patient only if the tumor is benign, it follows from Dr. Jones' beliefs that he is more likely to cure the patient if he does those things which are, if the tumor is benign, more (rather than less) likely to result in his curing the patient. Hence it is pragmatically rational (in the sense defined above) for Jones to guide his actions on the assumption that the tumor is benign. Thus, in general, *PRA* is a valid principle.

4. THE RELIGIOUS PERSON'S STANCE ON "GOD EXISTS"

Let us turn, at last, to religious faith. At the outset of this paper we said that one question at stake in the debate about faith is, What stance is a religious person committed to taking on the proposition "God exists"—*given* the fact that he is religious? We may now supply a rigorous answer to this question. A religious person is committed to making an action-guiding assumption that "God exists" for the purpose of pursuing a good relationship with God. He is "committed" to taking this stance in the sense that it is pragmatically rational for him to do so. The proof of this is as follows. Recall our conception of a religious person as someone who pursues the goal of having a good relationship with God. Now such a person believes he will succeed in having a good relationship with God only if God exists. Hence, by *PRA* it follows that it is pragmatically rational for a religious person to make an action-guiding assumption that God exists for the purpose of pursuing a good relationship with God. Now it would be improper to say that faith *consists in* this assumption, since faith may involve more than the religious person's stance on "God exists." However, to the extent that faith consists partly in that stance, we may say that faith consists partly in an action-guiding assumption that God exists for the purpose of pursuing a good relationship with God.

What is involved in having this sort of faith? To begin with, as with any action-guiding assumption, there are two components involved, namely, a cognitive and a practical aspect. The cognitive aspect consists in trying to figure out what actions are, if God exists, more (rather than less) likely to result in one's having a good relationship with God. The practical aspect involves trying to carry out those actions.

Now the precise nature of the actions dictated by this sort of faith will depend first and foremost on the religious person's conception of God. It is not our task here to account for how one arrives at a conception of God, much less to defend one conception in particular. But, for the sake of example, let us consider what actions would be dictated on a Biblical conception, where God assists those who pursue a good relationship with him, and indeed the success of the religious person's quest is dependent on God's assistance. On this conception of God, faith requires that the religious person conduct his pursuit on the assumption that indeed God will assist him. Moreover, on a Biblical conception, God responds at least on some occasions to **petitionary prayer.** Thus faith requires that the religious person at least on some occasions pray to God for assistance in his pursuit of God. Finally, on this conception, God turns away from those who do what is evil, so faith requires that the religious person avoid doing evil.

But the actions required by this sort of faith will depend not only on one's conception of God but also on one's personal experience, as well as one's historical and cultural background. On the present view, faith requires a religious person to interpret events in his own life, in the life of his community, and in the world at large in the context of the assumption that God exists, strictly for the purpose of reckoning how he should react to these events in order to promote his goal. For example, suppose a person has an extraordinary or even ordinary experience, in which it seems to him either very strongly or very faintly that God is in some way revealing himself. Or, to take another example, suppose a person witnesses unusual events (of the miraculous sort such as those described in the Bible or of the more mundane sort such as medically inexplicable recovery from a fatal disease) that seem to point toward the hand of God. Or, consider a person who only *hears of* or *reads about* accounts of such religious experience or unusual events. On the present view, faith requires a religious person to interpret these events on the assumption that God exists, for the purpose of pursuing a good relationship with God. A person in any of the above situations may conclude that, if God exists, God is communicating some message or directive to him. (Precisely what that message or directive might be will again depend on the particular circumstances.) And, should the person conclude that if God exists, some specific message or directive has been communicated, faith will also require that he try to incorporate that message or fulfill that directive in his pursuit of a good relationship with God.

This pragmatic conception of religious faith is rooted in the Bible. The Hebrew term usually translated as "faith" is *emunah,* which often connotes trust, reliance, or dependence.[4] Now there is no intention here to insist that the above is an *analysis* of the Biblical *emunah*. However, it is clear that a person who has *emunah* in God is a person who trusts in God, in (at least) the sense that he is willing to act in ways that count on God's existence. In particular, he is willing to pursue a good relationship with God, on the assumption that God exists. Thus, a person who has *emunah* in God must (at least) have the sort of pragmatic faith worked out above. Whether this is all that Biblical *emunah* amounts to is a question we cannot explore here. . . .

5. CONCLUDING REMARKS

. . . [O]n the present account, it is irrational to have faith without believing that there is some chance (however small) that God exists. Hence the rationality of faith does not require the rationality of the belief that God exists, but rather the rationality of the belief that there is some chance (however small) that God exists. On the other hand, faith does not *consist* in either of these beliefs, since it involves the assumption that God exists for the purpose of pursuing a good relationship with God. Hence one cannot show

[4]See, e.g., *Genesis,* 16:7; *Numbers* 20:12.

that it is rational to have faith *merely* by showing that it is rational to believe that God exists or that there is some chance that God exists. Finally, we have seen that *given* the goal of the religious person, and *given* his belief that he will attain that goal only if God exists, it is pragmatically rational for that person to make the action-guiding assumption. But (recalling a distinction made in section 3) this leaves open whether it is *objectively* pragmatically rational to have faith. Now clearly *the belief* of the religious person that he will attain the goal only if God exists is objectively rational. Thus one could show that his action-guiding assumption is *objectively* pragmatically rational, if one could show that it is objectively pragmatically rational to pursue the religious goal. It would then follow that faith is, at least in part, objectively pragmatically rational to have. Needless to say, the question of whether it is (or can be) objectively pragmatically rational to pursue the religious goal still remains to be explored.

STUDY QUESTIONS

1. Golding says that we are interested in whether it is rational to believe that God exists only because we are interested in whether it is rational to be religious.* Do you agree? Explain.
2. What is an action-guiding assumption? Give examples of cases in which such an assumption is made. Include the case of religious belief.
3. How is holding an action-guiding assumption that *P* for the purpose of pursuing goal *G* different from (i) hoping that *P* (ii) acting in the hope that *P* (iii) believing that *P?*
4. Does a person who pursues a goal *G* on an action-guiding assumption that *P* always act the same as someone who pursues *G* in the belief that *P?* Explain.
5. Explain the Principle of Rational Assumption (PRA).
6. Golding says that action-guiding assumptions have a cognitive and a practical aspect. What does he mean?
7. Golding maintains that not only how one acts, but also how one interprets events and experiences, is affected by one's action-guiding assumption that God exists. Illustrate this claim using examples from chapters 4, 5, and 6 of this book. For example, what impact does Golding's point have on the argument from religious experience or on the problem of evil?
8. *Suppose someone wants to be protected from attacks by extraterrestrial beings. The person believes it unlikely that there will be such an attack but believes there is some chance there will be. According to Golding's PRA, would it be rational for this person to build a shelter so as to be protected in case of attack, say complimentary things about extraterrestrials to curry their favor, and the like? If such actions would not be rational, how could Golding distinguish this case from the case of acting on the assumption that God exists?
9. *There are many different views about what God wants of us. How might this point affect Golding's argument? Give a response on behalf of Golding. (See Readings 7.7, 7.9, and 7.11.)
10. *Do you agree with Golding that faith involves an action-guiding assumption that God exists, rather than belief that God exists? Why or why not?

READING 7.6

The Wager

Blaise Pascal

Blaise Pascal (1623–1662) was an eminent mathematician who made vital contributions to geometry, number theory, and probability theory. On November 23, 1654, he had a mystical experience, which influenced him to devote his life to God and, in particular, the Jansenist version of Christianity. Contrary to his contemporary, René Descartes (1596–1650), Pascal thought that God's existence cannot be proved. Nevertheless, we know that God exists by faith, and having this faith can be ration-

ally defended by showing that it is rational and prudent to wager on God's existence. If God exists, and you believe in God, you gain infinite happiness; if God exists and you don't believe, you will suffer infinitely; if God exists, and you do believe in God, you will have surrendered a few earthly finite pleasures; if God does not exist, and you don't believe in God, you've gained a few earthly pleasures. (Some interpreters question whether the prospect of infinite suffering is really a part of the argument.) Given these payoffs, the smart course is to bet on God. Pascal admits that a person might not be able to directly will to believe that God exists, but he suggests that performing religious rituals will cause the person to believe that God exists. The logic of the wager is evaluated by William G. Lycan and George N. Schlesinger in the next selection.

If there is a God, He is infinitely incomprehensible, since, having neither parts nor limits, He has no affinity to us. We are then incapable of knowing either what He is or if He is. This being so, who will dare to undertake the decision of the question? Not we, who have no affinity to Him.

Who then will blame Christians for not being able to give a reason for their belief, since they profess a religion for which they cannot give a reason? They declare, in expounding it to the world, that it is a foolishness, *stultitiam;* and then you complain that they do not prove it! If they proved it, they would not keep their word; it is in lacking proofs that they are not lacking in sense. "Yes, but although this excuses those who offer it as such, and takes away from them the blame of putting it forward without reason, it does not excuse those who receive it." Let us then examine this point, and say, "God is, or He is not." But to which side shall we incline? Reason can decide nothing here. There is an infinite chaos which separated us. A game is being played at the extremity of this infinite distance where heads or tails will turn up. What will you wager? According to reason, you can do neither the one thing nor the other; according to reason, you can defend neither of the propositions.

Do not then reprove for error those who have made a choice; for you know nothing about it. "No, but I blame them for having made, not this choice, but a choice; for again both he who chooses heads and he who chooses tails are equally at fault, they are both in the wrong. The true course is not to wager at all."

Yes; but you must wager. It is not optional. You are embarked. Which will you choose then? Let us see. Since you must choose, let us see which interests you least. You have two things to lose, the true and the good; and two things to stake, your reason and your will, your knowledge and your happiness; and your nature has two things to shun, error and misery. Your reason is no more shocked in choosing one rather than the other, since you must of necessity choose. This is one point settled. But your happiness? Let us weigh the gain and the loss in wagering that God is. Let us estimate these two chances. If you gain, you gain all; if you lose, you lose nothing. Wager, then, without hesitation that He is.—"That is very fine. Yes, I must wager; but I may perhaps wager too much."—Let us see. Since there is an equal risk of gain and of loss, if you had only to gain two lives, instead of one, you might still wager. But if there were three lives to gain, you would have to play (since you are under the necessity of playing), and you would be imprudent, when you are forced to play, not to chance your life to gain three at a game where there is an equal risk of loss and gain. But there is an eternity of life and happiness. And this being so, if there were an infinity of chances, of which one only would be for you, you would still be right in wagering one to win two, and you would act stupidly, being obliged to play, by refusing to stake one life against three at a game in which out of an infinity of chances there is one for you, if there were an infinity of an infinitely happy life to gain. But there is here an infinity of an infinitely happy life to gain, a chance of gain against a finite number of chances of loss, and what you stake is finite. It is all divided; wherever the infinite is and there is not an infinity of chances of loss against that of gain, there is no time to hesitate, you must give all. And thus, when one is forced to play, he must renounce reason to preserve his life, rather

II. MISGUIDED OBJECTIONS

Just to get a better feel for the Wager, let us very quickly run through a few preliminary objections . . . .

(i) "But my beliefs are not under my control; if I don't believe, then I can't believe, any more than I can believe there to be a live swordfish in front of me just because someone offers me $1,000 if I can get myself to believe that." *Reply:* In the long run, most people's beliefs *are* under their control; as Pascal himself emphasized, behavior therapy is remarkably effective even upon intellectuals. Start going to church and observing its rituals; associate with intelligent and congenial religious people; stop reading philosophy and associating with cynics and logical positivists. To quote William James's pungent paraphrase of Pascal, [Reading 7.8] "Go then and take holy water, and have masses said; belief will come and stupefy your scruples." It may be that some people, of an indefatigably analytical and uncredulous temperament, simply cannot let themselves neglect the evidence and acquiesce in faith, just as some people simply cannot let themselves be hypnotized. But this is no reflection on the **prudential** rationality of the Wager; many people are psychologically incapable of doing what is demonstrably in their interest and known by them to be in their interest.[2]

(ii) "The Wager is cynical and mercenary; God wouldn't reward a 'believer' who makes it." *Reply:* Of course He wouldn't, just like that. Pascal's claim is rather that our interest lies in leaving our cynicism behind and eventually *becoming* believers, if we can. There is no particular reason to think that God would punish a truly sincere and devout believer just because of the historical origins of his or her belief. People are reportedly saved as a result of deathbed conversions, even after lives of the most appalling corruption, if their new belief is sincere and authentic.

(iii) "Pascal is wrong in conjecturing that the probability of theism is as high as .5. It isn't; it's minuscule." *Reply:* That doesn't matter; even if the probability of theism is .001, the expected payoffs are still infinite. "All right, then, the probability is *zero*. I'm *certain* there is no God." *Reply:* How certain? And on what grounds? We would need to see a very convincing argument that no God of even roughly the traditional sort *could* exist, and it would have to be better than most philosophical arguments. (How many philosophical arguments do we know that confer probability 1 on their conclusions?)

(iv) "But if I bet on theism and in fact there is no God, my life will have been based on a lie." *Reply:* But if one bets on atheism and in fact there is a God, one's life will have been based on a lie. (And one's *after*life will be based on the worm that dieth not and the fire that is not quenched.) "But Pascal is telling us, brazenly, to form a firm belief that is unsupported by evidence and may even go directly against the evidence. That is an **epistemic** vice, the shirking of an epistemic obligation. As a professional philosopher I couldn't live with myself knowing I had done that." *Reply:* Epistemic obligation is not moral obligation. No one suffers if (in this sort of case) one violates an epistemic norm.[3] No one could possibly care except (a) academic philosophers, (b) self-righteous textbook slaves, and (c) God Himself. As history abundantly shows, the first two of these may safely be ignored; the third is ultimately to be counted on Pascal's side (see the reply to objection [ii]). What does an epistemic peccadillo matter, compared to infinite joy or damnation?

(v) "What do you mean, '−20'? I *love* sin! And we're not talking about just a few Sunday mornings here, but proposing to bet an entire lifestyle." *Reply:* Does anyone *really* love sin so much as to be *rationally and without* **AKRASIA** willing to risk eternal damnation for it? That cannot be true of many people. Indeed (to make a slightly different point), a survey would probably show that religious people are on the average happier and more satisfied with their

[2]Someone experiences an ominous medical symptom, and does not—cannot—go to the doctor because he is paralyzed with fear. He ends up dead. Someone else does not—cannot—make Pascal's Wager because he is paralyzed with textbook rationality. He ends up dead. Permanently.

[3]Indeed, if Pascal is right in conjecturing that the probabilities are even, one may not even *be* violating any norm; it is arguable that when probabilities are even, one may believe as one likes. . . .

lives than are nonreligious people[4] (whether this happiness is *opiate* in some objectionable sense is a vexed question, resting on mixed **empirical** issues and philosophical concerns). How bad could a devout life be, compared to the (possible) alternative? . . .

III. THE MANY GODS OBJECTION

. . . Let us turn . . . to the Many Gods problem. Pascal assumes a very specific sort of god—roughly a Christian god who rewards His own partisans with infinite bliss and who perhaps sentences opponents and even neutrals to damnation of one truly awful sort or another.[5] But logical space contains countless possible gods of very different natures—all infinite, if you like—and if we can know nothing of infinitude then we cannot have reason to prefer any one of these gods to another. Unfortunately, their respective expected payoffs are diverse and conflicting: What if instead of the Christian God there is a Baal, a Moloch, a Wotan, or a Zeus, who prepares a particularly nasty fate for devout Christians? What if there is a very shy and reclusive god who does not want to be believed in and who enforces this desire by damning all believers to eternal torment? Etc., etc. Pascal assumed that *his* God has a .5 probability of existing, but this is grossly presumptuous in the face of all the other gods who cannot be ruled out **a priori.** Either Pascal's Christian God must take His place equiprobably alongside the indefinitely many other possible deities, in which case the probability of His existence is negligible, or Pascal's argument could be reiterated for every other god who offers infinite payoffs, in which case it proves too much and leads directly to contradiction due to incompatibly jealous gods.

IV. A FIRST ANSWER TO THE MANY GODS OBJECTION

A natural response is to say that for one reason or another all the various possible gods are *not* equiprobable. Intuitively, it is far more likely that the Christian God, the God of the Jews, or Allah exists, than that there is a vindictively shy god or a god who rewards all and only those who do not shave themselves or a god who wears pink bow ties that light up. For here, we believe, **empirical** evidence is relevant to a certain extent. There is *some* empirical reason for thinking that the Christian God or the God of Israel—or even Allah—exists, in the form of partially checkable scriptures, historical reports (made by ostensibly intelligent and impartial observers) of divine manifestations, and the like, even if this evidence is pathetically far from convincing; while there is simply no reason of any sort for thinking that there is a reclusive god or a divine rewarder of non–self-shaving or whatever. (We also think that the ability of a particular religion to attract and sustain millions of adherents over thousands of years is epistemically a mark in its favor, even if a very weak one.[6] More strongly, we suggest that on empirical grounds Pascal might justify, with fairly high probability, a conditional premise of the form "If there is any god at all, there is a god of type *G*," where '*G*' is replaced by some complex **disjunction** of **conjunctions** of traits of the deities of all the world's great religions. If this conditional premise is granted and if sufficiently many of the **disjuncts** have the infinite-payoff feature, then EUs are still on the side of accepting the disjunction [assuming one can manage it].)

There are still two powerful objections to this initial response. First, how are we to choose between the gods of the major religions? Why should we believe in the Christian God rather than Yahweh? (These deities may well be considered identical by

[4]Actual demographic surveys do show at least that religious people fare better with respect to divorce, suicide, and other indicators of troubled personal lives.

[5]There was nothing **dialectically** suspect about this at the time; Pascal was writing specifically for fellow Christians whose faith was wavering, stagnant, or lapsed.

[6]One might wish to join Peirce, and more recently D. M. Armstrong, in seeing consensus as a mark of epistemic probity, though the epistemic value attaches more properly to methods of producing belief than to beliefs themselves.

theorists, but their worship is not; they respectively require incompatible conduct.) For that matter, why should we believe in either of those rather than in Allah, or in one or more of the Hindu gods? There are probably more Muslims and more Hindus than there are genuinely religious Christians or Jews, so consensus is of no help in the present regard.

Here some fine-tuning is in order, though we cannot pursue the question in any detail. (i) Empirical indications are still germane. If one looks carefully, one may find that history provides more respectable evidence (however imperfect) for one of the major gods than for another. (ii) One must attend to the details of the respective payoffs; other things being equal, one should go for the deity that offers the more attractive afterlife and/or the nastiest form of damnation. (More on this shortly.) (iii) Given the facts taken account of in (i) and (ii), one must try for the lowest common denominator in terms of tolerance; that is, one must keep one's faith as ecumenical as one dares. Some gods are more jealous than others, of course; some deny salvation to any but the adherents of some crackpot sect, while others grant it to anyone who has led the right sort of life and had an appropriately respectful attitude toward something or other. So, overall, one must balance considerations (i), (ii), and (iii) against each other for each particular case and see how the resulting EUs come out. This is a very tricky but not completely unfeasible bit of comparison shopping. Of course, we may get it wrong and back the wrong god. In fact, given the multiplicity of major deities and the narrow tolerances involved in our attempt at judicious ecumenism, we *probably will* get it wrong. But a significant chance of infinite success offset by a greater chance of infinite failure is still better odds than *no* chance of success supplemented by a *still* greater chance of failure.

A second objection to our initial line is that when nonfinite payoffs are at stake, finite probabilities simply do not matter. If the reclusive god, for example, offers infinite bliss to those who deny him and eternal torture to his worshippers, then (so long as the probability of his existence is not a flat *zero,* which it is not) the EU of belief in him is itself still infinite and so equal to that of belief in the Christian God despite the far greater probability of the latter.

Our first reply to this is that if EUs are *equal,* then by **Bayesian principles** it doesn't matter what one does and one may follow one's inclinations. Moreover, so long as **prudence** does not rule on the matter, one would do best on *epistemically* rational grounds to go with the probabilities, and side with one's best traditional bet rather than with a crackpot or made-up god. Indeed, in this case we think a person should be rationally faulted for failing to prefer an objectively more probable god, so long as EUs are equal.

This response is complemented by our second general answer to the Many Gods Objection, to which we now turn.

V. LEMMA FOR A SECOND ANSWER TO THE MANY GODS OBJECTION: ST. ANSELM ON THE DIVINE ATTRIBUTES

Some people may see no empirical ground for distinguishing the probabilities of the various rival theistic hypotheses, and may find no other reason for preferring any one possible supernatural being to the others. Even so, it seems reasonable for such people to employ a further, common methodological principle, universally applied in more mundane situations which present us with indefinitely large choices among down-to-earth empirical hypotheses.

In science, **underdetermination** of theory is rife: when we can find one hypothesis accounting for a particular body of observational data (no matter how large), then we are invariably able to produce indefinitely many alternative and competing hypotheses, each capable of accounting for the same body of data. . . . As everyone knows, we escape . . . indecision by using the principle of **simplicity,** and choose the simplest of all such hypotheses.

For the case of theistic hypotheses, we suppose that one postulate is simpler than another if its statement requires fewer nonadventitious predicates (a predicate is adventitious if it is just *made up* by the theologian, in the manner of **'grue,'** to abbreviate a longer complex expression). Now, St. Anselm called our attention to the very remarkable predicate "absolutely perfect," which is **theological**ly unique in that it implies all the other predicates traditionally ascribed to God. In proclaiming the existence of an absolutely perfect or "greatest possible" being, the theist offers a complete description of the deity thus postulated. The theist's brief statement, that his object of worship necessarily exemplifies a maximally consistent set of great-making properties, enables one to determine for any property P whether the putative being does or does not possess P: if having P contributes to the excellence of a thing that does have P, then an absolutely perfect being has P; otherwise the being does not have P. (If there are evaluatively *neutral* properties that a divine being could exemplify, these presumably do not affect the rationality of our choice. We shall say a bit more below on the question of neutral properties.)

By contrast, a statement of the existence of any deity other than the absolutely perfect being will inevitably be more complex. For example: although there is a very considerable body of ancient Greek literature regarding Zeus, we are still far from having a complete description of Zeus's character. We are informed that Zeus, who weighs the lives of men and informs the Fates of his decisions, can nevertheless change his mind; but we have no notion of *just* how unsteadfast he is and in what ways. He is sometimes described as being asleep, but we have no idea how many hours of sleep he gets per day. We know he is not **omnipotent,** but we are given no detail here. And so on.

No one would suggest that Zeus constitutes the simplest alternative to **Anselmian theism.** But someone might be attracted by the hypothesis that there is a deity who is almost perfect except in such and such a respect, say, except for falling short of being 100 percent just. The trouble is that that characterization provides incomplete information; we would need some further specification of the precise ways in which that god may be unjust. . . .

VII. A THIRD ANSWER TO THE MANY GODS OBJECTION

A deeper and more authentic approach would take into account the special nature of the reward on which one is bid to wager. First, we are to realize that what Pascal is urging is for the gambler to set his eyes upon a prize of a sort entirely different from the "poisonous pleasures" Pascal advises him to abandon. The gratification to be pursued by the religious seeker is not something extrinsic to the devout life, but an organic outgrowth of it. It does not differ in kind from the seeking, as if one were to be handed a new IBM color-graphics monitor as a prize for having won the Carrboro marathon, but is the natural fruit of one's way of life. Theists in every age have anticipated the dissolving of their narrow selves in the ecstasy of a God-centered life here on earth and, more to Pascal's point, their eventual smooth translation into a disembodied existence in holy felicity—an eternal love of the divine. A human being becomes capable of this kind of love only after he or she has grasped the idea of God. [Moses] Maimonides puts it as follows:

> What is the proper love of God? It is the love of the Lord with a great and very strong love so that one's soul shall be tied to the love of the Lord, and one should be continually enraptured by it, like a love-sick individual, whose mind is at no time free from his passion for a particular woman, the thought of her filling his heart at all times, when sitting down or rising up, even when he is eating or drinking. Still more intense should be the love of God in the hearts of those who love Him.[7]

According to classical theologians, one who has spent one's life as a passionate servant of the Lord will have developed and perfected one's soul adequately to have acquired the capacity to partake in the transmundane bliss that awaits in the afterlife. The suitably groomed soul, when released from its earthly fetters, will bask in the radiance of the divine presence and delight in the adoring communion with a loving God (if this is a multiply mixed metaphor, it doesn't matter).

It is appropriate at this point to comment again upon objection (ii) considered in Section II above, the complaint that because of its calculating and mercenary character, the Wager is both morally

[7]Maimonides, *Mishneh Torah*, Hilkhot Teshuvash [Laws of Repentance] X.

repugnant and inefficacious, and incompatible with the spirit of any genuine religion. Many people would recoil from a wagerer just as they would from a hypocrite who went out of his way to brighten the mood of an enfeebled (but wealthy) elderly person for no loftier reason than to increase his chance of being mentioned in that person's will. Such misgivings could not easily be dismissed if Pascal had had in mind a pie-in-the-sky, **anthropocentric** sort of heaven such as that which Heinrich Heine sardonically claimed to be reserved for the righteous. According to Heine's mouth-watering description, Heaven is a place where roast geese fly around with gravy boats in their bills and there are brooks of boullion and champagne and everyone revels in eternal feasting and carousing. It would and should be hard to admire anyone who pursued a godly, righteous, and sober life mainly in the hope of gaining admission to that kind of paradise. But we are considering the Wager in the context of an infinitely more exalted afterlife. Suppose that we have always had great admiration for Smith because of the noteworthy humanitarian works he has performed, and that lately we have heard of further truly heroic acts of benevolence on his part that make his previous accomplishments pale into insignificance. Then we should hardly be condemned for making efforts to discover more information concerning Smith's further laudable deeds—even if we are fully conscious of the sentiments of Thomas Carlyle, who wrote, "Does not every true man feel that he is himself made higher by doing reverence to what is really above him?"[8] Most people would find our conduct neither ignoble nor stupid, even if our efforts to discover the grounds of Smith's greatly intensified worthiness were done explicitly for the sake of feeling ourselves made higher by doing reverence to a more exalted personage.

Let us return for a moment to the notion of expected utility. Rationality requires that when faced with a number of choices one is to bet on the hypothesis having the highest EU. In the special case in which the various outcomes are equiprobable, one's choice is then determined by the magnitudes of the respective payoffs. In Pascal's situation, then, where D ranges over possible deities: the degree of justified inclination to embark on a process leading to worshipping D = the probability that D exists × the magnitude of religious fulfillment to be gained by worshipping D provided D does exist. And when D_1, D_2, . . . are equiprobable, the degree of justified inclination and the rationality of one's choice must be determined by the second factor on the right-hand side.

It is the crux of our problem that for more than one deity there is an eternal and hence infinite payoff. Still, the very nature of the sublime gratification the believer aspires to ensures that its quality will vary with the character of the deity he or she bets on. When Carlyle spoke of the self-enhancement resulting from doing reverence to what is above oneself, he had in mind an entirely worldly context. But when the object of one's homage is a divine being, the uplift is immeasurably greater. Pascal wagered on the ecstasy to be derived from exalting a supereminent being and basking in its radiance, and naturally, the more glorious and sublime the being, the greater that worshipful ecstasy would be. Thus, Pascal's argument leads us to maximize religious benefit by positing that superbeing which is the very most worthy of worship, viz., the absolutely perfect being, which we take to be the God of Judeo-Christian theism and of some other, non-Western religions as well, minus some of the tendentious if traditional special features ascribed to Him by sectarian practitioners of those religions.

VIII. CONCLUSION

. . . We do not claim that our case is conclusive, or that the Wager is now dictated by reason. We do contend that at the present stage of investigation Pascal's argument is unrefuted and not unreasonable.

Let us pray.

STUDY QUESTIONS

1. Review what the authors call "misguided objections" to the wager argument and explain their responses.

[8]Thomas Carlyle, *On Heroes, Hero-Worship and the Heroic in History* (London: J. Fraser, 1841), p. 1.

2. *Lycan and Schlesinger say that, even if a person originally comes to believe in God for the sort of cynical and mercenary reasons given in the wager argument, the person later might become a "truly sincere and devout believer." Why would this happen, if the wager is the only rational grounds for belief? Also, should God make reward contingent on such a change in motivation?
3. Lycan and Schlesinger state that wagering on God would be rational even if *God exists* were to have a very low probability. Do you agree? Why or why not?
4. What reason do Lycan and Schlesinger give for Pascal's believing in a Christian God, on the basis of the wager, rather than in another God? *Do you think that their argument is convincing?

READING 7.8

The Will to Believe

William James

William James (1842–1909) was both an eminent psychologist and a leading figure in the American philosophical movement known as **pragmatism.** *In the 1896 lecture "The Will to Believe," presented to the philosophy clubs of Yale and Brown University, James argues, contrary to Clifford [Reading 7.1], that "our passional nature not only lawfully may, but must, decide an option between propositions, whenever it is a genuine option that cannot by its nature be decided on intellectual grounds." An option is considered genuine when it is forced rather than avoidable, living rather than dead, and momentous rather than trivial. James defines these terms in the essay; his point is that, in some cases, leaving a question open and not choosing between two hypotheses is itself a passional decision. It is attended with a risk of losing truth and is equivalent in its consequences to the outright rejection of a hypothesis.*

According to James, the choice between the religious hypothesis and its negation is a genuine option. If we don't choose to believe but, rather, choose to be **agnostic,** *we lose the good that belief in the religious hypothesis would bring. The faith-vetoer, no less than the person who embraces faith, makes a passional decision, for that person chooses to yield to the fear of making an error rather than to the hope of acquiring truth.*

I have brought with me tonight something like a sermon on justification by faith to read to you—I mean an essay in justification *of* faith, a defense of our right to adopt a believing attitude in religious matters, in spite of the fact that our merely logical intellect may not have been coerced. "The Will to Believe," accordingly, is the title of my paper.

I have long defended to my own students the lawfulness of voluntarily adopted faith; but as soon as they have got well imbued with the logical spirit, they have as a rule refused to admit my contention to be lawful philosophically, even though in point of fact they were personally all the time chock full of some faith or other themselves. I am all the while, however, so profoundly convinced that my own position is correct, that your invitation has seemed to me a good occasion to make my statements more clear. Perhaps your minds will be more open than those with which I have hitherto had to deal. . . .

I

Let us give the name of *hypothesis* to anything that may be proposed to our belief; and just as the electricians speak of live and dead wires, let us speak of any hypothesis as either *live* or *dead*. A live hypothesis is one which appeals as a real possibility to him to whom it is proposed. If I ask you to believe in the Mahdi, the notion makes no electric connection with your nature,—it refuses to scintillate with any credibility at all. As an hypothesis it is completely dead. To an Arab, however (even if he be not one of the Mahdi's followers), the hypothesis is among the mind's possibilities: it is alive. This shows that deadness and liveness in an hypothesis are not intrinsic properties, but relations to the individual thinker. They are measured by his willingness to act. The maximum of liveness in an hypothesis means willingness to act irrevocably. Practically, that means belief; but there is some believing tendency wherever there is willingness to act at all.

Next, let us call the decision between two hypotheses an *option*. Options may be of several kinds. They may be—1, *living* or *dead;* 2, *forced* or *avoidable;* 3, *momentous* or *trivial;* and for our purposes we may call an option a **genuine option** when it is of the forced, living, and momentous kind.

(1) A living option is one in which both hypotheses are live ones. If I say to you: "Be a theosophist or be a Mohammedan," it is probably a dead option, because for you neither hypothesis is likely to be alive. But if I say: "Be an **agnostic** or be a Christian," it is otherwise: trained as you are, each hypothesis makes some appeal, however small, to your belief.

(2) Next, if I say to you: "Choose between going out with your umbrella or without it," I do not offer you a genuine option, for it is not forced. You can easily avoid it by not going out at all. Similarly, if I say, "Either love me or hate me," "Either call my theory true or call it false," your option is avoidable. You may remain indifferent to me, neither loving nor hating, and you may decline to offer any judgment as to my theory. But if I say, "Either accept this truth or go without it," I put on you a forced option, for there is no standing place outside of the alternative. Every dilemma based on a complete logical **disjunction,** with no possibility of not choosing, is an option of this forced kind.

(3) Finally, if I were Dr. Nansen and proposed to you to join my North Pole expedition, your option would be momentous; for this would probably be your only similar opportunity, and your choice now would either exclude you from the North Pole sort of immortality altogether or put at least the chance of it into your hands. He who refuses to embrace a unique opportunity loses the prize as surely as if he tried and failed. *Per contra* [on the contrary, i.e., by contrast], the option is trivial when the opportunity is not unique, when the stake is insignificant, or when the decision is reversible if it later prove unwise. Such trivial options abound in the scientific life. A chemist finds an hypothesis live enough to spend a year in its verification: he believes in it to that extent. But if his experiments prove inconclusive either way, he is quit for his loss of time, no vital harm being done.

It will facilitate our discussion if we keep all these distinctions well in mind.

II

The next matter to consider is the actual psychology of human opinion. When we look at certain facts, it seems as if our passional and volitional nature lay at the root of all our convictions. When we look at others, it seems as if they could do nothing when the intellect had once said its say. Let us take the latter facts up first.

Does it not seem preposterous on the very face of it to talk of our opinions being modifiable at will? Can our will either help or hinder our intellect in its perceptions of truth? Can we, by just willing it, believe that Abraham Lincoln's existence is a myth, and that the portraits of him in *McClure's Magazine* are all of some one else? Can we, by any effort of our will, or by any strength of wish that it were true, believe ourselves well and about when we are roaring with rheumatism in bed, or feel certain that the sum of the two one-dollar bills in our pocket must be a hundred dollars? We can *say* any of these things, but we are absolutely impotent to believe them; and of just such things is the whole fabric of the truths that we do believe in made up,—**matters of fact,** immediate or remote, as Hume said, and **relations between ideas,** which are either there or not there for us if we see them so, and which if not there cannot be put there by any action of our own.

In Pascal's *Thoughts* there is a celebrated passage known in literature as Pascal's wager [See Reading 7.6.]. In it he tries to force us into Christianity by reasoning as if our concern with truth resembled our concern with the stakes in a game of chance. Translated freely his words are these: You must either believe or not believe that God is—which will you do? Your human reason cannot say. A game is going on between you and the nature of things which at the day of judgment will bring out either heads or tails. Weigh what your gains and your losses would be if you should stake all you have on heads, or God's existence: if you win in such case, you gain eternal beatitude; if you lose, you lose nothing at all. If there were an infinity of chances, and only one for God in this wager, still you ought to stake your all on God; for though you surely risk a finite loss by this procedure, any finite loss is reasonable, even a certain one is reasonable, if there is but the possibility of infinite gain. Go, then, and take holy water, and have masses said; belief will come and stupefy your scruples,—*Cela vous fera croire et vous abêtira* [lit., this will make you believe and stupefy you]. Why should you not? At bottom, what have you to lose?

You probably feel that when religious faith expresses itself thus, in the language of the gaming table, it is put to its last trumps. Surely Pascal's own personal belief in masses and holy water had far other springs; and this celebrated page of his is but an **argument** for others, a last desperate snatch at a weapon against the hardness of the unbelieving heart. We feel that a faith in masses and holy water adopted wilfully after such a mechanical calculation would lack the inner soul of faith's reality; and if we were ourselves in the place of the Deity, we should probably take particular pleasure in cutting off believers of this pattern from their infinite reward. It is evident that unless there be some pre-existing tendency to believe in masses and holy water, the option offered to the will by Pascal is not a living option. Certainly no Turk ever took to masses and holy water on its account; and even to us Protestants these means of salvation seem such foregone impossibilities that Pascal's logic, invoked for them specifically, leaves us unmoved. As well might the Mahdi write to us, saying, "I am the Expected One whom God has created in his effulgence. You shall be infinitely happy if you confess me; otherwise you shall be cut off from the light of the sun. Weigh, then, your infinite gain if I am genuine against your finite sacrifice if I am not!" His logic would be that of Pascal; but he would vainly use it on us, for the hypothesis he offers us is dead. No tendency to act on it exists in us to any degree.

The talk of believing by our volition seems, then, from one point of view, simply silly. From another point of view it is worse than silly, it is vile. When one turns to the magnificent edifice of the physical sciences, and sees how it was reared; what thousands of disinterested moral lives of men lie buried in its mere foundations; what patience and postponement, what choking down of preference, what submission to the icy laws of outer fact are wrought into its very stones and mortar; how absolutely impersonal it stands in its vast augustness,—then how besotted and contemptible seems every little sentimentalist who comes blowing his voluntary smoke-wreaths, and pretending to decide things from out of his private dream! Can we wonder if those bred in the rugged and manly school of science should feel like spewing such subjectivism out of their mouths? The whole system of loyalties which grow up in the schools of science go dead against its toleration; so that it is only natural that those who have caught the scientific fever should pass over to the opposite extreme, and write sometimes as if the incorruptibly truthful intellect ought positively to prefer bitterness and unacceptableness to the heart in its cup.

> It fortifies my soul to know
> That, though I perish, Truth is so—

sings Clough, while [Thomas H.] Huxley exclaims: "My only consolation lies in the reflection that, however bad our posterity may become, so far as they hold by the plain rule of not pretending to believe what they have no reason to believe, because it may be to their advantage so to pretend [the word 'pretend' is surely here redundant], they will not have reached the lowest depth of immorality." And that delicious *enfant terrible* [W. K.] Clifford writes: "Belief is desecrated when given to unproved and unquestioned statements for the solace and private pleasure of the believer. . . . Whoso would deserve well of his fellows in this matter will guard the purity of his belief with a very fanaticism of jealous care, lest at any time it should rest on an unworthy object, and catch a stain which can never be wiped away. . . . If [a] belief has been accepted on insufficient evidence [even though the belief be true, as Clifford on the same page explains] the pleasure is a stolen one. . . . It is sinful because it is stolen in defiance of our duty to mankind. That duty is to guard ourselves from such beliefs as from a pestilence which may shortly master our own body and then spread to the rest of the town. . . . It is wrong always, everywhere, and for every one, to believe anything upon insufficient evidence" [Reading 7.1–ed.].

III

All this strikes one as healthy, even when expressed, as by Clifford, with somewhat too much of robustious pathos in the voice. Free-will and simple wishing do seem, in the matter of our credences, to be only fifth wheels to the coach. Yet if any one should thereupon assume that intellectual insight is what remains after wish and will and sentimental preference have taken wing, or that pure reason is what then settles our opinions, he would fly quite as directly in the teeth of the facts.

It is only our already dead hypotheses that our willing nature is unable to bring to life again. But what has made them dead for us is for the most part a previous action of our willing nature of an antagonistic kind. When I say 'willing nature,' I do not mean only such deliberate volitions as may have set up habits of belief that we cannot now escape from,—I mean all such factors of belief as fear and hope, prejudice and passion, imitation and partisanship, the circumpressure of our caste and set. As a matter of fact we find ourselves believing, we hardly know how or why. Mr. Balfour gives the name of 'authority' to all those influences, born of the intellectual climate, that make hypotheses possible or impossible for us, alive or dead. Here in this room, we all of us believe in molecules and the conservation of energy, in democracy and necessary progress, in Protestant Christianity and the duty of fighting for 'the doctrine of the immortal Monroe,' all for no reasons worthy of the name. We see into these matters with no more inner clearness, and probably with much less, than any disbeliever in them might possess. His unconventionality would probably have some grounds to show for its conclusions; but for us, not insight, but the *prestige* of the opinions, is what makes the spark shoot from them and light up our sleeping magazines of faith. Our reason is quite satisfied, in nine hundred and ninety-nine cases out of every thousand of us, if it can find a few arguments that will do to recite in case our credulity is criticised by some one else. Our faith is faith in some one else's faith, and in the greatest matters this is most the case. Our belief in truth itself, for instance, that there is a truth, and that our minds and it are made for each other,—what is it but a passionate affirmation of desire, in which our social system backs us up? We want to have a truth; we want to believe that our experiments and studies and discussions must put us in a continually better and better position towards it; and on this line we agree to fight out our thinking lives. But if a **pyrrhonistic sceptic** asks us *how we know* all this, can our logic find a reply? No! certainly it cannot. It is just one volition against another,—we willing to go in for life upon a trust or assumption which he, for his part, does not care to make.[1]

As a rule we disbelieve all facts and theories for which we have no use. Clifford's cosmic emotions find no use for Christian feelings. Huxley belabors the bishops because there is no use for sacerdotalism in his scheme of life. [John Henry] Newman, on the contrary, goes over to Romanism, and finds all sorts of reasons good for staying there, because a priestly system is for him an organic need and delight. Why do so few 'scientists' even look at the evidence for telepathy, so called? Because they think, as a leading biologist, now dead, once said to me, that even if such a thing were true, scientists ought to band together to keep it suppressed and concealed. It would undo the uniformity of Nature and all sorts

[1]Compare the admirable page 310 in S. H. Hodgson's "Time and Space," London, 1865.

of other things without which scientists cannot carry on their pursuits. But if this very man had been shown something which as a scientist he might *do* with telepathy, he might not only have examined the evidence, but even have found it good enough. This very law which the logicians would impose upon us—if I may give the name of logicians to those who would rule out our willing nature here—is based on nothing but their own natural wish to exclude all elements for which they, in their professional quality of logicians, can find no use.

Evidently, then, our non-intellectual nature does influence our convictions. There are passional tendencies and volitions which run before and others which come after belief, and it is only the latter that are too late for the fair; and they are not too late when the previous passional work has been already in their own direction. Pascal's argument, instead of being powerless, then seems a regular clincher, and is the last stroke needed to make our faith in masses and holy water complete. The state of things is evidently far from simple; and pure insight and logic, whatever they might do ideally, are not the only things that really do produce our creeds.

IV

Our next duty, having recognized this mixed-up state of affairs, is to ask whether it be simply reprehensible and pathological, or whether, on the contrary, we must treat it as a normal element in making up our minds. The thesis I defend is, briefly stated, this: *Our passional nature not only lawfully may, but must, decide an option between propositions, whenever it is a genuine option that cannot by its nature be decided on intellectual grounds; for to say, under such circumstances, "Do not decide, but leave the question open," is itself a passional decision,—just like deciding yes or no,—and is attended with the same risk of losing the truth. . . .*

VII

One more point, small but important, and our preliminaries are done. There are two ways of looking at our duty in the matter of opinion,—ways entirely different, and yet ways about whose difference the theory of knowledge seems hitherto to have shown very little concern. *We must know the truth;* and *we must avoid error,*—these are our first and great commandments as would-be knowers; but they are not two ways of stating an identical commandment, they are two separable laws. Although it may indeed happen that when we believe the truth *A*, we escape as an incidental consequence from believing the falsehood *B*, it hardly ever happens that by merely disbelieving *B* we necessarily believe *A*. We may in escaping *B* fall into believing other falsehoods, *C* or *D*, just as bad as *B;* or we may escape *B* by not believing anything at all, not even *A*.

Believe truth! Shun error!—these, we see, are two materially different laws; and by choosing between them we may end, coloring differently our whole intellectual life. We may regard the chase for truth as paramount, and the avoidance of error as secondary; or we may, on the other hand, treat the avoidance of error as more imperative, and let truth take its chance. Clifford, in the instructive passage which I have quoted, exhorts us to the latter course. Believe nothing, he tells us, keep your mind in suspense forever, rather than by closing it on insufficient evidence incur the awful risk of believing lies. You, on the other hand, may think that the risk of being in error is a very small matter when compared with the blessings of real knowledge, and be ready to be duped many times in your investigation rather than postpone indefinitely the chance of guessing true. I myself find it impossible to go with Clifford. We must remember that these feelings of our duty about either truth or error are in any case only expressions of our passional life. Biologically considered, our minds are as ready to grind out falsehood as veracity, and he who says, "Better go without belief forever than believe a lie!" merely shows his own preponderant private horror of becoming a dupe. He may be critical of many of his desires and fears, but this fear he slavishly obeys. He cannot imagine any one questioning its binding force. For my own part, I have also a horror of being duped; but I can believe that worse things than being duped may happen to a man in this world: so Clifford's exhortation has to my ears a thoroughly fantastic sound. It is like a general informing his soldiers that it is better to keep out of battle forever than to risk a single wound. Not so are victories either over enemies or over nature gained. Our errors are surely not such awfully solemn things. In a world where we are so certain to incur them in spite of all our caution, a certain lightness of heart seems healthier than this excessive nervousness on their behalf. At any rate, it seems the fittest thing for the **empiricist** philosopher.

VIII

And now, after all this introduction, let us go straight at our question. I have said, and now repeat it, that not only as a matter of fact do we find our passional nature influencing us in our opinions, but that there are some options between opinions in which this influence must be regarded both as an inevitable and as a lawful determinant of our choice.

I fear here that some of you my hearers will begin to scent danger, and lend an inhospitable ear. Two first steps of passion you have indeed had to admit as necessary,—we must think so as to avoid dupery, and we must think so as to gain truth; but the surest path to those ideal consummations, you will probably consider, is from now onwards to take no further passional step.

Well, of course, I agree as far as the facts will allow. Wherever the option between losing truth and gaining it is not momentous, we can throw the chance of *gaining truth* away, and at any rate save ourselves from any chance of *believing falsehood,* by not making up our minds at all till objective evidence has come. In scientific questions, this is almost always the case; and even in human affairs in general, the need of acting is seldom so urgent that a false belief to act on is better than no belief at all. Law courts, indeed, have to decide on the best evidence attainable for the moment, because a judge's duty is to make law as well as to ascertain it, and (as a learned judge once said to me) few cases are worth spending much time over: the great thing is to have them decided on *any* acceptable principle, and got out of the way. But in our dealings with objective nature we obviously are recorders, not makers, of the truth; and decisions for the mere sake of deciding promptly and getting on to the next business would be wholly out of place. Throughout the breadth of physical nature facts are what they are quite independently of us, and seldom is there any such hurry about them that the risks of being duped by believing a premature theory need be faced. The questions here are always trivial options, the hypotheses are hardly living (at any rate not living for us spectators), the choice between believing truth or falsehood is seldom forced. The attitude of **sceptical** balance is therefore the absolutely wise one if we would escape mistakes. What difference, indeed, does it make to most of us whether we have or have not a theory of the Röntgen rays, whether we believe or not in mind-stuff, or have a conviction about the causality of conscious states? It makes no difference. Such options are not forced on us. On every account it is better not to make them, but still keep weighing reasons *pro et contra* [pro and con] with an indifferent hand.

I speak, of course, here of the purely judging mind. For purposes of discovery such indifference is to be less highly recommended, and science would be far less advanced than she is if the passionate desires of individuals to get their own faiths confirmed had been kept out of the game. See for example the sagacity which [Herbert] Spencer and [August] Weismann now display. On the other hand, if you want an absolute duffer in an investigation, you must, after all, take the man who has no interest whatever in its results: he is the warranted incapable, the positive fool. The most useful investigator, because the most sensitive observer, is always he whose eager interest in one side of the question is balanced by an equally keen nervousness lest he become deceived.[2] Science has organized this nervousness into a regular *technique*, her so-called method of verification; and she has fallen so deeply in love with the method that one may even say she has ceased to care for truth by itself at all. It is only truth as technically verified that interests her. The truth of truths might come in merely affirmative form, and she would decline to touch it. Such truth

[2]Compare Wilfrid Ward's essay, "The Wish to Believe," in his *Witnesses to the Unseen*, Macmillan & Co., 1893.

as that, she might repeat with Clifford, would be stolen in defiance of her duty to mankind. Human passions, however, are stronger than technical rules. "Le cœur a ses raisons," as Pascal says, "que la raison ne connaît pas" [The heart has its reasons that reason knows not]; and however indifferent to all but the bare rules of the game the umpire, the abstract intellect, may be, the concrete players who furnish him the materials to judge of are usually, each one of them, in love with some pet 'live hypothesis' of his own. Let us agree, however, that wherever there is no forced option, the dispassionately judicial intellect with no pet hypothesis, saving us, as it does, from dupery at any rate, ought to be our ideal.

The question next arises: Are there not somewhere forced options in our speculative questions, and can we (as men who may be interested at least as much in positively gaining truth as in merely escaping dupery) always wait with impunity till the coercive evidence shall have arrived? It seems ***a priori*** improbable that the truth should be so nicely adjusted to our needs and powers as that. In the great boarding-house of nature, the cakes and the butter and the syrup seldom come out so even and leave the plates so clean. Indeed, we should view them with scientific suspicion if they did.

IX

Moral questions immediately present themselves as questions whose solution cannot wait for **sensible** proof. A moral question is a question not of what sensibly exists, but of what is good, or would be good if it did exist. Science can tell us what exists; but to compare the *worths,* both of what exists and of what does not exist, we must consult not science, but what Pascal calls our heart. Science herself consults her heart when she lays it down that the infinite ascertainment of fact and correction of false belief are the supreme goods for man. Challenge the statement, and science can only repeat it oracularly, or else prove it by showing that such ascertainment and correction bring man all sorts of other goods which man's heart in turn declares. The question of having moral beliefs at all or not having them is decided by our will. Are our moral preferences true or false, or are they only odd biological phenomena, making things good or bad for *us,* but in themselves indifferent? How can your pure intellect decide? If your heart does not *want* a world of moral reality, your head will assuredly never make you believe in one. Mephistophelian **scepticism,** indeed, will satisfy the head's play-instincts much better than any rigorous idealism can. Some men (even at the student age) are so naturally cool-hearted that the moralistic hypothesis never has for them any pungent life, and in their supercilious presence the hot young moralist always feels strangely ill at ease. The appearance of knowingness is on their side, of *naïveté* and gullibility on his. Yet, in the inarticulate heart of him, he clings to it that he is not a dupe, and that there is a realm in which (as Emerson says) all their wit and intellectual superiority is no better than the cunning of a fox. Moral scepticism can no more be refuted or proved by logic than intellectual scepticism can. When we stick to it that there *is* truth (be it of either kind), we do so with our whole nature, and resolve to stand or fall by the results. The sceptic with his whole nature adopts the doubting attitude; but which of us is the wiser, **Omniscience** only knows.

Turn now from these wide questions of good to a certain class of questions of fact, questions concerning personal relations, states of mind between one man and another. *Do you like me or not?*—for example. Whether you do or not depends, in countless instances, on whether I meet you half-way, am willing to assume that you must like me, and show you trust and expectation. The previous faith on my part in your liking's existence is in such cases what makes your liking come. But if I stand aloof, and refuse to budge an inch until I have objective evidence, until you shall have done something apt, as the absolutists say, *ad extorquendum assensum meum* [to twist out my assent], ten to one your liking never comes. How many women's hearts are vanquished by the mere sanguine insistence of some man that they *must* love him! [H]e will not consent to the hypothesis that they cannot. The desire for a certain kind of truth here brings about that special truth's existence; and so it is in innumerable cases of other sorts. Who gains promotions, boons, appointments, but the man in whose life they are seen to play the part of live hypotheses, who discounts them, sacrifices other things for their sake before they have come, and takes risks for them in advance? His faith acts on the powers above him as a claim, and creates its own verification.

A social organism of any sort whatever, large or small, is what it is because each member proceeds to his own duty with a trust that the other members will simultaneously do theirs. Wherever a desired result is achieved by the cooperation of many independent persons, its existence as a fact is a pure consequence of the precursive faith in one another of those immediately concerned. A government, an army, a commercial system, a ship, a college, an athletic team, all exist on this condition, without which not only is nothing achieved, but nothing is even attempted. A whole train of passengers (individually brave enough) will be looted by a few highwaymen, simply because the latter can count on one another, while each passenger fears that if he makes a movement of resistance, he will be shot before any one else backs him up. If we believed that the whole carfull would rise at once with us, we should each severally rise, and train-robbing would never even be attempted. There are, then, cases where a fact cannot come at all unless a preliminary faith exists in its coming. *And where faith in a fact can help create the fact,* that would be an insane logic which should say that faith running ahead of scientific evidence is the 'lowest kind of immorality' into which a thinking being can fall. Yet such is the logic by which our scientific absolutists pretend to regulate our lives!

X

In truths dependent on our personal action, then, faith based on desire is certainly a lawful and possibly an indispensable thing.

But now, it will be said, these are all childish human cases, and have nothing to do with great cosmical matters, like the question of religious faith. Let us then pass on to that. Religions differ so much in their **accidents** that in discussing the religious question we must make it very generic and broad. What then do we now mean by the religious hypothesis? Science says things are; morality says some things are better than other things; and religion says essentially two things.

First, she says that the best things are the more eternal things, the overlapping things, the things in the universe that throw the last stone, so to speak, and say the final word. "Perfection is eternal,"—this phrase of Charles Secrétan seems a good way of putting this first affirmation of religion, an affirmation which obviously cannot yet be verified scientifically at all.

The second affirmation of religion is that we are better off even now if we believe her first affirmation to be true.

Now, let us consider what the logical elements of this situation are *in case the religious hypothesis in both its branches be really true*. (Of course, we must admit that possibility at the outset. If we are to discuss the question at all, it must involve a living option. If for any of you religion be a hypothesis that cannot, by any living possibility be true, then you need go no farther. I speak to the 'saving remnant' alone.) So proceeding, we see, first, that religion offers itself as a *momentous* option. We are supposed to gain, even now, by our belief, and to lose by our nonbelief, a certain vital good. Secondly, religion is a *forced* option, so far as that good goes. We cannot escape the issue by remaining sceptical and waiting for more light, because, although we do avoid error in that way *if religion be untrue,* we lose the good, *if it be true,* just as certainly as if we positively chose to disbelieve. It is as if a man should hesitate indefinitely to ask a certain woman to marry him because he was not perfectly sure that she would prove an angel after he brought her home. Would he not cut himself off from that particular angel-possibility as decisively as if he went and married some one else? Scepticism, then, is not avoidance of option; it is option of a certain particular kind of risk. *Better risk loss of truth than chance of error,*—that is your faith-vetoer's exact position. He is actively playing his stake as much as the believer is; he is backing the field against the religious hypothesis, just as the believer is backing the religious hypothesis against the field. To preach scepticism to us as a duty until 'sufficient evidence' for religion be found, is tantamount therefore to telling us, when in presence of the religious hypothesis, that to yield to our fear of its being error is wiser and better than to yield to our hope that it may be true. It is not intellect against all passions, then; it is only intellect with one passion laying down its law. And by what, forsooth, is the supreme wisdom of this passion warranted? Dupery for dupery, what proof is there that dupery through hope is so much worse than dupery through fear? I, for one, can see no proof; and I simply refuse obedience to the scientist's command to imitate his kind of option, in a case where my own stake is important enough to give me the right to choose my own form of risk. If religion be true and the evidence for it be still insufficient, I do not wish, by putting your extinguisher upon my nature (which feels to me as if it had after all some business in this matter), to forfeit my sole chance in life of getting upon the winning side,—that chance depending, of course, on my willingness to run the risk of acting as if my passional need of taking the world religiously might be prophetic and right.

All this is on the supposition that it really may be prophetic and right, and that, even to us who are discussing the matter, religion is a live hypothesis which may be true. Now, to most of us religion comes in a still further way that makes a veto on our active faith even more illogical. The more perfect and more eternal aspect of the universe is represented in our religion as having personal form. The universe is no longer a mere *It* to us, but a *Thou,* if we are religious; and any relation that may be possible from person to person might be possible here. For instance, although in one sense we are passive portions of the universe, in another we show a curious **autonomy,** as if we were small active centers on our own account. We feel, too, as if the appeal of religion to us were made to our own active good-will, as if evidence might be forever withheld from us unless we met the hypothesis half-way. To take a trivial illustration: just as a man who in a company of gentlemen made no advances, asked a warrant for every concession, and believed no one's word without proof, would cut himself off by such churlishness from all the social rewards that a more trusting spirit would earn,—so here, one who should shut himself up in snarling logicality and try to make the gods extort his recognition willy-nilly, or not get it at all, might cut himself off forever from his only opportunity of making the gods' acquaintance. This feeling, forced on us we know not whence, that by obstinately believing that there are gods (although not to do so would be so easy both for our logic and our life) we are doing the universe the deepest service we can, seems part of the living essence of the religious hypothesis. If the hypothesis *were* true in all its parts, including this one, then pure intellectualism, with its veto on our making willing advances, would be an absurdity; and some participation of our sympathetic nature would be logically required. I, therefore, for one, cannot see my way to accepting the **agnostic** rules for truth-seeking, or willfully agree to keep my willing nature out of the game. I cannot do so for this plain reason, that *a rule of thinking which would absolutely prevent me from acknowledging certain kinds of truth if those kinds of truth were really there, would be an irrational rule*. That for me is the long and short of the formal logic of the situation, no matter what the kinds of truth might materially be.

I confess I do not see how this logic can be escaped. But sad experience makes me fear that some of you may still shrink from radically saying with me, *in abstracto,* that we have the right to believe at our own risk any hypothesis that is live enough to tempt our will. I suspect, however, that if this is so, it is because you have got away from the abstract logical point of view altogether, and are thinking (perhaps without realizing it) of some particular religious hypothesis which for you is dead. The freedom to 'believe what we will' you apply to the case of some patent superstition; and the faith you think of is the faith defined by the schoolboy when he said, "Faith is when you believe something that you know ain't true." I can only repeat that this is misapprehension. *In concreto,* the freedom to believe can only cover living options which the intellect of the individual cannot by itself resolve; and living options never seem absurdities to him who has them to consider. When I look at the religious question as it really puts itself to concrete men, and when I think of all the possibilities which both practically and theoretically it involves, then this command that we shall put a stopper on our heart, instincts, and courage, and *wait*—acting of course meanwhile more or less as if religion were *not* true[3]—till doomsday, or till such time as our intellect and senses working together may have raked in evidence enough,—this command, I say, seems to me the queerest idol ever manufactured in the philosophic cave. Were we **scholastic** absolutists, there might be more excuse. If we had an infallible intellect with its objective certitudes, we might feel ourselves disloyal to such a perfect organ of knowledge in not trusting to it exclusively, in not waiting for its releasing word. But if we are empiricists, if we believe that no bell in us tolls to let us know for certain when truth is in our grasp, then it seems a piece of idle fantasticality to preach so solemnly our duty of waiting for the bell. Indeed we *may* wait if we will,—I hope you do not think that I am denying that,—but if we do so, we do so at our peril as much as if we believed. In either case we *act,* taking our life in our hands. . . .

STUDY QUESTIONS

1. James says that in some circumstances our passional nature "not only lawfully may, but must" decide between two hypotheses or propositions. What are those circumstances?
2. *In what cases besides religion can belief plausibly be said to be based on passion? If there are none, does the absence of examples outside of religious belief hurt James's case? Why or why not?
3. Explain the following quotation: "Dupery for dupery, what proof is there that dupery through hope is so much worse than dupery through fear?"
4. *James has often been accused of giving license (in "The Will to Believe") to wishful thinking. What do you think is meant by this charge? Do you agree with it? Why or why not?
5. *Compare and contrast James's pragmatic justification of religious belief with Pascal's.
6. *James writes: " . . . a rule of thinking which would absolutely prevent me from acknowledging certain kinds of truth if those kinds of truth were really there, would be an irrational rule." Do you agree that *any* such rule is irrational? Why or why not?

[3]Since belief is measured by action, he who forbids us to believe religion to be true, necessarily also forbids us to act as we should if we did believe it to be true. The whole defence of religious faith hinges upon action. If the action required or inspired by the religious hypothesis is in no way different from that dictated by the **naturalistic** hypothesis, then religious faith is a pure superfluity, better pruned away, and controversy about its legitimacy is a piece of idle trifling, unworthy of serious minds. I myself believe, of course, that the religious hypothesis gives to the world an expression which specifically determines our reactions, and makes them in a large part unlike what they might be on a purely naturalistic scheme of belief.

READING 7.9

An Evaluation of James's Argument

Michael Martin

Michael Martin (Boston University) believes that William James (Reading 7.8) ought to consider a wider range of options as "live." Rather than restricting live options to those which people take as a real possibility, he ought to define a live option as one that is not improbable in the light of available evidence. Buddhism, Christianity, Islam, Judaism, and Hinduism would then become live options for all Americans, and the choice of one from among them on **pragmatic** *grounds would need to be justified. In addition, James's statement of the religious hypothesis is unclear,* *especially when he says, "The best things are the more eternal things." Martin argues that there is little* **empirical** *reason to suppose that theists are happier and healthier than nontheists or that they live more rewarding lives. Martin also thinks that James should take probabilities, not only benefits, into account, as Pascal did. Next, Martin disputes James's claim that the verification of God's existence in one's experience is facilitated by belief in God. Finally, he objects that James's procedure does not seem to allow for disconfirmation of the religious hypothesis by means of experiment.*

One important thing to notice about James's argument is his subjective and relativistic definition of a live option. For James a live option to person P is simply one that appeals to P as a real possibility. But what appeals to a person as a real possibility may have nothing to do with what the evidence indicates and may be completely irrational. Indeed, certain options that appeal to a person as real possibilities may in fact be impossible, while ones that do not appeal as real possibilities may in the light of the evidence be at least as plausible as, or even more plausible than, the ones the person considers to be real possibilities. For example, granted that Buddhism would not appeal to an average American as a real possibility while Christianity would, it is hard to see why this is a reason for excluding Buddhism from serious consideration when this person is choosing a religion. Perhaps objective investigation would show that Christianity rests on historically dubious evidence and an incoherent **ontology** and that Buddhism does not suffer from these problems.

I suggest that James should have said that a live option is one that is not improbable in the light of the available evidence. Let us understand "live option" in this new sense, and let us assume with James that in matters of religion, options are live, forced, momentous, and not capable of intellectual resolution. On these assumptions there may be many more **genuine options** than James ever imagined. For example, Buddhism, Christianity, Islam, Judaism, and Hinduism would become genuine options for every person living in this country. Not only would there be the genuine options of the various living world religions but there would also be the genuine options of various concepts of gods or God within those religions. How is one to choose between them? By hypothesis **epistemic** arguments cannot help, and it is unclear how beneficial reasons can give a clear answer. How can one tell if one would be better off in this life believing that Christianity or Buddhism is true? And if one makes a choice, which form of Christianity or Buddhism is justified on beneficial grounds?

The second thing to notice is that although James uses rather specific examples (Christianity vs. **agnosticism**) to illustrate what a live option in the choice of religious hypothesis is, his actual statement of the religious hypothesis is extremely vague and unclear. Recall that the first part of James's religious hypothesis says that "the best things are the more eternal things, the overlapping things, the things in the universe that throw the last stone, so to speak, and say the final word," and the second part says that "we are better off even now if we believe" the first part of the hypothesis. This statement has prompted one commentator on James's work to remark:

> "Best" is vague, and "more eternal" comes close to being nonsense: either something is eternal or it is not. To add that the best things are "the overlapping things" and "throw the last stone, so to speak" only adds further mystification. Is James referring to God but embarrassed to say so?[1]

In any case, taken at their face value both parts of the religious hypothesis are **normative** statements. They seem to have no obvious **metaphysical** implication. The first part says, in effect, for any X and for any Y, if X is eternal and Y is not, X is better than Y. Let us call this statement B. The second part has the form, it is better to believe B than not to. But unless more is said, there is surely little

[1]Walter Kaufmann, *Critique of Religion and Philosophy* (New York: Harper & Brothers, 1958), p. 85.

warrant for either judgment. Mathematical entities such as numbers, at least on a Platonic view of such entities, are eternal. They are timeless and unchanging. But why are numbers better than all noneternal things? One would have thought it at least prima facie debatable that the set of all primes **[prime numbers]** was better than a millennium of world peace and love.

If we give James's religious hypothesis a more specific religious meaning, the first part can perhaps be stated as follows: For any X and for any Y, if X is a perfect and eternal being and Y is neither, X is better than Y. The second part of the hypothesis is that it is better to believe this than not to. On one interpretation the first part of the hypothesis is true by definition. A perfect being is surely better—that is, more perfect—than a less than perfect being. But on other interpretations the religious hypothesis is not true. The expression "is better" is usually used contextually. Something is better for some purposes but not for others. For example, a hammer is better than a pencil for driving a nail, but not for signing one's name. Surely, in this contextual sense, a perfect and eternal being is not always better than some noneternal and less than perfect being. For example, a hammer is better than God if one wants to drive a nail.

But let us concentrate on the sense of "better" that would make the first part of the religious hypothesis true by definition. Given this understanding of the first part of the religious hypothesis, atheists could accept the second part. Atheists could well admit that it is better to believe that an eternal and perfect being is more perfect than a noneternal and nonperfect being, since such a statement is trivially true and it is better to believe that trivially true statements are true than to believe that they are false. It does not follow from this admission that this being actually exists.

However, let us give the religious hypothesis a more metaphysical interpretation. Despite what his words suggest, let us understand James to mean that the religious hypothesis asserts two things:

(1) There exists a perfect and eternal being: God.
(2) It is better in this life to believe that (1) than not to.

One could approach the justification of (2) in a spirit similar to that of Pascal's wager [see Reading 7.6]. One might argue that if God exists, then believing in God will result in a better life in this world than not believing. If God does not exist, then believing in God will still bring about a better life in this world than not believing. So in any case it is better to believe in God. Why would one be better off in this life by believing in God than by not believing in God if God exists? Two reasons come to mind. First, if God exists and one believes in Him, He may tend to make one's life better than if one does not believe. On this intervention interpretation, God intervenes in the natural course of events and rewards the faithful. Second, it may just be true, given human nature and the way society is structured, that theists tend to live happier, healthier, and more rewarding lives than nontheists. Let us call this the natural law interpretation. On either the intervention interpretation or the natural law interpretation, belief in God, if God exists, would be preferable. Let us assume further that if God did not exist, given human nature and the way society is structured, theists would tend to live happier, healthier, and more rewarding lives than nontheists. The situation, then, would look like Figure 6,

	God exists	*God doesn't exist*
Believe in God	X_1	X_2
Do not believe in God	Y_1	Y_2

FIGURE 6

where X_1, X_2, Y_1, and Y_2 are finite values found in this life, such that $X_1 > Y_1$ and $X_2 > Y_2$.

The trouble with James's argument, interpreted in this way, is that there is little **empirical** reason to suppose that theists are happier and healthier, lead more rewarding lives, and so on than nontheists. It certainly seems to be true that nontheists are capable of living lives with as great an amount of happiness, self-fulfillment, and the like as theists. Nor does it seem to be true that if one is a theist it is more likely that one will achieve happiness and so on in this life than if one is a nontheist. Indeed, an argument could be given for just the opposite conclusion. For example, suppose one picked two children at random, one from a nontheistic family and one from a theistic family in the United States. Which one is more likely to live a healthy and productive life while growing up? From what we know of religious belief and its relation to education, health care, social class, economic level, and the like, the best guess is that the child from the theistic family is more likely to be ill, to have less education, and to end up in some unsatisfying job than the child from a family of nonbelievers. Insofar as health and happiness and a satisfying job are correlated (which seems likely), the child from the nonreligious family is likely to be happier than the child from the religious family as an adult. Further, if we consider two children picked at random from the world at large and not just from the United States, one from a religious family and one from a nonreligious family, the chances surely would improve that the child from a religious family will be worse off than the child from a nonreligious family. The reason is simple. Poverty, ignorance, and sickness are more prevalent in the world at large than in the United States, and we know that religious belief is associated with poverty and lack of education, as well as that poverty and ignorance are associated with disease. Thus one might say that if one had a choice and was interested in staying healthy, getting an education, and getting a challenging job, one should choose not to be born into a religious family.

It still might be maintained that, although theists are less likely to live productive and healthy lives than nontheists, theists are capable of a higher quality of happiness. For example, theists are capable of achieving a state of spiritual tranquility and serenity while nontheists are not, and this state is qualitatively better than any state of happiness that a nontheist can reach. In reply, the following points can be made. First, it is not clear that tranquility and serenity are better than, say, the satisfaction of a challenging job. Why should we consider tranquility and serenity a higher sort of happiness? Recall that tranquility and serenity of a sort can be achieved by means of drugs and frontal lobotomies, yet such a state is not particularly desirable. What makes the tranquility and serenity that are achieved by religious means so valuable? Second, even if tranquility and serenity achieved through spiritual insights are so valuable, it is not clear that nontheists cannot achieve them. Surely, this state of mind is not uniquely associated with belief in God. Certain sects of Buddhism, on most interpretations a nontheistic religion, aim to achieve this state of mind, and transcendental meditation claims great success in achieving tranquility and serenity although it makes no assumption about God in the theistic sense.

Let us admit for the sake of argument that theists are capable of achieving a higher degree of happiness, self-fulfillment, and the like than nontheists. It is still not clear that theism would be the best choice. For despite James's neglect of probabilities, they must be taken into account. Although a theist may be able to achieve a higher degree of happiness, and so on, in this life than a nontheist can, the probability of his or her doing so may be lower than that of a nontheist's achieving a more modest degree of happiness. If we compute the **expected value,** nontheists may be better off. For example, suppose the probability p_1 of achieving the sort of life that theists are capable of is 0.4 while the probability of achieving the sort of life nontheists are capable of is 0.7. Suppose further that the value of happiness that a theist can achieve is 500 while the value of happiness a nontheist can achieve is 300. Then the expected value EV of theistic belief is $0.4 \times 500 = 200$ while the EV of nontheistic belief is $0.7 \times 300 = 210$. Thus with these values and probabilities, nontheism would still be preferable to theism despite the assumption that a higher level of happiness is associated with theism. However, we have seen no reason to suppose that this assumption is true. . . .

Further, there are certain values associated with nonbelief that have nothing to do with happiness and the like. Once we bring these values into the computation of EV, we seem to tip the scales toward nonbelief even if belief is associated with more happiness. The possibility of less happiness and the like may be offset by these other values. . . . [N]onbelief puts responsibility for humanity's problems on humans. There is a certain value in self-reliance that may go far in outweighing the value of any happiness and the like that belief in God may produce. Thus it is by no means clear that we are better off even now in believing that God exists. Indeed, non-belief seems preferable when all the relevant values are taken into account.

Moreover, as we have seen, even on a generous interpretation of James, he seems to suppose that believing that the religious hypothesis is true involves accepting some undifferentiated theism. But as many religious scholars have noted, one does not have religious belief in the abstract; it is always relative to a certain religious tradition. For example, one does not believe in God per se but rather in the God of the Catholic Church or of Islam. Belief in these different Gods leads to very different ways of life, since different ritual, ethical codes, and religious practices are associated with different concepts of God in different religions. Oddly enough, when James discusses live and dead religious options he seems to be aware of the nature of religious belief, but he forgets this when he specifies the content of the religious hypothesis. Furthermore, there are religions in which belief in God, as we understand it, has no important role.

What would be the effect of bringing specific religious beliefs into James's scheme? For one thing, it would complicate the question of whether it would be better to believe the religious hypothesis even now. For there would not be a single religious hypothesis. The question would become whether it would be better even now to embrace religion R_1 or R_2 or R_3 and so on or to embrace none. There would be no **a priori** reason to suppose that in terms of conduciveness to happiness, health, or whatever, the preferred religion would be theistic or that, on the basis of such values, would be preferred to no religion at all.

So far we have not considered James's claim that there is an **epistemological** advantage in religious belief. Recall that James can be interpreted as saying at one point that the verification of God's existence in one's experience is facilitated by belief in God. Does this provide a beneficial reason to believe in God?

To see that it is not obvious that it does, recall first that this would be simply one advantage that would have to be weighed against possible disadvantages. Second, on a more plausible conception of live option, any option is live if it is not improbable in the light of the evidence. Therefore, there are surely live religious options where religious belief would not have this epistemological advantage and, indeed, where it would have a disadvantage. Consider a god who reveals himself to his believers less often than to people who are **skeptical.** After all, he might reason, his followers do not need convincing, whereas skeptics do. Belief in such a god would have a decided epistemological disadvantage. Further, there does not seem to be any more **epistemic** reason to believe in this god than in the sort of god that James has in mind. Indeed, James's God seems vindictive and ungenerous to withhold evidence from skeptics who may simply be more cautious than believers are. Why should going beyond what the evidence indicates be rewarded even when the reward is new evidence that vindicates the incautious attitude?

In addition to these problems, religious experience varies from one religious tradition to another, and it is often in conflict. If belief in the god of religion R_1 results in the confirmation of R_1, then would belief in the god of religion R_2 result in the confirmation of R_2? If so, since R_1 and R_2 may be incompatible with one another, beliefs in different gods may result in the confirmation of incompatible hypotheses.

Finally, James talks as if believing in God and seeing whether the hypothesis that God exists is confirmed in one's experience is like an experiment. But his procedure lacks an essential element of standard experimental procedure: he does not seem to allow for the *disconfirmation* of the hypothesis by the results of the experiment. Suppose one believes in some god and yet no evidence of his existence is revealed in one's experience. James does not entertain the possibility that this failure would count against the hypothesis that this god exists. . . .

STUDY QUESTIONS

1. How did William James define *live option?* What is Martin's objection to James's definition? What is Martin's own suggested definition? What impli-

cations does this definition have vis-á-vis the rationality of a person's embracing a particular theistic religion in America today?

2. Explain the problems Martin sees with James's view that "the best things are the more eternal things." *Can these problems be overcome in your opinion? How?
3. *Do you agree with Martin that any of the religions he mentions should be considered a live option for anybody deciding whether to embrace a religion? Why or why not? (You might answer this question either by considering his definition of *live option* or by considering whether all religions satisfy the definition.)
4. *Martin claims that if one believes in God, but no evidence of God's existence is revealed in one's experience, one's hypothesis that God exists is disconfirmed. Contrast this view with the one espoused by Michael J. Murray in Reading 5.5. Who do you think is right? Why?

ON EXISTENTIALIST APPROACHES

READING 7.10

Kierkegaard's Arguments Against Objective Reasoning in Religion

Robert Merrihew Adams

The Danish philosopher Søren Kierkegaard (1813–55) held that objective reasoning for religious commitment is undesirable because genuine religious commitment must have certain features that objective reasoning precludes. If a person has historical evidence in support of the truth of Christianity or philosophical proofs of God's existence, this precludes that person from believing in Christianity (or in God) in a proper religious fashion. Robert Merrihew Adams identifies three arguments given by Kierkegaard for this view:

1. The approximation argument: *Objective reasoning (such as historical reasoning) yields only an approximation, a high probability, of truth, and high probability is not sufficient for eternal happiness.*
2. The postponement argument: *Objective reasoning is revisable, open to correction and change in the face of newly discovered difficulties; religious commitment is unconditional.*
3. The passion argument: *Religious commitment requires infinite passion, and infinite passion requires risk and sacrifice; objective reasoning does not carry this element of risk.*

Adams's main replies to these arguments run as follows (the numbers correspond to the preceding arguments): (1) it may be objectively advantageous *to disregard small possibilities of error, so high probability is enough for eternal happiness; (2) faith does not require* unconditional *commitment but, rather, is consistent with humility and openness to change in belief; (3) the maximization of risk and sacrifice is not required in religious life. At the essay's end, Adams suggests an argument for belief in Christianity that resembles Pascal's wager (Reading 7.6).*

It is sometimes held that there is something in the nature of religious faith itself that renders it useless or undesirable to reason objectively in support of such faith, even if the reasoning should happen to have considerable plausibility. Søren Kierkegaard's *Concluding Unscientific Postscript* is probably the document most commonly cited as representative of this view. In the present essay I shall discuss three arguments for the view. I call them the Approximation Argument, the Postponement Argument, and the Passion Argument; and I suggest they can all be found in the *Postscript*. I shall try to show that the Approximation Argument is a bad argument. The other two will not be so easily disposed of, however. I believe they show that Kierkegaard's conclusion, or something like it, does indeed follow from a certain conception of religiousness—a conception which has some appeal, although for reasons which I shall briefly suggest, I am not prepared to accept it.

Kierkegaard uses the word "objective" and its cognates in several senses, most of which need not concern us here. We are interested in the sense in which he uses it when he says, "it is precisely a misunderstanding to seek an objective assurance," and when he speaks of "an objective uncertainty held fast in the appropriation-process of the most passionate inwardness" (pp. 41, 182).[1] Let us say that a piece of reasoning, *R,* is *objective reasoning* just in case every (or almost every) intelligent, fair-minded, and sufficiently informed person would regard *R* as showing or tending to show (in the circumstances in which *R* is used, and to the extent claimed in *R*) that *R*'s conclusion is true or probably true. Uses of "objective" and "objectively" in other contexts can be understood from their relation to this one; for example, an objective uncertainty is a proposition which cannot be shown by objective reasoning to be certainly true.

1. THE APPROXIMATION ARGUMENT

"Is it possible to base an eternal happiness upon historical knowledge?" is one of the central questions in the *Postscript,* and in the *Philosophical Fragments* to which it is a "postscript." Part of Kierkegaard's answer to the question is that it is not possible to base an eternal happiness on objective reasoning about historical facts.

> For nothing is more readily evident than that the greatest attainable certainty with respect to anything historical is merely an *approximation*. And an approximation, when viewed as a basis for an eternal happiness, is wholly inadequate, since the incommensurability makes a result impossible. (p. 25)

Kierkegaard maintains that it is possible, however, to base an eternal happiness on a belief in historical facts that is independent of objective evidence for them, and that that is what one must do in order to be a Christian. This is the Approximation Argument for the proposition that Christian faith cannot be based on objective reasoning.[2] (It is assumed that some belief about historical facts is an essential part of Christian faith, so that if religious faith cannot be based on objective historical reasoning, then Christian faith cannot be based on objective reasoning at all.) Let us examine the argument in detail.

Its first premise is Kierkegaard's claim that "the greatest attainable certainty with respect to anything historical is merely an approximation." I take him to mean that historical evidence, objectively considered, never completely excludes the possibility of error. "It goes without saying," he claims, "that it is impossible in the case of historical problems to reach an objective decision so certain that no doubt could disturb it" (p. 41). For Kierkegaard's purposes it does

[1]Søren Kierkegaard, *Concluding Unscientific Postscript,* translated by David F. Swenson; introduction, notes, and completion of translation by Walter Lowrie (Princeton: Princeton University Press, 1941). Page references in parentheses in the body of the present paper are to this work.

[2]The argument is not original with Kierkegaard. It can be found in works of G. E. Lessing and D. F. Strauss that Kierkegaard had read. See especially Thulstrup's quotation and discussion of a passage from Strauss in the commentary portion of Søren Kierkegaard, *Philosophical Fragments,* translated by David F. Swenson, second edition, translation revised by Howard V. Hong, with introduction and commentary by Niels Thulstrup (Princeton: Princeton University Press, 1962), pp. 149–51.

not matter how small the possibility of error is, so long as it is finitely small (that is, so long as it is not literally infinitesimal). He insists (p. 31) that his Approximation Argument makes no appeal to the supposition that the objective evidence for Christian historical beliefs is weaker than the objective evidence for any other historical belief. The argument turns on a claim about *all* historical evidence. The probability of error in our belief that there was an American Civil War in the nineteenth century, for instance, might be as small as $\frac{1}{10^{2,000,000}}$; that would be a large enough chance of error for Kierkegaard's argument.

It might be disputed, but let us assume for the sake of argument that there is some such finitely small probability of error in the objective grounds for all historical beliefs, as Kierkegaard held. This need not keep us from saying that we "know," and it is "certain," that there was an American Civil War. For such an absurdly small possibility of error is as good as no possibility of error at all, "for all practical intents and purposes," as we might say. Such a possibility of error is too small to be worth worrying about.

But would it be too small to be worth worrying about if we had an *infinite* passionate interest in the question about the Civil War? If we have an infinite passionate interest in something, there is no limit to how important it is to us. (The nature of such an interest will be discussed more fully in section 3 below.) Kierkegaard maintains that in relation to an infinite passionate interest *no* possibility of error is too small to be worth worrying about. "In relation to an eternal happiness, and an infinite passionate interest in its behalf (in which latter alone the former can exist), an iota is of importance, of infinite importance . . ." (p. 28). This is the basis for the second premise of the Approximation Argument, which is Kierkegaard's claim that "an approximation, when viewed as a basis for an eternal happiness, is wholly inadequate" (p. 25). "An approximation is essentially incommensurable with an infinite personal interest in an eternal happiness" (p. 26).

At this point in the argument it is important to have some understanding of Kierkegaard's conception of faith, and the way in which he thinks faith excludes doubt. Faith must be decisive: in fact it seems to consist in a sort of decision-making. "The conclusion of belief is not so much a conclusion as a resolution, and it is for this reason that belief excludes doubt."[3] The decision of faith is a decision to disregard the possibility of error—to act on what is believed, without hedging one's bets to take account of any possibility of error.

To disregard the possibility of error is not to be unaware of it, or fail to consider it, or lack anxiety about it. Kierkegaard insists that the believer must be keenly *aware* of the risk of error. "If I wish to preserve myself in faith I must constantly be intent upon holding fast the objective uncertainty, so as to remain out upon the deep, over seventy thousand fathoms of water, still preserving my faith" (p. 182).

For Kierkegaard, then, to ask whether faith in a historical fact can be based on objective reasoning is to ask whether objective reasoning can justify one in disregarding the possibility of error which (he thinks) historical evidence always leaves. Here another aspect of Kierkegaard's conception of faith plays its part in the argument. He thinks that in all genuine religious faith the believer is *infinitely* interested in the object of his faith. And he thinks it follows that objective reasoning cannot justify him in disregarding *any* possibility of error about the object of faith, and therefore cannot lead him all the way to religious faith where a historical fact is concerned. The farthest it could lead him is to the conclusion that *if* he had only a certain finite (though very great) interest in the matter, the possibility of error would be too small to be worth worrying about and he would be justified in disregarding it. But faith disregards a possibility of error that *is* worth worrying about, since an infinite interest is involved. Thus faith requires a "leap" beyond the evidence, a leap that cannot be justified by objective reasoning (cf. p. 90).

There is something right in what Kierkegaard is saying here, but his Approximation Argument is a bad argument. He is right in holding that grounds of doubt which may be insignificant for most practical purposes can be extremely troubling for the intensity of a religious concern, and that it may require great

[3]Kierkegaard, *Philosophical Fragments,* p. 104; cf. pp. 102–03.

abandon the belief in that event? If so, he is not totally committed to the belief in the relevant sense. But if he is determined to cling to his belief even if its objective justification is taken away, then he is not basing the belief on the objective justification—or at least he is not basing it solely on the justification.[5]

The conclusion to be drawn from these two premises is that authentic religious faith cannot be based on an inquiry in which one recognizes any possibility of a future need to revise the results. We ought to note that this conclusion embodies two important restrictions on the scope of the argument.

In the first place, we are not given an argument that authentic religious faith cannot *have* an objective justification that is subject to possible future revision. What we are given is an argument that the authentic believer's holding of his religious belief cannot *depend* entirely on such a justification.

In the second place, this conclusion applies only to those who *recognize* some **epistemic possibility** that the objective results which appear to support their belief may be overturned. I think it would be unreasonable to require, as part of total commitment, a determination with regard to one's response to circumstances that one does not recognize as possible at all. It may be, however, that one does not recognize such a possibility when one ought to.

Kierkegaard needs one further premise in order to arrive at the conclusion that authentic religious faith cannot without error be based on any objective empirical reasoning. This third premise is that in every objective empirical inquiry there is always, objectively considered, some epistemic possibility that the results of the inquiry will need to be revised in view of new evidence or new reasoning. I believe Kierkegaard makes this assumption; he certainly makes it with regard to historical inquiry. From this premise it follows that one is in error if in any objective empirical inquiry one does not recognize any possibility of a future need to revise the results. But if one does recognize such a possibility, then according to the conclusion already reached in the Postponement Argument, one cannot base an authentic religious faith on the inquiry.

Some philosophers might attack the third premise of this argument; and certainly it is controversial. But I am more inclined to criticize the first premise. There is undoubtedly something plausible about the claim that authentic religious faith must involve a commitment so complete that the believer is resolved not to abandon his belief under any circumstances that he regards as epistemically possible. If you are willing to abandon your ostensibly religious beliefs for the sake of objective inquiry, mightn't we justly say that objective inquiry is your real religion, the thing to which you are most deeply committed?

There is also something plausible to be said on the other side, however. It has commonly been thought to be an important part of religious ethics that one ought to be humble, teachable, open to correction, new inspiration, and growth of insight, even (and perhaps especially) in important religious beliefs. That view would have to be discarded if we were to concede to Kierkegaard that the heart of commitment in religion is an unconditional determination not to change in one's important religious beliefs. In fact I think there is something radically wrong with this conception of religious commitment. Faith ought not to be thought of as unconditional devotion to a belief. For in the first place the object of religious devotion is not a belief or attitude of one's own, but God. And in the second place it may be doubted that religious devotion to God can or should be completely unconditional. God's love for sinners is sometimes said to be completely unconditional, not being based on any excellence or merit of theirs. But religious devotion to God is generally thought to be based on His goodness and love. It is the part of the strong, not the weak, to love unconditionally. And in relation to God we are weak.

[5]Kierkegaard notes the possibility that in believing in God's existence "I make so bold as to defy all objections, even those that have not yet been made." But in that case he thinks the belief is not really based on the evidence of God's work in the world; "it is not from the works that I make my proof" (*Philosophical Fragments,* p. 52.).

3. THE PASSION ARGUMENT

In Kierkegaard's statements of the Approximation Argument and the Postponement Argument it is assumed that a system of religious beliefs might be objectively probable. It is only for the sake of argument, however, that Kierkegaard allows this assumption. He really holds that religious faith, by its very nature, needs objective *im*probability. "Anything that is almost probable, or probable, or extremely and emphatically probable, is something [one] can almost know, or as good as know, or extremely and emphatically almost *know*—but it is impossible to *believe*" (p. 189). Nor will Kierkegaard countenance the suggestion that religion ought to go beyond belief to some almost-knowledge based on probability. "Faith is the highest passion in a man. There are perhaps many in every generation who do not even reach it, but no one gets further."[6] It would be a betrayal of religion to try to go beyond faith. The suggestion that faith might be replaced by "probabilities and guarantees" is for the believer "a temptation to be resisted with all his strength" (p. 15). The attempt to establish religious beliefs on a foundation of objective probability is therefore no service to religion, but inimical to religion's true interests. The approximation to certainty which might be afforded by objective probability is rejected, not only for the reasons given in the Approximation Argument and Postponement Argument, but also from a deeper motive, "since on the contrary it behooves us to get rid of introductory guarantees of security, proofs from consequences, and the whole mob of public pawnbrokers and guarantors, so as to permit the absurd to stand out in all its clarity—in order that the individual may believe if he wills it; I merely say that it must be strenuous in the highest degree so to believe" (p. 190).

As this last quotation indicates, Kierkegaard thinks that religious belief ought to be based on a strenuous exertion of the will—a passionate striving. His reasons for thinking that objective probability is religiously undesirable have to do with the place of passion in religion, and constitute what I call the Passion Argument. The first premise of the argument is that the most essential and the most valuable feature of religiousness is passion, indeed an infinite passion, a passion of the greatest possible intensity. The second premise is that an infinite passion requires objective improbability. And the conclusion therefore is that that which is most essential and most valuable in religiousness requires objective improbability.

My discussion of this argument will have three parts. (a) First I will try to clarify, very briefly, what it is that is supposed to be objectively improbable. (b) Then we will consider Kierkegaard's reasons for holding that infinite passion requires objective improbability. In so doing we will also gain a clearer understanding of what a Kierkegaardian infinite passion is. (c) Finally I will discuss the first premise of the argument—although issues will arise at that point which I do not pretend to be able to settle by argument.

(a) What are the beliefs whose improbability is needed by religious passion? Kierkegaard will hardly be satisfied with the improbability of just any one belief; it must surely be at least an important belief. On the other hand it would clearly be preposterous to suppose that every belief involved in Christianity must be objectively improbable. (Consider, for example, the belief that the man Jesus did indeed live.) I think that what is demanded in the Passion Argument is the objective improbability of at least one belief which must be true if the goal sought by the religious passion is to be attained.

(b) We can find in the *Postscript* suggestions of several reasons for thinking that an infinite passion needs objective improbability. The two that seem to me most interesting have to do with (i) the risks accepted and (ii) the costs paid in pursuance of a passionate interest.

(i) One reason that Kierkegaard has for valuing objective improbability is that it increases the *risk* attaching to the religious life, and risk is so essential for the expression of religious passion that "without risk there is no faith" (p. 182). About the nature of an eternal happiness, the goal of religious striving, Kierkegaard says "there is nothing to be said . . .

[6]Søren Kierkegaard, *Fear and Trembling,* trans. Walter Lowrie, 2d ed. (Princeton: Princeton University Press, 1970; published in one volume with *The Sickness unto Death*), p. 131. Cf. *Postscript,* p. 31f.

except that it is the good which is attained by venturing everything absolutely" (p. 382).

> But what then does it mean to venture? A venture is the precise correlative of an uncertainty; when the certainty is there the venture becomes impossible. . . . If what I hope to gain by venturing is itself certain, I do not risk or venture, but make an exchange. . . . No, if I am in truth resolved to venture, in truth resolved to strive for the attainment of the highest good, the uncertainty must be there, and I must have room to move, so to speak. But the largest space I can obtain, where there is room for the most vehement gesture of the passion that embraces the infinite, is uncertainty of knowledge with respect to an eternal happiness, or the certain knowledge that the choice is in the finite sense a piece of madness: now there is room, now you can venture! (pp. 380–82)

How is it that objective improbability provides the largest space for the most vehement gesture of infinite passion? Consider two cases. (A) You plunge into a raging torrent to rescue from drowning someone you love, who is crying for help. (B) You plunge into a raging torrent in a desperate attempt to rescue someone you love, who appears to be unconscious and *may* already have drowned. In both cases you manifest a passionate interest in saving the person, risking your own life in order to do so. But I think Kierkegaard would say there is more passion in the second case than in the first. For in the second case you risk your life in what is, objectively considered, a smaller chance that you will be able to save your loved one. A greater passion is required for a more desperate attempt.

A similar assessment may be made of the following pair of cases. (A′) You stake everything on your faith in the truth of Christianity, knowing that it is objectively 99 per cent probable that Christianity is true. (B′) You stake everything on your faith in the truth of Christianity, knowing that the truth of Christianity is, objectively, possible but so improbable that its probability is, say, as small as $\frac{1}{10^{2,000,000}}$. There is passion in both cases, but Kierkegaard will say that there is more passion in the second case than in the first. For to venture the same stake (namely, everything) on a much smaller chance of success shows greater passion.

Acceptance of risk can thus be seen as a *measure* of the intensity of passion. I believe this provides us with one way of understanding what Kierkegaard means when he calls religious passion "infinite." An *infinite* passionate interest in x is an interest so strong that it leads one to make the greatest possible sacrifices in order to obtain x, on the smallest possible chance of success. The infinity of the passion is shown in that there is no sacrifice so great one will not make it, and no chance of success so small one will not act on it. A passion which is infinite in this sense requires, by its very nature, a situation of maximum risk for its expression.

It will doubtless be objected that this argument involves a misunderstanding of what a passionate interest is. Such an interest is a **disposition.** In order to have a great passionate interest it is not necessary actually to make a great sacrifice with a small chance of success; all that is necessary is to have such an intense interest that one *would* do so if an appropriate occasion should arise. It is therefore a mistake to say that there *is* more passion in case (B) than in case (A), or in (B′) than in (A′). More passion is *shown* in (B) than in (A), and in (B′) than in (A′); but an equal passion may exist in cases in which there is no occasion to show it.

This objection may well be correct as regards what we normally mean by "passionate interest." But that is not decisive for the argument. The crucial question is what part dispositions, possibly unactualized, ought to play in religious devotion. And here we must have a digression about the position of the *Postscript* on this question—a position that is complex at best and is not obviously consistent.

In the first place I do not think that Kierkegaard would be prepared to think of passion, or a passionate interest, as primarily a disposition that might remain unactualized. He seems to conceive of passion chiefly as an intensity in which one actually does and feels. "Passion is momentary" (p. 178), although capable of continual repetition. And what is momentary in such a way that it must be repeated rather than protracted is presumably an occurrence rather than a disposition. It agrees with this conception of passion that Kierkegaard idealizes a life of "persistent striving," and says that the religious task is to "exercise" the God-relationship and to give "existential expression" to the religious choice (pp. 110, 364, 367).

All of this supports the view that what Kierkegaard means by "an infinite passionate interest" is a pattern of actual decision-making, in which one continually exercises and expresses one's religiousness by making the greatest possible sacrifices on the smallest possible chance of success. In order to actualize such a pattern of life one needs chances of success that are as small as possible. That is the room that is required for "the most vehement gesture" of infinite passion.

But on the other hand Kierkegaard does allow a dispositional element in the religious life, and even precisely in the making of the greatest possible sacrifices. We might suppose that if we are to make the greatest possible sacrifices in our religious devotion, we must do so by abandoning all worldly interests and devoting all our time and attention to religion. That is what monasticism attempts to do, as Kierkegaard sees it; and (in the *Postscript,* at any rate) he rejects the attempt, contrary to what our argument to this point would have led us to expect of him. He holds that "resignation" (pp. 353, 367) or "renunciation" (pp. 362, 386) of *all* finite ends is precisely the first thing that religiousness requires; but he means a renunciation that is compatible with pursuing and enjoying finite ends (pp. 362–71). This renunciation is the practice of a sort of detachment; Kierkegaard uses the image of a dentist loosening the soft tissues around a tooth, while it is still in place, in preparation for pulling it (p. 367). It is partly a matter of not treating finite things with a desperate seriousness, but with a certain coolness or humor, even while one pursues them (pp. 368, 370).

This coolness is not just a disposition. But the renunciation also has a dispositional aspect. "Now if for any individual an eternal happiness is his highest good, this will mean that all finite satisfactions are volitionally relegated to the status of what may have to be renounced in favor of an eternal happiness" (p. 350). The volitional relegation is not a disposition but an act of choice. The object of this choice, however, appears to be a **dispositional state**—the state of being such that one *would* forgo any finite satisfaction *if* it *were* religiously necessary or advantageous to do so.

It seems clear that Kierkegaard, in the *Postscript,* is willing to admit a dispositional element at one point in the religious venture, but not at another. It is enough in most cases, he thinks, if one is *prepared* to cease for the sake of religion from pursuing some finite end; but it is not enough that one *would* hold to one's belief in the face of objective improbability. The belief must actually be improbable, although the pursuit of the finite need not actually cease. What is not clear is a reason for this disparity. The following hypothesis, admittedly somewhat speculative as interpretation of the text, is the best explanation I can offer.

The admission of a dispositional element in the religious renunciation of the finite is something to which Kierkegaard seems to be driven by the view that there is no alternative to it except idolatry. For suppose one actually ceases from all worldly pursuits and enters a monastery. In the monastery one would pursue a number of particular ends (such as getting up in the middle of the night to say the offices) which, although religious in a way ("churchy," one might say), are still finite. The absolute **telos** or end of religion is no more to be identified with them than with the ends pursued by an alderman (pp. 362–71). To pretend otherwise would be to make an idolatrous identification of the absolute end with some finite end. An existing person cannot have sacrificed everything by actually having ceased from pursuing *all* finite ends. For as long as he lives and acts he is pursuing some finite end. Therefore his renouncing *everything* finite must be at least partly dispositional.

Kierkegaard does not seem happy with this position. He regards it as of the utmost importance that the religious passion should come to expression. The problem of finding an adequate expression for a passion for an infinite end, in the face of the fact that in every concrete action one will be pursuing some finite end, is treated in the *Postscript* as the central problem of religion (see especially pp. 386–468). If the sacrifice of everything finite must remain largely dispositional, then perhaps it is all the more important to Kierkegaard that the smallness of the chance for which it is sacrificed should be fully actual, so that the infinity of the religious passion may be measured by an actuality in at least one aspect of the religious venture.

(ii) According to Kierkegaard, as I have argued, the intensity of a passion is measured in part by the smallness of the chances of success that one acts on. It can also be measured in part by its *costliness*—that is, by how much one gives up or suffers in acting on those chances. This second measure can also be made the basis of an argument for the claim that an infinite passion requires objective improbability. For the objective improbability of a religious belief, if recognized, increases the costliness of holding it. The risk involved in staking everything on an objectively improbable belief gives rise to an anxiety and mental suffering whose acceptance is itself a sacrifice. It seems to follow that if one is not staking everything on a belief one sees to be objectively improbable, one's passion is not infinite in Kierkegaard's sense, since one's sacrifice could be greater if one did adhere to an improbable belief.

Kierkegaard uses an argument similar to this. For God to give us objective knowledge of Himself, eliminating paradox from it, would be "to lower the price of the God-relationship."

> And even if God could be imagined willing, no man with passion in his heart could desire it. To a maiden genuinely in love it could never occur that she had bought her happiness too dear, but rather that she had not bought it dear enough. And just as the passion of the infinite was itself the truth, so in the case of the highest value it holds true that the price is the value, that a low price means a poor value. . . . (p. 207)

Kierkegaard here appears to hold, first, that an increase in the objective probability of religious belief would reduce its costliness, and second, that the value of a religious life is measured by its cost. I take it his reason for the second of these claims is that passion is the most valuable thing in a religious life and passion is measured by its cost. If we grant Kierkegaard the requisite conception of an infinite passion, we seem once again to have a plausible argument for the view that objective improbability is required for such a passion.

(c) We must therefore consider whether infinite passion, as Kierkegaard conceives of it, ought to be part of the religious ideal of life. Such a passion is a striving, or pattern of decision-making, in which, with the greatest possible intensity of feeling, one continually makes the greatest possible sacrifices on the smallest possible chance of success. This seems to me an impossible ideal. I doubt that any human being could have a passion of this sort, because I doubt that one could make a sacrifice so great that a greater could not be made, or have a (nonzero) chance of success so small that a smaller could not be had.

But even if Kierkegaard's ideal is impossible, one might want to try to approximate it. Intensity of passion might still be measured by the greatness of sacrifices made and the smallness of chances of success acted on, even if we cannot hope for a greatest possible or a smallest possible here. And it could be claimed that the most essential and valuable thing in religiousness is a passion that is very intense (though it cannot be infinite) by this standard—the more intense the better. This claim will not support an argument that objective improbability is absolutely required for religious passion. For a passion could presumably be very intense, involving great sacrifices and risks of some other sort, without an objectively improbable belief. But it could still be argued that objectively improbable religious beliefs enhance the value of the religious life by increasing its sacrifices and diminishing its chances of success, whereas objective probability detracts from the value of religious passion by diminishing its intensity.

The most crucial question about the Passion Argument, then, is whether maximization of sacrifice and risk is so valuable in religion as to make objective improbabiltiy a desirable characteristic of religious beliefs. Certainly much religious thought and feeling places a very high value on sacrifice and on passionate intensity. But the doctrine that it is desirable to increase without limit, or to the highest possible degree (if there is one) the cost and risk of a religious life is less plausible (to say the least) than the view that *some* degree of cost and risk may add to the value of a religious life. The former doctrine would set the religious interest at enmity with all other interests, or at least with the best of them. Kierkegaard is surely right in thinking that it would be impossible to live without pursuing some finite ends. But even so it would be possible to exchange the pursuit of better finite ends for the pursuit of worse ones—for example, by exchanging the pursuit of truth, beauty, and satisfying personal relationships for the self-flagellating pursuit of pain.

And a way of life would be the costlier for requiring such an exchange. Kierkegaard does not, in the *Postscript,* demand it. But the presuppositions of his Passion Argument seem to imply that such a sacrifice would be religiously desirable. Such a conception of religion is demonic. In a tolerable religious ethics some way must be found to conceive of the religious interest as inclusive rather than exclusive of the best of other interests—including, I think, the interest in having well-grounded beliefs.

4. PASCAL'S WAGER AND KIERKEGAARD'S LEAP

Ironically, Kierkegaard's views about religious passion suggest a way in which his religious beliefs could be based on objective reasoning—not on reasoning which would show them to be objectively probable, but on reasoning which shows them to be objectively advantageous. Consider the situation of a person whom Kierkegaard would regard as a genuine Christian believer. What would such a person want most of all? He would want above all else to attain the truth through Christianity. That is, he would desire both that Christianity be true and that he himself be related to it as a genuine believer. He would desire that state of affairs (which we may call *S*) so ardently that he would be willing to sacrifice everything else to obtain it, given only the smallest possible chance of success.

We can therefore construct the following argument, which has an obvious analogy to Pascal's Wager. Let us assume that there is, objectively, some chance, however small, that Christianity is true. This is an assumption which Kierkegaard accepts (p. 31), and I think it is plausible. There are two possibilities, then: either Christianity it true, or it is false. (Others might object to so stark a **disjunction,** but Kierkegaard will not.) If Christianity is false it is impossible for anyone to obtain *S,* since *S* includes the truth of Christianity. It is only if Christianity is true that anything one does will help one or hinder one in obtaining *S*. And if Christianity is true, one will obtain *S* just in case one becomes a genuine Christian believer. It seems obvious that one would increase one's chances of becoming a genuine Christian believer by becoming one now (if one can), even if the truth of Christian beliefs is now objectively uncertain or improbable. Hence it would seem to be advantageous for anyone who can to become a genuine Christian believer now, if he wants *S* so much that he would be willing to sacrifice everything else for the smallest possible chance of obtaining *S*. Indeed I believe that the argument I have given for this conclusion is a piece of objective reasoning, and that Christian belief is therefore *objectively* advantageous for anyone who wants *S* as much as a Kierkegaardian genuine Christian must want it.

Of course this argument does not tend at all to show that it is objectively probable that Christianity is true. It only gives a practical, prudential reason for believing, to someone who has a certain desire. Nor does the argument do anything to prove that such an absolutely overriding desire for *S* is reasonable.[7] It does show, however, that just as Kierkegaard's position has more logical structure than one might at first think, it is more difficult than he probably realized for him to get away entirely from objective justification.

STUDY QUESTIONS

1. What does Adams mean by *objective reasoning?*
2. Explain Kierkegaard's three arguments against the use of objective reasoning in religion.
3. Adams says that we sometimes disregard the possibility of error because it is practically advantageous to do so. First explain how this supplies a rejoinder to the approximation argument. Then give examples of your own, from outside the religious context, to illustrate his point.
4. In his examination of the postponement argument, Adams claims that there is a distinction between a person's having objective reasoning for believing something and the person's belief *depending* on having that reasoning. Give an example of your own to illustrate this distinction.

[7]It is worth noting, though, that a similar argument might still provide some less overriding justification of belief to someone who had a strong, but less overriding, desire for *S*.

5. Explain why passion requires risk, according to Kierkegaard.
6. *Adams says that Kierkegaard overstates the role of risk and sacrifice in religious life. In what ways does religious commitment require such risk and sacrifice? Do you think it requires a degree of *intellectual* risk?
7. *It has been said by contemporary philosopher Louis Pojman that, if Kierkegaard's view of religiosity is correct, the cult of the Charles Manson family (which savagely murdered eight people in 1969) was more religious than Roman Catholicism. Explain what Pojman meant by this remark.
8. *Some of the great religious thinkers, such as St. Anselm, St. Thomas Aquinas, and Maimonides, used objective reasoning to support belief in God. Could Kierkegaard regard them as truly religious, nonetheless? Explain.
9. *Is it reasonable of God to expect unconditional commitment? Discuss.

CLOSING THOUGHTS

READING 7.11

Suppose God Exists

Steven M. Cahn

Readings 7.3 and 7.5–7.8 maintained that, even if one lacks a good deductive or inductive argument for God's existence, it could be rational for one to believe that God exists and to lead a religious life. In "Suppose God Exists," Steven M. Cahn (City University of New York) argues quite differently: that, even if one were able to show through the **ontological, cosmological** *or* **design (teleological)** *arguments—or alternatively through a* **pragmatic** *argument—that it is rational to believe that the most perfect conceivable being, the all-good creator of the universe, exists, such arguments would be of limited value. They would not provide either specific moral principles by which we must abide or dictates about prayer and ritual that we must follow. Trying to deduce moral precepts from God's existence is another case of the so-called* **is-ought fallacy** *pointed to by David Hume: deducing* **normative** *judgments (ought-statements) from factual premises (is-statements). Such a deduction is not* **valid.** *Cahn provides several principles that one would assume could be deduced from the existence of God and then argues against them. Cahn concludes, as Hume does, that the existence of God "affords no inference that affects human life." His essay leads into chapter 8, which confronts the implications of the fact that there are so many alternative religious systems.*

For centuries philosophers have discussed the merits of the **ontological, cosmological, teleological,** and **pragmatic** arguments for believing in God. Let us, however, temporarily bypass these debates and assume that some versions of these arguments make it reasonable to believe in the existence of the most perfect conceivable Being, the all-good creator of the universe. What implications follow that would be relevant to our lives?

Most persons, either out of fear or respect, would wish to act in accord with God's will. None of the arguments for believing in God, however, provides any hint whatever as to which actions God wishes us to perform or what we ought to do to please or obey Him. We may affirm that God is all-good and yet have no way of knowing the highest moral standards. All we may presume is that, whatever these standards, God always acts in accordance with them. We might expect God to have implanted the correct moral intuitions in our minds, but this supposition is doubtful in view of the conflicts among people's intuitions. And even if some consensus prevailed, it might be only a means by which God tests us to see whether we have the courage to dissent from popular opinion.

Some would argue that, if God exists, then at least it follows that murder is immoral, since it would be immoral to destroy what God in His infinite wisdom created. This argument, however, fails on several grounds. First, God also created germs, viruses, and disease-carrying rats. Does it follow that since God created these things they ought not be eliminated? Second, if God arranged for us to live, He also arranged for us to die. Does it follow that by committing murder we are assisting the work of God? Third, God provided us with the mental and physical capacities to commit murder. Does it follow that God wishes us to commit murder?

Clearly, the attempt to deduce moral precepts from God's existence is but another case of trying to do what David Hume long ago pointed out to be logically impossible, *viz.,* the deduction of **normative** judgments from purely factual premises (*Treatise of Human Nature* III,1,1). No such deduction is **valid** and, thus, any moral principle is consistent with the existence of God.

Since the arguments for believing in God afford no means of distinguishing good from evil, no person can be sure how to obey God and do what is best in His eyes. We may hope our actions are in accord with God's standards, but no test is available to check. Some seemingly good persons suffer great ills, and some seemingly evil persons achieve great happiness. Perhaps in a future life these outcomes are reversed, but we have no way of ascertaining who, if anyone, is ultimately punished and who ultimately rewarded.

Holy books may be thought to provide such insights. But while many such books claim to embody the will of God, they conflict with one another. Which is to be believed? Which moral code is to be followed? Which prayers are to be recited? Which rituals are to be performed? Believing that God exists does not yield answers to these crucial questions.

Does God wish us to worship or serve Him? Perhaps, but perhaps not. Who knows what God wills? Might He not disapprove of all religious activity? Persons may devote themselves to the adoration of God, but He might look with more favor on those dedicated to quite different ends.

Orthodox believers traditionally proclaim that God is incomprehensible, inscrutable, beyond our powers of understanding. So be it. How, then, can we draw any implications from God's existence?

I conclude, as Hume apparently did at the end of his *Dialogues Concerning Natural Religion,* that the existence of God "affords no inference that affects human life."

STUDY QUESTIONS

1. According to Cahn, why does proving God's existence have no effect on human life?
2. *Citing Hume, Cahn argues that moral principles cannot be deduced from factual premises. Give other examples of this is-ought fallacy besides the theistic case.
3. Cahn implies that it is *always* fallacious to infer normative conclusions from factual premises. Nonetheless, he seems to think as well that there are special features of the theistic case that make such an inference *especially* problematic in that context. Explain what those features are.
4. *If people were to accept Cahn's view of moral principles, do you think that they would change their attitudes toward such crimes as murder and abuse? Why or why not?

FURTHER READING

Adams, Robert Merrihew. "The Virtue of Faith." *Faith and Philosophy* 1 (1984): 3–15. Repr. in Robert Merrihew Adams, *The Virtue of Faith,* 3–15. New York: Oxford University Press, 1987.

Audi, Robert, and William J. Wainwright, eds. *Rationality, Religious Belief, and Moral Commitment.* Ithaca, NY: Cornell University Press, 1986.

Davis, Stephen T. *Faith, Skepticism, and Evidence*. Lewisburg, PA: Bucknell University Press, 1978.

Delaney, C. F. *Rationality and Religious Belief*. Notre Dame, IN: University of Notre Dame Press, 1978.

Gale, Richard. *On the Nature and Existence of God*. New York: Cambridge University Press, 1991. Ch. 9.

Green, Ronald. *Religious Reason*. New York: Oxford University Press, 1978.

Helm, Paul, ed. *Faith and Reason*. Oxford, England: Oxford University Press, 1999.

Helm, Paul. *Faith With Reason*. Oxford, England: Clarendon Press, 2000.

Hester, Marcus, ed. *Faith, Reason, and Skepticism: Essays by William P. Alson, Robert Audi, Terence Penelhum, Richard H. Popkin*. Philadelphia: Temple University Press, 1992.

Hoitenga, D. *From Plato to Plantinga: An Introduction to Reformed Epistemology*. Albany, NY: SUNY Press, 1983.

Hook, Sidney, ed. *Religious Experience and Truth*. New York: New York University Press, 1961.

Jordan, Jeff, ed. *Gambling on God: Essays on Pascal's Wager*. Lanham, MD: Rowman & Littlefield, 1994.

Kenny, Anthony. *What Is Faith?: Essays in the Philosophy of Religion*. New York: Oxford University Press, 1992.

Lamm, Norman. "Faith and Doubt." In *Faith and Doubt: Studies in Traditional Jewish Thought,* pp. 1–41, New York: Ktav Publishing House, 1986.

Malcolm, Norman. "The Groundlessness of Religious Belief." In *Reason and Religion,* edited by Stuart Brown, pp. 143–57. Ithaca, NY: Cornell University Press, 1975.

Mavrodes, George, "It is Beyond the Power of Human Reason." *Philosophical Topics* 16, 2 (1988): pp. 75–88.

Penelhum, Terence, ed. *Faith*. New York: Macmillan, 1989.

Penelhum, Terence. *God and Skepticism*. Dordrecht: Reidel, 1983.

Plantinga, Alvin. *Warranted Christian Belief*. New York: Oxford University Press, 2000.

Plantinga, Alvin, and Nicholas Wolterstorff, eds. *Faith and Rationality; Reason and Belief in God*. Notre Dame, IN: University of Notre Dame Press, 1983.

Pojman, Louis. *Religious Belief and the Will*. London and New York: Routledge and Kegan Paul, 1986.

Quinn, Philip L. "Epistemic Parity and Religious Argument." In *Philosophical Perspectives 5: Philosophy of Religion,* edited by James E. Tomberlin, pp. 317–41. Atascadero, CA: Ridgeview, 1991.

Quinn, Philip L. "In Search of the Foundations of Theism." *Faith and Philosophy* 2 (1985): 469–86.

Shatz, David. "The Overexamined Life Is Not Worth Living." In *God and the Philosophers,* edited by Thomas V. Morris, pp. 263–85. New York: Oxford University Press, 1994.

Stich, Stephen P. "The Recombinant DNA Debate." *Philosophy and Public Affairs* 7 (1978). (Briefly discusses Pascal's wager.)

Swinburne, Richard. *Faith and Reason*. New York: Oxford University Press, 1981.

Trigg, Roger. *Reason and Commitment*. London: Cambridge University Press, 1973.

Wainwright, William J. *Reason and the Heart: A Prolegomenon to a Critique of Passional Reason*. Ithaca, NY and London: Cornell University Press, 1995.

Wolterstorff, Nicholas. "Once More: Evidentialism—This Time Social." *Philosophical Topics* 16, 2 (1988): pp. 53–74.

CHAPTER 8

The Diversity of World Religions

In this, the book's final chapter, it is time to rectify some oversimplifications in the way we have discussed issues thus far.

Until now, we have been treating theism as a single, mostly undifferentiated entity. The major theistic religions—Christianity, Judaism, and Islam—share, we said, certain beliefs. They hold in common that God exists; that God is **omnipotent, omniscient,** and **omnibenevolent;** that God created the world; and that God exercises providence over it. We have seen dissent among theists from these beliefs of classical theism—think of those who believe in a God whose knowledge or power is limited, in a **deistic** God who created the world but then withdrew from it, or in the deity of **process theology.** But these are the exceptions, not the rule. By and large, we have been able to identify core beliefs that unite the various theistic religions, and have not sought to identify beliefs that divide them.

In point of fact, however, the three major religions of the West seem to be in logical conflict with one another. If Christianity believes that God became human in the **Incarnation,** that Jesus is Christ the redeemer, and that God is a trinity, whereas Judaism as well as Islam deny these assertions, aren't Judaism and Islam logically incompatible with Christianity? If Islam affirms that Mohammed was a prophet of God, and the Koran a revealed book, whereas Christianity and Judaism reject this claim, are we not dealing with contradictory beliefs? The different religions have, it seems, incompatible views of revelation and salvation, about what God has communicated and about what way of life God wants people to lead. Wars have been fought over the truth of religious propositions. Going yet further, within each of the major religions there are many subgroups, known as denominations. Protestants and Roman Catholics disagree about such key issues as how to interpret Scripture and whether God is known on the basis of evidence or instead in another way. Anglican, Baptist, Lutheran, Methodist and Presbyterian groups disagree over **theological** doctrines. Within Judaism, the denominations of Orthodox, Conservative, and Reform have different views of revelation and of whether it is necessary to observe all the commandments given in the Torah. And even within denominations there are divisions—for example, between left, center, and right wings.

Besides glossing over differences among and within the major theistic religions, we have ignored to this point religions outside of Christianity, Judaism, and Islam. We have not discussed other personal gods, such as the *Vishnu* deity of Hinduism. We have ignored the notion that ultimate reality is not a personal being but, rather, Brahman—an impersonal, exhaustive, and ultimate reality—as in

Hinduism (the personal deities like *Vishnu* being but Brahman's refraction). Belief in Brahman entails that individuality and the existence of anything besides the ultimate unified reality are illusions; a person's life goal is to realize oneness with Brahman and, in doing so, lose individuality. We have also ignored Shinto and Taoism. We have ignored such ideas as that after a person dies the person is reincarnated as another person or as an animal. We have not discussed forms of Buddhism which deny there is *any* ultimate **metaphysical** reality. But our way of life in the contemporary world, a world of instant communication and easy travel, makes it impossible for traditional theists to shut their eyes to the rest of the world, to overlook the remarkable diversity in world religions. The actual state of world religion is crowded and confusing—a far cry from the simplistic treatment of theism we have adopted so far in this book.

Let us put aside the differences within theistic religions—that is, denominational differences within Christianity, Judaism, and Islam. Let us focus instead on the fact there are differences (1) between different theistic religions and (2) between theistic and nontheistic religions. Surely a thoughtful theist, call her Diane, will want to reflect on whether her religion is the only true one, and on whether it is the only religion that leads to salvation, liberation, fulfillment, or whatever else Diane thinks her religion achieves for her. Notice that we are not asking at this juncture whether the very existence of other religions logically should lead Diane to question whether her religion is the only true one and the only path to salvation. Notice also that we must not confuse the question of whether another religion is true or leads to salvation with the question of whether that religion should be tolerated. (We might readily tolerate beliefs with which we disagree.) We want to know, whether from within the standpoint of one religion, (1) another religion may lead to salvation, liberation, and fulfillment and (2) another religion may be true as well.

The question about whether other paths exist to salvation and other goals has been addressed within each religion. For example, many authorities of the Church have held that salvation can be achieved only through the Church, but other theologians, particularly in recent times, hold this is not so. Jewish authorities have generally agreed that people outside Judaism have a share in the world to come, although they have disagreed about the precise conditions under which this share is assured. Our theist, Diane, could decide to regard other religions in whatever way the authorities of her religion do.

What about our other question—whether it is logically possible that religions other than one's own are true? Surely an adherent of one religion may acknowledge that other religions contain *some* truths: after all, adherents of all three major Western religions concur that God exists and that God created the world. But can it be that the ultimate religious truth lies in a worldview that is neither what Diane's religion teaches nor what other religions teach but, instead, embraces both Diane's religion and all the others?

Let us lay out possible positions on these issues using terms made common by John Hick.

A religious **exclusivist** is someone who believes there is only one true religion (one's own) and only one path to salvation, liberation, and fulfillment (namely, the path prescribed by one's own religion). Because exclusivists hold this belief, they might proselytize so as to bring others to salvation, liberation, fulfillment, or whatever goal an exclusivist thinks is the aim of religion.

Exclusivism seems problematic. Considering first the issue of salvation, would a good God consign a person to hell if the person lived in a remote part of the world and had never heard of Diane's religion? The Jewish philosopher Moses Mendelssohn (1729–86) was incredulous at the suggestion that highly moral personalities such as Confucius and Solon would have no share in the afterlife. Diane's religion should allow that adherents of another faith, even if they have heard of Diane's religion, can attain salvation in some way, such as leading an ethical life. For this reason, exclusivism seems problematic. In addition, what gives one the **epistemic** right to regard *only* one's own religion as giving an accurate description of reality? If an adherent of religion X had been born into or raised in religion Y, that person would have been an adherent of Y. Why should an accident of birth or upbringing be given epistemic weight?

A religious **inclusivist** is someone who believes that, although other religions hold to false beliefs, one can achieve salvation while adhering to a religion other than the true one, perhaps even by being an ethical person with no religious commitment at all. For example, Catholic theologian Karl Rahner (1904–1984) held that, although Christianity is the one true religion, Christianity itself teaches that Jesus's work of salvation saves even those who have never heard of Christianity. Among the questions an inclusivist faces (and Rahner dealt with) is why Christians would be motivated to proselytize, given that the people whom they are seeking to convert can attain salvation anyway without converting.

Finally, a **religious pluralist** is one who believes that all religions are (in some sense) true. A prevalent form of pluralism maintains that all religions are manifestations of one divine reality. This view is asserted in Hinduism and is given elaborate expression today by John Hick. Hick believes that, although not every conception of God is valid, every conception of he divine that has come out of a great revelatory experience, that has been tested through a long tradition of worship, and that has sustained human faith over centuries is likely to represent a genuine encounter with the divine reality. We must distinguish reality as it is in itself from reality as it is perceived and experienced culturally. The ultimate reality is infinite and cannot be adequately described. But each religion has something partially correct to say about the ultimate reality. It is like the Eastern tale of an elephant being brought to blind men who had never encountered an elephant before. Each felt a different part of the elephant. One felt a leg and reported that an elephant is a great living pillar. Another felt a trunk and reported that an elephant is a great snake. Another felt a tusk and reported that an elephant is like a sharp ploughshare. All these descriptions were true, but each referred to only one aspect of the reality and expressed it in imperfect analogies. Just so, different religious traditions are responses to the same infinite divine reality and lead to different focused awarenesses of that reality, as well as to different metaphors and images to describe it. The development of different cultures leads over time to increasing differentiation of traditions, but the fact remains that the traditions represent an encounter with a single reality. The pluralist maintains that this analysis holds even for nontheistic religions (and maybe that it could somehow be extended to cover even religions, such as forms of Buddhism, that deny the existence of any ultimate metaphysical reality). Images in all the world's religions can have an impact on people's lives, bringing about personal transformation, liberation, and salvation by turning people away from a focus on the self and toward a focus on ultimate reality.

In short, for pluralists of Hick's type, it is not just that *within* each religion there is a single ultimate reality; rather, there is in fact a single ultimate reality on which *all* religions focus (albeit in their vastly different, culturally conditioned ways). One surmises that pluralists would not be fazed by the fact that many adherents of individual religions would reject pluralism's central assertion that all religions experience the same ultimate reality. These adherents, pluralists would say, are simply mistaken. Nor would pluralists take as decisive the fact that many adherents of particular religions would deny that the ultimate reality is different from the way it is described in their religion. Regarding this second point, not only might these adherents be mistaken, but Hick notes that religions themselves often distinguish between God in Himself and God as He appears to humans, so there is logical space in individual religions for pluralism to enter. Some pluralists view themselves as offering a version of Christianity (one that is Hindu-like), but insofar as it is confusing and maybe even self-defeating for a pluralist to regard pluralism as the view of *one particular religion,* and insofar as, Hinduism aside, the task of linking any particular religion with pluralism is daunting, we may for immediate purposes think of pluralism as a philosophical thesis that is independent of any particular religion. As a philosophical thesis, religious pluralism seeks both to explain religious diversity and to do justice to the epistemic difficulty of justifying one set of religious beliefs and practices as against another.

Pluralists face several problems. First, to worship a being requires more than experiencing that being—it requires having at least a partly correct concept of the being who is worshipped; otherwise, what makes the act one of worshipping *that* being? Given this, what would it mean to say that all religions worship the same God? Second, pluralism threatens to create **skepticism** about religious belief. If pluralists cannot know what the ultimate reality is like, how, then, can they postulate the reality? In fact, as mentioned earlier, some forms of Buddhism deny that there is an ultimate metaphysical reality.[1] Third, according to pluralists, what difference should it make to anyone what any particular religion holds? Are not all world religions equally inadequate or equally adequate? Why is what one believes important at all? These are some of the criticisms pluralists must address.

In the first of this chapter's selections, Avishai Margalit argues that an adherent of Judaism, Christianity, or Islam must be an exclusivist. Because the claims of Judaism, Christianity, and Islam are in logical conflict with one another, a believer in one religion must maintain that the others are false and—this is a further step—without value. John Hick, however, is a pluralist. The various religions—both theistic and nontheistic, Western and Eastern—use different sets of images to mediate the human encounter with ultimate reality. But all are responding to the same reality.

The next selection, by Alvin Plantinga, defends exclusivism against certain attacks. Among the considerations that are thought to support religious pluralism is that it is arrogant and therefore ethically improper for an adherent of a particular religion to regard other religions as false. Plantinga disputes this contention, arguing that, if we accept the pluralist's objection, we cannot believe anything, not even pluralism. In addition, Plantinga replies to Hick's argument from the **contingency** of religious belief (i.e., the argument that, if a believer were born in a different time and place, he or she would not adhere to the religion to which he or she, in fact, does adhere). Plantinga's retort is that, if the pluralist were born in a different time and place, he or she would not be a pluralist; thus, if contingency is a reason for abandoning one's belief, the pluralist should not be a pluralist.

The last essay is by Joseph Runzo, who defends a position we have not yet discussed—religious relativism. This position arises in response to deficiencies in Hick's pluralistic outlook, for example, that in Hick's one account what one believes is (it seems) inconsequential. Religious relativism maintains that the correctness of a religion is relative to the world view of its adherents. Thus, there can be more than one correct religion, but not from the internal perspective of a particular religion.

[1]The situation with respect to Buddhism is complex and defies easy description. Although Buddhist thinkers generally reject belief in God and are overtly atheistic, the development of ideas such as Buddha, Dharma and Nirvana lead, in the opinion of some if not many scholars, to an outlook that is not radically different from theism. See, for example, Edward Conze, *Buddhism: Its Essence and Development* (New York: Harper Torchbooks, 1975), at, e.g., pp. 110–111; Paul J. Griffiths, "Buddhism," in *A Companion to the Philosophy of Religion,* ed. Philip L. Quinn and Charles Taliaferro (Malden, MA and Oxford, England: Blackwell Publishers, 1997), 15–24, esp. pp. 22–23. In defending his pluralist outlook in his many writings, Hick stresses aspects of Buddhism that are similar to theism and that do suggest belief in an ultimate metaphysical reality.

READING 8.1

The Ring: On Religious Pluralism

Avishai Margalit

Does each of the three major religions of the West—Christianity, Islam, and Judaism—allow its adherents to ascribe intrinsic value to the others? **Religious pluralists** *answer that, yes, each religion may ascribe intrinsic value to the others. However, in this selection, Avishai Margalit (the Hebrew University, Jerusalem) formulates an* **argument** *against pluralists. Margalit takes off from an oft-told story in which a king leaves three rings to his three sons. Margalit argues that there are contradictions among the "constitutive revealed truths" of the three major religions (the three rings). Hence, each religion should see itself as the only true one—the only real ring—and ascribe no value to the others.*

A great asset of Margalit's article is that, even though he endorses the argument for a religious person's allowing for only one ring, he points out how some of his argument's premises could be or have been disputed. For example, Protestants do not view revelation as the revelation of propositions but, rather, as the revelation of God's presence. The view of revelation as revelation of presence plays a role in the pluralist viewpoint, as is evident in John Hick's writing (reading 8.2). Also, it could be argued that a good God would not give revelatory truths to only one group. Influenced by this consideration, some religions explicitly maintain that adherents of other religions can attain salvation. These last points provide ingredients for **inclusivism.** *Thus the article hints at how a case for* **inclusivism** *and pluralism can be built, even while asserting that a religious person is logically committed to* **exclusivism.**

Can Judaism, Christianity, and Islam be **pluralistic?** The question is not whether they can tolerate one another, but whether they can accept the idea that the other religions have intrinsic religious value. Christians, said Goethe, want to be accepted, not tolerated. This is presumably true of Jews and Muslims as well. The question is whether each of these groups is willing to accept the others, that is, to ascribe value to the others' lifestyle, so that, if they have the power, they will not only refrain from persecuting the others but will also encourage the flourishing of their way of life.

Put differently, do the three religions allow their adherents to ascribe intrinsic value to competing religious ways of life? In competing ways of life, beliefs and values essential to one of them contradict beliefs and values essential to the other. . . .

My question is about the possibility of interreligious rather than intrareligious **pluralism,** where the latter includes the acceptance of Protestants by Catholics, of Sunnis by Shiites, and of Reform Judaism by the Orthodox. If a religion can adopt a pluralistic stance with respect to other religions, this does not necessarily imply that it can also adopt such a stance toward heterodox streams within itself. Religious expectations from people perceived as belonging to one's own religion are liable to be much more demanding than those relating to people on the outside.

THE PARABLE OF THE RINGS

The lore of discussions about religious pluralism is accompanied by the folklore of the parable of the three rings, a story made famous by [Gotthold] Lessing in his play *Nathan the Wise* [1779]. This story has many different medieval ancestors, but I will jump through the rings regardless of historical precedence.

A king leaves a legacy of three rings to his three sons. Only one of the rings is real, and its owner is the king's legitimate heir. But the father has mercy on his other children and gives them imitation rings that look like the real one. The analogy is clear. The king is the Heavenly Father, who is the king of the universe, and the three sons are Moses, Jesus, and Muhammad. The real ring is the true revelation.

The story of the one real ring is an antipluralist story. There is one true religion, and the others are false. An imitation ring—for example, one with glass instead of a diamond—not only is valueless but can even have negative value if it pretends to be a real ring.

In the above version, the father did indeed leave two imitation rings and one real one, but no one else knows for certain which ring is the real one. This doubt should lead to an attitude of "respect and suspect," because it is possible that the truth is in another religion.

Another, more radical reading of the parable claims that none of the rings is real. The genuine ring is actually somewhere else. The three rings are only a means for discovering the genuine one. This version of the parable, in which the real ring is not one of the three, has two different interpretations. One is a mystic interpretation, which can be found, for example, in the writings of the thirteenth-century Jewish mystic [Abraham] Abulafia. This interpretation claims that the degree of religious perfection represented by the genuine ring cannot be attained by any of the three traditional religions. Religious perfection can be achieved only by the mystic, who is the sole possible owner of the real ring. The second interpretation of this version claims that the real ring is philosophy. Only philosophy permits the supreme religious knowledge that constitutes religious perfection. (Spinoza is probably the most radical advocate of the philosophical ring.) None of the three rings is real, but this does not mean that they are not effective, that is, able to promote the creation of a social order that enables the real ring to be found—in other words, a social and political order that permits doing philosophy.

Yet another version of the parable, that of Lessing in his play, is that none of the rings has intrinsic value in the sense that a gold ring has such a value, which is the worth of the gold it is made of. Rather, the worth of a ring is in the attitude of its owner. A religion is genuine in the sense that a wedding ring is. It is the person's belief in its significance that makes it effective, for example, by leading to love or good deeds. For someone who does not believe in it, the ring is worthless. All three rings can be valuable or valueless; their worth is in the eye of the beholder.

This last version of the parable raises the question of what it means for a ring to be genuine. Here there are three possibilities that need to be distinguished. One is that the ring is made out of the material it is supposed to be made of. A gold ring is genuine if it is made of eighteen-karat gold. The analogy to this is that the belief is true. The second possibility is that the ring is real if it is effective, if faith in it leads to desirable actions. The analogy here is to religious practice; a religion is genuine if it leads to the proper worship of God. The third possibility is that the ring is real if it truly determines who the father's legitimate heir or representative is. Here the analogy is to the question of who truly constitutes the source of religious authority—more precisely, who the true prophet is, from among the three claimants for legislative revelation.

Of course, there is yet another important version of the parable. A ring made of impure gold, which was the best available in its time, is replaced by a ring of purer, "more real" gold. This is a possible Christian or Muslim interpretation of the story, and the analogy is clear. The ring that was once "real" represents Judaism; now its time has passed, and the father has provided a "more real" ring, in all the senses of "real" I have discussed.

My ring stories do not have Boccaccio's mocking Renaissance charm or Lessing's moral sublimity, but their dry schematism has the advantage of suggesting, if only in parable form, the approaches *to* religion and *within* religion that bear on religious pluralism.

I intend to approach the discussion of religious pluralism indirectly. I will present an antipluralist **argument,** the argument of the one genuine ring. Possible rebuttals of the premises of this argument, if any, would then constitute a basis for the claim that religious pluralism is possible. Thus this possibility requires the rebuttal of at least one of the premises, and the stance of religious pluralism will be only as convincing as this rebuttal.

THE ONE-RING ARGUMENT

Premise 1: Revelation is propositional.

Premise 2: Revealed truths are constitutive of religion and of redemption through religion.

Premise 3: Religions acquire their intrinsic value by providing a framework for redemption (that is, for achieving religious perfection).

Premise 4: There are contradictions between the constitutive revealed truths of each pair of the three traditional religions.

Premise 5: The fact that the source of religious truths is revelation implies that false religious propositions are valueless (as opposed to scientific errors, for example, which could have value).

Premise 6: Premises 1–5 fit the historical reality of the three religions.

Conclusion: A religion based on constitutive, redemptive, revealed truths cannot ascribe value to a religion that contradicts these truths. Thus each religion sees itself as the only true religion and ascribes no value to the others. In other words, there is no room for religious pluralism.

I will now examine this argument.

PROPOSITIONAL REVELATION

. . . Premise (1) of the one-ring argument is that revelations are propositional. This contradicts a view that has become very widespread, especially in the twentieth century and particularly in Protestant thought. This view claims that revelation is not propositional but rather has to do with the divine presence in historical events. But even if one claims that revelations have an experiential nature, as encounters of divine significance, this does not necessarily, as I see it, prevent the revelation from having propositional content. Saying that Protestants oppose the idea that revelation is propositional does not necessarily mean claiming that they play their religion on the organ. Opposing the idea of propositional revelation is a way of expressing opposition to the notion of Church dogma rather than to the linguistic nature of revelation. According to the view of revelation as "non-propositional," it is a living dialogue rather than a list of commands and articles of faith. Revelation is meant to be an encounter with "the living God," not with an institution issuing **metaphysical** truths or authoritarian commands. Revelation for the believer is a "belief in," which cannot be reduced to a "belief that." It is in this sense that it is non-propositional, not in the sense that the revelatory encounter cannot be formulated in propositional language.

CONSTITUTIVE TRUTHS

The one-ring argument rests on the premise that the truths received in revelation are those that are constitutive of the religion, whether in the form of dogmas to be held or commands to be obeyed. . . .

. . . I distinguish between constitutive revelations, which reveal the religious path, and secondary (instructive) revelations, which bring strayers back to the known straight path. In Judaism the constitutive revelation is to Moses, whereas in Islam it is to Muhammad. The case of Jesus in Christianity is more complicated. In one sense Jesus *is* the revelation, but in another sense the revelation is to Jesus. In either sense, however, this revelation is constitutive of Christianity. In Judaism the distinction between constitutive and secondary revelations is a sharp one. "One must not obey a divine voice, because the Torah was already given at Mount Sinai." That is, any revelation that contradicts the constitutive one at Mount Sinai must be ignored. Moreover, anyone who claims to have received such a revelation is by definition a false prophet.

Premise (2) of the one-ring argument claims that there is a constitutive element in the religion that is given through revelation. . . .

One well-known argument against giving a constitutive status to the truths of revelation is the argument from God's benevolence: it is impossible that God should give revelatory truths to one person or group and keep these truths from other people. God's truths must be available to everyone. In a radical **(deistic)** formulation, this is an argument against revelation in general. In a more moderate formulation, it is an argument against truths that cannot be attained through reason and yet are constitutive of a religion. The idea is that constitutive truths should be subject to human understanding, whereas revelatory truths should serve only to delineate the conditions and the method of applying constitutive principles. Thus, for example, the necessity of giving thanks to God is a matter of reason and a basic principle. The particular way of giving thanks—that is, the method and timing of the prayers—is given by revelation.

In other words, what can be given through revelation is the religious lifestyle, not the principles. According to this view, the truths of revelation in the various religions do not stand in contradiction to one another.

INTRINSIC VALUE

. . . One place to examine the possibility of religious pluralism is in the willingness of each religion to grant members of the other religions citizenship in the world to come. It makes no difference for the present discussion whether "the world to come" is meant literally or metaphorically. Thus the test of whether a given religion allows for pluralism is whether that religion is willing to recognize the citizenship of members of other religions in the world to come. This test can be refined: is the ticket to the world to come offered *in spite* of, or *because* of, the candidate's being a member of another religion? This is obviously a distinction that makes a difference.

There is no salvation outside the Church, says an ancient Church doctrine. The Koran, for its part, says (sura 3, verse 18): "The only true faith in Allah is Islam." These statements seem to be judgments that other religions have no intrinsic value. But, as mentioned, the way to test the stringency of these pronouncements is to find out whether the members of other religions have a share in the world to come. Maimonides incorporated in his code the view that "the pious of the nations of the world have a share in the world-to-come" (*Mishneh Torah, Hilkhot Teshuvah* [Laws of Repentance] 3:5). This inclusion in the Heavenly Club is not enough to establish religious pluralism. The righteous among the gentiles can be included in spite of the fact that they belong to another religion, rather than because of it.

CONTRADICTORY TRUTHS

Premise (4) in the one-ring argument is that there are contradictions between the revealed truths of the different religions. This premise refers not to just any revealed truth but to important truths that are constitutive of the religion, especially those vital for redemption. If the Christian outlook is defined by the belief that Jesus is the Redeemer, and redemption requires this belief as a necessary component, then it is clear that Judaism denies it. Christianity, for its part, of course claims not only that there is nothing in the Jewish revelation that contradicts the belief in Jesus' redemptive role, but that the Bible as a source of revelation for the Jewish people attests to that very belief. This example demonstrates that the issue of contradiction here is not a matter for the logician but for the believer. Jewish believers might see a contradiction just where Christian believers see evidence supporting their belief. In order to say whether there is a contradiction between religions, it is necessary to specify for whom it is supposed to be a contradiction.

Another note might be in order here. It is not difficult to recognize the possibility of religious pluralism, even with respect to the religions based on historical revelation, if one believes that these revelations are addressed to different groups of people. The Jewish Midrash (*Exodus Rabbah 5*) says that the pronouncements made on Mount Sinai were conveyed to all the nations in seventy languages. If this is taken figuratively to mean that every nation received a different revelation, then there is no contradiction between them.

At any rate, the problem of religious pluralism arises when a contradiction is found between revelations, a contradiction in matters essential to the religion and particularly to the issue of redemption. If the area in which the contradiction is found is an issue that prevents redemption, then the competing religion must be considered lacking in intrinsic value. Not every element that is constitutive of a religion is necessarily vital for redemption. One might consider such a commandment as circumcision vital to Judaism without seeing it as a necessary condition for redemption. . . .

The issue of contradictions between the three revelatory religions is a complicated one. As mentioned, there is a lack of symmetry among the religions with respect to such contradictions. Christianity and Islam affirm the revelations of Judaism, but not vice versa. It sometimes seems as if the controversy between Judaism and Islam is not about the truths of revelation but about principles of the kind governing the firing of employees. Judaism holds the principle of "Last in, first out," Muhammad being the last one in this case. The Islamic principle, on the other hand, is "First in, first out," in this case, Moses. According to the latter principle, the revelation to Muhammad has priority because it came later than those to Moses and Jesus. Islam recognizes that the Torah and the New Testament were taken from the same heavenly tablets as the Koran, but because the Koran came last, it has the power to cancel what was said before.

What does it means to abrogate what was given in previous revelations? In Islam it is common to use a path metaphor: Islam is seen as the guide to the straight path. Thus we can present our question in terms of this metaphor. There is a difference between two of its usages. One is the idea that a short, straight path leading to the City of God was revealed to Muhammad, but the old paths, even though they are winding and full of pitfalls, still lead to the same place. The other idea is that the old paths were closed off after the new, straight one was revealed, and so they can no longer bring the traveler to the City of God. In the second case, unlike the first, using the old paths contradicts the only set of directions that can lead to redemption. The one-ring argument is based on the idea that all the other paths to redemption are closed off. In this sense, one can speak of a contradiction between the religions.

A move that is familiar to us from [Ludwig] Wittgenstein questions the whole idea that religious discourse can be presented in terms of contradictions. If I say the deposed interior minister will be put on trial during the coming year and you say he will not, then our assertions are contradictory. In contrast, if you claim that on the Day of Judgment I will be put on trial before the heavenly throne and I, as a nonbeliever, deny this, our disagreement cannot be described in terms of contradictions. A sentence about the Day of Judgment is a framework sentence, and framework sentences cannot be contradicted, because it is only within a framework that the idea of contradiction makes any sense. A person who rejects such a proposition is living within a different framework but does not hold a contradictory proposition.

As I see it, however, it is precisely between the religions of historical revelation that there is sufficient agreement, including agreement about many framework sentences, that sentences affirmed by one religion and negated by another can be seen as disagreements rather than misunderstandings. The idea is that in general not everything that seems formally to be a contradiction (one sentence negating another) actually is one. In most cases, it is a manifestation of misunderstanding rather than disagreement. In order for the disagreement between two views to be focused enough to constitute a contradiction, there must be a broad basis of agreement in their judgments. The broader and more varied the basis of agreement between two views, the more focused are the contradictions generated by the disagreements between them. Because this is indeed the situation with the religions of historical revelation, it is appropriate to speak of contradictions between them. . . .

REVELATION AND ERROR

Pluralism has a far-reaching requirement: ascribing value to forms of life based on error, precisely what is denied in premise (5). One way of justifying this requirement is to say that the possibility of choosing a mistaken path is necessary for the individual's **autonomy** and the community's self-definition.

Respecting the autonomy of individuals means respecting their choices even if these are mistaken.

Must we accept this claim? It seems that the same argument about error could be raised with respect to evil in general. After all, a necessary component of free choice is the possibility of doing what is bad. Then must we respect evil just because we respect free choice? No. For one thing, what is predominantly bad about evil is that it harms others. One reason for not tolerating evil, even if it is an expression of free choice—which is a good thing in itself—is because of the harm to others.

One antipluralist stance in the religious realm is based on the idea that error and evil should not be distinguished. Religious error constitutes sin if the person committing the error ought to have known better. Toleration of error is like toleration of evil, it is a manifestation of sloth, the worst of the seven deadly sins. In Judaism, Islam, and Catholicism, there is a conception of a religious collective that does not permit them to adopt the distinction between harm to oneself and harm to others. . . .

The one-ring argument relies on the assumption that, because the revelatory religions claim the authority of revelation for their basic truths, this renders whatever is done on the basis of error devoid of intrinsic value, whether it is the error of people whose revelation was false to begin with (i.e., not really a revelation) or of people whose revelation has become outdated. There is a specific reason for not ascribing value to religions based on error: it is because the truths constitutive of religion—those concerning the worship of the right God in the right way—are given by revelation, not reason.

We might call the specific argument about the connection between revelation and the worthlessness of a life based on error the crystal-ball argument. Suppose we have a crystal ball that tells us medical truths and suggests treatment methods. If the goal is curing people, an error in treatment resulting from not relying on the crystal ball would be a foolish act that should not be respected from any point of view. If, on the other hand, it is scientific medicine that is in question, then errors in theory of treatment could still be considered rational. What gives the errors value is the fact that they are the result of the rational act of hypothesis testing. In other words, the possibility of error has a constitutive function in scientific activity, and a society that relies on scientific rationality must be an open society that encourages competition among hypotheses, including those that bear a high risk of being false. When truth is given by revelation, or when medicine is a crystal-ball practice, errors are not a constitutive element in attaining truth. Errors have no value, and when they occur in a way of life, or in medical treatment, they become sins.

HISTORICAL FAITHFULNESS

Premise (6) of the one-ring argument is that the previous antipluralistic premises are faithful to the historical reality of the relations among the three religions. . . . The history of these religions is half as old as time. It may be presumed that in such a long history it will always be possible to find some quotation to support any position we want to ascribe to any of the three religions. It is therefore important to ascertain whether the quotation is an authentic one, and thus indicates a serious possibility, or whether it is merely an eccentric curiosity. In the realm of historical possibilities, it would seem that the **modal** rule, "what exists must be possible," does not always hold. If we ask, for example, whether there can be three popes at the same time, we will obviously get a negative answer. Even if there once were three popes, this is irrelevant to the present judgment. This is the sense of possibility that is not **empirical** but **normative.** A church headed by three popes is liable to be considered by believers to be so corrupt that the three popes will not be recognized as legitimate, even if there was nominally a time when three persons were called "pope." In order to ascertain what is possible in a long cultural tradition, judgment is sometimes more important than logic. For acquiring discerning judgment, the protagonist's point of view has an advantage over the spectator's.

As a spectator, I accept that there is a great deal of descriptive truth in the premises of the one-ring argument. I am therefore convinced that the burden of proof is on those who believe in the possibility of religious pluralism. Be that as it may, one thing is clear: the pagan Ovid got it right when he said, "A ring is worn thin by use."

STUDY QUESTIONS

1. Margalit describes various interpretations of the ring parable. Explain the interpretations and what each implies about whether religious pluralism is possible.
2. Outline the six premises and conclusions of the one-ring argument, explaining each premise.
3. As mentioned in the introduction to the selection, a valuable feature of Margalit's article is that it suggests how each premise of his argument can be denied. For each premise, explain on what basis it can be rejected. Which of these pluralist rejoinders do you find most compelling?
4. How is religious tolerance different from religious pluralism?
5. Margalit states that, "if a religion can adopt a pluralistic stance with respect to other religions, this does not necessarily imply that it can also adopt such a stance toward heterodox streams within itself." Why is this so, in his opinion?* Do you agree? Why or why not?
6. List the differences among all the religions you know about. Do these differences seem important to you? Why or why not?

READING 8.2

Towards a Philosophy of Religious Pluralism

John Hick

Through many books and articles, John Hick (Claremont Graduate School and University of Birmingham, England) has placed the topic of religious diversity high on the agenda of contemporary philosophers of religion and has become the chief exponent of **religious pluralism.** *Hick observes that many religions distinguish between God as God is in Himself, which eludes the grasp of the human mind, and God as God is experienced by humanity—as, for example, creator or redeemer. Hick suggests that, in like fashion, we must distinguish the ultimate reality as it is in itself (*an sich*) from the way this reality, this "God above the gods," is perceived and experienced in the context of human culture. Various religious traditions are responses to the same infinite divine reality, but they use different images to describe their experience.*

*Hick develops this idea by means of analogies. One is an analogy to sense perception as understood by Immanuel Kant. Images of God in religious awareness play the role that, according to Kant, is played in sense perception by our concepts and recognitional capacities. These concepts and capacities enable us to interpret input from things as they are in themselves (***noumena***). Hick puts forward the following structural analogy: God exists independently of our sense experience, but we experience the divine only under particular images. (Kant, to be sure, does not think that God is experienced; he denies that. Hick's point is just that there is an analogy between his view of religious experience and Kant's view of ordinary perception.) Hick maintains that this analysis holds even for nontheistic religions. At the end of the article, he suggests that, although all religions are experiencing the same reality, a particular religion may use images that are better, more adequate, than those in other religions.*

[THE PROBLEM OF RELIGIOUS PLURALISM]

From the point of view of **phenomenology,** or description, the fact of **religious pluralism** presents no philosophical problem. It just is the case that there are many different traditions of religious life and thought. Their histories, and their interactions with one another and with other aspects of the human story, have been traced in increasing detail during the last hundred and fifty years or so; and indeed knowledge of the religious life of mankind has now multiplied to the point at which it far exceeds the receptivity of any one mind. There is available to us a fascinating plethora of information concerning religious practices and beliefs, worship and ethics, creeds and theologies, myths, poetry, music and architecture, reported religious and mystical experiences, and the interactions of all these with one another. But simply as historical fact none of this raises a *problem* of religious pluralism. It is only when we add what can be called the basic religious conviction that a problem is generated.

By the basic religious conviction I mean the conviction that the realm of religious experience and belief is our human response to a transcendent divine reality or realities. It is the conviction, in other words, that religion is not, as a totality, illusion and self-deception. Whether this conviction is justified, and if so how that justification is to be spelled out, is the central issue in the philosophy of religion. . . . [O]n this occasion I propose to consider a further problem which arises if one adopts that basic religious conviction. One may actually share that conviction (as I do), or one may simply be interested to see what the implications of religious pluralism are for religious belief. But on whichever basis let us, for the purposes of the present discussion, assume hypothetically the truth of the basic religious conviction and ask ourselves how the facts of religious pluralism may then be understood.

The basic religious conviction normally takes the form of the claim that some one particular religion is a valid response to the divine, a response embodying true beliefs concerning the nature of reality. And the problem of religious pluralism arises from the fact that there are many such claims. In view of this variety of gospels it would seem on the face of it that they cannot all be true; and in that case may they not very well all be false? This is the problem that is generated by the fact of religious pluralism in conjunction with the basic religious conviction.

However in adopting the basic religious conviction we are not obliged to assume that all religious experience is straightforwardly **veridical** or all religious belief straightforwardly true. On the contrary our human nature and circumstances may well make their own contribution to our religious awareness, a contribution in which the range of individual and social mentalities and of cultural forms produces a corresponding variety of perceptions, or it may be of partial distortions, in our human consciousness of the divine. But we are nevertheless assuming that, basically, religion is a range of responses to reality—even if variously inadequate responses—rather than being pure projection or illusion.

Clearly this assumption must, unless good reasons to the contrary are produced, be applied to the entire realm of religions and not only to one favoured religion. I cannot then, as a Christian, solve the problem of religious pluralism by holding that my own religion is a response to the divine reality but that the others are merely human projections. . . . For it is evident, when one witnesses worship within the great world faiths, including Christianity, that the same sort of thing is going on in each, namely the directing of the worshippers' attention upon a (putative) higher and transcendent reality, in relation to which lies the human being's ultimate good. There may be clear and convincing criteria by which some forms of religion can be seen to be 'better' or 'higher' than others. But if we restrict our attention to the great world traditions the only criterion by which any of these could be judged to be the one and only true religion, with all the others dismissed as false, would be its own dogmatic assertion, in its more chauvinistic moments, to this effect.

Let us then look at the religious scene and consider how its pluralism is to be understood.

[GOD VS. HUMAN IMAGES OF GOD]

At the outset we encounter a terminological problem to which there seems to be no satisfactory solution. How are we to name the postulated transcendent reality to which we are assuming that religion is man's response? One is initially inclined to reject the word 'God' as too theistic—for the religious spectrum includes major non-theistic as well as theistic traditions—and to consider such alternatives as 'the Transcendent,' 'the Divine,' 'the Dharma,' the Absolute,' 'the Tao,' 'Being itself,' 'Brahman,' 'the ultimate divine Reality.' The fact is however that we have no fully tradition-neutral or tradition-transcending term. One is therefore obliged to use a term provided by a particular tradition, but to use it (or consciously to misuse it) in a way which moves beyond the bounds of that tradition. As a Christian I shall accordingly use the word 'God', but shall not use it in a straightforwardly theistic sense. There is of course a danger that either the writer or the reader may slip back without noticing it into the standard use of the term; and both must try to be vigilant against this. I shall then, in what follows, speak of God, but with the important proviso that it is an open question at this stage whether, and if so in what sense, God is personal. We shall in fact, I believe, be led to distinguish between God, and God as conceived and experienced by human beings. God is neither a person nor a thing, but is the transcendent reality which is conceived and experienced by different human mentalities in both personal and non-personal ways.

The general conception of a distinction between, on the one hand, the Godhead in its own infinite depths beyond human experience and comprehension and, on the other hand, the Godhead as finitely experienced by humanity, is both ancient and widespread. Perhaps its most explicit form is the Hindu distinction between *nirguna* Brahman, Brahman without attributes, beyond the scope of human language, and *saguna* Brahman, Brahman with attributes, known within human religious experience as Ishvara, the personal creator and governor of the universe. In the West the Christian mystic Meister Eckhart distinguished between the Godhead *(Deitas)* and God *(Deus);* and Rudolf Otto in his comparative study of Eckhart and Shankara says, "Herein lies the most extraordinary analogy between Eckhart and Sankara: high above God and the personal Lord abides the 'Godhead', having an almost identical relationship to God as that of Brahman to Isvara" (*Mysticism East and West,* New York: Meridian Books, p. 14). The Taoist scripture, the *Tao Te Ching,* begins by affirming that "The Tao that can be expressed is not the eternal Tao." The Jewish Kabbalist mystics distinguished between En Soph, the absolute divine reality beyond human description, and the God of the Bible; and among the Sufis, Al Haqq, the Real, seems to be a similar concept, as the abyss of Godhead underlying the personal Allah. More recently Paul Tillich has spoken of "the God above the God of theism" (*The Courage to Be,* p. 190) and has said that "God is the symbol of God" (*Dynamics of Faith,* p. 46). Whitehead, and the **process theologians** who have followed him, distinguish between the primordial and consequent natures of God, the former being his nature in himself, and the latter being constituted by his inclusion of and response to the world. And Gordon Kaufman has recently distinguished between the "real God" and the "available God," the former being an "utterly unknowable X" and the latter "essentially a mental or imaginative construction" (*God the Problem,* p. 86). A traditional Christian form of the distinction is that between God in himself, in his infinite self-existent being, beyond the grasp of the human mind, and God in relation to mankind, revealed as creator and redeemer. In one form or another such a distinction seems unavoidable for any view which is not willing to reduce God to a finite being, wholly knowable by the human mind and definable in human concepts. The infinite God must pass out into sheer mystery beyond the reach of our knowledge and comprehension, and is in this limitless transcendence *nirguna,* the ultimate Godhead, the God above the God of theism.

There are in fact, I would suggest, three main types of religious experience. The most common is the experience of God as a personal presence and will, known in I-Thou encounter. This experience is the heart of theistic religion, in the Eastern as well as in the Western traditions. The second type is the nature—or cosmic—mysticism in which the whole world or the whole universe is experienced as the manifestation or vehicle of divine reality—as in Wordsworth's famous lines:

> And I have felt
> A presence that disturbs me with the joy
> Of something far more deeply interfused
> Whose dwelling is the light of setting suns,
> And the round ocean and the living air,
> And the blue sky, and in the mind of man:
> A motion and a spirit, that impels
> All thinking things, all objects of all thought,
> And rolls through all things.

In such experiences God is not known as personal, nor yet as impersonal, but rather as more than personal—as living, as the ultimate source of value, and yet as altogether transcending the notion of an encountered person, on however tremendous a scale. And the third type is that in which the experiencing self is temporarily absorbed into the divine reality, becoming one with the One. Since personality is essentially interpersonal, so that one is a person only in relationship with other persons, there is no personal existence or encounter within this unitive moment. This is perhaps the mystical state *par excellence,* apparently experienced by some, but described by none; for it is beyond the scope of human language.

Now these are all finite experiences of finite creatures. (This is true even of the unitive experience; for the experiencer returns from it, still a finite individual, to try to speak of what has happened to him.) If we assume, with the major religious traditions, that God is infinite, then we have to say that these forms of religious experience are not experiences of the infinitude of God—which no finite experience could ever encompass—but of God as finitely experienced by particular human consciousnesses. And in understanding such a plurality of experiences we have to take account of the contribution of the human mind itself to all our awareness of our environment, divine as well as natural. I shall be arguing that these different forms of religious awareness are not necessarily competitive, in the sense that the validity of one entails the spuriousness of the others, but are better understood as different phenomenal experiences of the one divine **noumenon;** or in another language, different experiential transformations of the same transcendent informational input.

I shall return in due course to the non-personal forms of religious awareness; but let us first approach the idea of a divine phenomenon through the theistic type of religious experience.

If one were to list all the many gods whose names we know from the literature and traditions of India (such as Rudra, Agni, Mitra, Indra, Varuna . . .) and of the Near East (such as Osiris, Isis, Horus, Ra, Jahweh . . .) and of southern Europe (such as Jupiter, Apollo, Dionysus, Poseidon . . .) and of northern Europe (such as Odin, Thor, Balder, Vali, Woden . . .) and of Africa (such as Nabongo, Luhanga, Nyame, Lesa, Ruhanga . . .) and also of the Americas, Australasia, Northern Asia and the rest of the world, they would probably form a list as long as the telephone directory of a large city. What are we to say about all these gods? Do we say that they all exist? And what would it be for a named god, say Balder, with his distinctive characteristics, to exist? In any straightforward sense it would, I suggest, at least involve there being a consciousness, answering to this name, in addition to all the millions of human consciousnesses. Are we then to say that for each name in our directory of gods there is an additional consciousness enjoying the further set of attributes specified by the concept of that particular god? In most cases this would be theoretically possible since in most cases the gods are explicitly or implicitly finite beings whose powers and spheres of operation are at least approximately known; and many of them could co-exist without contradiction. On the other hand, the gods of the monotheistic faiths are thought of in each case as the one and only God, so that it is impossible for more than one of them to instantiate this concept. It does not seem, then, that we can possibly say that all the named gods, and particularly not all the most important ones, exist, at any rate not in any simple and straightforward sense. Nor, having assumed the basic religious conviction of the reality of the divine, can we say in any straightforward sense that they are all non-existent and man's whole supposed awareness of divine beings and powers illusory. Nor, again, as I have already indicated, can we take refuge in the claim that the God of one's own religion is real and all the others either illusory or, perhaps, non-divine demonic beings. Instead let us explore the possibility that the immediate object of theistic religious awareness is what I shall call an 'image' of God; and that the plurality of such images arises from the various ways in which the divine reality has impinged upon the human consciousness in its different circumstances.

But first we must establish the distinction between God and our human images of God. Within the Judaic-Christian tradition we see the need for such a distinction when we ask ourselves whether God is really male, as distinguished from female, or whether on the contrary God transcends the distinction between men and women but has commonly been thought of as male within patriarchal societies. I believe that most of us today will give the latter answer. Although in the Bible God is consistently referred to as 'He' and is described, metaphorically, as king, father, warrior, shepherd, etc., yet surely God is not in fact a larger or even an infinite man as distinguished from woman, but can be thought of equally appropriately in male and female terms. In this respect much Indian devotional language, in which God is addressed as mother as well as father, is to be preferred to the exclusively masculine language of the semitic faiths. But the point at the moment is that if God is not in reality male as distinguished from female, but is nevertheless imaged as such in many religious traditions, then we are obliged to draw a distinction between God and our human images of God—in this case between God and our distinctively masculine images of God.

But what, more precisely, do we mean by an 'image' of God? We can I think find partial analogies in the varied impressions of the same individual in the minds of different historians. Consider a personage, X, who lived in the past and who is therefore not directly accessible to us, about whom certain salient facts are known but such that any concrete impression of X's character leaves a good deal to the constructive imagination of the historian. Any such impression or, as I shall call it, image, represents an interpretation of the available data. Varying images of X may form in the minds of writers in different subsequent periods, with their different cultural backgrounds; and there may be both popular, often oversimplified, images and caricatures as well as more academic images. There are a number of famous historical figures to whom all this applies—for example, Mary Queen of Scots, King Charles I, Napoleon, Abraham Lincoln, Mahatma Gandhi, Stalin, Chairman Mao . . . In such cases the distinction seems inevitable between the historical individual *an sich* [in itself] and the images in terms of which he or she has become known to later consciousness. This is of course only a partial analogy; I am not suggesting that God existed in the past but does not exist today. The analogy is rather with the varying images in terms of which we may be aware of an historical figure. An image of this kind represents data moulded into concrete forms by the imagination in accordance with the selective attention of the historian. And the more a figure engages our interest by touching our own vital concerns—a concern, for example, for justice or freedom—the greater tends to be the subjective contribution to our image of him or her. And when we turn to those who are religiously significant to us, and who accordingly help to form the basic orientation of our lives, the subjective contribution generally increases yet further in importance. Because a saint, or messiah, or avatar, or bodhissatva, or arahant, or spiritual master or guru meets some spiritual need in us, and so has salvific power in our lives, our image of such a person naturally emphasises holiness, goodness, wisdom and remarkable powers; and further the image tends to expand as the tradition in which it is embedded develops. These images of saints—and I am referring to personality-impressions of them rather than to physical representations—extend the analogy in the direction of our images of God. Within Christianity, Catholic spirituality is particularly rich in examples. The faithful often address an individual saint, or Mary, Mother of Jesus, asking him or her to perform some miracle or to intercede for them with God the Father. In the case of Mary distinctive local versions are cherished within particular communities. Thus there is Our Lady of Lourdes, who appeared as a young girl eighteen times to Bernadette Soubirous in 1858, speaking to her on several occasions, thereby founding a place of pilgrimage and healing to which many thousands go each year. Or Our Lady of Fatima, in Portugal, who made prophecies about when the first world war was to end, about developments in Russia, and about another war in the future. And there is our Lady of Walsingham, and other local miraculous versions of Mary in many countries. Thus if we assume that the Virgin Mary is an existing personal being, now exalted into heaven but still actively concerned with the affairs of living men and women, we are led to distinguish between Mary herself and a variety of partially different human images of her. It does not however necessarily follow from the fact of their plurality that these images are false. The alternative possibility is that they arise from genuine encounters with Mary in which, as she has met the varying needs of different individuals and communities, different images of her have legitimately been formed. . . .

A further analogy, which may be illuminating to some even though possibly not to others, comes from **parapsychology.** One of the types of phenomena studied is that in which a medium goes into a trance and it seems that the still living consciousness of someone who has physically died—let us call him John Smith—communicates through the medium's vocal machinery. Sometimes the 'spirit' speaks in a way which is recognisably that of the John Smith whom he claims to be, and sometimes also his conversation includes items of information which could hardly have been known to the medium. To account for all this the theory has been advanced that the conscious, speaking, responding personality who is controlling the medium's vocal apparatus is a secondary personality, a fragment of the medium's mind which takes over in the trance state. This secondary personality plays roles suggested to it and indeed often puts considerable intelligence and skill into its productions—somewhat as in the case of hypnotised persons who may play on command the role of, say, guests at a banquet or of visitors from outer space. In the spiritualist seance it may be that the informational input which informs the performance is derived telepathically from the sitters. But the further possibility has been suggested that some of the input may come from the deceased individual John Smith, who is being impersonated by the medium's secondary personality. In that case John Smith is, in this doubtless frustratingly indirect and unreliable way, communicating with his friends on earth. If this is so, the sitters are in contact with a dramatic personation of John Smith, produced by a secondary personality of the medium, but based at least partly on information deriving from John Smith himself. Thus it is possible that he communicates at different times to different groups of sitters through varying dramatic images of himself formed in the minds of different mediums. Here again we are led to a distinction between John Smith *an sich* and a plurality of, in this case, speaking and responding images of him which are partly similar and partly different.

[INFORMATION AND THE INTERPRETATION OF EXPERIENCE]

I do not want to pursue here the possible functional analogy between spiritualist mediums and the prophets, avatars, gurus, etc., through whom God is believed to speak to mankind. I want instead to develop a different aspect of the theory of mediumship to which I have referred. In doing so it will be helpful to use the notion of information, not in the familiar propositional sense of 'items of information' but in the modern cybernetic sense of **cognitive** input which can be expressed in different modes and which can be transformed from one mode to another. The value of this concept lies precisely in its generality. Whatever influences or impacts from our surrounding world affect one's state as a self-directing part of that world constitute information: in the definition of Norbert Wiener, the father of **Cybernetics,** "Information is a name for the content of what is exchanged with the outer world as we adjust to it, and make our adjustment felt upon it" (*The Human Use of Human Beings,* London: Sphere Books, 1968, p. 19). Thus information passes in the form of light waves from a lighted object to the retina of the eye, is there transformed into chemical changes in the rods and cones, and then into electrical impulses passing up the strands of the optic nerve into the brain, and finally into the conscious experience of seeing the object which had been reflecting light into our eye. Or again, information flows along the wire from the aerial into the television set and is there transformed into a picture on the screen; or along the telephone wire to be transformed into the sound of a voice. In such cases the same information is being expressed in a variety of ways. And whenever there is transformation from one coding to another there is the possibility of distortion of the information. Indeed there is a general tendency for information to deteriorate as it functions. The picture on the TV screen may be distorted or blurred; and the machinery of the brain can likewise be damaged and produce a distorted version of the environment in consciousness. There are mechanical failures, comparable with the errors to which an electronic calculator is liable when its battery is insufficiently charged. But in addition to the mechanical transformation of information studied by cybernetics there is also, and more importantly, its interpretation by the mind into units or moments of meaning. For at the distinctively human level of consciousness we inhabit a more or less familiar and ordered world with recognisable characteristics to which we know how to respond. (There is of course also novelty and surprise, but always within the context of a familiar basic framework.) All our consciousness of objects and of situations is an experience of them as having a certain character such that it is appropriate to behave in relation to them, or within them, in this rather than in that way. Such awareness represents a fusion between, on the one hand, the information reaching us from our environment and, on the other hand, the system of concepts in terms of which that information comes to consciousness as organised and meaningful experience. In this procedure—which constitutes normal perception—the function of our system of concepts, or recognitional capacities, is to guide the pre-conscious interpretive process whereby sensory information is transformed into our actual consciousness of the world. The word 'meaning' is appropriate as pointing to the way in which our awareness of our environment, as having the character that we experience it to have, is related to our own practical responses to it. To say that the perceived world has meaning to us is to say that it is a world which we can inhabit by acting and reacting in accordance with its perceived character. . . .

This general account of cognition also applies to our awareness (whether veridical or illusory) of the religious meaning, of character, of situations. For our human commerce with God does not consist only or even mainly in our holding certain beliefs, but above all in experiencing the reality of God as the lord in whose presence one is, and in experiencing the power of God in the events of one's own life and of the wider history with which this is continuous. When for example Jeremiah perceived the Babylonian army, marching on Jerusalem, as God's agent to punish his unfaithful people, he was interpreting the events of his time in terms of his image of God. . . . Or when today a theistic believer has some degree of awareness of existing in the unseen presence of God, he is interpreting his total situation in religious terms. This interpretation comes to consciousness as the experience that in and through all his dealings with the world and with other people he is also having to do with the transcendent God; and this awareness is embodied in his . . . tendencies to engage in acts of worship, to think and feel in certain ways and to behave in accordance with associated ethical norms.

What part, then, is played in this religious awareness by images of God? Essentially the part, I suggest, that is played in sense perception by the concepts or recognitional capacities in terms of which we are conscious of the objects and situations constituting our physical environment.

It was above all Immanuel Kant, with his doctrine that we are necessarily aware of the world in terms of certain forms and categories inherent in the structure of a unitary finite consciousness, who has enabled the modern world to recognise the mind's own positive contribution to the meaningful character of its perceived environment. The view that I am proposing is in some respects Kantian and in other respects un-Kantian, and it may perhaps be useful at this point to bring out the analogies and disanalogies with the Kantian model. Kant is himself notoriously difficult to interpret, largely because the *Critique of Pure Reason* contains several different strands of argument whose mutual consistency can be questioned and whose relative importance can be variously estimated. The strand that I shall be using is the distinction between **phenomenon** and **noumenon,** but transposed from the problem of sense perception to that of the awareness of God. In using something analogous to Kant's phenomenon/noumenon distinction I am not opting for any view of the place of this distinction in the *Critique.* I am in fact not concerned at all with questions of Kantian interpretation or of the general assessment of Kant's critical philosophy. I am, rather, taking a structural model from his system and using it in a sphere—the **epistemology** of religion—which Kant treated in a very different way, and in relation to a problem within that sphere which had hardly begun to be recognised in his time. It should also be stressed that Kant himself would not have sanctioned the idea that we in any way *experience* God, even as divine phenomenon in distinction from divine noumenon. God was not for him a reality encountered in religious experience, but an object postulated by reason on the basis of its own practical functioning as moral agent. . . . However I am exploring here the different and very non-Kantian hypothesis that God *is* experienced by human beings, but experienced in a manner analogous to that in which, according to Kant, we experience the world—namely by informational input from external reality being interpreted by the mind in terms of its own categorial system and thus coming to consciousness as meaningful phenomenal experience. For Kant distinguished—in one strand of his thought—between the noumenal world, which exists independently of and outside man's perception of it, and the phenomenal world, which is that world as it appears to our human consciousness. All that we are entitled to say about the noumenal world is that it is the unknown reality whose informational input produces, in collaboration with the human mind, the phenomenal world of our experience. This happens through the medium of certain concepts which Kant calls the categories of the understanding. . . . Something analogous to this, I am suggesting, takes place in our awareness of God. For the religious person experiences the divine, not as a general idea, but under some specific and relatively concrete divine image. . . . It is the variations of the human cultural situation that concretise the notion of deity as specific images of God. And it is these images that inform man's actual religious experience, so that it is an experience specifically of the God of Israel, or of Allah, or of the Father of our Lord Jesus Christ, or of Vishnu or Shiva . . . .

It is desirable to avoid a possible misunderstanding which offers itself at this point. If the worshipper's thought of God only describes an image of God, and the worshipper's experience of God is only the experience of God as thus imaged, does it not follow that worship is directed to an illusion, a mere phenomenal appearance? The answer must echo Kant's statement that his distinction between phenomenon, or appearance, and noumenon, or reality, results in a 'transcendental idealism' which is at the same time an 'empirical realism' (*Critique of Pure Reason,* p. A 370–2). That is to say, the world as we perceive it is real, not illusory; but it is the appearance to us of that which exists in itself outside our experience of it. The perceptually organized world of colours, sounds and scents, of heat and cold, of solid tables and chairs and trees and animals is entirely real. And yet as humanly perceived it exists only for human perceivers. Animals with different sensory equipment and different forms of consciousness must perceive the world very differently. We are real beings in a real environment; but we experience that environment selectively, in terms of our special cognitive equipment. Something essentially similar has to be said about the human awareness of God. God as experienced by this or that individual or group is real, not illusory; and yet the experience of God is partial and is adapted to our human spiritual capacities. God as humanly known is not God *an sich* but God in relation to mankind, thought and experienced in terms of some particular limited tradition of religious awareness and response.

Thus in expounding this situation we have to try to keep two themes in balance: the **agnostic** theme that we only know God partially and imperfectly, and the positive theme that we really do know God as practically and savingly related to ourselves.

[GOD AS PERSONAL AND AS IMPERSONAL]

Let us now apply this thesis to what is perhaps the largest and most obvious contrast between different human awarenesses of the divine, namely as personal and as non-personal. . . .

We cannot . . . meaningfully attribute personality to the infinite and eternal existence of God *a se* [in Himself]. But on the other hand God is the ground, or creator, or source of personal life, and is in that sense 'more' rather than 'less' than a person. Further God is experienced by finite persons as (though not only as) the divine Thou existing over against them in I-Thou relationship. God is personal, then, in the sense that man's awareness of God as Person is a genuine encounter with the transcendent ground of all existence, including personal existence. Using another language, God experienced as personal is a valid transformation in human consciousness of informational input from the transcendent divine source. But we have to add the significant fact that God has been and is experienced by human beings not only as a person but as a number of different persons, each constituted by God's impingement upon a different human community with its own divine image formed through a particular strand of history. Thus the God of Israel is a specific personal deity with his own historical biography. His personal life—that is, his interactions with a group of finite persons—began with his self-revelation to Abraham and has continued in Jewish religious experience down to the present day. As such he has a distinctive personality, developed in interaction with his chosen people; he is a part of their history and they are part of his. And he is a recognisably different personality from, say, the Lord Krishna, because Krishna exists in relation to a different community, forming and formed by a different culture, and creating and created by a different history. Again, the God who speaks to mankind in the Qur'an is part of yet another history of divine-human relationship . . . I suggest that this pluralistic situation is rendered intelligible by the hypothesis of one infinite divine noumenon experienced in varying ways within different strands of human history, thereby giving rise to different divine personalities who are each formed in their interactions with a particular community or tradition.

But God is also non-personal. We have to affirm this both in the negative sense that personality is a function of personal interaction and therefore cannot be attributed to the eternal divine nature *a se;* and in the positive sense that God is validly experienced in non-personal as well as in personal ways. The varying divine personalities worshipped in their respective religious traditions, and likewise the varying non-personal forms in which God is known in yet other religious traditions, are all alike divine phenomena formed by the impact of God upon the plurality of human consciousnesses. I have concentrated here upon the awareness of God as personal; but the other aspect . . . is equally important.

It will be evident that the above is a significantly different hypothesis from one with which it nevertheless has a partial resemblance, namely the Hindu *advaitist* view that God, or Brahman, is non-personal, being known as such in the state of full enlightenment, and that the worship of personal Gods belongs to a lower and preliminary stage of the religious life which is eventually to be left behind. In distinction from this I am suggesting that God is to be thought of as the divine noumenon, experienced by mankind as a range of divine phenomena which take both theistic and non-theistic forms.

At first sight the distinction between divine noumenon and divine phenomena might seem to preclude any 'doctrine of God,' or account of the divine nature. For if we only know God as experienced by mankind, and if God is so experienced in a number of different ways, does not the noumenal or real God remain impenetrably hidden from us? Thus [Ludwig]

Feuerbach attacked the distinction between "God as he is in himself and God as he is for me" as a **sceptical** distinction (*The Essence of Christianity,* New York: Harper Torchbook edition, p. 17). And it is true that, on this view, we have to accept that the infinite divine reality is only knowable by man in so far as it impinges upon finite human consciousnesses, with their variously limited and conditioned capacities for awareness and response. But once we accept this, then the very plurality and variety of the human experiences of God provide a wider basis for **theology** than can the experience of any one religious tradition taken by itself. For whereas we can learn from one tradition that God is personal, as the noumenal ground of theistic experience, and from another tradition that God is the non-personal Void, as the noumenal ground of its form of mystical experience, we learn from the two together that God is the ground and source of both types of experience and is in that sense both personal and non-personal. . . .

[THE HISTORY OF RELIGIONS]

Let us now look, in the briefest possible way, at the application of this broad interpretive conception to the religious history of mankind. Man is a thoroughly historical creature, living through a changing continuum of **contingent** circumstances into which he has emerged from a primitive prehistoric condition which itself evolved out of lower forms of life. Thus the human awareness of God must be expected to have undergone development though changing historical circumstances, the cumulative growth of traditions, and the influence of those outstanding individuals, prophets and saints, who have in their own individual freedom been more open to God than the societies of which they were members. The influence of such spiritual and moral leaders is crucial; for we are not looking at a natural process of evolution but at a *history* with all the complex and sometimes conflicting contingencies generated by human freedom. In the earliest stages of this history God was reduced in human awareness to the dimensions of man's own image, so that the gods were, like human kings, often cruel and bloodthirsty; or to the dimensions of the tribe or nation, as the symbol of its unity and power; or again to the more ample dimensions of the forces of nature, such as the life-giving and yet burning radiance of the sun, or the destructive power of storm and earthquake, or the mysterious pervasive force of fertility, and the response that was required, the way of life which such awareness rendered appropriate, was a communal response. The anthropologists have taught us how closely knit primitive societies have been, and how little scope they offered for individual thought, whether in religion or in other aspects of life. It was only with the gradual emergence of individuality, in what [Karl] Jaspers has called the axial period, particularly from about 800 B.C., that higher conceptions of God developed, in correlation with a deeper sense of a moral claim upon human life. For it was the emergence of the individual, and in particular of the religious individual, that made possible the outstanding spiritual leaders on whose consciousness God impinged in new ways or with new intensity and power. The greatest of these became the founders of continuing religious traditions—Moses, Zoroaster, Confucius, Gautama, Jesus and later Mohammad. Others effected important developments within existing traditions—the Hebrew prophets; the writers of the Upanishads, of the Tao Te Ching, and of the Gita; Pythagoras, Socrates, Plato, Guru Nanak. These great traditions have continued to develop in larger and smaller ways through the centuries, ramifying out into the vast and complex ideological organisms which we know as the world religions. These religions are thus based upon different human perceptions of, and embody different human responses to, the infinite reality of God.

Let me now end by pointing forward to the next major question that arises if one opts for some such hypothesis as this. I have just referred to the different world religions, with their different images of God. Our question concerns the relative adequacy or value of these different images, both theistic and non-theistic. For it is clearly possible that they are not all equally adequate, but that some mediate God to mankind better than others. . . . How are we to evaluate these images? This is the large and difficult question that next arises.

STUDY QUESTIONS

1. Hick speaks of *the problem* of religious pluralism. What is the problem, and how does it arise? Explain in terms of what he calls the *fact* of religious pluralism and what he calls *the basic religious conviction.*
2. Explain Hick's response to the problem of religious pluralism.
3. What analogies does Hick use to develop his response? (Include the analogy to Kant and those he uses when developing the idea of having an image of *X*.)
4. Hick tells us that "it is evident, when one witnesses worship within the great world faiths, that the same sort of thing is going on." Do you agree? Why or why not?
5. Ludwig Feuerbach, as quoted by Hick, says that the distinction between "God as He is in Himself and God as He is for me" is a skeptical distinction. Why does he think this? How does Hick respond? Is the response satisfactory?
6. *Hick's critics have charged that someone who believes that the diverse world religions are different manifestations of a single reality can too easily abandon his or her own particular religion and switch to another. What do you think is meant by this charge? Is the charge persuasive, in your opinion?
7. *Hick seeks to rebut the objection that, according to his theory, no religion is superior to any other. Explain the reasoning behind this objection. How does Hick handle the objection? Develop his idea further. Do you think the objection stands?
8. *Do you think the world's religions are likely to eventually converge? Why or why not?

READING 8.3

A Defense of Religious Exclusivism

Alvin Plantinga

Alvin Plantinga (Notre Dame) defines religious **exclusivism** *as the view that the tenets of one particular religion are true and that any propositions incompatible with those tenets (such as propositions advanced by other religions) are false. In the essay from which this selection is excerpted, Plantinga replies to two kinds of objections to exclusivism: moral and* **epistemic.** *The moral objections are that contradicting others is either oppressive, imperialistic, arrogant, or egotistical. Plantinga responds that, if these charges were valid, they would preclude our believing, dissenting from, and even withholding assent from any proposition whatsoever. How, in particular, can the* **pluralist** *hold that it is wrong not to abstain from holding a particular belief, without being charged with the same moral fault (oppressiveness, imperialism, arrogance, or egotism) with which he or she charges others?*

In the second part of the paper, Plantinga turns to epistemic objections to exclusivism. The essay as abridged here includes just one of those epistemic objections: that, if a believer had been born somewhere else, his or her beliefs would be different from what they actually are, so the believer must not reject the beliefs of others. Plantinga argues that pluralists once again defeat themselves; had they been born elsewhere, they would not have been pluralists. Thus, by their own argument, they should not endorse pluralism. Although Plantinga thinks the arguments for pluralism are self-defeating, he concedes that the knowledge of views different from one's own can serve as an occasion for a renewed and more powerful working of the processes by which one forms belief.

When I was a graduate student at Yale, the philosophy department prided itself on diversity: and it was indeed diverse. There were **idealists, pragmatists, phenomenologists, existentialists, Whiteheadians,** historians of philosophy, a token **positivist,** and what could only be described as observers of the passing intellectual scene. In some ways, this was indeed something to take pride in; a student could behold and encounter real live representatives of many of the main traditions in philosophy. It also had an unintended and unhappy side effect, however. If anyone raised a philosophical question inside, but particularly outside, class, the typical response would be a catalog of some of the various different answers the world has seen: there is the Aristotelian answer, the existentialist answer, the **Cartesian** answer, [Martin] Heidegger's answer, perhaps the Buddhist answer, and so on. But the question 'what is the truth about this matter?' was often greeted with disdain as unduly naive. There are all these different answers, all endorsed by people of great intellectual power and great dedication to philosophy; for every argument *for* one of these positions, there is another *against* it; would it not be excessively naive, or perhaps arbitrary, to suppose that one of these is in fact *true,* the others being false? Or, if there really is a truth of the matter, so that one of them is true and conflicting ones false, wouldn't it be merely arbitrary, in the face of this embarrassment of riches, to *endorse* one of them as the truth, consigning the others to falsehood? How could you possibly know which was true?

Some urge a similar attitude with respect to the impressive variety of religions the world displays. There are theistic religions but also at least some nontheistic religions (or perhaps nontheistic strands of religion) among the enormous variety of religions going under the names 'Hinduism' and 'Buddhism'; among the theistic religions, there are strands of Hinduism and Buddhism and American Indian religion as well as Islam, Judaism, and Christianity; and all these differ significantly from one another. Isn't it somehow arbitrary, or irrational, or unjustified, or unwarranted, or even oppressive and imperialistic to endorse one of these as opposed to all the others? According to Jean Bodin, "each is refuted by all";[1] must we not agree? It is in this neighborhood that the so-called problem of **pluralism** arises. Of course, many concerns and problems can come under this rubric; the specific problem I mean to discuss can be thought of as follows. To put it in an internal and personal way, I find myself with religious beliefs, and religious beliefs that I realize aren't shared by nearly everyone else. For example, I believe both

> (1) The world was created by God, an almighty, all-knowing, and perfectly good personal being (one that holds beliefs; has aims, plans, and intentions; and can act to accomplish these aims)

and

> (2) Human beings require salvation, and God has provided a unique way of salvation through the **incarnation,** life, sacrificial death, and resurrection of his divine son.

Now there are many who do not believe these things. First, there are those who agree with me on (1) but not (2): there are non-Christian theistic religions. Second, there are those who don't accept either (1) or (2) but nonetheless do believe that there is something beyond the natural world, a something such that human well-being and salvation depend upon standing in a right relation to it. And third, in the West and since the Enlightenment, anyway, there are people—***naturalists,*** we may call them—who don't believe any of these three things. And my problem is this: when I become really aware of these other ways of looking at the world, these other ways of responding religiously to the world, what must or should I do? What is the right sort of attitude to take? What sort of impact should this awareness have on the beliefs I hold and the strength with which I hold them? My question is this: how should I think about the great religious diversity the world in fact displays? Can I sensibly remain an adherent of just one

[1] *Colloquium Heptaplomeres de rerum subimium arcanis abditis,* written by 1593 but first published in 1857. English translation by Marion Kuntz [*Colloquium of the Seven About Secrets of the Sublime*] (Princeton: Princeton University Press, 1975). The quotation is from the Kuntz translation, p. 256.

of these religions, rejecting the others? And here I am thinking specifically of *beliefs*. Of course, there is a great deal more to any religion or religious practice than just belief, and I don't for a moment mean to deny it. But belief is a crucially important part of most religions; it is a crucially important part of *my* religion; and the question I mean to ask here is what the awareness of religious diversity means or should mean for my religious beliefs.

Some speak here of a *new* awareness of religious diversity, and speak of this new awareness as constituting (for us in the West) a crisis, a revolution, an intellectual development of the same magnitude as the Copernican revolution of the sixteenth century and the alleged discovery of evolution and our animal origins in the nineteenth.[2] No doubt there is at least some truth to this. Of course, the fact is all along many Western Christians and Jews have known that there are other religions and that not nearly everyone shares *their* religion.[3] The ancient Israelites—some of the prophets, say—were clearly aware of Canaanitish religion; and the apostle Paul said that he preached "Christ crucified, a stumbling block to Jews and folly to the Greeks" (I Cor. 1:23). Other early Christians, the Christian martyrs, say, must have suspected that not everyone believed as they did. The church fathers, in offering defenses of Christianity, were certainly apprised of this fact; Origen, indeed, wrote an eight-volume reply to Celsus, who urged an argument similar to those put forward by contemporary pluralists. Aquinas, again, was clearly aware of those to whom he addressed the *Summa contra gentiles,* and the fact that there are non-Christian religions would have come as no surprise to the Jesuit missionaries of the sixteenth and seventeenth centuries or to the Methodist missionaries of the nineteenth. In more recent times, when I was a child, *The Banner,* the official publication of the Christian Reformed Church, contained a small column for children; it was written by 'Uncle Dick,' who exhorted us to save our nickels and send them to our Indian cousins at the Navaho mission in New Mexico. Both we and our elders knew that the Navahos had or had had a religion different from Christianity, and part of the point of sending the nickels was to try to rectify that situation.

Still, in recent years probably more of us Western Christians have become aware of the world's religious diversity; we have probably learned more about people of other religious persuasions, and we have come to see more clearly that they display what looks like real piety, devoutness, and spirituality. What is new, perhaps, is a more widespread sympathy for other religions, a tendency to see them as more valuable, as containing more by way of truth, and a new feeling of solidarity with their practitioners.

There are several possible reactions to awareness of religious diversity. One is to continue to believe what you have all along believed; you learn about this diversity but continue to believe, that is, take to be true, such propositions as (1) and (2) above, consequently taking to be false any beliefs, religious or otherwise, that are incompatible with (1) and (2). Following current practice, I call this **exclusivism;** the exclusivist holds that the tenets or some of the tenets of *one* religion—Christianity, let's say—are in fact true; he adds, naturally enough, that any propositions, including other religious beliefs, that are incompatible with those tenets are false. Now there is a fairly widespread belief that there is something seriously wrong with exclusivism. It is irrational, or egotistical and unjustified,[4] or intellectually

[2]Thus Joseph Runzo: "Today, the impressive piety and evident rationality of the belief systems of other religious traditions inescapably confronts Christians with a crisis—and a potential revolution." [Reading 8.4]

[3]As explained in detail in Robert Wilken, "Religious Pluralism and Early Christian Thought". . . . Wilken focuses on the third century; he explores Origen's response to Celsus and concludes that there are striking parallels between Origen's historical situation and ours. What is different today, I suspect, is not that Christianity has to confront other religions but that we now call this situation 'religious pluralism.'

[4]Thus Gary Gutting: "Applying these considerations to religious belief, we seem led to the conclusion that, because believers have many epistemic peers who do not share their belief in God . . . , they have no right to maintain their belief without a justification. If they do so, they are guilty of **epistemological** egoism." *Religious Belief and Religious Skepticism* (Notre Dame: University of Notre Dame Press, 1982), p. 90 (but see the following pages for an important qualification).

arrogant,[5] or elitist,[6] or a manifestation of harmful pride,[7] or even oppressive and imperialistic.[8] The claim is that exclusivism as such is or involves a vice of some sort: it is wrong or deplorable; and it is this claim I want to examine. I propose to argue that exclusivism need not involve either **epistemic** or moral failure and that furthermore something like it is wholly unavoidable, given our human condition.

These objections are not to the *truth* of (1) or (2) or any other proposition someone might accept in this exclusivist way (although, of course, objections of that sort are also put forward); they are instead directed to the *propriety* or *rightness* of exclusivism. And there are initially two different kinds of indictments of exclusivism: broadly moral or ethical indictments and broadly intellectual or epistemic indictments. These overlap in interesting ways, as we shall see below. But initially, anyway, we can take some of the complaints about exclusivism as *intellectual* criticisms: it is *irrational* or *unjustified* to think in an exclusivistic way. And the other large body of complaint is moral: there is something *morally* suspect about exclusivism: it is arbitrary, or intellectually arrogant, or imperialistic. As Joseph Runzo suggests, exclusivism is "neither tolerable nor any longer intellectually honest in the context of our contemporary knowledge of other faiths."[9] I want to consider both kinds of claims or criticisms; I propose to argue that the exclusivist is not as such necessarily guilty of any of these charges.

MORAL OBJECTIONS TO EXCLUSIVISM

I first turn to the moral complaints: that the exclusivist is intellectually arrogant, or egotistical, or self-servingly arbitrary, or dishonest, or imperialistic, or oppressive. But first three qualifications. An exclusivist, like anyone else, will probably be guilty of some or all of these things to at least some degree, perhaps particularly the first two; the question is, however, whether she is guilty of these things just by virtue of being an exclusivist. Second, I shall use the term 'exclusivism' in such a way that you don't count as an exclusivist unless you are rather fully aware of other faiths, have had their existence and their claims called to your attention with some force and perhaps fairly frequently, and have to some degree reflected on the problem of pluralism, asking yourself such questions as whether it is or could be really true that the Lord has revealed himself and his programs to us Christians, say, in a way in which he hasn't revealed himself to those of other faiths. Thus my grandmother, for example, would not have counted as an exclusivist. She had, of course, *heard* of the heathen, as she called them, but the idea that perhaps Christians could learn from them, and learn from them with respect to religious matters, had not so much as entered her head; and the fact that it *hadn't* entered her head, I take it, was not a matter of moral dereliction on her part. The same would go

[5]"Here my submission is that on this front the traditional doctrinal position of the Church has in fact militated against its traditional moral position, and has in fact encouraged Christians to approach other men immorally. Christ has taught us humility, but we have approached them with arrogance. . . . This charge of arrogance is a serious one." Wilfred Cantwell Smith, *Religious Diversity* (New York: Harper and Row, 1976), p. 13.

[6]Runzo, "Ethically, Religious Exclusivism has the morally repugnant result of making those who have privileged knowledge, or who are intellectually astute, a religious elite, while penalizing those who happen to have no access to the putatively correct religious view, or who are incapable of advanced understanding." . . . [Reading 8.4]

[7]"But natural pride, despite its positive contribution to human life, becomes harmful when it is elevated to the level of dogma and is built into the belief system of a religious community. This happens when its sense of its own validity and worth is expressed in doctrines implying an exclusive or a decisively superior access to the truth or the power to save." John Hick, "Religious Pluralism and Absolute Claims," in Leroy Rouner, ed. *Religious Pluralism* (Notre Dame: University of Notre Dame Press, 1984), p. 197.

[8]Thus John Cobb: "I agree with the liberal theists that even in Pannenberg's case, the quest for an absolute as a basis for understanding reflects the long tradition of Christian imperialism and triumphalism rather than the pluralistic spirit." "The Meaning of Pluralism for Christian Self-Understanding," in Rouner, *Religious Pluralism,* p. 171.

[9][See Reading 7.4—ed.]

for a Buddhist or Hindu peasant. These people are not, I think, plausibly charged with arrogance or other moral flaws in believing as they do.

Third, suppose I am an exclusivist with respect to (1), for example, but nonculpably believe, like Thomas Aquinas, say, that I have a knockdown, drag-out argument, a **demonstration** or conclusive proof of the proposition that there is such a person as God; and suppose I think further (and nonculpably) that if those who don't believe (1) were to be apprised of this argument (and had the ability and training necessary to grasp it, and were to think about the argument fairly and reflectively), they too would come to believe (1). Then I could hardly be charged with these moral faults. My condition would be like that of [Kurt] Gödel, let's say, upon having recognized that he had a proof for the incompleteness of arithmetic. True, many of his colleagues and peers didn't believe that arithmetic was incomplete, and some believed that it *was* complete; but presumably Gödel wasn't arbitrary or egotistical in believing that arithmetic is in fact incomplete. Furthermore, he would not have been at fault had he nonculpably but *mistakenly* believed that he had found such a proof. Accordingly, I shall use the term 'exclusivist' in such a way that you don't count as an exclusivist if you nonculpably think you know of a demonstration or conclusive **argument** for the beliefs with respect to which you are an exclusivist, or even if you nonculpably think you know of an argument that would convince all or most intelligent and honest people of the truth of that proposition. So an exclusivist, as I use the term, not only believes something like (1) or (2) and thinks false any proposition incompatible with it; she also meets a further condition C that is hard to state precisely and in detail (and in fact any attempt to do so would involve a long and at present irrelevant discussion of **ceteris paribus clauses**). Suffice it to say that C includes (1) being rather fully aware of other religions, (2) knowing that there is much that at the least looks like genuine piety and devoutness in them, and (3) believing that you know of no arguments that would necessarily convince all or most honest and intelligent dissenters of your own religious allegiances.

Given these qualifications, then, why should we think that an exclusivist is properly charged with these moral faults? I shall deal first and most briefly with charges of oppression and imperialism: I think we must say that they are on the face of it wholly implausible. I daresay there are some among you who reject some of the things I believe; I do not believe that you are thereby oppressing me, even if you do not believe you have an argument that would convince me. It is conceivable that exclusivism might in some way *contribute* to oppression, but it isn't in itself oppressive.

The important moral charge is that there is a sort of self-serving arbitrariness, an arrogance or egotism, in accepting such propositions as (1) or (2) under condition C; exclusivism is guilty of some serious moral fault or flaw. According to Wilfred Cantwell Smith, "except at the cost of insensitivity or delinquency, it is morally not possible actually to go out into the world and say to devout, intelligent, fellow human beings: '. . . we believe that we know God and we are right; you believe that you know God, and you are totally wrong.'"[10]

So what can the exclusivist have to say for herself? Well, it must be conceded immediately that if she believes (1) or (2), then she must also believe that those who believe something incompatible with them are mistaken and believe what is false. That's no more than simple logic. Furthermore, she must

[10]Smith, *Religious Diversity,* p. 14. A similar statement: "Nor can we reasonably claim that our own form of religious experience together with that of the tradition of which we are part, is **veridical** whilst others are not. We can of course claim this; and indeed virtually every religious tradition has done so, regarding alternative forms of religion either as false or as confused and inferior versions of itself. . . . Persons living within other traditions, then, are equally justified in trusting their own distinctive religious experience and in forming their beliefs on the basis of it. . . . let us avoid the implausibly arbitrary dogma that religious experience is all delusory with the single exception of the particular form enjoyed by the one who is speaking." John Hick, *An Interpretation of Religion* (New Haven, Yale University Press, 1989), p. 235.

also believe that those who do not believe as she does—those who believe neither (1) nor (2), whether or not they believe their negations—*fail* to believe something that is true, deep, and important, and that she *does* believe. She must therefore see herself as *privileged* with respect to those others—those others of both kinds. There is something of great value, she must think, that *she* has and *they* lack. They are ignorant of something—something of great importance—of which she has knowledge. But does this make her properly subject to the above censure?

I think the answer must be no. Or if the answer is yes, then I think we have here a genuine moral dilemma; for in our earthly life here below, as my Sunday School teacher used to say, there is no real alternative; there is no reflective attitude that is not open to the same strictures. These charges of arrogance are a philosophical tar baby: get close enough to them to use them against the exclusivist, and you are likely to find them stuck fast to yourself. How so? Well, as an exclusivist, I realize I can't convince others that they should believe as I do, but I nonetheless continue to believe as I do: and the charge is that I am as a result arrogant or egotistical, arbitrarily preferring my way of doing things to other ways.[11] But what are my alternatives with respect to a proposition like (1)? There seem to be three choices.[12] I can continue to hold it; I can withhold it, in Roderick Chisholm's sense, believing neither it nor its denial; and I can accept its denial. Consider the third way, a way taken by those pluralists who, like John Hick, hold that such propositions as (1) and (2) and their colleagues from other faiths are literally false although in some way still valid responses to the Real. This seems to me to be no advance at all with respect to the arrogance or egotism problem; this is not a way out. For if I do this, I will then be in the very same condition as I am now: I will believe many propositions others don't believe and will be in condition C with respect to those propositions. For I will then believe the denials of (1) and (2) (as well as the denials of many other propositions explicitly accepted by those of other faiths). Many others, of course, do not believe the denials of (1) and (2), and in fact believe (1) and (2). Further, I will not know of any arguments that can be counted on to persuade those who do believe (1) or (2) (or propositions accepted by the adherents of other religions). I am therefore in the condition of believing propositions that many others do not believe and furthermore am in condition C. If, in the case of those who believe (1) and (2), that is sufficient for intellectual arrogance or egotism, the same goes for those who believe their denials.

So consider the second option: *I* can instead *withhold* the proposition in question. I can say to myself; "the right course here, given that I can't or couldn't convince these others of what *I* believe, is to believe neither these propositions nor their denials." The pluralist objector to exclusivism can say that the right course under condition C, is to *abstain* from believing the offending proposition and also abstain from believing its denial; call him, therefore, 'the abstemious pluralist.' But does he thus really avoid the condition that, on the part of the exclusivist, leads to the charges of egotism and arrogance? Think, for a moment, about disagreement. Disagreement, fundamentally, is a matter of adopting conflicting propositional attitudes with respect to a given proposition. In the simplest and most familiar case, I disagree with you if there is some proposition p such that I believe p and you believe $-p$ [not $-p$]. But that's just the simplest case: there are also others. The one that is at present of interest is this: I believe p and you withhold it, fail to believe it. Call the first kind of disagreement 'contradicting'; call the second 'dissenting.'

[11]"The only reason for treating one's tradition differently from others is the very human but not very cogent reason that it is one's own!" Hick, *Interpretation of Religion,* p. 235.

[12]To speak of choice here suggests that I can simply choose which of these three attitudes to adopt; but is that at all realistic? Are my beliefs to that degree within my control? Here I shall set aside the question whether and to what degree my beliefs are subject to my control and within my power. Perhaps we have very little control over them: then the moral critic of exclusivism can't properly accuse the exclusivist of dereliction of moral duty, but he could still argue that the exclusivist's stance is unhappy, bad, a miserable state of affairs. Even if I can't help it that I am overbearing and conceited, my being that way is a bad state of affairs.

My claim is that if contradicting others (under the condition C spelled out above) is arrogant and egotistical, so is dissenting (under that same condition). For suppose you believe some proposition p but I don't: perhaps you believe it is wrong to discriminate against people simply on the grounds of race, but I, recognizing that there are many people who disagree with you, do not believe this proposition. I don't disbelieve it either, of course, but in the circumstances I think the right thing to do is to abstain from belief. Then am I not implicitly condemning your attitude, your *believing* the proposition, as somehow improper—native, perhaps, or unjustified, or in some other way less than optimal? I am implicitly saying that my attitude is the superior one; I think my course of action here is the right one and yours somehow wrong, inadequate, improper, in the circumstances at best second-rate. Also, I realize that there is no question, here, of *showing* you that your attitude is wrong or improper or naive; so am I not guilty of intellectual arrogance? Of a sort of egotism, thinking I know better than you, arrogating to myself a privileged status with respect to you? The problem for the exclusivist was that she was obliged to think she possessed a truth missed by many others; the problem for the abstemious pluralist is that he is obliged to think he possesses a virtue others don't, or acts rightly where others don't. If, in conditions C, one is arrogant by way of believing a proposition others don't, isn't one equally, under those reflective conditions, arrogant by way of withholding a proposition others don't?

Perhaps you will respond by saying that the abstemious pluralist gets into trouble, falls into arrogance, by way of implicitly saying or believing that his way of proceeding is *better* or *wiser* than other ways pursued by other people, and perhaps he can escape by abstaining from *that* view as well. Can't he escape the problem by refraining from believing that racial bigotry is wrong, and also refraining from holding the view that it is *better*, under the conditions that obtain, to withhold that proposition than to assert and believe it? Well, yes, he can; then he has no *reason* for his abstention; he doesn't believe that abstention is better or more appropriate; he simply does abstain. Does this get him off the egotistical hook? Perhaps. But then, of course, he can't, in consistency, also hold that there is something wrong with *not* abstaining, with coming right out and *believing* that bigotry is wrong; he loses his objection to the exclusivist. Accordingly, this way out is not available for the abstemious pluralist who accuses the exclusivist of arrogance and egotism.

Indeed, I think we can show that the abstemious pluralist who brings charges of intellectual arrogance against exclusivism is hoist with his own petard, holds a position that in a certain way is self-referentially inconsistent in the circumstances. For he believes

(3) If S knows that others don't believe p and that he is in condition C with respect to p, then S should not believe p;

this or something like it is the ground of the charges he brings against the exclusivist. But, the abstemious pluralist realizes that many do not accept (3); and I suppose he also realizes that it is unlikely that he can find arguments for (3) that will convince them; hence he knows that he is in condition C. Given his acceptance of (3), therefore, the right course for him is to abstain from believing (3). Under the conditions that do in fact obtain—namely, his knowledge that others don't accept it and that condition C obtains—he can't properly accept it.

I am therefore inclined to think that one can't, in the circumstances, properly hold (3) or any other proposition that will do the job. One can't find here some principle on the basis of which to hold that the exclusivist is doing the wrong thing, suffers from some moral fault—that is, one can't find such a principle that doesn't, as we might put it, fall victim to itself.

So the abstemious pluralist is hoist with his own petard; but even apart from this **dialectical** argument (which in any event some will think unduly cute), aren't the charges unconvincing and implausible? I must concede that there are a variety of ways in which I can be and have been intellectually arrogant and egotistic; I have certainly fallen into this vice in the past and no doubt am not free of it now. But am I really arrogant and egotistic just by virtue of believing what I know others don't believe, where I can't show them that I am right? Suppose I think the matter over, consider the objections as carefully as I can, realize that I am finite and furthermore a sinner, certainly no better than those with whom I disagree, and indeed inferior both morally and intellectually to many who do not believe what I do; but suppose it *still* seems clear to me that the proposition in question is true: can I really be behaving immorally in continuing to believe it? I am dead sure that it is wrong to try to advance my career by telling lies about my colleagues; I realize there are those who disagree; I also realize that in all likelihood there is no way I can find to show them that they are wrong; nonetheless, I think they *are* wrong. If I think this after careful reflection—if I consider the claims of those who disagree as sympathetically as I can, if I try level best to ascertain the truth here—and it *still* seems to me sleazy, wrong, and despicable to lie about my colleagues to advance my career, could I really be doing something immoral in continuing to believe as before? I can't see how. If, after careful reflection and thought, you find yourself convinced that the right propositional attitude to take to (1) and (2) in the face of the facts of religious pluralism is abstention from belief, how could you properly be taxed with egotism, either for so believing or for so abstaining? Even if you knew others did not agree with you? So I can't see how the moral charge against exclusivism can be sustained.

EPISTEMIC OBJECTIONS TO EXCLUSIVISM[13]

. . . [T]here is an oft-repeated pluralistic argument (an argument that goes back at least to John Stuart Mill's *On Liberty* and possibly all the way back to the third century) that seems to be designed to appeal to **reliabilist** intuitions. The conclusion of this argument is not always clear, but here is its premise, in John Hick's words:

> For it is evident that in some ninety-nine percent of cases the religion which an individual professes and to which he or she adheres depends upon the accidents of birth. Someone born to Buddhist parents in Thailand is very likely to be a Buddhist, someone born to Muslim parents in Saudi Arabia to be a Muslim, someone born to Christian parents in Mexico to be a Christian, and so on.[14]

As a matter of sociological fact, this may be right. Furthermore, it can certainly produce a sense of intellectual vertigo. But what is one to do with this fact, if fact it is, and what follows from it? Does it follow, for example, that I ought not to accept the religious views that I have been brought up to accept, or the ones that I find myself inclined to accept, or the ones that seem to me to be true? Or that the belief-producing processes that have produced those beliefs in me are unreliable? Surely not. Furthermore, self-referential problems once more loom; this argument is another philosophical tar baby.

For suppose we concede that if I had been born in Madagascar rather than Michigan, my beliefs would have been quite different.[15] (For one thing, I probably wouldn't believe that I was born in Michigan.) But, of course, the same goes for the pluralist. Pluralism isn't and hasn't been widely popular in the world at large; if the pluralist had been born in Madagascar, or medieval France, he probably wouldn't have been a pluralist. Does it follow that he shouldn't be a pluralist or that his pluralistic beliefs are produced in him by an unreliable belief-producing process? I doubt it. Suppose I hold

(4) If S's religious or philosophical beliefs are such that if S had been born elsewhere and elsewhen, she wouldn't have held them, then those beliefs are produced by unreliable belief-producing mechanisms and hence have no warrant;

or something similar: then once more I will be hoist with my own petard. For in all probability, someone

[13][Most of the original section has been omitted from this selection. Plantinga discusses various notions of justification, rationality, and warrant and argues that exclusivists are not irrational or unjustified in their beliefs, according to these definitions.—Ed.]

[14]*Interpretation of Religion,* p. 2.

[15]Actually, this conditional as it stands is probably not true; the point must be stated with more care. Given my parents and their proclivities, if I had been born in Madagascar, it would probably have been because my parents were (Christian) missionaries there.

born in Mexico to Christian parents wouldn't believe (4) itself. No matter what philosophical and religious beliefs we hold and withhold (so it seems), there are places and times such that if we had been born there and then, then we would not have displayed the pattern of holding and withholding of religious and philosophical beliefs we *do* display. As I said, this can indeed be vertiginous; but what can we make of it? What can we infer from it about what has warrant and how we should conduct our intellectual lives? That's not easy to say. Can we infer *anything at all* about what has warrant or how we should conduct our intellectual lives? Not obviously. . . .

. . . But don't the realities of religious pluralism count for anything at all? Is there nothing at all to the claims of the pluralists? Could that really be right? Of course not. For many or most exclusivists, I think, an awareness of the enormous variety of human religious response serves as a ***defeater*** for such beliefs as (1) and (2)—an *undercutting* defeater, as opposed to a *rebutting* defeater. It calls into question, to some degree or other, the sources of one's belief in (1) or (2). It doesn't or needn't do so by way of an *argument;* and indeed, there isn't a very powerful argument from the proposition that many apparently devout people around the world dissent from (1) and (2) to the conclusion that (1) and (2) are false. Instead, it works more directly; it directly reduces the level of confidence or degree of belief in the proposition in question. From a Christian perspective, this situation of religious pluralism and our awareness of it is itself a manifestation of our miserable human condition; and it may deprive us of some of the comfort and peace the Lord has promised his followers. It can also deprive the exclusivist of the *knowledge* that (1) and (2) are true, even if they are true and he *believes* that they are. Since degree of warrant depends in part on degree of belief, it is possible, though not necessary, that knowledge of the facts of religious pluralism should reduce an exclusivist's degree of belief and hence of warrant for (1) and (2) in such a way as to deprive him of knowledge of (1) and (2). He might be such that if he *hadn't* known the facts of pluralism, then he would have known (1) and (2), but now that he *does* know those facts, he doesn't know (1) and (2). In this way he may come to know less by knowing more.

Things *could* go this way with the exclusivist. On the other hand, they *needn't* go this way. Consider once more the moral parallel. Perhaps you have always believed it deeply wrong for a counselor to use his position of trust to seduce a client. Perhaps you discover that others disagree; they think it more like a minor peccadillo, like running a red light when there's no traffic; and you realize that possibly these people have the same internal markers for their beliefs that you have for yours. You think the matter over more fully, imaginatively recreate and rehearse such situations, become more aware of just what is involved in such a situation (the breach of trust, the breaking of implied promises, the injustice and unfairness, the nasty irony of a situation in which someone comes to a counselor seeking help but receives only hurt) and come to believe even more firmly the belief that such an action is wrong—which belief, indeed, can in this way acquire more warrant for you. But something similar can happen in the case of religious beliefs. A fresh or heightened awareness of the facts of religious pluralism could bring about a reappraisal of one's religious life, a reawakening, a new or renewed and deepened grasp and apprehension of (1) and (2). From Calvin's perspective, it could serve as an occasion for a renewed and more powerful working of the belief-producing processes by which we come to apprehend (1) and (2). In that way knowledge of the facts of pluralism could initially serve as a defeater, but in the long run have precisely the opposite effect.

STUDY QUESTIONS

1. What are the moral objections to pluralism? Why does Plantinga regard them as unconvincing?
2. What epistemic objection to pluralism does Plantinga consider in this selection? How does he reply?
3. Consider the following objection to Plantinga:

> Plantinga's replies to both the moral and epistemic objections in the excerpt are *tu quoque* (you, too) arguments. In a *tu quoque* reply, the person responding to the objection only tries to show that

the critic is guilty of the same charge that the critic is leveling, so that to be consistent the critic must not put the charge forward. Thus, with regard to the moral objection, that the exclusivist is being arrogant or imperialistic, Plantinga replies, in effect: so is the critic. Likewise, in responding to the epistemic objection, Plantinga says that the pluralist's objection to the exclusivist can be turned against the pluralist. But Plantinga does not explain why an exclusivist is not being arrogant or imperialistic, or why an exclusivist can be confident in his or her beliefs despite the fact that he or she holds those beliefs only because of an accident of birth.

Why should we not say that *both* the exclusivist and the pluralist are arrogant and imperialistic? And why should we not say that *both* the exclusivist and the pluralist should give up their beliefs because, had they been born in a different time and place, they would hold different beliefs? Discuss this objection—how would Plantinga reply? (Questions 4 and 5 are related to this question.)

4. *Suppose we grant Plantinga that believing one is right is not arrogant or imperialistic. Are there *any* circumstances in which a person *is* arrogant and imperialistic, as well as morally culpable, in holding a belief? If so, what are they? Give examples.
5. *Under what circumstances should a person abandon a belief because, had he or she been born in a different time and place, he or she would not hold the belief? Give examples.
6. *Contrast Plantinga with Hick. Are they addressing the same questions?
7. *What connections are there between Plantinga's view in this selection and his view in Reading 7.3?

READING 8.4

God, Commitment, and Other Faiths: Pluralism vs. Relativism

Joseph Runzo

Joseph Runzo (Chapman University) identifies six possible responses to the diversity of world religions and champions a position he calls religious relativism. The correctness of a religion, he asserts, is relative to the world view of its community of adherents. Runzo explains how relativism differs from John Hick's **religious pluralism.** *The latter is deficient because, by saying that all world religions are manifestations of a single divine reality, pluralism does not account for the importance of belief and the specific* **cognitive** *content of one's faith. It also lessens the dignity of each faith community by treating differences among religions as inconsequential. Furthermore, pluralism threatens to undermine the reality of God, particularly the God of history. Religious relativism has none of these objectionable features, yet it accepts the possibility that more than one religion is correct and leads to salvation. It recognizes that one's perspective is subject to sociohistorical conditioning and thus "recognizes that judgments about other faiths will necessarily be made within the perspective of one's own faith." Humility and a sense of fallibility result from this stance.*

. . . Religious beliefs, like many philosophical orientations, seem largely an accident of birth. If you are born in India, you are likely to be a Hindu; if born in France, you are likely to be a Christian. Moreover, on their own grounds, Buddhists and Muslims and adherents of other great religious faiths, seem rationally justified in their beliefs. This raises the *problem of* ***religious pluralism:*** the mutually conflicting systems of truth-claims of the world's religions, if taken separately, appear rationally justified—but are they *correct?* Is only one system of religious truth-claims correct, is more than one system correct, or are all religious systems mistaken?

. . . [A]n uncritical pluralism undermines the strength of commitment of faith. How then can we both remain fully committed to our most basic truth-claims about God, and at the same time take full account of religious pluralism? Christians today must be responsive to other faiths, but responsive *within* the Christian vision expressed in the Vatican II Declaration *Nostra Aetate:* ". . . all peoples comprise a single community, and have a single origin . . . God . . . One also is their final goal: God."

After explaining why the problem of religious pluralism is a problem of conflicting *truth*-claims, I will set out six possible responses, religious and non-religious, to the conflicting truth-claims of the world's religions. Then I will assess each response in turn from an external, religious (but not necessarily Christian) point of view, ultimately focusing on the Pluralist and Relativist responses. I will end by defending the Relativist response from an internal, Christian perspective, and explain how it incorporates strengths, without some of the salient weaknesses, of other possible responses to the conflicting truth-claims of the world religions.

I

In the *Dynamics of Faith,* [Paul] Tillich suggests that "The conflict between religions is not a conflict between forms of belief, but it is a conflict between expressions of our ultimate concern. . . . All decisions of faith are existential, not theoretical, decisions." It *would* be a gross distortion of faith to reduce it to merely theoretical concerns or to questions of belief. But in avoiding this intellectualist distortion of faith Tillich is mistaken to suggest that the conflict between religions is not a conflict between truth-claims. True, a religious way of life importantly involves such elements as ritual and symbols, and a moral ordering of one's life. But our beliefs, or more comprehensively, our world-views—i.e., the total **cognitive** web of our interrelated concepts, beliefs, and processes of rational thought—determine the very nature of our ultimate concern. For all experience, understanding, and praxis—whether it concerns the mundane or the *mysterium tremendum*—is structured by our world-views. Consequently, conflicts between religious traditions fundamentally stem from conflicts of belief, conflicts over specific claims about how meaning and value are to be achieved, and what is the desired **telos** for humankind.

In assessing the conflict of truth-claims among world religions it must be kept in mind that a religion is not itself true or false any more than any other human institution such as art, government, or law, is in and of itself true or false. A total institution—aesthetic, political, legal, or religious—is only more or less expedient, only more or less effective in meeting its intended goals. What is true or false, and what is most fundamentally in conflict between such systems, are the underlying, specific truth-claims within the systems. Now, in the conflict of religious truth-claims, all of the world's major religions agree that the divine, or the Absolute, or the Real, is One, transcends the natural order, and is ultimately inexpressible. As *Ecclesiastes* puts it, God "has put eternity into man's mind, yet so that he cannot find out what God has done from the beginning to the end." (Eccles. 3:11 . . .) But though they have this general point of agreement, and though each religious tradition includes truth-claims and even scriptural material which is expendable, there is a fundamental or "vital core" of beliefs in each religion which is definitive of that very tradition. And it is particular elements of this "vital core" of beliefs that are incompatible among world religions.

For instance, there is no intractable conflict between claims in the Muslim tradition that Mahdis will periodically appear to revive faith in God, and orthodox Christian claims that Jesus represents the final prophetic revelation of God. For Christians could come to accept, and Sunnis could come to reject, further prophetic revelations from God *via* Mahdis, without impugning the respective orthodox status of Jesus or Mohammed. But traditionally it *is* essential to monotheistic traditions, like Christianity, Islam, Judaism and Ramanujan Hinduism, that the correct human perception of the divine is the perception of a personal deity. In contrast, on a Hinayana (Theravada) Buddhist view, God does not exist, and in much of the Hindu tradition, the notion of a personal deity is talk about an illusory state of affairs bound to this life. Or, to take another trenchant conflict among religious truth-claims, consider some of the diverse notions of the relation of humanity to Ultimate Reality. In Hinayana Buddhism there is no real question of one's relation to ultimate reality, for the goal of liberation is the complete extinction of the ego; in Islām the basic human relation to God is one of slave to master; in orthodox Judaism the central relation is one of a servant to his or her God.

Thus, because they make essentially different truth-claims, different religious traditions are structured by *essentially* different world-views, offering *essentially* different paths to what is perceived as Ultimate Reality. Since a person's world-view, then, is inherently constitutive of their religious way of life, the question is whether the differences in *truth-claims* among the world religions, and the consequent differences in the (putative) paths to Ultimate Reality, are significant or ultimately irrelevant.

We can also see that the conflict among the world religions is fundamentally a conflict of *truth-claims* if we consider the meaning of "faith" and of "religion." Faith is the more encompassing notion. Faith can be either religious or non-religious: we speak of faith in the progress of science or in the inevitableness of **dialectical materialism,** as much as of Christian or Muslim faith. Therefore, I will use the term "faith" to refer to a person's fundamental commitment to any world-view, a commitment which is a total **dispositional state** of the person involving affective, conative, and cognitive elements.

Religion, on the other hand, involves a particular form of faith, focused within a specific religious tradition. To distinguish religious from non-religious faith, I will define a religion or religious tradition as a set of symbols and rituals, **myths** and stories, concepts and truth-claims, which a community believes gives ultimate meaning to life, *via* its connection to a transcendent God or Ultimate Reality *beyond* the natural order. Thus religion is a *human* construct (or institution) which fundamentally involves beliefs at two levels: (I) it involves the **meta-belief** that the religion in question does indeed refer to a transcendent reality which gives meaning to life, and (II) it involves specific beliefs—including vital core beliefs—about the nature of that ultimate reality and the way in which it gives meaning to life. The first sort of belief, (I), is shared by the world religions. The second sort of belief, (II), is the point of conflict among the world religions.

II

There are six possible responses, religious and non-religious, to the conflicting truth-claims of vital core beliefs among the world religions:

1. *Atheism:* all religions are mistaken.
2. *Religious Exclusivism:* only one world religion is correct, and all others are mistaken.
3. *Religious Inclusivism:* only one world religion is fully correct, but other world religions participate in or partially reveal some of the truth of the one correct religion.
4. *Religious Subjectivism:* each world religion is correct, and each is correct insofar as it is best for the individual who adheres to it.
5. *Religious Pluralism:* ultimately all world religions are correct, each offering a different, salvific path and partial perspective *vis-á-vis* the one Ultimate Reality.
6. *Religious Relativism:* at least one, and probably more than one, world religion is correct, and the correctness of a religion is relative to the world-view(s) of its community of adherents.

One obvious response to the conflicting truth-claims of the world's religions is the Atheist response, (1). Is it not most plausible, given the enormity of the conflict among truth-claims, that all religious traditions are simply false in different ways, rather than that one is correct, or that several are correct in different ways? . . .

At stake here is the basic religious presupposition that only reference to a transcendent divine or ultimate reality gives ultimate meaning to human life. This meta-belief (I) is supported in the various religious traditions by appeals to religious experience, purported transformations of people's lives, the claimed necessity of a "leap of faith," and so on. These are internal considerations which will not, of course, prove that the Atheist response (1) must be mistaken. But in this discussion we can set aside the Atheist response if we take the basic religious meta-belief (I) as a presupposition.

Turning to the second response, Exclusivism in its strongest form is exemplified by the traditional Roman Catholic dogma, *Extra ecclesiam nulla salus* [no salvation outside the Church]. Exclusivism is the view that salvation can only be found either (as in the dogma just cited) inside a particular *institutional* structure, or on the basis of a specified tradition of religious beliefs, symbols, and rituals. . . . But such unqualified Exclusivism seems untenable in the face of the problem of religious pluralism. In Ernst Troeltsch's words, regarding Christianity,

> a study of the non-Christian religions convinced me more and more that their naive claims to absolute validity are also genuinely such. I found Buddhism and Brahminism especially to be really humane and spiritual religions, capable of appealing in precisely the same way to the inner certitude and devotion of their followers as Christianity, . . .[1]

Principal considerations against Exclusivism within *any* religious tradition include the following: Historically, it is largely a matter of geographical accident whether one grows up as a Hindu or Buddhist, Christian or Muslim, etc. Theologically, a strict reading of Exclusivism condemns the vast majority of humanity to perdition, which certainly appears contrary to the notion of a loving God, as well as seeming to contradict the idea of an Absolute which is the telos of all humankind. Ethically, Religious Exclusivism has the morally repugnant result of making those who have privileged knowledge, or who are intellectually astute, a religious elite, while penalizing those who happen to have no access to the putatively correct religious views, or who are incapable of advanced understanding. Sociologically, Exclusivism is a concomitant of sectarianism, serving as a rationale for enforcing discipline and communal cohesion. **Epistemologically,** one could not *know* with certainty that there is only one correct set of religious truth-claims or only one institutional structure providing a path to salvation—a consideration exacerbated by the fact that all religions at some point make Exclusivist claims. And religiously, Exclusivism is highly presumptuous, ignoring the fact that religious truth-claims are human constructs, human attempts to know Ultimate Reality, subject to the limitations and fallibility of the human mind.

It is of course possible that the Exclusivism of some particular religious tradition is correct. But given these weighty considerations against Exclusivism, we must turn to responses (3)–(6), responses that hold that in some form each of the great world religions is at least in part correctly directed toward the divine or Absolute. The problem is how to avoid the serious moral, theological, **empirical,** and epistemological deficiencies of Exclusivism without dissipating the very cohesiveness and vitality of one's own religious tradition which Exclusivism properly seeks to protect.

III

A natural alternative to take to meet these concerns is Inclusivism. This has become an especially prominent view in Roman Catholic theology since Vatican II. Religious Inclusivists jointly hold two theses: That other religions convey part of the truth about Ultimate Reality and the relation of humanity to Ultimate Reality, but that only one's own tradition most fully provides an understanding of Ultimate Reality, and most adequately provides a path to salvation. Thus, *Nostra Aetate* states both that "The Catholic Church rejects nothing which is true and holy in [other] religions," and that the cross of Christ "is the sign of God's all-embracing love" and "the fountain from which every grace flows.". . .

Inclusivism is typically based on the notion that one's own religion most fully possesses a particular element which is most essential to religion. [R. C.] Zaehner looks to the integration of the personal and collective; [Immanuel] Kant holds that true

[1]Ernst Troeltsch, "The Place of Christianity Among the World Religions," in *Christian Thought: Its History and Applications,* ed. Baron R. Hugel (New York: Meridian Books, Living Age Books, 1957), p. 52.

religiosity is identical to the moral life; [Friedrich] Schleiermacher proposes that underlying genuine religion is "the feeling of absolute dependence"; Rudolph Otto emphasizes a **numinous** sense of the holy, a sense of the *mysterium tremendum; Nostra Aetate* declares that "from ancient times down to the present, there has existed among diverse peoples a certain perception of that hidden power which hovers over the course of things and over the events of human life"; and John Baillie suggests that all humans have a knowledge of God through a felt presence of the divine such that all people "already believe in him."

That other religious traditions, in accordance with the religious meta-belief (I), might provide some apprehension of Ultimate Reality, is not at issue here. Rather, Inclusivism supposes that a *particular* sort of apprehension and understanding of Ultimate Reality is elemental to all religion. However, in the first place we could not *know* that all humans have the same sort of elemental apprehension of Ultimate Reality. Second, the empirical evidence supports precisely the opposite supposition. Even in the broadest terms, the notion of an elemental apprehension of Ultimate Reality is understood in *personal* terms in the monotheistic traditions, while it is *non-personal* in Confucianism and in Hindu and Buddhist traditions. And third, each religion tends to see itself as the culmination of *the* elemental apprehension of Ultimate Reality: "other religions can have their own fulfillment theology. Sri Aurobindo sees the world religious process converging on Mother India rather than the Cosmic Christ, and Sir Muhammad Iqbal sees it converging upon a kind of ideal Islam."[2]

So when [Karl] Rahner, for example, says that the Christian has, "other things being equal, a still greater chance of salvation than someone who is merely an anonymous Christian,"[3] this can only be a statement of faith, not one of certain knowledge. Yet the strength of Inclusivism *is* this unequivocal faith—*within* an acceptance of other traditions—that one's own religion is **salvific.** Inclusivism expresses an appropriate religious disposition. But Inclusivism ultimately fails as a warranted epistemological thesis. This failure leads us to the pluralistic types of responses to the problem of religious pluralism.

IV

Subjectivism, Pluralism, and Relativism are all pluralistic responses to the conflicting truth-claims of world religions. All three views share a basic ***idealist epistemology:*** i.e., they share the basic assumption that the world we experience and understand is not the world independent of our perceiving but a world at least in part structured by our minds. Thus these pluralistic views share the epistemic view expressed in the Kantian dictum that "[**sensible**] intuitions without concepts are blind," a view sometimes expressed in the contemporary notion that all experiencing is experiencing-*as.* But further, they share the assumption that there is more than one set of human concepts—more than one world-view—which is valid for understanding the world. Thus they share the sort of *pluralist* epistemology expressed by William James in *The Varieties of Religious Experience:* "why in the name of common sense need we assume that only one . . . system of ideas can be true? The obvious outcome of our total experience is that the world can be handled according to many systems of ideas, . . . " The three pluralistic religious responses all hold that one's perception of religious truth is in some sense relative to one's world-view. Typically this view is supported on the grounds of the ineluctable enculturation or the historicity of all thought and experience, or . . . by suggesting a necessary connection between language, which varies from community to community, and truth, which consequently varies.

The most radical of the pluralistic responses to the conflicting truth-claims of the world religions is Subjectivism, where religious truth and salvation are literally as varied as individuals are diverse. As a general view in epistemology, subjectivism is a form of relativism about truth. It is the extreme epistemological

[2]Frank Whaling, *Christian Theology and World Religions: A Global Approach* (Basingstoke: Marshall Pickering, 1986), p. 87.
[3]Karl Rahner, *Theological Investigations* (London: Dalton, Longman, Todd; New York: Seabury Press, 1961–84), vol. 5, p. 132.

position that truth is relative to each individual's idiosyncratic world-view. Thus, on a Religious Subjectivist's view, religion is a radically private affair, often understood as purely a matter of one's individual relation to the divine or Absolute. But subjectivism, and therefore Religious Subjectivism, is conceptually incoherent. Truth-bearers are statements or propositions. Statements or propositions are comprised of concepts. And precisely what Wittgenstein's **"private-language"** argument demonstrates is that concepts are social constructions and cannot be purely private, individual understandings.[4] Thus, since statements and propositions are comprised of concepts, and concepts are social constructs, truth cannot be idiosyncratically individualistic. Religious Subjectivism, then, must be rejected.

The two remaining pluralistic views, Religious Pluralism and Religious Relativism, are often conflated. John Hick offers a concise description of Pluralism as the view that "There is not merely one way but a plurality of ways of salvation or liberation . . . taking place in different ways within the contexts of all the great religious traditions." Pluralism holds that there is only one Ultimate Reality, but that Ultimate Reality is properly, though only partially, understood in different ways. Following a metaphor which Hick employs, just as the historian does not have direct access to figures of history, and consequently different historians develop different perspectives on historical figures like Genghis Khan or Sun Yat-Sen because of historians' different methods of inquiry, cultural backgrounds, etc., so too, different religious traditions or different theologies, not having direct access to the divine, offer different enculturated "images" of the one Ultimate Reality. On the Pluralist account, there is no ultimate conflict between these different perspectives, since there still remains one set of truths, even if those truths are imperfectly and only partially understood within each perspective. Religious Pluralism, then, focuses on the viability of different religious *perspectives* on Ultimate Reality.

[4]Ludwig Wittgenstein, *Philosophical Investigations,* 3rd edition, trans. G. E. M. Anscombe (New York: Macmillan Co., 1953), I, 268 b.

Religious Relativism, in contrast, is directly a thesis about differences of religious *truth-claims.* The Religious Relativist minimally holds the general **epistemic** view, which I shall designate as "conceptual relativism," that first-order truth-claims about reality—e.g., that persons or that subatomic particles or that God exists—are relative to the world-view of a particular society. More precisely, a conceptual relativist definitively holds that, corresponding to differences of world-view, there are mutually incompatible, yet individually adequate, sets of conceptual-schema-relative truths. Thus for the Religious Relativist, unlike the Pluralist, truth itself is relative and plural.

However, Religious Pluralism and Religious Relativism do share two underlying Kantian theses. They share the Kantian **metaphysical** division (though the Kantian terminology may not be employed) between **noumena** and **phenomena,** distinguishing between God in Himself or the Absolute in itself, and God or the Absolute as humanly experienced. And as we have seen, they share the Kantian epistemic notion that all experience, and so all religious experience, is structured by the (culturally and historically conditioned) world-view of the percipient. Thus, Religious Pluralism and Religious Relativism hold that differences of religious perception cannot just be treated as a matter of some people simply being wrong about the nature of the divine Reality, but rather that such differences of perception are inherent to religious perception and conception. Given these points of fundamental agreement, which position, Pluralism or Relativism, better accounts for the conflicting truth-claims of the world religions?

V

John Hick has developed [a] rather impressive and comprehensive, Pluralist approach, in part by following out a key aspect of [Wilfred] Cantwell Smith's work, *viz.* the rejection of the idea that a religion is fundamentally a set of beliefs. Proposing instead that religion definitively concerns "the transformation of human existence from self-centredness to Reality-centredness,"[5] Hick essentially argues that the apparently conflicting truth-claims of the world's religions are, in the final analysis, irrelevant, and that the world religions can be reconciled, and the integrity of each preserved, through this more fundamental shared goal of moving from self- to Reality-centeredness.

Hick explicitly employs the two Kantian theses underlying both Pluralism and Relativism. He employs the Kantian thesis that all experience is structured by the mind by suggesting that specific forms of religious awareness "are formed by the presence of the divine Reality, . . . coming to consciousness in terms of the different sets of religious concepts and structures of religious meaning that operate within the different religious traditions" i.e., *as* divine *personae* (e.g., Yahweh, Allah, etc.) for theists and *as* divine *impersonae* (e.g., Brahman, the Dharma, the Tao, etc.) for non-theists. Regarding the **phenomenal/noumenal** distinction, he supports the distinction between personal and non-personal divine phenomena and the Eternal noumenon, on the basis of what he takes to be strong **inductive evidence** from religious experience.[6] And indeed we do find consistent differentiation in the world religions between Ultimate Reality as we experience it and as it is in itself. There is the Hindu distinction between *saguna* Brahman and *nirguna* Brahman; the Jewish Cabalistic distinction between the God of the Bible and En Soph; and in the Christian tradition, Eckhart's distinction between God *qua* Trinity and the Godhead itself, and more recently, Tillich's notion of "the God above the God of theism," and so on.

Hick does allow for the logical possibility that only one religion might be correct, but he thinks that the overwhelming facts of religious diversity make Religious Pluralism the most plausible response to the conflicting truth-claims of world religions. A comprehensive Religious Pluralism like Hick's fully confronts the diversity of religious truth-claims. As such, it is an admirable and helpful response to the challenge which these conflicting claims presents. But even so, Religious Pluralism has significant shortcomings.

VI

Religious Pluralism fails to adequately account for the necessary, central role of cognition in religious faith. Hick suggests that differences of belief among the world religions are

> of great philosophical importance as elements within our respective theories about the universe; but they are not of great *religious,* i.e. **soteriological,** importance. For different groups can hold incompatible sets of theories all of which constitute intellectual frameworks within which the process of salvation/liberation can proceed.[7]

Of course, even incompatible theories can serve as guides to the same religious goal. But from this it neither follows that systems of belief and theory are irrelevant to guiding one to that goal, nor that it is unimportant which *particular* belief system one holds for reaching that end. Rather, the cognitive content of religious faith is essential for providing a coherent and sufficiently comprehensive view of reality as a basis for purposive action and an effective, directive guide to "salvation/liberation." Further, the *specific* cognitive content of one's faith is of paramount importance since it is precisely what delimits one's *specific* path to salvation/liberation. And the specific path to salvation/liberation is not just a means to an end but is itself an integral part of the goal of salvation/liberation. This is expressed in the New Testament in the idea that the Kingdom of God is not future but begins in the lives of those who enter the new covenant now: "asked by the Pharisees when the kingdom was coming, he [Jesus] answered them, 'The kingdom of God is not coming with signs to be observed; . . . the kingdom of God is in the midst of you."' (Luke 17:20–21, . . .) Consequently since the specific path to salvation/liberation is itself part of that very salvation/liberation, a

[5]John Hick, *Problems of Religious Pluralism* (New York: St. Martin's Press, 1985), p. 29.

[6]See Hick, *God Has Many Names* (Philadelphia: Westminster Press, 1982), p. 91.

[7]Hick, *Problems of Religious Pluralism,* p. 99.

specific religious world-view is importantly constitutive of what makes a way of life a (particular) *religious* way of life.

Indeed, it would seem that specific religious cognitive content is essential to making it meaningful even to be committed at all to a religious way of life. True, de-emphasizing specific doctrines—such as the idea that the Christ-event is the definitive self-revelation of the divine—makes it easier to reconcile apparently conflicting religious truth-claims, especially the notion of a personal God with the notion of a non-personal Absolute. But the more such specific doctrines are set aside, the more questionable it becomes whether a *religious,* as opposed to a non-religious, commitment is what gives life ultimate significance. Insofar as the specificity of religious doctrines is de-emphasized, the basic religious meta-belief (I) that religion does indeed refer to a transcendent Reality which gives meaning to life becomes less plausible. The plausibility of (I) rests in large part on the evidence of religious experience. But as any hypothesis about the nature of reality is made more indefinite, the available inductive evidence to support that hypothesis is not increased, as for example Hick's defense of Religious Pluralism seems to suggest, but decreased. For, evidence for an indefinite hypothesis is correspondingly indefinite or ambiguous.

Another difficulty with Religious Pluralism is this. Exactly what a recognition of pluralism in general seems to acknowledge is that humans, and human conceptions, fundamentally differ. But then, to the extent that the differences of human conception embedded in the world religions are regarded as inconsequential, the dignity of the individual and the value of each distinct community of faith is lessened.

To see how this applies to Christianity, consider Maurice Wiles' observation that, "there are two fundamental characteristics of the conception of God . . . it must be a profoundly personal concept, . . . And secondly it is God in relation to us with which we have to do."[8] The Christian understanding that the universe is under the providence of a God who has revealed Himself as a personal being—One who understands and loves humanity—is and must be a conception of God as He manifests Himself *to us.* Yet this conception of an essentially *personal* God is not incidental but central to both corporate and individual Christian faith. Hick attempts to account for this by suggesting that among the world religions the Real is experienced as *either* personal or non-personal. While this Religious Pluralist view properly acknowledges that theistic understanding is an understanding of Ultimate Reality not *an sich* [in itself] but *as* it confronts us in history, it obviates the significance of the Christian understanding of a personal God as *somehow* correctly revealing the nature of Ultimate Reality in itself. A personal reality might have non-personal aspects, but it could not be identical to something which is non-personal. Hence, this Pluralist account entails that the monotheist's experience of a *personal* divine reality *cannot,* to that extent, correctly represent the nature of the Real in itself.

Finally, Religious Pluralism is deficient insofar as it unintentionally undermines the sense of the reality of God. It is part of the fundamental meta-belief (I) of religion that the God or the Absolute of which humans speak is real and not a metaphysical illusion or psychological delusion. But if the God of which monotheists speak is only an "image," only a perspective on an unknowable, **noumenal** reality, than the God of history will not be a real God. I will address this last point more fully below.

These deficiencies must be met if a pluralistic resolution to the conflicting truth-claims of the world religions is to be successful. Yet despite these shortcomings, Religious Pluralism has an obvious strength which must be retained for any successful pluralistic resolution. Religious Pluralism offers a reconciliation of the disparate world religious traditions which avoids the theologically unacceptable and epistemically unsupportable religious imperialism which we find in Exclusivism, and even in Inclusivism.

VII

If, then, we reject the religious imperialism of the Exclusivist and Inclusivist views that one's own tradition must be either the sole or at least the fullest arbiter of truth about the divine, we have two choices

[8]Hick, *Problems of Religious Pluralism,* pp. 93–94.

about how to deal with the irreducible plurality of religious conception and experience. We can either take the approach of Pluralism, treat the incompatible beliefs among differing religious world-views as ultimately inessential, and conclude that the great world religions simply offer different perspectives on Ultimate Reality. Or we can accept the doctrines which adherents of different world religions so ardently profess and passionately follow as *essential* to their faith. I have suggested that the former approach runs the danger of undermining the basic religious meta-belief (I), and reducing the substance of religious world-views to vacuity, obviating just those differences in the path to salvation/liberation which give significance to each individual religious tradition. If I am right about this, we are led to conclude that different religions have different constitutive sets of truth-claims, and that—while these sets of core truth-claims are mutually incompatible—each set of truth-claims is probably adequate in itself.

This is the Religious Relativist response to the problem of religious pluralism. Granted, the different religious world-views among the world's great religious tradition are complementary insofar as they have a commonality in the religious experiences and perceptions of humankind. But different religious world-views are, ultimately, irreducibly plural, with features that are incompatible if not contradictory *vis-á-vis* other religious world-views. Further, corresponding to each distinct religious world-view, there is a different set of possible religious *experiences.* For what can be experienced depends on what *can be* real or unreal, and what can be real—i.e., what is possible—is determined by the percipient's world-view. This means that each distinct religious world-view delineates a distinct possible divine reality—though just to the extent that religious world-views "overlap," characteristics of these distinct possible divine realities will overlap.

For instance, monotheistic truth-claims will be most directly about God *as* humans experience Him, for they are most directly about divine reality *relative to* a particular theistic world-view. But then each **theology,** as a product of human constructive reasoning, will delimit only one *possible* divine reality. There will be other *contrasting*—though not totally mutually exclusive—valid theologies, held by other sincere women and men of faith, delimiting other possible divine phenomenal realities.

Importantly, on this Religious Relativist account, "The" God of history, delimited by the strictures of a particular theology is *not,* if He exists, somehow unreal *vis-á-vis* the noumenal. God *qua* noumenal lies "behind," so to speak, the possible plurality of real phenomenal divine realities, delimited by different monotheistic world-views. But noumenal and phenomenal reality are two different categories of reality. And just as there is nothing unreal about nuclear weapons or pains or piano concertos because they are part of phenomenal reality, "The" God of history, "The" God one confronts, is not less real, if He exists, just because He is not in the category of the noumenal. What could be *more* real than that which we do experience? And to try to transcend our experience for something putatively "untainted" by human thought is not only the worst sort of degenerate Platonism, it is to turn away from the means we *do* have in experience for understanding the divine and our own humanity in relation to the divine.

Among the possible responses to the problem of religious pluralism, this Religious Relativist account of a possible plurality of phenomenal divine realities seems to offer the best explanation of the differing experiences and incompatible conceptions of the great religious traditions. . . .

First, Religious Relativism reasserts the central role which cognition has in a religious life. The path to salvation is itself part of the salvific process. And one's religious world-view, as a guide for attitudes and actions, is inseparable from that path. Moreover, if all experience is conceptualized, then one will quite literally not be able to have any experience of the divine without a world-view which, e.g., enables one to experience the world *as* under the providence of God, or *as* an environment for working out one's ***Karma,*** etc. But then, as Religious Relativism asserts, *specific* truth-claims are essential to a religious tradition and way of life, and the conflict among the claims of the world religions cannot be resolved by de-emphasizing those conflicting claims.

Second, it follows from this that Religious Relativism treats adherents of each religious tradition with fullest dignity. Regarding Christianity, we could say, as the Pluralist must, that the doctrine of the Incarnation cannot be taken literally and cannot mean for *any* Christian that Jesus uniquely manifests the presence of God. Or, we can allow that on *some* world-views this would be a perfectly rational view, delineating a world where Jesus *is* the definitive self-manifestation of God. Ironically, we fall back into a certain measure of the old absolutism that undergirds Exclusivism if we take the inflexible, even though Pluralist, first course. In contrast, Relativism not only allows with Pluralism that the world's great religions could have the same telos, it allows for the likelihood that more than one of the conflicting sets of *specific* truth-claims, which adherents of the differing world religions themselves regard as vital to their faith, is correct.

Third, that it is essential for the direct object of **theological** conception to be a *real* God seems to leave a Pluralist view like Hick's caught between two problematic options. As in his earlier work, the God of theology can be characterized as an "image" of God. But then the God of theology does not have the **ontological** status of an existent entity with causal properties in the phenomenal world. This will unintentionally reduce the sense of the reality of God, for what theology would then be most directly referring to would not be *God,* but a human *idea* of the noumenal. So to speak about *God,* would be to speak about something noumenal about which we can only know that we do not know its true character. In contrast, on Religious Relativism the God of theology can be a *real* God, not just a conception of or perspective on the divine. God *qua* phenomenal is not just, in Tillich's phrase, "a symbol for God."

On the other hand, the Pluralist might hold, as Hick does in his more recent work, that the divine phenomena just *are* the divine noumenon *as* experienced by humans via their particular religio-cultural perspectives. While this does indicate a more substantive ontological status for divine personae and impersonae, it threatens to collapse the phenomena/noumena distinction and runs counter to the basic idealist epistemology which underlies both Pluralism and Relativism. First, this suggests that the divine noumenon is itself experienced. One can postulate an unexperienced divine noumenon, and one can talk about divine phenomena which are (putatively) experienced. But this cannot amount to talk about the same thing—even if in different ways—for that would effectively be to eliminate the divine noumenon. And given an idealist epistemology, one cannot claim that the divine noumenon *is* experienced insofar as it appears to us in various ways, *even though* we cannot characterize the noumenal. For the conceptualization of all experience implies that what we experience can, in principle, be characterized.

Second, that a particular divine phenomenon somehow manifests the divine noumenon is a matter of faith. And while it could be a matter of reasonable faith for an individual to claim that the divine phenomenon which *they* experience somehow manifests Ultimate Reality in itself, it would not make sense to say that it was a matter of one's *faith* that the various divine phenomena, which adherents of all the great world religions feel that they experience, all *do* manifest Ultimate Reality. Rather this would amount to a hypothesis or theory about the world religions. And I do not see how we could know that this hypothesis is true; how could we know that the divine phenomena of all the great world religions *are* (or most probably are) the divine noumenon *as* experienced by humans? One's faith warrants one's own religious commitment; it cannot warrant the mutually conflicting commitments of others.

In contrast, on a Religious Relativist account, what is putatively experienced is not the noumenal Ultimate Reality, but e.g., the *real* God of history. Now, I do think that it is a mistake to suppose that one can *know* that specific claims which we make about phenomenal divine reality are also true of the divine noumenon, since this would obviate the very point of the noumena/phenomena distinction. But I think it is perfectly sensible to make the bare claim that there *is* a noumenal—*whatever* its character—which, so to speak, "lies behind" the phenomenal reality which we experience. Presumably there is no one-to-one correspondence between phenomena and noumena and hence no *direct* check from our successes and failures to the nature of the noumenal. But the greater the correspondence between our conception of the phenomenal and the character of the noumenal (whatever it is), the more our purposive activity, carried out within phenomenal reality as *we* understand it, will be successful and the closer—in principle—our understanding of the phenomenal will correspond to the noumenal. For the monotheist it is a matter of faith that, in this manner, one's *own* experience of the presence of "The" God of history does increase, on the whole, one's understanding of God in Himself.

VIII

One obvious point of resistance to this Religious Relativist account is the notion that there may be more than one phenomenal reality, and more than one phenomenal divine reality. But this notion initially seems strange only because we are used to thinking in terms of that one possible world which *we* regard as *the* (unique) actual world. Commonly, we treat any other conception of the actual world as simply false or mistaken. But if one accepts the idea that phenomenal reality is relative to a world-view, and that therefore there is a plurality of actual worlds corresponding to the plurality of distinct world-views, that does not undermine or alter what *we* call the actual world—i.e., the world delimited by *our* schemas.

Recognizing that others might be responding to a different phenomenal God is like recognizing that others might rationally claim to discern a cyclical recurrence of events in history where you discern none. One can accept that there *could* be states of affairs which others but not you experience, without thereby committing yourself to the existence of any *particular* such state of affairs. To have faith in only one real (phenomenal) God is to say that for *oneself* there is only one real God who lives and moves and has His being; for others there may be other real entities which are "The" God of *their* history. But just as any actual event or state of affairs is by definition an event or state of affairs in *your* actual world, any actual event which you acknowledge as an act of God is an act of the real God who confronts *you* within (your) history.

IX

Frank Whaling raises another possible objection to both Pluralism and Relativism. Whaling argues that these views avoid "the necessity of theological ordering of any sort," and that they have "the appearance of being a somewhat abstract exercise in the theology of religion, rather than a summing-up of where the Christian community around the world actually *is*."[9] The second, descriptive point, that Christians do not currently tend to be Religious Pluralists or Relativists, misses the question of whether Christians *ought* to move toward Pluralism or Relativism in the face of the challenge of the conflicting truth-claims of the world religions. But with respect to the first point, it *would* be a serious defect of any pluralistic response to the world religions if diverse religious truth-claims cannot be compared and assessed. Here Pluralism and Relativism offer two quite different approaches.

Pluralists most naturally approach the apparently conflicting truth-claims of world religions from the perspective of a "global theology."[10] That is, the Pluralist fundamentally attempts to look at religious traditions from an external, or inclusive point of view. But the unavoidable historicity and the inherent enculturation of our thought obviate the very possibility of being able to assume this purported global perspective. There can be no such thing as a "neutral" or "objective" perspective in either religious or non-religious matters. Hence, any attempt to assess other faiths from a genuinely global perspective is inherently impossible.

Religious Relativism, on the other hand, avoids this difficulty by suggesting an internal approach to assessing other faiths. Relativism, more fundamentally than Pluralism, recognizes the inextricably socio-historical conditioning of one's perspective, and hence fundamentally recognizes that judgments about *other* faiths will necessarily be made from the point of view of one's *own* faith. This is simply to

[9]Maurice Wiles, *Faith and the Mystery of God* (Philadelphia: Fortress Press, 1982), p. 120. . . .

[10]Whaling, *Christian Theology and World Religions,* pp. 95 and 98.

acknowledge an inherent condition of the human mind, and does not entail falling back into the religious imperialism we found in Exclusivism and Inclusivism. For there are general meta-criteria that can be applied across world-views to assess the acceptability of a world-view. These criteria include the internal coherence of a world-view, its comprehensiveness, thoroughness of explanation (e.g., that it does not depend on ad hoc hypotheses), the efficaciousness of the world-view in producing its intended end, considerations of parsimony, and so on. Thus Relativism, while not attempting to assume the stance of an impossible "neutral" global theology, can employ these meta-criteria to assess other faiths and so meet Whaling's objection. Further, this gives Relativism a strength that we observed in Religious Inclusivism. Religious Relativism, while recognizing that salvation *could* come to others in other traditions, supports the strength of commitment to one's own tradition.

X

While the Pluralist attempts to solve the problem of religious pluralism by setting aside conflicting truth-claims and emphasizing a universality and unity to all religions, the Religious Relativist can resolve the problem of religious pluralism by accepting these conflicting truth-claims as an appropriate manifestation of divine/human interaction. In the spirit of the **Leibnizian** notion that not just the quantity of good, but the *variety* of good things makes this "the best of all possible worlds"—the world that a good God would create—we *should* expect correct religious beliefs and **veridical** religious experiences to be as richly varied as human needs and human individuality. Contrary to the Pluralist conception, an ultimate uniformity of the central elements of all religious traditions is not an ultimate value. Where Pluralism tends to homogenize religion, if one believes that God indeed has providence over the world, then precisely what the evidence of the world we find ourselves in indicates is that a diversity of religious truth-claims is intrinsically valuable, and divinely valued. Rather than a problem to be solved, the conflicting truth-claims of the great religious traditions, and even conflicting systems *within* traditions, can be accepted as a profound indication of God's manifest love and delight in the diverse worlds of His creatures.

That our religious beliefs have a correlation to the transcendent divine reality is a matter of faith. Since our perception and understanding are ineluctably limited to our world-view, even if what we believe is true about God *qua* phenomenal turns out to be true also of God *qua* noumenal, we could never *know* that that was so. We cannot *know* that we possess the requisite conceptual resources to apply to God in Himself, or *know* that we have formed ideas which are true of God *qua* noumenal, or *know* that our ideas do properly refer to the noumenal God. But just because we cannot know these things to be true *vis-á-vis* the noumenal God, this clearly does not entail that they are not the case. I do not see how it could be shown that it is *impossible* that our concepts or beliefs do in fact correctly refer to the noumenal. Quite the contrary, it is a matter of reasonable faith that Christian religious experience and theological conception *do* provide the basis for proper reference and proper talk about God in Himself. Yet to acknowledge that we cannot transcend our world-views, and that they in turn are inescapably structured by our limiting socio-historical perspective, is to recognize the fundamental fallibility and finitude of even our noblest conceptions and highest values. There is thus a religiously appropriate humbleness which Religious Relativism brings to our claims to religious truth.

Faced with the inescapable challenge of the claims of other faiths, it may now be time for Christians to move toward a Christian Relativism. A Christian Relativism would combine the strengths of Exclusivism and Inclusivism, and of Pluralism, without their respective disadvantages. A Christian Relativism would enable us to say, on the one hand, that salvation through Christ is definitive, without committing us, on the other hand, to the unsupportable view that salvation is exclusively Christian. A Christian Relativism would sustain Christian commitment and support Christian claims to truth, without claiming to be the only truth.

STUDY QUESTIONS

1. Why does Runzo think that differences between religions are differences about truth claims?
2. Explain Runzo's distinction between faith and religion.
3. Why does Runzo reject exclusivism?
4. *Contrast Runzo's reasons for rejecting exclusivism with Alvin Plantinga's response to anti-exclusivist arguments in Reading 8.3. Who do you think is right? Why?
5. Explain Runzo's objections to Hick's religious pluralism.
6. Explain religious relativism. According to Runzo, how does it overcome the objections to pluralism?
7. *Runzo states that religious relativism recognizes that one's perspective is the result of socio-historical conditioning. In your opinion, does this recognition lessen the importance of what one believes, just as Runzo believes pluralism does? Why or why not?

FURTHER READING

Byrne, Peter. *Prolegomena to Religious Pluralism: Reference and Realism in Religion.* New York: St. Martin's Press, 1995.

D'Costa, Gavin. "The Impossibility of a Pluralist View of Religions." *Religious Studies* 32 (1996): 223–32.

Dean, Thomas, ed. *Religious Pluralism and Truth: Essays on Cross-cultural Philosophy of Religion.* Albany: State University of New York Press, 1995.

Gellman, Jerome. "In Defense of a Contented Religious Exclusivism." *Religious Studies* 36 (2000): 401–17.

Gellman, Jerome. "Religious Diversity and the Epistemic Justification of Religious Belief." *Faith and Philosophy* 10 (1993): 345–64.

Griffiths, Paul J. "Religious Diversity." *The Thomist* 52 (1988): 319–27.

Hamnett, Ian, ed. *Religious Pluralism and Unbelief.* New York: Routledge, 1990.

Hick, John. *God and the Universe of Faiths.* London: Macmillan, 1973.

Hick, John. *An Interpretation of Religion: Human Responses to the Transcendent.* New Haven, CT: Yale University Press, 1989.

Hick, John, ed. *Truth and Dialogue in World Religions: Conflicting Truth Claims.* Philadelphia: Westminster Press, 1974.

Hick, John, advisory ed. *Faith and Philosophy* 5, 4 (1998). (Special issue on religious pluralism.)

Hick, John, and Peter Hebblethwaite, eds. *Christianity and Other Religions.* Glasgow, Scotland: Collins, 1980.

Kellenberger, John, ed. *Inter-religious Models and Criteria.* New York: St. Martin's Press, 1993.

Lipner, Julius J. "Truth-Claims and Inter-religious Dialogue." *Religious Studies* 12 (1976): 217–30.

Mavrodes, George I. "The Gods Above the Gods: Can the High Gods Survive?" In *Reasoned Faith Essays in Philosophical Theology in Honor of Norman Kretzman,* edited by Eleonore Stump, pp. 179–203. Ithaca, NY, and London: Cornell University Press, 1993.

Mavrodes, George I. "Polytheism." In *The Rationality of Belief and the Plurality of Faiths,* edited by Thomas D. Senor, pp. 261–86, Ithaca, NY, and London: Cornell University Press, 1995.

Montefiore, Alan. "Ecumenical Movements and Truth." *Midwest Studies in Philosophy* 21 (1997): 145–58.

Quinn, Philip L. and Kevin Meeker, eds. *The Philosophical Challenge of Religious Diversity.* New York: Oxford University Press, 1999.

Rouner, L S., ed. *Religious Pluralism.* Notre Dame, IN: Notre Dame University Press, 1984.

Sharma, Arvind, ed. *God, Truth and Reality.* New York: St. Martin's Press, 1993.

Smith, William Cantwell. *Religious Diversity,* edited by William G. Oxtoby, New York: Harper & Row, 1976.

Smith, William Cantwell. *Towards a World Theology.* Philadelphia: Westminster, 1981.

van Inwagen, Peter. "Non Est Hick." In *The Rationality of Belief and the Plurality of Faiths,* edited by Thomas D. Senor, pp. 216–41. Ithaca, NY, and London: Cornell University Press, 1995. Repr. in van Inwagen, *God, Knowledge and Mystery.* Ithaca, NY, and London: Cornell University Press, 1995.

Yandell, Keith. "Religious Experience and Rational Appraisal." *Religious Studies* 8 (June 1974): 173–87.

Some of the Further Readings listed in chapter 4 under the heading "Mysticism and Arguments from Religious Experience" assess the diversity of religious experience in connection with arguments for the existence of God that are based on religious experience.

Glossary of Technical Terms

Generally, terms are explained in accordance with how they are used in the readings, sometimes using an author's own wording. Occasionally, however, additional meanings of a term are given as an aid to further reading in the field.

Glossary terms are bolded in the text only at their first occurrence in a selection. Occasionally, the first word of an entry appears in a reading without the rest of the entry, *e.g.*, the term **valid** may appear rather than **valid argument,** or **sufficient** rather than **sufficient condition.**

Because it occurs so frequently, the term *theism* is not bolded in the readings.

a posteriori Based on experience. A posteriori knowledge and a posteriori **arguments** contrast with **a priori** knowledge and **a priori** arguments.

a priori (1) Not based on experience. Usually used to describe a certain sort of knowledge: A priori knowledge is knowledge that is independent of experience, and contrasts with **a posteriori** knowledge. It is often thought that a priori knowledge is knowledge of necessary truths, and a posteriori knowledge is knowledge of contingent truths (see **contingent truth vs. necessary truth**), but this claim has been disputed. An a priori **argument** is an argument all of whose premises are known a priori and whose conclusion follows necessarily from the premises. (2) Colloquially, the term means antecedently or prior to investigation.

abreactive A term in psychoanalytic writing which means: Pertaining to the discharge of the emotional energy attached to a repressed idea, especially by the conscious verbalization of that idea to a therapist.

accident A property of a substance or thing without which it could still exist. Also called an accidental property. Contrasts with **essence.**

act (in Aquinas) Actuality

actuality vs. potentiality A distinction in Aristotelian philosophy between actually being in a certain state (motion, for example) and having the potential (or potency) to be in a certain state.

***ad hominem* argument** Literally, an **argument** against the person. In the abusive form of an *ad hominem* argument, one party in a debate argues against an opponent's position by attacking the other's personal traits, or accusing him or her of having ulterior motives in holding a particular position. In the circumstantial form of an *ad hominem* argument, person *A* replies to person *B*'s argument by saying that a premise *B* uses is put forward insincerely, is inconsistent with other assertions *B* has made, or is inconsistent with how *B* acts. In one variety of *ad hominem* argument, *A* might try to show that *B* should not believe that *p* by showing that not-*p* follows from claims *B* accepts, even though *A* does not accept those claims. *Ad hominem* arguments are generally but not always fallacious.

agnostic A person who suspends belief about the truth of a particular statement or proposition is an agnostic vis-á-vis that statement or proposition. In the case of religion, an agnostic is one who neither believes nor denies that God exists but, rather, suspends belief about this question. Generally, the agnostic thinks that there is not sufficient evidence for either *God exists* or *God does not exist.* However, a **fideist** might believe there is not sufficient evidence for either proposition yet still believe that God exists.

agnosticism The approach of an **agnostic** (to a particular question or assertion).

akedah In Hebrew, a binding; "the *akedah*" refers to the Binding of Isaac in Genesis 22.

akrasia Weakness of will—that is, action against one's better judgment.

alienation Used by, among others, George Hegel, Ludwig Feuerbach, and Karl Marx; it connotes estrangement or the act or process of becoming estranged. In Feuerbach's writing, human beings are alienated from themselves.

allegorical interpretation (of Scripture) An interpretation that construes the biblical text figuratively (technically, allegory is but one type of figurative interpretation; nevertheless the term is often used to cover any type of figurative interpretation).

allegorization The activity of using **allegorical interpretation.**

analogy (as a type of argument)–See **argument by analogy.**

analogy, theory of An approach to understanding sentences of the form *God is Q* that is associated with Thomas Aquinas. In the *analogy of proportionality,* such a statement is interpreted to mean that God's Q-ness is to God's nature as a human being's Q-ness is to human nature. In *analogy of causation, God is Q* expresses the proposition that God causes creatures to have Q.

analytically true True by definition or meaning.

anisotropy Lack of **isotropy.**

Anselmian theism Belief in the being described by **perfect being theology** (which is associated with Anselm of Canterbury). St. Anselm defines God as the being than whom none greater may be conceived.

Anselmian theist A theist who adopts **perfect being theology.**

antirealism The negation of **realism,** usually in sense (1) of that term.

anthropic principle Both atheists and theists invoke a principle by this name, but their respective principles are different. (1) As used by atheists, the anthropic principle is the principle that, given our presence in the universe as observers, it necessarily follows that the requisite conditions for intelligent life have been met. Therefore, we should not be surprised that we observe a universe with initial conditions, laws, and constants that allow for intelligent life. (2) As used by theists, the anthropic principle asserts that the initial conditions, laws, and constants of the universe are fine-tuned for the creation of human life, which suggests an intelligent God who designed the universe. (See also **fine-tuning.**)

anthropocentric Centered on human beings and their interests.

anthropocentrism The focusing on human beings and their interests.

anthropomorphic Reflecting **anthropomorphism.**

anthropomorphism Literally, form of humanity. (1) Narrowly defined: the view that God has human *form* (i.e., a body) (2) Broadly defined: the view that God has humanlike characteristics, such as bodily form and emotion. (See also **anthropopathism.**)

anthropopathism The view that God has humanlike emotions. (See also **anthropomorphism.**)

argument A set of claims (variously called statements or propositions), some of which are designated as premises and another as a conclusion, such that the conclusion is said to follow from the premises. For senses of *follow from* and the distinction between **deductive** and **inductive arguments,** see pp. 172–73.

argument by analogy An **argument** of the following type: since object *A* has properties $P_1 \ldots P_n$ and property *Q,* and object *B* is known to have $P_1 \ldots P_n$, therefore *B* probably has property *Q* as well. David Hume treats the **design argument** as an argument by analogy.

atheological Reflecting the view of an atheist.

autonomous Possessing **autonomy.**

autonomy Literally, self-legislation. In James Rachels's essay, an autonomous being is depicted as one who decides for him- or herself how to act and does not submit to the will of others.

bare particular An object without properties.

basic belief A belief not based on other beliefs but on which other beliefs are based.

Bayesian principles Named for eighteenth-century English clergyman Thomas Bayes. Bayesianism is an approach to scientific method which stresses that beliefs have degrees of strength and that a rational person's beliefs must conform to principles of probability theory.

begging the question Assuming in the course of an argument, explicitly or implicitly, the very conclusion one is arguing for. Arguments that beg the question are unpersuasive, but they are formally **valid,** since the conclusion *p* follows from the premise *p.*

behaviorism, logical/ philosophical The view that statements ascribing mental states to a person can be translated into statements that refer only to the person's body.

big bang theory (sometimes capitalized) The prevailing scientific theory that the universe originated as the result of a gigantic explosion. Contrasts with steady-state theory, the theory that the universe has always existed in the same state.

brute fact A fact that has no explanation. According to the **principle of sufficient reason,** there are no brute facts.

Cartesian Having to do with French philosopher René Descartes (1596–1650).

cause *in esse* See cause *in esse* vs. cause *in fieri.*

cause *in esse* vs. cause *in fieri* A cause *in fieri* is a factor that brings or helps bring an effect into existence; a cause *in esse* is a factor that sustains or helps sustain an effect in being.

cause *in fieri* See cause *in esse* vs. cause *in fieri.*

***ceteris paribus* clause** An "other things being equal" clause; *if A then B, ceteris paribus* means: if A then B, other things being equal.

coeval Of the same age or duration.

cognitive Having to do with cognition, that is, the process or state of knowing or believing.

compatibilism The view that free will is compatible with determinism. Contrasts with **incompatibilism.**

compatibilist As an adjective: reflecting **compatibilism;** as a noun: one who endorses **compatibilism.**

complement The complement of a property F is not-F; the complement of things that have the property F is things that do not have the property F.

composition To ascribe composition to God is to say he is not **simple** but rather composed of parts.

conjunction A conjunction is an *and* statement; **conjuncts** are the component statements of a conjunction. Thus, in the conjunction *p and q, p* and *q* are the conjuncts.

conjunct See **conjunction.**

consequent In a statement of the form, "If *p* then *q,*" *p* is the antecedent and *q* is the consequent.

constant conjunction When events, objects, or properties of type A are regularly succeeded (or accompanied) by events, objects, or properties of type B, we speak of the constant conjunction of type-A events, objects, or properties and type-B events, objects, or properties (or loosely, of the constant conjunction of A and B). According to David Hume, there is nothing more to causation than regular sequence, i.e., constant conjunction.

contingent being(s) A being (or beings) who might not have existed, as distinct from a **necessary being.**

contingent event (or circumstance) An event (or circumstance) that might not have occurred.

contingent truth See **contingent truth vs. necessary truth.**

contingent truth vs. necessary truth A contingent truth is a statement that is true but could be false; a necessary truth is a statement that is true but could not be false. Philosophers debate how *could be* is best explicated in these definitions.

continuous creation The doctrine that God recreates the world at each moment; sometimes used to imply that God *sustains* the universe at each moment.

contraposition Rearranging terms to produce the **contrapositive** of a statement.

contrapositive The contrapositive of a statement is the statement yielded by switching the subject and predicate terms, or the constituent propositions, in the original statement and then negating them. Thus, the contrapositive of *all A is B* is *all not-B is not-A,* and the contrapositive of *if p then q* is *if not-q, then not-p.*

conventionalism The view that certain statements, such as those in arithmetic, logic, and geometry, are true solely by virtue of people having decided to use certain terms in certain ways.

conventionalist As an adjective: reflecting **conventionalism;** as a noun: one who believes **conventionalism.**

cosmogony (1) The study of how the world originated. (2) Any theory that describes how the world originated.

cosmological arguments Arguments for the existence of God that are based on inferences from the existence of dependent beings in the universe. Cosmological arguments try to show there is a being, God, on which everything else depends. In cosmological arguments, God is variously characterized as First Cause, First Mover, Independent Being, Necessary Being, or Self-Existent Being, depending on the precise argument used and the terminological preferences of the arguer.

cosmologist Someone who studies **cosmology.**

cosmology The science that deals with the origin and structure of the cosmos, or, more specifically, of the physical universe.

counterexample An example that shows a generalization to be false.

counterfactual (1) As an adjective: contrary to fact; (2) as a noun: shorthand for counterfactual conditional, i.e., a conditional, or "if__ then___" statement, whose "if clause" is presupposed to be false, e. g., "If you were president, you would be famous around the world", "if you had worn a glove, you would not have burned your finger."

covering law model A model of scientific explanation according to which to explain an event, fact, or state-of-affairs is to subsume it under a law of nature. That is, a scientific explanation is a **deductive argument** in which a statement describing the event, fact, or state-of-affairs being explained (the **explanandum**) is deduced logically from a statement or statements describing laws of nature together with a statement or statements describing antecedent conditions. (The conjunction of these latter statements is called the **explanans.**)

creation science See **scientific creationism.**

creationism (1) **Scientific creationism;** (2) the view that God created the world.

creationist A believer in **creationism.**

critical realism The view that there is a world independent of our minds (a position called **realism**) but our beliefs about the world are always open to correction.

cybernetics The study of how information is communicated in physical systems such as computers and nervous systems. The term was coined by Norbert Wiener in 1947 (and derives from a Greek word for steersman).

decision theory A branch of philosophy and of probability theory that examines the nature of rational decisionmaking.

deductive argument Used variously to mean (1) an argument that is thought by the arguer to be **valid;** (2) an argument that is thought by the arguer to be **sound;** (3) an argument that is valid; (4) an argument that is sound.

defeasible Subject to being given up in the face of contrary evidence that generates **defeaters.** Generally used to characterize presumptions and hypotheses.

defeater Suppose that statement e_1 supports statement p but that, when e_2 is conjoined with e_1, the **conjunction** (e_1 *and* e_2) does not support p. Then e_2 is a defeater of a person's justification e_1 for believing that p. An *undercutting defeater* is generated by evidence for not-p. A *rebutting defeater* is generated by evidence which shows that a person's justification for believing that p is defective; it need not provide evidence for not-p.

definiens In a definition, the term being defined is the definiendum, and the explanation of the term is the definiens.

deism (1) The view that God created the world but does not intervene in it; (2) the view that human reason can arrive at all important religious truths; revelation does not occur, or, at least, is not needed. Sense (2) is the one prevalent during the rise of deism in the seventeenth and eighteenth centuries; sense (1) prevails today.

deistic Relating to or reflecting **deism.**

demonstrable Capable of being shown true by **demonstration.**

demonstration A medieval term for proof: that is, a **valid argument** with premises that are known to be true, indeed (in most usages of *demonstration*) are self-evidently true.

demonstrative (applied to an argument or proof) constituting a **demonstration.**

design arguments Arguments for God's existence that are based on inferences from the order exhibited in the world.

determinism The view that everything that happens is uniquely determined to happen by prior events and states of the universe; or that at every moment in time, the laws of nature and the complete history of the universe up until that moment jointly entail all the facts that happen then and thereafter. Usually associated with the view that natural causes are what produce events, but technically God's actions could be the cause of events (as in **predestination**), or God's states could determine events (as in **foreknowledge**) independently of laws and nature and of natural causes.

dialectic (1) In Søren Kierkegaard's and other existentialists' writings, back and forth movements between opposite beliefs, emotions, or attitudes. (2) The process of presenting arguments and debating their cogency.

dialectical Pertaining to **dialectic** (in either sense of that term).

dialectical materialism A distinctive version of **materialism** associated with, among others, Friedrich Engels, Karl Marx, and Vladimir Lenin.

dilemma An **argument** with the following form; p or *not-p;* if p, then q; if not-p, then q; therefore, q.

dipolar theism Associated with the philosopher Charles Hartshorne (1899–2000) and sometimes used to denote **process theism.** There are two poles, or aspects, of God: the abstract essence and the concrete actuality. The former is eternal, absolute, independent, and **immutable;** the latter is temporal, relative, dependent, and constantly changing.

direct realist theory of perception A theory of perception which endorses **realism** and according to which perceivers directly perceive objects outside the mind, rather than *inferring* their existence from the occurrence of sensory representations. According to this view, perception is unmediated.

disjunct See **disjunction.**

disjunction A disjunction is an *or* statement; **disjuncts** are the component statements of a disjunction. Thus, in the disjunction *p or q or r, p, q,* and *r* are the disjuncts.

disjunctive Expressed as a **disjunction,** i.e. a disjunctive statement is a disjunction.

disposition A tendency to act in specified ways in specified circumstances. Dispositions are expressed by means of hypothetical statements of the form: in circumstances C, object *O* behaves in way *W*. See also **dispositional state (or property).**

dispositional state (or property) A state (or property) like fragility, elasticity, or courage which is best understood by means of **dispositions.**

divine command theory (of ethics) Usually understood as the view that *right* and *wrong* are defined by what God commands or forbids, so that ethics is conceptually dependent on the command of God. This version of the divine command theory should be distinguished from the **epistemological** thesis that right and wrong can be known only through God's commands and prohibitions but are not *defined* in terms of God's commands and prohibitions.

divine relativity A term used in **process theology** (and coined by Charles Hartshorne). Perfection entails independence or absoluteness in some respects but dependence or relativity in other respects, for to promote the greatest good one must be informed by, and thus relativized by, the feelings of others.

doxastic Having to do with *doxa* (belief).

dualism Substance dualism is the view that there are two fundamentally different sorts of substances involved in a person: a mind and a body. **Property-dualism** is the view that there are two fundamentally different sorts of properties, mental and physical, even though there is no nonphysical substance.

dualist Reflecting **dualism.**

efficient causation The activity of an **efficient cause** bringing something into being.

efficient cause In Aristotelian philosophy, the efficient cause of a change *C* is the thing (or agent) that brings about *C,* and the efficient cause of an object *O* is the thing (or agent) that creates *O*. Efficient causes contrast with **final causes.**

eliminative materialism The view that there are no mental entities or properties; these are falsely postulated, as the powers of witches once were. See also **materialism.**

eminently In medieval philosophy, to possess a property eminently is to possess it in a higher form or degree than other things possess it.

empirical Based on sense experience.

empirically In an **empirical** manner, or from an empirical standpoint.

empiricism The view that all knowledge comes from sense experience (usually identified with experience produced by the five senses and introspection of one's own mental states). Empiricism denies **rationalism** in sense (1) of that term below.

empiricist As an adjective, reflecting **empiricism;** as a noun, a philosopher who believes empiricism.

epiphenomenalism The view that mental events are effects or byproducts of physical events but do not cause physical events.

epistemic Having to do with knowledge or the justification of belief.

epistemic possibility It is epistemically possible that *p* if, for all we know, it might be true that *p*. Epistemic possibility should be distinguished from **metaphysical possibility.**

epistemically In terms of **epistemic** considerations.

epistemically possible See **epistemic possibility.**

epistemological Having to do with knowledge (Greek: *episteme*) or with the justification of belief. Philosophers distinguish the epistemological questions of how one could or does know that *p* and whether one is justified in believing that *p,* from the **metaphysical** question of whether it is true that *p*.

epistemologically Relating to **epistemology.**

epistemology The theory of knowledge.

equivocal See **equivocal predication.**

equivocal predication A term *Q* is said to be predicated equivocally of subject A and subject B when *Q* has a different meaning in *A is Q* than it does in *B is Q*. Contrasts with **univocal predication.**

equivocally In a way reflecting **equivocal predication.**

eschatology Theory of the end of days.

essence A property or set of properties without which a substance or thing could not exist. Also called an essential property or essential properties. Contrasts with **accident.**

essentialism The view that objects have **essences.** Thus, theistic essentialism is the view that God has an essence.

eternal In perfect being theology, God often is said to exist outside of time. Nicholas Wolterstorff (Reading 1.9) contrasts the thesis that *God is eternal* (God is outside of time) with the thesis that *God is **everlasting*** (God exists in time but God's existence has no beginning or end).

eternity (1) The property of being **eternal;** (2) a time duration without beginning and/or without end.

etiology A description of causes.

everlasting Having no beginning or end. See, by contrast, **eternal.**

evidential problem of evil One of two major versions of what is called the problem of evil, the other being known as the **logical problem of evil.** According to the evidential version, whereas *God exists* is *logically compatible* with *evil exists, God exists* is *improbable,* given the truth of *evil exists.*

evidentialism (1) The view, represented by W. K. Clifford, that no one should believe anything without having adequate evidence for what is believed. (2) The view that a person should not believe that *p* to a degree that exceeds of evidence for believing that *p*.

evidentialist As an adjective: Reflecting **evidentialism.** As a noun: an adherent of **evidentialism.**

ex nihilo From nothing.

exclusivism (1) The view that salvation can be attained only by adherents of one religion, usually one's own. (2) The view that no religion besides one's own is true (though salvation is attainable by adherence to another religion). (3) The view that at most one religion leads to salvation. (4) The view that at most one religion is true. (An atheist or **agnostic** could subscribe to (3) and (4) but not (1) or (2).)

exclusivist As an adjective: reflecting **exclusivism.** As a noun: an adherent of **exclusivism.**

existential generalization (1) A statement asserting that something exists that has a certain property or properties. (2) A rule that allows one to infer that something has the property *Q* from the premise that a particular thing has *Q*.

existentialism A nineteenth- and twentieth-century philosophy that makes the individual central rather than the universal, accents individual freedom and responsibility, and highlights the absurd character of reality. Although some existentialists are atheists, there are also existentialist **theologians,** such as Søren Kierkegaard (1813–1855); they often espouse **fideism.**

existentialist As an adjective, pertaining to **existentialism;** as a noun: a proponent of **existentialism.**

existentially From the point of view of existence; or from the point of view of the meaning something has for human beings.

expected utility Suppose *S* is deciding whether to do *A* or to do *B* but does not know all the facts that are relevant to making the decision. To decide on the most rational action, *S* assigns probabilities to the various unknown facts, along with a utility or value to each possible outcome of the action. Then *S* applies a formula to arrive at the expected utility (also called expected value) of each action and does the action with the highest expected utility. The concept of expected utility is used to represent Pascal's reasoning in his wager argument. The formula for calculating expected utility is found in the Lycan-Schlesinger article (Reading 7.7).

explanandum In an explanation, a fact or event being explained; more precisely, a statement that describes the fact being explained.

extrovertive Outer directed; used to describe a type of mystical experience. An extrovertive mystical experience is directed outwards, i.e., the mystic discovers the divine in the world outside. Contrasts with **introvertive** mystical experience.

fallacy An **argument** that may appear to be **valid** but really is not. In both formal and informal logic, various types of fallacies are identified and given names; see, *e.g.,* **fallacy of equivocation.**

fallacy of equivocation The **fallacy** of inferring a conclusion from a set of premises when a term is used with one meaning in the premises and another in the conclusion, and the inference would be **valid** were the term used with the same meaning in both premises and conclusion.

falsifiability The property, ascribed to statements, hypotheses and theories, of being open to testing that could lead to their rejection as false. The philosopher Karl Popper (1902–1994) maintained that the distinguishing mark of scientific statements, hypotheses, and theories, as opposed to pseudoscientific ones, is that the scientific ones are falsifiable.

feminist theology A **theology** that describes God in terms and images associated with femininity.

fideism (1) The view that religious belief *is* based on faith and not reason. (2) The view that religious belief *should be* based on faith and not reason. The denial of **rationalism.**

fideist As an adjective: pertaining to **fideism;** as a noun: a proponent of **fideism.**

final causes An explanation of an event or phenomenon *E* by reference to final causes is an explanation in terms of the purposes of an intelligent agent. Thus, if one says that God designed the order in the world, one is explaining order by reference to final causes (in this case, God's purposes). Contrasts with **efficient causes.**

fine-tuning Fine-tuning is an alleged characteristic of the universe, to wit, that the basic laws of nature and cosmological constants are minutely adjusted to allow for life and/or intelligent life. The fine-tuning *argument* maintains that the existence of God provides the best explanation of fine-tuning.

fine-tuning argument See **fine-tuning.**

foreknowledge Knowledge of the future.

foundationalism The view that justified belief has foundations: in other words, that, in a system of justified beliefs, there are certain beliefs that are justified, but not on the basis of other beliefs, and that provide justificatory support for other beliefs.

free will theodicy An explanation of evil according to which evil, or at least the potential for evil, is necessary for the existence of free will.

functionalism The view that mental states are defined in terms of their functional roles—that is, their typical causes and effects (or input-output relations). For example, to be in pain is to be in a state of the kind that typically is caused in certain ways and causes certain effects.

future contingents (1) Facts about the future, or events or states-of-affairs in the future, that are not determined purely by the present, such as (on **incompatibilist** views of free will) an individual's freely doing or refraining from a certain action in the future. (2) Statements or propositions about such facts, events, or states-of-affairs. Philosophers ask whether God knows future-tensed statements like *Jack will shave his beard on March 28, 2007,* since if God does know such truths, it would seem that Jack's choice to shave his beard cannot be free.

G. E. Moore shift Suppose you are given an argument: *p, q,* therefore *r*. You are using the G. E. Moore shift (named for the twentieth-century British philosopher who used such an argument to combat **skepticism**) if, instead of arguing directly against *p,* you try to refute *p* by constructing another argument: not-*r, q,* therefore not-*p*. Sometimes this is called reversing an argument.

***gedanken* experiment** A thought experiment in which one imagines a hypothetical scenario and comes to a conclusion about what else would be true in that scenario.

genetic fallacy To commit this **fallacy** is to infer that a belief is false or true from a premise stating the causal origin of the belief, *in a case where this inference is fallacious;* that is, a case in which a statement about the truth or falsehood of the belief does not really follow from a statement about its causal origins. (Sometimes the origin of a belief *is* relevant to its truth or falsehood.)

genuine option In William James's "The Will to Believe," a genuine option is an option that is living, forced, and momentous. These terms are defined in James's essay (Reading 7.8).

genus See **genus and species.**

genus and species In reading 1.1 (by Aquinas), the general category or genus (in that selection, emotion) is distinguished from the species—that is, specific types of things falling under that category (such as anger or love). Usually the terms are used for biological classifications.

geocentrism The now rejected view that the earth is at the center of the universe.

Gnosticism An outlook that originated in the first and second centuries C.E., emphasizing a dualism of spirit and matter, liberation from material things, and the existence of inferior, even evil powers (including the creator of the world) that originated from the supreme power.

god of the gaps When someone postulates God as a means of filling in gaps of our understanding of nature, philosophers say that the person believes in the god of the gaps.

Gödel's law David Johnson uses this term to describe the principle of twentieth-century mathematician/logician Kurt Gödel that, if a property is positive, and nothing could have it without having a certain other property, then that other property is positive as well.

Goldbach's Conjecture The conjecture by Russian mathematician Christian Goldbach (1690–1764) (who lacked a proof for the proposition) that every even number (in modern formulations, every even number greater than 2) is the sum of two **prime numbers.**

grue An adjective made up by twentieth century philosopher Nelson Goodman. An object *x* is grue if and only if either *x* is first examined before temporal interval *T* and is green, or is not examined before *T* and is blue. Goodman used *grue* to make a point about what predicates are "projectible," that is, can be legitimately extrapolated in **inductive arguments.** *Green* is projectible, *grue* is not. We would not argue, *all hitherto examined emeralds are grue, therefore all emeralds are grue;* but we would argue, *all hitherto examined emeralds are green, therefore all emeralds are green.*

hard facts See **hard facts and soft facts.**

hard facts and soft facts A hard fact is a fact that is simply about the past; a soft fact is a fact about the past that is not simply about the past—for example, *In 1941, a war began between Japan and the United States that lasted five years.* Philosophers debate whether *God knew (believed) in 1821 that Booth would shoot Lincoln in 1865* is a hard fact or soft fact.

hardening (of the hearts) In the Bible, God is said to harden the hearts of certain individuals, resulting in their doing a wrong act. Thus, when God hardens the heart of Pharaoh, the king of Egypt who enslaves the Israelites in the biblical book Exodus, Pharaoh refuses to release the Israelites, despite the plagues being inflicted by God on Egypt.

heilgeschichte Sacred history, i.e., a history of the divine presence and activity in human history.

hellenization The process of being affected by Hellenistic (ancient Greek) influences. The charge of Hellenization in **theology** is that, in assigning to God such properties as **immutability, impassibility,** and timelessness, religious philosophers have been unduly influenced by Greek principles and conceptions of perfection.

hermeneutical Interpretive.

hermeneutics Method of interpretation or theory of interpretation.

heteronomous Imposed by another, as opposed to **autonomous** (imposed by oneself). If S does *A* only because someone else has commanded S to do *A,* S acts heteronomously.

hiddenness God is hidden in the sense that there is no unambiguous evidence that God exists. This fact leads to the question: if God exists, why is He hidden?

homology In evolutionary biology, a similarity of form, structure, or function based upon common evolutionary origins. For example, the forelimbs of humans and bats are homologous. Some similarities of form are *analogous* but not *homologous,* such as the wings of birds and those of insects.

idealism (1) The view that all that exists is mental. (2) The view that all reality is mind-dependent. Contrasts with **realism** in sense (1) of that entry.

idealist As an adjective, reflecting **idealism;** as a noun, an adherent of idealism.

identity theory The view that every mental property, state, or event is really a physical property, state, or event. This view usually is supported today by correlations that scientists have discovered between mental properties, states, and events, and physical ones.

illusion In Sigmund Freud's thought, an illusion is a belief that results from wishful thinking but that might be true nonetheless. A delusion, by contrast, is a belief that results from wishful thinking and is false.

imitatio dei The imitation or emulation of God.

immortality (of the soul) The continued and endless existence of a person after the death of the body.

immutability The property of being **immutable.**

immutable Unchangeable. In perfect being theology, God is said to be immutable and, for that reason along with others, **impassible.**

impassibility The property of being **impassible.**

impassible Incapable of experiencing passions or emotions; or, incapable of being affected by external influences. In **perfect being theology,** God is said to be impassible in both senses. Some purported advocates of impassibility, such as Aquinas, might assign to God some emotions, such as love and delight, while denying God has passions (see Reading 1.1).

Incarnation In Christian **theology,** the doctrine that God became incarnate in the body of Jesus.

incompatibilism The view that free will is incompatible with **determinism.**

incompatibilist As an adjective: reflecting **incompatibilism;** as a noun: one who endorses **incompatibilism.**

incorrigible A belief is incorrigible if and only if it is not subject to correction by further evidence.

inclusivism The view that only one religion is fully correct, but adherents of religions other than the true one can achieve salvation.

Induction (1) the pattern of inference used in an **inductive argument** (2) the (psychological) process of reasoning by means of an **inductive argument.**

inductive argument An **argument** from observed instances of a correlation (for example, of *a*-type events being followed by *b*-type events) to either: a universal generalization (*all* a-*type events are followed by* b-*type events*); or unobserved instances (*this* a-*type event will be followed by a* b-*type event*); or a non-universal statistical generalization, e.g., 90% of *a*-type events will be followed by *b*-type events. See also **deductive argument.**

inductive evidence Evidence that supports but does not logically entail the proposition for which it is evidence. (See **inductive argument.**)

ineffable Indescribable or inexpressible (or inexpressible in words).

infinite regress An infinite backward series. An infinite regress **argument** is an argument stating that it is the case that *p* because, if not-*p* were the case, the result would be an infinite regress. Infinite regress arguments discussed in this book include the argument that there must be a first mover because, if everything in motion were put into motion by something else, the result would be an infinite regress; and the argument that some beliefs are foundational (see **foundationalism**) because, if every belief had to be justified by another belief, the result would be an infinite regress.

instantiation (1) The application of a general statement to a particular instance. (2) An instance of a generalization. (3) When a particular object exemplifies a certain property, we say the property is instantiated.

intersubjective testing The testing of a claim by means that are accessible to other people. For example, a claim that *there is a banana on the table* may be tested by determining what other people observe; however, according to Levinson and Malino (Reading 4.13), the claim *I saw God,* as used by mystics, is not intersubjectively testable.

introvertive Inner directed; used to describe a type of mystical experience that is directed inward, i.e., the mystic discovers the divine reality in the deepest part of the self. Contrasts with **extrovertive** mystical experience.

isotropy Smoothness or evenness in all directions; used with reference to, *e.g.,* the facts that matter is distributed equally throughout the universe, and that the background temperature varies only slightly from region to region.

is-ought fallacy The (alleged) fallacy of inferring a normative (evaluative) conclusion (e.g., an ought-statement) from a factual premise or set of factual premises (is-statements). Associated with a statement by Scottish philosopher David Hume (1711–1776).

karma In Hindu and Buddhist thought, the law or force whereby right actions bring benefits and wrong actions bring adversity, in this or a future existence.

kerygma Message of the Gospel.

Leibnizian Having to do with philosopher-mathematician Gottfried Wilhelm Leibniz (1646–1716).

lemma A theorem proved in the course of proving, and for the purpose of proving, another theorem.

libertarian As an adjective: reflecting **libertarianism;** as a noun, one who endorses **libertarianism.**

libertarian free will The kind of free will that satisfies the conditions set forth in **libertarianism.**

libertarianism A form of **incompatibilism,** *viz.,* the view that (1) free will is incompatible with **determinism** and (2) human beings have free will. (Thus, libertarians hold that **determinism** is false.)

logical positivism A form of **positivism** popular in British and European philosophy in the first half of the twentieth century.

logical positivist An adherent of **logical positivism.**

logical problem of evil One of two major versions of what is called the problem of evil, the other being known as the **evidential problem of evil.** According to the logical version, *God exists* is *logically incompatible* with *evil exists.*

logical truth A truth that is true necessarily, by logic alone.

materialism (1) The view that all objects (or substances) and all their properties are material, so that there are no abstract objects, disembodied minds, or irreducibly mental properties. (2) The view that all objects (or substances) are material (which leaves room for non-material *properties*). See also **eliminative materialism, nonreductive materialism.**

materialistic Reflecting **materialism.**

matters of fact David Hume divides objects of inquiry into two categories: relations of ideas and matters of fact. In relations of ideas the truth of the negation of the proposition inquired into is inconceivable (as in math and geometry); in matters of fact the truth of the negation is conceivable. This distinction corresponds, roughly if not fully, to that between **necessary truths** and **contingent truths.**

memory criterion of personal identity A criterion according to which personal identity is determined by apparent memory: a person who has some experience e_2 at time t_2 is identical with a person who had some experience e_1 at an earlier time t_1 if and only if the person having e_2 has an apparent memory of e_1. Contrasts with a bodily criterion of personal identity.

metabelief A belief about beliefs.

metaethical thesis A thesis about the meanings of ethical terms, how ethical knowledge is acquired, and other questions that are distinct from questions of the type "is this-or-that action morally right?"

metaethics The branch of ethics that studies the meanings of ethical terms, the nature of ethical properties (good, bad, right, wrong), how ethical knowledge is acquired, and other questions pertaining to ethical concepts and the justification of ethical beliefs.

metaphysical Having to do with issues and concepts of **metaphysics.** Metaphysical questions are questions about what exists, metaphysical truths are truths about what exists, etc.

metaphysical possibility Real possibility, as opposed to mere **epistemic possibility.**

metaphysician One who develops views in **metaphysics.**

metaphysics (1) The branch of philosophy that seeks to describe the most general features of the world, such as existence, identity, physicality, mentality, and causality. (2) The study of entities and properties that are not physical. (3) A thinker's approach to issues in (1) and (2), e.g., "Locke's metaphysics." Locke's metaphysics, A metaphysical thesis (a thesis about what is the case) should be distinguished from an **epistemological** thesis (a thesis about whether and how we can know what is the case).

metonymically By means of a metonym, i.e., a figure of speech that uses the name of one thing to refer to another thing with which it is associated or of which it is an attribute. Example: "the crown" (used to refer to a government).

middle knowledge Knowledge of how every possible creature would freely act in any possible circumstance. A philosopher who says that God has simple **foreknowledge** (knowledge of what will *actually* happen) might nonetheless deny that God has middle knowledge. See also **Molinism.**

modal Having to do with necessity and possibility.

modal fallacy A **fallacy** involving the concepts of possibility and necessity.

modal logic A branch of logic that deals with the logic of possibility and necessity; for example, *if it is necessary that* p, *it is not possible that not*-p is a truth of modal logic.

Molinism A view associated with sixteenth-century Spanish Jesuit thinker Luis de Molina. Molinism attempts to affirm both that God controls everything that happens and that human beings have free will. It reconciles these two ostensibly contradictory doctrines by saying that God has **middle knowledge**—knowledge of how every possible creature would freely act in any possible circumstance. God creates or actualizes those individuals whose free choices will best help realize God's plans for the world.

Molinists Adherents of **Molinism.**

monism The view that reality is of one type, e.g., everything is physical, everything is mental, everything is neither physical nor mental.

myth A system of images, symbols, and stories used to talk about the divine or the otherworldly. (In this sense, a myth can be true.)

natural evil Evil not directly due to the actions of human beings.

natural religion A religion that is not based on revelation but rather on "natural" thought and observation, e.g., **arguments** for God's existence. Thus, David Hume's *Dialogues Concerning Natural Religion* examines whether the claims of traditional theism can be shown to be true without revelation.

natural selection According to Charles Darwin's theory of evolution, some variations among members of a species confer an advantage upon those members in the competition for survival. This part of the theory is called the theory of natural selection.

natural theologian One who engages in **natural theology.**

natural theology The enterprise of arguing for the existence of God and other tenets of theism from nontheistic premises. The various **arguments** for God's existence appraised in this book are part of natural theology.

naturalism A term with many meanings; in this book, *naturalism* usually refers to the view that only objects capable of being studied in the sciences exist (there are no supernatural entities) and that scientific method is the only means of acquiring truth. Many naturalists espouse **materialism.**

naturalist As an adjective: **naturalistic;** as a noun: an adherent of **naturalism.**

naturalist (or naturalistic) definition In **metaethics,** a naturalist definition is one that defines some ethical term (for example, *right, wrong*) as some "natural" property such as producing pleasure or producing pain.

naturalistic Reflecting **naturalism.**

necessary being Variously characterized as a being (1) that logically could not have failed to exist, (2) that exists by its own nature, or (3) whose existence is self-explained.

necessary condition *A* is a necessary condition of *B* when the following obtains: if *B*, then *A*. (See also **sufficient condition.**)

necessary and sufficient conditions See **necessary condition, sufficient condition.**

necessary truth See **contingent truth vs. necessary truth.**

negative existential claim A claim that a particular kind of thing does not exist—for example, *there is no justification for this animal's suffering*.

negative theology (1) Broadly speaking, the theory that we can say only what God is not and cannot characterize God positively. (2) More technically, the thesis that *God is Q* means that *God is not not-Q,* which for Maimonides means in turn that neither the concept of *Q* nor the concept of *not-Q* applies to God. (See Reading 2.1.)

nihilist One who embraces nihilism, the denial of the existence of something, e.g., values.

noetic Intellectual, pertaining to the mind.

nomic Lawlike (in the sense of a law of nature).

nominalism In medieval times, the view that properties or universals do not exist; predicates and common nouns are but names that refer to many particular things. Used in various additional ways in contemporary philosophy, with the upshot that only individuals exist. The term ***realism*** is usually used to denote the opposite of nominalism.

noncognitivism The view (in our context) that religious statements do not state facts but instead serve other functions, such as arousing emotions or influencing behavior. (One could also be a noncognitivist with regard to other areas, such as ethics.)

nonreductive materialism The view that mental properties are grounded in physical ones but are not identical to them.

non sequitur An argument in which the conclusion does not follow from the premises. Technically, any fallacious inference is a *non sequitur,* but the label is usually reserved for egregious instances of this sort.

normative Evaluative, as opposed to purely descriptive. Terms like *good, bad, right, wrong, justified* and *unjustified* are normative terms.

noumena See **noumena and phenomena.**

noumena and phenomena A distinction found in the writings of Immanuel Kant between, respectively, things as they really are (the noumena or **things in themselves**) and things as they appear to us due to the specific ways in which we human beings structure sensory input (the phenomena). The noumena are not accessible to our cognitive faculties.

noumenal Relating to **noumena.**

numinous German theologian Rudolph Otto (1869–1937) described the experience of God and other experiences as numinous, i.e., apart from the world of ordinary observation and non-rational.

Occam's razor See **Ockham's razor.**

occasionalism The view that God is the only true cause of things and that what people commonly call natural causes are merely the occasion for God's causal activity.

Ockham's razor A principle, associated with William of Ockham (1287–1347), that, in choosing between rival theories in science or **ontology,** one should choose the theory that is "simpler," other things being equal. Known also as the principle of parsimony and often expressed as (these are not Ockham's own words) "do not multiply entities without necessity."

omnibenevolent All-good.

omnidetermination God's bringing about every detail of creation.

omnipercipient Perceiving everything.

omnipotence The property of being **omnipotent.**

omnipotent All-powerful.

omniscience The property of being **omniscient.**

omniscient All-knowing.

ontological Having to do with being. To inquire into the ontological status of, for example, numbers, is to inquire whether numbers exist and if so what sort of entity a number is.

ontologically With regard to being.

ontological arguments Arguments for the existence of God that seek to prove that God exists from the very concept of God as the greatest conceivable being.

ontology Theory of being. To speak of "person S's ontology" is to speak of S's views about what exists and what does not exist.

open God See **openness of God.**

open view of God See **openness of God.**

openness of God A recent approach to God's nature that denies key elements of **perfect being theology.** In open God **theology,** for example, God does not know every detail of the future, is not **immutable,** and has emotions.

open question argument An argument by which Cambridge philosopher G. E. Moore (1873–1958) sought to refute **naturalistic** definitions of ethical terms. Suppose a naturalist says that *right* means having property *P*. Moore says the definition is incorrect because we can always intelligibly ask, "granted action *A* has *P*, but is *A* right?" Moore included in his critique not only definitions given by adherents of **utilitarianism** but also definitions given by proponents of **divine command theories.**

ordering In Thomas Aquinas's theory of **analogy,** a relationship—the details of which are debated by scholars and depend, *inter alia,* on the type of analogy being considered.

pantheism The view that God is everything; usually associated with the thesis that God is nature.

pantheistic Reflecting **pantheism.**

paradox An apparently **sound** line of **argument,** based on apparently true premises, that leads to a contradiction or other obviously false conclusion.

parapsychology The study of such phenomena as extrasensory perception, near-death experiences, and telekinesis.

parity arguments Arguments that seek to show that, although religious beliefs cannot be shown true by rational argument, they are nevertheless rational because other beliefs that are widely regarded as eminently rational likewise cannot be shown true by rational argument.

parousia (Second) advent of the redeemer.

perfect being theology An approach to characterizing God, adopted by Anselm and Aquinas, that assigns to God every property we judge to be a great-making (perfection-making) property. In perfect being theology, God is said to be **omniscient, omnipotent, omnibenevolent, eternal, immutable, and simple.**

peripatetics Philosophers in the tradition founded by Aristotle (d. 322). The term derives either from *peripatein* (walking about) or *peripatos* (collonade, where teaching took place).

petitionary prayer Prayer that requests God to do something.

phenomena See **noumena and phenomena.**

phenomenal Relating to how things appear.

phenomenally With respect to appearance(s), particularly sensory appearance(s).

phenomenological Pertaining to inner experience.

phenomenologist An adherent of **phenomenology** in sense (3) of that term.

phenomenology (1) Inner presentation; (2) description of consciousness; (3) the name of a 20th-21st century philosophical approach that focuses on the description of consciousness.

Pickwickian A Pickwickian sense of a term is an obscure or esoteric sense, one that pays attention to relatively insignificant features of the term.

Platonism The philosophy associated with Plato.

pluralism The view that seemingly contradictory viewpoints are all acceptable; for application to religion, see **religious pluralism.**

pluralist/pluralistic As an adjective: reflecting **pluralism;** as a noun, *pluralist* means an adherent of **pluralism.**

positivism A view that the only meaningful statements are statements that are subject to empirical testing (they can be empirically verified and/or falsified).

possible world The concept of a possible world is used to facilitate thinking about the **modal** notions necessity and possibility and related notions like **contingency.** For example, *it is possible that p* can be understood as *it is true that* p *in some possible world; it is necessary that p* can be understood as *it is true that p in all possible worlds.* While talking about possible worlds is very useful, the nature and **ontological** status of possible worlds (Do they really exist? what are they?) is a matter of considerable debate among philosophers.

posterior sense (of a term) See **prior and posterior predication.**

potency See **actuality vs. potentiality.**

potentia absoluta and potentia ordinata *Potentia absoluta* is God's power considered in abstraction from God's wisdom and goodness; *potentia ordinata* is God's power considered as controlled in its exercise by God's wisdom and goodness.

pragmatic Reflecting practical considerations such as those accented by **pragmatism.**

pragmatism An American philosophical movement that began in the late nineteenth century. For purposes of this text (and, in particular, the selection by William James [Reading 7.8]), the key feature of pragmatism is its stress on assessing beliefs by their practical consequences rather than the state of the evidence alone.

pragmatist An adherent of pragmatism.

predestination The doctrine that God has ordered from eternity everything that happens.

prime number A number that is divisible without remainder only by 1 and by itself (i.e., 2, 3, 5, 7, 11, 13 . . .). (Modern mathematicians do not treat 1 as a prime.)

principle of sufficient reason The thesis that every fact (or every positive fact, or every event, or every change—there are various versions) has an explanation. There are no **brute facts.**

prior and posterior predication Some philosophers (e.g., Gersonides) say that terms apply to God in the primary sense and to humans in the secondary sense. This means that God possesses these properties to a perfect degree and causes humans to possess them, but to a lesser degree.

prior sense (of a term) See **prior and posterior predication.**

private language A language in which a person communicates to him- or herself (about, e.g., inner states) but which others cannot understand. By means of the "private language argument," Ludwig Wittgenstein (1889–1951) argued that there cannot be a private language.

probabilistic argument An argument whose premises are said to confer high probability on the conclusion, though it is still logically possible for the premises to be true and the conclusion false.

process theism/process theology A theory of God pioneered by Alfred North Whitehead (1861–1947). In process theology, (1) the world and God are interdependent; (2) God is not **immutable** and not timeless, nor does God know the future completely, nor does God control everything—instead God persuades rather than coerces results.

projection A term used by Ludwig Feuerbach to denote the process by which human beings arrive at the concept of God; they project their own qualities onto another being, not realizing the qualities are really theirs.

property dualism See **dualism.**

proximate cause In a causal chain leading from *A* to *B* to *C* . . . to *Y* to *Z*, *Y* is the proximate (near, immediate) cause of *Z* while *A* is the remote (ultimate) cause. *B* . . . *X* are intermediate causes.

prudence Calculated self-interest.

prudential Based on considerations of **prudence;** in the case of belief, based on considerations of prudence rather than the state of the evidence alone.

punctuated equilibrium A term in evolutionary biology that refers to the thesis (held by Stephen Jay Gould and others) that evolution occurs through long periods of stasis, or little change, which are interrupted by rapid evolutionary changes. The thesis seems to explain the lack of transitional forms in parts of the fossil record.

Pure Act Pure actuality. (See **actuality vs. potentiality.**)

pyrrhonism A form of **skepticism** associated with the Hellenistic philosopher Pyrrho of Elis (365 B.C.E.–270 B.C.E.).

Pyrrhonistic skepticism See **Pyrrhonism.**

quantum mechanics See **quantum physics.**

quantum physics The branch of physics that studies atomic and subatomic particles.

question-begging See **begging the question.**

quiddity In medieval philosophy, whatness or essence.

random mutation In Darwin's theory of evolution, there are variations (mutations) in the characteristics of living things that occur randomly and lead to differentiations of species.

rationalism (1) The view that some knowledge is not derived from sense experience (this is the denial of **empiricism**). (2) The view that reason plays a positive role in religious life, such as by proving the existence of God; the denial of **fideism.**

rationalist As a noun: adherent of **rationalism;** as an adjective: pertaining to **rationalism.**

realism (1) The view that there are things whose existence is independent of the mind. Contrasts with **idealism** in sense (2) of that entry. (Some philosophers deny that *God exists* expresses a literal truth. They are antirealists with regard to God.) (2) The opposite of **nominalism:** according to realism, properties really do exist independently of the objects that are said to have those properties. Also called Platonism.

reductio ad absurdum An **argument** that tries to prove that *p* by showing that, if we assume not-*p,* a contradiction results.

reductive materialism The view that the mental can be reduced to the material.

reflective equilibrium A term originated by Nelson Goodman in connection with **deductive** and **inductive** reasoning, and later used by John Rawls in connection with **metaethics.** In Rawls's work, it refers to a mutual adjustment or equilibrium between judgments about ethical principles and ethical judgments about particular cases, an adjustment from which (in conjunction with other judgments), new conclusions are derived.

Reformed Adhering to views associated with the Reformed tradition of sixteenth century Protestantism; see for example **Reformed epistemology.**

Reformed epistemologist An adherent of **Reformed epistemology.**

Reformed epistemology An approach to the rationality or justification of religious belief which denies that religious beliefs must be justified by deriving them from nonreligious premises, as they are in **natural theology.** In Alvin Plantinga's version of Reformed epistemology, certain beliefs about God are *properly basic* and are rational or justified for that reason. The term derives from the Reformed tradition in sixteenth-century Protestantism.

reincarnation The view that, after a person dies, the person's soul or mind lives in another body.

relations of ideas See **matters of fact.**

reliabilism The view that a belief is justified if and only if it is formed by reliable processes, i.e., processes likely to yield truth.

reliabilist As a noun: adherent of **reliabilism;** as an adjective: having to do with reliabilism.

religious pluralism The view that all religions are correct, meaning either that all are true or (as used by some writers) that all lead to salvation, fulfillment, and liberation.

religious pluralist: as an adjective, reflecting **religious pluralism;** as a noun, a proponent of **religious pluralism.**

remote cause See **proximate cause.**

repression In psychoanalytic theory, a process by which painful or unacceptable desires, impulses, feelings, beliefs, and thoughts are excluded from consciousness, leaving them to operate only in the unconscious.

resurrection The bringing back to life of the body of a person who has died. When capitalized, the word usually refers to a period in the future when many people will be resurrected.

salvific Leading to salvation.

sceptic See under the spelling **skeptic.**

scepticism See under the heading **skepticism.**

scholastics Christian philosophers who taught in universities during the twelfth through fifteenth centuries.

scientific creationism The view that the biblical story of creation in chapter one of Genesis provides an account of origins that is superior *from a scientific standpoint* to the theory of evolution.

scientism The thesis that science is the only reliable guide to truth.

scientistic Reflecting **scientism.**

second law of thermodynamics A law stating that processes taking place in a closed system always tend toward a state of equilibrium; that is, there is an increase in entropy, which is a measure of disorder and breakdown in the system.

semantic-like relation A *semantic* relation is any relation between a linguistic symbol and the world, such as reference, denotation, or exemplification. A *semantic-like* relation is any relation between a linguistic *or non-*

linguistic symbol and the world; thus, a picture might bear a semantic-like relation to the world.

sensible Capable of being experienced through the senses.

severally necessary and jointly sufficient conditions Conditions C1 . . . Cn are severally necessary and jointly sufficient for event E if and only if each condition in C1 . . . Cn is a **necessary condition** of E and the conjunction C1 . . . Cn is a **sufficient condition** of E.

shamans Religious leaders of a tribal people who, in order to address social ills or heal diseases, employ trance states to communicate with the supernatural realm. The term originally meant holy men or women in the language of the Tungus, a Siberian tribe.

simple See **simplicity.**

simplicity (1) In medieval religious philosophy, a being is simple when it has no parts. Medieval philosophers often say that God is simple and therefore does not have separate attributes. (2) In science, the "economy" or "parsimony" of a theory. (See **Ockham's razor.**)

skeptic A person who accepts **skepticism.**

skepticism (1) The view that all claims to knowledge are false (except the claim to know that all claims to knowledge are false); (2) the view that all claims to knowledge in a certain domain are false. The term *religious skepticism* is often used to refer to the view of someone who doubts or denies the existence of God.

soft facts See **hard facts and soft facts.**

soteriological Pertaining to salvation or redemption.

soteriology A theory of salvation.

soul-making theodicy The **theodicy** which says that God is justified in allowing evil because evil is logically necessary for the development of human virtues such as sympathy, benevolence or charity, courage, and faith.

sound argument A **valid argument** all of whose premises are true.

special creation The thesis that at least some species did not arise by evolution; rather, God created them directly.

species See **genus and species.**

steady-state theory The theory that the universe has always existed in the same state. Contrasts with **big bang theory.**

stipulative definition A definition that is stipulated by the user of a term and does not necessarily reflect how the term is commonly used.

sub specie eternatis Under the aspect of eternity—that is, considered from a cosmic, eternal perspective.

substance Usually used in this book to refer to something, or to the part of a thing, that bears properties, in other words, in which properties inhere. Also used to refer to that which is capable of existing independently, and to what a thing is made of.

substance dualism See **dualism.**

sufficient condition *A* is a sufficient condition of *B* when the following obtains: if *A,* then *B*. (See also **necessary condition.**)

supervenience A property (or fact) *P* supervenes on properties (or facts) $Q_1 \ldots Q_n$ if and only if *P* is grounded in $Q_1 \ldots Q_n$—that is, it exists only because of $Q_1 \ldots Q_n$. For example, someone might hold that consciousness supervenes on neurophysiological facts or properties.

symmetrical relation A relation *R* is symmetrical when the following holds for every *a* and *b*: if *a* bears *R* to *b*, then *b* bears *R* to *a*. For example, if *a* is equal to *b*, then *b* is equal to *a*. So, the relation *is equal to* is symmetrical.

tautological A tautological statement is one that expresses a **tautology.**

tautology A statement whose denial is self-contradictory and which is therefore necessarily false. Except in parts of formal logic, most writers reserve the term for obvious and uninteresting **necessary truths.**

teleological Purposive.

teleological argument Another term for **design argument.**

teleological suspension of the ethical In the thought of Søren Kierkegaard, this refers to the suspension of the ethical for a higher *telos* (purpose) outside of the ethical—namely, fulfilling God's command. Abraham's willingness to sacrifice his son Isaac is the example on which Kierkegaard elaborates.

teleology Purposiveness.

telos Purpose.

theism The view that God exists.

theodicy Literally, God's justice. A theodicy is an attempt to provide a justification for God's allowing evil. The term was coined by Gottfried Wilhelm von Leibniz (1646–1716).

theologian One who explores **theology.**

theological Having to do with issues in **theology.**

theology (1) A theory of God, including, prominently, God's nature. (2) A discipline in which one draws inferences about God or the world from premises, some of which may be based on revelation. (See, however, **natural theology.**)

theophany An appearance by God, as in divine revelation.

thing-in-itself See **noumena and phenomena.**

Thomism A school of Catholic philosophy deriving from Thomas Aquinas.

Thomistic Having to do with Thomas Aquinas.

transitive relation A relation *R* is transitive when the following holds for every *a, b,* and *c;* if *a* bears *R* to *b,* and *b* bears *R* to *c,* then *a* bears *R* to *c*. (Example: if *a* is larger than *b,* and *b* is larger than *c,* then *a* is larger than *c*. So the relation "larger than" is transitive.)

truth functional A compound statement is truth functional if and only if the truth value (truth or falsehood) of the compound statement is determined completely by the truth value of the components. (Examples of truth-functional compound statements: **conjunction, disjunction.**)

underdetermination A theory or hypothesis *H* is underdetermined by the evidence (or data) if and only if there is a hypothesis *H′* that is incompatible with *H* but is equally well supported by the evidence supporting *H* or by parallel evidence.

universal generalization (1) A statement about everything—for example, that everything has a property *P* or that everything is such that, if it has property *P,* it has property *Q*. (2) A rule of logic that allows one to infer a statement about everything from a statement or statements about an arbitrarily chosen object, in a special sense of *arbitrarily chosen:* roughly, the object chosen has no special features that would make it different from others with regard to the properties being investigated.

universal instantiation (1) A rule of logic that allows one to infer a statement about a particular thing (*a is Q*) from a statement that is true of everything (*for every x, x is Q*). (2) **instantiation.**

univocal See **univocal predication.**

univocal predication A term *Q* is said to be predicated univocally of subject A and subject B when *Q* has the same meaning in *A is Q* as it does in *B is Q*. Contrasts with **equivocal predication.**

univocally In a way reflecting **univocal predication.**

utilitarian As an adjective, having to do with consequences (see **utilitarianism**); as a noun, a person who accepts **utilitarianism.**

utilitarianism A **metaethical** theory that defines *right action* in terms of what brings about good consequences (e.g., happiness, pleasure) and *wrong action* in terms of what brings about bad consequences (e.g., pain).

valid argument An **argument** in which it is logically impossible for the premises to be true and the conclusion false.

veil of ignorance In John Rawls's ethical theory, the principles of justice are those which people would choose were they under a veil of ignorance, i.e., were they to lack knowledge of their own circumstances, such as their gender, religious beliefs, and economic status.

veridicality A veridical experience (one that has veridicality) is an experience that represents reality accurately. This could mean either that the experience really *is* of the entity it seems to be an experience of or that the object of the experience really has the properties that the experience represents it as having.

verifiability criterion (of meaning) A criterion of meaningfulness advocated by a school called logical **positivism** according to which a statement is meaningful only if it can be verified in principle. The meaning of a statement is given by its verifiability conditions.

Whiteheadian Following Alfred North Whitehead (1861–1947).

Wittgensteinian fideism The view, associated with twentieth-century philosopher Ludwig Wittgenstein, that religion is a "form of life," with its own "language game," and therefore cannot be evaluated from an external perspective.

Credits

In many cases selections have been abridged and notes renumbered or reformatted.

Reading 1.1: From Thomas Aquinas, *On the Truth of the Catholic Faith, Summa Contra Gentiles,* Book One: God, chs. 89 & 90, pp. 271–277. Copyright © 1955. By permission of the A. C. Pegis Estate.

Reading 1.2: From *Anselm, Monologion and Proslogion, With the Replies of Gaunilo and Anselm,* translated with introduction and notes, by Thomas Williams, ch. 8 (p. 104). Copyright © 1995, 1996. Reprinted by permission of Hackett Publishing Company.

Reading 1.3: Robert Oakes, "The Wrath of God," *International Journal for the Philosophy of Religion* 27, 1990, pp. 129–140. Copyright © 1990. Reprinted by permission of Lawrence Erlbaum Associates, Inc.

Reading 1.4: Charles Taliaferro, "The Vanity of God," *Faith and Philosophy*, *6*, 1989, pp. 140–155. Copyright © 1989. Reprinted by permission.

Reading 1.5: Anne C. Minas, "God and Forgiveness," *Philosophical Quarterly*, *25*, 1975, pp. 138–150. Copyright © 1975 by The Editors of The Philosophical Quarterly. Reprinted by permission of Blackwell Publishers.

Reading 1.6: Peter Geach, "Omnipotence," *Philosophy*, *48*, 1973, pp. 7–20. Reprinted with the permission of Cambridge University Press.

Reading 1.7: From *Philosophy of Religion: An Introduction, 2nd edition*, by W. L. Rowe © 1993. Reprinted with permission of Wadsworth, a division of Thomson Learning. Fax 800–730–2215.

Reading 1.8: Adapted from *The Openness of God* by Clark Pinnock, Richard Rice, John Sanders, William Hasker and David Basinger. © 1994. Used by Permission of Intervarsity Press, P.O. Box 1400, Downers Grove, IL 60515.

Reading 1.9: Nicholas Wolterstorff, "God Everlasting," from *God and the Good: Essays in Honor of Henry Stob*, Clifton J. Orlebeke and Lewis B. Smedes, eds., © 1975 Wm. B. Eerdmans Publishing Co., Grand Rapids, MI. Used by permission: all rights reserved.

Reading 1.10: Reproduced from PROCESS THEOLOGY: AN INTRODUCTORY EXPOSITION by John B. Cobb, Jr. and David Ray Griffin. © 1976 The Westminster Press. Used by permission of Westminster John Knox Press.

Reading 2.1: Moses Maimonides, "Negative Theology," in *Guide of the Perplexed,* trans. by Shlomo Pines, Pt. 1, chs. 57–59, vol. 1, pp. 132–139. Reprinted by permission of the publisher, the University of Chicago Press.

Reading 2.2: Gersonides (Levi ben Gershom), from *Wars of the Lord, II,* trans. Seymour Feldman, pp. 108–112. Copyright © 1987. Reprinted by permission of the Jewish Publication Society.

Reading 2.4: From Thomas Aquinas, *Summa Theologiae* 1.13.5 and *Disputed Questions: On Truth* 2.11, as translated by James F. Ross in Ross, *Introduction to the Philosophy of Religion* (The MacMillan Company, 1969), pp. 159–63. Used by permission of James F. Ross.

Reading 2.5: Ira M. Schnall, "Philosophy, Poetry, and the Bible." Published for the first time. Used by permission of the author.

Reading 2.6: From George F. Hourani, *Averroes on the Harmony of Religion and Philosophy*, pp. 50–52. Copyright © 1961. Published by Luzac & Co., UK.

Reading 2.7: From Rudolph Bultmann, *Kerygma and Myth*, ed. H. W. Barisch, tr. R. M. Fuller, pp. 1–16. Copyright © 1961. Reprinted by permission of SPCK.

Reading 2.8: Adapted from "Doctrine," *Faith and Philosophy*, Vol. 14, No. 4, October 1997, and "Theological Impressionism," *Judaism*, Vol. 49, No. 2, Spring 2000. Used by permission of Howard K. Wettstein.

Reading 2.9: Patricia Altenbernd Johnson, "Feminist Christian Philosophy?," *Faith and Philosophy, 9*, 3, July 1992, pp. 320–334. Copyright © 1992. Reprinted by permission.

Reading 3.1: From Plato, *Euthyphro*, trans. G. M. A. Grube, pp. 18–21. Reprinted by permission of Hackett Publishing Company, Inc. All rights reserved.

Reading 3.2: From *Contemporary Jewish Religious Thought*, by Josef Stern, The Gale Group 1987. Copyright © 1987. Reprinted by permission of The Gale Group.

Reading 3.3: Michael J. Murray and Kurt Meyers, "Ask and It Will Be Given to You." *Religious Studies, 30*, pp. 311–330. Reprinted with the permission of Cambridge University Press.

Reading 3.4: From Plato, *Euthyphro,* trans. G. M. A. Grube. Reprinted by permission of Hackett Publishing Company, Inc. All rights reserved.

Reading 3.5: Janine Marie Idziak, *Divine Command Morality: Historical and Contemporary Readings*, pp. 3–5. 8-36. Copyright © 1979. Reprinted by permission of Edwin Mellen Press.

Reading 3.7: Hong and Hong (trans.), *Fear and Trembling*. Copyright © 1983 by Princeton University Press. Reprinted by permission of Princeton University Press.

Reading 3.8: James Rachels, "God and Human Attitudes," *Religious Studies*, 7, pp. 325–337, sects. 1, 3–6 only. Reprinted with the permission of Cambridge University Press.

Reading 4.1: From *Anselm, Monologion and Proslogion, With the Replies of Gaunilo and Anselm*, translated, with introduction and notes, by Thomas Williams, chs. 2 & 3 (pp. 99–101). Copyright © 1995, 1996. Reprinted by permission of Hackett Publishing Company.

Reading 4.2: From *Anselm, Monologion and Proslogion, With the Replies of Gaunilo and Anselm*, translated, with introduction and notes, by Thomas Williams (pp. 124–125). Copyright © 1995, 1996. Reprinted by permission of Hackett Publishing Company.

Reading 4.3: David Johnson, "A Modal Version of the Ontological Argument." Published for the first time. Used by permission of the author.

Reading 4.4: Thomas Aquinas, "The Five Ways," in *The Basic Writings of Saint Thomas Aquinas.* ed. Anton Pegis, 1945, pp. 25–27. Reprinted by permission of Hackett Publishing Company, Inc. All rights reserved.

Reading 4.5: Paul Edwards, "The Cosmological Argument," *The Rationalist Annual* (1959), pp. 63–77. Reprinted by Permission of Paul Edwards.

Reading 4.6: William Lane Craig, "Philosophical and Scientific Pointers to Creatio ex Nihilo," revised version, from *Journal of the American Scientific Affiliation 32,* March 1980. Reprinted by permission of the author.

Reading 4.7: From *Philosophy of Religion: An Introduction, 2nd edition,* by W. L. Rowe © 1993. Reprinted with permission of Wadsworth, an imprint of the Wadsworth Group, a division of Thomson Learning. Fax 800–730–2215.

Reading 4.9: From Stephen T. Davis, *God, Reason and Theistic Proofs.* © 1997 Stephen T. Davis, used by permission of Wm. B. Eerdmans Publishing Co., Grand Rapids, MI. All rights reserved.

Reading 4.10: Reprinted from Robert Hambourger, "The Argument from Design," in *Intention and Intentionality: Essays for G. E. M. Anscombe,* eds. Jenny Teichman and Cora Diamond. Copyright © 1979 by The Harvester Press, Ltd. Used by permission of the publisher, Cornell University Press.

Reading 4.11: © John Mackie 1982. Reprinted from *The Miracle of Theism: Arguments for and against the existence of God* by J. L. Mackie (1982) by permission of Oxford University Press.

Reading 4.12: Reprinted from Jerome I. Gellman: *Experience of God and the Rationality of Theistic Belief.* Copyright © 1997 by Cornell University. Used by permission of the publisher, Cornell University Press.

Reading 4.13: Jonathan Malino and Henry Levinson, "Who's Afraid of a BEE STING?" *Iyyun: Jerusalem Philosophical Quarterly, 48,* July 1999, pp. 293–297. Copyright © 1999. Reprinted by permission of *Iyyun: The Jerusalem Philosophical Quarterly.*

Reading 4.14: Evan Fales, "Scientific Explanations of Mystical Experiences: The Case of Saint Theresa," *Religious Studies, 32,* pp. 143–163, pt. I and pp. 297–313, pt. II. Reprinted with the permission of Cambridge University Press.

Reading 5.1: William L. Rowe, "The Problem of Evil and Some Varieties of Atheism," *American Philosophical Quarterly, 16,* pp. 335–341. Copyright © 1979. Reprinted by permission.

Reading 5.2: "The Inductive Argument from Evil and the Human Cognitive Condition," by William Alston appeared in *Philosophical Perspectives, 5, Philosophy of Religion, 1991* edited by James E. Tomberlin. Reprinted by permission of Ridgeview Publishing Company.

Reading 5.3: "The Mirror of Evil" by Eleonore Stump, from GOD AND THE PHILOSOPHERS: THE RECONCILIATION OF FAITH AND REASON, edited by Thomas V. Morris, copyright © 1996 by Thomas V. Morris. Used by permission of Oxford University Press, Inc.

Reading 5.4: © Richard Swinburne 1981. Reprinted from *Faith and Reason* by Richard Swinburne (1981) by permission of Oxford University Press.

Reading 5.5: Michael Murray, "Coercion and the Hiddenness of God," *American Philosophical Quarterly, 30,* 1993, pp. 27–38. Copyright © 1993. Reprinted by permission.

Reading 5.6: Xenophon, "Gods in the Image of Humans," Wallace Matson, trans., *A New History of Philosophy,* vol. 1, 1987, p. 22.

Reading 5.7: Baruch Spinoza, "How Human Ignorance Leads to Religion," in Samuel Shirley, trans., *The Ethics and Selected Letters,* pp. 57–66. Copyright © 1992. Reprinted by permission of Hackett Publishing Company, Inc. All rights reserved.

Reading 5.8: pp. 1–3, 27–35 from THE ESSENCE OF CHRISTIANITY by LUDWIG FEUERBACH. Copyright 1957 by Harper & Row, Publishers, Inc. Reprinted by permission of HarperCollins Publishers, Inc.

Reading 5.9: From THE FUTURE OF AN ILLUSION by Sigmund Freud, translated by James Strachey. Copyright © 1961 by James Strachey, renewed 1989 by Alix Strachey. Used by permission of W. W. Norton & Company, Inc., and The Random House Group Ltd.

Reading 5.10: From *Philosophy of Religion: An Introduction, 2nd edition,* by W. L. Rowe © 1993. Reprinted with permission of Wadsworth, a division of Thomson Learning. Fax 800–730–2215.

Reading 6.1: Excerpts from *Science & Religion* by John Haught/copyright © 1995// Used with permission of Paulist Press. www. paulistpress.com

Reading 6.2: From Alvin Plantinga, "When Faith and Reason Clash: Evolution and the Bible," from *Christian Scholar's Review,* Vol. XXI, No. 1, Sept. 1991, Special Issue: Creation/Evolution and Faith, p. 8. Copyright © 1991. Reprinted by permission of Christian Scholars' Review.

Reading 6.3: From Howard J. Van Till, "When Faith and Reason Cooperate," from *Christian Scholar's Review,* Vol. XXI, No. 1, Sept. 1991, Special Issue: Creation/Evolution and Faith, p. 33. Copyright © 1991. Reprinted by permission of Christian Scholars' Review.

Reading 6.4: Reprinted from *Reasoned Faith.* Eleonore Stump, ed. Copyright © 1978 by Cornell University. Used by permission of the publisher, Cornell University Press.

Reading 6.5: Robert Audi, "Theism and the Mind-Body Problem," in *Faith, Freedom and Rationality,* ed. J. Jordan and D. Howard-Snyder, pp. 155–169. Copyright © 1996. Reprinted by permission of Rowman & Littlefield Publishers.

Reading 6.6: © Richard Swinburne 1986. Reprinted from *The Evolution of the Soul* by Richard Swinburne (1986) by permission of Oxford University Press.

Reading 6.7: From THE POSSIBILITY OF RESURRECTION by PETER VAN INWAGEN. Copyright © 1998 by Westview Press. Reprinted by permission of Westview Press, a member of Perscus Books, L.L.C.

Reading 6.8: From *Evolution and Creation,* edited by Ernan McMullin. © 1986 by University of Notre Dame Press. Used by permission of the publisher.

Reading 6.10: From THE POSSIBILITY OF RESURRECTION by PETER VAN INWAGEN. Copyright © 1998 by Westview Press. Reprinted by permission of Westview Press, a member of Perscus Books, L.L.C.

Reading 6.12: Reprinted from David Johnson: *Hume, Holism, and Miracles.* Copyright © 1999 by

Cornell University. Used by permission of the publisher, Cornell University Press.

Reading 6.13: Stephen Griffith, "Miracles and the Shroud of Turin," *Faith and Philosophy, 13,* 1996, pp. 34–49. Copyright © 1996. Reprinted by permission.

Reading 7.2: Peter van Inwagen, "It is Wrong, Anywhere, Everywhere and for Anyone to Believe Anything on Insufficient Evidence: A Response to Clifford," from *Faith, Freedom and Rationality,* ed. J. Jordan and D. Howard-Snyder, pp. 137–153. Copyright © 1996. Reprinted by permission of Rowman & Littlefield Publishers.

Reading 7.3: Alvin Plantinga, "Rationality and Religious Belief," in *Contemporary Philosophy of Religion,* ed. S. M. Cahn and D. Shatz. Copyright © 1982. Published by Oxford University Press. Reprinted by permission of the author.

Reading 7.4: Terence Penelhum, "Do Religious Beliefs Need Grounds?," *Nederlands theologisch tijdschrift 40,* 1986, pp. 227–237.

Reading 7.5: Joshua Golding, "Toward a Pragmatic Conception of Religious Faith," *Faith and Philosophy, 7,* 1990, pp. 486–503. Copyright © 1990. Reprinted by permission.

Reading 7.6: Blaise Pascal, "The Wager," from *Pensées and the Provincial Letters,* trans. W. F. Trotter, published by Modern Library, a division of Random House, Inc. Copyright © 1941.

Reading 7.7: William G. Lycan and George N. Schlesinger, "You Bet Your Life: Pascal's Wager Defended." Reprinted by permission of the authors.

Reading 7.9: From "Evaluation of James's Argument" as it appears in *Atheism: A Philosophical Justification,* by Michael Martin. Reprinted by permission of Temple University Press. © 1990 by Temple University. All Rights Reserved.

Reading 7.10: Robert Merrihew Adams, "Kierkegaard's Arguments Against Objective Reasoning in Religion." *The Monist, 60,* no. 2, pp. 228–243. Copyright © 1977. THE MONIST. Peru, Illinois 61354. Reprinted by permission.

Reading 7.11: Steven M. Cahn, "Suppose God Exists." © 2001 by Steven M. Cahn. Published for the first time. Used by permission of the author.

Reading 8.1: Avishai Margalit: "The Ring: On Religious Pluralism." Copyright © 1996 by Princeton University Press. Reprinted by permission of Princeton University Press.

Reading 8.2: From John Hick, "Toward a Philosophy of Religious Pluralism," which first appeared in *Neue Zeitschrift fur Systematische Theologie und Religionsphilosophie, 22,* 1980, pp. 131–149. Copyright © 1980. Reprinted with the author's permission.

Reading 8.3: From Thomas D. Senor, editor, *The Rationality of Belief and the Plurality of Faith.* Copyright © 1995 by Cornell University. Used by permission of the publisher, Cornell University Press.

Reading 8.4: Joseph Runzo, "God, Commitment and Other Faiths," *Faith and Philosophy, 5,* October 1988, pp. 343–364. Copyright © 1988. Reprinted by permission of *Faith and Philosophy.*

Index

Abelard, Peter, 23
Abulafia, Abraham, 516
Acts and action
  Acts of God, 75
  miracles, 385–94
  religious language, 89
Actual infinite, 194, 195
Actuality
  concept of God, 3, 5, 6
  cosmological argument, 184
Adams, Marilyn McCord, 280–81, 285–86
Adams, Robert Merrihew, 57n5, 153, 154–55, 164, 428, 497–507
Ad hominem arguments, 38–39, 383
Adler, Rachel, 109n9
Adventure, and divine creative love, 78–80
Afikoman, 132
Agnosticism. *See also* Atheism
  faith, 433, 440, 477, 483, 484, 491, 493
  problem of evil, 275
  religious experience, 529
  theism and concept of mind, 373
Ahern, M. B., 277
Akedah, 158
Alienation, from human self, 317
Allegory, and religious language, 100–102
Allen, Diogenes, 357–58
Allusion, and rituals, 135
Alston, William P., 93, 251, 254, 255–56, 260, 265, 274–91, 332, 385–94
American Heritage Dictionary, The, 109
Amidah, 131, 134
Analogy, and religious language, 84, 93–95
Anger, and perfection of God, 6, 9–10
Anisotropy, 225
Anscombe, Elizabeth, 230
Anselmian theism, 20, 481
Anselm of Canterbury, St., 1, 5, 8, 10, 11, 72, 73, 107, 173, 176–77, 480–81
Antecedent free-will theodicies, 308
Anthropic Principle, 223, 227
Anthropocentrism, 9, 482
Anthropomorphism, 2n3, 11, 107, 212, 221, 321
Anthropopathism, 2
Antirealism, 342–43
A posteriori arguments, 207
Approximation argument, and faith, 497, 498–501
A priori arguments
  concept of God, 40
  design arguments, 206, 207
  faith, 479, 496
  miracles, 397
  science and religion, 335, 340, 369
  worship, 165
Aquinas, St. Thomas
  cosmological argument, 173, 183–84, 186
  faith, 446, 448, 449, 458, 463
  heaven, 301–2
  immortality of soul, 378n7
  literalism, 362
  moral agency, 168
  omnideterminism and divine agency, 387, 389
  perfection and concept of God, 3, 5–7, 10, 12, 37–38, 39–40, 41–42, 53, 56, 66–67, 68, 72–73, 75, 77
  religious exclusivism, 533
  religious language, 84, 93–95, 100
Arabic language, and allegorical interpretation of Koran, 101
Aristotelian theory, and resurrection, 383
Aristotle, 16–17, 41, 47, 51, 52, 96, 446
Armstrong, D. M., 479n6
Arnold, Matthew, 363
Asher ben Yehiel, 134–35
Atheism. *See also* Agnosticism
  coercion and divine hiddenness, 305–14
  concepts of heaven and hell, 299–305

Atheism—*Cont.*
evolutionary theory, 343–44, 350
expected utility of, 477
faith, 494
meta-belief, 542–43
problem of evil, 263, 267–91, 292–99
summary of case for, 263–65
Atheological argument, 277
Auden, W. H., 21
Audi, Robert, 332, 366–73
Augustine, St., 22, 56, 70, 77, 177, 342, 361, 451–52
Aurobindo, Sri, 544
Austin, James H., 259n7
Autonomy
faith, 491
miracles, 389–90
morality and moral agency, 128, 164, 167
prayer, 145
religion as wish fulfillment, 322
religious language, 114
religious pluralism, 519–20
Averroes, 84, 100–102
Avodah, 136
Ayala, Francisco J., 346
Ayer, A. J., 455

Badham, Paul & Linda, 376n2
Baillie, John, 544
Barbour, Ian, 333
Barrow, John, 227
Barth, Karl, 153
Basic beliefs, 460–62
Basinger, David, 59
Bayesian principles, 480
Beauvoir, Simone de, 117–18
Belenky, Mary Field, 117
Benevolence, and evil, 264n1. *See also* Omnibenevolence
Bentham, Jeremy, 153
Bernard, St., 19
Bible
concept of God, 65–69
concept of heaven, 302
divine hiddenness, 306
literalists, 335, 359–66
pragmatism and faith, 473
problem of evil, 293, 294, 296–97, 298–99
relationship between science and religion, 336, 342–53, 359–66
religious language, 84, 96–99, 100, 102–114
rituals, 158–59

Bible—*Cont.*
threats and coercion, 311, 313n3
Big Bang theory, and cosmology, 194, 199–201, 224–25, 228, 236, 331, 346, 388
Blackmore, Susan, 259n7
Bodin, Jean, 532
Body, and immortality of soul, 378–79. *See also* Mind-body relationship; Resurrection
Boethius, 52–53
Brahman, 511–12, 523, 529. *See also* Hinduism
Braithwaite, R. B., 98n2
Broad, C. D., 203, 241n2
Brown, Patterson, 153, 154
Browne, Malcolm W., 439–40
Brümmer, Vincent, 141, 145, 146–47
Brute facts, 174, 229
Bryan, William Jennings, 364
Buddhism, 495, 513, 514, 541
Bultmann, Rudolf, 84, 102–6
Butler, Joseph, 30, 378
Byron, Lord George, 99

Cahn, Steven M., 428, 508–9
Calvin, John, 55–56, 76, 257, 313, 454
Calvin College, 353
Calvinism, 54, 55–56
Camus, Albert, 166, 293
Cantor, Georg, 65, 196
Carlyle, Thomas, 482
Carnap, Rudolph, 108n8
Cartesianism, 369
Cartesian skepticism, 17
Catholic Church, 302. *See also* Christianity; Church
Causal determinism, 387–88
Causation
analogy of, 93
necessary and sufficient conditions, 153
psychological explanations of religion, 327–29
Causes *in esse* and *in fieri*, 187, 188, 189
Ceteris paribus clauses, 535
Chalcedon, Council of, 2
Chaucer, Geoffrey, 21
Chisholm, Roderick, 270n5, 455, 536
Choice, freedom of and concept of God, 44–45. *See also* Autonomy
Christianity. *See also* Calvinism; Catholic Church; Church, and corporate petitionary prayer; Reformation; Religion; Theism
beliefs in common with Islam and Judaism, 511

Christianity—*Cont.*
religious pluralism, 515–21, 541
Church, and corporate petitionary prayer, 148
Civilization, and psychological explanations of religious belief, 325–26
Clarke, Samuel, 173–74, 185, 186
Classical foundationalism, 445–52
Clifford, W. K., 17n1, 21, 425, 427, 428, 429–42, 444, 446, 483, 485–86, 487
Clones and cloning, 19
Cobb, John B., 3–4, 70–80, 534n8
Coercion, and divine hiddenness, 305–14
Cognition. *See also* Noncognitivism
atheism, 274–91
evil, 295
faith, 469
mind-body problem, 371
miracles, 391
religious experience, 526–27
religious pluralism, 540, 541
Coleridge, Samuel Taylor, 433
Community, and corporate petitionary prayer, 148
Compatibilism, 55, 372–73
Composition, and religious language, 86
Compossibility, and omniscience of God, 38
Concordism, and science, 336
Confirmation approach, to religion and science, 334, 339–41
Conflation, of science with religion, 336, 341
Conflict model, of religion and science, 334–35, 354–56
Conjunctions
design argument, 230
faith, 479
problem of evil, 268n2
Conscience, and voice of God, 168
Consequent free-will theodicies, 307
Consonance, and relation of science to religion, 338
Constant conjunction, 372
Constitutive truths, 517–18
Contact model, of religion and science, 334, 337–39
Contingency
beings, 190–91
cosmological arguments, 173, 184, 185
events, 387
moral agency, 167
petitionary prayer, 146
religious diversity, 514, 530
truth, 447
Contradictory truths, 518–19
Contraposition, 37, 39
Contrast approach, to religion and science, 334, 335–37
Controlling Power, and concept of God, 77, 78
Conventionalism, 37
Copleston, F. C., 189–90, 191
Corporate prayer, 146–48. *See also* Prayer
Corporeality, and religious language, 90
Cosmic Moralist, and concept of God, 77, 78–79
Cosmogony, 217, 219
Cosmological arguments, and theism, 172n1, 173–74, 183–84, 185–93, 204–6, 235, 236
Cosmology, 22, 102, 174, 222, 334, 336, 508–9
Counterexamples, and miracles, 407
Counterfactuals, 57, 58n7, 146
Covering-law model, 434
Craig, William L., 173, 194–204, 226, 228, 331
Creation, and concept of God, 18–19
Creation science, 355. *See also* Scientific creationism
Creel, Richard, 18
Critical realism, 339
Cudworth, Ralph, 152–54, 155, 156
Cullmann, Oscar, 63n1
Culverwell, Nathaniel, 154

Darwin, Charles, 175, 222, 223, 235–36, 334, 343–44, 349
Darwinism, 345
Davies, Paul, 202, 225, 228
Davis, Caroline Franks, 255, 260
Davis, Stephen T., 175, 222–29
Dawkins, Richard, 223, 343–44, 346
Death, survival of soul after, 374–80
Decision theory, 477
Deductive arguments, 172, 206, 224, 452
Defeasible claims, of miracles, 421
Dehellenization, 64
Deism, 75, 360, 511, 518
Demonstrations
arguments, 173
faith, 443, 446
religious exclusivism, 535
religious language, 87, 94, 100, 101
Demythologizing, of religious language, 102–6
Denotation, and rituals, 133, 134, 136
Deontology, and divine command morality, 154
Descartes, René, 19, 36, 37, 370, 408, 447, 449, 451, 474
Descriptive fideism, 424–25

Design arguments, 174–75, 206–34, 235–37, 501, 508–9
Determinism, 55–56, 386, 387–92, 434
Dialectical materialism, 542
Dialectics and dialectical arguments, 161, 537
Dipolar theism, 74
Disjuncts
atheism, 276–77
faith, 437, 479, 484, 507
Dispositional properties, of genes, 288–89
Dispositional state, 505, 542
Dispositions
faith, 451, 504
miracles, 388
Diversity, of world religions
exclusivism, 512, 515, 531–39
inclusivism, 512–13, 515
perspectives on, 511–14
pluralism, 513–14, 515–30, 540–51
relativism, 514, 540–51
Divine agency, and miracles, 387–92
Divine attributes, 91–92
Divine command theory of ethics, 127–28, 150, 152–57
Divine hiddenness, 265, 305–14
Divine image, 19
Divine intervention, 392–94
Divine relativity, 74
Divinization, and early Christianity, 23
Doctrine, and religious language, 107n5, 108–9, 111, 114
Dostoevsky, Fyodor, 127
Doxastic relation, and faith, 110, 439
Dualism
immortality of soul, 377–78
mind/body relationship, 331, 366
relationship between science and religion, 341
Durkheim, Emile, 266

Earth, thermal properties of, 225
Eckhart, Meister, 523
Eddy, Mary Baker, 120
Edwards, Jonathan, 49
Edwards, Paul, 173, 185–93
Efficient cause, 183, 184, 282
Eliminative materialism, 368–69
Eminence, and religious language, 94
Emotions, and perfection of God, 2, 3, 5, 9–15. *See also* Passions
Empiricism and empirical evidence
big bang model of universe, 203
design arguments, 231
Empiricism and empirical evidence—*Cont.*
evolutionary theory, 356
faith, 435, 479, 488, 493, 494, 501
immortality of soul, 377–78
logical problem of evil, 264
mind-body problem, 368
miracles, 421
mysticism, 254, 257
ontological arguments, 176
perfection and concept of God, 12
religious exclusivism, 543
religious experience, 240
religious pluralism, 520
science and religion, 331, 335, 336, 345
Enlightenment Humanism, 342, 343
Epistemic possibility, 180, 502
Epistemology
atheism, 275, 291
design argument, 230
faith, 425, 434, 435, 446, 448, 463, 478, 493, 496
imminence, 310–11
miracles, 402, 416
morality, 127, 153
mysticism, 255
perfection and concept of God, 17, 23
petitionary prayer, 144
religion and science, 335
religious exclusivism, 512, 531, 534, 538–39, 543
religious experience, 248, 528
religious language, 121
religious relativism, 545
resurrection, 385
Equivocality, and religious language, 83–84, 88, 89, 93, 94
Equivocal predication, 91
Error, and religious pluralism, 519–21
Eschatology
religious language, 105
rituals, 132
Essence, of God and religious language, 85
Essentialism
concept of God, 21–22
divine command morality, 154
Eternity. *See also* Infinity
concept of God, 3, 62, 63
prayer, 138
religious language, 96
Ethics. *See also* Morality
divine command theory of, 127–28, 150, 152–57

Ethics—*Cont.*
teleological suspension of, 159–63
Etiology, and mystic experiences, 252
Euclid, 65
Euthyphro (Plato), 127, 129–31, 149–51, 153, 168
Everlastingness, and concept of God, 3, 62–69
Evidentialism, and faith, 425–28, 429–42, 443–45, 457–64
Evidential problem, of evil, 263, 267
Evil. *See also* Theodicy
atheism, 267–91, 292–99
concept of God and passions, 6
logical and evidential problem of, 263–65
Evolution, theory of. *See also* Natural selection; Science
design arguments, 175, 222–29, 232–34, 235–37
relationship between science and religion, 332, 342–53, 354–58, 359–66
Ewing, A. C., 152, 153, 156, 193
Exclusivism, religious, 512, 515, 531–39, 542, 543
Exemplification, and Jewish rituals, 131, 133–34
Existential fideism, 428
Existential generalization, 275
Existentialism
antirealism, 343
ethics and morality, 159
faith, 497–507
religious language, 99, 102, 105–6
Ex nihilo, acts of creation, 362
Expected utility (EU), of faith, 477
Expected value (EV), of faith, 495
Experience, religious
arguments for theism, 175, 237–50, 251–60
information and interpretation of, 526–29
religious pluralism, 551
Explanandum, 236
Expression, and Jewish rituals, 131, 134, 136
Extroversion, and drug-induced experiences, 255

Faith
evidentialism, 425–28, 429–42, 443–45, 457–64
existentialism, 497–507
foundationalism, 425–26, 442–57
perspectives on, 424–28
pragmatism, 427, 464–82, 483–96, 508–9
relationship between science and religion, 355
teleological suspension of the ethical, 162–63
Fales, Evan, 175, 251–60
Fallacy, and concept of God, 40
Fallacy of equivocation, 94
False pride, 16
Falsifiability, and science, 335
Feagin, Susan, 14n7
Fear, and perfection of God, 6
Feminist philosophy, and religious language, 114–23
Fermi, Enrico, 412
Feuerbach, Ludwig, 265, 317–21, 529–30
Final causes, 208, 282, 315
Fine-tuning, and design argument, 223, 229
Fiorenza, Elizabeth Schüssler, 115, 118–19
Fitzpatrick, F. J., 277
Foreknowledge
concept of God, 3, 20, 43–53, 54–62
miracles, 391
Forgiveness, and concept of God, 25–34
Formalism, 180
Fossil record, 347–49
Foster, Michael, 42
Foundationalism, and faith, 425–26, 442–57, 460
Fraassen, B. C. van, 465n1
Freddoso, Alfred J., 57, 61n13
Freedom, foreknowledge and concept of God, 43–53. *See also* Autonomy
Free University of Amsterdam, 353
Free will, and concept of God, 44–45, 55. *See also* Autonomy
Free will theism, 61n14
Free will theodicy, 284, 307
Freud, Sigmund, 253, 265, 321–26, 327–29, 439
Friedman, Maurice, 112
Friendly atheism, 273–74
Friendship, and prayer, 144–45, 147
Functional integrity, 354, 356
Functionalism
faith, 441
mind-body problem, 369
Fundamentalism, and religious language, 96, 97
Future contingents, 43, 146

Galileo, 211, 334, 336
Gaunilo, 173, 178
Geach, Peter, 3, 34–42, 232, 233
Gedanken-experiment, 14
Gellman, Jerome I., 175, 237–46, 247–50
"G. E. Moore shift," 267, 271–72
Gender
concept of God, 80
images of God, 525

Gender—*Cont.*
religious language, 117–19, 121–23
Genes, dispositional properties of, 288–89
Genesiac literalism, 359–66. *See also* Literalism
Genetic fallacy, 266, 327, 328–29
Genuine options, and faith, 484, 493
Genus, of passions, 5, 6
Geocentrism, 362
Gereboff, Joel, 107n1
Gershom, Levi ben. *See* Gersonides, Levi
Gerson, Jean, 152
Gersonides, Levi, 83–84, 88–91
Gillen, F. J., 253
Gingerich, Owen, 331
Glanvill, Joseph, 155
Global reform, 293–94
Global theology, 550
Glock, Charles Y., 258
Gnosticism, 103, 106
God. *See also* Images; Omnibenevolence; Omnipercipitence; Omnipotence; Omniscience; Theism
faith and existence of, 467–73
perfect being theology and concept of, 1–80
as personal and impersonal, 529–30
religious language and subject of, 83–123
semideism and view of, 346
Gödel, Kurt, 179, 181n3, 183, 535
Gödel's law, 179, 181–82
God-of-the-gaps strategy, 259, 331, 356
"God's will," and prayer, 142–44
Goethe, Johann Wolfgang von, 19, 515
Goldbach's Conjecture, 180, 447
Golding, Joshua L., 428, 464–74
Goldstick, D., 152
Goodman, Nelson, 132
Gould, Stephen J., 345, 346, 347, 348
Gray, Elizabeth Dodson, 120
Greeley, Andrew M., 258
Gregory of Nyssa, 362
Gribbin, John, 200
Griffin, David Ray, 3–4, 70–80
Griffith, Stephen, 333, 414–22
Gutting, Gary, 533n4

Halbertal, Moshe, 107n4, 112, 113
HaLevi, Yehuda, 96n1
Hallie, Philip, 294, 296, 297, 299
Hambourger, Robert, 229–34
Hamilton, Sir William, 91
Hardening, of epistemic capacity, 313
Hard facts, 43, 50n4
Haroset, 132
Hart, Michael, 225
Hartshorne, Charles, 70–71, 74, 164n1
Hasker, William, 3, 54–62
Haught, John, 331–32, 334–41
Havdalah ceremony, 133
Hay, David, 258
Heaven, and theodicy, 299–305
Hegel, George, 72
Heidegger, Martin, 116
Heilsgeschichte, 122
Heine, Heinrich, 482
Hell, and theodicy, 299–305
Helm, Paul, 70
Henry, Carl F., 153
Hermeneutics
Genesiac literalism, 361
perfection and concept of God, 10
religious language, 115–17
Heschel, Abraham Joshua, 106, 107, 108, 109–10, 111
Heteronomousness
divine command ethics, 154
moral agency, 164
Hick, John, 279, 280, 513, 514, 521–30, 534n7, 535n10, 536, 538, 540, 545–46, 549
Hilbert, David, 195
Hinduism, 511–12, 513, 523, 529, 541–42
History, and religious pluralism, 530
Hobbes, Thomas, 26, 35, 36
Holland, R. F., 333n1
Homologies, and evolution, 347
Hope, and perfection of God, 6
Hoyle, Fred, 199–200, 203
Hubble, Edwin, 199
Huchingson, James E., 333
Human beings
evolution of, 233–34
image of God, 314
Humanism, 342, 343
Hume, David
design arguments, 174, 206–22
faith, 458, 459–60, 462, 484
mind-body problem, 368
miracles and science, 333, 392, 395–401, 402–9, 421–22
scientific study of religion, 260
skepticism, 271–72
Humility
perfection and concept of God, 16–18
worship and moral agency, 165

Huxley, Thomas H., 485, 486
Hypothesis, 172

Idealism, and mind-body problem, 371–72
Idealist epistemology, 544
Identity theory, and nature of mind, 367
Idolatry, and petitionary prayer, 139–42
Idziak, Janine Marie, 127, 152–57
Ignorance, and religious belief, 315–17
Illusion, and psychological explanations of religious belief, 322, 324–25, 327
Image, of God
  humans in, 314
  religious pluralism, 521, 523–26
Imitatio dei, 8
Immortality
  dualist theory of person, 331
  religious language, 100
Immutability
  concept of God, 2, 5, 6, 71
  design argument, 212
  prayer, 138
  religious language, 96
Impassibility
  concept of God, 2–3, 5–7, 8, 72
  prayer, 138
  religious language, 96
Incarnation, 16, 23, 42, 511, 532
Inclusivism, religious, 512–13, 515, 542, 543–44
Incompatibilism, 55, 267n1
Incorporeality, and concept of God, 12
Incorrigibility, and foundationalism, 443
Inductive arguments, 172, 206, 267, 274–91, 456
Inductive evidence, 546
Ineffability, of religious language, 83, 85, 88
Infallibility, and perfection of God, 12–14. *See also* Omniscience
Inference, 172
Infinite regress, 173, 183, 185
Infinity, and design arguments, 194, 195–99. *See also* Eternity
Information, and interpretation of religious experience, 526–29
In Memory of Her: A Feminist Theological Reconstruction of Christian Origins (Fiorenza), 118
Instantiation, 20
Intellectual fallability, 13
Intersubjective testing, 175, 246, 248–50
Intrinsic value, and religious pluralism, 518
Introversion, and drug-induced experiences, 255
Inwagen, Peter van, 332, 333, 359–66, 381–85,
Inwagen, Peter van—*Cont.*
  402–9, 427, 428, 433–42
Iqbal, Muhammad, 544
Islam
  beliefs in common with Christianity and Judaism, 511
  religious language, 101–2
  religious pluralism, 515–21, 541
Isotropy, 225
Is-ought fallacy, 508–9
Isserles, Rabbi Moses, 134

Jaki, S. L., 200
James, William, 17n1, 205, 258, 427, 428, 478, 483–96, 544
Jaspers, Karl, 530
Jefferson, Thomas, 407–8
Jerome, St., 362
Jewish Apocalyptic, 103, 106
Johnson, David, 173, 179–83, 333, 411–13
Johnson, Patricia Altenbernd, 84, 114–23
Johnson, Samuel, 363–64
Joy, and perfection of God, 6, 7
Judaism. *See also* Jewish Apocalyptic; Maimonides, Moses
  beliefs in common with Christianity and Islam, 511
  religious language, 107
  religious pluralism, 515–21
  rituals, 127, 131–36
Justification, and psychological explanations of religion, 327–29

Kalven, Janet, 115
Kant, Immanuel
  antirealism, 342, 343
  faith, 465n1
  moral agency, 164, 167
  perception and religious experience, 521, 527–28
  pride, 21n6
  religious inclusivism, 544
  universality of ethics, 159
Karma, 379, 548
Kaufman, Gordon, 523
Keats, John, 99
Kelvin,William Thomson, 384, 385
Kenny, Anthony, 203
Kerygma, 84, 103
Kierkegaard, Søren, 24n10, 128, 158, 159–63, 428, 457, 461, 462, 464, 497–507
Kneale, William, 63–64
Koran, and religious language, 100–102

Kretzmann, Norman, 69n4
Kripke, Saul, 1n1
Kuhn, Thomas, 338

Language, religious
analogy, 84, 93–95
Bible, 96–99, 102–14
demythologizing of, 102–6
divine attributes, 91–92
feminist philosophy, 114–23
Koran, 100–102
meaning of, 83–84
negative theology, 85–91
poetic imagery, 106–14
Leavis, F. R., 363
Leftow, Brian, 70
Lehrer, Keith, 329, 424
Leibniz, Gottfried Wilhelm, 181, 194, 551
Leslie, John, 225
Lessing, G. E., 498n2
Lessing, Nathan, 515–17
Levinson, Henry Samuel, 175, 246–50
Lewis, C. S., 38, 401–2
Lewis, David, 434, 436
Lewis, I. M., 251–52, 254, 256, 257–58
Libertarian free will, 55
Libertarianism, and voluntary actions, 308, 389
Lieberman, Saul, 133
Literalism, and religious language, 96. *See also* Genesiac literalism
Literature, and religious language, 99
Live option, and faith, 493
Locke, John, 45, 153, 154, 157, 449, 450
Logic. *See* Reasoning
Logical problem, of evil, 263–65
Logical truth, 37
Love, and concept of God, 72–80
Lulav ritual, 134–35
Luther, Martin, 56, 75–76, 361
Lycan, William G., 428, 476–82

McFague, Sallie, 120–21
Mackie, John L., 175, 235–37, 443
McMullin, Ernan, 361n1
McTaggart, J. M. E., 35, 36, 37
Maimonides, Moses, 10, 34, 83, 84, 85–87, 89n2, 97, 100, 111, 481, 518
Malcolm, Norman, 177, 194, 427, 458, 461, 462, 463
Malebranche, Nicholas, 332
Malino, Jonathan W., 175, 246–50
Mansel, H. L., 91, 92
Margalit, Avishai, 107n4, 112, 113, 514, 515–21
Marion, Jean-Luc, 19
Martin, Michael, 237, 242, 243, 245, 428, 492–96
Martyrdom, as model for redemptive suffering, 280–81, 285–86
Marx, Karl, 266
Mary, Virgin, 525–26
Materialism, 12, 367–68, 369
Maternal Thinking (Ruddick), 121
Matters of fact, 397, 484
Mavrodes, George, 37
Medawar, Peter, 343
Mendelssohn, Moses, 512
Mental illness, and mystical states, 260n8
Mercy, and St. Anselm on God as impassible, 8
Meta-belief, 542–43, 544
Metaethics, and divine command morality, 153, 156
Metaphor, and religious language, 101, 109
Metaphysical goodness, 309
Metaphysical possibilities, 180, 288, 384
Metaphysics
evil, 295
faith, 493
free action, 308
immortality of soul, 379–80
mind-body problem, 368, 372
morality, 127
naturalism and theory of evolution, 352
perfection and concept of God, 10, 18, 71
religious language, 84, 100
religious pluralism, 517, 545
religious relativism, 545
Methodological naturalism, 356–58
Metonymics, and ritual, 132–33
Meyers, Kurt, 127, 136–48
Middle knowledge, 54–62, 386, 391
Mill, John Stuart, 2, 84, 91–92, 284–85, 333, 409–13, 538
Milton, John, 433
Minas, Anne C., 3, 25–34
Mind-body relationship, 332, 366–73. *See also* Perception; Psychology
Miracles. *See also* Hume, David; Mill, John Stuart
evidence on origins of Shroud of Turin, 414–22
God's action in world, 385–94
laws of nature and credibility of reports, 395–401, 402–9

Miracles—*Cont.*
natural explanations and challenge to repeat, 409–13
petitionary prayer, 149
relationship between science and religion, 332–33
Modal fallacy, 40
Modal logic, 173, 179–83, 382, 520
Molina, Luis de, 54, 57, 386, 391
Molinism, 54–55, 57–59, 146
Moore, G. E., 271–72
Moral agency, and worship, 164–69
Moral arguments, and theism, 175
Moral evils, 263
Morality. *See also* Ethics
concept of God, 77–79
divine command morality, 152–57
piety, 149–51
religious exclusivism, 534–38
religious language, 91–92
religious life, 127–28
suspension of the ethical, 159–63
worship and agency, 164–69
Moral judgment, and perfection of God, 26–32
Moreland, J. P., 224
Morisy, Ann, 258
Morris, Thomas V., 1, 138–39
Mother, and religious language, 120–23
Mueller, Marvin, 414–15, 416, 418, 420
Murray, Michael J., 127, 136–48, 265, 305–14
Mysticism
religious pluralism, 524
scientific explanations of, 251–60
Mythology, and religious language, 102–6
Myths
evolutionary theory, 343
religious language, 104, 105
religious pluralism, 542

Nagel, Thomas, 21
Nahmanides, Moses, 97
Natural evil, 280
Naturalism
accounts of religious experience, 251
definitions of ethical terms, 156
evolutionary theory, 342, 345, 350, 355, 356–58
faith, 492n3
mind-body problem, 373
miracles, 392, 412, 415
religious exclusivism, 532
theory of, 223
Natural religion, 206
Natural selection, 222, 223, 232–33, 342, 344, 345, 360. *See also* Evolution, theory of
Natural theology. *See also* Theology
definition of, 171
faith, 444, 452, 458
science and religion, 332
Natural Theology (Paley, 1802), 174
Necessary being
concept of God, 2
cosmological arguments, 173, 184, 191
ontological arguments, 176
Necessary conditions. *See also* Sufficient conditions
atheism, 268, 269, 277, 309
concept of God, 18, 33, 37
divine command morality, 153
faith, 427, 444, 456, 468
petitionary prayer, 137
Necessary truths
concept of God, 2
cosmological arguments, 191
divine command morality, 155
faith, 435, 437, 447
moral agency, 167–68
rationality of arguments, 172
Negative existential claim, 277
Negative theology, 83, 84n2, 85–91
Neuropsychology, and mysticism, 259–60
New Encyclopedia Britannica (1979), 346
Newman, John Henry, 486
Nielsen, Kai, 156
Nietzsche, Friedrich, 306
Nihilism, 319
Noetic standards, and faith, 445
Nomic relation, 369
Nominalism, 434
Non-Applicability Reply, and religious experience, 244, 246
Noncognitivism. *See also* Cognition
mind-body problem, 373
religious language, 98n2, 126
Nonreductive materialism, 369
Nontautological statements, 166
Normative fideism, and faith, 425–28, 466, 493, 508–9
Normative possibility, and religious pluralism, 520
Noumena, 521, 528, 545, 546, 549–50
Nowell-Smith, P. H., 154
Numinous aspects, of divine nature, 11, 544
Nygren, Anders, 73

Oakes, Robert, 3, 9–15
Oberman, Heiko, 154
Objective reasoning, and faith, 497–507
Ockham. *See* William of Ockham
Ockham's razor, 216n1, 229, 370
Ogden, Schubert, 340
Omnibenevolence, of God
  concept of, 2
  major world religions, 511
  mind-body problem, 372
  religious language, 96
Omnideterminism, of God, 386, 387
Omnipercipitence, and concept of God, 30–31
Omnipotence, of God
  concept of, 2, 3, 20, 34–42, 55, 60, 75
  cosmological argument, 174
  divine command morality, 152
  evil, 263–64, 267, 268, 275, 276, 292
  faith, 481
  heaven, 301
  immortality of soul, 379, 380
  major world religions, 511
  mind-body problem, 371, 372
  miracles, 386, 389
  religious language, 96
  resurrection, 381
  survival after death, 374
  worship and moral agency, 164–65
Omniscience, of God
  concept of, 2, 3–4, 20, 25, 26, 55, 71
  cosmological argument, 174
  evil, 263–64, 267, 268, 275, 276, 292
  faith, 489
  heaven, 301
  mind-body problem, 372
  religious language, 96
  science and religion, 339
Ontological arguments, 8, 173, 176–77, 178, 179–83
Ontology
  faith, 493, 508–9
  miracles, 402
  morality, 127
  perfection and concept of God, 12, 22, 63, 71
  religious pluralism, 549
Open God, concept of, 3, 54–62
Open question argument, 155–56
Order, and concept of God, 79
Ordering, and religious language, 94
Origen, 533
Origin of Species (Darwin), 223
Oscillating model, of universe, 200–201, 228
Otto, Rudolph, 11, 523, 544
Out-of-body experiences, 376–77
Ovid, 521
Oxford English Dictionary, 25, 26, 27, 29
"Ozymandias" (Shelley), 99

Paley, William, 156, 174
Pantheism, 319
Paradoxes, and faith, 450
Parallel universes, 229
Parapsychology, 374, 375–77, 526
Parity arguments, and faith, 426–27, 457–64
Parody, and logic, 179
Parousia, of Christ, 105
Pascal, Blaise, 96, 427, 428, 457, 461, 462, 464, 474–82, 485, 489, 507
Passions. *See also* Emotions
  concept of God, 5–7
  faith, 497, 503–7
Patriarchy, and religious language, 117, 118, 119, 120, 121
Peirce, Charles Sanders, 479n6
Pelikan, Jaroslav, 362
Penelhum, Terence, 428, 457–64
Penfield, Wilder, 259
Penzias, A. A., 200
Perception. *See also* Mind-body relationship
  Appearance Theory, 239
  direct realist theory, 256n3
  religious experience, 521, 527–28
Perennial Naturalism, 342, 343
Perfect being theology, and concept of God, 1–4, 9
Perfection, and concept of God, 1–4
Peripatetics, 213
Peterson, Michael, 59
Petitionary prayer, 136–48, 473. *See also* Prayer
Phenomenology
  faith, 449, 453
  mind-body problem, 370
  miracles, 392
  religious pluralism, 522
Phenomenon, and noumenon, 528, 545, 546, 549–50
Phillips, D. Z., 427
Phillips, R. P., 187–88
Philosophical behaviorism, 368
Philosophy. *See* Epistemology; Existentialism; Feminist philosophy; Hume, David; Islam; Kant, Immanuel; Kierkegaard; Søren; Metaphysics; Reasoning
Physical evils, 263

Physics. *See* Big Bang theory; Quantum physics; Universe
Pickwickianism, 10–11
Pierce, Charles, 19
Piety, and Plato on morality, 149–51
Pike, Nelson, 164n1, 264
Plantinga, Alvin
  evolution and the Bible, 342–53, 354–58
  faith, 425, 426, 428, 442–57, 460, 461, 462, 463
  feminist Christian philosophy, 114, 115, 116, 117, 123
  middle knowledge, 57n3, 284–85
  moral significance of free actions, 309
  problem of evil, 264, 267n1
  religious diversity, 514
  religious exclusivism, 531–39
Plato, 64, 127, 129–31, 149–51, 153, 158, 374, 377
Platonism, 362
Plotinus, 85, 96
Pluralism, religious, 513–14, 515–30, 531, 540–51
Poetry, and Bible, 96, 99, 106–114
Pojman, Louis, 508
Politics, and faith, 436–37
Popper, Karl, 335
Positivism, and faith, 455
Posterior sense, and religious language, 89
Postponement argument, and faith, 497, 501–2
Potentia absoluta, 40
Potential infinite, 194, 195–99
Potentiality
  concept of God, 3, 5, 6, 11
  cosmological argument, 184
Potentia ordinata, 40
Practicalism, 121
Pragmatism, and faith, 427, 464–82, 483–96, 508–9
Prayer, and ritual, 136–48. *See also* Petitionary prayer; Worship
Predestination, foreknowledge and concept of God, 43–53
Price, Richard, 40, 156
Pride
  perfection and concept of God, 16–18
  worship, 165
Prime numbers, 494
Principle of Credulity (PC), 238n1
Principle of Rational Assumption (PRA), 471–72
Principle of Sufficient Reason (PSR), 174, 204–6, 230
Prior, Arthur, 40, 69n4
Prior and posterior predication, 89
Prior sense, and religious language, 89
"Private-language" argument, 545
Probability, of logical or deductive conclusions, 172
Process theology
  concept of God, 4, 61n14, 70–80, 511
  religious language, 123
  religious pluralism, 523
Projection, and psychological explanations of religious belief, 317–21
Proper name, God as, 1n1
Property dualism, 369
Prophets and prophecy, 54
Proportionality, analogy of, 93
Propositional revelation, 517
Prosopagnosia, 295
Providence, 43
Provine, William, 350
Provisional atheism, 358
Proximate causes, 387
Prudence, and faith, 480
Prudential rationality, 478
Psychology. *See also* Mind-body relationship
  mysticism, 252–54
  religious belief, 314–29
Punishment, and concept of God, 28, 29
Pyrrhonism and pyrrhonistic skepticism, 17, 486

Quantum mechanics, 277, 389
Quantum physics, 228, 333
Question-begging, 188, 236, 254, 278
Quiddity, and religious language, 85, 94
Quine van Orman, Willard, 37
Quinn, Philip L., 34, 153, 155, 447n2

Rachamim, 108n7
Rachels, James, 128, 164–69
Rahner, Karl, 513, 544
Rationalists, and ontological argument, 176
Rationality. *See also* Reasoning
  atheism, 270, 271
  beliefs in God's existence, 171–72
  faith, 442–57
Realism, and mind-body problem, 371. *See also* Antirealism
Reasoning, and faith, 497–507. *See also* *A posteriori* arguments; *A priori* arguments; Deductive arguments; Inductive arguments; Question-begging; Rationality; Sound argument; Valid argument

Redemption
concept of God, 22–24
religious language, 103
Reductio ad absurdum, 38, 173, 176
Reenactment, and rituals, 135–36
Reference, and rituals, 134, 135
Reflective equilibrium, 295
Reformation, and mysticism, 252n1
Reformed epistemology, and faith, 425–26, 443, 455, 456
Reichenbach, Bruce, 286, 288
Reincarnation, 375. *See also* Resurrection
Relativism, and religious diversity, 514, 540–51
Reliabilist intuitions, and religious exclusivism, 538
Religion. *See also* Agnosticism; Atheism; Buddhism; Christianity; Diversity; Hinduism; Islam; Judaism; Taoism; Theism; Theology
doctrine of resurrection, 381–85
human ignorance, 315–17
mind-body problem, 366–73
miracles, 385–94, 395–401, 402–22
as projection, 317–21
relationship between science and, 331–80
wish fulfillment, 321–26
Repentance, and perfection of God, 6, 31, 32
Representation, and Jewish rituals, 131, 132
Resentment, moral judgment and concept of God, 30–32
Resurrection. *See also* Reincarnation
doctrine of, 381–85
immortality of soul, 380
mind-body problem, 371
Revelation, and religious pluralism, 519–21
Ridley, Mark, 348n10
Rituals. *See also* Prayer; Worship
Bible, 158–59
gestures and symbols in Judaism, 131–36
prayer, 136–48
religious life, 126–27, 129–31
worship, 164–69
Rowe, William L.
concept of God, 3, 43–53
cosmological arguments, 174
Principle of Sufficient Reason, 204–6
problem of evil and atheism, 265, 266, 267–74, 276, 277, 281, 282–83, 285, 289–90
psychological causes of belief, 327–29
Ruddick, Sara, 121–23
Ruether, Rosemary, 120
Runzo, Joseph, 514, 533n2, 534, 540–51
Ruse, Michael, 344, 346
Rushd, Ibn. *See* Averroes
Russell, Bertrand, 191, 194, 450
Russell, Bruce, 276
Russell, Letty, 120
Rust, George, 155

Sabbath ritual, and Judaism, 136
Sabom, Michael B., 376n2
Sagan, Carl, 359, 364
Saganism, 359
Saint Thierry, William de, 19
Saint-Victor, Richard, 19
Salvific religion, 544
Sandage, Alan, 200
Santayana, George, 98n2
Sargant, William, 254
Sartre, Jean Paul, 343
Schafersman, Steven, 418n8
Scheffler, Israel, 132
Schleiermacher, Friedrich, 544
Schlesinger, George N., 235, 428, 476–82
Schnall, Ira M., 84, 96–99
Scholasticism
divine command morality, 152
faith, 492
omnipotence and concept of God, 35, 40
Schopenhauer, Arthur, 188–89
Schroeder, Gerald, 336
Science. *See also* Big Bang theory; Evolution, theory of; Quantum mechanics; Quantum physics; Universe
design arguments, 194–204
mind-body problem, 366–73
miracles, 385–94, 395–401, 402–22
mysticism, 251–60
relationship between religion and, 331–80
resurrection, 381–85
view of world, 104
Scientific creationism, 341. *See also* Creation science
Scientism, 337, 358
Scopes Trial (1925), 343, 364n5
Secrétan, Charles, 490
Segundo, Joan, 115, 116
Self-exemplification, and faith, 450
Self-replication, 222, 223
Semanticlike relations, 132
Semideism, and view of God, 346
Sensible objects, and faith, 446
Sensus divinitatus, 313
Shamans, and miracles, 404
Shavuot, 131, 135

Shelley, Percy Bysshe, 99
Shema, 131, 132
Shipman, Pat, 439
Shofar, 132, 133
Shroud of Turin, 414–22
Simple foreknowledge, theory of, 59–60
Simplicity
design argument, 212
faith, 480
perfect being theology and concept of God, 4, 20, 68, 74, 76
religious language, 85
Simpson, George Gaylord, 344, 348n11
Sin, and arguments for atheism, 277–78
Skepticism
atheism, 271–72, 277
faith, 426, 433, 434, 459, 488, 489, 496
human experiences of God, 530
relationship of religion and science, 334, 341
religious pluralism, 514
Slote, Michael, 24
Smart, J. J. C., 194
Smith, Wilfred Cantwell, 534n5, 535, 545
Social order, and concept of God, 79
Society of Christian Philosophers (SCP), 116
Soft facts, 43, 50n4
Soteriological importance, and religious pluralism, 546
Soul
doctrine of resurrection, 381–85
immortality of, 374–80
Soul-making theodicy, 123, 278–79, 292. *See also* Theodicy
Sound argument, 172, 176, 205
Spanish Inquisition, 252n1
Spanos, Nicholas P., 253
Special creations, 332, 343, 355
Species, of passions, 5, 6
Spencer, Baldwin, 253
Spencer, Herbert, 488
Spieth, Philip, 346
Spinoza, Benedict, 38, 39, 265, 315, 516
Spiritualism, 375–76
Starbuck, Edwin D., 258
Stark, Rodney, 258
Steady-state model, of universe, 200
Stek, John, 356–57
Stern, Josef, 127, 131–36
Stipulative definitions, 156, 180
Stowe, Harriet Beecher, 99
Strauss, D. F., 498n2
Stump, Eleonore, 137, 145, 147, 148, 265, 280, 292–99
Subjectivism, religious, 542, 544–45
Substance, and religious language, 94
Substance dualism, 366, 370
Sufficient conditions, 153, 244, 250, 268, 269, 309, 421, 427, 453, 456, 468. *See also* Necessary conditions
Sufis, 523
Sukkot, 131, 134–35
Superstition, and scientific view of world, 104n1
Supervenience, 369
Swift, Jonathan, 293
Swinburne, Richard, 180, 227, 237, 238n1, 242, 265, 299–305, 307, 332, 374–80
Symbols and symbolism
religious language, 119–20, 121
rituals, 132–33, 135
Sympathy, and evil, 264n1

Taliaferro, Charles, 3, 15–24
Talmud, and religious language, 107
Taoism, 80, 523
Tautology, and divine command morality, 156
Teleology and telos
design arguments, 223, 233
faith, 505, 508–9
suspension of the ethical, 159–63
Temporal array, 65
Tennant, F. R., 223
Teresa of Avila, 252, 253
Thanksgiving, and prayer, 139–42
Theism. *See also* Christianity; God; Religion; Theology; *specific topics*
atheism, 273
cosmological arguments, 173–74, 183–84, 185–93, 194–206
design arguments, 174–75, 206–34, 235–37
evidentialism and faith, 444–45
immortality of soul, 379
major world religions, 511, 512
mind-body problem, 366–73
ontological arguments, 173, 176–77, 178, 179–83
problem of evil, 263
rationality of beliefs in God's existence, 171–72
religious experience, 175, 237–50, 251–60

Theistic science, 353, 358
Theodicy. *See also* Evil; Soul-making theodicy
 atheism and, 264, 274–75, 274–91, 299–305, 307–8
 petitionary prayer, 146
 religious language, 122
Theologically Sophisticated Thesis (TST) and Theologically Naive Thesis (TNT), 9, 11, 12, 13–14, 15
Theology. *See also* Global theology; Natural theology; Negative theology; Perfect being theology; Process theology
 moral agency, 169
 religious language, 84, 96, 97, 104, 105, 107, 111–14, 117, 123
Theophany, 252
Thermal properties, of Earth, 225
Thermodynamics, second law of, 194, 201–2
Thomism, 5, 72, 93, 154, 187, 387
Thulstrup, Niels, 498n2
Tillich, Paul, 119–20, 121, 523, 541
Tillotson, John, 395
Timelessness, and concept of God, 2–3
Tinsley, Beatrice M., 201
Tipler, Frank, 227
Tolkien, J. L., 292, 293, 294
Transitive relation, 369
Trinkhaus, Erik, 439
Troeltsch, Ernst, 543
Truth-functional conditional, 181
Tu quoque reply, 539–40

Uncle Tom's Cabin (Stowe), 99
Underdetermination, and faith, 480
Universal generalization, 182
Universal instantiation, 445
Universe. *See also* Big Bang theory
 oscillating model of, 200–201, 228
 philosophical arguments on beginning of, 195–204
 World Ensemble thesis, 228, 229
Univocality, and religious language, 83–84, 88, 93
Utilitarianism, and concept of God, 29

Valid arguments, 172, 186, 205, 267, 272, 420, 508–9
Vanity, and concept of God, 15–24
Van Till, Howard, 342, 345, 354–58
Veil of ignorance, 22
Veridicality
 mysticism, 254
 religious exclusivism, 535n10
 religious experience, 246, 248–50, 551
 religious pluralism, 522
Verifiability criterion, 116, 455

Wainwright, William J., 255
Water, and design argument, 225–26
Weinberg, Steven, 363, 364
Weismann, August, 488
Wernham, James C. S., 465n1
Wettstein, Howard, 84, 98n2, 106–14
Whaling, Frank, 550, 551
Whilley, Basil, 351n15
Whitehead, Alfred North, 70, 72, 74, 76, 79, 523
Wieman, Henry Nelson, 80
Wiener, Norbert, 526
Wiles, Maurice, 547
Wilken, Robert, 533n3
William of Ockham, 49, 50, 154
Wilson, R. W., 200
Wish fulfillment, and religious belief, 321–26
Wittgenstein, Ludwig, 110, 126, 343, 427, 461, 519, 545
Wittgensteinian fideism, 427
Wolterstorff, Nicholas, 3, 62–69
Women's Ways of Knowing (Belenky et al.), 117
Wordsworth, William, 524
World Ensemble thesis, and universe, 228, 229
World views, and religious pluralism, 542
Worship. *See also* Prayer; Rituals
 perfection and concept of God, 20–22
 rituals and morality, 164–69
Wykstra, Stephen J., 263, 277

Xenophanes, 314

Zaehner, R. C., 543
Zeroa, 134
Zwingli, Ulrich, 56

Philosophy and faith